Is it in Force?
1996

Is it in Force?
1996

A Guide to the commencement
of statutes passed since
1st January 1971

Assistant Editor
Euan Callum, LLB

Revising Editors
Gillian Walsh, LLB
Dominic Shryane, BA

London
Butterworths
1996

United Kingdom	Butterworths a Division of Reed Elsevier (UK) Ltd, Halsbury House, 35 Chancery Lane, LONDON WC2A 1EL and 4 Hill Street, EDINBURGH EH2 3JZ
Australia	Butterworths, SYDNEY, MELBOURNE, BRISBANE, ADELAIDE, PERTH, CANBERRA and HOBART
Canada	Butterworths Canada Ltd, TORONTO and VANCOUVER
Ireland	Butterworth (Ireland) Ltd, DUBLIN
Malaysia	Malayan Law Journal Sdn Bhd, KUALA LUMPUR
New Zealand	Butterworths of New Zealand Ltd, WELLINGTON and AUCKLAND
Singapore	Butterworths Asia, SINGAPORE
South Africa	Butterworths Publishers (Pty) Ltd, DURBAN
USA	Michie, CHARLOTTESVILLE, Virginia

A CIP Catalogue record for this book is available from the British Library.

ISBN 0 406 064 237
0 406 064 059 (Scottish edition)

Typeset by Phoenix Photosetting, Chatham, Kent
Printed by Mackays of Chatham PLC, Chatham, Kent

Preface

Is it in Force? contains the information you need to establish the exact commencement dates of Acts of general application in England, Wales and Scotland and General Synod Measures passed between 1 January 1971 and 31 December 1995.

1 What's in *Is it in Force?*

The short title and chapter number of every Act is given, and unless an Act is of limited or local application only, or has been repealed, the following details are provided:

(a) the date on which the Act received the royal assent;
(b) a list of provisions which deal with the commencement of an Act or any part of an Act (including any commencement orders which have been made);
(c) in limited circumstances (see para 2 below), information on whether the commencement of provisions has been superseded by their repeal/substitution etc;
(d) any date or dates which have been appointed for the provisions of the Act to come into force;
(e) an indication where any provision is not in force.

2 How to use *Is it in Force?*

Acts passed during each calendar year are arranged alphabetically, and the years are dealt with in chronological order.

Each Act is dealt with according to its commencement provisions. Thus, an Act is treated as a single unit if the whole Act was brought into force on one date. An Act will only be treated on a section by section or subsection by subsection basis where the complexity of its commencement provisions demands this. It therefore follows that, whereas the repeal of a whole Act will always be noted, *partial* repeals, substitutions etc of many Acts (which are not otherwise broken down into parts) will not.

It should also be noted that saving and transitional provisions, non-textual amendments (eg extensions or applications) and textual amendments *within* sections, subsections etc, are not in general noted to any Act in this book. **For information about repeals, amendments, savings etc, reference should be made to the volumes of Halsbury's Statutes, and to the Cumulative Supplement and the Noter-up to that work.**

Where a provision of an Act applying both to England and Wales and to Scotland is brought into force on the same date by different provisions, it is noted thus:

11 Apr 1983 (SI 1982/1857; SI 1983/24)

Where such a provision is brought into force on different dates, it is noted thus:

1 Jul 1978 (EW) (SI 1977/2164); 1 Sep 1978 (S) (1978/816)

Where a provision of an Act which applies both to England and Wales and to Scotland is repealed, substituted etc in relation to one jurisdiction only, it is noted thus:

30 Dec 1986 (EW) (SI 1986/2145); repealed (S)

3 Finance Acts

Finance Acts are not dealt with in detail, as the dates from which their provisions take effect are usually stated clearly and unambiguously in the text of the Act, and charging provisions will normally state for which year or years of assessment they are to have effect.

The following information may be of use to readers when considering the effect of taxing provisions in Finance Acts which are expressed to have effect from a date prior to that on which the Act received royal assent:

(a) Income tax and corporation tax are annual taxes which have to be reimposed by Parliament for each year of assessment (Income and Corporation Taxes Act 1988, ss 1, 6).

(b) Under the rules of procedure of the House of Commons a ways and means resolution is a necessary preliminary to the imposition, increase or extension of income tax (but not for its alleviation).

(c) From 1993, the Chancellor of the Exchequer will normally open his budget in November or December (usually on a Tuesday) and at the conclusion of his speech move a set of ways and means resolutions which embody his proposals.

(d) The Provisional Collection of Taxes Act 1968, s 1, makes provision, subject to certain conditions, for statutory effect to be given to those resolutions in so far as they relate to income tax for a period ending on 5 May in the next calendar year (or at the end of 4 months after the date on which the resolution takes effect if the resolution is passed other than in November or December).

(e) If statutory effect is lost, or expires without an Act coming into operation to renew or vary the tax, or the provisions in the resolution are modified by the Act renewing or varying the tax, any money paid or overpaid must be repaid or made good (Provisional Collection of Taxes Act 1968, s 1(6), (7)).

(f) It may be desirable that some motions should have immediate effect without waiting for the conclusion of the Budget debate. The House of Commons may therefore resolve that *provisional* statutory effect shall be given to one or more motions which, if passed, would be resolutions to which statutory effect could be given under s 1 of the 1968 Act. Upon the House so resolving, the motions have statutory effect immediately, subject to that motion or a similar motion being agreed to by a confirmatory resolution of the House within the next 10 sitting days; the provisions of s 1 then apply. If not confirmed, the motion is of no effect and any money paid or overpaid must be repaid or made good; there is similar adjustment if the confirmatory resolution differs from the original motion (Provisional Collection of Taxes Act 1968, s 5). Motions regarding corporation tax and advance corporation tax (ACT) may also be given provisional statutory effect under s 5 of the 1968 Act.

4 General principles governing commencement of statutes

(a) 'Commencement' means the time when the Act comes into force (Interpretation Act 1978, s 5, Sch 1).

(b) Where no provision is made for the coming into force of an Act, it comes into force at the beginning of the day on which it receives the Royal Assent (Interpretation Act 1978, s 4(b)).

(c) Where provision is made for an Act to come into force on a particular day, it comes into force at the beginning of that day (Interpretation Act 1978, s 4(a)).
(d) Where an Act does not come into force immediately on its passing, and it confers power to make subordinate legislation, or to make appointments, give notices, prescribe forms or do any other thing for the purposes of the Act, then, unless the contrary intention appears, the power may be exercised, and any instrument made under it may be made so as to come into force, at any time after the passing of the Act so far as may be necessary or expedient for the purpose of (1) bringing the Act or any provision of the Act into force, or (2) giving full effect to the Act or any such provision at or after the time when it comes into force (Interpretation Act 1978, s 13).
(e) There is a general presumption that an enactment is not intended to have retrospective effect. Parliament undoubtedly has power to enact with retrospective effect, so the general presumption applies only unless the contrary is clearly stated (44(1) Halsbury's Laws (4th edn reissue) 1285).

Updating and the Is it in Force? Telephone Helpline

Is it in Force? is an annual publication. Each subsequent edition incorporates the most recent year's statutes and in addition deals with new commencement orders, repeals and amendments affecting material already published.

Interim updating is provided for subscribers to Halsbury's Statutes as part of their Service in the form of looseleaf pages filed following the guide card 'Is it in Force?' in the Noter-up Service binder.

Where a provision has not been noted as having been brought into force in either this volume or the current service issue, subscribers to Halsbury's Statutes are invited to call the **Is it in Force? Telephone Helpline** on 0171–400–2518 for the latest available information.

Queries on the content or scope of this work should be directed to the Managing Editor, Halsbury's Statutes, at Halsbury House, 35 Chancery Lane, London, WC2A 1EL.
Document Exchange (DX) Cursitor Street 1023.

BUTTERWORTHS

This book includes the effect of commencement orders published up to 1 February 1996.

Contents

1971

Administration of Estates Act 1971 (c 25)

RA: 12 May 1971

Commencement provisions: s 14(2)

s 1–7	1 Jan 1972 (s 14(2))
8	Repealed
9–12	1 Jan 1972 (s 14(2))
13	Repealed
14	12 May 1971 (s 14(2))
Sch 1, 2	1 Jan 1972 (s 14(2))

Air Corporations Act 1971 (c 5)

Whole Act repealed

Anguilla Act 1971 (c 63)

Whole Act repealed

Animals Act 1971 (c 22)

RA: 12 May 1971

Commencement provisions: s 13(3)

1 Oct 1971 (s 13(3))

Appropriation Act 1971 (c 67)

Whole Act repealed

Armed Forces Act 1971 (c 33)

RA: 27 May 1971

Commencement provisions: s 78(3); Armed Forces Act 1971 (Commencement) Order 1972, SI 1972/359

s 1	Repealed
2–25	1 Jul 1972 (SI 1972/359)
26	1 Jul 1972 (SI 1972/359); prospectively repealed (EW) by Civil Evidence Act 1995, s 15(2), Sch 2[1]
27–77	1 Jul 1972 (SI 1972/359)

Armed Forces Act 1971 (c 33)—*cont*

s 78	27 May 1971 (RA)
Sch 1–4	1 Jul 1972 (SI 1972/359)

[1] Any order made under Civil Evidence Act 1995, s 16(2), bringing the prospective repeal into force will be noted to that Act in the service to this work

Atomic Energy Authority Act 1971 (c 11)

RA: 16 Mar 1971

16 Mar 1971 (RA)

Attachment of Earnings Act 1971 (c 32)

RA: 12 May 1971

Commencement provisions: s 29(4)[1]; Administration of Justice Act 1970 (Commencement No 4) Order 1971, SI 1971/834 (made under Administration of Justice Act 1970, s 54)

2 Aug 1971 (SI 1971/834)

[1] s 29(4) provides that this Act is to come into force on the day appointed under Administration of Justice Act 1970, s 54, for the coming into force of Pt II of that Act

Banking and Financial Dealings Act 1971 (c 80)

RA: 16 Dec 1971

Commencement provisions: s 3(3)

s 1, 2	16 Dec 1971 (RA)
3	16 Jan 1972 (s 3(3))
4, 5	16 Dec 1971 (RA)
Sch 1, 2	16 Dec 1971 (RA)

Betting, Gaming and Lotteries (Amendment) Act 1971 (c 26)

Whole Act repealed

Carriage of Goods by Sea Act 1971 (c 19)

RA: 8 Apr 1971

Commencement provisions: s 6(5); Carriage of Goods by Sea Act 1971 (Commencement) Order 1977, SI 1977/981

23 Jun 1977 (SI 1977/981)

Civil Aviation Act 1971 (c 75)

Whole Act repealed

Civil Aviation (Declaratory Provisions) Act 1971 (c 6)

Whole Act repealed

Coal Industry Act 1971 (c 16)

RA: 30 Mar 1971

30 Mar 1971 (RA)

Whole Act repealed (in part prospectively) as follows: ss 1, 2 repealed by Coal Industry Act 1977, ss 7(10), 15, Sch 5; s 3 repealed by Coal Industry Act 1973, s 13(2), Sch 2; ss 4, 7(7), 8–10 prospectively repealed by Coal Industry Act 1994, s 67(8), Sch 11, Pts III, IV[1]; s 5 repealed by Overseas Development and Co-operation Act 1980, s 18(1), Sch 2, Pt I; ss 6, 7(1)–(6), (8) repealed by Coal Industry Act 1994, s 67(8), Sch 11, Pt II

[1] Order(s) made under Coal Industry Act 1994 bringing these prospective repeals into force will be noted to that Act in the service to this work

---

Coinage Act 1971 (c 24)

RA: 12 May 1971

Commencement provisions: s 14(2)

1 Sep 1971 (s 14(2))

Consolidated Fund Act 1971 (c 1)

Whole Act repealed

Consolidated Fund (No 2) Act 1971 (c 14)

Whole Act repealed

Consolidated Fund (No 3) Act 1971 (c 79)

Whole Act repealed

Consumer Protection Act 1971 (c 15)

Whole Act repealed

Copyright (Amendment) Act 1971 (c 4)

Whole Act repealed

Courts Act 1971 (c 23)

RA: 12 May 1971

Commencement provisions: s 59(2); Courts Act 1971 (Commencement) Order 1971, SI 1971/1151

s 1–15	Repealed
16–22	1 Jan 1972 (SI 1971/1151)
23	Repealed
24	Substituted by Supreme Court Act 1981, s 146 (qv)
25, 26	Repealed
27	Substituted by Deregulation and Contracting Out Act 1994, s 76, Sch 16, para 2 (qv)
28–30	1 Jan 1972 (SI 1971/1151)
31–40	Repealed
41–44	1 Jan 1972 (SI 1971/1151)
45–50	Repealed
51–55	1 Jan 1972 (SI 1971/1151)
56(1)–(3)	1 Jan 1972 (SI 1972/1151)
(4)	See Sch 11 below
57	1 Jan 1972 (SI 1971/1151)
58	Repealed
59	1 Oct 1971 (SI 1971/1151)
Sch 1	Repealed
2, 3	1 Jan 1972 (SI 1971/1151)
4	Repealed
5–10	1 Jan 1972 (SI 1971/1151)
11, Pt I	1 Oct 1971 (repeal of County Courts Act 1959, s 96(3)) (SI 1971/1151)
	1 Jan 1972 (remainder) (SI 1971/1151)
II, III	1 Jan 1972 (SI 1971/1151)
IV	1 Oct 1971 (repeal of Magistrates' Courts Act 1952, s 1(4); Criminal Appeal Act 1966, s 1(3)) (SI 1971/1151)
	1 Jan 1972 (remainder) (SI 1971/1151)

Criminal Damage Act 1971 (c 48)

RA: 14 Jul 1971

Commencement provisions: s 12(1)

14 Oct 1971 (s 12(1))

Dangerous Litter Act 1971 (c 35)

Whole Act repealed

Diplomatic and other Privileges Act 1971 (c 64)

RA: 27 Jul 1971

Commencement provisions: s 4(2); Commonwealth Countries and Republic of Ireland (Immunities and Privileges) Order 1971, SI 1971/1237[1]

Diplomatic and other Privileges Act 1971 (c 64)—*cont*

s 1	27 Jul 1971 (RA)
2	Repealed
3	27 Jul 1971 (RA)
4(1)	27 Jul 1971 (RA)
(2)	1 Sep 1971 (SI 1971/1237)[1]
Schedule	27 Jul 1971 (RA)

[1] SI 1971/1237 was made under Consular Relations Act 1968, s 12, as inserted by the Schedule to this Act

Education (Milk) Act 1971 (c 74)

Whole Act repealed

Education (Scotland) Act 1971 (c 42)

Whole Act repealed

Finance Act 1971 (c 68)

RA: 5 Aug 1971

See the note concerning Finance Acts at the front of this book

Fire Precautions Act 1971 (c 40)

RA: 27 May 1971

Commencement provisions: s 44(3); Fire Precautions Act 1971 (Commencement No 1) Order 1972, SI 1972/236; Fire Precautions Act 1971 (Commencement No 2) Order 1976, SI 1976/2006

s 1, 2	20 Mar 1972 (SI 1972/236)
3, 4	*Not in force*
5	20 Mar 1972 (SI 1972/236)
5A, 5B	Inserted by Fire Safety and Safety of Places of Sport Act 1987, s 1(4) (qv)
6–8	20 Mar 1972 (SI 1972/236)
8A	Inserted by Fire Safety and Safety of Places of Sport Act 1987, s 2(1) (qv)
8B	Inserted by Fire Safety and Safety of Places of Sport Act 1987, s 3 (qv)
9	20 Mar 1972 (SI 1972/236)
9A	Inserted by Health and Safety at Work etc Act 1974, s 78 (qv); substituted by Fire Safety and Safety of Places of Sport Act 1987, s 5 (qv)
9B, 9C	Inserted by Fire Safety and Safety of Places of Sport Act 1987, s 6 (qv)
9D–9F	Inserted by Fire Safety and Safety of Places of Sport Act 1987, s 7(1) (qv)
10	Substituted by Fire Safety and Safety of Places of Sport Act 1987, s 9(1) (qv)
10A, 10B	Inserted by Fire Safety and Safety of Places of Sport Act 1987, s 9(2) (qv)

Fire Precautions Act 1971 (c 40)—*cont*

s 11	Repealed
12(1)	1 Jan 1977 (SI 1976/2006)
(2)	*Not in force*
(3)–(8)	1 Jan 1977 (SI 1976/2006)
(9)	*Not in force*
(10)	1 Jan 1977 (SI 1976/2006)
(11)	*Not in force*
(12)	Repealed (*never in force*)
13, 14	20 Mar 1972 (SI 1972/236)
15	Repealed
16(1)(a)	20 Mar 1972 (SI 1972/236)
(b)	*Not in force*
(2)(a)	20 Mar 1972 (SI 1972/236)
(b)	*Not in force*
(3)	20 Mar 1972 (SI 1972/236)
17, 18	20 Mar 1972 (SI 1972/236)
19(1), (2)	20 Mar 1972 (SI 1972/236)
(3)(a), (b)	20 Mar 1972 (SI 1972/236)
(c)	*Not in force*
(d)	20 Mar 1972 (SI 1972/236)
(4)–(6)	20 Mar 1972 (SI 1972/236)
20–27	20 Mar 1972 (SI 1972/236)
27A	Inserted by Fire Safety and Safety of Places of Sport Act 1987, s 12(1) (qv)
28	1 Jan 1977 (SI 1976/2006)
28A	Inserted by Fire Safety and Safety of Places of Sport Act 1987, s 16(1), (2), Sch 1 (qv)
29–33	20 Mar 1972 (SI 1972/236)
34	*Not in force*
35	20 Mar 1972 (SI 1972/236)
36	*Not in force*
37–39	20 Mar 1972 (SI 1972/236)
40	20 Mar 1972 (except so far as relates to ss 3, 4, 12) (SI 1972/236)
	1 Jan 1977 (otherwise, except so far as relates to ss 3, 4, 12(2), (9)) (SI 1976/2006)
	Not in force (so far as relates to ss 3, 4, 12(2), (9))
41	20 Mar 1972 (SI 1972/236)
42	Repealed
43, 44	20 Mar 1972 (SI 1972/236)
Sch 1 Pt I, II	Repealed
III	*Not in force*
IV	Inserted by Housing (Financial Provisions) (Scotland) Act 1972, Sch 9, para 31(4) (qv)
2	Inserted by Fire Safety and Safety of Places of Sport Act 1987, s 16(2), Sch 1 (qv)

Friendly Societies Act 1971 (c 66)

RA: 27 Jul 1971

Commencement provisions: s 15(6); Friendly Societies Act 1971 (Commencement) Order 1971, SI 1971/1899

Whole Act repealed except ss 11(5), 15(4), (5), which came into force on 31 Dec 1971 (SI 1971/1899)

Guardianship of Minors Act 1971 (c 3)

Whole Act repealed

Highways Act 1971 (c 41)

Whole Act repealed

Hijacking Act 1971 (c 70)

Whole Act repealed

Hospital Endowments (Scotland) Act 1971 (c 8)

Whole Act repealed

Housing Act 1971 (c 76)

Whole Act repealed

Hydrocarbon Oil (Customs and Excise) Act 1971 (c 12)

Whole Act repealed

Immigration Act 1971 (c 77)

RA: 28 Oct 1971

Commencement provisions: ss 34(1), 35(1)–(3); Immigration Act 1971 (Commencement) Order 1972, SI 1972/1514

s 1	1 Jan 1973 (SI 1972/1514)
2	Substituted by British Nationality Act 1981, s 39(2) (qv)
3–24	1 Jan 1973 (SI 1972/1514)
25(1)	28 Nov 1971 (s 35(2))
(2)	1 Jan 1973 (SI 1972/1514)
(3)–(8)	28 Nov 1971 (s 35(2))
26, 27	1 Jan 1973 (SI 1972/1514)
28(1), (2)	28 Oct 1971 (so far as relates to Commonwealth Immigrants Act 1962, s 4A) (s 35(3))
	28 Nov 1971 (so far as relates to s 25(1) of this Act) (s 35(2))
	1 Jan 1973 (otherwise) (SI 1972/1514)
(3), (4)	1 Jan 1973 (SI 1972/1514)
29	28 Oct 1971 (RA)
30	Repealed
31–37	28 Oct 1971 (RA)
Sch 1	Repealed
2–5	1 Jan 1973 (SI 1972/1514)
6	28 Oct 1971 (s 34(1))

Industrial Relations Act 1971 (c 72)

Whole Act repealed

Industry Act 1971 (c 17)

Whole Act repealed

Interest on Damages (Scotland) Act 1971 (c 31)

RA: 12 May 1971

12 May 1971 (RA)

Investment and Building Grants Act 1971 (c 51)

Whole Act repealed

Land Commission (Dissolution) Act 1971 (c 18)

RA: 8 Apr 1971

Commencement provisions: s 1(2); Land Commission (Dissolution) (Appointed Day) Order 1971, SI 1971/670

s 1–7	8 Apr 1971 (RA)
Sch 1, Pt I, II	8 Apr 1971 (RA)
III	1 May 1971 (SI 1971/670)
2	8 Apr 1971 (RA)
3, Pt I	8 Apr 1971 (RA)
II	1 May 1971 (SI 1971/670)

Land Registration and Land Charges Act 1971 (c 54)

RA: 27 Jul 1971

Commencement provisions: s 15(5); Land Registration and Land Charges Act 1971 (Commencement No 1) Order 1971, SI 1971/1489

s 1, 2	1 Oct 1971 (SI 1971/1489)
3, 4	27 Jul 1971 (s 15(5))
5–11	Repealed
12, 13	27 Jul 1971 (s 15(5))
14(1)	27 Jul 1971 (s 15(5))
(2)(a)	27 Jul 1971 (s 15(5))
(b)	See Sch 2, Pt II below
15	27 Jul 1971 (s 15(5))
Sch 1	Repealed
2, Pt I	27 Jul 1971 (s 15(5))
II	1 Oct 1971 (except provisions specified below) (SI 1971/1489)
	2 Oct 1972 (so far as relates to Land Registration Act 1925, s 85(5)) (SI 1971/1489)
	Not in force (so far as it relates to Land Charges Act 1925, ss 16, 17(4) (repealed))

Law Reform (Jurisdiction in Delict) (Scotland) Act 1971 (c 55)

Whole Act repealed

Law Reform (Miscellaneous Provisions) Act 1971 (c 43)

RA: 1 Jul 1971

Commencement provisions: s 6(2)

Whole Act repealed (subject to a saving in the case of s 5(2)) except s 6 which came into force on 1 Aug 1971 (s 6(2))

Licensing (Abolition of State Management) Act 1971 (c 65)

Whole Act repealed

Local Authorities (Qualification of Members) Act 1971 (c 7)

Whole Act repealed

Medicines Act 1971 (c 69)

RA: 5 Aug 1971

5 Aug 1971 (RA)

Merchant Shipping (Oil Pollution) Act 1971 (c 59)

Whole Act repealed

Mineral Workings Act 1971 (c 71)

Whole Act repealed

Mineral Workings (Offshore Installations) Act 1971 (c 61)

RA: 27 Jul 1971

Commencement provisions: s 14(2); Mineral Workings (Offshore Installations) Act 1971 (Commencement) Order 1972, SI 1972/644

s 1	Repealed
2	Repealed[1]
3(1)–(3)	Repealed[1]
(4)	1 May 1972 (SI 1972/644)
4, 5	Repealed
6	Repealed[1]
7(1), (2)	Repealed[1]
(3)–(6)	1 May 1972 (SI 1972/644)
(7), (8)	Repealed[1]
8	Repealed
9(1)–(4)	1 May 1972 (SI 1972/644)

Mineral Workings (Offshore Installations) Act 1971 (c 61)—*cont*

s 9(5)	Repealed
10	Repealed
11–14	1 May 1972 (SI 1972/644)
Schedule	Repealed[1]

[1] Whole Act (and its subordinate legislation) are 'existing statutory provisions' to be progressively replaced by health and safety regulations and approved codes of practice (Offshore Safety Act 1992, s 1). Consequently, provisions for the making of regulations in relation to offshore installations under this Act were repealed, as from 23 Aug 1993, by Offshore Safety (Repeals and Modifications) Regulations 1993, SI 1993/1823, regs 3(1), (4), 6, but regulations made or having effect under the repealed provisions and in force immediately before that date were continued in force notwithstanding the repeals

Mines Management Act 1971 (c 20)

Whole Act repealed

Misuse of Drugs Act 1971 (c 38)

RA: 27 May 1971

Commencement provisions: s 40(3); Misuse of Drugs Act 1971 (Commencement No 1) Order 1971, SI 1971/2120; Misuse of Drugs Act 1971 (Commencement No 2) Order 1973, SI 1973/795

s 1	1 Feb 1972 (SI 1971/2120)
2–9	1 Jul 1973 (SI 1973/795)
9A	Inserted by Drug Trafficking Offences Act 1986, s 34 (qv)
10–23	1 Jul 1973 (SI 1973/795)
24	1 Jul 1973 (SI 1973/795); repealed (EW)
25	1 Jul 1973 (SI 1973/795)
26	Repealed
27–31	1 Jul 1973 (SI 1973/795)
32	1 Feb 1972 (SI 1971/2120)
33, 34	Repealed
35	1 Feb 1972 (SI 1971/2120)
36	1 Jul 1973 (SI 1973/795)
37, 38	1 Feb 1972 (SI 1971/2120)
39	1 Jul 1973 (SI 1973/795)
40	1 Feb 1972 (SI 1971/2120)
Sch 1	1 Feb 1972 (SI 1971/2120)
2–5	1 Jul 1973 (SI 1973/795)

Motor Vehicles (Passenger Insurance) Act 1971 (c 36)

Whole Act repealed

Mr Speaker King's Retirement Act 1971 (c 13)

Limited application only

National Insurance Act 1971 (c 50)

Whole Act repealed

National Savings Bank Act 1971 (c 29)

RA: 12 May 1971

Commencement provisions: s 29(2)

12 Jun 1971 (s 29(2))

New Towns Act 1971 (c 81)

Whole Act repealed

Nullity of Marriage Act 1971 (c 44)

Whole Act repealed

Oil in Navigable Waters Act 1971 (c 21)

Whole Act repealed

Pensions (Increase) Act 1971 (c 56)

RA: 27 Jul 1971

27 Jul 1971 (RA)

Pool Competitions Act 1971 (c 57)

Whole Act expired

Powers of Attorney Act 1971 (c 27)

RA: 12 May 1971

Commencement provisions: s 11(4)

1 Oct 1971 (s 11(4))

Prevention of Oil Pollution Act 1971 (c 60)

RA: 27 Jul 1971

Commencement provisions: s 34(2); Prevention of Oil Pollution Act 1971 (Commencement) Order 1973, SI 1973/203

1 Mar 1973 (SI 1973/203)

Rating Act 1971 (c 39)

RA: 27 May 1971

s 1–4	Repealed (with savings) in relation to financial years beginning in or after 1990, by Local Government Finance Act 1988, s 149, Sch 13, Pt I (qv)
5–11	27 May 1971 (RA)

Recognition of Divorces and Legal Separations Act 1971 (c 53)

Whole Act repealed

Redemption of Standard Securities (Scotland) Act 1971 (c 45)

RA: 1 Jul 1971

1 Jul 1971 (RA)

Rent (Scotland) Act 1971 (c 28)

RA: 12 May 1971

Whole Act repealed except Sch 18, Pt II, which came into force on 12 Aug 1971 (s 136(2) (repealed))

Rolls-Royce (Purchase) Act 1971 (c 9)

Whole Act repealed

Rural Water Supplies and Sewerage Act 1971 (c 49)

RA: 14 July 1971

14 Jul 1971 (RA)

Whole Act repealed (EW); *Whole Act repealed* (S) (prospectively) by Local Government etc (Scotland) Act 1994, s 180(2), Sch 14 (any order made under s 184(2), (3) of that Act bringing the prospective repeal into force will be noted to that Act in the service to this work

---

Sheriff Courts (Scotland) Act 1971 (c 58)

RA: 27 Jul 1971

Commencement provisions: s 47(2); Sheriff Courts (Scotland) Act 1971 (Commencement No 1) Order 1971, SI 1971/1582; Sheriff Courts (Scotland) Act 1971 (Commencement No 2) Order 1973, SI 1973/276; Sheriff Courts (Scotland) Act 1971 (Commencement No 3) Order 1976, SI 1976/236

s 1–5	1 Nov 1971 (SI 1971/1582)
5A	Inserted by Judicial Pensions and Retirement Act 1993, s 26(10), Sch 6, para 10 (qv)

Sheriff Courts (Scotland) Act 1971 (c 58)—*cont*

s 6–20	1 Nov 1971 (SI 1971/1582)
21	Repealed
22	1 Nov 1971 (SI 1971/1582)
23–30	1 Apr 1973 (SI 1973/276)
31	1 Sept 1976 (SI 1976/236)
32–34	1 Nov 1971 (SI 1971/1582)
35, 36	1 Sept 1976 (SI 1976/236)
36A, 36B	Inserted by Law Reform (Miscellaneous Provisions) (Scotland) Act 1985, s 18(2) (qv)
37, 38	1 Sept 1976 (SI 1976/236)
39, 40	Repealed
41, 42	1 Sept 1976 (SI 1976/236)
43	1 Nov 1971 (SI 1971/1582)
44(1), (2)	1 Nov 1971 (SI 1971/1582)
(3)	1 Apr 1973 (SI 1973/276)
45–47	1 Nov 1971 (SI 1971/1582)
Sch 1, para 1	1 Nov 1971 (SI 1971/1582)
2, 3	1 Sept 1976 (SI 1976/236)
4	Repealed
2, Pt I	1 Nov 1971 (repeals of or in Sheriffs of Edinburgh and Lanark Act 1822; Sheriff Courts (Scotland) Act 1907, ss 12, 13, 15, 16, 18, 19, 21, 25, 26; Sheriff Courts and Legal Officers (Scotland) Act 1927, s 14; Administration of Justice (Scotland) Act 1933, ss 31(2)–(5), 32, 34, 35; Sheriff Courts (Scotland) Act 1939; Administration of Justice (Scotland) Act 1948, s 4) (SI 1971/1582)
	1 April 1973 (otherwise) (SI 1973/276)
Pt II	1 Sept 1976 (SI 1976/236)

Shipbuilding Industry Act 1971 (c 46)

Whole Act repealed

Social Security Act 1971 (c 73)

Whole Act repealed

Statute Law (Repeals) Act 1971 (c 52)

RA: 27 Jul 1971

27 Jul 1971 (RA)

Teaching Council (Scotland) Act 1971 (c 2)

RA: 17 Feb 1971

Commencement provisions: s 5(2); Social Work (Scotland) Act 1968 (Commencement No 5) Order 1971, SI 1971/184

17 Feb 1971 (s 5(2)), except Schedule, para 2, which came into force on 15 Apr 1971 (SI 1971/184 (made under Social Work (Scotland) Act 1968, s 98))

Town and Country Planning Act 1971 (c 78)

Whole Act repealed

Tribunals and Inquiries Act 1971 (c 62)

Whole Act repealed

Unsolicited Goods and Services Act 1971 (c 30)

RA: 12 May 1971

Commencement provisions: s 7(2)

12 Aug 1971 (s 7(2))

Vehicles (Excise) Act 1971 (c 10)

Whole Act repealed (For savings, see Vehicle Excise and Registration Act 1994, s 64, Sch 4)

Water Resources Act 1971 (c 34)

Whole Act repealed (For savings, see Water Act 1989, s 190(2), (3), Sch 26, Pt VII, para 41, Sch 27, Pt I)

Welsh National Opera Company Act 1971 (c 37)

RA: 27 May 1971

27 May 1971 (RA)

Wild Creatures and Forest Laws Act 1971 (c 47)

RA: 1 Jul 1971

1 Jul 1971 (RA)

1972

Administration of Justice (Scotland) Act 1972 (c 59)

RA: 9 Aug 1972

Commencement provisions: s 5(3); Administration of Justice (Scotland) Act 1972 (Commencement) Order 1973, SI 1973/339

s 1	2 Apr 1973 (SI 1973/339)
2	Repealed
3	2 Apr 1973 (SI 1973/339)
4, 5	9 Aug 1972 (RA)

Admission to Holy Communion Measure 1972 (No 1)

RA: 10 Feb 1972

10 Feb 1972 (RA)

Affiliation Proceedings (Amendment) Act 1972 (c 49)

Whole Act repealed

Agriculture (Miscellaneous Provisions) Act 1972 (c 62)

RA: 9 Aug 1972

Commencement provisions: s 27(2), (3); Agriculture (Miscellaneous Provisions) Act 1972 (Commencement) Order 1972, SI 1972/1260

s 1–3	Repealed
4	9 Aug 1972 (RA)
5–7	Repealed
8–12	9 Aug 1972 (RA)
13	Repealed
14	9 Aug 1972 (RA)
15	Repealed
16, 17	9 Aug 1972 (RA)
18	15 Aug 1972 (SI 1972/1260); repealed (EW)
19–25	9 Aug 1972 (RA)
26(1), (2)	9 Aug 1972 (RA)
(3)	See Sch 6 below
(4)	9 Aug 1972 (RA)
27	9 Aug 1972 (RA)
Sch 1–3	Repealed
4, 5	9 Aug 1972 (RA)
6	9 Aug 1972 (except repeals of or in Agriculture Act 1947, ss 77, 78) (RA)

Agriculture (Miscellaneous Provisions) Act 1972 (c 62)—*cont*

Sch 6—*cont*	15 Aug 1972 (exception noted above) (SI 1972/1260) 1 Jan 1974 (repeals of or in Slaughterhouses Act 1954; Food and Drugs Act 1955, ss 65, 70(1), 75–78; Slaughterhouses Act 1958; London Government Act 1963, s 54(2)) (s 27(2))

Airports Authority Act 1972 (c 8)

Whole Act repealed

Appropriation Act 1972 (c 56)

Whole Act repealed

Benefices Measure 1972 (No 3)

RA: 10 Feb 1972

10 Feb 1972 (RA)

Betting and Gaming Duties Act 1972 (c 25)

Whole Act repealed

British Library Act 1972 (c 54)

RA: 27 Jul 1972

27 Jul 1972 (RA)

Carriage by Railway Act 1972 (c 33)

Whole Act repealed

Children Act 1972 (c 44)

RA: 27 Jul 1972

27 Jul 1972 (RA)

Chronically Sick and Disabled Persons (Scotland) Act 1972 (c 51)

RA: 27 Jul 1972

27 Jul 1972 (RA)

Civil Evidence Act 1972 (c 30)

RA: 12 Jun 1972

Commencement provisions: s 6(3); Civil Evidence Act 1972 (Commencement No 1) Order 1974, SI 1974/280; Civil Evidence Act 1972 (Commencement No 2) Order 1974, SI 1974/1137

s 1	1 Jun 1974 (for purpose of proceedings other than in bankruptcy in the Supreme Court; proceedings before tribunals to which strict rules of evidence apply; arbitrations and references (other than references under County Courts Act 1959, s 92 (now County Courts Act 1984, s 64)) to which strict rules of evidence apply; applications and appeals arising from the above) (SI 1974/280) 1 Sep 1974 (proceedings, other than in bankruptcy, in county courts) (SI 1974/1137) *Not in force* (otherwise) Section prospectively repealed by Civil Evidence Act 1995, s 15(2), Sch 2[1]
2, 3	1 Jan 1973 (s 6(3))
4(1)	1 Jan 1973 (s 6(3))
(2)–(5)	See note to s 1 above
5, 6	1 Jan 1973 (s 6(3))

[1] Any order made under Civil Evidence Act 1995, s 16(2), bringing the prospective repeal into force will be noted to that Act in the service to this work

Civil List Act 1972 (c 7)

RA: 24 Feb 1972

Commencement provisions: s 8(5), (6)

s 1–3	Effective as respects payments for 1972 onwards (s 8(5))
4(1)	1 Apr 1972 (s 8(6))
(2)	24 Feb 1972 (RA)
5–7	24 Feb 1972 (RA)
8(1)–(3)	24 Feb 1972 (RA)
(4)	See Schedule below
(5), (6)	24 Feb 1972 (RA)
Schedule	24 Feb 1972 (except repeal of Civil List Act 1952, s 13(1)) (RA) 1 Apr 1972 (exception noted above) (s 8(6))

Clergy Pensions (Amendment) Measure 1972 (No 5)

RA: 9 Aug 1972

9 Aug 1972 (RA)

Companies (Floating Charges and Receivers) (Scotland) Act 1972 (c 67)

Whole Act repealed

Consolidated Fund Act 1972 (c 13)

Whole Act repealed

Consolidated Fund (No 2) Act 1972 (c 23)

Whole Act repealed

Consolidated Fund (No 3) Act 1972 (c 78)

Whole Act repealed

Contracts of Employment Act 1972 (c 53)

Whole Act repealed

Counter-Inflation (Temporary Provisions) Act 1972 (c 74)

Whole Act repealed

Criminal Justice Act 1972 (c 71)

RA: 26 Oct 1972

Commencement provisions: s 66(6); Criminal Justice Act 1972 (Commencement No 1) Order 1972, SI 1972/1763; Criminal Justice Act 1972 (Commencement No 2) Order 1973, SI 1973/272; Criminal Justice Act 1972 (Commencement No 3) Order 1973, SI 1973/1472; Criminal Justice Act 1972 (Commencement No 4) Order 1973, SI 1973/1995; Criminal Justice Act 1972 (Commencement No 5) Order 1976, SI 1976/299

s 1–5	Repealed
6	1 Jan 1973 (SI 1972/1763)
7–23	Repealed
24(1), (2)	Repealed
(3)	1 Apr 1973 (SI 1973/272)
(4)	1 Apr 1973 (SI 1973/272) (EW); substituted (S) by Criminal Procedure (Scotland) Act 1975, s 461(1), Sch 9, para 48 (qv)
25–27	Repealed
28, 29	1 Jan 1973 (SI 1972/1763)
30	Repealed
31	1 Jan 1973 (SI 1972/1763)
32	Repealed
33	1 Jan 1973 (SI 1972/1763)
34	1 Apr 1976 (SI 1976/299)
35	Repealed
36	1 Oct 1973 (SI 1973/1472)
37–45	Repealed
46(1)	1 Jan 1973 (SI 1972/1763)
(2)	1 Jan 1973 (SI 1972/1763); prospectively repealed by Criminal Justice and Public Order Act 1994, s 168(3), Sch 11[1]
47	Repealed
48	1 Jan 1973 (SI 1972/1763)
49	*Not in force*
50	Repealed

Criminal Justice Act 1972 (c 71)—*cont*

51	1 Jan 1973 (SI 1972/1763)
52–57	Repealed
58–60	1 Jan 1973 (SI 1972/1763)
61, 62	Repealed
63(1)	Repealed
(2)	1 Jan 1973 (SI 1972/1763)
(3)	Repealed
64	See Schs 5, 6 below
65, 66	1 Jan 1973 (SI 1972/1763)
Sch 1–4	Repealed
5	1 Jan 1973 (amendments in Petty Sessions (Ireland) Act 1851; Incitement to Disaffection Act 1934; Dogs Amendment Act 1938; Prevention of Fraud (Investment) Act 1958; Criminal Justice Act 1967, ss 18(7), 67(1); Theft Act 1968; Children and Young Persons Act 1969, s 7(8); Immigration Act 1971) (SI 1972/1763)
	1 Mar 1973 (amendment in Criminal Justice Act 1967, s 60(2)) (SI 1973/272)
	1 Apr 1973 (amendment in Road Traffic Act 1972, s 105(2)) (SI 1973/272)
	Repealed (otherwise)
6	1 Jan 1973 (repeals of or in Forfeiture Act 1870; Summary Jurisdiction (Scotland) Act 1908; Protection of Animals Act 1911; Criminal Justice Act 1948; Costs in Criminal Cases Act 1952; Prison Act 1952; Magistrates' Courts Act 1952; First Offenders Act 1958; Criminal Justice Act 1961; Criminal Justice (Scotland) Act 1963; Administration of Justice Act 1964, s 22, Sch 3, para 19; Criminal Law Act 1967; Criminal Justice Act 1967, ss 39, 54; Firearms Act 1968; Theft Act 1968; Children and Young Persons Act 1969; Administration of Justice Act 1970; Courts Act 1971; Criminal Damage Act 1971) (SI 1972/1763)
	1 Mar 1973 (repeal in Criminal Justice Act 1967, s 60(2)) (SI 1973/272)
	1 Apr 1973 (repeals in Pt II so far as not already in force) (SI 1973/272)
	30 Mar 1974 (repeals in Pt I, except repeal of Aliens Restriction (Amendment) Act 1919, s 8) (SI 1973/1472)
	Not in force (otherwise; but note that many of the Acts in which repeals are made by this Act have been consolidated or otherwise superseded and those repeals will therefore never be brought into force)

[1] Any order made under Criminal Justice and Public Order Act 1994, s 172(2), bringing the prospective repeal into force will be noted to that Act in the service to this work

---

Deaconesses and Lay Ministry Measure 1972 (No 4)

RA: 9 Aug 1972

9 Aug 1972 (RA)

Defective Premises Act 1972 (c 35)

RA: 29 Jun 1972

Commencement provisions: s 7(2)

1 Jan 1974 (s 7(2))

Deposit of Poisonous Waste Act 1972 (c 21)

Whole Act repealed

Electricity Act 1972 (c 17)

Whole Act repealed

Employment Medical Advisory Service Act 1972 (c 28)

RA: 22 May 1972

Commencement provisions: s 9(2); Employment Medical Advisory Service Act 1972 (Commencement) Order 1973, SI 1973/28

1 Feb 1973 (SI 1973/28)

European Communities Act 1972 (c 68)

RA: 17 Oct 1972

Commencement provisions: See Sch 3 below

This Act largely came into force on receiving Royal Assent on 17 Oct 1972 but for most purposes it did not have practical effect until 1 Jan 1973 (the date the UK joined the European Communities). The repeals effected by Sch 3 have effect or are to have effect from dates appointed or to be appointed as follows:

Sch 3, Pt I	1 Jan 1974 (repeal of Import Duties Act 1958, ss 5(2), (3), (6), 9(4), (5) (words from 'and' onwards)) (Import Duties Act 1958 (Repeals) (Appointed Day) Order 1973, SI 1973/2176)
	1 Sep 1976 (repeals of Import Duties Act 1958, ss 5(5), 7(1)(c), 16(3), Schs 2, 6; European Free Trade Association Act 1960; Finance Act 1965, s 2 (except sub-s (5)); Finance Act 1966, ss 1(6), 9) (Customs Duties (Repeals) (Appointed Day) Order 1976, SI 1976/1304)
	1 Jan 1978 (repeals of Import Duties Act 1958, ss 1–3, 11, 12 (except part of sub-s (4)), Sch 1, Sch 4, para 1; Finance Act 1971, s 1(1)–(3)) (Customs Duties (Repeals) (Appointed Day) Order 1977, SI 1977/2028, as amended by SI 1987/2106)
II	1 Feb 1973 (repeals of Sugar Act 1956, ss 3(2)(b), 4(2), (3), 17(1) (from the beginning to words 'this section'), (3)–(5), 18(3), (4), 21, 22, 24–32, 33(2) (words 'except' to 'subsection'), (3), (5), Sch 4; South Africa Act 1962, Sch 2, para 5; Finance Act 1968, s 58) (Sugar Act 1956 (Repeals) (Appointed Day) (No 1) Order 1973, SI 1973/135)

European Communities Act 1972 (c 68)—*cont*

Sch 3, Pt II—*cont*	1 Jul 1973 (repeals of Sugar Act 1956, ss 7–16, 20(6), 33(1) (words 'regulations or'), (2) (words 'Every instrument containing any such regulations, and,'), 34 (words 'or the Commissioners'), 35(2) (definitions of 'Commissioners,' 'composite sugar products', 'distribution payments', 'distribution repayments', 'manufacture', 'refiner', 'surcharge', 'surcharge repayment'), (4)–(6), 36(2); Finance Act 1962, s 3(6) (words from 'the Sugar Act 1956' onwards), Sch 5, Pt II; Finance Act 1964, s 22; Finance Act 1966, s 52) (Sugar Act 1956 (Repeals) (Appointed Day) (No 2) Order 1973, SI 1973/1019)
	1 Aug 1975 (repeals of Sugar Act 1956, s 17(2), (6), (7), Sch 3, paras 2, 3; Agriculture Act 1957, ss 4, 36(2) (words 'and to sugar beet'); Agriculture (Miscellaneous Provisions) Act 1963, s 25) (Sugar Act 1956 (Repeals) (Appointed Day) (No 3) Order 1975, SI 1975/1164)
	5 May 1976 (repeals of Sugar Act 1956, ss 3(1) (words from 'including' onwards), 19, 20(1)–(5), (7), (8), 35(2) (definitions of 'the Consolidated Fund' and 'refined sugar'), Sch 3, para 4) (Sugar Act 1956 (Repeals) (Appointed Day) (No 4) Order 1976, SI 1976/548)
	1 Dec 1976 (repeals of Sugar Act 1956, ss 5, 23(5), 35(2) (definition of 'the Minister'); National Loans Act 1968, Sch 1, the entry for the Sugar Act 1956) (Sugar Act 1956 (Repeals) (Appointed Day) (No 5) Order 1976, SI 1976/2016)
	1 Sep 1981 (repeal of Sugar Act 1956, s 23(1)–(3), but without prejudice to the modification made by s 23(2) in the articles of the British Sugar Corporation) (Sugar Act 1956 (Repeals) (Appointed Day) (No 6) Order 1981, SI 1981/1192)
	Not in force (otherwise)
III	1 Sep 1978 (repeals of Plant Varieties and Seeds Act 1964, s 32; Trade Descriptions Act 1968, s 2(4)(a)) (Plant Varieties and Seeds Act 1964 (Repeals) (Appointed Day) Order 1978, SI 1978/1003)
	16 Aug 1982 (all repeals in 1964 Act save s 32 mentioned above; repeal of Agriculture (Miscellaneous Provisions) Act 1968, Sch 7) (Plant Varieties and Seeds Act 1964 (Repeals) (Appointed Day) Order 1982, SI 1982/1048)
IV	17 Oct 1972 (RA)

Field Monuments Act 1972 (c 43)

Whole Act repealed

Finance Act 1972 (c 41)

Budget Day: 21 Mar 1972

RA: 27 Jul 1972

See the note concerning Finance Acts at the front of this book

Gas Act 1972 (c 60)

Whole Act repealed except s 46 in relation to its operation as applied by the Gas Act 1965, s 22 (Gas Act 1986, s 67(3), (4), Sch 8, para 15, Sch 9, Pt I)

Harbours Development (Scotland) Act 1972 (c 64)

RA: 9 Aug 1972

9 Aug 1972 (RA)

Harbours (Loans) Act 1972 (c 16)

RA: 23 Mar 1972

23 Mar 1972 (RA)

Harbours, Piers and Ferries (Scotland) Act 1972 (c 29)

RA: 12 Jun 1972

12 Jun 1972 (RA)

Horserace Totalisator and Betting Levy Boards Act 1972 (c 69)

RA: 17 Oct 1972

Commencement provisions: s 3(3)

s 1, 2	17 Oct 1972 (RA)
3	*Not in force*
4–8	17 Oct 1972 (RA)

Housing Finance Act 1972 (c 47)

Whole Act repealed

Housing (Financial Provisions) (Scotland) Act 1972 (c 46)

RA: 27 Jul 1972

Commencement provisions: s 81(3); Housing (Financial Provisions) (Scotland) Act 1972 (Commencement) Order 1972, SI 1972/1130

Whole Act repealed except ss 69, 78, 81 and Sch 9, para 31, which came into force as follows:

s 69, 78, 81	3 Aug 1972 (SI 1972/1130)
Sch 9, para 31	27 Aug 1972 (s 81(3))

Industry Act 1972 (c 63)

RA: 9 Aug 1972

9 Aug 1972 (RA)

Iron and Steel Act 1972 (c 12)

Whole Act repealed

Island of Rockall Act 1972 (c 2)

RA: 10 Feb 1972

10 Feb 1972 (RA)

Land Charges Act 1972 (c 61)

RA: 9 Aug 1972

Commencement provisions: s 19(2); Land Charges Act 1972 (Commencement) Order 1972, SI 1972/2058

29 Jan 1973 (SI 1972/2058)

Legal Advice and Assistance Act 1972 (c 50)

Whole Act repealed

Local Employment Act 1972 (c 5)

RA: 10 Feb 1972

Commencement provisions: s 23(2)

10 Mar 1972 (s 23(2))

Local Government Act 1972 (c 70)

RA: 26 Oct 1972

Commencement provisions: ss 1(1), 20(1), 273; Local Government Act 1972 (Commencement No 1) (England) Order 1973, SI 1973/373; Local Government Act 1972 (Commencement No 2) (Wales) Order 1973, SI 1973/375

This Act largely came into force on receiving Royal Assent, and the whole Act was effective from 1 Apr 1974. The details of its commencement (whereby for administrative reasons slightly earlier dates were prescribed for the coming into force of certain provisions) are of only historical interest; consequently the section by section commencement dates are omitted here

Maintenance Orders (Reciprocal Enforcement) Act 1972 (c 18)

RA: 23 Mar 1972

Commencement provisions: s 49(2); Maintenance Orders (Reciprocal Enforcement) Act 1972 (Commencement No 1) Order 1974, SI 1974/517; Maintenance Orders (Reciprocal Enforcement) Act 1972 (Commencement No 2) Order 1975, SI 1975/377

s 1–21	1 Apr 1974 (SI 1974/517)
22(1)	1 Apr 1974 (SI 1974/517)
(2)(a)	*Not in force*
(b)	Repealed
(c)	*Not in force*
(d)	Repealed

Maintenance Orders (Reciprocal Enforcement) Act 1972 (c 18)—*cont*

s 23, 24	1 Apr 1974 (SI 1974/517)
25, 26	12 Apr 1975 (SI 1975/377)
27, 27A–27C, 28, 28A–28C	Substituted for existing ss 27, 28 (substituted by Domestic Proceedings and Magistrates' Courts Act 1978, s 57 (qv)), 28A (inserted by Domestic Proceedings and Magistrates' Courts Act 1978, s 58 (qv)) by Maintenance Orders (Reciprocal Enforcement) Act 1992, s 1(2), Sch 1, Pt II, para 13 (qv); s 28C prospectively substituted by ss 28C–28E by Children (Northern Ireland) Order 1995, SI 1995/755 (NI 2), art 185(1), Sch 9, para 72
28D, 28E	See note to ss 27, 27A–27C, 28, 28A–28C above
29	12 Apr 1975 (SI 1975/377); substituted by Maintenance Orders (Northern Ireland Consequential Amendments) Order 1980, SI 1980/564, art 4(3); prospectively substituted, together with s 29A, by ss 29, 29A, 29B by Children (Northern Ireland) Order 1995, SI 1995/755 (NI 2), art 185(1), Sch 9, para 72
29A	Inserted by Domestic Proceedings and Magistrates' Courts Act 1978, s 59 (qv); substituted by Maintenance Orders (Northern Ireland Consequential Amendments) Order 1980, SI 1980/564, art 4(4); prospectively substituted as noted to s 29 above
29B	See note to s 29 above
30–34	12 Apr 1975 (SI 1975/377)
34A	Inserted by Maintenance Enforcement Act 1991, s 10, Sch 1, para 19(2) (qv)
34B	Prospectively inserted by Family Law (Northern Ireland) Order 1993, SI 1993/1576 (NI 6), art 11, Sch 1, para 14(b)
35, 35A	Substituted for original s 35 by Maintenance Orders (Reciprocal Enforcement) Act 1992, s 1(2), Sch 1, Pt II, para 16 (qv); s 35A prospectively substituted by Children (Northern Ireland) Order 1995, SI 1995/755 (NI 2), art 185(1), Sch 9, para 75
36–38	12 Apr 1975 (SI 1975/377)
38A	Inserted by Maintenance Orders (Reciprocal Enforcement) Act 1992, s 1(2), Sch 1, Pt II, para 18 (qv)
39	12 Apr 1975 (SI 1975/377)
40	1 Apr 1974 (SI 1974/517)
41	Repealed (EW)
42, 43	1 Apr 1974 (SI 1974/517)
43A	Inserted (S) by Domestic Proceedings and Magistrates' Courts Act 1978, s 61 (qv)
44–49	1 Apr 1974 (SI 1974/517)
Schedule	1 Apr 1974 (SI 1974/517)

Matrimonial Proceedings (Polygamous Marriages) Act 1972 (c 38)

RA: 29 Jun 1972

29 Jun 1972 (RA)

Mineral Exploration and Investment Grants Act 1972 (c 9)

RA: 24 Feb 1972

24 Feb 1972 (RA)

Ministerial and other Salaries Act 1972 (c 3)

Whole Act repealed

Museums and Galleries Admission Charges Act 1972 (c 73)

RA: 26 Oct 1972

26 Oct 1972 (RA)

National Debt Act 1972 (c 65)

RA: 9 Aug 1972

9 Aug 1972 (RA)

National Health Service (Family Planning) Amendment Act 1972 (c 72)

Whole Act repealed

National Health Service (Scotland) Act 1972 (c 58)

RA: 9 Aug 1972

Commencement provisions: s 65(1) (repealed); National Health Service (Scotland) Act 1972 (Commencement No 1) Order 1972, SI 1972/1256; National Health Service (Scotland) Act 1972 (Commencement No 2) Order 1973, SI 1973/372; National Health Service (Scotland) Act 1972 (Commencement No 3) Order 1973, SI 1973/1421[1]; National Health Service (Scotland) Act 1972 (Commencement No 4) Order 1974, SI 1974/145

s 1–23	Repealed
24(1)	Repealed
(2)	1 Apr 1974 (SI 1974/145)
(3)	Repealed
25	Repealed
26, 27	1 Apr 1974 (SI 1974/145)
28	21 Aug 1972 (SI 1972/1256)
29–31	Repealed
32–36	1 Apr 1974 (SI 1974/145)
37–51	Repealed
52	1 Mar 1973 (SI 1973/372)
53	1 Apr 1974 (SI 1974/145)
54–60	Repealed
61(1)–(3)	1 Mar 1973 (SI 1973/372)
(4), (5)	Repealed
62, 63	Repealed
64(1)	See Sch 6 below

National Health Service (Scotland) Act 1972 (c 58)—*cont*

s 64(2)	Repealed
65	Repealed
Sch 1–3	Repealed
4	1 Apr 1974 (SI 1974/145)
5	Repealed
6, para 37–77, 82, 83(a), 84–93, 94(b), 95–97, 101, 102, 104, 119–122, 126, 127, 129, 135(a)–(c), 136(b), 138–140, 150, 154–156[2]	1 Apr 1974 (SI 1974/145)
6, para 156A[2]	Inserted by National Health Service Reorganisation Act 1973, s 57(1), Sch 4 (repealed)
Remainder	Repealed
7	Repealed

[1] Provisions brought into force by SI 1973/1421 are all now repealed

[2] These paragraphs of Sch 6, although repealed, are saved by National Health Service (Scotland) Act 1978, s 109, Sch 15, para 10 (qv)

National Insurance Act 1972 (c 57)

Whole Act repealed

National Insurance (Amendment) Act 1972 (c 36)

Whole Act repealed

National Insurance Regulations (Validation) Act 1972 (c 4)

Whole Act repealed

Northern Ireland Act 1972 (c 10)

Whole Act repealed

Northern Ireland (Border Poll) Act 1972 (c 77)

Whole Act repealed

Northern Ireland (Financial Provisions) Act 1972 (c 76)

Whole Act repealed

Northern Ireland (Temporary Provisions) Act 1972 (c 22)

RA: 30 Mar 1972

30 Mar 1972 (RA; note that s 1 expired on 1 Jan 1974, the commencement date for the Northern Ireland Constitution Act 1973, Pt II)

Overseas Investment and Export Guarantees Act 1972 (c 40)

Whole Act repealed

Parliamentary and other Pensions Act 1972 (c 48)

RA: 27 Jul 1972

27 Jul 1972 (RA)

Pensioners and Family Income Supplement Payments Act 1972 (c 75)

Whole Act repealed

Pensioners' Payments and National Insurance Contributions Act 1972 (c 80)

Whole Act repealed

Performers' Protection Act 1972 (c 32)

Whole Act repealed

Poisons Act 1972 (c 66)

RA: 9 Aug 1972

Commencement provisions: s 13(1); Medicines Act 1968 (Commencement No 7) Order 1977, SI 1977/2128

1 Feb 1978 (SI 1977/2128)

Police Act 1972 (c 39)

RA: 29 Jun 1972

29 Jun 1972 (RA)

Post Office (Borrowing) Act 1972 (c 79)

Whole Act repealed

Repair of Benefice Buildings Measure 1972 (No 2)

RA: 10 Feb 1972

This Measure came into force in different dioceses on different dates, as shown below, in accordance with orders of the Church Commissioners (and is in force for every diocese):

Bath and Wells	1 Jan 1973
Birmingham	1 Jan 1974
Blackburn	1 Jan 1974

Repeal of Benefice Buildings Measure 1972 (No 2)—*cont*

Bradford	1 Apr 1973
Bristol	1 Jan 1973
Canterbury	1 Jul 1973
Carlisle	1 Jan 1974
Chelmsford	1 Jan 1974
Chester	1 Jan 1974
Chichester	1 Jan 1974
Coventry	1 Apr 1973
Derby	1 Jan 1974
Durham	1 Jan 1974
Ely	1 Jan 1973
Exeter	1 Jan 1973
Gloucester	1 Jan 1974
Guildford	1 Jan 1974
Hereford	1 Apr 1973
Leicester	1 Apr 1974
Lichfield	1 Apr 1974
Lincoln	1 Jan 1974
Liverpool	1 Jan 1973
London	1 Jan 1974
Manchester	1 Jan 1974
Newcastle	1 Jan 1973
Norwich	1 Jan 1974
Oxford	1 Jan 1974
Peterborough	1 Apr 1974
Portsmouth	1 Jan 1974
Ripon	1 Jan 1974
Rochester	1 Jan 1973
St Albans	1 Jan 1973
St Edmundsbury and Ipswich	1 Jan 1974
Salisbury	1 Apr 1973
Sheffield	1 Jan 1974
Southwark	1 Jan 1974
Southwell	1 Jan 1974
Truro	1 Jan 1973
Wakefield	1 Jan 1974
Winchester	1 Apr 1973
Worcester	1 Jan 1974
York	1 Jan 1974

Road Traffic Act 1972 (c 20)

Whole Act repealed

Road Traffic (Foreign Vehicles) Act 1972 (c 27)

RA: 11 May 1972

Commencement provisions: s 8(2); Road Traffic (Foreign Vehicles) Act 1972 Commencement Order 1972, SI 1972/1018

31 Jul 1972 (SI 1972/1018)

Salmon and Freshwater Fisheries Act 1972 (c 37)

Whole Act repealed

Sierra Leone Republic Act 1972 (c 1)

RA: 10 Feb 1972

10 Feb 1972 (RA; but as Sierra Leone became a Republic before this date, this Act is deemed to have come into force on 19 Apr 1971 (s 1(4)))

Social Work (Scotland) Act 1972 (c 24)

RA: 11 May 1972

11 May 1972 (RA)

Whole Act prospectively repealed by Children (Scotland) Act 1995, s 105(5), Sch 5; any order made under s 105(1), (2) of that Act bringing the prospective repeal into force will be noted to that Act in the service to this work

---

Sound Broadcasting Act 1972 (c 31)

Whole Act repealed

Sri Lanka Republic Act 1972 (c 55)

RA: 27 Jul 1972

27 Jul 1972 (RA; but as Ceylon became a Republic before this date, this Act is deemed to have come into force on 22 May 1972 (s 1(6)))

Summer Time Act 1972 (c 6)

RA: 10 Feb 1972

Commencement provisions: s 6(2)

10 Mar 1972 (s 6(2))

Sunday Cinema Act 1972 (c 19)

Whole Act repealed

Sunday Theatre Act 1972 (c 26)

RA: 11 Apr 1972

Commencement provisions: s 6(3)

11 May 1972 (s 6(3))

Superannuation Act 1972 (c 11)

RA: 1 Mar 1972

Commencement provisions: s 30(4); Superannuation Act 1972 (Commencement No 1) Order 1972, SI 1972/325; Superannuation Act 1972 (Commencement No 2) Order 1972, SI 1972/384[1]

25 Mar 1972 (SI 1972/325)

[1] Provisions brought into force by SI 1972/384 are all now repealed

---

Town and Country Planning (Amendment) Act 1972 (c 42)

RA: 27 Jul 1972

Commencement provisions: s 12(2) (repealed)[1]

27 Jul 1972 (RA)

Whole Act repealed (EW)

[1] Provisions brought into force by s 12(2) are all now repealed

---

Town and Country Planning (Scotland) Act 1972 (c 52)

RA: 27 Jul 1972

Commencement provisions: ss 18, 279, 280; Town and Country Planning (Scotland) Act 1972 (Commencement No 1) (Orkney Islands Area) Order 1975, SI 1975/379; Town and Country Planning (Scotland) Act 1972 (Commencement No 2) Order 1975, SI 1975/380; Town and Country Planning (Scotland) Act 1972 (Commencement No 3) Order 1975, SI 1975/1203; Town and Country Planning (Scotland) Act 1972 (Commencement No 4) Order 1976, SI 1976/464

The Act mainly came into force on 27 Aug 1972 (s 280(1)), except for s 280, Sch 23 (so far as it relates to the repeal of Pt I of the Control of Office and Industrial Development Act 1965), any provisions conferring power to make regulations or orders or conferring power to revoke or vary any regulations or orders and any provisions relating to the exercise of such powers, and other provisions now repealed (together with other provisions insofar as they related to the repealed provisions), which came into force on 27 Jul 1972 (s 280(2)). Provision was made in s 18 for Pt II (dealing with development plans), with certain exceptions, to come into force on days appointed by the Secretary of State, with different days appointed for the commencement of the same provisions in different areas; see SI 1975/379, appointing 1 April 1975 for the Orkney Islands Area and SI 1975/380 appointing 16 May 1975 for the remainder of Scotland. In addition, ss 58(5), 59(1)–(3) came into force on 17 Jul 1975 by virtue of SI 1975/1203 and Sch 7 came into force on 1 Apr 1976 by virtue of SI 1976/464

Trade Descriptions Act 1972 (c 34)

Whole Act repealed

Trading Representations (Disabled Persons) Amendment Act 1972 (c 45)

RA: 27 Jul 1972

Commencement provisions: s 3(2)

1 Jan 1973 (s 3(2))

Transport (Grants) Act 1972 (c 15)

RA: 23 Mar 1972

23 Mar 1972 (RA)

Transport Holding Company Act 1972 (c 14)

RA: 23 Mar 1972

23 Mar 1972 (RA)

1973

Administration of Justice Act 1973 (c 15)

RA: 18 Apr 1973

Commencement provisions: s 20

s 1	1 Apr 1974 (s 20(1)(a))
2–4	Repealed
5	Substituted by Justices of the Peace Act 1979, s 71, Sch 2, para 22 (qv)
6	18 Apr 1973 (RA)
7	Repealed
8	18 May 1973 (s 20(1)(b))
9	18 Apr 1973 (RA)
10, 11	Repealed
12	18 Apr 1973 (RA)
13	Repealed
14	18 Apr 1973 (RA)
15–17	Repealed
18	18 May 1973 (s 20(1)(b))
19, 20	Repealed
21	18 Apr 1973 (RA)
Sch 1	1 Apr 1974 (s 20(1))
2	18 Apr 1973 (RA)
3–5	Repealed

Appropriation Act 1973 (c 40)

Whole Act repealed

Atomic Energy Authority (Weapons Group) Act 1973 (c 4)

RA: 6 Mar 1973

6 Mar 1973 (RA; but note that ss 1–5 had no effect until 1 Apr 1973, the day appointed for the purposes of s 1(1) by Atomic Energy Authority (Weapons Group) Act 1973 (Appointed Day) Order 1973, SI 1973/463)

Badgers Act 1973 (c 57)

Whole Act repealed

Bahamas Independence Act 1973 (c 27)

RA: 14 Jun 1973

Appointed day: 10 Jul 1973

Bangladesh Act 1973 (c 49)

RA: 25 Jul 1973

25 Jul 1973 (RA; but note that Bangladesh was recognised as an independent sovereign state on 4 Feb 1972, and most provisions of this Act are deemed to have had effect from that date)

Breeding of Dogs Act 1973 (c 60)

RA: 25 Oct 1973

Commencement provisions: s 7

1 Apr 1974 (s 7(3))

Channel Tunnel (Initial Finance) Act 1973 (c 66)

RA: 13 Nov 1973

13 Nov 1973 (RA)

Coal Industry Act 1973 (c 8)

RA: 22 Mar 1973

Commencement provisions: s 14(3)

22 Mar 1973 (RA; except for s 2(1) (repealed), and the provisions in Sch 2 (prospectively repealed) which relate to the Coal Industry Acts 1965, 1967 and 1971, which came into force on 1 Apr 1973 (s 14(3)))

Whole Act repealed (in part prospectively) as follows: ss 1, 11–14, Sch 1, para 1, Sch 2 prospectively repealed by Coal Industry Act 1994, s 67(8), Sch 11, Pt IV[1]; ss 2, 10, Sch 1, paras 2, 3 prospectively repealed by Coal Industry Act 1994, s 67(8), Sch 11, Pt III[1]; ss 3, 4, 6, 7, 9, Sch 1, para 4 repealed by Coal Industry Act 1977, ss 7(10), 15, Sch 5; s 5 repealed by National Coal Board (Finance) Act 1976, s 2(6); s 8 repealed by Coal Industry Act 1983, ss 2(3), 6(3), Schedule.

[1] Any order made under Coal Industry Act 1994 bringing these prospective repeals into force will be noted to that Act in the service to this work

Concorde Aircraft Act 1973 (c 7)

Whole Act repealed

Consolidated Fund Act 1973 (c 1)

Whole Act repealed

Consolidated Fund (No 2) Act 1973 (c 10)

Whole Act repealed

Costs in Criminal Cases Act 1973 (c 14)

Whole Act repealed

Counter-Inflation Act 1973 (c 9)

RA: 22 Mar 1973

The provisions of this Act were not intended to have permanent effect and are now repealed; note that the repeal of ss 17(6), (8), (9), 18(4), (5), 19, 20(4), (5)(i), (iii), 23(2), Sch 4, para 4 (except sub-para (2)(b)) takes effect from 1 Jan 2011 (Competition Act 1980, s 33(4), Sch 2)

Dentists (Amendment) Act 1973 (c 31)

Whole Act repealed

Domicile and Matrimonial Proceedings Act 1973 (c 45)

RA: 25 Jul 1973

Commencement provisions: s 17(5)

1 Jan 1974 (s 17(5))

Education Act 1973 (c 16)

RA: 18 Apr 1973

Commencement provisions: s 1(5); Education Act 1973 (Commencement) Order 1973, SI 1973/1661

s 1(1)	1 Feb 1974 (SI 1973/1661)
(2)(a)	18 Apr 1973 (RA)
(b)	Repealed
(c)	18 Apr 1973 (RA)
(3)–(5)	18 Apr 1973 (RA)
2(1), (1A)–(1C)	Substituted for original sub-s (1) by Education Reform Act 1988, s 112 (qv)
(2)–(5)	18 Apr 1973 (RA)
(5A)	Inserted by Education Act 1993, s 288 (qv)
(6)–(9)	18 Apr 1973 (RA)
3	18 Apr 1973 (RA)
4	Repealed
5	18 Apr 1973 (RA)
Sch 1	18 Apr 1973 (RA)
2, Pt I, II	18 Apr 1973 (RA)
III	1 Feb 1974 (SI 1973/1661)

Education (Scotland) Act 1973 (c 59)

Whole Act repealed

Education (Work Experience) Act 1973 (c 23)

RA: 23 May 1973

23 May 1973 (RA); *whole Act repealed (S)*

Employment Agencies Act 1973 (c 35)

RA: 18 Jul 1973

Commencement provisions: s 14(4); Employment Agencies Act 1973 (Commmencement) Order 1976, SI 1976/709

s 1–3	Repealed
3A–3D	Inserted by Deregulation and Contracting Out Act 1994, s 35, Sch 10, paras 1, 3 (qv)
4	Substituted, together with original s 3, by new s 3 (repealed)
5, 6	1 Jul 1976 (SI 1976/709)
7, 8	Repealed
9–13	1 Jul 1976 (SI 1976/709)
14	18 Jul 1973 (RA)
Schedule	1 Jul 1976 (SI 1976/709)

Employment and Training Act 1973 (c 50)

RA: 25 Jul 1973

Commencement provisions: s 15(2); Employment and Training Act 1973 (Commencement No 1) Order 1973, SI 1973/2063; Employment and Training Act 1973 (Commencement No 2) Order 1974, SI 1974/398; Employment and Training Act 1973 (Commencement No 3) Order 1974, SI 1974/1463; Employment and Training Act 1973 (Commencement No 4) Order 1975, SI 1975/689

Note that references to the Employment Service Agency and the Training Services Agency are repealed and accordingly no note is made of commencement dates relating to those Agencies

s 1	Repealed
2	Substituted by Employment Act 1988, s 25(1) (qv)
3	Repealed
4, 5	1 Jan 1974 (SI 1973/2063)
6, 7	Repealed
8–10	Substituted as from 1 Apr 1994 (ES) and 1 Apr 1995 (W) by Trade Union Reform and Employment Rights Act 1993, s 45 (qv); exception s 10(7) took effect from 30 Nov 1993
10A	Inserted as from 1 Apr 1994 (ES) and 1 Apr 1995 (W) by Trade Union Reform and Employment Rights Act 1993, s 46 (qv)
11	1 Jan 1974 (SI 1973/2063)
12(1)	1 Jan 1974 (SI 1973/2063)
(1A)	Inserted by Employment Act 1988, s 25(2), Sch 2, para 2 (qv)

Employment and Training Act 1973 (c 50)—*cont*

s 12(2)	Substituted by Social Security Act 1988, s 16, Sch 4, para 2 (qv)
(3)	Repealed
(4)	1 Jan 1974 (SI 1973/2063)
(5)	Repealed
(6)	1 Jan 1974 (SI 1973/2063)
13	1 Jan 1974 (SI 1973/2063)
14	See Schs 3, 4 below
15	1 Jan 1974 (SI 1973/2063)
Sch 1, 2	Repealed
3, para 1	1 Apr 1974 (SI 1974/398)
2	1 Oct 1974 (SI 1974/463)
3, 4	1 Jan 1974 (SI 1973/2063)
5, 6	Repealed
7(1)	1 Oct 1974 (SI 1974/463)
(2)	1 Apr 1974 (SI 1974/398)
(3)	1 Jan 1974 (SI 1973/2063)
8	1 Apr 1974 (SI 1974/398)
9, 10	Repealed
11(1)	1 Apr 1974 (SI 1974/398)
(2)	1 Jan 1974 (SI 1973/2063)
12–15	Repealed
4	1 Jan 1974 (repeals of or in Employment and Training Act 1948, ss 4, 20(2); Industrial Training Act 1964, ss 3(1), 6, 11, 13, Schedule, para 6(2); Chronically Sick and Disabled Persons Act 1970, s 13(2)) (SI 1973/2063) 1 Apr 1974 (repeal of Industrial Training Act 1964, ss 2(1)(f) (so far as relates to arrangements made by local education authorities in England and Wales), 5, 17) (SI 1973/2063) 1 Apr 1974 (repeals of or in Unemployment Insurance Act 1935, s 80; Employment and Training Act 1948, ss 3, 8–13, 14(2), 15 and Sch 1; Agriculture (Miscellaneous Provisions) Act 1949, s 8(5); London Government Act 1963, s 34; National Insurance (Industrial Injuries) Act 1965, s 72; Agriculture Act 1970, s 104; Local Government Act 1972, s 209) (SI 1974/398) 1 Oct 1974 (repeals of or in Disabled Persons (Employment) Act 1944, ss 2–4, 16 (in part); Employment and Training Act 1948, s 2(5), (8); National Insurance (Industrial Injuries) Act 1965, s 25(2)(c); Local Employment Act 1972, s 6) (SI 1974/1463) 16 May 1975 (repeal of Industrial Training Act 1964, s 2(1)(f) (so far as unrepealed)) (SI 1973/2063) 16 May 1975 (repeals of or in Employment and Training Act 1948 (so far as unrepealed); Criminal Justice Act 1967, in Sch 3, the entry relating to Employment and Training Act 1948; Employment Medical Advisory Service Act 1972, s 5(2)) (SI 1975/689)

Employment of Children Act 1973 (c 24)

RA: 23 May 1973

Commencement provisions: s 3(4)

Not in force

Fair Trading Act 1973 (c 41)

RA: 25 Jul 1973

Commencement provisions: s 140(3); Fair Trading Act 1973 (Commencement No 1) Order 1973, SI 1973/1545; Fair Trading Act 1973 (Commencement No 2) Order 1973, SI 1973/1652

s 1–28	1 Nov 1973 (SI 1973/1652)
29–32	14 Sep 1973 (SI 1973/1545)
33(1)	1 Nov 1973 (SI 1973/1652)
(2)(a), (b)	1 Nov 1973 (SI 1973/1652)
(c), (d)	14 Sep 1973 (SI 1973/1545)
34–42	1 Nov 1973 (SI 1973/1652)
43	Repealed
44–56	1 Nov 1973 (SI 1973/1652)
56A–56G	Inserted by Deregulation and Contracting Out Act 1994, s 7(1) (qv)
57(1)	1 Nov 1973 (SI 1973/1652)
(1A)	Inserted (retrospectively) by Deregulation and Contracting Out Act 1994, s 8
(2)–(4)	1 Nov 1973 (SI 1973/1652)
(5)–(7)	Inserted (retrospectively) by Deregulation and Contracting Out Act 1994, s 8
58–66	1 Nov 1973 (SI 1973/1652)
66A	Inserted by Companies Act 1989, s 150(1) (qv)
67–75	1 Nov 1973 (SI 1973/1652)
75A–75F	Inserted by Companies Act 1989, s 146 (qv)
75G–75K	Inserted by Companies Act 1989, s 147 (qv)
76–93	1 Nov 1973 (SI 1973/1652)
93A	Inserted by Companies Act 1989, s 148 (qv)
93B	Inserted by Companies Act 1989, s 151 (qv)
94	1 Nov 1973 (SI 1973/1652)
95–117	Repealed
118–123	14 Sep 1973 (SI 1973/1545)
124, 125	1 Nov 1973 (SI 1973/1652)
126	Repealed
127	1 Nov 1973 (SI 1973/1652)
128	Repealed
129	14 Sep 1973 (SI 1973/1545)
130, 131	1 Nov 1973 (SI 1973/1652)
132	14 Sep 1973 (SI 1973/1545)
133	1 Nov 1973 (SI 1973/1652)
134	14 Sep 1973 (SI 1973/1545)
135(1)	1 Nov 1973 (SI 1973/1652)
(2)(a), (b)	14 Sep 1973 (SI 1973/1545)
(c), (d)	1 Nov 1973 (SI 1973/1652)
(3)	Repealed
136	Repealed
137	14 Sep 1973 (SI 1973/1545)
138, 139	1 Nov 1973 (SI 1973/1652)

Fair Trading Act 1973 (c 41)—*cont*

s 140	14 Sep 1973 (SI 1973/1545)
Sch 1–9	1 Nov 1973 (SI 1973/1652)
10	Repealed
11–13	1 Nov 1973 (SI 1973/1652)

Finance Act 1973 (c 51)

Budget Day: 6 Mar 1973

RA: 25 Jul 1973

See the note concerning Finance Acts at the front of this book

Fire Precautions (Loans) Act 1973 (c 11)

RA: 29 Mar 1973

29 Mar 1973 (RA)

Fuel and Electricity (Control) Act 1973 (c 67)

Whole Act repealed (note, however, that the Act remains partly in force in Northern Ireland, and remains in force in its application to the Channel Islands and the Isle of Man so long as it extends there by Order in Council)

Furnished Lettings (Rent Allowances) Act 1973 (c 6)

Whole Act repealed

Gaming (Amendment) Act 1973 (c 12)

RA: 18 Apr 1973

18 Apr 1973 (RA)

Government Trading Funds Act 1973 (c 63)

RA: 25 Oct 1973

25 Oct 1973 (RA)

Guardianship Act 1973 (c 29)

RA: 5 Jul 1973

Commencement provisions: s 15(3); Guardianship Act 1973 (Commencement No 1) Order 1974, SI 1974/695; Guardianship Act 1973 (Commencement No 2) Order 1974, SI 1974/836

8 May 1974 (SI 1974/695, SI 1974/836)

Whole Act repealed (EW); whole Act prospectively repealed (S) by Children (Scotland) Act 1995, s 105(5), Sch 5; any order made under s 105(1), (2) of the 1995 Act bringing the prospective repeal into force will be noted to that Act in the service to this work

Hallmarking Act 1973 (c 43)

RA: 25 Jul 1973

Commencement provisions: s 24(2)

s 1–12	1 Jan 1975 (s 24(2))
13	1 Jan 1974 (s 24(2))
14–24	1 Jan 1975 (s 24(2))
Sch 1–3	1 Jan 1975 (s 24(2))
4	1 Jan 1974 (s 24(2))
5–7	1 Jan 1975 (s 24(2))

Heavy Commercial Vehicles (Controls and Regulations) Act 1973 (c 44)

Whole Act repealed

Housing (Amendment) Act 1973 (c 5)

Whole Act repealed

Independent Broadcasting Authority Act 1973 (c 19)

Whole Act repealed (except as extended to the Isle of Man)

Insurance Companies Amendment Act 1973 (c 58)

RA: 25 Jul 1973

Commencement provisions: s 57(3)–(8) (repealed)[1]

s 1–49	Repealed
50, 51	25 Jul 1973 (RA)
52–56	Repealed
57(1)	25 Jul 1973 (RA)
(2)–(8)	Repealed
Sch 1–5	Repealed

[1] Provisions brought into force by s 57(3)–(8) are all repealed

International Cocoa Agreement Act 1973 (c 46)

RA: 25 Jul 1973

Commencement provisions: s 2(2); International Cocoa Agreement Act 1973 (Commencement) Order 1973, SI 1973/1617

1 Oct 1973 (SI 1973/1617)

International Sugar Organisation Act 1973 (c 68)

RA: 19 Dec 1973

19 Dec 1973 (RA)

Land Compensation Act 1973 (c 26)

RA: 23 May 1973

Commencement provisions: s 89(2)

s 1–12	23 Jun 1973 (s 89(2))
12A	Inserted by Leasehold Reform, Housing and Urban Development Act 1993, s 187(1), Sch 21, para 5 (qv)
13	23 Jun 1973 (s 89(2))
14	Repealed
15–19	23 Jun 1973 (s 89(2))
20	23 May 1973 (RA)
20A	Inserted by Planning and Compensation Act 1991, s 70, Sch 15, para 5 (qv)
21–25	Repealed
26–29	23 May 1973 (RA)
29A	Inserted by Planning and Compensation Act 1991, s 69 (qv)
30	Substituted by Planning and Compensation Act 1991, s 68(3), (9) (qv)
31	Repealed
32–48	23 May 1973 (RA)
49	Repealed
50–52	23 May 1973 (RA)
52A	Inserted by Planning and Compensation Act 1991, s 63(2) (qv)
53–59	23 May 1973 (qv)
60	Repealed
61	23 May 1973 (RA)
62	Repealed
63	23 May 1973 (RA)
64–83	Repealed
84–89	23 May 1973 (RA)
Sch 1, 2	Repealed
3	23 May 1973 (RA)

Land Compensation (Scotland) Act 1973 (c 56)

RA: 25 Jul 1973

25 Jul 1973 (RA)

Law Reform (Diligence) (Scotland) Act 1973 (c 22)

Whole Act repealed

Local Government (Scotland) Act 1973 (c 65)

RA: 25 Oct 1973

Commencement provisions: s 238(2); Local Government (Scotland) Act 1973 (Commencement No 1) Order 1973, SI 1973/1886; Local Government (Scotland) Act 1973 (Commencement No 2) Order 1973, SI 1973/2181

Local Government (Scotland) Act 1973 (c 65)—*cont*

s 1, 2	20 Dec 1973 (SI 1973/2181); prospectively repealed by Local Government etc (Scotland) Act 1994, s 180(2), Sch 14[1]
3	20 Dec 1973 (sub-ss (1)–(5), (7)) and 16 May 1975 (sub-s (6)) (SI 1973/2181); prospectively repealed by Local Government etc (Scotland) Act 1994, s 180(2), Sch 14[1]
3A	Inserted by Local Government, Planning and Land Act 1980, s 27(1) (qv); prospectively repealed by Local Government etc (Scotland) Act 1994, s 180(2), Sch 14[1]
4, 5	20 Dec 1973 (SI 1973/2181); prospectively repealed by Local Government etc (Scotland) Act 1994, s 180(2), Sch 14[1]
6–10	Repealed
11(1)	12 Nov 1973 (SI 1973/1886); prospectively repealed by Local Government etc (Scotland) Act 1994, s 180(2), Sch 14[1]
(2)	Repealed
(3)	See Sch 3 below; prospectively repealed by Local Government etc (Scotland) Act 1994, s 180(2), Sch 14[1]
(4)	Repealed
12–19	20 Dec 1973 (SI 1973/2181)
20	20 Dec 1973 (SI 1973/2181); prospectively substituted by Local Government etc (Scotland) Act 1994, s 180(1), Sch 13, para 92(1), (4)[1]
21, 22	20 Dec 1973 (SI 1973/2181)
23	20 Dec 1973 (SI 1973/2181); prospectively substituted by Local Government etc (Scotland) Act 1994, s 180(1), Sch 13, para 92(1), (5)[1]
24–30	20 Dec 1973 (SI 1973/2181)
31(1)–(3)	20 Dec 1973 (SI 1973/2181)
(3A)	Prospectively inserted by Local Government etc (Scotland) Act 1994, s 180(1), Sch 13, para 92(1), (8)(b)[1]
(4)	20 Dec 1973 (SI 1973/2181); prospectively repealed by Local Government etc (Scotland) Act 1994, s 180, Sch 13, para 92(1), (8)(c), Sch 14[1]
32, 33	20 Dec 1973 (SI 1973/2181)
33A	Inserted by Local Government and Housing Act 1989, s 30(1) (qv)
34–43	20 Dec 1973 (SI 1973/2181)
44–45	Repealed
45A	Inserted by Local Government and Planning (Scotland) Act 1982, s 60(1)(b) (qv); repealed by Local Government and Housing Act 1989, s 194(4), Sch 12, Pt II (qv)
46–49	16 May 1975 (SI 1973/2181)
49A	Inserted by Local Government, Planning and Land Act 1980, s 26(3) (qv); repealed by Local Government and Housing Act 1989, s 194(4), Sch 12, Pt II (qv)
50	16 May 1975 (SI 1973/2181)
50A–50K	Inserted by Local Government (Access to Information) Act 1985, s 2(1) (qv)
51–53	20 Dec 1973 (SI 1973/2181)

Local Government (Scotland) Act 1973 (c 65)—*cont*

s 54	Repealed
55	20 Dec 1973 (SI 1973/2181)
56(1)	20 Dec 1973 (SI 1973/2181)
(2)	Substituted by Local Government and Planning (Scotland) Act 1982, s 32 (qv)
(3)–(5)	20 Dec 1973 (SI 1973/2181)
(6)	Substituted by Local Government Finance Act 1992, s 117(1), Sch 13, para 36 (subject to transitional provisions) (qv)
(7)	20 Dec 1973 (SI 1973/2181)
(8)–(10)	16 May 1975 (SI 1973/2181)
(11)–(13)	Repealed
(14), (15)	20 Dec 1973 (SI 1973/2181)
57–62	20 Dec 1973 (SI 1973/2181)
62A–62C	Inserted by Local Government etc (Scotland) Act 1994, s 20 (qv)
63	20 Dec 1973 (SI 1973/2181)
63A	Prospectively inserted by Local Government etc (Scotland) Act 1994, s 180(1), Sch 13, para 92(16)[1]
64(1)–(3)	20 Dec 1973 (SI 1973/2181)
(4), (5)	16 May 1975 (SI 1973/2181)
(6), (7)	20 Dec 1973 (SI 1973/2181)
65–68	20 Dec 1973 (SI 1973/2181)
69	16 May 1975 (SI 1973/2181)
70–74	20 Dec 1973 (SI 1973/2181)
74A	Repealed
75	16 May 1975 (SI 1973/2181)
76, 77	20 Dec 1973 (SI 1973/2181)
78	16 May 1975 (SI 1973/2181)
79–81	20 Dec 1973 (SI 1973/2181)
82, 83	16 May 1975 (SI 1973/2181)
84	20 Dec 1973 (SI 1973/2181)
85	16 May 1975 (SI 1973/2181)
86–89	20 Dec 1973 (SI 1973/2181)
90	Substituted by Local Government etc (Scotland) Act 1994, s 176 (qv)
90A	Inserted by Local Government and Planning (Scotland) Act 1982, s 11(2) (qv); prospectively repealed by Local Government etc (Scotland) Act 1994, s 180(2), Sch 14[1]
91	Repealed
92	16 May 1975 (SI 1973/2181)
93–96	20 Dec 1973 (SI 1973/2181)
97(1), (2)	20 Dec 1973 (SI 1973/2181)
(2A), (2B)	Inserted by National Health Service and Community Care Act 1990, s 36, Sch 7 (qv)
(3), (4)	20 Dec 1973 (SI 1973/2181)
(4A)–(4D)	Inserted by National Health Service and Community Care Act 1990, s 36, Sch 7 (qv)
(5), (6)	20 Dec 1973 (SI 1973/2181)
(6A)	Inserted by National Health Service and Community Care Act 1990, s 36, Sch 7 (qv)
(7)	20 Dec 1973 (SI 1973/2181)
97A, 97B	Inserted by Local Government Act 1988, s 35 (qv)
98–104	20 Dec 1973 (SI 1973/2181)

Local Government (Scotland) Act 1973 (c 65)—*cont*

s 104A	Inserted by National Health Service and Community Care Act 1990, s 36, Sch 7, para 11 (qv)
105, 106	20 Dec 1973 (SI 1973/2181)
107–108C	Repealed
109	16 May 1975 (SI 1973/2181); prospectively repealed by Local Government etc (Scotland) Act 1994, s 180(2), Sch 14[1]
110	20 Dec 1973 (SI 1973/2181); prospectively substituted by Local Government and Housing Act 1989, s 141(3); repealed by Local Government Finance Act 1992, s 117, Sch 13, para 38, Sch 14 (qv)
110A	Inserted by Local Government Finance Act 1988, s 137, Sch 12, Pt II, para 10; repealed, subject to transitional provisions, by Local Government Finance Act 1992, s 117, Sch13, para 38, Sch 14 (qv)
111	20 Dec 1973 (SI 1973/2181)
112–115	Repealed
116	20 Dec 1973 (SI 1973/2181); prospectively (sub-ss (1)–(5), (7), (8)) repealed by Local Government etc (Scotland) Act 1994, s 180(2), Sch 14[1]; repealed (sub-s (6)) 4 Jan 1995
117	Repealed
118	16 May 1975 (SI 1973/2181)
119–121	Repealed
122	See Sch 9 below
122A	Inserted by Local Government etc (Scotland) Act 1994, s 170 (qv)
123	16 May 1975 (SI 1973/2181); prospectively substituted by Local Government etc (Scotland) Act 1994, s 180(1), Sch 13, para 92(28)[1]
124	16 May 1975 (SI 1973/2181); prospectively substituted by Local Government etc (Scotland) Act 1994, s 31[1]
125	Repealed
126	16 May 1975 (SI 1973/2181); prospectively substituted by Local Government etc (Scotland) Act 1994, s 180(1), Sch 13, para 92(29)
127	16 May 1975 (SI 1973/2181); prospectively repealed by Local Government etc (Scotland) Act 1994, s 180(2), Sch 14[1]
128	16 May 1975 (SI 1973/2181)
129	Repealed
130	16 May 1975 (SI 1973/2181)
131, 132	16 May 1975 (SI 1973/2181); prospectively repealed by Local Government etc (Scotland) Act 1994, s 180(2), Sch 14[1]
133, 134	16 May 1975 (SI 1973/2181)
135(1)	16 May 1975 (SI 1973/2181)
(2)–(7)	20 Dec 1973 (SI 1973/2181)
(7A)	Prospectively inserted by Local Government etc (Scotland) Act 1994, s 180(1), Sch 13, para 92(34)(f)[1]
(8)	16 May 1975 (SI 1973/2181); prospectively repealed by Local Government etc (Scotland) Act 1994, s 180(2), Sch 14[1]

Local Government (Scotland) Act 1973 (c 65)—*cont*

s 135(9), (10)	16 May 1975 (SI 1973/2181)
	Section prospectively repealed by Environment Act 1995, s 120(3), Sch 24[2]
135A	Inserted by Natural Heritage (Scotland) Act 1991, s 27(1), Sch 10, para 6 (qv); prospectively repealed by Environment Act 1995, s 120(3), Sch 24[2]
136	16 May 1975 (SI 1973/2181); prospectively repealed by Control of Pollution Act 1974, s 109(2), Sch 4[3]
137, 138	16 May 1975 (SI 1973/2181)
139	Repealed
140	16 May 1975 (SI 1973/2181); prospectively repealed by Local Government etc (Scotland) Act 1994, s 180(2), Sch 14[1]
141	16 May 1975 (SI 1973/2181)
142, 143	16 May 1975 (SI 1973/2181); prospectively repealed by Local Government etc (Scotland) Act 1994, s 180(2), Sch 14[1]
144, 145	16 May 1975 (SI 1973/2181)
146(1)–(6)	16 May 1975 (SI 1973/2181)
(7)	20 Dec 1973 (SI 1973/2181); prospectively repealed by Local Government etc (Scotland) Act 1994, s 180(2), Sch 14[1]
(8)	16 May 1975 (SI 1973/2181)
(9)	20 Dec 1973 (SI 1973/2181)
(10)	16 May 1975 (SI 1973/2181)
147	Substituted by Local Government etc (Scotland) Act 1994, s 36 (qv)
148(1)	16 May 1975 (SI 1973/2181); prospectively repealed by Local Government etc (Scotland) Act 1994, s 180, Sch 13, para 92(40), Sch 14[1]
(2)–(7)	Repealed
(8)	See Sch 17 below
(9)	Repealed
149	Repealed
150	20 Dec 1973 (sub-s (3)) (SI 1973/2181) and 16 May 1975 (sub-ss (1), (2), (4)) (SI 1973/2181); sub-s (5) repealed; whole section prospectively substituted by Local Government etc (Scotland) Act 1973, s 180(1), Sch 13, para 92(43)[1]
151, 152	Repealed
153, 154	16 May 1975 (SI 1973/2181)
154A, 154B	Inserted by Local Government and Planning (Scotland) Act 1982, s 7 (qv); prospectively repealed by Local Government etc (Scotland) Act 1994, s 180(2), Sch 14[1]
155, 156	16 May 1975 (SI 1973/2181)
157	16 May 1975 (SI 1973/2181); repealed (1 Dec 1994) by Deregulation and Contracting Out Act 1994, s 81(1), Sch 17, and (prospectively) by Local Government etc (Scotland) Act 1994, s 180(2), Sch 14[1]
158	Repealed
159	16 May 1975 (SI 1973/2181); prospectively repealed by Local Government etc (Scotland) Act 1994, s 180(2), Sch 14[1]
160	Repealed

Local Government (Scotland) Act 1973 (c 65)—*cont*

s 161	16 May 1975 (SI 1973/2181); prospectively repealed by Local Government etc (Scotland) Act 1994, s 180(2), Sch 14[1]
162	Repealed
163	16 May 1975 (SI 1973/2181)
164	Repealed
165	20 Dec 1973 (SI 1973/2181)
166	16 May 1975 (SI 1973/2181)
167	Repealed
168	16 May 1975 (SI 1973/2181); prospectively repealed by Local Government etc (Scotland) Act 1994, s 180, Sch 13, para 92(51), Sch 14[1]
169, 170	16 May 1975 (SI 1973/2181)
170A, 170B	Inserted by Electricity Act 1989, s 102, Sch 13 (qv)
171	16 May 1975 (SI 1973/2181)
171A–171C	Inserted by Local Government etc (Scotland) Act 1994, s 171 (qv)
172	20 Dec 1973 (sub-s (2)) (SI 1973/2181) and 16 May 1975 (sub-ss (1), (3), (4)) (SI 1973/2181); prospectively substituted by Local Government etc (Scotland) Act 1994, s 180(1), Sch 13, para 92(57)[1]
173, 174	16 May 1975 (SI 1973/2181); prospectively repealed by Local Government etc (Scotland) Act 1994, s 180(2), Sch 14[1]
175	20 Dec 1973 (SI 1973/2181)
176, 177	16 May 1975 (SI 1973/2181); prospectively repealed by Local Government etc (Scotland) Act 1994, s 180(2), Sch 14[1]
178	Repealed
179	Substituted by Local Government and Planning (Scotland) Act 1982, s 66(2), Sch 3, para 24 (qv); prospectively repealed by Local Government etc (Scotland) Act 1994, s 180(2), Sch 14[1]
180	Repealed
181–183	16 May 1975 (SI 1973/2181); prospectively repealed by Local Government etc (Scotland) Act 1994, s 180(2), Sch 14[1]
184	16 May 1975 (SI 1973/2181)
185, 186	Repealed
187	16 May 1975 (SI 1973/2181)
188	16 May 1975 (SI 1973/2181); prospectively substituted by Local Government etc (Scotland) Act 1994, s 180(1), Sch 13, para 92(58)[1]
189	16 May 1975 (SI 1973/2181)
190–197	20 Dec 1973 (SI 1973/2181)
198, 199	16 May 1975 (SI 1973/2181)
200	16 May 1975 (SI 1973/2181); prospectively repealed by Environment Act 1995, s 120(3), Sch 24[2]
201, 202	16 May 1975 (SI 1973/2181)
202A–202C	Inserted by Civic Government (Scotland) Act 1982, ss 110(3), 137(2) (qv)
203, 204	16 May 1975 (SI 1973/2181)
205	Repealed
206, 207	16 May 1975 (SI 1973/2181)
208	20 Dec 1973 (SI 1973/2181)
209, 210	16 May 1975 (SI 1973/2181)

Local Government (Scotland) Act 1973 (c 65)—*cont*

s 210A	Inserted by Housing and Planning Act 1986, s 53, Sch 11, Pt II, para 39(4) (qv)
211–213	16 May 1975 (SI 1973/2181)
214	See Sch 27 below
215–217	20 Dec 1973 (SI 1973/2181)
218–221	Repealed
222, 223	20 Dec 1973 (SI 1973/2181); prospectively repealed by Local Government etc (Scotland) Act 1994, s 180(2), Sch 14[1]
224	12 Nov 1973 (SI 1973/1886); prospectively repealed by Local Government etc (Scotland) Act 1994, s 180(2), Sch 14[1]
225	20 Dec 1973 (sub-ss (1)–(7), (9), (10)) and 16 May 1975 (sub-s (8)) (SI 1973/2181); prospectively repealed by Local Government etc (Scotland) Act 1994, s 180(2), Sch 14[1]
226	20 Dec 1973 (SI 1973/2181); prospectively repealed by Local Government etc (Scotland) Act 1994, s 180(2), Sch 14[1]
227, 228	16 May 1975 (SI 1973/2181)
229	Repealed
230	20 Dec 1973 (SI 1973/2181); prospectively repealed by Local Government etc (Scotland) Act 1994, s 180(2), Sch 14[1]
231, 232	20 Dec 1973 (SI 1973/2181)
233	12 Nov 1973 (SI 1973/1886)
234–236	20 Dec 1973 (SI 1973/2181)
237(1)	See Sch 29 below
237(2)	20 Dec 1973 (SI 1973/2181)
238	20 Dec 1973 (SI 1973/2181)
Sch 1	20 Dec 1973 (SI 1973/2181); prospectively repealed by Local Government etc (Scotland) Act 1994, s 180(2), Sch 14[1]
2	12 Nov 1973 (SI 1973/1886); prospectively repealed by Local Government etc (Scotland) Act 1994, s 180(2), Sch 14[1]
3, para 1	16 May 1975 (SI 1973/2181)
2–18	Repealed
19	16 May 1975 (SI 1973/2181)
20–23	Repealed
4	20 Dec 1973 (SI 1973/2181)
5	20 Dec 1973 (SI 1973/2181); prospectively substituted by Local Government etc (Scotland) Act 1994, s 180(1), Sch 13, para 92(67)[1]
6, 7	20 Dec 1973 (SI 1973/2181)
7A	Inserted by Local Government (Access to Information) Act 1985, s 1(2), Sch 1, Pt II (qv)
8	20 Dec 1973 (SI 1973/2181)
9, para 1, 2	16 May 1975 (SI 1973/2181)
3–5	Repealed
6, 7	16 May 1975 (SI 1973/2181)
8	Repealed
9, 10	16 May 1975 (SI 1973/2181)
11	Repealed
12	16 May 1975 (SI 1973/2181)
13–15	Repealed

Local Government (Scotland) Act 1973 (c 65)—*cont*

Sch 9, para 16–43	16 May 1975 (SI 1973/2181)
44	20 Dec 1973 (in relation to regional and islands councils) (SI 1973/2181)
	16 May 1975 (otherwise) (SI 1973/2181)
45, 46	Repealed
47–52	16 May 1975 (SI 1973/2181)
53	16 May 1975 (SI 1973/2181); prospectively repealed by Local Government etc (Scotland) Act 1994, s 180(2), Sch 14[1]
54	20 Dec 1973 (in relation to any financial year commencing on or after 16 May 1975) (SI 1973/2181)
	16 May 1975 (otherwise) (SI 1973/2181)
55–57	16 May 1975 (SI 1973/2181)
58	20 Dec 1973 (in relation to any financial year commencing on or after 16 May 1975) (SI 1973/2181)
	16 May 1975 (otherwise) (SI 1973/2181)
59–61	16 May 1975 (SI 1973/2181)
62(a)	16 May 1974 (SI 1973/2181)
(b)	16 May 1975 (SI 1973/2181)
63	16 May 1975 (SI 1973/2181)
64	Repealed
65	20 Dec 1973 (SI 1973/2181)
66–72	20 Dec 1973 (in relation to any financial year commencing on or after 16 May 1975) (SI 1973/2181)
	16 May 1975 (otherwise) (SI 1973/2181)
73, 74	Repealed
10	16 May 1975 (SI 1973/2181); prospectively repealed by Local Government etc (Scotland) Act 1994, s 180(2), Sch 14[1]
11	Repealed
12	16 May 1975 (SI 1973/2181)
13, 14	16 May 1975 (SI 1973/2181); prospectively repealed by Local Government etc (Scotland) Act 1994, s 180, Sch 13, para 92(71), (72), Sch 14[1]
15, 16	16 May 1975 (SI 1973/2181)
17, para 1	16 May 1975 (SI 1973/2181)
2	16 May 1975 (SI 1973/2181); prospectively repealed by Local Government etc (Scotland) Act 1994, s 180(2), Sch 14[1]
3–63	Repealed
64	16 May 1975 (SI 1973/2181); prospectively repealed by Water Act 1983, s 11(3), Sch 5, Pt I[4]
18, 19	16 May 1975 (SI 1973/2181)
20	16 May 1975 (SI 1973/2181); prospectively repealed by Local Government etc (Scotland) Act 1994, s 180(2), Sch 14[1]
21	16 May 1975 (SI 1973/2181)
22	16 May 1975 (SI 1973/2181); prospectively repealed by Local Government etc (Scotland) Act 1994, s 180, Sch 13, para 92(74), Sch 14[1]
23	16 May 1975 (SI 1973/2181)
24, para 1–24	Repealed
25–27	16 May 1975 (SI 1973/2181)
28, 29	Repealed
30–32	16 May 1975 (SI 1973/2181)

Local Government (Scotland) Act 1973 (c 65)—*cont*

Sch 24, para 33	Repealed
34	16 May 1975 (SI 1973/2181)
35	Repealed
36–45	16 May 1975 (SI 1973/2181)
46	Repealed
47	16 May 1975 (SI 1973/2181)
25, 26	16 May 1975 (SI 1973/2181)
27, para 1–5	16 May 1975 (SI 1973/2181)
6, 7	Repealed
8–14	16 May 1975 (SI 1973/2181)
15	Repealed
16–29	16 May 1975 (SI 1973/2181)
30–32	16 May 1975 (SI 1973/2181); prospectively repealed by Environment Act 1995, s 120(3), Sch 24[2]
33–36	16 May 1975 (SI 1973/2181)
37, 38	16 May 1975 (SI 1973/2181); prospectively repealed by Environment Act 1995, s 120(3), Sch 24[2]
39–49	16 May 1975 (SI 1973/2181)
50	Repealed
51–77	16 May 1975 (SI 1973/2181)
78	Repealed
79–89	16 May 1975 (SI 1973/2181)
90	Repealed
91–96	16 May 1975 (SI 1973/2181)
97, 98	Repealed
99, 100	16 May 1975 (SI 1973/2181)
101	Repealed
102–113	16 May 1975 (SI 1973/2181)
114, 115	Repealed
116–127	16 May 1975 (SI 1973/2181)
128	Repealed
129–131	16 May 1975 (SI 1973/2181)
132	Repealed
133–139	16 May 1975 (SI 1973/2181)
140	Repealed
141–143	16 May 1975 (SI 1973/2181)
144	Repealed
145–148	16 May 1975 (SI 1973/2181)
149, 150	Repealed
151, 152	16 May 1975 (SI 1973/2181)
153	Repealed
154, 155	16 May 1975 (SI 1973/2181)
156, 157	Repealed
158	16 May 1975 (SI 1973/2181)
159	16 May 1975 (SI 1973/2181); prospectively repealed by Local Government etc (Scotland) Act 1994, s 180(2), Sch 14[1]
160, 161	16 May 1975 (SI 1973/2181)
162, 163	Repealed
164	16 May 1975 (SI 1973/2181)
165	Repealed
166, 167	16 May 1975 (SI 1973/2181)
168–170	Repealed
171–179	16 May 1975 (SI 1973/2181)
180	16 May 1975 (SI 1973/2181); prospectively repealed by Local Government etc (Scotland) Act 1994, s 180(2), Sch 14[1]

Local Government (Scotland) Act 1973 (c 65)—*cont*

Sch 27, para 181		16 May 1975 (SI 1973/2181)
	182	16 May 1975 (SI 1973/2181); prospectively repealed by Local Government etc (Scotland) Act 1994, s 180(2), Sch 14[1]
	183, 184	16 May 1975 (SI 1973/2181)
	185	16 May 1975 (SI 1973/2181); prospectively repealed by Children (Scotland) Act 1995, s 105(4), (5), Sch 4, para 22(1), (4), Sch 5[5]
	186	16 May 1975 (SI 1973/2181)
	187	20 Dec 1973 (SI 1973/2181); prospectively repealed by Children (Scotland) Act 1995, s 105(4), (5), Sch 4, para 22(1), (4), Sch 5[5]
	188–190	Repealed
	191–196	16 May 1975 (SI 1973/2181)
	197	Repealed
	198–200	16 May 1975 (SI 1973/2181)
	201	Repealed
	202–206	16 May 1975 (SI 1973/2181)
	207	Repealed
	208–211	16 May 1975 (SI 1973/2181)
28		Repealed
29		20 Dec 1973 (repeals of or in Representation of the People Act 1949, s 55(6); Valuation and Rating (Scotland) Act 1956, s 1 (in relation to regional and islands councils); Local Government (Scotland) Act 1966, s 2(2)(b)) (SI 1973/2181) 1 Apr 1974 (repeals of or in Representation of the People Act 1949, s 173(3), (8), Sch 3; Representation of the People Act 1969, ss 12(2), 13(5), 14, Schs 1, 2) (SI 1973/2181) 16 May 1974 (repeals of Rating Act 1966, ss 5–8; Rate Rebate Act 1973) (SI 1973/2181) 16 May 1975 (otherwise) (SI 1973/2181)

[1] Any order(s) made under Local Government etc (Scotland) Act 1994, s 184(2), (3), bringing this prospective change into force will be noted to that Act in the service to this work

[2] Any order(s) made under Environment Act 1995, s 125(3), bringing the prospective repeals into force will be noted to that Act in the service to this work

[3] Any order made under Control of Pollution Act 1974, s 109(2), bringing the prospective repeal into force will be noted to that Act in the service to this work

[4] Any order made under Water Act 1983, s 11(5), bringing the prospective repeal into force will be noted to that Act in the service to this work

[5] Any order(s) made under Children (Scotland) Act 1995, s 105, bringing the prospective repeals into force will be noted to that Act in the service to this work

London Cab Act 1973 (c 20)

RA: 23 May 1973

23 May 1973 (RA)

Maplin Development Act 1973 (c 64)

Whole Act repealed

Matrimonial Causes Act 1973 (c 18)

RA: 23 May 1973

Commencement provisions: s 55(2); Matrimonial Causes Act 1973 (Commencement) Order 1973, SI 1973/1972

1 Jan 1974 (SI 1973/1972)

National Health Service Reorganisation Act 1973 (c 32)

Whole Act repealed (S), subject to saving for certain amendments in Sch 4; *whole Act repealed (EW)*, subject to saving for s 44

National Insurance and Supplementary Benefit Act 1973 (c 42)

Whole Act repealed

National Theatre and Museum of London Act 1973 (c 2)

Whole Act repealed

Nature Conservancy Council Act 1973 (c 54)

RA: 25 Jul 1973

Commencement provisions: s 1(7) (repealed); Nature Conservancy Council (Appointed Day) Order 1973, SI 1973/1721

Whole Act repealed except ss 1(3), (9), 5, Sch 1, paras 1, 2, 4, 8, 9, 11, 13, Sch 2 which came into force on 25 Jul 1973 (RA; but note that this Act for the most part took effect from 1 Nov 1973, the day appointed by SI 1973/1721 on and after which the Nature Conservancy Council (now dissolved) was to discharge its functions under the Act)

Northern Ireland Assembly Act 1973 (c 17)

RA: 3 May 1973

3 May 1973 (RA; but note that the Assembly had no legislative powers until 1 Jan 1974, when the Northern Ireland Constitution Act 1973, Pt II, came into force)

Northern Ireland Constitution Act 1973 (c 36)

RA: 18 Jul 1973

Commencement provisions: ss 2, 41(1), 43(5), (6); Northern Ireland Constitution Act 1973 (Commencement No 1) Order 1973, SI 1973/1418; Northern Ireland Constitution (Devolution) Order 1973, SI 1973/2162

s 1–3	18 Jul 1973 (s 43(5))
4–16	1 Jan 1974 (SI 1973/2162)
17–23	1 Sep 1973 (SI 1973/1418)
24–43	18 Jul 1973 (s 43(5))
Sch 1–3	18 Jul 1973 (s 43(5))
4	1 Jan 1974 (SI 1973/2162)

Northern Ireland Constitution Act 1973 (c 36)—*cont*

Sch 5	18 Jul 1973 (s 43(5))
6, Pt I	18 Jul 1973 (s 41(1)(a))
II	1 Jan 1974 (s 41(1)(b); SI 1973/2162)

Northern Ireland Constitution (Amendment) Act 1973 (c 69)

RA: 19 Dec 1973

19 Dec 1973 (RA)

Northern Ireland (Emergency Provisions) Act 1973 (c 53)

RA: 25 Jul 1973

Commencement provisions: s 30(1)–(3)

8 Aug 1973 (s 30(1))

Overseas Pensions Act 1973 (c 21)

RA: 23 May 1973

23 May 1973 (RA)

Pakistan Act 1973 (c 48)

Whole Act repealed

Pensioners' Payments and National Insurance Act 1973 (c 61)

RA: 25 Oct 1973

Commencement provisions: s 8(1); Pensioners' Payments and National Insurance Act 1973 (Commencement) Order 1973, SI 1973/1969

25 Oct 1973 (RA; note that the only provision brought into force by SI 1973/1969 is repealed)

Whole Act repealed partly prospectively (s 7 and the Schedule), by Social Security Act 1986, s 86(2), Sch 11; any order made under the Social Security Act 1986, s 88, bringing the prospective repeal of s 7 and the Schedule into force will be noted to that Act in the service to this work

Powers of Criminal Courts Act 1973 (c 62)

RA: 25 Oct 1973

Commencement provisions: s 60(2); Powers of Criminal Courts Act 1973 (Commencement No 1) Order 1974, SI 1974/941

1 Jul 1974 (SI 1974/941), except s 6(3)(b), (6)(b), (10) (repealed)

Prescription and Limitation (Scotland) Act 1973 (c 52)

RA: 25 Jul 1973

Commencement provisions: s 25(2)

s 1–8	25 Jul 1976 (s 25(2))
8A	Inserted by Prescription and Limitation (Scotland) Act 1984, s 1 (qv)
9–16	25 Jul 1976 (s 25(2))
16A	Inserted by Consumer Protection Act 1987, s 6, Sch 1, Pt II, para 9 (qv)
17, 18	Substituted for original ss 17–19 by Prescription and Limitation (Scotland) Act 1984, ss 2, 5(1) (qv)
18A	Inserted by Law Reform (Miscellaneous Provisions) (Scotland) Act 1985, s 12(2) (qv)
19A	Inserted by Law Reform (Miscellaneous Provisions) (Scotland) Act 1980, s 23(a) (qv)
20, 21	Repealed
22	Substituted by Prescription and Limitation (Scotland) Act 1984, s 3 (qv)
22A–22D	Inserted by Consumer Protection Act 1987, s 6, Sch 1, Pt II, para 10 (qv)
23	Repealed
23A	Inserted by Prescription and Limitation (Scotland) Act 1984, ss 4, 5(2) (qv)
24, 25	25 Jul 1973 (s 25(2))
Sch 1–3	25 Jul 1976 (s 25(2))
4, Pt I	25 Jul 1976 (s 25(2))
II	25 Jul 1973 (s 25(2))
5, Pt I	25 Jul 1976 (s 25(2))
II	25 Jul 1973 (s 25(2))

Protection of Aircraft Act 1973 (c 47)

Whole Act repealed

Protection of Wrecks Act 1973 (c 33)

RA: 18 Jul 1973

18 Jul 1973 (RA)

Rate Rebate Act 1973 (c 28)

Whole Act repealed

Sea Fish Industry Act 1973 (c 3)

Whole Act repealed

Sea Fisheries (Shellfish) Act 1973 (c 30)

RA: 5 Jul 1973

Commencement provisions: s 2(2)

1 May 1974 (s 2(2))

Social Security Act 1973 (c 38)

RA: 18 Jul 1973

Commencement provisions: s 101(2); Social Security Act 1973 (Commencement) Order 1973, SI 1973/1249; Social Security Act 1973 (Commencement No 2) Order 1973, SI 1973/1433; Social Security Act 1973 (Commencement No 3) Order 1974, SI 1974/164; Social Security Act 1973 (Commencement No 4) Order 1974, SI 1974/823; Social Security Act 1973 (Commencement No 5) Order 1975, SI 1975/124

s 1–50	Repealed
51(1), (2)	Repealed
(3)(a)	5 Sept 1973 (for purposes of issue, cancellation, variation or surrender before, but with effect from dates not earlier than, 6 Apr 1975, of recognition certificates and for connected purposes) and 6 Apr 1975 (otherwise) (SI 1973/1433, as amended by SI 1974/823)
(b)	Repealed
(4)–(10)	Repealed
52–68	Repealed
69(1)–(6)	Repealed
(7)	*Not in force*
(8)	5 Sep 1973 (SI 1973/1433)
70–94	Repealed
95(1)	19 Jul 1973 (SI 1973/1249) (in relation to s 96) 28 Feb 1974 (otherwise) (SI 1974/164)
(2)	Repealed
(3)	28 Feb 1974 (SI 1974/164)
(4), (5)	Repealed
96(1)–(4)	19 July 1973 (SI 1973/1249)
(5)	Repealed
(6)	19 July 1973 (SI 1973/1249)
(7), (8)	Repealed
97(1), (2)	Repealed
(3)	Substituted by Social Security (Consequential Provisions) Act 1975, s 1(2), (3), Sch 1, Pt I, Sch 2, para 61 (qv)
(4)	Repealed
98(1)	5 Sep 1973 (SI 1973/1433)
(2)	Repealed
99(1)	Repealed
(2)	19 Jul 1973 (SI 1973/1249)
(3)	Repealed
(4)	19 Jul 1973 (SI 1973/1249)
(5)–(14)	Repealed
(15)–(17)	19 Jul 1973 (SI 1973/1249)
(18)	Repealed
100	See Schs 26, 27, 28 below

Social Security Act 1973 (c 38)—*cont*

s 101	19 Jul 1973 (SI 1973/1249)
Sch 1–26	Repealed
27, Pt I, para 1–5	Repealed
6	6 Apr 1975 (SI 1974/164)
7–9	Repealed
10	6 Apr 1975 (SI 1974/164)
11–14	Repealed or spent
15	6 Apr 1975 (SI 1974/164)
16	Spent
17	6 Apr 1975 (SI 1974/164)
18	Repealed
19	6 Apr 1975 (SI 1974/164)
20–23	Repealed
24	6 Apr 1975 (except the words 'or premiums' and 'or premium') (SI 1974/164) *Not in force* (exception noted above)
25–63	Repealed
64	6 Apr 1975 (except the words 'or premiums' and 'or premium') (SI 1974/164) *Not in force* (exception noted above)
65–71	Repealed
72	6 Apr 1975 (SI 1974/164)
73–77	Repealed
78	6 Apr 1975 (except the words 'or premiums' and 'or premium') (SI 1974/164) *Not in force* (exception noted above)
79	Repealed
80	6 Apr 1975 (except the words 'or premiums' and 'or premium' in sub-paras (a), (b) respectively) (SI 1974/164) *Not in force* (exception noted above)
81–84	Repealed
85	*Not in force*
86, 87	Repealed
88	*Not in force*
89–95	Repealed
96	6 Apr 1975 (SI 1974/164)
97, 98	Spent
Pt II, para 99–103	Repealed
104	6 Apr 1975 (SI 1974/164)
105, 106	Repealed
107	6 Apr 1975 (SI 1974/164)
108, 109	Repealed
110	Omitted from Queen's Printer's copy of the Act
111–120	Repealed
121	6 Apr 1975 (SI 1974/164)
122–176	Repealed or spent
28	28 Feb 1974/1 Apr 1974/1 Apr 1975/1 Apr 1976 (as provided by SI 1974/164) (entries relating to National Insurance Act 1965, ss 83(1)(c), (2)–(6), 84, 86, 87, 104(3), Sch 10; National Insurance (Industrial Injuries) Act 1965, ss 59(2)–(4), 60; National Insurance Act (Northern Ireland) 1966, ss 81(1)(c), (2)–(6), 82, 84; National Insurance (Industrial Injuries) Act (Northern Ireland) 1966, ss 57(2)–(4), 58) (SI 1974/164)

Social Security Act 1973 (c 38)—*cont*

Sch 28—*cont*	6 Apr 1975 (remaining entries, except those specified below) (SI 1974/164)
	Not in force (entries relating to Superannuation and other Trust Funds (Validation) Act 1927, ss 1–8, 10, 11(2) from 'but save as aforesaid' onwards; Superannuation and other Trust Funds (Validation) Act (Northern Ireland) 1928 (repealed))
	Repealed (entries relating to National Insurance Act 1967, s 4(4); National Insurance Act (Northern Ireland) 1967, s 5(4))

Statute Law (Repeals) Act 1973 (c 39)

RA: 18 Jul 1973

18 Jul 1973 (RA)

Statute Law Revision (Northern Ireland) Act 1973 (c 55)

RA: 25 Jul 1973

25 Jul 1973 (RA)

Succession (Scotland) Act 1973 (c 25)

RA: 23 May 1973

23 May 1973 (RA)

Supply of Goods (Implied Terms) Act 1973 (c 13)

RA: 18 Apr 1973

Commencement provisions: s 18(3)

s 1–7	Repealed
8–10	Substituted by Consumer Credit Act 1974, s 192(3)(a), Sch 4, para 35 (qv)
11	Substituted by Consumer Credit Act 1974, s 192(3)(a), Sch 4, para 35 (qv); section (as substituted) re-numbered sub-s (1) and sub-s (2) added by Sale and Supply of Goods Act 1994, s 7(1), Sch 2, para 4(1), (5) (qv)
11A	Inserted (E, W, NI) by Sale and Supply of Goods Act 1994, s 7(1), Sch 2, para 4(1), (6), (qv)
12	Substituted by Sale and Supply of Goods Act 1994, s 7(1), Sch 2, para 4(1), (7) (qv)
12A	Inserted (S) by Sale and Supply of Goods Act 1994, s 7(1), Sch 2, para 4(1), (8) (qv)
13	Repealed
14, 15	Substituted by Consumer Credit Act 1974, s 192(3)(a), Sch 4, para 36 (qv)
16–18	18 May 1973 (s 18(3))

Ulster Defence Regiment Act 1973 (c 34)

Whole Act repealed

Water Act 1973 (c 37)

RA: 18 Jul 1973

Commencement provisions: s 39(1)

s 1–33	Repealed (for savings in respect of ss 1–3, 5, 7–13, 14(1)–(3), (5), (8), 15–17, 20–22, 24, 24A, 26(1), 27–31, 32A, 33, see Water Act 1989, s 190(2), Sch 26)
34(1)	Repealed with savings by Water Act 1989, s 190(3), Sch 27, Pt II (qv)
(2)	18 Jul 1973 (RA); prospectively repealed by Water Act 1989, s 190(3), Sch 27, Pt II[1]
(3)	Repealed with savings by Water Act 1989, s 190(3), Sch 27, Pt II (qv)
35(1), (2)	Repealed
(3)	18 Jul 1973 (RA); prospectively repealed by Water Act 1989, s 190(3), Sch 27, Pt II[1]
36(1), (2)	18 Jul 1973 (RA; prospectively repealed by Water Act 1989, s 190(3), Sch 27, Pt II[1]
(3)	Repealed
37–39	Repealed
40(1)	18 Jul 1973 (RA)
(2)	See Sch 8 below
(3)	See Sch 9 below
(4), (5)	18 Jul 1973 (RA)
(6)	Repealed
Sch 1–5	Repealed (for savings in respect of Sch 3, Pts I, III, Sch 4A, see Water Act 1989, s 190(2), Sch 26, Pt I, para 1, Pt II, para 15, Pt VIII, para 52)
6, Pt I	Repealed
Pt II	18 Jul 1973 (RA); prospectively repealed by Water Act 1989, s 190(3), Sch 27, Pt II[1]
7	Repealed
8, 9	1 Apr 1974 (s 39(1))

[1] Any order(s) made under Water Act 1989, s 194(4), bringing the prospective repeal into force will be noted to that Act in the service to this work

1974

Appropriation Act 1974 (c 2)
Whole Act repealed

Appropriation (No 2) Act 1974 (c 31)
Whole Act repealed

Biological Weapons Act 1974 (c 6)
RA: 8 Feb 1974

8 Feb 1974 (RA)

Carriage of Passengers by Road Act 1974 (c 35)
RA: 31 Jul 1974

Commencement provisions: s 14(5)

s 1–6	*Not in force*
7–14	31 Jul 1974 (RA)
Schedule	*Not in force*

Charlwood and Horley Act 1974 (c 11)
RA: 8 Feb 1974

8 Feb 1974 (RA)

Church of England (Worship and Doctrine) Measure 1974 (No 3)
RA: 12 Dec 1974

Commencement provisions: s 7(2); Instrument of the Archbishops of 22 Jul 1975

1 Sep 1975 (Instrument of the Archbishops of 22 Jul 1975)

Consolidated Fund Act 1974 (c 1)
Whole Act repealed

Consolidated Fund (No 2) Act 1974 (c 12)
Whole Act repealed

Consolidated Fund (No 3) Act 1974 (c 15)
Whole Act repealed

Consolidated Fund (No 4) Act 1974 (c 57)

Whole Act repealed

Consumer Credit Act 1974 (c 39)

RA: 31 Jul 1974

Commencement provisions: s 192(2), (4); Consumer Credit Act 1974 (Commencement No 1) Order 1975, SI 1975/2123; Consumer Credit Act 1974 (Commencement No 2) Order 1977, SI 1977/325; Consumer Credit Act 1974 (Commencement No 3) Order 1977, SI 1977/802; Consumer Credit Act 1974 (Commencement No 4) Order 1977, SI 1977/2163; Consumer Credit Act 1974 (Commencement No 5) Order 1979, SI 1979/1685; Consumer Credit Act 1974 (Commencement No 6) Order 1980, SI 1980/50; Consumer Credit Act 1974 (Commencement No 7) Order 1981, SI 1981/280; Consumer Credit Act 1974 (Commencement No 8) Order 1983, SI 1983/1551; Consumer Credit Act 1974 (Commencement No 9) Order 1984, SI 1984/436; Consumer Credit Act 1974 (Commencement No 10) Order 1989, SI 1989/1128

With the exception of the provisions specified below, this Act came into force on 31 Jul 1974 (RA).

The orders mentioned here amend Sch 3 to the Act and appoint days as shown in the following table:—

Sch 3 para	*Subject matter*	*Appointed day*	*Order*
Sch 3, para 1	Consumer credit and consumer hire agreements made on and after the appointed day to be regulated agreements	1 Apr 1977	SI 1977/325
3	S 19(3)	19 May 1985	SI 1983/1551
5	S 21 not to apply to any description of business before the day appointed in relation to that description of business	1 Oct 1977 in the case of all consumer credit and consumer hire businesses except those consumer credit businesses carried on by individuals in the course of which only regulated consumer credit agreements for credit not exceeding £30 are made	SI 1977/325 (substituted by Consumer Credit Act 1974 (Commencement No 10) Order 1989, SI 1989/1128, art 3, Schedule)
		31 Jul 1989 in the case of any consumer credit business which is carried on by an individual and in the course of which only regulated consumer credit agreements for fixed-sum credit or running-account credit not exceeding £30 are made (provision amended but retaining 1977 references)	SI 1989/1128

Consumer Credit Act 1974 (c 39)—*cont*

Sch 3 para	*Subject matter*	*Appointed day*	*Order*
Sch 3, para 6	Ss 35, 36	2 Feb 1976	SI 1975/2123
7	S 40 not to apply to a regulated agreement made in the course of any business before the day specified or referred to in para 5(1) in relation to the description of business in question	See entry to para 5	SI 1977/325 (substituted by art 3, Sch 1 thereof)
8	Pt IV of the Act not to apply to any advertisement published before the day appointed for the purposes of this paragraph	6 Oct 1980	SI 1980/50
9	S 49	1 Oct 1977	SI 1977/802
10	S 50	1 Jul 1977	SI 1977/802
11	S 51	1 Jul 1977	SI 1977/802
12	S 56 to apply to regulated agreements where negotiations begin after the appointed day	16 May 1977	SI 1977/325
13	Ss 57–59, 61–65, 67–73	19 May 1985	SI 1983/1551
14	S 66	19 May 1985	SI 1983/1551
15	S 75 in relation to regulated agreements made on or after the appointed day	1 Jul 1977	SI 1977/802
16–18	Ss 76–81	19 May 1985	SI 1983/1551
19	S 82	1 Apr 1977	SI 1977/325
20–38	Ss 83–111	19 May 1985	SI 1983/1551
39	Ss 114–122 in respect of articles taken in pawn under a regulated consumer credit agreement only	19 May 1985	SI 1983/1551
40	Ss 123, 125	19 May 1985	SI 1984/436
41	S 126	19 May 1985	SI 1983/1551
42	Ss 137–140	16 May 1977	SI 1977/325
43	Pt IX (ss 127–136, 141–144)	19 May 1985	SI 1983/1551
44	S 21	3 Aug 1976	SI 1975/2123
		3 Aug 1976	SI 1977/325
		1 Jul 1978	SI 1977/2163
45	S 148(1)	3 Aug 1976	SI 1975/2123
		3 Aug 1976	SI 1977/325
		1 Jul 1978	SI 1977/2163
46	S 149	1 Jul 1978	SI 1977/2163
47	S 151(1), (2) not to apply to any advertisement published before the day appointed for the purposes of this paragraph	6 Oct 1980	SI 1980/50
48	Ss 157, 158 to apply to requests for information received on and after the appointed day	16 May 1977	SI 1977/325

The amendments made by the following paragraphs of Sch 4 take effect on the days appointed as shown below:—

Sch 4 para	*Subject matter*	*Appointed day*	*Order*
Sch 4, para 1	Amendment of Bills of Sale Act (1878) Amendment Act 1882	19 May 1985	SI 1983/1551
2	Amendment of Factors Act 1889	19 May 1985	SI 1983/1551
3, 4	Repealed		
5	Amendment of Law of Distress Amendment Act 1908 (except in relation to consumer hire agreements)	19 May 1985	SI 1983/1551

Consumer Credit Act 1974 (c 39)—*cont*

Sch 4 para	*Subject matter*	*Appointed day*	*Order*
Sch 4, para 6	Repealed		
7, 8	Amendment of Compensation (Defence) Act 1939	19 May 1985	SI 1983/1551
9	Amendment of Liability for War Damage (Miscellaneous Provisions) Act 1939	19 May 1985	SI 1983/1551
10	Repealed		
11	Amendment of Rag Flock and Other Filling Materials Act 1951	19 May 1985	SI 1983/1551
12–14	Amendment of Reserve and Auxiliary Forces (Protection of Civil Interests) Act 1951	19 May 1985	SI 1983/1551
15, 16	Repealed		
17	Spent		
18–21	Repealed		
22	Amendment of Hire-Purchase Act 1964	19 May 1985	SI 1983/1551
23	Amendment of Emergency Laws (Re-enactments and Repeals) Act 1964	19 May 1985	SI 1983/1551
24–26	Amendment of Trading Stamps Act 1964	6 Oct 1980	SI 1980/50
27	Repealed		
28	Amendment of Trade Descriptions Act 1968	1 Apr 1977	SI 1977/325
29	Repealed		
30, 31	Amendment of Administration of Justice Act 1970	19 May 1985	SI 1983/1551
32, 33	Repealed		
34	Spent		
35, 36	Amendment of Supply of Goods (Implied Terms) Act 1973	19 May 1985	SI 1983/1551
37	Amendment of Fair Trading Act 1973	19 May 1985	SI 1983/1551
38	Repealed		
39	Amendment of Bills of Sale (Ireland) Act (1879) Amendment Act 1883	19 May 1985	SI 1983/1551
40	Amendment of Liability for War Damage (Miscellaneous Provisions) Act (Northern Ireland) 1939	19 May 1985	SI 1983/1551
41, 42	Repealed		
43–45	Amendment of Trading Stamps Act (Northern Ireland) 1965	6 Oct 1980	SI 1980/50
46, 47	Repealed		
48	Repealed		
49	Amendment of Hire-Purchase Act (Northern Ireland) 1966	19 May 1985	SI 1983/1551
50	Repealed		
51	Amendment of miscellaneous transferred excise duties Act (Northern Ireland) 1972	1 Oct 1977	SI 1977/325

Consumer Credit Act 1974 (c 39)—*cont*

The following repeals take effect on the days appointed and to the extent shown below:—

UNITED KINGDOM (Sch 5, Pt I)

Short title	*Extent of repeal*	*Agreements in relation to which repeal not to have effect*	*Day appointed for coming into operation*	*Order*
Statutory Declarations Act 1835	S 12		19 May 1985	SI 1983/1551
Metropolitan Police Act 1839	S 50		19 May 1985	SI 1983/1551
Police Courts (Metropolis) Act 1839	In s 27 the words 'pawned, pledged' and the words 'or of any person who shall have advanced money upon the credit of such goods'. In s 28 the words 'pawned, pledged or' (in each place)		19 May 1985	SI 1983/1551
Pawnbrokers Act 1872	The whole Act, so far as unrepealed	Pledges taken in pawn before 19 May 1985	19 May 1985	SI 1983/1551
	S 13		6 Oct 1980	SI 1980/50
	Ss 37, 44 and Sch 6		1 Aug 1977	SI 1977/325
	In s 52, the words 'or by the refusal of a certificate for a licence'		1 Aug 1977	SI 1977/325
Commissioners for Oaths Act 1891	In s 1, the words 'or the Pawnbrokers Act 1872'		19 May 1985	SI 1983/1551
Betting and Loans (Infants) Act 1892	Ss 2–4		1 Jul 1977	SI 1977/802
	S 6, except as far as it extends to Northern Ireland		1 Jul 1977	SI 1977/802
	In s 7, the definitions of 'indictment' and 'summary conviction'		1 Jul 1977	SI 1977/802
Burgh Police (Scotland) Act 1892	In s 453, the words 'and all offences committed against the provisions of the Pawnbrokers Act 1872'		19 May 1985	SI 1983/1551
Local Government Act 1894	S 27(1)(b)		1 Aug 1977	SI 1977/325
Police (Property) Act 1897	In s 1(1), the words 'or section thirty-four of the Pawnbrokers Act 1872'		19 May 1985	SI 1983/1551
Money-lenders Act 1900	The whole Act, so far as unrepealed	Agreements made with, or any loan made by or security taken by, a moneylender before 19 May 1985	19 May 1985	SI 1983/1551

Consumer Credit Act 1974 (c 39)—*cont*

Short title	*Extent of repeal*	*Agreements in relation to which repeal not to have effect*	*Day appointed for coming into operation*	*Order*
Money-lenders Act 1900—*cont*	S 1	Agreements made before 16 May 1977 which are not personal credit agreements	16 May 1977	SI 1977/325
	S 4		6 Oct 1980	SI 1980/50
	S 5		1 Jul 1977	SI 1977/802
Law of Distress Amendment Act 1908	In s 4(1) the words 'bill of sale, hire purchase agreement or'		19 May 1985	SI 1983/1551
Money-lenders Act 1927	The whole Act, so far as unrepealed	Agreements made with, or any loan made by or security taken by a money-lender before 19 May 1985 (except s 8)	19 May 1985	SI 1983/1551
	Ss 1–3, 4(1) and in s 4(2), the words 'the provisions of the last fore-going section and of'		1 Aug 1977	SI 1977/325
	S 4(2)	Moneylending transactions made before 27 Jan 1980	27 Jan 1980	SI 1979/1685
	S 4(3)		6 Oct 1980	SI 1980/50
	S 5(1), (2), (4), (5), (6)	Moneylending transactions made before 27 Jan 1980	27 Jan 1980	SI 1979/1685
	S 5(3)	Moneylending transactions made before 1 Oct 1977	1 Oct 1977	SI 1977/802
	Ss 6–8		27 Jan 1980	SI 1979/1685
	S 9	Moneylending transactions made before 27 Jan 1980	27 Jan 1980	SI 1979/1685
	S 10	Agreements made before 16 May 1977 which are not personal credit agreements	16 May 1977	SI 1977/325
	Ss 11–14		27 Jan 1980	SI 1979/1685
	In s 13(2), the words 'Without prejudice to the powers of a court under section one of the Moneylenders Act, 1900'	In the case of the said words in s 13(2), agreements made before 16 May 1977 which are not personal credit agreements	16 May 1977	SI 1977/325
	In s 14(1)(a), the words ', and the rate of interest charged shall not exceed the rate of twenty per cent. per annum'.		30 Mar 1981	SI 1981/280
	S 15(2)		27 Jan 1980	SI 1979/1685
	S 16		27 Jan 1980	SI 1979/1685
	S 18(a), (b), (c)		1 Aug 1977	SI 1977/325

Consumer Credit Act 1974 (c 39)—*cont*

Short title	*Extent of repeal*	*Agreements in relation to which repeal not to have effect*	*Day appointed for coming into operation*	*Order*
Children and Young Persons Act 1933	S 8		19 May 1985	SI 1983/1551
Children and Young Persons (Scotland) Act 1937	S 19		19 May 1985	SI 1983/1551
Compensation (Defence) Act 1939	In s 18(1) the words from 'the expression "hire purchase agreement"' to 'omitted'		19 May 1985	SI 1983/1551
Liability for War Damage (Miscellaneous Provisions) Act 1939	Ss 4, 6(b)		19 May 1985	SI 1983/1551
Law Reform (Miscellaneous Provisions) (Scotland) Act 1940	In s 4(2), paras (b), (c)		19 May 1985	SI 1983/1551
Limitation (Enemies and War Prisoners) Act 1945	In s 2, the words 'subsection (1) of section thirteen of the Moneylenders Act 1927'; in s 4, the words 'subsection (1) of section thirteen of the Moneylenders Act 1927'		19 May 1985	SI 1983/1551
Companies Act 1948	S 201(2)(c)		1 Aug 1977	SI 1977/325
Finance Act 1949	In s 15, sub-ss (1)–(3), (6)–(8A)		1 Aug 1977	SI 1977/325
Customs and Excise Act 1952	In s 313(1) the words 'or section 15 of the Finance Act 1949'		1 Aug 1977	SI 1977/325
Pawnbrokers Act 1960	The whole Act	Pledges taken in pawn before 19 May 1985	19 May 1985	SI 1983/1551
Finance Act 1961	S 11(1) from 'or section 15 of the Finance Act 1949' onwards		1 Aug 1977	SI 1977/325
Administration of Justice Act 1964	S 9(3)(b)		1 Aug 1977	SI 1977/325
Hire-Purchase Act 1964	The whole Act, except Pt III and s 37		19 May 1985	SI 1983/1551
Emergency Laws (Re-enactments and Repeals) Act 1964	S 1(4)		19 May 1985	SI 1983/1551

Consumer Credit Act 1974 (c 39)—*cont*

Short title	*Extent of repeal*	*Agreements in relation to which repeal not to have effect*	*Day appointed for coming into operation*	*Order*
Trading Stamps Act 1964	In s 10(1) the definition of 'purchase'		6 Oct 1980	SI 1980/50
Hire-Purchase Act 1965	The whole Act	Hire-purchase agreements, conditional sale agreements and credit-sale agreements or guarantees and indemnities relating to such agreements provided by a guarantor, before 19 May 1985, unless the agreement would have been a regulated agreement if made on that day	19 May 1985	SI 1983/1551
Hire-Purchase (Scotland) Act 1965	The whole Act	Hire-purchase agreements, conditional sale agreements and credit-sale agreements or guarantees and indemnities relating to such agreements provided by a guarantor, before 19 May 1985, unless the agreement would have been a regulated agreement if made on that day	19 May 1985	SI 1983/1551
Local Government Act 1966	In Sch 3, Pt II, the entries relating to s 37 of the Pawnbrokers Act 1872 and s 1(1) of the Moneylenders Act 1927		1 Aug 1977	SI 1977/325
Local Government (Scotland) Act 1966	In Sch 4, Pt II, the entries relating to s 37 of the Pawnbrokers Act 1872 and s 1(1) of the Moneylenders Act 1927		1 Aug 1977	SI 1977/325
Advertisements (Hire-Purchase) Act 1967	The whole Act		6 Oct 1980	SI 1980/50
Companies Act 1967	Ss 123–125		19 May 1985	SI 1983/1551
Theft Act 1968	In Sch 2, Pt III, the entry relating to the Pawnbrokers Act 1872		1 Aug 1977	SI 1977/325

Consumer Credit Act 1974 (c 39)—*cont*

Short title	*Extent of repeal*	*Agreements in relation to which repeal not to have effect*	*Day appointed for coming into operation*	*Order*
Decimal Currency Act 1969	In Sch 2, para 2		19 May 1985	SI 1983/1551
Post Office Act 1969	In Sch 4, para 31		19 May 1985	SI 1983/1551
Courts Act 1971	In Sch 9, Pt I, the entry relating to the Pawnbrokers Act 1872		19 May 1985	SI 1983/1551
	In Sch 9, Pt I, the entry relating to the Moneylenders Act 1927		1 Aug 1977	SI 1977/325
Local Government Act 1972	S 213(1)(a), (b), (3)		1 Aug 1977	SI 1977/325
Local Government (Scotland) Act 1973	In Sch 27, para 96		1 Aug 1977	SI 1977/325
	In Sch 29, the entry relating to the Finance Act 1949		1 Aug 1977	SI 1977/325

NORTHERN IRELAND (Sch 5, Pt II)

Short title	*Extent of repeal*	*Agreements in relation to which repeal not to have effect*	*Day appointed for coming into operation*	*Order*
Charitable Pawn Offices (Ireland) Act 1842	The whole Act		1 Oct 1977	SI 1977/325
Moneylenders Act (Northern Ireland) 1933	The whole Act, so far as unrepealed	Agreements made with, or any loan made by or security taken by, a moneylender before 19 May 1985 (except s 8)	19 May 1985	SI 1983/1551
	Ss 1–3, 4(1)		1 Aug 1977	SI 1977/325
	In s 4(2) the words 'the provisions of sub-s (1) of this section and of' and, in paragraph (a) the words 'followed by the words "licensed moneylender"'		1 Aug 1977	SI 1977/325
	S 4(2)	Moneylending transactions made before 27 Jan 1980	27 Jan 1980	SI 1979/1685
	S 4(3)		6 Oct 1980	SI 1980/50
	S 5(1), (2), (4)–(6)	Moneylending transactions made before 27 Jan 1980	27 Jan 1980	SI 1979/1685

Consumer Credit Act 1974 (c 39)—*cont*

Short title	*Extent of repeal*	*Agreements in relation to which repeal not to have effect*	*Day appointed for coming into operation*	*Order*
Moneylenders Act (Northern Ireland) 1933 —*cont*	S 5(3)	Moneylending transactions made before 1 Oct 1977	1 Oct 1977	SI 1977/802
	Ss 6–8		27 Jan 1980	SI 1979/1685
	S 9	Moneylending transactions made before 27 Jan 1980	27 Jan 1980	SI 1979/1685
	Ss 10, 11	Agreements made before 16 May 1977 which are not personal credit agreements	16 May 1977	SI 1977/325
	Ss 12–16		27 Jan 1980	SI 1979/1685
	In s 13(2), the words 'Without prejudice to the powers of a court under section one of the Moneylenders Act 1900'	In the case of the said words in s 13(2), agreements made before 16 May 1977 which are not personal credit agreements	16 May 1977	SI 1977/375
	In s 4(1)(a), the words ', and the rate of interest charged shall not exceed the rate of twenty per cent per annum'.		30 Mar 1981	SI 1981/280
	Sch 1		27 Jan 1980	SI 1979/1685
Liability for War Damage (Miscellaneous Provisions) Act (Northern Ireland) 1939	In s 5(1) the definition of 'hire-purchase agreement'		19 May 1985	SI 1983/1551
Agriculture Act (Northern Ireland) 1949	S 7(2)		19 May 1985	SI 1983/1551
Pawnbrokers Act (Northern Ireland) 1954	The whole Act, so far as unrepealed	Pledges taken in pawn before 19 May 1985	19 May 1985	SI 1983/1551
	Ss 5–9		1 Aug 1977	SI 1977/325
	S 11		6 Oct 1980	SI 1980/50
Betting and Lotteries Act (Northern Ireland) 1957	S 3(1)(j)		1 Aug 1977	SI 1977/325
Companies Act (Northern Ireland) 1960	S 192(3)(c)		1 Aug 1977	SI 1977/325
Trading Stamps Act (Northern Ireland) 1965	In s 9 the definition of 'purchase'		6 Oct 1980	SI 1980/50

Consumer Credit Act 1974 (c 39)—*cont*

Short title	*Extent of repeal*	*Agreements in relation to which repeal not to have effect*	*Day appointed for coming into operation*	*Order*
Hire-Purchase Act (Northern Ireland) 1966	The whole Act so far as unrepealed, except Pt VI and s 68	Hire-purchase agreements, conditional sale agreements and credit-sale agreements or guarantees and indemnities relating to such agreements provided by a guarantor, before 19 May 1985, unless the agreement would have been a regulated agreement if made on that day	19 May 1985	SI 1983/1551
	Pt V and Sch 4		6 Oct 1980	SI 1980/50
Increase of Fines Act (Northern Ireland) 1967	In Pt I of the Schedule the entries relating to ss 4(2), (3), 5(5) of the Moneylenders Act (Northern Ireland) 1933		6 Oct 1980	SI 1980/50
	In Pt I of the Schedule the entry relating to s 16(1) of the Moneylenders Act (Northern Ireland) 1933		19 May 1985	SI 1983/1551
Criminal Justice (Miscellaneous Provisions) Act (Northern Ireland) 1968	In Sch 2 the entry relating to s 5(5) of the Moneylenders Act (Northern Ireland) 1933		6 Oct 1980	SI 1980/50
	In Sch 2 the entry relating to s 16(1) of the Moneylenders Act (Northern Ireland) 1933		19 May 1985	SI 1983/1551
Theft Act (Northern Ireland) 1969	In Sch 2, the entry relating to the Pawnbrokers Act (Northern Ireland) 1954		1 Aug 1977	SI 1977/325
Industrial and Provident Societies Act (Northern Ireland) 1969	S 96		19 May 1985	SI 1983/1551
Money-lenders (Amendment) (Northern Ireland) 1969	The whole Act	Agreements made with, or any loan made by or security taken by, a moneylender before 19 May 1985	19 May 1985	SI 1983/1551

Consumer Credit Act 1974 (c 39)—*cont*

Short title	*Extent of repeal*	*Agreements in relation to which repeal not to have effect*	*Day appointed for coming into operation*	*Order*
Judgments (Enforcement) Act (Northern Ireland) 1969	In Sch 4 the amendments of the Hire Purchase Act (Northern Ireland) 1966		19 May 1985	SI 1983/1551
Licensing Act (Northern Ireland) 1971	S 2(5)(b)		1 Aug 1977	SI 1977/325
Miscellaneous	Pt VI		1 Oct 1977	SI 1977/325
	Pt VII		1 Aug 1977	SI 1977/325
Transferred Duties Act (Northern Ireland) 1972	In Sch 4 the entry relating to the Pawnbrokers Act (Northern Ireland) 1954		1 Aug 1977	SI 1977/325

Contingencies Fund Act 1974 (c 18)

RA: 23 May 1974

23 May 1974 (RA)

Control of Pollution Act 1974 (c 40)

RA: 31 Jul 1974

Commencement provisions: s 109(2); Control of Pollution Act 1974 (Commencement No 1) Order 1974, SI 1974/2039; Control of Pollution Act 1974 (Commencement No 2) Order 1974, SI 1974/2169; Control of Pollution Act 1974 (Commencement No 3) Order 1975, SI 1975/230; Control of Pollution Act 1974 (Commencement No 4) Order 1975, SI 1975/2118; Control of Pollution Act 1974 (Commencement No 5) Order 1976, SI 1976/731; Control of Pollution Act 1974 (Commencement No 6) Order 1976, SI 1976/956; Control of Pollution Act 1974 (Commencement No 7) Order 1976, SI 1976/1080; Control of Pollution Act 1974 (Commencement No 8) Order 1977, SI 1977/336; Control of Pollution Act 1974 (Commencement No 9) Order 1977, SI 1977/476; Control of Pollution Act 1974 (Commencement No 10) Order 1977, SI 1977/1587; Control of Pollution Act 1974 (Commencement No 11) Order 1977, SI 1977/2164; Control of Pollution Act 1974 (Commencement No 12) Order 1978, SI 1978/816; Control of Pollution Act 1974 (Commencement No 13) Order 1978, SI 1978/954; Control of Pollution Act 1974 (Commencement No 14) Order 1981, SI 1981/196; Control of Pollution Act 1974 (Commencement No 15) (Scotland) Order 1982, SI 1982/624; Control of Pollution Act 1974 (Commencement No 15 (renumbered 16 by Order No 17 below)) Order 1983, SI 1983/1175; Control of Pollution Act 1974 (Commencement No 17) Order 1984, SI 1984/853; Control of Pollution Act 1974 (Commencement No 18) Order 1985, SI 1985/70; Control of Pollution Act 1974 (Commencement No 19) Order 1988, SI 1988/818; Control of Pollution Act 1974 (Commencement No 20) (Scotland) Order 1991, SI 1991/1173

s 1	Repealed (*never in force*)
2	Repealed

Control of Pollution Act 1974 (c 40)—*cont*

s 3–10	14 Jun 1976 (EW) (SI 1976/731); 1 Jan 1978 (S) (SI 1977/1587); repealed (1 May 1994 or, as respects specified activities, according to the state of affairs on 1 Apr 1995) by Environmental Protection Act 1990, s 162(2), Sch 16, Pt II (qv)
11	14 Jun 1976 (EW) (SI 1976/731); 1 Jan 1978 (S) (SI 1977/1587); repealed (S); prospectively repealed (EW) by Environmental Protection Act 1990, s 162(2), Sch 16, Pt II[1]
12	1 Jan 1976 (SI 1975/2118), 1 Apr 1977 (SI 1977/336) or 6 Jun 1988 (SI 1988/818); repealed (S); repealed (save insofar as it relates to industrial waste in EW) by Environmental Protection Act 1990, s 162(2), Sch 16, Pt II (qv)
13	1 Aug 1978 (SI 1978/954) (EW) and 6 Jun 1988 (SI 1988/818) (EW); sub-ss (1), (1A) substituted for original sub-s (1) by Local Government Planning and Land Act 1980, s 1(2), Sch 2, para 10 (qv); sub-ss (5), (5A) substituted for original sub-s (5) by ibid; sub-ss (7), (7A) substituted for original sub-s (7) by ibid
	Repealed (S); repealed (save insofar as it relates to industrial waste in EW) by Environmental Protection Act 1990, s 162(2), Sch 16, Pt II (qv)
14	1 Apr 1977 (SI 1977/336) or 6 Jun 1988 (SI 1988/818); repealed (prospectively in part) by Environmental Protection Act 1990, s 162(2), Sch 16, Pt II[1]
15	Repealed
16	14 Jun 1976 (EW) (SI 1976/731); 1 Jan 1978 (S) (SI 1977/1587); prospectively repealed by Environmental Protection Act 1990, s 162(2), Sch 16, Pt II[1]
17	1 Jan 1976 (EW) (SI 1975/2118); 18 Jul 1976 (S) (except s 17(3)(a)) (SI 1976/1080); 1 Jan 1978 (S) (s 17(3)(a)) (SI 1977/1587); prospectively repealed by Environmental Protection Act 1990, s 162, Sch 16, Pt II[1]
18	14 Jun 1976 (sub-ss (1), (2)) (EW) (SI 1976/731); 1 Jan 1978 (sub-ss (1), (2)) (S) (SI 1977/1587); 6 Jun 1988 (sub-s (3)) (EW) (SI 1988/818) *not in force* (sub-s (3)) (S); repealed (1 May 1994 or, as respects specified activities, according to the state of affairs on 1 Apr 1995) by Environmental Protection Act 1990, s 162(2), Sch 16, Pt II (qv)
19	1 Jan 1976 (EW) (SI 1975/2118) *not in force* (S); prospectively repealed by Environmental Protection Act 1990, s 162(2), Sch 16, Pt II[1]
20	1 Jan 1976 (EW) (SI 1975/2118) *not in force* (S); 1 Jan 1978 (S) (SI 1977/1587); prospectively repealed by Environmental Protection Act 1990, s 162(2), Sch 16, Pt II[1]
21	1 Jan 1976 (EW) (SI 1975/2118) *not in force* (S); prospectively repealed by Environmental Protection Act 1990, s 162, Sch 16, Pt II[1]
22(1), (2)	Repealed
(3), (4)	14 Jun 1976 (EW) (SI 1976/731); repealed (S)

Control of Pollution Act 1974 (c 40)—*cont*

s 22(5)	Repealed
23	14 Jun 1976 (EW) (SI 1976/731); repealed (S)
24(1)–(3)	*Not in force*; prospectively repealed by Litter Act 1983, s 12(3), Sch 2[2]
(4)	Repealed
25, 26	Repealed
27	1 Jan 1976 (sub-ss (1)(a), (2)) (EW) (SI 1975/2118); 18 Jul 1976 (sub-ss (1)(a), (2)) (S) (SI 1976/1080); 6 Jun 1988 (sub-s (1)(b)) (EW) (SI 1988/818); *not in force* (sub-s (1)(b)) (S); repealed (1 May 1994 or, as respects specified activities according to the state of affairs on 1 Apr 1995) by Environmental Protection Act 1990, s 162(2), Sch 16, Pt II (qv)
28	1 Jan 1976 (EW) (so far as applies to ss 12(6), 21(4), 26) (SI 1975/2118); prospectively repealed by Environmental Protection Act 1990, s 162, Sch 16, Pt II[1]
	6 Jun 1988 (EW) (otherwise, except so far as applies to s 15(2)) (SI 1988/818); prospectively repealed by Environmental Protection Act 1990, s 162, Sch 16, Pt II[1]
	Not in force (S); prospectively repealed by Environmental Protection Act 1990, s 162, Sch 16, Pt II[1]
29, 30	1 Jan 1976 (SI 1975/2118); prospectively repealed by Environmental Protection Act 1990, s 162, Sch 16, Pt II[1]
30Y, 30Z	Inserted, partly prospectively, (S) (as Pt IA) by Environment Act 1995, s 59 (qv)
31–42	Repealed (EW)
	Substituted (S) by ss 30A–30E, 31, 31A–31D, 32–42 (prospectively as to the substitution of s 33) by Water Act 1989, s 168, Sch 23, para 4[4]; ss 30F–30J prospectively inserted (S) by Environment Act 1995, s 106, Sch 16, paras 1, 2[3]; ss 31D, 32 prospectively repealed by Environment Act 1995, ss 106, 120(1), (3), Sch 16, paras 1, 3, Sch 22, para 29(1), (7), Sch 24[3]; s 38A prospectively inserted (S) by Environment Act 1995, s 120(1), Sch 22, para 29(1), (14)[3]; ss 42A, 42B prospectively substituted for s 42 by Environment Act 1995, s 120(1), Sch 22, para 29(1), (20)[3]
43	Repealed
44	12 Dec 1974 (SI 1974/2039)
45	Repealed
46–51	Repealed (EW)
	Substituted (S) (prospectively as to the substitution of ss 47, 48) by Water Act 1989, s 168, Sch 23, para 5[4]; ss 46A–46D prospectively inserted (S) by Environment Act 1995, s 120(1), Sch 22, para 29(1), (22)[3]; ss 49A, 49B prospectively inserted (S) by Environment Act 1995, s 120(1), Sch 22, para 29(1), (26)[3]
52	Repealed
53	Substituted by Water Act 1989, s 168, Sch 23, para 6 (qv); prospectively repealed by Environment Act 1995, ss 120(1), (3), Sch 22, para 29(1), (28), Sch 24[3]

Control of Pollution Act 1974 (c 40)—*cont*

s 54, 55	Repealed (EW); substituted (S) by Water Act 1989, s 168, Sch 23, para 6 (qv); prospectively repealed (S) by Environment Act 1995, ss 120(1), (3), Sch 22, para 29(1), (28), Sch 24[3]
55A	Inserted (S) by National Heritage (Scotland) Act 1991, s 27(1), Sch 10, para 7(1), (3) (qv)
56	Repealed (EW); substituted (S) by Water Act 1989, s 168, Sch 23, para 6 (qv)
57(a)	Repealed (EW); 18 Jul 1976 (S) (SI 1976/1080); prospectively repealed (S) by Environment Act 1995, s 120(3), Sch 24[3]
(b)	1 Jan 1976 (EW) (SI 1975/2118); 1 Aug 1982 (S) (SI 1982/624)
58	Repealed (EW)
	18 Jul 1976 (S) (SI 1976/1080) and 1 Aug 1982 (S) (SI 1982/624); prospectively repealed (S) by Environment Act 1995, s 120(3), Sch 24[3]
58A, 58B	Inserted (S) by Noise and Statutory Nuisance Act 1993, s 6(1), Sch 1, para 3 (qv); prospectively repealed (S) by Environment Act 1995, s 120(3), Sch 24[3]
59	Repealed (EW); 18 Jul 1976 (S) (SI 1976/1080); prospectively repealed (S) by Environment Act 1995, s 120(3), Sch 24[3]
59A	Inserted (S) by Noise and Statutory Nuisance Act 1993, s 6(1), Sch 1, para 5 (qv); prospectively repealed (S) by Environment Act 1995, s 120(3), Sch 24[3]
60, 61	1 Jan 1976 (EW) (SI 1975/2118); 1 Aug 1982 (S) (SI 1982/624)
62	1 Jan 1976 (EW) (SI 1975/2118); 18 Jul 1976 (S) (SI 1976/1080)
63–67	1 Jan 1976 (EW) (SI 1975/2118); 1 Aug 1982 (S) (SI 1982/624)
68	1 Jan 1976 (EW) (SI 1975/2118); 18 Jul 1976 (S) (SI 1976/1080)
69	1 Jan 1976 (EW) (SI 1975/2118); 18 Jul 1976 (S) (except so far as applies or refers to 'a noise reduction notice' or to s 65) (SI 1976/1080); 1 Aug 1982 (S) (so far as so applying or referring) (SI 1982/624)
70	1 Jan 1976 (EW) (SI 1975/2118); 18 Jul 1976 (S) (SI 1976/1080)
71	1 Jan 1976 (EW) (SI 1975/2118)
(1)	18 Jul 1976 (S) (SI 1976/1080)
(2)	1 Aug 1982 (S) (SI 1982/624)
(3)	18 Jul 1976 (S) (SI 1976/1080)
72	1 Jan 1976 (EW) (SI 1975/2118); 18 Jul 1976 (S) (SI 1976/1080)
73	1 Jan 1976 (EW) (SI 1975/2118); 18 Jul 1976 (S) (except definitions of 'noise abatement order', 'noise abatement zone' 'noise level register' and 'noise reduction notice') (SI 1976/1080); 1 Aug 1982 (S) (remainder) (SI 1982/624)
74	1 Jan 1976 (EW) (SI 1975/2118); 18 Jul 1976 (S) (SI 1976/1080)

Control of Pollution Act 1974 (c 40)—*cont*

s 75–84	Repealed
85	1 Jan 1976 (EW) (SI 1975/2118); 18 Jul 1976 (S) (SI 1976/1080)
86	Repealed
87	1 Jan 1976 (EW) (SI 1975/2118); 18 Jul 1976 (S) (SI 1976/1080)
88	14 Jun 1976 (EW) (SI 1976/731); 1 Jan 1978 (S) (SI 1977/1587)
89–93	1 Jan 1976 (EW) (SI 1975/2118); 18 Jul 1976 (S) (SI 1976/1080)
94	1 Jan 1976 (EW) (SI 1975/2118); 18 Jul 1976 (S) (except s 94(2)(a)(ii)) (SI 1976/1080); 31 Jan 1985 (S) (s 94(2)(a)(ii)) (SI 1985/70)
95	Substituted by Water Act 1989, s 190(1), Sch 25, para 48(10) (qv)
96	1 Jan 1976 (EW) (SI 1975/2118); 18 Jul 1976 (S) (SI 1976/1080)
97	1 Jan 1976 (SI 1975/2118)
98	1 Jan 1976 (EW) (SI 1975/2118); 18 Jul 1976 (S) (SI 1976/1080)
99	1 Jan 1976 (SI 1975/2118)
100	Repealed
101, 102	1 Jan 1976 (SI 1975/2118)
103	Repealed
104, 105	12 Dec 1974 (SI 1974/2039)
106	1 Jan 1976 (SI 1975/2118)
107	12 Dec 1974 (SI 1974/2039)
108	See Schs 3, 4 below
109	12 Dec 1974 (SI 1974/2039)
Sch 1	Substituted by Local Government, Planning and Land Act 1980, s 1(2), Sch 2, para 18 (qv)
1A	Inserted (S) by Water Act 1989, s 168, Sch 23, para 8 (qv)
2	1 Jan 1976 (SI 1975/2118)
3, para 1, 2	1 Jan 1975 (SI 1974/2169)
3, 4	Spent
5, 6	Repealed
7	*Not in force*
8–10	Repealed
11	31 Jan 1985 (SI 1985/70)
12	31 Jan 1985 (SI 1985/70); prospectively repealed by Environment Act 1995, s 120(3), Sch 24[3]
13	4 Jul 1984 (SI 1984/853); prospectively repealed by Environment Act 1995, s 120(3), Sch 24[3]
14, 15	4 Jul 1984 (SI 1984/853)
16	Repealed
17	4 Jul 1984 (SI 1984/853)
18	14 Jun 1976 (SI 1976/731)
19–22	Repealed
23, 24	31 Jan 1985 (SI 1985/70)
25	Repealed
26	1 Jan 1976 (EW) (SI 1975/2118); 18 Jul 1976 (S) (SI 1976/1080)
27–31	Repealed

Control of Pollution Act 1974 (c 40)—*cont*

Sch 4

1 Jan 1975 (repeals in Alkali and Works Regulation Act 1906) (SI 1974/2169)

3 Mar 1975 (repeal in Local Government (Scotland) Act 1973, s 135(3)) (SI 1975/230)

1 Jan 1976 (repeals of or in Clean Air Act 1956, s 16(1), proviso, para 1); Criminal Justice Act 1967, Sch 3, entries relating to Clean Air Act 1956, s 27(1), (2); Administration of Justice (Appeals) Act 1934; Public Health (Drainage of Trade Premises) Act 1937, ss 2(4), 3(2), 7(1) proviso, s 11, definition of 'interested body' in s 14(1); Rivers (Prevention of Pollution) Act 1951, s 4; Clean Air Act 1956, s 25(a), (b), the words 'manufacturing process or' in s 26, the amendments of the Alkali Act 1936, ss 3, 8, 18 in Sch 2; Noise Abatement Act 1960; Public Health Act 1961, ss 55(4), 57(3); London Government Act 1963, s 40(4)(*g*), Sch 11, Pt I, para 32; Criminal Justice Act 1967, entries relating to Public Health Act 1936, ss 94(2), 95(1)) (SI 1975/2118)

14 Jun 1976 (repeals of or in Public Health Act 1875; Trunk Roads Act 1936; Highways Act 1959; London Government Act 1963, Sch 11, Pt I, so far as it repeals para 14(1)(c)) (SI 1976/731)

18 Jul 1976 (repeals of or in Clean Air Act 1956, Sch 2; Noise Abatement Act 1960; Criminal Justice Act 1967, entry relating to Public Health (Scotland) Act 1897, s 22) (S) (SI 1976/1080)

20 Jul 1976 (repeals of or in Public Health (Drainage of Trade Premises) Act 1937; Public Health Act 1961, ss 55(1)–(3), (5)–(9), 56, 57(1), (2), (4)–(8), 58, 63(5)) (SI 1976/956)

1 Apr 1977 (as respects inner London boroughs, repeals of or in Public Health Act 1936, s 72(1)(b), (2) (in relation to cleansing of earthclosets, privys, ashpits or cesspools); London Government Act 1963, Sch 11, Pt I, para 14(1), to the extent that the Public Health Act 1936, s 72(1)(b), (2) relate to the cleansing of the above items) (SI 1977/336)

1 Apr 1977 (repeal of Public Health Act 1936, s 77) (SI 1977/476))

16 Mar 1981 (repeal of Deposit of Poisonous Waste Act 1972) (SI 1981/196)

31 Jan 1985 (repeals of or in Salmon Fisheries (Scotland) Act 1862; Sea Fisheries Regulation (Scotland) Act 1895; Public Health Act 1936, s 259(2); Rivers (Prevention of Pollution) Act 1951, except ss 5(1)(c), (6), (7), 11(1) (so far as defines 'stream'), (6), 12(1), (3); Rivers (Prevention of Pollution) (Scotland) Act 1951, except (in addition to provisions saved in col 3 of Sch 4) ss 18(6), 25(1)(c), (4), 26(2), (4), (7)–(9) and certain definitions in s 35(1); Clean Rivers (Estuaries and Tidal Waters) Act 1960; Rivers (Prevention of Pollution) Act 1961; Water Resources Act 1963, except s 79; Rivers

Control of Pollution Act 1974 (c 40)—*cont*

Sch 4–*cont* (Prevention of Pollution) (Scotland) Act 1965; Water Act 1973) (SI 1985/70)

6 Jun 1988 (repeals of or in Public Health Act 1936, ss 72(1)–(5), 73–76; London Government Act 1963, Sch 11, Pt I, paras 14, 16, 32; Local Government Act 1972, Sch 14, paras 5–8) (SI 1988/818)

31 May 1991 (repeals of or in Rivers (Prevention of Pollution) (Scotland) Act 1951, ss 25(1)(c), (4), 26(2), (7)–(9)) (S) (SI 1991/1173)

Not in force (remainder)

[1] Any order(s) made under Environmental Protection Act 1990, s 164(3), bringing the prospective repeal into force will be noted to that Act in the service to this work

[2] Any order(s) made under Litter Act 1983, s 13(2), bringing the prospective repeal into force will be noted to that Act in the service to this work

[3] Any order(s) made under Environment Act 1995, s 125(3), bringing the prospective amendments into force will be noted to that Act in the service to this work

[4] Any order(s) made under Water Act 1989, s 194(4), bringing the prospective substitution into force will be noted to that Act in the service to this work

---

Dumping at Sea Act 1974 (c 20)

Whole Act repealed

Ecclesiastical Jurisdiction (Amendment) Measure 1974 (No 2)

RA: 9 Jul 1974

9 Jul 1974 (RA)

Education (Mentally Handicapped Children) (Scotland) Act 1974 (c 27)

RA: 17 Jul 1974

17 Jul 1974 (RA; but note that the Act largely took effect from 16 May 1975, the day appointed by Education (Mentally Handicapped Children) (Scotland) Act 1974 (Commencement) Order 1975, SI 1975/307)

Finance Act 1974 (c 30)

Budget day: 26 Mar 1974

RA: 31 Jul 1974

See the note concerning Finance Acts at the front of this book

---

Friendly Societies Act 1974 (c 46)

RA: 31 Jul 1974

Commencement provisions: s 117(2); Friendly Societies Act 1974 (Commencement) Order 1975, SI 1975/204

Friendly Societies Act 1974 (c 46)—*cont*

s 1–7	1 Apr 1975 (SI 1975/204)
8	Repealed
9–14	1 Apr 1975 (SI 1975/204)
15	See note to s 15A below
15A	Substituted (subject to savings) for original s 15 by Friendly Societies Act 1992, s 95, Sch 16, paras 1, 6(1), (3) (qv)
16	1 Apr 1975 (SI 1975/204)
17	Repealed (subject to savings)
18–23	1 Apr 1975 (SI 1975/204)
23A	Inserted by Friendly Societies Act 1992, s 95, Sch 16, paras 1, 8 (qv)
24	Substituted by Friendly Societies Act 1992, s 95, Sch 16, paras 1, 9 (qv)
25	1 Apr 1975 (SI 1975/204)
26	Substituted by Friendly Societies Act 1992, s 95, Sch 16, paras 1, 10 (qv)
27, 28	Repealed
29–45	1 Apr 1975 (SI 1975/204); repealed in relation to registered friendly societies and registered branches of such societies by Friendly Societies Act 1992, s 95, Sch 16, paras 1, 12 (qv)
46–57	1 Apr 1975 (SI 1975/204)
57A	Inserted by Friendly Societies Act 1992, s 95, Sch 16, paras 1, 21 (qv)
58–63	1 Apr 1975 (SI 1975/204)
63A	Inserted by Friendly Societies Act 1992, s 95, Sch 16, paras 1, 22 (qv)
64	Repealed
65	1 Apr 1975 (SI 1975/204)
65A, 65B	Inserted by Friendly Societies Act 1992, s 95, Sch 16, paras 1, 23 (qv)
66–69	1 Apr 1975 (SI 1975/204)
70–73	Repealed
74	1 Apr 1975 (SI 1975/204); prospectively repealed by Friendly Societies Act 1992, ss 95, 120(2), Sch 16, paras 1, 24, Sch 22, Pt I[1]
75	Repealed (subject to savings)
76	1 Apr 1975 (SI 1975/204)
77	Repealed
78–83	1 Apr 1975 (SI 1975/204)
84	1 Apr 1975 (SI 1975/204); repealed in relation to registered friendly societies by Friendly Societies Act 1992, s 95, Sch 16, paras 1, 31 (qv)
84A	Inserted by Friendly Societies Act 1992, s 95, Sch 16, para 32 (qv)
85, 86	1 Apr 1975 (SI 1975/204)
87	Substituted by Friendly Societies Act 1992, s 95, Sch 16, paras 1, 34 (qv)
88, 89	Repealed
90	1 Apr 1975 (SI 1975/204); repealed in relation to registered friendly societies by Friendly Societies Act 1992, s 95, Sch 16, paras 1, 36 (qv)
91–94	1 Apr 1975 (SI 1975/204)
95	1 Apr 1975 (SI 1975/204); repealed in relation to registered friendly societies by Friendly Societies Act 1992, s 95, Sch 16, paras 1, 39 (qv)

Friendly Societies Act 1974 (c 46)—*cont*

s 95A	Inserted by Friendly Societies Act 1992, s 95, Sch 16, paras 1, 39 (qv)
96–105	1 Apr 1975 (SI 1975/204)
106	Repealed
107, 108	1 Apr 1975 (SI 1975/204)
109	31 Jul 1974 (so far as relates to regulations under s 115 (s 117(2)) 1 Apr 1975 (otherwise) (SI 1975/204)
110, 111	1 Apr 1975 (SI 1975/204)
112, 113	31 Jul 1974 (s 117(2))
114	1 Apr 1975 (SI 1975/204)
115	Repealed
116	1 Apr 1975 (SI 1975/204)
117	31 Jul 1974 (s 117(2))
Sch 1	Repealed
2	1 Apr 1975 (SI 1975/204)
3	Repealed
4	1 Apr 1975 (SI 1975/204)
5	Repealed
6	1 Apr 1975 (SI 1975/204); prospectively repealed by Friendly Societies Act 1992, s 120(2), Sch 22, Pt I[1]
6A	Inserted by Friendly Societies Act 1992, s 95, Sch 16, paras 1, 52 (qv)
7	1 Apr 1975 (SI 1975/204); spent
8	Repealed (subject to savings)
9–11	1 Apr 1975 (SI 1975/204)

[1] Any order(s) made under Friendly Societies Act 1992, s 126(2), bringing the prospective repeal into force will be noted to that Act in the service to this work

Health and Safety at Work etc Act 1974 (c 37)

RA: 31 Jul 1974

Commencement provisions: s 85(2); Health and Safety at Work etc Act 1974 (Commencement No 1) Order 1974, SI 1974/1439; Health and Safety at Work etc Act 1974 (Commencement No 2) Order 1975, SI 1975/344; Health and Safety at Work etc Act 1974 (Commencement No 3) Order 1975, SI 1975/1364; Health and Safety at Work etc Act 1974 (Commencement No 4) Order 1977, SI 1977/294; Health and Safety at Work etc Act 1974 (Commencement No 5) Order 1980, SI 1980/208; Health and Safety at Work etc Act 1974 (Commencement No 6) Order 1980, SI 1980/269

s 1	1 Oct 1974 (SI 1974/1439)
2–4	1 Apr 1975 (SI 1974/1439)
5	1 Apr 1975 (SI 1974/1439); prospectively repealed by Environmental Protection Act 1990, s 162, Sch 16, Pt I[1]
6–9	1 Apr 1975 (SI 1974/1439)
10(1)	1 Oct 1974 (in relation to the Commission) (SI 1974/1439) 1 Jan 1975 (in relation to the Executive) (SI 1974/1439)
(2)–(4)	1 Oct 1974 (SI 1974/1439)
(5)	1 Jan 1975 (SI 1974/1439)

Health and Safety at Work etc Act 1974 (c 37)—*cont*

s 10(6), (7)	1 Oct 1974 (in relation to the Commission) (SI 1974/1439) 1 Jan 1975 (in relation to the Executive) (SI 1974/1439)
(8)	Inserted by Employment Protection Act 1975, s 116, Sch 15, para 3 (qv)
11(1)–(3)	1 Oct 1974 (in relation to the Commission) (SI 1974/1439) 1 Jan 1975 (in relation to the Executive) (SI 1974/1439)
(4), (5)	1 Jan 1975
(6)	1 Oct 1974 (in relation to the Commission) (SI 1974/1439) 1 Jan 1975 (in relation to the Executive) (SI 1974/1439)
12, 13	1 Oct 1974 (SI 1974/1439)
14	1 Jan 1975 (SI 1974/1439)
15, 16	1 Oct 1974 (SI 1974/1439)
17–25	1 Jan 1975 (SI 1974/1439)
25A	Inserted by Consumer Protection Act 1987, s 36, Sch 3, para 3 (qv)
26, 27	1 Jan 1975 (SI 1974/1439)
27A	Inserted by Consumer Protection Act 1987, s 36, Sch 3, para 4 (qv)
28	1 Jan 1975 (SI 1974/1439)
29–32	Repealed
33(1)(a), (b)	1 Apr 1975 (SI 1974/1439)
(c)–(o)	1 Jan 1975 (SI 1974/1439)
(1A)	Inserted by Offshore Safety Act 1992, s 4(2) (qv)
(2)	1 Jan 1975 (SI 1974/1439)
(2A)	Inserted by Offshore Safety Act 1992, s 4(3) (qv)
(3), (4)	1 Jan 1975 (SI 1974/1439)
(5), (6)	Repealed
34–42	1 Jan 1975 (SI 1974/1439)
43	1 Oct 1974 (in relation to payments to the Commission) (SI 1974/1439) 1 Jan 1975 (otherwise) (SI 1974/1439)
44–46	1 Jan 1975 (SI 1974/1439)
47	1 Jan 1975 (except in relation to ss 2–8) (SI 1974/1439) 1 Apr 1975 (exception noted above) (SI 1974/1439)
48	1 Jan 1975 (except in relation to ss 2–9) (SI 1974/1439) 1 Apr 1975 (exception noted above) (SI 1974/1439)
49	1 Jan 1975 (SI 1974/1439)
50–52	1 Oct 1974 (SI 1974/1439)
53	1 Oct 1974, 1 Jan 1975 (in relation to other provisions in force on those dates) (SI 1974/1439) 1 Apr 1975 (otherwise) (SI 1974/1439)
54–60	1 Jan 1975 (SI 1974/1439)
61–74	Repealed
75	See Sch 7 below
76	Repealed
77(1)	1 Oct 1974 (SI 1974/1439)
(2)	1 Jan 1975 (SI 1974/1439)
78	1 Apr 1974 (SI 1974/1439)
79	Repealed
80–82	1 Oct 1974 (SI 1974/1439)
83	Repealed
84, 85	1 Oct 1974 (SI 1974/1439)

Health and Safety at Work etc Act 1974 (c 37)—*cont*

Sch 1	1 Oct 1974 (SI 1974/1439)
2, para 1–9	1 Oct 1974 (SI 1974/1439)
10–12	1 Jan 1975 (SI 1974/1439)
13–19	1 Oct 1974 (SI 1974/1439)
20	1 Jan 1975 (SI 1974/1439)
3	1 Oct 1974 (SI 1974/1439)
4–6	Repealed
7, para 1	27 Mar 1975 (SI 1975/344)
2(a), (b)	27 Mar 1975 (SI 1975/344)
(c)	*Not in force*
3	*Not in force*
4–6	27 Mar 1975 (SI 1975/344)
7	17 Mar 1980 (SI 1980/269)
8, 9	*Not in force*
8	1 Apr 1975 (SI 1974/1439)
9, 10	Repealed

[1] Any order made under Environmental Protection Act 1990, s 164(3), bringing the prospective repeal into force will be noted to that Act in the service to this work

Horticulture (Special Payments) Act 1974 (c 5)

RA: 8 Feb 1974

8 Feb 1974 (RA)

Housing Act 1974 (c 44)

RA: 31 Jul 1974

Commencement provisions: ss 18(6), 118(5), 131(3); Housing Act 1974 (Commencement No 1) Order 1974, SI 1974/1406; Housing Act 1974 (Commencement No 2) Order 1974, SI 1974/1562; Housing Act 1974 (Commencement No 3) Order 1974, SI 1974/1791; Housing Act 1974 (Commencement No 4) Order 1975, SI 1975/374; Housing Act 1974 (Commencement No 5) Order 1975, SI 1975/1113; Housing Act 1974 (Commencement No 6) Order 1979, SI 1979/1214

s 1–17	Repealed
18	Repealed (EW)
(1)	Repealed (S)
(2)–(6)	2 Dec 1974 (SI 1974/1791)
19–117	Repealed
118	31 Jul 1974 (s 118(5))
119–128	Repealed
129	20 Aug 1974 (SI 1974/1406); repealed (EW)
130	See Schs 13–15 below
131	20 Aug 1974 (SI 1974/1406)
Sch 1, 2	Repealed
3, Pt I, II	Repealed
III	2 Dec 1974 (SI 1974/1791); repealed (EW)
4–7	Repealed
8	31 Jul 1974 (s 118(5))
9–12	Repealed
13, para 1–37	Repealed
38–45	20 Aug 1974 (SI 1974/1406)

Housing Act 1974 (c 44)—*cont*

Sch 13, para 46(1)	1 Apr 1975 (SI 1975/374)
(2)	1 Apr 1975 (SI 1975/374) (repeal of Local Government (Scotland) Act 1973, Sch 12, para 11); spent otherwise
14, 15	Repealed

Housing (Scotland) Act 1974 (c 45)

Whole Act repealed

Independent Broadcasting Authority Act 1974 (c 16)

Whole Act repealed

Independent Broadcasting Authority (No 2) Act 1974 (c 42)

Whole Act repealed

Insurance Companies Act 1974 (c 49)

Whole Act repealed

Juries Act 1974 (c 23)

RA: 9 Jul 1974

Commencement provisions: s 23(3)

9 Aug 1974 (s 23(3))

Land Tenure Reform (Scotland) Act 1974 (c 38)

RA: 31 Jul 1974

Commencement provisions: s 24(2)

1 Sep 1974 (s 24(2))

Legal Aid Act 1974 (c 4)

Whole Act repealed

Local Government Act 1974 (c 7)

RA: 8 Feb 1974

Commencement provisions: s 43(2), (3); Local Government Act 1974 (Commencement No 1) Order 1974, SI 1974/335; Local Government Act 1974 (Commencement No 2) Order 1977, SI 1977/943; Local Government Act 1974 (Commencement No 3) Order 1978, SI 1978/1583

s 1(1)–(7)	8 Feb 1974 (RA)
(8)	Repealed
2–4	8 Feb 1974 (RA)

Local Government Act 1974 (c 7)—*cont*

s 5(1)	8 Feb 1974 (RA)
(2)	Repealed
(3), (4)	8 Feb 1974 (RA)
6	8 Feb 1974 (RA)
7	8 Feb 1974 (RA); prospectively repealed by Environment Act 1995, s 120(3), Sch 24[1]
8–10	8 Feb 1974 (RA)
11–22	Repealed
23	8 Feb 1974 (RA)
23A	Inserted by Local Government and Housing Act 1989, s 25(2) (qv)
24	Repealed
25–31	8 Feb 1974 (RA)
31A	Inserted by Local Government and Housing Act 1989, s 28(1) (qv)
32–34	8 Feb 1974 (RA)
35	1 Apr 1974 (SI 1974/335)
36	8 Feb 1974 (RA)
37, 38	Repealed
39	8 Feb 1974 (RA)
40	Repealed
41	8 Feb 1974 (RA)
42	4 Mar 1974 (SI 1974/335; see also Schs 7, 8 below)
43	8 Feb 1974 (RA)
Sch 1, Pt I	Repealed
II, III	8 Feb 1974 (RA)
2	8 Feb (RA)
3	Repealed
4, 5	8 Feb 1974 (RA)
6, para 1, 2	1 Apr 1974 (SI 1974/335)
3	Repealed
4	1 Apr 1974 (SI 1974/335)
5	Repealed
6	1 Apr 1974 (SI 1974/335)
7	Repealed
8	1 Apr 1974 (SI 1974/335)
9	Repealed
10	1 Apr 1974 (SI 1974/335)
11, 12	Repealed
13, 14	1 Apr 1974 (SI 1974/335)
15	Repealed
16–19	1 Apr 1974 (SI 1974/335)
20, 21	Repealed
22	1 Apr 1974 (SI 1974/335)
23	Repealed
24	1 Apr 1974 (SI 1974/335)
25	Repealed and spent
26	1 Apr 1974 (SI 1974/335)
7, para 1–13	Repealed
14, 15	1 Apr 1974 (SI 1974/335)
8	1 Apr 1974 (except as below) (SI 1974/335) 1 Oct 1974 (repeals in Weights and Measures Act 1963) (SI 1974/335) 1 Apr 1975 (repeals of or in Local Government Act 1966, s 27(2); Road Traffic Regulation Act 1967, ss 72(6)(a), 84B(8)(a); Transport Act 1968, s 34(2),

Local Government Act 1974 (c 7)—*cont*

Sch 8—*cont*	(3); Transport (London) Act 1969, ss 7(5), (6), 29(1)(a); Highways Act 1971; Town and Country Planning Act 1971, s 212(1)) (SI 1974/335)
	1 Jun 1977 (repeals of or in National Parks and Access to the Countryside Act 1949, s 98; Local Government Act 1966, ss 1–5, 10, Sch 1; General Rate Act 1967, s 49, Sch 9; Transport Act 1968, ss 13(7), 138(6); Transport (London) Act 1969, s 3(1); Housing Finance Act 1972; Local Government Act 1972, s 203(5), Sch 24, para 12; Rate Rebate Act 1973) (SI 1977/943)
	1 Apr 1979 (repeals of or in National Parks and Access to the Countryside Act 1949, s 97; Rating Act 1966, ss 9, 12(a); Local Government Act 1966, s 8; Countryside Act 1968, ss 33–36) (SI 1978/1583)

[1] Any order made under Environment Act 1995, s 125(3), bringing the prospective repeal into force will be noted to that Act in the service to this work

Lord Chancellor (Tenure of Office and Discharge of Ecclesiastical Functions) Act 1974 (c 25)

RA: 9 Jul 1974

9 Jul 1974 (RA)

Lord High Commissioner (Church of Scotland) Act 1974 (c 19)

RA: 27 Jun 1974

27 Jun 1974 (RA)

Merchant Shipping Act 1974 (c 43)

RA: 31 Jul 1974

Commencement provisions: s 24(2) (repealed); Merchant Shipping Act 1974 (Commencement No 1) Order 1974, SI 1974/1792; Merchant Shipping Act 1974 (Commencement No 2) Order 1975, SI 1975/866; Merchant Shipping Act 1974 (Commencement No 3) Order 1978, SI 1978/1466; Merchant Shipping Act 1974 (Commencement No 4) Order 1979, SI 1979/808

s 1–8A, 9–18	Repealed
19(1)	Repealed
(2)	1 Nov 1974 (SI 1974/1792)
(3)–(6)	Repealed
20	Repealed (with savings) by Merchant Shipping (Registration, etc) Act 1993, s 8(4), Sch 5, Pt II[1]
21–24	Repealed
Sch 1–5	Repealed

[1] This repeal came into force on 1 May 1994, but instruments made under s 20 and in force on that date remained in force until superseded by an instrument made under Sch 4, para 4 to the 1993 Act (Merchant Shipping (Registration, etc) Act

Merchant Shipping Act 1974 (c 43)—*cont*

1993 (Commencement No 1 and Transitional Provisions) Order 1993, SI 1993/3137, art 7(1), Sch 3). Sch 4, para 4 to the 1993 Act was repealed by Merchant Shipping Act 1995, s 314(1), Sch 12 and by virtue of Interpretation Act 1978, s 17(2)(b), such instruments remain in force until superseded by an instrument made under s 315 of the 1995 Act

Mines (Working Facilities and Support) Act 1974 (c 36)

RA: 31 Jul 1974

31 Jul 1974 (RA)

Ministers of the Crown Act 1974 (c 21)

Whole Act repealed

National Insurance Act 1974 (c 14)

RA: 13 May 1974

Commencement provisions: s 8(4), Sch 5 (repealed); National Insurance Act 1974 (Commencement) Order 1974, SI 1974/841

s 1–5	Repealed
6(1)–(4)	Repealed
(5)	Spent (on repeal of Sch 4)
7	Repealed
8(1)	13 May 1974 (Sch 5, para 1(1) (repealed))
(2)–(5)	Repealed
(6)	17 May 1974 (SI 1974/841)
Sch 1–6	Repealed

National Theatre Act 1974 (c 55)

RA: 29 Nov 1974

29 Nov 1974 (RA)

Northern Ireland Act 1974 (c 28)

RA: 17 Jul 1974

17 Jul 1974 (RA) (Interim period continued until 16 Jul 1996 (Northern Ireland Act 1974 (Interim Period Extension) Order 1995, SI 1995/1895))

Northern Ireland (Young Persons) Act 1974 (c 33)

Whole Act repealed

Pakistan Act 1974 (c 34)

Whole Act repealed

Parks Regulation (Amendment) Act 1974 (c 29)

RA: 17 Jul 1974

17 Jul 1974 (RA)

Pensioners' Payments Act 1974 (c 54)

Whole Act repealed

Pensions (Increase) Act 1974 (c 9)

RA: 8 Feb 1974

8 Feb 1974 (RA)

Policing of Airports Act 1974 (c 41)

Whole Act repealed

Prevention of Terrorism (Temporary Provisions) Act 1974 (c 56)

Whole Act repealed

Prices Act 1974 (c 24)

RA: 9 Jul 1974

9 Jul 1974 (RA)

Rabies Act 1974 (c 17)

Whole Act repealed

Railways Act 1974 (c 48)

RA: 31 Jul 1974

Commencement provisions: s 10(4)

s 1	1 Jan 1975 (s 10(4))
2, 3	Repealed
4	31 Jul 1974 (RA)
5–7	Repealed
8	31 Jul 1974 (RA); repealed by Railways Act 1993, ss 139(8), 152, Sch 14[1]
9	Repealed
10	31 Jul 1974 (RA)

[1] This repeal came into force on 15 Jul 1994, but not so as to affect the operation of s 8 in relation to any application for grant made pursuant to that section before that date but in respect of which no decision had been made by the Secretary of State before that date (Railways Act 1993 (Commencement No 5 and Transitional Provisions) Order 1994, SI 1994/1648, arts 2, 3(1))

Rehabilitation of Offenders Act 1974 (c 53)

RA: 31 Jul 1974

Commencement provisions: s 11(2)

1 Jul 1975 (s 11(2))

Rent Act 1974 (c 51)

RA: 31 Jul 1974

Commencement provisions: s 17(5)

14 Aug 1974 (s 17(5))

Whole Act repealed (S)

Representation of the People Act 1974 (c 10)

Whole Act repealed

Representation of the People (No 2) Act 1974 (c 13)

Whole Act repealed

Road Traffic Act 1974 (c 50)

RA: 31 Jul 1974

Commencement provisions: s 24(4); Road Traffic Act 1974 (Commencement No 1) Order 1974, SI 1974/2075; Road Traffic Act 1974 (Commencement No 2) (Section 20: Northern Ireland) Order 1975, SI 1975/264; Road Traffic Act 1974 (Commencement No 3) Order 1975, SI 1975/489; Road Traffic Act 1974 (Commencement No 4) Order 1975, SI 1975/756; Road Traffic Act 1974 (Commencement No 5) Order 1975, SI 1975/1154; Road Traffic Act 1974 (Commencement No 6) Order 1975, SI 1975/1479; Road Traffic Act 1974 (Commencement No 7) Order 1975, SI 1975/1653; Road Traffic Act 1974 (Commencement No 1) (Scotland) Order 1979, SI 1979/85; Road Traffic Act 1984 (Commencement No 8) Order 1984, SI 1984/811

s 1–17	Repealed
18	1 Jan 1975 (SI 1974/2075)
19–22	Repealed
23	1 Jan 1975 (SI 1974/2075)
24(1)	1 Jan 1975 (SI 1974/2075)
(2)	See Sch 6 below
(3)	See Sch 7 below
(4), (5)	1 Jan 1975 (SI 1974/2075)
Sch 1–5	Repealed
6, para 1–9	Repealed
10, 11	1 Jan 1975 (SI 1974/2075)
12–24	Repealed
7	1 Jan 1975 (repeals of or in Road Traffic Act 1960, s 133(4); Road Traffic Act 1962, Schs 1, 4; Road Traffic Regulation Act 1967, ss 9(10), 31(3), 42(4),

Road Traffic Act 1974 (c 50)—*cont*

Sch 7—*cont*
85(1); Criminal Justice Act 1967, Sch 3; Road Traffic Act 1972, ss 47, 48(3), 50, 51, 53(2), 62(2)(c), 64, 88(5) (without affecting regulations made under it), 162(1)(iii), 188; Road Traffic (Foreign Vehicles) Act 1972, ss 5, 7(7)) (SI 1974/2075)
1 Apr 1975 (repeals of or in Road Traffic Act 1972, s 65, Sch 4, Pt I) (SI 1975/489)
1 Sep 1975 (repeal of Road Traffic Regulation Act 1967, s 80(10), 24(3) thereof so far as relates to s 80(10)) (SI 1975/1154)
1 Jan 1976 (repeal of Road Traffic Act 1972, ss 104(1)–(3), (6)(a), 105(2)) (SI 1975/1479)
1 Aug 1984 (repeals of or in Road Traffic Act 1972, ss 68–80, 81(1), 82) (SI 1984/811)
Not in force (otherwise)

Slaughterhouses Act 1974 (c 3)

RA: 8 Feb 1974

Commencement provisions: s 48(3)

1 Apr 1974 (s 48(3))

Social Security Amendment Act 1974 (c 58)

Whole Act repealed

Solicitors Act 1974 (c 47)

RA: 31 Jul 1974

Commencement provisions: s 90(2); Solicitors Act 1974 (Commencement) Order 1975, SI 1975/534

1 May 1975 (SI 1975/534)

Solicitors (Amendment) Act 1974 (c 26)

Whole Act repealed

Statute Law (Repeals) Act 1974 (c 22)

RA: 27 Jun 1974

27 Jun 1974 (RA)

Statutory Corporations (Financial Provisions) Act 1974 (c 8)

RA: 8 Feb 1974

8 Feb 1974 (RA)

Synodical Government (Amendment) Measure 1974 (No 1)

RA: 9 Jul 1974

9 Jul 1974 (RA)

Town and Country Amenities Act 1974 (c 32)

RA: 31 Jul 1974

Commencement provisions: s 13(3), (4); Town and Country Amenities Act 1974 (Commencement) Order 1975, SI 1975/147; Town and Country Amenities Act 1974 (Commencement) (Scotland) Order 1975, SI 1975/1202

s 1–4	31 Aug 1974 (s 13(3))
5	31 Aug 1974 (s 13(3)); repealed (EW); prospectively repealed (S) by Housing and Planning Act 1986, s 53(2), Sch 12, Pt IV[1]
6, 7	31 Aug 1974 (s 13(3))
8	Repealed
9	17 Jul 1975 (SI 1975/1202)
10	Repealed
11–13	31 Aug 1974 (s 13(3))
Schedule	31 Aug 1974 (s 13(3))

[1] Any order made under Housing and Planning Act 1986, s 57(1), (2), bringing the prospective repeal into force will be noted to that Act in the service to this work

Trade Union and Labour Relations Act 1974 (c 52)

Whole Act repealed

1975

Air Travel Reserve Fund Act 1975 (c 36)

Whole Act repealed

Airports Authority Act 1975 (c 78)

Whole Act repealed

Appropriation Act 1975 (c 44)

Whole Act repealed

Arbitration Act 1975 (c 3)

RA: 25 Feb 1975

Commencement provisions: s 8; Arbitration Act 1975 (Commencement) Order 1975, SI 1975/1662

23 Dec 1975 (SI 1975/1662)

Biological Standards Act 1975 (c 4)

RA: 25 Feb 1975

Commencement provisions: s 9; Biological Standards Act 1975 (Commencement) Order 1976, SI 1976/885

1 Jul 1976 (SI 1976/885)

British Leyland Act 1975 (c 43)

Whole Act repealed

Child Benefit Act 1975 (c 61)

Whole Act repealed

Children Act 1975 (c 72)

RA: 12 Nov 1975

Commencement provisions: s 108(2)–(4) (repealed EW, NI); Children Act 1975 (Scotland) (Commencement No 1) Order 1977, SI 1977/227; Children Act 1975 (Scotland) (Commencement No 2) Order 1978, SI 1978/440; Children Act 1975 (Scotland) (Commencement No 3) Order 1982, SI 1982/33; Children Act 1975 (Scotland) (Commencement No 4) Order 1984, SI 1984/554; Children Act 1975 (Scotland) (Commencement No 5) Order 1984, SI 1984/1702; Children Act 1975 (Scotland) (Commencement No 6) Order 1985, SI 1985/1557

Whole Act repealed (EW, NI)

s 1–46	Repealed
47	1 Apr 1986 (SI 1985/1557); prospectively repealed by Children (Scotland) Act 1995, s 105(4), (5), Sch 4, para 26(1), (2), Sch 5[1]
48(1), (2)	1 Apr 1986 (SI 1985/1557); prospectively repealed by Children (Scotland) Act 1995, s 105(4), (5), Sch 4, para 26(1), (2), Sch 5[1]
(3), (4)	1 Sep 1984 (SI 1984/554); prospectively repealed by Children (Scotland) Act 1995, s 105(4), (5), Sch 4, para 26(1), (2), Sch 5[1]
49	1 Apr 1986 (SI 1985/1557); prospectively repealed by Children (Scotland) Act 1995, s 105(4), (5), Sch 4, para 26(1), (2), Sch 5[1]
50–52	1 Apr 1986 (SI 1985/1557)
53	1 Apr 1986 (SI 1985/1557); prospectively repealed by Children (Scotland) Act 1995, s 105(4), (5), Sch 4, para 26(1), (6), Sch 5[1]
54	Repealed
55	1 Apr 1986 (SI 1985/1557)
56–65	Repealed
66	30 Jun 1985 (SI 1984/1702)
67–69	Repealed
70	*Not in force*
71	Repealed
72	12 Nov 1975 (s 108(3))
73	7 Mar 1977 (SI 1977/227); prospectively repealed by Children (Scotland) Act 1995, s 105(4), (5), Sch 4, para 26(1), (8), Sch 5[1]
74	7 Mar 1977 (except insofar as substitutes Social Work (Scotland) Act 1968, s 16(1)(b), (4), (11)(d) and in s 16(5) the words 'or in the voluntary organisation as the case may be,') (SI 1977/227)
	15 Feb 1982 (remainder) (SI 1982/33)
	Prospectively repealed by Children (Scotland) Act 1995, s 105(4), (5), Sch 4, para 26(1), (8), Sch 5[1]
75	15 Feb 1982 (SI 1982/33); prospectively repealed by Children (Scotland) Act 1995, s 105(4), (5), Sch 4, para 26(1), (8), Sch 5[1]
76	7 Mar 1977 (SI 1977/227); prospectively repealed by Children (Scotland) Act 1995, s 105(4), (5), Sch 4, para 26(1), (8), Sch 5[1]
77	7 Mar 1977 (insofar as inserts Social Work (Scotland) Act 1968, s 18(4A)(a)) (SI 1977/227)
	1 Sep 1984 (remainder) (SI 1984/554)
	Prospectively repealed by Children (Scotland) Act 1995, s 105(4), (5), Sch 4, para 26(1), (8), Sch 5[1]

Children Act 1975 (c 72)—*cont*

s 78	30 Jan 1985 (SI 1984/1702); prospectively repealed by Children (Scotland) Act 1995, s 105(4), (5), Sch 4, para 26(1), (8), Sch 5[1]
79	7 Mar 1977 (SI 1977/227); prospectively repealed by Children (Scotland) Act 1995, s 105(4), (5), Sch 4, para 26(1), (8), Sch 5[1]
80	1 Sep 1984 (SI 1984/554); prospectively repealed by Children (Scotland) Act 1995, s 105(4), (5), Sch 4, para 26(1), (8), Sch 5[1]
81	7 Mar 1977 (SI 1977/227); prospectively repealed by Children (Scotland) Act 1995, s 105(4), (5), Sch 4, para 26(1), (8), Sch 5[1]
82	12 Nov 1975 (s 108(3)); prospectively repealed by Children (Scotland) Act 1995, s 105(4), (5), Sch 4, para 26(1), (8), Sch 5[1]
83, 84	1 Jan 1976 (s 108(4)); prospectively repealed by Children (Scotland) Act 1995, s 105(4), (5), Sch 4, para 26(1), (8), Sch 5[1]
85–88	Repealed
89	Repealed; also prospectively repealed by Children (Scotland) Act 1995, s 105(4), Sch 4, para 26(1), (8)[1]
90–98	Repealed
99, 100	1 Jan 1976 (s 108(4)); prospectively repealed by Children Act 1995, s 105(4), (5), Sch 4, para 26(1), (8), Sch 5[1]
101	Repealed
102	1 Sep 1984 (SI 1984/554); prospectively repealed by Children (Scotland) Act 1995, s 105(4), (5), Sch 4, para 26(1), (8), Sch 5[1]
103	1 Jan 1976 (s 108(4)); prospectively repealed by Children (Scotland) Act 1995, s 105(4), (5), Sch 4, para 26(1), (8), Sch 5[1]
104	1 Jan 1976 (s 108(4))
105	1 Jan 1976 (s 108(4)); prospectively repealed by Children (Scotland) Act 1995, ss 102, 105(5), Sch 5[1]
106, 107	1 Jan 1976 (s 108(4))
108, 109	12 Nov 1975 (s 108(3))
Sch 1	Repealed
2	1 Jan 1976 (s 108(4)); repealed except paras 5(3), 6(2)
3, para 1	Repealed
2	1 Jan 1976 (s 108(4))
3–47	Repealed
48, 49	1 Jan 1976 (s 108(4))
50	15 Feb 1982 (SI 1982/33)
51(a)	1 Jan 1976 (s 108(4))
(b)	15 Feb 1982 (SI 1982/33)
52(a)	7 Mar 1977 (SI 1977/227); prospectively repealed by Children (Scotland) Act 1995, s 105(4), (5), Sch 4, para 26(1), (10), Sch 5[1]
(b)	15 Feb 1982 (SI 1982/33); prospectively repealed by Children (Scotland) Act 1995, s 105(4), (5), Sch 4, para 26(1), (10), Sch 5[1]
(c), (d)	7 Mar 1977 (SI 1977/227); prospectively repealed by Children (Scotland) Act 1995, s 105(4), (5), Sch 4, para 26(1), (10), Sch 5[1]

Children Act 1975 (c 72)—*cont*

Sch 3, para 52(e)	15 Feb 1982 (SI 1982/33); prospectively repealed by Children (Scotland) Act 1995, s 105(4), (5), Sch 4, para 26(1), (10), Sch 5[1]
(f)(i)	7 Mar 1977 (SI 1977/227); prospectively repealed by Children (Scotland) Act 1995, s 105(4), (5), Sch 4, para 26(1), (10), Sch 5[1]
(ii)	1 Jan 1976 (s 108(4)); prospectively repealed by Children (Scotland) Act 1995, s 105(4), (5), Sch 4, para 26(1), (10), Sch 5[1]
(g)(i)	15 Feb 1982 (SI 1982/33); prospectively repealed by Children (Scotland) Act 1995, s 105(4), (5), Sch 4, para 26(1), (10), Sch 5[1]
(ii)	1 Jan 1976 (s 108(4)); prospectively repealed by Children (Scotland) Act 1995, s 105(4), (5), Sch 4, para 26(1), (10), Sch 5[1]
53(a)	7 Mar 1977 (SI 1977/227); prospectively repealed by Children (Scotland) Act 1995, s 105(4), (5), Sch 4, para 26(1), (10), Sch 5[1]
(b)(i), (ii)	7 Mar 1977 (SI 1977/227); prospectively repealed by Children (Scotland) Act 1995, s 105(4), (5), Sch 4, para 26(1), (10), Sch 5[1]
(iii)	15 Feb 1982 (SI 1982/33); prospectively repealed by Children (Scotland) Act 1995, s 105(4), (5), Sch 4, para 26(1), (10), Sch 5[1]
(c)	15 Feb 1982 (SI 1982/33); prospectively repealed by Children (Scotland) Act 1995, s 105(4), (5), Sch 4, para 26(1), (10), Sch 5[1]
54, 55	1 Jan 1976 (s 108(4)); prospectively repealed by Children (Scotland) Act 1995, s 105(4), (5), Sch 4, para 26(1), (10), Sch 5[1]
56	*Not in force*; prospectively repealed by Children (Scotland) Act 1995, s 105(4), (5), Sch 4, para 26(1), (10), Sch 5[1]
57	12 Nov 1975 (s 108(3)); prospectively repealed by Children (Scotland) Act 1995, s 105(4), (5), Sch 4, para 26(1), (10), Sch 5[1]
58–60	1 Jan 1976 (s 108(4))
61–83	Repealed
4, Pt I–III	1 Jan 1976 (s 108(4))
IV	7 Mar 1977 (except in relation to s 12(3) of 1958 Act) (SI 1977/227)
	1 Sep 1984 (remainder) (SI 1984/554)
V	7 Mar 1977 (SI 1977/227)
VI	Repealed
VII	15 Feb 1982 (except in relation to provisions of s 28(2) of 1958 Act) (SI 1982/33))
	Not in force (repeal of above-mentioned provisions; now spent)
VIII, IX	1 Sep 1984 (SI 1984/554)
X	Repealed
XI	1 Sep 1984 (SI 1984/554)
XII	Repealed

[1] Any order(s) made under Children (Scotland) Act 1995, s 105, bringing the prospective repeals into force, will be noted to that Act in the service to this work

Church Commissioners (Miscellaneous Provisions) Measure 1975 (No 1)

RA: 1 Aug 1975

1 Aug 1975 (RA)

Cinematograph Films Act 1975 (c 73)

Whole Act repealed

Civil List Act 1975 (c 82)

RA: 19 Dec 1975

19 Dec 1975 (RA)

Coal Industry Act 1975 (c 56)

RA: 1 Aug 1975

Commencement provisions: s 8(2)

1 Sep 1975 (s 8(2))

Community Land Act 1975 (c 77)

Whole Act repealed

Conservation of Wild Creatures and Wild Plants Act 1975 (c 48)

Whole Act repealed

Consolidated Fund Act 1975 (c 1)

Whole Act repealed

Consolidated Fund (No 2) Act 1975 (c 12)

Whole Act repealed

Consolidated Fund (No 3) Act 1975 (c 79)

Whole Act repealed

Criminal Jurisdiction Act 1975 (c 59)

RA: 7 Aug 1975

Commencement provisions: s 14(2), (3); Criminal Jurisdiction Act 1975 (Commencement No 1) Order 1975, SI 1975/1347; Criminal Jurisdiction Act 1975 (Commencement No 2) Order 1976, SI 1976/813

s 1	1 Jun 1976 (SI 1976/813)
2	21 Aug 1975 (SI 1975/1347) (only as respects an act done in Northern Ireland) 1 Jun 1976 (otherwise) (SI 1976/813)

Criminal Jurisdiction Act 1975 (c 59)—*cont*

s 3	1 Jun 1976 (SI 1976/813)
4	21 Aug 1975 (so far as relates to Sch 2, paras 2(2), (3)) (SI 1975/1347)
	1 Jun 1976 (otherwise) (SI 1976/813)
5–7	1 Jun 1976 (SI 1976/813)
8	Repealed
9–11	1 Jun 1976 (SI 1976/813)
12	7 Aug 1975 (s 14(2)); repealed (EW)
13	7 Aug 1975 (s 14(2))
14	7 Aug 1975 (except as noted below) (s 14(2))
	1 Jun 1976 (so far as s 14(5) relates to Sch 6, Pts III, IV) (SI 1976/813)
Sch 1	1 Jun 1976 (SI 1976/813)
2, para 1	Repealed
2(1)	Repealed
(2), (3)	21 Aug 1975 (SI 1975/1347)
3	Repealed
3, 4	1 Jun 1976 (SI 1976/813)
5	7 Aug 1975 (s 14(2))
6, Pt I, II	7 Aug 1975 (s 14(2))
III, IV	1 Jun 1976 (SI 1976/813)

Criminal Procedure (Scotland) Act 1975 (c 21)

Whole Act repealed

Diseases of Animals Act 1975 (c 40)

Whole Act repealed

District Courts (Scotland) Act 1975 (c 20)

RA: 27 Mar 1975

Commencement provisions: s 27(2)

s 1	16 May 1975 (s 27(2))
1A	Inserted by Law Reform (Miscellaneous Provisions) (Scotland) Act 1985, s 33 (qv)
2–4	Repealed
5	16 May 1975 (s 27(2))
6	Repealed
7	16 May 1975 (s 27(2))
8	27 Mar 1975 (RA)
9	16 May 1975 (s 27(2))
10, 11	27 Mar 1975 (RA)
12, 13	16 May 1975 (s 27(2))
13A	Inserted by Statute Law (Repeals) Act 1989, s 1(2), Sch 2, Pt 1, para 2 (qv)
14	27 Mar 1975 (RA)
15	16 May 1975 (s 27(2))
16, 17	27 Mar 1975 (RA)
18	16 May 1975 (s 27(2))
19	Repealed
20	27 Mar 1975 (RA)
21, 22	Repealed

District Courts (Scotland) Act 1975 (c 20)—*cont*

s 23	27 Mar 1975 (RA)
24, 25	16 May 1975 (s 27(2))
26, 27	27 Mar 1975 (RA)
Sch 1, 2	16 May 1975 (s 27(2))

Ecclesiastical Offices (Age Limit) Measure 1975 (No 2)

RA: 1 Aug 1975

Commencement provisions: s 7(4)

1 Jan 1976 (day appointed by Archbishops of Canterbury and York under s 7(4))

Education Act 1975 (c 2)

RA: 25 Feb 1975

Commencement provisions: s 5(4), (5)

s 1, 2	Repealed
3[1]	25 Feb 1975 (RA)
4[1]	See Schedule below
5[1]	25 Feb 1975 (RA)
Sch Pt I[1]	1 Sep 1975 (s 5(4))
II[1]	25 Feb 1975 (RA; but repeals do not affect contributions or grants in respect of expenditure on work begun before 6 Nov 1974; see s 5(5))

[1] Whole Act prospectively repealed by Education Act 1993, s 307(3), Sch 21, Pt II; any order made under s 308(3) of that Act bringing the prospective repeal into force will be noted to that Act in the service to this work

Employment Protection Act 1975 (c 71)

RA: 12 Nov 1975

Commencement provisions: s 129(3); Employment Protection Act 1975 (Commencement No 1) Order 1975, SI 1975/1938; Employment Protection Act 1975 (Commencement No 2) Order 1976, SI 1976/144; Employment Protection Act 1975 (Commencement No 3) Order 1976, SI 1976/321[1]; Employment Protection Act 1975 (Commencement No 4) Order 1976, SI 1976/530 (as amended by SI 1976/1379, SI 1977/82); Employment Protection Act 1975 (Commencement No 6) Order 1976, SI 1976/1996; Employment Protection Act 1975 (Commencement No 7) Order 1977, SI 1977/433[1]; Employment Protection Act 1975 (Commencement No 8) Order 1977, SI 1977/936; Employment Protection Act 1975 (Commencement No 9) Order 1977, SI 1977/2075[1]

s 1–96	Repealed
97	1 Jan 1976 (SI 1975/1938)
98–110	Repealed
111	1 Feb 1977 (SI 1976/1996)
112, 113	Repealed
114, 115	1 Jan 1976 (SI 1975/1938)
116	1 Jan 1976 (so far as relates to Sch 15, paras 2, 3, 9) (SI 1975/1938)
	1 Mar 1976 (otherwise) (SI 1975/1938)

Employment Protection Act 1975 (c 71)—*cont*

s 117–123	Repealed
124	1 Jan 1976 (SI 1975/1938)
125(1)	See Sch 16 below
(2)	See Sch 17 below
(3)	See Sch 18 below
126–128	Repealed
129	1 Jan 1976 (SI 1975/1938)
Sch 1–8	Repealed
9, 10	1 Jan 1976 (SI 1975/1938)
11, 12	Repealed
13, 14	1 Jan 1976 (SI 1975/1938)
15, para 1	1 Mar 1976 (SI 1975/1938)
2, 3	1 Jan 1976 (SI 1975/1938)
4–8	1 Mar 1976 (SI 1975/1938)
9	1 Jan 1976 (SI 1975/1938)
10–21	1 Mar 1976 (SI 1975/1938)
16, Pt I–III	Repealed
IV, para 1–5	Repealed
6	1 Jan 1976 (SI 1975/1938)
7–17	Repealed
18(1)	1 Jun 1976 (so far as relates to para 13(6) (10), (11)) (SI 1975/1938)
	1 Jan 1976 (otherwise) (SI 1976/530)
(2)	Repealed
(3)	1 Jan 1976 (so far as relates to para 13(6), (10), (11)) (SI 1975/1938)
	1 Jan 1976 (otherwise) (SI 1976/530)
17, para 1–11	Repealed
12	1 Jan 1976 (SI 1975/1938)
13	Repealed
14, 15	1 Jan 1976 (SI 1975/1938)
16, 17	Repealed
18, 19	1 Jan 1976 (SI 1975/1938)
18	1 Jan 1976 (so far as it relates to Conciliation Act 1896; Agricultural Wages (Scotland) Act 1949; Public Records Act 1958; Wages Councils Act 1959; Equal Pay Act 1970; Superannuation Act 1972; Employment Agencies Act 1973; Employment and Training Act 1973; Health and Safety at Work etc Act 1974, s 2(5); Trade Union and Labour Relations Act 1974, s 8(10), Sch 1, para 26(1), Sch 3, para 9(4), (6), (7); House of Commons Disqualification Act 1975, Sch 1, Pt III; Northern Ireland Assembly Disqualification Act 1975, Sch 1, Pt III; Sex Discrimination Act 1975) (SI 1975/1938)
	1 Feb 1976 (so far as relates to Trade Union Act 1913; Industrial Courts Act 1919; Road Haulage Wages Act 1938; National Health Service (Amendment) Act 1949; Trade Union (Amalgamations, etc) Act 1964; Remuneration of Teachers Act 1965; Remuneration of Teachers (Scotland) Act 1967; Transport Act 1968; Consumer Credit Act 1974; Trade Union and Labour Relations Act 1974, ss 8(1), (8), 30(1), Sch 3, paras 2(6), 3, 10(4), (6), 15; House of

Employment Protection Act 1975 (c 71)—*cont*

Sch 18—*cont*	Commons Disqualification Act 1975, Sch 1, Pt II; Northern Ireland Assembly Disqualification Act 1975, Sch 1, Pt II) (SI 1975/1938)
	1 Mar 1976 (remaining repeals in Health and Safety at Work etc Act 1974) (SI 1975/1938)
	1 Jun 1976 (so far as relates to Education (Scotland) Act 1962; Redundancy Payments Act 1965; Social Security Act 1973; remaining provisions relating to Trade Union and Labour Relations Act 1974, except Sch 1, para 9(1)(a)) (SI 1976/530)
	1 Jan 1977 (so far as relates to Terms and Conditions of Employment Act 1959) (SI 1976/1996)
	1 Feb 1977 (otherwise) (SI 1976/1996)

[1] Provisions brought into force by these orders are now all repealed or spent

---

Evidence (Proceedings in other Jurisdictions) Act 1975 (c 34)

RA: 22 May 1975

Commencement provisions: s 10(2); Evidence (Proceedings in other Jurisdictions) Act 1975 (Commencement) Order 1976, SI 1976/429

4 May 1976 (SI 1976/429)

Export Guarantees Act 1975 (c 38)

Whole Act repealed

Export Guarantees Amendment Act 1975 (c 19)

Whole Act repealed

Farriers (Registration) Act 1975 (c 35)

RA: 22 May 1975

Commencement provisions: s 19(2), (3); Farriers (Registration) Act 1975 (Commencement No 1) Order 1975, SI 1975/2018; Farriers (Registration) Act 1975 (Commencement No 2) Order 1978, SI 1978/1928; Farriers (Registration) Act 1975 (Commencement No 3) Order 1981, SI 1981/767

s 1–6	1 Jan 1976 (SI 1975/2018)
7	Substituted by Farriers (Registration) (Amendment) Act 1977, s 1(1), Schedule (qv)
8–15	1 Jan 1976 (SI 1975/2018)
15A	Inserted by Farriers (Registration) (Amendment) Act 1977, ss 1(1), 2(3), Schedule (qv)
16	1 Jun 1979 (EW) (SI 1978/1928); 1 Nov 1981 (S, except in Highland Region, Western Isles Islands Area, Orkney Islands Area, Shetland Islands Area and all other islands) (SI 1981/767)
	Not in force (exceptions noted above)
17–19	1 Jan 1976 (SI 1975/2018)
Sch 1–3	1 Jan 1976 (SI 1975/2018)

Finance Act 1975 (c 7)

RA: 13 Mar 1975

See the note concerning Finance Acts at the front of this book

Finance (No 2) Act 1975 (c 45)

Budget Day: 15 Apr 1975

RA: 1 Aug 1975

See the note concerning Finance Acts at the front of this book

General Rate Act 1975 (c 5)

Whole Act repealed

Guard Dogs Act 1975 (c 50)

RA: 1 Aug 1975

Commencement provisions: s 8(2); Guard Dogs Act 1975 (Commencement No 1) Order 1975, SI 1975/1767

s 1	1 Feb 1976 (SI 1975/1767)
2–4	*Not in force*
5	1 Feb 1976 (SI 1975/1767; but note *not in force* in relation to ss 2–4, 6)
6	*Not in force*
7, 8	1 Feb 1976 (SI 1975/1767)

Hearing Aid Council (Extension) Act 1975 (c 39)

RA: 3 Jul 1975

Commencement provisions: s 2(2); Hearing Aid Council (Extension) Act 1975 (Commencement) Order 1975, SI 1975/1882

29 Dec 1975 (SI 1975/1882)

House of Commons Disqualification Act 1975 (c 24)

RA: 8 May 1975

8 May 1975 (RA)

Housing Finance (Special Provisions) Act 1975 (c 67)

Whole Act repealed

Housing Rents and Subsidies Act 1975 (c 6)

Whole Act repealed

Housing Rents and Subsidies (Scotland) Act 1975 (c 28)

RA: 8 May 1975

Commencement provisions: s 17(4) (repealed)

Whole Act repealed except Sch 3, paras 9, 10, which came into force on 16 May 1975 (s 17(4))

Industrial and Provident Societies Act 1975 (c 41)

RA: 3 Jul 1975

Commencement provisions: s 3(4)

3 Aug 1975 (s 3(4))

Industrial Injuries and Diseases (Northern Ireland Old Cases) Act 1975 (c 17)

Whole Act repealed

Industrial Injuries and Diseases (Old Cases) Act 1975 (c 16)

Whole Act repealed

Industry Act 1975 (c 68)

RA: 12 Nov 1975

Commencement provisions: s 39(6), (7); Industry Act 1975 (Commencement) Order 1975, SI 1975/1881

20 Nov 1975 (SI 1975/1881)

Inheritance (Provision for Family and Dependants) Act 1975 (c 63)

RA: 12 Nov 1975

Commencement provisions: s 27(3)

1 Apr 1976 (s 27(3); note that Act only applies to persons dying on or after this date)

International Road Haulage Permits Act 1975 (c 46)

RA: 1 Aug 1975

Commencement provisions: s 5(2)

1 Sep 1975 (s 5(2))

Iron and Steel Act 1975 (c 64)

Whole Act repealed

Limitation Act 1975 (c 54)

Whole Act repealed

Litigants in Person (Costs and Expenses) Act 1975 (c 47)

RA: 1 Aug 1975

Commencement provisions: s 2(2); Litigants in Person (Costs and Expenses) Act 1975 (Commencement) Order 1976, SI 1976/364; Litigants in Person (Costs and Expenses) Act 1975 (Commencement) (Scotland) Order 1976, SI 1976/1432; Litigants in Person (Costs and Expenses) Act 1975 (Commencement) (Northern Ireland) Order 1977, SI 1977/509; Litigants in Person (Costs and Expenses) Act 1975 (Commencement No 2) (Scotland) Order 1980, SI 1980/1152; Litigants in Person (Costs and Expenses) Act 1975 (Commencement No 2) Order 1980, SI 1980/1158

1 Apr 1976 (as respects civil proceedings in a county court, the Supreme Court and the Lands Tribunal) (EW) (SI 1976/364)
1 Oct 1976 (as respects civil proceedings in the sheriff court, the Scottish Land Court, the Court of Session, the House of Lords on appeal from the Court of Session and the Lands Tribunal for Scotland) (S) (SI 1976/1432)
1 May 1977 (as respects civil proceedings in a county court, the Supreme Court and the Lands Tribunal) (NI) (SI 1977/509)
1 Sep 1980 (remainder) (EW) (SI 1980/1158)
(remainder) (S) (SI 1980/1152)

Local Government (Scotland) Act 1975 (c 30)

RA: 8 May 1975

Commencement provisions: s 39(2); Local Government (Scotland) Act 1975 (Commencement) Order 1975, SI 1975/824; Local Government (Scotland) Act 1975 (Commencement No 2) Order 1975, SI 1975/1055

s 1	16 May 1975 (SI 1975/824)
2(1)(a)–(c)	16 Sep 1975 (SI 1975/824)
(d)	1 Apr 1976 (SI 1975/824)
(e)	16 Sep 1975 (SI 1975/824)
(ee)	Inserted by Rating and Valuation (Amendment) (Scotland) Act 1984, s 21, Sch 2, para 13(2) (qv)
(f), (g)	16 Sep 1975 (SI 1975/824)
(gg), (ggg)	Inserted by SI 1991/646–649, 914–917, 940, 941, 943–950, 1992/864, 865, 1782–1796, 1994/911–913, 2068–2081, (sub-para (gg) only) 1995/366–373, 929, 930 in different terms, and for different purposes, as from 1 Apr 1990 (SI 1991/646–649, 916), as from 1 Apr 1991 (SI 1991/914, 915, 917, 940, 941, 943–950), as from 1 Apr 1992 (SI 1992/864, 865), as from 17 Jul 1992 (SI 1992/1782–1796), as from 1 Apr 1993 (SI 1994/911), as from 1 Apr 1994 (SI 1994/912, 913, 2068–2081) and as from 1 Apr 1995 (sub-para (gg) only) (SI 1995/366–373, 929, 930)
(h)	16 Sep 1975 (SI 1975/824)
(2)(a), (b)	16 Sept 1975 (SI 1975/824)
(c)	1 Apr 1976 (SI 1975/824)
(cc)	Inserted by Rating and Valuation (Amendment) (Scotland) Act 1984, s 21, Sch 2, para 14 (qv)
(d)	16 Sep 1975 (SI 1975/824)

Local Government (Scotland) Act 1975 (c 30)—*cont*

s 2(3)	16 Sep 1975 (SI 1975/824)
(4)	Repealed
3	16 Sep 1975 (SI 1975/824)
4	15 Aug 1975 (SI 1975/824); repealed (1 Apr 1996) by Local Government etc (Scotland) Act 1994, ss 29(1)(b), 180(2), Sch 14
5	1 Apr 1976 (SI 1975/824)
6	Substituted by Local Government (Scotland) Act 1978, s 1 (qv)
7	16 May 1975 (SI 1975/824)
7A	Inserted by Local Government Finance Act 1992, s 110(1) (qv)
7B	Prospectively substituted for s 7A by Local Government Finance Act 1992, s 110(2)[1]
8	1 Apr 1976 (SI 1975/824)
9	16 May 1975 (SI 1975/824)
9A	Inserted by Local Government Finance Act 1988, s 137, Sch 12, Pt II, para 13 (qv); substituted by Local Government Finance Act 1992, s 110(4) (qv)
10, 11	16 May 1975 (SI 1975/824)
12	See Sch 2 below
13	16 May 1975 (SI 1975/824); prospectively repealed by Local Government etc (Scotland) Act 1994, s 180(2), Sch 14[2]
14, 15	16 May 1975 (SI 1975/824)
15A	Inserted by Local Government etc (Scotland) Act 1994, s 168(1) (qv)
16–19	16 May 1975 (SI 1975/824)
20	Repealed
21–29	16 May 1975 (SI 1975/824)
29A	Inserted by Local Government and Housing Act 1989, s 29(1) (qv)
30–37	16 May 1975 (SI 1975/824)
38(1)	See Sch 6 below
(2)	See Sch 7 below
39	8 May 1975 (RA)
Sch 1	Repealed
2, para 1	16 May 1975 (SI 1975/824)
2	16 May 1975 (as respects rate support grants for the year 1976–77 and any subsequent year) (SI 1975/824)
3	(the new s 4(1)–(3), (6), (7)) 16 May 1975 (as respects rate support grants for the year 1975–76 and any subsequent year) (SI 1975/824)
	(the new s 4(4), (5)) 16 May 1975 (as respects rate support grants for the year 1976–77 and any subsequent year) (SI 1975/824)
4	16 May 1975 (as respects rate support grants for the year 1976–77 and any subsequent year) (SI 1975/824)
5	16 May 1975 (as respects rate support grants for the year 1975–76 and any subsequent year) (SI 1975/824)
6, 7	16 May 1975 (as respects rate support grants for the year 1976–77 and any subsequent year) (SI 1975/824)

Local Government (Scotland) Act 1975 (c 30)—*cont*

Sch 3–5	16 May 1975 (SI 1975/824)
6, Pt I, para 1	1 Apr 1976 (SI 1975/824)
2	16 May 1975 (SI 1975/824)
Pt II, para 1	16 May 1975 (SI 1975/824)
2, 3	1 Apr 1976 (SI 1975/824)
4, 5	16 May 1975 (SI 1975/824)
6	Repealed
7	1 Apr 1976 (SI 1975/824)
8	16 May 1975 (SI 1975/824)
9	1 Apr 1976 (SI 1975/824)
10	Repealed
11, 12	16 May 1975 (SI 1975/824)
13	Repealed
14	1 Apr 1976 (SI 1975/824)
15, 16	Repealed
17, 18	1 Apr 1976 (SI 1975/824)
19–21	16 May 1975 (SI 1975/824)
22	Repealed
23	16 May 1975 (SI 1975/824); prospectively repealed by Local Government etc (Scotland) Act 1994, s 180(2), Sch 14[2]
24	16 May 1975 (as respects rate support grants for the year 1976–77 and any subsequent year) (SI 1975/824)
25–31	16 May 1975 (SI 1975/824)
32	16 Sep 1975 (SI 1975/824)
33	16 May 1975 (SI 1975/824)
34	Repealed
35, 36	16 May 1975 (SI 1975/824)
37	1 Apr 1976 (SI 1975/824)
38	16 May 1975 (SI 1975/824)
39	Repealed
40–42	16 May 1975 (SI 1975/824)
43	Repealed
44, 45	16 May 1975 (SI 1975/824)
46	16 May 1975 (SI 1975/824); prospectively repealed by Local Government and Housing Act 1989, s 194, Sch 12, Pt II[3]
47–52	16 May 1975 (SI 1975/824)
53	16 May 1975 (SI 1975/824); prospectively repealed by Local Government etc (Scotland) Act 1994, s 180(2), Sch 14[2]
54–62	16 May 1975 (SI 1975/824)
7	16 May 1975 (except entries noted below) (SI 1975/824)
	16 May 1975 (as respects rate support grants for the year 1976–77 and any subsequent year (repeals of or in Local Government (Financial Provisions) (Scotland) Act 1963 ss 3, 9(4); Local Government (Scotland) Act 1966, s 13; Local Government (Scotland) Act 1973, Sch 9, para 54(b))) (SI 1975/824)
	21 Jun 1975 (repeal of Local Government (Scotland) Act 1947, s 231) (SI 1975/1055)
	15 Aug 1975 (repeal of Valuation and Rating (Scotland) Act 1956, s 5) (SI 1975/824)
	16 Sep 1975 (repeals of or in Lands Valuation (Scotland) Act 1854, ss 1, 5; Valuation and Rating

Local Government (Scotland) Act 1975 (c 30)—*cont*

Sch 7—*cont*

(Scotland) Act 1956, ss 9(1), (2), (4), (7), 13(2), Sch 2; Local Government (Financial Provisions) (Scotland) Act 1962, s 9, Sch 2, para 4) (SI 1975/824)

1 Apr 1976 (repeals of or in Lands Valuation (Scotland) Act 1854, ss 23, 24, 27; Valuation of Lands (Scotland) Acts Amendment Act 1894; Local Government (Scotland) Act 1947, s 232; Local Government Act 1948; Rating and Valuation (Scotland) Act 1952; Valuation and Rating (Scotland) Act 1956, ss 9(6), 10; Local Government (Financial Provisions) (Scotland) Act 1963, s 21; Local Government (Development and Finance) (Scotland) Act 1964, s 12; Rating Act 1966; Local Government (Scotland) Act 1966, Sch 2; Local Government (Scotland) Act 1973, Sch 9, para 57) (SI 1975/824)

1 Apr 1977 (repeal of Lands Valuation (Scotland) Act 1854, s 9) (SI 1975/824)

1 Apr 1978 (repeals of or in Lands Valuation (Scotland) Act 1854, s 42; Registration Amendment (Scotland) Act 1885; Local Government (Financial Provisions) (Scotland) Act 1963, s 13(1), (2)(b), (e), (3), (4), (6), (7), (8)) (SI 1975/824)

[1] Any order(s) made under Local Government Finance Act 1992, s 119(2), bringing the prospective substitution into force will be noted to that Act in the service to this work.

[2] Any order(s) made under Local Government etc (Scotland) Act 1994, s 184(2), (3), bringing the prospective amendment into force will be noted to that Act in the service to this work

[3] Any order made under Local Government and Housing Act 1989, s 195(2), (3), bringing the prospective repeal into force will be noted to that Act in the service to this work

---

Local Land Charges Act 1975 (c 76)

RA: 12 Nov 1975

Commencement provisions: s 20(3); Local Land Charges Act 1975 (Commencement) Order 1977, SI 1977/984

1 Aug 1977 (SI 1977/984)

Lotteries Act 1975 (c 58)

RA: 7 Aug 1975

Commencement provisions: s 20(6) (repealed); Lotteries Act 1975 (Commencement No 1) Order 1975, SI 1975/1413

Whole Act repealed except s 20(1), (3), Sch 4, para 6 which came into force on 5 Sep 1975 (SI 1975/1413)

Malta Republic Act 1975 (c 31)

RA: 8 May 1975

Independence Day: 13 Dec 1974

Mental Health (Amendment) Act 1975 (c 29)

Whole Act repealed

Ministerial and other Salaries Act 1975 (c 27)

RA: 8 May 1975

8 May 1975 (RA)

Ministers of the Crown Act 1975 (c 26)

RA: 8 May 1975

8 May 1975 (RA)

Mobile Homes Act 1975 (c 49)

RA: 1 Aug 1975

Commencement provisions: s 10(2)

1 Oct 1975 (s 10(2))

Moneylenders (Crown Agents) Act 1975 (c 81)

Whole Act repealed

New Towns Act 1975 (c 42)

RA: 3 Jul 1975

Whole Act repealed except for s 2(3) (S), which came into force on 3 Jul 1975 (RA)

Northern Ireland Assembly Disqualification Act 1975 (c 25)

RA: 8 May 1975

8 May 1975 (RA)

Northern Ireland (Emergency Provisions) (Amendment) Act 1975 (c 62)

RA: 7 Aug 1975

Commencement provisions: s 21(1)

21 Aug 1975 (s 21(1))

Northern Ireland (Loans) Act 1975 (c 83)

RA: 19 Dec 1975

19 Dec 1975 (RA)

Nursing Homes Act 1975 (c 37)

Whole Act repealed

OECD Support Fund Act 1975 (c 80)

RA: 19 Dec 1975

19 Dec 1975 (RA)

Offshore Petroleum Development (Scotland) Act 1975 (c 8)

RA: 13 Mar 1975

13 Mar 1975 (RA)

Oil Taxation Act 1975 (c 22)

RA: 8 May 1975

8 May 1975 (RA)

Note: Petroleum Revenue Tax (levied in accordance with Pt I (ss 1–12, Schs 1–8) of this Act, abolished for new oil and gas fields ('non-taxable fields') with effect from 16 Mar 1993, by Finance Act 1993, s 185)

Petroleum and Submarine Pipelines Act 1975 (c 74)

RA: 12 Nov 1975

Commencement provisions: s 49(2); Petroleum and Submarine Pipe-lines Act 1975 (Commencement) Order 1975, SI 1975/2120

1 Jan 1976 (SI 1975/2120)

Policyholders Protection Act 1975 (c 75)

RA: 12 Nov 1975

12 Nov 1975 (RA)

Prices Act 1975 (c 32)

RA: 8 May 1975

8 May 1975 (RA)

Public Service Vehicles (Arrest of Offenders) Act 1975 (c 53)

RA: 1 Aug 1975

1 Aug 1975 (RA) although note s 1, in part, *not in force* in pursuance of s 2(3); *whole Act prospectively repealed* by Transport and Works Act 1992, s 68(1), Sch 4, Pt I; any order made under s 70 of that Act, bringing the prospective repeal of this Act into force will be noted to that Act in the service to this work

---

Recess Elections Act 1975 (c 66)

RA: 12 Nov 1975

Commencement provisions: s 5(7)

12 Dec 1975 (s 5(7))

Referendum Act 1975 (c 33)

Whole Act repealed

Remuneration, Charges and Grants Act 1975 (c 57)

Whole Act repealed

Reservoirs Act 1975 (c 23)

RA: 8 May 1975

Commencement provisions: s 29; Reservoirs Act 1975 (Commencement No 1) Order 1983, SI 1983/1666; Reservoirs Act 1975 (Commencement No 2) Order 1985, SI 1985/176; Reservoirs Act 1975 (Commencement No 3) Order 1986, SI 1986/466; Reservoirs Act 1975 (Commencement No 4) Order 1986, SI 1986/2202

s 1	30 Nov 1983 (SI 1983/1666)
2, 3	1 Apr 1985 (SI 1985/176)[1]
4, 5	30 Nov 1983 (SI 1983/1666)
6–10	1 Apr 1986 (SI 1986/466)[2]
11	1 Apr 1985 (SI 1985/176)[1]
12–14	1 Apr 1986 (SI 1986/466)[2]
15(1)–(3)	1 Apr 1986 (SI 1986/466)[2]
(4)	1 Apr 1985 (so far as applied by s 16(5)) (SI 1985/176)[1]
	1 Apr 1986 (otherwise) (SI 1986/466)[2]
(5)	1 Apr 1986 (SI 1986/466)[2]
16	1 Apr 1985 (SI 1985/176)[1]
17(1)(a)	1 Apr 1985 (SI 1985/176)[1]
(b)–(d)	1 Apr 1986 (SI 1986/466)[2]
(e)	1 Apr 1985 (SI 1985/176)[1]
(2)	1 Apr 1985 (SI 1985/176)[1]
(3)	1 Apr 1986 (SI 1986/466)[2]
(4)–(9)	1 Apr 1985 (SI 1985/176)[1]
18	1 Apr 1985 (SI 1985/176)[1]
19, 20	1 Apr 1986 (SI 1986/466)[2]
21(1)–(4)	1 Apr 1986 (SI 1986/466)[2]
(5), (6)	1 Apr 1985 (so far as relate to the provision of information to persons appointed under s 16(3)) (SI 1985/176)[1]
	1 Apr 1986 (otherwise) (SI 1986/466)[2]
22	1 Apr 1985 (so far as relates to provisions brought into force by SI 1983/1666 or 1985/176) (SI 1985/176)[1]
	1 Apr 1986 (otherwise) (SI 1986/466)[2]
23	1 Apr 1986 (SI 1986/466)[2]
24	1 Apr 1985 (SI 1985/176)[1]
25–28	1 Apr 1986 (SI 1986/466)[2]
29, 30	30 Nov 1983 (SI 1983/1666)
Sch 1	30 Nov 1983 (SI 1983/1666)
2	1 Apr 1986 (SI 1986/466)[2]

[1] Brought into force in the areas of Metropolitan Counties or Greater London on 1 Apr 1986 (SI 1986/466)

[2] Brought into force in the areas of Metropolitan Counties or Greater London on 1 Apr 1987 (SI 1986/2202)

Safety of Sports Grounds Act 1975 (c 52)

RA: 1 Aug 1975

Commencement provisions: s 19(6); Safety of Sports Grounds Act 1975 (Commencement) Order 1975, SI 1975/1375

1 Sep 1975 (SI 1975/1375)

Salmon and Freshwater Fisheries Act 1975 (c 51)

RA: 1 Aug 1975

Commencement provisions: s 43(4)

1 Aug 1975 (s 43(4))

Scottish Development Agency Act 1975 (c 69)

RA: 12 Nov 1975

Commencement provisions: ss 8(6), 15(5), 28(2); Scottish Development Agency Act 1975 (Commencement) Order 1975, SI 1975/1898

Whole Act repealed (by Enterprise and New Towns (Scotland) Act 1990, s 38(2), Sch 5), except ss 1, 20, 28, Sch 1, paras 1–6, 11–14, 16, 17, which came into force on 15 December 1975 (SI 1975/1898)

Sex Discrimination Act 1975 (c 65)

RA: 12 Nov 1975

Commencement provisions: s 83(2), (4), (5); Sex Discrimination Act 1975 (Commencement) Order 1975, SI 1975/1845 (amended by SI 1975/2112)

s 1–5	12 Nov 1975 (RA)
6, 7	29 Dec 1975 (SI 1975/1845)
8(1)–(5)	29 Dec 1975 (SI 1975/1845)
(6)	See Sch 1 below
9–13	29 Dec 1975 (SI 1975/1845)
14	Substituted by Employment Act 1989, s 7(1) (qv)
15–20	29 Dec 1975 (SI 1975/1845)
21	Repealed
22	29 Dec 1975 (SI 1975/1845; note however that this section and s 25, so far as relate to admission of pupils to educational establishments for certain purposes, do not apply to offers of, or applications for, admission on date before 1 Sep 1976)
22A	Inserted (EW) by Further and Higher Education Act 1992, s 93(1), Sch 8, Pt II, paras 75, 77 (qv)
23	29 Dec 1975 (SI 1975/1845)
23A	Inserted (EW) by Further and Higher Education Act 1992, s 93(1), Sch 8, Pt II, paras 75, 78 (qv)
23B	Inserted (S) (prospectively in part) by Further and Higher Education (Scotland) Act 1992, s 62(2), Sch 9, para 4(1), (3)[1]
23C	Inserted (EW) by Education Act 1993, s 307(1), Sch 19, para 57 (qv)
23D	Inserted (EW) by Education Act 1994, s 24, Sch 2, para 5(1), (3) (qv)
24	29 Dec 1975 (SI 1975/1845)
25	29 Dec 1975 (SI 1975/1845; see note to s 22 above)
26–35	29 Dec 1975 (SI 1975/1845)
35A	Inserted by Courts and Legal Services Act 1990, s 64(1) (qv)
35B	Inserted by Courts and Legal Services Act 1990, s 65(2) (qv)
36, 37	29 Dec 1975 (SI 1975/1845)

Sex Discrimination Act 1975 (c 65)—*cont*

s 38	29 Dec 1975 (SI 1975/1845 as amended by SI 1975/2112; but note not unlawful to publish or cause to be published printed advertisement before 1 Apr 1976 if printed or made up for publication before 15 Dec 1975)
39–50	29 Dec 1975 (SI 1975/1845)
51	Substituted by Employment Act 1989, s 3(3) (qv)
51A	Inserted by Employment Act 1989, s 3(3) (qv)
52	29 Dec 1975 (SI 1975/1845)
52A	Inserted by Employment Act 1989, s 3(4) (qv)
53	12 Nov 1975 (SI 1975/1845)
54, 55	29 Dec 1975 (SI 1975/1845)
56	1 Jan 1976 (SI 1975/1845)
56A	Inserted by Race Relations Act 1976, s 79(4), Sch 4, para 1 (qv)
57–61	29 Dec 1975 (SI 1975/1845)
62	Substituted by Race Relations Act 1976, s 79(4), Sch 4, para 3 (qv)
63–76	29 Dec 1975 (SI 1975/1845)
77–85	12 Nov 1975 (RA)
85A	Inserted by Trade Union and Labour Relations (Consolidation) Act 1992, s 300(2), Sch 2, para 6 (qv)
85B	Inserted by Trade Union Reform and Employment Rights Act 1993, s 49(1), Sch 7, para 9 (qv)
86, 87	12 Nov 1975 (RA)
Sch 1	29 Dec 1975 (SI 1975/1845; but note so far as Schedule amends Equal Pay Act 1970, s 6, and as regards that Act as set out in Pt II of this Schedule, it came into force on 6 April 1978 (SI 1975/1845). In interim period SI 1975/1845 provided for substituted para 3 of this Schedule for the purposes of s 8(6) of this Act)
2, 3	29 Dec 1975 (SI 1975/1845)
4	12 Nov 1975 (RA)
5, 6	29 Dec 1975 (SI 1975/1845)

[1] Any order(s) made under Further and Higher Education (Scotland) Act 1992 s 63(2), bringing the insertion, by Sch 9, para 4(3) to that Act, of s 23B into force, so far as not already in force, will be noted to that Act in the service to this work

---

Social Security Act 1975 (c 14)

Whole Act repealed

Social Security Benefits Act 1975 (c 11)

RA: 13 Mar 1975

Commencement provisions: s 14(5), Sch 5; Social Security Benefits Act 1975 (Commencement) (No 1) Order 1975, SI 1975/400; Social Security Benefits (1975 Act) (Commencement No 1) (Northern Ireland) Order 1975, SR (NI) 1975/60; Social Security Benefits Act 1975 (Commencement) (No 2) Order 1975, SI 1975/1336; Social Security Benefits (1975 Act) (Commencement No 2) (Northern Ireland) Order 1975, SR (NI) 1975/243

s 1–11	Repealed
12	24 Mar 1975 (SI 1975/400)
13	24 Mar 1975 (SR (NI) 1975/60)
14(1), (2)	24 Mar 1975 (SI 1975/400, SR (NI) 1975/60)
(3)	Repealed

Social Security Benefits Act 1975 (c 11)—*cont*

s 14(4), (5)	24 Mar 1975 (SI 1975/400, SR (NI) 1975/60)
(6)	See Sch 6 below
Sch 1–3	Repealed
4, 5	24 Mar 1975 (SI 1975/400, SR (NI) 1975/60)
6, Pt I	SI 1975/400 brought following repeals into force on dates as indicated:

(a) provisions of the National Insurance (Industrial Injuries) Act 1965—
(i) ss 19(3)(d), 21(4)(part) .... 6 Apr 1975
(ii) Sch 5, para 1 (parts) .... 7 Apr 1975
(b) Supplementary Benefit Act 1966, Sch 2, para 2(2) .... 7 Apr 1975
(c) provisions of the Family Allowances and National Insurance Act 1968.................. 8 Apr 1975
(d) provision of the National Insurance Act 1969.................. 6 Apr 1975
(e) provision of the National Insurance Act 1971.................. 6 Apr 1975
(f) provisions of the Social Security Act 1973—
(i) ss 9(3)(parts), 24(8)(part), 25(11)(part), 39, Sch 11, Sch 13, paras 4, 9(part) .... 24 Mar 1975
(ii) s 14(6)(c)(part).................. 16 May 1975
(iii) s 32(4)(a)(parts).................. 7 Apr 1975
(iv) Sch 28, Pt I, so much as relates to the National Insurance Act 1967, s 4(4) .... 6 Apr 1975
(g) provisions of the National Insurance Act 1974—
(i) ss 1(1), 7(a), Sch 1 .... 6 Apr 1975
(ii) s 3(1), (2), Sch 3 in the case of—
(aa) injury benefit (including increase for dependants) ..... 10 Apr 1975
(bb) disablement benefit (including increases of disablement pension), increase of unemployability supplement under s 13A, maximum under s 29(1)(a) of aggregate of weekly benefits payable for successive accidents and maximum disablement gratuity under s 12(3) .... 9 Apr 1975
(cc) widow's pension under s 19, widower's pension under s 20 and allowances in respect of children of deceased's family under s 21.. 7 Apr 1975
(dd) benefit under the Industrial Injuries and Diseases (Old Cases) Act 1967............... 9 Apr 1975

Social Security Benefits Act 1975 (c 11)—*cont*

Sch 6, Pt I—*cont*

(iii) s 5, Sch 4, para 22 .... 24 Mar 1975

SR (NI) 1975/60 brought following repeals into force in Northern Ireland on the dates indicated:

Provisions of the Social Security Act 1973—

(i) ss 9(3)(parts), 24(8)(part), 25(11)(part), Sch 13, paras 4, 9 (parts) ...... 24 Mar 1975

(ii) s 14(6)(c)(part) .... 6 May 1975

(iii) s 32(4)(a)(parts) .... 7 Apr 1975

(iv) Sch 28, Pt II, so much as relates to the National Insurance Act (Northern Ireland) 1967, s 5(4) .... 6 Apr 1975

SI 1975/1336 brought following repeals into force on 17 Nov 1975:

(i) Supplementary Benefit Act 1966, Sch 2, para 23(1)

(ii) Family Income Supplements Act 1970, s 13(3)

(iii) Social Security Act 1973, Sch 27, para 70(d), (e)

(iv) National Insurance and Supplementary Benefit Act 1973, Sch 4, para 8

(v) National Insurance Act 1974, Sch 4, para 14

SR (NI) 1975/243 brought following repeals into force in Northern Ireland on 17 Nov 1975:

(i) Social Security Act 1973, Sch 7, para 161(d), (e)

(ii) National Insurance and Supplementary Benefit Act 1973, Sch 4, para 8

(iii) National Insurance Act 1974, Sch 4, para 56

Pt II

SR (NI) 1975/60 brought following repeals into force in Northern Ireland on the dates indicated:

(a) provisions of the National Insurance (Industrial Injuries) Act (Northern Ireland) 1966—

(i) ss 19(3)(d), 21(4)(part) .... 6 Apr 1975

(ii) Sch 5, para 1(parts) .... 7 Apr 1975

(b) Supplementary Benefits &c (Northern Ireland) 1966, Sch 2, para 2(2) .... 7 Apr 1975

(c) provisions of the Family Allowances and National Insurance (No 2) Act (Northern Ireland) 1968 .... 8 Apr 1975

(d) provision of the National Insurance &c (No 2) Act (Northern Ireland) 1969 .... 6 Apr 1975

(e) provision of the Social Services (Parity) Order (Northern Ireland) 1971 .... 6 Apr 1975

(f) provisions of the National Insurance Measure (Northern Ireland) 1974—

(i) s 1(1), Sch 1 .... 6 Apr 1975

(ii) s 3(1), (2) and Sch 3 in the case of—

(aa) injury benefit (including increases for dependants) .... 10 Apr 1975

(bb) disablement benefit (including increases of disablement pension), increases of

Social Security Benefits Act 1975 (c 11)—*cont*

Sch 6, Pt II—*cont*

unemployability supplement under s 13A, maximum under s 29(1)(a) of aggregate of weekly benefits payable for successive accidents and maximum disablement gratuity under s 12(4) .... 9 Apr 1975

(cc) widow's pension under s 19, widower's pension under s 20 and allowances in respect of children of deceased's family under s 21 .... 7 Apr 1975

(dd) benefit under the Workmen's Compensation (Supplementation) Act (Northern Ireland) 1966..... 9 Apr 1975

(iii) Sch 4, para 2(b) so far as it relates to the Social Security Act 1973, Sch 13, para 5(2) ..... 16 May 1975

SR (NI) 1975/243 brought following repeals into force in Northern Ireland on 17 Nov 1975:

(i) Supplementary Benefits Act (Northern Ireland) 1966, Sch 2, para 23(1)

(ii) Family Income Supplements Act (Northern Ireland) 1971, s 13(3)

Social Security (Consequential Provisions) Act 1975 (c 18)

RA: 20 Mar 1975

Commencement provisions: s 3(2)

This Act came into force, subject to s 3(3)–(5), as soon as all the provisions mentioned in s 3(1) of this Act came into force, which for most purposes was 6 Apr 1975

Social Security (Northern Ireland) Act 1975 (c 15)

RA: 20 Mar 1975

Commencement provisions: s 158(3)

This Act came into force, subject to Social Security (Consequential Provisions) Act 1975, s 3(5), on 6 Apr 1975

Whole Act, except ss 97(4), 158 and Sch 10, paras 5(2), 6, 7, 7A *repealed* (1 Jul 1992) by Social Security (Consequential Provisions) (Northern Ireland) Act 1992, s 3, Sch 1

Social Security Pensions Act 1975 (c 60)

RA: 7 Aug 1975

Commencement provisions: s 67(1), (2), (3); Social Security Pensions Act 1975 (Commencement No 1) Order 1975, SI 1975/1318; Social Security Pensions Act 1975

Social Security Pensions Act 1975 (c 60)—*cont*

(Commencement No 2) Order 1975, SI 1975/1572; Social Security Pensions Act 1975 (Commencement No 3) Order 1975, SI 1975/1689; Social Security Pensions Act 1975 (Commencement No 4) Order 1975, SI 1975/2079; Social Security Pensions Act 1975 (Commencement No 5) Order 1976, SI 1976/141; Social Security Pensions Act 1975 (Commencement No 6) Order 1976, SI 1976/1173; Social Security Pensions Act 1975 (Commencement No 7) Order 1976, SI 1976/2129; Social Security Pensions Act 1975 (Commencement No 8) Order 1977, SI 1977/778; Social Security Pensions Act 1975 (Commencement No 9) Order 1977, SI 1977/1403; Social Security Pensions Act 1975 (Commencement No 10) Order 1977, SI 1977/1617; Social Security Pensions Act 1975 (Commencement No 11) Order 1977, SI 1977/2028; Social Security Pensions Act 1975 (Commencement No 12) Order 1978, SI 1978/367; Social Security Pensions Act 1975 (Commencement No 13) Order 1979, SI 1979/171; Social Security Pensions Act 1975 (Commencement No 14) Order 1979, SI 1979/367 (revoked); Social Security Pensions Act 1975 (Commencement No 15) Order 1979, SI 1979/394; Social Security Pensions Act 1975 (Commencement No 16) Order 1979, SI 1979/1030

s 1–58B		Repealed
59		6 Apr 1979 (SI 1975/1689)
59A		Inserted by Social Security Act 1979, s 11(4) (qv)
59B–60B		Repealed
61		7 Aug 1975 (SI 1975/1318)
61A		Inserted by Social Security (Consequential Provisions) Act 1992, s 4, Sch 2, para 37 (qv); repealed by Pension Schemes Act 1993, s 188(1), Sch 5, Pt I (qv)
61B		Inserted by Social Security (Consequential Provisions) Act 1992, s 4, Sch 2, para 37 (qv)
62–64		7 Aug 1975 (SI 1975/1318)
65(1)		See Sch 4 below
	(2)	7 Aug 1975 (SI 1975/1318)
	(3)	See Sch 5 below
	(4)	Repealed
	(5)	7 Aug 1975 (SI 1975/1318)
66		Repealed
67, 68		7 Aug 1975 (SI 1975/1318)
Sch 1–3A		Repealed
4, para 1–3		Repealed
	4	6 Apr 1979 (SI 1975/1689)
	5–9	Repealed
	10	6 Apr 1979 (SI 1975/1689)
	11, 12	Repealed
	13	7 Aug 1975 (SI 1975/1318)
	14	Repealed
	15	6 Apr 1978 (SI 1975/1689)
	16	7 Aug 1975 (SI 1975/1318)
	17	Repealed
	18, 19	6 Apr 1979 (SI 1975/1689)
	20	Repealed
	21	Spent
	22–33	Repealed
	34	Spent
	35–64	Repealed
	65	Spent
	66–71	Repealed

Social Security Pensions Act 1975 (c 60)—*cont*

Sch 5 — 7 Aug 1975 (repeals of or in Public Records Act 1958; Income and Corporation Taxes Act 1970; Attachment of Earnings Act 1971; Social Security Act 1973, Pt III, ss 85, 86, 89(4), 98, Schs 18–20; Social Security Act 1975, ss 27(6), 133(6), Sch 20; Social Security (Consequential Provisions) Act 1975, Sch 2, paras 53–59, 63, 64(a), Sch 3; House of Commons Disqualification Act 1975) (SI 1975/1318)

21 Nov 1975 (repeals of or in Contracts of Employment Act 1972; Social Security Act 1973, ss 1, 23, 51–62, 88, 89(3), 91, 92, 99, Schs 15, 22, 23; National Insurance Act 1974; Social Security (Consequential Provisions) Act 1975, Sch 2, paras 51, 62, 64(b), 65) (SI 1975/1689)

6 Apr 1977 (repeals of or in Social Security Act 1975, ss 4, 5, 7(2)(c), 130, 167) (SI 1975/1689)

6 Apr 1978 (repeals of or in Social Security Act 1973, s 93, Sch 24; Social Security Act 1975, ss 6, 7(2)(a), (b), (3), 8, 9, 120; Social Security (Consequential Provisions) Act 1975, Sch 2, paras 1(b), 2(b), 7(a)) (SI 1975/1689)

6 Apr 1979 (repeals of or in Pensions (Increase) Act 1971; Superannuation Act 1972; Parliamentary and other Pensions Act 1972; Pensions (Increase) Act 1974; Social Security Act 1975, ss 28, 29, Schs 4, 7; Social Security (Consequential Provisions) Act 1975, Sch 2, para 47) (SI 1975/1689)

Repealed (otherwise)

Statute Law (Repeals) Act 1975 (c 10)

RA: 13 Mar 1975

13 Mar 1975 (RA)

Statutory Corporations (Financial Provisions) Act 1975 (c 55)

RA: 1 Aug 1975

1 Aug 1975 (RA)

Supply Powers Act 1975 (c 9)

RA: 13 Mar 1975

Commencement provisions: s 9(2)

13 Apr 1975 (s 9(2))

Unsolicited Goods and Services (Amendment) Act 1975 (c 13)

RA: 20 Mar 1975

Commencement provisions: s 4(2), (3); Unsolicited Goods and Services (Amendment) Act 1975 (Commencement No 1) Order 1975, SI 1975/731

Unsolicited Goods and Services (Amendment) Act 1975 (c 13)—*cont*

s 1[1]	20 Mar 1975 (s 4(2))
2(1)	*Not in force*
(2)	30 May 1975 (SI 1975/731)
3, 4	20 Mar 1975 (s 4(2))

[1] Note that any regulations made by virtue of s 1 of this Act (inserts Unsolicited Goods and Services Act 1971, s 3A) shall not come into force before the commencement of s 2 of this Act

Welsh Development Agency Act 1975 (c 70)

RA: 12 Nov 1975

Commencement provisions: s 29(2); Welsh Development Agency Act 1975 (Commencement) Order 1975, SI 1975/2028

s 1, 2	1 Jan 1976 (SI 1975/2028)
3	Repealed
4–11	1 Jan 1976 (SI 1975/2028)
12	Repealed
13–15	1 Jan 1976 (SI 1975/2028)
16	Substituted by Derelict Land Act 1982, s 2(1) (qv)
17–28	1 Jan 1976 (SI 1975/2028)
29	12 Nov 1975 (RA)
Sch 1–3	1 Jan 1976 (SI 1975/2028)

1976

Adoption Act 1976 (c 36)

RA: 22 Jul 1976

Commencement provisions: s 74(2); Children Act 1975 and the Adoption Act 1976 (Commencement) Order 1983, SI 1983/1946; Children Act 1975 and the Adoption Act 1976 (Commencement No 2) Order 1987, SI 1987/1242

s 1–9	1 Jan 1988 (SI 1987/1242)
10	Repealed
11–20	1 Jan 1988 (SI 1987/1242)
21	Substituted by Children Act 1989, s 88, Sch 10, para 9 (qv)
22, 23	1 Jan 1988 (EW) (SI 1987/1242); repealed (S)
24, 25	1 Jan 1988 (SI 1987/1242)
26	Repealed
27–33	1 Jan 1988 (SI 1987/1242)
34	Repealed
35–39	1 Jan 1988 (SI 1987/1242)
40	Repealed
41–51	1 Jan 1988 (SI 1987/1242)
51A	Inserted by Children Act 1989, s 88, Sch 10, para 21 (qv)
52–57	1 Jan 1988 (SI 1987/1242)
57A	Inserted by Children Act 1989, s 88, Sch 10, para 25 (qv)
58	1 Jan 1988 (SI 1987/1242)
58A	27 May 1984 (inserted by Health and Social Services and Social Security Adjudications Act 1983, s 9, Sch 2, para 35 (qv); note that SI 1983/1946 brought the section into force as noted here, but that the insertion was actually made as from the 15 Aug 1983; see the Health and Social Services and Social Security Adjudications Act 1983 (Commencement No 1) Order 1983, SI 1983/974)
59–65	1 Jan 1988 (SI 1987/1242)
65A	Inserted by Children Act 1989, s 88, Sch 10, para 29 (qv)
66–72	1 Jan 1988 (SI 1987/1242)
73(1)	1 Jan 1988 (SI 1987/1242)
(2)	See Sch 3 below
(3)	See Sch 4 below
74	27 May 1984 (SI 1983/1946)
Sch 1, 2	1 Jan 1988 (SI 1987/1242)
3, para 1–8	Repealed or superseded
9, 10	1 Jan 1988 (SI 1987/1242)
11–14	Repealed or superseded
15	1 Jan 1988 (SI 1987/1242)

Adoption Act 1976 (c 36)—*cont*

Sch 3, para 16	Repealed
17	1 Jan 1988 (SI 1987/1242)
18–22	Repealed or superseded
23, 24	1 Jan 1988 (SI 1987/1242)
25–44	Repealed
4	15 Aug 1983 (repeal of Adoption Act 1958, s 33; see Health and Social Services and Social Security Adjudications Act 1983, s 9, Sch 2, para 1 and SI 1983/974, noted to s 58A above)
	1 Jan 1988 (otherwise except repeal of Children Act 1975, Sch 3, paras 6, 26, 63) (SI 1987/1242)
	Not in force (exception noted above; but the whole of the Children Act 1975 was repealed (EW) by Children Act 1989, s 108(7), Sch 15)

Agriculture (Miscellaneous Provisions) Act 1976 (c 55)

RA: 15 Nov 1976

Commencement provisions: s 27(2), (3); Agriculture (Miscellaneous Provisions) Act 1976 (Commencement No 1) Order 1977, SI 1977/39; Agriculture (Miscellaneous Provisions) Act 1976 (Commencement No 2) Order 1978, SI 1978/402

s 1	15 Nov 1976 (RA)
2	Repealed
3	1 Feb 1977 (SI 1977/39)
4, 5	15 Nov 1976 (RA)
6	15 Nov 1976 (RA); repealed (EW)
7	15 Nov 1976 (RA)
8–12	Repealed
13, 14	7 Apr 1978 (SI 1978/402); repealed (S)
15	15 Nov 1976 (RA)
16-24	Repealed
25–27	15 Nov 1976 (RA)
Sch 1	1 Feb 1977 (SI 1977/39)
2	15 Nov 1976 (RA); repealed (EW)
3	15 Nov 1976 (RA)
3A	Repealed
4, Pt I	15 Nov 1976 (RA)
II	15 Nov 1976 (except repeals in Agriculture Act 1967) (RA)
	1 Feb 1977 (exception noted above) (SI 1977/39)

Appropriation Act 1976 (c 43)

Whole Act repealed

Armed Forces Act 1976 (c 52)

RA: 26 Oct 1976

Commencement provisions: s 22(7)–(9); Armed Forces Act 1976 (Commencement) Order 1977, SI 1977/897

s 1	Repealed
2–9	1 Jul 1977 (SI 1977/897)

Armed Forces Act 1976 (c 52)—*cont*

s 10	26 Oct 1976 (s 22(7))
11–16	1 Jul 1977 (SI 1977/897)
17(1)	26 Oct 1976 (s 22(7))
(2)	1 Jul 1977 (SI 1977/897)
18, 19	1 Jul 1977 (SI 1977/897)
20(a)	26 Oct 1976 (s 22(7))
(b)	1 Jul 1977 (SI 1977/897)
21	26 Oct 1976 (s 22(7))
22(1)–(4)	26 Oct 1976 (s 22(7))
(5)	See Sch 9 below
(6)	See Sch 10 below
(7)–(9)	26 Oct 1976 (s 22(7))
Sch 1–8	1 Jul 1977 (SI 1977/897)
9, para 1	1 Jul 1977 (SI 1977/897)
2	Repealed
3	1 Jul 1977 (SI 1977/897)
4	26 Oct 1976 (s 22(7))
5–8	1 Jul 1977 (SI 1977/897)
9	Repealed
10	1 Jul 1977 (SI 1977/897)
11	26 Oct 1976 (s 22(7))
12	Repealed
13–18	1 Jul 1977 (SI 1977/897)
19	Repealed
20(1)	1 Jul 1977 (SI 1977/897)
(2)	26 Oct 1976 (s 22(7))
(3)	1 Jul 1977 (SI 1977/897)
(4), (5)	26 Oct 1976 (s 22(7))
21, 22	1 Jul 1977 (SI 1977/897)
10	26 Oct 1976 (repeals of or in Naval Knights of Windsor (Dissolution) Act 1892; Armed Forces Act 1971, s 1; House of Commons Disqualification Act 1975, s 10(4); Northern Ireland Assembly Disqualification Act 1975, s 5(3)) (s 22(7)) 1 Jul 1977 (otherwise) (SI 1977/897)

Atomic Energy Authority (Special Constables) Act 1976 (c 23)

RA: 10 Jun 1976

10 Jun 1976 (RA)

Bail Act 1976 (c 63)

RA: 15 Nov 1976

Commencement provisions: s 13(2); Bail Act 1976 (Commencement) Order 1978, SI 1978/132

s 1–3	17 Apr 1978 (SI 1978/132)
3A	Inserted by Criminal Justice and Public Order Act 1994, s 27(3) (qv)
4, 5	17 Apr 1978 (SI 1978/132)
5A	Inserted by Criminal Justice and Public Order Act 1994, s 27(4), Sch 3, para 2 (qv)

Bail Act 1976 (c 63)—*cont*

s 5B	Inserted by Criminal Justice and Public Order Act 1994, s 30 (qv)
6–9	17 Apr 1978 (SI 1978/132)
10, 11	Repealed
12	17 Apr 1978 (SI 1978/132)
13	15 Nov 1976 (RA)
Sch 1–4	17 Apr 1978 (SI 1978/132)

Cathedrals Measure 1976 (No 1)

RA: 25 Mar 1976

25 Mar 1976 (RA)

Chronically Sick and Disabled Persons (Amendment) Act 1976 (c 49)

RA: 26 Oct 1976

26 Oct 1976 (RA)

Church of England (Miscellaneous Provisions) Measure 1976 (No 3)

RA: 15 Nov 1976

Commencement provisions: s 8(3)

15 Dec 1976 (s 8(3))

Companies Act 1976 (c 69)

Whole Act repealed

Congenital Disabilities (Civil Liability) Act 1976 (c 28)

RA: 22 Jul 1976

22 Jul 1976 (RA)

Consolidated Fund Act 1976 (c 2)

Whole Act repealed

Consolidated Fund (No 2) Act 1976 (c 84)

Whole Act repealed

Crofting Reform (Scotland) Act 1976 (c 21)

RA: 10 Jun 1976

10 Jun 1976 (RA)

Damages (Scotland) Act 1976 (c 13)

RA: 13 Apr 1976

Commencement provisions: s 12(3)

13 May 1976 (s 12(3))

Dangerous Wild Animals Act 1976 (c 38)

RA: 22 Jul 1976

Commencement provisions: s 10(2)

22 Oct 1976 (s 10(2))

Development Land Tax Act 1976 (c 24)

Whole Act repealed

Development of Rural Wales Act 1976 (c 75)

RA: 22 Nov 1976

Commencement provisions: s 35(2); Development of Rural Wales (Commencement No 1) Order 1976, SI 1976/2038; Development of Rural Wales (Commencement No 2) Order 1977, SI 1977/116

s 1	1 Jan 1977 (SI 1976/2038)
2	1 Apr 1977 (SI 1977/116)
3(1)	1 Apr 1977 (SI 1977/116)
(2)(a)	11 Feb 1977 (SI 1977/116)
(b)	1 Apr 1977 (SI 1977/116)
(3), (4)	11 Feb 1977 (SI 1977/116)
(5)–(8)	1 Apr 1977 (SI 1977/116)
4–6	1 Apr 1977 (SI 1977/116)
7	Repealed
8–10	1 Apr 1977 (SI 1977/116)
11	1 Jan 1977 (SI 1976/2038)
12, 13	1 Apr 1977 (SI 1977/116)
13A	Inserted (EW) by New Towns and Urban Development Corporations Act 1985, s 11, Sch 2, para 1 (qv)
14(1)(a)	1 Jan 1977 (SI 1976/2038)
(b)	1 Apr 1977 (SI 1977/116)
(2)–(6)	1 Apr 1977 (SI 1977/116)
15–17	1 Apr 1977 (SI 1977/116)
18	1 Apr 1977 (SI 1977/116); superseded for years 1981–82 to 1985–86 by Housing Act 1980, s 96(1),

Development of Rural Wales Act 1976 (c 75)—*cont*

s 18—*cont*	Sch 11, Pt I (repealed); and for years from 1986–87 by Housing Act 1985, ss 421–427A; repeal of this section by Housing Act 1980, s 152(3), Sch 26 has never been brought into force by an order made under s 153(4) of the 1980 Act; any order so made will be noted to that Act in the service to this work
19, 20	Repealed
21, 22	1 Apr 1977 (SI 1977/116)
23(1)–(3)	1 Jan 1977 (SI 1976/2038)
(4)	1 Apr 1977 (SI 1977/116)
24	11 Feb 1977 (SI 1977/116)
25–28	1 Apr 1977 (SI 1977/116)
29(1), (2)	1 Jan 1977 (SI 1976/2038)
(3)	11 Feb 1977 (SI 1977/116)
(4)–(6)	1 Apr 1977 (SI 1977/116)
30	1 Apr 1977 (SI 1977/116)
31	Repealed by Finance Act 1985, s 98(6), Sch 27, Pt X, in relation to a disposal (as defined in s 93(1) of that Act) taking place on or after 19 Mar 1985 1 Apr 1977 (SI 1977/116) (so far as unrepealed)
32–34	1 Apr 1977 (SI 1977/116)
35	22 Nov 1976 (RA)
Sch 1	1 Jan 1977 (SI 1976/2038)
2, para 1, 2	1 Apr 1977 (SI 1977/116)
3–5	11 Feb 1977 (SI 1977/116)
6	1 Apr 1977 (SI 1977/116)
3, para 1(1)	1 Apr 1977 (SI 1977/116)
(2)	11 Feb 1977 (SI 1977/116)
(3)–(5)	1 Apr 1977 (SI 1977/116)
(6)	1 Apr 1977 (SI 1977/116); prospectively repealed by Local Government (Wales) Act 1994, s 66(6), (8), Sch 16, para 53(4)(a), Sch 18[1]
2–38	1 Apr 1977 (SI 1977/116)
39	Substituted by Telecommunications Act 1984, s 109(1), Sch 4, para 67(4) (qv)
40–50	1 Apr 1977 (SI 1977/116)
51, 52	Repealed
53–56	1 Apr 1977 (SI 1977/116)
4, Pt I	Repealed
II	1 Apr 1977 (SI 1977/116)
5, Pt I	1 Apr 1977 (SI 1977/116); prospectively repealed by Housing Act 1980, s 152(3), Sch 26: see note to s 18 above
II	1 Apr 1977 (SI 1977/116)
III	Repealed
6, para 1	11 Feb 1977 (SI 1977/116)
2	1 Apr 1977 (SI 1977/116)
3–5	11 Feb 1977 (SI 1977/116)
6	1 Apr 1977 (SI 1977/116)
7	1 Apr 1977 (SI 1977/116)

[1] Any order made under Local Government (Wales) Act 1994, s 66(2)–(4), bringing this prospective repeal into force will be noted to that Act in the service to this work

Divorce (Scotland) Act 1976 (c 39)

RA: 22 Jul 1976

Commencement provisions: s 14(2)

1 Jan 1977 (s 14(2)), except s 8 (repealed)

Dock Work Regulation Act 1976 (c 79)

Whole Act repealed

Domestic Violence and Matrimonial Proceedings Act 1976 (c 50)

RA: 26 Oct 1976

Commencement provisions: s 5(2); Domestic Violence and Matrimonial Proceedings Act 1976 (Commencement) Order 1977, SI 1977/559

1 Jun 1977 (SI 1977/559)

Drought Act 1976 (c 44)

Whole Act repealed

Ecclesiastical Judges and Legal Officers Measure 1976 (No 2)

RA: 25 Mar 1976

Commencement provisions: s 9(2)

25 Apr 1976 (s 9(2))

Education Act 1976 (c 81)

RA: 22 Nov 1976

Whole Act repealed except ss 6, 11, 12, which came into force on 22 Nov 1976 (RA)

Education (School-leaving Dates) Act 1976 (c 5)

RA: 25 Mar 1976

Commencement provisions: s 3(5)

s 1	25 Mar 1976 (RA)
2	Repealed
3	25 Mar 1976 (RA)
Schedule	25 Mar 1976 (except repeal in Social Security Act 1975, Sch 20) (RA) 6 Apr 1976 (repeal mentioned above) (s 3(4))

Education (School-leaving Dates) Act 1976 (c 5)—*cont*

Whole Act prospectively repealed by Education Act 1993, s 307(1), (3), Sch 19, para 63, Sch 21, Pt II; any order made under s 308(3) of that Act bringing the prospective repeal into force will be noted to that Act in the service to this work

Education (Scotland) Act 1976 (c 20)

Whole Act repealed

Electricity (Financial Provisions) (Scotland) Act 1976 (c 61)

Whole Act repealed

Endangered Species (Import and Export) Act 1976 (c 72)

RA: 22 Nov 1976

Commencement provisions: s 13(3)

3 Feb 1977 (s 13(3))

Endowments and Glebe Measure 1976 (No 4)

RA: 22 Nov 1976

Commencement provisions: s 49(2); Order of the Church Commissioners dated 11 Aug 1977

s 1–8	1 Apr 1978 (order dated 11 Aug 1977)
9	22 Nov 1976 (s 49(2))
10–15	1 Apr 1978 (order dated 11 Aug 1977)
16	22 Nov 1976 (s 49(2))
17, 18	1 Apr 1978 (order dated 11 Aug 1977)
19(1)	1 Apr 1978 (order dated 11 Aug 1977)
(2)–(4)	22 Nov 1976 (s 49(2))
20–30	1 Apr 1978 (order dated 11 Aug 1977)
31, 32	22 Nov 1976 (s 49(2))
33	1 Apr 1978 (order dated 11 Aug 1977)
34	22 Nov 1976 (s 49(2))
35–42	1 Apr 1978 (order dated 11 Aug 1977)
43, 44	Repealed
45–49	1 Apr 1978 (order dated 11 Aug 1977)
Sch 1–8	1 Apr 1978 (order dated 11 Aug 1977)

Energy Act 1976 (c 76)

RA: 22 Nov 1976

Commencement provisions: s 23(2); Energy Act 1976 (Commencement No 1) Order 1976, SI 1976/1964; Energy Act 1976 (Commencement No 2) Order 1976, SI 1976/2127; Energy Act 1976 (Commencement No 3) Order 1977, SI 1977/652

s 1–6	30 Nov 1976 (SI 1976/1964)
7, 8	Repealed
9	Substituted for original ss 9–11 by Oil and Gas (Enterprise) Act 1982, s 37, Sch 3, para 37 (qv)

Energy Act 1976 (c 76)—*cont*

s 10, 11	See the note to s 9 above
12	1 May 1977 (SI 1977/652)
13	Repealed
14, 15	1 Jan 1977 (SI 1976/2127)
16	Repealed
17–21	30 Nov 1976 (so far as relate to ss 1–6, 13, Sch 1 or provisions made under them) (SI 1976/1964) 1 Jan 1977 (so far as relate to ss 7, 14–16 or provisions made under them or to obligations specified in Sch 3) (SI 1976/2127) 1 May 1977 (otherwise) (SI 1977/652)
22	See Sch 4 below
23	30 Nov 1976 (SI 1976/1964)
Sch 1	30 Nov 1976 (SI 1976/1964)
2, 3	As ss 17–21 above
4	30 Nov 1976 (repeal of Fuel and Electricity (Control) Act 1973) (SI 1976/1964) 1 May 1977 (otherwise) (SI 1977/652)

Explosives (Age of Purchase etc) Act 1976 (c 26)

RA: 22 Jul 1976

Commencement provisions: s 2(3)

22 Aug 1976 (s 2(3))

Fair Employment (Northern Ireland) Act 1976 (c 25)

RA: 22 Jul 1976

Commencement provisions: s 59(5), (6); Fair Employment (Northern Ireland) Act 1976 (Commencement) Order 1976, SI 1976/1182

1 Sep 1976 (ss 1–3, 5, 37(1), (2), (4), (5), 56(1), 57(1)–(3), (6), (8), (11), (12), 58(1) (so far as it relates to Sch 6, paras 2–4), 59(1)–(3), (5), Sch 1, Sch 6, paras 2–4) and 1 Dec 1976 (remaining provisions) (SI 1976/1182)

Fatal Accidents Act 1976 (c 30)

RA: 22 Jul 1976

Commencement provisions: s 7(2)

1 Sep 1976 (s 7(2); note the Act does not apply to any cause of action arising on a death before that date; also that ss 1, 2–4 were substituted, and s 1A inserted (1 Jan 1983) by Administration of Justice Act 1982, s 3(1))

Fatal Accidents and Sudden Deaths Inquiry (Scotland) Act 1976 (c 14)

RA: 13 Apr 1976

Commencement provisions: s 10(5); Fatal Accidents and Sudden Deaths Inquiry (Scotland) Act 1976 Commencement Order 1977, SI 1977/190

1 Mar 1977 (SI 1977/190)

Finance Act 1976 (c 40)

Budget day: 6 Apr 1976

RA: 29 Jul 1976

See the note concerning Finance Acts at the front of this book

Fishery Limits Act 1976 (c 86)

RA: 22 Dec 1976

Commencement provisions: s 12(2)

1 Jan 1977 (s 12(2))

Food and Drugs (Control of Food Premises) Act 1976 (c 37)

Whole Act repealed

Freshwater and Salmon Fisheries (Scotland) Act 1976 (c 22)

RA: 10 Jun 1976

10 Jun 1976 (RA)

Health Services Act 1976 (c 83)

Whole Act repealed

Housing (Amendment) (Scotland) Act 1976 (c 11)

Whole Act repealed

Industry (Amendment) Act 1976 (c 73)

Whole Act repealed

Industrial Common Ownership Act 1976 (c 78)

RA: 22 Nov 1976

22 Nov 1976 (RA)

Insolvency Act 1976 (c 60)

RA: 15 Nov 1976

Commencement provisions: s 14(5); Insolvency Act 1976 (Commencement No 1) Order 1976, SI 1976/1960; Insolvency Act 1976 (Commencement No 2) Order 1977, SI 1977/363; Insolvency Act 1976 (Commencement No 3) Order 1977, SI 1977/1375; Insolvency Act 1976 (Commencement No 4) Order 1978, SI 1978/139

s 1–11	Repealed
12	1 Mar 1978 (SI 1978/139)

Insolvency Act 1976 (c 60)—*cont*

s 13	20 Dec 1976 (SI 1976/1960)
14	See Sch 3 below
Sch 1	Repealed
2	1 Apr 1977 (SI 1977/363)
3	1 Oct 1977 (repeals of Bankruptcy Act 1914, s 92(3); Companies Act 1948, s 249(3)) (SI 1977/1375) 1 Mar 1978 (otherwise) (SI 1978/139)

International Carriage of Perishable Foodstuffs Act 1976 (c 58)

RA: 15 Nov 1976

Commencement provisions: s 21(2); International Carriage of Perishable Foodstuffs Act 1976 (Commencement) Order 1979, SI 1979/413

1 Oct 1979 (SI 1979/413)

Iron and Steel (Amendment) Act 1976 (c 41)

Whole Act repealed

Land Drainage Act 1976 (c 70)

RA: 15 Nov 1976

Commencement provisions: s 118(2)

Whole Act repealed except ss 105, 116(1) (part), 117(2), 118, Sch 5, Sch 7, paras 3, 5, which came into force on 17 Jan 1977 (s 118(2); Land Drainage (Amendment) Act 1976 (Commencement) Order 1976, SI 1976/2244 (made under Land Drainage (Amendment) Act 1976, s 10(5) (repealed))

Land Drainage (Amendment) Act 1976 (c 17)

Whole Act repealed

Legitimacy Act 1976 (c 31)

RA: 22 Jul 1976

Commencement provisions: s 12(2)

22 Aug 1976 (s 12(2))

Licensing (Amendment) Act 1976 (c 18)

RA: 27 May 1976

27 May 1976 (RA)

Licensing (Scotland) Act 1976 (c 66)

RA: 15 Nov 1976

Commencement provisions: s 141(2); Licensing (Scotland) Act 1976 (Commencement No 1) Order 1976, SI 1976/2068; Licensing (Scotland) Act 1976 (Commencement No 2) Order 1977, SI 1977/212; Licensing (Scotland) Act 1976 (Commencement No 3) Order 1977, SI 1977/718

s 1, 2	1 Mar 1977 (SI 1977/212)
3–7	1 Jul 1977 (SI 1977/718)
8	1 Mar 1977 (SI 1977/212)
9–16	1 Jul 1977 (SI 1977/718)
16A	Inserted by Law Reform (Miscellaneous Provisions) (Scotland) Act 1990, s 53(1) (qv)
17–21	1 Jul 1977 (SI 1977/718)
22	Repealed
23–46	1 Jul 1977 (SI 1977/718)
47–52	Repealed
53	Substituted by Law Reform (Miscellaneous Provisions) (Scotland) Act 1990, ss 45(1), 46 (qv)
54(1)	13 Dec 1976 (SI 1976/2068)
(2)	1 Jul 1977 (SI 1977/718)
(3)–(5)	13 Dec 1976 (SI 1976/2068)
55	Repealed
56–59	13 Dec 1976 (SI 1976/2068)
60	1 Mar 1977 (SI 1977/212)
61	Repealed
62	1 Jul 1977 (SI 1977/718)
63	1 May 1977 (SI 1977/718)
63A	Inserted by Deregulation and Contracting Out Act 1994, s 18(2) (qv)
64–66	1 Jul 1977 (SI 1977/718)
67	13 Dec 1976 (SI 1976/2068)
68–90	1 Jul 1977 (SI 1977/718)
90A	Inserted by Law Reform (Miscellaneous Provisions) (Scotland) Act 1990, s 52 (qv)
91–93	1 Jul 1977 (SI 1977/718)
94	Repealed
95–97	1 Jul 1977 (SI 1977/718)
97A	Inserted by Law Reform (Miscellaneous Provisions) (Scotland) Act 1990, s 54(1) (qv)
98–118	1 Jul 1977 (SI 1977/718)
119	1 May 1977 (SI 1977/718)
120–130	1 Jul 1977 (SI 1977/718)
131, 132	Repealed
133(1)–(3)	1 Jul 1977 (SI 1977/718)
(4)	1 Oct 1977 (SI 1977/718)
134, 135	1 Jul 1977 (SI 1977/718)
136(1)	1 Jul 1977 (SI 1977/718)
(2)	See Sch 8 below
137, 138	1 Jul 1977 (SI 1977/718)
139	13 Dec 1976 (so far as necessary for purposes of SI 1976/2068) (SI 1976/2068)
	1 Mar 1977 (so far as necessary for purposes of SI 1977/212) (SI 1977/212)
	1 Jul 1977 (otherwise) (SI 1977/718)

Licensing (Scotland) Act 1976 (c 66)—*cont*

s 140(1)	Repealed
(2)	13 Dec 1976 (SI 1976/2068)
(3)	Repealed
(4)–(8)	13 Dec 1976 (SI 1976/2068)
141	15 Nov 1976 (s 141(2))
Sch 1, 2	1 Jul 1977 (SI 1977/718)
3	Repealed
4	1 Jul 1977 (SI 1977/718)
5	13 Dec 1976 (entries relating to ss 54(1)(a), (b), 57(7), (8), 58(7), (8), 59(7)) (SI 1976/2068)
	1 Mar 1977 (entry relating to s 2) (SI 1977/212)
	1 May 1977 (entry relating to s 119) (SI 1977/718)
	1 Jul 1977 (otherwise) (SI 1977/718)
6, 7	1 Jul 1977 (SI 1977/718)
8	13 Dec 1976 (repeals of Licensing (Scotland) Act 1959, ss 121, 126; Licensing (Scotland) Act 1962, ss 3(3), 4–8) (SI 1976/2068)
	1 Mar 1977 (repeal of Licensing (Scotland) Act 1959, s 29) (SI 1977/212)
	1 May 1977 (repeal of Licensing (Scotland) Act 1959, s 130; Licensing (Scotland) Act 1962, s 20) (SI 1977/718)
	1 Jul 1977 (otherwise, except repeals noted below) (SI 1977/718)
	1 Oct 1977 (repeals of Betting, Gaming and Lotteries Act 1963, Sch 1, para 24(2); Gaming Act 1968, Sch 2, paras 33(2), (3), 34(2)) (SI 1977/718)

Local Government (Miscellaneous Provisions) Act 1976 (c 57)

RA: 15 Nov 1976

Commencement provisions: ss 45, 83(2); Local Government (Miscellaneous Provisions) Act 1976 (Commencement) Order 1977, SI 1977/68

s 1–6	Repealed
7	14 Feb 1977 (SI 1977/68)
8–10	Repealed
11–27	14 Feb 1977 (SI 1977/68)
28	Repealed (except in relation to any body which is not mentioned in Local Government and Housing Act 1989, s 39(1)(a)–(j), and has not been prescribed by regulations under s 39(3) of the 1989 Act)
29–33	14 Feb 1977 (SI 1977/68)
34	Repealed
35, 36	14 Feb 1977 (SI 1977/68)
37	Repealed
38–42	14 Feb 1977 (SI 1977/68)
43	Repealed
44	14 Feb 1977 (SI 1977/68)
45–80	Came into force for different areas on different dates in accordance with resolutions of district councils (see s 45)
81–83	14 Feb 1977 (SI 1977/68)
Sch 1, 2	14 Feb 1977 (SI 1977/68)

Lotteries and Amusements Act 1976 (c 32)

RA: 22 Jul 1976

Commencement provisions: s 25(9)

s 1–8	1 May 1977 (s 25(9))
9	Repealed
9A	Inserted by National Lottery etc Act 1993, s 50(1) (qv)
10	Substituted by National Lottery etc Act 1993, s 51 (qv)
11–25	1 May 1977 (s 25(9))
Sch 1	1 May 1977 (s 25(9))
1A	Inserted by National Lottery etc Act 1993, s 48(6), Sch 7, Pt II (qv)
2	1 May 1977 (s 25(9))
2A	Inserted by National Lottery etc Act 1993, s 50(2), Sch 9 (qv)
3–5	1 May 1977 (s 25(9))

Maplin Development Authority (Dissolution) Act 1976 (c 51)

Whole Act repealed

Motor-Cycle Crash-Helmets (Religious Exemption) Act 1976 (c 62)

Whole Act repealed

National Coal Board (Finance) Act 1976 (c 1)

RA: 4 Mar 1976

4 Mar 1976 (RA)

Whole Act repealed (in part prospectively) as follows: ss 1, 3 repealed by Coal Industry Act 1977, s 15, Sch 5, Pt II; ss 2, 4 prospectively repealed by Coal Industry Act 1994, s 67(8), Sch 11, Pt III; any order made under Coal Industry Act 1994, s 68(4), (5), bringing these prospective repeals into force will be noted to that Act in the service to this work

National Health Service (Vocational Training) Act 1976 (c 59)

Whole Act repealed

National Insurance Surcharge Act 1976 (c 85)

Whole Act repealed

New Towns (Amendment) Act 1976 (c 68)

Whole Act repealed

Parliamentary and Other Pensions and Salaries Act 1976 (c 48)

RA: 12 Oct 1976

12 Oct 1976, but certain provisions were retrospective in effect (see, in particular, s 6 which has effect as from 1 Jan 1975 (s 6(5)); the other provisions with retrospective effect have been repealed)

Police Act 1976 (c 46)

RA: 6 Aug 1976

Commencement provisions: s 13(1); Police Act 1976 (Commencement No 1) Order 1976, SI 1976/1998; Police Act 1976 (Commencement No 2) Order 1977, SI 1977/576

s 1(1)–(4)	Repealed
(5)	8 Dec 1976 (SI 1976/1998)
2–13	Repealed
14(1)	8 Dec 1976 (SI 1976/1998)
(2)	Repealed
Schedule	8 Dec 1976 (SI 1976/1998)

Police Pensions Act 1976 (c 35)

RA: 22 Jul 1976

22 Jul 1976 (RA)

Post Office (Banking Services) Act 1976 (c 10)

RA: 25 Mar 1976

25 Mar 1976 (RA)

Prevention of Terrorism (Temporary Provisions) Act 1976 (c 8)

Whole Act repealed

Protection of Birds (Amendment) Act 1976 (c 42)

Whole Act repealed

Race Relations Act 1976 (c 74)

RA: 22 Nov 1976

Commencement provisions: s 79(2); Race Relations Act 1976 (Commencement No 1) Order 1977, SI 1977/680; Race Relations Act 1976 (Commencement No 2) Order 1977, SI 1977/840

s 1–12	13 Jun 1977 (SI 1977/840)
13	Substituted by Employment Act 1989, s 7(2) (qv)
14–17	13 Jun 1977 (SI 1977/840)
17A	Inserted (EW) by Further and Higher Education Act 1992, s 93(1), Sch 8, Pt II, paras 84, 86 (qv)

Race Relations Act 1976 (c 74)—*cont*

s 18	13 Jun 1977 (SI 1977/840)
18A	Inserted (EW) by Further and Higher Education Act 1992, s 93(1), Sch 8, Pt II, paras 84, 87 (qv)
18B	Inserted (S) (in part prospectively) by Further and Higher Education (Scotland) Act 1992, s 62(2), Sch 9, para 5(1), (3)[1]
18C	Inserted (EW) by Education Act 1993, s 307(1), Sch 19, para 65 (qv)
18D	Inserted (EW) by Education Act 1994, s 24, Sch 2, para 6(1) (3) (qv)
19	13 Jun 1977 (SI 1977/840)
19A	Inserted by Housing and Planning Act 1986, s 55 (qv)
20–26	13 Jun 1977 (SI 1977/840)
26A, 26B	Inserted by Courts and Legal Services Act 1990, ss 64(2), 65(2) respectively (qv)
27–69	13 Jun 1977 (SI 1977/840)
70	Repealed
71, 72	13 Jun 1977 (SI 1977/840)
73–75	28 Apr 1977 (SI 1977/680)
75A, 75B	Inserted by Trade Union and Labour Relations (Consolidation) Act 1992, s 300(2), Sch 2, paras 7, 10 (qv)
76	13 Jun 1977 (SI 1977/840)
77, 78	28 Apr 1977 (SI 1977/680)
79(1)	28 Apr 1977 (SI 1977/680)
(2)	22 Nov 1976 (RA)
(3)–(5)	28 Apr 1977 (SI 1977/840)
(6)	Repealed
(7)	22 Nov 1976 (RA)
80	28 Apr 1977 (SI 1977/680)
Sch 1	13 Jun 1977 (SI 1977/840)
2	28 Apr 1977 (SI 1977/680)
3	Repealed
4	28 Apr 1977 (SI 1977/680)

Note

S 43(1)–(4), Sch 1 of this Act came into force on 28 Apr 1977 (SI 1977/680) for the purposes of bringing into existence the Commission for Racial Equality and enabling it to make preparatory arrangements for the exercise of its powers

[1] Any order(s) made under Further and Higher Education (Scotland) Act 1992, s 63(2), bringing the insertion, by Sch 9, para 5(3) to, that Act, of s 18B into force, so far as not already in force, will be noted to that Act in the service to this work

Rating (Caravan Sites) Act 1976 (c 15)

RA: 13 Apr 1976

13 Apr 1976 (RA; but mainly effective for rate periods beginning after Mar 1976, see s 1(9))

Note

This Act made provision for the rating of caravan sites under the system of rating governed by General Rate Act 1967 (repealed with savings). Regulations made under Local Government Finance Act 1988 contain provision corresponding to that made by this Act in relation to the system of non-domestic rating governed by the 1988 Act

Rating (Charity Shops) Act 1976 (c 45)

RA: 6 Aug 1976

6 Aug 1976 (RA); *whole Act repealed or spent (EW)*

Rent (Agriculture) Act 1976 (c 80)

RA: 22 Nov 1976

Commencement provisions: s 1(5), (6); Rent (Agriculture) Act 1976 (Commencement No 1) Order 1976, SI 1976/2124; Rent (Agriculture) Act 1976 (Commencement No 2) Order 1977, SI 1977/1268

1 Jan 1977 (SI 1976/2124; but note that in relation to forestry workers the Act came into force on 1 Oct 1976, by virtue of s 1(5)(b), Sch 3, Pt II, SI 1977/1268)

Representation of the People (Armed Forces) Act 1976 (c 29)

Whole Act repealed

Resale Prices Act 1976 (c 53)

RA: 26 Oct 1976

Commencement provisions: s 30(3); Resale Prices Act 1976 (Commencement) Order 1976, SI 1976/1876

15 Dec 1976 (SI 1976/1876)

Restrictive Practices Court Act 1976 (c 33)

RA: 22 Jul 1976

Commencement provisions: s 12(3); Restrictive Practices Court Act 1976 (Commencement) Order 1976, SI 1976/1896

15 Dec 1976 (SI 1976/1896)

Restrictive Trade Practices Act 1976 (c 34)

RA: 22 Jul 1976

Commencement provisions: s 45(3); Restrictive Trade Practices Act 1976 (Commencement) Order 1976, SI 1976/1877

15 Dec 1976 (SI 1976/1877)

Retirement of Teachers (Scotland) Act 1976 (c 65)

Whole Act repealed

Road Traffic (Drivers' Ages and Hours of Work) Act 1976 (c 3)

RA: 25 Mar 1976

Commencement provisions: s 4(2)–(4); Road Traffic (Drivers' Ages and Hours of Work) Act 1976 (Commencement No 1) Order 1976, SI 1976/471; Road Traffic (Drivers' Ages and Hours of Work) Act 1976 (Commencement No 2) Order 1978, SI 1978/6

s 1	Repealed
2	4 Jan 1978 (SI 1978/6)
3, 4	25 Mar 1976 (s 4(2))
Sch 1, 2	Repealed
3, Pt I	25 Mar 1976 (s 4(2))
II	4 Jan 1978 (SI 1978/6)

Sexual Offences (Amendment) Act 1976 (c 82)

RA: 22 Nov 1976

Commencement provisions: s 7(4); Sexual Offences (Amendment) Act 1976 (Commencement) Order 1978, SI 1978/485

s 1–4	22 Dec 1976 (s 7(4))
5(1)(a)	22 Dec 1976 (s 7(4))
(b)	22 Apr 1978 (SI 1978/485)
(c)–(e)	22 Dec 1976 (s 7(4))
(2)–(6)	22 Dec 1976 (s 7(4))
6	Repealed
7	22 Dec 1976 (s 7(4))

Sexual Offences (Scotland) Act 1976 (c 67)

RA: 15 Nov 1976

Commencement provisions: s 22(2)

15 Dec 1976 (s 22(2))

Seychelles Act 1976 (c 19)

RA: 27 May 1976

Appointed day: 29 Jun 1976

Solicitors (Scotland) Act 1976 (c 6)

Whole Act repealed

Statute Law (Repeals) Act 1976 (c 16)

RA: 27 May 1976

27 May 1976 (RA)

Statute Law Revision (Northern Ireland) Act 1976 (c 12)

RA: 13 Apr 1976

13 Apr 1976 (RA)

Stock Exchange (Completion of Bargains) Act 1976 (c 47)

RA: 12 Oct 1976

Commencement provisions: s 7(4); Stock Exchange (Completion of Bargains) Act 1976 (Commencement Order) 1979, SI 1979/55

12 Feb 1979 (SI 1979/55)

Supplementary Benefit (Amendment) Act 1976 (c 56)

Whole Act repealed

Supplementary Benefits Act 1976 (c 71)

RA: 15 Nov 1976

Commencement provisions: s 36(3)

Whole Act repealed except ss 35, 36, Schs 6–8 which came into force on 15 Nov 1976 (s 36(3); note that repeals of provisions of Sch 8, Pt II did not come into force until those provisions had themselves come into force)

Theatres Trust Act 1976 (c 27)

RA: 22 Jul 1976

Commencement provisions: s 6(2); Theatres Trust Act (Appointed Day) Order 1976, SI 1976/2236

21 Jan 1977 (SI 1976/2236)

Note

The Act was extended to Scotland by the Theatres Trust (Scotland) Act 1978, s 1(1) (qv) and came into force there on the passing of that Act

---

Trade Union and Labour Relations (Amendment) Act 1976 (c 7)

Whole Act repealed

Trinidad and Tobago Republic Act 1976 (c 54)

RA: 26 Oct 1976

Appointed day: 26 Oct 1976 (Trinidad and Tobago Republic Appointed Day Order 1976, SI 1976/1914)

Trustee Savings Banks Act 1976 (c 4)

Whole Act repealed

Note that the repeal of this Act is subject to transitional provisions and savings contained in Trustee Savings Banks Act 1981, s 55(2), Sch 7

Valuation and Rating (Exempted Classes) (Scotland) Act 1976 (c 64)

RA: 15 Nov 1976

15 Nov 1976 (RA)

Water Charges Act 1976 (c 9)

Whole Act repealed

Weights and Measures &c Act 1976 (c 77)

RA: 22 Nov 1976

Commencement provisions: s 15(2)

Whole Act repealed, except ss 12–14, 15(1)–(3) and Sch 6, which came into force on 22 Dec 1976 (s 15(2))

1977

Administration of Justice Act 1977 (c 38)

RA: 29 Jul 1977

Commencement provisions: s 32(5)–(7); Administration of Justice Act 1977 (Commencement No 1) Order 1977, SI 1977/1405; Administration of Justice Act 1977 (Commencement No 2) Order 1977, SI 1977/ 1490; Administration of Justice Act 1977 (Commencement No 3) Order 1977, SI 1977/1589; Administration of Justice Act 1977 (Commencement No 4) Order 1977, SI 1977/2202; Administration of Justice Act 1977 (Commencement No 5) Order 1978, SI 1978/810; Administration of Justice Act 1977 (Commencement No 6) Order 1979, SI 1979/972; Administration of Justice Act 1977 (Commencement No 7) Order 1980, SI 1980/1981

s 1	Spent (EW); repealed (S)
2	29 Aug 1977 (s 32(5))
3	See Sch 3 below
4, 5	29 Aug 1977 (s 32(5))
6	Repealed
7	29 Aug 1977 (s 32(5))
8–10	Repealed
11	29 Aug 1977 (s 32(5)); prospectively repealed by Administration of Justice Act 1982, s 75, Sch 9, Pt I; any order made under Administration of Justice Act 1982, s 76, bringing the prospective repeal into force will be noted to that Act in the service to this work (this section amended provisions of Administration of Justice Act 1965 which were repealed by Administration of Justice Act 1982, s 75, Sch 9, Pt I, on 13 Jun 1991, and is therefore spent)
12	Spent
13–16	Repealed
17(1)	Repealed
(2)	29 Aug 1977 (s 32(5))
18	Repealed
19(1)	Repealed
(2)	Spent
(3), (4)	Repealed
(5)	3 Jul 1978 (SI 1978/810)
20, 21	Repealed
22	29 Aug 1977 (s 32(5))
23	17 Oct 1977 (SI 1977/1589)
24	29 Aug 1977 (s 32(5))
25	Repealed
26	29 Aug 1977 (s 32(5))
27	Repealed
28	15 Sep 1977 (SI 1977/1490)
29	29 Aug 1977 (s 32(5))

Administration of Justice Act 1977 (c 38)—*cont*

s 30	Repealed
31, 32	29 Jul 1977 (RA)
Sch 1	Repealed
2	29 Aug 1977 (s 32(5))
3, para 1–10	1 Jan 1981 (SI 1980/1981)
11, 12	1 Sept 1977 (SI 1977/1405)
4	17 Oct 1977 (SI 1977/1589)
5, Pt I–IV	29 Aug 1977 (s 32(5))
V	17 Oct 1977 (SI 1977/1589)
VI	29 Jul 1977 (s 32(6))

Agricultural Holdings (Notices to Quit) Act 1977 (c 12)

Whole Act repealed

Aircraft and Shipbuilding Industries Act 1977 (c 3)

RA: 17 Mar 1977

17 Mar 1977 (RA)

Note

Under ss 19, 56, vesting date for aircraft industry was 29 Apr 1977 (under Aircraft and Shipbuilding Industries (Aircraft Industry Vesting Date) Order 1977, SI 1977/539) and for shipbuilding industry was 1 Jul 1977 (under Aircraft and Shipbuilding Industries (Shipbuilding Industry Vesting Date) Order 1977, SI 1977/540)

Appropriation Act 1977 (c 35)

Whole Act repealed

British Airways Board Act 1977 (c 13)

Whole Act repealed

Coal Industry Act 1977 (c 39)

RA: 29 Jul 1977

Commencement provisions: s 16(2)

29 Aug 1977 (s 16(2))

Whole Act repealed (in part prospectively) as follows: ss 1, 7, 9–16, Schs 1, 3, Sch 4, paras 1–3, Sch 5 repealed by Coal Industry Act 1994, s 67(8), Sch 11, Pts II–IV (prospectively in the case of ss 1, 7, 9(5) (part), 10, 11(1)–(6), (8), 12–16, Schs 1, 3, Sch 4, paras 1(1)–(4), (6), (7), 2, 3, Sch 5)[1]; ss 2, 3 repealed by Coal Industry Act 1983, ss 2(3), 6(3), Schedule; ss 4, 5, 8 repealed by Coal Industry Act 1980, ss 5, 11(2); s 6, Sch 2, Sch 4, para 5 repealed by Coal Industry Act 1987, ss 4(1), 10(3), Sch 3, Pt I; Sch 4, para 4 repealed by Overseas Development and Co-operation Act 1980, s 18(1), Sch 2, Pt I

[1] Order(s) made under Coal Industry Act 1994 bringing the prospective repeals into force will be noted to that Act in the service to this work

---

Consolidated Fund Act 1977 (c 1)

Whole Act repealed

Consolidated Fund (No 2) Act 1977 (c 52)

Whole Act repealed

Control of Food Premises (Scotland) Act 1977 (c 28)

Whole Act repealed

Control of Office Development Act 1977 (c 40)

Whole Act repealed

Covent Garden Market (Financial Provisions) Act 1977 (c 2)

Limited application only

Criminal Law Act 1977 (c 45)

RA: 29 Jul 1977

Commencement provisions: s 65(7); Criminal Law Act 1977 (Commencement No 1) Order 1977, SI 1977/1365; Criminal Law Act 1977 (Commencement No 2) Order 1977, SI 1977/1426; Criminal Law Act 1977 (Commencement No 3) Order 1977, SI 1977/1682; Criminal Law Act 1977 (Commencement No 4) (Scotland) Order 1977, SI 1977/1744; Criminal Law Act 1977 (Commencement No 5) Order 1978, SI 1978/712; Criminal Law Act 1977 (Commencement No 6) (Scotland) Order 1978, SI 1978/900; Criminal Law Act 1977 (Commencement No 7) Order 1980, SI 1980/487; Criminal Law Act 1977 (Commencement No 8) (Scotland) Order 1980, SI 1980/587; Criminal Law Act 1977 (Commencement No 9) Order 1980, SI 1980/1632; Criminal Law Act 1977 (Commencement No 10) (Scotland) Order 1980, SI 1980/1701; Criminal Law Act 1977 (Commencement No 11) Order 1982, SI 1982/243; Criminal Law Act 1977 (Commencement No 12) Order 1985, SI 1985/579

s 1(1)	1 Dec 1977 (SI 1977/1682); substituted by Criminal Attempts Act 1981, s 5, except as to agreements entered into before 27 Aug 1981 (ie date of commencement of 1981 Act) when the conspiracy continued to exist after that date
(1A), (1B)	Inserted by Computer Misuse Act 1990, s 7 (qv)
(2)	1 Dec 1977 (SI 1977/1682)
(3)	Repealed
(4)	1 Dec 1977 (SI 1977/1682)
(5), (6)	Inserted by Computer Misuse Act 1990, s 7 (qv)
1A	Prospectively inserted by Criminal Justice Act 1993, s 5(1)[1]
2–4	1 December 1977 (SI 1977/1682)
5(1)–(9)	1 Dec 1977 (SI 1977/1682)
(10)(a)	1 Dec 1977 (SI 1977/1682)

Criminal Law Act 1977 (c 45)—*cont*

s 5(10)(b)	8 Sep 1977 (SI 1977/1365)
(11)	Repealed
6(1)	1 Dec 1977 (SI 1977/1682)
(1A)	Inserted by Criminal Justice and Public Order Act 1994, s 72(1), (2) (qv)
(2)	1 Dec 1977 (SI 1977/1682)
(3)	Repealed
(4)–(7)	1 Dec 1977 (SI 1977/1682)
7	Substituted by Criminal Justice and Public Order Act 1994, s 73 (qv)
8–10	1 Dec 1977 (SI 1977/1682)
11	Repealed
12	1 Dec 1977 (SI 1977/1682)
12A	Inserted by Criminal Justice and Public Order Act 1994, s 74 (qv)
13	1 Dec 1977 (SI 1977/1682)
14	Repealed
15(1)	17 Jul 1978 (SI 1978/712)
(2), (3)	Repealed
(4)	17 Jul 1978 (SI 1978/712; SI 1978/900)
(5)	17 Jul 1978 (SI 1978/712)
16–27	Repealed
28	17 Jul 1978 (SI 1978/712)
29	Repealed
30(1), (2)	17 Jul 1978 (SI 1978/712)
(3)	17 Jul 1978 (SI 1978/712; SI 1978/900)
(4)	Repealed
31(1)	8 Sep 1977 (SI 1977/1365)
(2)–(6)	17 Jul 1978 (SI 1978/712)
(7)	Repealed
(8), (9)	17 Jul 1978 (SI 1978/712)
(10)	17 Jul 1978 (SI 1978/712; SI 1978/900)
(11)	17 Jul 1978 (SI 1978/712)
32(1)	17 Jul 1978 (SI 1978/712)
(2)	Repealed
(3)	17 Jul 1978 (SI 1978/712; SI 1978/900)
33	8 Sep 1977 (SI 1977/1365)
34, 35	Repealed
36	Repealed or spent
37	17 Jul 1978 (SI 1978/712)
38	Repealed
38A	Inserted by Criminal Justice (Scotland) Act 1980, s 51 (qv)
38B	Inserted by Criminal Justice Act 1982, s 52 (qv)
39	12 May 1980 (SI 1980/487; SI 1980/587)
40	1 Dec 1980 (SI 1980/1632; SI 1980/1701)
41–45	Repealed
46	17 Jul 1978 (SI 1978/712)
47	Repealed
48	20 May 1985 (SI 1985/579)
49	1 Dec 1977 (SI 1977/1682)
50	Repealed
51, 52	8 Sep 1977 (SI 1977/1365)
53	1 Dec 1977 (SI 1977/1682)
54	8 Sep 1977 (SI 1977/1365)
55, 56	Repealed
57	8 Sep 1977 (SI 1977/1365)

Criminal Law Act 1977 (c 45)—*cont*

s 58	Repealed or spent
59–62	Repealed
63(1)	8 Sep 1977 (SI 1977/1365)
(2)	8 Sep 1977 (so far as relates to ss 33, 51, 52, 55, 65, Schs 12 (part), 13 (part), 14) (SI 1977/1365) 1 Dec 1977 (so far as relates to s 50, Schs 12 (part), 13 (part)) (SI 1977/1744) 17 Jul 1978 (so far as relates to ss 15(2)–(4), 30(3), 31(10), 32(3), Schs 9, para 3(3), 12 (part), 13 (part)) (SI 1978/900) 12 May 1980 (so far as relates to ss 38, 39, Sch 13 (part)) (SI 1980/587) 1 Dec 1980 (so far as relates to s 40, Schs 7, 12 (part), 13 (part)) (SI 1980/1701)
64	17 Jul 1978 (SI 1978/712)
65	8 Sep 1977 (SI 1977/1365)
Sch 1	17 Jul 1978 (SI 1978/712)
2–4	Repealed
5	17 Jul 1978 (SI 1978/712)
6	8 Sep 1977 (SI 1977/1365)
7, 8	Repealed
9	29 Mar 1982 (SI 1982/243) (except para 3(3)) and 17 Jul 1978 (SI 1978/900) (para 3(3)); now spent on repeal of s 47
10, 11	Repealed
12	8 Sep 1977 (so far as relates to Offences Against the Person Act 1861; Explosive Substances Act 1883; Sexual Offences Act 1956, Sch 2, Pt II, paras 14, 15; Housing (Scotland) Act 1966; Children and Young Persons Act 1969, s 13(3); Powers of Criminal Courts Act 1973, ss 15(2), 17(3); Adoption Act 1976; Bail Act 1976, ss 3(8), 5) (SI 1977/1365) 1 Dec 1977 (so far as relates to Metropolitan Police Courts Act 1839; Public Stores Act 1875; Obscene Publications Act 1959; Criminal Justice Act 1961; Criminal Justice Act 1967, ss 60, 91; Theft Act 1968; Finance Act 1972; Criminal Justice Act 1972; Administration of Justice Act 1973; Powers of Criminal Courts Act 1973, ss 1, 2(5); Legal Aid Act 1974 (repealed); Juries Act 1974; Bail Act 1976, s 7(4)) (EW) (SI 1977/1682) 1 Dec 1977 (so far as relates to Public Stores Act 1875; Prison Act 1952 (in its application to persons for the time being in Scotland); Criminal Justice Act 1961, ss 26, 28, 29, 39(1); Criminal Justice Act 1967, s 60; Road Traffic Act 1972, s 179) (S) (SI 1977/1744) 1 Jan 1978 (so far as relates to Coroners Act 1887; Births and Deaths Registration Act 1953; Bail Act 1976, s 2(2)) (SI 1977/1682) 17 Jul 1978 (so far as relates to Night Poaching Act 1828; Accessories and Abettors Act 1861; Sexual Offences Act 1956, Sch 2, Pt II, paras 17, 18; Criminal Law Act 1967; Firearms Act 1968; Children and Young Persons Act 1969, ss 15, 16;

Criminal Law Act 1977 (c 45)—*cont*

Sch 12—*cont*

Powers of Criminal Courts Act 1973, s 9(1); Health and Safety at Work etc Act 1974; Rehabilitation of Offenders Act 1974) (EW) (SI 1978/712)

17 Jul 1978 (so far as relates to Night Poaching Act 1828; Health and Safety at Work etc Act 1974; Rehabilitation of Offenders Act 1974) (S) (SI 1978/900)

Repealed or spent (remainder)

13

8 Sep 1977 (repeals of or in Criminal Justice Act 1848, s 19(3); Criminal Justice Act 1967, Sch 3, Pt I; Children and Young Persons Act 1969, s 13(3); Powers of Criminal Courts Act 1973, Sch 3, para 9; Bail Act 1976, Sch 2, para 38) (SI 1977/1365)

8 Sep 1977 (repeals of or in Exchange Control Act 1947, Sch 5, Pt II, para 3(1); Customs and Excise Act 1952, s 285(1); Magistrates' Courts Act 1952, Sch 3, para 3; Land Commission Act 1967, s 82(5); Criminal Justice Act 1967, s 93) (SI 1977/1426)

1 Dec 1977 (repeals of or in Forcible Entry Act 1381; Statutes concerning forcible entries and riots confirmed; Forcible Entry Acts, 1429, 1588, 1623; Metropolitan Police Courts Act 1839, s 24; Offences against the Person Act 1861, s 4; Public Stores Act 1875, ss 7, 9, 10; Conspiracy and Protection of Property Act 1875, s 3; Justices of the Peace Act 1949, s 43(3); Obscene Publications Act 1959, s 1(3); Criminal Justice Act 1961, ss 26(6), 28(2); Licensing Act 1964, s 30(5); Road Traffic Regulation Act 1967, ss 43(2), 80(5), (11); Criminal Justice Act 1967, ss 60(6)(a), (8)(d), 91(5); Transport Act 1968, s 131(2); Road Traffic Act 1972, Sch 4, Pt I; Criminal Justice Act 1972, s 34(1); Powers of Criminal Courts Act 1973, ss 2(8)(a), 49(1)–(3), 50(1)–(3), 51, 57(1), Sch 1, para 3(2)(b), Sch 3, paras 11, 12, 18(1)(b); Road Traffic Act 1974, Sch 5, Pts II, III) (SI 1977/1682; SI 1977/1744)

1 Jan 1978 (repeals of or in Prosecution of Offences Act 1879, s 5; Coroners Act 1887, ss 4(2), (3), 5, 9, 10, 16, 18(4), (5), 20; City of London Fire Inquests Act 1888; Interpretation Act 1889, s 27; Indictments Act 1915, s 8(3); Coroners (Amendment) Act 1926, ss 13(2)(a), (d), 25; Suicide Act 1961, Sch 1; Criminal Justice Act 1967, s 22(4); Administration of Justice Act 1970, Sch 9, Pt I, para 4; Courts Act 1971, s 57(2); and Bail Act 1976, ss 2(2), 10, Sch 2, paras 4, 37(4)) (SI 1977/1682)

17 Jul 1978 (repeals of or in Night Poaching Act 1828, ss 4, 11; Truck Act 1831, s 10; Conspiracy and Protection of Property Act 1875, ss 5, 7, 9, 19(1), (2); Cruelty to Animals Act 1876, ss 15, 17; Newspaper Libel and Registration Act 1881, s 5; Truck Amendment Act 1887, s 13(1), (3); Witnesses (Public Inquiries) Protection Act 1892,

Criminal Law Act 1977 (c 45)—*cont*

Sch 13—*cont*

ss 3, 6, para 2; Criminal Justice Act 1925, s 28(3); Water Act 1945, Sch 3, s 71(1); Exchange Control Act 1947, Sch 5, Pt II, para 2(3); Children Act 1948, s 29(5); Customs and Excise Act 1952, s 283(2)(a); Magistrates' Courts Act 1952, ss 18, 19, 24, 25, 32, 104, 125, 127(2), Sch 1, Sch 2, para 8; Protection of Animals (Amendment) Act 1954, s 3; Sexual Offences Act 1956, Sch 2, Pt II, Sch 3; Police, Fire and Probation Officers Remuneration Act 1956; Magistrates' Courts Act 1957, s 1(1)(a); Prevention of Fraud (Investments) Act 1958, s 13(2); Obscene Publications Act 1959, s 2(2), (3); Films Act 1960, s 45(3); Criminal Justice Act 1961, ss 8(1), 11(2); Criminal Justice Administration Act 1962, ss 12(3), 13, Sch 3, Sch 4, Pt II; Penalties for Drunkenness Act 1962, s 1(2)(a), (b); Public Order Act 1963, s 1(1); Building Control Act 1966, s 1(8); Industrial Development Act 1966, s 8(10); Veterinary Surgeons Act 1966, ss 19(2), 20(6); Finance Act 1967, Sch 7, para 4; Criminal Law Act 1967, ss 4(5), 5(4); Sexual Offences Act 1967, ss 4(2), 5(2), 7(2)(b), 9; Road Traffic Regulation Act 1967, s 91; Criminal Justice Act 1967, ss 27, 35, 43, 92(8), 106(2)(f), Sch 3, Pt II; Firearms Act 1968, s 57(4); Theft Act 1968, s 29(2), Sch 2, Pt III; Transport Act 1968, Sch 8, para 8; Decimal Currency Act 1969, Sch 2, para 21; Development of Tourism Act 1969, Sch 2, para 3(2), (4); Children and Young Persons Act 1969, ss 3(1)(b), (6), 6(1), (2), 12(2)(a), (3)(b)–(e), 15(1), 34(5), Sch 5, para 56; Auctions (Bidding Agreements) Act 1969, s 1(2), (4); Administration of Justice Act 1970, s 51(1); Courts Act 1971, Sch 8, paras 15(1), 16, 20, 34(1); Misuse of Drugs Act 1971, s 26(4); Road Traffic Act 1972, Sch 5, Pt IV, para 3; Gas Act 1972, s 43(2)(b); Industry Act 1972, Sch 1, para 4(2), (5); Criminal Justice Act 1972, s 47; Costs in Criminal Cases Act 1973, s 20(3); Hallmarking Act 1973, Sch 3, para 2(2), (5); Powers of Criminal Courts Act 1973, s 30(1), (2); Control of Pollution Act 1974, s 87(3); Housing Act 1974, Sch 13, para 2; Road Traffic Act 1974, Sch 5, Pt IV, para 4(1)–(3), (4)(a); Trade Union and Labour Relations Act 1974, s 29(7); District Courts (Scotland) Act 1975, ss 3(3), 27(1), Sch 1, para 26; Criminal Procedure (Scotland) Act 1975, s 403(4); Protection of Birds (Amendment) Act 1976) (SI 1978/712; SI 1978/900)

12 May 1980 (repeals of or in Magistrates' Courts Act 1952, s 102(3); Criminal Procedure (Scotland) Act 1975, ss 17, 325, 463(1)(a), (b)) (SI 1980/487; SI 1980/587)

1 Dec 1980 (repeals of or in Criminal Justice (Scotland) Act 1963, ss 26, 53(1), Sch 3, Pt II; Criminal Justice Act 1967, s 106(2)(f), Sch 6, paras 14–16, 21; Administration of Justice Act 1970,

Criminal Law Act 1977 (c 45)—*cont*

Sch 13—*cont*	s 41(6)(a); Courts Act 1971, s 59(5)(e), Sch 8, paras 34(3), 48(a); Powers of Criminal Courts Act 1973, ss 33, 58(a), Sch 5, paras 6, 8; Criminal Procedure (Scotland) Act 1975, ss 403(1), (5), 463(1); District Courts (Scotland) Act 1975, Sch 1, para 26) (SI 1980/1632; SI 1980/1701)
	29 Mar 1982 (repeals of or in Criminal Procedure (Scotland) Act 1975, Sch 9, paras 15, 35) (SI 1982/243)
14	8 Sep 1977 (SI 1977/1365)

[1] Any order(s) made under Criminal Justice Act 1993, s 78(3), bringing the prospective insertion into force will be noted to that Act in the service to this work

Farriers (Registration) (Amendment) Act 1977 (c 31)

RA: 22 Jul 1977

Commencement provisions: s 2(2), (3)

s 1, 2	22 Oct 1977 (s 2(2))
Schedule, para 1–4	22 Oct 1977 (s 2(2))
5	22 Jan 1978 (s 2(3))
6, 7	22 Oct 1977 (s 2(2))

Finance Act 1977 (c 36)

Budget Day: 29 Mar 1977

RA: 29 Jul 1977

See the note concerning Finance Acts at the front of this book

Finance (Income Tax Reliefs) Act 1977 (c 53)

Whole Act repealed

General Rate (Public Utilities) Act 1977 (c 11)

RA: 30 Mar 1977

30 Mar 1977 (RA)

Whole Act repealed, with savings, by Local Government Finance (Repeals, Savings and Consequential Amendments) Order 1990, SI 1990/776, art 3, Sch 1

Housing (Homeless Persons) Act 1977 (c 48)

Whole Act repealed

Incumbents (Vacation of Benefices) Measure 1977 (No 1)

RA: 30 Jun 1977

Commencement provisions: s 21(3)

s 1	Inserted by Incumbents (Vacation of Benefices) (Amendment) Measure 1993, s 1 (qv)
1A	30 Dec 1977 (s 21(3)); original s 1 renumbered s 1A by Incumbents (Vacation of Benefices) (Amendment) Measure 1993, s 1 (qv)
2–4	30 Dec 1977 (s 21(3))
5	Substituted by Incumbents (Vacation of Benefices) (Amendment) Measure 1993, s 14(1), Sch 3, para 3 (qv)
6, 7	30 Dec 1977 (s 21(3))
7A	Inserted by Incumbents (Vacation of Benefices) (Amendment) Measure 1993, s 5 (qv)
8, 9	30 Dec 1988 (s 21(3))
9A	Inserted by Incumbents (Vacation of Benefices) (Amendment) Measure 1993, s 6 (qv)
10–12	30 Dec 1977 (s 21(3))
13	Substituted by Incumbents (Vacation of Benefices) (Amendment) Measure 1993, s 8 (qv)
14	30 Dec 1977 (s 21(3))
15	Repealed
16, 17	30 Dec 1977 (s 21(3))
18	Substituted by Incumbents (Vacation of Benefices) (Amendment) Measure 1993, s 9 (qv)
19	30 Dec 1997 (s 21(3))
19A	Inserted by Incumbents (Vacation of Benefices (Amendment) Measure 1993, s 10 (qv)
20, 21	30 Dec 1977 (s 21(3))
Sch 1	Original Schedule renumbered as Sch 1 and substituted by Incumbents (Vacation of Benefices) (Amendment) Measure 1993, s 12, Sch 1 (qv)
2	Inserted by Incumbents (Vacation of Benefices) (Amendment) Measure 1993, s 12, Sch 1 (qv)

Insurance Brokers (Registration) Act 1977 (c 46)

RA: 29 Jul 1977

Commencement provisions: s 30(3), (4); Insurance Brokers (Registration) Act 1977 (Commencement No 1) Order 1977, SI 1977/1782; Insurance Brokers (Registration) Act 1977 (Commencement No 2) Order 1978, SI 1978/1393; Insurance Brokers (Registration) Act 1977 (Commencement No 3) Order 1980, SI 1980/1824

s 1	1 Dec 1977 (SI 1977/1782)
2–5	20 Oct 1978 (SI 1978/1393)
6–8	1 Dec 1977 (SI 1977/1782)
9	20 Oct 1978 (SI 1978/1393)
10–12	1 Dec 1977 (SI 1977/1782)
13–18	20 Oct 1978 (SI 1978/1393)
19(1)–(3)	20 Oct 1978 (SI 1978/1393)
(4)–(6)	1 Dec 1977 (SI 1977/1782)

Insurance Brokers (Registration) Act 1977 (c 46)—*cont*

s 20	20 Oct 1978 (SI 1978/1393)
21	1 Dec 1977 (SI 1977/1782)
22–24	1 Dec 1981 (SI 1980/1824)
25–30	1 Dec 1977 (SI 1977/1782)
Schedule	1 Dec 1977 (SI 1977/1782)

International Finance, Trade and Aid Act 1977 (c 6)

Whole Act repealed

Job Release Act 1977 (c 8)

RA: 30 Mar 1977

30 Mar 1977 (RA)

Note: s 1(4) of the Act stated that it would have effect for a period of eighteen months from Royal Assent unless further extended by order made by the Secretary of State; the last such order extended the Act to 29 Sep 1988 (SI 1987/1339)

Licensing (Amendment) Act 1977 (c 26)

RA: 22 Jul 1977

Commencement provisions: s 2(2)

22 Aug 1977 (s 2(2))

Local Authorities (Restoration of Works Powers) Act 1977 (c 47)

RA: 29 Jul 1977

29 Jul 1977 (RA)

Marriage (Scotland) Act 1977 (c 15)

RA: 26 May 1977

Commencement provisions: s 29(2)

s 1–23	1 Jan 1978 (s 29(2))
23A	Inserted (retrospectively) by Law Reform (Miscellaneous Provisions) (Scotland) Act 1980, s 22(1)(d) (qv)
24–28	1 Jan 1978 (s 29(2))
29	26 May 1977 (RA)
Sch 1–3	1 Jan 1978 (s 29(2))

Merchant Shipping (Safety Convention) Act 1977 (c 24)

Whole Act repealed

Minibus Act 1977 (c 25)

Whole Act repealed

National Health Service Act 1977 (c 49)

RA: 29 Jul 1977

Commencement provisions: s 130(5)

29 Aug 1977 (s 130(5))

New Towns Act 1977 (c 23)

Whole Act repealed

New Towns (Scotland) Act 1977 (c 16)

RA: 26 May 1977

26 May 1977 (RA)

Northern Ireland (Emergency Provisions) (Amendment) Act 1977 (c 34)

Whole Act repealed

Nuclear Industry (Finance) Act 1977 (c 7)

RA: 30 Mar 1977

30 Mar 1977 (RA)

Passenger Vehicles (Experimental Areas) Act 1977 (c 21)

Whole Act repealed

Patents Act 1977 (c 37)

RA: 29 Jul 1977

Commencement provisions: s 132(5); Patents Act 1977 (Commencement No 1) Order 1977, SI 1977/2090; Patents Act 1977 (Commencement No 2) Order 1978, SI 1978/586; Patents (Amendment) Rules 1987, SI 1987/288, r 4 (made for the purposes of ss 77(9), 78(8))

s 1–28	1 Jun 1978 (SI 1978/586)
28A	Inserted by Copyright, Designs and Patents Act 1988, s 295, Sch 5, para 7 (qv)
29–31	1 Jun 1978 (SI 1978/586)
32	Substituted by Patents, Designs and Marks Act 1986, s 1, Sch 1, para 4 (qv)
33, 34	1 Jun 1978 (SI 1978/586)
35	Repealed
36–50	1 Jun 1978 (SI 1978/586)

Patents Act 1977 (c 37)—*cont*

s 51	Substituted by Copyright, Designs and Patents Act 1988, s 295, Sch 5, para 14 (qv)
52	1 Jun 1978 (SI 1978/586)
53(1)	*Not in force*
(2)–(5)	1 Jun 1978 (SI 1978/586)
54–57	1 Jun 1978 (SI 1978/586)
57A	Inserted by Copyright, Designs and Patents Act 1988, s 295, Sch 5, para 16(1) (qv)
58, 59	1 Jun 1978 (SI 1978/586)
60(1)–(3)	1 Jun 1978 (SI 1978/586)
(4)	*Not in force*
(5)–(7)	1 Jun 1978 (SI 1978/586)
61–63	1 Jun 1978 (SI 1978/586)
64	Substituted by Copyright, Designs and Patents Act 1988, s 295, Sch 5, para 17 (qv)
65–75	1 Jun 1978 (SI 1978/586)
76	Substituted by Copyright, Designs and Patents Act 1988, s 295, Sch 5, para 20 (qv)
77(1), (2)	1 Jun 1978 (SI 1978/586)
(3)	Substituted by Copyright, Designs and Patents Act 1988, s 295, Sch 5, para 21 (1), (2) (qv)
(4), (4A)	Substituted for original sub-s (4) by Copyright, Designs and Patents Act 1988, s 295, Sch 5, para 21(1), (3) (qv)
(5)	1 Jun 1978 (SI 1978/586)
(6)	1 Sep 1987 (SI 1987/288)
(7)	29 Jul 1977 (RA)
(8)	1 Jun 1978 (SI 1978/586)
(9)	29 Jul 1977 (RA)
78(1)–(4)	1 Jun 1978 (SI 1978/586)
(5), (5A)	Substituted for original sub-s (5) by Copyright, Designs and Patents Act 1988, s 295, Sch 5, para 22 (qv)
(6)	1 Jun 1978 (SI 1978/586)
(7)	1 Sep 1987 (SI 1987/288)
(8)	29 Jul 1977 (RA)
79–83	1 Jun 1978 (SI 1978/586)
84, 85	Repealed
86, 87	*Not in force*
88	Repealed (*never in force*)
89–89B	Substituted for original s 89 by Copyright, Designs and Patents Act 1988, s 295, Sch 5, para 25 (qv)
90–95	1 Jun 1978 (SI 1978/586)
96	Repealed
97–99	1 Jun 1978 (SI 1978/586)
99A, 99B	Inserted by Copyright, Designs and Patents Act 1988, s 295, Sch 5, para 26 (qv)
100, 101	1 Jun 1978 (SI 1978/586)
102, 102A	Substituted for original s 102 by Copyright, Designs and Patents Act 1988, s 295, Sch 5, para 27 (qv)
103	1 Jun 1978 (SI 1978/586)
104	Repealed
105–113	1 Jun 1978 (SI 1978/586)
114, 115	Repealed
116–125	1 Jun 1978 (SI 1978/586)
125A	Inserted by Copyright, Designs and Patents Act 1988, s 295, Sch 5, para 30 (qv)

Patents Act 1977 (c 37)—*cont*

s 126	1 Jun 1978 (SI 1978/586)
127(1)–(4)	1 Jun 1978 (SI 1978/586)
(5)	See Sch 3 below
(6), (7)	1 Jun 1978 (SI 1978/586)
128, 129	1 Jun 1978 (SI 1978/586)
130	31 Dec 1977 (SI 1977/2090)
131	1 Jun 1978 (SI 1978/586)
132(1)–(4)	1 Jun 1978 (SI 1978/586)
(5)	29 Jul 1977 (RA)
(6)	1 Jun 1978 (SI 1978/586)
(7)	See Sch 6 below
Sch 1, 2	1 Jun 1978 (SI 1978/586)
3	29 Jul 1977 (repeal of Patents Act 1949, s 41) (RA) 1 Jun 1978 (otherwise) (SI 1978/586)
4, 5	1 Jun 1978 (SI 1978/586)
6	29 Jul 1977 (repeal of Patents Act 1949, s 41) (RA) 31 Dec 1977 (repeal of Patents Act 1949, s 88) (SI 1977/2090) 1 Jun 1978 (otherwise) (SI 1978/586)

Pensioners Payments Act 1977 (c 51)

Whole Act repealed

Presumption of Death (Scotland) Act 1977 (c 27)

RA: 22 Jul 1977

Commencement provisions: s 20(2); Presumption of Death (Scotland) Act 1977 (Commencement) Order 1978, SI 1978/159

s 1–19	1 Mar 1978 (SI 1978/159)
20	22 Jul 1977 (RA)
Sch 1, 2	1 Mar 1978 (SI 1978/159)

Price Commission Act 1977 (c 33)

RA: 22 Jul 1977

Commencement provisions: s 24(2) (repealed)

Whole Act repealed, except ss 16, 17, by the Competition Act 1980, s 33(4), Sch 2 (the repeal of s 15(4) and Sch 2, para 4(b), (d) being as from 1 Jan 2011). S 17 repealed by Statute Law (Repeals) Act 1989, s 1(1), Sch 1, Pt II. S 16 came into force on 1 Aug 1977 (s 24(2))

Post Office Act 1977 (c 44)

Whole Act repealed

Protection from Eviction Act 1977 (c 43)

RA: 29 Jul 1977

Commencement provisions: s 13(2)

29 Aug 1977 (s 13(2))

Redundancy Rebates Act 1977 (c 22)

Whole Act repealed

Rent Act 1977 (c 42)

RA: 29 Jul 1977

Commencement provisions: s 156(2)

29 Aug 1977 (s 156(2))

Rent (Agriculture) Amendment Act 1977 (c 17)

RA: 26 May 1977

Commencement provisions: s 2(2)

9 Jun 1977 (s 2(2))

Rentcharges Act 1977 (c 30)

RA: 22 Jul 1977

Commencement provisions: s 18(2); Rentcharges Act 1977 (Commencement) Order 1978, SI 1978/15

s 1–3	22 Aug 1977 (s 18(2))
4–11	1 Feb 1978 (SI 1978/15)
12–15	22 Aug 1977 (s 18(2))
16	1 Feb 1978 (SI 1978/15)
17(1)	22 Aug 1977 (in relation to Sch 1, para 2) (s 18(2)) 1 Feb 1978 (otherwise) (SI 1978/15)
(2)	See Sch 2 below
(3)	22 Aug 1977 (s 18(2))
(4), (5)	1 Feb 1978 (SI 1978/15)
(6)	22 Aug 1977 (s 18(2))
18	22 Aug 1977 (s 18(2))
Sch 1, para 1	1 Feb 1978 (SI 1978/15)
2	22 Aug 1977 (s 18(2))
3, 4	1 Feb 1978 (SI 1978/15)
2	1 Feb 1978 (repeal of Inclosure Act 1854, s 10; Law of Property Act 1925, s 191) (SI 1978/15) 22 Aug 1977 (otherwise) (s 18(2))

Representation of the People Act 1977 (c 9)

Whole Act repealed

Restrictive Trade Practices Act 1977 (c 19)

RA: 30 Jun 1977

30 Jun 1977 (RA)

Returning Officers (Scotland) Act 1977 (c 14)

Whole Act repealed

Roe Deer (Close Seasons) Act 1977 (c 4)

Whole Act repealed

Social Security (Miscellaneous Provisions) Act 1977 (c 5)

RA: 30 Mar 1977

Commencement provisions: s 25(2), (3), (4); Social Security (Miscellaneous Provisions) Act 1977 (Commencement No 1) Order 1977, SI 1977/617; Social Security (Miscellaneous Provisions) Act 1977 (Commencement No 2) Order 1977, SI 1977/618

s 1–11	Repealed
12	25 Apr 1977 (SI 1977/618)
13	Repealed
14	Repealed or spent
15–21	Repealed
22	Repealed or spent
23	25 Apr 1977 (SI 1977/618)
24(1)	30 Mar 1977 (RA)
(2)	Repealed
(3)	30 Mar 1977 (RA)
(4)	Repealed
(5)	30 Mar 1977 (RA)
(6)	See Sch 2 below
25	30 Mar 1977 (RA)
Sch 1	Repealed
2	30 Mar 1977 (repeals of or in Social Security Act 1975, ss 30(2), 45(4), 66(5), 124(1)(d)) (RA)
	6 Apr 1977 (repeals of or in Employment Protection Act 1975, s 113; Supplementary Benefits Act 1976, Sch 7, para 41) (SI 1977/617)
	25 Apr 1977 (repeals of or in Tribunals and Inquiries Act 1971; Social Security Act 1975, s 1(5), 129(3); Social Security (NI) Act 1975; Social Security Pensions Act 1975; Employment Protection Act 1975, s 40(3); Supplementary Benefits Act 1976, s 29) (SI 1977/618)
	27 Jun 1977 (repeals of or in Social Security Act 1975, Sch 20) (SI 1977/618)
	1 Jul 1977 (repeals of or in Industrial Injuries and Diseases (Old Cases) Act 1975) (SI 1977/618)

Statute Law (Repeals) Act 1977 (c 18)

RA: 16 Jun 1977

16 Jun 1977 (RA)

Torts (Interference with Goods) Act 1977 (c 32)

RA: 22 Jul 1977

Commencement provisions: s 17(2); Torts (Interference with Goods) Act 1977 (Commencement No 1) Order 1977, SI 1977/1910; Torts (Interference with Goods) Act 1977 (Commencement No 2) Order 1978, SI 1978/627; Torts (Interference with Goods) Act 1977 (Commencement No 3) Order 1980, SI 1980/2024[1]

s 1–11	1 Jun 1978 (SI 1978/627)
12–16	1 Jan 1978 (SI 1977/1910)
17(1), (2)	1 Jan 1978 (SI 1977/1910)
(3)	1 Jun 1978 (SI 1978/627)
Sch 1	1 Jan 1978 (SI 1977/1910)
2	1 Jun 1978 (SI 1978/627)

[1] Note that Torts (Interference with Goods) Act 1977 (Commencement No 3) Order 1980, SI 1980/2024, brought this Act into force, so far as not already in force by virtue of SI 1977/1910, in Northern Ireland on 1 Jan 1981 (SI 1978/627 applied to England and Wales only)

Town and Country Planning (Amendment) Act 1977 (c 29)

Whole Act repealed

Town and Country Planning (Scotland) Act 1977 (c 10)

RA: 30 Mar 1977

30 Mar 1977 (RA)

Transport (Financial Provisions) Act 1977 (c 20)

Whole Act repealed

Unfair Contract Terms Act 1977 (c 50)

RA: 26 Oct 1977

Commencement provisions: s 31(1)

1 Feb 1978 (s 31(1); note that this Act does not apply to contracts before this date but applies to liability for loss or damage suffered on or after that date (s 31(2)))

Water Charges Equalisation Act 1977 (c 41)

Whole Act repealed

1978

Adoption (Scotland) Act 1978 (c 28)

RA: 20 Jul 1978

Commencement provisions: s 67(2); Adoption (Scotland) Act 1978 Commencement Order 1984, SI 1984/1050

s 1, 2	1 Feb 1985 (SI 1984/1050)
3–5	1 Sep 1984 (SI 1984/1050)
6	1 Sep 1984 (SI 1984/1050); prospectively substituted by Children (Scotland) Act 1995, s 95[1]
6A	Prospectively inserted by Children (Scotland) Act 1995, s 96[1]
7	1 Sep 1984 (SI 1984/1050)
8	1 Sep 1984 (SI 1984/1050); prospectively repealed by Children (Scotland) Act 1995, ss 98(1), 105(5), Sch 2, paras 1, 4, Sch 5
9	1 Sep 1984 (SI 1984/1050)
10	Repealed
11–20	1 Sep 1984 (subject to transitional provisions) (SI 1984/1050)
21	Substituted by Children Act 1989, s 88, Sch 10, para 37 (qv)
22	1 Sep 1984 (subject to transitional provisions) (SI 1984/1050)
22A	Prospectively inserted by Children (Scotland) Act 1995, s 98(1), Sch 2, paras 1, 15[1]
23–25	1 Sep 1984 (subject to transitional provisions) (SI 1984/1050)
25A	Prospectively inserted by Children (Scotland) Act 1995, s 98(1), Sch 2, paras 1, 18[1]
26	1 Sep 1984 (subject to transitional provisions) (SI 1984/1050); prospectively repealed by Children (Scotland) Act 1995, s 105(5), Sch 5[1]
27–31	1 Sep 1984 (subject to transitional provisions) (SI 1984/1050)
32–37	1 Sep 1984 (subject to transitional provisions) (SI 1984/1050); prospectively repealed by Children (Scotland) Act 1995, ss 98(1), 105(5), Sch 2, paras 1, 21, Sch 5[1]
38, 39	1 Sep 1984 (subject to transitional provisions) (SI 1984/1050)
40	Repealed
41–51	1 Sep 1984 (subject to transitional provisions) (SI 1984/1050)
51A, 51B	Prospectively inserted by Children (Scotland) Act 1995, s 98(1), Sch 2, paras 1, 25[1]

Adoption (Scotland) Act 1978 (c 28)—*cont*

s 52–67	1 Sep 1984 (subject to transitional provisions) (SI 1984/1050)
Sch 1–4	1 Sep 1984 (SI 1984/1050)

[1] Any order(s) made under Children (Scotland) Act 1995, s 105, bringing the prospective amendents into force will be noted to that Act in the service to this work

Appropriation Act 1978 (c 57)

Whole Act repealed

Chronically Sick and Disabled Persons (Northern Ireland) Act 1978 (c 53)

Applies to Northern Ireland only

Church of England (Miscellaneous Provisions) Measure 1978 (No 3)

RA: 30 Jun 1978

Commencement provisions: s 13(4)

30 Jul 1978 (s 13(4))

Civil Aviation Act 1978 (c 8)

Whole Act repealed

Civil Liability (Contribution) Act 1978 (c 47)

RA: 31 Jul 1978

Commencement provisions: s 10(2)

1 Jan 1979 (s 10(2))

Commonwealth Development Corporation Act 1978 (c 2)

RA: 23 Mar 1978

Commencement provisions: s 19(2)

23 Apr 1978 (s 19(2))

Community Service by Offenders (Scotland) Act 1978 (c 49)

RA: 31 Jul 1978

Commencement provisions: s 15(2); Community Service by Offenders (Scotland) Act 1978 (Commencement No 1) Order 1978, SI 1978/1944; Community Service by Offenders (Scotland) Act 1978 (Commencement No 2) Order 1980, SI 1980/268

Community Service by Offenders (Scotland) Act 1978 (c 49)—*cont*

s 1–5	Repealed
5A	Prospectively inserted by Criminal Justice (Scotland) Act 1995, s 40(3); repealed by Criminal Procedure (Consequential Provisions) (Scotland) Act 1995, s 6(1), Sch 5 (qv)[1]
6, 6A, 6B, 7, 8	Repealed
9	1 Feb 1979 (SI 1978/1944)
10–13	Repealed
14	1 Feb 1979 (SI 1978/1944)
15	Repealed
Sch 1	Repealed
2	1 Feb 1979 (SI 1978/1944)

[1] As to retention of prospective nature of amendments made by Criminal Justice (Scotland) Act 1995, see Criminal Procedure (Consequential Provisions) (Scotland) Act 1995, s 4, Sch 3, paras 3, 16

Consolidated Fund Act 1978 (c 7)

Whole Act repealed

Consolidated Fund (No 2) Act 1978 (c 59)

Whole Act repealed

Consumer Safety Act 1978 (c 38)

Whole Act repealed

Co-operative Development Agency Act 1978 (c 21)

Whole Act repealed

Dioceses Measure 1978 (No 1)

RA: 2 Feb 1978

Commencement provisions: s 25(2)

2 May 1978 (s 25(2))

Dividends Act 1978 (c 54)

Whole Act repealed

Domestic Proceedings and Magistrates' Courts Act 1978 (c 22)

RA: 30 Jun 1978

Commencement provisions: s 89(3); Domestic Proceedings and Magistrates' Courts Act 1978 (Commencement No 1) Order 1978, SI 1978/997; Domestic Proceedings and Magistrates' Courts Act 1978 (Commencement No 2) Order 1978, SI 1978/1489; Domestic Proceedings and Magistrates' Courts Act 1978 (Commencement No 1)

Domestic Proceedings and Magistrates' Courts Act 1978 (c 22)—*cont*
(Scotland) Order 1978, SI 1978/1490; Domestic Proceedings and Magistrates' Courts Act 1978 (Commencement No 3) Order 1979, SI 1979/731; Domestic Proceedings and Magistrates' Courts Act 1978 (Commencement No 4) Order 1980, SI 1980/1478; Domestic Proceedings and Magistrates' Courts Act 1978 (Commencement No 2) (Scotland) Order 1980, SI 1980/2036; Children Act 1975 and the Domestic Proceedings and Magistrates' Courts Act 1978 (Commencement) Order 1985, SI 1985/779

s 1, 2	1 Feb 1981 (SI 1980/1478)
3	Substituted by Matrimonial and Family Proceedings Act 1984, s 9 (qv)
4, 5	1 Feb 1981 (SI 1980/1478)
6	Substituted by Matrimonial and Family Proceedings Act 1984, s 10 (qv)
7	1 Feb 1981 (SI 1980/1478)
8	Substituted by Children Act 1989, s 108(5), Sch 13, para 36 (qv)
9–15	Repealed
16–18	1 Nov 1979 (SI 1979/731)
19, 20	1 Feb 1981 (SI 1980/1478)
20ZA	Inserted by Maintenance Enforcement Act 1991, s 5 (qv)
20A	Inserted by Family Law Reform Act 1987, s 33(1), Sch 2, para 69 (qv); substituted by Children Act 1989, s 108(5), Sch 15, para 39(1) (qv)
21	Repealed
22, 23	1 Feb 1981 (SI 1980/1478)
24	Repealed
25–27	1 Feb 1981 (SI 1980/1478)
28	1 Nov 1979 (SI 1979/731)
29(1), (2)	1 Nov 1979 (SI 1979/731)
(3)	1 Feb 1981 (SI 1980/1478)
(4)	Repealed
(5)	1 Nov 1979 (SI 1979/731)
30	1 Nov 1979 (SI 1979/731)
31, 32	1 Feb 1981 (SI 1980/1478)
33, 34	Repealed
35	1 Feb 1981 (SI 1980/1478)
36–53	Repealed
54	1 Feb 1981 (SI 1980/1478)
55	23 Oct 1978 (SI 1978/1490)
56	1 Feb 1981 (SI 1980/1478)
57, 58	Repealed
59, 60	1 Feb 1981 (SI 1980/1478)
61	23 Oct 1978 (SI 1978/1490)
62, 63	1 Feb 1981 (SI 1980/1478)
64–72	Repealed
73	20 Nov 1978 (SI 1978/1489)
74	20 Nov 1978 (EW) (SI 1978/1489); repealed (S)
75–86	Repealed
87	23 Oct 1978 (S) (SI 1978/1490) 20 Nov 1978 (EW) (SI 1978/1489)
88(1)–(4)	1 Nov 1979 (SI 1979/731)
(5)	18 Jul 1978 (SI 1978/997)
89(1)	18 Jul 1978 (SI 1978/997)
(2)(a)	23 Oct 1978 (S) (so far as brings Sch 2, paras 17, 18 into force) (SI 1978/1490)

Domestic Proceedings and Magistrates' Courts Act 1978 (c 22)—*cont*

s 89(2)(a)—*cont*	29 Nov 1978 (EW) (SI 1978/1489) 1 Feb 1981 (S) (otherwise) (SI 1980/2036)
(b)	18 Jul 1978 (SI 1978/997)
(3)–(6)	18 Jul 1978 (SI 1978/997)
90	18 Jul 1978 (SI 1978/997)
Sch 1	18 Jul 1978 (SI 1978/997)
2, para 1, 2	1 Feb 1981 (SI 1980/1478)
3–5	Repealed
6	1 Feb 1981 (SI 1980/1478)
7	Spent
8	Repealed
9	1 Feb 1981 (SI 1980/1478)
10, 11	Spent
12	1 Nov 1979 (SI 1979/731)
13, 14	1 Feb 1981 (SI 1980/1478)
15	Repealed
16	Spent
17–20	Repealed or spent
21–25	Repealed
26	1 Feb 1981 (SI 1980/1478)
27	Repealed
28	1 Feb 1981 (SI 1980/1478)
29–31	Repealed
32, 33	1 Feb 1981 (SI 1980/1478)
34–36	Repealed
37	1 Feb 1981 (SI 1980/1478)
38, 39	1 Nov 1979 (SI 1979/731)
40	Spent
41–50	Repealed
51	20 Nov 1978 (SI 1978/1489)
52	Repealed
53	20 Nov 1978 (SI 1978/1489)
54	Spent
3	18 Jul 1978 (repeal in Administration of Justice Act 1964, s 2) (SI 1978/997) 20 Nov 1978 (repeals of or in Adoption (Hague Convention) Act (Northern Ireland) 1969, s 7(2); Children Act 1975, Sch 3, para 26; Adoption Act 1976, Sch 1, para 6) (SI 1978/1489) 1 Nov 1979 (repeals of or in National Assistance Act 1948, s 43(7); Magistrates' Courts Act 1952, ss 57(4), 60(1), (2)(a), 61, 62, 121(2); Matrimonial Proceedings (Magistrates' Courts) Act 1960, s 8(3); Criminal Justice Act 1961, Sch 4; Maintenance Orders (Reciprocal Enforcement) Act 1972, s 17(1)–(3), Schedule, para 1; Affiliation Proceedings (Amendment) Act 1972, s 3(1), (2); Children Act 1975, s 21(3), Sch 3, para 12; Adoption Act 1976, s 64(c), Sch 3, para 4; Supplementary Benefits Act 1976, s 18(7), Sch 7) (SI 1979/731) 1 Feb 1981 (repeals of or in Maintenance Orders Act 1950, s 2(3); Magistrates' Courts Act 1952, s 59; Affiliation Proceedings Act 1957, s 7(1)–(3); Matrimonial Proceedings (Magistrates' Courts) Act 1960 except s 8(3) (repealed as above);

Domestic Proceedings and Magistrates' Courts Act 1978 (c 22)—*cont*

Sch 3—*cont*	Administration of Justice Act 1964, Sch 3, para 27; Matrimonial Causes Act 1965, s 42; Criminal Justice Act 1967, Sch 3 (entry relating to Matrimonial Proceedings (Magistrates' Courts) Act 1960); Family Law Reform Act 1969, s 5(2); Local Authority Social Services Act 1970, Sch 1 (entry relating to Matrimonial Proceedings (Magistrates' Courts) Act 1960); Matrimonial Proceedings and Property Act 1970, ss 30(1), 31–33; Guardianship of Minors Act 1971, ss 9(3), 14(4); Misuse of Drugs Act 1971, s 34; Maintenance Orders (Reciprocal Enforcement) Act 1972, s 27(3); Local Government Act 1972, Sch 23, para 10; Matrimonial Causes Act 1973, s 27(8); Guardianship Act 1973, ss 2(5), 3(2), 8, Sch 2, para 1(2); Legal Aid Act 1974, Sch 1, para 3(a); Children Act 1975, ss 17(1), 91; Adoption Act 1976, s 26(1)) (SI 1980/1478)

Education (Northern Ireland) Act 1978 (c 13)

Whole Act repealed

Employment (Continental Shelf) Act 1978 (c 46)

RA: 31 Jul 1978

31 Jul 1978 (RA)

Whole Act prospectively repealed by Oil and Gas (Enterprise) Act 1982, s 37, Sch 4; any order made under s 38(2) of the 1982 Act bringing the prospective repeal into force will be noted to that Act in the service to this work

Employment Protection (Consolidation) Act 1978 (c 44)

RA: 31 Jul 1978

Commencement provisions: s 160(2)

s 1–6	Substituted (subject to savings) for ss 1, 2, 2A, 4, 5, 5A, 6 by Trade Union Reform and Employment Rights Act 1993, ss 26, 50, Sch 4, Sch 9, para 3 (qv) (original s 3 repealed by Employment Act 1982, s 21(3), Sch 4 (qv); s 2A originally inserted by Employment Act 1989, s 13(1), (3) (qv); s 5A originally inserted by Employment Act 1982, s 20, Sch 2, para 8(4) (qv))
7	Repealed
8–22	1 Nov 1978 (s 160(2))
22A	Inserted by Trade Union Reform and Employment Rights Act 1993, s 28, Sch 5, para 1 (qv)
22AA	Inserted (26 Oct 1995) by Collective Redundancies and Transfer of Undertakings (Protection of Employment) (Amendment) Regulations 1995, SI 1995/2587, reg 12(1)

Employment Protection (Consolidation) Act 1978 (c 44)—*cont*

s 22B, 22C	Inserted by Trade Union Reform and Employment Rights Act 1993, s 28, Sch 5, para 1 (qv)
23–28	Repealed
29–31	1 Nov 1978 (s 160(2))
31A	Inserted by Employment Act 1980, s 13 (qv)
31AA	Inserted (26 Oct 1995) by Collective Redundancies and Transfer of Undertakings (Protection of Employment) (Amendment) Regulations 1995, SI 1995/2587, reg 13(1)
32	Substituted by Trade Union and Labour Relations (Consolidation) Act 1992, s 300(2), Sch 2, para 13 (qv)
33–48	Substituted by new Pt III (ss 33–37, 37A, 38, 38A, 39–47) by Trade Union Reform and Employment Rights Act 1993, ss 23, 25, Schs 2, 3, with effect from 10 Jun 1994 but only in relation to women whose expected week of childbirth began on or after 16 Oct 1994 (Trade Union Reform and Employment Rights Act 1993 (Commencement No 3 and Transitional Provisions) Order 1994, SI 1994/1365); original ss 34–44 were repealed by Social Security Act 1986, s 86, Sch 11 (qv)
49–56	1 Nov 1978 (s 160(2))
56A	Inserted by Employment Act 1980, s 12 (qv)
57	1 Nov 1978 (s 160(2))
57A	Inserted by Trade Union Reform and Employment Rights Act 1993, s 28, Sch 5, para 3 (qv)
57AA	Inserted (26 Oct 1995) by Collective Redundancies and Transfer of Undertakings (Protection of Employment) (Amendment) Regulations 1995, SI 1995/2587, reg 14(1)
58, 58A	Repealed
59	1 Nov 1978 (s 160(2))
60	1 Nov 1978 (s 160(2)); substituted (subject to transitional provisions) by Trade Union Reform and Employment Rights Act 1993, s 24(1) (qv)
60A	Inserted by Trade Union Reform and Employment Rights Act 1993, s 29(1) (qv)
61	1 Nov 1978 (s 160(2))
62, 62A	Repealed
63, 64	1 Nov 1978 (s 160(2))
64A	Repealed
65–71	1 Nov 1978 (s 160(2))
72	Substituted by Trade Union and Labour Relations (Consolidation) Act 1992, s 300(2), Sch 2, para 16 (qv)
72A	Repealed
73–75	1 Nov 1978 (s 160(2))
75A	Inserted (with savings) by Trade Union Reform and Employment Rights Act 1993, s 28, Sch 5, para 9 (qv); (original s 75A inserted by Employment Act 1982, s 5(3) (qv) and repealed by Trade Union and Labour Relations (Consolidation) Act 1992, s 300(1), Sch 1 (qv))
76	1 Nov 1978 (s 160(2))
76A–76C	Repealed

Employment Protection (Consolidation) Act 1978 (c 44)—*cont*

s 77, 77A, 78, 78A, 79	Inserted by Trade Union Reform and Employment Rights Act 1993, s 28, Sch 5, para 10 (qv); (original ss 77, 78, 79 repealed by Trade Union and Labour Relations (Consolidation) Act 1992, s 300(1), Sch 1 (qv))
80–93	1 Nov 1978 (s 160(2))
94, 95	Repealed
96	1 Nov 1978 (s 160(2))
97	Repealed
98–102	1 Nov 1978 (s 160(2))
103–105	Repealed
106, 107	1 Nov 1978 (s 160(2))
108	Substituted by Employment Act 1989, s 29(3), Sch 6, para 22 (qv)
109	Repealed
110–112	1 Nov 1978 (s 160(2))
113	Repealed
114–120	1 Nov 1978 (s 160(2))
121	Repealed
122	1 Nov 1978 (s 160(2))
123	Repealed
124–136	1 Nov 1978 (s 160(2))
136A	Inserted by Trade Union Reform and Employment Rights Act 1993, s 42 (qv)
137, 138	1 Nov 1978 (s 160(2))
138A	Prospectively inserted by Trade Union Reform and Employment Rights Act 1993, s 31(2)[1]
139(1)	1 Nov 1978 (s 160(2))
(2)–(9)	1 Jan 1979 (s 160(2))
139A	Inserted by Trade Union Reform and Employment Rights Act 1993, s 49(1), Sch 7, para 11 (qv)
140–142	1 Nov 1978 (s 160(2))
143	Repealed
144	1 Nov 1978 (s 160(2))
145	Repealed
146	1 Nov 1978 (s 160(2))
146A	Inserted by Trade Union Reform and Employment Rights Act 1993, s 49(1), Sch 7, para 5 (qv)
147	Repealed
148–150	1 Nov 1978 (s 160(2))
151	Substituted by Employment Act 1982, s 20, Sch 2, para 7(1) (qv)
152–160	1 Nov 1978 (s 160(2))
Sch 1–4	1 Nov 1978 (s 160(2))
5, 6	Repealed
7–15	1 Nov 1978 (s 160(2))
16, para 1, 2	Repealed
3	Purported to amend Iron and Steel Act 1949, ss 40(3), 41(3) (repealed)
4, 5	Repealed
6	1 Nov 1978 (s 160(2))
7	Repealed
8	1 Nov 1978 (s 160(2))
9	Repealed
10	1 Nov 1978 (s 160(2))

Employment Protection (Consolidation) Act 1978 (c 44)—*cont*

Sch 16, para 11, 12	Repealed
13	1 Nov 1978 (s 160(2))
14	Repealed
15–17	1 Nov 1978 (s 160(2))
18, 19	Repealed
20(1)	Repealed
(2)	1 Nov 1978 (s 160(2))
21	Repealed
22	1 Nov 1978 (s 160(2))
23, 24	Repealed
25(1)	1 Nov 1978 (s 160(2))
(2)	Repealed
(3), (4)	1 Nov 1978 (s 160(2))
26	1 Nov 1978 (s 160(2))
27	Repealed
28	1 Nov 1978 (s 160(2))
29	Repealed
30	1 Nov 1978 (s 160(2))
31–33	Repealed
34	1 Nov 1978 (s 160(2))
17	1 Nov 1978 (except repeals in Employment Protection Act 1975, s 122) 1 Jan 1979 (exception noted above) (s 160(2))

[1] Any order made under Trade Union Reform and Employment Rights Act 1993, s 52, bringing the prospective insertion into force will be noted to that Act in the service to this work

Employment Subsidies Act 1978 (c 6)

Whole Act lapsed (31 Dec 1991) in accordance with terms of s 3(4)

European Parliamentary Elections Act 1978 (c 10)

RA: 5 May 1980

5 May 1980 (RA)

Export Guarantees and Overseas Investment Act 1978 (c 18)

Whole Act repealed

Finance Act 1978 (c 42)

Budget Day: 11 Apr 1978

RA: 31 Jul 1978

See the note about Finance Acts at the front of this book

Gun Barrel Proof Act 1978 (c 9)

RA: 5 May 1978

Commencement provisions: s 9(3); Gun Barrel Proof Act 1978 (Commencement No 1) Order 1978, SI 1978/1587; Gun Barrel Proof Act 1978 (Commencement No 2) Order 1980, SI 1980/640

s 1	5 Jun 1980 (SI 1980/640)
2–7	1 Dec 1978 (SI 1978/1587)
8(1)	1 Dec 1978 (so far as relates to Sch 3) (SI 1978/1587) 5 Jun 1980 (otherwise) (SI 1980/640)
(2)	1 Dec 1978 (SI 1978/1587)
(3)	5 Jun 1980 (SI 1980/640)
9	1 Dec 1978 (SI 1978/1587)
Sch 1, 2	5 Jun 1980 (SI 1980/640)
3, para 1(a)	5 Jun 1980 (SI 1980/640)
(b)	1 Dec 1978 (except definition of 'convention proof mark') (SI 1978/1587) 5 Jun 1980 (exception noted above) (SI 1980/640)
2–9	1 Dec 1978 (SI 1978/1587)
10(1)	1 Dec 1978 (SI 1978/1587)
(2)	5 Jun 1980 (SI 1980/640)
11–14	1 Dec 1978 (SI 1978/1587)
15(1), (2)	1 Dec 1978 (SI 1978/1587)
(3)	5 Jun 1980 (SI 1980/640)
16	1 Dec 1980 (except words 'or which is or at any time was a convention proof mark'), (SI 1978/1587) 5 Jun 1980 (exception noted above) (SI 1980/640)
17–20	1 Dec 1978 (SI 1978/1587)
4	1 Dec 1978 (SI 1978/1587)

Homes Insulation Act 1978 (c 48)

Whole Act repealed

Home Purchase Assistance and Housing Corporation Guarantee Act 1978 (c 27)

Whole Act repealed

House of Commons (Administration) Act 1978 (c 36)

RA: 20 Jul 1978

Commencement provisions: s 5(5)

s 1	20 Jul 1978 (RA)
2	1 Jan 1979 (s 5(5))
3–5	20 Jul 1978 (RA)
Sch 1	20 Jul 1978 (RA)
2, para 1, 2	20 Jul 1978 (RA)
3	1 Jan 1979 (s 5(5))
4, 5	Repealed
3	1 Jan 1979 (s 5(5))

Housing (Financial Provisions) (Scotland) Act 1978 (c 14)

RA: 25 May 1978

Commencement provisions: s 19(2), (3) (repealed)

Whole Act repealed, except for Sch 2, paras 12–14, 39, which came into force on 25 Jun 1978 (s 19(2))

Import of Live Fish (Scotland) Act 1978 (c 35)

RA: 20 Jul 1978

20 Jul 1978 (RA)

Independent Broadcasting Authority Act 1978 (c 43)

Whole Act repealed

Industrial and Provident Societies Act 1978 (c 34)

RA: 20 Jul 1978

Commencement provisions: s 3(3)

20 Aug 1978 (s 3(3))

Inner Urban Areas Act 1978 (c 50)

RA: 31 Jul 1978

31 Jul 1978 (RA)

Internationally Protected Persons Act 1978 (c 17)

RA: 30 Jun 1978

Commencement provisions: s 5(5); Internationally Protected Persons Act 1978 (Commencement) Order 1979, SI 1979/455

24 May 1979 (SI 1979/455)

Interpretation Act 1978 (c 30)

RA: 20 Jul 1978

Commencement provisions: s 26

1 Jan 1979 (s 26)

Iron and Steel (Amendment) Act 1978 (c 41)

Whole Act repealed

Judicature (Northern Ireland) Act 1978 (c 23)

RA: 30 Jun 1978

Commencement provisions: s 123(2); Judicature (Northern Ireland) Act 1978 (Commencement No 1) Order 1978, SI 1978/1101; Judicature (Northern Ireland) Act 1978 (Commencement No 2) Order 1978, SI 1978/1829; Judicature (Northern Ireland) Act 1978 (Commencement No 3) Order 1979, SI 1979/124; Judicature (Northern Ireland) Act 1978 (Commencement No 4) Order 1979, SI 1979/422

s 1–26	18 Apr 1979 (SI 1979/422)
27	18 Apr 1979 (SI 1979/422); prospectively repealed by Children (Northern Ireland) Order 1995, SI 1995/755 (NI 2), art 185(2), Sch 10
28	Repealed
29–33	18 Apr 1979 (SI 1979/422)
33A	Inserted by Administration of Justice Act 1982, s 69(1), Sch 7, Pt I (qv)
34–38	18 Apr 1979 (SI 1979/422)
39, 40	Repealed
41–51	18 Apr 1979 (SI 1979/422)
52, 53	21 Aug 1978 (SI 1978/1101)
54–56	2 Jan 1979 (SI 1978/1829) (Note that s 54(2)–(4), (6), 55(3), 56(1)–(3) came into force on 21 Aug 1978 so far as they apply to the Crown Court Rules Committee and Crown Court Rules (SI 1978/1101))
57–72	18 Apr 1979 (SI 1979/422)
73	Substituted (1 Nov 1982) by Supreme Court (Departments and Officers) (Northern Ireland) Order 1982, SR 1982/300, art 5(1)
74	18 Apr 1979 (SI 1979/422)
75	Substituted (1 Nov 1982) by SR 1982/300, art 4 (see s 73 above)
76–82	18 Apr 1979 (SI 1979/422)
83	Repealed
84–94	18 Apr 1979 (SI 1979/422)
94A	Inserted by Administration of Justice Act 1982, s 70, Sch 8, para 11 (qv)
95, 96	Repealed
97, 98	18 Apr 1979 (SI 1979/422)
99	21 Aug 1978 (SI 1978/1101)
100	18 Apr 1979 (SI 1979/422)
101	Repealed
102–106	18 Apr 1979 (SI 1979/422)
107	21 Aug 1978 (SI 1978/1101)
108–115	18 Apr 1979 (SI 1979/422)
116	21 Aug 1978 (SI 1978/1101)
117	18 Apr 1979 (SI 1979/422)
117A	Inserted by Administration of Justice Act 1982, s 70, Sch 8, para 12 (qv)
118–121	21 Aug 1978 (SI 1978/1101)
122	See Schs 5–7 below
123	21 Aug 1978 (SI 1978/1101)
Sch 1–4	18 Apr 1979 (SI 1979/422)
5, Pt I, para 1, 2	18 Apr 1979 (SI 1979/422)
3, 4	2 Jan 1979 (SI 1978/1829)

Judicature (Northern Ireland) Act 1978 (c 23)—*cont*

Sch 5, Pt II	21 Aug 1978 (amendments to Bills of Sale (Ireland) Act 1879; Deeds of Arrangement Act 1887; Deeds of Arrangement Amendment Act 1890) (SI 1978/1101)
	2 Jan 1979 (amendments to Probates and Letters of Administration Act (Ireland) 1857; Juries Act (Ireland) 1871, s 18; Bankruptcy (Ireland) Amendment Act 1872, ss 57, 124; Bills of Sale (Ireland) Act 1879, s 4; Land Law (Ireland) Act 1887; Foreign Judgments (Reciprocal Enforcement) Act 1933; Trade Marks Act 1938; Exchange Control Act 1947; Representation of the People Act 1949, s 163; Arbitration Act 1950; Arbitration (International Investment Disputes) Act 1966; Criminal Appeal (Northern Ireland) Act 1968, ss 49, 50 (definition 'rules of court'); Administration of Justice Act 1969, ss 20(5), 21(4); Social Security (Northern Ireland) Act 1975) (SI 1978/1829)
	18 Apr 1979 (all other amendments to Acts of UK Parliament) (SI 1979/422)
	21 Aug 1978, 2 Jan 1979, 21 Feb 1979, 18 Apr 1979 and 1 Sep 1979 (Acts of Irish Parliament and Parliament of Northern Ireland; Orders in Council)
6	18 Apr 1979 (SI 1979/422); except para 3, and para 10 so far as it relates to para 3, which came into force on 2 Jan 1979 (SI 1978/1829); and except para 7 and, para 10 so far as it relates to para 7, which came into force on 21 Aug 1978 (SI 1978/1101)
7, Pt I	21 Aug 1978 (repeal of Supreme Court of Judicature Act (Ireland) 1877) (SI 1978/1101)
	2 Jan 1979 (repeals of or in Law of Property Amendment Act 1860, s 10; Settled Estates Act 1877, s 42; Bills of Sale (Ireland) Act 1879, s 21; Conveyancing Act 1881, ss 48(5), 72(5); Deeds of Arrangement Act 1887, s 18; Deeds of Arrangement Amendment Act 1890, s 3; Administration of Justice Act 1920, ss 11, 12(2); Representation of the People Act 1949, s 160; Arbitration Act 1950, s 42(4); Administration of Justice Act 1960, s 9(2); Northern Ireland Act 1962, ss 7–9, Sch 1; Criminal Appeal (Northern Ireland) Act 1968, s 49) (SI 1978/1829)
	18 Apr 1979 (all other repeals to Acts of UK Parliament) (SI 1979/422)
II, III	21 Aug 1978, 2 Jan 1979 and 18 Apr 1979 (Acts of Irish Parliament and Parliament of Northern Ireland; Orders in Council)

Local Government Act 1978 (c 39)

RA: 20 Jul 1978

20 Jul 1978 (RA)

Local Government (Scotland) Act 1978 (c 4)

RA: 23 Mar 1978

Commencement provisions: s 8(3)

23 Mar 1978 (RA), except Schedule, para 2 (repealed)

Medical Act 1978 (c 12)

Whole Act repealed

National Health Service (Scotland) Act 1978 (c 29)

RA: 20 Jul 1978

Commencement provisions: s 110(4)

1 Jan 1979 (s 110(4))

Northern Ireland (Emergency Provisions) Act 1978 (c 5)

Whole Act repealed

Nuclear Safeguards and Electricity (Finance) Act 1978 (c 25)

RA: 30 Jun 1978

30 Jun 1978 (RA)

Oaths Act 1978 (c 19)

RA: 30 Jun 1978

Commencement provisions: s 8(5)

1 Aug 1978 (s 8(5))

Parliamentary Pensions Act 1978 (c 56)

Whole Act repealed

Parochial Registers and Records Measure 1978 (No 2)

RA: 2 Feb 1978

Commencement provisions: s 27(2)

1 Jan 1979 (day appointed by the Archbishops of Canterbury and York under s 27(2))

Participation Agreements Act 1978 (c 1)

RA: 23 Feb 1978

23 Feb 1978 (RA)

Pensioners Payments Act 1978 (c 58)

Whole Act repealed

Protection of Children Act 1978 (c 37)

RA: 20 Jul 1978

Commencement provisions: s 9(3)

s 1–7	20 Aug 1978 (s 9(3))
8, 9	20 Jul 1978 (s 9(3))

Rating (Disabled Persons) Act 1978 (c 40)

RA: 20 Jul 1978

Commencement provisions: s 9(4)

1 Apr 1979 (s 9(4))

Whole Act repealed (EW) except s 9, Sch 2 (by Local Government Finance (Repeals, Savings and Consequential Amendments) Order 1990, SI 1990/776, art 3(1), Sch 1, as from 1 Apr 1990)

Refuse Disposal (Amenity) Act 1978 (c 3)

RA: 23 Mar 1978

Commencement provisions: s 13(2)

23 Apr 1978 (s 13(2))

Representation of the People Act 1978 (c 32)

Whole Act repealed

Scotland Act 1978 (c 51)

Whole Act repealed

Shipbuilding (Redundancy Payments) Act 1978 (c 11)

RA: 5 May 1978

5 May 1978 (RA)

Whole Act prospectively repealed by Statute Law (Repeals) Act 1993, s 1(1), Sch 1, Pt IX; any order made under Statute Law (Repeals) Act 1993, s 4(3), bringing the prospective repeal into force will be noted to that Act in the service to this work

---

Solomon Islands Act 1978 (c 15)

RA: 25 May 1978

Independence Day: 7 Jul 1978

State Immunity Act 1978 (c 33)

RA: 20 Jul 1978

Commencement provisions: s 23(5); State Immunity Act 1978 (Commencement) Order 1978, SI 1978/1572

22 Nov 1978 (SI 1978/1572; note that Pts I, II of this Act do not apply to proceedings in respect of matters that occurred before 22 Nov 1978 (s 23(3), (4)))

Statute Law (Repeals) Act 1978 (c 45)

RA: 31 Jul 1978

31 Jul 1978 (RA)

Suppression of Terrorism Act 1978 (c 26)

RA: 30 Jun 1978

Commencement provisions: s 9(3); Suppression of Terrorism Act 1978 (Commencement) Order 1978, SI 1978/1063

21 Aug 1978 (SI 1978/1063)

Theatres Trust (Scotland) Act 1978 (c 24)

RA: 30 Jun 1978

30 Jun 1978 (RA)

Theft Act 1978 (c 31)

RA: 20 Jul 1978

Commencement provisions: s 7(2)

20 Oct 1978 (s 7(2))

Transport Act 1978 (c 55)

RA: 2 Aug 1978

Commencement provisions: s 24(1); Transport Act 1978 (Commencement No 1) Order 1978, SI 1978/1150; Transport Act 1978 (Commencement No 2) Order 1978, SI 1978/1187; Transport Act 1978 (Commencement No 3) Order 1978, SI 1978/1289

s 1–8	Repealed
9	1 Nov 1978 (SI 1978/1187)
10	1 Sep 1978 (SI 1978/1187)
11, 12	Repealed
13	1 Sep 1978 (SI 1978/1187)
14	Repealed
15	4 Aug 1978 (SI 1978/1150)
16, 17	Repealed
18	4 Aug 1978 (SI 1978/1150)
19, 20	Repealed
21	4 Aug 1978 (SI 1978/1150)
22	Spent
23	4 Aug 1978 (SI 1978/1150)
24(1)–(3)	4 Aug 1978 (SI 1978/1150)
(4)	See Sch 4 below
25	*Not in force*[1]
Sch 1, 2	Repealed
3, Pt A	Repealed
Pt B	1 Nov 1978 (SI 1978/1187)
4	1 Sep 1978 (repeals except in Transport Act 1968, Sch 2, para 3, Road Traffic Act 1972, s 57(7)) (SI 1978/1187)
	4 Aug 1978 (repeal in Transport Act 1968, Sch 2, para 3) (SI 1978/1150)
	1 Nov 1978 (repeal in Road Traffic Act 1972, s 57(7)) (SI 1978/1187)

[1] The fact that s 25 has not been brought into force appears to be due to an oversight

---

Trustee Savings Banks Act 1978 (c 16)

Whole Act repealed

Tuvalu Act 1978 (c 20)

RA: 30 Jun 1978

Independence Day: 1 Oct 1978

Wales Act 1978 (c 52)

Whole Act repealed

1979

Administration of Justice (Emergency Provisions) (Scotland) Act 1979 (c 19)

Whole Act repealed

Agricultural Statistics Act 1979 (c 13)

RA: 4 Apr 1979

Commencement provisions: s 8(2)

22 Apr 1979 (s 8(2))

Alcoholic Liquor Duties Act 1979 (c 4)

RA: 22 Feb 1979

Commencement provisions: s 93(2)

1 Apr 1979 (s 93(2))

Ancient Monuments and Archaeological Areas Act 1979 (c 46)

RA: 4 Apr 1979

Commencement provisions: s 65(2); Ancient Monuments and Archaeological Areas Act 1979 (Commencement No 1) Order 1979, SI 1979/786; Ancient Monuments and Archaeological Areas Act 1979 (Commencement No 2) Order 1981, SI 1981/1300; Ancient Monuments and Archaeological Areas Act 1979 (Commencement No 3) Order 1981, SI 1981/1466; Ancient Monuments and Archaeological Areas Act 1979 (Commencement No 4) Order 1982, SI 1982/362

s 1	9 Oct 1981 (EW) (SI 1981/1300) 30 Nov 1971 (S) (SI 1981/1466)
1A	Inserted by National Heritage Act 1983, s 33, Sch 4, para 26 (qv)
2–6	9 Oct 1981 (EW) (SI 1981/1300) 30 Nov 1981 (S) (SI 1981/1466)
6A	Inserted by National Heritage Act 1983, s 33, Sch 4, para 32 (qv)
7–32	9 Oct 1981 (EW) (SI 1981/1300) 30 Nov 1981 (S) (SI 1981/1466)
33–41	14 Apr 1982 (EW) (SI 1982/362); *not in force* (S)
42–47	9 Oct 1981 (except so far as relate to Pt II) (EW) (SI 1981/1300) 30 Nov 1981 (S) (SI 1981/1466)

Ancient Monuments and Archaeological Areas Act 1979 (c 46)—*cont*

s 42–47—*cont*	14 Apr 1982 (so far as relate to Pt II) (EW) (SI 1982/362)
48, 49	16 Jul 1979 (EW) (SI 1979/786)
	30 Nov 1981 (S) (SI 1981/1466)
50–52	9 Oct 1981 (except so far as relate to Pt II) (EW) (SI 1981/1300)
	30 Nov 1981 (S) (SI 1981/1466)
	14 Apr 1982 (so far as relate to Pt II) (EW) (SI 1982/362)
52A	Inserted (EW) by Norfolk and Suffolk Broads Act 1988, s 2(5), Sch 3, Pt I, para 30(1) (qv)
53–62	9 Oct 1981 (except so far as relate to Pt II) (EW) (SI 1981/1300)
	30 Nov 1981 (S) (SI 1981/1466)
	14 Apr 1982 (so far as relate to Pt II) (EW) (SI 1982/362)
63	Repealed
64	9 Oct 1981 (except so far as relates to Pt II) (EW) (SI 1981/1300)
	30 Nov 1981 (S) (SI 1981/1466)
	14 Apr 1982 (so far as relates to Pt II) (EW) (SI 1982/362)
65	4 Apr 1979 (RA)
Sch 1	9 Oct 1981 (EW) (SI 1981/1300)
	30 Nov 1981 (S) (SI 1981/1466)
2	14 Apr 1982 (EW) (SI 1982/362); *not in force* (S)
3–5	9 Oct 1981 (EW) (except so far as relate to Pt II) (SI 1981/1300)
	30 Nov 1981 (S) (SI 1981/1466)
	14 Apr 1982 (EW) (so far as relate to Pt II) (SI 1982/362)

Appropriation Act 1979 (c 24)

Whole Act repealed

Appropriation (No 2) Act 1979 (c 51)

Whole Act repealed

Arbitration Act 1979 (c 42)

RA: 4 Apr 1979

Commencement provisions: s 8(2); Arbitration Act 1979 (Commencement) Order 1979, SI 1979/750

1 Aug 1979 (except in relation to arbitrations commenced before that date; if all the parties to a reference to arbitration which commenced before that date agree in writing that the Act should apply to that arbitration, the Act applies from 1 Aug 1979 or the date of the agreement, whichever is the later) (SI 1979/750)

Banking Act 1979 (c 37)

RA: 4 Apr 1979

Commencement provisions: s 52(3), (4); Banking Act 1979 (Commencement No 1) Order 1979, SI 1979/938; Banking Act 1979 (Commencement No 2) Order 1982, SI 1982/188; Banking Act 1979 (Commencement No 3) Order 1985, SI 1985/797

s 1–37	Repealed
38	1 Oct 1979 (SI 1979/938)
39–46	Repealed
47	1 Oct 1979 (SI 1979/938)
48–50	Repealed
51(1)	19 Feb 1982 (so far as relates to the provisions of Sch 6 coming into force on that date) (SI 1982/188) 1 Jul 1985 (so far as relates to the provisions of Sch 6 coming into force on that date) (SI 1985/797)
(2)	Spent
52	1 Oct 1979 (SI 1979/938)
Sch 1–5	Repealed
6, para 1–3	19 Feb 1982 (SI 1982/188)
4–8	Repealed
9	1 Jul 1985 (SI 1985/797)
10	Spent
11, 12	Repealed
13–15	19 Feb 1982 (SI 1982/188)
16–18	Repealed
19	19 Feb 1982 (SI 1982/188)
7	Repealed

Capital Gains Tax Act 1979 (c 14)

Whole Act repealed

Carriage by Air and Road Act 1979 (c 28)

RA: 4 Apr 1979

Commencement provisions: ss 2(2), 7(2); Carriage by Air and Road Act 1979 (Commencement No 1) Order 1980, SI 1980/1966

s 1	*Not in force*
2	4 Apr 1979 (does not apply to loss which occurred before that date) (s 2(2))
3(1), (2)	*Not in force*
(3)	28 Dec 1980 (SI 1980/1966)
(4)	*Not in force*
4(1)	*Not in force*
(2)	28 Dec 1980 (SI 1980/1966)
(3)	*Not in force*
(4)	28 Dec 1980 (so far as relates to amendment of Carriage of Goods by Road Act 1965 by s 4(2)) (SI 1980/1966) *Not in force* (otherwise)
5	28 Dec 1980 (so far as relates to amendment of Carriage of Goods by Road Act 1965 by s 4(2)) (SI 1980/1966) *Not in force* (otherwise)
6(1)(a)	*Not in force*

Carriage by Air and Road Act 1979 (c 28)—*cont*

s 6(1)(b)	28 Dec 1980 (SI 1980/1966)
(c)	*Not in force*
(2)–(4)	*Not in force*
7	4 Apr 1979 (RA)
Sch 1, 2	*Not in force*

Charging Orders Act 1979 (c 53)

RA: 6 Dec 1979

Commencement provisions: s 8(2); Charging Orders Act 1979 (Commencement) Order 1980, SI 1980/627

3 Jun 1980 (SI 1980/627)

Confirmation to Small Estates (Scotland) Act 1979 (c 22)

RA: 29 Mar 1979

Commencement provisions: s 3(2); Confirmation to Small Estates (Scotland) Act 1979 (Commencement) Order 1980, SI 1980/734

s 1, 2	1 Jul 1980 (SI 1980/734)
3	29 Mar 1979 (RA)
Schedule	1 Jul 1980 (SI 1980/734)

Consolidated Fund Act 1979 (c 20)

Whole Act repealed

Consolidated Fund (No 2) Act 1979 (c 56)

Whole Act repealed

Credit Unions Act 1979 (c 34)

RA: 4 Apr 1979

Commencement provisions: s 33(2); Credit Unions Act 1979 (Commencement No 1) Order 1979, SI 1979/936; Credit Unions Act 1979 (Commencement No 2) Order 1980, SI 1980/481

s 1, 2	20 Aug 1979 (SI 1979/936)
3(1)	20 Aug 1979 (SI 1979/936)
(2), (3)	*Not in force*
(4)	20 Aug 1979 (SI 1979/936)
4–14	20 Aug 1979 (SI 1979/936)
15	1 Oct 1980 (SI 1980/481)
16–24	20 Aug 1979 (SI 1979/936)

Credit Unions Act 1979 (c 34)—*cont*

s 25	Repealed
26–31	20 Aug 1979 (SI 1979/936)
32, 33	4 Apr 1979 (s 33(2))
Sch 1, 2	20 Aug 1979 (SI 1979/936)
3	Repealed

Criminal Evidence Act 1979 (c 16)

RA: 22 Mar 1979

Commencement provisions: s 2(2)

22 Apr 1979 (s 2(2))

Crown Agents Act 1979 (c 43)

RA: 4 Apr 1979

4 Apr 1979 (RA; but note that most of the provisions of the Act became effective from 1 Jan 1980, the day appointed by the Crown Agents Act 1979 (Appointed Day) Order 1979, SI 1979/1672, made under s 1(1)), which is prospectively repealed by the Crown Agents Act 1995, s 13(2), Sch 2, Pt II, as from the day on which the Crown Agents are dissolved in accordance with s 8(4) of the 1995 Act (qv))

Customs and Excise Duties (General Reliefs) Act 1979 (c 3)

RA: 22 Feb 1979

Commencement provisions: ss 20(2), 59(7), 62(2)

1 Apr 1979 (s 20(2))

Customs and Excise Management Act 1979 (c 2)

RA: 22 Feb 1979

Commencement provisions: ss 59(7), 62(2), 178(3)

1 Apr 1979 (s 178(3)) except ss 59, 62(2) which are *not in force*

Education Act 1979 (c 49)

RA: 26 Jul 1979

26 Jul 1979 (RA)

Electricity (Scotland) Act 1979 (c 11)

RA: 22 Mar 1979

Commencement provisions: s 47(4)

Whole Act repealed by Electricity Act 1989, s 112(4), Sch 18, the repeal being brought into force on 31 Mar 1990 by Electricity Act 1989 (Commencement No 2) Order 1990, SI 1990/117, except as regards s 1, in Sch 1, paras 2–5, in para 6 the words 'Each of the Boards shall be a body corporate' and the words

Electricity (Scotland) Act 1979 (c 11)—*cont*

'shall have power to regulate their own procedure' and paras 7–11, the repeal of which remains prospective; the excepted provisions came into force on 22 Apr 1979 (s 47(4)); any order(s) made under Electricity Act 1989, s 113(2), bringing the prospective repeal of the excepted provisions into force will be noted to that Act in the service to this work

Estate Agents Act 1979 (c 38)

RA: 4 Apr 1979

Commencement provisions: s 36(2); Estate Agents Act 1979 (Commencement No 1) Order 1981, SI 1981/1517

s 1–15	3 May 1982 (SI 1981/1517)
16, 17	*Not in force*
18	3 May 1982 (SI 1981/1517)
19	*Not in force*
20, 21	3 May 1982 (SI 1981/1517)
22	*Not in force*
23–34	3 May 1982 (SI 1981/1517)
35	Repealed
36	3 May 1982 (SI 1981/1517)
Sch 1, 2	3 May 1982 (SI 1981/1517)

European Parliament (Pay and Pensions) Act 1979 (c 50)

RA: 26 Jul 1979

26 Jul 1979 (RA)

European Communities (Greek Accession) Act 1979 (c 57)

RA: 20 Dec 1979

20 Dec 1979 (RA; but note that the accession of Greece to the European Communities did not take effect until 1 Jan 1981)

Exchange Equalisation Account Act 1979 (c 30)

RA: 4 Apr 1979

Commencement provisions: s 5(3)

5 May 1979 (s 5(3))

Excise Duties (Surcharges or Rebates) Act 1979 (c 8)

RA: 22 Feb 1979

Commencement provisions: s 5(2)

1 Apr 1979 (s 5(2))

Films Act 1979 (c 9)

Whole Act repealed

Finance Act 1979 (c 25)

Whole Act repealed

Finance (No 2) Act 1979 (c 47)

Budget Day: 12 Jun 1979

RA: 26 Jul 1979

See the note concerning Finance Acts at the front of this book

---

Forestry Act 1979 (c 21)

RA: 29 Mar 1979

Commencement provisions: s 3(3)

30 May 1979 (s 3(3))

House of Commons (Redistribution of Seats) Act 1979 (c 15)

Whole Act repealed

Hydrocarbon Oil Duties Act 1979 (c 5)

RA: 22 Feb 1979

Commencement provisions: s 29(2)

1 Apr 1979 (s 29(2))

Independent Broadcasting Authority Act 1979 (c 35)

Whole Act repealed

Industry Act 1979 (c 32)

RA: 4 Apr 1979

4 Apr 1979 (RA)

International Monetary Fund Act 1979 (c 29)

RA: 4 Apr 1979

Commencement provisions: s 7(2)

5 May 1979 (s 7(2))

Isle of Man Act 1979 (c 58)

RA: 20 Dec 1979

Commencement provisions: s 14(6), (7)

s 1–5	1 Apr 1980 (s 14(6))
6, 7	20 Dec 1979 (subject to the proviso that no Order in Council and no provision by virtue of s 6(5) or 7(5) be made by or under an Act of Tynwald so as to come into force before 1 Apr 1980) (s 14(7))
8, 9	1 Apr 1980 (s 14(6))
10	20 Dec 1979 (s 14(7))
11	20 Dec 1979 (subject to the proviso that no Order in Council be made under this section so as to come into force before 1 Apr 1980) (s 14(7))
12–14	1 Apr 1980 (s 14(6))
Sch 1, 2	1 Apr 1980 (s 14(6))

Justices of the Peace Act 1979 (c 55)

RA: 6 Dec 1979

Commencement provisions: s 72(2)

6 Mar 1980 (s 72(2))

Kiribati Act 1979 (c 27)

RA: 19 Jun 1979

Independence Day: 12 Jul 1979

Land Registration (Scotland) Act 1979 (c 33)

RA: 4 Apr 1979

Commencement provisions: s 30(2); Land Registration (Scotland) Act 1979 (Commencement No 1) Order 1980, SI 1980/1412; Land Registration (Scotland) Act 1979 (Commencement No 2) Order 1982, SI 1982/520; Land Registration (Scotland) Act 1979 (Commencement No 3) Order 1983, SI 1983/745; Land Registration (Scotland) Act 1979 (Commencement No 4) Order 1985, SI 1985/501; Land Registration (Scotland) Act 1979 (Commencement No 5) Order 1992, SI 1992/815; Land Registration (Scotland) Act 1979 (Commencement No 6) Order 1992, SI 1992/2060; Land Registration (Scotland) Act 1979 (Commencement No 7) Order 1993, SI 1993/922; Land Registration (Scotland) Act 1979 (Commencement No 8) Order 1994, SI 1994/2588; Land Registration (Scotland) Act 1979 (Commencement No 9) Order 1995, SI 1995/2547

s 1	4 Apr 1979 (s 30(2))
2(1), (2)	6 Apr 1981 (in the area, for the purpose of registration of writs, of the County of Renfrew) (SI 1980/1412)
	4 Oct 1982 (in the area, for the purpose of registration of writs, of the County of Dunbarton) (SI 1982/520)

Land Registration (Scotland) Act 1979 (c 33)—*cont*

s 2(1), (2)—*cont*	3 Jan 1984 (in the area, for the purpose of registration of writs, of the County of Lanark) (SI 1983/745)
	30 Sep 1985 (in the area, for the purpose of registration of writs, of the Barony and Regality of Glasgow) (SI 1985/501)
	1 Oct 1992 (in the area, for the purpose of registration of writs, of the County of Clackmannan) (SI 1992/815)
	1 Apr 1993 (in the area, for the purpose of registration of writs, of the County of Stirling) (SI 1992/2060)
	1 Oct 1993 (in the area, for the purpose of registration of writs, of the County of West Lothian) (SI 1993/922)
	1 Apr 1995 (in the area, for the purpose of registration of writs, of the County of Fife) (SI 1994/2588)
	1 Apr 1996 (in the areas, for the purpose of registration of writs, of the Counties of Aberdeen and Kincardine) (SI 1995/2547)
	Not in force (otherwise)
(3)–(6)	6 Apr 1981 (SI 1980/1412)
3(1), (2)	6 Apr 1981 (SI 1980/1412)
(3)	6 Apr 1981 (in the area, for the purpose of registration of writs, of the County of Renfrew) (SI 1980/1412)
	4 Oct 1982 (in the area for the purpose of registration of writs, of the County of Dunbarton) (SI 1982/520)
	3 Jan 1984 (in the area, for the purpose of registration of writs, of the County of Lanark) (SI 1983/745)
	30 Sep 1985 (in the area, for the purpose of registration of writs, of the Barony and Regality of Glasgow) (SI 1985/501)
	1 Oct 1992 (in the area, for the purpose of registration of writs, of the County of Clackmannan) (SI 1992/815)
	1 Apr 1993 (in the area, for the purpose of registration of writs, of the County of Stirling) (SI 1992/2060)
	1 Oct 1993 (in the area, for the purpose of registration of writs, of the County of West Lothian) (SI 1993/922)
	1 Apr 1995 (in the area, for the purpose of registration of writs, of the County of Fife) (SI 1994/2588)
	1 Apr 1996 (in the areas, for the purpose of registration of writs, of the Counties of Aberdeen and Kincardine) (SI 1995/2547)
	Not in force (otherwise)
(4)–(7)	6 Apr 1981 (SI 1980/1412)
4–15	6 Apr 1981 (SI 1980/1412)
16–22	4 Apr 1979 (s 30(2))
22A	Inserted by Law Reform (Miscellaneous Provisions) Act 1985, s 2 (qv)

Land Registration (Scotland) Act 1979 (c 33)—*cont*

s 23	4 Apr 1979 (s 30(2))
24–29	4 Apr 1979 (so far as relate to ss 1, 16–23, 30) (s 30(2))
	6 Apr 1981 (otherwise) (SI 1980/1412)
30	4 Apr 1979 (s 30(2))
Sch 1	4 Apr 1979 (s 30(2))
2–4	4 Apr 1979 (so far as relate to ss 1, 16–23, 30) (s 30(2))
	6 Apr 1981 (otherwise) (SI 1980/1412)

Leasehold Reform Act 1979 (c 44)

RA: 4 Apr 1979

4 Apr 1979 (RA)

Legal Aid Act 1979 (c 26)

Whole Act repealed

Matches and Mechanical Lighters Duties Act 1979 (c 6)

Whole Act repealed

Merchant Shipping Act 1979 (c 39)

Whole Act repealed: note however s 47, which was repealed with savings by Merchant Shipping (Registration, etc) Act 1993, s 8(4), Sch 5, Pt II, as from 1 May 1994, but instruments made under s 47 and in force on that date remained in force until superseded by an instrument made under Sch 4, para 4 to the 1993 Act (Merchant Shipping (Registration, etc) Act 1993 (Commencement No 1 and Transitional Provisions) Order 1993, SI 1993/3137, art 7(1), Sch 3). Sch 4, para 4 to the 1993 Act was repealed by Merchant Shipping Act 1995, s 314(1), Sch 12, and by virtue of Interpretation Act 1978, s 17(2)(b), such instruments remain in force until superseded by an instrument made under s 315 of the 1995 Act

---

Nurses, Midwives and Health Visitors Act 1979 (c 36)

RA: 4 Apr 1979

Commencement provisions: s 24(2); Nurses, Midwives and Health Visitors Act 1979 (Commencement No 1) Order 1980, SI 1980/893; Nurses, Midwives and Health Visitors Act 1979 (Commencement No 2) Order 1982, SI 1982/963; Nurses, Midwives and Health Visitors Act 1979 (Commencement No 3) Order 1982, SI 1982/1565; Nurses, Midwives and Health Visitors Act 1979 (Commencement No 4) Order 1983, SI 1983/668

s 1	1 Nov 1980 (SI 1980/893)
2	1 Jul 1983 (SI 1983/668)
3(1)	1 Nov 1980 (so far as relates to the Finance Committee and s 3(2)) (SI 1980/893)
	1 Dec 1982 (otherwise) (SI 1982/1565)

Nurses, Midwives and Health Visitors Act 1979 (c 36)—*cont*

s 3(2)	1 Nov 1980 (SI 1980/893)
(3)	1 Dec 1982 (SI 1982/1565)
(4)(a)	1 Nov 1980 (so far as relates to the Finance Committee and s 3(2)) (SI 1980/893)
	1 Dec 1982 (otherwise) (SI 1982/1565)
(b)	1 Dec 1982 (SI 1982/1565)
4	1 Jul 1983 (SI 1983/668)
5	15 Sep 1980 (SI 1980/893)
6	1 Jul 1983 (SI 1983/668)
7–9	Repealed
10, 11	1 Jul 1983 (SI 1983/668)
11A	Inserted (1 Jul 1983) by Nursing and Midwifery Qualifications (EEC Recognition) Order 1983, SI 1983/884, art 4
12	1 Jul 1983 (SI 1983/668)
12A	Inserted by Nurses, Midwives and Health Visitors Act 1992, s 9 (qv)
13–17	1 Jul 1983 (SI 1983/668)
18	Repealed
19(1), (2)	1 Jul 1983 (SI 1983/668)
(3)(a)	Repealed
(b), (c)	1 Jul 1983 (SI 1983/668)
(d)	Added by Nurses, Midwives and Health Visitors Act 1992, s 13(2)(b) (qv)
(4)	Repealed
(5)	15 Sep 1980 (so far as relates to National Boards) (SI 1980/893)
	1 Nov 1980 (otherwise) (SI 1980/893)
20	15 Sep 1980 (so far as relates to National Boards) (SI 1980/893)
	1 Nov 1980 (otherwise) (SI 1980/893)
21(1)	1 Jul 1983 (SI 1983/668)
(2)	4 Apr 1979 (s 24(2))
(3)	1 Jul 1983 (SI 1983/668)
(4)	Repealed
22	1 Jul 1983 (SI 1983/668)
22A, 22B	Inserted (1 Jul 1983) by Nursing and Midwifery Qualifications (EEC Recognition) Order 1983, SI 1983/884, art 6
23(1)–(3)	15 Sep 1980 (SI 1980/893)
(4), (5)	1 Jul 1983 (SI 1983/668)
24	4 Apr 1979 (s 24(2))
Sch 1	Substituted by Nurses, Midwives and Health Visitors Act 1992, s 1(2), Sch 1 (qv)
2, Pt I	Repealed
II, para 2–4	Repealed
5	15 Sep 1980 (SI 1980/893)
6	Repealed
7	15 Sep 1983 (SI 1980/893); prospectively repealed by Nurses, Midwives and Health Visitors Act 1992, s 16(2), Sch 3[1]
8	Repealed
3	1 Jul 1983 (SI 1983/668)
4	Repealed
5	1 Jul 1983 (SI 1983/668)

Nurses, Midwives and Health Visitors Act 1979 (c 36)—*cont*

Sch 6	15 Sep 1980 (SI 1980/893)
7, 8	1 Jul 1983 (SI 1983/668)

[1] Any order(s) made under Nurses, Midwives and Health Visitors Act 1992, s 17(3), bringing the prospective repeal into force will be noted to that Act in the service to this work

Pensioners' Payments and Social Security Act 1979 (c 48)

Whole Act repealed

Pneumoconiosis etc (Workers' Compensation) Act 1979 (c 41)

RA: 4 Apr 1979

Commencement provisions: s 10(3)

4 Jul 1979 (s 10(3))

Price Commission (Amendment) Act 1979 (c 1)

Whole Act repealed

Prosecution of Offences Act 1979 (c 31)

Whole Act repealed

Public Health Laboratory Service Act 1979 (c 23)

RA: 29 Mar 1979

29 Mar 1979 (RA)

Public Lending Right Act 1979 (c 10)

RA: 22 Mar 1979

Commencement provisions: s 5(3); Public Lending Right Act 1979 (Commencement) Order 1980, SI 1980/83

1 Mar 1980 (SI 1980/83)

Representation of the People Act 1979 (c 40)

Whole Act repealed

Sale of Goods Act 1979 (c 54)

RA: 6 Dec 1979

Commencement provisions: s 64(2)

1 Jan 1980 (s 64(2))

Shipbuilding Act 1979 (c 59)

RA: 20 Dec 1979

20 Dec 1979 (RA)

Social Security Act 1979 (c 18)

RA: 22 Mar 1979

Commencement provisions: s 21(2), (3); Social Security Act 1979 (Commencement No 1) Order 1979, SI 1979/369; Social Security Act 1979 (Commencement No 2) Order 1979, SI 1979/1031; Social Security Act 1986, s 72

s 1	22 Mar 1979 (RA)
2–10	Repealed
11	6 Apr 1979 (s 21(3))
12–15	Repealed
16	22 Mar 1979 (RA); repealed (EW)
17–19	Repealed
20, 21	22 Mar 1979 (RA)
Sch 1, 2	Repealed
3, para 1–11	Repealed
12	Spent
13	22 Mar 1979 (RA)
14–16	Repealed
17	Spent
18	Repealed
19	Spent
20	6 Apr 1979 (s 21(3))
21	22 Mar 1979 (RA)
22	6 Apr 1979 (s 21(3))
23–29	Repealed
30	Repealed or spent
31, 32	Repealed

Southern Rhodesia Act 1979 (c 52)

RA: 14 Nov 1979

Appointed Day: 18 Apr 1980

Tobacco Products Duty Act 1979 (c 7)

RA: 22 Feb 1979

Commencement provisions: s 12(2)

1 Apr 1979 (s 12(2))

Vaccine Damage Payments Act 1979 (c 17)

RA: 22 Feb 1979

22 Feb 1979 (RA)

Wages Councils Act 1979 (c 12)

Whole Act repealed

Weights and Measures Act 1979 (c 45)

Whole Act repealed

Zimbabwe Act 1979 (c 60)

RA: 20 Dec 1979

Independence Day: 18 Apr 1980

1980

Anguilla Act 1980 (c 67)

RA: 16 Dec 1980

16 Dec 1980 (RA; but note the Anguilla (Appointed Day) Order 1980, SI 1980/1953, appointing 19 Dec 1980 for the purposes of s 1(1) (repealed))

Appropriation Act 1980 (c 54)

Whole Act repealed

Bail etc (Scotland) Act 1980 (c 4)

Whole Act repealed

Bees Act 1980 (c 12)

RA: 20 Mar 1980

Commencement provisions: s 5(2); Bees Act 1980 (Commencement) Order 1980, SI 1980/791

10 Jun 1980 (SI 1980/791)

Betting, Gaming and Lotteries (Amendment) Act 1980 (c 18)

Whole Act repealed

British Aerospace Act 1980 (c 26)

RA: 1 May 1980

1 May 1980 (RA; but note Act largely took effect on 1 Jan 1981, the day appointed under s 14(1))

Broadcasting Act 1980 (c 64)

Whole Act repealed

Child Care Act 1980 (c 5)

Whole Act repealed

Civil Aviation Act 1980 (c 60)

RA: 13 Nov 1980

Commencement provisions: ss 10(1), 12 (repealed); Civil Aviation Act 1980 (Commencement) Order 1981, SI 1981/671; Civil Aviation Act 1980 (Appointed Day) Order 1983, SI 1983/1940

s 1	13 Nov 1980 (RA), but not effective until 1 Apr 1984, the day appointed under s 10(1) by SI 1983/1940
2	Spent
3–10	13 Nov 1980 (RA), but not effective until 1 Apr 1984, the day appointed under s 10(1) by SI 1983/1940
11–19	Repealed
20	13 Nov 1980 (RA)
21–26	Repealed
27	13 Nov 1980 (RA)
28	See Sch 3 below
29–31	13 Nov 1980 (RA)
Sch 1, 2	13 Nov 1980 (RA)
3	13 Nov 1980 (except repeal of Civil Aviation Act 1971, s 24(2)) (RA)
	22 May 1981 (exception noted above) (SI 1981/671)

Coal Industry Act 1980 (c 50)

RA: 8 Aug 1980

8 Aug 1980 (RA)

Whole Act repealed (in part prospectively) as follows: ss 1, 2, 7–11 prospectively repealed by Coal Industry Act 1994, s 67(8), Sch 11, Pts III, IV[1]; s 3 repealed by Coal Industry Act 1985, s 5(2); ss 4, 5 repealed by Coal Industry Act 1983, ss 2(3), 6(3), Schedule; s 6 repealed by Coal Industry Act 1987, s 10(3), Sch 3, Pt I

[1] Orders made under Coal Industry Act 1994 bringing these prospective repeals into force will be noted to that Act in the service to this work

Companies Act 1980 (c 22)

Whole Act repealed

Competition Act 1980 (c 21)

RA: 3 Apr 1980

Commencement provisions: s 33(5); Competition Act 1980 (Commencement No 1) Order 1980, SI 1980/497; Competition Act 1980 (Commencement No 2) Order 1980, SI 1980/978

s 1	Repealed
2	12 Aug 1980 (SI 1980/978)
3(1)	12 Aug 1980 (SI 1980/978)

Competition Act 1980 (c 21)—*cont*

s 3(2)–(6)	Repealed, subject to transitional provisions, by Deregulation and Contracting Out Act 1994, ss 12(2), (3), (7), 81(1), Sch 4, paras 5–8, Sch 17 (qv)
(7), (8)	1 May 1980 (as applied by s 13(7)) (SI 1980/497) 12 Aug 1980 (otherwise) (SI 1980/978)
(9), (10)	Repealed, subject to transitional provisions, by Deregulation and Contracting Out Act 1994, ss 12(2), (3), (7), 81(1), Sch 4, paras 5–8, Sch 17 (qv)
4–10	12 Aug 1980 (SI 1980/978)
11(1), (2)	4 Apr 1980 (SI 1980/497)
(3)(a)	4 Apr 1980 (SI 1980/497)
(aa)	Inserted by Railways Act 1993, s 152(1), Sch 12, para 12(1)(qv)
(b)	Substituted by Transport Act 1985, s 114(1) (qv)
(bb)	Inserted by London Regional Transport Act 1984, s 71(3)(a), Sch 6, para 15 (qv)
(c)	Substituted by Water Act 1989, s 190(1), Sch 25, para 59(1) (qv)
(cc)	Prospectively inserted (S) by Local Government etc (Scotland) Act 1994, s 72[1]
(d), (e)	4 Apr 1980 (SI 1980/497)
(f)	4 Apr 1980 (except so far as relates to s 11(3)(b)) (SI 1980/497) 12 Aug 1980 (exception noted above) (SI 1980/978)
(4), (5)	12 Aug 1980 (SI 1980/978)
(6)–(11)	4 Apr 1980 (SI 1980/497)
12, 13	1 May 1980 (SI 1980/497)
14	Repealed
15(1)	1 May 1980 (SI 1980/497)
(2)(a)	Repealed
(b)	12 Aug 1980 (SI 1980/978)
(c)	4 Apr 1980 (for purposes of s 11) (SI 1980/497) 12 Aug 1980 (otherwise) (SI 1980/978)
(3), (4)	12 Aug 1980 (SI 1980/978)
(5)	4 Apr 1980 (for purposes of s 11) (SI 1980/497) 12 Aug (otherwise) (SI 1980/978)
16	4 Apr 1980 (for purposes of reports under s 11) (SI 1980/497) 12 Aug 1980 (otherwise) (SI 1980/978)
17(1)	4 Apr 1980 (for purposes of reports under s 11) (SI 1980/497) 1 May 1980 (for purposes of reports under s 13) (SI 1980/497) 12 Aug 1980 (otherwise) (SI 1980/978)
(2)	4 Apr 1980 (for purposes of reports under s 11) (SI 1980/497) 12 Aug 1980 (otherwise) (SI 1980/978)
(3)–(5)	4 Apr 1980 (for purposes of reports under s 11) (SI 1980/497) 1 May 1980 (for purposes of reports under s 13) (SI 1980/497) 12 Aug 1980 (otherwise) (SI 1980/978)
(6)	1 May 1980 (for purposes of reports under s 12) (SI 1980/497) 12 Aug 1980 (otherwise) (SI 1980/978)

Competition Act 1980 (c 21)—*cont*

s 18	1 May 1980 (SI 1980/497)
19	4 Apr 1980 (SI 1980/497)
20–22	1 May 1980 (SI 1980/497)
23	4 Apr 1980 (SI 1980/497)
24–30	1 May 1980 (SI 1980/497)
31(1)	4 Apr 1980 (SI 1980/497)
(2)	12 Aug 1980 (SI 1980/978)
(3)	1 May 1980 (for purposes of s 12) (SI 1980/497) 12 Aug 1980 (otherwise) (SI 1980/978)
(4)	1 May 1980 (SI 1980/497)
32	4 Apr 1980 (SI 1980/497)
33(1), (2)	4 Apr 1980 (SI 1980/497)
(3)	1 May 1980 (SI 1980/497)
(4)	See Sch 2 below
(5)–(8)	4 Apr 1980 (SI 1980/497)
Sch 1	Repealed
2	4 Apr 1980 (except as noted below) (SI 1980/457) 1 Jan 2011 (repeals of Counter-Inflation Act 1973, ss 17(6), (8), (9), 18(4), (5), 19, 20(4), (5)(i), (iii), (7), 23(2), Sch 4, para 4 (except sub-para 2(b)); Price Commission Act 1977, s 15(4), Sch 2, para 4(b), (d)) (SI 1980/497)

[1] Order(s) made under Local Government etc (Scotland) Act 1994 bringing this prospective insertion into force will be noted to that Act in the service to this work

---

Concessionary Travel for Handicapped Persons (Scotland) Act 1980 (c 29)

RA: 23 May 1980

23 May 1980 (RA)

Consolidated Fund Act 1980 (c 14)

Whole Act repealed

Consolidated Fund (No 2) Act 1980 (c 68)

Whole Act repealed

Consular Fees Act 1980 (c 23)

RA: 1 May 1980

1 May 1980 (RA)

Coroners Act 1980 (c 38)

Whole Act repealed

Criminal Appeal (Northern Ireland) Act 1980 (c 47)

RA: 1 Aug 1980

Commencement provisions: s 52(2)

1 Sep 1980 (s 52(2))

Criminal Justice (Scotland) Act 1980 (c 62)

RA: 13 Mar 1980

Commencement provisions: s 84(2); Criminal Justice (Scotland) Act 1980 (Commencement No 1) Order 1981, SI 1981/50; Criminal Justice (Scotland) Act 1980 (Commencement No 2) Order 1981, SI 1981/444; Criminal Justice (Scotland) Act 1980 (Commencement No 3) Order 1981, SI 1981/766; Criminal Justice (Scotland) Act 1980 (Commencement No 4) Order 1981, SI 1981/1751; Criminal Justice (Scotland) Act 1980 (Commencement No 5) Order 1983; SI 1983/1580

s 1–3	Repealed
3A–3D	Inserted by Law Reform (Miscellaneous Provisions) (Scotland) Act 1985, s 35 (qv)
4–44	Repealed
45	15 Nov 1983 (SI 1983/1580)
46–50	Repealed
51	1 Jun 1981 (SI 1981/766)
52–55	Repealed
56, 57	1 Feb 1981 (SI 1981/50)
58–78	Repealed
79	1 Feb 1981 (SI 1981/50)
80	Repealed
81, 82	1 Feb 1981 (SI 1981/50)
83	See Schs 6–8 below
84(1)–(4)	1 Feb 1981 (SI 1981/50)
(5)	1 Feb 1981 (for purposes of extending to England and Wales ss 22, 84(1)–(5), Sch 6, paras 2, 8, Sch 7, paras 8, 9, 11(a), 24(c), 58, 79, Sch 8 (so far as repeals Criminal Procedure (Scotland) Act 1975, s 365)) (SI 1981/50)
	1 Apr 1981 (for purposes of extending to England and Wales s 66, Sch 6, para 9) (SI 1981/444)
	1 Jun 1981 (for purposes of extending to England and Wales s 51, Sch 6, para 10) (SI 1981/766)
	15 Nov 1983 (for purposes of extending to England and Wales Sch 7, paras 6(a), 10, 24(a), (b)(i), (ii), (d)(i), (ii), Sch 8 (so far as repeals Criminal Justice Act 1961, s 32(2)(b) and words in ss 32(2)(f), 38(3)(a))) (SI 1983/1580)
(6)	1 Feb 1981 (for purposes of extending to Northern Ireland ss 22, 84(1)–(4), (6), Sch 6, paras 2, 8, Sch 7, paras 8, 9, 11(a), 77) (SI 1981/50)
	1 Apr 1981 (for purposes of extending to Northern Ireland s 66, Sch 6, para 9) (SI 1981/444)
	1 Jun 1981 (for purposes of extending to Northern Ireland s 51, Sch 6, para 10) (SI 1981/766)
	15 Nov 1983 (for purposes of extending to Northern Ireland Sch 7, paras 6(a), 10, Sch 8 (so far as repeals Criminal Justice Act 1961, s 32(2)(b) and words in ss 32(2)(f), 38(3)(a))) (SI 1983/1580)

Criminal Justice (Scotland) Act 1980 (c 62)—*cont*

s 84(7)	15 Nov 1983 (for purposes of extending to Channel Islands and Isle of Man s 84(1)–(4), (7), Sch 7, paras 6(a), 10(a), Sch 8 (so far as repeals the Criminal Justice Act 1961, s 32(2)(b))) (SI 1983/1580)
Sch 1–5	Repealed
6, para 1–8	1 Feb 1981 (SI 1981/50)
9	1 Apr 1981 (SI 1981/444)
10	1 Jun 1981 (SI 1981/766)
7, para 1–7	Repealed
8, 9	1 Feb 1981 (SI 1981/50)
10	15 Nov 1983 (SI 1983/1580)
11(a)	1 Feb 1981 (SI 1981/50)
(b)	Spent
12	Repealed
13	1 Feb 1981 (SI 1981/50)
14, 15	Repealed
16	1 Feb 1981 (SI 1981/50)
17–20	Repealed
21	1 Feb 1981 (SI 1981/50); prospectively repealed by Children (Scotland) Act 1995, s 105(4), (5), Sch 4, para 29(1), (3), Sch 5[1]
22	1 Feb 1981 (SI 1981/50); prospectively repealed by Transport Act 1981, s 40(4), Sch 12, Pt III[2]
23	Repealed
24(a)	1 Apr 1981 (SI 1981/444)
(b)(i)	1 Apr 1981 (SI 1981/444)
(ii)	15 Nov 1983 (SI 1983/1580)
(c)	1 Feb 1981 (SI 1981/50)
(d)(i)	15 Nov 1983 (SI 1983/1580)
(ii)	1 Apr 1981 (SI 1981/444)
25–78	Repealed
79	1 Feb 1981 (SI 1981/50)
8	1 Feb 1981 (repeals of or in Treason Act 1708, s 7; Treason Act 1800; Conspiracy and Protection of Property Act 1875, s 11; Burgh Police (Scotland) Act 1892, s 382; Children and Young Persons Act 1933, s 26(5); Treason Act 1945; Criminal Justice (Scotland) Act 1949, ss 21, 75(3)(e); Prisons (Scotland) Act 1952, ss 7(4), 19, 31(4), 35(5)(a); Road Traffic Act 1960, s 246; Penalties for Drunkenness Act 1962, s 1(2)(a), (b); Road Traffic Regulation Act 1967, s 93; Criminal Justice Act 1961, s 70(1); Firearms Act 1968, Sch 6, Pt II, para 1; Road Traffic Act 1972, Sch 4, Pt IV, para 3; Social Security Act 1975, s 147(6); Criminal Procedure (Scotland) Act 1975, ss 141, 191(1), 193(2), 195, 197–202, 228, 285, 289D(3)(c), 296(5), 310, 314(3), 337(e), 346, 365, 392(1), 399(1), 405, 410, 411(2), 417, 434(3), 460(5), (6), Schs 4, 7B, para 1; Child Benefit Act 1975, s 11(8); Licensing (Scotland) Act 1976, s 128(2); Sexual Offences (Scotland) Act 1976, ss 7, 16; Supplementary Benefits Act 1976, s 26(5); Criminal Law Act 1977, Sch 11, paras 11–13; Customs and Excise Management Act 1979, s 149(2)) (SI 1981/50)

Criminal Justice (Scotland) Act 1980 (c 62)—*cont*

Sch 8—*cont*	1 Apr 1981 (repeals of or in Railways Clauses Consolidation (Scotland) Act 1845, s 144; Protection of Animals (Scotland) Act 1912, s 4; Criminal Justice Act 1967, s 60(6), (8); Immigration Act 1971, s 6(5); Criminal Procedure (Scotland) Act 1975, ss 229, 232, 234(1), (3), 236, 240, 245(3), 247, 253(2), 257, 263(1), 265(3), 272, 274(1), 277, 444(6), 445, 447(2), 448(9), 454(2), Sch 9, para 40) (SI 1981/444)
	1 Jan 1982 (repeals of or in Criminal Procedure (Scotland) Act 1887, Schs F, G; Criminal Procedure (Scotland) Act 1975, ss 68(3), 74(3), 105–107, 120–122) (SI 1981/1751)
	15 Nov 1983 (repeals of or in Prisons (Scotland) Act 1952, ss 32, 33, 37(2); Criminal Justice Act 1961, ss 32(2)(b), (f), 38(3)(a); Criminal Justice (Scotland) Act 1963, ss 2, 4, 5, 9(1), (2), 11, 50(1); Rehabilitation of Offenders Act 1975, s 5(2); Criminal Procedure (Scotland) Act 1975, ss 204, 208–11, 218, 414, 416, 418–420) (SI 1983/1580)
Remainder	Repealed or spent

[1] Any order(s) made under Children (Scotland) Act 1995, s 105(1), (2), bringing this prospective repeal into force will be noted to that Act in the service to this work

[2] Any order(s) made under Transport Act 1981, s 40(4), bringing this prospective repeal into force will be noted to that Act in the service to this work

---

Deaconesses and Lay Workers (Pensions) Measure 1980 (No 1)

RA: 20 Mar 1980

20 Mar 1980 (RA)

Deer Act 1980 (c 49)

Whole Act repealed

Diocese in Europe Measure 1980 (No 2)

RA: 30 Jun 1980

Commencement provisions: s 7(2)

2 Jul 1980 (s 7(2) (following establishment of Diocese in Europe))

Education Act 1980 (c 20)

RA: 3 Apr 1980

Commencement provisions: s 37(2); Education Act 1980 (Commencement No 1) Order 1980, SI 1980/489; Education Act 1980 (Commencement No 2) Order 1980, SI 1980/959; Education Act 1980 (Commencement No 3) Order 1981, SI 1981/789; Education Act 1980 (Commencement No 4) Order 1981, SI 1981/1064

Education Act 1980 (c 20)—*cont*

s 1	5 May 1980 (SI 1980/489)
2–4	Repealed
5	1 Jul 1981 (SI 1981/789)
6–9	1 Oct 1980 (SI 1980/959)
10, 11	Repealed
12(1)(a)–(d)	1 Aug 1980 (SI 1980/489)
(e)	5 May 1980 (SI 1980/489)
(1A), (1B)	Inserted by Education Act 1993, s 229(1) (qv)
(2)	5 May 1980 (SI 1980/489)
(2A)	Inserted by Education Reform Act 1988, s 31(4) (qv)
(3)	5 May 1980 (SI 1980/489)
(4)	1 Aug 1980 (SI 1980/489)
(5)–(9)	5 May 1980 (SI 1980/489)
13	1 Aug 1980 (SI 1980/489)
14(1), (2)	5 May 1980 (SI 1980/489)
(3)	1 Aug 1980 (SI 1980/489)
(4)	Repealed
15	Repealed
16(1)	5 May 1980 (SI 1980/489)
(1A)	Inserted by Education Act 1993, s 307(1), Sch 19, para 78 (qv)
(2), (3)	1 Aug 1980 (SI 1980/489)
(3A), (3B)	Inserted by Education Reform Act 1988, s 237(1), Sch 12, Pt III, para 81 (qv)
(4), (5)	1 Aug 1980 (SI 1980/489)
(6), (7)	5 May 1980 (SI 1980/489)
17, 18	1 Oct 1980 (SI 1980/959)
19	5 May 1980 (SI 1980/489)
20	5 May 1980 (SI 1980/489); repealed (S)
21	5 May 1980 (SI 1980/489)
22	14 April 1980 (SI 1980/489)
23	Repealed
24	1 May 1980 (SI 1980/489)
25	Repealed
26	5 May 1980 (SI 1980/489)
27	Repealed
28–30	5 May 1980 (SI 1980/489)
31, 32	Repealed
33(1)	Repealed
(2)	5 May 1980 (SI 1980/489); repealed (S)
(3)	1 Sep 1981 (SI 1981/1064)
34	1 Oct 1980 (SI 1980/959)
35	14 Apr 1980 (SI 1980/489); repealed (S)
36	14 Apr 1980 (SI 1980/489)
37	14 Apr 1980 (SI 1980/489); repealed (S)
38(1)–(3)	14 Apr 1980 (SI 1980/489)
(4)	1 Oct 1980 (SI 1980/959)
(5)	1 Aug 1980 (SI 1980/489)
(5A)	Inserted by Education Reform Act 1988, s 31(6) (qv)
(6)	See Sch 7 below
(7)	14 Apr 1980 (SI 1980/489)
	Whole section repealed (S)
Sch 1	5 May 1980 (SI 1980/489)
2	1 Oct 1980 (SI 1980/959)
3	1 Aug 1980 (SI 1980/489)

Education Act 1980 (c 20)—*cont*

Sch 4	1 Oct 1980 (SI 1980/959)
5	5 May 1980 (SI 1980/489)
6	Repealed
7	14 Apr 1980 (repeals of or in Education Act 1944, s 49; Education (Scotland) Act 1962, ss 53, 55; Education (Milk) Act 1971; Education (Scotland) Act 1976, s 3; Education Act 1976, s 9) (SI 1980/489)
	5 May 1980 (repeals of or in Education Act 1944, ss 8(2)(b), 9(1), 11, 12, 31(1), 32, 53(1), 61(2), 66, 82-84, 90, 97, 100(1), 114, Sch 1, Pt I, para 3, Sch 3, para 3; Education (Miscellaneous Provisions) Act 1953, s 6(1); Local Government Act 1958, Sch 8, para 16(2); London Government Act 1963, ss 31(1)–(3), 33; Local Government Act 1966, s 14; Education Act 1973, s 4; Education Act 1975, ss 1, 2, 5(4); Education Act 1976, ss 5, 7, 8) (SI 1980/489)
	1 Aug 1980 (repeals of or in Education Act 1944, s 13; Education Act 1946, Sch 2, Pt II; Education (Miscellaneous Provisions) Act 1948, ss 6, 7; Education (Miscellaneous Provisions) Act 1953, ss 7, 9, 16, Sch 1; London Government Act 1963, s 31(9); Education Act 1968, ss 1(2), 3, 5, Sch 1, para 7, Sch 3, Pt A; Education Act 1976, s 4) (SI 1980/489)
	1 Aug 1981 (repeals of Education Act 1944, s 21(2), Sch 4) (SI 1981/789)
	1 Sep 1981 (repeal of Sex Discrimination Act 1975, Sch 2, para 2) (SI 1981/1064)

Education (Scotland) Act 1980 (c 44)

RA: 1 Aug 1980

Commencement provisions: s 137(2)–(4); Education (Scotland) Act 1980 (Commencement) Order 1980, SI 1980/1287[1]

s 1(1), (2)	1 Sep 1980 (s 137(2))
(2A)	Inserted by Further and Higher Education (Scotland) Act 1992, s (qv)
(3)	1 Sep 1980 (s 137(2), (3))[2]
(4), (5)	1 Sep 1980 (s 137(2))
2–4	1 Sep 1980 (s 137(2))
5	Repealed
6–9	1 Sep 1980 (s 137(2))
10, 11	1 Sep 1980 (s 137(2), (3))[2]
12–14	1 Sep 1980 (s 137(2))
14ZA	Inserted by Further and Higher Education (Scotland) Act 1992, s 62, Sch 9, para 7(1), (2) (qv)
14A	Inserted by Education (Scotland) Act 1981, s 12 (qv)
15–19	1 Sep 1980 (s 137(2))
19A	Inserted by Education (Amendment) (Scotland) Act 1984, s 1 (qv)
20–22	1 Sep 1980 (s 137(2))
22A–22D	Inserted by Education (Scotland) Act 1981, s 6 (qv)

Education (Scotland) Act 1980 (c 44)—*cont*

s 23(1)	1 Sep 1980 (s 137(2), (3))[2]
(1A)–(1C)	Prospectively inserted by Local Government etc (Scotland) Act 1994, s 32(1), (2)[3]
(2), (3)	1 Sep 1980 (s 137(2), (3))[2]
(3A)	Prospectively inserted by Local Government etc (Scotland) Act 1994, s 32(1), (3)[3]
(4)	1 Sep 1980 (s 137(2), (3))[2]
(5)–(7)	Repealed
24–28	1 Sep 1980 (s 137(2))
28A–28H	Inserted by Education (Scotland) Act 1981, s 1(1) (qv)
28I–28K	Prospectively inserted by Education (Schools) Act 1992, s 17 (qv)
29	Repealed
30–44	1 Sep 1980 (s 137(2))
45–48	Repealed
48A	Inserted by Education (No 2) Act 1986, s 48 (qv)
49	1 Sep 1980 (s 137(2))
50(1)(a), (b)	1 Sep 1980 (s 137(2), (3))[2]
(c)	Repealed
(1A)	Inserted by Self-Governing Schools etc (Scotland) Act 1989, s 82(1), Sch 10, para 8(10)(b) (qv)
(2)	1 Sep 1980 (s 137(2), (3))[2]
(3), (4)	Inserted by Education (Scotland) Act 1981, s 2(2)(b) (qv)
51	1 Sep 1980 (s 137(2))
52	1 Sep 1980 (s 137(2), (3))[2]
53–56	1 Sep 1980 (s 137(2))
57, 58	1 Sep 1980 (s 137(2), (3))[2]
59	Repealed
60–65F	Substituted for ss 60–65 by Education (Scotland) Act 1981, s 4(1), Sch 8 (qv)
65G	Inserted by Self-Governing Schools etc (Scotland) Act 1989, s 71(2) (qv)
66	1 Sep 1980 (s 137(2), (3))[2]
67	1 Sep 1980 (s 137(2))
68	1 Sep 1980 (s 137(2), (3))[2]
69–71	1 Sep 1980 (s 137(2))
72(1)	1 Sep 1980 (s 137(2))
(2)	1 Sep 1980 (s 137(2), (3))[2]
73–75	1 Sep 1980 (s 137(2))
75A, 75B	Inserted by Education (Scotland) Act 1981, s 5(1) (qv)
76	1 Sep 1980 (s 137(2))
77	Repealed
78	1 Sep 1980 (s 137(2)); prospectively repealed by Local Government etc (Scotland) Act 1994, s 180, Sch 13, para 118(1), (4), Sch 14[3]
79–85	1 Sep 1980 (s 137(2))
86, 87	1 Sep 1980 (s 137(2), (3))[2]
87A, 87B	Inserted by Self-Governing Schools etc (Scotland) Act 1989, s 74 (qv)
88	Repealed
89, 90	1 Sep 1980 (s 137(2))
91–93	Substituted by Education (Scotland) Act 1981, s 14(1), Sch 8 (qv)
94–97	Repealed

Education (Scotland) Act 1980 (c 44)—*cont*

s 97A–97D	Inserted by Education (Scotland) Act 1981, s 14(1), Sch 8 (qv)
98–107	1 Sep 1980 (s 137(2))
108(1)	1 Sep 1980 (s 137(2))
(2)	1 Sep 1980 (s 137(2)); renumbered s 108A by Education (Scotland) Act 1981, Sch 6, para 7(b) (qv)
108A	See s 108(2) above
109–112	1 Sep 1980 (s 137(2))
113	Repealed
114	1 Sep 1980 (s 137(2))
115, 116	Repealed
117	1 Sep 1980 (s 137(2))
118	Substituted by Education (Scotland) Act 1981, Sch 6, para 16, Sch 8 (qv)
118A	Inserted by Education (Scotland) Act 1981, Sch 6, para 17 (qv)
119–123	1 Sep 1980 (s 137(2))
124	Repealed
125	1 Sep 1980 (s 137(2))
125A	Inserted by Children (Scotland) Act 1995, s 35 (qv)
126	1 Sep 1980 (s 137(2))
127(1), (2)	1 Sep 1980 (s 137(2))
(3), (4)	*Not in force*
(5)	Repealed
(6)	1 Sep 1980 (s 137(2))
128–137	1 Sep 1980 (s 137(2))
Sch A1	Inserted by Education (Scotland) Act 1981, s 1(2), Sch 1 (qv)
A2	Inserted by Education (Scotland) Act 1981, s 4(3), Schs 3, 8 (qv)
1	1 Sep 1980 (s 137(2))
1A	Inserted by Education (Scotland) Act 1981, s 5(3), Sch 4 (qv)
1B	Inserted by Education (Scotland) Act 1981, s 14(2), Sch 5 (qv)
2–5	1 Sep 1980 (s 137(2))
6, paras 1–15	Repealed
16	Added (retrospectively) by Local Government (Miscellaneous Provisions) (Scotland) Act 1981, s 38

[1] This order, made under s 137(4), (5), appointed 1 Sep 1980 for the coming into force of s 23(5)–(7) (now repealed) of this Act

[2] So far as relating to junior colleges (or, in the case of s 1(3), as originally enacted, so far as relating to compulsory further education and junior colleges), the commencement of the provision(s) was postponed under paras 1–15 (now repealed) of Sch 6, until a day appointed under s 137(3); no day was appointed before the Self-Governing Schools etc (Scotland) Act 1989 removed references to junior colleges in the provision(s)

[3] Any orders made under Local Government etc (Scotland) Act 1994, s 184(2), (3), bringing the prospective change into force will be noted to that Act in the service to this work

Employment Act 1980 (c 42)

RA: 1 Aug 1980

Commencement provisions: s 21(2); Employment Act 1980 (Commencement No 1) Order 1980, SI 1980/1170; Employment Act 1980 (Commencement No 2) Order 1980, SI 1980/1926

s 1–5	Repealed
6	1 Oct 1980 (SI 1980/1170)
7	Repealed
8, 9	1 Oct 1980 (SI 1980/1170)
10	Repealed
11	1 Oct 1980 (SI 1980/1170); repealed by Trade Union Reform and Employment Rights Act 1993, s 51, Sch 10 (qv), as from 10 Jun 1994, in relation only to women whose expected week of childbirth begins on or after 16 Oct 1994
12–14	1 Oct 1980 (SI 1980/1170)
15–19	Repealed
20(1)	1 Aug 1980 (RA)
(2)	See Sch 1 below
(3)	See Sch 2 below
21	1 Aug 1980 (RA)
Sch 1, para 1	15 Aug 1980 (SI 1980/1170)
2–7	Repealed
8	1 Oct 1980 (SI 1980/1170)
9, 10	Repealed
11	1 Oct 1980 (SI 1980/1170)
12	Repealed
13	1 Oct 1980 (SI 1980/1170)
14, 15	Repealed
16	8 Sep 1980 (SI 1980/1170)
17	8 Sep 1980 (so far as relates to s 4) (SI 1980/1170) 1 Oct 1980 (otherwise) (SI 1980/1170)
18	1 Oct 1980 (SI 1980/1170)
19	Repealed
20	15 Aug 1980 (SI 1980/1170)
21	Repealed
22, 23	1 Oct 1980 (SI 1980/1170)
24	Repealed
25	1 Oct 1980 (SI 1980/1170)
26	8 Sep 1980 (SI 1980/1170)
27	1 Oct 1980 (SI 1980/1170)
28, 29	8 Sep 1980 (SI 1980/1170)
30	Repealed
31	1 Oct 1980 (SI 1980/1170)
32	Repealed
33	1 Oct 1980 (SI 1980/1170)
2	15 Aug 1980 (except repeals of or in Trade Union and Labour Relations Act 1974; Employment Protection Act 1975, s 127(1)(g); Trade Union and Labour Relations (Amendment) Act 1976, s 2; Employment Protection (Consolidation) Act 1978, ss 23, 25(1), 33(3), 66(1), 73(1)(c), (8), 135(1), 154(1)) (SI 1980/1170) 8 Sep 1980 (repeals of Trade Union and Labour Relations Act 1974, s 13(3); Employment

Employment Act 1980 (c 42)—*cont*

Sch 2—*cont*	Protection (Consolidation) Act 1978, ss 23, 25(1), 135(1)) (SI 1980/1170)
	1 Oct 1980 (otherwise except repeals of or in Trade Union and Labour Relations Act 1974; Trade Union and Labour Relations (Amendment) Act 1976, s 2) (SI 1980/1170)
	22 Dec 1980 (exceptions noted above) (SI 1980/1926)

Note transitional provisions in SI 1980/1170

Films Act 1980 (c 41)

Whole Act repealed

Finance Act 1980 (c 48)

Budget Day: 26 Mar 1980

RA: 1 Aug 1980

See the note concerning Finance Acts at the front of this book

Foster Children Act 1980 (c 6)

Whole Act repealed

Gaming (Amendment) Act 1980 (c 8)

RA: 20 Mar 1980

20 Mar 1980 (RA)

Gas Act 1980 (c 37)

Whole Act repealed

Health Services Act 1980 (c 53)

RA: 8 Aug 1980

Commencement provisions: s 26(2), (3); Health Services Act 1980 (Commencement No 1) Order 1980, SI 1980/1257; Health Services Act 1980 (Commencement No 2) Order 1981, SI 1981/306; Health Services Act 1980 (Commencement No 3) Order 1981, SI 1981/884; Health Services Act 1980 (Commencement No 4) Order 1983, SI 1983/303

s 1	8 Aug 1980 (RA)
2	Repealed
3	8 Aug 1980 (RA)
4	Repealed
5–9	8 Aug 1980 (RA)
10–15	Repealed
16	1 Aug 1981 (SI 1981/884)
17–19	Repealed

Health Services Act 1980 (c 53)—*cont*

s 20	8 Aug 1980 (RA)
21	1 Apr 1983 (SI 1983/303)
22	Repealed
23, 24	8 Aug 1980 (RA)
25(1)	8 Aug 1980 (RA)
(2)	1 Apr 1981 (SI 1981/306)
(3)	8 Aug 1980 (RA)
(4)	See Sch 7 below
26	8 Aug 1980 (RA)
Sch 1, 2	8 Aug 1980 (RA)
3	Repealed
4	1 Aug 1981 (SI 1981/884)
5	1 Apr 1981 (SI 1981/306)
6	8 Aug 1980 (RA)
7	8 Aug 1980 (except repeals in Nursing Homes Registration (Scotland) Act 1938; Nursing Homes Act 1975; Nurses, Midwives and Health Visitors Act 1979) (RA) 1 Aug 1981 (exception noted above) (SI 1981/884)

Highlands and Islands Air Services (Scotland) Act 1980 (c 19)

RA: 3 Apr 1980

Commencement provisions: s 5(2)

15 Dec 1980 (s 5(2))

Highways Act 1980 (c 66)

RA: 13 Nov 1980

Commencement provisions: s 345(2)

1 Jan 1981 (s 345(2))

Housing Act 1980 (c 51)

RA: 8 Aug 1980

Whole Act repealed (S)

Commencement provisions: s 153; Housing Act 1980 (Commencement No 1) Order 1980, SI 1980/1406; Housing Act 1980 (Commencement No 2) Order 1980, SI 1980/1466; Housing Act 1980 (Commencement No 3) Order 1980, SI 1980/1557; Housing Act 1980 (Commencement No 4) Order 1980, SI 1980/1693; Housing Act 1980 (Commencement No 5) Order 1980, SI 1980/1706; Housing Act 1980 (Commencement No 6) Order 1980, SI 1980/1781; Housing Act 1980 (Commencement No 7) Order 1981, SI 1981/119; Housing Act 1980 (Commencement No 8) Order 1981, SI 1981/296; Rent Rebates and Rent Allowances (England and Wales) (Appointed Day) Order 1981, SI 1981/297

s 1–50	Repealed
51	28 Nov 1980 (SI 1980/1706)
52	28 Nov 1980 (SI 1980/1706); repealed, subject to saving, by Housing Act 1988, s 140(2), Sch 18, Note 2 (qv)

Housing Act 1980 (c 51)—*cont*

s 53–55	28 Nov 1980 (SI 1980/1706)
56–58	6 Oct 1980 (SI 1980/1706); ss 56–58 (including ss 56A–56D which were inserted by Housing and Planning Act 1986, s 12(2)) repealed, subject to saving, by Housing Act 1988, s 140(2), Sch 18, Note 3 (qv)
59(1)	Repealed
(2)	28 Nov 1980 (SI 1980/1706)
(3)	See Sch 6 below
60	Repealed
61–77	28 Nov 1980 (SI 1980/1706)
78, 79	20 Oct 1980 (SI 1980/1557)
80	Repealed
81–86	3 Oct 1980 (SI 1980/1406)
87	Repealed
88, 89	3 Oct 1980 (SI 1980/1406)
90–137	Repealed
138	8 Aug 1980 (s 153(3))
139	Repealed
140	8 Aug 1980 (s 153(3)); repealed, subject to saving, by Housing and Planning Act 1986, ss 18, 24(3), Sch 4, paras 7, 11(2), Sch 12, Pt I (qv)
141	3 Oct 1980 (except in relation to Sch 21, para 7) (SI 1980/1406)
	Not in force (exception noted above)
142	31 Mar 1981 (SI 1981/119)
143	3 Oct 1980 (SI 1980/1406)
144–147	Repealed
148	3 Oct 1980 (SI 1980/1406)
149	Repealed
150, 151	8 Aug 1980 (s 153(3))
152(1)	See Sch 25 below
(2)	8 Aug 1980 (s 153(3))
(3)	See Sch 26 below
153	8 Aug 1980 (RA)
154, 155	8 Aug 1980 (s 153(3))
Sch 1–4A	Repealed
5	6 Oct 1980 (SI 1980/1466)
6	*Not in force*—it has been stated that amendments made by this Schedule will not be brought into operation (Regulated Tenancies (Procedure) Regulations 1980, SI 1980/1696 (made under Rent Act 1977, s 74))
7–10	28 Nov 1980 (SI 1980/1706)
11–20	Repealed
21, para 1, 2	3 Oct 1980 (SI 1980/1406)
3	Repealed
4–6	3 Oct 1980 (SI 1980/1706)
7	*Not in force*
8	3 Oct 1980 (SI 1980/1406)
22	31 Mar 1981 (SI 1981/119)
23, 24	Repealed
25, para 1–3	28 Nov 1980 (SI 1980/1706)
4–6	Spent
7–31	Repealed
32, 33	28 Nov 1980 (SI 1980/1706)

Housing Act 1980 (c 51)—*cont*

Sch 25, para	34	Repealed
	35	28 Nov 1980 (SI 1980/1706)
	36	Repealed
	37–45	28 Nov 1980 (SI 1980/1706)
	46	Repealed
	47–60	28 Nov 1980 (SI 1980/1706)
	61	3 Oct 1980 (SI 1980/1406)
	62, 63	Repealed
	64–68	8 Aug 1980 (s 153(3))
	69	Repealed
	70	Spent on repeal of s 114 of this Act
	71	Repealed
	72, 73	Spent
	74	Repealed
	75	8 Aug 1980 (s 153(3))
	76	Repealed
	77, 78	8 Aug 1980 (s 153(3))
26		3 Oct 1980 (repeals of or in Housing Act 1957, ss 5, 43(4), 113(5), 119(3); Housing (Financial Provisions) Act 1958, s 43(1); Housing Act 1961, s 20; Housing Act 1964, ss 65(1A), 66; Housing Subsidies Act 1967, ss 24(5), 26A; Leasehold Reform Act 1967, Sch 1, para 7(1)(b); Housing Act 1969, s 61(6); Housing Finance Act 1972, ss 90–91A; Local Government Act 1972, Sch 22, para 2; Housing Act 1974, ss 5(3), 13(4), (5)(a), 14, 19(1), 30(5), 31, 32(1), (4), (8), 33(6), 104, 114(1), (6), (7); Criminal Law Act 1977, Schs 6, 12) (SI 1980/1406)
		27 Oct 1980 (repeals of or in Housing Act 1961, s 16; Housing Act 1969, s 60; Housing Act 1974, ss 56(1)(d), 57(6), 62(3), 64(7), 67(2)(b), (4), 84) (SI 1980/1557)
		28 Mar 1980 (repeals of or in Landlord and Tenant Act 1927, s 16; Reserve and Auxiliary Forces (Protection of Civil Interests) Act 1951, ss 16(2)(c), 19(5); Landlord and Tenant Act 1954, s 43(1)(c); Housing Act 1964, Sch 4, para 2; Tribunals and Inquiries Act 1971, ss 7(3), 13(1), Sch 1, para 28(a); Rent (Agriculture) Act 1976, Sch 4, Case X, Sch 6, paras 1, 7; Rent Act 1977 except repeals in Sch 12, paras 4, 9) (SI 1980/1706)
		15 Dec 1980 (repeals of or in Housing Act 1957, s 96(e); Housing (Financial Provisions) Act 1958, ss 14, 15; Housing Act 1969, ss 28A, 29B, 30, 35(1), (3)–(7), 38, 86(5); Chronically Sick and Disabled Persons Act 1970, s 3(1); Local Employment Act 1972, Sch 3; Housing (Amendment) Act 1973, ss 1(1), 2; Housing Act 1974, ss 38(2)(a), 42, 50, 52–55, 56(2)(d), 71(3)(a), Sch 5, Pt I, Pt II, para 4; Housing Rents and Subsidies Act 1975, Sch 1, paras 1–11, 12(4)(a), Sch 5, paras 8(3), 18; Remuneration, Charges and Grants Act 1975, s 9; Local Land Charges Act 1975, Sch 1) (SI 1980/1781)
		31 Mar 1981 (repeal of Leasehold Reform Act 1967, s 21(5), Sch 2, para 8(2)) (SI 1981/119)

Housing Act 1980 (c 51)—*cont*

Sch 26—*cont*

1 Apr 1981 (repeals of Housing Finance Act 1972, ss 8, 20(5), (7), 24(5), 26(1), Sch 3, Pt II, Sch 4, paras 1(3)(a), 16, 17) (SI 1981/296)

Not in force (repeals of or in Housing Act 1957, ss 91, 105, 106; Housing (Financial Provisions) Act 1958, s 45; New Towns Act 1959, s 4; Housing Subsidies Act 1967, ss 24, 24B, 26, 28A; Town and Country Planning Act 1968, s 39; Housing Act 1974, s 79, Schs 8, 11; Housing Rents and Subsidies Act 1975, ss 1(3), 2, 4; New Towns (Amendment) Act 1976, s 9; Supplementary Benefits Act 1976, Sch 7, para 28; Development of Rural Wales Act 1976, ss 18, 22, Sch 5; Rent Act 1977, Sch 12, paras 4, 9)

Import of Live Fish (England and Wales) Act 1980 (c 27)

RA: 15 May 1980

15 May 1980 (RA)

Imprisonment (Temporary Provisions) Act 1980 (c 57)

RA: 29 Oct 1980

29 Oct 1980 (RA)

Industry Act 1980 (c 33)

RA: 30 Jun 1980

30 Jun 1980 (RA)

Insurance Companies Act 1980 (c 25)

RA: 1 May 1980

Commencement provisions: s 5(2); Insurance Companies Act 1980 (Commencement) Order 1980, SI 1980/678

Whole Act repealed except ss 4(1), 5, Sch 3, paras 4, 9, 15(b), 17, 18, 20 which came into force on 1 Jun 1980 (SI 1980/678); Sch 3, para 4 is prospectively repealed by Children (Northern Ireland) Order 1995, SI 1995/755 (NI 2), art 185(2), Sch 10

Iran (Temporary Powers) Act 1980 (c 28)

Whole Act repealed

Law Reform (Miscellaneous Provisions) (Scotland) Act 1980 (c 55)

RA: 29 Oct 1980

Commencement provisions: s 29(2); Law Reform (Miscellaneous Provisions) (Scotland) Act 1980 (Commencement) Order 1980, SI 1980/1726

Law Reform (Miscellaneous Provisions) (Scotland) Act 1980 (c 55)—*cont*

s 1–11	22 Dec 1980 (SI 1980/1726)
12	Repealed
13, 14	22 Dec 1980 (SI 1980/1726)
15	Repealed
16–25	22 Dec 1980 (SI 1980/1726)
26	Repealed
27, 28	22 Dec 1980 (SI 1980/1726)
29	29 Oct 1980 (RA)
Sch 1, 2	22 Dec 1980 (SI 1980/1726)
3	Repealed

Licensed Premises (Exclusion of Certain Persons) Act 1980 (c 32)

RA: 30 Jun 1980

30 Jun 1980 (RA)

Licensing (Amendment) Act 1980 (c 40)

RA: 17 Jul 1980

Commencement provisions: s 4(2); Licensing (Amendment) Act 1980 (Commencement) Order 1982, SI 1982/1383

s 1	17 Jul 1980 (RA)
2, 3	1 Oct 1982 (SI 1982/1383)
4	17 Jul 1980 (RA)

Limitation Act 1980 (c 58)

RA: 13 Nov 1980

Commencement provisions: s 41(2), (3); Limitation Act 1980 (Commencement) Order 1981, SI 1981/588

1 May 1981 (s 41(2); note that s 35 also came into force on that date by virtue of SI 1981/588)

Limitation Amendment Act 1980 (c 24)

RA: 1 May 1980

Whole Act repealed except ss 10, 14(1), (5) which came into force on 1 Aug 1980 (s 14(3) (repealed))

Local Government, Planning and Land Act 1980 (c 65)

RA: 13 Nov 1980

Commencement provisions: ss 23(3), 47, 68(8), 85, 86(8)–(11), 178; Local Government, Planning and Land Act 1980 (Commencement No 1) Order 1980, SI 1980/1871; Local Government, Planning and Land Act 1980 (Commencement No 2) Order 1980, SI 1980/1893; Local Government, Planning and Land Act 1980 (Commencement No 3) Order 1980, SI 1980/2014; Local Government,

Local Government, Planning and Land Act 1980 (c 65)—*cont*

Planning and Land Act 1980 (Commencement No 4) Order 1981, SI 1981/194; Local Government, Planning and Land Act 1980 (Commencement No 5) Order 1981, SI 1981/341; Local Government, Planning and Land Act 1980 (Commencement No 6) Order 1981, SI 1981/1251; Local Government, Planning and Land Act 1980 (Commencement No 7) Order 1981, SI 1981/1618; Local Government, Planning and Land Act 1980 (Commencement No 8) (Scotland) Order 1982, SI 1982/317[1]; Local Government, Planning and Land Act 1980 (Commencement No 8) Order 1983, SI 1983/94; Community Land Act 1975 (Appointed Day for Repeal) Order 1983, SI 1983/673; Local Government, Planning and Land Act 1980 (Commencement No 9) Order 1984, SI 1984/1493

s 1–4	13 Nov 1980 (RA)
5–14	1 Apr 1981 (EW) (SI 1981/341) 1 Apr 1982 (S) (SI 1982/317)
15(1)	1 Apr 1981 (EW) (SI 1981/341) 1 Apr 1982 (S) (SI 1982/317)
(2), (3)	1 Apr 1981 (EW) (SI 1981/341); *not in force* (S)
16(1)	1 Apr 1981 (EW) (but in its application to relevant work, 1 Apr 1982) (SI 1981/341) 1 Apr 1982 (S) (SI 1982/317)
(1A)	Inserted by Local Government Act 1992, s 11, Sch 1, para 4(2) (qv)
(2), (3)	1 Apr 1981 (EW) (SI 1981/341); 1 Apr 1982 (S) (SI 1982/317); prospectively repealed by Local Government Act 1992, s 29(2), Sch 4, Pt I[2]
(4)–(6)	Repealed
17	1 Apr 1981 (EW) (SI 1981/341); 1 Apr 1982 (S) (SI 1982/317); repealed, subject to transitional provisions, by Local Government Act 1988, ss 32, 41, Sch 6, para 7, Sch 7, Pt III (qv)
18, 19	1 Apr 1981 (EW) (SI 1981/341) 1 Apr 1982 (S) (SI 1982/317)
19A, 19B	Inserted by Local Government Act 1988, s 32, Sch 6, para 9 (qv)
20–22	1 Apr 1981 (EW) (SI 1981/341) 1 Apr 1982 (S) (SI 1982/317)
23–27	13 Nov 1980 (RA)
28	13 Nov 1980 (s 47(7)); repealed, with savings, by Local Government Finance (Repeals, Savings and Consequential Amendments) Order 1990, SI 1990/776, art 3, Sch 1[3]
29(1)–(3)	13 Nov 1980, but not to have effect for rate periods beginning before first date after 13 Nov 1980, on which new valuation lists were to come into force[4] (s 47(4), (7)); repealed, with savings, by Local Government Finance (Repeals, Savings and Consequential Amendments) Order 1990, SI 1990/776, art 3, Sch 1[3]
29(4), (5)	13 Nov 1980 (s 47(7)); repealed, with savings, by Local Government Finance (Repeals, Savings and Consequential Amendments) Order 1990, SI 1990/776, art 3, Sch 1[3]
30	13 Nov 1980 (s 47(7)); repealed, with savings, by Local Government Finance (Repeals, Savings and Consequential Amendments) Order 1990, SI 1990/776, art 3, Sch 1[3]

Local Government, Planning and Land Act 1980 (c 65)—*cont*

s 31	13 Nov 1980, but only to have effect for rate periods beginning after 1 Apr 1981 (s 47(2), (7)); repealed, with savings, by Local Government Finance (Repeals, Savings and Consequential Amendments) Order 1990, SI 1990/776, art 3, Sch 1[3]
32	13 Nov 1980 (s 47(7))
33, 34	13 Nov 1980, but only to have effect for any rate passed beginning after 31 Mar 1981 (s 47(1), (7); SI 1980/2014); repealed, with savings, by Local Government Finance (Repeals, Savings and Consequential Amendments) Order 1990, SI 1990/776, art 3, Sch 1[3]
35, 36	13 Nov 1980 (s 47(7)); repealed, with savings, by Local Government Finance (Repeals, Savings and Consequential Amendments) Order 1990, SI 1990/776, art 3, Sch 1[3]
37	13 Nov 1980, but only to have effect for any rate period beginning after 31 Mar 1981 (s 47(1), (7); SI 1980/2014); repealed, with savings, by Local Government Finance (Repeals, Savings and Consequential Amendments) Order 1990, SI 1990/776, art 3, Sch 1[3]
38–40	13 Dec 1980 (s 47(3)); repealed, with savings, by Local Government Finance (Repeals, Savings and Consequential Amendments) Order 1990, SI 1990/776, art 3, Sch 1[3]
41–43	13 Nov 1980 (s 47(7)); repealed, with savings, by Local Government Finance (Repeals, Savings and Consequential Amendments) Order 1990, SI 1990/776, art 3, Sch 1[3]
44	13 Nov 1980, but only to have effect for rate periods beginning after 31 Mar 1981 (s 47(1), (7); SI 1980/2014); repealed, with savings, by Local Government Finance (Repeals, Savings and Consequential Amendments) Order 1990, SI 1990/776, art 3, Sch 1[3]
45, 46	Repealed
47	13 Nov 1980 (RA)
48–61	13 Nov 1980 (RA) but the commencing year for purposes of Part VI of this Act was that beginning 1 Apr 1981 (SI 1980/1893)
62	Substituted (retrospectively) by Rate Support Grants Act 1986, s 3, Sch 1, para 11
63	13 Nov 1980 (RA); commencing year began 1 Apr 1981 (SI 1980/1893)
63A	Inserted by Local Government Act 1985, s 83(2) (qv)
64	Repealed
65	Substituted by Local Government Finance Act 1987, s 11(1), Sch 4, para 4 (with effect as noted in para 12(3) of that Schedule) (qv)
66, 67	13 Nov 1980 (RA); commencing year began 1 Apr 1981 (SI 1980/1893)
68(1)	13 Nov 1980 (RA); commencing year began 1 Apr 1981 (SI 1980/1893)
(2)	11 Dec 1980 (s 68(8); SI 1980/1893)

Local Government, Planning and Land Act 1980 (c 65)—*cont*

s 68(3)–(6)	Repealed
(7)–(9)	13 Nov 1980 (RA)
69	13 Nov 1980 (RA)
70	13 Nov 1980 (RA); repealed (EW), with a saving, by Criminal Justice and Public Order Act 1994, s 80(5) (qv)
71–85	Repealed
86(1)–(7)	Repealed
(8)–(11)	13 Jan 1981 (s 86(8), (11))
87	13 Nov 1980 (RA); repealed (EW)
88–90	Repealed
91, 92	13 Nov 1980 (RA)
93–96	Brought into force area by area on different dates as follows: 31 Dec 1980 (Birmingham, Bradford, Bristol, Coventry, Dudley, Ealing, Gateshead, Leeds, Liverpool, Manchester, Middlesborough, Newcastle-under-Lyme, Newcastle-upon-Tyne, Preston, Salford, Sefton, Stockport, Stoke, Trafford, Wandsworth, Wirral) (SI 1980/1871) 19 Mar 1981 (Derby, Leicester, Newham, North Bedfordshire, Nottingham, Portsmouth, Sandwell, Sheffield, South Staffordshire, Southwark, Tower Hamlets, Walsall) (SI 1981/194) 2 Oct 1981 (Knowsley, St Helens) (SI 1981/1251) 11 Dec 1981 (areas of all other councils of districts in England, all other London boroughs and the City of London) (SI 1981/1618) 3 Mar 1983 (Alyn and Deeside, Cardiff, Newport, Swansea, Vale of Glamorgan, Wrexham, Maelor) (SI 1983/94) 24 Oct 1984 (areas of all other district councils in Wales) (SI 1984/1493)
96A	Inserted by Local Government Act 1988, s 31, Sch 5, para 2(1) (qv)
97	Substituted by Local Government Act 1988, s 31, Sch 5, para 3 (qv)
98, 99	See ss 93–96 above
99A	Inserted by Local Government Act 1988, s 31, Sch 5, para 6 (qv)
100	See ss 93–96 above
101	See Sch 17 below
102–104	13 Nov 1980 (RA)
105	Repealed
106–116	13 Nov 1980 (RA)
117	Repealed
118	13 Nov 1980 (RA)
119	Repealed
120	13 Nov 1980 (RA); repealed in part as to EW and now applies to S only
121	13 Nov 1980 (RA) but effective from 12 Dec 1975 (s 121(1))
122	13 Nov 1980 (RA)
123	13 Nov 1980 (RA) but effective from 12 Dec 1975 (s 123(1))
124, 125	13 Nov 1980 (RA)

Local Government, Planning and Land Act 1980 (c 65)—*cont*

s 126–130	Repealed
131–149	13 Nov 1980 (RA)
150	Repealed
151–153	13 Nov 1980 (RA)
154	Substituted by Social Security and Housing Benefits Act 1982, s 48(5), Sch 4, para 36 (qv)
155, 156	13 Nov 1980 (RA)
157, 157A, 157B	Substituted for original s 157 by Leasehold Reform, Housing and Urban Development Act 1993, s 178 (qv)
158	Repealed
159–165	13 Nov 1980 (RA)
165A	Inserted by Leasehold Reform, Housing and Urban Development Act 1993, s 180(2) (qv)
166–172	13 Nov 1980 (RA)
173(a)	13 Dec 1980 (s 178(3))
(b)	13 Dec 1981 (s 178(2))
174	13 Feb 1981 (s 178(1))
175–178	13 Dec 1980 (s 178(3))
179, 180	13 Nov 1980 (RA)
181, 182	Repealed
183–186	13 Nov 1980 (RA)
187–190	Repealed
191–197	13 Nov 1980 (RA)
Sch 1–10	13 Nov 1980 (RA)
11–15	Repealed
16	13 Nov 1980 (RA)
17, Pt I	13 Nov 1980 (RA)
II	13 Nov 1980 (repeals of Community Land Act 1975, except as noted below) (RA)
	1 Jun 1983 (repeals of Community Land Act 1975, ss 1, 2, 6(1) (part), (6), 7, 26, 40, 43, 44 (except part of sub-s (3)), 51–58 of, and Sch 2 to, 1975 Act) (SI 1983/673)
III, IV	13 Nov 1980 (RA)
18–24	13 Nov 1980 (RA)
25, Pt I	Repealed
II–IV	13 Nov 1980 (RA)
26–32	13 Nov 1980 (RA)
33, para 1–3	13 Nov 1980 (RA)
4	Effective from 25 Mar 1981 when power to prescribe appropriate multiplier first exercised (s 47(5), (6); Landlord and Tenant Act 1954 (Appropriate Multiplier) Regulations 1981, SI 1981/69)
5	13 Nov 1980 (RA)
6	Repealed
7	13 Nov 1980 (RA)
8	Repealed
9	13 Nov 1980 (RA); repealed, with savings, by Local Government Finance (Repeals, Savings and Consequential Amendments) Order 1990, SI 1990/776, art 3, Sch 1[3]
10	13 Nov 1980, but not to have effect for rate periods beginning before first date after 13 Nov 1980, on which new valuation lists were to come into force[4] (s 47(4), (7)); repealed, with savings, by

Local Government, Planning and Land Act 1980 (c 65)—*cont*

Sch 33, para 10—*cont*	Local Government Finance (Repeals, Savings and Consequential Amendments) Order 1990, SI 1990/776, art 3, Sch 1[3]
11	13 Nov 1980 (RA); repealed, with savings, by Local Government Finance (Repeals, Savings and Consequential Amendments) Order 1990, SI 1990/776, art 3, Sch 1[3]
12	Repealed
13	13 Nov 1980 (RA) but note para 13(2) only effective for applications after 12 Dec 1975
14	Effective when power to prescribe multipliers is exercised (s 47(5), (6)) (It is thought that the coming into force of Landlord and Tenant Act 1954 (Appropriate Multiplier) Regulations 1981, SI 1981/69, brought this paragraph into effect on 25 Mar 1981)
34, Pt I–VIII	13 Nov 1980 (RA)
IX	Rate periods beginning after 31 Mar 1981 (repeals of General Rate Act 1967, ss 4(2), 5(1)(g), 48(4), 50(2), Sch 10; Decimal Currency Act 1969; GLC (General Powers) Act 1973; Local Government Act 1974) (s 47(1); SI 1980/2014)
	Rate periods beginning after first date after 13 Nov 1980 on which new valuation lists in force (repeals of General Rate Act 1967, ss 19, 30) (s 47(4)(d))
	13 Nov 1980 (repeals of General Rate Act 1967, s 20, Schs 1, 2; General Rate Act 1975; Rating (Caravan Sites) Act 1976) (RA)
X	13 Nov 1980 (RA)
XI	13 Nov 1980 (RA) but note Sch 17 above in relation to repeal of Community Land Act 1975
XII–XVI	13 Nov 1980 (RA)

[1] No commencement orders under this Act, which affect Scotland, were made prior to this order; certain provisions of this Act, not subject to commencement order, were already in force in Scotland

[2] Orders made under Local Government Act 1992 bringing these prospective repeals into force will be noted to that Act in the service to this work

[3] This Order, made consequent upon (inter alia) Local Government Finance Act 1988 (which established new systems of community charges and non-domestic rates to replace the rating system) came into force on 1 Apr 1990

[4] The New Valuation Lists Order 1987, SI 1987/921 (made under General Rate Act 1967, s 68(1) (repealed), as substituted by s 28 of this Act), specified 1 Apr 1990 as the date on which new valuation lists were to come into force; that Order was revoked by SI 1988/2146, made under Local Government Finance Act 1988; SI 1988/2146 was itself revoked and replaced by SI 1992/1643, made under Sch 6, para 2(3)(b) to 1988 Act. Accordingly, SI 1987/921 was ineffective to bring s 29(1)–(3) of, and Sch 33, para 10(1) to, this Act into force

---

Magistrates' Courts Act 1980 (c 43)

RA: 1 Aug 1980

Commencement provisions: s 155(7)

6 Jul 1981 (s 155(7))

Married Women's Policies of Assurance (Scotland) (Amendment) Act 1980 (c 56)

RA: 29 Oct 1980

29 Oct 1980 (RA)

National Health Service (Invalid Direction) Act 1980 (c 15)

Whole Act repealed

National Heritage Act 1980 (c 17)

RA: 31 Mar 1980

31 Mar 1980 (RA)

New Hebrides Act 1980 (c 16)

RA: 20 Mar 1980

Commencement provisions: s 4(2); New Hebrides Order 1980, SI 1980/1079

s 1	Repealed
2	30 Jul 1980 (SI 1980/1079)
3	Repealed
4	20 Mar 1980 (RA)
Sch 1, 2	30 Jul 1980 (SI 1980/1079)

New Towns Act 1980 (c 36)

Whole Act repealed

Overseas Development and Co-operation Act 1980 (c 63)

RA: 13 Nov 1980

Commencement provisions: s 19(2)
14 Dec 1980 (s 19(2))

Papua New Guinea, Western Samoa and Nauru (Miscellaneous Provisions) Act 1980 (c 2)

RA: 31 Jan 1980

Commencement provisions: s 3(3)

s 1(1)	Repealed
(2)	31 Jan 1980 (RA)
(3)	Repealed
2	Repealed
3(1)	See Schedule below
(2)	Repealed
(3)	See Schedule below
4	31 Jan 1980 (RA)

Papua New Guinea, Western Samoa and Nauru (Miscellaneous Provisions) Act 1980 (c 2)—*cont*

Sch, para 1	16 Sep 1975 (retrospective; s 3(3))
2	31 Jan 1980 (RA)
3	16 Sep 1975 (retrospective; s 3(3))
4, 5	Repealed
6–14	31 Jan 1980 (RA)

Petroleum Revenue Tax Act 1980 (c 1)

RA: 31 Jan 1980

Commencement provisions: s 3(3)

s 1, 2(1), (2)	Effective for chargeable periods ending on or after 31 Dec 1979 (s 3(3))
2(3)	Repealed
3	31 Jan 1980 (RA); repealed in relation to chargeable periods beginning on or after 18 Aug 1989
Schedule	Effective for chargeable periods ending on or after 31 Dec 1979 (s 3(3))

(*Note:* Petroleum Revenue Tax abolished for new oil and gas fields ('non-taxable fields') with effect from 16 Mar 1993, by Finance Act 1993, s 185)

Police Negotiating Board Act 1980 (c 10)

RA: 20 Mar 1980

Commencement provisions: s 3(2)

20 May 1980 (s 3(2))

Port of London (Financial Assistance) Act 1980 (c 31)

Whole Act repealed

Protection of Trading Interests Act 1980 (c 11)

RA: 20 Mar 1980

20 Mar 1980 (RA)

Representation of the People Act 1980 (c 3)

Whole Act repealed

Reserve Forces Act 1980 (c 9)

RA: 20 Mar 1980

Commencement provisions: s 158(4)

20 Apr 1980 (s 158(4))

Residential Homes Act 1980 (c 7)

Whole Act repealed

Sea Fish Industry Act 1980 (c 35)

Whole Act repealed

Slaughter of Animals (Scotland) Act 1980 (c 13)

RA: 20 Mar 1980

20 Mar 1980 (RA)

Social Security Act 1980 (c 30)

RA: 23 May 1980

Commencement provisions: s 21(5); Social Security Act 1980 (Commencement No 1) Order 1980, SI 1980/729; Social Security Act 1980 (Commencement No 2) Order 1981, SI 1981/1438; Social Security Act 1980 (Commencement No 3) Order 1983, SI 1983/1002; Social Security Act 1980 (Commencement No 4) Order 1984, SI 1984/1492

s 1–3	Repealed
4(1), (2)	23 May 1980 (s 21(5))
(3)–(6)	Repealed
5	Repealed
6(1)	24 Nov 1980 (SI 1980/729)
(2)	Repealed
(3)	24 Nov 1980 (SI 1980/729)
(4)	Spent
7	Repealed
8	23 May 1980 (SI 1980/729)
9(1)–(5)	Repealed
(6)	24 Nov 1980 (SI 1980/729)
(7)	Repealed
10, 11	Repealed
12	23 May 1980 (s 21(5))
13–15	Repealed
16	23 May 1980 (s 21(5))
17, 18	Repealed
19–21	23 May 1980 (s 21(5))
Sch 1	Repealed
2, Pt I, paras 1–30	Repealed
31(a)	24 Nov 1980 (SI 1980/729)
(b), (c)	Repealed
(d)–(g)	24 Nov 1980 (SI 1980/729)
(h)	Repealed
32	24 Nov 1980 (SI 1980/729)
II	24 Nov 1980 (SI 1980/729)
3	Repealed
4, para 1, 2	24 Nov 1980 (SI 1980/729)
3	Spent
4	Repealed

Social Security Act 1980 (c 30)—*cont*

Sch 4, para 5–7	24 Nov 1980 (SI 1980/729)
8	Spent
9, 10	Repealed
11–13	24 Nov 1980 (SI 1980/729)
14	Repealed
5, Pt I	23 May 1980 (s 21(5))
II	14 Jul 1980 (repeals of or in Social Security Act 1975, ss 44(5)(b), 47(2)(b), Sch 4, Pt IV; Social Security (Miscellaneous Provisions) Act 1977, s 8(3)) (SI 1980/729)
	24 Nov 1980 (repeals of or in Polish Resettlement Act 1947; National Assistance Act 1948; Legal Aid (Scotland) Act 1967; Social Work (Scotland) Act 1968; Merchant Shipping Act 1970; Family Income Supplements Act 1970, ss 7(2), 10(2)(h); Housing (Financial Provisions) (Scotland) Act 1972; Housing Finance Act 1972; Legal Aid Act 1974; Social Security Act 1975, ss 138, 139, 142(5), 168(4), Sch 15; Social Security (Consequential Provisions) Act 1975; House of Commons Disqualification Act 1975; Northern Ireland Assembly Disqualification Act 1975; Social Security Pensions Act 1975; Child Benefit Act 1975; Supplementary Benefits Act 1976; National Insurance Surcharge Act 1976; Social Security (Miscellaneous Provisions) Act 1977, ss 14(1)–(4), (7)–(10), 15, 24(4); Employment Protection (Consolidation) Act 1978; Social Security Act 1979; Legal Aid Act 1979; Reserve Forces Act 1980) (SI 1980/729)
	23 Nov 1981 (repeals of or in Social Security Act 1975, ss 44(3)(b), (6), 47 (so far as not already repealed), 66(1)(c), (8)) (SI1981/1438)
	21 Nov 1983 (repeals of Social Security Act 1975, ss 44(5) (so far as not already repealed), 66(1)(b), Sch 20; Family Income Supplements Act 1970, s 17(1)) (SI 1983/1002)
	26 Nov 1984 (repeal of Social Security Act 1975, ss 41(1), 65(4), 158, Sch 19) (SI 1984/1492)

Social Security (No 2) Act 1980 (c 39)

Whole Act repealed

Solicitors (Scotland) Act 1980 (c 46)

RA: 1 Aug 1980

Commencement provisions: s 67(3)

1 Sep 1980 (s 67(3))

Statute Law Revision (Northern Ireland) Act 1980 (c 59)

RA: 13 Nov 1980

13 Nov 1980 (RA)

Tenants' Rights, Etc (Scotland) Act 1980 (c 52)

RA: 8 Aug 1980

Commencement provisions: s 86(4); Tenants' Rights, etc (Scotland) Act 1980 (Commencement) Order 1980, SI 1980/1387

s 1–32	Repealed
33	1 Dec 1980 (SI 1980/1387)
34–36	Repealed
37	1 Dec 1980 (SI 1980/1387)
38	Repealed
39	1 Dec 1980 (SI 1980/1387)
40	Repealed
41	1 Dec 1980 (SI 1980/1387)
42–45	Repealed
46	1 Dec 1980 (SI 1980/1387)
47, 48	Repealed
49	1 Dec 1980 (SI 1980/1387)
50–63	Repealed
64, 65	1 Dec 1980 (SI 1980/1387)
66–73	Repealed
74	3 Oct 1980 (SI 1980/1387)
75–85	Repealed
86	3 Oct 1980 (SI 1980/1387)
Sch A1, 1–4	Repealed
5	3 Oct 1980 (except repeals of or in Reserve and Auxiliary Forces (Protection of Civil Interests) Act 1951, ss 16(1), (2)(c), (4)(b), 17(2)(a), (b), 18(2)(a), (b), 19(5); Rent (Scotland) Act 1971, ss 4(1), 5(4), (5), 7(1), (2), 9(1), 24, 25(1), 29, 30, 36, Pt V, ss 70–76, 80(2), 81, 82, 84, 85, 97(2), 100, 106(8), 110(1)(b), (2), 111(1), 113–115, 122(1)(b), 123(2), (3), 125(2), 129(2), 133, 135(1), Sch 2, Sch 3, Case 5, Case 6, Case 9, Schs 8, 10–12, 14, 16, 17, 19, paras 9, 10, 14(1) (c), 19(1); Fire Precautions Act 1971, Sch, Pt III, paras 1(1), (2)(a), (6), (7), 4; Housing (Financial Provisions) (Scotland) Act 1972, ss 61(3), 62(2), (4), 64, 65, Sch 7, paras 1–7; Local Government (Scotland) Act 1973, Sch 13, paras 4, 5, 7; Housing Act 1974, s 18(2), (5); Rent Act 1974, s 1(3); Criminal Procedure (Scotland) Act 1975, Sch 7C; Housing Rents and Subsidies (Scotland) Act 1975, ss 7–11, Schs 2, 3, para 5) (SI 1980/1387)
	1 Dec 1980 (exceptions noted above) (SI 1980/1387)

Tenants' Rights, Etc (Scotland) (Amendment) Act 1980 (c 61)

Whole Act repealed

Transport Act 1980 (c 34)

RA: 30 Jun 1980

Commencement provisions: s 70; Transport Act 1980 (Commencement No 1) Order 1980, SI 1980/913; Transport Act 1980 (Commencement No 2) Order 1980, SI 1980/1353; Transport Act 1980 (Commencement No 3) Order 1980, SI 1980/1424; Transport Act 1980 (Commencement No 4) Order 1981, SI 1981/256

Transport Act 1980 (c 34)—*cont*

s 1–31	Repealed
32(1)–(4)	Repealed
(5)	6 Oct 1980 (SI 1980/1353)
33	Repealed
34	Spent
35–41	Repealed
42	Repealed except for sub-ss (1), (2)(b)(iii), which came into force on 6 Oct 1980 (SI 1980/1353)
43(1)	See Sch 5, Pt II below
(2)	Repealed
44	Repealed
45–50	30 Jun 1980 (s 70(3), but generally of no effect until 1 Oct 1980, the day appointed under s 45(2) by SI 1980/1380)
51(1)	30 Jun 1980 (s 70(3))
(2)	1 Oct 1980 (appointed day under SI 1980/1380)
52	30 Jun 1980 (s 70(3))
52A	Inserted by Railways Act 1993, s 134(1), Sch 11, para 9(2) (qv)
52B–52D	Inserted by Railways Act 1993, s 134(1), Sch 11, para 9(3) (qv)
53–60	30 Jun 1980 (s 70(3))
61	Repealed
62	6 Oct 1980 (SI 1980/1353)
63	Repealed
64	31 Jul 1980 (SI 1980/913)
65	6 Oct 1980 (SI 1980/913)
66–68	30 Jun 1980 (s 70(3))
69	See Sch 9 below
70	30 Jun 1980 (s 70(3))
Sch 1–3	Repealed
4	6 Oct 1980 (SI 1980/913)
5, Pt I	Repealed
II	6 Oct 1980 (amendments of Local Government (Miscellaneous Provisions) Act 1953; Transport Act 1962; Road Traffic Act 1972; Road Traffic (Foreign Vehicles) Act 1972 (paras 1(b), 2 only); Local Government (Miscellaneous Provisions) Act 1976 (para 2 only); Energy Act 1976 (sub-paras (a) and (c) only)) (SI 1980/913)
	1 Apr 1981 (amendments of Road Traffic (Foreign Vehicles) Act 1972 (paras 1(a), 3); Road Traffic Act 1974; Local Government (Miscellaneous Provisions) Act 1976 (para 1); Energy Act 1976 (sub-para (b))) (SI 1981/256)
	Remainder repealed
6	30 Jun 1980 (s 70(3); but not generally effective until 1 Oct 1980, the date appointed under s 45(2) by SI 1980/1380)
7	1 Oct 1980 (appointed day under SI 1980/1380)
8	30 Jun 1980 (s 70(3))
9, Pt I	31 Jul 1980 (repeals of Road Traffic Act 1960, ss 144, 145(1), 147(1)(d), 154, 155, 158, 160(1)(f), 163(1); Transport (London) Act 1969, s 24(2), (3); Local Government (Scotland) Act 1973, Sch 18, para 30; Road Traffic Act 1974, Sch 6, para 2;

Transport Act 1980 (c 34)—*cont*

Sch 9, Pt I—*cont*	Energy Act 1976, Sch 1, para 2) (SI 1980/913)
	6 Oct 1980 (repeals of Education (Miscellaneous Provisions) Act 1953, s 12; Transport Charges &c (Miscellaneous Provisions) Act 1954, s 2, Sch 1; Public Service Vehicles (Travel Concessions) Act 1955, s 1(7); Local Government (Omnibus Shelters and Queue Barriers) (Scotland) Act 1958, s 7(1); Road Traffic Act 1960, ss 117, 118, 119(3)(a), 128(2), 134-139, 139A, 140, 143(1)–(3), (4), (9) (in so far as relate to road service licences), 149, 156(1), 160 (repeals in heads (a) and (c)), 234, 240, 247(2), 257(1), (definition of 'road service licence'), 258, Schs 12, 17; Transport Act 1962, Sch 2, Part I; London Government Act 1963, ss 9(6)(b), 14(6)(d), Sch 5, Part I, para 25; Finance Act 1965, s 92(8); Road Traffic Regulation Act 1967, s 1(3), Sch 6; Transport Act 1968, ss 21(1), 30, 138(1)(a), (3)(a), 145(1), 159(1); Transport (London) Act 1969, ss 23(6), (7), 24(4)(b), (d), Sch 3, paras 8, 11; Tribunals and Inquiries Act 1971, s 13(5), (6)(a), Sch 1, para 30(a) (in so far as relate to road service licences); European Communities Act 1972, Sch 4, para 10; Local Government Act 1972, s 186(3); Local Government (Scotland) Act 1973, Sch 18, paras 26, 31–35; Road Traffic Act 1974, Sch 5, Part I (except the entries relating to Road Traffic Act 1960, ss 127, 128(3), 132(3), 148(2), 239), Sch 6, para 1, Sch 7; Transport Act 1978, ss 6, 7(1), (2), 8, Schs 1, 2) (SI 1980/1353)
	1 Apr 1981 (repeal of Road Traffic Act 1960, ss 127, 129, 130(2), 132, 133, 133A, 143 (so far as unrepealed), 153(2), 257(1) (definition of 'owner'); Transport Act 1968, s 35(1), (2), (3)(a); Tribunals and Inquiries Act 1971, s 13(5), (6)(a), Sch 1, para 30(a) (so far as unrepealed); Road Traffic Act 1972, s 44(4); Road Traffic Act 1974, Sch 2, paras 1, 3–5, Sch 5, Pt I (entries relating to Road Traffic Act 1960, ss 127, 128(3), 132(2)); Transport Act 1978, s 5(10)) (SI 1981/256)
II	30 Jun 1980 (s70(3))
III	1 Oct 1980 (date appointed by SI 1980/1380)
IV	1 Apr 1981 (SI 1981/256)

Water (Scotland) Act 1980 (c 45)

RA: 1 Aug 1980

1 Aug 1980 (RA)

1981

Acquisition of Land Act 1981 (c 67)

RA: 30 Oct 1981

Commencement provisions: s 35(2)

30 Jan 1982 (s 35(2))

Animal Health Act 1981 (c 22)

RA: 11 Jun 1981

Commencement provisions: s 97(3)

11 Jul 1981 (s 97(3))

Appropriation Act 1981 (c 51)

Whole Act repealed

Armed Forces Act 1981 (c 55)

RA: 28 Jul 1981

Commencement provisions: ss 1(5), 29(1)–(3), (5), Sch 5, Pt II, para 1; Armed Forces Act 1981 (Commencement No 1) Order 1981, SI 1981/1503; Armed Forces Act 1981 (Commencement No 2) Order 1982, SI 1982/497

s 1	Repealed
2–5	1 May 1982 (SI 1982/497)
6	1 Nov 1981 (SI 1981/1503)
7	28 Jul 1981 (s 29(4))
8	1 May 1982 (SI 1982/497)
9	Repealed
10–13	1 May 1982 (SI 1982/497)
14	1 May 1982 (SI 1982/497); prospectively repealed by Armed Forces Act 1991, ss 19(7), 26(2), Sch 3[1]
15–17	28 Jul 1981 (s 29(4))
18	1 May 1982 (SI 1982/497)
19–22	28 Jul 1981 (s 29(4))
23, 24	1 May 1982 (SI 1982/497)
25–27	28 Jul 1981 (s 29(4))
28(1)	1 May 1982 (SI 1982/497)
(2)	28 Jul 1981 (s 29(4))
29, 30	28 Jul 1981 (s 29(4))
Sch 1, 2	1 May 1982 (SI 1982/497)
3	28 Jul 1981 (s 29(4))

Armed Forces Act 1981 (c 55)—*cont*

Sch 4	1 May 1982 (SI 1982/497)
5, Pt I	28 Jul 1982 (s 29(5), Sch 5, para 2)
II	28 Jul 1982 (repeals of or in Naval Agency and Distribution Act 1864, s 17; Naval and Marine Pay and Pensions Act 1865, s 12; Army Pensions Act 1914; Naval Discipline Act 1957, s 93; Armed Forces Act 1976, Sch 9) (s 29(5), Sch 5, para 1)
	1 Sep 1981 (repeal of Armed Forces Act 1976, s 1) (s 29(5), Sch 5, para 2)
	1 May 1982 (repeals of or in Greenwich Hospital Act 1885, s 4; Colonial Naval Defence Act 1931, s 2(1); Colonial Naval Defence Act 1949, s 1(4); Army Act 1955, ss 82(2)(b), 99(2), 131(2), 153(3), 209(3), Sch 7, para 6; Air Force Act 1955, ss 82(2)(b), 99(2), 131(2), 153(3), 209(3); Naval Discipline Act 1957, ss 51(1), (2), 101(2); Army and Air Force Act 1961, s 26(3); Criminal Justice (Scotland) Act 1963, s 9(3), (4); Armed Forces Act 1976, Sch 9, para 12) (s 29(1); SI 1982/497)

[1] Any order made under Armed Forces Act 1991, s 27(2), (3), bringing the prospective repeal into force will be noted to that Act in the service to this work

Atomic Energy (Miscellaneous Provisions) Act 1981 (c 48)

RA: 27 Jul 1981

27 Jul 1981 (RA)

Belize Act 1981 (c 52)

RA: 28 Jul 1981

Commencement provisions: s 6(2); Belize Independence Order 1981, SI 1981/1107

21 Sep 1981 (Independence Day; SI 1981/1107)

Betting and Gaming Duties Act 1981 (c 63)

RA: 30 Oct 1981

30 Oct 1981 (RA)

British Nationality Act 1981 (c 61)

RA: 30 Oct 1981

Commencement provisions: s 53(2), (3); British Nationality Act 1981 (Commencement) Order 1982, SI 1982/933

s 1–48	1 Jan 1983 (SI 1982/933)
49	Repealed
50–52	1 Jan 1983 (SI 1982/933)
53	30 Oct 1981 (s 53(3))
Sch 1–9	1 Jan 1983 (SI 1982/933)

British Telecommunications Act 1981 (c 38)

RA: 27 Jul 1981

27 Jul 1981 (RA; note, however, that many provisions of the Act did not come into force until 1 Oct 1981, the date appointed by British Telecommunications Act 1981 (Appointed Day) Order 1981, SI 1981/1274, made under s 1(2) (repealed))

Broadcasting Act 1981 (c 68)

Whole Act repealed

Companies Act 1981 (c 62)

Whole Act repealed

Consolidated Fund Act 1981 (c 4)

Whole Act repealed

Consolidated Fund (No 2) Act 1981 (c 70)

Whole Act repealed

Compulsory Purchase (Vesting Declarations) Act 1981 (c 66)

RA: 30 Oct 1981

Commencement provisions: s 17(2)

30 Jan 1982 (s 17(2))

Contempt of Court Act 1981 (c 49)

RA: 27 Jul 1981

Commencement provisions: s 21(2), (3)

27 Aug 1981 (s 21(3) with the exception of the provisions relating to legal aid (namely, s 13, Sch 2, Pts I, II) which, in relation to EW, S, were *not in force* and are now repealed)

Countryside (Scotland) Act 1981 (c 44)

RA: 27 Jul 1981

Commencement provisions: s 18(2); Countryside (Scotland) Act 1981 (Commencement) Order 1981, SI 1981/1614

s 1	1 Apr 1982 (SI 1981/1614)
2–4	5 Nov 1981 (SI 1981/1614)
5	Repealed
6–14	5 Nov 1981 (SI 1981/1614)
15	See Sch 2 below
16–18	5 Nov 1981 (SI 1981/1614)
Sch 1	5 Nov 1981 (SI 1981/1614)
2	5 Nov 1981 (except repeal of Countryside (Scotland) Act 1967, ss 67, 68) (SI 1981/1614) 1 Apr 1982 (exception noted above) (SI 1981/1614)

Criminal Attempts Act 1981 (c 47)

RA: 27 Jul 1981

Commencement provisions: s 11(1)

27 Aug 1981 (s 11(1))

Criminal Justice (Amendment) Act 1981 (c 27)

RA: 2 Jul 1981

Commencement provisions: s 2(2)

2 Oct 1981 (s 2(2))

Deep Sea Mining (Temporary Provisions) Act 1981 (c 53)

RA: 28 Jul 1981

Commencement provisions: s 18(2); Deep Sea Mining (Temporary Provisions) Act 1981 (Appointed Day) Order 1982, SI 1982/52

25 Jan 1982 (SI 1982/52)

Disabled Persons Act 1981 (c 43)

RA: 27 Jul 1981

Commencement provisions: ss 6(6), 9(2)

s 1	27 Oct 1981 (s 9(2))
2, 3	Repealed
4, 5	27 Oct 1981 (s 9(2))
6	*Not in force*
7–9	27 Oct 1981 (s 9(2))

Disused Burial Grounds (Amendment) Act 1981 (c 18)

RA: 21 May 1981

21 May 1981 (RA)

Education Act 1981 (c 60)

RA: 31 Jul 1981

Commencement provisions: s 20(2); Education Act 1981 (Commencement No 1) Order 1981, SI 1981/1711; Education Act 1981 (Commencement No 2) Order 1983, SI 1983/7

Whole Act except ss 2(1), 11(1), 17, the definition of 'principal Act' in s 20(1), ss 20(2), (3), 21, Sch 2, para 1, Sch 3 paras 3, 4, 6, 7, 8(1), (2)(b), (d), 11, 12, 14, Sch 4, *repealed* by Education Act 1993, 307(1), (3), Sch 19, para 82, Sch 21, Pt I (qv)

s 1	Repealed
2(1)	1 Apr 1983 (SI 1983/7)
(2)–(7)	Repealed
3–10	Repealed
11(1)	1 Apr 1983 (SI 1983/7) (spent)
(2), (3)	Repealed
12–16	Repealed
17	1 Apr 1983 (SI 1983/7)
18, 19	Repealed
20(1)	5 Jan 1982 (SI 1981/1711); repealed other than definition of 'principal Act'
(2), (3)	5 Jan 1982 (SI 1981/1711)
21(1), (2)	5 Jan 1982 (SI 1981/1711)
(3), (4)	1 Apr 1983 (SI 1983/7)
(5)	5 Jan 1982 (SI 1981/1711)
Sch 1	Repealed
2, para 1	1 Apr 1983 (SI 1983/7)
2–8	Repealed
3, para 1, 2	Repealed
3, 4	1 Apr 1983 (SI 1983/7)
5	Repealed
6–8	1 Apr 1983 (SI 1983/7)
9, 10	Repealed
11, 12	1 Apr 1983 (SI 1983/7)
13	Repealed
14	1 Apr 1983 (SI 1983/7)
15, 16	Repealed
4	1 Apr 1983 (SI 1983/7)

Education (Scotland) Act 1981 (c 58)

RA: 30 Oct 1981

Commencement provisions: s 22(2), (3); Education (Scotland) Act 1981 (Commencement No 1) Order 1981, SI 1981/1557; Education (Scotland) Act 1981 (Commencement No 2) Order 1982, SI 1982/951; Education (Scotland) Act 1981 (Commencement No 3) Order 1982, SI 1982/1737; Education (Scotland) Act 1981 (Commencement No 4) Order 1983, SI 1983/371

Education (Scotland) Act 1981 (c 58)—*cont*

s 1(1)	15 Feb 1982 (so far as inserts Education (Scotland) Act 1980, ss 28A, 28B (except s 28B(1)(d)), and s 28G so far as relates to those sections) (SI 1981/1557)
	15 Mar 1982 (so far as inserts Education (Scotland) Act 1980, ss 28C, 28D, 28E (except s 28E(2)), 28F and s 28G so far as relates to those sections) (SI 1981/1557)
	1 Jan 1983 (so far as inserts Education (Scotland) Act 1980, ss 28B(1)(d), 28E(2)) (SI 1982/951)
	9 Mar 1983 (so far as inserts Education (Scotland) Act 1980, s 28G so far as relates to ss 28B(1)(d), 28E(2) and Sch A1) (SI 1983/371)
	5 Apr 1983 (so far as inserts Education (Scotland) Act 1980, s 28H) (SI 1982/1737)
(2)	15 Mar 1982 (SI 1981/1557)
(3), (4)	15 Feb 1982 (SI 1981/1557)
2	15 Feb 1982 (SI 1981/1557)
3, 4	1 Jan 1983 (SI 1982/951)
5	16 Aug 1982 (SI 1982/951)
6–8	1 Dec 1981 (SI 1981/1557)
9–12	30 Oct 1981 (SI 1981/1557)
13(1)–(7)	1 Jan 1982 (SI 1981/1557)
(8)	16 Aug 1982 (SI 1982/951)
14	1 Jan 1982 (SI 1981/1557)
15	10 Nov 1981 (SI 1981/1557)
16	1 Jan 1983 (SI 1982/1737)
17–20	30 Oct 1981 (SI 1981/1557)
21(1)	See Sch 7 below
(2)	See Sch 8 below
(3)	See Sch 9 below
22	30 Oct 1981 (SI 1981/1557)
Sch 1	15 Mar 1982 (SI 1981/1557)
2, 3	1 Jan 1983 (SI 1982/951)
4	16 Aug 1982 (SI 1982/951)
5	1 Jan 1982 (SI 1981/1557)
6	10 Nov 1981 (SI 1981/1557)
7, para 1–3	30 Oct 1981 (SI 1981/1557)
4	1 Dec 1981 (SI 1981/1557)
5	30 Oct 1981 (SI 1981/1557)
6	15 Feb 1982 (so far as relates to Education (Scotland) Act 1980, ss 50, 51) (SI 1981/1557)
	1 Jan 1983 (so far as relates to Education (Scotland) Act 1980, ss 1(5)(c), (d), 28A(1) (as it has effect under the 1980 Act, Sch A2), 60–65F) (SI 1982/951)
7	15 Feb 1982 (SI 1981/1557)
8, para 1	1 Jan 1983 (SI 1982/951)
2	15 Feb 1982 (SI 1981/1557)
3	15 Mar 1982 (SI 1981/1557)
4	1 Jan 1983 (SI 1982/951)
5	30 Oct 1981 (SI 1981/1557)
6	1 Jan 1982 (SI 1981/1557)
7	30 Oct 1981 (SI 1981/1557)

Education (Scotland) Act 1981 (c 58)—*cont*

Sch 9	30 Oct 1981 (repeals of or in Education (Scotland) Act 1980, ss 98(1), 132(1), Sch 2, paras 1, 3, 4) (SI 1981/1557) 10 Nov 1981 (repeals of or in Education (Scotland) Act 1980, ss 104(2), 105(5), 108(2), 110(3), 111(1), (2), (3), (4), (5), 112(6), 113, 114(1), 115, 116, 117 (proviso), 121(b)) (SI 1981/1557) 1 Dec 1981 (repeals of or in Education (Scotland) Act 1980, ss 7(1)(c), (8), 17(1), 22(1), (4), proviso (ii), 29) (SI 1981/1557) 1 Jan 1982 (repeals in Education (Scotland) Act 1980, s 129(3), (4)(e), (5)) (SI 1981/1557) 15 Feb 1982 (repeals of or in Education (Scotland) Act 1980, ss 23(2), proviso, 28(2)) (SI 1981/1557) 16 Aug 1982 (repeal of Education (Scotland) Act 1980, s 129(6)) (SI 1982/951) 1 Jan 1983 (repeals of or in Education (Scotland) Act 1980, ss 4(b), (c), 5, 59, 135(1)) (SI 1982/951) 1 Jan 1983 (repeal of Education (Scotland) Act 1980, s 66(2)) (SI 1982/1737)

Employment and Training Act 1981 (c 57)

RA: 31 Jul 1981

Commencement provisions: s 11(3); Employment and Training Act 1981 (Commencement) Order 1982, SI 1982/126

s 1–8	Repealed
9–11	31 Jul 1981 (RA)
Sch 1	Repealed
2	31 Jul 1981 (RA)
3	31 Jul 1981 (except entry relating to Industrial Training Act 1964, Schedule) (RA) 1 Apr 1982 (entry relating to Industrial Training Act 1964, Schedule, except for the purposes of specified industrial training boards, but note whole of 1964 Act except s 16 was repealed as from 29 Jun 1982, except as applied to agricultural training boards) (SI 1982/126)

Energy Conservation Act 1981 (c 17)

RA: 21 May 1981

21 May 1981 (RA)

English Industrial Estates Corporation Act 1981 (c 13)

Whole Act repealed

European Parliamentary Elections Act 1981 (c 8)

RA: 19 Mar 1981

19 Mar 1981 (RA)

Film Levy Finance Act 1981 (c 16)

Whole Act repealed

Finance Act 1981 (c 35)

Budget day: 10 Mar 1981

RA: 27 Jul 1981

See the note about Finance Acts at the front of this book

Fisheries Act 1981 (c 29)

RA: 2 Jul 1981

Commencement provisions: s 46(3), (4); Fisheries Act 1981 (Commencement No 1) Order 1981, SI 1981/1357; Fisheries Act 1981 (Commencement No 2) Order 1981, SI 1981/1640

s 1–14	1 Oct 1981 (SI 1981/1357)
15–30	2 Aug 1981 (s 46(3))
31	18 Nov 1981 (SI 1981/1640)
32–45	2 Aug 1981 (s 46(3))
46	2 Aug 1981 (generally) (s 46(3)) 1 Oct 1981 (for the purposes of Sch 5, Pt I) (SI 1981/1357)
Sch 1–3	1 Oct 1981 (SI 1981/1357)
4	2 Aug 1981 (s 46(3))
5, Pt I	1 Oct 1981 (SI 1981/1357)
II	2 Aug 1981 (s 46(3))

Food and Drugs (Amendment) Act 1981 (c 26)

Whole Act repealed

Forestry Act 1981 (c 39)

RA: 27 Jul 1981

27 Jul 1981 (RA)

Forgery and Counterfeiting Act 1981 (c 45)

RA: 27 Jul 1981

Commencement provisions: s 33

28 Oct 1981 (s 33)

Friendly Societies Act 1981 (c 50)

RA: 27 Jul 1981

27 Jul 1981 (RA)

Gas Levy Act 1981 (c 3)

RA: 19 Mar 1981

19 Mar 1981 (RA)

Horserace Betting Levy Act 1981 (c 30)

RA: 2 Jul 1981

2 Jul 1981 (RA)

House of Commons Members' Fund and Parliamentary Pensions Act 1981 (c 7)

RA: 19 Mar 1981

19 Mar 1981 (RA)

Housing (Amendment) (Scotland) Act 1981 (c 72)

Whole Act repealed

Indecent Displays (Control) Act 1981 (c 42)

RA: 27 Jul 1981

Commencement provisions: s 5(5)

27 Oct 1981 (s 5(5))

Industrial Diseases (Notification) Act 1981 (c 25)

RA: 2 Jul 1981

2 Jul 1981 (RA)

Industry Act 1981 (c 6)

RA: 19 Mar 1981

Commencement provisions: s 7(2)

s 1	Repealed
2(1)–(3)	Repealed
(4)	19 Mar 1981 (RA)
3, 4	19 Mar 1981 (RA)
5, 6	Repealed
7	19 Mar 1981 (RA)
Schedule	19 Mar 1981 (RA)

Insurance Companies Act 1981 (c 31)

RA: 2 Jul 1981

Commencement provisions: s 37(1) (repealed); Insurance Companies Act 1981 (Commencement) Order 1981, SI 1981/1657

1 Jan 1982 (SI 1981/1657)

Whole Act repealed except ss 36(1), 38, Sch 4, Pt II (which make minor and consequential amendments)

International Organisations Act 1981 (c 9)

RA: 15 Apr 1981

15 Apr 1981 (RA)

Iron and Steel Act 1981 (c 46)

Whole Act repealed

Iron and Steel (Borrowing Powers) Act 1981 (c 2)

Whole Act repealed

Judicial Pensions Act 1981 (c 20)

RA: 21 May 1981

Commencement provisions: s 37(2)

21 Jun 1981 (s 37(2))

Licensing (Alcohol Education and Research) Act 1981 (c 28)

RA: 2 Jul 1981

Commencement provisions: s 13(3); Licensing (Alcohol Education and Research) Act 1981 (Commencement) Order 1981, SI 1981/1324

1 Oct 1981 (SI 1981/1324)

Licensing (Amendment) Act 1981 (c 40)

RA: 27 Jul 1981

Commencement provisions: s 3(2); Licensing (Amendment) Act 1981 (Commencement) Order 1982, SI 1982/1383

1 Oct 1982 (SI 1982/1383)

Local Government and Planning (Amendment) Act 1981 (c 41)

Whole Act repealed

Local Government (Miscellaneous Provisions) (Scotland) Act 1981 (c 23)

RA: 11 Jun 1981

Commencement provisions: s 43(2)–(4); Local Government (Miscellaneous Provisions) (Scotland) Act 1981 (Commencement No 1) Order 1981, SI 1981/1402

s 1	11 Jun 1981 (RA)
2–4	Repealed
5	1 Apr 1982 (s 43(3))
6	Repealed
7, 8	1 Apr 1982 (s 43(3))
9, 10	Repealed
11	1 Jan 1982 (s 43(2)); prospectively repealed by Local Government etc (Scotland) Act 1994, s 180(2), Sch 14[1]
12, 13	11 Jun 1981 (RA)
14–23	Repealed
24–26	11 Jun 1981 (RA)
27	11 Jun 1981 (RA); prospectively repealed by Local Government etc (Scotland) Act 1994, s 180(2), Sch 14[1]
28	11 Jun 1981 (RA)
29	1 Oct 1981 (SI 1981/1402)
30–33	11 Jun 1981 (RA)
34, 35	Repealed
36	11 Jun 1981 (RA)
37	*Not in force*
38–40	11 Jun 1981 (RA)
41	See Sch 4 below
42, 43	11 Jun 1981 (RA)
Sch 1–3	11 Jun 1981 (RA)
4	11 Jun 1981 (except repeals of Local Government (Financial Provisions etc) (Scotland) Act 1962, s 4(2); Social Work (Scotland) Act 1968, s 7) (RA)
	1 Oct 1981 (repeal of Social Work (Scotland) Act 1968, s 7) (SI 1981/1402)
	1 Apr 1982 (repeal of Local Government (Financial Provisions etc) (Scotland) Act 1962, s 4(2)) (s 43(3))

[1] Any order made under Local Government etc (Scotland) Act 1994, s 184(2), (3), bringing the prospective repeal into force will be noted to that Act in the service to this work

---

Matrimonial Homes and Property Act 1981 (c 24)

RA: 2 Jul 1981

Commencement provisions: s 9; Matrimonial Homes and Property Act 1981 (Commencement No 1) Order 1981, SI 1981/1275; Matrimonial Homes and Property Act 1981 (Commencement No 2) Order 1983, SI 1983/50

Matrimonial Homes and Property Act 1981 (c 24)—*cont*

s 1–3	Repealed
4(1)	14 Feb 1983 (SI 1983/50)
(2)–(4)	Repealed
5, 6	Repealed
7–9	1 Oct 1981 (SI 1981/1275)
10(1)	1 Oct 1981 (SI 1981/1275)
(2)	14 Feb 1983 (SI 1983/50)
(3)	1 Oct 1981 (SI 1981/1275)
Sch 1, 2	Repealed
3	14 Feb (SI 1983/50)

Matrimonial Homes (Family Protection) (Scotland) Act 1981 (c 59)

RA: 30 Oct 1981

Commencement provisions: s 23(3); Matrimonial Homes (Family Protection) (Scotland) Act 1981 (Commencement) Order 1982, SI 1982/972

s 1–9	1 Sep 1982 (SI 1982/972)
10	Repealed
11–22	1 Sep 1982 (SI 1982/972)
23	30 Oct 1981 (RA)

Merchant Shipping Act 1981 (c 10)

Whole Act repealed

National Film Finance Corporation Act 1981 (c 15)

Whole Act repealed

New Towns Act 1981 (c 64)

RA: 30 Oct 1981

Commencement provisions: s 82(4)

30 Nov 1981 (s 82(4))

Nuclear Industry (Finance) Act 1981 (c 71)

Whole Act repealed

Parliamentary Commissioner (Consular Complaints) Act 1981 (c 11)

RA: 15 Apr 1981

15 Apr 1981 (RA)

Ports (Financial Assistance) Act 1981 (c 21)

RA: 11 Jun 1981

11 Jun 1981 (RA)

Public Passenger Vehicles Act 1981 (c 14)

RA: 15 Apr 1981

Commencement provisions: s 89(2); Public Passenger Vehicles Act 1981 (Commencement) Order 1981, SI 1981/1387

s 1	30 Oct 1981 (s 89(2); SI 1981/1387)
2	Repealed
3	30 Oct 1981 (s 89(2); SI 1981/1387)
4, 5	Substituted by Transport Act 1985, s 3(2) (qv)
6	30 Oct 1981 (s 89(2); SI 1981/1387)
7	Repealed
8(1), (1A), (2)	Repealed
(3)	30 Oct 1981 (s 89(2); SI 1981/1837)
9	Repealed
9A	Inserted by Transport Act 1985, s 33 (qv)
10–14	30 Oct 1981 (s 89(2); SI 1981/1387)
14A	Inserted by Transport Act 1985, s 25 (qv)
15–17	30 Oct 1981 (s 89(2); SI 1981/1387)
17A	Inserted by Transport Act 1985, s 5 (qv)
18–21	30 Oct 1981 (s 89(2); SI 1981/1387)
22–23A	Repealed
24–26	30 Oct 1981 (s 89(2); SI 1981/1387)
27, 28	Repealed
29	30 Oct 1981 (s 89(2); SI 1981/1387)
30–45	Repealed
46	30 Oct 1981 (s 89(2); SI 1981/1387)
47–49	Repealed
49A	Inserted by Deregulation and Contracting Out Act 1994, s 65(1) (qv)
50, 51	Substituted by Transport Act 1985, s 31 (qv)
52, 53	30 Oct 1981 (s 89(2); SI 1981/1387)
54	Substituted by Transport Act 1985, s 4 (qv)
55, 56	30 Oct 1981 (s 89(2); SI 1981/1387)
56A	Inserted by Deregulation and Contracting Out Act 1994, s 65(3) (qv)
57–61	30 Oct 1981 (s 89(2); SI 1981/1387)
62, 63	Repealed
64–66	30 Oct 1981 (s 89(2); SI 1981/1387)
66A	Prospectively inserted by Transport Act 1982, s 24(4)[1]
67–89	30 Oct 1981 (s 89(2); SI 1981/1387)
Sch 1	30 Oct 1981 (s 89(2); SI 1981/1387)
2	Substituted by Transport Act 1985, s 3(3), Sch 2, Pt I (qv)
3	30 Oct 1981 (s 89(2); SI 1981/1387)
4, 5	Repealed
6–8	30 Oct 1981 (s 89(2); SI 1981/1387)

[1] Any order made under Transport Act 1982, s 76(2), bringing the prospective insertion into force will be noted to that Act in the service to this work

---

Redundancy Fund Act 1981 (c 5)

Whole Act repealed

Representation of the People Act 1981 (c 34)

RA: 2 Jul 1981

2 Jul 1981 (RA)

Social Security Act 1981 (c 33)

RA: 2 Jul 1981

Commencement provisions: s 8(3); Social Security Act 1981 Commencement Order 1981, SI 1981/953

s 1–6	Repealed or spent
7	10 Aug 1981 (SI 1981/953)
8(1)	2 Jul 1981 (RA)
(2)	Repealed
(3)	2 Jul 1981 (RA)
(4)	10 Aug 1981 (SI 1981/953)
(5)	Repealed
(6)	2 Jul 1981 (RA)
Sch 1, 2	Repealed

Social Security (Contributions) Act 1981 (c 1)

Whole Act repealed

Statute Law (Repeals) Act 1981 (c 19)

RA: 21 May 1981

21 May 1981 (RA)

Supreme Court Act 1981 (c 54)

RA: 28 Jul 1981

Commencement provisions: s 153(2), (3)

s 1–28	1 Jan 1982 (s 153(2))
28A	Inserted by Statute Law (Repeals) Act 1993, s 1(2), Sch 2, para 9 (qv)
29–32	1 Jan 1982 (s 153(2))
32A	Inserted by Administration of Justice Act 1982, s 6(1) (qv)
33–35	1 Jan 1982 (s 153(2)); repealed so far as apply to county courts
35A	Inserted by Administration of Justice Act 1982, s 15(1), Sch 1, Pt I (qv)
36–40	1 Jan 1982 (s 153(2))
40A	Inserted by Administration of Justice Act 1982, s 55(1), Sch 4, Pt I (qv)
41–43	1 Jan 1982 (s 153(2))
43A	Inserted by Courts and Legal Services Act 1990, s 100 (qv)
44–46	1 Jan 1982 (s 153(2))

Supreme Court Act 1981 (c 54)—*cont*

s 46A	Inserted by Merchant Shipping Act 1995, s 314(2), Sch 13, para 59(1), (4) (qv)
47–50	1 Jan 1982 (s 153(2))
51	Substituted by Courts and Legal Services Act 1990, s 4(1) (qv)
52–56	1 Jan 1982 (s 153(2))
56A, 56B	Inserted by Criminal Justice and Public Order Act 1994, s 52(6), (8), (9) (qv)
57–71	1 Jan 1982 (s 153(2))
72	28 Jul 1981 (s 153(3))
73–82	1 Jan 1982 (s 153(2))
83	Substituted by Courts and Legal Services Act 1990, s 67 (qv)
84–93	1 Jan 1982 (s 153(2))
94	Repealed
95–102	1 Jan 1982 (s 153(2))
103	Repealed
104–125	1 Jan 1982 (s 153(2))
126	1 Jan 1982 (s 153(2)); prospectively repealed by Administration of Justice Act 1982, s 75, Sch 9, Pt I[1]
127–138	1 Jan 1982 (s 153(2))
138A, 138B	Inserted by Statute Law (Repeals) Act 1989, s 1(2), Sch 2, Pt I, para 4 (qv)
139–142	1 Jan 1982 (s 153(2))
143, 144	Repealed
145–148	1 Jan 1982 (s 153(2))
149	Repealed
150, 151	1 Jan 1982 (s 153(2))
152(1)	1 Jan 1982 (s 153(2))
(2)	Spent
(3)–(5)	1 Jan 1982 (s 153(2))
153	28 Jul 1981 (s 153(3))
Sch 1	1 Jan 1982 (s 153(2))
2	Substituted by Courts and Legal Services Act 1990, s 71(2), Sch 10, para 49 (qv)
3	Repealed
4–7	1 Jan 1982 (s 153(2))

[1] Any order made under Administration of Justice Act 1982, s 76(5), (6), bringing the prospective repeal into force will be noted to that Act in the service to this work

Town and Country Planning (Minerals) Act 1981 (c 36)

Whole Act repealed or spent

Transport Act 1962 (Amendment) Act 1981 (c 32)

Whole Act repealed

Transport Act 1981 (c 56)

RA: 31 Jul 1981

Commencement provisions: ss 5, 15(1), (2), 18(3), 31 (repealed), 32(2), 35(5), 40(4); Transport Act 1981 (Commencement No 1) Order 1981, SI 1981/1331; Transport

Transport Act 1981 (c 56)—*cont*

Act 1981 (Dissolution of National Ports Council) (Appointed Day) Order 1981, SI 1981/1364; Transport Act 1981 (Commencement No 2) Order 1981, SI 1981/1617; Transport Act 1981 (Dissolution of National Ports Council) (Final) Order 1981, SI 1981/1665; Transport Act 1981 (Commencement No 3) Order 1982, SI 1982/300; Transport Act 1981 (Commencement No 4) Order 1982, SI 1982/310; Transport Act 1981 (Commencement No 5) Order 1982, SI 1982/866; Transport Act 1981 (Commencement No 6) Order 1982, SI 1982/1341; Transport Act 1981 (Commencement No 7) Order 1982, SI 1982/1451; Transport Act 1981 (Commencement No 8) Order 1982, SI 1982/1803; Transport Act 1981 (Commencement No 9) Order 1983, SI 1983/576; Transport Act 1981 (Commencement No 10) Order 1983, SI 1983/930; Transport Act 1981 (Commencement No 11) Order 1983, SI 1983/1089; Transport Act 1981 (Commencement No 12) Order 1988, SI 1988/1037; Transport Act 1981 (Commencement No 13) Order 1988, SI 1988/1170

s 1–4	Repealed
5	31 Jul 1981 (RA)
	31 Dec 1982 (appointed day for reconstitution of the British Transport Docks Board (s 5; SI 1982/1887)
6–15	31 Jul 1981 (RA)
	1 Oct 1981 (date on which the functions of the National Ports Council were determined) (s 15(1); SI 1981/1364)
	1 Dec 1981 (date on which the National Ports Council was dissolved) (s 15(2); SI 1981/1665)
16, 17	31 Jul 1981 (RA)
18	See Sch 6 below
19–31	Repealed
32	25 Aug 1983 (EW) (s 32(2); SI 1983/1089); repealed (S)
33, 34	Repealed
35(1), (2)	1 Apr 1982 (s 35(5); SI 1982/310)
(3)	12 Oct 1981 (s 35(5); SI 1981/1331)
(3A)	Prospectively inserted by Local Government (Wales) Act 1994, s 22(1), Sch 7, Pt II, para 37[1]
(4), (5)	12 Oct 1981 (s 35(5); SI 1981/1331)
36	Repealed
37–43	31 Jul 1981 (RA)
Sch 1	Repealed
2–5	31 Jul 1981 (RA)
6, para 1–9	1 Oct 1981 (s 18(2); SI 1981/1364)
10	2 Aug 1983 (s 18(3); SI 1983/930)
11–15	1 Oct 1981 (s 18(2); SI 1981/1364)
7, 8	Repealed
9, para 1–24	Repealed
25	6 May 1983 (s 31; SI 1983/576)
10	25 Aug 1983 (EW) (s 32(2); SI 1983/1089); repealed (S)
11	Repealed
12, Pt I	31 Dec 1982 (ss 5(4), 40(2))
II	1 Oct 1981 (except repeal of entry for National Ports Council in House of Commons Disqualification Act 1975, Sch 1, Pt II) (ss 5(3), 15(1))
	1 Dec 1981 (exception noted above) (s 15(1))

Transport Act 1981 (c 56)—*cont*

Sch 12, Pt III	31 Jul 1981 (repeals of or in Railway Fires Act (1905) Amendment Act 1923; Public Passenger Vehicles Act 1981) (s 40(4))
	12 Oct 1981 (repeal of Town Police Clauses Act 1847, s 39) (s 40(4); SI 1981/1331)
	1 Apr 1982 (repeal in Metropolitan Public Carriage Act 1869) (s 40(4); SI 1982/310)
	1 Nov 1982 (repeals of or in Road Traffic Act 1972, ss 93(3), (5), 177(2)) (s 40(4); SI 1982/1451)
	6 May 1983 (repeals of or in Road Traffic Act 1972, ss 89, 90, 189, Sch 4, Pt V, para 1) (s 40(4); SI 1983/576)
	25 Aug 1983 (repeal of entry relating to Road Traffic Act 1974, s 17) (EW) (s 40(4); SI 1983/1089)
	Not in force (repeals of or in Road Traffic Act 1974, Sch 3; British Railways (No 2) Act 1975, s 21; London Transport Act 1977, s 13(1); British Railways Act 1977, s 14(1); Criminal Justice (Scotland) Act 1980, Sch 7, para 22)

[1] Any order made under Local Government (Wales) Act 1994, s 66(2), bringing the prospective insertion into force will be noted to that Act in the service to this work

---

Trustee Savings Banks Act 1981 (c 65)

Whole Act repealed

Water Act 1981 (c 12)

RA: 15 Apr 1981

Commencement provisions: ss 2(5), 6(8); Water Act 1981 (Commencement No 1) Order 1981, SI 1981/1755

s 1	15 Apr 1981 (RA)
2–6	Repealed
7	15 Apr 1981 (RA)

Wildlife and Countryside Act 1981 (c 69)

RA: 30 Oct 1981

Commencement provisions: s 74(2), (3); Wildlife and Countryside Act 1981 (Commencement No 1) Order 1982, SI 1982/44; Wildlife and Countryside Act 1981 (Commencement No 2) Order 1982, SI 1982/327; Wildlife and Countryside Act 1981 (Commencement No 3) Order 1982, SI 1982/990; Wildlife and Countryside Act 1981 (Commencement No 4) Order 1982, SI 1982/1136; Wildlife and Countryside Act 1981 (Commencement No 5) Order 1982, SI 1982/1217; Wildlife and Countryside Act 1981 (Commencement No 6) Order 1983, SI 1983/20; Wildlife and Countryside Act 1981 (Commencement No 7) Order 1983, SI 1983/87

s 1–11	28 Sep 1982 (SI 1982/1217)
12	16 Feb 1982 (SI 1982/44)
13–19	28 Sep 1982 (SI 1982/1217)

Wildlife and Countryside Act 1981 (c 69)—*cont*

s 19A	Inserted (S) by Prisoners and Criminal Proceedings (Scotland) Act 1993, s 36 (qv)
20–27	28 Sep 1982 (SI 1982/1217)
27A	Inserted by Environmental Protection Act 1990, s 132, Sch 9, para 11(8) (qv)
28	30 Nov 1981 (s 74(2))
29–31	6 Sep 1982 (SI 1982/1136)
32	28 Feb 1983 (SI 1983/87)
33–37	30 Nov 1981 (s 74(2))
38	Repealed
39, 40	30 Nov 1981 (s 74(2))
41	28 Feb 1983 (SI 1983/87)
42–45	30 Nov 1981 (s 74(2))
46	19 Aug 1982 (SI 1982/990); prospectively repealed by Environment Act 1995, s 120(3), Sch 24[1]
47	1 Apr 1982 (SI 1982/327)
48	Repealed
49–52	30 Nov 1981 (s 74(2))
53–59	28 Feb 1983 (SI 1983/20)
60, 61	Repealed
62–66	28 Feb 1983 (SI 1983/20)
67–70	30 Nov 1981 (s 74(2))
70A	Inserted by Wildlife and Countryside (Service of Notices) Act 1985 s 1(1) (qv)
71	30 Nov 1981 (s 74(2))
72(1)	Repealed
(2), (3)	30 Nov 1981 (s 74(2))
(4)	28 Sep 1982 (SI 1982/1217)
(5)	30 Nov 1981 (s 74(2))
(6)	28 Sep 1982 (SI 1982/1217)
(7)–(9)	30 Nov 1981 (s 74(2))
(10)	30 Nov 1981 (s 74(2)); prospectively repealed by Environment Act 1995, s 120(3), Sch 24[1]
(11)–(13)	30 Nov 1981 (s 74(2))
(14)	28 Sep 1982 (SI 1982/1217)
73(1)	See Sch 17
(2), (3)	30 Nov 1981 (s 74(2))
(4)	Repealed
74	30 Nov 1981 (s 74(2))
Sch 1–6	28 Sep 1982 (SI 1982/1217)
7	16 Feb 1982 (SI 1982/44)
8–10	28 Sep 1982 (SI 1982/1217)
11	30 Nov 1981 (so far as relates to orders under s 34) (s 74(2)) 6 Sep 1982 (so far as relates to orders under s 29) (SI 1982/1136)
12	30 Nov 1981 (s 74(2))
13	1 Apr 1982 (SI 1982/327)
14–16	28 Feb 1983 (SI 1983/20)
17, Pt I	30 Nov 1981 (s 74(2))
II	16 Feb 1982 (repeals of or in Deer Act 1963, Sch 2; Conservation of Seals Act 1970, s 10(1); Badgers Act 1973, ss 6, 7, 8(2)(c), 11) (SI 1982/44) 1 Apr 1982 (repeals of or in National Parks and Access to the Countryside Act 1949, ss 2, 4, 95; Countryside Act 1968, s 3) (SI 1982/327)

Wildlife and Countryside Act 1981 (c 69)—*cont*

Sch 17, Pt II—*cont* 28 Sep 1982 (repeals of or in Protection of Animals (Scotland) Act 1912, s 9; Protection of Birds Act 1954 (Amendment) Act 1964; Protection of Birds Act 1967; Countryside Act 1968, s 1; Local Government Act 1972, Sch 29, para 37; Water Act 1973, Sch 8, para 67; Nature Conservancy Council Act 1973, s 5(3), Sch 1, paras 3, 5, 7, 12; Local Government (Scotland) Act 1973, Sch 27, Pt II, paras 115, 168; Criminal Procedure (Scotland) Act 1975, Sch 7C; Conservation of Wild Creatures and Wild Plants Act 1975; Statute Law (Repeals) Act 1976, Sch 2, Pt II; Endangered Species (Import and Export) Act 1976, s 13(6); Criminal Law Act 1977, Sch 6; Customs and Excise Management Act 1979, Sch 4, para 12; Animal Health Act 1981, Sch 5, para 1; Zoo Licensing Act 1981, s 4(5)) (SI 1982/1217)

28 Feb 1983 (repeals of or in National Parks and Access to the Countryside Act 1949, ss 27–35, 38; London Government Act 1963, s 60(1)–(4); Countryside Act 1968, Sch 3; Courts Act 1971, Sch 8, para 31, Sch 9, Pt II; Town and Country Planning Act 1971, Sch 20; Local Government Act 1972, Sch 17; Highways Act 1980, ss 31(10), 340(2)(d)) (SI 1983/20)

[1] Any order(s) made under Environment Act 1995, s 125(3), bringing the prospective repeals into force will be noted to that Act in the service to this work

---

Zoo Licensing Act 1981 (c 37)

RA: 27 Jul 1981

Commencement provisions: s 23(2); Zoo Licensing Act 1981 (Commencement) Order 1984, SI 1984/423

30 Apr 1984 (SI 1984/423)

1982

Administration of Justice Act 1982 (c 53)

RA: 28 Oct 1982

Commencement provisions: s 76; Administration of Justice Act 1982 (Commencement No 1) Order 1983, SI 1983/236; Administration of Justice Act 1982 (Commencement No 2) Order 1984, SI 1984/1142; Administration of Justice Act 1982 (Commencement No 3) Order 1984, SI 1984/1287; Administration of Justice Act 1982 (Commencement No 4) Order 1985, SI 1985/858; Administration of Justice Act 1982 (Commencement No 5) Order 1986, SI 1986/2259; Administration of Justice Act 1982 (Commencement No 6) Order 1991, SI 1991/1245; Administration of Justice Act 1982 (Commencement No 7) Order 1991, SI 1991/1786

s 1–5	1 Jan 1983 (s 76(11))
6	1 Jul 1985 (SI 1985/858)
7–11	1 Jan 1983 (s 76(11))
12	1 Sep 1984 (SI 1984/1287)
13	1 Jan 1983 (s 76(11))
14(1)	1 Jan 1983 (s 76(11))
(2)	1 Sep 1984 (SI 1984/1287)
(3), (4)	1 Jan 1983 (s 76(11))
15, 16	1 Apr 1983 (SI 1983/236)
17–22	1 Jan 1983 (s 76(11))
23–25	*Not in force*
26	1 Jan 1983 (s 76(11))
27, 28	*Not in force*
29–33	Repealed
34	1 Sep 1984 (SI 1984/1142)
35	Spent
36	Repealed
37	1 Jan 1983 (s 76(11))
38–47	2 Jan 1987 (SI 1986/2259)
48	*Not in force*
49–51	1 Jan 1983 (s 76(11))
52	28 Oct 1982 (s 76(9), (10))
53	1 Jan 1983 (s 76(11))
54	1 Apr 1983 (SI 1983/236)
55, 56	1 Jan 1983 (s 76(11))
57	1 Apr 1983 (SI 1983/236)
58, 59	1 Jan 1983 (s 76(11))
60	Repealed
61	1 Jan 1983 (s 76(11))
62	Repealed
63	1 Jan 1983 (s 76(11))
64, 65	28 Oct 1982 (s 76(9), (10))
66, 67	1 Jan 1983 (s 76(11))
68	See Sch 6 below

Administration of Justice Act 1982 (c 53)—*cont*

s 69	1 Jun 1983 (SI 1983/236)
70	See Sch 8 below
71	Repealed
72	1 Jan 1983 (s 76(11))
73(1)–(7)	1 Jan 1983 (s 76(11))
(8)	Spent
(9)	1 Jan 1983 (s 76(11))
74	Repealed
75	See Sch 9 below
76–78	28 Oct 1982 (s 76(9), (10))
Sch 1	1 Apr 1983 (SI 1983/236)
2	*Not in force*
3–5	1 Jan 1983 (s 76(11))
6, para 1–9	1 Jan 1983 (s 76(11))
10	1 Sep 1991 (SI 1991/1786)
7	1 Jun 1983 (SI 1983/236)
8, para 1–5	1 Jan 1983 (s 76(11))
6–8	13 Jun 1991 (SI 1991/1245)
9–12	1 Jan 1983 (s 76(11))
9, Pt I	1 Jan 1983 (except repeals noted below) (s 76(11))
	1 Apr 1983 (repeal in Judicial Trustees Act 1896) (SI 1983/236)
	1 Jun 1983 (repeal of Law Reform (Miscellaneous Provisions) Act (Northern Ireland) 1937, s 17) (SI 1983/236)
	1 Sep 1984 (repeal in County Courts Act 1959, s 148) (SI 1984/1142)
	1 Sep 1984 (repeal in Damages (Scotland) Act 1976) (SI 1984/1287)
	2 Jan 1987 (repeal of County Courts Act 1959, ss 99(3), 168–174A, 176) (SI 1986/2259)
	13 Jun 1991 (repeals of Administration of Justice Act 1965, ss 1–16; Judicature (Northern Ireland) Act 1978, s 83) (SI 1991/1245)
	Not in force (repeals of or in Prevention of Fraud (Investments) Act 1958; Administration of Justice Act 1977; Supreme Court Act 1981, s 126)
II	1 Jan 1983 (revocation of or in SI 1967/761; SI 1977/1251) (s 76(11))
	Not in force (revocation in SI 1979/1575)

Agricultural Training Board Act 1982 (c 9)

RA: 29 Mar 1982

Commencement provisions: s 12(3)

29 Jun 1982 (s 12(3))

Appropriation Act 1982 (c 40)

Whole Act repealed

Aviation Security Act 1982 (c 36)

RA: 23 Jul 1982

Commencement provisions: s 41(2)

23 Oct 1982 (s 41(2))

Canada Act 1982 (c 11)

RA: 29 Mar 1982

29 Mar 1982 (RA)

Children's Homes Act 1982 (c 20)

Whole Act repealed

Cinematograph (Amendment) Act 1982 (c 33)

Whole Act repealed

Civic Government (Scotland) Act 1982 (c 45)

RA: 28 Oct 1982

Commencement provisions: s 137(2)–(4); Civic Government (Scotland) Act 1982 (Commencement) Order 1983, SI 1983/201 (as amended by SI 1984/573, SI 1984/774)

s 1–8	1 Apr 1983 (for purpose only of enabling preliminary arrangements to be made for when provisions fully effective in operation) (SI 1983/201) 1 Jul 1984 (otherwise) (SI 1983/201)
9–23	1 Apr 1983 (for purpose only of enabling preliminary arrangements to be made for when provisions fully effective in operation) (SI 1983/201) 1 Jul 1984 (otherwise, except in relation to areas of local authorities noted below) (SI 1983/201, as amended by SI 1984/744) 2 Aug 1984 (as respects the area of Lochaber District Council) (SI 1984/744) 20 Aug 1984 (as respects the area of the City of Glasgow District Council) (SI 1984/744) 20 Sep 1984 (as respects the area of Wigtown District Council) (SI 1984/744) 1 Nov 1984 (as respects the area of Cunninghame District Council) (SI 1984/744)
24–27	As noted to ss 9–23 above, and in addition: 1 Jan 1985 (as respects the area of Monklands District Council) (SI 1984/744)

Civic Government (Scotland) Act 1982 (c 45)—*cont*

s 28–37	1 Apr 1983 (for purpose only of enabling preliminary arrangements to be made for when provisions fully effective in operation) (SI 1983/201)
	1 Jul 1984 (otherwise) (SI 1983/201)
38–41	As noted to ss 9–23, 24–27 above
41A	Inserted by Fire Safety and Safety of Places of Sport Act 1987, s 44 (qv)
42–44	As noted to ss 9–23, 24–27 above
45–52	1 Apr 1983 (SI 1983/201)
52A	Inserted by Criminal Justice Act 1988, s 161 (qv)
53–61	1 Apr 1983 (SI 1983/201)
62–66	1 Apr 1983 (for purpose only of enabling preliminary arrangements to be made for when provisions fully effective in operation) (SI 1983/201)
	1 Jul 1984 (otherwise) (SI 1983/201)
67–109	1 Apr 1983 (SI 1983/201)
110(1)	1 Apr 1983 (so far as relates to s 110(2)) (SI 1983/201)
	1 Jul 1984 (otherwise) (SI 1983/201)
(2)	1 Apr 1983 (SI 1983/201)
(3)	1 Jul 1984 (SI 1983/201)
111–118	1 Apr 1983 (SI 1983/201)
119	18 Apr 1984 (for purpose only of enabling preliminary arrangements to be made for when provisions fully effective in operation) (SI 1983/201, as amended by SI 1984/573)
	1 Jul 1984 (otherwise) (SI 1983/201)
120–123	1 Apr 1983 (SI 1983/201)
124, 125	1 Apr 1983 (SI 1983/201); repealed (1 Apr 1992) subject to transitional and saving provisions by Environmental Protection Act 1990, s 162(1), (2), Sch 16, Pt II
126(1)	Repealed
(2)	1 Apr 1983 (SI 1983/201)
(3)	Repealed
127	1 Apr (SI 1983/201)
128(1)	Repealed
(2), (3)	1 Apr 1983 (SI 1983/201)
129–133	1 Apr 1983 (SI 1983/201)
134–136	28 Oct 1982 (s 137(2))
137(1)–(6)	28 Oct 1982 (s 137(2))
(7)	See Sch 3 below
(8)	See Sch 4 below
(9)	28 Oct 1982 (s 137(2))
Sch 1	1 Apr 1983 (for purpose only of enabling preliminary arrangements to be made for when provisions fully effective in operation) (SI 1983/201)
	1 Jul 1984 (otherwise) (SI 1983/201)
2	1 Apr 1983 (SI 1983/201)
3, para 1	Repealed
2, 3	1 Apr 1983 (SI 1983/201)
4	Repealed
5	1 Jul 1984 (SI 1983/201)
4	1 Apr 1983 (repeals of or in Vagrancy Act 1824, s 4; Prevention of Crime Act 1871, ss 7, 15; Licensing

Civic Government (Scotland) Act 1982 (c 45)—*cont*

Sch 4—*cont*	(Scotland) Act 1903; Dogs Act 1906, s 3(6), (7); Countryside (Scotland) Act 1967, ss 56, 57(1), (2); Theatres Act 1968, s 2(4)(c); Sexual Offences (Scotland) Act 1976, s 13(3)) (SI 1983/201)
	1 Jul 1984 (otherwise) (SI 1983/201)

Civil Aviation Act 1982 (c 16)

RA: 27 May 1982

Commencement provisions: s 110(2)

27 Aug 1982 (s 110(2))

Civil Aviation (Amendment) Act 1982 (c 1)

RA: 2 Feb 1982

2 Feb 1982 (RA)

Civil Jurisdiction and Judgments Act 1982 (c 27)

RA: 13 Jul 1982

Commencement provisions: s 53(1), Sch 13, Pt I; Civil Jurisdiction and Judgments Act 1982 (Commencement No 1) Order 1984, SI 1984/1553; Civil Jurisdiction and Judgments Act 1982 (Commencement No 2) Order 1986, SI 1986/1781; Civil Jurisdiction and Judgments Act 1982 (Commencement No 3) Order 1986, SI 1986/2044

s 1–3	1 Jan 1987 (SI 1986/2044)
3A, 3B	Inserted by Civil Jurisdiction and Judgments Act 1991, s 1(1) (qv)
4–23	1 Jan 1987 (SI 1986/2044)
24(1)(a)	24 Aug 1982 (s 53(1), Sch 13, Pt I)
(b)	1 Jan 1987 (SI 1986/2044)
(2)(a)	24 Aug 1982 (s 53(1), Sch 13, Pt I)
(b)	1 Jan 1987 (SI 1986/2044)
(3)	24 Aug 1982 (s 53(1), Sch 13, Pt I)
25	1 Jan 1987 (SI 1986/2044)
26	1 Nov 1984 (SI 1984/1553)
27, 28	1 Jan 1987 (SI 1986/2044)
29–34	24 Aug 1982 (s 53(1), Sch 13, Pt I)
35(1)	14 Nov 1986 (SI 1986/1781)
(2)	1 Jan 1987 (SI 1986/2044)
(3)	24 Aug 1982 (s 53(1), Sch 13, Pt I)
36, 37	1 Jan 1987 (SI 1986/2044)
38	24 Aug 1982 (s 52(1), Sch 13, Pt I)
39	1 Jan 1987 (SI 1986/2044)
40	24 Aug 1982 (s 53(1), Sch 13, Pt I)
41–48	1 Jan 1987 (SI 1986/2044)
49–52	24 Aug 1982 (s 53(1), Sch 13, Pt I)
53(1)	13 Jul 1982 (s 53(1), Sch 13, Pt I)
(2)	24 Aug 1982 (so far as relates to Sch 13, Pt II, paras 7–10) (s 53(1), Sch 13, Pt I)

Civil Jurisdiction and Judgments Act 1982 (c 27)—*cont*

s 53(2)—*cont*	1 Nov 1984 (so far as relates to Sch 13, Pt II, para 6) (SI 1984/1553)
	1 Jan 1987 (otherwise) (SI 1986/2044)
54	24 Aug 1982 (so far as relates to repeal in Foreign Judgments (Reciprocal Enforcement) Act 1933, s 4) (s 53(1), Sch 13, Pt I)
	1 Jan 1987 (otherwise) (SI 1986/2044)
55	13 Jul 1982 (s 53(1), Sch 13, Pt I).
Sch 1–3	Substituted (1 Dec 1991) by Civil Jurisdiction and Judgments Act 1982 (Amendment) Order 1990, SI 1990/2591, art 12(1)–(3), Schs 1–3
3A	Inserted (1 Oct 1989) by Civil Jurisdiction and Judgments Act 1982 (Amendment) Order 1989, SI 1989/1346, art 9(3), Sch 3
3B	Inserted (1 Dec 1991) by Civil Jurisdiction and Judgments Act 1982 (Amendment) Order 1990, SI 1990/2591, art 12(4), Sch 4
3C	Inserted by Civil Jurisdiction and Judgments Act 1991, s 1(3), Sch 1 (qv)
4–9	1 Jan 1987 (SI 1986/2044)
10	14 Nov 1986 (SI 1986/1781)
11, 12	1 Jan 1987 (SI 1986/2044)
13, Pt I	13 Jul 1982 (s 53(1), Sch 13, Pt I, para 2)
II, para 1–5	1 Jan 1987 (SI 1986/2044)
6	1 Nov 1984 (SI 1984/1553)
7–10	24 Aug 1982 (s 53(1), Sch 13, Pt I, para 2)
14	24 Aug 1982 (repeals in Foreign Judgments (Reciprocal Enforcement) Act 1933, s 4) (s 53(1), Sch 13, Pt I)
	1 Jan 1987 (otherwise) (SI 1986/2044)

Clergy Pensions (Amendment) Measure 1982 (No 2)

RA: 23 Jul 1982

23 Jul 1982 (RA)

Coal Industry Act 1982 (c 15)

RA: 7 Apr 1982

7 Apr 1982 (RA)

Whole Act repealed (in part prospectively) as follows: ss 1, 2, 4 repealed by Coal Industry Act 1983, s 6(3), Sch; ss 3, 5, 6 prospectively repealed by Coal Industry Act 1994, s 67(8), Sch 11, Pt III[1]

[1] Orders made under Coal Industry Act 1994 bringing these prospective repeals into force will be noted to that Act in the service to this work

---

Commonwealth Development Corporation Act 1982 (c 54)

RA: 22 Dec 1982

22 Dec 1982 (RA)

Consolidated Fund Act 1982 (c 8)

Whole Act repealed

Copyright Act 1956 (Amendment) Act 1982 (c 35)

Whole Act repealed

Criminal Justice Act 1982 (c 48)

RA: 28 Oct 1982

Commencement provisions: s 80; Criminal Justice Act 1982 (Commencement No 1) Order 1982, SI 1982/1857; Criminal Justice Act 1982 (Scotland) (Commencement No 1) Order 1983, SI 1983/24; Criminal Justice Act 1982 (Commencement No 2) Order 1983, SI 1983/182; Criminal Justice Act 1982 (Scotland) (Commencement No 2) Order 1983, SI 1983/758

s 1	24 May 1983 (SI 1983/182)
1A–1C	Inserted by Criminal Justice Act 1988, s 123(1), (4) (qv)
2	Repealed
3	24 May 1983 (SI 1983/182)
4–7	Repealed
8–13	24 May 1983 (SI 1983/182)
14, 15	Repealed
16–21	24 May 1983 (SI 1983/182)
22–25	Repealed
26	21 Jan 1983 (SI 1982/1857)
27	Repealed
28	Spent
29	24 May 1983 (SI 1983/182)
30, 31	31 Jan 1983 (SI 1982/1857)
32	28 Oct 1982 (s 80(1))
33, 34	Repealed
35–40	11 Apr 1983 (SI 1982/1857)
41, 42	11 Apr 1983 (SI 1982/1857; SI 1983/24)
43–45	Repealed
46	11 Apr 1983 (SI 1982/1857)
47(1)	11 Apr 1983 (SI 1982/1857)
(2)	11 Apr 1983 (SI 1982/1857; SI 1983/24)
48	11 Apr 1983 (SI 1982/1857)
49	Repealed
50	11 Apr 1983 (SI 1982/1857; SI 1983/24)
51	24 May 1983 (SI 1983/182)
52	31 Jan 1983 (SI 1982/1857)
53–56	Repealed
57(1)	28 Oct 1982 (s 80(1))
(2)	Repealed
58	24 May 1983 (SI 1983/182; SI 1983/758)
59–61	24 May 1983 (SI 1983/182)
62	Repealed
63	31 Jan 1983 (SI 1982/1857)
64	31 Jan 1983 (SI 1982/1857; SI 1983/24)
65	31 Jan 1983 (SI 1982/1857); repealed, with savings, by Probation Service Act 1993, s 32(2), (3), Sch 3, para 1, Sch 4 (qv)

Criminal Justice Act 1982 (c 48)—*cont*

s 66, 67	31 Jan 1983 (SI 1982/1857)
68(1)	24 May 1983 (SI 1983/182)
(2)	24 May 1983 (SI 1983/182; SI 1983/758)
69	24 May 1983 (SI 1983/182)
70, 71	31 Jan 1983 (SI 1982/1857)
72	24 May 1983 (SI 1983/182)
73	31 Jan 1983 (SI 1983/24)
74, 75	28 Oct 1982 (s 80(1)); repealed (except in relation to Channel Islands and Isle of Man) by Criminal Justice Act 1988, s 170(2), Sch 16
76	28 Oct 1982 (s 80(1))
77	See Schs 14, 15 below
78	See Sch 16 below
79	See Sch 17 below
80, 81	28 Oct 1982 (s 80(1))
Sch 1	28 Oct 1982 (s 80(1))
2–4	11 Apr 1983 (SI 1982/1857)
5–7	Repealed
8	24 May 1983 (SI 1983/182; SI 1983/758)
9	24 May 1983 (SI 1983/182)
10	31 Jan 1983 (SI 1982/1857; SI 1983/24))
11	Repealed
12	24 May 1983 (SI 1983/182)
13	24 May 1983 (SI 1983/182; SI 1983/758)
14, para 1	31 Jan 1983 (SI 1982/1857)
2	Repealed
3	31 Jan 1983 (SI 1983/24)
4	24 May 1983 (SI 1983/182)
5	31 Jan 1983 (SI 1982/1857)
6, 7	24 May 1983 (SI 1983/182)
8(a)	24 May 1983 (SI 1983/182; SI 1983/758); prospectively repealed by Criminal Justice and Public Order Act 1994, s 168(3), Sch 11[1]
(b), (c)	24 May 1983 (SI 1983/182); prospectively repealed by Criminal Justice and Public Order Act 1994, s 168(3), Sch 11[1]
9	24 May 1983 (SI 1983/182)
10(a)	31 Jan 1983 (SI 1982/1857)
(b)	24 May 1983 (SI 1983/182)
11–13	24 May 1983 (SI 1983/182; SI 1983/758)
14	24 May 1983 (SI 1983/182)
15–17	24 May 1983 (SI 1983/182; SI 1983/758)
18(a)	24 May 1983 (SI 1983/182; SI 1983/758); repealed (S)
(b)	31 Jan 1983 (SI 1982/1857; SI 1983/24); repealed (S)
(c)	24 May 1983 (SI 1983/182; SI 1983/758); repealed (S)
19	24 May 1983 (SI 1983/182; SI 1983/758); repealed (S)
20	28 Oct 1982 (s 80(1)); repealed (S)
21	31 Jan 1983 (SI 1982/1857; SI 1983/24); repealed (S)
22	31 Jan 1983 (SI 1982/1857)
23	24 May 1983 (SI 1983/182)
24	24 May 1983 (SI 1983/182; SI 1983/758)
25	Repealed
26	24 May 1983 (SI 1983/182)
27	Spent
28	24 May 1983 (SI 1983/182)
29	24 May 1983 (SI 1983/182; SI 1983/758)

Criminal Justice Act 1982 (c 48)—*cont*

Sch 14, para 30	24 May 1983 (SI 1983/182)
31	31 Jan 1983 (SI 1982/1857; SI 1983/24)
32	Repealed
33, 34	24 May 1983 (SI 1983/182)
35	Spent
36, 37	24 May 1983 (SI 1983/182; SI 1983/758)
38	24 May 1983 (SI 1983/182)
39	24 May 1983 (SI 1983/182; SI 1983/758)
40, 41	31 Jan 1983 (SI 1982/1857)
42, 43	31 Jan 1983 (SI 1982/1857; SI 1983/24)
44	Spent
45, 46	Repealed
47–56	24 May 1983 (SI 1983/182)
57	Spent
58–60	24 May 1983 (SI 1983/182)
15, para 1	11 Apr 1983 (SI 1983/24)
2–5	Repealed
6, 7	11 Apr 1983 (SI 1983/24); prospectively repealed by Environment Act 1995, s 120(3), Sch 24[2]
8–13	11 Apr 1983 (SI 1983/24)
14	Repealed
15	31 Jan 1983 (SI 1983/24)
16	Repealed
17	11 Apr 1983 (SI 1983/24)
18, 19	31 Jan 1983 (SI 1983/24)
20, 21	11 Apr 1983 (SI 1983/24)
22	Repealed
23–29	11 Apr 1983 (SI 1983/24)
30	31 Jan 1983 (SI 1983/24)
16	28 Oct 1982 (repeal of Imprisonment (Temporary Provisions) Act 1980) (s 80(1))
	31 Jan 1983 (repeals of or in Merchant Shipping Act 1894, s 680(1); Prison Act 1952, s 55(3); Criminal Justice Act 1967, s 95(1); Immigration Act 1971, s 6(5); Powers of Criminal Courts Act 1973, ss 2, 4, 23(1), 47(d), 48–51, 57(1), Sch 1, para 7, Sch 3; Criminal Procedure (Scotland) Act 1975, s 421(1); Criminal Law Act 1977, Sch 9, para 10, Sch 12 (repeals in the entry relating to Powers of Criminal Courts Act 1973 only); Customs and Excise Management Act 1979, ss 147(5), 156(3); Criminal Justice (Scotland) Act 1980, s 55; Magistrates' Courts Act 1980, s 108(3)(a); Animal Health Act 1981, s 70) (SI 1982/1857; SI 1983/24)
	11 Apr 1983 (repeals of or in Sea Fisheries (Scotland) Amendment Act 1885, s 4; Electric Lighting (Clauses) Act 1899, Sch; Housing (Scotland) Act 1966, s 185(2); Criminal Procedure (Scotland) Act 1975, ss 8(2), 289D(2), (3A), 291(1); Criminal Law Act 1977, s 31; National Health Service (Scotland) Act 1978, Sch 9, para 1(1), Sch 10, para 7(2)(b); Electricity (Scotland) Act 1979, s 41(1)(b); Merchant Shipping Act 1979, s 43; Water (Scotland) Act 1980, Sch 4, para 10(3); Criminal Justice (Scotland) Act 1980, ss 7(3), 8, 46(1), Sch 7, para 50) (SI 1982/1857; SI 1983/24)

Criminal Justice Act 1982 (c 48)—*cont*

Sch 16—*cont*	24 May 1983 (otherwise except as noted below) (SI 1983/182; SI 1983/758)
	Not in force (repeal of Criminal Justice Act 1961, s 38(5)(c), (d))
17, para 1–14	24 May 1983 (SI 1983/182)
15	28 Oct 1982 (s 80(1))
16, 17	Repealed
18	31 Jan 1983 (SI 1983/24)

[1] Any order(s) made under Criminal Justice and Public Order Act 1994, s 172(2), (3), bringing the prospective repeal into force will be noted to that Act in the service to this work

[2] Any order(s) made under Environment Act 1995, s 125(3), bringing the prospective repeal into force will be noted to that Act in the service to this work

Currency Act 1982 (c 3)

RA: 2 Feb 1982

2 Feb 1982 (RA)

Deer Amendment (Scotland) Act 1982 (c 19)

RA: 28 Jun 1982

Commencement provisions: s 16(3), (4); commencement order made 27 Jun 1984 (not a statutory instrument)

s 1–10	28 Jul 1982 (s 16(3))
11	1 Jan 1985 (commencement order made 27 Jun 1984)
12–16	28 Jul 1982 (s 16(3))
Sch 1, 2	28 Jul 1982 (s 16(3))
3	28 Jul 1982 (except repeal of Sale of Venison (Scotland) Act 1968) (s 16(3))
	1 Jan 1985 (exception noted above) (commencement order made 27 Jun 1984)

Derelict Land Act 1982 (c 42)

RA: 30 Jul 1982

Commencement provisions: s 5(3)

30 Aug 1982 (s 5(3))

Duchy of Cornwall Management Act 1982 (c 47)

RA: 28 Oct 1982

28 Oct 1982 (RA)

Electricity (Financial Provisions) (Scotland) Act 1982 (c 56)

Whole Act repealed

Employment Act 1982 (c 46)

RA: 28 Oct 1982

Commencement provisions: s 22; Employment Act 1982 (Commencement) Order 1982, SI 1982/1656

s 1–19	Repealed
20	2 Jan 1983 (SI 1982/1656; but note the amendments made by Sch 2 do not apply in the circumstances set out in sub-ss (2)–(4))
21(1)	Substituted by Trade Union and Labour Relations (Consolidation) Act 1992, s 300(2), Sch 2, para 30 (qv)
(2)	See Sch 3 below
(3)	See Sch 4 below
22	1 Dec 1982 (SI 1982/1656)
Sch 1	Repealed
2	2 Jan 1983 (SI 1982/1656; see the note to s 20 above)
3	1 Dec 1982 (subject to transitional and supplementary provisions) (SI 1982/1656)
4	1 Dec 1982 (subject to transitional and supplementary provisions) (except repeals noted below) (SI 1982/1656)
	2 Jan 1983 (repeals of or in Employment Protection (Consolidation) Act 1978, ss 3, 4(4)(b), 5, 7, 73(3), 81(4), 143, 147, 149, Sch 4, paras 2, 7, Sch 13, para 13, Sch 16, para 23(9)) (SI 1982/1656)

Finance Act 1982 (c 39)

Budget day: 9 Mar 1982

RA: 30 Jul 1982

See the note concerning Finance Acts at the front of this book

Fire Service College Board (Abolition) Act 1982 (c 13)

Whole Act repealed

Firearms Act 1982 (c 31)

RA: 13 Jul 1982

Commencement provisions: s 4(3); Firearms Act 1982 (Commencement) Order 1983, SI 1983/1440

1 Nov 1983 (SI 1983/1440)

Food and Drugs (Amendment) Act 1982 (c 26)

Whole Act repealed

Forfeiture Act 1982 (c 34)

RA: 13 Jul 1982

Commencement provisions: s 7(2); Forfeiture Act 1982 Commencement Order 1982, SI 1982/1731

s 1–3	13 Oct 1982 (s 7(2))
4	31 Dec 1982 (SI 1982/1731)
5	13 Oct 1982 (s 7(2))
6, 7	13 Jul 1982 (RA)

Gaming (Amendment) Act 1982 (c 22)

RA: 28 Jan 1982

Commencement provisions: s 3(2)

28 Aug 1982 (s 3(2))

Harbours (Scotland) Act 1982 (c 17)

RA: 27 May 1982

27 May 1982 (RA)

Hops Marketing Act 1982 (c 5)

RA: 25 Feb 1982

25 Feb 1982 (RA); note that for practical purposes the majority of the Act came into effect on 1 Apr 1982, the day appointed for the revocation of the Hops Marketing Scheme under s 1(2)

Industrial Development Act 1982 (c 52)

RA: 28 Oct 1982

Commencement provisions: s 20(2)

28 Jan 1983 (s 20(2))

Industrial Training Act 1982 (c 10)

RA: 29 Mar 1982

Commencement provisions: s 21(3)

29 Jun 1982 (s 21(3))

Industry Act 1982 (c 18)

Whole Act repealed

Insurance Companies Act 1982 (c 50)

RA: 28 Oct 1982

Commencement provisions: ss 99(1), 100(2), Sch 4, para 6

s 1–5	28 Jan 1983 (s 100(2))
6	Substituted (1 Jul 1994) by Insurance Companies (Third Insurance Directives) Regulations 1994, SI 1994/1696, reg 6
7–12	28 Jan 1983 (s 100(2))
12A	Inserted (1 Jul 1994) by Insurance Companies (Third Insurance Directives) Regulations 1994, SI 1994/1696, reg 11
13–21	28 Jan 1983 (s 100(2))
21A	Inserted by Financial Services Act 1986, s 135(1) (qv)
22–31	28 Jan 1983 (s 100(2))
31A	Inserted by Financial Services Act 1986, s 136(1) (qv)
32–34	28 Jan 1983 (s 100(2))
34A	Prospectively inserted by Insurance (Reserves) Act 1995, s 1(1)[1]
35	28 Jan 1983 (s 100(2))
35A, 35B	Inserted (1 Jul 1994) by Insurance Companies (Third Insurance Directives) Regulations 1994, SI 1994/1696, regs 17, 18
36	*Not in force*
37–40	28 Jan 1983 (s 100(2))
40A	Inserted (1 Jul 1994) by Insurance Companies (Third Insurance Directives) Regulations 1994, SI 1994/1696, reg 22
41–43	28 Jan 1983 (s 100(2))
43A	Inserted (1 Jul 1994) by Insurance Companies (Third Insurance Directives) Regulations 1994, SI 1994/1696, reg 23
44	28 Jan 1983 (s 100(2))
44A	Inserted by Companies Act 1989, s 77(3) (qv)
45–47	28 Jan 1983 (s 100(2))
47A	Inserted by Companies Consolidation (Consequential Provisions) Act 1985, s 25; substituted (1 Jul 1994) by Insurance Companies (Third Insurance Directives) Regulations 1994, SI 1994/1696, reg 26(1)
47B	Inserted by Companies Consolidation (Consequential Provisions) Act 1985, s 25 (qv)
48	28 Jan 1983 (s 100(2))
49	Substituted (1 Jul 1994) for ss 49–52 by Insurance Companies (Third Insurance Directives) Regulations 1994, SI 1994/1696, reg 28(1)
49A–52	See note to s 49 above
52A	Inserted (1 Jul 1990) by Insurance Companies (Amendment) Regulations 1990, SI 1990/1333, reg 9(2)
52B	Inserted (1 Jul 1994) by Insurance Companies (Third Insurance Directives) Regulations 1994, SI 1994/1696, reg 30
53–61	28 Jan 1983 (s 100(2))
61A, 61B	Inserted (1 Jul 1994) by Insurance Companies (Third Insurance Directives) Regulations 1994, SI 1994/1696, regs 34, 35(1)

Insurance Companies Act 1982 (c 50)—*cont*

s 62, 63	28 Jan 1983 (s 100(2))
63A	Repealed
64–72	28 Jan 1983 (s 100(2))
72A, 72B	Inserted (1 Jul 1994) by Insurance Companies (Third Insurance Directives) Regulations 1994, SI 1994/1696, regs 40(1), 41
73	Repealed
74–78	28 Jan 1983 (s 100(2))
79	Repealed
80, 81	28 Jan 1983 (s 100(2))
81A	Inserted by Insurance Companies (Amendment) Regulations 1990, SI 1990/1333, reg 10; substituted (1 Jul 1994) by Insurance Companies (Third Insurance Directives) Regulations 1994, SI 1994/1696, reg 45(1)
81B	Substituted (1 Jul 1994) for ss 81B–81J (inserted by Insurance Companies (Amendment) Regulations 1990, SI 1990/1333, reg 10, Insurance Companies (Amendment) Regulations 1992, SI 1992/2890, reg 7(6)) by Insurance Companies (Third Insurance Directives) Regulations 1994, SI 1994/1696, reg 46(1)
81C–81J	See note to s 81B above
82, 83	28 Jan 1983 (s 100(2))
83A	Inserted (19 Nov 1992) by Insurance Companies (Amendment) Regulations 1992, SI 1992/2890, reg 8
84–94	28 Jan 1983 (s 100(2))
94A	Inserted by Insurance (Fees) Act 1985, s 1 (qv)
94B	Inserted (1 Jul 1990) as s 94A by Insurance Companies (Amendment) Regulations 1990, SI 1990/1333, reg 6(1); renumbered (19 Nov 1992) by Insurance Companies (Amendment) Regulations 1992, SI 1992/2890, reg 9(2).
95, 96	28 Jun 1983 (s 100(2))
96A, 96B	Inserted (1 Jul 1990) by Insurance Companies (Amendment) Regulations 1990, SI 1990/1333, regs 2(1), 4
96C–96F	Inserted (1 Jul 1994) by Insurance Companies (Third Insurance Directives) Regulations 1994, SI 1994/1696, regs 52–55
97–100	28 Jan 1983 (s 100(2))
Sch 1, 2	28 Jan 1983 (s 100(2))
2A–2E	Inserted (1 Jul 1994) by Insurance Companies (Third Insurance Directives) Regulations 1994, SI 1994/1696, regs 5(3), 26(2), 28(2), 35(2), 40(2), Schs 1–5
2F, 2G	Inserted (1 Jul 1994), subject to transitional provisions, by Insurance Companies (Third Insurance Directives) Regulations 1994, SI 1994/1696, regs 45(2), 46(2), 69, 70, Schs 6, 7
3	Repealed
3A, Pt I	Inserted (1 Jul 1990) as Sch 3A by Insurance Companies (Amendment) Regulations 1990, SI 1990/1333, reg 6(2); renumbered (20 May 1993) by Insurance Companies (Amendment) Regulations 1993, SI 1993/174, reg 5(4)

Insurance Companies Act 1982 (c 50)—*cont*

Sch 3A, Pt II	Inserted (20 May 1993) by Insurance Companies (Amendment) Regulations 1993, SI 1993/174, reg 5(5)
4–6	28 Jan 1983 (s 100(2)

[1] Any order made under Insurance (Reserves) Act 1995, s 4(2), bringing the prospective insertion into force will be noted to that Act in the service to this work

Iron and Steel Act 1982 (c 25)

RA: 13 Jul 1982

Commencement provisions: s 39(2)

13 Oct 1982 (s 39(2))

Whole Act repealed, partly prospectively (s 1, Sch 1), except ss 33 (part), 34 (part), by British Steel Act 1988, s 16(3), Sch 2[1]

[1] The repeals of s 1, Sch 1, by British Steel Act 1988, s 16(3), Sch 2, Pt II, come into force on a day to be appointed by order under s 10 of that Act for the dissolution of the British Steel Corporation (s 17(4)); any such order will be noted to that Act in the service to this work

Lands Valuation Amendment (Scotland) Act 1982 (c 57)

RA: 22 Dec 1982

22 Dec 1982 (RA)

Legal Aid Act 1982 (c 44)

Whole Act repealed

Local Government and Planning (Scotland) Act 1982 (c 43)

RA: 30 Jul 1982

Commencement provisions: s 69(2); Local Government and Planning (Scotland) Act 1982 (Commencement No 1) Order 1982, SI 1982/1137; Local Government and Planning (Scotland) Act 1982 (Commencement No 2) Order 1982, SI 1982/1397; Local Government and Planning (Scotland) Act 1982 (Commencement No 3) Order 1984, SI 1984/239

s 1–4	Repealed
5	1 Sep 1982 (SI 1982/1137)
6	1 Apr 1983 (SI 1982/1397); prospectively repealed by Local Government etc (Scotland) Act 1994, s 180(2), Sch 14[1]
7	1 Nov 1982 (so far as inserts Local Government (Scotland) Act 1973, s 154B) (SI 1982/1397) and 1 Apr 1983 (so far as inserts Local Government (Scotland) Act 1973, s 154A) (SI 1982/1397); prospectively repealed by Local Government etc (Scotland) Act 1994, s 180(2), Sch 14[1]

Local Government and Planning (Scotland) Act 1982 (c 43)—*cont*

s 8	1 Sep 1982 (SI 1982/1137)
9	1 Apr 1983 (SI 1982/1397); prospectively substituted by Local Government etc (Scotland) Act 1994, s 180(1), Sch 13, para 128(1), (2)[1]
10–13	1 Apr 1983 (SI 1982/1397)
14(1), (2)	1 Apr 1983 (SI 1982/1397)
(3)	Prospectively inserted by Local Government etc (Scotland) Act 1994, s 180(1), Sch 13, para 128(1), (3)(c)[1]
15, 16	1 Apr 1983 (SI 1982/1397)
17	1 Apr 1983 (SI 1982/1397); prospectively substituted by Local Government etc (Scotland) Act 1994, s 180(1), Sch 13, para 128(1), (6)[1]
18–28	1 Apr 1983 (SI 1982/1397)
29	1 Nov 1982 (SI 1982/1397)
30, 31	1 Apr 1983 (SI 1982/1397)
32	1 Nov 1982 (SI 1982/1397)
33, 34	1 Sep 1982 (SI 1982/1137); prospectively repealed by Local Government etc (Scotland) Act 1994, s 180(2), Sch 14[1]
35	1 Sep 1982 (SI 1982/1137)
36–40	1 Nov 1982 (SI 1982/1397)
41	14 May 1984 (SI 1984/239)
42, 43	1 Nov 1982 (SI 1982/1397)
44	14 May 1984 (SI 1984/239)
45, 46	1 Nov 1982 (SI 1982/1397)
47(a)	14 May 1984 (SI 1984/239)
(b), (c)	1 Nov 1982 (SI 1982/1397)
48	See Sch 2 below
49, 50	1 Sep 1982 (SI 1982/1137)
51–55	Repealed
56	1 Sep 1982 (SI 1982/1137); prospectively repealed by Local Government etc (Scotland) Act 1994, s 180(2), Sch 14[1]
57	1 Apr 1983 (SI 1982/1397)
58–60	1 Nov 1982 (SI 1982/1397)
61–65	1 Sep 1982 (SI 1982/1137)
66(1)	See Sch 3 below
(2)	See Sch 4 below
67, 68	1 Sep 1982 (SI 1982/1137)
69	30 Jul 1982 (RA)
Sch 1, Pt I	1 Apr 1983 (SI 1982/1397); prospectively repealed by Local Government etc (Scotland) Act 1994, s 180, Sch 13, para 128(1), (15), Sch 14[1]
II	1 Apr 1983 (SI 1982/1397)
2, para 1–4	1 Nov 1982 (SI 1982/1397)
5	14 May 1984 (SI 1984/239)
6, 7	1 Nov 1982 (SI 1982/1397)
8–12	14 May 1984 (SI 1984/239)
13–16	1 Nov 1982 (SI 1982/1397)
17–20	14 May 1984 (SI 1984/239)
21, 22	1 Nov 1982 (SI 1982/1397)
23	14 May 1984 (SI 1984/239)
24	1 Nov 1982 (SI 1982/1397)
25–27	14 May 1984 (SI 1984/239)
28–41	1 Nov 1982 (SI 1982/1397)

Local Government and Planning (Scotland) Act 1982 (c 43)—*cont*

Sch 2, para 42	14 May 1984 (SI 1984/239)
43	1 Nov 1982 (SI 1982/1397)
3, para 1, 2	1 Apr 1983 (SI 1982/1397)
3(a)	1 Sep 1982 (SI 1982/1137)
(b)	1 Apr 1983 (SI 1982/1397)
4	1 Nov 1982 (SI 1982/1397)
5–7	Repealed
8–11	1 Nov 1982 (SI 1982/1397)
12	1 Apr 1983 (SI 1982/1397)
13–15	1 Nov 1982 (SI 1982/1397)
16	1 Apr 1983 (SI 1982/1397); prospectively repealed by Local Government etc (Scotland) Act 1994, s 180(2), Sch 14[1]
17	1 Sep 1982 (SI 1982/1137)
18–20	Repealed
21	1 Apr 1983 (SI 1982/1397)
22, 23	1 Nov 1982 (SI 1982/1397)
24	14 May 1984 (SI 1984/239)
25–28	1 Nov 1982 (SI 1982/1397)
29–33	Repealed
34	1 Nov 1982 (SI 1982/1397)
35, 36	Repealed
37, 38	1 Apr 1983 (SI 1982/1397)
39, 40	Repealed
41	1 Apr 1983 (SI 1982/1397)
42	1 Sep 1982 (SI 1982/1137)
43	Repealed
4	1 Sep 1982 (repeals of or in Local Government (Scotland) Act 1966, s 5(1), Sch 1, Pt II, paras 2, 3; Local Government (Scotland) Act 1973, ss 216(2)–(5), 218, 221, 224(1)–(4), (6); Local Government (Scotland) Act 1975, Sch 1, paras 2, 2A, 3, 4, 4A; Electricity (Scotland) Act 1979, Sch 4, paras 1, 3, 5, 6; Tenants' Rights, Etc (Scotland) Act 1980, ss 1(1), 4(3)) (SI 1982/1137)
	1 Nov 1982 (repeals of or in Requisitioned Land and War Works Act 1945, s 52; Civic Restaurants Act 1947; Requisitioned Land and War Works Act 1948, Sch, para 10; Highlands and Islands Development (Scotland) Act 1965, s 10(1), (3); Countryside (Scotland) Act 1967, ss 14(5), 34(5), 35A, Sch 3, paras 1(2), 2(1)–(3), 4; Social Work (Scotland) Act 1968, s 6(1)(d); Town and Country Planning (Scotland) Act 1972, ss 12(1), (2), 37(1), 54(2), 61(7), 84(6), 85(8), 92(1), 93(5)(b), 154(2), 164(6), 167C(2)(b), 215(1), 231(1)(b), (3)(f), 262(2), (3), 262A(3), (4), 262B(3), Sch 10, para 11(1); Local Government (Scotland) Act 1973, ss 49(2)(a), 164, Sch 22, Pt II, para 5, 8, 9; Safety of Sports Grounds Act 1975, s 11; Scottish Development Agency Act 1975, s 10(1); Refuse Disposal (Amenity) Act 1978, s 8(1); Water (Scotland) Act 1980, Sch 3, para 7(5), Sch 4, para 23; Countryside (Scotland) Act 1981, s 5) (SI 1982/1397)
	1 Apr 1983 (repeals of or in Public Parks (Scotland) Act 1878; Burgh Police (Scotland) Act 1892,

Local Government and Planning (Scotland) Act 1982 (c 43)—*cont*

Sch 4—*cont*	ss 107, 110, 112, 116, 277, 288, 307, 308; Public Health (Scotland) Act 1897, ss 29, 39; Burgh Police (Scotland) Act 1903, s 44; Physical Training and Recreation Act 1937, ss 4(1)–(4), 5, 7, 10(4)–(7), (11); Food and Drugs (Scotland) Act 1956, s 26(3); Physical Training and Recreation Act 1958; Caravan Sites and Control of Development Act 1960, s 32(1)(h)(iii); Social Work (Scotland) Act 1968, s 85; Agriculture Act 1970, ss 95, 96; Local Government (Scotland) Act 1973, ss 55, 91, 137(2), 139, 158, 162, 178, 219, 220, Sch 23, para 2(a); Control of Pollution Act 1974, ss 22, 23, Sch 4; Education (Scotland) Act 1980, s 1(3)(b), (5)(b)(iii); Local Government, Planning and Land Act 1980, s 70(4)) (SI 1982/1397)
	14 May 1984 (otherwise) (SI 1984/239)

[1] Any order(s) made under Local Government etc (Scotland) Act 1994, s 184(2), (3), bringing the prospective change into force will be noted to that Act in the service to this work

---

Local Government Finance Act 1982 (c 32)

RA: 13 Jul 1982

Commencement provisions: See notes to individual provisions below

s 1	13 Jul 1982 (RA, but only effective for financial years 1 Apr 1982 onwards); repealed (1 Apr 1990), with savings, by Local Government Finance (Repeals, Savings and Consequential Amendments) Order 1990, SI 1990/776, art 3, Sch 1
2–4	13 Jul 1982 (RA; but only effective for financial years 1 Apr 1982 onwards)
5	13 Jul 1982 (RA; but only effective for financial years 1 Apr 1982 onwards); sub-s (1) repealed by Local Government and Housing Act 1989, s 194(2), Sch 12, Pt I (qv), except in relation to any bodies which have not been prescribed by regulations under s 39(3) of that Act; sub-ss (2), (3) repealed by Local Government Act 1985, s 102(2), Sch 17 (qv)
6	13 Jul 1982 (RA; but only effective for financial years 1 Apr 1982 onwards); repealed (1 Apr 1990), with savings, by Local Government Finance (Repeals, Savings and Consequential Amendments) Order 1990, SI 1990/776, art 3, Sch 1
7	13 Jul 1982 (RA)
8–10	13 Jul 1982 (RA; s 8 only effective in relation to block grant for years 1 Apr 1982 onwards, except s 8(2) so far as relates to consultation; s 8(4A) effective in relation to years 1 Apr 1987 onwards;

Local Government Finance Act 1982 (c 32)—*cont*

s 8–10—*cont*	s 8(8) which only applies to years 1 Apr 1983 onwards; s 10 (and Sch 2) only effective for years 1 Apr 1983 onwards)
11–18	13 Jul 1982 (RA, s 11 (and Sch 3) only effective from 21 Jan 1983 (s 33(2); Accounts and Audit (First Appointed Day) Order 1982, SI 1982/1881); ss 12–18 only effective for periods beginning on or after 1 Apr 1983 (s 33(3); Accounts and Audit (Second Appointed Day) Order 1983, SI 1983/165))
18A	Inserted by Local Government Finance (Publicity for Auditors' Reports) Act 1991, s 1(1), (2) (qv)
19–25	13 Jul 1982 (RA; ss 19–25 only effective for periods beginning on or after 1 Apr 1983 (s 33(3); Accounts and Audit (Second Appointed Day) Order 1983, SI 1983/165))
25A	Inserted by Local Government Act 1988, s 30, Sch 4 (qv)
25AA	Inserted by Local Government Finance Act 1988, s 137, Sch 12, Pt I, para 3(1), (3) (qv)
25B–25D	Inserted by Local Government Act 1988, s 30, Sch 4 (qv)
26–28	13 Jul 1982 (RA; s 11 (and Sch 3) only effective from 21 Jan 1983 (s 33(2); Accounts and Audit (First Appointed Day) Order 1982, SI 1982/1881)
28A	Repealed
28B	Inserted by Police and Magistrates' Courts Act 1994, s 43, Sch 4, Pt I, para 28 (qv)
29–31	13 Jul 1982 (RA; s 11 (and Sch 3) only effective from 21 Jan 1983 (s 33(2); Accounts and Audit (First Appointed Day) Order 1982, SI 1982/1881); s 31 (so far as it relates to ss 12–25) only effective for periods beginning on or after 1 Apr 1983 (s 33(3); Accounts and Audit (Second Appointed Day) Order 1983, SI 1983/165)
32	Repealed
33–36	13 Jul 1982 (RA; s 11 (and Sch 3) only effective from 21 Jan 1983 (s 33(2); Accounts and Audit (First Appointed Day) Order 1982, SI 1982/1881))
37–39	13 Jul 1982 (RA)
Sch 1	13 Jul 1982 (RA; but only effective for financial years 1 Apr 1982 onwards)
2	See ss 8–10 above
3	See ss 11–18 above
4	Repealed
5	13 Jul 1982 (RA; only effective for periods 1 Apr 1983 onwards)
6, Pt I	Effective for financial years 1 Apr 1982 onwards (s 38(2))
II	Effective for financial years 1 Apr 1981 onwards (s 38(3))
III	Effective for financial years 1 Apr 1983 onwards (s 38(4))
IV	Effective for periods 1 Apr 1983 onwards (s 38(5))

Local Government (Miscellaneous Provisions) Act 1982 (c 30)

RA: 13 Jul 1982

Commencement provisions: ss 1(12), 7(3), 25(3), 40(10), 47(3), Sch 3, para 30(1); Local Government (Miscellaneous Provisions) Act 1982 (Commencement No 1) Order 1982, SI 1982/1119; Local Government (Miscellaneous Provisions) Act 1982 (Commencement No 2) Order 1982, SI 1982/1160

Note

Certain provisions of this Act must be adopted by local authority resolution to have effect in particular areas

s 1	1 Jan 1983 (s 1(12))
2–6	13 Jul 1982 (RA)
7(1), (2)	13 Oct 1982 (s 7(3))
(3), (4)	13 Jul 1982 (RA)
8–17	13 Jul 1982 (RA)
18, 19	Repealed
20–23	13 Jul 1982 (RA)
24–26	Repealed
27	13 Jul 1982 (RA)
28	Repealed
29–34	13 Jul 1982 (RA)
35, 36	Repealed
37–39	13 Jul 1982 (RA)
40	13 Sep 1982 (s 40(10))
41	13 Jul 1982 (RA)
42	Repealed
43–46	13 Jul 1982 (RA)
47(1)	13 Jul 1982 (RA)
(2), (3)	See Sch 7 below
(4)	13 Jul 1982 (RA)
48, 49	13 Jul 1982 (RA)
Sch 1, 2	1 Jan 1983 (s 1(12))
3	13 Jul 1982 (except in relation to sex cinemas) (RA)
	13 Oct 1982 (in relation to sex cinemas) (SI 1982/1119)
4–6	13 Jul 1982 (RA)
7, Pt I, II	1 Jan 1983 (s 47(3))
III–XV	13 Jul 1982 (RA)
XVI	13 Jul 1982 (except as noted below) (RA)
	1 Sep 1982 (repeal of Health and Safety at Work etc Act 1974, s 63) (SI 1982/1160)

Mental Health (Amendment) Act 1982 (c 51)

RA: 28 Oct 1982

Commencement provisions: s 69

s 1–33	Repealed
34	30 Sep 1983 (s 69(1))
35–63	Repealed
64	30 Sep 1983 (s 69(1))
65(1)	See Sch 3 below
(2)	See Sch 4 below

Mental Health (Amendment) Act 1982 (c 51)—*cont*

s 66	Repealed
67–69	30 Sep 1983 (s 69(1))
Sch 1, 2	Repealed
3, Pt I	30 Sep 1983 (s 69(1))
II	Repealed
4, Pt I	30 Sep 1983 (s 69(1))
II	28 Oct 1984 (s 69(4))
5, para 1	30 Sep 1983 (s 69(1))
2–15	Repealed

Merchant Shipping (Liner Conferences) Act 1982 (c 37)

RA: 23 Jul 1982

Commencement provisions: s 15(2); Merchant Shipping (Liner Conferences) Act 1982 (Commencement) Order 1985, SI 1985/182

14 Mar 1985 (SI 1985/182)

National Insurance Surcharge Act 1982 (c 55)

Whole Act repealed (with respect to earnings paid on or after 6 April 1985)

New Towns Act 1982 (c 7)

RA: 25 Feb 1982

25 Feb 1982 (RA)

Whole Act repealed (EW)

Northern Ireland Act 1982 (c 38)

RA: 23 Jul 1982

23 Jul 1982 (RA)

Oil and Gas (Enterprise) Act 1982 (c 23)

RA: 28 Jun 1982

Commencement provisions: s 38(2); Oil and Gas (Enterprise) Act 1982 (Commencement No 1) Order 1982, SI 1982/895; Oil and Gas (Enterprise) Act 1982 (Commencement No 2) Order 1982, SI 1982/1059; Oil and Gas (Enterprise) Act 1982 (Commencement No 3) Order 1982, SI 1982/1431; Oil and Gas (Enterprise) Act 1982 (Commencement No 4) Order 1987, SI 1987/2272

s 1–7	Repealed
8	1 Apr 1983 (SI 1982/1431)
9–17	Repealed
18	23 Jul 1982 (SI 1982/895)
19, 20	1 Oct 1982 (SI 1982/1059)
21	Repealed
22	1 Feb 1988 (SI 1987/2272)

Oil and Gas (Enterprise) Act 1982 (c 23)—*cont*

s 23(1)	1 Feb 1988 (SI 1987/2272)
(2)–(4)	31 Dec 1982 (amendments to Social Security Act 1975, Patents Act 1977 and Social Security and Housing Benefits Act 1982) (SI 1982/1431) 1 Feb 1988 (otherwise) (SI 1987/2272)
(5)	1 Feb 1988 (SI 1987/2272)
(6)	31 Dec 1982 (amendments to Social Security Act 1975, Patents Act 1977 and Social Security and Housing Benefits Act 1982) (SI 1982/1431) 1 Feb 1988 (otherwise) (SI 1987/2272)
24	1 Nov 1982 (SI 1982/1431)
25	1 Oct 1982 (SI 1982/1059)
26	1 Nov 1982 (SI 1982/1431)
27(1)(a)	1 Feb 1988 (SI 1987/2272)
(b), (c)	1 Oct 1982 (SI 1982/1059)
(d)	Repealed
(2)	1 Oct 1982 (SI 1982/1059)
(3)	1 Oct 1982 (SI 1982/1059); repealed, so far as relates to prosecutions for offences under Mineral Workings (Offshore Installations) Act 1971 or Petroleum Act 1987, s 23, by Offshore Safety Act 1992, s 3(1)(d) (qv)
(4)	1 Oct 1982 (SI 1982/1059); repealed so far as relates to prosecutions for offences under Mineral Workings (Offshore Installations) Act 1971 or Petroleum Act 1987, s 23, by Offshore, and Pipelines, Safety (Northern Ireland) Order 1992, SI 1992/1728, art 8, Sch 2
(5)–(7)	1 Oct 1982 (SI 1982/1059)
28	1 Oct 1982 (SI 1982/1059)
29	23 Jul 1982 (SI 1982/895)
30, 31	1 Oct 1982 (SI 1982/1059)
32	2 Jul 1982 (SI 1982/895)
33, 34	Repealed
35, 36	2 Jul 1982 (SI 1982/895)
37	See Schs 3, 4 below
38	2 Jul 1982 (SI 1982/895)
Sch 1	Repealed
2	1 Oct 1982 (SI 1982/1059)
3, para 1	1 Oct 1982 (SI 1982/1059)
2, 3	1 Feb 1988 (SI 1987/2272)
4	1 Oct 1982 (SI 1982/1059)
5, 6	Repealed
7–11	1 Nov 1982 (SI 1982/1431)
12–21	Repealed
22	18 Aug 1982 (SI 1982/1059)
23	Repealed
24	*Not in force*
25–29	Repealed
30, 31	1 Nov 1982 (SI 1982/1431)
32, 33	Repealed
34	1 Feb 1988 (SI 1987/2272)
35, 36	*Not in force*
37	18 Aug 1982 (SI 1982/1059)
38	*Not in force*
39	31 Dec 1982 (SI 1982/1431)

Oil and Gas (Enterprise) Act 1982 (c 23)—*cont*

Sch 3, para 40	*Not in force*; substituted by Trade Union and Labour Relations (Consolidation) Act 1992, s 300(2), Sch 2, para 29(1), (2) (qv)
41	Repealed
42, 43	1 Feb 1988 (SI 1987/2272)
44	Repealed
45	*Not in force;* added by Trade Union and Labour Relations (Consolidation) Act 1992, s 300(2), Sch 2, para 29(1), (3), (4) (qv)
4	18 Aug 1982 (repeals in Petroleum (Production) Act 1934; Gas Act 1972 (except repeal in s 7(2)); Oil Taxation Act 1975; Energy Act 1976; Gas Act 1980) (SI 1982/1059)
	1 Oct 1982 (repeals in Continental Shelf Act 1964, s 2; Mineral Workings (Offshore Installations) Act 1971, s 10 (except in relation to offences within sub-s (1)(a)); Petroleum and Submarine Pipe-lines Act 1975, ss 22, 26, 41; Customs and Excise Management Act 1979) (SI 1982/1059)
	1 Nov 1982 (repeals of or in Mineral Workings (Offshore Installations) Act 1971, ss 6(2), 12(1); Petroleum and Submarine Pipe-lines Act 1975, ss 1(3)(c), 3(3), 44(1)–(4), 45(3)) (SI 1982/1431)
	31 Dec 1982 (repeals of or in Petroleum and Submarine Pipe-lines Act 1975, ss 2(4)(d), 7(2), 14(4)(b), 40(2)(a), (c), (3)(a), (c)) (SI 1982/1431)
	1 Apr 1983 (repeals of Petroleum and Submarine Pipe-lines Act 1975, s 40(1), (4), 40(3) (so far as not brought into force on 31 Dec 1982)) (SI 1982/1431)
	1 Feb 1988 (repeals of Continental Shelf Act 1964, ss 3, 11(3); Mineral Workings (Offshore Installations) Act 1971, ss 8, 9(5), 10 (so far as not already repealed)) (SI 1987/2272)
	Not in force (otherwise)

Pastoral (Amendment) Measure 1982 (No 1)

Whole Measure repealed

Planning Inquiries (Attendance of Public) Act 1982 (c 21)

Whole Act repealed

Reserve Forces Act 1982 (c 14)

RA: 7 Apr 1982

7 Apr 1982 (RA)

Shipbuilding Act 1982 (c 4)

Whole Act repealed

Social Security and Housing Benefits Act 1982 (c 24)

RA: 28 Jun 1982

Commencement provisions: s 48(3); Social Security and Housing Benefits Act 1982 (Commencement No 1) Order 1982, SI 1982/893; Social Security and Housing Benefits Act 1982 (Commencement No 2) Order 1982, SI 1982/906

s 1–9	Repealed
10	6 Apr 1983 (SI 1982/893)
11–38	Repealed
39	6 Apr 1983 (SI 1982/893)
40, 41	Repealed
42	28 Jun 1982 (s 48(3))
43	30 Aug 1982 (SI 1982/893)
44	Repealed
45–47	28 Jun 1982 (s 48(3))
48(1)	28 Jun 1982 (s 48(3))
(2)	Repealed
(3), (4)	28 Jun 1982 (s 48(3))
(5), (6)	See Schs 4, 5 below
(7)	28 Jun 1982 (s 48(3))
Sch 1	Repealed
2, paras 1–12	Repealed
13	6 Apr 1983 (SI 1982/893)
3	Repealed
4, para 1–35	Repealed or spent
36	4 Apr 1983 (SI 1982/906)
37	28 Jun 1982 (RA)
38, 39	Repealed
5	30 Jun 1982 (repeals of or in Social Security Act 1975, s 4(2), Sch 11, para 2) (SI 1982/893)
	6 Apr 1983 (remaining repeals in Social Security Act 1975, except words in s 65(4); repeals of or in Child Benefit Act 1975, Sch 4, para 39; Social Security Act 1980, Sch 1; Social Security (No 2) Act 1980, s 3(2)) (SI 1982/893)
	4 Apr 1983 (otherwise except repeals in Social Security Act 1975, s 65(4); Social Security Pensions Act 1975, Sch 4, para 22) (SI 1982/906)
	Note: It is unclear why the outstanding repeals were not brought into force; the whole of Social Security Act 1975 was repealed (1 Jul 1992) by Social Security (Consequential Provisions) Act 1992, s 3, Sch 1; Social Security Pensions Act 1975, Sch 4, para 22 amended Housing Finance Act 1972, Sch 3, which was repealed (4 Apr 1983) by Sch 5 to this Act

Social Security (Contributions) Act 1982 (c 2)

Whole Act repealed

Stock Transfer Act 1982 (c 41)

RA: 30 Jul 1982

Commencement provisions: s 6(2); Stock Transfer Act 1982 (Commencement) Order 1985, SI 1985/1137

s 1–3	23 Jul 1985 (SI 1985/1137)
4	Repealed
5(1)	Repealed
(2)	30 Oct 1982 (s 6(2)); prospectively repealed by Local Government etc (Scotland) Act 1994, s 180(2), Sch 14[1]
6	30 Oct 1982 (s 6(2))
Sch 1, 2	23 Jul 1985 (SI 1985/1137)

[1] Any order made under Local Government etc (Scotland) Act 1994, s 184(2), (3), bringing the prospective repeal into force will be noted to that Act in the service to this work

---

Supply of Goods and Services Act 1982 (c 29)

RA: 13 Jul 1982

Commencement provisions: s 20(3); Supply of Goods and Services Act 1982 (Commencement) Order 1982, SI 1982/1770

s 1–5	4 Jan 1983 (s 20(3))
5A	Inserted by Sale and Supply of Goods Act 1994, s 7(1), Sch 2, para 6(1), (5) (qv)
6–10	4 Jan 1983 (s 20(3))
10A	Inserted by Sale and Supply of Goods Act 1994, s 7(1), Sch 2, para 6(1), (9) (qv)
11	4 Jan 1983 (s 20(3))
11A–11L	Inserted (S) by Sale and Supply of Goods Act 1994, s 6, Sch 1, para 1 (qv)
12–16	4 Jul 1983 (SI 1982/1770)
17	4 Jan 1983 (s 20(3))
18, 19	4 Jan 1983 (so far as relate to ss 1–11) (s 20(3)) 4 Jul 1983 (so far as relate to ss 12–16) (SI 1982/1770)
20	13 Jul 1982 (RA)
Schedule	Spent

Taking of Hostages Act 1982 (c 28)

RA: 13 Jul 1982

Commencement provisions: s 6; Taking of Hostages Act 1982 (Commencement) Order 1982, SI 1982/1532

26 Nov 1982 (SI 1982/1532)

Transport Act 1982 (c 49)

RA: 28 Oct 1982

Commencement provisions: s 76; Transport Act 1982 (Commencement No 1) Order 1982, SI 1982/1561; Transport Act 1982 (Commencement No 2) Order 1982, SI 1982/1804; Transport Act 1982 (Commencement No 3) Order 1983, SI 1983/276; Transport Act 1982 (Commencement No 4) Order 1983, SI 1983/577; Transport Act 1982 (Scotland) (Commencement No 1) Order 1983, SI 1983/650; Transport Act 1982 (Commencement No 5) Order 1984, SI 1984/175; Transport Act 1982 (Commencement No 6) Order 1986, SI 1986/1326; Transport Act 1982 (Scotland) (Commencement No 2) Order 1986, SI 1986/1874

s 1–7	Repealed
8–15	*Not in force*
16	Repealed
17, 18	*Not in force*
19	Repealed
20	*Not in force*: substituted by Road Traffic Act 1991, s 48, Sch 4, para 20 (qv)
21–26	*Not in force*
27–64	Repealed
65	11 Apr 1983 (SI 1983/276)
66	*Not in force*
67	20 Dec 1982 (SI 1982/1804)
68	1 Nov 1982 (SI 1982/1561)
69	Repealed
70	1 Nov 1982 (SI 1982/1561)
71	20 Dec 1982 (SI 1982/1804)
72(a)	*Not in force*
(b)	Repealed
73	30 Jun 1983 (S) (SI 1983/650) 1 Oct 1986 (EW) (SI 1986/1326)
74	See Schs 5, 6 below
75, 76	30 Jun 1983 (S) (SI 1983/650) 1 Oct 1986 (EW) (SI 1986/1326)
Sch 1–4	Repealed
5, para 1–4	Repealed
5	*Not in force*
6–16	Repealed
17	*Not in force*
18, 19	Repealed
20	*Not in force*
21	Repealed
22–24	*Not in force*
25, 26	Repealed
6	1 Nov 1982 (repeal of Road Traffic Regulation Act 1967, s 72(2), (4)) (SI 1982/1561) 1 Jun 1984 (repeals in Transport Act 1968) (SI 1984/175) *Not in force* (otherwise, although most remaining repeals by Sch 6 have been superseded)

Transport (Finance) Act 1982 (c 6)

RA: 25 Feb 1982

25 Feb 1982 (RA)

Travel Concessions (London) Act 1982 (c 12)

Whole Act repealed

1983

Agricultural Holdings (Amendment) (Scotland) Act 1983 (c 46)

Whole Act repealed

Agricultural Marketing Act 1983 (c 3)

RA: 1 Mar 1983

Commencement provisions: s 9(3); Agricultural Marketing Act 1983 (Commencement) Order 1983, SI 1983/366

23 Mar 1983 (SI 1983/366)

Appropriation Act 1983 (c 27)

Whole Act repealed

Appropriation (No 2) Act 1983 (c 48)

Whole Act repealed

British Fishing Boats Act 1983 (c 8)

RA: 28 Mar 1983

28 Mar 1983 (RA)

British Nationality (Falkland Islands) Act 1983 (c 6)

RA: 28 March 1983

Commencement provisions: s 5(2)

1 Jan 1983 (retrospective: s 5(2))

British Shipbuilders Act 1983 (c 15)

RA: 9 May 1983

Commencement provisions: s 3(4)

9 Jul 1983 (s 3(4))

British Shipbuilders (Borrowing Powers) Act 1983 (c 58)

RA: 21 Dec 1983

21 Dec 1983 (RA)

Car Tax Act 1983 (c 53)

RA: 26 Jul 1983

Commencement provisions: s 11(2)

26 Oct 1983 (s 11(2)) (**Note:** car tax abolished with effect from 13 November 1992 by Car Tax (Abolition) Act 1992, but 1983 Act has not been repealed)

Church of England (Miscellaneous Provisions) Measure 1983 (No 2)

RA: 9 May 1983

Commencement provisions: s 13(3)

9 Jun 1983 (s 13(3))

Civil Aviation (Eurocontrol) Act 1983 (c 11)

RA: 11 Apr 1983

Commencement provisions: s 4(2); Civil Aviation (Eurocontrol) Act 1983 (Commencement No 1) Order 1983, SI 1983/1886; Civil Aviation (Eurocontrol) Act 1983 (Commencement No 2) Order 1985, SI 1985/1915

s 1, 2	1 Jan 1986 (SI 1985/1915)
3(1)	1 Jan 1986 (SI 1985/1915)
(2)	1 Jan 1984 (s 4(2); SI 1983/1886)
4	1 Jan 1984 (s 4(2); SI 1983/1886)

Coal Industry Act 1983 (c 60)

RA: 21 Dec 1983

21 Dec 1983 (RA)

Whole Act repealed (in part prospectively) as follows: ss 1, 2, 4–6 and Schedule prospectively repealed by Coal Industry Act 1994, s 67(8), Sch 11, Pt III[1]; s 3 repealed by Coal Industry Act 1987, s 10(3), Sch 3, Pt I

[1] Any order made under Coal Industry Act 1994, s 68(4), (5), bringing the prospective repeals into force will be noted to that Act in the service to this work

---

Companies (Beneficial Interests) Act 1983 (c 50)

Whole Act repealed

Consolidated Fund Act 1983 (c 1)

Whole Act repealed

Consolidated Fund (No 2) Act 1983 (c 5)

Whole Act repealed

Consolidated Fund (No 3) Act 1983 (c 57)

Whole Act repealed

Conwy Tunnel (Supplementary Powers) Act 1983 (c 7)

RA: 28 Mar 1983

Local application only

Copyright (Amendment) Act 1983 (c 42)

Whole Act repealed

Coroners' Juries Act 1983 (c 31)

Whole Act repealed

County Courts (Penalties for Contempt) Act 1983 (c 45)

RA: 13 May 1983

13 May 1983 (RA)

Currency Act 1983 (c 9)

RA: 28 Mar 1983

28 Mar 1983 (RA)

Dentists Act 1983 (c 38)

Whole Act repealed

Diseases of Fish Act 1983 (c 30)

RA: 13 May 1983

Commencement provisions: s 11(2); Diseases of Fish Act 1983 (Commencement) Order 1984, SI 1984/302

s 1–10	1 Apr 1984 (SI 1984/302)
11	13 May 1983 (RA)
Schedule	1 Apr 1984 (SI 1984/302)

Divorce Jurisdiction, Court Fees and Legal Aid (Scotland) Act 1983 (c 12)

RA: 11 Apr 1983

Commencement provisions: s 7(2), (3); Divorce Jurisdiction, Court Fees and Legal Aid (Scotland) Act 1983 (Commencement) Order 1984, SI 1984/253

s 1	1 May 1984 (SI 1984/253)
2, 3	Repealed
4, 5	1 Apr 1984 (SI 1984/253)
6(1)	See Sch 1 below
(2)	See Sch 2 below
7	11 Jun 1983 (s 7(2))
Sch 1, para 1	1 May 1984 (SI 1984/253)
2–5	Repealed
6	1 Apr 1984 (certain purposes) (SI 1984/253) 1 May 1984 (otherwise) (SI 1984/253)
7, 8	Repealed
9, 10	1 Apr 1984 (SI 1984/253)
11	Repealed
12	1 May 1984 (SI 1984/253)
13–17	Repealed
18–20	1 May 1984 (SI 1984/253)
21	Repealed
22	1 May 1984 (SI 1984/253)
23	Repealed
24	1 May 1984 (SI 1984/253)
2	1 Apr 1984 (repeals of or in Court of Session Act 1821, s 31; Sheriff Courts (Scotland) Act 1907, s 40; Church of Scotland (Property and Endowments) Act 1925, s 1(3); Juries Act 1949, s 26(1); Legal Aid (Scotland) Act 1967, s 16(1)(b)(i), (2), (4); Legal Advice and Assistance Act 1972, ss 3(3), 5(6)) (SI 1984/253) 1 May 1984 (otherwise) (SI 1984/253)

Education (Fees and Awards) Act 1983 (c 40)

RA: 13 May 1983

13 May 1983 (RA)

Energy Act 1983 (c 25)

RA: 9 May 1983

Commencement provisions: s 37(1); Energy Act 1983 (Commencement No 1) Order 1983, SI 1983/790; Energy Act 1983 (Commencement No 2) Order 1988, SI 1988/1587

s 1–26	Repealed
27–34	1 Sep 1983 (SI 1983/790)
35(a)	1 Jun 1983 (SI 1983/790)
(b)	1 Sep 1983 (SI 1983/790)
36	See Sch 4 below
37(1), (2)	1 Jun 1983 (SI 1983/790)
(3)	1 Sep 1983 (SI 1983/790)

Energy Act 1983 (c 25)—*cont*

s 38	1 Jun 1983 (SI 1983/790)
Sch 1–3	Repealed
4, Pt I	1 Jun 1983 (repeals of or in Electric Lighting (Clauses) Act 1899, Schedule, ss 2, 52, 54(2); Electric Lighting Act 1909, s 23; Electricity (Supply) Act 1919, ss 11, 36; Electricity (Supply) Act 1922, s 23; Electricity Supply (Meters) Act 1936, s 1(1), (3); Acquisition of Land (Authorisation Procedure) Act 1946, Sch 4; Electricity Act 1947 (except for s 60, in Sch 4, Pt I, the entry relating to the Electricity (Supply) Act 1946, s 24, and in Sch 4, Pt III, the entry relating to the Electric Lighting (Clauses) Act 1899, Schedule, s 60); South of Scotland Electricity Order Confirmation Act 1956, s 40; Electricity Act 1957 (except in Sch 4, Pt I, the entry relating to the Electricity Act 1947, s 60); North of Scotland Electricity Order Confirmation Act 1958, s 27; Post Office Act 1969, Sch 4, para 11; Energy Act 1976, s 14(6)(b); Electricity (Scotland) Act 1979 (except reference to Electricity Act 1947, s 60 in Sch 10, para 13); Acquisition of Land Act 1981, Sch 4, para 1) (SI 1983/790) 1 Oct 1988 (repeals of or in Electric Lighting (Clauses) Act 1899, Schedule, ss 10, 38, 60, 69(1), (2); Electricity Act 1947, s 60, in Sch 4, Pt III, the entry relating to the Electric Lighting (Clauses) Act 1899, Schedule, s 60; Electricity Act 1957, in Sch 4, Pt I, the entry relating to Electricity Act 1947, s 60; Post Office Act 1969, Sch 4, para 8 (c), (g); Electricity (Scotland) Act 1979, in Sch 10, para 13, the reference to Electricity Act 1947, s 60) (SI 1988/1587) *Not in force* (repeals of or in Electric Lighting Act 1888; Electricity (Supply) Act 1926, s 24; Electricity Act 1947, in Sch 4, Pt I, the entry relating to Electricity (Supply) Act 1926, s 24; Electricity Reorganisation (Scotland) Act 1954, s 1(3), Sch 1, Pt III; Post Office Act 1969, Sch 4, para 8(b)) (*Note*: of the above repeals, the repeal of Post Office Act 1969, Sch 4, para 8(b) became spent by virtue of Telecommunications Act 1984, s 109(6), Sch 7, Pt I; and the repeals of or in the 1888, 1926, 1947 and 1954 Acts will become spent on coming into force of Electricity Act 1989, s 112(4), Sch 18 (qv))
II	1 Sep 1983 (SI 1983/790)

Finance Act 1983 (c 28)

Budget day: 15 Mar 1983

RA: 13 May 1983

See the note about Finance Acts at the front of this book

Finance (No 2) Act 1983 (c 49)

RA: 26 Jul 1983

See the note about Finance Acts at the front of this book

Health and Social Services and Social Security Adjudications Act 1983 (c 41)

RA: 13 May 1983

Commencement provisions: s 32(1), (2); Health and Social Services and Social Security Adjudications Act 1983 (Commencement No 1) Order 1983, SI 1983/974; Health and Social Services and Social Security Adjudications Act 1983 (Commencement No 2) Order 1983, SI 1983/1862; Health and Social Services and Social Security Adjudications Act 1983 (Commencement No 3) Order 1984, SI 1984/216; Health and Social Services and Social Security Adjudications Act 1983 (Commencement No 4) Order 1984, SI 1984/957; Health and Social Services and Social Security Adjudications Act 1984 (Commencement No 5) Order 1984, SI 1984/1347; Health and Social Services and Social Security Adjudications Act 1983 (Scotland) (Commencement No 1) Order 1985, SI 1985/704; Health and Social Services and Social Security Adjudications Act 1983 (Commencement No 6) Order 1992, SI 1992/2974

s 1	15 Aug 1983 (so far as relates to (i) National Health Service Act 1977, s 28A(2)(a)–(d), but only for the purpose of giving effect to s 28B(1)(a) of that Act, and (ii) s 28B of the 1977 Act) (SI 1983/974) 1 Apr 1984 (so far as relates to new s 28A of the 1977 Act) (SI 1984/216)
2	1 May 1985 (SI 1985/704)
3	15 Aug 1983 (SI 1983/974)
4	1 Jan 1984 (SI 1983/974)
5, 6	Repealed
7(1)	15 Aug 1983 (SI 1983/974); prospectively repealed by Children (Scotland) Act 1995, s 105(5), Sch 5[1]
(2), (3)	30 Jan 1984 (SI 1983/1862); prospectively repealed by Children (Scotland) Act 1995, s 105(5), Sch 5[1]
8	30 Jan 1984 (SI 1983/1862)
9	See Sch 2 below
10	1 Apr 1984 (SI 1983/974)
11	1 Oct 1984 (so far as relates to Sch 4, para 24 (repealed)) (SI 1984/957) 1 Jan 1985 (otherwise) (SI 1984/1347))
12	See Sch 5 below
13, 14	15 Aug 1983 (SI 1983/974)
15, 16	1 Oct 1984 (SI 1983/974)
17, 18	1 Jan 1984 (SI 1983/974)
19	Repealed
20	15 Aug 1983 (SI 1983/974)
21–24	12 Apr 1993 (SI 1992/2974)
25	See Sch 8 below
26–28	15 Aug 1983 (SI 1983/974)
29(1)	See Sch 9, Pt I below
(2)	See Sch 9, Pt II below
30(1)	See Sch 10, Pt I below
(2)	See Sch 10, Pt II below
(3)	Repealed

Health and Social Services and Social Security Adjudications Act 1983 (c 41)—*cont*

s 31	15 Aug 1983 (SI 1983/974)
32–34	13 May 1983 (s 32(1))
Sch 1	Repealed
2, para 1–3	Repealed
4–6	15 Aug 1983 (SI 1983/974); prospectively repealed by Children (Scotland) Act 1995, s 105(4), (5), Sch 4, para 32, Sch 5[1]
7	15 Aug 1983 (SI 1983/974)
8	15 Aug 1983 (SI 1983/974); prospectively repealed by Children (Scotland) Act 1995, s 105(4), (5), Sch 4, para 32, Sch 5[1]
9–14	Repealed
15, 16	15 Aug 1983 (SI 1983/974)
17, 18	1 Jan 1984 (SI 1983/974)
19	15 Aug 1983 (SI 1983/974)
20–24	Repealed
25, 26	Spent
27, 28	Repealed
29–33	15 Aug 1983 (SI 1983/974)
34	Repealed
35	15 Aug 1983 (SI 1983/974)
36	15 Aug 1983 (SI 1983/974)
37	Repealed
38–45	15 Aug 1983 (SI 1983/974)
46–62	Repealed
3	1 Apr 1984 (SI 1983/974)
4	Repealed
5, para 1	15 Aug 1983 (SI 1983/974)
2	1 Apr 1984 (SI 1984/216)
3	15 Aug 1983 (SI 1983/974)
6, 7	15 Aug 1983 (SI 1983/974)
8	Repealed (except paras 1(3)(a), 29, which came into force on 23 Apr 1984 (SI 1984/216))
9, Pt I, para 1	Repealed
2	15 Aug 1983 (SI 1983/974)
3	1 Apr 1984 (SI 1983/974)
4–7	Repealed
8	15 Aug 1983 (SI 1983/974)
9–17	Repealed
18	23 Apr 1984 (SI 1984/216)
19	1 Jan 1985 (SI 1984/1347)
20	Repealed
21	15 Aug 1983 (SI 1983/974)
22	1 Jan 1984 (SI 1983/974)
23	1 Apr 1984 (SI 1983/974)
24, 25	15 Aug 1983 (SI 1983/974)
26	Repealed
27	1 Jan 1985 (SI 1984/1347)
28	Repealed
II	1 Jan 1984 (SI 1983/974)
10, Pt I	15 Aug 1983 (repeals of or in Public Health Act 1936; Food and Drugs Act 1955; Health Services and Public Health Act 1968, ss 48(2), 64 (so far as relates to Scotland); Social Work (Scotland) Act 1968, s 31(2); Radiological Protection Act 1970; Powers

Health and Social Services and Social Security Adjudications Act 1983 (c 41)—*cont*

Sch 10, Pt I—*cont*

of Criminal Courts Act 1973; Children Act 1975, s 109(3); Adoption Act 1976; Criminal Law Act 1977; National Health Service Act 1977, ss 8(1A), 9, 100(2), 128(1), Sch 5; Adoption (Scotland) Act 1978; Employment Protection (Consolidation) Act 1978; Child Care Act 1980, ss 71, 79(5)(h); Health Services Act 1980, ss 1, 4(1) (but only for the purpose of giving effect to new s 28B(1)(a) of National Health Service Act 1977), Sch 1; Overseas Development and Co-operation Act 1980) (SI 1983/974, as partly revoked by SI 1983/1862)

1 Jan 1984 (repeals of or in National Assistance Act 1948; Local Government Act 1966; Health Services and Public Health Act 1968, s 45(2); Social Work (Scotland) Act 1968, ss 14(2), 78(1)(b); Children and Young Persons Act 1969; Local Government Act 1972; National Health Service Act 1977, Sch 8; Domestic Proceedings and Magistrates' Courts Act 1978; Child Care Act 1980, ss 10(2), 36(1), 39(2), 43(3), 44(5), 45(1)(ii), 87(1), Schs 1, 5; Residential Homes Act 1980 (but only for the purposes of the repeal of s 8 of that Act); Criminal Justice Act 1982) (SI 1983/974, as partly revoked by SI 1983/1862)

30 Jan 1984 (repeals of or in Social Work (Scotland) Act 1968, s 59A(1), (3); Children Act 1975, s 72) (SI 1983/1862)

1 Apr 1984 (repeals of or in Health Visiting and Social Work (Training) Act 1962; Local Authority Social Services Act 1970; National Health Service Act 1977, Sch 15; Nurses, Midwives and Health Visitors Act 1979) (SI 1983/974, as partly revoked by SI 1983/1862)

1 Apr 1984 (repeal of Health Services Act 1980, s 4(1) for remaining purposes) (SI 1984/216)

23 Apr 1984 (repeals of or in Family Income Supplements Act 1970; Tribunals and Inquiries Act 1971; Social Security Act 1975; House of Commons Disqualification Act 1975; Child Benefit Act 1975; Supplementary Benefits Act 1976; Social Security (Miscellaneous Provisions) Act 1977; Social Security and Housing Benefits Act 1982) (SI 1984/216)

1 Jan 1985 (repeals of or in Nursing Homes Act 1975; Child Care Act 1980, s 58, Sch 3; Residential Homes Act 1980 (except s 8, repealed on 1 Jan 1984); Children's Homes Act 1982) (SI 1984/1347, as amended by SI 1984/1767)

1 May 1985 (repeal of Health Services Act 1980, s 4(2)) (SI 1985/704)

II — 15 Aug 1983 (SI 1983/974)

[1] Any order(s) under Children (Scotland) Act 1995, s 105, bringing the prospective repeals into force will be noted to that Act in the service to this work

Importation of Milk Act 1983 (c 37)

Whole Act repealed

International Monetary Arrangements Act 1983 (c 51)

RA: 26 Jul 1983

Commencement provisions: s 3(2); International Monetary Arrangements Act 1983 (Commencement) Order 1983, SI 1983/1643

s 1	14 Nov 1983 (SI 1983/1643)
2, 3	26 Jul 1983 (RA)

International Transport Conventions Act 1983 (c 14)

RA: 11 Apr 1983

Commencement provisions: s 11(3); International Transport Convention Act 1983 (Certification of Commencement of Convention) Order 1985, SI 1985/612

s 1	1 May 1985 (SI 1985/612)
2–10	11 Apr 1983 (RA)
11	11 Apr 1983 (RA; sub-s (2) effective from 1 May 1985, the day on which the Convention comes into force as regards the United Kingdom) (s 11(3); SI 1985/612)
Sch 1, 2	11 Apr 1983 (RA)
3	1 May 1985 (SI 1985/612)

Level Crossings Act 1983 (c 16)

RA: 9 May 1983

Commencement provisions: s 2(2)

9 Aug 1983 (s 2(2))

Licensing (Occasional Permissions) Act 1983 (c 24)

RA: 9 May 1983

Commencement provisions: s 5(2)

9 Aug 1983 (s 5(2))

Litter Act 1983 (c 35)

RA: 13 May 1983

Commencement provisions: s 13(2), (3)

s 1, 2	Repealed
3	13 Aug 1983 (s 13(3))

Litter Act 1983 (c 35)—*cont*

s 4	*Not in force*; sub-s (4) substituted by Local Government etc (Scotland) Act 1994, s 180(1), Sch 13, para 132(1), (2), as from a day to be appointed by order made under s 184(2), (3) of that Act; any order so made will be noted to that Act in the service to this work
5–9	13 Aug 1983 (s 13(3))
10	13 Aug 1983 (s 13(3)); section re-numbered s 10(1) and s 10(2) added by Local Government (Wales) Act 1994, s 22(3), Sch 9, para 12, as from a day to be appointed by order made under s 66(3) of that Act; any order so made will be noted to that Act in the service to this work
11	13 Aug 1983 (s 13(3))
12(1)	Repealed
(2)	13 Aug 1983 (s 13(3))
(3)	See Sch 2 below
13	13 Aug 1983 (s 13(3))
Sch 1	13 Aug 1983 (s 13(3))
2	13 Aug 1983 (except repeal of Control of Pollution Act 1974, s 24(1)–(3)) (s 13(2))
	Not in force (exception noted above)

Local Authorities (Expenditure Powers) Act 1983 (c 52)

RA: 26 Jul 1983

26 Jul 1983 (RA)

Whole Act repealed (EW)

Marriage Act 1983 (c 32)

RA: 13 May 1983

Commencement provisions: s 12(5); Marriage Act 1983 (Commencement) Order 1984, SI 1984/413

1 May 1984 (SI 1984/413)

Matrimonial Homes Act 1983 (c 19)

RA: 9 May 1983

Commencement provisions: s 13(2)

9 Aug 1983 (s 13(2))

Medical Act 1983 (c 54)

RA: 26 Jul 1983

Commencement provisions: s 57(2)

26 Oct 1983 (s 57(2))

Mental Health Act 1983 (c 20)

RA: 9 May 1983

Commencement provisions: s 149(2), (3); Mental Health Act 1983 Commencement Order 1984, SI 1984/1357

s 1–20	30 Sep 1983 (s 149(2))
21, 21A, 21B	Substituted (for s 21) by Mental Health (Patients in the Community) Act 1995, s 2(2) (qv)
22–25	30 Sep 1983 (s 149(2))
25A–25J	Inserted by Mental Health (Patients in the Community) Act 1995, s 1(1) (qv)
26	30 Sep 1983 (s 149(2))
27	Substituted by Children Act 1989, s 108(5), Sch 13, para 48 (qv)
28–34	30 Sep 1983 (s 149(2))
35, 36	1 Oct 1984 (SI 1984/1357)
37	30 Sep 1983 (s 149(2))
38	1 Oct 1984 (SI 1984/1357)
39	30 Sep 1983 (s 149(2))
39A	Inserted by Criminal Justice Act 1991, s 27(1) (qv)
40(1), (2)	30 Sep 1983 (s 149(2))
(3)	1 Oct 1984 (SI 1984/1357)
(4), (5)	30 Sep 1983 (s 149(2))
(6)	Inserted by Mental Health (Patients in the Community) Act 1995, s 2(4) (qv)
41–54	30 Sep 1983 (s 149(2))
54A	Inserted by Criminal Justice Act 1991, s 27(2) (qv)
55–123	30 Sep 1983 (s 149(2)
124	Repealed
125–149	30 Sep 1983 (s 149(2))
Sch 1–6	30 Sep 1983 (s 149(2))

Mental Health (Amendment) (Scotland) Act 1983 (c 39)

RA: 13 May 1983

Commencement provisions: s 41(2) (repealed); Mental Health (Amendment) (Scotland) Act 1983 (Commencement No 1) Order 1983, SI 1983/1199; Mental Health (Amendment) (Scotland) Act 1983 (Commencement No 2) Order 1983, SI 1983/1920

Whole Act repealed, subject to savings for the provisions mentioned below

s 7(2)	16 Aug 1983 (SI 1983/1199)
22(2)	30 Sep 1984 (SI 1983/1920)
34–36	30 Sep 1984 (SI 1983/1920)
Sch 2, para 1	30 Sep 1984 (SI 1983/1920)
38	31 Mar 1984 (SI 1983/1920)

Merchant Shipping Act 1983 (c 13)

Whole Act repealed

Miscellaneous Financial Provisions Act 1983 (c 29)

RA: 13 May 1983

Commencement provisions: s 9(1), (2); Miscellaneous Financial Provisions Act 1983 (Commencement of Provisions) Order 1983, SI 1983/1338

s 1	1 Apr 1984 (SI 1983/1338)
2	13 Jul 1983 (s 9(2))
3	Repealed
4–7	13 Jul 1983 (s 9(2))
8	1 Apr 1984 (SI 1983/1338)
9–11	13 Jul 1983 (s 9(2))
Sch 1	1 Apr 1984 (SI 1983/1338)
2	13 Jul 1983 (s 9(2))
3	1 Apr 1984 (SI 1983/1338)

Mobile Homes Act 1983 (c 34)

RA: 13 May 1983

Commencement provisions: s 6(3)

20 May 1983 (s 6(3))

National Audit Act 1983 (c 44)

RA: 13 May 1983

Commencement provisions: s 15(2), (3)

s 1–15	1 Jan 1984 (s 15(2))
Sch 1–4	1 Jan 1984 (s 15(2))
5	1 Jan 1984 (repeal of Exchequer and Audit Departments Act 1866, s 24; Exchequer and Audit Departments Act 1921, in s 1(2), the proviso, ss 3(3), (4), 8(1)) (s 15(2))
	1 Oct 1984 (repeal of Exchequer and Audit Departments Act 1921, s 8(2)) (s 15(3))

National Heritage Act 1983 (c 47)

RA: 13 May 1983

Commencement provisions: s 41(1)–(3); National Heritage Act 1983 (Commencement No 1) Order 1983, SI 1983/1062; National Heritage Act 1983 (Commencement No 2) Order 1983, SI 1983/1183; National Heritage Act 1983 (Commencement No 3) Order 1983, SI 1983/1437; National Heritage Act 1983 (Commencement No 4) Order 1984, SI 1984/208, National Heritage Act 1983 (Commencement No 5) Order 1984, SI 1984/217; National Heritage Act 1983 (Commencement No 6) Order 1984, SI 1984/225

s 1(1)	30 Sep 1983 (SI 1983/1062)
(2)	See Sch 1, Pt I below
2, 3	1 Apr 1984 (SI 1984/225)

National Heritage Act 1983 (c 47)—*cont*

s 4(1)–(4)	1 Apr 1984 (SI 1984/225)
(5)	13 Jul 1983 (s 41(3))
(6)	1 Apr 1984 (SI 1984/225)
(7)	13 Jul 1983 (s 41(3))
(8)	1 Apr 1984 (SI 1984/225)
5–7	1 Apr 1984 (SI 1984/225)
8	Repealed
9(1)	30 Sep 1983 (SI 1983/1062)
(2)	See Sch 1, Pt II below
10, 11	1 Apr 1984 (SI 1984/225)
12(1)–(4)	1 Apr 1984 (SI 1984/225)
(5), (6)	13 Jul 1983 (s 41(3))
(7)	1 Apr 1984 (SI 1984/225)
13–15	1 Apr 1984 (SI 1984/225)
16	Repealed
17	1 Oct 1983 (SI 1983/1437)
18	1 Apr 1984 (SI 1984/208)
18A	Inserted by Museums and Galleries Act 1992, s 11(2), Sch 8, Pt II, para 13(4) (qv)
19(1)–(3)	1 Apr 1984 (SI 1984/208)
(4), (5)	13 Jul 1983 (s 41(3))
(6)	1 Apr 1984 (SI 1984/208)
20, 21	1 Apr 1984 (SI 1984/208)
22	1 Oct 1983 (SI 1983/1437)
23	8 Aug 1983 (SI 1983/1183)
24–28	1 Apr 1984 (SI 1984/217)
29	8 Aug 1983 (SI 1983/1183)
30, 31	13 Jul 1983 (s 41(3))
32	1 Oct 1983 (SI 1983/1437)
33(1), (2)	1 Apr 1984 (SI 1984/208)
(2A)	Inserted by Planning and Compensation Act 1991, s 29(1) (qv)
(2B)	Inserted by Leasehold Reform, Housing and Urban Development Act 1993, s 187(1), Sch 21, para 9 (qv)
(3), (4)	1 Apr 1984 (SI 1984/208)
(5)	1 Oct 1983 (SI 1983/1437)
(6)–(8)	1 Apr 1984 (SI 1984/208)
34	1 Apr 1984 (SI 1984/208)
35	1 Oct 1983 (SI 1983/1437)
36, 37	1 Apr 1984 (SI 1984/208)
38	1 Oct 1983 (SI 1983/1437)
39	1 Apr 1984 (SI 1984/208)
40(1)	See Sch 5 below
(2)	See Sch 6 below
41–43	13 Jul 1983 (s 41(3))
Sch 1, Pt I, para 1–8	30 Sep 1983 (SI 1983/1062)
9	Repealed
10	30 Sep 1983 (SI 1983/1062)
II 11–18	30 Sep 1983 (SI 1983/1062)
19	Repealed
20	30 Sep 1983 (SI 1983/1062)
III 21–30	1 Oct 1983 (SI 1983/1437)
IV 31–40	8 Aug 1983 (SI 1983/1183)
2	13 Jul 1983 (s 41(3))
3	1 Oct 1983 (SI 1983/1437)

National Heritage Act 1983 (c 47)—*cont*

Sch 4, para 1–11	1 Apr 1984 (SI 1984/208)
12	Spent
13–21	Repealed
22	1 Apr 1984 (SI 1984/208)
23, 24	Repealed
25–71	1 Apr 1984 (SI 1984/208)
5, para 1, 2	Repealed
3	8 Aug 1983 (so far as relates to Royal Botanic Gardens, Kew) (SI 1983/1183)
	30 Sep 1983 (so far as relates to Science Museum and Victoria and Albert Museum) (SI 1983/1062)
	1 Oct 1983 (so far as relates to Armouries, the Historic Buildings and Monuments Commission for England and Board of Trustees of the Armouries) (SI 1983/1437)
4–7	Repealed
6	3 Aug 1983 (repeal in National Gallery and Tate Gallery Act 1954, s 4(2)) (SI 1983/1062)
	1 Apr 1984 (repeals in Historic Buildings and Ancient Monuments Act 1953; Town and Country Planning (Amendment) Act 1972; Ancient Monuments and Archaeological Areas Act 1979) (SI 1984/208)
	1 Apr 1984 (repeals in Patents and Designs Act 1907, s 47(1); Public Records Act 1958, Sch 1, para 3 (entries in Pt I of the Table relating to Victoria and Albert Museum and Science Museum) (SI 1984/225)

Nuclear Material (Offences) Act 1983 (c 18)

RA: 9 May 1983

Commencement provisions: s 8(2); Nuclear Material (Offences) Act 1983 (Commencement) Order 1991, SI 1991/1716

s 1–4	2 Oct 1991 (SI 1991/1716)
5	Repealed
5A	Prospectively inserted by Criminal Justice Act 1988, s 170(1), Sch 15, para 95 (repealed)
6	2 Oct 1991 (SI 1991/1716)
7(1)	Repealed
(2)	24 Jul 1991 (in relation to any Order in Council) (SI 1991/1716)
	2 Oct 1991 (otherwise) (SI 1991/1716)
8	2 Oct 1991 (SI 1991/1716)
Schedule	2 Oct 1991 (SI 1991/1716)

Oil Taxation Act 1983 (c 56)

RA: 1 Dec 1983

1 Dec 1983 (RA) (though largely effective from 1 Jul 1982)

Pastoral Measure 1983 (No 1)

RA: 9 May 1983

Commencement provisions: s 94(4)

1 Nov 1983 (s 94(4))

Pet Animals Act 1951 (Amendment) Act 1983 (c 26)

RA: 9 May 1983

Commencement provisions: s 2(2)

9 Nov 1983 (s 2(2))

Petroleum Royalties (Relief) Act 1983 (c 59)

RA: 21 Dec 1983

Commencement provisions: s 2(2)

21 Feb 1984 (s 2(2))

Pig Industry Levy Act 1983 (c 4)

RA: 1 Mar 1983

1 Mar 1983 (RA)

Pilotage Act 1983 (c 21)

Whole Act repealed

Plant Varieties Act 1983 (c 17)

RA: 9 May 1983

Commencement provisions: s 6(3)

9 Jul 1983 (s 6(3))

Ports (Reduction of Debt) Act 1983 (c 22)

RA: 9 May 1983

9 May 1983 (RA)

Representation of the People Act 1983 (c 2)

RA: 8 Feb 1983

Commencement provisions: s 207(2); Representation of the People Act 1983 (Commencement) Order 1983, SI 1983/153

15 Mar 1983 (SI 1983/153)

Road Traffic (Driving Licences) Act 1983 (c 43)

Whole Act repealed

Social Security and Housing Benefits Act 1983 (c 36)

Whole Act repealed

Solvent Abuse (Scotland) Act 1983 (c 33)

RA: 13 May 1983

Commencement provisions: s 3(2)

13 July 1983 (s 3(2))

Whole Act prospectively repealed by Children (Scotland) Act 1995, s 105(5), Sch 5; any order made under s 105(1), (2) of that Act bringing the prospective repeal into force will be noted to that Act in the service to this work

---

Transport Act 1983 (c 10)

RA: 28 Mar 1983

Commencement provisions: s 10(1)(a)–(c)

This Act came into force on Royal Assent, subject to certain provisions of Pt I taking effect; see the relevant provisions as noted below:

s 1	28 Mar 1983 (s 10(1))
2	Effective in relation to any accounting period of an Executive ending after 31 Mar 1983 (s 10(1)(a))
3, 4	1 Apr 1983 (s 10(1)(b))
5	Effective in relation to any year beginning on or after 1 Apr 1984 (s 10(1)(c))
6(1), (2)	1 Apr 1983 (s 10(1)(b))
(3), (4)	Repealed
(5), (6)	1 Apr 1983 (s 10(1)(b))
(7)	Effective in relation to any accounting period of an Executive ending after 31 Mar 1983 (s 10(1)(a))
7, 8	28 Mar 1983 (s 10(1))
9(1)	See Schedule below
(2)	Repealed
(3)	Effective in relation to any accounting period of an Executive ending after 31 Mar 1983 (s 10(1)(a))
(4), (5)	Repealed
10	28 Mar 1983 (s 10(1))
11, 12	28 Mar 1983 (RA)
Schedule	31 Mar 1983 (repeals in Transport (London) Act 1969, ss 5, 7) (s 10(1)(a))
	1 Apr 1983 (repeals in Transport (London) Act 1969, s 11) (s 10(1)(b))

Value Added Tax Act 1983 (c 55)

Whole Act repealed (for transitional provisions and savings, see Value Added Tax Act 1994, Sch 13)

Water Act 1983 (c 23)

RA: 9 May 1983

Commencement provisions: ss 3(1), 9(2), 11(4), (5); Water Act 1983 (Commencement No 1) Order 1983, SI 1983/1173; Water Act 1983 (Water Space Amenity Commission Appointed Day) Order 1983, SI 1983/1174; Water Act 1983 (Commencement No 2) Order 1983, SI 1983/1234; Water Act 1983 (National Water Council Appointed Day) Order 1983, SI 1983/1235; Water Act 1983 (Dissolution of the National Water Council) Order 1983, SI 1983/1927; Water Act 1983 (Representation of Consumers' Interests) (Appointed Date) Order 1984, SI 1984/71

s 1(1)	Repealed
(2)	1 Oct 1983 (SI 1983/1234); prospectively repealed by Water Act 1989, s 190(3), Sch 27, Pt II[1]
(3)	Repealed
2	Repealed
3, 4	9 May 1983 (s 11(4))
5–7	Repealed
8	10 Aug 1983 (SI 1983/1173)
9, 10	9 May 1983 (s 11(4))
11(1)	9 May 1983 (s 11(4))
(2), (3)	See Schs 4, 5 below
(4)–(7)	9 May 1983 (s 11(4))
Sch 1	Repealed
2	9 May 1983 (s 11(4))
3	Repealed
4, para 1–6	Repealed
7	1 Oct 1983 (SI 1983/1234)
8, 9	9 May 1983 (s 11(4))
5, Pt I	10 Aug 1983 (repeals of or in Development of Rural Wales Act 1976, Sch 7, para 11; Water Charges Equalisation Act 1977; Local Government Planning and Land Act 1980, s 158(1), (2); New Towns Act 1981, Sch 12, para 12) (SI 1983/1173)
	1 Oct 1983 (repeals of or in Water Act 1973, ss 23, 24(12)(a), 25(5)(a), Sch 3, para 40, sub-para (1)(b) and word 'and' immediately preceding it, and sub-para (5)) (SI 1983/1174)
	1 Oct 1983 (repeals of or in Public Bodies (Admission to Meetings) Act 1960; Local Government Act 1972; Water Act 1973, ss 6, 17(5); House of Commons Disqualification Act 1975, Sch 1, Pt III; Local Government, Planning and Land Act 1980, s 25(4)) (SI 1983/1234)
	1 Oct 1983 (repeals of or in Public Health Act 1961, s 9(3); Water Act 1973, ss 4, 5(3), 26(2)–(4), 29(2), 30(6), 38(1), Sch 3, Sch 8, para 90; House of Commons Disqualification Act 1975, Sch 1, Pt III; Land Drainage Act 1976, Sch 5, para 8(1); Water (Scotland) Act 1980, Sch 10) (SI 1983/1235)

Water Act 1983 (c 23)—*cont*

Sch 5, Pt I—*cont*	*Not in force* (repeal of Local Government (Scotland) Act 1973, Sch 17, para 64)
II	9 May 1983 (revocation of SI 1982/944) (s 11(4))
	1 Oct 1983 (otherwise) (SI 1983/1234)

[1] Any order made under Water Act 1989, s 194(4), (5), bringing the prospective repeal into force will be noted to that Act in the service to this work

1984

Agricultural Holdings Act 1984 (c 41)

Whole Act repealed

Agriculture (Amendment) Act 1984 (c 20)

RA: 24 May 1984

Commencement provisions: s 3(2)

24 Jul 1984 (s 3(2))

Anatomy Act 1984 (c 14)

RA: 24 May 1984

Commencement provisions: s 13(3); Anatomy Act 1984 (Commencement) Order 1988, SI 1988/81

14 Feb 1988 (SI 1988/81)

Animal Health and Welfare Act 1984 (c 40)

RA: 12 Jul 1984

Commencement provisions: s 17(2)–(4); Animal Health and Welfare Act 1984 (Commencement No 1) Order 1985, SI 1985/1267

s 1–4		12 Sep 1984 (s 17(2))
5		Repealed
6–12		12 Sep 1984 (s 17(2))
13		16 Aug 1985 (SI 1985/1267)
14–17		12 Sep 1984 (s 17(2))
Sch 1,	para 1	12 Sep 1984 (s 17(2))
	2	Repealed
	3	16 Aug 1985 (SI 1985/1267)
	4	12 Sep 1984 (s 17(2))
2		12 Sep 1984 (except repeals in Medicines Act 1968) (s 17(2))
		16 Aug 1985 (exception noted above) (SI 1985/1267)

Appropriation Act 1984 (c 44)

Whole Act repealed

Betting, Gaming and Lotteries (Amendment) Act 1984 (c 25)

RA: 26 Jun 1984

Commencement provisions: s 4(2); Betting, Gaming and Lotteries (Amendment) Act 1984 (Commencement) Order 1986, SI 1986/102

s 1	26 Aug 1984 (s 4(2))
2	10 Mar 1986 (SI 1986/102)
3	26 Aug 1984 (s 4(2))
4	26 Jun 1984 (RA)

Building Act 1984 (c 55)

RA: 31 Oct 1984

Commencement provisions: s 134; Building Act 1984 (Commencement No 1) Order 1985, SI 1985/1602; Building Act 1984 (Appointed Day and Repeal) Order 1985, SI 1985/1603

s 1–11	1 Dec 1984 (s 134(2))
12, 13	1 Dec 1984 (so far as enable regulations to be made) (s 134(1)(a))
	Not in force (otherwise)
14, 15	1 Dec 1984 (s 134(2))
16	1 Dec 1984 (11 Nov 1985 being the appointed day under sub-s (13)) (SI 1985/1603)
17–19	1 Dec 1984 (s 134(2))
20	*Not in force*
21–25	1 Dec 1984 (s 134(2))
26–30	Repealed
31	1 Dec 1984 (so far as enables regulations to be made) (s 134(1)(a))
	Not in force (otherwise)
32	1 Dec 1984 (s 134(2))
33	*Not in force*
34–37	1 Dec 1984 (s 134(2))
38	1 Dec 1984 (so far as enables regulations to be made) (s 134(1)(a))
	Not in force (otherwise)
39–41	1 Dec 1984 (s 134(2))
42(1)–(3)	*Not in force*
(4)–(6)	1 Dec 1984 (so far as enable regulations to be made) (s 134(1)(a))
	Not in force (otherwise)
(7)	1 Dec 1984 (but no day appointed)
43(1), (2)	*Not in force*
(3)	*Not in force* (except so far as enables regulations to be made) (s 134(1)(a))
44, 45	*Not in force*
46–49	1 Dec 1984 (s 134(2))
50(1)	1 Dec 1984 (s 134(2))
(2), (3)	11 Nov 1985 (SI 1985/1602)
(4)–(8)	1 Dec 1984 (s 134(2))
51–68	1 Dec 1984 (s 134(2))
69	Repealed (for savings see Water Act 1989, s 190(2), Sch 26, Pt II, para 20(2))
70–108	1 Dec 1984 (s 134(2))

Building Act 1984 (c 55)—*cont*

s 109	Repealed
110–132	1 Dec 1984 (s 134(2))
133(1)	1 Dec 1984 (s 134(2))
(2)	1 Dec 1984 (except so far as relates to Town and Country Planning Act 1947 and Atomic Energy Authority Act 1954) (s 134(2)) *Not in force* (otherwise)(s 134(1)(c))
134	1 Dec 1984 (s 134(2))
135	1 Dec 1984 (s 134(2))
Sch 1, para 1–8	1 Dec 1984 (s 134(2))
9	*Not in force*
10, 11	1 Dec 1984 (s 134(2))
2–6	1 Dec 1984 (s 134(2))
7	*Not in force* (repeals of or in Town and Country Planning Act 1947; Atomic Energy Authority Act 1954) (s 134(1)(c)) 1 Dec 1984 (otherwise) (s 134(2))

Cable and Broadcasting Act 1984 (c 46)

Whole Act repealed

Capital Transfer Tax Act 1984 (c 51)

RA: 31 Jul 1984

Commencement provisions: s 274(1)

1 Jan 1985 (s 274(1))

Notes

This Act does not apply to transfers of value made before 1985 or to other events before then on which tax is or would be chargeable. Note also s 275 of, and Sch 7 to, the Act in relation to continuity and construction of references to old and new law

On and after 25 Jul 1986 the tax charged under this Act is known as inheritance tax and this Act may be cited as the Inheritance Tax Act 1984 (Finance Act 1986, s 100)

Child Abduction Act 1984 (c 37)

RA: 12 Jul 1984

Commencement provisions: s 13(2)

12 Oct 1984 (s 13(2))

Consolidated Fund Act 1984 (c 1)

Whole Act repealed

Consolidated Fund (No 2) Act 1984 (c 61)

Whole Act repealed

Co-operative Development Agency and Industrial Development Act 1984 (c 57)

RA: 31 Oct 1984

Commencement provisions: s 7(1); Co-operative Development Agency and Industrial Development Act 1984 (Commencement) Order 1984, SI 1984/1845

s 1, 2	Repealed
3	31 Oct 1984 (s 7(1))
4, 5	29 Nov 1984 (SI 1984/1845)
6	See Sch 2 below
7, 8	31 Oct 1984 (s 7(1))
Sch 1	29 Nov 1984 (SI 1984/1845)
2, Pt I	31 Oct 1984 (s 7(1))
II	31 Dec 1990 (see note below)
III	29 Nov 1984 (SI 1984/1845)

Note

The days appointed for the winding up and dissolution of the Co-operative Development Agency were 30 Sep 1990 and 31 Dec 1990, by the Co-operative Development Agency (Winding up and Dissolution) Order 1990 (SI 1990/279)

County Courts Act 1984 (c 28)

RA: 26 Jun 1984

Commencement provisions: s 150

1 Aug 1984 (s 150)

Cycle Tracks Act 1984 (c 38)

RA: 12 Jul 1984

Commencement provisions: s 9(2)

12 Sep 1984 (s 9(2))

Data Protection Act 1984 (c 35)

RA: 12 Jul 1984

Commencement provisions: s 42; Data Protection Act 1984 (Appointed Day) Order 1985, SI 1985/1055

12 Jul 1984 (RA)

Note

Although this Act in general came into force on the date of Royal Assent, no application for registration under Pt II (ss 4–20) of the Act was to be made until 11 Nov 1985 (ie the day appointed by SI 1985/1055 for the purposes of s 42(1) of the Act) and certain provisions of the Act did not to apply, or fully apply, until six months, or two years, after that date (s 42)

Dentists Act 1984 (c 24)

RA: 26 Jun 1984

Commencement provisions: s 55(1)–(3); Dentists Act 1984 (Commencement) Order 1984, SI 1984/1815

s 1	1 Oct 1984 (s 55(1))
2(1)–(3)	1 Oct 1984 (s 55(1))
(4), (5)	1 Jan 1985 (SI 1984/1815)
3–27	1 Oct 1984 (s 55(1))
28	1 Jan 1985 (SI 1984/1815)
29, 30	1 Jan 1985 (so far as relate to proceedings before Health Committee or any direction or order given or made by that Committee) (SI 1984/1815)
	1 Oct 1984 (otherwise) (s 55(1))
31	1 Jan 1985 (SI 1984/1815)
32	1 Oct 1984 (s 55(1))
33	As noted to ss 29, 30 above
34–48	1 Oct 1984 (s 55(1))
49	26 Jul 1984 (s 55(2))
50–53	1 Oct 1984 (s 55(1))
54(1)	See Sch 5 below
(2)	See Sch 6, Pt I below
(3)	See Sch 6, Pt II below
55, 56	1 Oct 1984 (s 55(1))
Sch 1, para 1–7	1 Oct 1984 (s 55(1))
8(1)	1 Oct 1984 (s 55(1))
(2)	1 Jan 1985 (SI 1984/1815)
(3)–(12)	1 Oct 1984 (s 55(1))
2	1 Oct 1984 (s 55(1))
3, para 1, 2	As noted to ss 29, 30 above
3	1 Jan 1985 (SI 1984/1815)
4, 5	As noted to ss 29, 30 above
6	1 Jan 1985 (SI 1984/1815)
7, 8	As noted to ss 29, 30 above
9	Repealed
4, 5	1 Oct 1984 (s 55(1))
6, Pt I	26 Jul 1984 (repeal of Dentists Act 1983, s 29) (s 55(2))
	1 Oct 1984 (otherwise) (s 55(1))
II	1 Oct 1984 (s 55(1))
7	1 Oct 1984 (s 55(1))

Education (Amendment) (Scotland) Act 1984 (c 6)

RA: 13 Mar 1984

Commencement provisions: s 2

13 May 1984 (s 2)

Education (Grants and Awards) Act 1984 (c 11)

RA: 12 Apr 1984

Commencement provisions: s 6(2)

12 Jun 1984 (s 6(2))

Finance Act 1984 (c 43)

Budget Day: 13 Mar 1984

RA: 26 Jul 1984

See the note concerning Finance Acts at the front of this book

---

Food Act 1984 (c 30)

RA: 26 Jun 1984

Commencement provisions: s 136(4)

26 Sep 1984 (s 136(4))

Foreign Limitation Periods Act 1984 (c 16)

RA: 24 May 1984

Commencement provisions: s 7(2); Foreign Limitation Periods Act 1984 (Commencement) Order 1985, SI 1985/1276

1 Oct 1985 (SI 1985/1276)

Fosdyke Bridge Act 1984 (c 17)

RA: 24 May 1984

Local application only

Foster Children (Scotland) Act 1984 (c 56)

RA: 31 Oct 1984

Commencement provisions: s 23(2)

31 Jan 1985 (s 23(2))

Friendly Societies Act 1984 (c 62)

RA: 20 Dec 1984

20 Dec 1984 (RA)

Health and Social Security Act 1984 (c 48)

RA: 26 Jul 1984

Commencement provisions: s 27; Health and Social Security Act 1984 (Commencement No 1) Order 1984, SI 1984/1302; Health and Social Security Act 1984 (Commencement No 1) Amendment Order 1984, SI 1984/1467; Health and Social Security Act 1984 (Commencement No 2) Order 1986, SI 1986/974

s 1(1), (2)	Repealed
(3)	1 Jul 1986 (SI 1986/974)
(4)	1 Apr 1985 (SI 1984/1302)
(5)(a)	1 Jul 1986 (SI 1986/974)
(b)	1 Apr 1985 (SI 1984/1302)
(6), (7)	1 Jul 1986 (SI 1986/974)
2–4	Repealed
5(1)	Repealed
(2)	1 Apr 1985 (SI 1984/1302)
(3)	Repealed
(4)	See Sch 3 below
(5), (6)	Repealed
(7), (8)	26 Sep 1984 (SI 1984/1302)
6(1)	Repealed
(2)	1 Apr 1985 (SI 1984/1302)
(3)	26 Sep 1984 (SI 1984/1302)
(4)	26 Jul 1984 (s 27(2))
7(1)–(3)	*Not in force*
(4)	26 Jul 1984 (s 27(2))
8	Repealed
9, 10	26 Jul 1984 (s 27(2))
11–14	Repealed
15	26 Jul 1984 (s 27(2))
16–20	Repealed
21	See Sch 7 below
22	Repealed
23	26 Jul 1984 (s 27(2))
24	See Sch 8 below
25–29	26 Jul 1984 (s 27(2))
Sch 1	1 Jul 1986 (SI 1986/974)
2	Repealed
3, para 1	26 Sep 1984 (SI 1984/1302)
2	Repealed
3–6	1 Apr 1985 (SI 1984/1302)
7	Repealed
8	1 Apr 1985 (SI 1984/1302)
9–11	Repealed
12	26 Sep 1984 (SI 1984/1302); prospectively repealed by National Health Service and Community Care Act 1990, s 66(2), Sch 10[1]
13, 14	Repealed
15	1 Apr 1985 (SI 1984/1302)
16, 17	Repealed
4–6	Repealed
7, para 1–8	Repealed
9	Spent
8	26 Sep 1984 (repeal in Social Security Pensions Act 1975, s 38(3)) (s 27(3))
	26 Sep 1984 (repeals of or in National Health

Health and Social Security Act 1984 (c 48)—*cont*

Sch 8—*cont*

Service Act 1977, ss 45(2), (3), 97(1)(a), (c), (2); National Health Service (Scotland) Act 1978, s 85(1); Health Services Act 1980, s 18, Sch 1, paras 30, 79, 88, 99; Social Security Act 1980, s 3(5)) (SI 1984/1302)

1 Nov 1984 (repeal in Opticians Act 1958, s 13(3)) (spent) (SI 1984/1302)

26 Nov 1984 (repeals of or in Social Security Act 1975, ss 12(1)(d), 41(2)(d), (3), Sch 4, Pt IV, para 3) (SI 1984/1302)

28 Nov 1984 (repeal of Child Benefit Act 1975, Sch 4, para 25) (SI 1984/1302)

29 Nov 1984 (repeals of or in Social Security Act 1975, s 57(2), Sch 4, Pt IV, para 1(a), (c); Social Security (Miscellaneous Provisions) Act 1977, s 22(2); Social Security and Housing Benefits Act 1982, Sch 4, para 18(4)) (SI 1984/1302)

1 Apr 1985 (repeals of or in Tribunals and Inquiries Act 1971, Sch 1 (repealed); National Health Service Act 1977, ss 12(b), 15(1), (2), 39(c), 98(2), Sch 5, paras 9(1)–(3), 10; National Health Service (Scotland) Act 1978, s 26(2)(c); Health Services Act 1980, ss 1(6), 2, Sch 1, paras 35, 37, 56, 57, 69, 77(b), 82(2), (3), 87, 89–98) (SI 1984/1302)

6 Apr 1985 (repeal in Social Security Pensions Act 1975, s 4(1)) (SI 1984/1302)

1 Jul 1986 (repeals of or in National Health Service Act 1977, ss 44, 46, 72, 81–83, Sch 5, paras 1, 2, 6(3)(e), (5)(iv), Sch 12; National Health Service (Scotland) Act 1978, ss 26 (except sub-s (2)(c)), 29, 64, 73–75, Schs 8, 11; Health Services Act 1980, Sch 5) (SI 1986/974)

Not in force (otherwise)

[1] Any order(s) made under National Health Service and Community Care Act 1990 bringing the prospective repeal into force will be noted to that Act in the service to this work

---

Housing and Building Control Act 1984 (c 29)

RA: 26 Jun 1984

Commencement provisions: s 66(3)

26 Aug 1984 (s 66(3))

Housing Defects Act 1984 (c 50)

Whole Act repealed

Inheritance Tax Act 1984 (c 51)

See entry for Capital Transfer Tax Act 1984 ante

Inshore Fishing (Scotland) Act 1984 (c 26)

RA: 26 Jun 1984

Commencement provisions: s 11(2); Inshore Fishing (Scotland) Act 1984 (Commencement) Order 1985, SI 1985/961

26 Jul 1985 (SI 1985/961)

Juries (Disqualification) Act 1984 (c 34)

RA: 12 Jul 1984

Commencement provisions: s 2(3); Juries (Disqualification) Act 1984 (Commencement) Order 1984, SI 1984/1599

1 Dec 1984 (SI 1984/1599)

Law Reform (Husband and Wife) (Scotland) Act 1984 (c 15)

RA: 24 May 1984

Commencement provisions: s 10(2)

24 Jul 1984 (s 10(2))

Local Government (Interim Provisions) Act 1984 (c 53)

RA: 31 Jul 1984

Commencement provisions: s 1(1) (repealed); Local Government (Interim Provisions) Act 1984 (Appointed Day) Order 1985, SI 1985/2 (appointed 1 Feb 1985 for the coming into force of Pt II (ss 2, 3 (now repealed)) of this Act)

Whole Act repealed, except ss 4, 6(3), 10, 11 and 13, which came into force on 31 Jul 1984 (RA)

London Regional Transport Act 1984 (c 32)

RA: 26 Jun 1984

Commencement provisions: s 72(2)–(6); London Regional Transport (Appointed Day) Order 1984, SI 1984/877

s 1–12	29 Jun 1984 (SI 1984/877)
13, 14	Repealed by Local Government Finance Act 1988, s 149, Sch 13, Pt III, in accordance with s 127 of that Act (qv) and subject to any regulations made under that section
15–31	29 Jun 1984 (SI 1984/877)
31A	Inserted by Railways Act 1993, s 152(1), Sch 12, para 17 (qv)
32–35	29 Jun 1984 (SI 1984/877)
36–39	Repealed
40(1)	26 Jun 1984 (s 72(4))

London Regional Transport Act 1984 (c 32)—*cont*

s 40(2)	26 Jun 1984 (s 72(4)); substituted (savings) by Railways Act 1993, s 152(1), Sch 12, para 18(2) (qv)
(3)	26 Jun 1984 (s 72(4))
(4), (5)	29 Jun 1984 (SI 1984/877)
(6)	Repealed
(7)–(11)	29 Jun 1984 (SI 1984/877)
(12)	See Sch 3 below
41	Repealed
42(1), (2)	29 Jun 1984 (SI 1984/877)
(3)–(5)	Repealed
(6)	29 Jun 1984 (SI 1984/877)
43–45	Repealed
46–53	29 Jun 1984 (SI 1984/877)
54–58	Repealed
59	29 Jun 1984 (SI 1984/877)
60	26 Jun 1984 (s 72(3))
61–63	29 Jun 1984 (SI 1984/877)
64(1)–(6)	Repealed
(7)	29 Jun 1984 (SI 1984/877)
(8)	Repealed
65–67	29 Jun 1984 (SI 1984/877)
68, 69	26 Jun 1984 (s 72(3))
70	29 Jun 1984 (SI 1984/877)
71(1)	29 Jun 1984 (SI 1984/877)
(2)	See Sch 5 below
(3)	See Schs 6, 7 below
(4)–(7)	29 Jun 1984 (SI 1984/877)
72	26 Jun 1984 (s 72(3))
Sch 1, 2	29 Jun 1984 (SI 1984/877)
3	26 Jun 1984 (s 72(4))
4	29 Jun 1984 (SI 1984/877)
5, para 1–6	29 Jun 1984 (SI 1984/877)
7	26 Jun 1984 (s 72(3))
8(1)–(5)	26 Jun 1984 (s 72(3))
(6)–(8)	29 Jun 1984 (SI 1984/877)
(9)	26 Jun 1984 (s 72(3))
(10)(a)	26 Jun 1984 (s 72(3))
(b)	29 Jun 1984 (SI 1984/877)
9–19	29 Jun 1984 (SI 1984/877)
6	29 Jun 1984 (SI 1984/877)
7	1 Apr 1985 (repeals of or in London Government Act 1963, Sch 2; Local Government, Planning and Land Act 1980, Sch 13, para 9) (s 72(6)) 29 Jun 1984 (otherwise) (SI 1984/877)

Lotteries (Amendment) Act 1984 (c 9)

RA: 12 Apr 1984

Commencement provisions: s 2(2)

12 Jun 1984 (s 2(2))

Matrimonial and Family Proceedings Act 1984 (c 42)

RA: 12 Jul 1984

Commencement provisions: s 47; Matrimonial and Family Proceedings Act 1984 (Commencement No 1) Order 1984, SI 1984/1589; Matrimonial and Family Proceedings Act 1984 (Commencement No 2) Order 1985, SI 1985/1316; Matrimonial and Family Proceedings Act 1984 (Commencement No 3) Order 1986, SI 1986/635; Matrimonial and Family Proceedings Act 1984 (Commencement No 4) Order 1986, SI 1986/1049; Matrimonial and Family Proceedings Act 1984 (Commencement No 3) (Scotland) Order 1986, SI 1986/1226; Matrimonial and Family Proceedings Act 1984 (Commencement No 5) Order 1991, SI 1991/1211

s 1–9	12 Oct 1984 (s 47(1))
10	1 Oct 1986 (SI 1986/1049)
11	12 Oct 1984 (s 47(1))
12–25	16 Sep 1985 (SI 1985/1316)
26	Repealed
27	16 Sep 1985 (SI 1985/1316)
28, 29	1 Sep 1986 (SI 1986/1226)
29A	Inserted (S) by Family Law (Scotland) Act 1985, Sch 1, para 12 (qv)
30, 31	1 Sep 1986 (SI 1986/1226)
32–39	28 Apr 1986 (SI 1986/635)
40, 41	14 Oct 1991 (SI 1991/1211)
42, 43	28 Apr 1986 (SI 1986/635)
44	12 Oct 1984 (SI 1984/1589)
45	*Not in force*; prospectively repealed by Children (Northern Ireland) Order 1995, SI 1995/755 (NI 2), art 185(2), Sch 10
46	See Schs 1–3 below
47, 48	12 Jul 1984 (s 47(1))
Sch 1, para 1(a)	16 Sep 1985 (SI 1985/1316)
(b)	1 Sep 1986 (SI 1986/1226)
2	12 Oct 1984 (SI 1984/1589)
3	28 Apr 1986 (SI 1986/635)
4	12 Oct 1984 (SI 1984/1589)
5	16 Sep 1985 (SI 1985/1316)
6, 7	1 Sep 1986 (SI 1986/1226)
8	16 Sep 1985 (SI 1985/1316)
9	Repealed
10–13	12 Oct 1984 (SI 1984/1589)
14	Repealed
15	16 Sep 1985 (SI 1985/1316)
16, 17	28 Apr 1986 (SI 1986/635)
18, 19	Repealed
20(a)	*Not in force*
(b)	28 Apr 1986 (SI 1986/635)
21	1 Oct 1986 (SI 1986/1049)
22	12 Oct 1984 (SI 1984/1589)
23	Repealed
24–26	1 Oct 1986 (SI 1986/1049)
27	12 Oct 1984 (SI 1984/1589)
28	1 Sep 1986 (SI 1986/1226)
29	Repealed
30	28 Apr 1986 (SI 1986/635)
31	Repealed

Matrimonial and Family Proceedings Act 1984 (c 42)—*cont*

Sch 2, para 1, 2	12 Oct 1984 (s 47(1))
3	*Not in force*
3	12 Oct 1984 (repeal of Matrimonial Causes Act 1973, ss 43(9), 44(6)) (SI 1984/1589)
	28 Apr 1986 (repeals of or in Matrimonial Causes Act 1967; Guardianship of Minors Act 1971; Courts Act 1971; Matrimonial Causes Act 1973, s 45, Sch 2; Domicile and Matrimonial Proceedings Act 1973; Children Act 1975; Adoption Act 1976; Domestic Proceedings and Magistrates' Courts Act 1978; Matrimonial Homes and Property Act 1981; Matrimonial Homes Act 1983; County Courts Act 1984) (SI 1986/635)
	14 Oct 1991 (otherwise) (SI 1991/1211)

Mental Health (Scotland) Act 1984 (c 36)

RA: 12 Jul 1984

Commencement provisions: s 130

30 Sep 1984 (s 130)

Merchant Shipping Act 1984 (c 5)

Whole Act repealed; s 13 was repealed with savings by Merchant Shipping (Registration, etc) Act 1993, s 8(4), Sch 5, Pt II, as from 1 May 1994, but instruments made under that section and in force on that date remained in force until superseded by an instrument made under Sch 4, para 4 to the 1993 Act (Merchant Shipping (Registration, etc) Act 1993 (Commencement No 1 and Transitional Provisions) Order 1993, SI 1993/3137, art 7(1), Sch 3). Sch 4, para 4 to the 1993 Act was repealed by Merchant Shipping Act 1995, s 314(1), Sch 12, and by virtue of Interpretation Act 1978, s 17(2)(b), such instruments remain in force until superseded by an instrument made under s 315 of the 1995 Act

---

Occupiers' Liability Act 1984 (c 3)

RA: 13 Mar 1984

Commencement provisions: s 4(2)

13 May 1984 (s 4(2))

Ordnance Factories and Military Services Act 1984 (c 59)

RA: 31 Oct 1984

31 Oct 1984 (RA)

Parliamentary Pensions etc Act 1984 (c 52)

RA: 31 Jul 1984

Commencement provisions: ss 1(5), 2(8), 4(5), 5(6) (repealed)

s 1–11	Repealed[1]
12	31 Jul 1984 (RA)
13	Repealed
14, 15	31 Jul 1984 (RA)[1]
16	Repealed[1]
17	31 Jul 1984 (RA)
Schedule	Repealed[1]

[1] Ss 1–11, 15(2)(a), 16 and the Schedule repealed by Parliamentary and other Pensions Act 1987, s 6(2), Sch 4 (qv), but by s 2(a) of, Sch 2 to, that Act, ss 3(4)–(6), 4(3)–(6), 5(1), (2) and 6 of this Act continued to have effect as if contained in regulations made under and in accordance with s 2 of the 1987 Act. The Parliamentary Pensions (Consolidation and Amendment) Regulations 1993, SI 1993/3253 (made under s 2 of the 1987 Act, and in force from 21 Jan 1994), revoked and replaced (with savings), ss 3(4)–(6), 4(3)–(6), 5(1), (2) and 6 of this Act

Pensions Commutation Act 1984 (c 7)

RA: 13 Mar 1984

Commencement provisions: s 3(2); Pensions Commutation Act 1984 (Commencement) Order 1984, SI 1984/1140

20 Aug 1984 (SI 1984/1140)

Police and Criminal Evidence Act 1984 (c 60)

RA: 31 Oct 1984

Commencement provisions: s 121; Police and Criminal Evidence Act 1984 (Commencement No 1) Order 1984, SI 1984/2002; Police and Criminal Evidence Act 1984 (Commencement No 2) Order 1984, SI 1985/623; Police and Criminal Evidence Act 1984 (Commencement No 3) Order 1985/1934; Police and Criminal Evidence Act 1984 (Commencement No 4) Order 1991, SI 1991/2686; Police and Criminal Evidence Act 1984 (Commencement No 5) Order 1992, SI 1992/2802

s 1	1 Jan 1985 (so far as relates to search for stolen articles in localities in which, on 31 Dec 1984, an enactment (other than one contained in a public general Act or one relating to statutory undertakers) applies conferring power on a constable to search for stolen or unlawfully obtained goods) (SI 1984/2002)
	1 Jan 1986 (otherwise) (SI 1985/1934)
2–6	1 Jan 1986 (SI 1985/1934)
7(1)	1 Jan 1986 (SI 1985/1934)
(2)(a)	1 Jan 1986 (SI 1985/1934)
(b)	1 Jan 1985 (SI 1984/2002)
(3)	1 Jan 1985 (SI 1984/2002)

Police and Criminal Evidence Act 1984 (c 60)—*cont*

s 8–22	1 Jan 1986 (SI 1985/1934)
23	1 Jan 1985 (SI 1984/2002)
24–36	1 Jan 1986 (SI 1985/1934)
37(1)–(10)	1 Jan 1986 (SI 1985/1934)
(11)–(14)	Repealed
(15)	1 Jan 1986 (SI 1985/1934)
38–46	1 Jan 1986 (SI 1985/1934)
46A	Inserted by Criminal Justice and Public Order Act 1994, s 29(1), (2), (5) (qv)
47(1)	1 Jan 1986 (SI 1985/1934)
(1A)	Inserted by Criminal Justice and Public Order Act 1994, s 27(1)(b) (qv)
(2)–(4)	1 Jan 1986 (SI 1985/1934)
(5)	Repealed
(6)–(8)	1 Jan 1986 (SI 1985/1934)
48–51	1 Jan 1986 (SI 1985/1934)
52	Repealed
53–58	1 Jan 1986 (SI 1985/1934)
59	Repealed
60(1)(a)	1 Jan 1986 (SI 1985/1934)
(b)	29 Nov 1991 (in the following police areas: Avon and Somerset, Bedfordshire, Cambridgeshire, Cheshire, City of London, Cleveland, Cumbria, Derbyshire, Devon and Cornwall, Dorset, Durham, Dyfed-Powys, Essex, Gloucestershire, Greater Manchester, Gwent, Hampshire, Hertfordshire, Humberside, Kent, Lancashire, Leicestershire, Lincolnshire, Merseyside, Metropolitan Police District, Norfolk, Northamptonshire, Northumbria, North Wales, North Yorkshire, Nottinghamshire, South Wales, South Yorkshire, Staffordshire, Suffolk, Surrey, Sussex, Warwickshire, West Mercia, West Midlands, West Yorkshire, Wiltshire) (SI 1991/2686)
	9 Nov 1992 (in the Thames Valley police area) (SI 1992/2802)
(2)	29 Nov 1991 (SI 1991/2686)
61(1)–(7)	1 Jan 1986 (SI 1985/1934)
(7A)	Inserted by Criminal Justice and Public Order Act 1994, s 168(2), Sch 10, para 56(a) (qv)
(8), (9)	1 Jan 1986 (SI 1985/1934)
62(1)	1 Jan 1986 (SI 1985/1934)
(1A)	Inserted by Criminal Justice and Public Order Act 1994, s 54(1), (2) (qv)
(2)–(7)	1 Jan 1986 (SI 1985/1934)
(7A)	Inserted by Criminal Justice and Public Order Act 1994, s 168(2), Sch 10, para 57(a) (qv)
(8)–(11)	1 Jan 1986 (SI 1985/1934)
(12)	Inserted by Criminal Justice and Public Order Act 1994, s 168(2), Sch 10, para 62(4)(a) (qv)
63(1)–(3)	1 Jan 1986 (SI 1985/1934)
(3A), (3B)	Inserted by Criminal Justice and Public Order Act 1994, s 55(1), (2) (qv)
(4)–(8)	1 Jan 1986 (SI 1985/1934)
(8A)	Inserted by Criminal Justice and Public Order Act 1994, s 55(1), (4) (qv)

Police and Criminal Evidence Act 1984 (c 60)—*cont*

s 63(8B)	Inserted by Criminal Justice and Public Order Act 1994, s 168(2), Sch 10, para 59(a) (qv)
(9)	1 Jan 1986 (SI 1985/1934)
(10)	Inserted by Criminal Justice and Public Order Act 1994, s 55(1), (6) (qv)
(10)	A second sub-s (10) is inserted by Criminal Justice and Public Order Act 1994, s 168(2), Sch 10, para 62(4)(b) (qv)
63A	Inserted by Criminal Justice and Public Order Act 1994, s 56 (qv)
64(1)–(3)	1 Jan 1986 (SI 1985/1934)
(3A), (3B)	Inserted by Criminal Justice and Public Order Act 1994, s 57(1), (3) (qv)
(4)	1 Jan 1986 (SI 1985/1934)
(5)	Substituted by Criminal Justice Act 1988, s 148 (qv)
(6)	1 Jan 1986 (SI 1985/1934)
(6A), (6B)	Inserted by Criminal Justice Act 1988, s 148 (qv)
(7)	1 Jan 1986 (SI 1985/1934)
65	1 Jan 1986 (SI 1985/1934)
66, 67	1 Jan 1985 (SI 1984/2002)
68	Repealed
69–82	1 Jan 1986 (SI 1985/1934)
83, 84	29 Apr 1985 (SI 1985/623)
85(1)–(7)	29 Apr 1985 (SI 1985/623)
(8)	29 Apr 1985 (SI 1985/623); prospectively repealed by Police and Magistrates' Courts Act 1994, ss 44, 93, Sch 5, Pt II, para 25(a), Sch 9, Pt I[1]
(9), (10)	29 Apr 1985 (SI 1985/623)
86–89	29 Apr 1985 (SI 1985/623)
90(1)–(5)	29 Apr 1985 (SI 1985/623)
(6)	29 Apr 1985 (SI 1985/623); prospectively repealed by Police and Magistrates' Courts Act 1994, ss 35(1), (5), 93, Sch 9, Pt I[1]
(7)	29 Apr 1985 (SI 1985/623)
(8)	29 Apr 1985 (SI 1985/623); prospectively repealed by Police and Magistrates' Courts Act 1994, ss 35(1), (7), 93, Sch 9, Pt I[1]
(9), (10)	29 Apr 1985 (SI 1985/623)
91	29 Apr 1985 (SI 1985/623); prospectively repealed by Police and Magistrates' Courts Act 1994, ss 44, 93, Sch 5, Pt II, para 28, Sch 9, Pt I[1]
92	29 Apr 1985 (SI 1985/623); prospectively repealed by Police and Magistrates' Courts Act 1994, ss 37(b), 38, 93, Sch 9, Pt I[1]
93(1)–(5)	29 Apr 1985 (SI 1985/623)
(6)	29 Apr 1985 (SI 1985/623); prospectively substituted by Police and Magistrates' Courts Act 1994, ss 36(1), (6), 38[1]
(7), (8)	29 Apr 1985 (SI 1985/623); prospectively substituted by new sub-s (7) by Police and Magistrates' Courts Act 1994, ss 36(1), (7), 38[1]
94	29 Apr 1985 (SI 1985/623); prospectively repealed by Police and Magistrates' Courts Act 1994, ss 37(c), 38, 93, Sch 9, Pt I[1]
95, 96	29 Apr 1985 (SI 1985/623)
97(1)–(3)	29 Apr 1985 (SI 1985/623)

Police and Criminal Evidence Act 1984 (c 60)—*cont*

s 97(4)	29 Apr 1985 (SI 1985/623); prospectively repealed by Police and Magistrates' Courts Act 1994, ss 37(d), 38, 93, Sch 9, Pt I[1]
(5), (6)	29 Apr 1985 (SI 1985/623)
98–100	29 Apr 1985 (SI 1985/623)
101	29 Apr 1985 (SI 1985/623); prospectively repealed by Police and Magistrates' Courts Act 1994, ss 37(e), 38, 93, Sch 9, Pt I[1]
102	29 Apr 1985 (SI 1985/623); prospectively substituted by Police and Magistrates' Courts Act 1994, s 44, Sch 5, Pt II, para 33[1]
103	29 Apr 1985 (SI 1985/623); prospectively repealed by Police and Magistrates' Courts Act 1994, s 93, Sch 9, Pt I[1]
104(1), (2)	29 Apr 1985 (SI 1985/623); prospectively repealed by Police and Magistrates' Courts Act 1984, ss 37(f), 38, 93, Sch 9, Pt I[1]
(3), (4)	29 Apr 1985 (SI 1985/623)
105(1), (2)	29 Apr 1985 (SI 1985/623)
(3)	29 Apr 1985 (SI 1985/623); prospectively substituted by Police and Magistrates' Courts Act 1994, s 44, Sch 5, Pt II, para 34(1), (3)[1]
(4), (5)	29 Apr 1985 (SI 1985/623)
106	1 Jan 1985 (SI 1984/2002)
107	1 Jan 1986 (SI 1985/1934)
108(1)	1 Mar 1985 (SI 1984/2002)
(2), (3)	Repealed
(4)–(6)	1 Mar 1985 (SI 1984/2002)
109(a), (b)	29 Apr 1985 (SI 1985/623)
(c)	1 Jan 1985 (SI 1984/2002)
110, 111	1 Mar 1985 (SI 1984/2002)
112	1 Jan 1985 (SI 1984/2002)
113(1), (2)	1 Jan 1986 (SI 1985/1934)
(3)–(13)	1 Jan 1985 (SI 1984/2002)
114	1 Jan 1986 (SI 1985/1934)
115	1 Jan 1985 (SI 1984/2002)
116	29 Apr 1985 (SI 1985/623)
117	1 Jan 1986 (SI 1985/1934)
118	1 Jan 1985 (SI 1984/2002)
119	See Schs 6, 7 below
120–122	31 Oct 1984 (RA)
Sch 1–3	1 Jan 1986 (SI 1985/1934)
4, 5	29 Apr 1985 (SI 1985/623)
6, para 1–12	1 Jan 1986 (SI 1985/1934)
13–16	Repealed
17–21	1 Jan 1986 (SI 1985/1934)
22, 23	Repealed
24–26	1 Jan 1986 (SI 1985/1934)
27	Repealed
28, 29	1 Jan 1986 (SI 1985/1934)
30–33	1 Mar 1985 (SI 1984/2002)
34	1 Jan 1986 (SI 1985/1934)
35	29 Apr 1985 (SI 1985/623)
36–40	1 Jan 1986 (SI 1985/1934)
41	Repealed

Police and Criminal Evidence Act 1984 (c 60)—*cont*

Sch 7	1 Mar 1985 (repeals in Police (Scotland) Act 1967) (SI 1984/2002, as amended by SI 1985/623)
	29 Apr 1985 (repeals of or in Police Act 1964; Superannuation Act 1972; House of Commons Disqualification Act 1975; Northern Ireland Assembly Disqualification Act 1975; Police Act 1976) (SI 1985/623)
	1 Jan 1986 (otherwise) (SI 1985/1934)

[1] Any order(s) made under Police and Magistrates' Courts Act 1994, s 94, bringing the prospective change into force will be noted to that Act in the service to this work

---

Prescription and Limitation (Scotland) Act 1984 (c 45)

RA: 26 Jul 1984

Commencement provisions: s 7(2)

26 Sep 1984 (s 7(2))

Prevention of Terrorism (Temporary Provisions) Act 1984 (c 8)

Whole Act repealed

Public Health (Control of Disease) Act 1984 (c 22)

RA: 26 Jun 1984

Commencement provisions: s 79(2)

26 Sep 1984 (s 79(2))

Rates Act 1984 (c 33)

RA: 26 Jun 1984

Commencement provisions: s 18

s 1–8	26 Jun 1984 (RA) (but maximum rate or precept may only be prescribed from financial year 1 Apr 1985 onwards (s 18(1)))
9	26 Jun 1984 (RA)
10, 11	*Not in force*
12	26 Jun 1984 (RA)
13	Repealed
14	26 Jun 1984 (RA)
15	Repealed, with savings, by Local Government Finance (Repeals, Savings and Consequential Amendments) Order 1990, SI 1990/776, art 3, Sch 1
16(1)	See Sch 1 below
(2)	See Sch 2 below
(3)	26 Jun 1984 (RA)
17–19	26 Jun 1984 (RA)

Rates Act 1984 (c 33)—*cont*

Sch 1, para 1	26 Jun 1984 (RA)
2–22	Repealed, with savings, by Local Government Finance (Repeals, Savings and Consequential Amendments) Order 1990, SI 1990/776, art 3, Sch 1
23	Effective for any financial year from 1 Apr 1983 (para 23(2))
24	Effective for any financial year from 1 Apr 1984 (para 24(2))
2	Repealed, with savings, by Local Government Finance (Repeals, Savings and Consequential Amendments) Order 1990, SI 1990/776, art 3, Sch 1

Rating and Valuation (Amendment) (Scotland) Act 1984 (c 31)

RA: 26 Jun 1984

Commencement provisions: s 23(1)

s 1–4	Repealed
5	26 Aug 1984 (s 23(1)(c))
6–8	Repealed
9–13	1 Apr 1985 (s 23(1)(b))
14	26 Aug 1984 (s 23(1)(c))
15	Repealed
16	26 Aug 1984 (s 23(1)(c))
17–19	1 Apr 1985 (s 23(1)(b))
20	26 Aug 1984 (s 23(1)(c))
21(1)	See Sch 2 below
(2)	Repealed
22	26 Aug 1984 (s 23(1)(c))
23	26 Jun 1984 (s 23(1)(a))
Sch 1	Repealed
2, para 1–6	26 Aug 1984 (s 23(1)(c))
7	Repealed
8	26 Aug 1984 (s 23(1)(c))
9	1 Apr 1985 (s 23(1)(b))
10, 11	26 Aug 1984 (s 23(1)(c))
12	Repealed
13–15	1 Apr 1985 (s 23(1)(b))
16	26 Aug 1984 (s 23(1)(c))
17	1 Apr 1985 (s 23(1)(b))
18	Repealed
3	Repealed

Registered Homes Act 1984 (c 23)

RA: 26 Jun 1984

Commencement provisions: s 59(2); Registered Homes Act 1984 (Commencement) Order 1984, SI 1984/1348

1 Jan 1985 (except s 1 so far as relates to an establishment which is a school referred to in s 1(5)(f), for which the date is 1 Jan 1986) (SI 1984/1348)

Rent (Scotland) Act 1984 (c 58)

RA: 31 Oct 1984

Commencement provisions: s 118(2)

31 Jan 1985 (s 118(2))

Repatriation of Prisoners Act 1984 (c 47)

RA: 26 Jul 1984

Commencement provisions: s 9(2); Repatriation of Prisoners (Commencement) Order 1985, SI 1985/550

15 Apr 1985 (SI 1985/550)

Restrictive Trade Practices (Stock Exchange) Act 1984 (c 2)

Whole Act repealed

Road Traffic (Driving Instruction) Act 1984 (c 13)

Whole Act repealed

Road Traffic Regulation Act 1984 (c 27)

RA: 26 Jun 1984

Commencement provisions: s 145(1), (2); Road Traffic Regulation Act 1984 (Commencement No 1) Order 1986, SI 1986/1147

s 1–13	26 Sep 1984 (s 145(1))
13A	Inserted by Road Traffic Act 1991, s 81, Sch 7, para 4 (qv)
14, 15	Substituted by Road Traffic (Temporary Restrictions) Act 1991, s 1(1), Sch 1 (qv)
16(1)	26 Sep 1984 (s 145(1))
(2), (2A)	Substituted for original sub-s (2) by Road Traffic (Temporary Restrictions) Act 1991, s 1(2) (qv)
(3), (4)	Repealed
16A–16C	Inserted by Road Traffic Regulation (Special Events) Act 1994, s 1(1) (qv)
17(1)	Substituted by New Roads and Street Works Act 1991, s 168(1), Sch 8, Pt II, para 28(1), (2) (qv)
(2)–(4)	26 Sep 1984 (s 145(1))
(5)	Substituted by New Roads and Street Works Act 1991, s 168(1), Sch 8, Pt II, para 28(1), (4) (qv)
(6)	26 Sep 1984 (s 145(1))
17A	Inserted by New Roads and Street Works Act 1991, s 168(1), Sch 8, Pt II, para 29 (qv)
18–28	26 Sep 1984 (s 145(1))
29	Substituted for original ss 29, 30 by New Roads and Street Works Act 1991, s 168(1), Sch 8, Pt II, para 37 (qv)
30	See note to s 29 above
31–35	26 Sep 1984 (s 145(1))
35A, 35B	Inserted by Parking Act 1989, ss 2, 3 (qv)
35C	Inserted by Road Traffic Act 1991, s 41 (qv)

Road Traffic Regulation Act 1984 (c 27)—*cont*

36–46	26 Sep 1984 (s 145(1))
46A	Inserted by Road Traffic Act 1991, s 42 (qv)
47–49	26 Sep 1984 (s 145(1))
50	Repealed
51	Substituted by Road Traffic Regulation (Parking) Act 1986, s 2(1) (qv)
52, 53	26 Sep 1984 (s 145(1))
54	26 Sep 1984 (s 145(1)); prospectively repealed by Local Government (Wales) Act 1994, ss 22(1), 66(8), Sch 7, Pt II, para 38(5), Sch 18[1]
55–63	26 Sep 1984 (s 145(1))
63A	Inserted by Road Traffic Act 1991, s 44(1) (qv)
64–77	26 Sep 1984 (s 145(1))
78	Repealed
79–89	26 Sep 1984 (s 145(1))
90, 91	Repealed
92, 93	26 Sep 1984 (s 145(1))
94	Substituted by Local Government Act 1985, s 8, Sch 5, para 4 (qv)
95–97	26 Sep 1984 (s 145(1))
98	Repealed
99–106	26 Sep 1984 (s 145(1))
106A	Inserted by Road Traffic Act 1991, s 75 (qv)
107–112	26 Sep 1984 (s 145(1))
113, 114	Repealed
115–117	26 Sep 1984 (s 145(1))
118	Repealed
119	26 Sep 1984 (s 145(1))
120, 121	Repealed
121A	Inserted by New Roads and Street Works Act 1991, s 168(1), Sch 8, Pt II, para 70 (qv)
122	26 Sep 1984 (s 145(1))
122A	Inserted by New Roads and Street Works Act 1991, ss 24 (EW), 44 (S) (qv)
123	Repealed
124–132	26 Sep 1984 (s 145(1))
132A	Inserted (S) by Roads (Scotland) Act 1984, s 127; now repealed
133–140	26 Sep 1984 (s 145(1))
141	Repealed
141A	Inserted by Road Traffic Act 1991, s 46(1) (qv)
142–147	26 Sep 1984 (s 145(1))
Sch 1, 2	26 Sep 1984 (s 145(1))
3	Repealed
4–6	26 Sep 1984 (s 145(1))
7	Repealed
8, para 1, 2	26 Sep 1984 (s 145(1))
3	*Not in force*
4–6	26 Sep 1984 (s 145(1))
9–11	26 Sep 1984 (s 145(1))
12	Superseded
13, 14	26 Sep 1984 (s 145(1))

[1] Any order made under Local Government (Wales) Act 1994, s 66(3), bringing the prospective repeal into force will be noted to that Act in the service to this work

Roads (Scotland) Act 1984 (c 54)

RA: 31 Oct 1984

Commencement provisions: s 157(2), (3); Roads (Scotland) Act 1984 (Commencement No 1) Order 1985, SI 1985/1953; Roads (Scotland) Act 1984 (Commencement No 2) Order 1989, SI 1989/1094; Roads (Scotland) Act 1984 (Commencement No 3) Order 1990, SI 1990/2622

s 1–12	1 Jan 1985 (s 157(2))
12A–12F	Inserted by Local Government etc (Scotland) Act 1994, s 38(1), (2) (qv)
13–20	1 Jan 1985 (s 157(2))
20A	Inserted (15 Jul 1988) by Environmental Assessment (Scotland) Regulations 1988, SI 1988/1221, regs 69, 70
21–35	1 Jan 1985 (s 157(2))
36–39	1 Aug 1989 (so far as relates to areas of Tayside and Lothian Regional Councils) (SI 1989/1084)
	8 Jan 1991 (otherwise) (SI 1990/2622)
39A–39C	Inserted by Traffic Calming Act 1992, s 2(1), Sch 2 (qv)
40	1 Aug 1989 (so far as relates to areas of Tayside and Lothian Regional Councils) (SI 1989/1084)
	8 Jan 1991 (otherwise) (SI 1990/2622)
41–55	1 Jan 1985 (s 157(2))
55A	Inserted (15 Jul 1988) by Environmental Assessment (Scotland) Regulations 1988, SI 1988/1221, regs 69, 71
56–61	1 Jan 1985 (s 157(2))
61A	Inserted by New Roads and Street Works Act 1991, s 168(1), Sch 8, Pt III, para 88 (qv)
62–81	1 Jan 1985 (s 157(2))
81A	Inserted by Local Government etc (Scotland) Act 1994, s 39 (qv)
82–113	1 Jan 1985 (s 157(2))
113A	Inserted by Local Government etc (Scotland) Act 1994, s 147 (qv)
114–125	1 Jan 1985 (s 157(2))
126	1 Jan 1986 (SI 1985/1953)
127	Repealed
128–132	1 Jan 1985 (s 157(2))
133	Repealed
134–155	1 Jan 1985 (s 157(2))
156(1), (2)	1 Jan 1985 (s 157(2))
(3)	See Sch 11 below
157	31 Oct 1984 (RA)
Sch 1–6	1 Jan 1985 (s 157(2))
7	1 Jan 1986 (SI 1985/1953)
8–10	1 Jan 1985 (s 157(2))
11	1 Jan 1985 (except repeal of Road Traffic Regulation Act 1984, Sch 10, paras 14–16) (s 157(2))
	1 Jan 1986 (exception noted above) (SI 1985/1953)

Somerset House Act 1984 (c 21)

RA: 26 Jun 1984

26 Jun 1984 (RA)

Telecommunications Act 1984 (c 12)

RA: 12 Apr 1984

Commencement provisions: s 60(1), 69(2), 110(2)–(5); Telecommunications Act 1984 (Appointed Day) (No 1) Order 1984, SI 1984/749; Telecommunications Act 1984 (Appointed Day) (No 2) Order 1984, SI 1984/876; British Telecommunications (Dissolution) Order 1994, SI 1994/2162

s 1	18 Jun 1984 (SI 1984/749)
2–21	5 Aug 1984 (SI 1984/876)
22	5 Aug 1984 (SI 1984/876); repealed in relation to applicable terminal equipment by Telecommunications Terminal Equipment Regulations 1992, SI 1992/2423, reg 2(1), as from 6 Nov 1992
23–27	5 Aug 1984 (SI 1984/876)
27A, 27B	Inserted by Competition and Service (Utilities) Act 1992, s 1 (qv)
27C	Inserted by Competition and Service (Utilities) Act 1992, s 2 (qv)
27D	Inserted by Competition and Service (Utilities) Act 1992, s 3 (qv)
27E	Inserted by Competition and Service (Utilities) Act 1992, s 4 (qv)
27F	Inserted by Competition and Service (Utilities) Act 1992, s 5(1) (qv)
27G	Inserted (prospectively in the case of sub-s (8)) by Competition and Service (Utilities) Act 1992, s 6(1) (qv)[1]
27H	Inserted (prospectively in the case of sub-s (4)) by Competition and Service (Utilities) Act 1992, s 7 (qv)[1]
27I	Inserted by Competition and Service (Utilities) Act 1992, s 7 (qv)
27J	Inserted by Competition and Service (Utilities) Act 1992, s 8 (qv)
27K	Inserted by Competition and Service (Utilities) Act 1992, s 9 (qv)
27L	Inserted by Competition and Service (Utilities) Act 1992, s 10 (qv)
28–30	5 Aug 1984 (SI 1984/876)
31	Repealed, with savings, by Local Government Finance (Repeals, Savings and Consequential Amendments) Order 1990, SI 1990/776, art 3, Sch 1
32–44	5 Aug 1984 (SI 1984/876)
45	Substituted by Interception of Communications Act 1985, s 11(1), Sch 2 (qv)
46	5 Aug 1984 (SI 1984/876)
46A	Inserted by Competition and Service (Utilities) Act 1992, s 49 (qv)

Telecommunications Act 1984 (c 12)—*cont*

s 47–55	5 Aug 1984 (SI 1984/876)
56–59	Repealed
60–73	6 Aug 1984 (SI 1984/876)
74, 75	16 Jul 1984 (SI 1984/876)
76	Repealed
77	16 Jul 1984 (SI 1984/876)
78	Repealed
79–83	16 Jul 1984 (SI 1984/876)
84	16 Jul 1984 (SI 1984/876); repealed in relation to applicable terminal equipment by Telecommunications Terminal Equipment Regulations 1992, SI 1992/2423, reg 2(1), as from 6 Nov 1992
85–92	16 Jul 1984 (SI 1984/876)
93–95	5 Aug 1984 (SI 1984/876)
96	*Not in force*
97–99	5 Aug 1984 (SI 1984/876)
100	Repealed
101–107	5 Aug 1984 (SI 1984/876)
108	18 Jun 1984 (SI 1984/749)
109(1)	5 Aug 1984 (SI 1984/876)
(2), (3)	5 Aug 1984 (SI 1984/876)
(4)	See Sch 5 below
(5)	5 Aug 1984 (SI 1984/876)
(6)	See Sch 7 below
(7)	5 Aug 1984 (SI 1984/876)
110	18 Jun 1984 (SI 1984/749)
Sch 1	18 Jun 1984 (SI 1984/749)
2	5 Aug 1984 (SI 1984/876)
3	16 Jul 1984 (SI 1984/876)
4	5 Aug 1984 (SI 1984/876)
5, Pt I	5 Aug 1984 (SI 1984/876)
II	6 Aug 1984 (SI 1984/876)
6	6 Aug 1984 (SI 1984/876)
7, Pt I	5 Aug 1984 (SI 1984/876)
II	6 Aug 1984 (SI 1984/876)
III	6 Sep 1994 (SI 1994/2162)
IV	16 Jul 1984 (SI 1984/876)

[1] Any order made under Competition and Service (Utilities) Act 1992, s 56(2), bringing the prospective insertion into force will be noted to that Act in the service to this work

---

Tenant's Rights, Etc (Scotland) Amendment Act 1984 (c 18)

Whole Act repealed

Tourism (Overseas Promotion) (Scotland) Act 1984 (c 4)

RA: 13 Mar 1984

Commencement provisions: s 3

13 May 1984 (s 3)

Town and Country Planning Act 1984 (c 10)

RA: 12 Apr 1984

Commencement provisions: s 7(2)

12 Aug 1984 (s 7(2)); *whole Act repealed (EW)*

Trade Marks (Amendment) Act 1984 (c 19)

Whole Act repealed

Trade Union Act 1984 (c 49)

Whole Act repealed

Video Recordings Act 1984 (c 39)

RA: 12 Jul 1984

Commencement provisions: s 23(2); Video Recordings Act 1984 (Commencement No 1) Order 1985, SI 1985/883; Video Recordings Act 1984 (Scotland) (Commencement No 1) Order 1985, SI 1985/904; Video Recordings Act 1984 (Commencement No 2) Order 1985, SI 1985/1264; Video Recordings Act 1984 (Scotland) (Commencement No 2) Order 1985, SI 1985/1265; Video Recordings Act 1984 (Commencement No 3) Order 1986, SI 1986/1125; Video Recordings Act 1984 (Scotland) (Commencement No 3) Order 1986, SI 1986/1182; Video Recordings Act 1984 (Commencement No 4) Order 1987, SI 1987/123; Video Recordings Act 1984 (Scotland) (Commencement No 4) Order 1987, SI 1987/160; Video Recordings Act 1984 (Commencement No 5) Order 1987, SI 1987/1142; Video Recordings Act 1984 (Scotland) (Commencement No 5) Order 1987, SI 1987/1249; Video Recordings Act 1984 (Commencement No 6) Order 1987, SI 1987/2155; Video Recordings Act 1984 (Scotland) (Commencement No 6) Order 1987, SI 1987/2273; Video Recordings Act 1984 (Commencement No 7) Order 1988, SI 1988/1018; Video Recordings Act 1984 (Scotland) (Commencement No 7) Order 1988, SI 1988/1079

s 1	10 Jun 1985 (SI 1985/883; SI 1985/904)
2, 3	1 Sep 1985 (SI 1985/1264; SI 1985/1265)
4	10 Jun 1985 (SI 1985/883; SI 1985/904)
4A, 4B	Inserted by Criminal Justice and Public Order Act 1994, s 90 (qv)
5	10 Jun 1985 (SI 1985/883; SI 1985/904)
6	1 Sep 1985 (SI 1985/1264; SI 1985/1265)
7, 8	10 Jun 1985 (SI 1985/883; SI 1985/904)
9, 10[1]	1 Sep 1985 (for the purpose of prohibiting the supply, the offer to supply or the possession for the purpose of supply of a video recording containing a video work where— (a) a video recording containing such video work has not been sold, let on hire or offered for sale or hire in the United Kingdom to the public before 1 Sep 1985; and (b) no classification certificate in respect of such video work has been issued) (SI 1985/1264; SI 1985/1265)

Video Recordings Act 1984 (c 39)—*cont*

s 9, 10[1]—*cont*

1 Sep 1986 (for the purpose of prohibiting the supply, the offer to supply or the possession for the purpose of supply of a video recording which has been sold, let on hire or offered for sale in the UK to the public in video form before 1 Sep 1985 where—

(a) its visual images, when shown as a moving picture, are not substantially the same as the moving picture produced on showing a film registered, or deemed to have been registered, under Films Act 1960, Pt II, on or after 1 Jan 1940;

(b) its visual images are accompanied by sound which comprises or includes words predominantly in the English language; and

(c) no classification certificate has been issued in respect of it.

Where such a video recording also contains another video work which does not satisfy the above requirements these sections are only brought into force for the above purpose in respect of the video work which does satisfy the requirements) (SI 1986/1125; SI 1986/1182)

1 Mar 1987 (for the purpose of prohibiting the supply, the offer to supply, or the possession for the purpose of supply of a video recording which has been sold, let on hire or offered for sale in the UK to the public in video form before 1 Sep 1985 where—

(a) its visual images, when shown as a moving picture, are substantially the same as the moving picture produced on showing a film registered, or deemed to have been registered, under Part II of Films Act 1960 on or after 1 Jan 1980;

(b) its visual images are accompanied by sound which comprises or includes words predominantly in the English language; and

(c) no classification certificate has been issued in respect of it.

Where such a video recording also contains another video work which does not satisfy the above requirements these sections are only brought into force for the above purpose in respect of the video work which does satisfy the requirements) (SI 1987/123; SI 1987/160)

1 Sep 1987 (for the purpose of prohibiting the supply, the offer to supply or the possession for the purpose of supply of a video recording which has been sold, let on hire or offered for sale in the UK to the public in video form before 1 Sep 1985 where—

(a) its visual images, when shown as a moving picture, are substantially the same as the moving picture produced on showing a film registered, or deemed to have been registered, under Part II of the Films Act 1960 on or after 1 Jan 1975;

Video Recordings Act 1984 (c 39)—*cont*

s 9, 10[1]—*cont*	(b) its visual images are accompanied by sound which comprises or includes words predominantly in the English language; and (c) no classification certificate has been issued in respect of it. Where such a video recording also contains another video work which does not satisfy the above requirements these sections are only brought into force for the above purposes in respect of the video work which does satisfy the requirements) (SI 1987/1142; SI 1987/1249)
	1 Mar 1988 (for the purpose of prohibiting the supply, the offer to supply or the possession for the purpose of supply of a video recording which has been sold, let on hire or offered for sale in the UK to the public in video form before 1 Sep 1985 where— (a) its visual images, when shown as a moving picture, are substantially the same as the moving picture produced on showing a film registered under Part II of Films Act 1960 on or after 1 Jan 1970; (b) its visual images are accompanied by sound which comprises or includes words predominantly in the English language; and (c) no classification certificate has been issued in respect of it. Where such a video recording also contains another video work which does not satisfy the above requirements these sections are only brought into force for the above purposes in respect of the video work which does satisfy the requirements) (SI 1987/2155; SI 1987/2273)
	1 Sep 1988 (otherwise) (SI 1988/1018; SI 1988/1079)
11(1), (2)	1 Sep 1985 (SI 1985/1264; SI 1985/1265)
(3)	Inserted by Criminal Justice and Public Order Act 1994, s 88(1), (4) (qv)
12(1)–(4)	1 Sep 1985 (SI 1985/1264; SI 1985/1265)
(4A)	Inserted by Criminal Justice and Public Order Act 1994, s 88(1), (5) (qv)
(5), (6)	1 Sep 1985 (SI 1985/1264; SI 1985/1265)
13(1), (2)	1 Sep 1985 (SI 1985/1264; SI 1985/1265)
(3)	Inserted by Criminal Justice and Public Order Act 1994, s 168(2), Sch 10, para 52(1), (2) (qv)
14(1)–(4)	1 Sep 1985 (SI 1985/1264; SI 1985/1265)
(5)	Inserted by Criminal Justice and Public Order Act 1994, s 88(1), (6) (qv)
14A	Inserted by Video Recordings Act 1993, s 2 (qv)
15	Substituted by Criminal Justice and Public Order Act 1994, s 168(2), Sch 10, para 52(1), (3) (qv)
16	1 Sep 1985 (SI 1985/1264; SI 1985/1265)
16A	Inserted by Criminal Justice Act 1988, s 162 (qv)
16–16D	Inserted (s 16C in relation to Scotland only) by Criminal Justice and Public Order Act 1994, s 91(1), (3) (qv)
17	1 Sep 1985 (SI 1985/1264; SI 1985/1265)
18	Repealed
19	1 Sep 1985 (SI 1985/1264)

Video Recordings Act 1984 (c 39)—*cont*

s 20	Repealed
21	1 Sep 1985 (SI 1985/1264; SI 1985/1265)
22, 23	10 Jun 1985 (SI 1985/883; SI 1985/904)

[1] Ie ss 9(1), (2), 10(1), (2); ss 9(3), 10(3) added by Criminal Justice and Public Order Act 1994, s 88(1)–(3) (qv)

1985

Administration of Justice Act 1985 (c 61)

RA: 30 Oct 1985

Commencement provisions: s 69(2)–(4); Administration of Justice Act 1985 (Commencement No 1) Order 1986, SI 1986/364; Administration of Justice Act 1985 (Commencement No 2) Order 1986, SI 1986/1503; Administration of Justice Act 1985 (Commencement No 3) Order 1986, SI 1986/2260; Administration of Justice Act 1985 (Commencement No 4) Order 1987, SI 1987/787; Administration of Justice Act 1985 (Commencement No 5) Order 1988, SI 1988/1341; Administration of Justice Act 1985 (Commencement No 6) Order 1989, SI 1989/287; Administration of Justice Act 1985 (Commencement No 7) Order 1991, SI 1991/2683

s 1	Repealed
2	12 Mar 1986 (except so far as relates to the investigation of any complaint made to the Law Society relating to the quality of any professional services provided by a solicitor) (SI 1986/364) 1 Jan 1987 (exception noted above) (SI 1986/2260)
3	Repealed
4, 5	12 Mar 1986 (SI 1986/364)
6(1)–(3)	11 May 1987 (SI 1987/787)
(4)	1 Dec 1987 (SI 1987/787)
(5)	11 May 1987 (SI 1987/787)
7, 8	12 Mar 1986 (SI 1986/364)
9, 10	1 Jan 1992 (SI 1991/2683)
11	11 May 1987 (SI 1987/787)
12	12 Mar 1986 (SI 1986/364)
13	1 Oct 1986 (SI 1986/1503)
14–21	11 May 1987 (SI 1987/787)
22, 23	1 Oct 1986 (SI 1986/1503)
24–33	11 May 1987 (SI 1987/787)
34(1), (2)	11 May 1987 (SI 1987/787)
(3)	*Not in force*
35–37	11 May 1987 (SI 1987/787)
38	1 Oct 1986 (SI 1986/1503)
39	11 May 1987 (SI 1987/787)
40	1 Apr 1989 (SI 1989/287)
41, 42	Substituted by Legal Aid Act 1988, s 33 (qv)
43, 44	1 Apr 1989 (SI 1989/287)
45, 46	Repealed
47	1 Oct 1986 (SI 1986/1503)
48	1 Jan 1987 (SI 1986/2260)
49	30 Dec 1985 (s 69(4))
50	28 Apr 1986 (SI 1986/364)
51	1 Oct 1986 (SI 1986/1503)
52	30 Dec 1985 (s 69(4))

Administration of Justice Act 1985 (c 61)—*cont*

s 53	1 Oct 1988 (SI 1988/1341)
54	30 Dec 1985 (s 69(4))
55	1 Oct 1986 (SI 1986/1503)
56–59	30 Dec 1985 (s 69(4))
60	Repealed
61, 62	30 Dec 1985 (s 69(4))
63	Repealed
64, 65	30 Dec 1985 (s 69(4))
66	Repealed
67(1)	See Sch 7 below
(2)	See Sch 8 below
68, 69	30 Oct 1985 (s 69(3))
Sch 1	12 Mar 1986 (SI 1986/364)
2	1 Jan 1992 (SI 1991/2683)
3	12 Mar 1986 (SI 1986/364)
4–6	11 May 1987 (SI 1987/787)
7, para 1–5	Repealed
6	*Not in force*
7	1 Oct 1986 (SI 1986/1503)
8	30 Dec 1985 (s 69(4))
8, Pt I	30 Oct 1985 (s 69(3))
II	30 Dec 1985 (s 69(4))
III	12 Mar 1986 (repeals in Solicitors Act 1974) (SI 1986/364)
	1 Oct 1986 (repeals in Supreme Court Act 1981; County Courts Act 1984) (SI 1986/1503)
	Not in force (otherwise)
9	30 Oct 1985 (s 69(3))

Agricultural Training Board Act 1985 (c 36)

RA: 16 Jul 1985

Commencement provisions: s 4(2)

16 Sep 1985 (s 4(2))

Appropriation Act 1985 (c 55)

Whole Act repealed

Bankruptcy (Scotland) Act 1985 (c 66)

RA: 30 Oct 1985

Commencement provisions: s 78(2); Bankruptcy (Scotland) Act 1985 (Commencement) Order 1985, SI 1985/1924; Bankruptcy (Scotland) Act 1985 (Commencement No 2) Order 1986, SI 1986/1913

s 1–1C	Substituted for original s 1 by Bankruptcy (Scotland) Act 1993, s 1 (qv)
2	Substituted by Bankruptcy (Scotland) Act 1993, s 2 (qv)

Bankruptcy (Scotland) Act 1985 (c 66)—*cont*

s 3(1)–(4)	1 Apr 1986 (SI 1985/1924)
(5)–(7)	Inserted by Bankruptcy (Scotland) Act 1993, s 11, Sch 1, para 1 (qv)
4	1 Apr 1986 (SI 1985/1924)
5(1)	1 Apr 1986 (SI 1985/1924)
(2)–(2C)	Substituted for original sub-s (2) by Bankruptcy (Scotland) Act 1993, s 3(1), (2) (qv)
(3), (4)	1 Apr 1986 (SI 1985/1924)
(4A)	Inserted by Bankruptcy (Scotland) Act 1993, s 3(1), (4) (qv)
(5), (6)	1 Apr 1986 (SI 1985/1924)
(6A)	Inserted by Bankruptcy (Scotland) Act 1993, s 3(1), (6) (qv)
(7), (8)	1 Apr 1986 (SI 1985/1924)
(9), (10)	Inserted by Bankruptcy (Scotland) Act 1993, s 3(1), (7) (qv)
6–11	1 Apr 1986 (SI 1985/1924)
12(1)	Substituted by Bankruptcy (Scotland) Act 1993, s 4(1), (2) (qv)
(1A)	Inserted by Bankruptcy (Scotland) Act 1993, s 4(1), (3) (qv)
(2)	1 Apr 1986 (SI 1985/1924)
(3), (3A)	Substituted for original sub-s (3) by Bankruptcy (Scotland) Act 1993, s 4(1), (4) (qv)
(4)	Substituted by Bankruptcy (Scotland) Act 1993, s 4(1), (5) (qv)
13	Substituted by Bankruptcy (Scotland) Act 1993, s 11, Sch 1, para 2 (qv)
14–18	1 Apr 1986 (SI 1985/1924)
19	Substituted by Bankruptcy (Scotland) Act 1993, s 11, Sch 1, para 7 (qv)
20(1)	Substituted by Bankruptcy (Scotland) Act 1993, s 11, Sch 1, para 8(1), (2) (qv)
(2)–(5)	1 Apr 1986 (SI 1985/1924)
(5A)	Inserted by Bankruptcy (Scotland) Act 1993, s 11, Sch 1, para 8(1), (4) (qv)
20A	Inserted by Bankruptcy (Scotland) Act 1993, s 11, Sch 1, para 9 (qv)
21(1)	1 Apr 1986 (SI 1985/1924)
(1A)	Inserted by Bankruptcy (Scotland) Act 1993, s 11, Sch 1, para 10(1), (3) (qv)
(2), (3)	1 Apr 1986 (SI 1985/1924)
(4)	Inserted by Bankruptcy (Scotland) Act 1993, s 11, Sch 1, para 10(1), (4) (qv)
21A, 21B	Inserted by Bankruptcy (Scotland) Act 1993, s 5 (qv)
22, 23	1 Apr 1986 (SI 1985/1924)
23A	Inserted by Bankruptcy (Scotland) Act 1993, s 6(1) (qv)
24(1)	Substituted by Bankruptcy (Scotland) Act 1993, s 11, Sch 1, para 12(1), (2) (qv)
(2)(a)–(d)	1 Apr 1986 (SI 1985/1924)
(e), (f)	Inserted by Bankrutpcy (Scotland) Act 1993, s 11, Sch 1, para 12(1), (3) (qv)
(3)	1 Apr 1986 (SI 1985/1924)
(3A), (3B)	Inserted by Bankruptcy (Scotland) Act 1993, s 11, Sch 1, para 12(1), (4) (qv)
(4)	1 Apr 1986 (SI 1985/1924)

Bankruptcy (Scotland) Act 1985 (c 66)—*cont*

s 24(4A)	Inserted by Bankruptcy (Scotland) Act 1993, s 11, Sch 1, para 12(1), (6) (qv)
(5)	1 Apr 1986 (SI 1985/1924)
25(1), (2)	1 Apr 1986 (SI 1985/1924)
(2A)	Inserted by Bankruptcy (Scotland) Act 1993, s 11, Sch 1, para 13(1), (2) (qv)
(3)–(6)	1 Apr 1988 (SI 1985/1924)
25A	Inserted by Bankruptcy (Scotland) Act 1993, s 7 (qv)
26(1)–(5)	1 Apr 1986 (SI 1985/1924)
(5A)	Inserted by Bankruptcy (Scotland) Act 1993, s 11, Sch 1, para 14(1), (4) (qv)
26A	Inserted by Bankruptcy (Scotland) Act 1993, s 11, Sch 1, para 15 (qv)
27(1)–(4)	1 Apr 1986 (SI 1985/1924)
(4A)	Inserted by Bankruptcy (Scotland) Act 1993, s 11, Sch 1, para 16(1), (2) (qv)
(5)–(7)	1 Apr 1986 (SI 1985/1924)
(7A)	Inserted by Bankruptcy (Scotland) Act 1993, s 11, Sch 1, para 16(1), (3) (qv)
28(1), (1A)	Substituted for original sub-s (1) by Bankruptcy (Scotland) Act 1993, s 11, Sch 1, para 17(1), (2) qv
(2)–(4)	1 Apr 1986 (SI 1985/1924)
(5)	Substituted by Bankruptcy (Scotland) Act 1993, s 11, Sch 1, para 17(1), (4) (qv)
(6), (7)	1 Apr 1986 (SI 1985/1924)
(8)	Inserted by Bankruptcy (Scotland) Act 1993, s 11, Sch 1, para 17(1), (5) (qv)
29–36	1 Apr 1986 (SI 1985/1924)
36A–36C	Prospectively inserted by Pensions Act 1995, s 95(2)[1]
37–50	1 Apr 1986 (SI 1985/1924)
51(1)	1 Apr 1986 (SI 1985/1924)
(2)	29 Dec 1986 (SI 1986/1913)
(3)–(7)	1 Apr 1986 (SI 1985/1924)
52(1), (2), (2A)	Substituted for original sub-ss (1), (2) by Bankruptcy (Scotland) Act 1993, s 11, Sch 1, para 21 (qv)
(3)–(5)	1 Apr 1986 (SI 1985/1924)
(6)	Repealed
(7)–(9)	1 Apr 1986 (SI 1985/1924)
53(1)	1 Apr 1986 (SI 1985/1924)
(2), (2A)	Substituted for original sub-s (2) by Bankruptcy (Scotland) Act 1993, s 11, Sch 1, para 22(1), (2) (qv)
(3)–(10)	1 Apr 1986 (SI 1985/1924)
54	1 Apr 1986 (SI 1985/1924)
55(1), (2)	1 Apr 1986 (SI 1985/1924)
(3)	Inserted (retrospectively) by Bankruptcy (Scotland) Act 1993, s 11, Sch 1, para 23(1), (3), (4)
56	1 Apr 1986 (SI 1985/1924)
57(1)–(4)	1 Apr 1986 (SI 1985/1924)
(4A)	Inserted by Bankruptcy (Scotland) Act 1993, s 11, Sch 1, para 24(1), (2) (qv)
(5)–(7)	1 Apr 1986 (SI 1985/1924)
(8)	Inserted by Bankruptcy (Scotland) Act 1993, s 11, Sch 1, para 24(1), (3) (qv)
58	1 Apr 1986 (SI 1985/1924)
58A	Inserted by Bankruptcy (Scotland) Act 1993, s 11, Sch 1, para 26 (qv)
59–69	1 Apr 1986 (SI 1985/1924)

Bankruptcy (Scotland) Act 1985 (c 66)—*cont*

s 69A	Inserted by Bankruptcy (Scotland) Act 1993, s 8 (qv)
70, 71	1 Apr 1986 (SI 1985/1924)
72	1 Feb 1986 (SI 1985/1924)
72A	Inserted by Bankruptcy (Scotland) Act 1993, s 11, Sch 1, para 28 (qv)
73(1)	1 Feb 1986 (except definition of 'preferred debt') (SI 1985/1924)
	29 Dec 1986 (definition of 'preferred debt') (SI 1986/1913)
(2)–(5)	1 Feb 1986 (SI 1985/1924)
(6)	Added by Bankruptcy (Scotland) Act 1993, s 11, Sch 1, para 29 (qv)
74, 75	1 Apr 1986 (SI 1985/1924)
76	1 Feb 1986 (SI 1985/1924)
77	1 Apr 1986 (SI 1985/1924)
78	30 Oct 1985 (RA)
Sch 1	1 Apr 1986 (SI 1985/1924)
2, para 1	1 Apr 1986 (SI 1985/1924)
2, 2A	Substituted for original para 2 by Bankruptcy (Scotland) Act 1993, s 11, Sch 1, para 30(1), (3) (qv)
3, 4	Substituted by Bankruptcy (Scotland) Act 1993, s 11, Sch 1, para 30(1), (4), (5) (qv)
5–7	1 Apr 1986 (SI 1985/1924)
7A	Inserted by Bankruptcy (Scotland) Act 1993, s 11, Sch 1, para 30(1), (8) (qv)
8	1 Apr 1986 (SI 1985/1924)
9	Substituted by Bankruptcy (Scotland) Act 1993, s 11, Sch 1, para 30(1), (10) (qv)
2A	Inserted by Bankruptcy (Scotland) Act 1993, s 6(2) (qv)
3	29 Dec 1986 (SI 1986/1913)
4–6	1 Apr 1986 (SI 1985/1924)
7, para 1	1 Apr 1986 (SI 1985/1924)
2	Repealed
3–6	1 Apr 1986 (SI 1985/1924)
7	Repealed
8, 9	1 Apr 1986 (SI 1985/1924)
10	Repealed
11, 12	1 Apr 1986 (SI 1985/1924)
13	Repealed
14(1), (2)	1 Apr 1986 (SI 1985/1924)
(3)	Repealed
(4)	1 Apr 1986 (SI 1985/1924)
15–18	1 Apr 1986 (SI 1985/1924)
19–22	Repealed
23–25	1 Apr 1986 (SI 1985/1924)
8	1 Apr 1986 (repeals of or in Bankruptcy Act 1621; Bankruptcy Act 1696; Titles to Land Consolidation (Scotland) Act 1868; Married Women's Property (Scotland) Act 1881; Judicial Factors (Scotland) Act 1889; Merchant Shipping Act 1894; Bankruptcy (Scotland) Act 1913 (except repeal of s 118); Married Women's Property (Scotland) Act 1920; Conveyancing (Scotland) Act 1924; Third Parties (Rights Against Insurers) Act 1930; Industrial Assurance and Friendly Societies Act 1948; Post

Bankruptcy (Scotland) Act 1985 (c 66)—*cont*

Sch 8—*cont*	Office Act 1969; Road Traffic Act 1972; Insolvency Act 1976; Banking Act 1979; Sale of Goods Act 1979; Law Reform (Miscellaneous Provisions) (Scotland) Act 1980; Matrimonial Homes (Family Protection) (Scotland) Act 1981; Companies Act 1985) (SI 1985/1924)
	29 Dec 1986 (otherwise) (SI 1986/1913)

[1] Any order made under Pensions Act 1995, s 180, bringing the prospective insertion into force will be noted to that Act in the service to this work

---

Betting, Gaming and Lotteries (Amendment) Act 1985 (c 18)

RA: 9 May 1985

Commencement provisions: s 3(2), (3); Betting, Gaming and Lotteries (Amendment) Act 1985 (Commencement) Order 1985, SI 1985/1475

s 1	9 Jul 1985 (s 3(2))
2(1)	9 Jul 1985 (s 3(2))
(2)	Repealed
(3), (4)	28 Oct 1985 (SI 1985/1475)
(5)	9 Jul 1985 (s 3(2))
(6)	Repealed
3	9 Jul 1985 (s 3(2))
Schedule	9 Jul 1985 (s 3(2))

Brunei and Maldives Act 1985 (c 3)

RA: 11 Mar 1985

11 Mar 1985 (RA)

Business Names Act 1985 (c 7)

RA: 11 Mar 1985

Commencement provisions: s 10

1 Jul 1985 (s 10)

Charities Act 1985 (c 20)

Whole Act repealed (with savings)

Charter Trustees Act 1985 (c 45)

RA: 16 Jul 1985

16 Jul 1985 (RA)

Child Abduction and Custody Act 1985 (c 60)

RA: 25 Jul 1985

Commencement provisions: s 29(2); Child Abduction and Custody Act 1985 (Commencement) Order 1986, SI 1986/1048

1 Aug 1986 (SI 1986/1048)

Cinemas Act 1985 (c 13)

RA: 27 Mar 1985

Commencement provisions: s 25(2)

27 Jun 1985 (s 25(2))

Coal Industry Act 1985 (c 27)

RA: 13 Jun 1985

13 Jun 1985 (RA)

Whole Act repealed (in part prospectively) as follows: s 1 repealed by Coal Industry Act 1994, s 67(8), Sch 11, Pt II; s 2 repealed by Coal Industry Act 1987, s 10(3), Sch 3, Pt I; ss 3–5 prospectively repealed by Coal Industry Act 1994, s 67(8), Sch 11, Pt III (any order bringing the prospective repeals into force will be noted to the 1994 Act in the service to this work)

Companies Act 1985 (c 6)

RA: 11 Mar 1985

Commencement provisions: ss 243(6), 746

1 Jul 1985 (s 746), except s 243(3), (4) (which provision has now been replaced)

Companies Consolidation (Consequential Provisions) Act 1985 (c 9)

RA: 11 Mar 1985

Commencement provisions: s 34

1 Jul 1985 (s 34)

Company Securities (Insider Dealing) Act 1985 (c 8)

Whole Act repealed

Consolidated Fund Act 1985 (c 1)

Whole Act repealed

Consolidated Fund (No 2) Act 1985 (c 11)

Whole Act repealed

Consolidated Fund (No 3) Act 1985 (c 74)

Whole Act repealed

Controlled Drugs (Penalties) Act 1985 (c 39)

RA: 16 Jul 1985

Commencement provisions: s 2(1)

16 Sep 1985 (s 2(1))

Copyright (Computer Software) Amendment Act 1985 (c 41)

Whole Act repealed

Dangerous Vessels Act 1985 (c 22)

RA: 23 May 1985

Commencement provisions: s 8(2)

23 Jul 1985 (s 8(2))

Elections (Northern Ireland) Act 1985 (c 2)

RA: 24 Jan 1985

Commencement provisions; s 7(2), (3); Elections (Northern Ireland) Act 1985 (Commencement) Order 1985, SI 1985/1221

s 1–3	24 Jan 1985 (so far as gives effect to s 5(1)) (s 7(3)) 6 Aug 1985 (otherwise) (SI 1985/1221)
4	6 Aug 1985 (SI 1985/1221)
5(1)	24 Jan 1985 (s 7(3))
(2), (3)	6 Aug 1985 (SI 1985/1221)
6, 7	24 Jan 1985 (s 7(3))

Enduring Powers of Attorney Act 1985 (c 29)

RA: 26 Jun 1985

Commencement provisions: s 14(2); Enduring Powers of Attorney Act 1985 (Commencement) Order 1986, SI 1986/125

10 Mar 1986 (SI 1986/125)

European Communities (Finance) Act 1985 (c 64)

Whole Act repealed

European Communities (Spanish and Portuguese Accession) Act 1985 (c 75)

RA: 19 Dec 1985

19 Dec 1985 (RA); but note that the accession of Spain and Portugal to the European Communities did not take effect until 1 Jan 1986

Family Law (Scotland) Act 1985 (c 37)

RA: 16 Jul 1985

Commencement provisions: s 29(2), (3); Family Law (Scotland) Act 1985 (Commencement No 1) Order 1986, SI 1986/1237; Family Law (Scotland) Act 1985 (Commencement No 2) Order 1988, SI 1988/1887

s 1–12	1 Sep 1986 (SI 1986/1237)
12A	Prospectively inserted by Pensions Act 1995, s 167(3)[1]
13–24	1 Sep 1986 (SI 1986/1237)
25	30 Nov 1988 (SI 1988/1887)
26–29	1 Sep 1986 (SI 1986/1237)
Sch 1, 2	1 Sep 1986 (SI 1986/1237)

[1] Orders made under Pensions Act 1995, s 180, bringing the prospective insertion into force will be noted to that Act in the service to this work

Films Act 1985 (c 21)

RA: 23 May 1985

Commencement provisions: s 8(2)

s 1	23 May 1985 (RA)
2	Repealed
3	23 May 1985 (RA)
4	Repealed
5	23 May 1985 (RA)
6	23 Jul 1985 (s 8(2))
7(1)	See Sch 2 below
(2)	Repealed
(3), (4)	23 May 1985 (RA)
(5), (6)	Repealed
(7)	23 May 1985 (RA)
8	23 May 1985 (RA)
Sch 1	23 Jul 1985 (s 8(2))
2	23 May 1985 (except repeals noted below) (RA)
	23 Jul 1985 (repeals in Finance Act 1982; Finance Act 1984) (s 8(2))

Finance Act 1985 (c 54)

Budget Day: 19 Mar 1985

RA: 25 Jul 1985

See the note concerning Finance Acts at the front of this book

Food and Environment Protection Act 1985 (c 48)

RA: 16 Jul 1985

Commencement provisions: s 27; Food and Environment Protection Act 1985 (Commencement No 1) Order 1985, SI 1985/1390; Food and Environment Protection Act 1985 (Commencement No 2) Order 1985, SI 1985/1698

s 1–4	16 Jul 1985 (s 27(2))
5–13	1 Jan 1986 (SI 1985/1698)
14	Substituted by Environmental Protection Act 1990, s 147 (qv)
15	1 Jan 1986 (SI 1985/1698)
16, 17	5 Sep 1985 (SI 1985/1390)
18	Substituted by Pesticides (Fees and Enforcement) Act 1989, s 1(2) (qv)
19	5 Sep 1985 (SI 1985/1390)
20–26	16 Jul 1985 (so far as relate to Pt I (ss 1–4)) (s 27(2)) 1 Jan 1986 (otherwise) (SI 1985/1698)
27, 28	16 Jul 1985 (s 27(2))
Sch 1	16 Jul 1985 (s 27(2))
2	16 Jul 1985 (so far as relates to Pt I (ss 1–4)) (s 27(2)) 5 Sep 1985 (so far as relates to Pt III (ss 16–19)) (SI 1985/1390) 1 Jan 1986 (otherwise) (SI 1985/1698)
3	1 Jan 1986 (SI 1985/1698)
4	1 Jan 1986 (SI 1985/1698; prospectively repealed by Environmental Protection Act 1990, s 162(2), Sch 16, Pt VIII)[1]
5	5 Sep 1985 (SI 1985/1390)

[1] Any order made under Environmental Protection 1990, s 164, bringing the prospective repeal into force will be noted to that Act in the service to this work

Further Education Act 1985 (c 47)

RA: 16 Jul 1985

Commencement provisions: s 7; Further Education Act 1985 (Commencement) (No 1) Order 1985, SI 1985/1429; Further Education Act 1985 (Commencement No 2) (Scotland) Order 1987, SI 1987/1335

s 1–3	16 Sep 1985 (s 7(3))
4	16 Sep 1985 (EW) (SI 1985/1429) 17 Aug 1987 (S) (SI 1987/1335)
5–8	16 Jul 1985 (s 7(2))

Gaming (Bingo) Act 1985 (c 35)

RA: 16 Jul 1985

Commencement provisions: s 5(2); Gaming (Bingo) Act 1985 (Commencement) Order 1986, SI 1986/832

9 Jun 1986 (SI 1986/832)

Hill Farming Act 1985 (c 32)

RA: 26 Jun 1985

Commencement provisions: s 2(3)

26 Aug 1985 (s 2(3))

Hong Kong Act 1985 (c 15)

RA: 11 Mar 1985

11 Mar 1985 (RA)

Hospital Complaints Procedure Act 1985 (c 42)

RA: 16 Jul 1985

Commencement provisions: s 2(2); Hospital Complaints Procedure Act 1985 (Commencement) Order 1989, SI 1989/1191

11 Jul 1989 (SI 1989/1191)

Housing Act 1985 (c 68)

RA: 30 Oct 1985

Commencement provisions: s 625(2)

1 Apr 1986 (s 625(2))

Housing Associations Act 1985 (c 69)

RA: 30 Oct 1985

Commencement provisions: s 107(2)

1 Apr 1986 (s 107(2))

Housing (Consequential Provisions) Act 1985 (c 71)

RA: 30 Oct 1985

Commencement provisions: s 6(2)

1 Apr 1986 (s 6(2))

Industrial Development Act 1985 (c 25)

RA: 13 Jun 1985

Commencement provisions: s 6(4)

s 1, 2	13 Aug 1985 (s 6(4)); prospectively repealed by Leasehold Reform, Housing and Urban Development Act 1993, s 187(2), Sch 22[1]

Industrial Development Act 1985 (c 25)—*cont*

s 3	1 Apr 1986 (s 6(4)); prospectively repealed by Leasehold Reform, Housing and Urban Development Act 1993, s 187(2), Sch 22[1]
4	13 Aug 1985 (s 6(4)); prospectively repealed by Leasehold Reform, Housing and Urban Development Act 1993, s 187(2), Sch 22[1]
5, 6	13 Aug 1985 (s 6(4))
Schedule	13 Aug 1985 (s 6(4))

[1] Any order(s) made under Leasehold Reform, Housing and Urban Development Act 1993, s 188(2), (3), bringing the prospective repeal into force will be noted to that Act in the service to this work

Insolvency Act 1985 (c 65)

RA: 30 Oct 1985

Commencement provisions: s 236(2); Insolvency Act 1985 (Commencement No 1) Order 1986, SI 1986/6; Insolvency Act 1985 (Commencement No 2) Order 1986, SI 1986/185; Insolvency Act 1985 (Commencement No 3) Order 1986, SI 1986/463; Insolvency Act 1985 (Commencement No 4) Order 1986, SI 1986/840; Insolvency Act 1985 (Commencement No 5) Order 1986, SI 1986/1924

s 1–216	Repealed
217(1)–(3)	Repealed
(4)	29 Dec 1986 (SI 1986/1924)
218–220	29 Dec 1986 (SI 1986/1924)
221–234	Repealed
235(1)	1 Mar 1986 (SI 1986/185)
(2)–(5)	Repealed
236(1), (2)	1 Feb 1986 (SI 1986/6)
(3)–(5)	Repealed
Sch 1, para 1–5	Repealed
6	1 Jul 1986 (SI 1986/840)
2–5	Repealed
6, para 1, 2	Repealed
3, 4	28 Apr 1986 (SI 1986/463)
5–7	Repealed
8	29 Dec 1986 (SI 1986/1924)
9	Repealed
10–13	29 Dec 1986 (SI 1986/1924)
14–17	Repealed
18, 19	29 Dec 1986 (SI 1986/1924)
20–23	Repealed
24	1 Mar 1986 (so far as relates to the making of rules under s 106 in relation to England and Wales) (SI 1986/185) 29 Dec 1986 (otherwise) (SI 1986/1924)
25–45	Repealed
46, 47	29 Dec 1986 (SI 1986/1924)
48–52	Repealed
7	Repealed
8, para 1–7	29 Dec 1986 (SI 1986/1924)
8, 9	Repealed
10–15	29 Dec 1986 (SI 1986/1924)

Insolvency Act 1985 (c 65)—*cont*

Sch 8, para	16	Repealed
	17	Spent
	18–23	29 Dec 1986 (SI 1986/1924)
	24	Repealed
	25	29 Dec 1986 (SI 1986/1924)
	26	Repealed
	27	1 Apr 1986 (so far as relates to the awarding by a court in Scotland of the sequestration of an individual's estate) (SI 1986/463) 29 Dec 1986 (otherwise) (SI 1986/1924)
	28	Repealed
	29, 30	Repealed
	31	29 Dec 1986 (SI 1986/1924)
	32	Spent
	33–35	29 Dec 1986 (SI 1986/1924)
	36	1 Apr 1986 (SI 1986/185)
	37(1)–(3)	29 Dec 1986 (SI 1986/1924)
	(4)	1 Mar 1986 (so far as relates to the making of rules under s 106 in relation to England and Wales) (SI 1986/185) 29 Dec 1986 (otherwise) (SI 1986/1924)
	38–40	29 Dec 1986 (SI 1986/1924)
9, 10		Repealed

Insurance (Fees) Act 1985 (c 46)

RA: 16 Jul 1985

16 Jul 1985 (RA)

Interception of Communications Act 1985 (c 56)

RA: 25 Jul 1985

Commencement provisions: s 12(2); Interception of Communications Act 1985 (Commencement) Order 1986, SI 1986/384

10 Apr 1986 (SI 1986/384)

Intoxicating Substances (Supply) Act 1985 (c 26)

RA: 13 Jun 1985

Commencement provisions: s 2(2)

13 Aug 1985 (s 2(2))

Landlord and Tenant Act 1985 (c 70)

RA: 30 Oct 1985

Commencement provisions: s 40(2)

1 Apr 1986 (s 40(2))

Law Reform (Miscellaneous Provisions) (Scotland) Act 1985 (c 73)

RA: 30 Oct 1985

Commencement provisions: s 60(3), (4); Law Reform (Miscellaneous Provisions) (Scotland) Act 1985 (Commencement No 1) Order 1985, SI 1985/1908; Law Reform (Miscellaneous Provisions) (Scotland) Act 1985 (Commencement No 2) Order 1985, SI 1985/2055; Law Reform (Miscellaneous Provisions) (Scotland) Act 1985 (Commencement No 3) Order 1986, SI 1986/1945; Law Reform (Miscellaneous Provisions) (Scotland) Act 1985 (Commencement No 4) Order 1988, SI 1988/1819

s 1–13		30 Dec 1985 (s 60(3))
14, 15		8 Dec 1986 (SI 1986/1945)
16		Repealed
17		30 Dec 1985 (s 60(3))
18		30 Nov 1988 (SI 1988/1819)
19		8 Dec 1986 (SI 1986/1945)
20		30 Dec 1985 (s 60(3))
21		Repealed
22–25		30 Dec 1985 (s 60(3))
26–29		30 Oct 1985 (s 60(3))
30–32		Repealed
33, 34		30 Dec 1985 (s 60(3))
35		1 Jan 1986 (SI 1985/1908)
36–40		Repealed
41		30 Dec 1985 (s 60(3))
42–45		Repealed
46–49		30 Dec 1985 (s 60(3))
50		1 Feb 1986 (SI 1985/1908)
51–53		30 Dec 1985 (s 60(3))
54		30 Oct 1985 (s 60(3))
55–58		30 Dec 1985 (s 60(3))
59(1)		See Sch 2 below
(2)		30 Dec 1985 (s 60(3))
60		30 Oct 1985 (s 60(3))
Sch 1		30 Dec 1985 (s 60(3))
2, para	1–7	30 Dec 1985 (s 60(3))
	8	Repealed
	9–11	30 Dec 1985 (s 60(3))
	12, 13	8 Dec 1986 (SI 1986/1945)
	14, 15	30 Dec 1985 (s 60(3))
	16–20	Repealed
	21, 22	30 Dec 1985 (s 60(3))
	23	Repealed
	24	8 Dec 1986 (SI 1986/1945)
	25	30 Dec 1985 (s 60(3))
	26, 27	Repealed
	28–30	30 Oct 1985 (s 60(3))
	31	30 Dec 1985 (s 60(3))
	32	30 Oct 1985 (s 60(3))
3		30 Oct 1985 (s 60(3))
4		30 Dec 1985 (s 60(3))

Licensing (Amendment) Act 1985 (c 40)

RA: 16 Jul 1985

16 Jul 1985 (RA)

Local Government Act 1985 (c 51)

RA: 16 Jul 1985

This Act largely came into force on the date of Royal Assent, but the effective date of operation for many of its provisions (except as otherwise provided) is 1 Apr 1986 (the date of abolition of the Greater London Council and the metropolitan county councils). In addition certain provisions come into force in different areas on dates appointed by order before and after 1 Apr 1986

Local Government (Access to Information) Act 1985 (c 43)

RA: 16 Jul 1985

Commencement provisions: s 5

1 Apr 1986 (s 5)

London Regional Transport (Amendment) Act 1985 (c 10)

RA: 11 Mar 1985

11 Mar 1985 (RA)

Milk (Cessation of Production) Act 1985 (c 4)

RA: 11 Mar 1985

Commencement provisions: s 7(2)

s 1–5	11 May 1985 (s 7(2))
6	11 Mar 1985 (RA)
7	11 May 1985 (s 7(2))

Mineral Workings Act 1985 (c 12)

RA: 27 Mar 1985

Commencement provisions: s 11(2)–(4)

s 1	1 Apr 1985 (s 11(2))
2	Repealed
3–6	1 Apr 1985 (s 11(2))
7, 8	27 May 1985 (s 11(3))
9, 10	1 Apr 1985 (s 11(2))
11	27 Mar 1985 (s 11(4))
Sch 1, 2	1 Apr 1985 (s 11(2))

Motor-Cycle Crash-Helmets (Restriction of Liability) Act 1985 (c 28)

Whole Act repealed

National Heritage (Scotland) Act 1985 (c 16)

RA: 4 Apr 1985

Commencement provisions: s 25(1); National Heritage (Scotland) Act 1985 Commencement Order 1985, SI 1985/851

s 1	4 Jun 1985 (SI 1985/851)
2–5	1 Oct 1985 (SI 1985/851)
6(1)–(4)	1 Oct 1985 (SI 1985/851)
(5)–(7)	4 Jun 1985 (SI 1985/851)
7–9	1 Oct 1985 (SI 1985/851)
10	4 Jun 1985 (SI 1985/851)
11–15	1 Apr 1986 (SI 1985/851)
16	4 Jun 1985 (SI 1985/851)
17	4 Jun 1985 (so far as adds paras 1–7, 9 of Schedule to National Galleries of Scotland Act 1906) (SI 1985/851)
	1 Apr 1986 (so far as adds para 8 of that Schedule) (SI 1985/851)
18(1)–(5)	4 Jun 1985 (SI 1985/851)
(6)	1 Apr 1986 (SI 1985/851)
19(1)	1 Oct 1985 (SI 1985/851)
(2), (3)	4 Jun 1985 (SI 1985/851)
20–23	4 Jun 1985 (SI 1985/851)
24	See Sch 2 below
25	4 Apr 1985 (RA)
Sch 1, Pt I, para 1–3	4 Jun 1985 (SI 1985/851)
4(1)–(5)	4 Jun 1985 (SI 1985/851)
(6)	1 Oct 1985 (SI 1985/851)
5–7	4 Jun 1985 (SI 1985/851)
8	Repealed
9, 10	4 Jun 1985 (SI 1985/851)
Pt II, para 11–18	4 Jun 1985 (SI 1985/851)
19	Repealed
20, 21	4 Jun 1985 (SI 1985/851)
2, Pt I, para 1	1 Apr 1986 (SI 1985/851)
2	Repealed
3, 4	1 Oct 1985 (SI 1985/851)
Pt II	4 Jun 1985 (repeal of words in National Library of Scotland Act 1925, s 2(f)) (SI 1985/851)
	1 Oct 1985 (repeal of or in National Museum of Antiquities of Scotland Act 1954; National Gallery and Tate Gallery Act 1954, Sch 1) (SI 1985/851)
	1 Apr 1986 (repeal of National Library of Scotland Act 1925, s 10) (SI 1985/851)

New Towns and Urban Development Corporations Act 1985 (c 5)

RA: 11 Mar 1985

Commencement provisions: s 15(2)

s 1, 2	11 May 1985 (s 15(2))
3, 4	11 May 1985 (s 15(2)); prospectively repealed by Local Government and Housing Act 1989, s 194(4), Sch 12, Pt II[1]
5	11 Mar 1985 (RA)

New Towns and Urban Development Corporations Act 1985 (c 5)—*cont*

s 6–11	11 May 1985 (s 15(2))
12	Repealed
13–15	11 May 1985 (s 15(2))
Sch 1, 2	11 May 1985 (s 15(2))
3, para 1–6	11 May 1985 (s 15(2))
7	11 Mar 1985 (RA); prospectively repealed by Local Government and Housing Act 1989, s 194(4), Sch 12, Pt II[1]
8–16	11 May 1985 (s 15(2))

[1] Any order(s) made under Local Government and Housing Act 1989, s 195(2), bringing the prospective repeal into force will be noted to that Act in the service to this work

Northern Ireland (Loans) Act 1985 (c 76)

RA: 19 Dec 1985

19 Dec 1985 (RA)

Oil and Pipelines Act 1985 (c 62)

RA: 30 Oct 1985

Commencement provisions: s 8(2), (3); Oil and Pipelines Act 1985 (Commencement) Order 1985, SI 1985/1748; Oil and Pipelines Act 1985 (Appointed Day) Order 1985, SI 1985/1749; British National Oil Corporation (Dissolution) Order 1986, SI 1986/585

s 1, 2	1 Dec 1985 (SI 1985/1748)
3	1 Dec 1985 (SI 1985/1749)
4–8	1 Dec 1985 (SI 1985/1748)
Sch 1	1 Dec 1985 (SI 1985/1748)
2	1 Dec 1985 (SI 1985/1749)
3	1 Dec 1985 (SI 1985/1748)
4, Pt I	1 Dec 1985 (SI 1985/1749)
II	27 Mar 1986 (SI 1986/585)

Ports (Finance) Act 1985 (c 30)

RA: 26 Jun 1985

Commencement provisions: s 7(2); Ports (Finance) Act 1985 (Commencement) Order 1985, SI 1985/1153

s 1	Repealed
2	5 Aug 1985 (SI 1985/1153)
3–5	1 Jan 1986 (SI 1985/1153)
6, 7	5 Aug 1985 (SI 1985/1153)
Schedule	5 Aug 1985 (SI 1985/1153)

Prohibition of Female Circumcision Act 1985 (c 38)

RA: 16 Jul 1985

Commencement provisions: s 4(2)

16 Sep 1985 (s 4(2))

Prosecution of Offences Act 1985 (c 23)

RA: 23 May 1985

Commencement provisions: s 31(2); Prosecution of Offences Act 1985 (Commencement No 1) Order 1985, SI 1985/1849; Prosecution of Offences Act 1985 (Commencement No 2) Order 1986, SI 1986/1029; Prosecution of Offences Act 1985 (Commencement No 3) Order 1986, SI 1986/1334

s 1, 2	1 Apr 1986 (in the counties of Durham, Greater Manchester, Merseyside, Northumberland, South Yorkshire, Tyne and Wear, West Midlands and West Yorkshire only) (SI 1985/1849)
	1 Oct 1986 (otherwise) (SI 1986/1029)
3	1 Apr 1986 (in the counties noted to ss 1, 2 above only; but s 3(2) (a), (c), (d) does not apply in relation to proceedings transferred (whether on appeal or otherwise) to an area where those provisions are in force from an area where they are not) (SI 1985/1849)
	1 Oct 1986 (otherwise) (SI 1986/1029)
4–7	1 Apr 1986 (in the counties noted to ss 1, 2 above only) (SI 1985/1849)
	1 Oct 1986 (otherwise) (SI 1986/1029)
7A	Inserted by Courts and Legal Services Act 1990, s 114 (qv)
8	1 Apr 1986 (in the counties noted to ss 1, 2 above only) (SI 1985/1849)
	1 Oct 1986 (otherwise) (SI 1986/1029)
9	5 Apr 1987 (SI 1986/1029)
10	1 Apr 1986 (in the counties noted to ss 1, 2 above only) (SI 1985/1849)
	1 Oct 1986 (otherwise) (SI 1986/1029)
11–13	23 May 1985 (s 31(2))
14	1 Apr 1986 (in the counties noted to ss 1, 2 above only) (SI 1985/1849)
	1 Oct 1986 (otherwise) (SI 1986/1029)
15	23 May 1985 (so far as applies in relation to ss 11–13) (s 31(2))
	1 Oct 1986 (otherwise) (SI 1986/1029)
16–19	1 Oct 1986 (SI 1986/1334)
19A	Inserted by Courts and Legal Services Act 1990, s 111 (qv)
20, 21	1 Oct 1986 (SI 1986/1334)
22	1 Oct 1986 (SI 1986/1029)
23	1 Apr 1986 (in the counties noted to ss 1, 2 above only) (SI 1985/1849)
	1 Oct 1986 (otherwise) (SI 1986/1029)
24	1 Apr 1986 (SI 1985/1849)

Prosecution of Offences Act 1985 (c 23)—*cont*

s 25, 26	1 Apr 1986 (in the counties noted to ss 1, 2 above only) (SI 1985/1849) 1 Oct 1986 (otherwise) (SI 1986/1029)
27	Repealed
28	1 Apr 1986 (SI 1985/1849)
29, 30	23 May 1985 (s 31(2))
31(1)–(4)	23 May 1985 (s 31(2))
(5), (6)	1 Apr 1986 (SI 1985/1849)
(7)	23 May 1985 (s 31(2))
Sch 1, para 1	Repealed
2, 3	1 Apr 1986 (in the counties noted to ss 1, 2 above only) (SI 1985/1849) 1 Oct 1986 (otherwise) (SI 1986/1029)
4, 5	1 Apr 1986 (SI 1985/1849)
6–10	1 Oct 1986 (otherwise) (SI 1986/1334)
11	*Not in force*
2	1 Apr 1986 (repeals of or in Perjury Act 1911; Administration of Justice (Miscellaneous Provisions) Act 1933; Industrial Development Act 1966; Transport Act 1968; European Communities Act 1972; Bail Act 1976; Representation of the People Act 1983) (SI 1985/1849) 1 Apr 1986 (in the counties noted to ss 1, 2 above only) (repeals of or in Prosecution of Offences Act 1979; Magistrates' Courts Act 1980, s 25) (SI 1985/1849) 1 Oct 1986 (in counties other than those noted above) (repeals of or in Prosecution of Offences Act 1979; Magistrates' Courts Act 1980, s 25) (SI 1986/1029) 1 Oct 1986 (repeals of or in Indictments Act 1915; Criminal Justice Act 1967; Criminal Appeal Act 1968; Administrtaion of Justice Act 1970; Costs in Criminal Cases Act 1973; Administration of Justice Act 1973; Magistrates' Courts Act 1980, s 30(3); Legal Aid Act 1982) (SI 1986/1334) *Not in force* (repeal in Supreme Court Act 1981, s 77)

Rating (Revaluation Rebates) (Scotland) Act 1985 (c 33)

RA: 26 Jun 1985

Commencement provisions: s 3(1)

26 Aug 1985 (s 3(1))

Rent (Amendment) Act 1985 (c 24)

RA: 23 May 1985

23 May 1985 (RA)

Representation of the People Act 1985 (c 50)

RA: 16 Jul 1985

Commencement provisions: s 29(2), (3); Representation of the People Act 1985 (Commencement No 1) Order 1985, SI 1985/1185; Representation of the People Act 1985 (Commencement No 2) Order 1986, SI 1986/639; Representation of the

Representation of the People Act 1985 (c 50)—*cont*

People Act 1985 (Commencement No 3) Order 1986, SI 1986/1080; Representation of the People Act 1985 (Commencement No 4) Order 1987, SI 1987/207

s 1–4	11 Jul 1986 (SI 1986/1080)
5–11	16 Feb 1987 (SI 1986/1080)
12(1), (2)	11 Jul 1986 (SI 1986/1080)
(3)	16 Feb 1987 (SI 1986/1080)
(4)	11 Jul 1986 (SI 1986/1080)
13, 14	1 Oct 1985 (SI 1985/1185)
15, 16	16 Feb 1987 (SI 1986/1080)
17	1 Sep 1985 (SI 1985/1185)
18	1 Oct 1985 (SI 1985/1185)
19(1)–(5)	16 Feb 1987 (SI 1986/1080)
(6)(a)	1 Oct 1985 (SI 1985/1185)
(b), (c)	16 Feb 1987 (SI 1986/1080)
20	1 Oct 1985 (SI 1985/1185)
21	16 Feb 1987 (SI 1986/1080)
22	Substituted by Welsh Language Act 1993, s 35(5) (qv)
23, 24	1 Oct 1985 (SI 1985/1185)
25(1)	16 Jul 1985 (s 29(3))
(2)	1 Oct 1985 (SI 1985/1185)
26	1 Oct 1985 (SI 1985/1185)
27(1)	16 Jul 1985 (s 29(3))
(2), (3)	1 Oct 1985 (SI 1985/1185)
28	1 Oct 1985 (SI 1985/1185)
29	16 Jul 1985 (s 29(3))
Sch 1	*Not in force*
2	16 Feb 1987 (SI 1986/1080)
3	1 Oct 1985 (SI 1985/1185)
4, para 1–6	1 Oct 1985 (SI 1985/1185)
7	16 Feb 1987 (SI 1986/1080)
8	1 Oct 1985 (SI 1985/1185)
9	16 Feb 1987 (SI 1986/1080)
10–17	1 Oct 1985 (SI 1985/1185)
18	16 Jul 1985 (s 29(3))
19–33	1 Oct 1985 (SI 1985/1185)
34	30 Mar 1987 (except for the purposes of an election, notice of which is published before that date) (SI 1987/207)
35–68	1 Oct 1985 (SI 1985/1185)
69	21 Apr 1986 (SI 1986/639)
70–72	1 Oct 1985 (SI 1985/1185)
73	16 Feb 1987 (SI 1986/1080)
74–78	1 Oct 1985 (SI 1985/1185)
79, 80	16 Feb 1987 (SI 1986/1080)
81–83	1 Oct 1985 (SI 1985/1185)
84–86	16 Feb 1987 (SI 1986/1080)
87–89	1 Oct 1985 (SI 1985/1185)
90	Repealed
5	16 Jul 1985 (repeals in Police and Criminal Evidence Act 1984) (s 29(3))
	1 Oct 1985 (repeals of or in Meeting of Parliament Act 1797, ss 3–5; Representation of the People Act 1918; Local Government Act 1972, s 243(3); Representation of the People Act 1983, ss 18(2)(b),

Representation of the People Act 1985 (c 50)—*cont*

Sch 5—*cont*

(6)(b), 39(8), 49(1)(d), (2)(c), 51, 52(2), 53(2), 55, 56(1)(c), (6), 76(3), 103(2), 104(b), 106(4), 108(3), (4), 124(a), (b), 125(a), 126(3), 136(4), (5), (7), 140(5), (7), 141(3), (4), 142, 148(4)(a), 156(2)–(4), 161, 162, 163(1)(b), 168(5), (6), 169, 171, 172, 173(a), 176(1), (3), 181(3), (6), 187(1), 190, 191(1)(a), 192, 196, 199, 202(1), 203(4)(a), Sch 1, rule 5, para (1), rule 23, para (2)(c), (3), Appendix of Forms, Sch 2, para 9, Sch 7, paras 8, 9) (SI 1985/1185)

16 Feb 1987 (repeals of or in City of London (Various Powers) Act 1957; Representation of the People Act 1983, ss 19–22, 32–34, 38, 40(1), 43(2)(b), 44, 49(3), 61, Sch 1, rr 2(3), 27, 40(1)(b), Sch 2, para 5(4), Sch 8) (SI 1986/1080)

Not in force (otherwise)

Reserve Forces (Safeguard of Employment) Act 1985 (c 17)

RA: 9 May 1985

Commencement provisions: s 23(3)

9 Aug 1985 (s 23(3))

Road Traffic (Production of Documents) Act 1985 (c 34)

Whole Act repealed

Sexual Offences Act 1985 (c 44)

RA: 16 Jul 1985

Commencement provisions: s 5(4)

16 Sep 1985 (s 5(4))

Shipbuilding Act 1985 (c 14)

RA: 27 Mar 1985

27 Mar 1985 (RA)

Whole Act repealed by Statute Law (Repeals) Act 1993, s 1, Sch 1, Pt IX (partly (repeal of s 1) as from a day to be appointed by order under s 4(3) of that Act; any such order will be noted to the 1993 Act in the service to this work)

Social Security Act 1985 (c 53)

RA: 22 Jul 1985

Commencement provisions: s 32; Social Security Act 1985 (Commencement No 1) Order 1985, SI 1985/1125; Social Security Act 1985 (Commencement No 2) Order 1985, SI 1985/1364

Social Security Act 1985 (c 53)—*cont*

s 1–7	Repealed
8(1)	Repealed
(2), (3)	22 Jul 1985 (s 32(2))
9–20	Repealed
21	See Sch 4 below
22	Repealed
23–25	22 Jul 1985 (s 32(2))
26	Repealed (savings) by Pension Schemes Act 1993, s 188(1), Sch 5 (qv)
27	Repealed
28(1)	22 Jul 1985 (s 32(2))
(2)	Repealed
29(1)	See Sch 5 below
(2)	See Sch 6 below
30	Repealed
31–33	22 Jul 1985 (s 32(2))
Sch 1–3	Repealed
4, para 1	16 Sep 1985 (SI 1985/1125)
2–7	Repealed
5, para 1–5	Repealed
6	6 Oct 1985 (SI 1985/1125); repealed (prospectively in the case of para (b)) by Social Security Act 1986, s 86(2), Sch 11[1]
7–15	Repealed
16	6 Oct 1985 (SI 1985/1125); prospectively repealed by Social Security Act 1986, s 86(2), Sch 11[1]
17–32	Repealed
33	6 Oct 1985 (SI 1985/1364)
34–38	Repealed
39	6 Oct 1985 (SI 1985/1125)
40	6 Oct 1985 (SI 1985/1364)
6	22 Jul 1985 (repeals of or in Social Security Pensions Act 1975, s 41D; Social Security (Miscellaneous Provisions) Act 1977, s 22(7); Social Security Act 1981; Health and Social Security Act 1984) (s 32(2))
	23 Jul 1985 (repeals of or in Social Security Act 1975, s 28(2); Social Security Act 1979, Sch 1, para 11) (SI 1985/1125)
	5 Aug 1985 (repeals of or in Social Security Act 1975, ss 79, 82, 90) (s 32(3))
	16 Sep 1985 (repeals of or in Social Security Act 1975, ss 45(3), (4), 125(1), 126A(1); Social Security (Miscellaneous Provisions) Act 1977, s 5(1); Social Security and Housing Benefits Act 1982, s 24, Sch 2, paras 7–11) (SI 1985/1125; SI 1985/1364)
	6 Oct 1985 (repeals of or in Social Security Pensions Act 1975, ss 41B(4), 59(5)(b), Sch 4, para 36(b); Social Security (Contributions) Act 1982, s 1(5), Sch 1, para 1(3)) (SI 1985/1125; SI 1985/1364)
	25 Nov 1985 (repeals of or in Social Security Act 1975, s 39(2), Sch 4, Pt III, para 5) (SI 1985/1125)
	1 Jan 1986 (repeals of or in Social Security Act 1973, Sch 16, para 6(1)(a); Social Security Pensions Act 1975, ss 26(2), 34(4), 41A(4)(i), 66; Social Security

Social Security Act 1985 (c 53)—*cont*

Sch 6—*cont*	(Miscellaneous Provisions) Act 1977, s 22(9)–(11); Social Security Act 1980, s 3(6), (7)) (SI 1985/1364)
	6 Apr 1986 (remaining repeals in Social Security and Housing Benefits Act 1982) (SI 1985/1125)

[1] Any order(s) made under Social Security Act 1986, s 88, bringing the prospective repeal into force will be noted to that Act in the service to this work; but note para 1 of the Report of the Law Commission and the Scottish Law Commission on the Consolidation of the Legislation relating to Social Security (Law Com No 203; Scot Law Com No 132; Cm 1726), in relation to the repeal of Sch 5, para 6(b); the prospective nature of the repeal of Sch 5, para 16 is preserved by Social Security (Consequential Provisions) Act 1992, s 6, Sch 4, paras 1–3

Sporting Events (Control of Alcohol etc) Act 1985 (c 57)

RA: 25 Jul 1985

25 Jul 1985 (RA)

Surrogacy Arrangements Act 1985 (c 49)

RA: 16 Jul 1985

16 Jul 1985 (RA)

Town and Country Planning (Amendment) Act 1985 (c 52)

RA: 22 Jul 1985

Commencement provisions: s 3(3)

22 Sep 1985 (s 3(3))

Town and Country Planning (Compensation) Act 1985 (c 19)

RA: 9 May 1985

9 May 1985 (RA)

Transport Act 1985 (c 67)

RA: 30 Oct 1985

Commencement provisions: s 140(2); Transport Act 1985 (Commencement No 1) Order 1985, SI 1985/1887; Transport Act 1985 (Commencement No 2) Order 1986, SI 1986/80; Transport Act 1985 (Commencement No 3) Order 1986, SI 1986/414; Transport Act 1985 (Commencement No 4) Order 1986, SI 1986/1088; Transport Act 1985 (Commencement No 5) Order 1986, SI 1986/1450; Transport Act 1985 (Commencement No 6) Order 1986, SI 1986/1794 (as amended by SI 1988/2294); Transport Act 1985 (Commencement No 7) Order 1987, SI 1987/1228

s 1(1), (2)	26 Oct 1986 (SI 1986/1794)
(3)	See Sch 1 below
2, 3	6 Jan 1986 (SI 1985/1887)

Transport Act 1985 (c 67)—*cont*

s 4	6 Jan 1986 (to extent necessary to replace Public Passenger Vehicles Act 1981, s 54 with sub-ss (1), (2) only of the new s 54) (SI 1985/1887)
	26 Oct 1986 (otherwise) (SI 1986/1794)
5	6 Jan 1986 (SI 1985/1887)
6	26 Oct 1986 (SI 1986/1794)
7–9	14 Jul 1986 (SI 1986/1088)
10, 11	1 Aug 1986 (SI 1986/1088)
12(1), (2)	6 Jan 1986 (SI 1985/1887)
(3)	Repealed
(4)–(13)	6 Jan 1986 (SI 1985/1887)
13	6 Jan 1986 (to the extent that supplements s 12 of this Act) (SI 1985/1887)
	1 Aug 1986 (otherwise) (SI 1986/1088)
14, 15	1 Jan 1987 (SI 1986/1794)
16	6 Jan 1986 (SI 1985/1887)
17	1 Aug 1986 (SI 1986/1088)
18	1 Aug 1986 (so far as relates to the use of any vehicle under a permit granted under s 22 or the driving of any vehicle so used) (SI 1986/1088)
	13 Aug 1987 (otherwise) (SI 1987/1228)
19–21	13 Aug 1987 (SI 1987/1228)
22, 23	1 Aug 1986 (SI 1986/1088)
24(1)	26 Oct 1986 (SI 1986/1794)
(2)	Repealed
25–27	26 Oct 1986 (SI 1986/1794)
28(1), (2)	26 Oct 1986 (SI 1986/1794)
(2A)	Inserted by Deregulation and Contracting Out Act 1994, s 67 (qv)
(3)–(6)	26 Oct 1986 (SI 1986/1794)
(6A)	Inserted by Deregulation and Contracting Out Act 1994, s 67 (qv)
(7)	26 Oct 1986 (SI 1986/1794)
29, 30	6 Jan 1986 (SI 1985/1887)
31	15 Sep 1986 (SI 1986/1450)
32	6 Jan 1986 (to the extent that applies to Public Passenger Vehicles Act 1981, s 28) (SI 1985/1887)
	26 Oct 1986 (otherwise) (SI 1986/1794)
33	1 Aug 1986 (SI 1986/1088)
34	6 Jan 1986 (SI 1985/1887)
35–46	26 Oct 1986 (SI 1986/1794)
47–53	Repealed
54–56	6 Jan 1986 (SI 1985/1887)
57(1)–(5)	6 Jan 1986 (SI 1985/1887)
(6)	See Sch 3 below
58	30 Oct 1985 (s 140(2))
59–80	6 Jan 1986 (SI 1985/1887)
81(1), (2)	6 Jan 1986 (SI 1985/1887)
(2A)	Prospectively inserted by Local Government (Wales) Act 1994, s 22(1), Sch 7, Pt II, para 39[1]
(3)–(5)	6 Jan 1986 (SI 1985/1887)
(5A)	Prospectively inserted by Local Government (Wales) Act 1994, s 22(1), Sch 7, Pt II, para 39[1]
(6), (7)	6 Jan 1986 (SI 1985/1887)
82–84	6 Jan 1986 (SI 1985/1887)
85, 86	13 Aug 1987 (SI 1987/1228)
87–92	6 Jan 1986 (SI 1985/1887)

Transport Act 1985 (c 67)—*cont*

s 93(1)–(7), (8)(a)	14 Feb 1986 (SI 1986/80)
(8)(b)	1 Apr 1986 (SI 1986/414)
(9), (10)	14 Feb 1986 (SI 1986/80)
94–101	14 Feb 1986 (SI 1986/80)
102	1 Apr 1986 (SI 1986/414)
103	14 Feb 1986 (SI 1986/80)
104	15 Sep 1986 (SI 1986/1450)
105(1), (2)	14 Feb 1986 (SI 1986/80)
(2A)	Prospectively inserted by Local Government (Wales) Act 1994, s 22(1), Sch 7, Pt II, para 39[1]
(3)	14 Feb 1986 (SI 1986/80)
106	6 Jan 1986 (SI 1985/1887)
107	1 Apr 1986 (SI 1985/1887)
108, 109	1 Apr 1986 (SI 1986/414)
110	6 Jan 1986 (SI 1985/1887)
111	26 Oct 1986 (SI 1986/1794)
112, 113	6 Jan 1986 (SI 1985/1887)
114, 115	26 Jul 1986 (SI 1986/1088)
116(1)	1 Apr 1986 (SI 1986/414)
(2), (3)	26 Jul 1986 (SI 1986/1088)
117	15 Sep 1986 (SI 1986/1450)
118–125	6 Jan 1986 (SI 1985/1887)
126(1), (2)	1 Aug 1986 (so far as relate to fees chargeable in respect of applications for, and the grant of, permits under s 22) (SI 1986/1088) 26 Oct 1986 (otherwise, except so far as sub-s (1) relates to applications for and the grant of permits under s 19) (SI 1986/1794) 13 Aug 1987 (otherwise) (SI 1987/1228)
(3)(a)	26 Oct 1986 (SI 1986/1794)
(b)	14 Jul 1986 (SI 1986/1088)
(c)	26 Oct 1986 (SI 1986/1794)
127(1), (2)	1 Aug 1986 (SI 1986/1088)
(3)	6 Jan 1986 (SI 1985/1887)
(4)	6 Jan 1986 (so far as relates to s 30(2)) (SI 1985/1887) 1 Aug 1986 (so far as relates to s 23(5)) (SI 1986/1088) 26 Oct 1986 (otherwise) (SI 1986/1794)
(5)–(7)	6 Jan 1986 (SI 1985/1887)
128–130	6 Jan 1986 (SI 1985/1887)
131(1)–(5)	Repealed
(6), (7)	6 Jan 1986 (SI 1985/1887)
132–136	6 Jan 1986 (SI 1985/1887)
137(1), (2)	6 Jan 1986 (SI 1985/1887)
(2A)	Prospectively inserted by Local Government (Wales) Act 1994, s 22(1), Sch 7, Pt II, para 39[1]
(3)–(8)	6 Jan 1986 (SI 1985/1887)
138	6 Jan 1986 (SI 1985/1887)
139(1)–(3)	See Schs 6–8 below
(4), (5)	6 Jan 1986 (SI 1985/1887)
140	30 Oct 1985 (s 140(2))
Sch 1, para 1, 2	6 Jan 1986 (SI 1985/1887)
3(1), (2)	6 Jan 1986 (SI 1985/1887)
(3)	26 Oct 1986 (SI 1986/1794)

Transport Act 1985 (c 67)—*cont*

Sch 1, para 3(4)	6 Jan 1986 (except omission of words 'or Part III') (SI 1985/1887)
	26 Oct 1986 (exception noted above) (SI 1986/1794)
(5)	6 Jan 1986 (SI 1985/1887)
4	6 Jan 1986 (SI 1985/1887)
5	Repealed
6	6 Jan 1986 (SI 1985/1887)
7–11	26 Oct 1986 (SI 1986/1794)
12	6 Jan 1986 (SI 1985/1887)
13	6 Jan 1986 (except omission of definitions of 'excursion or tour', 'road service licence', 'trial area') (SI 1985/1887)
	26 Oct 1986 (exceptions noted above) (SI 1986/1794)
14	6 Jan 1986 (SI 1985/1887)
15(1)	6 Jan 1986 (SI 1985/1887)
(2), (3)	26 Oct 1986 (SI 1986/1794)
(4), (5)	6 Jan 1986 (SI 1985/1887)
16	6 Jan 1986 (SI 1985/1887)
2	6 Jan 1986 (SI 1985/1887)
3, para 1–7	6 Jan 1986 (SI 1985/1887)
8	1 Apr 1986 (SI 1986/414)
9–23	6 Jan 1986 (SI 1985/1887)
24	6 Jan 1986 (to the extent that relates to Local Government Act 1972, s 202(1), (4)–(7) only) (SI 1985/1887)
	1 Apr 1986 (otherwise) (SI 1986/414)
25	6 Jan 1986 (SI 1985/1887)
26	1 Apr 1986 (SI 1986/414)
27, 28	6 Jan 1986 (SI 1985/1887)
29	Repealed
30–33	6 Jan 1986 (SI 1985/1887)
4	15 Sep 1986 (SI 1986/1450)
5	6 Jan 1986 (SI 1985/1887)
6, para 1–5	Spent
6–11	6 Jan 1986 (SI 1985/1887)
12	30 Oct 1985 (s 140(2))
13	6 Jan 1986 (SI 1985/1887)
14	26 Oct 1986 (SI 1986/1794)
15	6 Jan 1986 (SI 1985/1887)
16–18	26 Oct 1986 (SI 1986/1794)
19	6 Jan 1986 (SI 1985/1887)
20	Spent
21	6 Jan 1986 (SI 1985/1887)
22, 23	14 Feb 1986 (SI 1986/80) (also purportedly brought into force, to the extent that not already in force, by SI 1986/414)
24, 25	15 Sep 1986 (SI 1986/1450)
26	6 Jan 1986 (SI 1985/1887)
7, para 1	6 Jan 1986 (SI 1985/1887)
2	1 Aug 1986 (SI 1986/1088)
3	1 Apr 1986 (SI 1986/414)
4	6 Jan 1986 (SI 1985/1887)
5	26 Oct 1986 (SI 1986/1794)
6	6 Jan 1986 (SI 1985/1887)
7, 8	15 Sep 1986 (SI 1986/1450)
9	1 Apr 1986 (SI 1986/414)
10–14	6 Jan 1986 (SI 1985/1887)

Transport Act 1985 (c 67)—*cont*

Sch 7, para 15	Repealed
16	26 Oct 1986 (SI 1986/1794)
17	1 Apr 1986 (SI 1986/414)
18	6 Jan 1986 (SI 1985/1887)
19	1 Apr 1986 (SI 1986/414)
20	6 Jan 1986 (SI 1985/1887)
21(1)	6 Jan 1986 (SI 1985/1887)
(2), (3)	Repealed
(4)	6 Jan 1986 (except words 'sub-section (1A) below and') (SI 1985/1887) 26 Oct 1986 (exception noted above) (SI 1986/1794)
(5)	26 Oct 1986 (SI 1986/1794)
(6)	6 Jan 1986 (SI 1985/1887)
(7)	Repealed
(8)	6 Jan 1986 (SI 1985/1887)
(9), (10)	26 Oct 1986 (SI 1986/1794)
(11)	15 Sep 1986 (SI 1986/1450)
(12)	6 Jan 1986 (SI 1985/1887)
22	1 Apr 1986 (SI 1986/414)
23	6 Jan 1986 (SI 1985/1887)
24	1 Apr 1986 (SI 1986/414)
25, 26	26 Oct 1986 (SI 1986/1794)
8	6 Jan 1986 (repeals of or in Road Traffic Act 1930; Transport Act 1962, ss 4, 92; Finance Act 1965; Transport Act 1968, ss 9, 10(2), 11(1), 12(3)(d), 14(3), 15, 15(A)(1), 16(2), 17–19, 20, 21, 22, 24(3), 29(4), 34, 36, 54, 59(3), 90, 103(1), 159(1), Sch 5; Post Office Act 1969; Local Government Act 1972, ss 80(4), 202, Sch 24, Pt II; Local Government Act 1974; Energy Act 1976, Sch 1, para 1(2); Transport Act 1978; Transport Act 1980; Public Passenger Vehicles Act 1981, ss 1, 2, 28, 46, 53(1) (word 'the' before words 'traffic commissioners'), 56, 60, 61(2), 62, 81(2), 82(1) (definitions of 'contract carriage', 'express carriage', 'express carriage service', 'stage carriage' and 'stage carriage service'), 83, Sch 1, paras 3, 4; Transport Act 1982, s 73(4); Transport Act 1983, s 9(2); Road Traffic Regulation Act 1984, Sch 13, para 49; London Regional Transport Act 1984, s 28, Sch 6, paras 3, 6) (SI 1985/1887) 1 Apr 1986 (repeals of or in Finance Act 1970; Local Government Act 1972, s 202(2), (3); Local Government (Scotland) Act 1973, s 150; Transport Act 1983, s 3; Local Government Act 1985) (SI 1986/414) 26 Jul 1986 (repeal of London Regional Transport Act 1984, Sch 6, para 15(1)(a)) (SI 1986/1088) 15 Sep 1986 (repeals of or in Transport Act 1962, s 57, Sch 10; Transport Act 1968, s 88, Sch 10) (SI 1986/1450) 26 Oct 1986 (otherwise except those of or in Town Police Clauses Act 1847 (which entry is now itself repealed); Public Passenger Vehicles Act 1981, ss 42–44, 52, 67, 76 (words 'except sections 42 to 44' and word 'thereof')) (SI 1986/1794) 13 Aug 1987 (otherwise except repeal of words

Transport Act 1985 (c 67)—*cont*

Sch 8—*cont*	'such number of' and 'as they think fit' in Town Police Clauses Act 1847, s 37 (which repeal entry is now itself repealed)) (SI 1987/1228)

[1] Any order made under Local Government (Wales) Act 1994, s 66, bringing the prospective insertion into force will be noted to that Act in the service to this work

Trustee Savings Banks Act 1985 (c 58)

RA: 25 Jul 1985

Commencement provisions: ss 1(4), 2(4), 4(3)–(5), 7(2), Sch 1, Pt III, para 13; Trustee Savings Banks Act 1985 (Appointed Day) (No 1) Order 1985, SI 1986/1219; Trustee Savings Banks Act 1985 (Appointed Day) (No 2) Order 1986, SI 1986/1220; Trustee Savings Banks Act 1985 (Appointed Day) (No 3) Order 1986, SI 1986/1222; Trustee Savings Banks Act 1985 (Appointed Day) (No 4) Order 1986, SI 1986/1223; Trustee Savings Banks Act 1985 (Appointed Day) (No 6) Order 1988, SI 1988/1168; Trustee Savings Banks Act 1985 (Appointed Day) (No 7) Order 1990, SI 1990/1982 (*Note:* No (Appointed Day) (No 5) Order was made)

s 1–5	25 Sep 1985 (s 7(2)) (but note 21 July 1986 was the vesting day appointed under s 1(4) (SI 1986/1222); 31 Oct 1990 was the day appointed under s 2(4) on which the Trustee Savings Bank Central Board ceased to exist (SI 1990/1982)
6	Repealed
7	25 Sep 1985 (s 7(2))
Sch1, para 1–7	25 Sept 1985 (s 7(2))
8, 9	Repealed
10, 11	25 Sept 1985 (s 7(2))
12	25 Sept 1985 (s 7(2)); but this paragraph never had any effect
13	20 Jul 1986 (SI 1986/1219)
2	25 Sep 1985 (s 7(2))
3	Repealed
4	20 Jul 1986 (repeals of or in Finance Act 1921; Finance Act 1946; Finance Act 1969; National Savings Bank Act 1971; Trustee Savings Banks Act 1981, Sch 7, para 10, para 12(a) (words '4 to 7')) (SI 1986/1220)
	21 Jul 1986 (repeals of or in Bankers' Books Evidence Act 1879; Consolidated Fund (Permanent Charges Redemption) Act 1883; Savings Banks Act 1887; Bankruptcy Act 1914; Agricultural Credits Act 1928; Agricultural Credits (Scotland) Act 1929; Government Annuities Act 1929; Payment of Wages Act 1960; Companies Act (Northern Ireland) 1960; Trustee Investments Act 1961; Clergy Pensions Measure 1961; Building Societies Act 1962; Administration of Estates (Small Payments) Act 1965; Building Societies Act (Northern Ireland) 1967; Payment

Transport Act 1985 (c 67)—*cont*

Sch 4—*cont* of Wages Act (Northern Ireland) 1970; Friendly Societies Act (Northern Ireland) 1970; Northern Ireland Constitution Act 1973; Pensions (Increase) Act 1974; Friendly Societies Act 1974; Solicitors Act 1974; Financial Provisions (Northern Ireland) Order 1976; Home Purchase Assistance and Housing Corporation Guarantee Act 1978; Credit Unions Act 1979, s 31(1)(b) in definition of 'authorised bank'; Banking Act 1979; Solicitors (Scotland) Act 1980; British Telecommunications Act 1981; Trustee Savings Banks Act 1981, ss 1, 2, 3(1), (2), 4, 5, 6(1), 7(3), (5), (6), 8–11, 13 (words 'to the Central Board and' and ', and shall furnish such particulars of that person as the Central Board may direct'), 14, 15(1)–(8), (11), 16(1), (3), (4), 17, 18, 19(1)–(4), 20–22, 25(1) (the words 'to the Central Board and'), (2), 26–50, 52, 55(1), (3), Schs 1, 2, paras 1(a), (c), (3), (4), 4, 11, 13–16, Schs 4, 6, Sch 7, para 5–8, 9(1), 11, 12, (so far as unrepealed), 13–15, Sch 8; Housing (Northern Ireland) Order 1981; Companies (Northern Ireland) Order 1982; Companies Act 1985) (SI 1986/1223)

5 Jul 1988 (repeal of Trustee Savings Banks Act 1981, ss 12, 13 (so far as unrepealed), 23, 24, 25 (so far as unrepealed), 51, 53, Schs 3, 5, Sch 7, para 9(2); Insolvency Act 1986, s 220(3)) (SI 1988/1168)

31 Oct 1990 (repeal of Trustee Savings Banks Act 1981, ss 3(3), 6(2), 7(1), (2), (4), 15(9), (10), 16(2), 19(5), 54, 55(2), (4), 56, 57, Sch 2 (so far as unrepealed), Sch 7, paras 1–4) (SI 1990/1982)

Water (Fluoridation) Act 1985 (c 63)

RA: 30 Oct 1985

30 Oct 1985 (RA); *Whole Act repealed (EW)*

Weights and Measures Act 1985 (c 72)

RA: 30 Oct 1985; Weights and Measures Act 1985 (Commencement) Order 1992, SI 1992/770 (revoked); Weights and Measures Act 1985 (Revocation) Order 1993, SI 1993/2698 (revoked Weights and Measures Act 1985 (Commencement) Order 1992, SI 1992/770, which appointed 1 Apr 1994 as the date on which s 43 (now repealed) was to come into force))

Commencement provisions: ss 43(2) (repealed), 99(2)

s 1–42	30 Jan 1986 (s 99(2))
43	Repealed (*never in force*)
44–59	30 Jan 1986 (s 99(2))
60, 61	Repealed
62–99	30 Jan 1986 (s 99(2))
Sch 1–8	30 Jan 1986 (s 99(2))

Weights and Measures Act 1985 (c 72)—*cont*

Sch 9	Repealed
10–13	30 Jan 1986 (s 99(2))

Wildlife and Countryside (Amendment) Act 1985 (c 31)

RA: 26 Jun 1985

Commencement provisions: s 5(3)

26 Aug 1985 (s 5(3))

Wildlife and Countryside (Service of Notices) Act 1985 (c 59)

RA: 25 Jul 1985

25 Jul 1985 (RA)

1986

Advance Petroleum Revenue Tax Act 1986 (c 68)

RA: 18 Dec 1986

18 Dec 1986 (RA)

(*Note:* Petroleum Revenue Tax (levied in accordance with Oil Taxation Act 1975, Pt I (ss 1–12, Schs 1–8) abolished for new oil and gas fields ('non-taxable fields') with effect from 16 Mar 1993, by Finance Act 1993, s 185)

Agricultural Holdings Act 1986 (c 5)

RA: 18 Mar 1986

Commencement provision: s 102(2)

18 Jun 1986 (s 102(2))

(*Note:* By virtue of the Agricultural Tenancies 1995, s 4, this Act does not apply in relation to any tenancy beginning on or after 1 September 1995, with the exception of specified tenancies of an agricultural holding)

Agriculture Act 1986 (c 49)

RA: 25 Jul 1986

Commencement provisions: s 24(2), (3); Agriculture Act 1986 (Commencement) (No 1) Order 1986, SI 1986/1484; Agriculture Act 1986 (Commencement) (No 2) (Scotland) Order 1986, SI 1986/1485; Agriculture Act 1986 (Commencement No 3) Order 1986, SI 1986/1596; Agriculture Act 1986 (Commencement No 4) Order 1986, SI 1986/2301; Agriculture Act 1986 (Commencement No 5) Order 1991, SI 1991/2635

s 1–7	25 Sep 1986 (s 24(2))
8(1)	*Not in force*
(2)	8 Sep 1986 (SI 1986/1596)
(3)–(6)	*Not in force*
9	25 Sep 1986 (s 24(2))
10	31 Dec 1986 (SI 1986/2301)
11	25 Sep 1986 (s 24(2))
12	25 Jul 1986 (RA)
13	25 Sep 1986 (SI 1986/1484)
14	25 Sep 1986 (SI 1986/1485)
15	25 Sep 1986 (SI 1986/1484)
16	25 Sep 1986 (SI 1986/1485)
17	25 Sep 1986 (s 24(2))
18(1)–(12)	25 Sep 1986 (s 24(2))
(13)	25 Jul 1986 (RA)

Agriculture Act 1986 (c 49)—*cont*

s 19, 20	25 Sep 1986 (s 24(2))
21	Repealed
22, 23	25 Sep 1986 (s 24(2))
23A	Inserted (S) by Agricultural Holdings (Scotland) Act 1991, s 88(1), Sch 11, para 45 (qv)
24	25 Sep 1986 (s 24(2))
Sch 1	25 Sep 1986 (SI 1986/1484)
2	25 Sep 1986 (SI 1986/1485)
3	25 Sep 1986 (s 24(2))
4	25 Sep 1986 (except repeals consequential on ss 8–10) (s 24(2))
	31 Dec 1986 (repeals consequential on ss 9, 10) (SI 1986/2301)
	21 Nov 1991 (repeals in House of Commons Disqualification Act 1975; Northern Ireland Assembly Disqualification Act 1975) (SI 1991/2635)
	Not in force (repeals consequential on s 8)

Airports Act 1986 (c 31)

RA: 8 Jul 1986

Commencement provisions: s 85(2)–(6); Airports Act 1986 (Commencement No 1 and Appointed Day) Order 1986, SI 1986/1228; Airports Act 1986 (Commencement No 2) Order 1986, SI 1986/1487

s 1	8 Jul 1986 (s 85(2))
2	1 Aug 1986 (SI 1986/1228)
3	8 Jul 1986 (s 85(2))
4–9	1 Aug 1986 (SI 1986/1228)
10	Repealed
11	1 Aug 1986 (SI 1986/1228)
12–35	8 Sep 1986 (s 85(4))
36–56	1 Oct 1986 (SI 1986/1487)
57–62	31 Jul 1986 (SI 1986/1228)
63–66	1 Apr 1986 (SI 1986/1228)
67	1 Oct 1986 (SI 1986/1487)
68	8 Sep 1986 (SI 1986/1228)
69	1 Oct 1986 (SI 1986/1487)
70, 71	Repealed
72	8 Sep 1986 (s 85(4))
73, 74	1 Oct 1986 (SI 1986/1487)
75	8 Jul 1986 (s 85(2))
76(1), (2)	Repealed
(3), (4)	8 Jul 1986 (s 85(2))
(5)	Repealed
77(1)–(4)	1 Aug 1986 (SI 1986/1228)
(5), (6)	8 Jul 1986 (s 85(2))
78	8 Sep 1986 (s 85(4))
79–82	8 Jul 1986 (s 85(2))
83(1)	See Sch 4 below
(2)	1 Aug 1986 (SI 1986/1228)
(3)	1 Oct 1986 (SI 1986/1487)
(4)	1 Aug 1986 (SI 1986/1228)

Airports Act 1986 (c 31)—*cont*

s 83(5)	See Sch 6 below
84	8 Sep 1986 (s 85(4))
85	8 Jul 1986 (s 85(2))
Sch 1	1 Oct 1986 (SI 1986/1487)
2	31 Jul 1986 (SI 1986/1228)
3	1 Aug 1986 (SI 1986/1228)
4, para 1	Repealed
2	31 Jul 1986 (SI 1986/1228)
3–8	1 Oct 1986 (SI 1986/1487)
9	1 Aug 1986 (SI 1986/1228)
10	1 Aug 1986 (except the expression '60(3)(o)') (SI 1986/1228)
	1 Apr 1987 (exception noted above) (SI 1986/1487)
5	1 Aug 1986 (SI 1986/1228)
6, Pt I	1 Aug 1986 (SI 1986/1228)
II	1 Aug 1986 (repeals of or in Civil Aviation Act 1982, ss 27, 29, 32, 33, 37, 40, 58, 99, Sch 5, Sch 13, Pt II (entries relating to ss 32(5), 33(1), 37, 40(2)), Sch 14; Criminal Justice Act 1982) (SI 1986/1228)
	1 Oct 1986 (repeal in Fair Trading Act 1973) (SI 1986/1487)
	1 Apr 1987 (repeals of or in Local Government, Planning and Land Act 1980; Civil Aviation Act 1982, s 38, Sch 13, Pt II, entry relating to s 61(6)) (SI 1986/1487)

Animals (Scientific Procedures) Act 1986 (c 14)

RA: 20 May 1986

Commencement provisions: s 30(3); Animals (Scientific Procedures) Act (Commencement) Order 1986, SI 1986/2088; Animals (Scientific Procedures) (1986 Act) (Commencement No 1) Order (Northern Ireland) 1986, SR 1986/364 (NI); Animals (Scientific Procedures) Act (Commencement No 2) Order 1989, SI 1989/2306; Animals (Scientific Procedures) (1986 Act) (Commencement No 2) Order (Northern Ireland) 1989, SR 1989/496 (NI)

s 1–6	1 Jan 1987 (SI 1986/2088)
7	1 Jan 1990 (SI 1989/2306; SR 1989/496)
8, 9	1 Jan 1987 (SI 1986/2088)
10(1), (2)	1 Jan 1987 (SI 1986/2088)
(3)	1 Jan 1990 (SI 1989/2306; SR 1989/496)
(3A)	Inserted (1 Oct 1993) by Animals (Scientific Procedures) Act 1986 (Amendment) Regulations 1993, SI 1993/2102, reg 2(1), (3)
(4)–(7)	1 Jan 1987 (SI 1986/2088)
11–28	1 Jan 1987 (SI 1986/2088)
29	1 Jan 1987 (SR 1986/364) (NI)
30	1 Jan 1987 (SI 1986/2088)
Sch 1	1 Jan 1987 (SI 1986/2088)
2	1 Jan 1990 (SI 1989/2306; SR 1989/496)
3, 4	1 Jan 1987 (SI 1986/2088)

Appropriation Act 1986 (c 42)

Whole Act repealed

Armed Forces Act 1986 (c 21)

RA: 26 Jun 1986

Commencement provisions: s 17(2), (3); Armed Forces Act 1986 (Commencement No 1) Order 1986, SI 1986/2071; Armed Forces Act 1986 (Commencement No 2) Order 1986, SI 1986/2124; Armed Forces Act 1986 (Commencement No 3) Order 1987, SI 1987/1998

s 1	Repealed
2	1 Jan 1987 (SI 1986/2124)
3	1 Jan 1987 (SI 1986/2124); prospectively repealed (EW) by Civil Evidence Act 1995, s 15(2), Sch 2[1]
4–8	1 Jan 1987 (SI 1986/2124)
9	31 Dec 1987 (SI 1987/1998)
10–12	1 Jan 1987 (SI 1986/2124)
13	1 Jan 1987 (SI 1986/2124); prospectively repealed by Armed Forces Act 1991, s 26, Sch 3[2]
14	30 Dec 1986 (SI 1986/2071)
15	26 Jun 1986 (RA)
16(1)	1 Jan 1987 (SI 1986/2124)
(2)	See Sch 2 below
(3)	1 Jan 1987 (SI 1986/2124)
17	26 Jun 1986 (RA)
Sch 1	1 Jan 1987 (SI 1986/2124)
2	1 Sep 1986 (repeal of Armed Forces Act 1981, s 1) (s 17(3))
	30 Dec 1986 (repeal of Army Act 1955, s 213(a)) (SI 1986/2071)
	1 Jan 1987 (otherwise) (SI 1986/2124)

[1] Any order made under Civil Evidence Act 1995, s 16(2), bringing the prospective repeal into force will be noted to that Act in the service to this work

[2] Any order made under Armed Forces Act 1991, s 27, bringing the prospective repeal into force will be noted to that Act in the service to this work

---

Atomic Energy Authority Act 1986 (c 3)

RA: 19 Feb 1986

Commencement provisions: s 10(2)

1 Apr 1986 (s 10(2))

Australia Act 1986 (c 2)

RA: 17 Feb 1986

Commencement provisions: s 17(2); Australia Act 1986 (Commencement) Order 1986, SI 1986/319 3 Mar 1986 (at 5 am GMT) (SI 1986/319)

Bishops (Retirement) Measure 1986 (No 1)

RA: 18 Mar 1986

Commencement provisions: s 13(3)

1 Jun 1986 (the day appointed by the Archbishops of Canterbury and York under s 13(3))

British Council and Commonwealth Institute Superannuation Act 1986 (c 51)

RA: 25 Jul 1986

Commencement provisions: s 3(2); British Council and Commonwealth Institute Superannuation Act 1986 (Commencement No 1) Order 1986, SI 1986/1860; British Council and Commonwealth Institute Superannuation Act 1986 (Commencement No 2) Order 1987, SI 1987/588 10 Nov 1986 (in relation to British Council) (SI 1986/1860) 1 Apr 1987 (in relation to Commonwealth Institute) (SI 1987/588)

British Shipbuilders (Borrowing Powers) Act 1986 (c 19)

Whole Act repealed

Building Societies Act 1986 (c 53)

RA: 25 Jul 1986

Commencement provisions: s 126(2)–(4); Building Societies Act 1986 (Commencement No 1) Order 1986, SI 1986/1560; Building Societies Act 1986 (Commencement No 2) Order 1989, SI 1989/1083

s 1–4	25 Sep 1986 (s 126(2))
5, 6	1 Jan 1987 (SI 1986/1560)
7	25 Sep 1986 (so far as relates to orders under s 7(9)) (SI 1986/1560) 1 Jan 1987 (otherwise) (SI 1986/1560)
8, 9	1 Jan 1987 (SI 1986/1560)
10–14	1 Jan 1987 (SI 1986/1560)
14A	Inserted by Deregulation and Contracting Out Act 1994, s 17(1) (qv)
15–17	1 Jan 1987 (SI 1986/1560)
18	25 Sep 1986 (so far as relates to designation orders under s 18(2)(c)) (SI 1986/1560) 1 Jan 1987 (otherwise, except so far as empowers building societies to invest in, or support, corresponding European bodies) (SI 1986/1560) 1 Jan 1988 (exception noted above) (SI 1986/1560)
19–23	1 Jan 1987 (SI 1986/1560)
24, 25	1 Jan 1987 (SI 1986/1560)
25A	Inserted (1 Jul 1995) by Credit Institutions (Protection of Depositors) Regulations 1995, SI 1995/1442, reg 38 (subject to transitional and savings provisions contained in reg 53(1), (4) thereof)
26–29	1 Jan 1987 (SI 1986/1560)

Building Societies Act 1986 (c 53)—*cont*

s 29A	Inserted (1 Jul 1995) by Credit Institutions (Protection of Depositors) Regulations 1995, SI 1995/1442, reg 43
30–34	1 Jan 1987 (SI 1986/1560)
35	*Not in force*; prospectively repealed by Courts and Legal Services Act 1990, s 125(7), Sch 20[1]
36(1)–(4)	1 Jan 1987 (SI 1986/1560)
(5), (6)	1 Jan 1988 (SI 1986/1560)
(7)	1 Jan 1987 (SI 1986/1560)
(8), (9)	1 Jan 1988 (SI 1986/1560)
(10)	1 Jan 1987 (SI 1986/1560)
(11)(a)	1 Jan 1987 (SI 1986/1560)
(b), (c)	1 Jan 1988 (SI 1986/1560)
(d)	1 Jan 1987 (SI 1986/1560)
(e), (f)	1 Jan 1988 (SI 1986/1560)
(12)	1 Jan 1988 (SI 1986/1560)
37	1 Jan 1987 (SI 1986/1560)
38–40	25 Sep 1986 (so far as relate to procedure following directions under Sch 20, para 11(5)(c)) (SI 1986/1560) 1 Jan 1987 (otherwise) (SI 1986/1560)
41–45	1 Jan 1987 (SI 1986/1560)
45A	Inserted (1 Jan 1993) by Banking Coordination (Second Council Directive) Regulations 1992, SI 1992/3218, reg 74
46–82	1 Jan 1987 (SI 1986/1560)
83(1)–(5)	1 Jul 1987 (SI 1986/1560)
(6)–(15)	1 Jan 1987 (SI 1986/1560)
84(1)–(7)	1 Jan 1987 (SI 1986/1560)
(8)–(10)	1 Jul 1987 (SI 1986/1560)
(11)	1 Jan 1987 (SI 1986/1560)
85	1 Jan 1987 (SI 1986/1560)
86–89	1 Jan 1988 (SI 1986/1560)
90	1 Jan 1987 (so far as relates to Sch 15, paras 58, 59) (SI 1986/1560) 1 Jan 1988 (otherwise) (SI 1986/1560)
91, 92	1 Jan 1988 (SI 1986/1560)
93–96	1 Jan 1987 (SI 1986/1560)
97–102	1 Jan 1988 (SI 1986/1560)
102A	Inserted by Building Societies (Joint Account Holders) Act 1995, s 1(1) (qv), with effect in any case where the vesting date (as defined by s 100 of this Act) falls after 1 May 1995
103(1)	1 Jan 1987 (so far as relates to societies dissolved by ss 93(5) or 94(10)) (SI 1986/1560) 1 Jan 1988 (otherwise) (SI 1986/1560)
(2)–(9)	1 Jan 1987 (SI 1986/1560)
104–108	1 Jan 1987 (SI 1986/1560)
109(1)	25 Sep 1986 (so far as it relates to the exemption from stamp duties of any instrument referred to in s 109(1)(e) and required or authorised to be given, issued, signed, made or produced in pursuance of this Act) (SI 1986/1560) 1 Jan 1987 (otherwise) (SI 1986/1560) (Formerly s 109, renumbered (29 Jul 1988) as s 109(1) by Finance Act 1988, s 145, Sch 12, para 8)

Building Societies Act 1986 (c 53)—*cont*

s 109(2)	Added (29 Jul 1988) by Finance Act 1988, s 145, Sch 12, para 8
110, 111	1 Jan 1987 (SI 1986/1560)
112(1)	25 Sep 1986 (SI 1986/1560)
(2)	1 Jan 1987 (SI 1986/1560)
(3), (4)	25 Sep 1986 (SI 1986/1560)
113	25 Sep 1986 (so far as relates to a memorandum or rules agreed upon under Sch 20, para 2) (SI 1986/1560)
	1 Jan 1987 (otherwise) (SI 1986/1560)
114	1 Jan 1987 (SI 1986/1560)
115, 116	25 Sep 1986 (SI 1986/1560)
117	1 Jan 1987 (SI 1986/1560)
118	25 Sep 1986 (SI 1986/1560)
118A	Inserted (1 Jan 1993) by Banking Coordination (Second Council Directive) Regulations 1992, SI 1992/3218, reg 80
119	25 Sep 1986 (SI 1986/1560)
120(1)	1 Jan 1987 (SI 1986/1560)
(2)	See Sch 19 below
(3)	1 Jan 1987 (SI 1986/1560)
(4)	See Sch 20 below
121	25 Jul 1986 (s 126(3))
122, 123	25 Sep 1986 (SI 1986/1560)
124	*Not in force*; prospectively repealed by Courts and Legal Services Act 1990, s 125(7), Sch 20[1]
125, 126	25 Jul 1986 (s 126(3))
Sch 1	25 Sep 1986 (s 126(2))
2, para 1–29	1 Jan 1987 (SI 1986/1560)
30	1 Jan 1988 (SI 1986/1560)
31–36	1 Jan 1987 (SI 1986/1560)
3–7	1 Jan 1987 (SI 1986/1560)
8	Substituted (30 Aug 1988) by Building Societies (Commercial Assets and Services) Order 1988, SI 1988/1141, art 5, Sch 5
9–14	1 Jan 1987 (SI 1986/1560)
15, para 1–33	1 Jan 1988 (SI 1986/1560)
34–55E	Substituted (1 Oct 1991) for original paras 34–55 by Insolvency (Northern Ireland) Order 1989, SI 1989/2405 (NI 19), art 381, Sch 9, Pt II(1), para 45(c)
56, 57	1 Jan 1988 (SI 1986/1560)
58, 59	1 Jan 1987 (SI 1986/1560)
16	1 Jan 1987 (SI 1986/1560)
17	1 Jan 1988 (SI 1986/1560)
18	1 Jan 1987 (SI 1986/1560)
19, Pt I	1 Jan 1987 (except repeals of or in Building Societies Act 1874; Building Societies Act 1894; Building Societies Act 1960, Sch 5; Building Societies Act 1962, ss 2831, Pt VII) (SI 1986/1560)
	1 Jan 1988 (otherwise, except repeal of 1962 Act, ss 28–31) (SI 1986/1560)
	17 Jul 1989 (repeal of 1962 Act, ss 28–31) (SI 1989/1083)
II	1 Jan 1987 (SI 1986/1560)

Building Societies Act 1986 (c 53)—*cont*

Sch 19, Pt III		1 Jan 1987 (except repeal of Building Societies Act (Northern Ireland) 1967, ss 28–31, Pt VII) (SI 1986/1560)
		1 Jan 1988 (repeal of 1967 Act, Pt VII) (SI 1986/1560)
		17 Jul 1989 (repeal of 1967 Act, ss 28–31) (SI 1989/1083)
20, para	1, 2	25 Sep 1986 (SI 1986/1560)
	3–6	1 Jan 1987 (SI 1986/1560)
	7	25 Jul 1986 (s 126(3))
	8–11	25 Sep 1986 (SI 1986/1560)
	12	Ceased to have effect
	13–16	1 Jan 1987 (SI 1986/1560)
	17	25 Sep 1986 (SI 1986/1560)
	18	1 Jan 1987 (SI 1986/1560)
21		*Not in force*; prospectively repealed by virtue of Courts and Legal Services Act 1990, s 125(7), Sch 20[1]

[1] Any order made under Courts and Legal Services Act 1990, s 124(3), bringing the prospective repeal into force will be noted to that Act in the service to this work

Children and Young Persons (Amendment) Act 1986 (c 28)

Whole Act repealed

Civil Protection in Peacetime Act 1986 (c 22)

RA: 26 Jun 1986

Commencement provisions: s 3(2)

26 Aug 1986 (s 3(2))

Commonwealth Development Corporation Act 1986 (c 25)

RA: 26 Jun 1986

26 Jun 1986 (RA)

Company Directors Disqualification Act 1986 (c 46)

RA: 25 Jul 1986

Commencement provisions: s 25

29 Dec 1986 (s 25)

Consolidated Fund Act 1986 (c 4)

Whole Act repealed

Consolidated Fund (No 2) Act 1986 (c 67)

Whole Act repealed

Consumer Safety (Amendment) Act 1986 (c 29)

Whole Act repealed

Corneal Tissue Act 1986 (c 18)

RA: 26 Jun 1986

Commencement provisions: s 2(2)

26 Aug 1986 (s 2(2))

Crown Agents (Amendment) Act 1986 (c 43)

RA: 25 Jul 1986

25 Jul 1986 (RA); whole Act prospectively repealed by Crown Agents Act 1995, s 13(2), Sch 2, Pt I. Any order made under s 1(1) thereof bringing the prospective repeal into force will be noted to that Act in the service to this work

---

Deacons (Ordination of Women) Measure 1986 (No 4)

RA: 7 Nov 1986

Commencement provisions: s 5(2)

16 Feb 1987 (the day appointed by the Archbishops of Canterbury and York under s 5(2))

Disabled Persons (Services, Consultation and Representation) Act 1986 (c 33)

RA: 8 Jul 1986

Commencement provisions: s 18(2); Disabled Persons (Services, Consultation and Representation) Act 1986 (Commencement No 1) Order 1987, SI 1987/564; Disabled Persons (Services, Consultation and Representation) Act 1986 (Commencement No 2) Order 1987, SI 1987/729; Disabled Persons (Services, Consultation and Representation) Act 1986 (Commencement No 3) (Scotland) Order 1987, SI 1987/911; Disabled Persons (Services, Consultation and Representation) Act 1986 (Commencement No 4) Order 1988, SI 1988/51; Disabled Persons (Services, Consultation and Representation) Act 1986 (Commencement No 5) (Scotland) Order 1988, SI 1988/94; Disabled Persons (Services, Consultation and Representation) Act 1986 (Commencement No 5) Order 1989, SI 1989/2425

s 1–3	*Not in force*
4(a)	1 Apr 1987 (EW) (SI 1987/564) 1 Oct 1987 (S) (SI 1987/911)
(b)	*Not in force*
(c)	1 Apr 1987 (EW) (SI 1987/564) 1 Oct 1987 (S) (SI 1987/911)

Disabled Persons (Services, Consultation and Representation) Act 1986 (c 33)—*cont*

s 5(1), (2)	1 Feb 1988 (SI 1988/51)
(3), (3A)–(3C), (4)	Substituted for original sub-ss (3), (4) by Further and Higher Education Act 1992, s 93(1), Sch 8, Pt II, para 91(1), (2) (qv)
(5)–(10)	1 Feb 1988 (SI 1988/51)
6(1)	Substituted by Further and Higher Education Act 1992, s 93(1), Sch 8, Pt II, para 92 (qv)
(2)	1 Feb 1988 (SI 1988/51)
7	*Not in force*
8(1)	1 Apr 1987 (EW) (SI 1987/564) 1 Oct 1987 (S) (SI 1987/911)
(2), (3)	*Not in force*
9, 10	1 Apr 1987 (EW) (SI 1987/564) 1 Jun 1987 (S) (SI 1987/911)
11	1 Jun 1987 (S) (SI 1987/911) 18 Dec 1989 (EW) (SI 1989/2425)
12	1 Jun 1987 (SI 1987/911)
13	1 Feb 1988 (SI 1988/94)
14	1 Jun 1987 (SI 1987/911)
15	Repealed *(never in force)*
16–18	17 Apr 1987 (EW) (SI 1987/729) 1 Jun 1987 (S) (SI 1987/911)

Dockyard Services Act 1986 (c 52)

RA: 25 Jul 1986

Commencement provisions: s 5(2)

25 Sep 1986 (s 5(2))

Drainage Rates (Disabled Persons) Act 1986 (c 17)

Whole Act repealed

Drug Trafficking Offences Act 1986 (c 32)

RA: 8 Jul 1986

Commencement provisions: s 40(2) (repealed); Drug Trafficking Offences Act 1986 (Commencement No 1) Order 1986, SI 1986/1488; Drug Trafficking Offences Act 1986 (Commencement No 2) (Scotland) Order 1986, SI 1986/1546; Drug Trafficking Offences Act 1986 (Commencement No 3) Order 1986, SI 1986/2145, Drug Trafficking Offences Act 1986 (Commencement No 4) (Scotland) Order 1986, SI 1986/2266

Whole Act repealed, except ss 24(6), 32, 34, 40(1), (3), (4) (but now substituted), (5), which came into force as follows: s 24(6) on 30 Sep 1986 (SI 1986/1488); s 32 on 12 Jan 1987 (SI 1986/2145); s 34 on 30 Sep 1986 (SI 1986/1488; SI 1986/1546); s 40(1), (3) on 30 Sep 1986 (SI 1986/1488; SI 1986/1546); s 40(4) substituted (3 Feb 1995) by Drug Trafficking Act 1994, s 65(1), Sch 1, para 11; s 40(5) on 30 Sep 1986 (SI 1986/1488; SI 1986/1546)

Ecclesiastical Fees Measure 1986 (No 2)

RA: 18 Mar 1986

Commencement provisions: s 12(3)

1 Sep 1986 (the day appointed by the Archbishops of Canterbury and York under s 12(3))

Education Act 1986 (c 40)

RA: 18 Jul 1986

Commencement provisions: s 6(2)

s 1	18 Sep 1986 (s 6(2))
2–6	18 Jul 1986 (RA)

Education (No 2) Act 1986 (c 61)

RA: 7 Nov 1986

Commencement provisions: s 66(1)–(4); Education (No 2) Act 1986 (Commencement No 1) Order 1986, SI 1986/2203; Education (No 2) Act 1986 (Commencement No 2) Order 1987, SI 1987/344; Education (No 2) Act 1986 (Commencement No 3) Order 1987, SI 1987/1159

s 1–4	1 Sep 1987 (SI 1987/344)
4A	Inserted by Education Act 1993, s 271(1) (qv)
5–16	1 Sep 1987 (SI 1987/344)
16A	Inserted by Further and Higher Education Act 1992, s 12(3) (qv)
17	7 Jan 1987 (SI 1986/2203)
18, 19	1 Sep 1987 (SI 1987/344)
20	Repealed
21	Substituted by Education Reform Act 1988, s 115 (qv)
22–28	1 Sep 1987 (SI 1987/344)
29	Repealed
30, 31	7 Jan 1987 (SI 1986/2203)
32	1 Sep 1987 (SI 1987/344)
33	7 Jan 1987 (SI 1986/2203)
34–41	1 Sep 1987 (SI 1987/344)
42	Substituted by Education Act 1993, s 238(9), Sch 13, para 5 (qv)
43	1 Sep 1987 (SI 1987/344)
44–46	7 Jan 1987 (SI 1986/2203)
46A	Inserted by Education Reform Act 1988, s 237(1), Sch 12, Pt I, para 34 (qv)
47(1)	15 Aug 1987 (SI 1987/344)
(1A), (1B)	Inserted by Education Act 1993, s 293(2) (qv)
(2)–(10)	15 Aug 1987 (SI 1987/344)
(11)	7 Jan 1987 (SI 1986/2203)
48	15 Aug 1987 (SI 1987/344)
49	7 Jan 1987 (s 66(2))
50–53	7 Jan 1987 (SI 1986/2203)
54, 55	1 Apr 1987 (SI 1986/2203)

Education (No 2) Act 1986 (c 61)—*cont*

s 56	7 Jan 1987 (SI 1986/2203)
57, 58	1 Sep 1987 (SI 1987/344)
59	7 Jan 1987 (s 66(2))
60	7 Nov 1986 (s 66(1))
61, 62	1 Sep 1987 (SI 1987/344)
63–66	7 Nov 1986 (s 66(1))
67(1)–(3)	7 Nov 1986 (s 66(1))
(4)	See Sch 4 below
(5)	See Sch 5 below
(6)	See Sch 6 below
(7)	7 Nov 1986 (s 66(1))
Sch 1–3	1 Sep 1987 (SI 1987/344)
4, para 1	1 Apr 1987 (SI 1986/2203)
2, 3	1 Sep 1987 (SI 1987/344)
4	Repealed
5	7 Jan 1987 (SI 1986/2203)
6, 7	Repealed
5	1 Sep 1987 (SI 1987/344)
6, Pt I	7 Jan 1987 (repeals of or in Education Act 1944, ss 4, 5, 67; London Government Act 1963, s 31(7)(a); Education Act 1980, ss 31, 32, Sch 6; Education (Scotland) Act 1980; Local Government, Planning and Land Act 1980) (SI 1986/2203) 1 Sep 1987 (repeals of or in Education Act 1944, ss 1721, 23, 24(1), 27(3); Education Act 1962; Education (No 2) Act 1968; Education Act 1980, ss 2–4, 35(1)) (SI 1987/344) 1 Sep 1987 (repeals of or in London Government Act 1963, s 31(8); Local Government Act 1966, Sch 5, para (6)) (SI 1987/1159)
II	7 Jan 1987 (SI 1986/2203)

Education (Amendment) Act 1986 (c 1)

Whole Act repealed or spent

European Communities (Amendment) Act 1986 (c 58)

RA: 7 Nov 1986

7 Nov 1986 (RA; but note that the repeals and revocations in the Schedule took effect on 1 Jul 1987, the day on which the Single European Act came into force; see Art 33(2) thereof, Cmnd 9758)

Family Law Act 1986 (c 55)

RA: 7 Nov 1986

Commencement provisions: s 69(2), (3); Family Law Act 1986 (Commencement No 1) Order 1988, SI 1988/375

s 1	4 Apr 1988 (SI 1988/375)
2, 2A	Substituted for original s 2 by Children Act 1989, s 108(5), Sch 13, para 64 (qv)

Family Law Act 1986 (c 55)—*cont*

s 3	4 Apr 1988 (SI 1988/375)
4	Repealed
5, 6	4 Apr 1988 (SI 1988/375)
7	Substituted by Children Act 1989, s 108(5), Sch 13, para 67 (qv)
8–18	4 Apr 1988 (SI 1988/375)
19	4 Apr 1988 (SI 1988/375); prospectively substituted by new ss 19, 19A by Children (Northern Ireland) Order 1995, SI 1995/755 (NI 2), art 185(1), Sch 9, para 124
20	4 Apr 1988 (SI 1988/375)
21	4 Apr 1988 (SI 1988/375); prospectively repealed by Children (Northern Ireland) Order 1995, SI 1995/755 (NI 2), art 185(2), Sch 10
22, 23	4 Apr 1988 (SI 1988/375)
24	4 Apr 1988 (SI 1988/375); prospectively substituted by Children (Northern Ireland) Order 1995, SI 1995/755 (NI 2), art 185(1), Sch 9, para 127
25	4 Apr 1988 (SI 1988/375)
26	4 Apr 1988 (SI 1988/375); prospectively substituted by Children (Scotland) Act 1995, s 105(4), Sch 4, para 41(1), (6)[1]
27–55	4 Apr 1988 (SI 1988/375)
56	Substituted by Family Law Reform Act 1987, s 22 (qv)
57–63	4 Apr 1988 (SI 1988/375)
64	Repealed
65	7 Jan 1987 (s 69(2))
66	7 Jan 1987 (s 69(2)); prospectively repealed by Children (Northern Ireland) Order 1995, SI 1995/755 (NI 2), art 185(2), Sch 10
67	7 Jan 1987 (s 69(2))
68, 69	4 Apr 1988 (SI 1988/375)
Sch 1, para 1	Repealed
2	4 Apr 1988 (SI 1988/375); prospectively repealed by Children (Northern Ireland) Order 1995, SI 1995/755 (NI 2), art 185(2), Sch 10
3–9	4 Apr 1988 (SI 1988/375)
10, 11	Repealed
12	4 Apr 1988 (SI 1988/375)
13	Repealed
14, 15	4 Apr 1988 (SI 1988/375)
16, 17	Repealed
18, 19	Spent
20	Repealed
21, 22	4 Apr 1988 (SI 1988/375)
23	Repealed
24–31	4 Apr 1988 (SI 1988/375)
32, 33	4 Apr 1988 (SI 1988/375); prospectively repealed by Children (Northern Ireland) Order 1995, SI 1995/755 (NI 2), art 185(2), Sch 10
34	4 Apr 1988 (SI 1988/375)
2	4 Apr 1988 (SI 1988/375)

[1] Any order made under Children (Scotland) Act 1995, s 105(1), (2), bringing the prospective repeal into force will be noted to that Act in the service to this work

Finance Act 1986 (c 41)

Budget Day: 18 Mar 1986

RA: 25 Jul 1986

See the note concerning Finance Acts at the front of this book

Financial Services Act 1986 (c 60)

RA: 7 Nov 1986

Commencement provisions: s 211(1), (2); Financial Services Act 1986 (Commencement No 1) Order 1986, SI 1986/1940; Financial Services Act 1986 (Commencement No 2) Order 1986, SI 1986/2031; Financial Services Act 1986 (Commencement No 3) Order 1986, SI 1986/2246; Financial Services Act 1986 (Commencement) (No 4) Order 1987, SI 1987/623; Financial Services Act 1986 (Commencement) (No 5) Order 1987, SI 1987/907; Financial Services Act 1986 (Commencement) (No 6) Order 1987, SI 1987/1997; Financial Services Act 1986 (Commencement) (No 7) Order 1987, SI 1987/2158; Financial Services Act 1986 (Commencement) (No 8) Order 1988, SI 1988/740; Financial Services Act 1986 (Commencement) (No 9) Order 1988, SI 1988/995; Financial Services Act 1986 (Commencement) (No 10) Order 1988, SI 1988/1960; Financial Services Act 1986 (Commencement) (No 11) Order 1988, SI 1988/2285; Financial Services Act 1986 (Commencement) (No 12) Order 1989, SI 1989/1583; Financial Services Act 1986 (Commencement) (No 13) Order 1995, SI 1995/1538

s 1	See Sch 1 below
2	18 Dec 1986 (SI 1986/2246)
3, 4	29 Apr 1988 (SI 1988/740)
5	12 Jan 1987 (so far as necessary to identify agreements to which s 5(1) applies for the purposes of s 132, so far as that section is in force by virtue of SI 1986/2246) (SI 1986/2246)
	29 Apr 1988 (otherwise) (SI 1988/740)
6, 7	29 Apr 1988 (SI 1988/740)
8–11	4 Jun 1987 (SI 1987/907)
12	1 Dec 1987 (SI 1987/1997)
13, 14	4 Jun 1987 (SI 1987/907)
15	4 Jun 1987 (except so far as has effect of conferring authorisation) (SI 1987/907)
	29 Apr 1988 (otherwise) (SI 1988/740)
16–19	4 Jun 1987 (SI 1987/907)
20	1 Dec 1987 (SI 1987/1997)
21	4 Jun 1987 (SI 1987/907)
22	29 Apr 1988 (SI 1988/740)
23	Substituted by Friendly Societies Act 1992, s 98(a), Sch 18, Pt I, para 1 (qv)
24	29 Apr 1988 (for purposes of Sch 15, para 10) (SI 1988/740)
	1 Oct 1989 (otherwise) (SI 1989/1583)
25	29 Apr 1988 (SI 1988/740)
26–30	1 Jan 1988 (SI 1987/2158)
31(1)–(3)	29 Apr 1988 (SI 1988/740)
(4)	1 Jan 1988 (so far as necessary to enable the Secretary of State to issue and revoke certificates) (SI 1987/2158)
	29 Apr 1988 (otherwise) (SI 1988/740)

Financial Services Act 1986 (c 60)—*cont*

s 31(5)	29 Apr 1988 (SI 1988/740)
32–34	29 Apr 1988 (SI 1988/740)
35	18 Dec 1986 (so far as relevant for the purposes of s 105) (SI 1986/2246) 29 Apr 1988 (otherwise) (SI 1988/740)
36(1)	29 Apr 1988 (SI 1988/740)
(2), (3)	4 Jun 1987 (SI 1987/907)
37	4 Jun 1987 (except so far as has effect in relation to a body or association of the kind described in s 40(1)) (SI 1987/907) 23 Nov 1987 (exception noted above) (SI 1987/1997)
38(1)	29 Apr 1988 (SI 1988/740)
(2), (3)	4 Jun 1987 (SI 1987/907)
39	4 Jun 1987 (except so far as has effect in relation to a body or association of the kind described in s 40(1)) (SI 1987/907) 23 Nov 1987 (exception noted above) (SI 1987/1997)
40	23 Nov 1987 (SI 1987/1997)
41	4 Jun 1987 (SI 1987/907)
42	18 Dec 1986 (for purposes of s 105) (SI 1986/2246) 29 Apr 1988 (otherwise) (SI 1988/740)
43	1 Jan 1988 (SI 1987/2158)
44	29 Apr 1988 (SI 1988/740)
45	18 Dec 1986 (for purposes of s 105) (SI 1986/2246) 29 Apr 1988 (otherwise) (SI 1988/740)
46	4 Jun 1987 (SI 1987/907)
47	29 Apr 1988 (SI 1988/740)
47A	Inserted by Companies Act 1989, s 192 (qv)
47B	Prospectively inserted by Companies Act 1989, s 192; any order made under Companies Act 1989, s 215(2), bringing the prospective insertion into force will be noted to that Act in the service to this work
48–52	4 Jun 1987 (SI 1987/907)
53	*Not in force*
54, 55	4 Jun 1987 (SI 1987/907)
56	4 Jun 1987 (so far as necessary in order to enable regulations to be made under s 56(1)) (SI 1987/907) 29 Apr 1988 (otherwise) (SI 1988/740)
57	29 May 1988 (so far as it relates to an advertisement issued for valuable consideration in a newspaper, journal, magazine or other periodical publication which is published at intervals of less than seven days except in relation to an advertisement issued on or after 29 May 1988 in an edition of a newspaper, magazine, journal or other publication first issued before that date) (SI 1988/740) 29 Jul 1988 (so far as relates to an advertisement issued for valuable consideration either (i) in any newspaper, journal, magazine or other publication which is published at intervals of seven or more days; or (ii) by way of sound broadcasting or television, by the exhibition of cinematographic films or by the distribution of recordings *except* in relation to an advertisement

Financial Services Act 1986 (c 60)—*cont*

s 57—*cont*	issued on or after 29 Jul 1988 in an edition of a newspaper, magazine, journal or other publication first issued before that date) (SI 1988/740)
	6 May 1988 (so far as relates to an advertisement which is *neither* (a) issued for valuable consideration in a newspaper, journal, magazine or other periodical published at intervals of less than seven days, *nor* (b) issued for valuable consideration either (i) in any newspaper, journal, magazine or other publication published at intervals of seven or more days, or (ii) by way of sound broadcasting or television by the exhibition of cinematographic films or by the distribution of recordings, and which is issued or caused to be issued by a person who is not an authorised person *except* in relation to an advertisement issued on or after 6 May 1988 in an edition of a newspaper, magazine, journal or other publication first issued before 6 May 1988) (SI 1988/740)
	29 Apr 1988 (exception noted above) (SI 1988/740)
58(1)(a)–(c)	29 Apr 1988 (SI 1988/740)
(d)(i)	29 Apr 1988 (SI 1988/740)
(ii)	29 Apr 1988 (except so far as relates to an advertisement required or permitted to be published by an approved exchange under Pt V of the Act) (SI 1988/740)
	Not in force (exception noted above)
(2)	Repealed *(never in force)*
(3)–(6)	29 Apr 1988 (SI 1988/740)
59–61	29 Apr 1988 (SI 1988/740)
62(1)	1 Dec 1987 (except so far as s 62(1) applies to a contravention such as is mentioned in s 62(2)) (SI 1987/1997)
	3 Oct 1988 (exception noted above) (SI 1987/1997)
(2)–(4)	1 Dec 1987 (SI 1987/1997)
62A	Inserted by Companies Act 1989, s 193(1) (qv)
63	23 Apr 1987 (SI 1987/623)
63A, 63B	Inserted by Companies Act 1989, s 194 (qv)
63C	Inserted by Companies Act 1989, s 195 (qv)
64–75	29 Apr 1988 (SI 1988/740)
76	29 Apr 1988 (except so far as has effect in relation to (a) a collective investment scheme which takes the form of an open-ended investment company units in which are either included in the Official List of the International Stock Exchange of the United Kingdom and the Republic of Ireland Limited or are offered on terms such that any agreement for their acquisition is conditional upon their admission to that List; or (b) any prospectus issued by or on behalf of an open-ended investment company which complies with Chapter II of Part III of Companies Act 1985 or the corresponding provisions of Companies (Northern Ireland) Order 1986 and the issue of which in the United Kingdom does not

Financial Services Act 1986 (c 60)—*cont*

s 76—*cont*

contravene s 74 or 75 of Companies Act 1985 or the corresponding provisions of Companies (Northern Ireland) Order 1986 as the case may be) (SI 1988/740)

31 Dec 1988 (otherwise, except so far as has effect in relation to (a) an open-ended investment company units in which are either included in the Official List of the International Stock Exchange of the United Kingdom and the Republic of Ireland Limited or are offered on terms such that any agreement for their acquisition is conditional upon such listing being an open-ended investment company which either (i) is managed in and authorised under the law of a country or territory in respect of which an order under s 87 of Financial Services Act 1986 is in force on 31 Dec 1988 and which is of a class specified in that order; or (ii) is constituted in a member State in respect of which an order under para 10 of Sch 15 to Financial Services Act 1986 is in force on 31 Dec 1988 and which meets the requirements specified in that order; or (b) any prospectus issued by or on behalf of an open-ended investment company which fulfils the conditions described in head (a)(i) or (a)(ii) immediately above being a prospectus which complies with Chapter II of Part III of Companies Act 1985 or the corresponding provisions of Companies (Northern Ireland) Order 1986 and the issue of which in the United Kingdom does not contravene s 74 or 75 of Companies Act 1985 or the corresponding provisions of Companies (Northern Ireland) Order 1986 as the case may be) (SI 1988/1960, as amended by SI 1988/2285) (and also except so far as has effect in relation to (a) an open-ended investment company managed in and authorised under the law of Bermuda units in which are, on 31 Dec 1988, included in the Official List of the International Stock Exchange of the United Kingdom and the Republic of Ireland Limited; or (b) any prospectus issued by or on behalf of an open-ended investment company which fulfils the conditions described in head (a) immediately above, being a prospectus which complies with Chapter II of Part III of Companies Act 1985 or the corresponding provisions of Companies (Northern Ireland) Order 1986 and the issue of which in the United Kingdom does not contravene s 74 or 75 of Companies Act 1985 or the corresponding provisions of Companies (Northern Ireland) Order 1986 (as the case may be) (SI 1988/2285)

28 Feb 1989 (so far as has effect in relation to an open-ended investment company falling within head (a) immediately above but which is not a scheme of a class specified in the Schedule to Financial Services (Designated Countries and

Financial Services Act 1986 (c 60)—*cont*

s 76—*cont*	Territories) (Overseas Collective Investment Schemes) (Bermuda) Order 1988, SI 1988/2284, or to any prospectus which falls within head (b) immediately above issued by or on behalf of any such company) (SI 1988/2285)
	1 Mar 1989 (otherwise, except so far as has effect in relation to (a) an open-ended investment company which fulfils the conditions described in head (a) immediately above and which is a scheme of a class specified in the Schedule to Financial Services (Designated Countries and Territories) (Overseas Collective Investment Schemes) (Bermuda) Order 1988, SI 1988/2284, or (b) any prospectus issued by or on behalf of such an open-ended investment company, being a prospectus which fulfils the conditions described in head (b) immediately above) (SI 1988/1960)
	1 May 1989 (exception noted above) (SI 1988/2285)
77–85	29 Apr 1988 (SI 1988/740)
86	29 Apr 1988 (for purposes of Sch 15, para 10) (SI 1988/740)
	1 Oct 1989 (otherwise) (SI 1989/1583)
87–95	29 Apr 1988 (SI 1988/740)
96	1 Dec 1987 (SI 1987/1997)
97–101	29 Apr 1988 (SI 1988/740)
102, 103	4 Jun 1987 (SI 1987/9907)
104(1)	29 Apr 1988 (SI 1988/740)
(2), (3)	4 Jun 1987 (SI 1987/907)
(4)	29 Apr 1988 (SI 1988/740)
105, 106	18 Dec 1986 (SI 1986/2246)
107	4 Jun 1987 (SI 1987/907)
107A	Inserted by Companies Act 1989, s 206(1), Sch 23, para 11 (qv)
108, 109	29 Apr 1988 (SI 1988/740)
110	4 Jun 1987 (SI 1987/907)
111	29 Apr 1988 (SI 1988/740)
112(1)–(4)	4 Jun 1987 (SI 1987/907)
(5)	1 Jan 1988 (so far as has effect in relation to applications under s 26) (SI 1987/2158)
	29 Apr 1988 (otherwise) (SI 1988/740)
113(1)	4 Jun 1987 (SI 1987/907)
(2)	29 Apr 1988 (SI 1988/740)
(3)	Substituted by Friendly Societies Act 1992, s 98(a), Sch 18, Pt I, para 2 (qv)
(4)–(8)	29 Apr 1988 (SI 1988/740)
114–118	12 Jan 1987 (SI 1986/2246)
119, 120	4 Jun 1987 (SI 1987/907)
121	12 Jan 1987 (SI 1986/2246)
122	12 Jan 1987 (for purposes of s 121) (SI 1986/2246)
	4 Jun 1987 (otherwise) (SI 1987/907)
123	12 Jan 1987 (for purposes of any provision brought into force by SI 1986/2246) (SI 1986/2246)
	4 Jun 1987 (otherwise) (SI 1987/907)
124	12 Jan 1987 (SI 1986/2246)
125(1)–(7)	4 Jun 1987 (SI 1987/907)
(8)	1 Jul 1988 (SI 1988/995)
126	12 Jan 1987 (SI 1986/2246)

Financial Services Act 1986 (c 60)—*cont*

s 127	4 Jun 1987 (SI 1987/907)
128	12 Jan 1987 (SI 1986/2246)
128A–128C	Inserted by Companies Act 1989, s 196 (qv)
129	See Sch 10 below
130, 131	29 Apr 1988 (SI 1988/740)
132(1)–(5)	12 Jan 1987 (SI 1986/2246)
(6) (first part)	12 Jan 1987 (for purposes of any contract of insurance which is not an agreement to which s 5(1) applies) (SI 1986/2246) 29 Apr 1988 (otherwise) (SI 1988/740)
(second part)	12 Jan 1987 (for purposes of any reinsurance contract entered into in respect of a contract of insurance which is not an agreement to which s 5(1) applies) (SI 1986/2246) 29 Apr 1988 (otherwise) (SI 1988/740)
133	29 Apr 1988 (SI 1988/740)
134	Repealed (partly never in force)
135, 136	29 Apr 1988 (SI 1988/740)
137	12 Jan 1987 (SI 1986/2246)
138(1), (2)	4 Jun 1987 (SI 1987/907)
(3)	12 Jan 1987 (SI 1986/2246)
(4)	29 Apr 1988 (SI 1988/740)
(5)	12 Jan 1987 (SI 1986/2246)
(6)	4 Jun 1987 (SI 1987/907)
139(1)(a)	29 Apr 1988 (SI 1988/740)
(b)	12 Jan 1987 (SI 1986/2246)
(2)	29 Apr 1988 (SI 1988/740)
(3), (4)	Repealed
(5)	29 Apr 1988 (SI 1988/740)
140	See Sch 11 below
141	12 Jan 1987 (SI 1986/2246)
142–153	12 Jan 1987 (for all purposes relating to the admission of securities offered by or on behalf of a minister of the Crown or a body corporate controlled by a minister of the Crown or a subsidiary of such a body corporate to the Official List in respect of which an application is made after that date) (SI 1986/2246) 16 Feb 1987 (for purposes relating to the admission of securities in respect of which an application is made after that date, other than those referred to in the preceding paragraph, and otherwise for all purposes) (SI 1986/2246)
154(1)	12 Jan 1987 (for all purposes relating to the admission of securities offered by or on behalf of a minister of the Crown or a body corporate controlled by a minister of the Crown or a subsidiary of such a body corporate to the Official List in respect of which an application is made after that date) (SI 1986/2246) 16 Feb 1987 (for purposes relating to the admission of securities in respect of which an application is made after that date, other than those referred to in the preceding paragraph, and otherwise for all purposes) (SI 1986/2246)
(2)–(4)	29 Apr 1988 (SI 1988/740)

Financial Services Act 1986 (c 60)—*cont*

s 154(5)	12 Jan 1987 (for all purposes relating to the admission of securities offered by or on behalf of a minister of the Crown or a body corporate controlled by a minister of the Crown or a subsidiary of such a body corporate to the Official List in respect of which an application is made after that date) (SI 1986/2246)
	16 Feb 1987 (for purposes relating to the admission of securities in respect of which an application is made after that date, other than those referred to in the preceding paragraph, and otherwise for all purposes) (SI 1986/2246)
154A	Inserted (19 Jun 1995) by Public Offers of Securities Regulations 1995, SI 1995/1537, reg 17, Sch 2, Pt I, para 2(3)
155, 156	12 Jan 1987 (for all purposes relating to the admission of securities offered by or on behalf of a minister of the Crown or a body corporate controlled by a minister of the Crown or a subsidiary of such a body corporate to the Official List in respect of which an application is made after that date) (SI 1986/2246)
	16 Feb 1987 (for purposes relating to the admission of securities in respect of which an application is made after that date, other than those referred to in the preceding paragraph, and otherwise for all purposes) (SI 1986/2246)
156A, 156B	Inserted (19 Jun 1995) by Public Offers of Securities Regulations 1995, SI 1995/1537, reg 17, Sch 2, Pt I, para 2(4)
157	Repealed
158–171	Repealed *(never in force for more than limited purposes)*
172	30 Apr 1987 (SI 1986/2246)
173–176	Repealed
177	15 Nov 1986 (SI 1986/1940)
178(1)	15 Nov 1986 (SI 1986/1940)
(2)(a)	15 Nov 1986 (SI 1986/1940)
(b)	29 Apr 1988 (SI 1988/740)
(3)–(9)	29 Apr 1988 (SI 1988/740)
(10)	12 Jan 1987 (SI 1986/2246)
179	15 Nov 1986 (for purposes of information obtained by a person mentioned in s 179(3)(h) so far as that provision applies to a person appointed or authorised to exercise any powers under s 177, or by a person mentioned in s 179(3)(i) who is an officer or servant of any such person) (SI 1986/1940)
	18 Dec 1986 (otherwise) (SI 1986/2246)
180	15 Nov 1986 (SI 1986/2246)
181	12 Jan 1987 (SI 1986/2246)
182	See Sch 13 below
183	23 Apr 1987 (so far as relates to notices relating to the carrying on of insurance business or of a deposittaking business as a recognised bank or licensed institution within the meaning of the Banking Act 1979) (SI 1987/623)
	29 Apr 1988 (otherwise) (SI 1988/740)

Financial Services Act 1986 (c 60)—*cont*

s 184(1)–(3)	23 Apr 1987 (so far as relate to notices relating to the carrying on of insurance business) (SI 1987/623)
	29 Apr 1988 (otherwise) (SI 1988/740)
(4)	29 Apr 1988 (SI 1988/740)
(5)	23 Apr 1987 (SI 1987/623)
(6)	29 Apr 1988 (SI 1988/740)
(7)	23 Apr 1987 (SI 1987/623)
(8)	29 Apr 1988 (SI 1988/740)
185	23 Apr 1987 (SI 1987/623)
186(1)–(5)	23 Apr 1987 (so far as relate to provisions brought into force by SI 1987/623) (SI 1987/623)
	29 Apr 1988 (otherwise) (SI 1988/740)
(6)	29 Apr 1988 (SI 1988/740)
(7)	23 Apr 1987 (so far as relates to provisions brought into force by SI 1987/623) (SI 1987/623)
	29 Apr 1988 (otherwise) (SI 1988/740)
187(1), (2)	4 Jun 1987 (SI 1987/907)
(3), (4)	12 Jan 1987 (SI 1986/2246)
(5)–(7)	4 Jun 1987 (SI 1987/907)
188	Substituted by Companies Act 1989, s 200(1) (qv)
189	See Sch 14 below
190, 191	4 Jun 1987 (SI 1987/907)
192	Substituted by Companies Act 1989, s 201 (qv)
193	Repealed
194	29 Apr 1988 (SI 1988/740)
195	7 Nov 1986 (s 211(2)); repealed by s 212(3) of, and Sch 17 to, this Act, as from a day to be appointed under s 211(1) of this Act; any order made under that section bringing the prospective repeal into force will be noted thereto in the service to this work
196	1 Dec 1987 (SI 1987/1997)
197	29 Apr 1988 (SI 1988/740)
198(1)	Repealed
(2)(a)	15 Nov 1986 (SI 1986/1940)
(b)	18 Dec 1986 (SI 1986/2246)
(3)	Repealed
199(1), (2)	Substituted by Companies Act 1989, s 76(2) (qv)
(3)–(6)	15 Nov 1986 (for purposes relating to offences under Company Securities (Insider Dealing) Act 1985, ss 1, 2, 4, 5) (SI 1986/1940)
	29 Apr 1988 (otherwise) (SI 1988/740)
(7)	12 Jan 1987 (SI 1986/2246)
(8)	Substituted by Companies Act 1989, s 76(7) (qv)
(8A)	Inserted by Criminal Justice Act 1993, s 79(13), Sch 5, para 12(2) (qv)
(9)	15 Nov 1986 (for purposes relating to offences under Company Securities (Insider Dealing) Act 1985, ss 1, 2, 4, 5) (SI 1986/1940)
	29 Apr 1988 (otherwise) (SI 1988/740)
200(1)(a)	4 Jun 1987 (so far as has effect in relation to an application for a recognition order under Ch III or IV of Pt 1) (SI 1987/907)
	1 Jan 1988 (so far as has effect in relation to an application for authorisation under s 26) (SI 1987/2158)
	29 Apr 1988 (otherwise) (SI 1988/740)

Financial Services Act 1986 (c 60)—*cont*

s 200(1)(b)	15 Nov 1986 (so far as relates to a requirement imposed by or under s 177) (SI 1986/2246) 12 Jan 1987 (so far as relates to a requirement imposed by or under any provision brought into force on 12 Jan 1987 by SI 1986/2246) (SI 1986/2246) 4 Jun 1987 (so far as relates to a requirement imposed by or under any provision brought into force by SI 1987/907) (SI 1987/907) 1 Jan 1988 (so far as relates to a requirement imposed by or under any provision brought into force by SI 1987/2158) (SI 1987/2158) 29 Apr 1988 (otherwise) (SI 1988/740)
(2)	29 Apr 1988 (SI 1988/740)
(3), (4)	4 Jun 1987 (SI 1987/907)
(5)	15 Nov 1986 (so far as relates to a requirement imposed by or under s 177) (SI 1986/1940) 18 Dec 1986 (so far as relates to a requirement imposed by or under s 105) (SI 1986/2246) 12 Jan 1987 (so far as relates to a requirement imposed by or under any provision brought into force on 12 Jan 1987 by SI 1986/2246) (SI 1986/2246) 4 Jun 1987 (so far as relates to a provision brought into force by SI 1987/907) (SI 1987/907) 1 Jan 1988 (so far as relates to any provision brought into force by SI 1987/2158 (SI 1987/2158) 29 Apr 1988 (otherwise) (SI 1988/740)
(6)–(8)	4 Jun 1987 (so far as relates to a provision brought into force by SI 1987/907) (SI 1987/907) 29 Apr 1988 (otherwise) (SI 1988/740)
201(1)	15 Nov 1986 (so far as relates to a provision brought into force by SI 1986/1940) (SI 1986/1940) 18 Dec 1986 (otherwise) (SI 1986/2246)
(2)	29 Apr 1988 (SI 1988/740)
(3)	23 Apr 1987 (SI 1987/623)
(4)	12 Jan 1987 (SI 1986/2246)
202, 203	15 Nov 1986 (for purposes of any provision brought into force by SI 1986/1940) (SI 1986/1940) 18 Dec 1986 (otherwise) (SI 1986/2246)
204	12 Jan 1987 (SI 1986/2246
205, 205A	Substituted for original s 205 by Companies Act 1989, s 206(1), Sch 23, para 18 (qv)
206(1)–(3)	4 Jun 1987 (SI 1987/907)
(4)	15 May 1987 (SI 1987/907)
207	15 Nov 1986 (for purposes of any provision brought into force by SI 1986/1940) (SI 1986/1940) 18 Dec 1986 (otherwise) (SI 1986/2246)
208	29 Apr 1988 (so far as has effect in relation to the application of s 130) (SI 1988/740) *Not in force* (otherwise)
209, 210	15 Nov 1986 (for purposes of any provision brought into force by SI 1986/1940) (SI 1986/1940)

Financial Services Act 1986 (c 60)—*cont*

s 209, 210—*cont*	18 Dec 1986 (otherwise) (SI 1986/2246)
211(1), (2)	7 Nov 1986 (RA)
(3)	See Sch 15 below
212(1)	27 Nov 1986 (SI 1986/2031)
(2)	See Sch 16 below
(3)	See Sch 17 below
Sch 1, para 1–22	18 Dec 1986 (SI 1986/2246)
23	1 Dec 1987 (SI 1987/1997)
24	18 Dec 1986 (SI 1986/2246)
25(1)	18 Dec 1986 (SI 1986/2246)
(2), (3)	18 Jan 1988 (SI 1987/2158)
25A	Inserted (27 Feb 1988) by Financial Services Act 1986 (Restriction of Scope of Act) Order 1988, SI 1988/318, art 5 (revoked); substituted (1 Jun 1992) by Financial Services Act 1986 (Extension of Scope of Act) Order 1992, SI 1992/273, art 2
25B	Inserted (27 Feb 1988) by Financial Services Act 1986 (Restriction of Scope of Act) Order 1988, SI 1988/318, art 6
26–29	18 Dec 1986 (SI 1986/2246)
30	Substituted by Companies Act 1989, s 23, Sch 10, Pt II, para 36 (qv)
31–33	18 Dec 1986 (SI 1986/2246)
34, 35	Inserted (26 Mar 1990) by Financial Services Act 1986 (Restriction of Scope of Act and Meaning of Collective Investment Scheme) Order 1990, SI 1990/349, art 7
2–4	4 Jun 1987 (SI 1987/907)
5	1 Jan 1988 (SI 1987/2158)
6	1 Dec 1987 (SI 1987/1997)
7–9	12 Jan 1987 (SI 1986/2246)
10, para 1	12 Jan 1987 (SI 1986/2246)
2	29 Apr 1988 (SI 1988/740)
3(1), (2)	4 Jun 1987 (SI 1987/907)
(3)	12 Jan 1987 (SI 1986/2246)
(4)	4 Jun 1987 (SI 1987/907)
4(1), (2)	4 Jun 1987 (SI 1987/907)
(2A)	Inserted by Companies Act 1989, s 206(1), Sch 23, para 25 (qv)
(3), (4)	4 June 1987 (SI 1987/907)
(5)	29 Apr 1988 (SI 1988/740)
(6)	12 Jan 1987 (SI 1986/2246)
5(1), (2)	29 Apr 1988 (SI 1988/740)
(3), (4)	1 Jul 1988 (SI 1988/995)
6, 7	29 Apr 1988 (SI 1988/740)
8(1)–(5)	29 Apr 1988 (SI 1988/740)
(6)	12 Jan 1987 (SI 1986/2246)
9	29 Apr 1988 (SI 1988/740)
10	12 Jan 1987 (SI 1986/2246)
11, para 1	12 Jan 1987 (SI 1986/2246)
2–5	4 Jun 1987 (SI 1987/907)
6	1 Dec 1987 (SI 1987/1997)
7	Repealed
8–13	4 Jun 1987 (SI 1987/907)
13A	Inserted by Companies Act 1989, s 206(1), Sch 23, para 32 (qv)

Financial Services Act 1986 (c 60)—*cont*

Sch 11, para 13B		Prospectively inserted by Companies Act 1989, s 206(1), Sch 23, para 32; any order made under Companies Act 1989, s 206(2), (3) bringing the prospective insertion into force will be noted to that Act in the service to this work
	14–16	4 Jun 1987 (SI 1987/907)
	17	*Not in force*
	18, 19	4 Jun 1987 (SI 1987/907)
	20	Substituted by Companies Act 1989, s 206(1), Sch 23, para 35 (qv)
	21	29 Apr 1988 (SI 1988/740)
	22(1)–(3)	29 Apr 1988 (SI 1988/740)
	(4)	1 Dec 1987 (except for purposes of making a contravention of the kind described in para 22(4)(d) actionable at the suit of a person of the kind described in that paragraph) (SI 1987/1997)
		3 Oct 1988 (exception noted above) (SI 1987/1997)
	(5)	1 Dec 1987 (SI 1987/1997)
	22A	Inserted by Companies Act 1989, s 193(3) (qv)
	22B–22D	Inserted by Companies Act 1989, s 206(1), Sch 23, para 36 (qv)
	23	29 Apr 1988 (SI 1988/740)
	24	4 Jun 1987 (SI 1987/907)
	25, 26	29 Apr 1988 (SI 1988/740)
	27	Repealed
	28	12 Jan 1987 (SI 1986/2246)
	29	Substituted by Companies Act 1989, s 206(1), Sch 23, para 37 (qv)
	30, 31	12 Jan 1987 (SI 1986/2246)
	31A	Inserted by Friendly Societies Act 1992, s 98(a), Sch 18, Pt II, para 19 (qv)
	32, 33	12 Jan 1987 (SI 1986/2246)
	34	Substituted by Companies Act 1989, s 206(1), Sch 23, para 40 (qv)
	35–37	12 Jan 1987 (SI 1986/2246)
	38	4 Jun 1987 (SI 1987/907)
	39	1 Jan 1988 (SI 1987/2158)
	40	12 Jan 1987 (SI 1986/2246)
	40A	Inserted by Friendly Societies Act 1992, s 98(a), Sch 18, Pt II, para 21 (qv)
	41	12 Jan 1987 (SI 1986/2246)
	42	4 Jun 1987 (SI 1987/907)
	43	Repealed
	44	12 Jan 1987 (SI 1986/2246)
	45	Substituted by Friendly Societies Act 1992, s 98(a), Sch 18, Pt II, para 22 (qv)
11A		Inserted (19 Jun 1995) by Public Offers of Securities Regulations 1995, SI 1995/1537, reg 17, Sch 2, Pt I, para 2(2), Sch 3
12		30 Apr 1987 (SI 1986/2246)
13, para 1, 2		18 Dec 1986 (SI 1986/2246)
	3, 4	Repealed
	5	18 Dec 1986 (SI 1986/2246)
	6	15 Nov 1986 (for purposes of anything done or which may be done under or by virtue of any provision brought into force by SI 1986/1940) (SI 1986/1940)

Financial Services Act 1986 (c 60)—*cont*

Sch 13, para 6—*cont* | 18 Dec 1986 (otherwise) (SI 1986/2246)
7 | 15 Nov 1986 (for purposes of anything done or which may be done under or by virtue of any provision brought into force by SI 1986/1940) (SI 1986/1940)
27 Nov 1986 (otherwise) (SI 1986/2031)
8 | 27 Nov 1986 (SI 1986/2031)
9 | 15 Nov 1986 (for purposes of anything done or which may be done under or by virtue of any provision brought into force by SI 1986/1940) (SI 1986/1940)
27 Nov 1986 (otherwise) (SI 1986/2031)
10 | Spent
11 | 15 Nov 1986 (for purposes of anything done or which may be done under or by virtue of any provision brought into force by SI 1986/1940) (SI 1986/1940)
27 Nov 1986 (otherwise) (SI 1986/2031)
12 | 27 Nov 1986 (SI 1986/2031)
13, 14 | 15 Nov 1986 (for purposes of anything done or which may be done under or by virtue of any provision brought into force by SI 1986/1940) (SI 1986/1940)
27 Nov 1986 (otherwise) (SI 1986/2031)

14 | 12 Jan 1987 (so far as makes provision as to the application of:
(i) Rehabilitation of Offenders Act 1974, s 4(1), in relation to the determination of proceedings of the kind specified in Sch 14, Pt I, para 4;
(ii) s 4(2) of the 1974 Act in relation to a question put by or on behalf of a person specified in Sch 14, Pt II, para 5, first column;
(iii) s 4(3)(b) of the 1974 Act in relation to action taken by the competent authority or by a person specified in Sch 14, Pt III, para 3, first column) (SI 1986/2246)

1 Dec 1987 (so far as makes provision as to the application of:
(i) Rehabilitation of Offenders Act 1974, s 4(1), in relation to the determination of proceedings of the kind described in Sch 14, Pt 1, paras 2, 3 and 6; Rehabilitation of Offenders (Northern Ireland) Order 1978, art 5(1), in relation to the determination of proceedings of the kind described in those paras and in Sch 14, Pt I, para 4;
(ii) s 4(2) of the 1974 Act, in relation to a question put by or on behalf of a person specified in Sch 14, Pt II, para 6, first column; Rehabilitation of Offenders (Northern Ireland) Order 1978, art 5(2) in relation to a question put by or on behalf of a person specified in Sch 14, Pt II, para 5 or 6, first column;

Financial Services Act 1986 (c 60)—*cont*

Sch 14—*cont*	(iii) s 4(2) of the 1974 Act and art 5(2) of the 1978 Order, in relation to a question put by or on behalf of a person specified in Sch 14, Pt II, para 2 or 3, first column; or to a question put by or on behalf of a person specified in Sch 14, Pt II, para 4, first column insofar as it relates to persons described in paras 2(a), (b) or (c) or 3(a), (b) or (c) or to a question put by or on behalf of a person specified in para 8 of that column;
	(iv) s 4(3)(b) of the 1974 Act in relation to action taken by a person of a kind described in sub-para (c) above and art 5(3)(b) of the 1978 Order in relation to action taken by a person described in sub-para (c) above or specified in Sch 14, Pt III, para 3, first column (SI 1987/1977)
	1 Jan 1988 (otherwise, except for the purposes of Rehabilitation of Offenders Act 1974 (Exceptions) (Amendment No 2) Order 1986, art 1(2)(b), and Rehabilitation of Offenders (Exceptions) (Amendment) Order (Northern Ireland) 1987, art 1(2)(b)) (SI 1987/2158)
	Not in force (exception noted above)
15, para 1(1)–(3)	27 Feb 1988 (SI 1987/2158)
(4)	29 Apr 1988 (SI 1988/740)
(5)	27 Feb 1988 (SI 1987/2158)
2, 3	29 Apr 1988 (SI 1988/740)
4–6	4 Jun 1987 (SI 1987/907)
7	29 Apr 1988 (SI 1988/740)
8	Repealed
9–11	29 Apr 1988 (SI 1988/740)
12	12 Jan 1987 (SI 1986/2246)
13	27 Nov 1986 (SI 1986/2031)
14, 15	29 Apr 1988 (SI 1988/740)
16	27 Feb 1988 (in relation to Sch 15, para 1(1)–(3), (5)) (SI 1987/2158)
	29 Apr 1988 (otherwise) (SI 1988/740)
16, para 1	Repealed
2	29 Apr 1988 (SI 1988/740)
3	Spent
4–9	29 Apr 1988 (SI 1988/740)
10, 11	Repealed
12	29 Apr 1988 (SI 1988/740)
13	30 Apr 1987 (SI 1986/2246)
14	Spent
15	29 Apr 1988 (SI 1988/740)
16	Repealed *(never in force)*
17(a), (b)	29 Apr 1988 (SI 1988/740)
(c)	12 Jan 1987 (so far as relates to Companies Act 1985, s 173(2)(a)) (SI 1986/2246)
	29 Apr 1988 (otherwise) (SI 1988/740)
(d)	29 Apr 1988 (SI 1988/740)
18–21	29 Apr 1988 (SI 1988/740)
22	Repealed
23–26	29 Apr 1988 (SI 1988/740)
27(a)	29 Apr 1988 (SI 1988/740)

Financial Services Act 1986 (c 60)—*cont*

Sch 16, para 27(b)	4 Jun 1987 (SI 1987/907)
28	Repealed
29, 30	29 Apr 1988 (SI 1988/740)
31	*Not in force*
32(a), (b)	29 Apr 1988 (SI 1988/740)
(c)	12 Jan 1987 (so far as it relates to Companies (Northern Ireland) Order 1986, art 173(2)(a)) (SI 1986/2246)
	29 Apr 1988 (otherwise) (SI 1988/740)
(d)	29 Apr 1988 (SI 1988/740)
33–36	29 Apr 1988 (SI 1988/740)
37	Repealed
38–42	29 Apr 1988 (SI 1988/740)
43	Repealed
17	27 Nov 1986 (repeals of or in Banking Act 1979, s 20; Companies Act 1985, ss 433, 446(5); Companies Consolidation (Consequential Provisions) Act 1985, Sch 2 (entry relating to Banking Act 1979, s 20); Companies (Consequential Provisions) (Northern Ireland) Order 1986, Sch 2 (entry relating to Banking Act 1979, s 20)) (SI 1986/2031)
	12 Jan 1987 (repeals of or in Banking Act 1979, Sch 1; Company Securities (Insider Dealing) Act 1985, s 3) (SI 1986/2246)
	12 Jan 1987 (for all purposes relating to the admission of securities offered by or on behalf of a minister of the Crown or a body corporate controlled by a minister of the Crown or a subsidiary of such a body corporate, to the Official List in respect of which an application is made after that date) (repeals of or in Companies Act 1985, Pt III, ss 81–87, 97, 693, 709, Schs 3, 22, 24 and corresponding provisions of Companies (Northern Ireland) Order 1986, to the extent which they would apply in relation to any investment which is listed or the subject of an application for listing in accordance with Pt IV of the Act) (SI 1986/2246)
	16 Feb 1987 (repeals noted above for all other purposes) (SI 1986/2246)
	30 Apr 1987 (repeals of or in Industry Act 1975; Scottish Development Agency Act 1975 (entry now repealed); Welsh Development Agency Act 1975; Aircraft and Shipbuilding Industries Act 1977) (SI 1986/2246)
	29 Apr 1988 (otherwise, except repeals of or in such provisions of Prevention of Fraud (Investments) Act (Northern Ireland) 1940 as are necessary for the purposes of Sch 15, para 1(3) to this Act as it applies by virtue of para 16 of that Schedule; such provisions of Prevention of Fraud (Investments) Act 1958 as are necessary for the purposes of Sch 15, para 1(3) to this Act; Tribunals and Inquiries Act 1971; House of Commons Disqualification Act 1975; Restrictive Trade Practices (Stock Exchange) Act 1984; Company Securities (Insider

Financial Services Act 1986 (c 60)—*cont*

Sch 17—*cont*

Dealing) Act 1985, s 13; to the extent not yet repealed, and except insofar as is necessary to have the effect that those provisions cease to apply to a prospectus offering for subscription, or to any form of application for, units in a body corporate which is a recognised scheme, Companies Act 1985, Pt III, ss 81 to 87, 97, 449(1)(d), 693, 709, 744, so far as relates to the definition 'prospectus issued generally', Schs 3, 22, 24, and corresponding provisions of Companies (Northern Ireland) Order 1986; s 195 of this Act) (SI 1988/740)

1 Jul 1988 (repeal of Restrictive Trade Practices (Stock Exchange) Act 1984) (SI 1988/995)

31 Dec 1988 (so far as necessary to have the effect that, to the extent that they do apply, Companies Act 1985, Pt III, s 693, Sch 3, and corresponding provisions of Companies (Northern Ireland) Order 1986 cease to apply to a prospectus offering for subscription, or to any application form for, units in an open-ended investment company which does not fulfil the conditions described in head (a)(i) or (a)(ii) mentioned against s 76 above, except in relation to a prospectus offering for subscription, or to any application form for, units in an open-ended investment company which is managed in and authorised under the law of Bermuda units in which are, on 31 Dec 1988, included in the Official List of the International Stock Exchange of the United Kingdom and the Republic of Ireland Limited) (SI 1988/1960 (amending SI 1988/740); SI 1988/2285)

28 Feb 1989 (so far as necessary to have the effect that, to the extent that they do apply, Companies Act 1985, Pt III, s 693, Sch 3, and corresponding provisions of Companies (Northern Ireland) Order 1986 cease to apply to a prospectus offering for subscription, or to any application form for, units in an open-ended investment company managed in and authorised under the law of Bermuda units in which are, on 31 Dec 1988, included in the Official List of the International Stock Exchange of the United Kingdom and the Republic of Ireland Limited but which is not a scheme of a class specified in the Schedule to the Financial Services (Designated Countries and Territories) (Overseas Collective Investment Schemes) (Bermuda) Order 1988, SI 1988/2284) (SI 1988/2285)

1 Mar 1989 (so far as necessary to have the effect that to the extent that they do apply, Companies Act 1985, Pt III, s 693, Sch 3, and corresponding provisions of Companies (Northern Ireland) Order 1986 cease to apply to a prospectus offering for subscription, or to any application form for, units in an open-ended investment

Financial Services Act 1986 (c 60)—*cont*

Sch 17—*cont*

company which does fulfil the conditions described in head (a)(i) or (a)(ii) mentioned against s 76 above) (SI 1988/1960 (amending SI 1988/740), as amended by SI 1988/2285)

1 May 1989 (so far as necessary to have the effect that, to the extent that they do apply, Companies Act 1985, Pt III, s 693, Sch 3, and corresponding provisions of Companies (Northern Ireland) Order 1986 cease to apply to a prospectus offering for subscription, or to any application form for, units in an open-ended investment company managed in and authorised under the law of Bermuda units in which are, on 31 Dec 1988, included in the Official List of the International Stock Exchange of the United Kingdom and the Republic of Ireland Limited and which is a scheme of a class specified in Financial Services (Designated Countries and Territories) (Overseas Collective Investment Schemes) (Bermuda) Order 1988, SI 1988/2284, Schedule) (SI 1988/2285)

1 Oct 1989 (repeals of or in Prevention of Fraud (Investments) Act (Northern Ireland) 1940 (for all remaining purposes); Prevention of Fraud (Investments) Act 1958 (for all remaining purposes); Tribunals and Inquiries Act 1971; House of Commons Disqualification Act 1975) (SI 1989/1583)

19 Jun 1995 (repeals of (i) Companies Act 1985, Pt III, Sch 3, Sch 22 (entry relating to Pt III), Sch 24 (entries relating to ss 56(4), 61, 64(5), 70(1), 78(1))—those repeals brought into force for all remaining purposes except for repeals of ss 58, 59, 60 (so far as necessary for purposes of ss 81, 83, 246, 248, 744), Sch 3, para 2 (so far as necessary for purposes of s 83(1)(a)) and s 62 (so far as necessary for purposes of s 744); and (ii) corresponding provisions of Companies (Northern Ireland) Order 1986, SI 1986/1032 (NI 6)) (SI 1995/1538)

Not in force (otherwise)

Forestry Act 1986 (c 30)

RA: 8 Jul 1986

Commencement provisions: s 2(1)

8 Sep 1986 (s 2(1))

Gaming (Amendment) Act 1986 (c 11)

RA: 2 May 1986

Commencement provisions: s 3(3); Gaming (Amendment) Act 1986 (Commencement) Order 1988, SI 1988/1250

19 Sep 1988 (SI 1988/1250)

Gas Act 1986 (c 44)

RA: 25 Jul 1986

Commencement provisions: ss 3, 49(1), 57(2), 68(2)–(5); Gas Act 1986 (Commencement No 1) Order 1986, SI 1986/1315; Gas Act 1986 (Appointed Day) Order 1986, SI 1986/1316; Gas Act 1986 (Transfer Date) Order 1986, SI 1986/1318; Gas Act 1986 (Commencement No 2) Order 1986, SI 1986/1809; British Gas Corporation (Dissolution) Order 1990, SI 1990/147

s 1	18 Aug 1986 (SI 1986/1315)
2	23 Aug 1986 (SI 1986/1315)
3	23 Aug 1986 (s 68(2); SI 1986/1316)
4	23 Aug 1986 (s 68(2); SI 1986/1316); prospectively substituted by Gas Act 1995, s 1[1]
4A	Prospectively inserted by Gas Act 1995, s 2[1]
5	Substituted by Gas (Exempt Supplies) Act 1993, s 1 (qv); prospectively further substituted by Gas Act 1995, s 3(1), subject to savings and transitional provisions (see 1995 Act, s 17(1), Sch 5, Pt II, paras 16–18)[1]
6	23 Aug 1986 (s 68(2); SI 1986/1316); prospectively repealed by Gas Act 1995, ss 3(3), 17(5), Sch 6[1]
6A	Inserted by Gas (Exempt Supplies) Act 1993, s 2 (qv); prospectively substituted by Gas Act 1995, s 4, subject to savings and transitional provisions (see 1995 Act, s 17(1), Sch 5, Pt I, Pt II, paras 14, 16, 17)[1]
7	23 Aug 1986 (s 68(2); SI 1986/1316); prospectively substituted by Gas Act 1995, s 5, subject to savings and transitional provisions (see 1995 Act, s 17(1), Sch 5, Pt I, Pt II, paras 15, 29)[1]
7A, 7B	Prospectively inserted by Gas Act 1995, ss 6(1), 7, subject to savings and transitional provisions (see 1995 Act, s 17(1), Sch 5, Pt I, Pt II, paras 14–16, 19)[1]
8	23 Aug 1986 (s 68(2); SI 1986/1316); prospectively substituted by Gas Act 1995, s 8(1)[1]
8AA	Prospectively inserted by Gas Act 1995, s 10(1), Sch 3, para 1[1]
8A	Inserted by Competition and Service (Utilities) Act 1992, s 37 (qv)
8B	Prospectively inserted by Gas Act 1995, s 9(1)[1]
9–13	23 Aug 1986 (s 68(2); SI 1986/1316); prospectively substituted by Gas Act 1995, s 10(1), Sch 3, paras 3–7, subject in the case of s 10 to savings and transitional provisions (see 1995 Act, s 17(1), Sch 5, Pt II, para 20)[1]
14	23 Aug 1986 (s 68(2); SI 1986/1316); prospectively repealed by Gas Act 1995, ss 10(1), 17(5), Sch 3, para 8, Sch 6[1]
14A	Inserted by Competition and Service (Utilities) Act 1992, s 16 (qv); prospectively repealed by Gas Act 1995, ss 10(1), 17(5), Sch 3, para 9, Sch 6[1]
15	23 Aug 1986 (s 68(2); SI 1986/1316); prospectively repealed by Gas Act 1995, ss 9(3), 17(5), Sch 6[1]
15A	Prospectively inserted by Competition and Service (Utilities) Act 1992, s 17[2]

Gas Act 1986 (c 44)—*cont*

s 15B	Inserted by Competition and Service (Utilities) Act 1992, s 15 (qv); prospectively repealed by Gas Act 1995, ss 10(1), 17(5), Sch 3, para 11, Sch 6[1]
16, 17	23 Aug 1986 (s 68(2); SI 1986/1316); prospectively substituted by Gas Act 1995, s 10(1), Sch 3, paras 12, 13, subject in the case of s 17 to savings and transitional provisions (see 1995 Act, s 17(1), Sch 5, Pt II, para 22)[1]
18	23 Aug 1986 (s 68(2); SI 1986/1316)
18A	Prospectively inserted by Gas Act 1995, s 10(1), Sch 3, para 15[1]
19	23 Aug 1986 (s 68(2); SI 1986/1316); prospectively substituted by Gas Act 1995, s 10(1), Sch 3, para 16[1]
20	23 Aug 1986 (s 68(2); SI 1986/1316); prospectively repealed by Gas Act 1995, ss 10(1), 17(5), Sch 3, para 17, Sch 6[1]
21, 22	23 Aug 1986 (s 68(2); SI 1986/1316)
22A	Prospectively inserted by Gas Act 1995, s 10(1), Sch 3, para 20[1]
23	23 Aug 1986 (s 68(2); SI 1986/1316); prospectively substituted by Gas Act 1995, s 10(1), Sch 3, para 21[1]
24–26	23 Aug 1986 (s 68(2); SI 1986/1316)
27	23 Aug 1986 (s 68(2); SI 1986/1316); prospectively substituted by Gas Act 1995, s 10(1), Sch 3, para 25[1]
27A	Prospectively inserted by Gas Act 1995, s 10(1), Sch 3, para 26[1]
28–32	23 Aug 1986 (s 68(2); SI 1986/1316)
32A	Inserted by Competition and Service (Utilities) Act 1992, s 18 (qv)
33	23 Aug 1986 (s 68(2); SI 1986/1316)
33A, 33B	Inserted by Competition and Service (Utilities) Act 1992, s 11 (qv); prospectively repealed as from end of period of four years beginning with the appointed day, or two years after an order is made by the Secretary of State, by Gas Act 1995, s 10(2)–(5)[1]
33BB	Prospectively inserted by Gas Act 1995, s 10(1), Sch 3, para 36, subject to savings and transitional provisions (see 1995 Act, s 17(1), Sch 5, Pt II, para 21); prospectively repealed as from end of period of four years beginning with the appointed day, or two years after an order is made by the Secretary of State, by Gas Act 1995, s 10(2)–(5)[1]
33C	Inserted by Competition and Service (Utilities) Act 1992, s 12 (qv); prospectively repealed as from end of period of four years beginning with the appointed day, or two years after an order is made by the Secretary of State, by Gas Act 1995, s 10(2)–(5)[1]
33D	Inserted by Competition and Service (Utilities) Act 1992, s 13 (qv); prospectively repealed as from end of period of four years beginning with the appointed day, or two years after an order is made by the Secretary of State, by Gas Act 1995, s 10(2)–(5)[1]

Gas Act 1986 (c 44)—*cont*

s 33E	Inserted by Competition and Service (Utilities) Act 1992, s 14 (qv); prospectively repealed as from end of period of four years beginning with the appointed day, or two years after an order is made by the Secretary of State, by Gas Act 1995, s 10(2)–(5)[1]
34–36	23 Aug 1986 (s 68(2); SI 1986/1316)
36A, 36B	Prospectively inserted by Gas Act 1995, s 10(1), Sch 3, paras 43, 44[1]
37	23 Aug 1986 (s 68(2); SI 1986/1316); prospectively substituted by Gas Act 1995, s 10(1), Sch 3, para 45[1]
38	23 Aug 1986 (s 68(2); SI 1986/1316)
38A	Prospectively inserted by Gas Act 1995, s 10(1), Sch 3, para 47[1]
39–48	23 Aug 1986 (s 68(2); SI 1986/1316)
49–57	24 Aug 1986 (s 68(3); SI 1986/1318)
58	Repealed
59–61	24 Aug 1986 (s 68(3); SI 1986/1318)
62	14 Nov 1986 (SI 1986/1809)
63	23 Aug 1986 (SI 1986/1315); prospectively repealed by Gas Act 1995, ss 11(6), 17(5), Sch 6[1]
64	23 Aug 1986 (SI 1986/1315)
65	18 Aug 1986 (SI 1986/1315)
66	23 Aug 1986 (s 68(2); SI 1986/1316)
67(1), (2)	23 Aug 1986 (s 68(2); SI 1986/1316)
(3)	See Sch 8 below
(4)	See Sch 9 below
68	18 Aug 1986 (SI 1986/1315)
Sch 1	18 Aug 1986 (SI 1986/1315)
2	23 Aug 1986 (SI 1986/1315)
2A	Prospectively inserted by Gas Act 1995, s 3(2), Sch 1[1]
2B	Prospectively inserted by Gas Act 1995, s 9(2), Sch 2[1]
3, 4	23 Aug 1986 (s 68(2); SI 1986/1316)
5	23 Aug 1986 (s 68(2); SI 1986/1316); prospectively repealed by Gas Act 1995, ss 9(3), 17(5), Sch 6[1]
6	24 Aug 1986 (s 68(3); SI 1986/1318)
7	23 Aug 1986 (s 68(2); SI 1986/1316)
8, Pt I	23 Aug 1986 (s 68(3); SI 1986/1316)
II	24 Aug 1986 (s 68(3); SI 1986/1318)
9, Pt I	23 Aug 1986 (s 68(2); SI 1986/1316)
II	24 Aug 1986 (s 68(3); SI 1986/1318)
III	28 Feb 1990 (SI 1990/147)

[1] Any order made under Gas Act 1995, s 18(2), (3), bringing the prospective amendments into force will be noted to that Act in the service to this work

[2] Any order made under Competition and Service (Utilities) Act 1992, s 56(2), bringing the prospective insertion into force will be noted to that Act in the service to this work

Health Service Joint Consultative Committee (Access to Information) Act 1986 (c 24)

RA: 26 Jun 1986

Commencement provisions: s 4(2)

26 Aug 1986 (s 4(2))

Highways (Amendment) Act 1986 (c 13)

RA: 2 May 1986

Commencement provisions: s 2(2)

2 Jul 1986 (s 2(2))

Horticultural Produce Act 1986 (c 20)

RA: 26 Jun 1986

Commencement provisions: s 7(3)

26 Aug 1986 (s 7(3))

Housing and Planning Act 1986 (c 63)

RA: 7 Nov 1986

Commencement provisions: s 57(1), (2); Housing and Planning Act 1986 (Commencement No 1) Order 1986, SI 1986/2262; Housing and Planning Act 1986 (Commencement No 2) Order 1987, SI 1987/178 (revoked); Housing and Planning Act 1986 (Commencement No 3) Order 1987, SI 1987/304; Housing and Planning Act 1986 (Commencement No 4) Order 1987, SI 1987/348; Housing and Planning Act 1986 (Commencement No 5) Order 1987, SI 1987/754; Housing and Planning Act 1986 (Commencement No 6) Order 1987, SI 1987/1554 (revoking); Housing and Planning Act 1986 (Commencement No 7) (Scotland) Order 1987, SI 1987/1607; Housing and Planning Act 1986 (Commencement No 8) Order 1987, SI 1987/1759; Housing and Planning Act 1986 (Commencement No 9) Order 1987, SI 1987/1939; Housing and Planning Act 1986 (Commencement No 10) Order 1987, SI 1987/2277; Housing and Planning Act 1986 (Commencement No 11) Order 1988, SI 1988/283; Housing and Planning Act 1986 (Commencement No 12) Order 1988, SI 1988/1787; Housing and Planning Act 1986 (Commencement No 13) Order 1989, SI 1989/430; Housing and Planning Act 1986 (Commencement No 14) Order 1990, SI 1990/511; Housing and Planning Act 1986 (Commencement No 15) Order 1990, SI 1990/614; Housing and Planning Act 1986 (Commencement No 16) Order 1990, SI 1990/797 (bringing into force enabling provision in relation to Sch 11, paras 39, 40 only); Housing and Planning Act 1986 (Commencement No 17 and Transitional Provisions) Order 1992, SI 1992/1753; Housing and Planning Act 1986 (Commencement No 18 and Transitional Provisions) (Scotland) Order 1993, SI 1993/273

s 1	Repealed
2	7 Jan 1987 (SI 1986/2262)
3	Repealed
4	7 Jan 1987 (SI 1986/2262)

Housing and Planning Act 1986 (c 63)—*cont*

s 5	13 Jul 1992 (SI 1992/1753)
6	11 Mar 1988 (SI 1988/283)
7	Repealed
8	5 Apr 1989 (SI 1989/430)
9	13 May 1987 (SI 1987/754)
10, 11	7 Jan 1987 (SI 1986/2262)
12	Repealed
13, 14	7 Jan 1987 (SI 1986/2262)
15	17 Feb 1988 (SI 1987/2277); prospectively repealed by Local Government and Housing Act 1989, s 194, Sch 12, Pt II[1]
16, 17	7 Jan 1987 (SI 1986/2262)
18	See Sch 4 below
19	Repealed
20	7 Jan 1987 (SI 1986/2262); prospectively repealed by Local Government and Housing Act 1989, s 194, Sch 12, Pt II[1]
21	7 Nov 1986 (s 57(1))
22, 23	7 Jan 1987 (SI 1986/2262)
24(1), (2)	See Sch 5 below (note sub-s (1)(j) came into force on 7 Nov 1986) (s 57(1))
(3)	See Sch 12, Pt I below
25	Repealed
26	1 Oct 1987 (SI 1987/1607)
27	Substituted by Leasehold Reform, Housing and Urban Development Act 1993, s 174 (qv)
28, 29	7 Jan 1987 (SI 1986/2262)
30–34	Repealed
35, 36	18 Feb 1993 (so far as confers power or imposes duty on Secretary of State to make regulations, or makes provision with respect to exercise of any such power or duty) (SI 1993/273)
	1 May 1993 (otherwise) (subject to transitional provisions) (SI 1993/273)
37	See Sch 7, Pt II below
38	18 Feb 1993 (so far as confers power or imposes duty on Secretary of State to make regulations, or makes provision with respect to exercise of any such power or duty) (SI 1993/273)
	1 May 1993 (otherwise) (SI 1993/273)
39	11 Dec 1987 (SI 1987/1939)
40	1 Apr 1987 (SI 1987/348)
41	Repealed
42	17 Nov 1988 (SI 1988/1787)
43	31 Mar 1990 (SI 1990/614)
44–46	Repealed
47, 48	7 Jan 1987 (SI 1986/2262)
49(1)	See Sch 11, Pt I below
(2)	See Sch 12, Pt III below
50, 51	1 Oct 1987 (SI 1987/1607)
52	7 Nov 1986 (s 57(1))
53(1)	See Sch 11, Pt II below
(2)	See Sch 12, Pt IV below
54, 55	7 Jan 1987 (SI 1986/2262)
56–59	7 Nov 1986 (s 57(1))
Sch 1	11 Mar 1988 (SI 1988/283)

Housing and Planning Act 1986 (c 63)—*cont*

Sch 2	5 Apr 1989 (SI 1989/430)
3	17 Feb 1988 (SI 1988/2277); prospectively repealed by Local Government and Housing Act 1989, s 194, Sch 12, Pt II[1]
4, para 1–9	11 Dec 1987 (SI 1987/1939)
10	Repealed
11	11 Dec 1987 (SI 1987/1939)
5, para 1–4	7 Jan 1987 (SI 1986/2262)
5	Repealed
6, 7	7 Jan 1987 (SI 1986/2262)
8	Repealed
9	17 Feb 1988 (SI 1987/2277)
10–13	7 Nov 1986 (s 57(1))
14	Repealed
15	7 Jan 1987 (SI 1986/2262)
16	*Not in force*
17	Repealed
18, 19	17 Aug 1992 (SI 1992/1753)
20	Repealed
21–26	7 Jan 1987 (SI 1986/2262)
27	17 Aug 1992 (so far as relates to definitions 'consent' and 'management agreement and manager') (SI 1992/1753)
	Not in force (otherwise)
28	7 Jan 1987 (SI 1986/2262)
29	17 Aug 1992 (subject to transitional provisions) (SI 1992/1753)
30	7 Jan 1987 (SI 1986/2262)
31	17 Aug 1992 (SI 1992/1753)
32, 33	7 Jan 1987 (SI 1986/2262)
34–38	17 Aug 1992 (subject to transitional provisions) (SI 1992/1753)
39	7 Jan 1987 (SI 1986/2262)
40	17 Aug 1992 (subject to transitional provisions) (SI 1992/1753)
41, 42	7 Jan 1987 (SI 1986/2262)
6, Pt I, II	Repealed
III, IV	1 Oct 1987 (SI 1987/1607)
7, Pt I	Repealed
II, para 1–3	1 May 1993 (SI 1993/273)
4	18 Feb 1993 (SI 1993/273)
5–8	1 May 1993 (SI 1993/273)
8	11 Dec 1987 (SI 1987/1939)
9, Pt I, para 1–5	Repealed
6	1 Apr 1987 (SI 1987/348)
7–12	Repealed
II	1 Oct 1987 (SI 1987/1607)
10	Repealed
11, Pt I, para 1–24	Repealed
25	7 Jan 1987 (SI 1986/2262
26, 27	Repealed
II, para 28–38	7 Jan 1987 (SI 1986/2262)
39, 40	31 Mar 1990 (SI 1990/511)
41–56	7 Jan 1987 (SI 1986/2262)
57, 58	*Not in force*
59–62	7 Jan 1987 (SI 1986/2262)

Housing and Planning Act 1986 (c 63)—*cont*

Sch 12, Pt I	7 Nov 1986 (repeals in Housing (Consequential Provisions) Act 1985 specified in first part of Sch 12, Pt I) (s 57(1))
	7 Jan 1987 (repeals of or in Housing Rents and Subsidies (Scotland) Act 1975; Rent Act 1977, s 70; Housing Act 1980, s 56; New Towns Act 1981; Housing Act 1985, ss 30, 46, 127, Schs 4, 6; Housing (Consequential Provisions) Act 1985, Sch 2, paras 27, 35(3), 45(2)) (SI 1986/2262)
	11 Dec 1987 (repeals of or in Housing Act 1980, s 140; Local Government Planning and Land Act 1980, s 156(3); Local Government Act 1985, Sch 13, para 14(d), Sch 14, para 58(e)) (SI 1987/1939)
	Not in force (otherwise)
II	11 Dec 1987 (SI 1987/1939)
III	7 Jan 1987 (repeals of or in Electric Lighting (Clauses) Act 1899; Electricity (Supply) Act 1926; Requisitioned Land and War Works Act 1945; Town and Country Planning Act 1947; Electricity Act 1947; Requisitioned Land and War Works Act 1948; Electricity Act 1957; Town and Country Planning Act 1971, ss 29A, B, 66–86, 88B, 105, 147, 151, 165, 169, 180, 185, 191, 237, 250–252, 260, 287(4), (5), (7), 290, Schs 12, 13, 21, 24; Town and Country Planning (Amendment) Act 1972; Local Government Act 1972, s 182; Local Government Act 1974; Town and Country Amenities Act 1974, s 3; Control of Office Development Act 1977; Local Government, Planning and Land Act 1980 (except s 88); Industrial Development Act 1982; Local Government Act 1985, s 3) (SI 1986/2262)
	1 Apr 1987 (repeals of or in Town and Country Planning Act 1971, s 55(4); Town and Country Amenities Act 1974, s 5; National Heritage Act 1983; Local Government Act 1985, Sch 2, para 1(8)) (SI 1987/348)
	2 Nov 1987 (repeals of or in Local Government Act 1972, s 183(2), Sch 16, paras 1–3; Local Government, Planning and Land Act 1980, s 88; Local Government (Miscellaneous Provisions) Act 1982, Sch 6, para 7(b)) (SI 1987/1759)
	17 Nov 1988 (repeals of or in Public Expenditure and Receipts Act 1968; Local Government Act 1972, s 250(4); Land Drainage Act 1976; Road Traffic Regulation Act 1984) (SI 1988/1787)
	31 Mar 1990 (repeal in Acquisition of Land Act 1981, Sch 4, para 1) (SI 1990/614)
	Not in force (otherwise)
IV	7 Jan 1987 (repeals of or in Town and Country Planning (Scotland) Act 1972, ss 29, 63, 64–83, 85, 136, 140, 154, 164, 174, 180, 226, 231, 233, 237–239, 247, 273 (4), (5), (7), (8), 275, Schs 19, 22; Local Government Planning and Land Act

Housing and Planning Act 1986 (c 63)—*cont*

Sch 12, Pt IV—*cont*	1980; Industrial Development Act 1982) (SI 1986/2262)
	Not in force (otherwise)

[1] Any order made under Local Government and Housing Act 1989, s 195(2), bringing the prospective repeal into force will be noted to that Act in the service to this work

Housing (Scotland) Act 1986 (c 65)

RA: 7 Nov 1986

Commencement provisions: s 26(2); Housing (Scotland) Act 1986 (Commencement) Order 1986, SI 1986/2137

s 1–12	Repealed
13	7 Jan 1987 (SI 1986/2137)
14–16	Repealed
17	7 Jan 1987 (SI 1986/2137)
18	Repealed
19, 20	7 Jan 1987 (SI 1986/2137)
21	Repealed
22–25	7 Jan 1987 (SI 1986/2137)
26	7 Nov 1986 (RA)
Sch 1	Repealed
2, para 1	7 Jan 1987 (SI 1986/2137)
2	Repealed
3, 4	7 Jan 1987 (SI 1986/2137)
3	7 Jan 1987 (SI 1986/2137)

Incest and Related Offences (Scotland) Act 1986 (c 36)

RA: 18 Jul 1986

Commencement provisions: s 3(2); Incest and Related Offences (Scotland) Act 1986 (Commencement) Order 1986, SI 1986/1803

1 Nov 1986 (SI 1986/1803)

Industrial Training Act 1986 (c 15)

RA: 20 May 1986

Commencement provisions: s 2(2)

20 Jul 1986 (s 2(2))

Insolvency Act 1986 (c 45)

RA: 25 Jul 1986

Commencement provisions: s 443; Insolvency Act 1985 (Commencement No 5) Order 1986, SI 1986/1924

29 Dec 1986 (s 443; SI 1986/1924)

Land Registration Act 1986 (c 26)

RA: 26 Jun 1986

Commencement provisions: s 6(4); Land Registration Act 1986 (Commencement) Order 1986, SI 1986/2117

1 Jan 1987 (SI 1986/2117)

Latent Damage Act 1986 (c 37)

RA: 18 Jul 1986

Commencement provisions: s 5(3)

18 Sep 1986 (s 5(3))

Law Reform (Parent and Child) (Scotland) Act 1986 (c 9)

RA: 26 Mar 1986

Commencement provisions: s 11(2); Law Reform (Parent and Child) (Scotland) Act 1986 (Commencement) Order 1986, SI 1986/1983

8 Dec 1986 (SI 1986/1983)

Legal Aid (Scotland) Act 1986 (c 47)

RA: 25 Jul 1986

Commencement provisions: s 46(2); Legal Aid (Scotland) Act 1986 (Commencement No 1) Order 1986, SI 1986/1617; Legal Aid (Scotland) Act 1986 (Commencement No 2) Order 1987, SI 1987/289; Legal Aid (Scotland) Act 1986 (Commencement No 3) Order 1992, SI 1992/1226

s 1(1)	1 Oct 1986 (SI 1986/1617)
(2)	1 Apr 1987 (SI 1987/289)
(3)–(6)	1 Oct 1986 (SI 1986/1617)
2(1)	1 Apr 1987 (SI 1987/289)
(2), (3)	1 Oct 1986 (SI 1986/1617)
3(1), (2)	1 Oct 1986 (SI 1986/1617)
(3)	1 Apr 1987 (SI 1987/289)
(4)–(6)	1 Oct 1986 (SI 1986/1617)
4–25	1 Apr 1987 (SI 1987/289)
26–28	*Not in force*
29	1 Apr 1987 (SI 1987/289); prospectively substituted by Children (Scotland) Act 1995, s 92[1]
30	1 Jul 1992 (SI 1992/1226)
31–39	1 Apr 1987 (SI 1987/289)
40(1)(a)	1 Apr 1987 (SI 1987/289)
(b)	1 Oct 1986 (SI 1986/1617)
(2)(a)	1 Apr 1987 (SI 1987/289)
(b)	1 Oct 1986 (SI 1986/1617)
(3), (4)	1 Apr 1987 (SI 1987/289)
41	1 Oct 1986 (SI 1986/1617)
42, 43	1 Apr 1987 (SI 1987/289)

Legal Aid (Scotland) Act 1986 (c 47)—*cont*

s 43A	Inserted by Law Reform (Miscellaneous Provisions) (Scotland) Act 1990, s 38 (qv)
44	1 Apr 1987 (SI 1987/289)
45(1)	See Sch 3 below
(2), (3)	1 Apr 1987 (SI 1987/289)
46	25 Jul 1986 (RA)
Sch 1	1 Oct 1986 (SI 1986/1617)
2	1 Apr 1987 (SI 1987/289)
3, para 1, 2	1 Apr 1987 (SI 1987/289)
3, 4	1 Oct 1986 (SI 1986/1617)
5–9	1 Apr 1987 (SI 1987/289)
4, 5	1 Apr 1987 (SI 1987/289)

[1] Any order made under Children (Scotland) Act 1995, s 105, bringing the prospective substitution into force will be noted to that Act in the service to this work

Local Government Act 1986 (c 10)

RA: 26 Mar 1986

Commencement provisions: s 12(2); Local Government Act 1986 (Commencement) Order 1987, SI 1987/2003

s 1	26 Mar 1986 (s 12(2)); repealed by Local Government Finance Act 1988, s 149, Sch 13, Pt I (qv), with effect for financial years beginning in or after 1990
2	1 Apr 1986 (s 12(2))
2A	Inserted by Local Government Act 1988, s 28 (qv)
3, 4	1 Apr 1986 (s 12(2))
5	1 Apr 1988 (SI 1987/2003)
6	1 Apr 1986 (s 12(2))
7	26 Mar 1986 (s 12(2))
8	Repealed
9, 10	26 Mar 1986 (s 12(2))
11	Repealed
12	26 Mar 1986 (s 12(2))

Marriage (Prohibited Degrees of Relationship) Act 1986 (c 16)

RA: 20 May 1986

Commencement provisions: s 6(5); Marriage (Prohibited Degrees of Relationship) Act 1986 (Commencement) Order 1986, SI 1986/1343

1 Nov 1986 (SI 1986/1343)

Marriage (Wales) Act 1986 (c 7)

RA: 18 Mar 1986

18 Mar 1986 (RA)

Museum of London Act 1986 (c 8)

RA: 26 Mar 1986

Commencement provisions: s 7(2)

1 Apr 1986 (RA)

National Health Service (Amendment) Act 1986 (c 66)

RA: 7 Nov 1986

Commencement provisions: s 8(4), (5); National Health Service (Amendment) Act 1986 (Commencement No 1) Order 1987, SI 1987/399

s 1, 2	Repealed
3	1 Apr 1987 (SI 1987/399)
4	7 Nov 1986 (RA)
5	7 Nov 1986 (except so far as inserts National Health Service (Scotland) Act 1978, s 13B) (RA)
	Not in force (exception noted above)
6–8	7 Nov 1986 (RA)

Outer Space Act 1986 (c 38)

RA: 18 Jul 1986

Commencement provisions: s 15(2); Outer Space Act 1986 (Commencement) Order 1989, SI 1989/1097

31 Jul 1989 (SI 1989/1097)

Parliamentary Constituencies Act 1986 (c 56)

RA: 7 Nov 1986

Commencement provisions: s 9(2)

7 Feb 1986 (s 9(2))

Patents, Designs and Marks Act 1986 (c 39)

RA: 18 Jul 1986

Commencement provisions: s 4(6), (7); Patents, Designs and Marks Act 1986 (Commencement No 1) Order 1986, SI 1986/1274; Patents, Designs and Marks Act 1986 (Commencement No 2) Order 1988, SI 1988/1824

s 1	See Sch 1 below
2	Repealed
3	See Sch 3 below
4(1)–(3)	18 Jul 1986 (RA)
(4)	Repealed
(5)–(7)	18 Jul 1986 (RA)
Sch 1, para 1, 2	Repealed

Patents, Designs and Marks Act 1986 (c 39)—*cont*

Sch 1, para 3, 4	1 Jan 1989 (SI 1988/1824)
2	Repealed
3, Pt I	1 Oct 1986 (repeals in Trade Marks Act 1938) (SI 1986/1274)
	1 Jan 1989 (repeals of Registered Designs Act 1949, s 24; Patents Act 1977, s 35) (SI 1988/1824)
II	1 Oct 1986 (s 4(7))

Patronage (Benefices) Measure 1986 (No 3)

RA: 18 Jul 1986

Commencement provisions: s 42(3)

The provisions of this Measure were brought into force on the following dates by an instrument made by the Archbishops of Canterbury and York and dated 31 Dec 1986 (made under s 42(3))

s 1, 2	1 Oct 1987
3–5	1 Jan 1989
6	1 Oct 1987
7–25	1 Jan 1989
26, 27	1 Jan 1987
28–34	1 Jan 1989
35(1)–(3)	1 Oct 1987
(4)–(9)	1 Jan 1989
36, 37	1 Oct 1987
38, 39	1 Jan 1987
40	1 Oct 1987
41	1 Jan 1989
42	1 Jan 1987
Sch 1	1 Oct 1987
2	1 Jan 1989
3	1 Jan 1987
4	1 Jan 1989
5	1 Jan 1987 (repeal of Benefices (Diocesan Boards of Patronage) Measure 1932)
	1 Jan 1989 (otherwise)

Prevention of Oil Pollution Act 1986 (c 6)

Whole Act repealed

Protection of Children (Tobacco) Act 1986 (c 34)

RA: 8 Jul 1986

Commencement provisions: s 3(3)

8 Oct 1986 (s 3(3))

Protection of Military Remains Act 1986 (c 35)

RA: 8 Jul 1986

Commencement provisions: s 10(2)

8 Sep 1986 (s 10(2))

Public Order Act 1986 (c 64)

RA: 7 Nov 1986

Commencement provisions: s 41(1); Public Order Act 1986 (Commencement No 1) Order 1986, SI 1986/2041; Public Order Act 1986 (Commencement No 2) Order 1987, SI 1987/198; Public Order Act 1986 (Commencement No 3) Order 1987, SI 1987/852

s 1–4	1 Apr 1987 (SI 1987/198)
4A	Inserted by Criminal Justice and Public Order Act 1994, s 154 (qv)
5–10	1 Apr 1987 (SI 1987/198)
11	1 Jan 1987 (SI 1986/2041)
12–14	1 Apr 1987 (SI 1987/198)
14A, 14B	Inserted by Criminal Justice and Public Order Act 1994, s 70 (qv)
14C	Inserted by Criminal Justice and Public Order Act 1994, s 71 (qv)
15	1 Apr 1987 (SI 1987/198)
16	1 Jan 1987 (SI 1986/2041)
17–29	1 Apr 1987 (SI 1987/198)
30–37	1 Aug 1987 (SI 1987/852); repealed (with savings) by Football Spectators Act 1989, s 27(5), as from the day to be appointed by order made under s 27(2) thereof for the commencement of s 2 of that Act; any order so made will be noted to that Act in the service to this work
38	1 Jan 1987 (SI 1986/2041)
39	Repealed
40(1)	See Sch 1 below
(2)	See Sch 2 below
(3)	See Sch 3 below
(4), (5)	1 Apr 1987 (SI 1987/198)
41–43	1 Jan 1987 (SI 1986/2041)
Sch 1	1 Jan 1987 (SI 1986/2041)
2, para 1	Repealed
2	1 Apr 1987 (SI 1987/198)
3(1), (2)	1 Jan 1987 (SI 1986/2041)
(3)–(6)	1 Apr 1987 (SI 1987/198)
4	1 Apr 1987 (SI 1987/198)
5, 6	Repealed
7	1 Apr 1987 (SI 1987/198)
3	1 Jan 1987 (repeals in Erith Tramways and Improvement Act 1903; Middlesex County Council Act 1944; County of South Glamorgan Act 1976; County of Merseyside Act 1980; West Midlands County Council Act 1980; Cheshire County Council Act 1980; Isle of Wight Act

Public Order Act 1986 (c 64)—*cont*

Sch 3—*cont*	1980; Greater Manchester Act 1981; East Sussex Act 1981; Civic Government (Scotland) Act 1982, s 62; Sporting Events (Control of Alcohol etc) Act 1985) (SI 1986/2041)
	1 Apr 1987 (otherwise) (SI 1987/198)

Public Trustee and Administration of Funds Act 1986 (c 57)

RA: 7 Nov 1986

Commencement provisions: s 6(2); Public Trustee and Administration of Funds Act 1986 Commencement Order 1986, SI 1986/2261

2 Jan 1987 (SI 1986/2261)

Rate Support Grants Act 1986 (c 54)

RA: 21 Oct 1986

21 Oct 1986 (RA)

Road Traffic Regulation (Parking) Act 1986 (c 27)

RA: 8 Jul 1986

Commencement provisions: s 3(3)

8 Sep 1986 (s 3(3))

Safety at Sea Act 1986 (c 23)

Whole Act repealed

Salmon Act 1986 (c 62)

RA: 7 Nov 1986

Commencement provisions: s 43(1), (2); Salmon Act 1986 (Commencement and Transitional Provisions) Order 1992, SI 1992/1973

s 1–3	7 Jan 1987 (s 43(1))
4	Repealed
5–20	7 Jan 1987 (s 43(1))
21	1 Jan 1993 (subject to transitional provisions) (SI 1992/1973)
22–43	7 Jan 1987 (s 43(1))
Sch 1–5	7 Jan 1987 (s 43(1))

Sex Discrimination Act 1986 (c 59)

RA: 7 Nov 1986

Commencement provisions: s 10(2)–(4); Sex Discrimination Act (Commencement) Order 1986, SI 1986/2313; Sex Discrimination Act 1986 (Commencement No 2) Order 1988, SI 1988/99

s 1	7 Feb 1987 (s 10(2))
2, 3	7 Nov 1987 (s 10(4))
4, 5	7 Nov 1986 (RA)
6(1)–(4)	7 Feb 1987 (s 10(2))
(4A)–(4D)	Inserted by Trade Union Reform and Employment Rights Act 1993, s 32 (qv)
(5)–(7)	7 Feb 1987 (s 10(2))
7	Repealed
8	27 Feb 1987 (SI 1986/2313)
9(1)	7 Feb 1987 (s 10(2))
(2)	7 Nov 1986 (RA)
(3)	7 Feb 1987 (s 10(2))
10	7 Nov 1986 (RA)
Schedule	
Pt I	7 Nov 1986 (RA)
II	7 Feb 1987 (s 10(2))
III	27 Feb 1987 (repeals of or in Baking Industry (Hours of Work) Act 1954; Mines and Quarries Act 1954, ss 125, 126, 128, 131; Factories Act 1961; Civil Evidence Act 1968; Health and Safety at Work etc Act 1974; Sex Discrimination Act 1975; Companies Consolidation (Consequential Provisions) Act 1985) (SI 1986/2313)
	26 Feb 1988 (repeals in Hours of Employment (Conventions) Act 1936; Mines and Quarries Act 1954, Sch 4) (SI 1988/99)

Social Security Act 1986 (c 50)

RA: 25 Jul 1986

Commencement provisions: s 88; Social Security Act 1986 (Commencement No 1) Order 1986, SI 1986/1609; Social Security Act 1986 (Commencement No 2) Order 1986, SI 1986/1719; Social Security Act (Commencement No 3) Order 1986, SI 1986/1958; Social Security Act 1986 (Commencement No 4) Order 1986, SI 1986/1959 (as amended by SI 1987/354); Social Security Act 1986 (Commencement No 5) Order 1987, SI 1987/354 (also amending SI 1986/1959); Social Security Act 1986 (Commencement No 6) Order 1987, SI 1987/543; Social Security Act 1986 (Commencement No 7) Order 1987, SI 1987/1096 (as amended by SI 1987/1853); Social Security Act 1986 (Commencement No 8) Order 1987, SI 1987/1853 (also amending SI 1987/1096); Social Security Act 1986 (Commencement No 9) Order 1988, SI 1988/567 (also amending SI 1987/1096)

s 1–8	Repealed
9(1)–(7)	Repealed
(8), (9)	6 Apr 1988 (SI 1987/543)
10–29	Repealed
30(1)–(9)	Repealed

Social Security Act 1986 (c 50)—*cont*

s 30(10)	25 Jul 1986 (s 88(5))
(11)	Repealed
31–36	Repealed
37(1)	Repealed
(2)	25 Jul 1986 (s 88(5))
38	Repealed
39	See Sch 3 below
40–53	Repealed
54(1)	6 Apr 1987 (SI 1986/1958)
(2)	Repealed
55	Repealed
56, 57	6 Apr 1987 (SI 1986/1959)
58–69	Repealed
70(1)	Repealed
(2)	25 Jul 1986 (s 88(5))
71–75	Repealed
76	25 Jul 1986 (s 88(5))
77	11 Apr 1988 (SI 1987/1853)
78–81	Repealed
82	6 Apr 1987 (SI 1987/1853)
83(1)	25 Jul 1986 (s 88(5))
(2), (3)	Repealed
(4)	Substituted by Social Security Act 1990, s 21(1), Sch 6, para 8(9) (qv)
(5), (6)	25 Jul 1986 (s 88(5))
84(1)	25 Jul 1986 (s 88(5))
(2), (3)	Repealed
(4)	25 Jul 1986 (s 88(5))
85(1), (2)	25 Jul 1986 (s 88(5))
(3), (4)	Repealed
(5), (6)	25 Jul 1986 (s 88(5))
(7)–(12)	Repealed
(13)	25 Jul 1986 (s 88(5))
86(1)	See Sch 10 below
(2)	See Sch 11 below
87–90	25 Jul 1986 (s 88(5))
Sch 1, 2	Repealed
3, para 1–16	Repealed
17	1 Oct 1986 (SI 1986/1609)
4–8	Repealed
9	6 Apr 1987 (SI 1986/1958)
10, para 1	6 Apr 1987 (SI 1987/354)
2–10	Repealed
11	6 Apr 1987 (SI 1987/354)
12–31	Repealed
32, 33	11 Apr 1988 (SI 1987/1853)
34	Repealed
35, 36	11 Apr 1988 (SI 1987/1853)
37	11 Apr 1988 (SI 1987/1853); prospectively repealed by Children (Northern Ireland Consequential Amendments) Order 1995, SI 1995/756, art 15, Schedule, in accordance with Children (Northern Ireland) Order 1995, SI 1995/755 (NI 2), art 1(2), (3)
38, 39	11 Apr 1988 (SI 1987/1853)
40	Repealed

Social Security Act 1986 (c 50)—*cont*

Sch 10, para 41–43	11 Apr 1988 (SI 1987/1853)
44	1 Apr 1988 (so far as relates to housing benefit in a case where rent is payable at intervals of one month or any other interval which is not a week or a multiple thereof or in a case where payments by way of rates are not made together with payments of rent at weekly intervals or multiples thereof) (SI 1987/1853)
	4 Apr 1988 (otherwise) (SI 1987/1853)
45–48	Repealed
49	1 Apr 1988 (so far as relates to housing benefit in a case where rent is payable at intervals of one month or any other interval which is not a week or a multiple thereof or in a case where payments by way of rates are not made together with payments of rent at weekly intervals or multiples thereof) (SI 1987/1853); and 4 Apr 1988 (otherwise) (SI 1987/1853); *spent (EW)*
50	11 Apr 1988 (SI 1987/1853)
51	Repealed
52, 53	1 Apr 1988 (so far as relates to housing benefit in a case where rent is payable at intervals of one month or any other interval which is not a week or a multiple thereof or in a case where payments by way of rates are not made together with payments of rent at weekly intervals or multiples thereof) (SI 1987/1853)
	4 Apr 1988 (otherwise) (SI 1987/1853)
54	Repealed
55	11 Apr 1988 (SI 1987/1853)
56	Repealed
57	11 Apr 1988 (SI 1987/1853)
58–60	1 Apr 1988 (so far as relates to housing benefit in a case where rent is payable at intervals of one month or any other interval which is not a week or a multiple thereof or in a case where payments by way of rates are not made together with payments of rent at weekly intervals or multiples thereof) (SI 1987/1853)
	4 Apr 1988 (otherwise) (SI 1987/1853)
61	11 Apr 1988 (SI 1987/1853)
62–74	Repealed
75	6 Apr 1987 (SI 1986/1959); repealed (10 Jun 1994) by Trade Union Reform and Employment Rights Act 1993, s 51, Sch 10 (qv) (in relation only to women whose expected week of childbirth began on or after 16 Oct 1994)
76	6 Apr 1987 (SI 1986/1959)
77, 78	Repealed
79–81	6 Apr 1987 (SI 1986/1959)
82–92	Repealed
93	1 Oct 1986 (SI 1986/1609); now superseded
94(a)	25 Jul 1986 (s 88(5))
(b)	26 Jun 1987 (SI 1987/1096)
95–101	Repealed
102	26 Jun 1987 (SI 1987/1096)
103(a), (b)	Repealed

Social Security Act 1986 (c 50)—*cont*

Sch 10, para 103(c)	6 Apr 1987 (SI 1986/1959); now superseded
104–107	Repealed
108(a)	Repealed
(b)	11 Apr 1988 (except so far as substitutes words for reference in Forfeiture Act 1982, s 4(5), to Family Income Supplements Act 1970 and Supplementary Benefits Act 1976) (SI 1987/1096) 11 Apr 1988 (exception noted above) (SI 1987/1853)
11	25 Jul 1986 (repeals of or in Social Security Act 1975, ss 37, 141; Social Security Pensions Act 1975, s 52D, Sch 1A; Social Security (Miscellaneous Provisions) Act 1977, s 22(2) (reference to Social Security Act 1975, s 37(3)(b)); Social Security Act 1980, s 10; Social Security and Housing Benefits Act 1982, s 29) (s 88(5)) 1 Oct 1986 (repeals of or in Statute Law Revision (Consequential Repeals) Act 1965; Social Security Act 1975, ss 12(3), 28, 34, 37A, 57, 60, 124–126A, Schs 14, 20 (definition of 'Up-rating Order'); Social Security Pensions Act 1975, ss 22, 23; Child Benefit Act 1975, ss 5, 17(3), (4); Social Security Act 1979, s 13, Social Security Act 1980, s 1; Social Security (No 2) Act 1980, ss 1, 2; Social Security Act 1981, s 1; Social Security and Housing Benefits Act 1982, ss 7, 42; Social Security and Housing Benefits Act 1983; Social Security Act 1985, ss 15, 16, Sch 5, para 10) (SI 1986/1609) 1 Nov 1986 (repeals of or in Social Security Act 1973, s 99; Social Security Pensions Act 1975, ss 30, 32–34, 36, 37, 39, 41, 44A, 46, 49, 66, Schs 2, 4, paras 31, 32(a); Social Security Act 1985, Sch 5, paras 19, 28) (SI 1986/1719) 6 Apr 1987 (repeals of or in Supplementary Benefit Act 1966; Social Work (Scotland) Act 1968; Income and Corporation Taxes Act 1970; Family Income Supplements Act 1970, ss 8(5), (6), 12; Local Government Act 1972; Social Security Act 1973, s 92, Sch 23; National Insurance Act 1974, s 6(1) (the words 'or the Social Security and Housing Benefits Act 1982'); Social Security Act 1975, ss 13(1), 21, 32, 92, 95, 100, 104, 106, 107, 110, 114, 119(1)(2A), (5), (6), 135(2)(g), 136, 144, 145, 146(3)(c), (5), 147, 164, Sch 3, Pt I, para 7, Pt II, paras 8(3), 12, Sch 4, Pt II, Sch 8, Sch 16, para 4; Industrial Injuries and Diseases (Old Cases) Act 1975, ss 9, 10; Social Security (Consequential Provisions) Act 1975, Sch 2, paras 5, 35; Social Security Pensions Act 1975, s 19, Sch 4, para 17; Child Benefit Act 1975, ss 9–11, 24, Sch 4, paras 11, 31; Adoption Act 1976; Supplementary Benefits Act 1976, s 20(1), (2), (5)–(7); Social Security (Miscellaneous Provisions) Act 1977, s 19; Social Security Act 1979, ss 6, 8; Child Care Act 1980; Social Security Act 1980, ss 5, 14, 15, 17, 20, Sch 1, paras 9, 10, Sch 2, paras 19(a), (b), (d), 21, Sch 3, Pt II, paras 16–18;

Social Security Act 1986 (c 50)—*cont*

Sch 11—*cont*

Social Security Act 1981, Sch 1, paras 1–5; Social Security and Housing Benefits Act 1982, ss 8, 9, 11–16, 19–21, 25, 41, Schs 2, 3, Sch 4, paras 26, 38; Health and Social Services and Social Security Adjudications Act 1983, Sch 8, paras 18, 31, Sch 9; Public Health (Control of Disease) Act 1984; Health and Social Security Act 1984, Sch 4, para 12; Social Security Act 1985, s 17, Sch 4, Sch 5, paras 37, 38; Insolvency Act 1985; Bankruptcy (Scotland) Act 1985) (SI 1986/1959, as amended by SI 1987/354)

6 Apr 1987 (repeals of or in Social Security Act 1975, ss 1(1)(b), 122(4), 134(5)(b); Employment Protection Act 1975, s 40(2), (4); Supplementary Benefits Act 1976, s 26; Social Security (Miscellaneous Provisions) Act 1977, s 18(1)(c), (2)(a), (b); Employment Protection (Consolidation) Act 1978 (except ss 123(5), 127(3), 132(6)); Social Security Act 1979, ss 3(2), 12, Sch 3, para 16; Social Security Act 1985, Sch 5, para 7) (SI 1987/354)

7 Apr 1987 (repeals of or in Family Income Supplement Act 1970, s 8(3), (4); Social Security Act 1975, ss 86, 119(3), (4)(b)–(d); Social Security (Consequential Provisions) Act 1975, Sch 2, para 41; Social Security Pensions Act 1975, Sch 4, para 13; Child Benefit Act 1975, ss 7, 8 (except in relation to Social Security Act 1975, ss 82(3)), 17(5), (6), Sch 4, paras 5, 29, 33; Supplementary Benefits Act 1979, s 7, Sch 3, para 9; Social Security Act 1980, s 4, Sch 1, para 12, Sch 2, paras 11, 19(c); Social Security and Housing Benefits Act 1982; Sch 4, para 22; Health and Social Services and Social Security Adjudications Act 1983, Sch 8, para 17) (SI 1986/1959)

26 Jun 1987 (repeals of or in Attachment of Earnings Act 1971; Social Security (Consequential Provisions) Act 1975, Sch 2, para 44; Social Security and Housing Benefits Act 1982, s 45(2)(a)) (SI 1987/1096)

4 Jan 1988 (repeals of or in Social Security Act 1975, ss 146(1), 151(1), 152(8); Employment Protection (Consolidation) Act 1978, ss 123(5), 127(3)) (SI 1987/543)

1 Apr 1988 or 4 Apr 1988 (repeals of or in Social Security Act 1980, Sch 3, Pt II, para 15B; Social Security and Housing Benefits Act 1982, Pt II, ss 45(1), (2)(b), (c), (3), 47, Sch 4, paras 5, 19, 27, 28, 35(1), (2); Social Security Act 1985, ss 22, 32(2)) (SI 1987/1853)

6 Apr 1988 (repeal of or in Social Security Pensions Act 1975, s 6(2)) (SI 1987/543)

11 Apr 1988 (repeals of or in Pensioners and Family Income Supplement Payments Act 1972 (except s 3 and s 4 so far as it refers to expenses attributable to s 3); Pensioners' Payments and National Insurance Contributions Act 1972;

Social Security Act 1986 (c 50)—*cont*

Sch 11—*cont*

Pensioners' Payments and National Insurance Act 1973 (except s 7 and the Schedule); Pensioners' Payments Act 1974; Social Security Act 1975, ss 12(1)(h), (2), 13(1) (entry relating to widow's allowance), (5)(a), 25(3), 26(3), 41(2)(e), (2C), 50(2), 79–81, 82, 84(3), 88(a), 90, 101(3), Sch 3, Pt II, paras 8(2), 9, 10, Sch 4, Pt I, para 5, Pt IV, para 4, Pt V, paras 6, 11, Sch 20 (definitions of 'Relative', 'Shortterm benefit'); Industrial Injuries and Diseases (Old Cases) Act 1975, s 4(4); Social Security Pensions Act 1975, s 56K(4), Sch 4, para 51; Child Benefit Act 1975, ss 6, 8 (so far as not already in force), 15(1), Sch 4, paras 3, 4, 6, 27; Social Security (Miscellaneous Provisions) Act 1977, ss 9, 17(2), 22(2), (reference to Social Security Act 1975, s 24(2)); Pensioners' Payments Act 1977; Pensioners' Payments Act 1978; Pensioners' Payments and Social Security Act 1979; Social Security (No 2) Act 1980, s 4(2); Social Security and Housing Benefits Act 1982, s 44(1)(f), Sch 4, para 14; Health and Social Security Act 1984, ss 22, 27(2), Sch 4, paras 3, 14, Sch 5, paras 5, 6; Social Security Act 1985, ss 27, 32(2) ('section 15'), Sch 5, para 6(a)) (SI 1987/1096)

11 Apr 1988 (repeals of or in National Assistance Act 1948; Family Income Supplements Act 1970 (so far as it is not already repealed); Pensioners and Family Income Supplement Payments Act 1972 (so far as it is not already repealed); National Insurance Act 1974, s 6(1); Social Security Act 1975, ss 67(2)(b), 143(1); Supplementary Benefits Act 1976, ss 111, 13–19, 21, 24, 25, 27, 31–34, Sch 1, Sch 5, para 1(2), Sch 7, paras 1(b), (d), 3(a), 5, 19, 21, 23, 24, 31, 33, 37; Social Security (Miscellaneous Provisions) Act 1977, s 18(1); Employment Protection (Consolidation) Act 1978, s 132(6); Social Security Act 1979, Sch 3, paras 1, 2, 24–27; Social Security Act 1980, ss 7, 8(1), 9(7), 18(1), Sch 2, paras 1–10, 12–18, 22–30, Sch 3, Pt II, paras 11, 15; Social Security (No 2) Act 1980, s 6; Social Security Act 1981, s 4, Sch 1, paras 8, 9; Social Security and Housing Benefits Act 1982, ss 38, 44(1)(a), Sch 4, paras 2, 4, 23–25; Health and Social Services and Social Security Adjudications Act 1983, s 19(2), Sch 8, Pt III, Pt IV (so far as that Pt is not already repealed); Law Reform (Parent and Child) (Scotland) Act 1986) (SI 1987/1853)

11 Apr 1988 (repeals of or in Social Security Act 1975, ss 67, 68, 70–75, 117(4), (5)) (SI 1988/567)

Not in force (repeals of or in Social Security Act 1975, ss 13(5A), 50(5), 91(2), 135(6), Sch 16, para 3 and Social Security Pensions Act 1975, s 6(5), Sch 4, paras 41, 42 and Social Security (Consequential Provisions) Act 1975, Sch 3, para 18, all of which provisions have now been

Social Security Act 1986 (c 50)—*cont*

Sch 11—*cont*	repealed by Social Security (Consequential Provisions) Act 1992, s 3, Sch 1, as from 1 Jul 1992; also repeals of Social Security Act 1985, Sch 5, paras 6(b), 16, as to which see note 1 to that Act ante)

Statute Law (Repeals) Act 1986 (c 12)

RA: 2 May 1986

2 May 1986 (RA)

Wages Act 1986 (c 48)

RA: 25 Jul 1986

Commencement provisions: s 33(2)(5); Wages Act 1986 (Commencement) Order 1986, SI 1986/1998

s 1–11	1 Jan 1987 (SI 1986/1998)
12–27	Repealed (with savings in relation to ss 16, 19, 20)
28	1 Aug 1986 (s 33(5))
29	25 Jul 1986 (s 33(2))
30	1 Jan 1987 (so far as relates to Pt 1 (ss 1–11)) (SI 1986/1998)
	25 Sep 1986 (so far as relates to Pt II (ss 12–26)) (s 33(4))
31	25 Jul 1986 (s 33(2))
32(1)	See Sch 4 below
(2)	See Sch 5 below
(3)	25 Jul 1986 (s 33(2))
33	25 Jul 1986 (s 33(2))
Sch 1	1 Jan 1987 (SI 1986/1998)
2, 3	Repealed
4, para 1–3	Repealed
4	25 Sep 1986 (s 33(4))
5–8	Repealed
9, 10	1 Jan 1987 (SI 1986/1998)
11	Repealed
5, Pt I	1 Aug 1986 (s 33(3))
II	25 Sep 1986 (s 33(4))
III	1 Jan 1987 (SI 1986/1998)
6, para 1–9	Repealed
10	25 Jul 1986 (s 33(2))

1987

Abolition of Domestic Rates etc (Scotland) Act 1987 (c 47)

RA: 15 May 1987

Commencement provisions: s 35(2); Abolition of Domestic Rates etc (Scotland) Act 1987 Commencement Order 1987, SI 1987/1489

★*Whole Act repealed*, in part prospectively, by Local Government Finance Act 1992, s 117(2), Sch 14 (qv)

s 1, 2	14 Sep 1987 (SI 1987/1489)★
3A	Repealed
3B	Substituted for s 3A by Local Government and Housing Act 1989, s 141(1) (qv)★
4, 5	14 Sep 1987 (SI 1987/1489)★
6–8	14 Sep 1987 (certain purposes) (SI 1987/1489) 1 Apr 1989 (remaining purposes) (SI 1987/1489)★
9	Repealed
9A	Inserted by Local Government and Housing Act, s 143(1) (qv)★
10, 11	14 Sep 1987 (certain purposes) (SI 1987/1489) 1 Apr 1989 (remaining purposes) (SI 1987/1489)★
11A	Inserted by Local Government Finance Act 1988, s 137, Sch 12, Pt II, para 21 (qv)★
11B	Repealed
12–17	14 Sep 1987 (SI 1987/1489)★
18	1 Oct 1988 (SI 1987/1489)★
18A	Inserted by Local Government Finance Act 1988, s 137, Sch 12, Pt II, para 28 (qv)★
19, 20	1 Oct 1988 (SI 1987/1489)★
20A	Inserted by Local Government Finance Act 1988, s 137, Sch 12, Pt II, para 30 (qv)★
20B	Inserted by Local Government Finance Act 1988, s 137, Sch 12, Pt II, para 31 (qv)★
20C	Inserted by Local Government and Housing Act 1989, s 145, Sch 6, para 27 (qv)★
21–23	14 Sep 1987 (SI 1987/1489)★
23A	Inserted by Local Government and Housing Act 1989, s 144 (qv)★
24	14 Sep 1987 (SI 1987/1489); prospectively repealed by Local Government Finance Act 1988, s 149, Sch 13, Pt IV★[1,2]
25(1)	14 Sep 1987 (SI 1987/1489)★
(2), (3)	14 Sep 1987 (certain purposes) (SI 1987/1489) 1 Apr 1989 (remaining purposes) (SI 1987/1489)★
26(1)	14 Sep 1987 (SI 1987/1489)★
(2)	14 Sep 1987 (certain purposes) (SI 1987/1489) 1 Apr 1989 (remaining purposes) (SI 1987/1489)★

Abolition of Domestic Rates etc (Scotland) Act 1987 (c 47)—*cont*

s 27		14 Sep 1987 (SI 1987/1489)*
28		Repealed
29–33		14 Sep 1987 (SI 1987/1489)*
34		14 Sep 1987 (certain purposes) (SI 1987/1489) 1 Apr 1989 (certain purposes) (SI 1987/1489) 1 Apr 1994 (remaining purposes) (SI 1987/1489)*
35		14 Sep 1987 (SI 1987/1489)*
Sch *1, para	1–14	14 Sep 1987 (SI 1987/1489)*
	15	14 Sep 1987 (certain purposes) (SI 1987/1489) 1 Apr 1989 (remaining purposes) (SI 1987/1489)
	16	1 Apr 1989 (SI 1987/1489)
	17	14 Sep 1987 (certain purposes) (SI 1987/1489) 1 Apr 1989 (remaining purposes) (SI 1987/1489)
	18	1 Apr 1989 (SI 1989/1489)
	19	Repealed
	20	14 Sep 1987 (SI 1987/1489)
	21	14 Sep 1987 (certain purposes) (SI 1987/1489) 1 Apr 1989 (remaining purposes) (SI 1987/1489)
	22	14 Sep 1987 (SI 1987/1489)
	23(a)	14 Sep 1987 (certain purposes) (SI 1987/1489) 1 Apr 1989 (remaining purposes) (SI 1987/1489)
	(b)	14 Sep 1987 (SI 1987/1489)
	24	1 Apr 1989 (SI 1987/1489)
	25, 26	14 Sep 1987 (SI 1987/1489)
	27	1 Apr 1989 (SI 1987/1489)
	28	14 Sep 1987 (certain purposes) (SI 1987/1489) 1 Apr 1989 (remaining purposes) (SI 1987/1489)
	29–31	1 Apr 1989 (SI 1987/1489)
	32	14 Sep 1987 (certain purposes) (SI 1987/1489) 1 Apr 1989 (remaining purposes) (SI 1987/1489)
	33	14 Sep 1987 (SI 1987/1489)
	34–36	1 Apr 1989 (SI 1987/1489)
	37, 38	14 Sep 1987 (certain purposes) (SI 1987/1489) 1 Apr 1989 (remaining purposes) (SI 1987/1489)
	39	1 Apr 1989 (SI 1987/1489)
*1A		Inserted by Local Government Finance Act 1988, s 137, Sch 12, Pt II, para 35 (qv)
*2–4		14 Sep 1987 (SI 1987/1489)
*5, para	1	14 Sep 1987 (certain purposes) (SI 1987/1489) 1 Apr 1989 (remaining purposes) (SI 1987/1489)
	2–5	Repealed
	6–8	14 Sep 1987 (certain purposes) (SI 1987/1489) 1 Apr 1989 (remaining purposes) (SI 1987/1489)
	9, 10	Repealed
	11–13	14 Sep 1987 (certain purposes) (SI 1987/1489) 1 Apr 1989 (remaining purposes) (SI 1987/1489)
	14, 15	Repealed
	16	14 Sep 1987 (certain purposes) (SI 1987/1489) 1 Apr 1989 (remaining purposes) (SI 1987/1489)
	17–19	Repealed
	19A	Inserted by Local Government and Housing Act 1989, s 145, Sch 6, para 21 (qv)
	20	14 Sep 1987 (certain purposes) (SI 1987/1489) 1 Apr 1989 (remaining purposes) (SI 1987/1489)
	21	Repealed

Abolition of Domestic Rates etc (Scotland) Act 1987 (c 47)—*cont*

Sch ★5, para 22	14 Sep 1987 (certain purposes) (SI 1987/1489)
	1 Apr 1989 (remaining purposes) (SI 1987/1489)
23, 24	1 Apr 1989 (SI 1987/1489)
25	Repealed
26	14 Sep 1987 (certain purposes) (SI 1987/1489)
	1 Apr 1989 (remaining purposes) (SI 1987/1489)
27	1 Apr 1989 (SI 1987/1489)
28, 29	14 Sep 1987 (certain purposes) (SI 1987/1489)
	1 Apr 1989 (remaining purposes) (SI 1987/1489)
30(a)	14 Sep 1987 (certain purposes) (SI 1987/1489)
	1 Apr 1989 (remaining purposes) (SI 1987/1489)
(b), (c)	1 Apr 1989 (SI 1987/1489)
31–37	14 Sep 1987 (certain purposes) (SI 1987/1489)
	1 Apr 1989 (remaining purposes) (SI 1987/1489)
38	1 Apr 1989 (SI 1987/1489)
39–41	14 Sep 1987 (certain purposes) (SI 1987/1489)
	1 Apr 1989 (remaining purposes) (SI 1987/1489)
42–46	1 Apr 1989 (SI 1987/1489)
47–49	14 Sep 1987 (certain purposes) (SI 1987/1489)
	1 Apr 1989 (remaining purposes) (SI 1987/1489)
★6	14 Sep 1987 (certain purposes) (SI 1987/1489)
	1 Apr 1989 (certain purposes) (SI 1987/1489)
	1 Apr 1994 (remaining purposes) (SI 1987/1489)

[1] The 1 Apr 1990 date appointed for the repeal by Local Government Finance Act 1988 (Commencement) (Scotland) Order 1988, SI 1988/1456, was cancelled before it took effect by Local Government Finance Act 1988 (Commencement) (Scotland) Amendment Order 1990, SI 1990/573, and the repeal is again prospective

---

Access to Personal Files Act 1987 (c 37)

RA: 15 May 1987

15 May 1987 (RA)

Agricultural Training Board Act 1987 (c 29)

RA: 15 May 1987

Commencement provisions: s 2(2)

15 Jul 1987 (s 2(2))

AIDS (Control) Act 1987 (c 33)

RA: 15 May 1987

15 May 1987 (RA)

Animals (Scotland) Act 1987 (c 9)

RA: 9 Apr 1987

Commencement provisions: s 9(2)

9 June 1987 (s 9(2))

Appropriation Act 1987 (c 17)

Whole Act repealed

Appropriation (No 2) Act 1987 (c 50)

Whole Act repealed

Banking Act 1987 (c 22)

RA: 15 May 1987

Commencement provisions: s 110(2); Banking Act 1987 (Commencement No 1) Order 1987, SI 1987/1189; Banking Act 1987 (Commencement No 2) Order 1987, SI 1987/1664; Banking Act 1987 (Commencement No 3) Order 1988, SI 1988/502; Banking Act 1987 (Commencement No 4) Order 1988, SI 1988/644

s 1–12	1 Oct 1987 (SI 1987/1664)
12A	Inserted (1 Jun 1993) by Banking Coordination (Second Council Directive) Regulations 1992, SI 1992/3218, reg 29
13–26	1 Oct 1987 (SI 1987/1664)
26A	Inserted (1 Jun 1993) by Banking Coordination (Second Council Directive) Regulations 1992, SI 1992/3218, reg 32(1)
27–36	1 Oct 1987 (SI 1987/1664)
36A	Inserted (1 Jun 1993) by Banking Coordination (Second Council Directive) Regulations 1992, SI 1992/3218, reg 33
37	1 Oct 1987 (SI 1987/1664)
37A	Inserted (1 Jun 1993) by Banking Coordination (Second Council Directive) Regulations 1992, SI 1992/3218, reg 35
38	1 Apr 1988 (SI 1988/502)
39–58	1 Oct 1987 (SI 1987/1664)
59	Substituted (1 Jul 1995) by Credit Institutions (Protection of Depositors) Regulations 1995, SI 1995/1442, reg 31 (subject to transitional and savings provisions contained in reg 53(1), (3) thereof)
60–81	1 Oct 1987 (SI 1987/1664)
82–85	15 Jul 1987 (SI 1987/1189)
86	Substituted (1 Jun 1993) by Banking Coordination (Second Council Directive) Regulations 1992, SI 1992/3218, reg 41
87	15 Jul 1987 (SI 1987/1189)
88–90	1 Oct 1987 (SI 1987/1664)
91	15 May 1987 (s 110(2))
92–101	1 Oct 1987 (SI 1987/1664)

Banking Act 1987 (c 22)—*cont*

s 102	15 Jul 1987 (SI 1987/1189)
103–105	1 Oct 1987 (SI 1987/1664)
105A	Inserted by Companies Act 1989, s 23, Sch 10, Pt II, para 37(3) (qv)
106	15 Jul 1987 (SI 1987/1189)
107	See Sch 5 below
108(1)	See Sch 6 below
(2)	See Sch 7 below
109, 110	15 Jul 1987 (SI 1987/1189)
Sch 1–4	1 Oct 1987 (SI 1987/1664)
5, para 1–13	1 Oct 1987 (SI 1987/1664)
14	15 Jul 1987 (SI 1987/1189)
6, para 1–3	1 Oct 1987 (SI 1987/1664)
4	Repealed
5–7	1 Oct 1987 (SI 1987/1664)
8	1 Oct 1987 (SI 1987/1664); prospectively repealed by Crown Agents Act 1995, s 13(2), Sch 2, Pt I[1]
9–12	1 Oct 1987 (SI 1987/1664)
13	Repealed
14, 15	1 Oct 1987 (SI 1987/1664)
16	Repealed
17–23	1 Oct 1987 (SI 1987/1664)
24	Repealed
25	1 Oct 1987 (SI 1987/1664)
26(1)–(4)	1 Oct 1987 (SI 1987/1189)
(5)	15 Jul 1987 (SI 1987/1189)
(6)–(8)	1 Oct 1987 (SI 1987/1664)
27–28	1 Oct 1987 (SI 1987/1664)
7	15 Jul 1987 (repeals of or in Banking Act 1979, s 20; Building Societies Act 1986, s 54(4), (5); Financial Services Act 1986, Sch 13, para 4) (SI 1987/1189)
	1 Oct 1987 (otherwise, except repeal of Financial Services Act 1986, s 193) (SI 1987/1664)
	29 Apr 1988 (exception noted above) (SI 1988/644)

[1] Any order made under Crown Agents Act 1995, s 1(1), bringing the prospective repeal into force will be noted to that Act in the service to this work

Billiards (Abolition of Restrictions) Act 1987 (c 19)

Whole Act repealed

British Shipbuilders (Borrowing Powers) Act 1987 (c 52)

RA: 23 Jul 1987

23 Jul 1987 (RA)

Broadcasting Act 1987 (c 10)

Whole Act repealed

Channel Tunnel Act 1987 (c 53)

RA: 23 Jul 1987

23 Jul 1987 (RA)

Chevening Estate Act 1987 (c 20)

RA: 15 May 1987

Commencement provisions: s 5(2); Chevening Estate Act 1987 (Commencement) Order 1987, SI 1987/1254

1 Sep 1987 (SI 1987/1254)

Coal Industry Act 1987 (c 3)

RA: 5 Mar 1987

Commencement provisions: s 10(2)

s 1[2]	5 Mar 1987 (RA)
2	Repealed
3, 4	5 Mar 1987 (RA); prospectively repealed by Coal Industry Act 1994, s 67(8), Sch 11, Pt III[1]
5	5 Mar 1987 (RA)
6	5 May 1987 (s 10(2)); prospectively repealed, subject to transitional provisions, by Coal Industry Act 1994, s 67(7), (8), Sch 10, para 11, Sch 11, Pt III[1]
7, 8	5 May 1987 (s 10(2)); prospectively repealed by Coal Industry Act 1994, s 67(8), Sch 11, Pt III[1]
9	5 Mar 1987 (RA); prospectively repealed by Coal Industry Act 1994, s 67(8), Sch 11, Pt III[1]
10	5 Mar 1987 (RA)
Sch 1[2]	5 Mar 1987 (RA)
2,3	5 Mar 1987 (RA); prospectively repealed by Coal Industry Act 1994, s 67(8), Sch 11, Pt III[1]

[1] Orders made under Coal Industry Act 1994 bringing these prospective repeals into force will be noted to that Act in the service to this work

[2] S 1 and Sch 1, so far as previously unrepealed and except insofar as amend Housing Act 1985, are prospectively repealed by Coal Industry Act 1994, s 67(8), Sch 11, Pt IV; any order bringing these prospective repeals into force will be noted to that Act in the service to this work

---

Consolidated Fund Act 1987 (c 8)

Whole Act repealed

Consolidated Fund (No 2) Act 1987 (c 54)

Whole Act repealed

Consolidated Fund (No 3) Act 1987 (c 55)

Whole Act repealed

Consumer Protection Act 1987 (c 43)

RA: 15 May 1987

Commencement provisions: s 50(2), (4), (5); Consumer Protection Act 1987 (Commencement No 1) Order 1987, SI 1987/1680; Consumer Protection Act 1987 (Commencement No 2) Order 1988, SI 1988/2041; Consumer Protection Act 1987 (Commencement No 3) Order 1988, SI 1988/2076

s 1–9	1 Mar 1988 (SI 1987/1680)
10–19	1 Oct 1987 (SI 1987/1680)
20–26	1 Mar 1989 (subject to transitional provisions in relation to s 20(1), (2)) (SI 1988/2076)
27–35	1 Oct 1987 (for purposes of or in relation to Pt II) (SI 1987/1680)
	1 Mar 1989 (otherwise) (SI 1988/2076)
36	1 Mar 1988 (SI 1987/1680)
37–40	1 Oct 1987 (for purposes of or in relation to Pt II) (SI 1987/1680)
	1 Mar 1989 (otherwise) (SI 1988/2076)
41(1)	1 Oct 1987 (for purposes of or in relation to Pt II) (SI 1987/1680)
	1 Mar 1989 (otherwise) (SI 1988/2076)
(2)	1 Oct 1987 (for purposes of or in relation to Pt II) (SI 1987/1680)
	1 Mar 1988 (for purposes of or in relation to Pt I) (SI 1987/1680)
	1 Mar 1989 (otherwise) (SI 1988/2076)
(3)–(5)	1 Oct 1987 (for purposes of or in relation to Pt II) (SI 1987/1680)
	1 Mar 1989 (otherwise) (SI 1988/2076)
(6)	1 Oct 1987 (for purposes of or in relation to Pt II) (SI 1987/1680)
	1 Mar 1988 (for purposes of or in relation to Pt I) (SI 1987/1680)
	1 Mar 1989 (otherwise) (SI 1988/2076)
42–44	1 Oct 1987 (so far as have effect for purposes of or in relation to Pt II) (SI 1987/1680)
	1 Mar 1989 (otherwise) (SI 1988/2076)
45, 46	1 Oct 1987 (so far as have effect for purposes of or in relation to Pt II) (SI 1987/1680)
	1 Mar 1988 (so far as have effect for purposes of or in relation to Pt I) (SI 1987/1680)
	1 Mar 1989 (otherwise) (SI 1988/2076)
47	1 Oct 1987 (for purposes of or in relation to Pt II) (SI 1987/1680)
	1 Mar 1989 (otherwise) (SI 1988/2076)
48(1)	See Sch 4 below
(2)(a)	31 Dec 1988 (SI 1988/2041)
(b)	1 Oct 1987 (SI 1987/1680)
(3)	See Sch 5 below
49, 50	1 Oct 1987 (SI 1987/1680)
Sch 1	1 Mar 1988 (SI 1987/1680)

Consumer Protection Act 1987 (c 43)—*cont*

Sch 2		1 Oct 1987 (SI 1987/1680)
3		1 Mar 1988 (SI 1987/1680)
4, para	1, 2	1 Oct 1987 (SI 1987/1680)
	3	1 Mar 1989 (SI 1988/2076)
	4	1 Oct 1987 (SI 1987/1680)
	5	1 Mar 1988 (SI 1987/1680)
	6, 7	1 Oct 1987 (SI 1987/1680)
	8	Repealed
	9–11	1 Oct 1987 (SI 1987/1680)
	12	1 Mar 1988 (SI 1987/1680)
	13	1 Oct 1987 (SI 1987/1680)
5		1 Oct 1987 (repeals of or in Fabrics (Misdescription) Act 1913; Criminal Justice Act 1967; Fines Act (Northern Ireland) 1967; Local Government Act 1972; Local Government (Scotland) Act 1973; Explosives (Age of Purchase etc) Act 1976; Consumer Safety Act 1978; Magistrates' Courts Act 1980; Telecommunications Act 1984; Food Act 1984; Consumer Safety (Amendment) Act 1986; Airports Act 1986; Gas Act 1986) (SI 1987/1680)
		1 Mar 1988 (repeals of or in Prescription and Limitation (Scotland) Act 1973; Health and Safety at Work etc Act 1974) (SI 1987/1680)
		31 Dec 1988 (repeal of Trade Descriptions Act 1972) (SI 1988/2041)
		1 Mar 1989 (repeal of Trade Descriptions Act 1968, s 11) (SI 1988/2076)

Criminal Justice Act 1987 (c 38)

RA: 15 May 1987

Commencement provisions: s 16; Criminal Justice Act 1987 (Commencement No 1) Order 1987, SI 1987/1061; Criminal Justice Act 1987 (Commencement No 2) Order 1988, SI 1988/397; Criminal Justice Act 1987 (Commencement No 3) Order 1988, SI 1988/1564

s 1	20 Jul 1987 (for purposes of appointment of person to be Director of the Serious Fraud Office, staff for Office and doing of such other things necessary or expedient for establishment of Office) (SI 1987/1061)
	6 Apr 1988 (otherwise) (SI 1988/397)
2, 3	6 Apr 1988 (SI 1988/397)
4, 5	31 Oct 1988 (SI 1988/1564)
6	Substituted by Criminal Justice Act 1988, s 144(1), (5) (qv)
7–11	31 Oct 1988 (SI 1988/1564)
12	20 Jul 1987 (except in relation to things done before that date) (SI 1987/1061)
13	15 May 1987 (s 16(3))
14	20 Jul 1987 (SI 1987/1061)
15	See Sch 2 below
16–18	15 May 1987 (s 16(3))

Criminal Justice Act 1987 (c 38)—*cont*

Sch 1	See s 1 above
2, para 1–5	31 Oct 1988 (SI 1988/1564)
6	6 Apr 1988 (SI 1988/397)
7, 8	Repealed
9	31 Oct 1988 (SI 1988/1564)
10, 11	31 Oct 1988 (SI 1988/1564); prospectively repealed by Criminal Justice and Public Order Act 1994, s 168(3), Sch 11[1]
12	31 Oct 1988 (SI 1988/1564)
13	6 Apr 1988 (SI 1988/397)
14–16	31 Oct 1988 (SI 1988/1564)

[1] Orders made under Criminal Justice and Public Order Act 1994, s 172(2), (3), bringing these prospective repeals into force will be noted to that Act in the service to this work

Criminal Justice (Scotland) Act 1987 (c 41)

RA: 15 May 1987

Commencement provisions: s 72(2); Criminal Justice (Scotland) Act 1987 (Commencement No 1) Order 1987, SI 1987/1468; Criminal Justice (Scotland) Act 1987 (Commencement No 2) Order 1987, SI 1987/1594; Criminal Justice (Scotland) Act 1987 (Commencement No 3) Order 1987, SI 1987/2119; Criminal Justice (Scotland) Act 1987 (Commencement No 4) Order 1988, SI 1988/483; Criminal Justice (Scotland) Act 1987 (Commencement No 5) Order 1988, SI 1988/482; Criminal Justice (Scotland) Act 1987 (Commencement No 6) Order 1988, SI 1988/1710

s 1–47	Repealed[1]
48, 49	1 Oct 1987 (SI 1987/1594)
50	1 Apr 1988 (SI 1988/482)
51–55	1 Jan 1988 (SI 1987/2119)
56–68	Repealed
69	1 Oct 1987 (SI 1987/1594)
70	See Schs 1, 2 below
71	1 Apr 1988 (SI 1988/482)
72	15 May 1987 (s 72(2))
Sch 1, para 1, 2	1 Sep 1987 (SI 1987/1468)
3–19	Repealed
2	1 Sep 1987 (repeals of or in Circuit Courts (Scotland) Act 1709; Heritable Jurisdiction (Scotland) Act 1746; Circuit Courts (Scotland) Act 1828; Justiciary (Scotland) Act 1848; Circuit Clerks (Scotland) Act 1898; Criminal Procedure (Scotland) Act 1975, ss 5(1), 87, 88, 113, 115–119) (SI 1987/1468)
	1 Oct 1987 (repeals of or in Road Traffic Act 1974, Sch 3, para 10(4); Criminal Procedure (Scotland) Act 1975, s 263(2)) (SI 1987/1594)
	1 Jan 1988 (repeals of or in Road Traffic Act 1972; Criminal Procedure (Scotland) Act 1976, s 300(5); Sexual Offences (Scotland) Act 1976; Community Service by Offenders (Scotland) Act 1978) (SI 1987/2119)

Criminal Justice (Scotland) Act 1987 (c 41)—*cont*

Sch 2—*cont*	1 Apr 1988 (repeals of or in Children and Young Persons (Scotland) Act 1937; Social Work (Scotland) Act 1968; Criminal Procedure (Scotland) Act 1975, s 193B; Law Reform (Miscellaneous Provisions) (Scotland) Act 1985; Drug Trafficking Offences Act 1986) (SI 1988/482)
	12 Oct 1988 (repeals of or in Criminal Procedure (Scotland) Act 1975, ss 289B(3), (4), 289D(1A), (2)–(4)) (SI 1988/1710)

[1] As to retention of prospective nature of amendments made by Criminal Justice (Scotland) Act 1995 to this Act, see Criminal Procedure (Consequential Provisions) (Scotland) Act 1995, s 4, Sch 3, paras 3, 16

Crossbows Act 1987 (c 32)

RA: 15 May 1987

Commencement provisions: s 8(2)

s 1–6	15 Jul 1987 (s 8(2))
7, 8	15 May 1987 (RA)

Crown Proceedings (Armed Forces) Act 1987 (c 25)

RA: 15 May 1987

15 May 1987 (RA)

Debtors (Scotland) Act 1987 (c 18)

RA: 15 May 1987

Commencement provisions: s 109(2); Debtors (Scotland) Act 1987 (Commencement No 1) Order 1987, SI 1987/1838; Debtors (Scotland) Act 1987 (Commencement No 2) Order 1988, SI 1988/1818

s 1–67	30 Nov 1988 (SI 1988/1818)
68	Repealed
69–74	30 Nov 1988 (SI 1988/1818)
75, 76	2 Nov 1987 (SI 1987/1838)
77–96	30 Nov 1988 (SI 1988/1818)
97	2 Nov 1987 (SI 1987/1838)
98–108	30 Nov 1988 (SI 1988/1818)
109	15 May 1987 (RA)
Sch 1–8	30 Nov 1988 (SI 1988/1818)

Deer Act 1987 (c 28)

Whole Act repealed

Diplomatic and Consular Premises Act 1987 (c 46)

RA: 15 May 1987

Commencement provisions: s 9(2); Diplomatic and Consular Premises Act 1987 (Commencement No 1) Order 1987, SI 1987/1022; Diplomatic and Consular Premises Act 1987 (Commencement No 2) Order 1987, SI 1987/2248; Diplomatic and Consular Premises Act 1987 (Commencement No 3) Order 1987, SI 1988/106

s 1–5	1 Jan 1988 (SI 1987/2248)
6, 7	11 Jun 1987 (SI 1987/1022)
8	1 Jan 1988 (SI 1987/2248)
9	3 Feb 1988 (SI 1988/106)
Sch 1	1 Jan 1988 (SI 1987/2248)
2	11 Jun 1987 (SI 1987/1022)

Family Law Reform Act 1987 (c 42)

RA: 15 May 1987

Commencement provisions: s 34(2); Family Law Reform Act 1987 (Commencement No 1) Order 1988, SI 1988/425; Family Law Reform Act 1987 (Commencement No 2) Order 1989, SI 1989/382

s 1	4 Apr 1988 (SI 1988/425)
2	1 Apr 1989 (SI 1989/382)
3–7	Repealed
8	1 Apr 1989 (SI 1989/382)
9–16	Repealed
17	1 Apr 1989 (SI 1989/382)
18–22	4 Apr 1988 (SI 1988/425)
23	*Not in force*
24, 25	1 Apr 1989 (SI 1989/382)
26–29	4 Apr 1988 (SI 1988/425)
30	1 Apr 1989 (SI 1989/382)
31	4 Apr 1988 (SI 1988/425)
32	*Not in force*[1]
33	See Schs 2–4 below
34	4 Apr 1988 (SI 1988/425)
Sch 1	Spent
2, para 1	1 Apr 1989 (SI 1989/382)
2–4	4 Apr 1988 (SI 1988/425)
5–8	1 Apr 1989 (SI 1989/382)
9, 10	4 Apr 1988 (SI 1988/425)
11	Repealed
12, 13	1 Apr 1989 (SI 1989/382)
14	Repealed
15	1 Apr 1989 (SI 1989/382)
16(a), (b)	1 Apr 1989 (SI 1989/382)
(c)	4 Apr 1988 (SI 1988/425)
17, 18	1 Apr 1989 (SI 1989/382)
19	4 Apr 1988 (SI 1988/425)
20	Repealed
21–25	*Not in force*
26, 27	1 Apr 1989 (SI 1989/382)

Family Law Reform Act 1987 (c 42)—*cont*

Sch 2, para 28–43	Spent
44, 45	1 Apr 1989 (SI 1989/382)
46	Repealed
47–50	1 Apr 1989 (SI 1989/382)
51	Repealed
52	1 Apr 1989 (SI 1989/382)
53–58	Spent
59	Repealed
60–66	Spent
67, 68	Repealed
69–72	1 Apr 1989 (SI 1989/382)
73, 74	4 Apr 1988 (SI 1988/425)
75–79	Spent
80–90	1 Apr 1989 (SI 1989/382)
91–95	Repealed
96	4 Apr 1988 (SI 1988/425)
3, para 1	4 Apr 1988 (SI 1988/425)
2–7	1 Apr 1988 (SI 1989/382)
8–10	4 Apr 1988 (SI 1988/425)
11, 12	Repealed
4	4 Apr 1988 (repeals of or in Domestic and Appellate Proceedings (Restriction of Publicity) Act 1968, s 2(1); Family Law Reform Act 1969, ss 14, 15, 17; Interpretation Act 1978, Sch 2, para 4) (SI 1988/425) 1 Apr 1989 (otherwise) (SI 1989/382)

[1] Provisions not brought into force consequent on errors in Sch 1

Finance Act 1987 (c 16)

RA: 15 May 1987

See the note concerning Finance Acts at the front of this book

Finance (No 2) Act 1987 (c 51)

RA: 23 Jul 1987

See the note concerning Finance Acts at the front of this book

Fire Safety and Safety of Places of Sport Act 1987 (c 27)

RA: 15 May 1987

Commencement provisions: s 50(2); Fire Safety and Safety of Places of Sport Act 1987 (Commencement No 1) Order 1987, SI 1987/1762; Fire Safety and Safety of Places of Sport Act 1987 (Commencement No 2) Order 1988, SI 1988/485; Fire Safety and Safety of Places of Sport Act 1987 (Commencement No 3) (Scotland) Order 1988, SI 1988/626; Fire Safety and Safety of Places of Sport Act 1987 (Commencement No 4) Order 1988, SI 1988/1806; Fire Safety and Safety of Places of Sport Act 1987 (Commencement No 5) Order 1989, SI 1989/75; Fire Safety and Safety of Places of Sport Act 1987 (Commencement No 6) Order 1990, SI 1990/1984; Fire Safety and Safety of Places of Sport Act 1987 (Commencement No 7) Order 1993, SI 1993/1411

Fire Safety and Safety of Places of Sport Act 1987 (c 27)—*cont*

s 1, 2	1 Apr 1989 (SI 1989/75)
3, 4	1 Jan 1988 (SI 1987/1762)
5–7	1 Apr 1989 (SI 1989/75)
8, 9	1 Jan 1988 (SI 1987/1762)
10	*Not in force*
11–14	1 Jan 1988 (SI 1987/1762)
15	1 Aug 1993 (SI 1993/1411)
16(1)	1 Jan 1988 (SI 1987/1762)
(2)	See Sch 1 below
(3)	1 Jan 1988 (SI 1987/1762)
17	1 Jan 1988 (SI 1987/1762)
18(1)	See s 18(2)–(4) below
(2)	1 Jan 1988 (so far as it amends Fire Precautions Act 1971, s 40(1)(a), by the insertion of a reference to '5(2A)') (SI 1987/1762) 1 Apr 1989 (otherwise) (SI 1989/75)
(3)	1 Jan 1988 (so far as amends Fire Precautions Act 1971, s 40(1)(b), by the insertion of references to '8B' and '10B') (SI 1987/1762) 1 Apr 1989 (otherwise) (SI 1989/75)
(4)	1 Apr 1989 (SI 1989/75)
19–25	1 Jan 1988 (SI 1987/1762)
26–41	1 Jan 1989 (SI 1988/1806)
42, 43	1 Jun 1988 (SI 1988/485)
44	1 Jun 1988 (SI 1988/626)
45	1 Jun 1988 (SI 1988/485)
46	1 Jan 1988 (SI 1987/1762)
47	31 Dec 1990 (SI 1990/1984)
48	1 Jun 1988 (SI 1988/626)
49	See Schs 4, 5 below
50(1)–(3)	1 Jan 1988 (SI 1987/1762)
(4)–(7)	1 Jan 1988 (so far as have effect in relation to Pt II of this Act) (SI 1987/1762) 1 Jan 1989 (otherwise) (SI 1988/1806)
Sch 1	1 Jan 1988 (so far as gives effect to Fire Precautions Act 1971, Sch 2, Pt I, Pt II, para 3(1), (2), (3) (so far as para 3(3) has effect in relation to the references to the occupier in ss 5(2A), 7(3A), 7(4), 8B(1) of the 1971 Act)) (SI 1987/1762) 1 Apr 1989 (otherwise) (SI 1989/75)
2	1 Jan 1988 (SI 1987/1762)
3	1 Jun 1988 (SI 1988/485)
4	1 Jan 1988 (repeals of or in Fire Precautions Act 1971, ss 2, 12(1), 43(1), (2); Safety of Sports Grounds Act 1975) (SI 1987/1762) 1 Jun 1988 (repeals in London Government Act 1963, Sch 12) (SI 1988/485) 1 Apr 1989 (repeal of Health and Safety at Work etc Act 1974, s 78(4)) (SI 1989/75) 1 Aug 1993 (repeals in Fire Precautions Act 1971, ss 5(3)(c), 6(1)(d)) (SI 1993/1411)
5, para 1	1 Jan 1988 (SI 1987/1762)
2	1 Apr 1989 (SI 1989/75)
3–7	1 Jan 1988 (SI 1987/1762)
8	1 Jun 1988 (SI 1988/485)

Fire Safety and Safety of Places of Sport Act 1987 (c 27)—*cont*

Sch 5, para 9	1 Jan 1988 (SI 1987/1762)
10	1 Jun 1988 (SI 1988/485)

Gaming (Amendment) Act 1987 (c 11)

RA: 9 Apr 1987

Commencement provisions: s 2(2); Gaming (Amendment) Act 1987 (Commencement) Order 1987, SI 1987/1200

1 Aug 1987 (SI 1987/1200)

Housing (Scotland) Act 1987 (c 26)

RA: 15 May 1987

Commencement provisions: s 340(2)

15 Aug 1987 (s 340(2))

Immigration (Carriers' Liability) Act 1987 (c 24)

RA: 15 May 1987

Commencement provisions: s 2(4)

Act has effect in relation to persons arriving in UK after 4 Mar 1987 except persons arriving by voyage or flight for which they embarked before that date (s 2(4))

Irish Sailors and Soldiers Land Trust Act 1987 (c 48)

RA: 15 May 1987

Commencement provisions: s 3(2); Irish Sailors and Soldiers Land Trust Act 1987 (Commencement) Order 1987, SI 1987/1909

4 Nov 1987 (SI 1987/1909)

Landlord and Tenant Act 1987 (c 31)

RA: 15 May 1987

Commencement provisions: s 62(2); Landlord and Tenant Act 1987 (Commencement No 1) Order 1987, SI 1987/2177; Landlord and Tenant Act 1987 (Commencement No 2) Order 1988, SI 1988/480; Landlord and Tenant Act 1987 (Commencement No 3) Order 1988, SI 1988/1283)

s 1–20	1 Feb 1988 (SI 1987/2177)
21–40	18 Apr 1988 (SI 1988/480)
41	1 Sep 1988 (SI 1988/1283)
42	1 Apr 1989 (SI 1988/1283)
43, 44	1 Sep 1988 (SI 1988/1283)
45	Repealed
46–50	1 Feb 1988 (SI 1987/2177)

Landlord and Tenant Act 1987 (c 31)—*cont*

s 51	Repealed
52–60	1 Feb 1988 (so far as relate to ss 1–20, 45–51) (SI 1987/2177)
	18 Apr 1988 (so far as relate to ss 21–40) (SI 1988/480)
	1 Sep 1988 (otherwise) (SI 1988/1283)
61(1)	See Sch 4 below
(2)	See Sch 5 below
62	1 Feb 1988 (SI 1987/2177)
Sch 1, Pt I	1 Feb 1988 (SI 1987/2177)
II	18 Apr 1988 (SI 1988/480)
2, 3	1 Sep 1988 (SI 1988/1283)
4, para 1, 2	18 Apr 1988 (SI 1988/480)
3(a)	1 Sep 1988 (SI 1988/1283)
(b)	1 Feb 1988 (SI 1987/2177)
4–6	1 Sep 1988 (SI 1988/1283)
7	Repealed
5	1 Sep 1988 (SI 1988/1283)

Licensing (Restaurant Meals) Act 1987 (c 2)

Whole Act repealed

Local Government Act 1987 (c 44)

RA: 15 May 1987

Commencement provisions: ss 1, 2(3), (4), 3(7)

s 1, 2	Repealed
3	15 Jul 1987 (s 3(7))
4	15 May 1987 (RA)
Schedule	Repealed

Local Government Finance Act 1987 (c 6)

RA: 12 Mar 1987

12 Mar 1987 (RA)

Ministry of Defence Police Act 1987 (c 4)

RA: 5 Mar 1987

Commencement provisions: s 8(2)

5 May 1987 (s 8(2))

Minors' Contracts Act 1987 (c 13)

RA: 9 Apr 1987

Commencement provisions: s 5(2)

9 June 1987 (s 5(2))

Motor Cycle Noise Act 1987 (c 34)

RA: 15 May 1987

Commencement provisions: s 2(3); Motor Cycle Noise Act 1987 (Commencement) Order 1995, SI 1995/2367

1 Aug 1996 (SI 1995/2367)

Northern Ireland (Emergency Provisions) Act 1987 (c 30)

Whole Act repealed

Parliamentary and Health Service Commissioners Act 1987 (c 39)

RA: 15 May 1987

Commencement provisions: s 10(3)

15 Jul 1987 (s 10(3))

Parliamentary and other Pensions Act 1987 (c 45)

RA: 15 May 1987

Commencement provisions: s 7(2); Parliamentary and other Pensions Act 1987 (Commencement No 1) Order 1987, SI 1987/1311; Parliamentary and other Pensions Act 1987 (Commencement No 2) Order 1989, SI 1989/892

s 1–3	24 May 1989 (SI 1989/892)
4(1)	23 Jul 1987 (SI 1987/1311)
(2)	24 May 1989 (SI 1989/892)
(3)	23 Jul 1987 (SI 1987/1311)
5–7	24 May 1989 (SI 1989/892)
Sch 1–4	24 May 1989 (SI 1989/892)

Petroleum Act 1987 (c 12)

RA: 9 Apr 1987

Commencement provisions: s 31(1), (2); Petroleum Act 1987 (Commencement No 1) Order 1987, SI 1987/820; Petroleum Act 1987 (Commencement No 2) Order 1987, SI 1987/1330

s 1–16	9 Jun 1987 (s 31(1))
17, 18	30 Jun 1987 (SI 1987/820)
19, 20	9 Jun 1987 (s 31(1))

Petroleum Act 1987 (c 12)—*cont*

s 21–24	1 Sep 1987 (SI 1987/1330)
25–32	9 Jun 1987 (s 31(1))
Sch 1, 2	30 Jun 1987 (SI 1987/820)
3	9 Jun 1987 (except repeals of or in Oil and Gas (Enterprise) Act 1982, ss 21, 27) (s 31(1))
	1 Sep 1987 (exception noted above) (SI 1987/1330)

Pilotage Act 1987 (c 21)

RA: 15 May 1987

Commencement provisions: s 33(2), (3); Pilotage Act 1987 (Commencement No 1) Order 1987, SI 1987/1306; Pilotage Act 1987 (Commencement No 2) Order 1987, SI 1987/2138; Pilotage Act 1987 (Commencement No 3) Order 1988, SI 1988/1137; Pilotage Act 1987 (Commencement No 4) Order 1991, SI 1991/1029

s 1–23	1 Oct 1988 (SI 1988/1137)
24, 25	1 Sep 1987 (SI 1987/1306)
26	1 Oct 1988 (SI 1988/1137)
27	Repealed
28	1 Sep 1987 (SI 1987/1306)
29	1 Aug 1988 (SI 1988/1137)
30, 31	1 Sep 1987 (SI 1987/1306)
32(1)–(3)	1 Sep 1987 (SI 1987/1306)
(4)	1 Oct 1988 (SI 1988/1137)
(5)	See Sch 3 below
33	1 Sep 1987 (SI 1987/1306)
Sch 1, para 1–4	1 Sep 1987 (SI 1987/1306)
5, 6	1 Oct 1988 (SI 1988/1137)
2	1 Oct 1988 (SI 1988/1137)
3	1 Feb 1988 (repeal of Pilotage Act 1983, s 15(1)(i)) (SI 1987/2138)
	1 Oct 1988 (otherwise, except repeal of Pilotage Act 1983, ss 1(1), 2, 4, 5(4), 8, Sch 1) (SI 1988/1137)
	30 Apr 1991 (exception noted above) (SI 1991/1029)

Prescription (Scotland) Act 1987 (c 36)

RA: 15 May 1987

15 May 1987 (RA)

Protection of Animals (Penalties) Act 1987 (c 35)

RA: 15 May 1987

Commencement provisions: s 2(3)

15 Jul 1987 (s 2(3))

Rate Support Grants Act 1987 (c 5)

RA: 12 Mar 1987

12 Mar 1987 (RA)

Recognition of Trusts Act 1987 (c 14)

RA: 9 Apr 1987

Commencement provisions: s 3(2); Recognition of Trusts Act 1987 (Commencement) Order 1987, SI 1987/1177

1 Aug 1987 (SI 1987/1177)

Register of Sasines (Scotland) Act 1987 (c 23)

RA: 15 May 1987

Commencement provisions: s 3(1)

15 Jul 1987 (s 3(1))

Registered Establishments (Scotland) Act 1987 (c 40)

RA: 15 May 1987

Commencement provisions: s 8(2); commencement order dated 26 Sep 1988 (not a statutory instrument)

17 Oct 1988 (commencement order dated 26 Sep 1988)

Reverter of Sites Act 1987 (c 15)

RA: 9 Apr 1987

Commencement provisions: s 9(2); Reverter of Sites (Commencement) Order 1987, SI 1987/1260

17 Aug 1987 (SI 1987/1260)

Scottish Development Agency Act 1987 (c 56)

Whole Act repealed

Social Fund (Maternity and Funeral Expenses) Act 1987 (c 7)

Whole Act repealed

Teachers' Pay and Conditions Act 1987 (c 1)

Whole Act repealed

Territorial Sea Act 1987 (c 49)

RA: 15 May 1987

Commencement provisions: s 4(2); Territorial Sea Act 1987 (Commencement) Order 1987, SI 1987/1270

1 Oct 1987 (SI 1987/1270)

Urban Development Corporations (Financial Limits) Act 1987 (c 57)

RA: 17 Dec 1987

Commencement provisions: s 2(2)

17 Feb 1988 (s 2(2))

1988

Access to Medical Reports Act 1988 (c 28)

RA: 29 Jul 1988

Commencement provisions: s 10(2)

1 Jan 1989 (s 10(2))

Appropriation Act 1988 (c 38)

Whole Act repealed

Arms Control and Disarmament (Privileges and Immunities) Act 1988 (c 2)

RA: 9 Feb 1988

9 Feb 1988 (RA)

British Steel Act 1988 (c 35)

RA: 29 Jul 1988

Commencement provisions: ss 1(1), 10(2), 17(2)–(4); British Steel Act 1988 (Appointed Day) Order 1988, SI 1988/1375

s 1	5 Sep 1988 (SI 1988/1375)
2	29 Jul 1988 (s 17(2))
3–14	5 Sep 1988 (SI 1988/1375)
15(1)	29 Jul 1988 (s 17(2))
(2)	5 Sep 1988 (SI 1988/1375)
16(1), (2)	5 Sep 1988 (SI 1988/1375)
(3)	See Sch 2 below
(4)	5 Sep 1988 (SI 1988/1375)
17	29 Jul 1988 (RA)
Sch 1	5 Sep 1988 (SI 1988/1375)
2, Pt I	5 Sep 1988 (SI 1988/1375)
II	*Not in force*
3	5 Sep 1988 (SI 1988/1375)

Church Commissioners (Assistance for Priority Areas) Measure 1988 (No 2)

RA: 3 May 1988

Commencement provisions: s 4(3)

4 May 1988 (the day appointed by the Archbishops of Canterbury and York under s 4(3))

Church of England (Ecumenical Relations) Measure 1988 (No 3)

RA: 29 Jul 1988

Commencement provisions: s 9(3)

1 Nov 1988 (the day appointed by the Archbishops of Canterbury and York under s 9(3))

Church of England (Legal Aid and Miscellaneous Provisions) Measure 1988 (No 1)

RA: 9 Feb 1988

Commencement provisions: s 15(2)

The provisions of this Measure were brought into force on the following dates by an instrument made by the Archbishops of Canterbury and York and dated 19 Apr 1988 (made under s 15(2))

Pt I (ss 1–4)	1 Aug 1988; repealed (subject to transitional provisions) by Church of England (Legal Aid) Measure 1994, ss 5, 7(1) (qv)
II, III (ss 5–15)	1 May 1988
Sch 1	1 Aug 1988; repealed (subject to transitional provisions) by Church of England (Legal Aid) Measure 1994, ss 5, 7(1) (qv)
2, para 1, 2	1 Aug 1988
3	1 May 1988
4	1 Aug 1988
3	1 May 1988 (repeals of or in Pluralities Act 1838, ss 97, 98; Parochial Church Councils (Powers) Measure 1956, s 7; Clergy (Ordination and Miscellaneous Provisions) Measure 1964, ss 10, 12)
	1 Aug 1988 (otherwise)

Church of England (Pensions) Measure 1988 (No 4)

RA: 27 Oct 1988

Commencement provisions: s 19(2)

The provisions of this Measure were brought into force on the following dates by an instrument made by the Archbishops of Canterbury and York and dated 31 Oct 1988 (made under s 19(2))

Church of England (Pensions) Measure 1988 (No 4)—*cont*

s 1–4	Repealed
5	1 Dec 1988
6	Repealed
7–14	1 Dec 1988
15	Repealed
16	1 Nov 1988
17–19	1 Dec 1988
Sch 1	Repealed
2, 3	1 Dec 1988

Civil Evidence (Scotland) Act 1988 (c 32)

RA: 29 Jul 1988

Commencement provisions: s 11(2); Civil Evidence (Scotland) Act 1988 (Commencement) Order 1989, SI 1989/556

3 Apr 1989 (SI 1989/556)

Community Health Councils (Access to Information) Act 1988 (c 24)

RA: 29 Jul 1988

Commencement provisions: s 3(2)

1 Apr 1989 (s 3(2))

Consolidated Fund Act 1988 (c 6)

Whole Act repealed

Consolidated Fund (No 2) Act 1988 (c 55)

Whole Act repealed

Consumer Arbitration Agreements Act 1988 (c 21)

RA: 28 Jun 1988

Commencement provisions: s 9(2); Consumer Arbitration Agreements Act 1988 (Appointed Day No 1) Order 1988, SI 1988/1598; Consumer Arbitration Agreements Act 1988 (Appointed Day No 2) Order 1988, SI 1988/2291

s 1–5	Have effect in relation to contracts made on or after 1 Oct 1988 (SI 1988/1598)
6–8	Have effect in relation to contracts made on or after 1 Feb 1989 (SI 1988/2291)
9	28 Jun 1988 (RA)

Copyright, Designs and Patents Act 1988 (c 48)

RA: 15 Nov 1988

Commencement provisions: s 305; Copyright, Designs and Patents Act 1988 (Commencement No 1) Order 1989, SI 1989/816 (as amended by SI 1989/1303); Copyright, Designs and Patents Act 1988 (Commencement No 2) Order 1989, SI 1989/955 (as amended by SI 1989/1032); Copyright, Designs and Patents Act 1988 (Commencement No 3) Order 1989, SI 1989/1032 (amends SI 1989/955); Copyright, Designs and Patents Act 1988 (Commencement No 4) Order 1989, SI 1989/1303 (amends SI 1989/816); Copyright, Designs and Patents Act 1988 (Commencement No 5) Order 1990, SI 1990/1400; Copyright, Designs and Patents Act 1988 (Commencement No 6) Order 1990, SI 1990/2168

s 1–36	1 Aug 1989 (SI 1989/816)
37–43	9 Jun 1989 (for purposes of making regulations) (SI 1989/955; SI 1989/1032) 1 Aug 1989 (otherwise) (SI 1989/816)
44–46	1 Aug 1989 (SI 1989/816)
47	9 Jun 1989 (for purposes of making orders) (SI 1989/955; SI 1989/1032) 1 Aug 1989 (otherwise) (SI 1989/816)
48–50	1 Aug 1990 (SI 1989/816)
50A–50C	Inserted in relation to agreements entered into on or after 1 Jan 1993 by Copyright (Computer Programs) Regulations 1992, SI 1992/3233, regs 2, 8, 12(2)
51	1 Aug 1990 (SI 1989/816)
52	9 Jun 1989 (for purposes of making orders) (SI 1989/955; SI 1989/1032) 1 Aug 1989 (otherwise) (SI 1989/816)
53–60	1 Aug 1989 (SI 1989/816)
61	9 Jun 1989 (for purposes of making orders) (SI 1989/955; SI 1989/1032) 1 Aug 1989 (otherwise) (SI 1989/816)
62–73	1 Aug 1989 (SI 1989/816)
74, 75	9 Jun 1989 (for purposes of making orders) (SI 1989/955; SI 1989/1032) 1 Aug 1989 (otherwise) (SI 1989/816)
76–99	1 Aug 1989 (SI 1989/816)
100	9 Jun 1989 (for purposes of making orders) (SI 1989/955; SI 1989/1032) 1 Aug 1989 (otherwise) (SI 1989/816)
101–107	1 Aug 1989 (SI 1989/816)
107A	Prospectively inserted by Criminal Justice and Public Order Act 1994, s 165(1), (2)[1]
108–111	1 Aug 1989 (SI 1989/816)
112	9 Jun 1989 (for purposes of making regulations) (SI 1989/955; SI 1989/1032) 1 Aug 1989 (otherwise) (SI 1989/816)
113–135	1 Aug 1989 (SI 1989/816)
135A–135G	Inserted by Broadcasting Act 1990, s 175 (qv)
136–149	1 Apr 1989 (SI 1989/816)
150	9 Jun 1989 (for purposes of making rules) (SI 1989/955; SI 1989/1032) 1 Aug 1989 (otherwise) (SI 1989/816)
151	1 Aug 1989 (SI 1989/816)

Copyright, Designs and Patents Act 1988 (c 48)—*cont*

s 152	9 Jun 1989 (for purposes of making rules) (SI 1989/955; SI 1989/1032) 1 Aug 1989 (otherwise) (SI 1989/816)
153–158	1 Aug 1989 (SI 1989/816)
159	9 Jun 1989 (for purposes of making orders) (SI 1989/955; SI 1989/1032) 1 Aug 1989 (otherwise) (SI 1989/816)
160–167	1 Aug 1989 (SI 1989/816)
168	9 Jun 1989 (for purposes of making orders) (SI 1989/955; SI 1989/1032) 1 Aug 1989 (otherwise) (SI 1989/816)
169	1 Aug 1989 (SI 1989/816)
170	See Sch 1 below
171–173	1 Aug 1989 (SI 1989/816)
174	9 Jun 1989 (for purposes of making orders) (SI 1989/955; SI 1989/1032) 1 Aug 1989 (otherwise) (SI 1989/816)
175–188	1 Aug 1989 (SI 1989/816)
189	See Sch 2 below
190–195	1 Aug 1989 (SI 1989/816)
196	9 Jun 1989 (for purposes of making orders) (SI 1989/955; SI 1989/1032) 1 Aug 1989 (otherwise) (SI 1989/816)
197, 198	1 Aug 1989 (SI 1989/816)
198A	Prospectively inserted by Criminal Justice and Public Order Act 1994, s 165(1), (3)[1]
199–207	1 Aug 1989 (SI 1989/816)
208	9 Jun 1989 (for purposes of making orders) (SI 1989/955; SI 1989/1032) 1 Aug 1989 (otherwise) (SI 1989/816)
209–249	1 Aug 1989 (SI 1989/816)
250	9 Jun 1989 (for purposes of making rules) (SI 1989/955; SI 1989/1032) 1 Aug 1989 (otherwise) (SI 1989/816)
251–255	1 Aug 1989 (SI 1989/816)
256	9 Jun 1989 (for purposes of making orders) (SI 1989/955; SI 1989/1032) 1 Aug 1989 (otherwise) (SI 1989/816)
257–271	1 Aug 1989 (SI 1989/816)
272	See Sch 3 below
273	See Sch 4 below
274–281	10 Jul 1990 (for the purpose of making rules expressed to come into force on or after 13 Aug 1990) (SI 1990/1400) 13 Aug 1990 (otherwise) (SI 1990/1400)
282–284	10 Jul 1990 (for the purpose of making rules expressed to come into force on or after 13 Aug 1990) (SI 1990/1400); and 13 Aug 1990 (otherwise) (SI 1990/1400); repealed (with savings) by Trade Marks Act 1994, ss 105, 106(2), Sch 3, para 22(1), Sch 5 (qv)
285, 286	10 Jul 1990 (for the purpose of making rules expressed to come into force on or after 13 Aug 1990) (SI 1990/1400) 13 Aug 1990 (otherwise) (SI 1990/1400)
287–289	1 Aug 1989 (SI 1989/816)

Copyright, Designs and Patents Act 1988 (c 48)—*cont*

s 290	1 Aug 1989 (SI 1989/816); prospectively repealed by Courts and Legal Services Act 1990, s 125(7), Sch 20[2]
291, 292	1 Aug 1989 (SI 1989/816)
293, 294	15 Jan 1989 (s 305(2))
295	See Sch 5 below
296(1), (2)	1 Aug 1989 (SI 1989/816)
(2A)	Inserted in relation to agreements entered into on or after 1 Jan 1993 by Copyright (Computer Programs) Regulations 1992, SI 1992/3233, regs 2, 10, 12(2)
(3)–(6)	1 Aug 1989 (SI 1989/816)
296A	Inserted in relation to agreements entered into on or after 1 Jan 1993 by Copyright (Computer Programs) Regulations 1992, SI 1992/3233, regs 2, 11, 12(2)
297	1 Aug 1989 (SI 1989/816)
297A	Inserted by Broadcasting Act 1990, s 179 (qv)
298, 299	1 Aug 1989 (SI 1989/816)
300	Repealed
301	See Sch 6 below
302	1 Aug 1989 (SI 1989/816)
303(1)	See Sch 7 below
(2)	See Sch 8 below
304(1)–(3)	1 Aug 1989 (SI 1989/816)
(4)	28 Jul 1989 (SI 1989/816; SI 1989/1303)
(5)	1 Aug 1989 (SI 1989/816)
(6)	28 Jul 1989 (SI 1989/816; SI 1989/1303)
305	15 Nov 1988 (RA)
306	1 Aug 1989 (SI 1989/816)
Sch 1, para 1–33	1 Aug 1989 (SI 1989/816)
34	9 Jun 1989 (for purposes of making rules) (SI 1989/955; SI 1989/1032)
	1 Aug 1989 (otherwise) (SI 1989/816)
35–46	1 Aug 1989 (SI 1989/816)
2	1 Aug 1989 (SI 1989/816)
3, para 1–20	1 Aug 1989 (SI 1989/816)
21	13 Aug 1990 (SI 1990/1400)
22–38	1 Aug 1989 (SI 1989/816)
4	13 Aug 1990 (SI 1990/1400)
5, para 1–11	1 Nov 1990 (for purposes of making rules) (SI 1990/2168)
	7 Jan 1991 (otherwise) (SI 1990/2168)
12–16	1 Aug 1989 (SI 1989/816)
17–23	1 Nov 1990 (for purposes of making rules) (SI 1990/2168)
	7 Jan 1991 (otherwise) (SI 1990/2168)
24	Repealed
25, 26	1 Nov 1990 (for purposes of making rules) (SI 1990/2168)
	7 Jan 1991 (otherwise) (SI 1990/2168)
27	13 Aug 1990 (SI 1990/1400)
28	1 Nov 1990 (for purposes of making rules) (SI 1990/2168)
	7 Jan 1991 (otherwise) (SI 1990/2168)
29	15 Nov 1988 (s 305(1))

Copyright, Designs and Patents Act 1988 (c 48)—*cont*

Sch 5, para 30	1 Nov 1990 (for purposes of making rules) (SI 1990/2168)
	7 Jan 1991 (otherwise) (SI 1990/2168)
6	15 Nov 1988 (s 305(1))
7, para 1–13	1 Aug 1989 (SI 1989/816)
14	Repealed
15	13 Aug 1990 (SI 1990/1400)
16, 17	1 Aug 1989 (SI 1989/816)
18(1)	1 Aug 1989 (SI 1989/1400)
(2)	13 Aug 1990 (SI 1990/1400)
(3)	1 Aug 1989 (SI 1989/816)
19, 20	1 Aug 1989 (SI 1989/816)
21	13 Aug 1990 (SI 1990/1400)
22–25	1 Aug 1989 (SI 1989/816)
26	Repealed
27, 28	1 Aug 1989 (SI 1989/816)
29, 30	Repealed
31	1 Aug 1989 (SI 1989/816); prospectively repealed by Companies Act 1989, s 212, Sch 24[3]
32–34	1 Aug 1989 (SI 1989/816)
35	1 Aug 1989 (SI 1989/816); prospectively repealed by Companies (No 2) (Northern Ireland) Order 1990, SI 1990/1504 (NI 10), art 113, Sch 6
36	1 Aug 1989 (SI 1989/816)
8	1 Aug 1989 (except repeals of or in of Registered Designs Act 1949, s 32; Patents Act 1977 (other than s 49(3), Sch 5, para 1, 3)) (SI 1989/816)
	13 Aug 1990 (repeals of or in Registered Design Act 1949, s 32; Patents Act 1977, ss 84, 85, 104, 105, 114, 115, 123(2)(k), 130(1)) (SI 1990/1400)
	7 Jan 1991 (repeals of or in Patents Act 1977 (so far as not already in force)) (SI 1990/2168)

[1] Any order made under Criminal Justice and Public Order Act 1994, s 172, bringing the prospective insertion into force will be noted to that Act in the service to this work

[2] Any order made under Courts and Legal Services Act 1990, s 124(3), bringing the prospective repeal into force will be noted to that Act in the service to this work

[3] Any order made under Companies Act 1989, s 215, bringing the prospective repeal into force will be noted to that Act in the service to this work

Coroners Act 1988 (c 13)

RA: 10 May 1988

Commencement provisions: s 37(2)

10 Jul 1988 (s 37(2))

Court of Session Act 1988 (c 36)

RA: 29 Jul 1988

Commencement provisions: s 53(2)

29 Sep 1988 (s 53(2))

Criminal Justice Act 1988 (c 33)

RA: 29 Jul 1988

Commencement provisions: ss 166(4), 171; Land Registration Act 1988, s 3(2); Extradition Act 1989, s 38(4)1; Criminal Justice Act 1988 (Commencement No 1) Order 1988, SI 1988/1408; Criminal Justice Act 1988 (Commencement No 2) Order 1988, SI 1988/1676; Criminal Justice Act 1988 (Commencement No 3) Order 1988, SI 1988/1817; Criminal Justice Act 1988 (Commencement No 4) Order 1988, SI 1988/2073; Criminal Justice Act 1988 (Commencement No 5) Order 1989, SI 1989/1; Criminal Justice Act 1988 (Commencement No 6) Order 1989, SI 1989/50; Criminal Justice Act 1988 (Commencement No 7) Order 1989, SI 1989/264; Criminal Justice Act 1988 (Commencement No 8) Order 1989, SI 1989/1085; Criminal Justice Act 1988 (Commencement No 9) Order 1989, SI 1989/1595; Criminal Justice Act 1988 (Commencement No 10) Order 1990, SI 1990/220; Criminal Justice Act 1988 (Commencement No 11) Order 1990, SI 1990/1145; Land Registration Act 1988 (Commencement) Order 1990, SI 1990/1359; Criminal Justice Act 1988 (Commencement No 12) Order 1990, SI 1990/2084

s 1–21	Repealed
22	5 Jun 1990 (SI 1990/1145)
23–28	3 Apr 1989 (except in relation to a trial, or proceedings before a magistrates' court acting as examining justices, which began before that date) (SI 1989/264)
29	Repealed
30, 31	3 Apr 1989 (except in relation to a trial, or proceedings before a magistrates' court acting as examining justices, which began before that date) (SI 1989/264)
32(1)(a)	26 Nov 1990 (in relation only to proceedings for murder, manslaughter or any other offence of killing any person; proceedings being conducted by the Director of the Serious Fraud Office under Criminal Justice Act 1987, s 1(5); and proceedings for serious and complex fraud where there has been given a notice of transfer under s 4 of that Act) (subject to transitional provisions set out in SI 1990/2084, art 3) (SI 1990/2084)
	Not in force (otherwise)
(b)	Substituted by Criminal Justice Act 1991, s 55(2) (qv)
(1A)	Inserted by Criminal Justice Act 1991, s 55(3) (qv)
(2)	5 Jan 1989 (SI 1988/2073)
(3)	26 Nov 1990 (in relation only to proceedings for murder, manslaughter or any other offence of killing any person; proceedings being conducted by the Director of the Serious Fraud Office under Criminal Justice Act 1987, s 1(5); and proceedings for serious and complex fraud where there has been given a notice of transfer under s 4 of that Act) (subject to transitional provisions set out in SI 1990/2084, art 3) (SI 1990/2084)
	Not in force (otherwise)
(3A), (3B)	Inserted by Criminal Justice Act 1991, s 55(4) (qv)
(4), (5)	5 Jan 1989 (SI 1988/2073)
(6)	Added by Criminal Justice Act 1991, s 55(6) (qv)
32A	Inserted by Criminal Justice Act 1991, s 54 (qv)

Criminal Justice Act 1988 (c 33)—*cont*

s 33	12 Oct 1988 (SI 1988/1676)
33A	Inserted by Criminal Justice Act 1991, s 52(1) (qv)
34	12 Oct 1988 (SI 1988/1676)
34A	Inserted by Criminal Justice Act 1991, s 55(7) (qv)
35, 36	1 Feb 1989 (SI 1989/1)
37–42	12 Oct 1988 (SI 1988/1676)
43	31 Jul 1989 (SI 1989/1085)
44–47	29 Sep 1988 (s 171(6))
48	Repealed
49	12 Oct 1988 (SI 1988/1676)
50	5 Jan 1989 (SI 1988/2073)
51–57	12 Oct 1988 (SI 1988/1676)
58	Repealed
59	12 Oct 1988 (SI 1988/1676)
60–62	5 Jan 1989 (SI 1988/2073)
63	Repealed
64	29 Sep 1988 (s 171(6))
65	5 Jun 1990 (SI 1990/1145
66, 67	29 Jul 1988 (s 171(5))
68	Repealed
69	29 Sep 1988 (s 171(6))
70	12 Oct 1988 (SI 1988/1676)
71, 72	3 Apr 1989 (SI 1989/264)
72AA	Inserted (EW) by Proceeds of Crime Act 1995, s 2 (qv)
72A	Inserted (EW) by Criminal Justice Act 1993, s 28 (qv)
73	3 Apr 1989 (SI 1989/264)
73A	Inserted (EW) by Proceeds of Crime Act 1995, s 4 (qv)
74	3 Apr 1989 (SI 1989/264)
74A	Inserted (EW) by Proceeds of Crime Act 1995, s 5 (qv)
74B	Inserted (EW) by Proceeds of Crime Act 1995, s 6 (qv)
74C	Inserted (EW) by Proceeds of Crime Act 1995, s 7 (qv)
75	3 Apr 1989 (SI 1989/264)
75A	Inserted (EW) by Proceeds of Crime Act 1995, s 9 (qv), subject to a saving contained in s 16(6) thereof
76–89	3 Apr 1989 (SI 1989/264)
90–93	3 Apr 1989 (SI 1989/264); prospectively repealed by Criminal Justice (Scotland) Act 1995, s 117, Sch 6, Pt II, para 186(1), (5), Sch 7, Pt II[2]
93A	Inserted by Criminal Justice Act 1993, s 29 (qv)
93B	Inserted by Criminal Justice Act 1993, s 30 (qv)
93C	Inserted by Criminal Justice Act 1993, s 31 (qv)
93D	Inserted by Criminal Justice Act 1993, s 32 (qv)
93E	Inserted (S) by Criminal Justice Act 1993, s 33 (qv)
93F	Inserted by Criminal Justice Act 1993, s 35 (qv)
93G	Inserted by Criminal Justice Act 1993, s 77, Sch 4, paras 1, 3 (qv)
93H	Inserted (EW) by Proceeds of Crime Act 1995, s 11 (qv)
93I	Inserted (EW) by Proceeds of Crime Act 1995, s 12 (qv)

Criminal Justice Act 1988 (c 33)—*cont*

s 93J	Inserted (EW) by Proceeds of Crime Act 1995, s 13 (qv)
94	3 Apr 1989 (SI 1989/264)
95	3 Apr 1989 (SI 1989/264); prospectively repealed by Criminal Justice (Scotland) Act 1995, s 117, Sch 6, Pt II, para 186(1), (5), Sch 7, Pt II[2]
96, 97	12 Oct 1988 (SI 1988/1676)
98	Repealed
99	3 Apr 1989 (SI 1989/264)
100	3 Apr 1989 (SI 1989/264); ceased to have effect on 3 Dec 1990 by virtue of s 100(7) and SI 1990/1359
101, 102	3 Apr 1989 (SI 1989/264)
103(1)	Repealed
(2)	See Sch 5, Pt II below
104–107	12 Oct 1988 (SI 1988/1676)
108–117	Repealed *(never in force)*
118	5 Jan 1989 (SI 1988/2073)
119	15 Feb 1990 (SI 1989/1085)
120	5 Jan 1989 (SI 1988/2073)
121, 122	12 Oct 1988 (SI 1988/1676)
123	1 Oct 1988 (SI 1988/1408)
124	1 Nov 1988 (SI 1988/1817)
125	1 Oct 1988 (SI 1988/1408)
126	Repealed
127, 128	1 Oct 1988 (SI 1988/1408)
129	29 Jul 1988 (s 171(5))
130	5 Jan 1989 (SI 1988/2073)
131	12 Oct 1988 (SI 1988/1676)
132	Repealed
133	12 Oct 1988 (SI 1988/1676)
134, 135	29 Sep 1988 (s 171(6))
136, 137	Repealed
138(1)	29 Sep 1988 (s 171(6))
(2), (3)	Repealed
139, 140	29 Sep 1988 (s 171(6))
141–144	29 Jul 1988 (s 171(5))
145	12 Oct 1988 (SI 1988/1676)
146	See Sch 13 below
147, 148	12 Oct 1988 (SI 1988/1676)
149	Repealed
150	*Not in force*
151(1)–(4)	*Not in force*
(5)	3 Apr 1989 (SI 1989/264)
152–154	5 Jan 1989 (SI 1988/2073)
155–157	12 Oct 1988 (SI 1988/1676)
158	29 Sep 1988 (s 171(6))
159	31 Jul 1989 (SI 1989/1085)
160, 161	29 Sep 1988 (s 171(6)
162	1 Sep 1988 (s 171(7))
163, 164	12 Oct 1988 (SI 1988/1676)
165	Repealed
166(1)	29 Jul 1988 (s 171(5))
(2), (3)	1 Oct 1986 (retrospective; s 166(4))
(4), (5)	29 Jul 1988 (s 171(5))
167–169	29 Jul 1988 (s 171(5))
170(1)	See Sch 15 below
(2)	See Sch 16 below

Criminal Justice Act 1988 (c 33)—*cont*

s 171–173	29 Jul 1988 (s 171(5))
Sch 1	Repealed
2	3 Apr 1989 (except in relation to a trial, or proceedings before a magistrates' court acting as examining justices, which began before that date) (SI 1989/264)
3	1 Feb 1989 (SI 1989/1)
4	3 Apr 1989 (SI 1989/264)
5, Pt I, para 1–17	Repealed
18–23	23 Jan 1989 (SI 1989/50)
6, 7	Repealed *(never in force)*
8	1 Oct 1988 (SI 1988/1408)
9	1 Nov 1988 (SI 1988/1817)
10	1 Oct 1988 (SI 1988/1408)
11	Repealed
12	12 Oct 1988 (SI 1988/1676)
13	31 Jul 1989 (SI 1989/1085)
14	Repealed
15, para 1–4	12 Oct 1988 (SI 1988/1676)
5, 6	3 Apr 1989 (SI 1989/264)
7	29 Jul 1988 (s 171(5)); ceased to have effect on 3 Dec 1990 by virtue of para 7(2) and SI 1990/1359
8	12 Oct 1988 (SI 1988/1676)
9	29 Jul 1988 (s 171(5))
10	12 Oct 1988 (SI 1988/1676)
11, 12	1 Oct 1988 (SI 1988/1408)
13–15	29 Jul 1988 (s 171(5))
16	*Not in force*
17	29 Jul 1988 (so far as relating to para 19) (s 171(5))
	12 Oct 1988 (so far as relating to para 18) (SI 1988/1676)
18	12 Oct 1988 (SI 1988/1676); repealed (S); ceased to have effect (EW)
19	29 Jul 1988 (s 171(5))
20	12 Oct 1988 (so far as relating to paras 21–24, 26–29, 31) (SI 1988/1676)
	31 Jul 1989 (so far as relating to paras 25, 30, 32) (SI 1989/1085)
21–24	12 Oct 1988 (SI 1988/1676)
25	31 Jul 1989 (SI 1989/1085)
26–29	12 Oct 1988 (SI 1988/1676)
30	31 Jul 1989 (SI 1989/1085)
31	12 Oct 1988 (SI 1988/1676)
32	31 Jul 1989 (SI 1989/1085)
33	12 Oct 1988 (SI 1988/1676)
34	Repealed
35	1 Oct 1988 (SI 1988/1408)
36	29 Jul 1988 (s 171(5))
37	Repealed
38	1 Oct 1988 (so far as relating to para 38) (SI 1988/1408)
	12 Oct 1988 (so far as relating to paras 39, 41) (SI 1988/1676)
	Not in force (so far as relating to para 40)
39	12 Oct 1988 (SI 1988/1676)
40	*Not in force*

Criminal Justice Act 1988 (c 33)—*cont*

Sch 15, para	41	12 Oct 1988 (SI 1988/1676)
	42	Repealed
	43	12 Oct 1988 (SI 1988/1676); ceased to have effect
	44	31 Jul 1989 (except in relation to any register of electors or any part of any such register required to be used for elections in the twelve months ending on 15 Feb 1990) (SI 1990/1085)
	45	29 Jul 1988 (s 171(5))
	46	5 Jan 1989 (SI 1988/2073)
	47	3 Apr 1989 (SI 1989/264)
	48	29 Jul 1988 (s 171(5))
	49	12 Oct 1988 (SI 1988/1676)
	50, 51	29 Jul 1988 (s 171(5))
	52	12 Oct 1988 (SI 1988/1676)
	53	29 Sep 1988 (s 171(6))
	54, 55	Repealed
	56	1 Feb 1989 (SI 1989/1)
	57	Repealed
	58, 59	12 Oct 1988 (SI 1988/1676)
	60–62	29 Sep 1988 (s 171(6))
	63	12 Oct 1988 (SI 1988/1676)
	64	29 Jul 1988 (s 171(5)); ceased to have effect
	65	29 Jul 1988 (so far as relating to paras 67, 70) (s 171(5)) 29 Sep 1988 (so far as relating to para 66) (s 171(6)) 12 Oct 1988 (otherwise) (SI 1988/1676)
	66	29 Sep 1988 (s 171(6))
	67	29 Jul 1988 (s 171(5))
	68, 69	12 Oct 1988 (SI 1988/1676)
	70	29 Jul 1988 (s 171(5))
	71	1 Feb 1989 (so far as relating to para 76) (SI 1989/1) 3 Apr 1989 (so far as relating to paras 72, 74, 75, 77) (SI 1989/264) 31 Jul 1989 (so far as relating to para 73) (SI 1989/1085)
	72	3 Apr 1989 (SI 1989/264)
	73	31 Jul 1989 (SI 1989/1085)
	74, 75	3 Apr 1989 (SI 1989/264)
	76	1 Feb 1989 (SI 1989/1)
	77	3 Apr 1989 (SI 1989/264)
	78	31 Jul 1989 (SI 1989/1085)
	79	31 Jul 1989 (SI 1989/1085); but note already in force 1 Feb 1989 (SI 1989/1)
	80	1 Feb 1989 (SI 1989/1)
	81	Repealed
	82	12 Oct 1988 (SI 1988/1676)
	83–88	Repealed
	89–91	29 Jul 1988 (s 171(5))
	92–96	Repealed
	97–104	29 Jul 1988 (s 171(5))
	105	Repealed
	106–110	3 Apr 1989 (SI 1989/264)
	111–117	29 Jul 1988 (s 171(5))
	118	12 Oct 1988 (SI 1988/1676)
16		29 Jul 1988 (repeals of or in Criminal Justice Act 1967, s 49; Children and Young Persons Act 1969, s 29; Criminal Justice Act 1987) (s 171(5))

Criminal Justice Act 1988 (c 33)—*cont*

Sch 16—*cont*

29 Sep 1988 (repeals of or in Prevention of Corruption Act 1916; Criminal Justice Act 1967, Sch 3; Criminal Justice Act 1972, s 28(3); Sexual Offences (Amendment) Act 1976; Protection of Children Act 1978; Cable and Broadcasting Act 1984; Police and Criminal Evidence Act 1984, s 24(2)(e)) (s 171(6))

1 Oct 1988 (repeals of or in Prison Act 1952; Criminal Justice Act 1961; Firearms Act 1968 (EW only); Children and Young Persons Act 1969, ss 16(10), 22(5), 34(1)(f); Powers of Criminal Courts Act 1973, s 57(3); Criminal Law Act 1977, Sch 12; Reserve Forces Act 1980; Criminal Justice Act 1982, ss 47, 12(1)(5), (8), (9), 14, 20(1), Sch 8, paras 3(c), 7(d); Repatriation of Prisoners Act 1984 (EW only)) (SI 1988/1408)

12 Oct 1988 (repeals of or in Criminal Law Act 1826, s 30; Offences Against the Person Act 1861, ss 42–44; Criminal Justice Act 1925, s 39; Children and Young Persons Act 1933, ss 1(5), (6), 38(1), Sch 1; Children and Young Persons (Scotland) Act 1937, s 12(5), (6); Criminal Appeal Act 1968, ss 10(3)(d), 42; Road Traffic Act 1972, s 100; Criminal Justice Act 1972, Sch 5; Powers of Criminal Courts Act 1973, ss 22(5), 34A(1)(c), Sch 3, paras 2(4)(b), 7, Sch 5, para 29; Juries Act 1974, s 16(2); Criminal Law Act 1977, Sch 5, para 2, Sch 6; Magistrates' Courts Act 1980; Criminal Justice Act 1982, ss 43, 74, 75, 80(1); Video Recordings Act 1984, s 15(2), (4), (5); Police and Criminal Evidence Act 1984, s 65; Cinemas Act 1985, Sch 2, para 11; Local Government Act 1985, s 15(5); Coroners Act 1988, Sch 3, para 14) (SI 1988/1676)

1 Nov 1988 (repeals of or in Prisons (Scotland) Act 1952; Firearms Act 1968 (s only); Fire Precautions Act 1971, s 40(2)(b); Repatriation of Prisoners Act 1984 (s only)) (SI 1988/1817)

5 Jan 1989 (repeals of or in Offences Against the Person Act 1861, ss 46, 47; Juries Act 1974, s 12(1)(a); Criminal Law Act 1977, s 43; Drug Trafficking Offences Act 1986, s 6(1)(b), (3), (5)) (SI 1988/2073)

23 Jan 1989 (repeals of or in Drug Trafficking Offences Act 1986, ss 10(1), 15(5)(b), (c), 17(1), 38(11)) (SI 1989/50)

3 Apr 1989 (repeals of or in Police and Criminal Evidence Act 1984, s 68, Sch 3, paras 1–7, 13) (except in relation to a trial, or proceedings before a magistrates' court acting as examining justices, which began before that date) (SI 1989/264)

3 Apr 1989 (repeals of or in Administration of Justice Act 1970, s 41(8); Insolvency Act 1985, Sch 8, para 24; Drug Trafficking Offences Act 1986, ss 19, 25) (SI 1989/264)

31 Jul 1989 (repeal in Criminal Appeal Act 1968, s 7(1)) (SI 1989/1085)

Criminal Justice Act 1988 (c 33)—*cont*

Sch 16—*cont*	*Not in force* (otherwise)

[1] Extradition Act 1989, s 38(4) provided for s 136(1) of, and Sch 1, para 4 to, this Act to come into force immediately before 27 Sep 1989 and those provisions were then repealed on that date by s 37(1) of, and Sch 2 to, the 1989 Act

[2] Any order made under Criminal Justice (Scotland) Act 1995, s 118, bringing the prospective repeals into force will be noted to that Act in the service to this work

Dartford-Thurrock Crossing Act 1988 (c 20)

Local application only

Duchy of Lancaster Act 1988 (c 10)

RA: 3 May 1988

3 May 1988 (RA)

Education Reform Act 1988 (c 40)

RA: 29 Jul 1988

Commencement provisions: s 236; Education Reform Act 1988 (Commencement No 1) Order 1988, SI 1988/1459; Education Reform Act 1988 (Commencement No 2) Order 1988, SI 1988/1794; Education Reform Act 1988 (Commencement No 3) Order 1988, SI 1988/2002; Education Reform Act 1988 (Commencement No 4) Order 1988, SI 1988/2271 (as amended by SI 1989/501, SI 1990/391); Education Reform Act 1988 (Commencement No 5) Order 1989, SI 1989/164; Education Reform Act 1988 (Commencement No 6) Order 1989, SI 1989/501 (also amends SI 1988/2271); Education Reform Act 1988 (Commencement No 7) Order 1989, SI 1989/719; Education Reform Act 1988 (Commencement No 8 and Amendment) Order 1990, SI 1990/391 (also amends SI 1988/2271); Education Reform Act 1988 (Commencement No 9) Order 1991, SI 1991/409

s 1	29 Jul 1988 (s 236(1))
2(1)(a)	29 Sep 1988 (s 236(3))
(aa), (ab)	Inserted by Education Act 1993, s 241(1) (qv)
(b)	29 Jul 1988 (s 236(1))
(2)	29 Jul 1988 (s 236(1))
(3)	29 Sep 1988 (s 236(3))
3, 4	29 Jul 1988 (s 236(1))
5	1 Aug 1989 (SI 1989/164)
6	29 Sep 1988 (s 236(3))
7	1 Aug 1989 (except in relation to ILEA schools) (SI 1988/2271)
	1 Aug 1990 (exception noted above) (SI 1988/2271)
8, 9	29 Sep 1988 (s 236(3))
10(1)	29 Sep 1988 (s 236(3))
(2)	1 Aug 1989 (SI 1989/164)
(3)	1 Aug 1989 (in relation to pupils at schools in England in the first, second and third key stage who do not have a statement of special educational needs) (SI 1989/164)
	1 Aug 1989 (so far as regards the core subjects, in relation to pupils at schools in Wales in the first,

Education Reform Act 1988 (c 40)—*cont*

s 10(3)—*cont*	second and third key stage who do not have a statement of special educational needs) (SI 1989/501)
	1 Aug 1990 (in relation to pupils at schools in England in the first, second and third key stage who have a statement of special educational needs and, so far as regards the core subjects, in relation to pupils at such schools in the first year of the fourth key stage) (SI 1989/164)
	1 Aug 1990 (so far as regards the core subjects and other foundation subjects, in relation to pupils at schools in Wales in the first, second and third key stage (and who, in the former case, have a statement of special educational needs); and, so far as regards the core subjects in relation to pupils at schools in Wales in the first year of the fourth key stage) (SI 1989/501)
	1 Aug 1991 (so far as regards the core subjects, in relation to pupils at schools in England in the second year of the fourth key stage) (SI 1989/164)
	1 Aug 1991 (so far as regards the core subjects, in relation to pupils at schools in Wales in the second year of the fourth key stage) (SI 1989/501)
11	29 Sep 1988 (s 236(3))
12	1 Mar 1989 (except in relation to ILEA county schools) (SI 1989/164)
	1 Apr 1990 (exception noted above) (SI 1989/164)
12A	Inserted by Education Act 1993, s 257 (qv)
13	29 Sep 1988 (s 236(3))
14, 15	29 Jul 1988 (s 236(1))
16	1 Aug 1989 (SI 1989/164)
17	1 Nov 1988 (SI 1988/1794)
17A	Inserted by Education Act 1993, s 241(3) (qv)
18, 19	1 Nov 1988 (SI 1988/1794)
20–22	29 Jul 1988 (s 236(1))
23(1)	29 Jul 1988 (s 236(1))
(2)	1 Sep 1989 (except in relation to ILEA schools) (SI 1989/164)
	1 Apr 1990 (exception noted above) (SI 1989/164)
24	31 Mar 1990 (SI 1990/391)
25	29 Jul 1988 (s 236(1))
26	1 Sep 1989 (for the purpose of enabling proposals to be made under s 26(4)–(6) for fixing the number of pupils in any age group which it is intended to admit to a secondary school in school year beginning next after 4 Aug 1990, and for purposes of s 26(7), (8), (10)) (SI 1988/1459)
	4 Aug 1990 (remaining purposes so far as relate to secondary schools) (SI 1988/1459)
	1 Sep 1991 (for the purpose of enabling proposals to be made under s 26(4)–(6) for fixing the number of pupils in any age group which it is intended to admit to a primary school in the school year beginning next after 1 Aug 1992, and for the purposes of s 26(7), (8), (10)) (SI 1991/409)
	1 Aug 1992 (for remaining purposes so far as relate to primary schools) (SI 1991/409)

Education Reform Act 1988 (c 40)—*cont*

s 27(1)–(3)	1 Sep 1988 (so far as relate to secondary schools) (SI 1988/1459)
	12 Mar 1991 (so far as relate to primary schools and subject, in the case of s 27(2), to transitional provisions) (SI 1991/409)
(4)–(8)	1 Sep 1988 (for purpose of enabling orders reducing any standard number applying to a secondary school to be made under s 27(5) and applications for such orders to be made as mentioned in s 27(6)) (SI 1988/1459)
	1 Sep 1989 (for purpose of enabling orders increasing any standard number applying to a secondary school to be made under s 27(5) and applications for such orders to be made as mentioned in s 27(7)) (SI 1988/1459)
	4 Aug 1990 (remaining purposes, so far as relate to secondary schools) (SI 1988/1459)
	1 May 1991 (for purpose of enabling orders reducing any standard number applying to a primary school to be made under s 27(5) and applications for such orders to be made as mentioned under s 27(6)) (SI 1991/409)
	1 Sep 1991 (for purpose of enabling orders increasing any standard numbers applying to a primary school to be made under s 27(5) and applications for such orders to be made as mentioned in s 27(7)) (SI 1991/409)
	12 Mar 1991 (for remaining purposes, so far as relate to primary schools) (SI 1991/409)
(9)	1 Sep 1988 (so far as relates to secondary schools) (SI 1988/1459)
	12 Mar 1991 (so far as relates to primary schools) (SI 1991/409)
28	1 Sep 1988 (so far as relates to secondary schools) (SI 1988/1459)
	12 Mar 1991 (so far as relates to primary schools) (SI 1991/409)
29	1 May 1991 (SI 1991/409)
30	1 Sep 1988 (SI 1988/1459)
31(1)	4 Aug 1990 (so far as relates to secondary schools) (SI 1988/1459)
	1 Aug 1992 (so far as relates to primary schools) (SI 1991/409)
(2)	1 Sep 1989 (so far as relates to the publication of admission arrangements for secondary schools for the school year beginning next after 4 Aug 1990 and subsequent school years) (SI 1988/1459)
	1 Sep 1991 (so far as relates to publication of admission arrangements for primary schools for the school year beginning next after 1 Aug 1992 and subsequent school years) (SI 1991/409)
(3)	1 Aug 1991 (SI 1991/409)
(4)–(6)	1 May 1991 (SI 1991/409)
32	1 Sep 1988 (so far as relates to secondary schools) (SI 1988/1459)
	12 Mar 1991 (so far as relates to primary schools) (SI 1991/409)

Education Reform Act 1988 (c 40)—*cont*

s 33, 34	29 Jul 1988 (s 236(1))
35	Substituted by Education Act 1993, s 274(2) (qv)
36–42	29 Jul 1988 (s 236(1))
42A	Inserted by Education Act 1993, s 275(2) (qv)
43	Substituted by Education Act 1993, s 276 (qv)
44–51	29 Jul 1988 (s 236(1))
52–99	Repealed
100(1)	Repealed
(2)	29 Jul 1988 (s 236(1))
(3)	Repealed
(4)	29 Jul 1988 (s 236(1))
101–104	Repealed
105	29 Jul 1988 (s 236(1))
106–111	1 Apr 1989 (SI 1988/1794)
112, 113	29 Jul 1988 (s 236(1))
114	30 Nov 1988 (SI 1988/2002)
115	1 May 1989 (SI 1989/164)
116	29 Jul 1988 (s 236(1))
117, 118	1 Apr 1989 (SI 1988/1794)
119	29 Jul 1988 (s 236(1))
120	1 Apr 1989 (SI 1988/2271)
121	21 Nov 1988 (except Southampton Institute of Higher Education) (SI 1988/1794) 1 Feb 1989 (exception noted above) (SI 1988/2271)
122	21 Nov 1988 (SI 1988/1794)
122A	Inserted by Further and Higher Education Act 1992, s 74(1) (qv)
123, 124	21 Nov 1988 (SI 1988/1794)
124A–124D	Inserted by Further and Higher Education Act 1992, s 71(1) (qv)
125–129	21 Nov 1988 (SI 1988/1794)
129A, 129B	Inserted by Further and Higher Education Act 1992, s 73(1) (qv)
130	21 Nov 1988 (SI 1988/1794)
131, 132	Repealed
133	1 Nov 1988 (SI 1988/1794)
134	Repealed
135	21 Nov 1988 (SI 1988/1794)
136	1 Nov 1988 (SI 1988/1794)
137, 138	29 Jul 1988 (s 236(1))
139–155	Repealed
156	29 Jul 1988 (s 236(1)); repealed in relation to designated institutions by Further and Higher Education Act 1992, ss 73(2), 85(1), 93(2), Sch 9 (qv)
157–199	29 Jul 1988 (s 236(1))
200	Repealed
201–208	29 Jul 1988 (s 236(1))
209	31 Mar 1990 (SI 1990/391)
210, 211	1 May 1989 (SI 1989/719)
212, 213	29 Jul 1988 (s 236(1))
214–216	30 Nov 1988 (SI 1988/2002)
217	29 Jul 1988 (s 236(1))
218	1 Apr 1989 (SI 1988/2002)
219(1)(a)	1 Jan 1989 (SI 1988/2271)
(b)	Repealed
(2)(a)	1 Jan 1989 (SI 1988/2271)

Education Reform Act 1988 (c 40)—*cont*

s 219(2)(b)	29 Jul 1988 (s 236(1))
(c)	1 Jan 1989 (SI 1988/2271)
(d), (e)	Repealed
(3)(a)	1 Jan 1989 (SI 1988/2271)
(b)	29 Jul 1988 (s 236(1))
(c)(i)	1 Jan 1989 (SI 1989/2271)
(ii)	Repealed
220	1 Nov 1988 (SI 1988/1794)
221–225	29 Jul 1988 (s 236(1))
226	21 Nov 1988 (SI 1988/1794)
227(1)	29 Jul 1988 (s 236(1))
(2)–(4)	Repealed
228, 229	21 Nov 1988 (SI 1988/1794)
230–236	29 Jul 1988 (s 236(1))
237(1)	See Sch 12 below
(2)	See Sch 13 below
238	29 Jul 1988 (s 236(1))
Sch 1	29 Sep 1988 (s 236(3))
2–4	29 Jul 1988 (s 236(1))
5	Repealed
6	29 Jul 1988 (s 236(1))
7	21 Nov 1988 (SI 1988/1794)
7A	Inserted by Further and Higher Education Act 1992, s 71(4), Sch 6 (qv)
8	29 Jul 1988 (so far as relating to the Education Assets Board) (s 236(1)); and 1 Nov 1988 (otherwise) (SI 1988/1754); repealed in relation to Universities Funding Council and Polytechnics and Colleges Funding Council, by Further and Higher Education Act 1992, s 93(1), Sch 8, Pt I, paras 27, 60 (qv)
9–11	29 Jul 1988 (s 236(1))
12, para 1, 2	29 Jul 1988 (s 236(1))
3	Spent
4–8	29 Jul 1988 (s 236(1))
9, 10	Repealed
11	29 Jul 1988 (s 236(1))
12	Repealed
13–25	29 Jul 1988 (s 236(1))
26–28	Repealed
29–32	29 Jul 1988 (s 236(1))
33	Repealed
34–37	29 Jul 1988 (s 236(1))
38–40	Repealed
41–46	1 Apr 1990 (s 236(4))
47–49	Repealed
50–53	1 Apr 1990 (s 236(4))
54–57	1 Apr 1989 (SI 1988/2271)
58	1 Mar 1989 (SI 1989/164)
59	1 Apr 1989 (SI 1988/2271)
60	29 Jul 1988 (s 236(1))
61, 62	1 Apr 1989 (SI 1988/2271)
63, 64	Repealed
65	1 Apr 1989 (SI 1988/2271)
66	Spent

Education Reform Act 1988 (c 40)—*cont*

Sch 12, para 67	29 Jul 1988 (s 236(1)) (NB also brought into force on 1 Jan 1989 by SI 1988/2271)
68	Repealed
69	1 Apr 1989 (SI 1988/2271)
70	Repealed
71–76	1 Apr 1989 (SI 1988/2271)
77	*Not in force* (by virtue of amendment made to SI 1988/2271) (SI 1989/501)
78, 79	1 Apr 1989 (SI 1988/2271)
80	21 Nov 1988 (SI 1988/1794)
81, 82	29 Jul 1988 (s 236(1))
83–85	Repealed
86–98	1 Apr 1989 (SI 1988/2271)
99	1 Aug 1989 (SI 1988/2271)
100, 101	1 Apr 1989 (SI 1988/2271)
102	29 Jul 1988 (s 236(1))
103–105	1 Apr 1989 (SI 1988/2271)
106	31 Mar 1990 (SI 1990/391)
107	1 Apr 1989 (SI 1988/2271)
13, Pt I	1 Apr 1990 (s 236(5))
II	30 Nov 1988 (repeals of Education Act 1967, s 3; Education Act 1980, Sch 3, para 14) (SI 1988/2002)
	1 Jan 1989 (repeals of Education Act 1944, ss 25, 29(2)–(4); Education Act 1946, s 7; Education (No 2) Act 1968 (subject to transitional provisions)) (SI 1988/2271)
	1 Apr 1989 (repeal of Education Act 1944, s 61) (SI 1988/1794)
	1 Apr 1989 (repeals of Education Act 1980, s 27; Education Act 1981, Sch 3, para 5) (SI 1988/2002)
	1 Apr 1989 (repeals of or in Education Act 1944, ss 8(1)(b), 42–46, 50, 52(1), 54, 60, 62(2), 69, 84, 114; Education Act 1946, s 8(3); London Government Act 1963, s 31(1), (4); Industrial Training Act 1964, s 16; Local Government Act 1972, ss 81(4)(a), 104(2); Sex Discrimination Act 1975, ss 24(2)(a), 25(6)(c)(ii); Race Relations Act 1976, ss 19(6)(c)(ii), 78(1); Education (No 2) Act 1986, s 56) (SI 1988/2271)
	1 Aug 1989 (repeals of or in Education (No 2) Act 1986, ss 17(1), (4), 18(3), (4), (6), (8), 19(3), 20) (SI 1988/2271)
	1 May 1989 (repeals of or in Education Act 1946, s 1(1); Employment Protection (Consolidation) Act 1978, s 29(1)(e); Education Act 1980, s 35(5), Sch 1, para 25; Local Government, Planning and Land Act 1980, Sch 10, Pt I; Local Government Act 1985, s 22; Education (No 2) Act 1986, ss 29, 47(5)(a)(ii), Sch 4, para 4; Local Government Act 1987, s 2) (SI 1989/719)
	31 Mar 1990 (repeals in Local Government Act 1974) (SI 1990/391)
	Not in force (repeal in Education Act 1980, s 35(3))

Electricity (Financial Provisions) (Scotland) Act 1988 (c 37)

Whole Act repealed

Employment Act 1988 (c 19)

RA: 26 May 1988

Commencement provisions: s 34(2); Employment Act 1988 (Commencement No 1) Order 1988, SI 1988/1118; Employment Act 1988 (Commencement No 2) Order 1988, SI 1988/2042

s 1–24	Repealed
25, 26	26 May 1988 (RA)
27	Repealed
28, 29	26 May 1988 (RA)
30	Repealed
31	26 May 1988 (RA)
32(1)	26 May 1988 (RA)
(2)	Repealed
33(1)	See Sch 3 below
(2)	See Sch 4 below
34(1)	26 May 1988 (RA)
(2), (3)	Repealed
(4), (5)	26 May 1988 (RA)
(6)(a), (b)	Repealed
(c)	26 May 1988 (RA)
Sch 1	Repealed
2	26 May 1988 (RA)
3, Pt I, para 1–6	Repealed
II, para 7–10	Repealed
11(1)	Repealed
(2)	26 May 1988 (RA)
12(1)	Repealed
(2)	26 May 1988 (RA)
(3)	Repealed
13	26 May 1988 (RA)
14(1)	26 May 1988 (RA)
(2)	Repealed
15	26 May 1988 (RA)
4	26 May 1988 (repeals of or in Parliamentary Commissioner Act 1967, Sch 2; Employment and Training Act 1973, ss 4(2), 5(1), (4), 11(3), 12(4); Social Security Act 1975, s 20(1); House of Commons Disqualification Act 1975, Sch 1, Pt III; Northern Ireland Assembly Disqualification Act 1975, Sch 1, Pt III; Employment Protection Act 1975, Sch 14, para 2(1); Social Security (Miscellaneous Provisions) Act 1977, s 22(6); Social Security (No 2) Act 1980, s 7(7)) (RA)
	26 Jul 1988 (repeals of or in Trade Union Act 1913, s 4(1F); Trade Union (Amalgamations, etc) Act 1964, s 4(6), Sch 1; Employment Protection (Consolidation) Act 1978, ss 23(1), (2A), (2B)[1], 58(1), (3)–(12)[1], 58A, 153(1); Employment Act 1980, s 15(2); Employment Act 1982, s 10(1), (2), Sch 3, para 16; Trade Union Act 1984, ss 3, 6(6), 9(1)) (SI 1988/1118)

Employment Act 1988 (c 19)—*cont*

Sch 4—*cont*	26 Jul 1989 (repeals of or in Trade Union Act 1984, ss 1(1)(3), 8(1)) (SI 1988/1118)

[1] (*Note:* Repeal of Employment Protection (Consolidation) Act 1978, ss 23(2A), (2B), 58(3)–(12) effected on 26 July 1988 by virtue of the bringing into force on that date of s 11 (now repealed) (SI 1988/1118))

Environment and Safety Information Act 1988 (c 30)

RA: 29 Jul 1988

Commencement provisions: s 5(2)

1 Apr 1989 (s 5(2))

European Communities (Finance) Act 1988 (c 46)

Whole Act repealed

Farm Land and Rural Development Act 1988 (c 16)

RA: 10 May 1988

10 May 1988 (RA)

Finance Act 1988 (c 39)

Budget Day: 15 Mar 1988

RA: 29 Jul 1988

See the note concerning Finance Acts at the front of this book

Firearms (Amendment) Act 1988 (c 45)

RA: 15 Nov 1988

Commencement provisions: s 27(3); Firearms (Amendment) Act 1988 (Commencement No 1) Order 1988, SI 1988/2209; Firearms (Amendment) Act 1988 (Commencement No 2) Order 1989, SI 1989/853 (amended by SI 1989/1673); Firearms (Amendment) Act 1988 (Commencement No 3) Order 1990, SI 1990/2620

s 1	1 Feb 1989 (subject to transitional provisions) (SI 1988/2209)
2(1), (2)	1 Jul 1989 (subject to transitional provisions) (SI 1989/853)
(3)	1 Jul 1989 (SI 1989/853)
3(1)	1 Jul 1989 (SI 1989/853)
(2)	1 Jul 1989 (subject to transitional provisions) (SI 1989/853)
4(1)	1 Jul 1989 (SI 1989/853)
(2)(a)	1 Jul 1989 (SI 1989/853)
(b)	1 Jul 1989 (subject to transitional provisions) (SI 1989/853)

Firearms (Amendment) Act 1988 (c 45)—*cont*

s 4(3)	1 Jul 1989 (subject to transitional provisions) (SI 1989/853)
(4), (5)	1 Jul 1989 (SI 1989/853)
5, 6	1 Jul 1990 (SI 1989/853)
7(1)	1 Feb 1989 (subject to transitional provisions) (SI 1988/2209)
(2)	1 Jul 1989 (subject to transitional provisions) (SI 1989/853)
(3)	1 Jul 1989 (SI 1989/853)
8–10	1 Feb 1988 (SI 1988/2209)
11	1 Jul 1989 (SI 1989/853)
12	1 Feb 1989 (SI 1989/2209)
13(1)	1 Jul 1989 (SI 1989/853)
(2)–(5)	1 Feb 1989 (SI 1988/2209)
14	1 Feb 1989 (SI 1988/2209)
15	1 Jul 1989 (SI 1989/853)
16	1 Feb 1989 (SI 1988/2209)
17, 18	1 Oct 1989 (SI 1989/853)
18A	Inserted (1 Jan 1993) by Firearms Acts (Amendment) Regulations 1992, SI 1992/2823, reg 9
19	See Schedule below
20(1), (2)	1 Jul 1989 (for purpose of enabling the Secretary of State to make an order under Firearms Act 1968, s 6(1A), which is to come into force on the date on which this section comes into force for all other purposes) (SI 1989/853 as amended by Firearms (Amendment) Act 1988 (Commencement No 2) Order (Amendment) Order 1989, SI 1989/1673, art 3)
	2 Apr 1991 (otherwise) (SI 1990/2620)
(3)	2 Apr 1991 (SI 1990/2620)
21, 22	1 Feb 1989 (SI 1988/2209)
23(1)–(3)	1 Feb 1989 (SI 1988/2209)
(4)–(6)	1 Jul 1989 (SI 1989/853)
(7)	1 Feb 1989 (SI 1988/2209)
(8)	1 Oct 1989 (except in relation to a person who is in Great Britain on 1 Oct 1989) (SI 1989/853)
	31 Oct 1989 (exception noted above) (SI 1989/853)
24(1)	1 Feb 1989 (SI 1988/2209)
(2)	1 Jul 1989 (SI 1989/853)
25	1 Feb 1989 (SI 1988/2209)
26, 27	15 Nov 1988 (s 27(3))
Schedule	1 Jul 1989 (SI 1989/853)

Foreign Marriage (Amendment) Act 1988 (c 44)

RA: 2 Nov 1988

Commencement provisions: s 7(3); Foreign Marriage (Amendment) Act 1988 (Commencement) Order 1990, SI 1990/522

12 Apr 1990 (SI 1990/522)

Health and Medicines Act 1988 (c 49)

RA: 15 Nov 1988

Commencement provisions: ss 19(2), 26(1)–(5); Health and Medicines Act 1988 (Commencement No 1) Order 1988, SI 1988/2107; Health and Medicines Act 1988 (Commencement No 2) Order 1989, SI 1989/111; Health and Medicines Act 1988 (Commencement No 3) Order 1989, SI 1989/337; Health and Medicines Act 1988 (Commencement No 4) Order 1989, SI 1989/826 ; Health and Medicines Act 1988 (Commencement No 5) Order 1989, SI 1989/1174 (revoked); Health and Medicines Act 1988 (Commencement No 6) Order 1989, SI 1989/1229 (revoking SI 1989/1174); Health and Medicine Act 1988 (Commencement No 7) Order 1989, SI 1989/1896; Health and Medicines Act 1988 (Commencement No 8) Order 1989, SI 1989/1984

s 1–6	15 Nov 1988 (s 26(3), (4))
7	15 Jan 1989 (s 26(1)(5))
8(1)(a)	15 Oct 1989 (except words 'or section 19 of the National Health Service (Scotland) Act 1978') (SI 1989/1896)
	31 Oct 1989 (exception noted above) (SI 1989/1984)
(b)	9 Jun 1989 (SI 1989/826)
(2)	9 Jun 1989 (except words '(a) or') (SI 1989/826)
	15 Oct 1989 (words '(a) or' except so far as they have effect for the purposes of any list maintained under National Health Service (Scotland) Act 1978, s 19) (SI 1989/1896)
	31 Oct 1989 (exception noted above) (SI 1989/1984)
(3)–(7)	9 Jun 1989 (SI 1989/826)
9	1 Apr 1990 (SI 1989/826)
10	15 Jan 1989 (s 26(1)–(5))
11(1)	7 Mar 1989 (SI 1989/337)
(2)	1 Apr 1989 (SI 1989/337)
(3)	7 Mar 1989 (for purposes of regulations as to charges authorised by National Health Service Act 1977, s 78(1A)) (SI 1989/337)
	1 Apr 1989 (otherwise) (SI 1989/337)
(4)	7 Mar 1989 (SI 1989/337)
(5)	1 Apr 1989 (SI 1989/337)
(6)	7 Mar 1989 (for purposes of regulations as to charges authorised by National Health Service (Scotland) Act 1978, s 70(1A)) (SI 1989/337)
	1 Apr 1989 (otherwise) (SI 1989/337)
(7)	1 Jan 1989 (SI 1989/2107)
(8)	1 Apr 1989 (SI 1989/337)
12(1)–(3)	1 Apr 1989 (SI 1989/337)
(4), (5)	Repealed
13(1)	7 Mar 1989 (for purposes of adding National Health Service Act 1977, s 38(2)–(6) and of adding s 38(7) thereof up to the words 'are to be made' thereto) (SI 1989/337)
	1 Apr 1989 (otherwise) (SI 1989/337)
(2)	7 Mar 1989 (for purposes of any regulations made to come into force on or after 1 Apr 1989) (SI 1989/337)
	1 Apr 1989 (otherwise) (SI 1989/337)
(3)	7 Mar 1989 (SI 1989/337)

Health and Medicines Act 1988 (c 49)—*cont*

s 13(4)	7 Mar 1989 (for purposes of adding National Health Service (Scotland) Act 1978, s 26(1A)–(1E) and of adding s 26(1F) thereof up to the words 'are to be made' thereto) (SI 1989/337)
	1 Apr 1989 (otherwise) (SI 1989/337)
(5)	7 Mar 1989 (SI 1989/337)
(6), (7)	Repealed
14	Repealed
15, 16	15 Jan 1989 (s 26(1)–(5))
17(1), (2)	15 Jan 1989 (s 26(1)–(5))
(3)	15 Nov 1988 (s 26(3), (4))
18	15 Jan 1989 (s 26(1)–(5))
19	26 Nov 1987 (retrospective; s 192))
20	15 Jan 1989 (s 26(1)–(5))
21, 22	15 Nov 1988 (s 26(3), (4))
23, 24	15 Jan 1989 (s 26(1)–(5))
25(1)	See Sch 2 below
(2)	See Sch 3 below
26–28	15 Nov 1988 (s 26(3), (4))
Sch 1	15 Nov 1988 (s 26(3), (4))
2, para 1	15 Jan 1989 (so far as relates to paras 2, 6, 7) (s 26(1)–(5))
	7 Mar 1989 (so far as relates to para 8(1), (2)) (SI 1989/337)
	1 Apr 1989 (so far as relates to paras 5, 8(3)) (SI 1989/337)
	9 Jun 1989 (so far as relates to para 4) (SI 1989/826)
	15 Oct 1989 (so far as relates to para 3) (SI 1989/1896)
2	15 Jan 1989 (s 26(1)(5))
3	15 Oct 1989 (SI 1989/1896)
4	9 Jun 1989 (SI 1989/826)
5	1 Apr 1989 (SI 1989/337)
6, 7	15 Jan 1989 (s 26(1)–(5))
8(1)	7 Mar 1989 (for purposes of any regulations made to come into force on or after 1 Apr 1989) (SI 1989/337)
	1 Apr 1989 (otherwise) (SI 1989/337)
(2)	7 Mar 1989 (SI 1989/337)
(3)	1 Apr 1989 (SI 1989/337)
9	15 Jan 1989 (so far as relates to paras 13, 14) (s 26(1)–(5)
	7 Mar 1989 (so far as relates to para 15(1), (2)) (SI 1989/337)
	1 Apr 1989 (so far as relates to paras 12, 15(3)) (SI 1989/337)
	9 Jun 1989 (so far as relates to para 11) (SI 1989/826)
	31 Oct 1989 (so far as relates to para 10) (SI 1989/1984)
10	31 Oct 1989 (SI 1989/1984)
11	Repealed
12	1 Apr 1989 (SI 1989/337)
13, 14	15 Jan 1989 (s 26(1)(5))
15(1)	7 Mar 1989 (for purposes of any regulations made to come into force on or after 1 Apr 1989) (SI 1989/337)
	1 Apr 1989 (otherwise) (SI 1989/337)

Health and Medicines Act 1988 (c 49)—*cont*

Sch 2, para 15(2)	7 Mar 1989 (SI 1989/337)
(3)	1 Apr 1989 (SI 1989/337)
3	15 Nov 1988 (repeal of National Health Service Act 1977, s 28(4)) (s 26(3), (4)) 1 Jan 1989 (repeals of or in National Health Service Act 1977, s 79(1)(d) and word 'or' preceding it; National Health Service (Scotland) Act 1978, s 71(1)(d) and word 'or' preceding it) (SI 1989/2107) 15 Jan 1989 (repeals of or in Health Services and Public Health Act 1968, s 63(3); National Health Service Act 1977, ss 5(1)(a), 58, 61, 62, 63(2), 66A; National Health Service (Scotland) Act 1978, ss 39, 50, 53, 54, 55(2), 58A; Health Services Act 1980, ss 10, 11) (s 26(1)–(5)) 27 Feb 1989 (repeals of or in National Health Service Act 1966; Superannuation Act 1972; Health Services Act 1980, ss 17, 19; Health and Social Security Act 1984, s 8; Companies Consolidation (Consequential Provisions) Act 1985) (SI 1989/111) 1 Apr 1989 (otherwise) (SI 1989/337)

Housing Act 1988 (c 50)

RA: 15 Nov 1988

Commencement provisions: ss 132(8), 141(2), (3); Housing Act 1988 (Commencement No 1) Order 1988, SI 1988/2056; Housing Act 1988 (Commencement No 2) Order 1988, SI 1988/2152; Housing Act 1988 (Commencement No 3) Order 1989, SI 1989/203; Housing Act 1988 (Commencement No 4) Order 1989, SI 1989/404; Housing Act 1988 (Commencement No 5 and Transitional Provisions) Order 1991, SI 1991/954; Housing Act 1988 (Commencement No 6) Order 1992, SI 1992/324

s 1–14	15 Jan 1989 (s 141(3))
14A, 14B	Inserted (1 Apr 1993) by Local Government Finance (Housing) (Consequential Amendments) Order 1993, SI 1993/651, art 2(2), Sch 2, para 8
15–39	15 Jan 1989 (s 141(3))
40(1)	15 Jan 1989 (s 141(3))
(2)	Repealed
(3)	15 Jan 1989 (s 141(3))
(4), (5)	15 Jan 1989 (s 141(3)); prospectively repealed by Courts and Legal Services Act 1990, s 125(7), Sch 20[1]
41(1)	Repealed
(2)–(4)	15 Jan 1989 (s 141(3))
41A	Inserted by Social Security (Consequential Provisions) Act 1992, s 4, Sch 2, para 103 (qv)
41B	Inserted (1 Apr 1993) by Local Government Finance (Housing) (Consequential Amendments) Order 1993, SI 1993/651, art 2(1), Sch 1, para 18 (as substituted by Local Government Finance (Housing) (Consequential Amendments) (Amendment) Order 1993, SI 1993/1120, art 2)

Housing Act 1988 (c 50)—*cont*

s 42–45	15 Jan 1989 (s 141(3))
46(1)	1 Dec 1988 (SI 1988/2056)
(2)	See Sch 5 below
(3)–(5)	1 Apr 1989 (SI 1989/404)
47(1)	1 Apr 1989 (SI 1989/404)
(2)	1 Dec 1988 (SI 1988/2056)
(3)–(5)	1 Apr 1989 (SI 1989/404)
(6)	1 Dec 1988 (so far as relates to s 47(2)) (SI 1988/ 2056)
	1 Apr 1989 (otherwise) (SI 1989/404)
48	1 Apr 1989 (SI 1989/404)
49	15 Jan 1989 (SI 1988/2152)
50–56	1 Apr 1989 (SI 1989/404)
57	15 Jan 1989 (SI 1988/2152)
58	1 Apr 1989 (SI 1989/404)
59(1)	15 Jan 1989 (SI 1988/2152)
(2), (3)	See Sch 6 below
(4)	1 Apr 1989 (SI 1989/404)
60–84	15 Nov 1988 (RA)
84A	Inserted by Leasehold Reform, Housing and Urban Development Act 1993, s 125(5) (qv)
85–92	15 Nov 1988 (RA)
93	5 Apr 1989 (SI 1989/404)
94	15 Jan 1989 (SI 1988/2152)
95–105	5 Apr 1989 (SI 1989/404)
106	15 Jan 1989 (SI 1988/2152)
107	5 Apr 1989 (SI 1989/404)
108	See Sch 12 below
109, 110	5 Apr 1989 (SI 1989/404)
111–114	15 Jan 1989 (SI 1988/2152)
115–118	15 Jan 1989 (s 141(3))
119	See Sch 13 below
120	15 Jan 1989 (s 141(3))
121(1)–(3)	15 Jan 1989 (s 141(3))
(4)–(6)	Repealed
(7)	Substituted by Social Security (Consequential Provisions) Act 1992, s 4, Sch 2, para 140 (qv)
122	10 Mar 1989 (SI 1989/203)
123	15 Jan 1989 (s 141(3))
124	10 Mar 1989 (SI 1989/203)
125, 126	15 Jan 1989 (s 141(3))
127	5 Apr 1989 (SI 1989/404)
128	21 Feb 1992 (SI 1992/324)
129	1 Apr 1989 (SI 1989/404)
130	15 Jan 1989 (s 141(3))
131	15 Jan 1989 (s 141(3)); prospectively repealed by Local Government and Housing Act 1989, s 194, Sch 12, Pt II[2]
132	9 Jun 1988 (retrospective; s 132(8))
133, 134	15 Nov 1988 (RA; s 141(2), (3))
135(1)	21 Feb 1992 (SI 1992/324)
(2)	See Sch 16 below
(3)	21 Feb 1992 (SI 1992/324)
136	Repealed
137	15 Jan 1989 (s 141(3))
138, 139	15 Nov 1988 (RA; s 141(2), (3))
140(1)	See Sch 17 below

Housing Act 1988 (c 50)—*cont*

s 140(2)	See Sch 18 below
141	15 Nov 1988 (RA; s 141(2), (3))
Sch 1–4	15 Jan 1989 (s 141(3))
5	1 Dec 1988 (SI 1988/2056)
6, para 1	15 Jan 1989 (for the purposes only of s 59(1) of the Act and Housing Associations Act 1985, s 36A) (SI 1988/2152)
	1 Apr 1989 (otherwise) (SI 1989/404)
2–7	1 Apr 1989 (SI 1989/404)
8(1)	1 Apr 1989 (SI 1989/404)
(2)	15 Jan 1989 (SI 1988/2152)
9–24	1 Apr 1989 (SI 1989/404)
25	15 Jan 1989 (SI 1988/2152)
26(a)	15 Jan 1989 (SI 1988/2152)
(b), (c)	1 Apr 1989 (SI 1989/404)
27	*Not in force*
28	1 Apr 1989 (SI 1989/404)
29	1 Apr 1989 (except for purposes of hostel deficit grant payable under Housing Associations Act 1985, s 55) (SI 1989/404)
30–37	1 Apr 1989 (SI 1989/404)
7–11	15 Nov 1988 (RA)
12	5 Apr 1989 (SI 1989/404)
13	15 Jan 1989 (subject to transitional provisions) (SI 1988/2152)
14, 15	15 Jan 1989 (s 141(3))
16	21 Feb 1992 (SI 1992/324)
17, para 1–16	15 Jan 1989 (SI 1988/2152)
17(1)	5 Apr 1989 (SI 1989/404)
(2)	15 Jan 1989 (SI 1988/2152)
18	Repealed
19–37	15 Jan 1989 (subject to transitional provision for para 21) (SI 1988/2152)
38, 39	5 Apr 1989 (SI 1989/404)
40	15 Jan 1989 (SI 1988/2152)
41	10 Mar 1989 (SI 1989/203)
42–65	15 Jan 1989 (SI 1988/2152)
66	1 Apr 1989 (SI 1989/404)
67–70	15 Jan 1989 (SI 1988/2152)
71, 72	Repealed
73–76	2 Jan 1989 (SI 1988/2152)
77, 78	2 Jan 1989 (SI 1988/2152)
79	*Not in force*
80–84	15 Jan 1989 (SI 1988/2152)
85–88	2 Jan 1989 (SI 1988/2152)
89	1 Apr 1989 (SI 1989/404)
90	2 Jan 1989 (SI 1988/2152)
91, 92	1 Dec 1988 (SI 1988/2056)
93	Repealed (retrospectively to 1 Dec 1988)
94–96	1 Dec 1988 (SI 1988/2056)
97	1 Apr 1989 (SI 1989/404)
98–102	1 Dec 1988 (SI 1988/2056)
103	1 Apr 1989 (SI 1989/404)
104, 105	1 Dec 1988 (SI 1988/2056)
106–113	1 Apr 1989 (SI 1989/404)
114–116	1 Dec 1988 (SI 1988/2056)

Housing Act 1988 (c 50)—*cont*

Sch 18	2 Jan 1989 (repeal in Housing (Scotland) Act 1988, s 38) (SI 1988/2152) 15 Jan 1989 (repeals of or in Reserve and Auxiliary Forces (Protection of Civil Interests) Act 1951; Rent (Agriculture) Act 1976; Rent Act 1977; Protection from Eviction Act 1977; Housing Act 1980; Local Government Act 1985; Housing Act 1985; Housing and Planning Act 1986, ss 7, 12, 13, Sch 4; Landlord and Tenant Act 1987, ss 3, 4, 60; Housing (Scotland) Act 1988, Sch 9, para 6) (subject to transitional provisions) (SI 1988/2152) 1 Apr 1989 (repeals of or in Housing Associations Act 1985, except s 55 and ss 56, 57 in relation to hostel deficit grants; Housing and Planning Act 1986 (so far as not yet in force); Housing (Scotland) Act 1986; Landlord and Tenant Act 1987 (so far as not yet in force); Local Government Act 1988; Housing (Scotland) Act 1988 (so far as not yet in force)) (SI 1989/404) 1 Apr 1991 (repeals of or in Housing Associations Act 1985, ss 55–57, except in relation to hostel deficit grant payable to an association for a period which expires before 1 Apr 1991) (SI 1991/954) *Not in force* (otherwise)

[1] Any order made under Courts and Legal Services Act 1990, s 124, bring the prospective repeal into force will be noted to that Act in the service to this work

[2] Any order made under Local Government and Housing Act 1989, s 195(2), bringing the prospective repeal into force will be noted to that Act in the service to this work

Housing (Scotland) Act 1988 (c 43)

RA: 2 Nov 1988

Commencement provisions: s 74(2); Housing (Scotland) Act 1988 Commencement Order 1988, SI 1988/2038

s 1(1)	1 Dec 1988 (SI 1988/2038)
(2)	See Sch 1 below
(3)	1 Dec 1988 (SI 1988/2038)
2	1 Dec 1988 (SI 1988/2038)
3(1)	1 Dec 1988 (SI 1988/2038)
(2)	1 Apr 1989 (SI 1988/2038)
(3)	See Sch 2 below
(4)	1 Dec 1988 (SI 1988/2038)
4(1)–(3)	1 Dec 1988 (SI 1988/2038)
(4)	Repealed
(5)–(7)	1 Dec 1988 (SI 1988/2038)
5–11	1 Dec 1988 (SI 1988/2038)
12(1)	2 Jan 1989 (SI 1988/2038)
(2)	See Sch 4 below
13–24	2 Jan 1989 (SI 1988/2038)
25A, 25B	Inserted (1 Apr 1993) by Local Government Finance (Housing) (Consequential Amendments) (Scotland) Order 1993, SI 1993/658, art 2, Sch 2, para 5

Housing (Scotland) Act 1988 (c 43)—*cont*

s 26–35	2 Jan 1989 (SI 1988/2038)
36–40	2 Jan 1989 (s 74(2)(b))
41–45	2 Jan 1989 (SI 1988/2038)
46(1), (2)	2 Jan 1989 (SI 1988/2038)
(3), (4)	See Sch 6 below
47, 48	2 Jan 1989 (SI 1988/2038)
48A	Inserted by Social Security (Consequential Provisions) Act 1992, s 4, Sch 2, para 102 (qv)
49–55	2 Jan 1989 (SI 1988/2038)
56–64	1 Apr 1989 (SI 1988/2038)
65	2 Jan 1989 (s 74(2)(b))
66	2 Jan 1989 (SI 1988/2038)
67	2 Jan 1989 (s 74(2)(b))
68	2 Jan 1989 (SI 1988/2038)
69	2 Nov 1988 (s 74(2)(a))
70	2 Jan 1989 (SI 1988/2038)
71	2 Jan 1989 (s 74(2)(b))
72(1)	See Schs 7, 8 below
(2)	See Sch 9 below
(3)	See Sch 10 below
73	1 Dec 1988 (SI 1988/2038)
74	2 Nov 1988 (s 74(2)(a))
Sch 1	1 Dec 1988 (SI 1988/2038)
2, para 1, 2	1 Apr 1989 (SI 1988/2038)
3(a)	1 Dec 1988 (SI 1988/2038)
(b)	1 Apr 1989 (SI 1988/2038)
4–17	1 Apr 1989 (SI 1988/2038)
3	Repealed
4–6	2 Jan 1989 (SI 1988/2038)
7	2 Nov 1988 (s 74(2)(a))
8	2 Jan 1989 (s 74(2)(b))
9, para 1–6	2 Jan 1989 (SI 1988/2038)
7	Repealed
8–16	2 Jan 1989 (SI 1988/2038)
17	1 Apr 1989 (SI 1988/2038)
18–21	2 Apr 1989 (SI 1988/2038)
10	2 Jan 1989 (repeals of or in Housing (Scotland) Act 1987, ss 62(11)–(13), 151) (s 74(2)(b)) 1 Apr 1989 (repeal of Housing (Scotland) Act 1987, Sch 16, para 1(b)) (s 74(2)(c)) 2 Jan 1989 (repeals of or in Rent (Scotland) Act 1984, ss 66(1), 68, 70(2), 71(1)) (SI 1988/2038) 1 Apr 1989 (otherwise)[1] (SI 1988/2038)

[1] (*Note:* entry relating to Housing Associations Act 1985 in Sch 10 was repealed on 1 Apr 1989 by Housing Act 1988, s 140, Sch 18)

Immigration Act 1988 (c 14)

RA: 10 May 1988

Commencement provisions: s 12(3), (4); Immigration Act 1988 (Commencement No 1) Order 1988, SI 1988/1133; Immigration Act 1988 (Commencement No 2) Order 1991, SI 1991/1001; Immigration Act 1988 (Commencement No 3) Order 1994, SI 1994/1923

Immigration Act 1988 (c 14)—*cont*

s 1–5	1 Aug 1988 (subject to exceptions in relation to ss 1, 2, 4) (SI 1988/1133)
6	10 Jul 1988 (s 12(3))
7(1)	20 Jul 1994 (SI 1994/1923)
(2), (3)	10 Jul 1988 (s 12(3))
8–12	10 Jul 1988 (s 12(3))
Schedule,	
para 1	1 May 1991 (SI 1991/1001)
2–10	10 Jul 1988 (s 12(3))

Income and Corporation Taxes Act 1988 (c 1)

RA: 9 Feb 1988

Commencement provisions: as provided for by s 843. In general, the Act came into force in relation to tax for the year 1988–89 and subsequent years of assessment, and for company accounting periods ending after 5 April 1988; but this is subject to a contrary intention, in particular as provided by ss 96, 380–384, 393, 394 (repealed), 400, 470(3)[1], 703, 729(12)[2], 812

[1] Appointed day for the purposes of s 470(3): 29 Apr 1988 (Income and Corporation Taxes Act 1988 (Appointed Day) Order 1988, SI 1988/745)

[2] Appointed day for the purposes of s 729(12): 9 Jun 1988 (SI 1988/1002) (Income and Corporation Taxes Act 1988 (Appointed Day No 2) Order 1988, SI 1988/1002)

Landlord and Tenant Act 1988 (c 26)

RA: 29 Jul 1988

Commencement provisions: s 7(2)

29 Sep 1988 (s 7(2))

Land Registration Act 1988 (c 3)

RA: 15 Mar 1988

Commencement provisions: s 3(2); Land Registration Act 1988 (Commencement) Order 1990, SI 1990/1359

3 Dec 1990 (SI 1990/1359)

Legal Aid Act 1988 (c 34)

RA: 29 Jul 1988

Commencement provisions: s 47; Legal Aid Act 1988 (Commencement No 1) Order 1988, SI 1988/1361; Legal Aid Act 1988 (Commencement No 2) (Scotland) Order 1988, SI 1988/1388; Legal Aid Act 1988 (Commencement No 3) Order 1989, SI 1989/288; Legal Aid Act 1988 (Commencement No 4) Order 1991, SI 1991/790

s 1, 2	1 Apr 1989 (SI 1989/288)

Legal Aid Act 1988 (c 34)—*cont*

s 3(1)	20 Aug 1988 (SI 1988/1361)
(2)–(4)	1 Apr 1989 (SI 1989/288)
(5)–(10)	20 Aug 1988 (SI 1988/1361)
4–26	1 Apr 1989 (SI 1989/288)
27, 28	Repealed
29	1 May 1991 (SI 1991/790)
30(1), (2)	Repealed
(3)	1 May 1991 (SI 1991/790)
31–34	1 Apr 1989 (SI 1989/288)
35	Repealed
36–43	1 Apr 1989 (SI 1989/288)
44	See Sch 4 below
45(1)	See Sch 5 below
(2)	See Sch 6 below
(3)	See Schs 5, 6 below
(4)	See Sch 7 below
46	29 Jul 1988 (s 47(4))
47	29 Jul 1988 (RA)
Sch 1	20 Aug 1988 (SI 1988/1361)
2, 3	1 Apr 1989 (SI 1989/288)
4, para 1, 2	29 Jul 1988 (SI 1988/1388)
3	*Not in force*
4	29 Jul 1988 (SI 1988/1388)
5	*Not in force*
6–9	29 Jul 1988 (SI 1988/1388)
5	1 Apr 1989 (SI 1989/288)
6	29 Jul 1988 (repeal of Legal Aid Act 1974, s 21) (s 47(4))
	1 Apr 1989 (otherwise) (SI 1989/288)
7, para 1–5	1 Apr 1989 (SI 1989/288)
6–8	20 Aug 1988 (SI 1988/1361)
9–11	1 Apr 1989 (SI 1989/288)
8	29 Jul 1988 (s 47(4))

Licensing Act 1988 (c 17)

RA: 19 May 1988

Commencement provisions: s 20(3); Licensing Act 1988 (Commencement No 1) Order 1988, SI 1988/1187; Licensing Act 1988 (Commencement No 2) Order 1988, SI 1988/1333

s 1	22 Aug 1988 (SI 1988/1333)
2	1 Aug 1988 (SI 1988/1187)
3	22 Aug 1988 (SI 1988/1333)
4	1 Aug 1988 (SI 1988/1187)
5	22 Aug 1988 (SI 1988/1333)
6–8	1 Aug 1988 (SI 1988/1187)
9	22 Aug 1988 (SI 1988/1333)
10	1 Aug 1988 (SI 1988/1187)
11	22 Aug 1988 (SI 1988/1333)
12	1 Mar 1989 (SI 1988/1333)
13, 14	22 Aug 1988 (SI 1988/1333)
15	1 Mar 1989 (SI 1988/1333)
16–18	1 Aug 1988 (SI 1988/1187)

Licensing Act 1988 (c 17)—*cont*

s 19(1)	See Sch 3 below
(2)	See Sch 4 below
20	1 Aug 1988 (SI 1988/1187)
Sch 1, 2	22 Aug 1988 (SI 1988/1333)
3, para 1	22 Aug 1988 (SI 1988/1333)
2	1 Aug 1988 (SI 1988/1187)
3–6	1 Mar 1989 (SI 1988/1333)
7	22 Aug 1988 (SI 1988/1333)
8(a)	22 Aug 1988 (SI 1988/1333)
(b)	1 Aug 1988 (SI 1988/1187)
9	22 Aug 1988 (SI 1988/1333)
10	1 Aug 1988 (SI 1988/1187)
11–14	22 Aug 1988 (SI 1988/1333)
15(a)	22 Aug 1988 (SI 1988/1333)
(b)	1 Mar 1989 (SI 1988/1333)
16–18	1 Aug 1988 (SI 1988/1187)
19	22 Aug 1988 (SI 1988/1333)
4	1 Aug 1988 (repeals of or in Licensing Act 1964, ss 9(5), 71(3), 72(2), 73(1), 92(4), 169) (SI 1988/1187)
	22 Aug 1988 (repeals of or in Licensing Act 1964, ss 2(3)(b), 6(4), 7, 60, 62(2), 80(2), 95, 151(5), Sch 2, para 9; Finance Act 1967; Criminal Law Act 1977; Magistrates' Courts Act 1980; Licensing (Restaurant Meals) Act 1987) (SI 1988/1333)

Licensing (Retail Sales) Act 1988 (c 25)

RA: 29 Jul 1988

Commencement provisions: s 4(2); Licensing (Retail Sales) Act 1988 (Commencement) Order 1988, SI 1988/1670

1 Nov 1988 (SI 1988/1670)

Local Government Act 1988 (c 9)

RA: 24 Mar 1988

Commencement provisions: passim; Local Government Act 1988 (Commencement No 1) Order 1988, SI 1988/979; Local Government Act 1988 (Commencement No 2) (Scotland) Order 1988, SI 1988/1043

s 1–3	24 Mar 1988 (RA)
4	24 Mar 1988 (RA; but applies only where it is proposed to enter into the works contract on or after 1 Apr 1989: s 4(7))
5–8	24 Mar 1988 (RA) (in relation to s 6, see s 6(3))
9–11	24 Mar 1988 (RA; apply in relation to work carried out in or after financial year beginning in 1989: ss 9(1), 10(1), 11(1))
12–16	24 Mar 1988 (RA)
17–22	7 Apr 1988 (s 23)
23–26	24 Mar 1988 (RA)
27–30	24 May 1988 (ss 27(3), 28(2), 29(2), 30(3))

Local Government Act 1988 (c 9)—*cont*

s 31	See Sch 5 below
32	24 May 1988 (RA); but see Sch 6 below
33	11 Feb 1988 (s 33(4))
34	The day any authority or body concerned was established (s 34(2))
35	24 May 1988 (s 35(5))
36	Repealed
37	24 Mar 1988 (RA)
38	24 May 1988 (s 38(4))
39	24 May 1988 (s 39(6))
40	24 Mar 1988 (RA)
41	24 Mar 1988 (RA); but see Sch 7 below
42	24 Mar 1988 (RA)
Sch 1	24 Mar 1988 (RA)
2	7 Apr 1988 (s 23)
3	24 May 1988 (s 29(2))
4	24 May 1988 (s 30(3))
5, para 1	24 May 1988 (s 31(2))
2	*Not in force*
3–6	24 May 1988 (s 31(2))
6, para 1–3	24 Jun 1988 (SI 1988/979; SI 1988/1043)
4	1 Oct 1988 (SI 1988/979; SI 1988/1043)
5–7	24 Jun 1988 (SI 1988/979; SI 1988/1043)
8(1)	24 Mar 1988 (s 32(3))
(2)	24 Jun 1988 (SI 1988/979; SI 1988/1043)
(3)	24 Mar 1988 (s 32(3))
(4)	24 Jun 1988 (SI 1988/979; SI 1988/1043)
9	24 Jun 1988 (SI 1988/979; SI 1988/1043)
10(1)	24 Jun 1988 (SI 1988/979; SI 1988/1043)
(2)	1 Oct 1988 (SI 1988/979; SI 1988/1043)
(3), (4)	24 Jun 1988 (SI 1988/979; SI 1988/1043)
(5)	Repealed
(6)	24 Jun 1988 (so far as inserts Local Government, Planning and Land Act 1980, s 20(5)) (SI 1988/979; SI 1988/1043)
	1 Oct 1988 (so far as inserts Local Government, Planning and Land Act 1980, s 20(6)) (SI 1988/979; SI 1988/1043)
(7)	24 Jun 1988 (SI 1988/979; SI 1988/1043)
11	24 Mar 1988 (s 32(3))
7, Pt I	7 Apr 1988 (s 23)
II	24 May 1988 (s 29(2))
III	24 Jun 1988 or 1 Oct 1988 (dependent on relationship to s 32 and Sch 6 noted above) (SI 1988/979; SI 1988/1043)
IV	29 May 1988 (Sch 7, Pt IV)

Local Government Finance Act 1988 (c 41)

RA: 29 Jul 1988

Commencement provisions: ss 111(5), 131(8), 132(6), 143(1), (2), 150, Schs 12, 13; Local Government Finance Act 1988 (Commencement) (Scotland) Order 1988, SI 1988/1456 (partially revoked by SI 1990/573); Local Government Finance Act 1988 Commencement (Scotland) Amendment Order 1990, SI 1990/573 (partially revokes SI 1988/1456)

Local Government Finance Act 1988 (c 41)—*cont*

s 1–40	29 Jul 1988 (RA); repealed, with savings, by Local Government Finance Act 1992, ss 117(2), 118, Sch 14 (qv)
41	29 Jul 1988 (RA)
41A	Inserted by Local Government (Wales) Act 1994, s 37 (qv)
42–44	29 Jul 1988 (RA)
44A	Inserted (retrospective to 29 Jul 1988) by Local Government and Housing Act 1989, s 139, Sch 5, para 22 (qv)
45, 46	29 Jul 1988 (RA)
46A	Inserted (retrospective to 29 Jul 1988) by Local Government and Housing Act 1989, s 139, Sch 5, para 25 (qv)
47–56	29 Jul 1988 (RA)
57	Substituted (retrospective to 29 Jul 1988) by Local Government and Housing Act 1989, s 139, Sch 5, para 31 (qv)
58	29 Jul 1988 (RA)
59	Substituted (retrospective to 29 July 1988) by Local Government and Housing Act 1989, s 139, Sch 5, para 32 (qv)
60–67	29 Jul 1988 (RA)
68–73	29 Jul 1988 (RA); repealed, with savings, by Local Government Finance Act 1992, s 117(2), 118(1), Sch 14 (qv)
74	29 Jul 1988 (RA)
74A	Inserted as from 16 Jan 1990 by Local Government and Housing Act 1989, s 139, Sch 5, paras 1, 54, 79(3); repealed, with savings, by Local Government Finance Act 1992, ss 117(2), 118(1), Sch 14 (qv)
75	29 Jul 1988 (RA)
75A	Inserted as from 16 Jan 1990 by Local Government and Housing Act 1989, s 139, Sch 5, paras 1, 56, 79(1); repealed, with savings, by Local Government Finance Act 1992, ss 117(2), 118(1), Sch 14 (qv)
76	29 Jul 1988 (RA)
77	29 Jul 1988 (RA); repealed (except as regards a case where a notice has been served before 16 Nov 1989; see Local Government and Housing Act 1989, ss 139, 194(4), Sch 5, paras 1, 57, 79(3), Sch 12, Pt II)
78	29 Jul 1988 (RA)
78A	Inserted by Local Government Finance Act 1992, s 104, Sch 10, Pt II, para 10 (qv)
79	29 Jul 1988 (RA)
80, 81	29 Jul 1988 (RA); repealed, with savings, by Local Government Finance Act 1992, ss 104, 117(2), 118(1), Sch 10, Pt II, para 12, Sch 14 (qv)
82	29 Jul 1988 (RA); substituted (savings) by Local Government Finance Act 1992, ss 104, 118(1), Sch 10, Pt II, para 13 (qv)
83	29 Jul 1988 (RA)

Local Government Finance Act 1988 (c 41)—*cont*

s 84	29 Jul 1988 (RA); repealed, with savings, by Local Government Finance Act 1992, ss 104, 117(2), 118(1), Sch 10, Pt II, para 14, Sch 14 (qv)
84A–84C	Inserted by Local Government Finance Act 1992, s 104, Sch 10, Pt II, para 15 (qv)
85–88	29 Jul 1988 (RA)
88A, 88B	Substituted for s 88A (as inserted (16 Nov 1989) by Local Government and Housing Act 1989, s 139, Sch 5, para 61), by Local Government Finance Act 1992, s 104, Sch 10, Pt II, para 18 (qv)
89	29 Jul 1988 (RA)
89A	Inserted by Local Government (Wales) Act 1994, s 38(11), Sch 12, para 2 (qv)
90	29 Jul 1988 (RA); substituted (savings) by Local Government Finance Act 1992, ss 104, 118(1) Sch 10, Pt III, para 20 (qv)
91–94	29 Jul 1988 (RA)
95, 96	29 Jul 1988 (RA); repealed, with savings, by Local Government Finance Act 1992, ss 104, 117(2), 118(1), Sch 10, Pt III, para 21, Sch 14 (qv)
97	29 Jul 1988 (RA); substituted (savings) by Local Government Finance Act 1992, ss 104, 118(1), Sch 10, Pt III, para 22 (qv)
98	29 Jul 1988 (RA)
99	29 Jul 1988 (RA); substituted (savings) by Local Government Finance Act 1992, s 104, 118(1), Sch 10, Pt III, para 24 (qv)
100–110	29 Jul 1988 (RA); repealed, with savings, by Local Government Finance Act 1992, ss 117(2), 118(1), Sch 14 (qv)[1]
111–116	29 Sep 1988 (s 111(5))
117, 118	29 Jul 1988 (RA)
119	Repealed
120–126	29 Jul 1988 (RA)
127	29 Jul 1988 (RA) (subject to prescribed savings made under s 127(2); section forbids levies under London Regional Transport Act 1984, s 13, after 31 Mar 1990)
128	22 Aug 1988 (SI 1988/1456); prospectively repealed by Local Government etc (Scotland) Act 1994, s 180(2), Sch 14[2]
129–134	Repealed
135–139	29 Jul 1988 (RA)
139A	Inserted by Local Government and Housing Act 1989, s 139, Sch 5, para 68 (qv)
140, 141	29 Jul 1988 (RA)
141A, 141B	Inserted (retrospective to 29 Jul 1988) by Local Government and Housing Act 1989, s 139, Sch 5, paras 1, 71 (repealed), 79(3); repealed, with savings, by Local Government Finance Act 1992, ss 117(2), 118(1), Sch 14 (qv)
142–145	29 Jul 1988 (RA)
145A	Inserted (retrospective to 29 Jul 1988) by Local Government and Housing Act 1989, s 139, Sch 5, paras 1, 73 (repealed), 79(3); repealed, with savings, by Local Government Finance Act 1992, ss 117(2), 118(1), Sch 14 (qv)

Local Government Finance Act 1988 (c 41)—*cont*

s 146–149	29 Jul 1988 (RA)
150	22 Aug 1988 (SI 1988/1456)
151, 152	29 Jul 1988 (RA)
Sch 1–4	29 Jul 1988 (RA); repealed, with savings, by Local Government Finance Act 1992, ss 117(2), 118(1), Sch 14 (qv)
4A	Inserted (retrospective to 29 Jul 1988) by Local Government and Housing Act 1989, s 139, Sch 5, para 36
5–7	29 Jul 1988 (RA)
7A	Inserted (retrospective to 29 Jul 1988) by Local Government and Housing Act 1989, s 139, Sch 5, para 40
8–11	29 Jul 1988 (RA)
12, Pt I, para 1	31 Mar 1990 (as regards qualifying dates after that date) (Sch 12, Pt I, para 1(2))
2	31 Mar 1990 (as regards any time after that date) (Sch 12, Pt I, para 2(2))
3(1)	29 Jul 1988 (RA)
(2)	1 Apr 1990 (Sch 12, Pt I, para 3(5))
(3)	29 Jul 1988 (RA)
(4)	1 Apr 1990 (Sch 12, Pt I, para 3(5))
(5)	29 Jul 1988 (RA)
II, para 4	22 Aug 1988 (SI 1988/1456)
5	Repealed
6	22 Aug 1988 (SI 1988/1456); prospectively repealed by Local Government etc (Scotland) Act 1994, s 180(2), Sch 14[2]
7	1 Apr 1990 (SI 1988/1456)
8	Repealed
9	22 Aug 1988 (SI 1988/1456)
10	Repealed
11, 12	1 Apr 1990 (SI 1988/1456)
13	Repealed
14	22 Aug 1988 (SI 1988/1456)
15–17	Repealed
18–21	22 Aug 1988 (only for the purposes of and in relation to the community charge and the community water charge in respect of the financial year 1989–90 and each subsequent financial year) (SI 1988/1456); and 1 Apr 1989 (otherwise) (SI 1988/1456); prospectively repealed by Local Government Finance Act 1992, s 117(2), Sch 14[3]
22	22 Aug 1988 (SI 1988/1456); prospectively repealed by Local Government Finance Act 1992, s 117(2), Sch 14[3]
23	Repealed
24–26	22 Aug 1988 (SI 1988/1456); prospectively repealed by Local Government Finance Act 1992, s 117(2), Sch 14[3]
27	Repealed
28	22 Aug 1988 (SI 1988/1456); prospectively repealed by Local Government Finance Act 1992, s 117(2), Sch 14[3]

Local Government Finance Act 1988 (c 41)—*cont*

Sch 12, Pt II, para 29, 30	1 Oct 1988 (SI 1988/1456); prospectively repealed by Local Government Finance Act 1992, s 117(2), Sch 14[3]
31–34	22 Aug 1988 (SI 1988/1456); prospectively repealed by Local Government Finance Act 1992, s 117(2), Sch 14[3]
35	22 Aug 1988 (only for the purposes of and in relation to the personal community charge and the personal community water charge in respect of the financial year 1989–90 and each subsequent financial year) (SI 1988/1456); 1 Apr 1989 (otherwise) (SI 1988/1456); prospectively repealed by Local Government Finance Act 1992, s 117(2), Sch 14[3]
36	22 Aug 1988 (SI 1988/1456); prospectively repealed by Local Government Finance Act 1992, s 117(2), Sch 14[3]
37	Repealed
38	22 Aug 1988 (SI 1988/1456); prospectively repealed by Local Government Finance Act 1992, s 117(2), Sch 14[3]
III, para 39	1 Apr 1989 (S); 1 Apr 1990 (EW) (Sch 12, Pt III, para 39(2), (3))
40	29 Jul 1988 (RA)
41	Repealed
42	1 Apr 1989 (S); 1 Apr 1990 (EW) (Sch 12, Pt III, para 42(2), (3))
12A	Inserted (retrospective to 29 Jul 1988) by Local Government and Housing Act 1989, s 139, Sch 5, paras 1, 74 (repealed), 79(3); repealed, with savings, by Local Government Finance Act 1992, ss 117(2), 118(1), Sch 14 (qv)
13, Pt I	1 Apr 1990 (subject to any saving under s 117(8)) (Sch 13, Pt I)
II	1 Apr 1990 (Sch 13, Pt II)
III	See s 127 above
IV	22 Aug 1988 (repeals of or in Abolition of Domestic Rates Etc (Scotland) Act 1987, ss 4(1), 11(11), 17(5), 30(2), Sch 2) (SI 1988/1456) 15 Sep 1988 (repeals in s 2 of 1987 Act) (SI 1988/1456) 1 Oct 1988 (repeals in s 20 of 1987 Act) (SI 1988/1456) 1 Apr 1989 (repeal in Acquisition of Land (Authorisation Procedure) (Scotland) Act 1947, s 5) (SI 1988/1456) 1 Apr 1990 (otherwise, except repeal in Abolition of Domestic Rates Act (Scotland) Act 1987, s 24) (SI 1988/1456, as amended by SI 1990/573) *Not in force* (exception noted above)

[1] S 101 previously repealed by Local Government Finance and Valuation Act 1991, s 1(1), subject to savings in s 1(3) thereof

[2] Any order made under Local Government etc (Scotland) Act 1994, s 184, bringing the prospective repeal into force will be noted to that Act in the service to this work

[3] Any order made under Local Government Finance Act 1992, s 119, bringing the prospective repeal into force will be noted to that Act in the service to this work

Malicious Communications Act 1988 (c 27)

RA: 29 Jul 1988

Commencement provisions: s 3(2)

s 1	29 Sep 1988 (s 3(2))
2, 3	29 Jul 1988 (RA)

Matrimonial Proceedings (Transfers) Act 1988 (c 18)

RA: 19 May 1988

19 May 1988 (RA)

Merchant Shipping Act 1988 (c 12)

RA: 3 May 1988

Commencement provisions: s 58(2)–(4); Merchant Shipping Act 1988 (Commencement No 1) Order 1988, SI 1988/1010; Merchant Shipping Act 1988 (Commencement No 2) Order 1988, SI 1988/1907; Merchant Shipping (Transitional Provisions—Fishing Vessels) Order 1988, SI 1988/1911[1]; Merchant Shipping Act 1988 (Commencement No 3) Order 1989, SI 1989/353; Merchant Shipping Act 1988 (Commencement No 4) Order 1994, SI 1994/1201

s 1–35	Repealed
36, 37	4 Jul 1988 (SI 1988/1010)
38–49	Repealed
50, 51	4 Jul 1988 (SI 1988/1010); repealed (as from 1 May 1994, with savings for any instrument made under s 50) by Merchant Shipping (Registration, etc) Act 1993, s 8(4), Sch 5, Pt II (repealed)
52	Repealed
53	4 Jul 1988 (SI 1988/1010); repealed (as from 1 Jan 1996, except for the purposes of s 37) by Merchant Shipping Act 1995, s 314(1), Sch 12 (qv)
54	Repealed
55	4 Jul 1988 (SI 1988/1010); repealed (as from 1 Jan 1996, except for the purposes of s 37) by Merchant Shipping Act 1995, s 314(1), Sch 12 (qv)
56	4 Jul 1988 (SI 1988/1010)); repealed (as from 1 May 1994, with savings for instruments made under the section) by Merchant Shipping (Registration, etc) Act 1993, s 8(4), Sch 5, Pt II (repealed)
57(1)	Repealed
(2)	4 Jul 1988 (SI 1988/1010)
(3)–(5)	Repealed
58(1)–(3)	4 Jul 1988 (SI 1988/1010)
(4)	Spent
(5)	4 Jul 1988 (SI 1988/1010)
Sch 1–8	Repealed

[1] Specifies how certain references in documents under law in force before commencement of the 1988 Act are to be construed after commencement;

Merchant Shipping Act 1988 (c 12)—*cont*

provided that no fishing vessels to be registered under law in force before commencement during the period 17–30 Nov 1988 inclusive; and provided that no entries relating to fishing vessels to be made in registers of ships kept under Merchant Shipping Act 1894, Pt I except entries closing the registry

Motor Vehicles (Wearing of Rear Seat Belts by Children) Act 1988 (c 23)

RA: 28 Jun 1988

Commencement provisions: s 3(2)

s 1	Repealed
2, 3	28 Jun 1988 (RA)

Multilateral Investment Guarantee Agency Act 1988 (c 8)

RA: 24 Mar 1988

Commencement provisions: s 9(2); Multilateral Investment Guarantee Agency Act 1988 (Commencement) Order 1988, SI 1988/715

12 Apr 1988 (SI 1988/715)

Norfolk and Suffolk Broads Act 1988 (c 4)

Local application only

Protection Against Cruel Tethering Act 1988 (c 31)

RA: 29 Jul 1988

Commencement provisions: s 2(2)

29 Sep 1988 (s 2(2))

Protection of Animals (Amendment) Act 1988 (c 29)

RA: 29 Jul 1988

Commencement provisions: s 3(4)

29 Sep 1988 (s 3(4))

Public Utility Transfers and Water Charges Act 1988 (c 15)

RA: 10 May 1988

Commencement provisions: s 8(2) (repealed); Public Utility Transfers and Water Charges Act 1988 (Commencement No 1) Order 1988, SI 1988/879; Public Utility Transfers and Water Charges Act 1988 (Commencement No 2) Order 1988, SI 1988/1165

Public Utility Transfers and Water Charges Act 1988 (c 15)—*cont*

s 1	10 May 1988 (RA); prospectively repealed by Water Act 1989, s 190(3), Sch 27, Pt II; any order made under Water Act 1989, s 194(4), bringing the prospective repeal into force will be noted to that Act in the service to this work
2, 3	Repealed
4	18 May 1988 (SI 1988/879); repealed by Water Act 1989, s 190(3), Sch 27, Pt I (qv), but continues to apply in accordance with Water Consolidation (Consequential Provisions) Act 1991, s 2, Sch 2, para 11(1)
5	Repealed
6, 7	18 May or 11 Jul 1988 (SI 1988/879); and 1 Oct 1988 (SI 1988/1165); repealed, with savings for orders made under s 6, by Water Act 1989, s 190(2), (3), Sch 26, para 54(3), Sch 27, Pt I (qv)
8(1)	10 May 1988 (RA); prospectively repealed by Water Act 1989, s 190(3), Sch 27, Pt II; any order made under Water Act 1989, s 194(4), bringing the prospective repeal into force will be noted to that Act in the service to this work
(2)	Repealed
(3)	10 May 1988 (RA); prospectively repealed by Water Act 1989, s 190(3), Sch 27, Pt II; any order made under Water Act 1989, s 194(4), bringing the prospective repeal into force will be noted to that Act in the service to this work
Sch 1–3	Repealed

Rate Support Grants Act 1988 (c 51)

RA: 15 Nov 1988

15 Nov 1988 (RA)

Regional Development Grants (Termination) Act 1988 (c 11)

RA: 3 May 1988

3 May 1988 (RA)

Road Traffic Act 1988 (c 52)

RA: 15 Nov 1988

Commencement provisions: s 197(2)

15 May 1989 (subject, in the case of ss 15, 195(3), (4), to transitory modifications specified in Road Traffic (Consequential Provisions) Act 1988, Sch 5 (now repealed) which applied until 21 Jul 1989 (Road Traffic Act 1988 (Appointed Day for Section 15) Order 1989, SI 1989/1086) or 1 Sep 1989 (Road Traffic Act 1988 (Appointed Day for Section 15) (No 2) Order 1989, SI 1989/1260)) (s 197(2))

Road Traffic (Consequential Provisions) Act 1988 (c 54)

RA: 15 Nov 1988

Commencement provisions: s 8(2), (3)

s 1–3	15 May 1989 (s 8(2), (3))
4	See Schs 2, 3 below
5	15 May 1989 (s 8(2), (3))
6	Repealed
7, 8	15 May 1989 (s 8(2), (3))
Sch 1	15 May 1989 (s 8(2), (3))
2, para 1	Repealed
2–7	15 May 1989 (s 8(2), (3))
8, 9	Repealed
10–14	15 May 1989 (s 8(2), (3))
15–20	*Not in force*
21–33	Repealed
3, para 1–5	15 May 1989 (s 8(2), (3))
6(1)–(5)	Repealed
(6)–(8)	15 May 1989 (s 8(2), (3))
7	15 May 1989 (s 8(2), (3))
8	Repealed
9–14	15 May 1989 (s 8(2), (3))
15	Repealed
16–31	15 May 1989 (s 8(2), (3))
32	Repealed
33	15 May 1989 (s 8(2), (3))
34	Repealed
35, 36	15 May 1989 (s 8(2), (3))
37(1), (2)	Repealed
(3)	15 May 1989 (s 8(2), (3))
38, 39	15 May 1989 (s 8(2), (3))
4	15 May 1989 (s 8(2), (3))
5	Repealed

Road Traffic Offenders Act 1988 (c 53)

RA: 15 Nov 1988

Commencement provisions: s 99(2)–(5)

s 1–19	15 May 1989 (s 99(2)–(5))
20	Substituted by Road Traffic Act 1991, s 23 (qv)
21–23	15 May 1989 (s 99(2)–(5))
24	Substituted by Road Traffic Act 1991, s 24 (qv)
25	15 May 1989 (s 99(2)–(5))
26	Substituted by Road Traffic Act 1991, s 25 (qv)
27(1)	15 May 1989 (s 99(2)–(5))
(2)	Repealed
(3)	15 May 1989 (s 99(2)–(5))
(4)	15 May 1989 (EW) (s 99(2)–(5)) *Not in force* (S)
28	Substituted by Road Traffic Act 1991, s 27 (qv)
29	Substituted by Road Traffic Act 1991, s 28 (qv)

Road Traffic Offenders Act 1988 (c 53)—*cont*

s 30	15 May 1989 (EW) (s 99(2)–(5))
	15 May 1989 (so far as relates to ss 7577) (S) (s 99(2)–(5))
	Not in force (otherwise) (S)
31–33	15 May 1989 (s 99(2)–(5))
33A	Prospectively inserted (S) by Criminal Justice (Scotland) Act 1995, s 117(1), Sch 6, Pt II, para 188; 1995 Act repealed (1 Apr 1996) by Criminal Procedure (Consequential Provisions) (Scotland) Act 1995, s 6(1), Sch 5; same s 33A prospectively inserted (S) by s 5 of, Sch 4, para 71(1), (6) to, latter Act[1]
34	15 May 1989 (s 99(2)–(5))
34A–34C	Inserted by Road Traffic Act 1991, s 30 (qv)
35	15 May 1989 (s 99(2)–(5))
36	Substituted by Road Traffic Act 1991, s 32 (qv)
37–41	15 May 1989 (s 99(2)–(5))
41A	Inserted by Road Traffic Act 1991, s 48, Sch 4, para 97 (qv)
42–47	15 May 1989 (s 99(2)–(5))
48	Substituted by Road Traffic Act 1991, s 48, Sch 4, para 101 (qv)
49–51	15 May 1989 (s 99(2)–(5))
52(1)–(3)	15 May 1989 (s 99(2)–(5))
(4)	*Not in force*
53	Substituted by Road Traffic Act 1991, s 48, Sch 4, para 102 (qv)
54–58	15 May 1989 (EW) (s 99(2)–(5))
	Not in force (S)
59(1)–(5)	*Not in force*
(6)	Repealed
60	Repealed
61	15 May 1989 (EW) (s 99(2)–(5)); *not in force* (S)
62–74	15 May 1989 (s 99(2)–(5))
75–77	Substituted by Road Traffic Act 1991, s 34 (qv)
78–99	15 May 1989 (s 99(2)(5))
Sch 1–5	15 May 1989 (s 99(2)–(5))

[1] As to retention of prospective nature of amendments made by Criminal Justice (Scotland) Act 1995, see Criminal Procedure (Consequential Provisions) (Scotland) Act 1995, s 4, Sch 3, paras 3, 16

School Boards (Scotland) Act 1988 (c 47)

RA: 15 Nov 1988

Commencement provisions: s 24(2); School Boards (Scotland) Act 1988 (Commencement) Order 1989, SI 1989/272

s 1–23	1 Apr 1989 (SI 1989/272)
24	15 Nov 1988 (RA)
Sch 1–3	1 Apr 1989 (SI 1989/272)
4, para 1–5	1 Nov 1989 (SI 1989/272)
6	1 Apr 1989 (SI 1989/272)
7	1 Nov 1989 (SI 1989/272)

Scotch Whisky Act 1988 (c 22)

RA: 28 Jun 1988

Commencement provisions: s 5(2); Scotch Whisky Act 1988 (Commencement and Transitional Provisions) Order 1990, SI 1990/997

s 1–3	30 Apr 1990 (SI 1990/997)
4, 5	28 Jun 1988 (RA; note that SI 1990/997 also purports to bring s 5 into force on 30 Apr 1990)

Social Security Act 1988 (c 7)

RA: 15 Mar 1988

Commencement provisions: s 18(1)–(4); Social Security Act 1988 (Commencement No 1) Order 1988, SI 1988/520; Social Security Act 1988 (Commencement No 2) Order 1988, SI 1988/1226; Social Security Act 1988 (Commencement No 3) Order 1988, SI 1988/1857

s 1–11	Repealed
12	15 Mar 1988 (s 18(1), (2))
13, 14	17 Mar 1988 (SI 1988/520)
15	15 Mar 1988 (s 18(1), (2))
15A	Inserted by Social Security Act 1990, s 21(1), Sch 6, para 8(10) (qv)
16(1)	See Sch 4 below
(2)	See Sch 5 below
17	Repealed
18–20	15 Mar 1988 (s 18(1), (2))
Sch 1–3	Repealed
4, para 1	6 Apr 1988 (SI 1988/520)
2	12 Sep 1988 (SI 1988/1226)
3–20	Repealed
21	6 Apr 1988 (SI 1988/520)
22–30	Repealed
5	15 Mar 1988 (repeals of or in Social Security Act 1975, ss 45, 45A, 46, 47B, 66; Social Security Act 1980, Sch 1; Social Security Act 1985, s 13(4)(a)) (s 18(1), (2))
	6 Apr 1988 (repeals in Social Security Act 1986, s 50(1)) (SI 1988/520)
	11 Apr 1988 (repeals of or in Emergency Laws (Re-enactments and Repeals) Act 1964; Health Services and Public Health Act 1968; Social Security Act 1975, ss 59A, 69; Adoption Act 1976; National Health Service Act 1977; Adoption (Scotland) Act 1978; National Health Service (Scotland) Act 1978; Social Security Act 1985, s 14; Social Security Act 1986, ss 20(6), 23(8), 32, 33(1), 34(1)(a), 51(2), 52(6), 53(10), 63(7), 84(1), Sch 3) (SI 1988/520)
	2 Oct 1988 (repeals in Social Security Act 1975, Sch 3) (SI 1988/520)
	12 Sep 1988 (repeal of Social Security Act 1986, Sch 10, para 45) (SI 1988/1226)

Solicitors (Scotland) Act 1988 (c 42)

RA: 29 Jul 1988

Commencement provisions: s 7(2)

29 Jan 1989 (s 7(2))

Welsh Development Agency Act 1988 (c 5)

Whole Act repealed

1989

Antarctic Minerals Act 1989 (c 21)

RA: 21 Jul 1989

Commencement provisions: s 20(2)

Not in force

Appropriation Act 1989 (c 25)

Whole Act repealed

Atomic Energy Act 1989 (c 7)

RA: 25 May 1989

Commencement provisions: s 7(2); Atomic Energy Act 1989 (Commencement) Order 1989, SI 1989/1317

1 Sep 1989 (SI 1989/1317)

Brunei (Appeals) Act 1989 (c 36)

RA: 16 Nov 1989

Commencement provisions: s 2(2); Brunei (Appeals) Act 1989 (Commencement) Order 1989, SI 1989/2450

1 Feb 1990 (SI 1989/2450)

Children Act 1989 (c 41)

RA: 16 Nov 1989

Commencement provisions: s 108(2), (3); Children Act 1989 (Commencement and Transitional Provisions) Order 1991, SI 1991/828; Children Act 1989 (Commencement No 2—Amendment and Transitional Provisions) Order 1991, SI 1991/1990

s 1–4	14 Oct 1991 (SI 1991/828)
5(1)–(10)	14 Oct 1991 (SI 1991/828)
(11), (12)	1 Feb 1992 (SI 1991/828, SI 1991/1990)
(13)	14 Oct 1991 (SI 1991/828)
6–87	14 Oct 1991 (SI 1991/828)
87A, 87B	Inserted (EW) by Deregulation and Contracting Out Act 1994, s 38 (qv)

Children Act 1989 (c 41)—*cont*

s 88(1)		See Sch 10 below
(2)		14 Oct 1991 (SI 1991/828)
89		16 Nov 1989 (s 108(2))
90–95		14 Oct 1991 (SI 1991/828)
96(1), (2)		14 Oct 1991 (SI 1991/828)
(3)–(7)		16 Nov 1989 (s 108(2))
97–107		14 Oct 1991 (SI 1991/828)
108		16 Nov 1989 (RA)
Sch 1–9		14 Oct 1991 (SI 1991/828)
10, para	1–20	14 Oct 1991 (SI 1991/828)
	21	1 May 1991 (SI 1991/828)
	22–46	14 Oct 1991 (SI 1991/828)
11		14 Oct 1991 (SI 1991/828)
12, para	1–3	14 Oct 1991 (SI 1991/828)
	4	Repealed
	5–7	14 Oct 1991 (SI 1991/828)
	8	Repealed
	9	14 Oct 1991 (SI 1991/828)
	10	Repealed
	11–17	14 Oct 1991 (SI 1991/828)
	18	Repealed
	19, 20	14 Oct 1991 (SI 1991/828)
	21	Repealed
	22, 23	14 Oct 1991 (SI 1991/828)
	24, 25	Repealed
	26–34	14 Oct 1991 (SI 1991/828)
	35	16 Nov 1989 (s 108(2))
	36	Repealed
	37–45	14 Oct 1991 (SI 1991/828)
13–15		14 Oct 1991 (SI 1991/828)

Civil Aviation (Air Navigation Charges) Act 1989 (c 9)

RA: 25 May 1989

25 May 1989 (RA)

Common Land (Rectification of Registers) Act 1989 (c 18)

RA: 21 Jul 1989

21 Jul 1989 (RA)

Companies Act 1989 (c 40)

RA: 16 Nov 1989

Commencement provisions: s 215(1)–(3); Companies Act 1989 (Commencement No 1) Order 1990, SI 1990/98; Companies Act 1989 (Commencement No 2) Order 1990, SI 1990/142; Companies Act 1989 (Commencement No 3, Transitional Provisions and Transfer of Functions under the Financial Services Act 1986) Order 1990, SI 1990/354 (which contains transitional provisions in relation to self-regulating organisations and professional bodies); Companies Act 1989 (Commencement No 4, Transitional and Saving Provisions) Order 1990, SI 1990/355, as amended by SI 1990/1707, SI 1990/2569, SI 1993/3246;

Companies Act 1989 (c 40)—*cont*

Companies Act 1989 (Commencement No 5 and Transitional and Saving Provisions) Order 1990, SI 1990/713; Companies Act 1989 (Commencement No 6 and Transitional and Savings Provisions) Order 1990, SI 1990/1392, as amended by SI 1990/1707; Companies Act 1989 (Commencement No 7, Transitional and Saving Provisions) Order 1990, SI 1990/1707; Companies Act 1989 (Commencement No 8 and Transitional and Saving Provisions) Order 1990, SI 1990/2569; Companies Act 1989 (Commencement No 9 and Saving and Transitional Provisions) Order 1991, SI 1991/488; Companies Act 1989 (Commencement No 10 and Saving Provisions) Order 1991, SI 1991/878; Companies Act 1989 (Commencement No 11) Order 1991, SI 1991/1452; Companies Act 1989 (Commencement No 12 and Transitional Provision) Order 1991, SI 1991/1996; Companies Act 1989 (Commencement No 13) Order 1991, SI 1991/2173; Companies Act 1989 (Commencement No 14 and Transitional Provision) Order 1991, SI 1991/2945; Companies Act 1989 (Commencement No 15 and Transitional and Savings Provisions) Order 1995, SI 1995/1352; Companies Act 1989 (Commencement No 16) Order 1995, SI 1995/1591

s 1	1 Mar 1990 (so far as relates to s 15 below) (SI 1990/142)
	1 Apr 1990 (so far as relates to any section or part thereof brought into force by SI 1990/355) (SI 1990/355)[1]
	7 Jan 1991 (so far as relates to any section or part thereof brought into force by SI 1990/2569)
	1 Jul 1992 (so far as relates to s 11) (subject to transitional provisions) (SI 1991/2945)
2–6	1 Apr 1990 (SI 1990/355)[1]
7	1 Apr 1990 (except so far as relates to Companies Act 1985, s 233(5)) (SI 1990/355)[1]
	7 Jan 1991 (exception noted above) (SI 1990/2569)[8]
8–10	1 Apr 1990 (SI 1990/355)[1]
11	1 Apr 1990 (except so far as relates to Companies Act 1985, s 242A) (SI 1990/355)[1]
	1 Jul 1992 (exception noted above) (subject to transitional provisions) (SI 1991/2945)
12	7 Jan 1991 (SI 1990/2569)[8]
13, 14	1 Apr 1990 (SI 1990/355)[1]
15	1 Mar 1990 (SI 1990/142)
16–22	1 Apr 1990 (SI 1990/355)[1]
23	See Sch 10 below
24	1 Mar 1990 (for purposes of ss 30–33, 37–40, 41(1), (3)–(6), 42–45, 47(1), 48(1), (2), 49–54, Schs 11, 12, 14) (SI 1990/142)
	1 Oct 1991 (otherwise) (SI 1991/1996)
25–27	1 Oct 1991 (SI 1991/1996)
28	1 Oct 1991 (subject to transitional provisions in SI 1991/1996, art 4) (SI 1991/1996)
29	1 Oct 1991 (SI 1991/1996)
30	1 Mar 1990 (SI 1990/142)
31	1 Mar 1990 (so far as relates to recognition of supervisory bodies under Sch 11 and for the purpose of enabling the Secretary of State to approve a qualification under s 31(4), (5)) (SI 1990/142)
	1 Oct 1991 (otherwise) (SI 1991/1996)
32, 33	1 Mar 1990 (SI 1990/142)
34	1 Oct 1991 (SI 1991/1996)

Companies Act 1989 (c 40)—*cont*

s 35, 36	26 Jun 1991 (SI 1991/1452)
37–40	1 Mar 1990 (SI 1990/142)
41(1)	1 Mar 1990 (for purposes of an application under this section or under provisions specified under s 24 above or of any requirement imposed under such provisions) (SI 1990/142) 1 Oct 1991 (otherwise) (SI 1991/1996)
(2)	1 Oct 1991 (SI 1991/1996)
(3)	1 Mar 1990 (SI 1990/142)
(4)	1 Mar 1990 (for purposes of an application under this section or under provisions specified under s 24 above or of any requirement imposed under such provisions) (SI 1990/142) 1 Oct 1991 (otherwise) (SI 1991/1996)
(5), (6)	1 Mar 1990 (for purposes of s 41(3)) (SI 1990/142) 1 Oct 1991 (otherwise) (SI 1991/1996)
42–44	1 Mar 1990 (for purposes of ss 30–33, 37–40, 41(1), (3)–(6), 42–45, 47(1), 48(1), (2), 49–54, Schs 11, 12, 14) (SI 1990/142) 1 Oct 1991 (otherwise) (SI 1991/1996)
45	1 Mar 1990 (SI 1990/142)
46	*Not in force*
47(1)	1 Mar 1990 (SI 1990/142)
(2)–(6)	*Not in force*
48(1), (2)	1 Mar 1990 (SI 1990/142)
(3)	*Not in force*
49	1 Mar 1990 (for purposes of ss 30–33, 37–40, 41(1), (3)–(6), 42–45, 47(1), 48(1), (2), 49–54, Schs 11, 12, 14) (SI 1990/142) 1 Oct 1991 (otherwise) (SI 1991/1996)
50, 51	1 Mar 1990 (SI 1990/142)
52–54	1 Mar 1990 (for purposes of ss 30–33, 37–40, 41(1), (3)–(6), 42–45, 47(1), 48(1), (2), 49–54, Schs 11, 12, 14) (SI 1990/142) 1 Oct 1991 (otherwise) (SI 1991/1996)
55–64	21 Feb 1990 (SI 1990/142)
65(1)	21 Feb 1990 (SI 1990/142)
(2)	21 Feb 1990 (except so far as refers to Part VII (ss 154–191) and so far as s 65(2)(g) refers to a body established under s 46) (SI 1990/142) 25 Apr 1991 (so far as not already in force, except so far as s 65(2)(g) refers to a body established under s 46) (SI 1991/878) *Not in force* (exception noted above)
(3)–(7)	21 Feb 1990 (SI 1990/142)
66–74	21 Feb 1990 (SI 1990/142)
75(1)	21 Feb 1990 (SI 1990/142)
(2)	25 Jan 1990 (SI 1990/98)
(3)(a)–(c)	21 Feb 1990 (except so far as refers to Part VII (ss 154–191) and so far as s 75(3)(c) refers to a body established under s 46) (SI 1990/142) 25 Apr 1991 (so far as not already in force, except so far as s 75(3)(c) refers to a body established under s 46) (SI 1991/878) *Not in force* (exception noted above)
(d)	25 Jan 1990 (SI 1990/98)

Companies Act 1989 (c 40)—*cont*

s 75(3)(e), (f)	21 Feb 1990 (except so far as refers to Part VII (ss 154–191)) (SI 1990/142)
	25 Apr 1991 (exception noted above) (SI 1991/878)
(4)	25 Jan 1990 (so far as relates to s 75(3)(d) above) (SI 1990/98)
	21 Feb 1990 (otherwise) (SI 1990/142)
(5), (6)	21 Feb 1990 (SI 1990/142)
(7)	25 Jan 1990 (SI 1990/98)
76–79	21 Feb 1990 (SI 1990/142)
80	21 Feb 1990 (except so far as refers to Pt VII (ss 154–191)) (SI 1990/142)
	25 Apr 1991 (exception noted above) (SI 1991/878)
81(1)	21 Feb 1990 (SI 1990/142)
(2)	21 Feb 1990 (except so far as refers to Part VII (ss 154–191)) (SI 1990/142)
	25 Apr 1991 (exception noted above) (SI 1991/878)
(3), (4)	21 Feb 1990 (SI 1990/142)
(5)	21 Feb 1990 (except so far as refers to Pt VII (ss 154191)) (SI 1990/142)
	25 Apr 1991 (exception noted above) (SI 1991/878)
82–86	21 Feb 1990 (SI 1990/142)
87(1)–(3)	21 Feb 1990 (SI 1990/142)
(4)	21 Feb 1990 (except so far as refers to Pt VII (ss 154–191)) (SI 1990/142)
	25 Apr 1991 (exception noted above) (SI 1991/878)
(5), (6)	21 Feb 1990 (SI 1990/142)
88–91	21 Feb 1990 (SI 1990/142)
92–107	*Not in force*
108–110	4 Feb 1991 (SI 1990/2569)[8]
111	Repealed
112	4 Feb 1991 (SI 1990/2569)[8]
113, 114	1 Apr 1990 (SI 1990/355)
115	1 Apr 1990 (SI 1990/355)[2]
116, 117	1 Apr 1990 (SI 1990/355)
118–123	1 Apr 1990 (SI 1990/355)[2]
124	Repealed
125	7 Jan 1991 (SI 1990/2569)
126	1 Jul 1991 (SI 1991/488)[9]
127(1), (2)	7 Jan 1991 (SI 1990/2569)
(3)	1 Jul 1991 (SI 1991/488)
(4)	7 Jan 1991 (SI 1990/2569)
(5), (6)	1 Jul 1991 (SI 1991/488)
(7)	7 Jan 1991 (so far as inserts in Companies Act 1985, Sch 22, a reference to ss 706, 707, 715A of the 1985 Act, as inserted by ss 125, 127(1) of this Act) (SI 1990/2569)
	1 Jul 1991 (otherwise) (SI 1991/488)
128	*Not in force*
129	1 Nov 1990 (SI 1990/1392)
130	31 Jul 1990 (SI 1990/1392)
131	1 Apr 1990 (not to be construed as affecting any right, privilege, obligation or liability acquired, accrued or incurred before 1 Apr 1990; see SI 1990/355, art 11) (SI 1990/355)
132	1 Apr 1990 (SI 1990/355)
133	*Not in force*
134(1)–(3)	31 May 1990 (SI 1990/713)

Companies Act 1989 (c 40)—*cont*

s 134(4)	1 Nov 1991 (SI 1991/1996)
(5), (6)	31 May 1990 (SI 1990/713)
135	7 Jan 1991 (SI 1990/2569)
136	1 Apr 1990 (SI 1990/355; see, however, saving in art 12 thereof)
137(1)	1 Apr 1990 (SI 1990/355)
(2)	1 Apr 1990 (for the purposes of a director's report of a company within the meaning of Companies Act 1985, s 735 (except in relation to a financial year commencing before 23 Dec 1989; see SI 1990/355, art 13)) (SI 1990/355)
	Not in force (otherwise)
138	31 Jul 1990 (SI 1990/1392)[4]
139	1 Oct 1990 (SI 1990/1707)[7]
140(1)–(6)	3 Jul 1995 (subject to transitional provisions and savings) (SI 1995/1352)
(7), (8)	*Not in force*
141	16 Nov 1989 (s 215(1))
142	*Not in force*
143	1 Nov 1991 (SI 1991/1996)
144	1 Nov 1990 (SI 1990/1392)[5]
145	See Sch 19 below
146	1 Apr 1990 (SI 1990/142)
147–150	16 Nov 1989 (s 215(1))
151	1 Apr 1990 (SI 1990/142)
152	1 Mar 1990 (SI 1990/142)
153	See Sch 20 below
154–156	25 Mar 1991 (Pt VII (ss 154–191, Schs 21, 22) brought into force only insofar as is necessary to enable regulations to be made under ss 155(4), (5), 156(1) (so far as it relates to Sch 21), 158(4), (5), 160(5), 173(4), (5), 174(2)–(4), 185, 186, 187(3), Sch 21, para 2(3)) (SI 1991/488)
	25 Apr 1991 (otherwise) (SI 1991/878)
157	25 Mar 1991 (see note to ss 154–156) (SI 1991/488)
	25 Apr 1991 (otherwise) (SI 1991/878)[10]
158, 159	25 Mar 1991 (see note to ss 154–156) (SI 1991/488)
	25 Apr 1991 (otherwise) (SI 1991/878)
160	25 Mar 1991 (see note to ss 154–156) (SI 1991/488)
	25 Apr 1991 (so far as not already in force, except insofar as imposing a duty (i) on any person where conflict with enactments in force in Northern Ireland relating to insolvency would arise, and (ii) on a relevant office-holder appointed under the general law of insolvency for the time being in force in Northern Ireland) (SI 1991/878)[10]
	1 Oct 1991 (exception noted above) (SI 1991/2173)
161	25 Mar 1991 (see note to ss 154–156) (SI 1991/488)
	25 Apr 1991 (otherwise) (SI 1991/878)
162	25 Mar 1991 (see note to ss 154–156) (SI 1991/488)
	25 Apr 1991 (otherwise, except so far as would require an exchange or clearing house to supply a copy of a report to any relevant office-holder appointed under the general law of insolvency for the time being in force in Northern Ireland) (SI 1991/878)
	1 Oct 1991 (exception noted above) (SI 1991/2173)

Companies Act 1989 (c 40)—*cont*

s 163–165	25 Mar 1991 (see note to ss 154–156) (SI 1991/488)
	25 Apr 1991 (otherwise) (SI 1991/878)
166	25 Mar 1991 (see note to ss 154–156) (SI 1991/488)
	25 Apr 1991 (so far as not already in force, except where would enable a direction to be given, where an order, appointment or resolution corresponding to those mentioned in s 166(6) has been made or passed in relation to the person in question under the general law of insolvency for the time being in force in Northern Ireland) (SI 1991/878)[10]
	1 Oct 1991 (exception noted above) (SI 1991/2173)
167	25 Mar 1991 (see note to ss 154–156) (SI 1991/488)
	25 Apr 1991 (otherwise, except where enabling an application to be made by a relevant office-holder appointed by, or in consequence of, or in connection with, an order or resolution corresponding to those mentioned in s 167(1) made or passed under the general law of insolvency for the time being in force in Northern Ireland) (1991/878)
	1 Oct 1991 (exception noted above) (SI 1991/2173)
168	25 Mar 1991 (see note to ss 154–156) (SI 1991/488)
	25 Apr 1991 (otherwise) (SI 1991/878)
169(1)–(3)	25 Mar 1991 (see note to ss 154–156) (SI 1991/488)
	25 Apr 1991 (otherwise) (SI 1991/878)
(4)	25 Mar 1991 (see note to ss 154–156) (SI 1991/488)
	Not in force (otherwise)
(5)	25 Mar 1991 (see note to ss 154–156) (SI 1991/488)
	25 Apr 1991 (otherwise) (SI 1991/878)
170	25 Mar 1991 (see note to ss 154–156) (SI 1991/488)
	Not in force (otherwise)
171	25 Mar 1991 (see note to ss 154–156) (SI 1991/488)
	4 Jul 1995 (otherwise) (SI 1995/1591)
172	25 Mar 1991 (see note to ss 154–156) (SI 1991/488)
	Not in force (otherwise)
173	25 Mar 1991 (see note to ss 154–156) (SI 1991/488)
	25 Apr 1991 (otherwise) (SI 1991/878)
174, 175	25 Mar 1991 (see note to ss 154–156) (SI 1991/488)
	25 Apr 1991 (otherwise) (SI 1991/878)[10]
176	25 Mar 1991 (see note to ss 154–156) (SI 1991/488)
	4 Jul 1995 (otherwise) (SI 1995/1591)
177	25 Mar 1991 (see note to ss 154–156) (SI 1991/488)
	25 Apr 1991 (otherwise) (SI 1991/878)[10]
178	25 Mar 1991 (see note to ss 154–156) (SI 1991/488)
	Not in force (otherwise)
179, 180	25 Mar 1991 (see note to ss 154–156) (SI 1991/488)
	25 Apr 1991 (otherwise) (SI 1991/878)[10]
181	25 Mar 1991 (see note to ss 154–156) (SI 1991/488)
	4 Jul 1995 (otherwise) (SI 1995/1591)
182, 183	25 Mar 1991 (see note to ss 154–156) (SI 1991/488)
	25 Apr 1991 (otherwise) (SI 1991/878)
184(1)	25 Mar 1991 (see note to ss 154–156) (SI 1991/488)
	25 Apr 1991 (so far as not already in force, except so far as has effect in relation to any relevant office-holder appointed under general law of insolvency

Companies Act 1989 (c 40)—*cont*

s 184(1)—*cont*	for the time being in force in Northern Ireland) (SI 1991/878)
	1 Oct 1991 (exception noted above) (SI 1991/2173)
(2)–(5)	25 Mar 1991 (see note to ss 154–156) (SI 1991/488)
	25 Apr 1991 (otherwise) (SI 1991/878)
185, 186	25 Mar 1991 (see note to ss 154–156) (SI 1991/488)
	Not in force (otherwise)
187–191	25 Mar 1991 (see note to ss 154–156) (SI 1991/488)
	25 Apr 1991 (otherwise) (SI 1991/878)
192	15 Mar 1990 (so far as relates to Financial Services Act 1986, s 47A) (SI 1990/354)
	Not in force (otherwise)
193(1)	15 Mar 1990 (so far as relates to regulations under Financial Services Act 1986, s 62A) (SI 1990/354)
	1 Apr 1991 (otherwise) (SI 1991/488)[9]
(2)	1 Apr 1991 (SI 1991/488)[9]
(3)	15 Mar 1990 (so far as relates to regulations under Financial Services Act 1986, Sch 11, para 22A) (SI 1990/354)
	1 Apr 1991 (otherwise) (SI 1991/488)[9]
(4)	1 Apr 1991 (SI 1991/488)[9]
194–197	15 Mar 1990 (SI 1990/354)
198, 199	Repealed
200	15 Mar 1990 (SI 1990/354)
201	25 Apr 1991 (SI 1991/878)[10]
202	16 Nov 1989 (s 215(1))
203–205	15 Mar 1990 (SI 1990/354)
206(1)	See Sch 23 below
(2)–(4)	15 Mar 1990 (SI 1990/354)
207	1 Nov 1990 (SI 1990/1392, as amended by SI 1990/1707)
208	1 Mar 1990 (SI 1990/142)
209	Repealed
210	1 Apr 1990 (SI 1990/142)
211(1)	1 Oct 1991 (SI 1991/1996)
(2)	31 Jul 1990 (SI 1990/1392)[6]
(3)	31 Jul 1990 (SI 1990/1392)
212	See Sch 24 below
213, 214	2 Feb 1990 (SI 1990/142)
215, 216	16 Nov 1989 (RA; see however SI 1990/98 which purports to bring s 216 into force on 25 Jan 1990)
Sch 1–9	1 Apr 1990 (SI 1990/355)[1]
10[3], para 1–10	1 Apr 1990 (SI 1990/355)[1]
11	Repealed
12–18	1 Apr 1990 (SI 1990/355)[1]
19	1 Aug 1990 (SI 1990/355)[1]
20–23	1 Apr 1990 (SI 1990/355)[1]
24(1)	1 Apr 1990 (SI 1990/355)[1]
(2)	1 Apr 1990 (except so far as relates to Companies Act 1985, s 245(1), (2)) (SI 1990/355)[1]
	7 Jan 1991 (exception noted above)[1] (SI 1990/2569)[8]
(3)	1 Apr 1990 (except so far as relates to Companies Act 1985, s 233(5)) (SI 1990/355)[1]
	7 Jan 1991 (exception noted above)[1] (SI 1990/2569)
(4)	1 Apr 1990 (SI 1990/355)[1]
25, 26	1 Apr 1990 (SI 1990/355)[1]

Companies Act 1989 (c 40)—*cont*

Sch 10[3], para 27	1 Apr 1990 (SI 1990/355)[1]; prospectively repealed by Coal Industry Act 1994, s 67(8), Sch 11, Pt IV[11]
28	1 Apr 1990 (SI 1990/355)[1]
29	1 Apr 1990 (SI 1990/355)[1]; prospectively repealed by Crown Agents Act 1995, s 13(2), Sch 2, Pt I[12]
30–34	1 Apr 1990 (SI 1990/355)[1]
35(1)	1 Apr 1990 (SI 1990/355)[1]
(2)(a)	1 Apr 1990 (SI 1990/355)[1]
(b)	7 Jan 1991 (SI 1990/2569)
(3)	1 Apr 1990 (SI 1990/355)[1]
36–39	1 Apr 1990 (SI 1990/355)[1]
11, 12	1 Mar 1990 (SI 1990/142)
13	*Not in force*
14	1 Mar 1990 (SI 1990/142)
15, 16	*Not in force*
17	31 Jul 1990 (SI 1990/1392)
18	1 Nov 1990 (SI 1990/1392)[5]
19, para 1	1 Mar 1990 (SI 1990/142)
2–6	1 Oct 1990 (SI 1990/1707)[7]
7	1 Oct 1990 (SI 1990/1707)
8, 9	1 Mar 1990 (SI 1990/142)
10	7 Jan 1991 (SI 1990/2569)
11	4 Feb 1991 (SI 1990/2569)
12	1 Mar 1990 (SI 1990/142)
13	*Not in force*
14	1 Oct 1990 (SI 1990/1707)
15–18	1 Apr 1990 (SI 1990/355)
19	1 Mar 1990 (SI 1990/142)
20	3 Jul 1995 (SI 1995/1352)
21	1 Mar 1990 (SI 1990/142)
20, para 1	1 Apr 1990 (SI 1990/142)
2–12	16 Nov 1989 (s 215(1))
13	1 Apr 1990 (SI 1990/142)
14–16	16 Nov 1989 (s 215(1))
17	1 Apr 1990 (SI 1990/142)
18–20	16 Nov 1989 (s 215(1))
21	1 Apr 1990 (SI 1990/142)
22–25	16 Nov 1989 (s 215(1))
26	1 Apr 1990 (SI 1990/142)
21, 22	25 Mar 1991 (see note to ss 154–156) (SI 1991/488) 25 Apr 1991 (otherwise) (SI 1991/878)
23, para 1–31	15 Mar 1990 (SI 1990/354)
32	15 Mar 1990 (so far as relates to Financial Services Act 1986, Sch 11, para 13A) (SI 1990/354) *Not in force* (otherwise)
33–43	15 Mar 1990 (SI 1990/354)
24	16 Nov 1989 (repeals of or in Fair Trading Act 1973, ss 71, 74, 88, 89, Sch 9) (s 215(1)) 21 Feb 1990 (repeals of or in Companies Act 1985, ss 435, 440, 443, 446, 447, 449, 452, 735A; Financial Services Act 1986, ss 94, 105, 179, 180, 198(1); Banking Act 1987, s 84(1)) (SI 1990/142) 1 Mar 1990 (repeals of or in Company Directors Disqualification Act 1986, s 21(2)) (SI 1990/142) 1 Mar 1990 (repeal in Financial Services Act 1986, s 199(9)) (SI 1990/355)

Companies Act 1989 (c 40)—*cont*

Sch 24—*cont*

15 Mar 1990 (repeals of or in Financial Services Act 1986, ss 48, 55, 119, 159, 160, Sch 11, paras 4, 10, 14) (SI 1990/354)

1 Apr 1990 (repeals of or in Fair Trading Act 1973, ss 46(3), 85) (SI 1990/142)

1 Apr 1990 (repeals of or in Harbours Act 1964, s 42(6) (subject to transitional or saving provisions); Companies Act 1985, ss 716, 717, 744 (definition of 'authorised institution'), 746, Schs 2, 4, 9, 11, 22 (entry relating to ss 384–393), 24 (except entries relating to ss 245(1), (2), 365(3), 389(10)) (subject to transitional or saving provisions); Insolvency Act 1985, Sch 6, paras 23, 45; Insolvency Act 1986, Sch 13, Pt 1 (entries relating to ss 222(4), 225); Financial Services Act 1986, Sch 16, para 22) (SI 1990/355)

31 May 1990 (repeals of or in Companies Act 1985, ss 201, 202(1), 209(1)(j)) (SI 1990/713)

31 Jul 1990 (repeals of or in Companies Act 1985, s 651(1), Sch 22 (entry relating to s 36(4)); Building Societies Act 1986, Schs 15, 18) (SI 1990/1392)

1 Oct 1990 (repeals of or in Companies Act 1985, ss 466(2), 733(3), Sch 22 (entries relating to ss 363365), Sch 24 (entries relating to s 365(3)); Insolvency Act 1986, Sch 13, Pt I (entry relating to s 733(3)) (SI 1990/1707)7

7 Jan 1991 (repeals of or in Companies Act 1985, s 708(1)(b), Sch 15, 24 (entries relating to s 245(1), (2))) (SI 1990/2569)[7,8]

1 Jul 1991 (repeal of Companies Act 1985, ss 712, 715) (SI 1991/488)

1 Oct 1991 (repeals of or in Companies Act 1985, ss 389, 460(1); Financial Services Act 1986, s 196(3); Income and Corporation Taxes Act 1988, s 565(6)(b)) (SI 1991/1996)

1 Nov 1991 (repeals of or in Companies Act 1985, ss 169(5), 175(6)(b), 191(1), (3)(a), (b), 219(1), 288(3), 318(7), 356(1), (2), (4), 383(1)–(3), Sch 13, para 25) (SI 1991/1996)

3 Jul 1995 (repeals of or in Companies Act 1985, ss 464(5)(c), 744 (definition 'annual return')) (SI 1995/1352)

Not in force (otherwise)

Note: Erroneous repeal of Financial Services Act 1986, s 199(1), by s 212, Sch 24, brought into force on 21 Feb 1990 by SI 1990/142, art 7(d), was revoked by SI 1990/355, art 16, as from 1 March 1990

[1] subject to transitional and saving provisions set out in SI 1990/355, arts 6–9, Sch 2, as amended by SI 1990/2569, art 8, SI 1993/3246, reg 5(2), the principal effect being (with certain exceptions) that the existing rules relating to accounts and reports of companies continue to apply for financial years of a company commencing before 23 December 1989

[2] subject to transitional and saving provisions set out in SI 1990/355, art 10, Sch 4, as amended by SI 1990/1707, art 8, with regard to annual returns and auditors

[3] see, as to transitional and savings provisions, SI 1990/355, art 8, Sch 3

Companies Act 1989 (c 40)—*cont*

[4] subject to the saving provision set out in SI 1990/1392, art 5

[5] subject to the transitional provisions set out in SI 1990/1392, art 6

[6] subject to the saving provision set out in SI 1990/1392, art 7

[7] subject to transitional and saving provisions set out in SI 1990/1707, arts 4–6

[8] subject to transitional and saving provisions set out in SI 1990/2569, arts 6, 7

[9] subject to the transitional and saving provisions set out in SI 1991/488, arts 3 and 4

[10] subject to saving provisions set out in SI 1991/878, art 3

[11] Orders made under Coal Industry Act 1994, s 68, bringing the prospective repeal into force will be noted to that Act in the service to this work

[12] Orders made under Crown Agents Act 1995, s 1(1), bringing the prospective repeal into force will be noted to that Act in the service to this work

Consolidated Fund Act 1989 (c 2)

Whole Act repealed

Consolidated Fund (No 2) Act 1989 (c 46)

Whole Act repealed

Continental Shelf Act 1989 (c 35)

RA: 27 Jul 1989

27 Jul 1989 (RA)

Control of Pollution (Amendment) Act 1989 (c 14)

RA: 6 Jul 1989

Commencement provisions: s 11(2); Control of Pollution (Amendment) Act 1989 (Commencement) Order 1991, SI 1991/1618

s 1(1), (2)	1 Apr 1992 (SI 1991/1618)
(3)	16 Jul 1991 (SI 1991/1618)
(4)–(6)	1 Apr 1992 (SI 1991/1618)
2	16 Jul 1991 (SI 1991/1618)
3	16 Jul 1991 (so far as relates to making of regulations) (SI 1991/1618) 14 Oct 1991 (otherwise) (SI 1991/1618)
4(1)–(5)	14 Oct 1991 (SI 1991/1618)
(6)	16 Jul 1991 (SI 1991/1618)
(7), (8)	14 Oct 1991 (SI 1991/1618)
(9)	Prospectively added by Environment Act 1995, s 120(1), Sch 22, para 37(1), (3)[1]
5(1), (2)	1 Apr 1992 (SI 1991/1618)
(3)	16 Jul 1991 (so far as relates to making of regulations) (SI 1991/1618) 1 Apr 1992 (otherwise) (SI 1991/1618)
(4), (5)	1 Apr 1992 (SI 1991/1618)

Control of Pollution (Amendment) Act 1989 (c 14)—*cont*

s 5(6)	16 Jul 1991 (so far as relates to making of regulations) (SI 1991/1618) 1 Apr 1992 (otherwise) (SI 1991/1618)
(7)	1 Apr 1992 (SI 1991/1618)
6	16 Jul 1991 (so far as relates to making of regulations) (SI 1991/1618) 14 Oct 1991 (otherwise) (SI 1991/1618)
7	14 Oct 1991 (SI 1991/1618)
8–10	16 Jul 1991 (SI 1991/1618)
10A	Prospectively inserted by Environment Act 1995, s 118(1)[1]
11	16 Jul 1991 (SI 1991/1618)

[1] Orders made under Environment Act 1995, s 125(3), bringing the prospective addition and insertion into force will be noted to that Act in the service to this work

Control of Smoke Pollution Act 1989 (c 17)

Whole Act repealed

Dangerous Dogs Act 1989 (c 30)

RA: 27 Jul 1989

Commencement provisions: s 2(4)

27 Aug 1989 (s 2(4))

Disabled Persons (Northern Ireland) Act 1989 (c 10)

RA: 25 May 1989

Commencement provisions: s 12(2); Disabled Persons (1989 Act) (Commencement No 1) Order (Northern Ireland) 1989, SR 1989/474; Disabled Persons (1989 Act) (Commencement No 2) Order (Northern Ireland) 1990, SR 1990/456

s 1–3	*Not in force*
4	1 Apr 1991 (except para (b)) (SR 1990/456) *Not in force* (exception noted above)
5, 6	1 Apr 1991 (SR 1990/456)
7	*Not in force*
8(1)	1 Apr 1991 (SR 1990/456)
(2), (3)	*Not in force*
9, 10	7 Dec 1989 (SR 1989/474)
11(1)	7 Dec 1989 (SR 1989/474)
(1A)	Prospectively inserted by Children (Northern Ireland) Order 1995, SI 1995/755 (NI 2), art 185(1), Sch 9, para 170(2)
(2), (3)	7 Dec 1989 (SR 1989/474)
(4)	1 Apr 1991 (SR 1990/456)
12	7 Dec 1989 (SR 1989/474)

Dock Work Act 1989 (c 13)

RA: 3 Jul 1989

Commencement provisions: s 8(3), (4); National Dock Labour Board (Date of Dissolution) Order 1990, SI 1990/1158

s 1–6	3 Jul 1989 (s 8(3))
7(1)	See Sch 1 below
(2)–(5)	3 Jul 1989 (s 8(3))
8	3 Jul 1989 (s 8(3))
Sch 1, Pt I	3 Jul 1989 (s 8(3))
II	30 Jun 1990 (SI 1990/1158)
2	3 Jul 1989 (s 8(3))

Elected Authorities (Northern Ireland) Act 1989 (c 3)

RA: 15 Mar 1989

Commencement provisions: s 13(2); Elected Authorities (Northern Ireland) Act 1989 (Commencement No 1) Order 1989, SI 1989/1093

s 1(1)	15 Mar 1989 (RA)
(2)	16 Feb 1990 (SI 1989/1093)
(3), (4)	15 Mar 1989 (RA)
2–4	15 Mar 1989 (RA)
5	*Not in force*
6, 7	15 Mar 1989 (RA)
8(1)	15 Mar 1989 (RA)
(2)	*Not in force*
9–13	15 Mar 1989 (RA)
Sch 1	15 Mar 1989 (so far as relates to Representation of the People Act 1983, ss 3, 4) (RA) 27 Jun 1989 (so far as relates to Representation of the People Act 1983, ss 53, 201, 202(1), Sch 2) (SI 1989/1093) 16 Feb 1990 (so far as relates to Representation of the People Act 1983, ss 49, 50) (SI 1989/1093) 1 Aug 1989 (otherwise) (SI 1989/1093)
2, 3	15 Mar 1989 (RA)

Electricity Act 1989 (c 29)

RA: 27 Jul 1989

Commencement provisions: s 113(2); Electricity Act 1989 (Commencement No 1) Order 1989, SI 1989/1369; Electricity Act 1989 (Commencement No 2) Order 1990, SI 1990/117

s 1, 2	1 Sep 1989 (SI 1989/1369)
3–5	31 Mar 1990 (SI 1990/117)
6(1)–(8)	31 Mar 1990 (SI 1990/117)
(9)	1 Sep 1989 (for the purpose of the interpretation of s 2(7)) (SI 1989/1369) 31 Mar 1990 (otherwise) (SI 1990/117)

Electricity Act 1989 (c 29)—*cont*

s 6(10), (11)	31 Mar 1990 (SI 1990/117)
7–42	31 Mar 1990 (SI 1990/117)
42A, 42B	Inserted by Competition and Service (Utilities) Act 1992, ss 21, 22 (qv)
43, 44	31 Mar 1990 (SI 1990/117)
44A	Prospectively inserted by Competition and Service (Utilities) Act 1992, s 23[1]
45–63	31 Mar 1990 (SI 1990/117)
64	1 Oct 1989 (definition of 'prescribed' for purposes of Schs 14, 15) (SI 1989/1369)
	31 Mar 1990 (otherwise) (SI 1990/117)
65–69	1 Oct 1989 (SI 1989/1369)
70	See Sch 10 below
71–84	31 Mar 1990 (SI 1990/117)
85	1 Mar 1990 (SI 1990/117)
86	1 Sep 1989 (SI 1989/1369)
87, 88	31 Mar 1990 (SI 1990/117)
89	1 Oct 1989 (SI 1989/1369)
90	31 Mar 1990 (SI 1990/117)
91, 92	1 Oct 1989 (SI 1989/1369)
93	31 Mar 1990 (SI 1990/117)
94, 95	1 Oct 1989 (SI 1989/1369)
96	31 Mar 1990 (SI 1990/117)
97	See Sch 12 below
98–103	31 Mar 1990 (SI 1990/117)
104	See Sch 14 below
105	See Sch 15 below
106, 107	1 Sep 1989 (SI 1989/1369)
108, 109	31 Mar 1990 (SI 1990/117)
110, 111	1 Sep 1989 (SI 1989/1369)
112(1)–(3)	31 Mar 1990 (SI 1990/117)
(4)	See Sch 18 below
113	1 Sep 1989 (SI 1989/1369)
Sch 1, 2	1 Sep 1989 (SI 1989/1369)
3–9	31 Mar 1990 (SI 1990/117)
10	1 Oct 1989 (SI 1989/1369)
11	31 Mar 1990 (SI 1990/117)
12	1 Oct 1989 (SI 1989/1369)
13	31 Mar 1990 (SI 1990/117)
14	1 Oct 1989 (SI 1989/1369)
15	1 Oct 1989 (SI 1989/1369)
16	31 Mar 1990 (SI 1990/117)
17, para 1, 2	31 Mar 1990 (SI 1990/117)
3(a)	31 Mar 1990 (SI 1990/117)
(b)	*Not in force*
4–40	31 Mar 1990 (SI 1990/117)
18	31 Mar 1990 (except repeals of or in Electricity Act 1947, ss 1(2), (3), 3(1), (7), (8), 64(3), (4), 67(1), 69, Sch 1, column 1; Electricity Act 1957, ss 2(1), 3(1), (6), (7), 40(1), 42, Sch 4, Pt I; House of Commons Disqualification Act 1975, Sch 1, Pt II; Electricity (Scotland) Act 1979, s 1, Sch 1, paras 26; National Audit Act 1983, Sch 4; Income and Corporation Taxes Act 1988, s 511(1)–(3), (6)) (SI 1990/117)
	Not in force (exception noted above)

Electricity Act 1989 (c 29)—*cont*

[1] Orders made under Competition and Service (Utilities) Act 1992, s 56, bringing the prospective insertion into force will be noted to that Act in the service to this work

Employment Act 1989 (c 38)

RA: 16 Nov 1989

Commencement provisions: s 30(2)–(4); Employment Act 1989 (Commencement and Transitional Provisions) Order 1990, SI 1990/189

s 1–7	16 Jan 1990 (s 30(3))
8	16 Nov 1989 (s 30(2))
9(1), (2)	16 Jan 1990 (s 30(3))
(3)	26 Feb 1990 (SI 1990/189)
(4)–(6)	16 Jan 1990 (s 30(3))
10(1), (2)	See Sch 3 below
(3)–(6)	16 Nov 1989 (s 30(2))
11, 12	16 Nov 1989 (s 30(2))
13, 14	Repealed
15	26 Feb 1990 (subject to transitional provisions) (SI 1990/189)
16–19	16 Jan 1990 (s 30(3))
20	26 Feb 1990 (SI 1990/189)
21	16 Jan 1990 (s 30(3))
22–28	16 Nov 1989 (s 30(2))
29(1), (2)	16 Nov 1989 (s 30(2))
(3)	See Sch 6 below
(4)	See Sch 7 below
(5)	See Sch 8 below
(6)	See Sch 9 below
30	16 Nov 1989 (s 30(2))
Sch 1, 2	16 Jan 1990 (s 30(3))
3, Pt I, II	16 Jan 1990 (except repeals of or in Employment of Women, Young Persons and Children Act 1920, s 1(3), Sch, Pt II; Factories Act 1961, s 119A) (s 30(3)) 26 Feb 1990 (repeals of or in Employment of Women, Young Persons and Children Act 1920, s 1(3), Sch, Pt II) (SI 1990/189) *Not in force* (otherwise)
III	16 Jan 1990 (s 30(3))
4, 5	16 Nov 1989 (s 30(2))
6, para 1, 2	26 Feb 1990 (SI 1990/189)
3–5	Repealed
6	*Not in force*
7, 8	16 Jan 1990 (s 30(3))
9–12	16 Nov 1989 (s 30(2))
13	Repealed
14, 15	16 Nov 1989 (s 30(2))
16	16 Jan 1990 (s 30(3))
17	16 Nov 1989 (s 30(2))
18–20	Repealed
21–25	16 Jan 1990 (s 30(3))
26	26 Feb 1990 (SI 1990/189)

Employment Act 1989 (c 38)—*cont*

Sch 6, para 27–29	16 Nov 1989 (s 30(2))
30	16 Jan 1990 (s 30(3))
7, Pt I	16 Nov 1989 (s 30(2))
II	16 Jan 1990 (s 30(3))
III	26 Feb 1990 (except repeals of or in Factories Act 1961, s 119A; Employment Medical Advisory Service Act 1972, s 5(1), s 8(1) (so far as relates to Factories Act 1961, s 119A); Employment and Training Act 1973, Sch 3, para 6) (SI 1990/189)
8	16 Jan 1990 (s 30(3))
9	16 Nov 1989 (s 30(2))

Extradition Act 1989 (c 33)

RA: 27 Jul 1989

Commencement provisions: s 38(2), (3)

s 1–6	27 Sep 1989 (s 38(2))
7(1), (2)	27 Sep 1989 (s 38(2))
(2A)	Inserted by Criminal Justice and Public Order Act 1994, s 158(1), (3) (qv)
(3)	27 Jul 1989 (s 38(3))
(4)–(6)	27 Sep 1989 (s 38(2))
(7)	Added by Criminal Justice and Public Order Act 1994, s 168(1), Sch 9, para 37(1) (qv)
8, 9	27 Sep 1989 (s 38(2))
10(1), (2)	27 Sep 1989 (s 38(2))
(3)	27 Jul 1989 (s 38(3))
(4)–(13)	27 Sep 1989 (s 38(2))
11–13	27 Sep 1989 (s 38(2))
14(1)	27 Sep 1989 (s 38(2))
(2), (3)	27 Jul 1989 (s 38(3))
(4)	27 Sep 1989 (s 38(2))
15–37	27 Sep 1989 (s 38(2))
38	27 Jul 1989 (s 38(3))
Sch 1, para 1–8	27 Sep 1989 (s 38(3))
9(1)	27 Sep 1989 (s 38(2))
(2)	27 Jul 1989 (s 38(3))
(3), (4)	27 Sep 1989 (s 38(2))
10–20	27 Sep 1989 (s 38(2))
2	27 Sep 1989 (s 38(2))

Fair Employment (Northern Ireland) Act 1989 (c 32)

RA: 27 Jul 1989

Commencement provisions: Fair Employment (Northern Ireland) Act 1989 (Commencement) Order 1989, SI 1989/1928

s 1(1), (2)	1 Jan 1990 (SI 1989/1928)
(3)	1 Nov 1989 (SI 1989/1928)
2–28	1 Jan 1990 (SI 1989/1928)
29	1 Nov 1989 (SI 1989/1928)
30	Repealed

Fair Employment (Northern Ireland) Act 1989 (c 32)—*cont*

s 31–46	1 Jan 1990 (SI 1989/1928)
47	1 Nov 1989 (SI 1989/1928)
48	1 Jan 1990 (SI 1989/1928)
49	1 Jan 1990 (except for purposes of acts done before 1 Jan 1990) (SI 1990/1928)
50–56	1 Jan 1990 (SI 1989/1928)
57	1 Nov 1989 (SI 1989/1928)
58–60	1 Jan 1990 (SI 1989/1928)
Sch 1	1 Jan 1990 (SI 1989/1928)
2, para 1–14	1 Jan 1990 (SI 1989/1928)
15	1 Jan 1990 (except for purposes of any complaint or act to which s 50(2) applies) (SI 1989/1928)
16(1), (2)	1 Jan 1990 (SI 1989/1928)
(3)(a)	1 Jan 1990 (SI 1989/1928)
(b)	1 Jan 1990 (except for purposes of any complaint or act to which s 50(2) applies) (SI 1989/1928)
17	1 Jan 1990 (except for purposes of any complaint or act to which s 50(2) applies) (SI 1989/1928)
18–20	1 Jan 1990 (SI 1989/1928)
21(a), (b)	1 Jan 1990 (SI 1989/1928)
(c)	1 Jan 1990 (except for purposes of any complaint or act to which s 50(2) applies) (SI 1989/1928)
(d)–(f)	1 Jan 1990 (SI 1989/1928)
22, 23	1 Jan 1990 (SI 1989/1928)
24–26	1 Jan 1990 (except for purposes of any complaint or act to which s 50(2) applies) (SI 1989/1928)
27–31	1 Jan 1990 (SI 1989/1928)
32, 33	1 Jan 1990 (except for purposes of any complaint or act to which s 50(2) applies) (SI 1989/1928)
3	1 Jan 1990 (except repeals of or in Fair Employment (Northern Ireland) Act 1976, ss 44–48, 51, 53(4), 57(1) (definitions of 'complainant', 'the county court', 'finding' and 'the injured person'), 59(2), Sch 1, para 11, for the purposes of any complaint or act to which s 50(2) of this Act applies) (SI 1989/1928)

Finance Act 1989 (c 26)

RA: 27 Jul 1989

See the note concerning Finance Acts at the front of this book

---

Football Spectators Act 1989 (c 37)

RA: 16 Nov 1989

Commencement provisions: s 27(2), (3); Football Spectators Act 1989 (Commencement No 1) Order 1990, SI 1990/690; Football Spectators Act 1989 (Commencement No 2) Order 1990, SI 1990/926; Football Spectators Act 1989 (Commencement No 3) Order 1991, SI 1991/1071; Football Spectators Act 1989 (Commencement No 4) Order 1993, SI 1993/1690

s 1(1), (2)	22 Mar 1990 (SI 1990/690)
(3)	*Not in force*
(4)(a)	22 Mar 1990 (SI 1990/690)
(b)	*Not in force*

Football Spectators Act 1989 (c 37)—*cont*

s 1(5), (6)	*Not in force*
(7)–(11)	22 Mar 1990 (SI 1990/690)
2–7	*Not in force*
8	1 Jun 1990 (SI 1990/690)
9	1 Aug 1993 (SI 1993/1690)
10(1)–(5)	1 Jun 1990 (SI 1990/690)
(6), (7)	*Not in force*
(8)(a), (b)	1 Jun 1990 (SI 1990/690)
(c)	*Not in force*
(9)–(11)	1 Jun 1990 (SI 1990/690)
(12)(a), (b)	*Not in force*
(c), (d)	1 Jun 1990 (SI 1990/690)
(13)–(17)	1 Jun 1990 (SI 1990/690)
11, 12	1 Jun 1990 (SI 1990/690)
13	3 Jun 1991 (SI 1991/1071)
14	22 Mar 1990 (SI 1990/690)
15–21	24 Apr 1990 (SI 1990/690)
22(1)	22 Mar 1990 (SI 1990/690)
(2)–(8)	24 Apr 1990 (SI 1990/690)
(9)	22 Mar 1990 (SI 1990/690)
(10), (11)	24 Apr 1990 (SI 1990/690)
(12)	22 Mar 1990 (SI 1990/690)
23–26	24 Apr 1990 (SI 1990/690)
27	16 Nov 1989 (RA)
Sch 1	24 Apr 1990 (SI 1990/926)
2	1 Jun 1990 (SI 1990/690)

Hearing Aid Council (Amendment) Act 1989 (c 12)

RA: 3 Jul 1989

Commencement provisions: s 6(2)

s 1–4	3 Sep 1989 (s 6(2))
5	1 Jan 1990 (s 6(2))
6	3 Sep 1989 (s 6(2))

Human Organ Transplants Act 1989 (c 31)

RA: 27 Jul 1989

Commencement provisions: s 7(3); Human Organ Transplants Act 1989 (Commencement) Order 1989, SI 1989/2106

s 1	28 Jul 1989 (s 7(3))
2(1)	1 Apr 1990 (SI 1989/2106)
(2)–(7)	27 Jul 1989 (RA)
3–7	27 Jul 1989 (RA)

International Parliamentary Organisations (Registration) Act 1989 (c 19)

RA: 21 Jul 1989

21 Jul 1989 (RA)

Law of Property (Miscellaneous Provisions) Act 1989 (c 34)

RA: 27 Jul 1989

Commencement provisions: s 5; Law of Property (Miscellaneous Provisions) Act 1989 (Commencement) Order 1990, SI 1990/1175

s 1(1)–(7)	31 Jul 1990 (SI 1990/1175)
(8)	See Sch 1 below
(9)–(11)	31 Jul 1990 (SI 1990/1175)
2, 3	27 Sep 1989 (s 5)
4	See Sch 2 below
5, 6	27 Jul 1989 (RA)
Sch 1	31 Jul 1990 (SI 1990/1175)
2	27 Sep 1989 (repeal of Law of Property Act 1925, s 40) (s 5)
	31 Jul 1990 (otherwise) (SI 1990/1175)

Licensing (Amendment) Act 1989 (c 20)

RA: 21 Jul 1989

Commencement provisions: s 2(2)

21 Sep 1989 (s 2(2))

Local Government and Housing Act 1989 (c 42)

RA: 16 Nov 1989

Commencement provisions: ss 154(3), 195(2), (3) (and individually as noted below: passim); Local Government and Housing Act 1989 (Commencement No 1) Order 1989, SI 1989/2180; Local Government and Housing Act 1989 (Commencement No 2) Order 1989, SI 1989/2186; Local Government and Housing Act 1989 (Commencement No 3) Order 1989, SI 1989/2445; Local Government and Housing Act 1989 (Commencement No 4) Order 1990, SI 1990/191; Local Government and Housing Act 1989 (Commencement No 5 and Transitional Provisions) Order 1990, SI 1990/431; Local Government and Housing Act 1989 (Commencement No 6 and Miscellaneous Provisions) Order 1990, SI 1990/762; Local Government and Housing Act 1989 (Commencement No 7) Order 1990, SI 1990/961; Local Government and Housing Act 1989 (Commencement No 8 and Transitional Provisions) Order 1990, SI 1990/1274, as amended by SI 1990/1335; Local Government and Housing Act 1989 (Commencement No 9 and Saving) Order 1990, SI 1990/1552; Local Government and Housing Act 1989 (Commencement No 10) Order 1990, SI 1990/2581; Local Government and Housing Act 1989 (Commencement No 11 and Savings) Order 1991, SI 1991/344; Local Government and Housing Act 1989 (Commencement No 12) Order 1991, SI 1991/953; Local Government and Housing Act 1989 (Commencement No 13) Order 1991, SI 1991/2940; Local Government and Housing Act 1989 (Commencement No 14) Order 1992, SI 1992/760; Local Government and Housing Act 1989 (Commencement No 15) Order 1993, SI 1993/105; Local Government and Housing Act 1989 (Commencement No 16) Order 1993, SI 1993/2410; Local Government and Housing Act 1989 (Commencement No 17) Order 1995, SI 1995/841

Abbreviation: "orders etc" means "so far as confers on Secretary of State powers to make orders, regulations or determinations, to give or make directions, to specify

Local Government and Housing Act 1989 (c 42)—*cont*

matters, to require information, to impose conditions or to give guidance or approvals, or make provision with respect to the exercise of any such power"

s 1(1)–(4)	1 Mar 1990 (SI 1989/2445)
(5), (6)	29 Nov 1989 (SI 1989/2186)
(7), (8)	1 Mar 1990 (SI 1989/2445)
2	29 Nov 1989 (SI 1989/2186)
3	16 Nov 1989 (RA)
4–7	16 Jan 1990 (ss 4(7), 5(9), 6(8), 7(3))
8	16 Nov 1989 (RA)
9	16 Jan 1990 (orders etc) (SI 1989/2445) 1 Aug 1990 (EW) (otherwise) (SI 1990/1552) *Not in force* (S) (otherwise)
10	1 Apr 1990 (SI 1990/431)
11	16 Nov 1989 (RA; note s 11(4))
12	16 Jan 1990 (s 12(3))
13	16 Jan 1990 (orders etc) (SI 1989/2445) 1 Aug 1990 (so far as not already in force, except in relation to a parish or community council until 1 Jan 1991) (SI 1990/1552)
14	*Not in force*
15	16 Jan 1990 (orders etc) (SI 1989/2445) 1 Aug 1990 (EW) (otherwise) (SI 1990/1552) *Not in force* (S) (otherwise)
16	1 Aug 1990 (EW) (SI 1990/1552) *Not in force*(S)
17	16 Jan 1990 (orders etc) (SI 1989/2445) 1 Aug 1990 (EW) (otherwise) (SI 1990/1552) *Not in force* (S) (otherwise)
18	16 Jan 1990 (SI 1989/2445)
19	16 Jan 1990 (orders etc) (SI 1989/2445) 8 May 1992 (otherwise) (SI 1992/760)
20	16 Jan 1990 (SI 1989/2445)
21	16 Nov 1989 (RA
22	16 Jan 1990 (SI 1989/2445)
23	1 Apr 1990 (SI 1990/431)
24	16 Nov 1989 (RA) (note s 24(3))
25–29	1 Apr 1990 (SI 1990/431)
30(1)	3 May 1990 (SI 1990/961)
(2)	3 May 1990 (so far as amends the Local Government Act 1972, s 83(1)) (SI 1990/961) 1 Jan 1991 (otherwise) (SI 1990/2581)
31	16 Jan 1990 (SI 1989/2445)
32	3 May 1990 (SI 1990/961)
33–35	16 Jan 1990 (orders etc) (SI 1989/2445) 1 Apr 1990 (otherwise) (SI 1990/762)
36	16 Jan 1990 (orders etc) (SI 1989/2445) 1 Apr 1990 (otherwise) (SI 1990/431)
37, 38	1 Apr 1990 (SI 1990/431)
39–66	16 Jan 1990 (SI 1989/2445)
67–70	16 Jan 1990 (orders etc) (SI 1989/2445) 7 Oct 1993 (otherwise) (SI 1993/2410)
71(1)	16 Jan 1990 (orders etc) (SI 1989/2445) 1 Apr 1995 (for purposes of sub-ss (4)–(6) only) (SI 1995/841) *Not in force* (otherwise)

Local Government and Housing Act 1989 (c 42)—*cont*

s 71(2), (3)	16 Jan 1990 (orders etc) (SI 1989/2445)
	Not in force (otherwise)
(4)	16 Jan 1990 (orders etc) (SI 1989/2445)
	1 Apr 1995 (subject to a transitional provision) (otherwise) (SI 1995/841)
(5)	16 Jan 1990 (orders etc) (SI 1989/2445)
	1 Apr 1995 (for purposes of para (a) only) (subject to a transitional provision) (SI 1995/841)
	Not in force (otherwise)
(6)	16 Jan 1990 (orders etc) (SI 1989/2445)
	1 Apr 1995 (SI 1995/841) (otherwise)
(7)	16 Jan 1990 (orders etc) (SI 1989/2445)
	Not in force (otherwise)
(8)	16 Jan 1990 (orders etc) (SI 1989/2445)
	1 Apr 1995 (SI 1995/841) (otherwise)
72	16 Jan 1990 (orders etc) (SI 1989/2445)
	7 Oct 1993 (otherwise) (SI 1993/2410)
73	7 Oct 1993 (SI 1993/2410)
74	16 Nov 1989 (RA)
75	See Sch 4 below
76–80	16 Nov 1989 (RA)
81	Repealed
82–88	16 Nov 1989 (RA)
89–92	16 Jan 1990 (orders etc) (SI 1989/2445)
	1 Apr 1990 (otherwise) (SI 1990/431)
93, 94	1 Apr 1990 (SI 1990/431)
95, 96	16 Jan 1990 (orders etc) (SI 1989/2445)
	1 Apr 1990 (otherwise) (SI 1990/431)
97	1 Apr 1990 (SI 1990/431)
98	16 Jan 1990 (orders etc) (SI 1989/2445)
	1 Apr 1990 (otherwise) (SI 1990/431)
99	16 Jan 1990 (SI 1989/2445)
100	1 Apr 1990 (SI 1990/431)
101(1)–(4)	1 Jul 1990 (SI 1990/1274)
(5)(a)	1 Jul 1990 (SI 1990/1274)
(b)	*Not in force*
102	16 Jan 1990 (orders etc) (SI 1989/2445)
	1 Jul 1990 (otherwise) (SI 1990/1274)
103	1 Jul 1990 (SI 1990/1274)
104	16 Jan 1990 (orders etc) (SI 1989/2445)
	1 Jul 1990 (otherwise) (SI 1990/1274)
105–108	1 Jul 1990 (SI 1990/1274)
109, 110	16 Jan 1990 (orders etc) (SI 1989/2445)
	1 Jul 1990 (otherwise) (SI 1990/1274)
111, 112	1 Jul 1990 (SI 1990/1274)
113	1 Jul 1990 (subject to transitional provisions) (SI 1990/1274)
114	1 Jul 1990 (SI 1990/1274)
115	16 Jan 1990 (orders etc) (SI 1989/2445)
	1 Jul 1990 (otherwise) (SI 1990/1274)
116–120	1 Jul 1990 (SI 1990/1274)
121	16 Jan 1990 (orders etc) (SI 1989/2445)
	1 Jul 1990 (otherwise) (SI 1990/1274)
122–126	1 Jul 1990 (SI 1990/1274)
127	16 Jan 1990 (orders etc) (SI 1989/2445)
	1 Jul 1990 (otherwise) (SI 1990/1274)
128, 129	1 Jul 1990 (SI 1990/1274)

Local Government and Housing Act 1989 (c 42)—*cont*

s 130	16 Jan 1990 (orders etc) (SI 1989/2445)
	1 Jul 1990 (otherwise) (SI 1990/1274)
131	16 Jan 1990 (orders etc) (SI 1989/2445)
	1 Apr 1990 (otherwise) (SI 1990/431)
132(1)–(4)	16 Jan 1990 (orders etc) (SI 1989/2445)
	1 Apr 1990 (so far as relate to s 131 and not already in force) (SI 1990/431)
(5)	16 Jan 1990 (orders etc) (SI 1989/2445)
	1 Jul 1990 (otherwise, subject to transitional provisions) (SI 1990/1274)
133–136	1 Jul 1990 (SI 1990/1274)
137, 138	16 Jan 1990 (SI 1989/2445)
139	See Sch 5 below
140, 141	Repealed (with savings)
142	1 Dec 1989 (for purposes of, and in relation to, the financial year 1990–91 and each subsequent financial year) (SI 1989/2180)
	Prospectively repealed by Local Government Finance Act 1992, s 117(2), Sch 14[1]
143, 144	1 Dec 1989 (SI 1989/2180); prospectively repealed by Local Government Finance Act 1992, s 117(2), Sch 14[1]
145	See Sch 6 below
146	Repealed
147–149	16 Nov 1989 (RA)
150–152	16 Jan 1990 (s 152(7))
153	16 Nov 1989 (RA)
154	1 Jan 1992 (SI 1991/2940)
155	1 Apr 1990 (s 155(7))
156	1 Apr 1990 (SI 1990/431)
157, 158	16 Nov 1989 (RA)
159	1 Dec 1989 (SI 1989/2180)
160	See Sch 8 below
161	16 Nov 1989 (RA)
162	16 Jan 1990 (SI 1989/2445)
163	16 Nov 1989 (RA)
164	Repealed
165(1)	See Sch 9 below
(2)	1 Apr 1990 (SI 1990/431)
(3)–(9)	1 Mar 1990 (SI 1990/191)
166	16 Nov 1989 (RA)
167, 168	16 Jan 1990 (SI 1989/2445)
169(1)	1 Apr 1990 (SI 1990/431)
(2)(a)	1 Apr 1990 (SI 1990/431)
(b), (c)	1 Jul 1990 (SI 1990/1274)
(d)	1 Apr 1990 (SI 1990/431)
(3)–(9)	1 Apr 1990 (SI 1990/431)
170	1 Apr 1990 (SI 1989/2180)
171	16 Jan 1990 (SI 1989/2445)
172(1)–(5)	1 Mar 1990 (SI 1989/2445)
(6)–(8)	16 Jan 1990 (SI 1989/2445)
(9)	1 Mar 1990 (SI 1989/2445)
173	1 Mar 1990 (SI 1989/2445)
174	16 Nov 1989 (RA)
175	16 Jan 1990 (SI 1989/2445)
176–178	16 Jan 1990 (SI 1989/2180)
179	1 Dec 1989 (SI 1989/2180)

Local Government and Housing Act 1989 (c 42)—*cont*

s 180	16 Jan 1990 (SI 1989/2445)
181	16 Nov 1989 (RA)
182	16 Jan 1990 (SI 1989/2445)
183	1 Apr 1990 (SI 1990/431)
184	16 Nov 1989 (RA)
185	16 Jan (SI 1989/2180)
186	1 Apr 1990 (SI 1990/431)
187, 188	16 Nov 1989 (RA)
189	16 Nov 1989 (RA); prospectively repealed by Criminal Justice Act 1991, s 101(2), Sch 132
190–193	16 Nov 1989 (RA)
194(1)	See Sch 11 below
(2)–(4)	See Sch 12 below
195	16 Nov 1989 (RA)
Sch 1	16 Jan 1990 (orders etc) (SI 1989/2445) 1 Aug 1990 (EW) (otherwise) (SI 1990/1552) *Not in force* (S) (otherwise)
2	16 Jan 1990 (orders etc) (SI 1989/2445) 1 Apr 1990 (otherwise) (SI 1990/431)
3	16 Jan 1990 (SI 1989/2445)
4	16 Nov 1989 (RA)
5, para 1*	16 Nov 1989 (RA)
2–18	Repealed
19–42*	16 Nov 1989 (RA)
43	Repealed
44–48*	16 Nov 1989 (RA)
49–54	Repealed
55*	16 Nov 1989 (RA)
56	Repealed
57*	16 Nov 1989 (RA)
58, 59	Repealed
60	16 Jan 1990 (SI 1989/2445)
61	Repealed
62*	16 Nov 1989 (RA)
63–65	Repealed
66	16 Jan 1989 (para 79(1))
67–69*	16 Nov 1989 (RA)
70, 71	Repealed
72*	16 Nov 1989 (RA)
73, 74	Repealed
75, 76*	16 Nov 1989 (RA)
77, 78	Repealed
79, 80*	16 Nov 1989 (RA)
6, para 1, 2	1 Apr 1990 (SI 1989/2180)
3, 4	1 Dec 1989 (for purposes of, and in relation to, the financial year 1990–91 and each subsequent financial year) (SI 1989/2180)
5, 6	1 Dec 1989 (SI 1989/2180)
7, 8	Repealed
9	1 Apr 1990 (SI 1989/2180)
10	1 Apr 1990 (SI 1989/2180); prospectively repealed by Local Government Finance Act 1992, s 117(2), Sch 14[1]
11, 12	1 Dec 1989 (SI 1989/2180); prospectively repealed by Local Government Finance Act 1992, s 117(2), Sch 14[1]

Local Government and Housing Act 1989 (c 42)—*cont*

Sch 6, para 13–15	1 Apr 1990 (SI 1989/2180); prospectively repealed by Local Government Finance Act 1992, s 117(2), Sch 14[1]
16, 17	1 Dec 1989 (SI 1989/2180); prospectively repealed by Local Government etc (Scotland) Act 1994, s 180(2), Sch 14[3]
18, 19	1 Apr 1990 (SI 1989/2180); prospectively repealed by Local Government etc (Scotland) Act 1994, s 180(2), Sch 14[3]
20, 21	Repealed
22	1 Apr 1990 (SI 1989/2180); prospectively repealed by Local Government Finance Act 1992, s 117(2), Sch 14[1]
23	1 Dec 1989 (SI 1989/2180)
24–27	1 Dec 1989 (SI 1989/2180); prospectively repealed by Local Government Finance Act 1992, s 117(2), Sch 14[1]
28, 29	1 Dec 1989 (for purposes of, and in relation to, the financial year 199091 and each subsequent financial year) (SI 1989/2180)
	Prospectively repealed by Local Government Finance Act 1992, s 117(2), Sch 14[1]
7	16 Nov 1989 (RA)
8	*Not in force*
9, para 1(1)–(5)	1 Apr 1990 (SI 1990/431)
(6)	1 Jul 1990 (SI 1990/1274)
2	1 Apr 1990 (SI 1990/431)
3	1 Jul 1990 (SI 1990/1274)
4–43	1 Apr 1990 (SI 1990/431)
44	16 Jan 1990 (for purposes of Housing Act 1985, s 369) (SI 1989/2445)
	1 Apr 1990 (otherwise) (SI 1990/431)
45–55	1 Apr 1990 (SI 1990/431)
56(1), (2)	16 Jan 1990 (SI 1989/2445)
(3), (4)	1 Apr 1990 (SI 1990/431)
57, 58	1 Jul 1990 (SI 1990/1274)
59	1 Apr 1990 (SI 1990/431)
60	1 Jul 1990 (SI 1990/1274)
61–63	1 Apr 1990 (SI 1990/431)
64, 65	1 Jul 1990 (SI 1990/1274)
66–70	1 Apr 1990 (SI 1990/431)
71(a), (b)	1 Apr 1990 (SI 1990/431)
(c), (d)	1 Jul 1990 (SI 1990/1274)
72–83	1 Apr 1990 (SI 1990/431)
84	16 Jan 1990 (orders etc) (SI 1989/2445)
	1 Apr 1990 (otherwise) (SI 1990/431)
85	1 Apr 1990 (except so far as relating to Housing Act 1985, s 605(1)(e)) (SI 1990/431)
	1 Jul 1990 (exception noted above) (SI 1990/1274)
86–91	1 Apr 1990 (SI 1990/431)
10	1 Apr 1990 (SI 1990/431)
11, para 1, 2	1 Apr 1990 (SI 1990/431)
3	*Not in force*
4	Repealed
5–13	1 Apr 1990 (SI 1990/431)
14	25 Jan 1993 (SI 1993/105)

Local Government and Housing Act 1989 (c 42)—*cont*

Sch 11, para 15	*Not in force*; prospectively repealed by Children (Scotland) Act 1995, s 105(5), Sch 5[4]
16	1 Apr 1990 (SI 1990/431)
17, 18	*Not in force*
19, 20	Repealed
21	*Not in force*
22, 23	1 Apr 1990 (SI 1990/431)
24, 25	*Not in force*
26	27 Feb 1991 (in relation only to the power to make regulations relating to prescribed amount in Local Government Act 1972, s 173(1)) (SI 1991/344) 1 Apr 1991 (otherwise) (SI 1991/344)
27	1 Apr 1990 (orders etc) (SI 1990/431) 1 Apr 1991 (otherwise) (SI 1991/344)
28(1), (2)	1 Jul 1990 (orders etc) (SI 1990/1274) 1 Apr 1991 (otherwise) (SI 1991/344)
(3)	16 Jan 1990 (orders etc) (SI 1989/2445) 1 Apr 1991 (otherwise) (SI 1991/344)
(4)	16 Jan 1990 (SI 1989/2445)
29	1 Apr 1991 (SI 1991/344)
30	8 May 1992 (SI 1992/760)
31–33	1 Apr 1990 (SI 1990/431)
34	1 Apr 1991 (SI 1991/344)
35(1), (2)	*Not in force*
(3)	16 Jan 1990 (orders etc) (SI 1989/2445) *Not in force* (otherwise)
(4)	16 Jan 1990 (SI 1989/2445)
36	*Not in force*
37	16 Jan 1990 (SI 1989/2445)
38–41	1 Apr 1990 (SI 1990/431)
42	16 Jan 1990 (SI 1989/2445)
43	*Not in force*; prospectively repealed by Local Government etc (Scotland) Act 1994, s 180(2), Sch 14[3]
44–48	1 Apr 1990 (SI 1990/431)
49	16 Jan 1990 (SI 1989/2445)
50	1 Apr 1990 (SI 1990/431)
51	Repealed
52	1 Jul 1990 (SI 1990/1274)
53(1)	16 Jan 1990 (SI 1989/2445)
(2)	1 Apr 1990 (SI 1990/431)
54	1 Apr 1990 (SI 1990/431)
55–57	*Not in force*
58	16 Jan 1990 (SI 1989/2445)
59	1 Apr 1990 (SI 1990/431)
60	*Not in force*
61	1 Dec 1989 (SI 1989/2180)
62	1 Apr 1990 (SI 1990/431)
63	1 Jul 1990 (SI 1990/1274)
64, 65	1 Apr 1990 (SI 1990/431)
66–69	1 Jul 1990 (SI 1990/1274)
70–76	1 Apr 1990 (SI 1990/431)
77–84	16 Jan 1990 (SI 1989/2445)
85–87	1 Apr 1990 (SI 1990/431)
88	16 Jan 1990 (orders etc) (SI 1989/2445) 1 Apr 1990 (otherwise) (SI 1990/431)
89	16 Jan 1990 (SI 1989/2445)

Local Government and Housing Act 1989 (c 42)—*cont*

Sch 11, para	90, 91	1 Jul 1990 (SI 1990/1274)
	92	*Not in force*
	93, 94	16 Jan 1990 (SI 1989/2180)
	95	1 Dec 1989 (SI 1989/2180)
	96	1 Apr 1990 (SI 1990/431)
	97	*Not in force*
	98	Repealed
	99, 100	16 Jan 1990 (SI 1989/2180)
	101, 102	1 Apr 1990 (SI 1990/431)
	103	16 Jan 1990 (SI 1989/2445)
	104–106	16 Nov 1989 (RA)
	107	16 Jan 1990 (SI 1989/2445)
	108	1 Apr 1990 (SI 1990/431)
	109–112	16 Jan 1990 (SI 1989/2445)
	113	Repealed
12, Pt I		1 Apr 1990 (SI 1990/431)
II		1 Dec 1989 (repeals of or in Valuation and Rating (Scotland) Act 1956, s 22(4); Local Government (Scotland) Act 1973, s 110A(2); Local Government Finance Act 1988, s 128(2), Sch 12, para 16; Housing (Scotland) Act 1988, s 2(6)) (SI 1988/2180)
		16 Jan 1990 (repeals of or in Housing (Scotland) Act 1987, s 61(10)(a)(v)) (SI 1989/2180)
		16 Jan 1990 (repeals of or in Race Relations Act 1976, s 47; Housing Act 1985, ss 107, 417–420, 423(2), 434, 459, Sch 14; Social Security Act 1986, s 30(10); Housing and Planning Act 1986, s 1; Housing (Scotland) Act 1987, s 80; Housing Act 1988, s 129(5)(b)) (SI 1989/2445)
		1 Mar 1990 (repeals of or in Housing Act 1985, ss 312–314, Sch 12 (in relation to any financial year beginning on or after 1 Apr 1990)) (SI 1990/191)
		1 Apr 1990 (repeals of or in Local Government (Financial Provisions etc) (Scotland) Act 1962, s 4(3), (4), Sch 1; Water (Scotland) Act 1980, s 40(7); Local Government Finance Act 1988, Sch 12, para 37) (SI 1989/2180)
		1 Apr 1990 (repeals of or in Land Compensation Act 1961, s 10, Sch 2; Local Government Act 1972, ss 101, 110; Land Compensation Act 1973, ss 29, 37, 39, 73; Local Government Act 1974, ss 23, 24, 25, 34; Housing Act 1974, Sch 13; Housing Act 1985, so far as not already in force *except* those of or in ss 370–372, 374, 379(1), 381(4) (figure '370'), 460–520, 524–526, 567, 569); Housing (Consequential Provisions) Act 1985, Sch 2; Housing and Planning Act 1986, s 42(1)(d), Sch 5; Local Government Act 1988, s 25, Sch 3; Housing Act 1988, s 130(2)) (SI 1990/431)
		1 Jul 1990 (repeals of or in Local Authorities (Expenditure Powers) Act 1983; Housing Act 1985, ss 370–372, 374, 379(1), 381(4) (figure '370'), 460–520, 567, 569) (subject to transitional provisions) (SI 1990/1274)

Local Government and Housing Act 1989 (c 42)—*cont*

Sch12, Pt II—*cont*	1 Aug 1990 (repeals of or in Local Government Act 1972, s 102(3) (except in relation to a parish or community council until 1 Jan 1991); Local Government Act 1985, s 33) (SI 1990/1552)
	1 Apr 1991 (repeals of or in Local Government Act 1972, ss 177, 177A, 178; Local Government (Scotland) Act 1973, ss 45, 45A, 49A; Education Act 1980; Local Government, Planning and Land Act 1980; Local Government Act 1985, Sch 14; Local Government Act 1986; Norfolk and Suffolk Broads Act 1988) (SI 1991/344)
	Not in force (otherwise)

**Note* Certain amendments made by Sch 5 above (except those made by paras 7, 8, 12, 49(3), 52, 54, 57, 60, 63, 66 or 68) to Local Government Finance Act 1988 are, by virtue of para 79(3) thereof, retrospective in effect

[1] Orders made under Local Government Finance Act 1992, s 119, bringing the prospective repeals into force will be noted to that Act in the service to this work

[2] Orders made under Criminal Justice Act 1991, s 102, bringing the prospective repeal into force will be noted to that Act in the service to this work

[3] Orders made under Local Government etc (Scotland) Act 1994, s 184, bringing the prospective repeal into force will be noted to that Act in the service to this work

[4] Orders made under Children (Scotland) Act 1995, s 105(1), (2), bringing the prospective repeal into force will be noted to that Act in the service to this work

---

National Maritime Museum Act 1989 (c 8)

RA: 5 May 1989

Commencement provisions: s 3(3); National Maritime Museum Act 1989 (Commencement) Order 1989, SI 1989/1028

7 Jul 1989 (SI 1989/1028)

Official Secrets Act 1989 (c 6)

RA: 11 May 1989

Commencement provisions: s 16(6); Official Secrets Act 1989 (Commencement) Order 1990, SI 1990/199

1 Mar 1990 (SI 1990/199)

Opticians Act 1989 (c 44)

RA: 16 Nov 1989

Commencement provisions: s 38

16 Feb 1990 (s 38)

Parking Act 1989 (c 16)

RA: 21 Jul 1989

Commencement provisions: s 5(2); Parking Act 1989 (Commencement) Order 1990, SI 1990/933)

16 May 1990 (SI 1990/933)

Pesticides (Fees and Enforcement) Act 1989 (c 27)

RA: 27 Jul 1989

Commencement provisions: s 3(2)

s 1	27 Jul 1989 (RA)
2	27 Sep 1989 (s 3(2))
3	27 Jul 1989 (RA)

Petroleum Royalties (Relief) and Continental Shelf Act 1989 (c 1)

RA: 7 Feb 1989

7 Feb 1989 (RA)

Police Officers (Central Service) Act 1989 (c 11)

RA: 3 Jul 1989

3 Jul 1989 (RA)

Prevention of Terrorism (Temporary Provisions) Act 1989 (c 4)

RA: 15 Mar 1989

Commencement provisions: s 27(1), (2), (3), (4) (see as to expiry of certain provisions on 22 Mar 1990, s 27(5), (10)–(12)); Prevention of Terrorism (Temporary Provisions) Act 1989 (Commencement No 1) Order 1989, SI 1989/1361; Prevention of Terrorism (Temporary Provisions) Act 1989 (Commencement No 2) Order 1990, SI 1990/215

Continuance orders: Prevention of Terrorism (Temporary Provisions) Act 1989 (Continuance) Order 1991, SI 1991/549; Northern Ireland (Emergency and Prevention of Terrorism Provisions) (Continuance) Order 1991, SI 1991/779; Prevention of Terrorism (Temporary Provisions) Act 1989 (Continuance) Order 1992, SI 1992/495; Northern Ireland (Emergency and Prevention of Terrorism Provisions) (Continuance) Order 1992, SI 1992/1413; Prevention of Terrorism (Temporary Provisions) Act 1989 (Continuance) Order 1993, SI 1993/747; Northern Ireland (Emergency and Prevention of Terrorism Provisions) (Continuance) Order 1993, SI 1993/1522; Prevention of Terrorism (Temporary Provisions) Act 1989 (Continuance) Order 1994, SI 1994/835; Northern Ireland (Emergency and Prevention of Terrorism Provisions) (Continuance) Order 1994, SI 1994/1569; Prevention of Terrorism (Temporary Provisions) Act 1989 (Continuance) Order 1995, SI 1995/816; Northern Ireland (Emergency and Prevention of Terrorism Provisions) (Continuance) Order 1995, SI 1995/1566

Prevention of Terrorism (Temporary Provisions) Act 1989 (c 4)—*cont*

The provisions of Pts I to V (ss 120, Schs 1–7) and s 27(6)(c) (except so far as Pt III (ss 9–13, Sch 4) and Pt V (ss 17–20, Sch 7) have effect in Northern Ireland and relate to proscribed organisations for the purposes of, or offences or orders under, Northern Ireland (Emergency Provisions) Act 1978, s 21 (repealed)) were continued in force for twelve months from 22 Mar 1991 (SI 1991/549); the latest relevant Order is SI 1995/816, by which those provisions (except so far as Pts III, V have effect in Northern Ireland and relate to proscribed organisations for the purposes of Northern Ireland (Emergency Provisions) Act 1991, s 28, or offences or orders under that section) are continued in force for twelve months from 22 Mar 1995

The provisions of Pts III (ss 9–13, Sch 4), V (ss 17–20, Sch 7), so far as they have effect in Northern Ireland and relate to proscribed organisations for the purposes of, or offences or orders under, Northern Ireland (Emergency Provisions) Act 1978, s 21 (repealed), were continued in force for twelve months from 22 Mar 1991 (SI 1991/779); the latest relevant Order is SI 1995/1566 by which those provisions, so far as they have effect in Northern Ireland and relate to proscribed organisations for the purposes of Northern Ireland (Emergency Provisions) Act 1991, s 28, or offences or orders under that section, are continued in force for twelve months from 16 Jun 1995

s 1–13	22 Mar 1989 (s 27(1))
13A	Inserted by Criminal Justice and Public Order Act 1994, s 81(1) (qv)
14–16	22 Mar 1989 (s 27(1))
16A, 16B	Inserted by Criminal Justice and Public Order Act 1994, s 82(1) (qv)
17, 18	22 Mar 1989 (s 27(1))
18A	Inserted by Criminal Justice Act 1993, s 51 (qv)
19	22 Mar 1989 (s 27(1))
19A	Inserted by Criminal Justice Act 1993, s 77, Sch 4, para 4 (qv)
20	22 Mar 1989 (s 27(1))
21–24	Repealed
25–28	22 Mar 1989 (s 27(1)) (ss 27(2), 28 in effect in force on 16 Mar 1989 for purposes of ss 22–24)
Sch 1, 2	22 Mar 1989 (s 27(1))
3	1 Sep 1989 (in relation to a person detained under s 14, Sch 2, para 7 or Sch 5, para 6, after 31 Aug 1989, or a person given notice under Sch 5, para 2(4), after 31 Aug 1989 but not detained under Sch 5, para 6) (SI 1989/1361) 5 Mar 1990 (otherwise) (SI 1990/215)
4, para 1–7	22 Mar 1989 (s 27(1))
8, 9	1 Sep 1989 (SI 1989/1361)
10	5 Mar 1990 (SI 1990/1361)
11–16	22 Mar 1989 (s 27(1))
16A	Prospectively inserted by Criminal Justice (Scotland) Act 1995, s 117(1), Sch 6, Pt II, para 189(1), (3)[1]
17	22 Mar 1989 (s 27(1))
18, 19	1 Sep 1989 (SI 1989/1361)
20	5 Mar 1990 (SI 1990/215)
21–25	22 Mar 1989 (s 27(1))
25A, 25B	Inserted by Northern Ireland (Emergency Provisions) Act 1991, s 70(3), Sch 7, para 5(9) (qv)

Prevention of Terrorism (Temporary Provisions) Act 1989 (c 4)—*cont*

Sch 4, para 26, 27	22 Mar 1989 (s 27(1))
28, 29	1 Sep 1989 (SI 1989/1361)
30	5 Mar 1990 (SI 1990/215)
31–33	22 Mar 1989 (s 27(1))
34	5 Mar 1990 (SI 1990/215)
35	22 Mar 1989 (s 27(1))
5–8	22 Mar 1989 (s 27(1))
9	22 Mar 1989 (except repeal of Sch 7, para 9 of this Act) (s 27(1))
	3 Dec 1990 (repeal of Sch 7, para 9 of this Act, which came into force on the coming into force of Land Registration Act 1988 (qv)) (s 27(4))

[1] Orders made under Criminal Justice (Scotland) Act 1995, s 118, bringing the prospective insertion into force will be noted to that Act in the service to this work

Prisons (Scotland) Act 1989 (c 45)

RA: 16 Nov 1989

Commencement provisions: s 46(2)

16 Feb 1990 (s 46(2))

Representation of the People Act 1989 (c 28)

RA: 27 Jul 1989

Commencement provisions: s 8(2); Representation of the People Act 1989 (Commencement No 1) Order 1989, SI 1989/1318; Representation of the People Act 1989 (Commencement No 2) Order 1990, SI 1990/519

s 1–4	1 Apr 1990 (SI 1990/519)
5–8	1 Sep 1989 (SI 1989/1318)

Road Traffic (Driver Licensing and Information Systems) Act 1989 (c 22)

RA: 21 Jul 1989

Commencement provisions: s 17(2); Road Traffic (Driver Licensing and Information Systems) Act 1989 (Commencement No 1) Order 1989, SI 1989/1843; Road Traffic (Driver Licensing and Information Systems) Act 1989 (Commencement No 2) Order 1990, SI 1990/802; Road Traffic (Driver Licensing and Information Systems) Act 1989 (Commencement No 3) Order 1990, SI 1990/2228; Road Traffic (Driver Licensing and Information Systems) Act 1989 (Commencement No 4) Order 1990, SI 1990/2610

s 1(1)–(5)	1 Apr 1991 (SI 1990/2610)
(6)	See Sch 1 below
(7)	1 Jun 1990 (so far as relates to definitions 'the 1981 Act', 'the 1988 Act') (SI 1990/802)
	1 Apr 1991 (otherwise) (SI 1990/2610)
2	1 Apr 1991 (SI 1990/2610)
3	1 Jun 1990 (SI 1990/802)

Road Traffic (Driver Licensing and Information Systems) Act 1989 (c 22)—*cont*

s 4	1 Apr 1991 (SI 1990/2610)
5(1)	1 Jun 1990 (except so far as relates to s 5(5)) (SI 1990/802)
	1 Apr 1991 (exception noted above) (SI 1990/2610)
(2)–(4)	1 Jun 1990 (SI 1990/802)
(5)	1 Apr 1991 (SI 1990/2610)
(6)–(10)	1 Jun 1990 (SI 1990/802)
6	1 Dec 1990 (SI 1990/2228)
7	See Sch 3 below
8–15	1 Jun 1990 (SI 1990/802)
16	See Sch 6 below
17	8 Nov 1989 (SI 1989/1843)
Sch 1, para 1–9	1 Apr 1991 (SI 1990/2610)
10	Repealed
11	1 Jun 1990 (SI 1990/802); prospectively repealed by s 16 of, and Sch 6 to, this Act (qv)
12	1 Apr 1991 (SI 1990/2610)
2	1 Apr 1991 (SI 1990/2610)
3, para 1–5	1 Apr 1991 (SI 1990/2610)
6	1 Dec 1990 (SI 1990/2228)
7	1 Jun 1990 (SI 1990/802)
8(a)	1 Apr 1991 (SI 1991/2610)
(b)(i)	1 Apr 1991 (SI 1990/2610)
(ii), (iii)	1 Jun 1990 (SI 1990/802)
(c)–(e)	1 Apr 1991 (SI 1990/2610)
9(a), (c)	1 Apr 1991 (SI 1990/2610)
(b), (d)	1 Jun 1990 (SI 1990/802)
10	1 Dec 1990 (SI 1990/2228)
11(a)	Repealed
(b)	1 Jun 1990 (SI 1990/802)
(c)	1 Dec 1990 (SI 1990/2228)
(d)	1 Jun 1990 (SI 1990/802)
12(a)	1 Apr 1991 (SI 1990/2610)
(b), (c)	1 Jun 1990 (SI 1990/802)
13	Spent
14	1 Jun 1990 (SI 1990/802)
15(a)	1 Jun 1990 (SI 1990/802)
(b)–(d)	1 Apr 1991 (SI 1990/2610)
(e)	1 Jun 1990 (so far as relates to definitions 'NI driving licence', 'NI licence') (SI 1990/802)
	1 Apr 1991 (so far as relates to definition 'passenger carrying vehicle') (SI 1990/2610)
(f)	1 Jun 1990 (SI 1990/802)
(g)	1 Dec 1990 (SI 1990/2228)
16, 17	1 Jun 1990 (SI 1990/802)
18(a)	1 Apr 1991 (SI 1990/2610)
(b)–(d)	1 Dec 1990 (SI 1990/2228)
19	1 Jun 1990 (SI 1990/802)
20	1 Apr 1991 (SI 1990/2610)
21	Repealed
22, 23	1 Apr 1991 (SI 1990/2610)
24, 25	1 Jun 1990 (SI 1990/802)
26	8 Nov 1989 (SI 1989/1843)
27(a)–(c)	1 Apr 1991 (SI 1990/2610)
(d)	1 Jun 1990 (SI 1990/802)

Road Traffic (Driver Licensing and Information Systems) Act 1989 (c 22)—*cont*

Sch 3, para 27(e)	1 Apr 1991 (SI 1990/2610)
28(a), (b)	1 Jun 1990 (SI 1990/802)
(c), (d)	1 Apr 1991 (SI 1990/2610)
29	8 Nov 1989 (so far as relates to offences under Sch 1, para 10(4), (5)) (SI 1989/1843)
	1 Apr 1991 (otherwise) (SI 1990/2610)
30(a)	1 Jun 1990 (SI 1990/802)
(b), (c)	1 Apr 1991 (SI 1990/2610)
(d)	8 Nov 1989 (so far as relates to offences under Sch 1, para 10(4), (5)) (SI 1989/1843)
	1 Apr 1991 (otherwise) (SI 1990/2610)
4, 5	1 Jun 1990 (SI 1990/802)
6	1 Jun 1990 (repeals of or in Road Traffic Act 1988, s 97(1); Road Traffic Offenders Act 1988, s 45(3), Sch 2, Pt I (entry relating to s 45 of that Act)) (SI 1990/802)
	1 Dec 1990 (repeals in Road Traffic Act 1988, s 97(3)) (SI 1990/2228)
	1 Apr 1991 (otherwise, except repeal of Road Traffic (Driver Licensing and Information Systems) Act 1989, Sch 1, para 11) (SI 1990/2610)
	Not in force (exception noted above)

Security Service Act 1989 (c 5)

RA: 27 Apr 1989

Commencement provisions: s 7(2); Security Service Act 1989 (Commencement) Order 1989, SI 1989/2093

18 Dec 1989 (SI 1989/2093)

Self-Governing Schools etc (Scotland) Act 1989 (c 39)

RA: 16 Nov 1989

Commencement provisions: s 81; Self-Governing Schools etc (Scotland) Act 1989 (Commencement) Order 1990, SI 1990/86; Self-Governing Schools etc (Scotland) Act 1989 (Commencement No 2) Order 1990, SI 1990/1108

s 1–53	16 Nov 1989 (s 81(1))
54–66	Repealed
67	1 Feb 1990 (SI 1990/86)
68	16 Nov 1989 (s 81(1))
69(1), (2)	1 Feb 1990 (SI 1990/86)
(3)	16 Nov 1989 (s 81(1))
70	*Not in force*
71	16 Nov 1989 (s 81(1))
72	1 Jun 1990 (SI 1990/1108)
73–76	1 Feb 1990 (SI 1990/86)
77–81	16 Nov 1989 (s 81(1))
82(1)	16 Nov 1989 (s 81(1))
(2)	1 Feb 1990 (SI 1990/86)
83	16 Nov 1989 (s 81(1))

Self-Governing Schools etc (Scotland) Act 1989 (c 39)—*cont*

Sch 1–9	16 Nov 1989 (s 81(1))
10, para 1, 2	1 Feb 1990 (SI 1990/86)
3	16 Nov 1989 (s 81(1))
4	Repealed
5–7	16 Nov 1989 (s 81(1))
8(1)–(6)	16 Nov 1989 (s 81(1))
(7)	1 Feb 1990 (SI 1990/86)
(8)	16 Nov 1989 (s 81(1))
(9)–(11)	1 Feb 1990 (SI 1990/86)
(12)	16 Nov 1989 (s 81(1))
(13)–(21)	1 Feb 1990 (SI 1990/86)
(22)	16 Nov 1989 (s 81(1))
9, 10	16 Nov 1989 (s 81(1))
11	1 Feb 1990 (SI 1990/86)

Social Security Act 1989 (c 24)

RA: 21 Jul 1989

Commencement provisions: s 33(2), (3); Social Security Act 1989 (Commencement No 1) Order 1989, SI 1989/1238; Social Security Act 1989 (Commencement No 2) Order 1989, SI 1989/1262; Social Security Act 1989 (Commencement No 3) Order 1990, SI 1990/102; Social Security Act 1989 (Commencement No 4) Order 1990, SI 1990/312 (correcting defect in SI 1990/102); Social Security Act 1989 (Commencement No 5) Order 1994, SI 1994/1661

s 1–3	Repealed
4	21 Jul 1989 (RA)
5	9 Oct 1989 (SI 1989/1238)
6	21 Jul 1989 (RA)
7–21	Repealed
22(1)–(6)	Repealed
(7)	See Sch 4 below
(8)	Repealed
23	See Sch 5 below
24	See Sch 6 below
25(1)–(3)	1 Mar 1990 (for purposes of regulations expressed to come into force on 1 Jan 1991) (SI 1990/102) 1 Jan 1991 (otherwise) (SI 1990/102)
(4)–(6)	1 Jan 1991 (SI 1990/102)
26	See Sch 7 below
27	Repealed
28–30	21 Jul 1989 (RA)
31(1)	See Sch 8 below
(2)	See Sch 9 below
(3)	21 Jul 1989 (RA)
32	Repealed
33	21 Jul 1989 (RA)
Sch 1–3	Repealed
4, para 1–21	Repealed
22, 23	3 Sep 1990 (SI 1990/102)
24	Repealed
5, para 1	23 Jun 1994 (for purpose of giving effect to paras 5, 6 so far as brought into force by SI 1994/1661) (SI 1994/1661) *Not in force* (otherwise)

Social Security Act 1989 (c 24)—*cont*

Sch 5, para 2(1), (2)	23 Jun 1994 (for purpose of giving effect to paras 5, 6 so far as brought into force by SI 1994/1661) (SI 1994/1661) *Not in force* (otherwise)
(3)	*Not in force*
(4)(a), (b)	*Not in force*
(c)	23 Jun 1994 (for purpose of giving effect to paras 5, 6 so far as brought into force by SI 1994/1661) (SI 1994/1661) *Not in force* (otherwise)
(d)–(g)	*Not in force*
(5)	23 Jun 1994 (for purpose of giving effect to paras 5, 6 so far as brought into force by SI 1994/1661) (SI 1994/1661) *Not in force* (otherwise)
(6)–(8)	*Not in force*
(9)	23 Jun 1994 (for purpose of giving effect to paras 5, 6 so far as brought into force by SI 1994/1661) (SI 1994/1661) *Not in force* (otherwise)
3(1)	23 Jun 1994 (for purpose of giving effect to paras 5, 6 so far as brought into force by SI 1994/1661) (SI 1994/1661) *Not in force* (otherwise)
(2)	*Not in force*
(3), (4)	23 Jun 1994 (for purpose of giving effect to paras 5, 6 so far as brought into force by SI 1994/1661) (SI 1994/1661) *Not in force* (otherwise)
4	*Not in force*; prospectively repealed by Pensions Act 1995, ss 151, 177, Sch 5, para 13(2), Sch 7, Pt III[1]
5(1)	23 Jun 1994 (SI 1994/1661)
(2)(a)	23 Jun 1994 (SI 1994/1661)
(b), (c)	*Not in force*
(3)	23 Jun 1994 (SI 1994/1661)
6(1), (2)	23 Jun 1994 (SI 1994/1661)
(3)(a)	23 Jun 1994 (SI 1994/1661)
(b), (c)	*Not in force*
(4)	23 Jun 1994 (SI 1994/1661)
7(a)–(c)	23 Jun 1994 (for purpose of giving effect to paras 5, 6 so far as brought into force by SI 1994/1661) (SI 1994/1661) *Not in force* (otherwise)
(d)	*Not in force*
(e)	23 Jun 1994 (for purpose of giving effect to paras 5, 6 so far as brought into force by SI 1994/1661) (SI 1994/1661) *Not in force* (otherwise)
8	*Not in force*
9, 10	23 Jun 1994 (for purpose of giving effect to paras 5, 6 so far as brought into force by SI 1994/1661) (SI 1994/1661) *Not in force* (otherwise)
11	Repealed
12	*Not in force*
13	Repealed

Social Security Act 1989 (c 24)—*cont*

Sch 5, para 14	*Not in force*; prospectively repealed by Pensions Act 1995, s 177, Sch 7, Pt I[1]
15	Repealed
6, para 1–5	Repealed
6, 7	21 Jul 1989 (RA); prospectively repealed by Social Security Act 1990, ss 21(2), 23, Sch 7[1]
8–20	Repealed
21	21 Jul 1989 (RA)
7	Repealed
8, para 1–7	Repealed
8(1)	Repealed
(2)	21 Jul 1989 (RA); prospectively repealed by Social Security Act 1990, ss 21(2), 23, Sch 7[2]
9	Repealed
10	21 Jul 1989 (RA)
11	Repealed
12, 13	21 Jul 1989 (RA)
14–18	Repealed
19	25 Jul 1989 (SI 1989/1262 (superseding SI 1989/1238))
9	21 Jul 1989 (repeals consequential on the bringing into force of provisions listed in s 33(3)(a)–(f) on 21 Jul 1989) (RA)
	1 Oct 1989 (repeals of or in Social Security Act 1973, s 51(7); Social Security Act 1975, ss 14(6), 15(6)(a), 27(3)–(5), 28(1)(a), 29(5)(a), 30(1), (3), (6)(a), 39(1)(b), 41(1), 48(2), (3), Sch 20 (in definition 'week'); Social Security Pensions Act 1975, ss 8(1), 11, 45(3), Sch 4, para 39; Social Security (Miscellaneous Provisions) Act 1977, s 21(1); Social Security Act 1979, Sch 1, para 17; Social Security and Housing Benefits Act 1982; Social Security Act 1986, ss 50(1), 63(1)(a)(ii), Sch 6, para 3, Sch 10, para 96) (SI 1989/1238)
	5 Oct 1989 (repeals of or in Social Security Act 1975, s 4(6F); Social Security Contributions Act 1982, s 4(4), Sch 1, para 1(4)) (SI 1989/1238)
	9 Oct 1989 (repeals of or in Merchant Shipping Act 1970, s 17(10); Social Security Act 1975, ss 20(1A), 26(7); Social Security Act 1986, s 26(3) and second paragraph of rubric at end of Sch 9) (SI 1989/1238)
	1 Feb 1990 (repeal of Social Security (Contributions) Act 1982, s 4(4)) (SI 1990/312)
	6 Apr 1990 (repeals of or in Social Security Act 1975, ss 100(3), 101(6), (7), 112(4), (5), Sch 10, para 1(7), 2(2), Sch 11, para 4, Sch 13, para 8, 9, Sch 20, definition of 'local office') (SI 1990/102)
	Not in force (otherwise)

[1] Orders made under Pensions Act 1995, ss 135, 180 bringing the prospective repeals into force will be noted to that Act in the service to this work

[2] Orders made under Social Security Act 1990 bringing the prospective repeals into force will be noted to that Act in the service to this work

Statute Law (Repeals) Act 1989 (c 43)

RA: 16 Nov 1989

Commencement provisions: s 3(2); Statute Law (Repeals) Act 1989 (Commencement) Order 1992, SI 1992/1275

s 1–3	16 Nov 1989 (RA)
Sch 1	16 Nov 1989 (except repeal of Federation of Malaya Independence Act 1957, s 3; Malaysia Act 1963, s 5) (RA)
	1 Jun 1992 (exceptions noted above) (SI 1992/1275)
2	16 Nov 1989 (RA)

Transport (Scotland) Act 1989 (c 23)

RA: 21 Jul 1989

Commencement provisions: s 12(2)

s 1–17	21 Sep 1989 (s 12(2))
18	21 Jul 1989 (s 12(2))

Water Act 1989 (c 15)

RA: 6 Jul 1989

Commencement provisions: s 194(2)–(5); Water Act 1989 (Commencement No 1) Order 1989, SI 1989/1146; Water Authorities (Transfer of Functions) (Appointed Day) Order 1989, SI 1989/1530; Water Act 1989 (Commencement No 2 and Transitional Provisions) Order 1989, SI 1989/1557; Water Act 1989 (Commencement No 3) (Scotland) Order 1989, SI 1989/1561; Water Act 1989 (Commencement No 4) Order 1989, SI 1989/2278

Abbreviation: "rel sub leg" means "so far as relating to the making of subordinate legislation"

s 1(1)–(5)	Repealed
(6)	See Sch 1 below
2, 3	Repealed
4	6 Jul 1989 (rel sub leg) (s 194(2))
	7 Jul 1989 (otherwise) (EW) (SI 1989/1146)
	1 Sep 1989 (otherwise) (NI) (SI 1989/1557)
	1 Sep 1989 (otherwise) (S) (SI 1989/1561)
5(1)–(4)	Repealed
(5)	See Sch 3 below
6(1)–(7)	Repealed
(8)	1 Sep 1989 (SI 1989/1146; SI 1989/1530; SI 1989/1561)
7–10	Repealed
11(1)–(8)	Repealed
(9)	7 Jul 1989 (EW) (SI 1989/1146)
	1 Sep 1989 (NI) (SI 1989/1557)
12	Repealed
13	6 Jul 1989 (rel sub leg) (S) (s 194(2))
	1 Sep 1989 (so far as relates to schemes under Sch 5) (S) (SI 1989/1561)

Water Act 1989 (c 15)—*cont*

s 13—*cont*	*Not in force* (otherwise) (S)
	Repealed (EW)
14–22	Repealed
23	1 Sep 1989 (S) (s 194(3))
	Repealed (EW)
24–68	Repealed
69	1 Sep 1989 (s 194(3))
70(1), (2)	1 Sep 1989 (s 194(3))
(3)–(5)	Repealed
71–82	Repealed
83	6 Jul 1989 (rel sub leg) (s 194(2))
	1 Sep 1989 (otherwise) (s 194(3))
84	1 Sep 1989 (s 194(3))
85, 86	6 Jul 1989 (rel sub leg) (s 194(2))
	1 Sep 1989 (otherwise) (s 194(3))
87, 88	1 Sep 1989 (s 194(3))
89	6 Jul 1989 (rel sub leg) (s 194(2))
	1 Sep 1989 (otherwise) (s 194(3))
90, 91	1 Sep 1989 (s 194(3))
92	6 Jul 1989 (rel sub leg) (s 194(2))
	1 Sep 1989 (otherwise) (s 194(3))
93, 94	1 Sep 1989 (s 194(3))
95	6 Jul 1989 (rel sub leg) (s 194(2))
	1 Sep 1989 (otherwise) (s 194(3))
96	1 Sep 1989 (s 194(3))
97–135	Repealed
136	1 Sep 1989 (S) (s 194(3))
	Repealed (EW)
137(1)–(8)	Repealed
(9)	6 Jul 1989 (rel sub leg) (s 194(2))
	1 Sep 1989 (otherwise) (s 194(3))
(10), (11)	Repealed
138	Repealed
139(1)–(5)	Repealed
(6)	1 Sep 1989 (s 194(3))
140	Repealed
141(1)–(4)	1 Sep 1989 (S) (s 194(3))
	Repealed (EW)
(5), (6)	1 Sep 1989 (s 194(3))
(7)	1 Sep 1989 (S) (s 194(3))
	Repealed (EW)
142(1)	Repealed
(2)	1 Sep 1989 (s 194(3))
143–167	Repealed
168	See Sch 22 below
169	See Sch 23 below
170, 171	Repealed
172	1 Sep 1989 (S) (SI 1989/1561)
	Repealed (EW)
173	6 Jul 1989 (rel sub leg) (s 194(2))
	1 Sep 1989 (otherwise) (SI 1989/1146; SI 1989/1530)
174(1)–(7)	6 Jul (rel sub leg) (s 194(2))
	7 Jul 1989 (otherwise) (SI 1989/1146)
(8)	Added by Water Consolidation (Consequential Provisions) Act 1991, s 2(1), Sch 1, para 50(1), (2)(e) (qv)
175	1 Sep 1989 (SI 1989/1146; SI 1989/1530)

Water Act 1989 (c 15)—*cont*

s 176	Repealed
177	7 Jul 1989 (SI 1989/1146)
178–182	Repealed
183, 184	1 Sep 1989 (SI 1989/1146; SI 1989/1530)
185	6 Jul 1989 (s 194(2))
186	Repealed
187	7 Jul 1989 (SI 1989/1146)
188	Repealed
189(1)	6 Jul 1989 (definitions of 'the 1945 Act', 'the 1973 Act', 'the Authority', 'contravention', 'the Director', 'disposal' (and cognate expressions), 'enactment', 'holding company', 'information', 'local statutory provision', 'the Minister', 'modifications' (and cognate expressions), 'sewer', 'statutory water company', 'subordinate legislation', 'successor company', 'transfer date', 'water authority') (rel sub leg) (s 194(2))
	Repealed (otherwise)
	7 Jul 1989 (definitions listed above) (otherwise) (SI 1989/1146)
(2)–(5)	Repealed
(6), (7)	6 Jul 1989 (rel sub leg) (s 194(2))
	7 Jul 1989 (otherwise) (SI 1989/1146)
(8)	Repealed
(9), (10)	6 Jul 1989 (rel sub leg) (s 194(2))
	7 Jul 1989 (otherwise) (SI 1989/1146)
190	See Schs 25–27 below (6 Jul 1989 (rel sub leg)) (s 194(2))
191(1)–(5)	6 Jul 1989 (s 194(2))
(6)	7 Jul 1989 (SI 1989/1146)
192	7 Jul 1989 (SI 1989/1146)
193	6 Jul 1989 (rel sub leg) (s 194(2))
	7 Jul 1989 (otherwise) (SI 1989/1146)
194	6 Jul 1989 (s 194(2))
Sch 1, para 1–10	Repealed
11	7 Jul 1989 (EW) (SI 1989/1146)
	1 Sep 1989 (NI) (SI 1989/1557)
	1 Sep 1989 (S) (SI 1989/1561)
	Prospectively repealed by Environment Act 1995, s 120(3), Sch 24[1]
12	7 Jul 1989 (SI 1989/1146); prospectively repealed by Environment Act 1995, s 120(3), Sch 24[1]
13	7 Jul 1989 (EW) (SI 1989/1146)
	1 Sep 1989 (NI) (SI 1989/1557)
	1 Sep 1989 (S) (SI 1989/1561)
	Prospectively repealed by Environment Act 1995, s 120(3), Sch 24[1]
14–23	Repealed
2	6 Jul 1989 (rel sub leg) (s 194(2))
	7 Jul 1989 (otherwise) (EW) (SI 1989/1146)
	1 Sep 1989 (otherwise) (NI) (SI 1989/1557)
	1 Sep 1989 (otherwise) (S) (SI 1989/1561)
3, para 1–5	Repealed
6, 7	7 Jul 1989 (EW) (SI 1989/1146)
	1 Sep 1989 (NI) (SI 1989/1557)
	1 Sep 1989 (S) (SI 1989/1561)

Water Act 1989 (c 15)—*cont*

Sch 4, para 1–5	Repealed
6	1 Sep 1989 (SI 1989/1146; SI 1989/1530; SI 1989/1557; SI 1989/1561)
5	6 Jul 1989 (rel sub leg) (S) (s 194(2))
	1 Sep 1989 (otherwise) (S) (s 194(3))
	Repealed (EW)
6, 7	Repealed
8, para 1	Repealed
2(1)–(10)	Repealed
(11)	1 Sep 1989 (s 194(3))
(12)	Repealed
3–5	Repealed
6, 7	1 Sep 1989 (s 194(3))
9–14	Repealed
15, para 1	1 Sep 1989 (S) (s 194(3))
	Repealed (EW)
2–13	Repealed
14	1 Sep 1989 (S) (s 194(3))
	Repealed (EW)
15–41	Repealed
16	Repealed
17, para 1	1 Sep 1989 (s 194(3))
2	6 Jul 1989 (s 194(2))
3	1 Sep 1989 (s 194(3))
4	*Not in force*
5–9	1 Sep 1989 (s 194(3))
18–21	Repealed
22	1 Sep 1989 (s 194(3))
23	1 Sep 1989 (except so far as relates to Control of Pollution Act 1974, s 33) (S) (s 194(3))
	31 May 1991 (exception noted above) (S) (SI 1991/1172)
	Not in force (so far as relates to Control of Pollution Act 1984, ss 33 (EW), 47, 48)
24	Repealed
25	1 Sep 1989 (for transitional provisions, see SI 1989/1557, art 6) (SI 1989/1146; SI 1989/1530; SI 1989/1557; SI 1989/1561)
26	6 Jul 1989 (rel sub leg) (s 194(2))
	1 Sep 1989 (otherwise) (s 194(3))
27, Pt I	1 Sep 1989 (s 194(3))
II	1 Sep 1989 (repeals of or in Water Act 1945, s 41(7), Sch 3, ss 75–77; Rating and Valuation (Miscellaneous Provisions) Act 1955, s 11; Trustee Investments Act 1961, Sch 4, para 3; Water Act 1973, ss 34(1), (3), 35(1), (2), Sch 6, Pt I, Sch 8, para 50) (SI 1989/1557; note savings therein)
	1 Apr 1990 (repeals of or in Water Act 1945, s 59(3), Sch 3, ss 74, 81) (SI 1989/1557)
	Not in force (otherwise)

[1] Orders made under Environment Act 1995, s 125(3), bringing the prospective repeals into force will be noted to that Act in the service to this work

1990

Access to Health Records Act 1990 (c 23)

RA: 13 Jul 1990

Commencement provisions: s 12(2)

1 Nov 1991 (s 12(2))

Agricultural Holdings (Amendment) Act 1990 (c 15)

RA: 29 Jun 1990

Commencement provisions: s 3(2)

29 Jul 1990 (s 3(2))

Appropriation Act 1990 (c 28)

Whole Act repealed

Australian Constitution (Public Record Copy) Act 1990 (c 17)

RA: 29 Jul 1990

29 Jul 1990 (RA)

Aviation and Maritime Security Act 1990 (c 31)

RA: 26 Jul 1990

Commencement provisions: s 54(2)

s 1	26 Sep 1990 (s 54(2))
2–4	26 Jul 1990 (RA)
5	26 Sep 1990 (s 54(2))
6, 7	26 Jul 1990 (RA)
8	See Sch 1 below
9–17	26 Sep 1990 (s 54(2))
18–36	26 Jul 1990 (RA)
37–40	26 Sep 1990 (s 54(2))
41–44	26 Jul 1990 (RA)
45	See Sch 2 below
46–52	26 Jul 1990 (RA)
53(1)	See Sch 3 below
(2)	See Sch 4 below
54	26 Jul 1990 (RA)

Aviation and Maritime Security Act 1990 (c 31)—*cont*

Sch 1, para 1	26 Sep 1990 (s 54(2))
2(1)–(5)	26 Jul 1990 (RA)
(6)	26 Sep 1990 (s 54(2))
(7)	26 Jul 1990 (RA)
3	26 Jul 1990 (RA)
4–6	26 Sep 1990 (s 54(2))
7–10	26 Jul 1990 (RA)
11(1)–(4)	26 Jul 1990 (RA)
(5)	26 Sep 1990 (s 54(2))
2	26 Jul 1990 (RA)
3	26 Sep 1990 (s 54(2))
4	26 Jul 1990 (except repeals of or in Criminal Jurisdiction Act 1975, Aviation Security Act 1982, ss 11(5)(a), 14(7)(a), 20(5); Extradition Act 1989) (RA) 26 Sep 1990 (exception noted above) (s 54(2))

British Nationality (Hong Kong) Act 1990 (c 34)

RA: 26 Jul 1990

Commencement provisions: s 6(4); British Nationality (Hong Kong) Act 1990 (Commencement) Order 1990, SI 1990/2210

s 1(1)	See Sch 1 below
(2), (3)	7 Nov 1990 (SI 1990/2210)
(4)	See Sch 2 below
(5)	7 Nov 1990 (SI 1990/2210)
2(1)	7 Nov 1990 (SI 1990/2210)
(2)	*Not in force*
(3)	7 Nov 1990 (SI 1990/2210)
3–6	7 Nov 1990 (SI 1990/2210)
Sch 1, 2	7 Nov 1990 (SI 1990/2210)

Broadcasting Act 1990 (c 42)

RA: 1 Nov 1990

Commencement provisions: s 204(2); Broadcasting Act 1990 (Commencement No 1 and Transitional Provisions) Order 1990, SI 1990/2347

s 1(1), (2)	1 Dec 1990 (SI 1990/2347)
(3)	See Sch 1 below
2(1)	1 Jan 1991 (SI 1990/2347)
(2)–(6)	1 Dec 1990 (SI 1990/2347)
3–9	1 Dec 1990 (SI 1990/2347)
10	1 Jan 1991 (SI 1990/2347)
11	1 Dec 1990 (SI 1990/2347)
12–22	1 Jan 1991 (SI 1990/2347)
23(1)–(5)	1 Jan 1993 (SI 1990/2347)
(6)	See Sch 3 below
24, 25	1 Jan 1993 (SI 1990/2347)
26	1 Jan 1991 (SI 1990/2347)
27	1 Jan 1993 (SI 1990/2347)
28–33	1 Jan 1991 (SI 1990/2347)

Broadcasting Act 1990 (c 42)—*cont*

s 34, 35	1 Jan 1991 (for purposes of enabling conditions of type specified in ss 34(2), 35(1) to be included in a Channel 3 or Channel 5 licence or a licence to provide Channel 4) (SI 1990/2347)
	1 Jan 1993 (otherwise) (SI 1990/2347)
36–42	1 Jan 1991 (SI 1990/2347)
43	1 Dec 1990 (SI 1990/2347)
44	1 Jan 1991 (SI 1990/2347)
45–47	1 Dec 1990 (SI 1990/2347)
48–55	1 Jan 1991 (SI 1990/2347)
56(1), (2)	1 Jan 1991 (SI 1990/2347)
(3)	See Sch 6 below
57–70	1 Jan 1991 (SI 1990/2347)
71	1 Dec 1990 (SI 1990/2347)
72–82	1 Jan 1991 (SI 1990/2347)
83(1), (2)	1 Dec 1990 (SI 1990/2347)
(3)	See Sch 8 below
84–125	1 Jan 1991 (SI 1990/2347)
126, 127	1 Dec 1990 (SI 1990/2347)
128, 129	1 Jan 1991 (SI 1990/2347)
130–133	1 Dec 1990 (SI 1990/2347)
134–140	1 Jan 1991 (SI 1990/2347)
141	1 Dec 1990 (SI 1990/2347)
142(1)–(3)	1 Jan 1991 (SI 1990/2347)
(4)	See Sch 13 below
143–150	1 Jan 1991 (SI 1990/2347)
151(1), (2)	1 Jan 1991 (SI 1990/2347)
(3)	See Sch 14 below
152–161	1 Jan 1991 (SI 1990/2347)
162(1)	1 Jan 1991 (SI 1990/2347)
(2)	See Sch 15 below
163–170	1 Jan 1991 (SI 1990/2347)
171	See Sch 16 below
172–174	1 Jan 1991 (SI 1990/2347)
175	1 Feb 1991 (SI 1990/2347)
176	See Sch 17 below
177–179	1 Jan 1991 (SI 1990/2347)
180	See Sch 18 below
181, 182	1 Jan 1991 (SI 1990/2347)
183	See Sch 19 below
184	1 Jan 1991 (SI 1990/2347)
185	1 Jan 1991 (for purposes of enabling conditions of type specified in s 185(3) to be included in a Channel 3 or Channel 5 licence or a licence to provide Channel 4) (SI 1990/2347)
	1 Jan 1993 (otherwise) (SI 1990/2347)
186	1 Jan 1991 (SI 1990/2347)
187	1 Jan 1993 (SI 1990/2347)
188–197	1 Jan 1991 (SI 1990/2347)
198–202	1 Dec 1990 (SI 1990/2347)
203(1)	See Sch 20 below
(2)	1 Jan 1991 (SI 1990/2347)
(3)	See Sch 21 below
(4)	See Sch 22 below
204	1 Dec 1990 (SI 1990/2347)
Sch 1, 2	1 Dec 1990 (SI 1990/2347)

Broadcasting Act 1990 (c 42)—*cont*

Sch 3	1 Jan 1993 (SI 1990/2347)
4–7	1 Jan 1991 (SI 1990/2347)
8, 9	1 Dec 1990 (SI 1990/2347)
10–16	1 Jan 1991 (SI 1990/2347)
17	1 Jan 1991 (for purposes of enabling publication of information about programmes to be included in a programme service on or after that date) (SI 1990/2347)
	1 Mar 1991 (otherwise) (SI 1990/2347)
18	1 Apr 1991 (SI 1990/2347)
19	1 Jan 1991 (SI 1990/2347)
20, para 1–13	1 Jan 1991 (SI 1990/2347)
14	Repealed
15–21	1 Jan 1991 (SI 1990/2347)
22	Repealed
23–35	1 Jan 1991 (SI 1990/2347)
36	1 Jan 1991 (except so far as replaces the reference to the Independent Broadcasting Authority until that Authority is dissolved by order under s 127(3)) (SI 1990/2347)
	Not in force (exception noted above)
37	Repealed
38–54	1 Jan 1991 (SI 1990/2347)
21	1 Dec 1990 (repeal of or in Cable and Broadcasting Act 1984, s 8(1)(a), (b)) (SI 1990/2347)
	1 Jan 1991 (all remaining repeals except repeals of or in Wireless Telegraphy (Blind Persons) Act 1955; Wireless Telegraphy Act 1967; entries for Cable Authority and Independent Broadcasting Authority in House of Commons Disqualification Act 1975, Sch 1, Pt II; Northern Ireland Assembly Disqualification Act 1975, Sch 1, Pt II) (subject to transitional provisions; see SI 1990/2347, art 3(3)) (SI 1990/2347)
	1 Apr 1991 (repeals of or in Wireless Telegraphy (Blind Persons) Act 1955; Wireless Telegraphy Act 1967) (SI 1990/2347)
	Not in force (entries for Cable Authority and Independent Broadcasting Authority in House of Commons Disqualification Act 1975, Sch 1, Pt II; Northern Ireland Assembly Disqualification Act 1975, Sch 1, Pt II)
22, para 1–3	1 Dec 1990 (SI 1990/2347)
4–7	1 Jan 1991 (SI 1990/2347)

Caldey Island Act 1990 (c 44)

RA: 1 Nov 1990

1 Nov 1990 (RA)

Capital Allowances Act 1990 (c 1)

RA: 19 Mar 1990

Commencement provisions: s 164

Capital Allowances Act 1990 (c 1)—*cont*

Act (which is a consolidation) has effect, generally, as respects allowances and charges falling to be made for chargeable periods ending after 5 April 1990 and applies in relation to expenditure incurred in chargeable periods ending before 6 April 1990

Care of Cathedrals Measure 1990 (No 2)

RA: 26 Jul 1990

Commencement provisions: s 21(2)

The provisions of this Measure were brought into force on the following dates by an instrument made by the Archbishops of Canterbury and York and dated 28 Sep 1990 (made under s 21(2))

s 1, 2	1 Mar 1991
3(1), (2)	1 Mar 1991
(3)	See Sch 1 below
4(1), (2)	1 Mar 1991
(3)	See Sch 2 below
5–12	1 Mar 1991
13	1 Oct 1990
14, 15	1 Mar 1991
16	Repealed
17–21	1 Oct 1990
Sch 1, 2	1 Mar 1991

Civil Aviation Authority (Borrowing Powers) Act 1990 (c 2)

RA: 19 Mar 1990

19 Mar 1990 (RA)

Clergy (Ordination) Measure 1990 (No 1)

RA: 22 Feb 1990

22 Feb 1990 (RA)

Coal Industry Act 1990 (c 3)

RA: 19 Mar 1990

Commencement provisions: s 6(2)

Whole Act repealed (in part prospectively)

s 1	19 Mar 1990 (RA); prospectively repealed by Coal Industry Act 1994, s 67(8), Sch 11, Pt III[1]
2	Repealed
3	19 Mar 1990 (RA); prospectively repealed by Coal Industry Act 1994, s 67(8), Sch 11, Pt III[1]
4, 5	Repealed

Coal Industry Act 1990 (c 3)—*cont*

s 6(1)	19 Mar 1990 (RA); prospectively repealed by Coal Industry Act 1994, s 67(8), Sch 11, Pt III[1]
(2)	Repealed
(3)	19 Mar 1990 (RA); prospectively repealed by Coal Industry Act 1994, s 67(8), Sch 11, Pt III[1]

[1] Any order made under Coal Industry Act 1994, s 68(4), (5), bringing the prospective repeals into force will be noted to that Act in the service to this work

Computer Misuse Act 1990 (c 18)

RA: 26 Jun 1990

Commencement provisions: s 18(2)

29 Aug 1990 (s 18(2))

Consolidated Fund Act 1990 (c 4)

Whole Act repealed

Consolidated Fund (No 2) Act 1990 (c 46)

Whole Act repealed

Contracts (Applicable Law) Act 1990 (c 36)

RA: 26 Jul 1990

Commencement provisions: s 7; Contracts (Applicable Law) Act 1990 (Commencement No 1) Order 1991, SI 1991/707

s 1	1 Apr 1991 (SI 1991/707)
2(1)	1 Apr 1991 (so far as relates to the Rome Convention and the Luxembourg Convention as defined in s 1) (SI 1991/707) *Not in force* (otherwise)
(1A)	Inserted (20 May 1993) by Insurance Companies (Amendment) Regulations 1993, SI 1993/174, reg 9; substituted (1 Jan 1994) by Friendly Societies (Amendment) Regulations 1993, SI 1993/2519, reg 6(5)
(2), (3)	1 Apr 1991 (SI 1991/707)
(4)	See Schs 1–3 below
3(1), (2)	Not in force
(3)(a)	1 Apr 1991 (SI 1991/707)
(b)	*Not in force*
4	1 Apr 1991 (SI 1991/707)
5	See Sch 4 below
6–9	1 Apr 1991 (SI 1991/707)
Sch 1–3	1 Apr 1991 (SI 1991/707)

Contracts (Applicable Law) Act 1990 (c 36)—*cont*

Sch 3A	Inserted by Contracts (Applicable Law) Act 1990 (Amendment) Order 1994, SI 1994/1900, art 9, Schedule[1]
4	1 Apr 1991 (SI 1991/707)

[1] That order came into force on 1 Sep 1994, the date on which the Convention on the accession of Spain and Portugal to the Rome Convention and to the Brussels Protocol entered into force in respect of the United Kingdom, which date was notified in the *London Gazette*, 16 Aug 1994 (art 1)

Courts and Legal Services Act 1990 (c 41)

RA: 1 Nov 1990

Commencement provisions: s 124; Courts and Legal Services Act 1990 (Commencement No 1) Order 1990, SI 1990/2170; Courts and Legal Services Act 1990 (Commencement No 2) Order 1990, SI 1990/2484; Courts and Legal Services Act 1990 (Commencement No 3) Order 1991, SI 1991/608; Courts and Legal Services Act 1990 (Commencement No 4) Order 1991, SI 1991/985; Courts and Legal Services Act 1990 (Commencement No 5) Order 1991, SI 1991/1364; Courts and Legal Services Act 1990 (Commencement No 6) Order 1991, SI 1991/1883; Courts and Legal Services Act 1990 (Commencement No 7) Order 1991, SI 1991/2730; Courts and Legal Services Act 1990 (Commencement No 8) Order 1992, SI 1992/1221; Courts and Legal Services Act 1990 (Commencement No 9) Order 1993, SI 1993/2132; Courts and Legal Services Act 1990 (Commencement No 10) Order 1995, SI 1995/641

s 1	1 Nov 1990 (RA)
2, 3	1 Jul 1991 (SI 1991/1364)
4	1 Oct 1991 (SI 1991/1883)
5	1 Nov 1990 (RA)
6	1 Jan 1991 (s 124(2)(a))
7(1)	23 Jul 1993 (except so far as relates to s 7(2)) (SI 1993/2132)
	1 Oct 1993 (exception noted above) (SI 1993/2132)
(2)	1 Oct 1993 (SI 1993/2132)
(3), (4)	23 Jul 1993 (SI 1993/2132)
8	1 Jan 1991 (s 124(2)(a))
9	1 Jan 1991 (SI 1990/2484)
10(1)	Substituted by Maintenance Enforcement Act 1991, s 11(1), Sch 2, para 11 (qv)
(2)	1 Jul 1991 (SI 1991/1364)
(3)–(5)	Repealed
11	1 Jan 1991 (s 124(2)(a))
12–14	*Not in force*
15	1 Jul 1991 (SI 1991/1364)
16	1 Jan 1991 (s 124(2)(a))
17, 18	1 Apr 1991 (SI 1991/608)
19(1)–(8)	1 Apr 1991 (SI 1991/608)
(9)	See Sch 1 below
20(1)	1 Apr 1991 (SI 1991/608)
(2)	See Sch 2 below
(3)	1 Apr 1991 (SI 1991/608)
21(1)–(5)	1 Jan 1991 (SI 1990/2484)
(6)	See Sch 3 below
22, 23	1 Jan 1991 (SI 1990/2484)
24(1), (2)	1 Jan 1991 (SI 1990/2484)

Courts and Legal Services Act 1990 (c 41)—*cont*

s 24(3)	1 Apr 1991 (SI 1991/608)
25–28	1 Jan 1991 (SI 1990/2484)
29	1 Apr 1991 (SI 1991/608)
30(1), (2)	1 Apr 1991 (SI 1991/608)
(3)	See Sch 4, Pt III below
(4)–(6)	1 Apr 1991 (SI 1991/608)
31(1), (2)	1 Jan 1991 (SI 1990/2484)
(3)–(9)	1 Apr 1991 (SI 1991/608)
32(1), (2)	1 Jan 1991 (SI 1990/2484)
(3)–(9)	1 Apr 1991 (SI 1991/608)
33(1), (2)	1 Jan 1991 (SI 1990/2484)
(3)–(9)	1 Apr 1991 (SI 1991/608)
34(1)–(7)	1 Apr 1991 (SI 1991/608)
(8)	See Sch 5 below
35	1 Apr 1991 (SI 1991/608)
36–39	*Not in force*
40	1 Apr 1991 (SI 1991/608)
41(1)–(10)	*Not in force*
(11)	See Sch 6 below
42	*Not in force*
43(1)–(3)	*Not in force*
(4)	See Sch 7 below
(5)–(12)	*Not in force*
44–52	*Not in force*
53(1)–(6)	1 Apr 1991 (except in relation to exemptions under s 55) (SI 1991/608) *Not in force* (exception noted above)
(7)	See Sch 8 below
(8), (9)	1 Apr 1991 (except in relation to exemptions under s 55) (SI 1991/608) *Not in force* (exception noted above)
54	*Not in force*
55(1)–(3)	*Not in force*
(4)	See Sch 9 below
56, 57	1 Jul 1991 (SI 1991/1364)
58	23 Jul 1993 (SI 1993/2132)
59	1 Apr 1991 (SI 1991/608)
60–62	1 Jan 1991 (SI 1990/2484)
63(1)(a)	1 Apr 1991 (SI 1991/608)
(b), (c)	*Not in force*
(2)	1 Apr 1991 (SI 1991/608)
(3)	*Not in force*
64, 65	1 Jan 1991 (s 124(2)(a))
66–68	1 Jan 1991 (SI 1990/2484)
69	1 Apr 1991 (SI 1991/608)
70	1 Jan 1991 (except so far as relates to authorised practitioners) (SI 1990/2484) *Not in force* (exception noted above)
71(1)	1 Jan 1991 (SI 1990/2484)
(2)	See Sch 10 below
(3)–(8)	1 Jan 1991 (SI 1990/2484)
72, 73	1 Jan 1991 (s 124(2)(a))
74(1)–(3)	1 Jan 1991 (SI 1990/2484)
(4)–(7)	1 Jul 1991 (SI 1991/1364)
75	See Sch 11 below
76–78	1 Jan 1991 (SI 1990/2484)
79(1)	1 Jan 1992 (SI 1991/2730)

Courts and Legal Services Act 1990 (c 41)—*cont*

s 79(2)	See Sch 12 below
80	1 Jan 1992 (SI 1991/2730)
81	See Sch 13 below
82	6 Mar 1995 (SI 1995/641)
83, 84	1 Jan 1991 (SI 1990/2484)
85	1 Jan 1991 (s 124(2)(a))
86	1 Jul 1991 (SI 1991/1364)
87, 88	1 Jan 1991 (s 124(2)(a))
89(1)–(7)	14 Oct 1991 (SI 1991/1883)
(8)	See Sch 14 below
(9)	14 Oct 1991 (SI 1991/1883)
90–92	1 Jan 1991 (s 124(2)(a))
93(1), (2)	1 Apr 1991 (SI 1991/608)
(3)	See Sch 15 below
(4)	1 Apr 1991 (SI 1991/608)
94–98	1 Jan 1991 (s 124(2)(a))
99–101	1 Apr 1991 (SI 1991/608)
102	1 Jan 1992 (SI 1991/2730)
103	1 Apr 1991 (SI 1991/608)
104–107	*Not in force*
108–110	1 Jan 1991 (s 124(2)(a))
111	1 May 1991 (SI 1991/985)
112	1 Oct 1991 (SI 1991/1883)
113–115	1 Apr 1991 (SI 1991/608)
116(1)	See Sch 16, Pt I below
(2)	See Sch 16, Pt II below
(3)	1 Jan 1992 (SI 1991/2730)
117	1 Jul 1991 (SI 1991/1364)
118	1 Jan 1991 (SI 1990/2484)
119–124	1 Nov 1990 (RA)
125(1)	1 Nov 1990 (RA)
(2)	See Sch 17 below
(3)	See Sch 18 below
(4), (5)	1 Oct 1991 (SI 1991/1883)
(6)	See Sch 19 below
(7)	See Sch 20 below
Sch 1, 2	1 Apr 1991 (SI 1991/608)
3	1 Jan 1991 (SI 1990/2484)
4, 5	1 Apr 1991 (SI 1991/608)
6, 7	*Not in force*
8	1 Apr 1991 (except in relation to exemptions under s 55) (SI 1991/608)
	Not in force (exception noted above)
9	*Not in force*
10, 11	1 Jan 1991 (SI 1990/2484)
12	1 Jan 1992 (SI 1991/2730)
13	*Not in force*
14	14 Oct 1991 (SI 1991/1883)
15	1 Apr 1991 (SI 1991/608)
16, Pt I, para 1–7	14 Oct 1991 (SI 1991/1883)
8	1 Jan 1991 (SI 1990/2484)
9–33	14 Oct 1991 (SI 1991/1883)
II, para 34–42	14 Oct 1991 (SI 1991/1883)
17, para 1	1 Jan 1991 (s 124(2)(b))
2, 3	1 Nov 1990 (RA)

Courts and Legal Services Act 1990 (c 41)—*cont*

Sch 17, para	4	1 Apr 1991 (SI 1991/608)
	5	*Not in force*
	6	1 Jul 1991 (SI 1991/1364)
	7, 8	1 Apr 1991 (SI 1991/608)
	9	1 Jan 1991 (SI 1990/2484)
	10	1 Apr 1991 (SI 1991/608)
	11, 12	1 Jan 1991 (s 124(2)(b))
	13	1 Apr 1991 (SI 1991/608)
	14	14 Oct 1991 (SI 1991/1883)
	15	1 Jan 1991 (SI 1990/2484)
	16	1 Jan 1991 (s 124(2)(b))
	17, 18	1 Jul 1991 (SI 1991/1364)
	19	*Not in force*
	20	1 Jan 1991 (s 124(2)(b))
18, para	1	1 Jan 1991 (so far as relates to the Legal Services Ombudsman) (SI 1990/2484) 1 Apr 1991 (so far as relates to Lord Chancellor's Advisory Committee on Legal Education and Conduct) (SI 1991/608) *Not in force* (otherwise)
	2	Repealed
	3	1 Jan 1991 (SI 1990/2484)
	4	*Not in force*
	5	1 Apr 1991 (SI 1991/608)
	6	*Not in force*
	7, 8	1 Jan 1991 (s 124(2)(c))
	9, 10	1 Jul 1991 (SI 1991/1364)
	11, 12	*Not in force*
	13	1 Jun 1992 (SI 1992/1221)
	14–16	1 Jan 1991 (s 124(2)(c))
	17, 18	1 Jul 1991 (SI 1991/1364)
	19	*Not in force*
	20	1 Jan 1991 (SI 1990/2484)
	21	14 Oct 1991 (SI 1991/1883)
	22, 23	*Not in force*
	24	Repealed
	25	1 Jan 1991 (SI 1990/2484)
	26–30	1 Jan 1992 (SI 1991/2730)
	31	*Not in force*
	32	1 Jan 1991 (SI 1990/2484)
	33–35	1 Jan 1992 (SI 1991/2730)
	36–40	1 Jan 1991 (SI 1990/2484)
	41	1 Apr 1991 (SI 1991/608)
	42	1 Jan 1991 (SI 1990/2484)
	43–46	1 Jul 1991 (SI 1991/1364)
	47	1 Jan 1991 (SI 1990/2484)
	48, 49	1 Apr 1991 (SI 1991/608)
	50, 51	1 Jan 1991 (SI 1990/2484)
	52	1 Apr 1991 (SI 1991/608)
	53	1 May 1991 (SI 1991/985)
	54	14 Oct 1991 (SI 1991/1883)
	55	1 Jan 1991 (s 124(2)(c))
	56	1 Apr 1991 (SI 1991/608)
	57	1 Jan 1991 (s 124(2)(c))
	58–63	1 Apr 1991 (SI 1991/608)
19, para	1	1 Jan 1991 (s 124(2)(d))
	2–8	1 Jan 1991 (SI 1990/2484)

Courts and Legal Services Act 1990 (c 41)—*cont*

Sch 19, para 9		1 Jan 1992 (SI 1991/2730)
	10, 11	1 Jan 1991 (SI 1990/2484)
	12, 13	1 Jul 1991 (SI 1991/1364)
	14, 15	1 Apr 1991 (SI 1991/608)
	16	1 Jan 1991 (SI 1990/2484)
	17	1 Apr 1991 (SI 1991/608)
20		1 Nov 1990 (repeal of Administration of Justice Act 1956, s 53) (SI 1990/2170)
		1 Jan 1991 (repeals of or in Public Notaries Act 1801, ss 10, 14; Summary Jurisdiction Act 1857; Naval Agency and Distribution Act 1864; War Pensions (Administrative Provisions) Act 1919; Pensions Appeal Tribunals Act 1943; Lands Tribunal Act 1949; Courts-Martial (Appeals) Act 1951; Barristers (Qualification for Office) Act 1961; Superannuation (Miscellaneous Provisions) Act 1967; Superannuation (Miscellaneous Provisions) Act (Northern Ireland) 1969; Courts Act 1971; Administration of Justice Act 1973; Solicitors Act 1974, ss 3–5, 7, 20(2)(c), 39, 45, 82, Sch 3, para 7; Social Security Act 1975; House of Commons Disqualification Act 1975; Ministerial and other Salaries Act 1975; Justices of the Peace Act 1979; Social Security Act 1980; Judicial Pensions Act 1981, s 33, Sch 1, Pt I; Supreme Court Act 1981, ss 12(4), 94, 100(5), 101(2), 102(6), 103(6); County Courts Act 1984, ss 10, 60(1), (2); Prosecution of Offences Act 1985, s 4(5); Administration of Justice Act 1985, ss 3(1), 63, Sch 1, paras 4, 11, Sch 2, paras 8, 15, Sch 7, para 4; Coroners Act 1988) (SI 1990/2484)
		1 Apr 1991 (repeals of or in Commissioners for Oaths Act 1889, s 1; Arbitration Act 1950, s 12(6)(b); Solicitors Act 1974, ss 2(2), 44A, 47A, 81(5); County Courts Act 1984, s 143(2); Prosecution of Offences Act 1985, s 15(1); Administration of Justice Act 1985, ss 1, 3(2), 26(3), 65(5), Sch 2, para 19, Sch 3, para 8, Sch 7, para 5) (SI 1991/608)
		1 Jul 1991 (repeals of or in Public Notaries Act 1801, ss 1–5, 7–9; Public Notaries Act 1833; Public Notaries Act 1843; Small Debts Act 1845; Welsh Church Act 1914; Administration of Justice Act 1956, s 37; Administration of Justice Act 1969, s 29; County Courts Act 1984, ss 19, 20, 22, 29, 34, 43, 44, 89(3), 105, 106, Sch 1) (SI 1991/1364)
		14 Oct 1991 (repeals of or in Maintenance Orders Act 1950; Family Law Reform Act 1969; Children and Young Persons Act 1969; Administration of Justice Act 1970; Maintenance Orders (Reciprocal Enforcement of Orders) Act 1972; Domestic Proceedings and Magistrates' Courts Act 1978; Magistrates' Courts Act 1980; Matrimonial and Family Proceedings Act 1984; Family Law Reform Act 1987; Children Act 1989) (SI 1991/1883)

Courts and Legal Services Act 1990 (c 41)—*cont*

Sch 20—*cont*	1 Jan 1992 (repeals of or in Judicial Pensions Act 1981, ss 18(3), 20(6), 22(5), 24, 25, Sch 1, para 15(3)) (SI 1991/2730)
	1 Jun 1992 (repeals of or in Solicitors Act 1974, ss 7, 33(4); County Courts Act 1984, s 45; Administration of Justice Act 1985, s 9(8), Sch 2, para 4(2)) (SI 1992/1221)
	1 Oct 1993 (repeal of words in Supreme Court Act 1981, s 18) (SI 1993/2132)
	Not in force (otherwise)

Criminal Justice (International Co-operation) Act 1990 (c 5)

RA: 5 Apr 1990

Commencement provisions: s 32(2); Criminal Justice (International Co-operation) Act 1990 (Commencement No 1) Order 1991, SI 1991/1072; Criminal Justice (International Co-operation) Act 1990 (Commencement No 2) Order 1991, SI 1991/2108

s 1, 2	10 Jun 1991 (SI 1991/1072)
3(1), (2)	10 Jun 1991 (SI 1991/1072)
(3)	23 Apr 1991 (for purpose of making any Order in Council, order, rules, or regulations) (SI 1991/1072)
	10 Jun 1991 (otherwise) (SI 1991/1072)
(4)–(10)	10 Jun 1991 (SI 1991/1072)
4(1), (2)	10 Jun 1991 (SI 1991/1072)
(2A), (2B)	Inserted by Criminal Justice and Public Order Act 1994, s 164(1) (qv)
(3)–(5)	10 Jun 1991 (SI 1991/1072)
(6)	See Sch 1 below
5, 6	10 Jun 1991 (SI 1991/1072)
7(1)–(6)	10 Jun 1991 (SI 1991/1072)
(7)	23 Apr 1991 (for purpose of making any Order in Council, order, rules, or regulations) (SI 1991/1072)
	10 Jun 1991 (otherwise) (SI 1991/1072)
(8), (9)	10 Jun 1991 (SI 1991/1072)
8(1)–(4)	10 Jun 1991 (SI 1991/1072)
(5)	23 Apr 1991 (for purpose of making any Order in Council, order, rules, or regulations) (SI 1991/1072)
	10 Jun 1991 (otherwise) (SI 1991/1072)
(6)	10 Jun 1991 (SI 1991/1072)
9, 10	23 Apr 1991 (for purpose of making any Order in Council, order, rules, or regulations) (SI 1991/1072)
	10 Jun 1991 (otherwise) (SI 1991/1072)
11	10 Jun 1991 (SI 1991/1072)
12(1)–(4)	1 Jul 1991 (SI 1991/1072)
(5)	23 Apr 1991 (for purpose of making any Order in Council, order, rules, or regulations) (SI 1991/1072)
	1 Jul 1991 (otherwise) (SI 1991/1072)

Criminal Justice (International Co-operation) Act 1990 (c 5)—*cont*

s 13	23 Apr 1991 (for purpose of making any Order in Council, order, rules, or regulations) (SI 1991/1072) 1 Jul 1991 (otherwise) (SI 1991/1072)
14	1 Jul 1991 (1991/1072); repealed (EW) (with savings) by Drug Trafficking Act 1994, ss 66, 67(1), 68(7), Schs 2, 3 (qv)[1]
15(1)	1 Jul 1991 (SI 1991/1072)
(2)	Substituted by Drug Trafficking Act 1994, s 65(1), Sch 1, para 27(3) (qv)
(3)	1 Jul 1991 (SI 1991/1072) Section repealed (S)
16	1 Jul 1991 (SI 1991/1072); repealed (with savings) by Drug Trafficking Act 1994, ss 66, 67(1), Schs 2, 3 (qv)
17	1 Jul 1991 (SI 1991/1072); prospectively repealed by Criminal Justice (Scotland) Act 1995, s 117, Sch 6, Pt II, para 190(3), Sch 7, Pt II[2]
18–23	1 Jul 1991 (SI 1991/1072)
23A	Inserted by Criminal Justice Act 1993, s 77, Sch 4, para 5 (qv); repealed (EW) (with savings) by Drug Trafficking Act 1994, ss 66, 67(1), 68(7), Schs 2, 3 (qv)
24	1 Jul 1991 (SI 1991/1072)
25, 26	23 Sep 1991 (SI 1991/2108); repealed (with savings) by Drug Trafficking Act 1994, ss 66, 67(1), Schs 2, 3 (qv)
26A	Prospectively inserted (EW) by Criminal Justice Act 1993, s 25(1) (repealed) *(never in force)*; repealed by Drug Trafficking Act 1994, s 67(1), Sch 3 (qv)
26B	Prospectively inserted (S) by Criminal Justice Act 1993, s 25(1) (repealed) (never in force); repealed by Drug Trafficking Act 1994, s 67(1), Sch 3 (qv)
27	23 Sep 1991 (SI 1991/2108); repealed (with savings) by Drug Trafficking Act 1994, ss 66, 67(1), Schs 2, 3 (qv)
28	23 Apr 1991 (sub-s (2), for the purpose of making any Order in Council, order, rules, or regulations) (SI 1991/1072) and 23 Sep 1991 (sub-ss (1), (2) (for all remaining purposes), (3)) (SI 1991/2108); repealed (with savings) by Drug Trafficking Act 1994, ss 66, 67(1), Schs 2, 3 (qv)
29	23 Apr 1991 (sub-s (2), for the purpose of making any Order in Council, order, rules, or regulations) (SI 1991/1072) and 23 Sep 1991 (sub-ss (1), (2) (for all remaining purposes), (3)) (SI 1991/2108); repealed (with savings) by Drug Trafficking Act 1994, ss 66, 67(1), Schs 2, 3 (qv)
30(1)	10 Jun 1991 (SI 1991/1072)
(2)	Repealed
(3)	Prospectively added (EW) by Criminal Justice Act 1993, s 25(5) (repealed) *(never in force)*; repealed by Drug Trafficking Act 1994, s 67(1), Sch 3 (qv)
31(1)	See Sch 4 below
(2)	Repealed
(3)	See Sch 5 below
(4)	1 Jul 1991 (SI 1991/1072)

Criminal Justice (International Co-operation) Act 1990 (c 5)—*cont*

s 32(1)–(3)	10 Jun 1991 (SI 1991/1072)
(4)	23 Apr 1991 (for purpose of making any Order in Council, order, rules, or regulations) (SI 1991/1072) 10 Jun 1991 (otherwise) (SI 1991/1072)
Sch 1	10 Jun 1991 (SI 1991/1072)
2	23 Apr 1991 (for purpose of making any Order in Council, order, rules, or regulations) (SI 1991/1072) 1 Jul 1991 (otherwise) (SI 1991/1072)
3, para 1(1)(a), (b)	1 Jul 1991 (SI 1991/1072)
(c)	23 Apr 1991 (for purpose of making any Order in Council, order, rules, or regulations) (SI 1991/1072) 1 Jul 1991 (otherwise) (SI 1991/1072)
(2), (3)	1 Jul 1991 (SI 1991/1072)
2–9	1 Jul 1991 (SI 1991/1072)
4, para 1	1 Jul 1991 (SI 1991/1072)
2	10 Jun 1991 (SI 1991/1072)
3	1 Jul 1991 (SI 1991/1072)
4, 5	Repealed
6–8	10 Jun 1991 (SI 1991/1072)
5	10 Jun 1991 (repeals of or in Extradition Act 1873, s 5; Evidence (Proceedings in Other Jurisdictions) Act 1975, s 5; Suppression of Terrorism Act 1978, s 1(3)(d) (and the word 'and' immediately preceding it), (4), (5)(b) (and the word 'and' immediately preceding it); Criminal Justice Act 1988, s 29) (SI 1991/1072) 1 Jul 1991 (otherwise) (SI 1991/1072)

[1] S 14(3), (5) previously repealed (15 Feb 1994) by Criminal Justice Act 1993, s 79(14), Sch 6, Pt I

[2] Any order made under Criminal Justice (Scotland) Act 1995, s 118, bringing the prospective repeal into force will be noted to that Act in the service to this work

---

Education (Student Loans) Act 1990 (c 6)

RA: 26 Apr 1990

26 Apr 1990 (RA)

Employment Act 1990 (c 38)

RA: 1 Nov 1990

Commencement provisions: s 18(2)–(4); Employment Act 1990 (Commencement and Transitional Provisions) Order 1990, SI 1990/2378; Employment Act 1990 (Commencement and Transitional Provisions) Amendment Order 1991, SI 1991/89 (corrects defect in SI 1990/2378)

s 1–12	Repealed
13	1 Feb 1991 (SI 1990/2378)
14, 15	1 Nov 1990 (s 18(2))
16(1)	See Sch 2 below
(2)	See Sch 3 below

Employment Act 1990 (c 38)—*cont*

s 17	1 Nov 1990 (s 18(2))
18	1 Nov 1990 (RA)
Sch 1	Repealed
2, para 1(1)	1 Feb 1991 (SI 1990/2378)
(2)	Repealed
(3)–(6)	1 Jan 1991 (SI 1990/2378)
2, 3	Repealed
3	1 Jan 1991 (repeals of or in Employment Act 1980; Employment Act 1982; Trade Union Act 1984; Employment Act 1988) (subject to transitional provisions) (SI 1990/2378) 1 Feb 1991 (otherwise) (SI 1990/2378)

Enterprise and New Towns (Scotland) Act 1990 (c 35)

RA: 26 Jul 1990

Commencement provisions: s 39(1), (3); Enterprise and New Towns (Scotland) Act 1990 Commencement Order 1990, SI 1990/1840

s 1	1 Oct 1990 (for purpose of establishing Scottish Enterprise and Highlands and Islands Enterprise, and bringing into force Sch 1) (SI 1990/1840) 1 Apr 1990 (otherwise) (SI 1990/1840)
2–14	1 Apr 1991 (SI 1990/1840)
14A	Inserted by Trade Union Reform and Employment Rights Act 1993, s 47(5) (qv)
15–18	1 Apr 1991 (SI 1990/1840)
19, 20	26 Jul 1990 (for purposes of Sch 3, paras 4, 5) (s 39(1), (3)) 1 Apr 1991 (otherwise) (SI 1990/1840)
21(1)–(3)	1 Apr 1991 (SI 1990/1840)
(4)	1 Oct 1990 (SI 1990/1840)
(5)	Prospectively inserted by Local Government etc (Scotland) Act 1994, s 180(1), Sch 13, para 164(1), (2)(b); any order made under s 184(2), (3) of that Act bringing the prospective insertion into force will be noted to that Act in the service to this work
22	1 Oct 1990 (SI 1990/1840)
23(1)–(3)	1 Apr 1991 (SI 1990/1840)
(4)	See Sch 3 below
24	1 Apr 1991 (SI 1990/1840)
25(1)	See Sch 2 below
(2)–(4)	1 Apr 1991 (SI 1990/1840)
26(1), (2)	1 Oct 1990 (SI 1990/1840)
(3), (4)	1 Apr 1991 (SI 1990/1840)
27	1 Oct 1990 (SI 1990/1840)
28	1 Apr 1991 (SI 1990/1840)
29, 30	1 Oct 1990 (SI 1990/1840)
31, 32	1 Apr 1991 (SI 1990/1840)
33–35	1 Oct 1990 (SI 1990/1840)
36, 37	26 Jul 1990 (s 39(1), (3))
38(1)	See Sch 4 below
(2)	See Sch 5 below

Enterprise and New Towns (Scotland) Act 1990 (c 35)—*cont*

s 38(3), (4)	1 Apr 1991 (SI 1990/1840)
39	26 Jul 1990 (RA)
40	1 Apr 1991 (SI 1990/1840)
Sch 1	1 Oct 1990 (SI 1990/1840)
2, para 1	1 Oct 1990 (SI 1990/1840)
2–6	1 Apr 1991 (SI 1990/1840)
3, para 1–3	1 Apr 1991 (SI 1990/1840)
4, 5	26 Jul 1990 (s 39(1), (3))
6–9	1 Apr 1991 (SI 1990/1840)
4, para 1	1 Oct 1990 (SI 1990/1840)
2–5	1 Apr 1991 (SI 1990/1840)
6	1 Oct 1990 (SI 1990/1840)
7–18	1 Apr 1991 (SI 1990/1840)
5	26 Jul 1990 (s 39(1), (3))

Entertainments (Increased Penalties) Act 1990 (c 20)

RA: 13 Jul 1990

13 Jul 1990 (RA)

Environmental Protection Act 1990 (c 43)

RA: 1 Nov 1990

Commencement provisions: ss 130(4), 131(3), 164(2), (3); Environmental Protection Act 1990 (Commencement No 1) Order 1990, SI 1990/2226; Environmental Protection Act 1990 (Commencement No 2) Order 1990, SI 1990/2243; Environmental Protection Act 1990 (Commencement No 3) Order 1990, SI 1990/2565; Environmental Protection Act 1990 (Commencement No 4) Order 1990, SI 1990/2635 (also amends SI 1990/2565); Environmental Protection Act 1990 (Commencement No 5) Order 1991, SI 1991/96; Environmental Protection Act 1990 (Commencement No 6 and Appointed Day) Order 1991, SI 1991/685; Environmental Protection Act 1990 (Commencement No 7) Order 1991, SI 1991/1042; Environmental Protection Act 1990 (Commencement No 8) Order 1991, SI 1991/1319; Environmental Protection Act 1990 (Commencement No 9) Order 1991, SI 1991/1577; Environmental Protection Act 1990 (Commencement No 10) Order 1991, SI 1991/2829; Environmental Protection Act 1990 (Commencement No 11) Order 1992, SI 1992/266; Environmental Protection Act 1990 (Commencement No 12) Order 1992, SI 1992/3253; Environmental Protection Act 1990 (Commencement No 13) Order 1993, SI 1993/274; Environmental Protection Act 1990 (Commencement No 14) Order 1994, SI 1994/780; Environmental Protection Act 1990 (Commencement No 15) Order 1994, SI 1994/1096, as amended by SI 1994/2487, SI 1994/3234; Environmental Protection Act 1990 (Commencement No 15) (Amendment) Order 1994, SI 1994/2487 (amending SI 1994/1096); Environmental Protection Act 1990 (Commencement No 16) Order 1994, SI 1994/2854; Environmental Protection Act 1990 (Commencement No 15) (Amendment No 2) Order 1994, SI 1994/3234 (amending SI 1994/1096); Environmental Protection Act 1990 (Commencement No 17) Order 1995, SI 1995/2152

s 1, 2	1 Jan 1991 (SI 1990/2635)

Environmental Protection Act 1990 (c 43)—*cont*

s 3	19 Dec 1991 (SI 1990/2635)
4	1 Jan 1991 (SI 1990/2635)
5	1 Jan 1991 (SI 1990/2635); prospectively repealed by Environment Act 1995, s 120(1), (3), Sch 22, para 47, Sch 24[1]
6	1 Jan 1991 (SI 1990/2635)
7–15	1 Jan 1991 (SI 1990/2635)
16–18	1 Jan 1991 (SI 1990/2635); prospectively repealed by Environment Act 1995, s 120(1), (3), Sch 22, para 55, Sch 24[1]
19–28	1 Jan 1991 (SI 1990/2635)
29, 30	31 May 1991 (SI 1991/1319)
31	31 May 1991 (SI 1991/1319); prospectively repealed by Environment Act 1995, s 120(1), (3), Sch 22, para 63, Sch 24[1]
32	See Sch 2 below
33(1)(a), (b)	See note at end of entry for this Act
(c)	1 Apr 1992 (SI 1991/2829)
(2)	1 Apr 1992 (so far as relates to s 33(1)(c)) (SI 1991/2829)
	See note at end of entry for this Act (otherwise)
(3), (4)	13 Dec 1991 (SI 1991/2829)
(5)	See note at end of entry for this Act
(6)–(9)	1 Apr 1992 (so far as relates to s 33(1)(c)) (SI 1991/2829)
	See note at end of entry for this Act (otherwise)
34(1)–(3)	1 Apr 1992 (SI 1991/2829)
(3A)	Prospectively inserted by Environment Act 1995, s 120(1), Sch 22, para 65[1]
(4)	1 Apr 1992 (SI 1991/2829)
(4A)	Inserted by Deregulation and Contracting Out Act 1994, s 33 (qv)
(5)	13 Dec 1991 (SI 1991/2829)
(6)	1 Apr 1992 (SI 1991/2829)
(7)–(9)	13 Dec 1991 (SI 1991/2829)
(10)	1 Apr 1992 (SI 1991/2829)
(11)	13 Dec 1991 (SI 1991/2829)
35(1)–(5)	See note at end of entry for this Act
(6)	18 Feb 1993 (SI 1993/274)
(7)	See note at end of entry for this Act
(7A)–(7C)	Prospectively inserted by Environment Act 1995, s 120(1), Sch 22, para 66[1]
(8)–(12)	See note at end of entry for this Act
35A	Prospectively inserted by Environment Act 1995, s 120(1), Sch 22, para 67[1]
36(1)	18 Feb 1993 (SI 1993/274)
(1A)	Prospectively inserted by Environment Act 1995, s 120(1), Sch 22, para 68(1), (2)[1]
(2)–(4)	See note at end of entry for this Act
(5), (6)	See note at end of entry for this Act; prospectively repealed by Environment Act 1995, s 120(1), (3), Sch 22, para 68(1), (4), Sch 24[1]
(7)–(9)	See note at end of entry for this Act
(9A)	Prospectively inserted by Environment Act 1995, s 120(1), Sch 22, para 68(1), (5)[1]

Environmental Protection Act 1990 (c 43)—*cont*

s 36(10)	See note at end of entry for this Act; prospectively substituted (by sub-ss (10–(14)) by Environment Act 1995, s 120(1), Sch 22, para 68(1), (6); sub-s (12), as so substituted, prospectively repealed by Environment Act 1995, s 120(3), Sch 24[1]
36A	Prospectively inserted by Environment Act 1995, s 120(1), Sch 22, para 69[1]
37(1), (2)	See note at end of entry for this Act
(3)	18 Feb 1993 (so far as enables Secretary of State to give directions) (SI 1993/274)
	See note at end of entry for this Act (otherwise)
(4)–(6)	See note at end of entry for this Act
(7)	Prospectively added by Environment Act 1995, s 120(1), Sch 22, para 70(3)[1]
37A	Prospectively inserted by Environment Act 1995, s 120(1), Sch 22, para 71[1]
38(1)–(6)	See note at end of entry for this Act
(7)	18 Feb 1993 (so far as enables Secretary of State to give directions) (SI 1993/274)
	See note at end of entry for this Act (otherwise)
(8), (9)	See note at end of entry for this Act
(9A)–(9C)	Prospectively inserted by Environment Act 1995, s 120(1), Sch 22, para 72(1)[1]
(10)–(12)	See note at end of entry for this Act
(13)	Prospectively added by Environment Act 1995, s 120(1), Sch 22, para 72(2)[1]
39(1), (2)	See note at end of entry for this Act
(3)	18 Feb 1993 (SI 1993/274)
(4)–(7)	See note at end of entry for this Act
(8)	See note at end of entry for this Act; prospectively repealed by Environment Act 1995, s 120(1), (3), Sch 22, para 73(1), (4), Sch 24[1]
(9)–(11)	See note at end of entry for this Act
(12)–(14)	Prospectively added by Environment Act 1995, s 120(1), Sch 22, para 73(1), (6); para (13) (as so added) prospectively repealed by Environment Act 1995, s 120(3), Sch 24[1]
40(1), (2)	See note at end of entry for this Act
(3)	18 Feb 1993 (SI 1993/274)
(4)–(6)	See note at end of entry for this Act
41(1)	16 Mar 1994 (SI 1994/780)
(2)	18 Feb 1993 (SI 1993/274)
(3)	16 Mar 1994 (SI 1994/780)
(4), (5)	18 Feb 1993 (SI 1993/274)
(6)–(8)	16 Mar 1994 (SI 1994/780)
	Section prospectively repealed by Environment Act 1995, s 120(1), (3), Sch 22, para 75, Sch 24[1]
42(1)	See note at end of entry for this Act
(2)	See note at end of entry for this Act; prospectively repealed by Environment Act 1995, s 120(1), (3), Sch 22, para 76(1), (2), Sch 24[1]
(3)–(6)	See note at end of entry for this Act
(6A)	Prospectively inserted by Environment Act 1995, s 120(1), Sch 22, para 76(1), (7)[1]
(7)	See note at end of entry for this Act
(8)	18 Feb 1993 (so far as enables Secretary of State to give directions) (SI 1993/274)
	See note at end of entry for this Act (otherwise)

Environmental Protection Act 1990 (c 43)—*cont*

s 43(1), (2)	See note at end of entry for this Act
(2A)	Prospectively inserted by Environment Act 1995, s 120(1), Sch 22, para 77[1]
(3)–(7)	See note at end of entry for this Act
(8)	18 Feb 1993 (SI 1993/274)
44	See note at end of entry for this Act; prospectively substituted by Environment Act 1995, s 112, Sch 19, para 4(1)[1]
44A, 44B	Prospectively inserted by Environment Act 1995, s 92(1)[1]
45(1)	14 Feb 1992 (so far as enables orders or regulations to be made) (SI 1992/266) 1 Apr 1992 (otherwise) (SI 1992/266)
(2)	14 Feb 1992 (so far as enables orders or regulations to be made) (SI 1992/266) 1 Apr 1992 (otherwise) (S) (SI 1992/266) *Not in force* (otherwise) (EW)
(3)–(12)	14 Feb 1992 (so far as enable orders or regulations to be made) (SI 1992/266) 1 Apr 1992 (otherwise) (SI 1992/266)
46, 47	1 Apr 1992 (SI 1992/266)
48(1)–(6)	1 Apr 1992 (SI 1992/266)
(7)	*Not in force*
(8), (9)	1 Apr 1992 (SI 1992/266)
49	1 Aug 1991 (SI 1991/1577)
50	31 May 1991 (SI 1991/1319); prospectively repealed by Environment Act 1995, s 120(1), (3), Sch 22, para 78, Sch 24 (for savings, see, in particular, 1995 Act, s 120(2), Sch 23, Pt I, para 16)[1]
51	31 May 1991 (SI 1991/1319)
52(1)	1 Apr 1992 (SI 1992/266)
(2)	*Not in force*
(3)–(7)	1 Apr 1992 (SI 1992/266)
(8)	13 Dec 1991 (so far as relates to s 52(1), (3)) (SI 1991/2829) *Not in force* (otherwise)
(9)–(11)	1 Apr 1992 (SI 1992/266)
53	1 Apr 1992 (SI 1992/266)
54(1)–(13)	1 May 1994 (SI 1994/1096)
(14)	18 Feb 1993 (SI 1993/274)
(15)–(17)	1 May 1994 (SI 1994/1096) Section prospectively repealed by Environment Act 1995, s 120(3), Sch 24[1]
55, 56	1 Apr 1992 (SI 1992/266)
57	See note at end of entry for this Act
58, 59	1 May 1994 (SI 1994/1096)
60	31 May 1991 (so far as relates to anything deposited at a place for the deposit of waste, or in a receptacle for waste, provided by a waste disposal contractor under arrangements made with a waste disposal authority) (SI 1991/1319) 1 May 1994 (otherwise) (SI 1994/1096)
61	*Not in force*; prospectively repealed by Environment Act 1995, s 120(1), (3), Sch 22, para 79, Sch 24[1]
62	11 Aug 1995 (SI 1995/2152)
63(1)	18 Feb 1993 (SI 1993/274)

Environmental Protection Act 1990 (c 43)—*cont*

s 63(2)	*Not in force*; prospectively substituted by Environment Act 1995, s 120(1), Sch 22, para 81[1]
(3), (4)	*Not in force*
64(1)	18 Feb 1993 (SI 1993/274)
(2)	1 May 1994 (SI 1994/1096)
(2A)	Prospectively inserted by Environment Act 1995, s 120(1), Sch 22, para 82(1), (2)[1]
(3)	1 May 1994 (SI 1994/1096)
(4)	18 Feb 1993 (SI 1993/274)
(5)	1 May 1994 (SI 1994/1096); prospectively substituted by Environment Act 1995, s 120(1), Sch 22, para 82(1), (4)[1]
(6), (7)	1 May 1994 (SI 1994/1096)
(8)	18 Feb 1993 (SI 1993/274)
65(1)	1 May 1994 (SI 1994/1096)
(2)	18 Feb 1993 (so far as enables Secretary of State to give directions) (SI 1993/274) 1 May 1994 (otherwise) (SI 1994/1096)
(3), (4)	1 May 1994 (SI 1994/1096)
66(1)–(5)	1 May 1994 (SI 1994/1096)
(6)	1 May 1994 (SI 1994/1096); prospectively substituted by Environment Act 1995, s 120(1), Sch 22, para 83(2)[1]
(7)	18 Feb 1993 (so far as enables Secretary of State to give directions) (SI 1993/274) 1 May 1994 (otherwise) (SI 1994/1096)
(8)–(11)	1 May 1994 (SI 1994/1096)
67	1 May 1994 (SI 1994/1096); prospectively repealed by Environment Act 1995, s 120(1), (3), Sch 22, para 84, Sch 24[1]
68	31 May 1991 (SI 1991/1319); prospectively repealed by Environment Act 1995, s 120(1), (3), Sch 22, para 85, Sch 24[1]
69, 70	1 Apr 1992 (SI 1991/2829); prospectively repealed by Environment Act 1995, s 120(1), (3), Sch 22, para 85, Sch 24[1]
71	31 May 1991 (SI 1991/1319)
72	31 May 1991 (SI 1991/1319); prospectively repealed by Environment Act 1995, s 120(1), (3), Sch 22, para 87, Sch 24[1]
73(1)–(5)	1 Apr 1992 (SI 1992/266)
(6)–(9)	1 May 1994 (SI 1994/1096)
74(1)–(5)	1 May 1994 (SI 1994/1096)
(6)	18 Feb 1993 (SI 1993/274)
(7)	1 May 1994 (SI 1994/1096)
75	31 May 1991 (SI 1991/1319)
76	*Not in force*; prospectively substituted by Environment Act 1995, s 118(3)[1]
77	31 May 1991 (SI 1991/1319)
78	13 Dec 1991 (SI 1991/2829)
78A–78YC	Inserted, partly prospectively, by Environment Act 1995, s 57 (qv)
79, 80	1 Jan 1991 (s 164(2))
80A	Inserted (EW) by Noise and Statutory Nuisance Act 1993, s 3(6) (qv)
81	1 Jan 1991 (s 164(2))

Environmental Protection Act 1990 (c 43)—*cont*

s 81A, 81B	Inserted (EW) by Noise and Statutory Nuisance Act 1993, s 10(2) (qv)
82	1 Jan 1991 (s 164(2))
83	1 Jan 1991 (s 164(2)); prospectively repealed by Environment Act 1995, s 120(3), Sch 24[1]
84	1 Jan 1991 (s 164(2))
85	Repealed
86(1)	13 Feb 1991 (EW) (SI 1991/96) 1 Apr 1991 (S) (SI 1991/1042)
(2)(a)	14 Jan 1991 (SI 1991/96)
(aa)	Prospectively inserted by Local Government (Wales) Act 1994, s 22(3), Sch 9, para 17(1), (6)[2]
(b)–(e)	14 Jan 1991 (SI 1991/96)
(3)	1 Apr 1991 (SI 1991/1042)
(4), (5)	13 Feb 1991 (EW) (SI 1991/96) 1 Apr 1991 (S) (SI 1991/1042)
(6)–(8)	14 Jan 1991 (SI 1991/96)
(9)(a), (b)	13 Feb 1991 (SI 1991/96)
(bb)	Prospectively inserted by Local Government (Wales) Act 1994, s 22(3), Sch 9, para 17(1), (7)[2]
(c)	13 Feb 1991 (SI 1991/96)
(10)	1 Apr 1991 (SI 1991/1042)
(11)	14 Jan 1991 (SI 1991/96)
(12)	1 Jun 1991 (SI 1991/1042)
(13)	13 Feb 1991 (EW) (SI 1991/96) 1 Apr 1991 (S) (SI 1991/1042)
(14), (15)	14 Jan 1991 (SI 1991/96)
87(1), (2)	13 Feb 1991 (EW) (SI 1991/96) 1 Apr 1991 (S) (SI 1991/1042)
(3)(a)–(e)	13 Feb 1991 (EW) (SI 1991/96) 1 Apr 1991 (S) (SI 1991/1042)
(f)	1 Jun 1991 (SI 1991/1042)
(4)–(6)	13 Feb 1991 (EW) (SI 1991/96) 1 Apr 1991 (S) (SI 1991/1042)
(7)	1 Apr 1991 (SI 1991/1042)
88(1)–(4)	13 Feb 1991 (EW) (SI 1991/96) 1 Apr 1991 (S) (SI 1991/1042)
(5)	14 Jan 1991 (SI 1991/96)
(6)	13 Feb 1991 (EW) (SI 1991/96) 1 Apr 1991 (S) (SI 1991/1042)
(7)	14 Jan 1991 (SI 1991/96)
(8)	13 Feb 1991 (EW) (SI 1991/96) 1 Apr 1991 (S) (SI 1991/1042)
(9)(a)	13 Feb 1991 (EW) (SI 1991/96) 1 Apr 1991 (S) (SI 1991/1042)
(b)	14 Jan 1991 (SI 1991/96)
(c), (d)	13 Feb 1991 (EW) (SI 1991/96) 1 Apr 1991 (S) (SI 1991/1042) Prospectively repealed by Environment Act 1995, s 120(3), Sch 24[1]
(e)	13 Feb 1991 (EW) (SI 1991/96)
(10)	13 Feb 1991 (EW) (SI 1991/96) 1 Apr 1991 (S) (SI 1991/1042)
89(1)(a)–(f)	1 Apr 1991 (SI 1991/1042)
(g)	1 Jun 1991 (SI 1991/1042)
(2), (3)	1 Apr 1991 (SI 1991/1042)
(4)	14 Jan 1991 (SI 1991/96)

Environmental Protection Act 1990 (c 43)—*cont*

s 89(5), (6)	1 Apr 1991 (SI 1991/1042)
(7)–(9)	13 Nov 1990 (SI 1990/2243)
(10)	1 Apr 1991 (SI 1991/1042)
(11)–(13)	13 Nov 1990 (SI 1990/2243)
(14)	1 Apr 1991 (SI 1991/1042)
90(1), (2)	14 Jan 1991 (SI 1991/96)
(3)–(6)	1 Jun 1991 (SI 1991/1042)
(7)	14 Jan 1991 (SI 1991/96)
91(1)(a)–(f)	1 Apr 1991 (SI 1991/1042)
(g)	1 Jun 1991 (SI 1991/1042)
(2)–(13)	1 Apr 1991 (SI 1991/1042)
92(1)(a)–(c)	1 Apr 1991 (SI 1991/1042)
(d)	1 Jun 1991 (SI 1991/1042)
(2)–(10)	1 Apr 1991 (SI 1991/1042)
93	1 Apr 1991 (SI 1991/1042)
94(1), (2)	14 Jan 1991 (SI 1991/96)
(3)–(9)	1 Apr 1991 (SI 1991/1042)
95	1 Apr 1991 (SI 1991/1042)
96(1)	1 Apr 1991 (SI 1991/1042)
(2), (3)	14 Jan 1991 (SI 1991/96)
97	1 Jan 1991 (s 164(2))
98(1)	13 Feb 1991 (EW) (SI 1991/96) 1 Apr 1991 (S) (SI 1991/1042)
(2)	13 Feb 1991 (SI 1991/96)
(3), (4)	1 Apr 1991 (SI 1991/1042)
(5), (6)	13 Feb 1991 (EW) (SI 1991/96) 1 Apr 1991 (S) (SI 1991/1042)
99	See Sch 4 below
100–105	Repealed
106(1)–(3)	1 Feb 1993 (SI 1992/3253)
(4), (5)	1 Apr 1991 (SI 1991/1042)
(6), (7)	1 Feb 1993 (SI 1992/3253)
107(1)–(7)	1 Feb 1993 (SI 1992/3253)
(8)	1 Apr 1991 (SI 1991/1042)
(9)–(11)	1 Feb 1993 (SI 1992/3253)
108(1)(a)	1 Feb 1993 (so far as relates to import or acquisition of genetically modified organisms) (SI 1992/3253) *Not in force* (otherwise)
(b)	1 Apr 1991 (SI 1991/1042)
(2)	*Not in force*
(3)(a)	*Not in force*
(b)	1 Apr 1991 (SI 1991/1042)
(4)	*Not in force*
(5)	1 Apr 1991 (SI 1991/1042)
(6)	*Not in force*
(7)	1 Apr 1991 (SI 1991/1042)
(8)	*Not in force*
(9)	1 Apr 1991 (SI 1991/1042)
(10)	1 Jan 1993 (SI 1992/3253)
109	*Not in force*
110	1 Feb 1993 (so far as relates to import, acquisition, release or marketing of genetically modified organisms) (SI 1992/3253) *Not in force* (otherwise)
111(1), (2)	1 Apr 1991 (SI 1991/1042)
(3)	*Not in force*
(4), (5)	1 Apr 1991 (SI 1991/1042)

Environmental Protection Act 1990 (c 43)—*cont*

s 111(6)	1 Feb 1993 (SI 1992/3253)
(6A)	Inserted (1 Feb 1993) by Genetically Modified Organisms (Deliberate Release) Regulations 1992, SI 1992/3280, reg 13
(7)	1 Apr 1991 (SI 1991/1042)
(8)–(10)	1 Feb 1993 (SI 1992/3253)
(11)	1 Apr 1991 (SI 1991/1042)
112(1), (2)	1 Feb 1993 (SI 1992/3253)
(3), (4)	*Not in force*
(5)–(7)	1 Feb 1993 (SI 1992/3253)
113	1 Apr 1991 (SI 1991/1042)
114(1)–(3)	1 Apr 1991 (SI 1991/1042)
(4), (5)	1 Feb 1993 (SI 1992/3253)
115(1)–(3)	1 Feb 1993 (SI 1992/3253)
(4)	1 Apr 1991 (SI 1991/1042)
(5)–(10)	1 Feb 1993 (SI 1992/3253)
116	1 Feb 1993 (so far as relates to import, acquisition, release or marketing of genetically modified organisms) (SI 1992/3253)
	Not in force (otherwise)
117	1 Feb 1993 (SI 1992/3253)
118(1)(a)	1 Feb 1993 (SI 1992/3253)
(b)	*Not in force*
(c)	1 Feb 1993 (SI 1992/3253)
(d)	*Not in force*
(e)–(l)	1 Feb 1993 (SI 1992/3253)
(m)	1 Feb 1993 (so far as relates to s 111) (SI 1992/3253)
	Not in force (otherwise)
(n), (o)	1 Feb 1993 (SI 1992/3253)
(2)–(10)	1 Feb 1993 (SI 1992/3253)
119–121	1 Feb 1993 (SI 1992/3253)
122(1)(a), (b)	1 Apr 1991 (so far as empower Secretary of State to make regulations) (SI 1991/1042)
	Not in force (otherwise)
(c)–(h)	1 Apr 1991 (so far as empower Secretary of State to make regulations) (SI 1991/1042)
	1 Feb 1993 (otherwise) (SI 1992/3253)
(2), (3)	1 Feb 1993 (SI 1992/3253)
(4)	1 Apr 1991 (SI 1991/1042)
123(1)–(6)	1 Feb 1993 (SI 1992/3253)
(7)	1 Apr 1991 (SI 1991/1042)
(8)	1 Feb 1993 (SI 1992/3253)
(9)	1 Apr 1991 (SI 1991/1042)
124–126	1 Apr 1991 (SI 1991/1042)
127	1 Feb 1993 (SI 1992/3253)
128(1)–(4)	5 Nov 1990 (save for amendments) (SI 1990/2226)
	1 Apr 1991 (otherwise) (SI 1991/685)
(5)	See Schs 6, 7 below
129	5 Nov 1990 (SI 1990/2226)
130	1 Apr 1991 (SI 1991/685)
131	5 Nov 1990 (SI 1990/2226)[3]
132(1)(a)	1 Apr 1991 (SI 1991/685)[3]
(b)–(e)	5 Nov 1990 (save for amendments) (SI 1990/2226)[3]
	1 Apr 1991 (otherwise) (SI 1991/685)[3]
(2), (3)	5 Nov 1990 (SI 1990/2226)[3]
133, 134	5 Nov 1990 (SI 1990/2226)[3]
135(1), (2)	5 Nov 1990 (SI 1990/2226)

Environmental Protection Act 1990 (c 43)—*cont*

s 135(3)	See Sch 10, Pt I below
136(1), (2)	5 Nov 1990 (SI 1990/2226)
(3)	See Sch 10, Pt II below
137(1)–(3)	5 Nov 1990 (SI 1990/2226)
(4)	See Sch 10, Pt III below
138	5 Nov 1990 (SI 1990/2226)
139	See Sch 11 below
140(1)–(4)	1 Jan 1991 (s 164(2))
(5)	See Sch 12 below
(6)–(11)	1 Jan 1991 (s 164(2))
141	1 Jan 1991 (s 164(2))
142(1), (2)	1 Jan 1991 (s 164(2))
(3)	See Sch 12 below
(4)–(7)	1 Jan 1991 (s 164(2))
143(1)	14 Feb 1992 (EW) (SI 1992/266)
	Not in force (S)
(2)–(4)	*Not in force*
(5), (6)	14 Feb 1992 (EW) (SI 1992/266)
	Not in force (S)
	Section prospectively repealed by Environment Act 1995, s 120(1), (3), Sch 22, para 91, Sch 24[1]
144	See Sch 13 below
145, 146	1 Jan 1991 (s 164(2))
147	31 May 1991 (SI 1991/1319)
148	Repealed
149–151	14 Feb 1992 (so far as enable orders or regulations to be made) (SI 1992/266)
	1 Apr 1992 (otherwise) (SI 1992/266)
152	10 Jul 1991 (SI 1991/1577)
153–155	1 Jan 1991 (s 164(2))
156	1 Apr 1991 (SI 1991/1042)
157	1 Jan 1991 (s 164(2))
158	1 Apr 1991 (SI 1991/1042)
159	1 Jan 1991 (SI 1990/2635)
160, 161	1 Jan 1991 (s 164(2))
162(1)	See Sch 15 below
(2)	See Sch 16 below
(3)	1 Apr 1992 (SI 1992/266)
(4)	*Not in force*
(5)	1 Jan 1991 (s 164(2))
163	1 Jan 1991 (s 164(2))
164	1 Nov 1990 (RA)
Sch 1	1 Jan 1991 (SI 1990/2635)
2	31 May 1991 (SI 1991/1319)
2A	Prospectively inserted by Environment Act 1995, s 92(2), Sch 12[1]
2B	Prospectively inserted by Environment Act 1995, s 120(1), Sch 22, para 95[1]
3, 4	1 Jan 1991 (s 164(2))
5	Repealed
6–9	5 Nov 1990 (save for amendments) (SI 1990/2226)
	1 Apr 1991 (otherwise) (SI 1991/685)
10, 11	5 Nov 1990 (SI 1990/2226)
12	1 Jan 1991 (s 164(2))
13, Pt I	1 Jan 1992 (SI 1991/2829)
II, para 11, 12	18 Feb 1993 (SI 1993/274)

Environmental Protection Act 1990 (c 43)—*cont*

Sch 13, Pt II, para 13	1 May 1993 (SI 1993/274)
14	1 Jan 1991 (s 164(2)); repealed, subject to an exception, by Merchant Shipping Act 1995, s 314(1), Sch 12 (qv)
15, para 1	Repealed
2	1 Apr 1991 (SI 1991/1042)
3	1 Apr 1992 (SI 1992/266)
4, 5	1 Jan 1991 (s 164(2))
6–8	Repealed
9	1 Jan 1991 (s 164(2))
10(1)	1 Apr 1992 (SI 1991/2829)
(2)	Repealed
(3)	14 Jan 1991 (SI 1991/96)
11	1 Apr 1991 (SI 1991/1042)
12	Repealed
13, 14	1 Apr 1991 (SI 1991/1042)
15(1), (2)	*Not in force*
(3)–(5)	14 Jan 1991 (SI 1991/96)
(6)–(9)	Repealed
16(1)	1 Apr 1991 (SI 1991/1042)
(2)	1 Apr 1991 (so far as inserts Control of Pollution Act 1974, s 31(2)(b)(v)) (SI 1991/1042)
	Not in force (otherwise)
(3)	1 Apr 1991 (SI 1991/1042)
	Para prospectively repealed by Environment Act 1995, s 120(3), Sch 24[1]
17	*Not in force*
18	Repealed
19	1 Apr 1992 (SI 1992/266)
20	1 Apr 1991 (SI 1991/1042)
21	18 Feb 1993 (SI 1993/274)
22	1 Jan 1991 (so far as inserts Public Health (Control of Disease) Act 1984, s 7(4)(m)) (s 164(2))
	1 Apr 1991 (otherwise) (SI 1991/1042)
23	Repealed
24	1 Jan 1991 (s 164(2))
25	*Not in force*
26	See note at end of entry for this Act
27	1 May 1994 (SI 1994/1096)
28–30	Repealed
31(1)–(3)	31 May 1991 (SI 1991/1319)
(4)(a)	31 May 1991 (SI 1991/1319)
(b)	1 Jan 1991 (s 164(2))
(c)	31 May 1991 (SI 1991/1319); prospectively repealed by Environment Act 1995, s 120(3), Sch 24[1]
(5)(a)	1 Apr 1992 (SI 1991/2829)
(b)	31 May 1991 (SI 1991/1319)
(c)	31 May 1991 (SI 1991/1319); prospectively repealed by Environment Act 1995, s 120(3), Sch 24[1]
(6)	1 Apr 1992 (SI 1991/2829)
16, Pt I	Repeal of Alkali, &c Works Regulation Act 1906 brought into force, for purposes of application of the 1906 Act to activities which fall within a description of a process which has been but has ceased to be a prescribed process (a) on 1 Dec 1994, or, if later, (b) on the date on which that

Environmental Protection Act 1990 (c 43)—*cont*

Sch 16, Pt I—*cont*	description of process ceases to be a prescribed process (SI 1994/2854)
	Not in force (otherwise)
II	31 May 1991 (repeals of or in Control of Pollution Act 1974, s 2; Control of Pollution (Amendment) Act 1989, ss 7(2), 9(1)) (SI 1991/1319)
	1 Apr 1992 (repeal of Control of Pollution (Amendment) Act 1989, s 9(2)) (SI 1991/2829)
	1 Apr 1992 (repeals of or in Control of Pollution Act 1974, ss 12, 13, 14(1)(5), (7)(11) (except so far as relate to industrial waste in England and Wales), 15; Civic Government (Scotland) Act 1982) (SI 1992/266)
	1 May 1994 (repeal of Control of Pollution Act 1974, s 1) (SI 1994/1096)
	1 May 1994 (S) (repeal of Control of Pollution Act 1974, s 11) (SI 1994/1096)
	In relation to repeal of Control of Pollution Act 1974, ss 310, 18, 27, see note at end of entry for this Act
	Not in force (otherwise)
III	1 Jan 1991 (s 164(2))
IV	1 Apr 1991 (SI 1991/1042)
V	1 Jan 1991 (SI 1990/2635)
VI	1 Apr 1991 (repeals of or in Countryside Act 1968; Wildlife and Countryside Act 1981) (SI 1991/685)
	1 Apr 1992 (repeals in Nature Conservancy Council Act 1973) (SI 1991/2829
	Not in force (otherwise)
VII	1 Jan 1992 (repeals in Planning (Hazardous Substances) Act 1990) (SI 1991/2829)
	18 Feb 1993 (repeals in Town and Country Planning (Scotland) Act 1972) (SI 1993/274)
	1 May 1993 (repeal in Housing and Planning Act 1986) (SI 1993/274)
	Not in force (otherwise)
VII	*Not in force*
IX	1 Jan 1991 (repeal of Control of Pollution Act 1974, s 100) (s 164(2))
	1 Apr 1992 (repeals of or in Dogs Act 1906; Civic Government (Scotland) Act 1982; Local Government Act 1988) (SI 1992/266)
	18 Feb 1993 (repeals of Criminal Justice Act 1982, s 43; Criminal Justice Act 1988, s 58) (SI 1993/274)
	Not in force (otherwise)

Ss 33 (so far as not already in force), 3540 (so far as not already in force), 42 (so far as not already in force), 43 (so far as not already in force), 44, 57, 162(1) (so far as relates to Sch 15, para 26), (2) (so far as relates to repeals in Sch 16, Pt II of Control of Pollution Act 1974, ss 310, 18, 27) all brought into force on 1 May 1994 by SI 1994/1096, save for purposes of their application to certain activities specified in art 2(2) of that Order. In relation to such activities, those provisions come into force in accordance with art 3 of the Order, as amended by SI 1994/2487, SI 1994/3234

[1] Any orders made under Environment Act 1995, s 125(3), bringing the prospective repeals, insertions, substitutions and additions into force will be noted to that Act in the service to this work

Environmental Protection Act 1990 (c 43)—*cont*

[2] Any orders made under Local Government (Wales) Act 1994, s 66, bringing the prospective insertion into force will be noted to that Act in the service to this work

[3] 1 Apr 1991 was the day appointed by SI 1991/685 as the day on and after which the Nature Conservancy Councils exercised functions under ss 132–134

Finance Act 1990 (c 29)

Budget Day: 20 Mar 1990

RA: 26 Jul 1990

See the note concerning Finance Acts at the front of this book

Food Safety Act 1990 (c 16)

RA: 29 Jun 1990

Commencement provisions: s 60(2)–(4); Food Safety Act 1990 (Commencement No 1) Order 1990, SI 1990/1383; Food Safety Act 1990 (Commencement No 2) Order 1990, SI 1990/2372; Food Safety Act 1990 (Commencement No 3) Order 1992, SI 1992/57

s 1(1), (2)	3 Jul 1990 (for purposes of ss 13, 51) (SI 1990/1383) 1 Dec 1990 (otherwise) (SI 1990/2372)
(3), (4)	3 Jul 1990 (for purposes of s 13) (SI 1990/1383) 1 Dec 1990 (otherwise) (SI 1990/2372)
2, 3	3 Jul 1990 (for purposes of s 13) (SI 1990/1383) 1 Dec 1990 (otherwise) (SI 1990/2372)
4(1)	1 Dec 1990 (SI 1990/2372)
(2)	3 Jul 1990 (for purposes of s 13) (SI 1990/1383) 1 Dec 1990 (otherwise) (SI 1990/2372)
5, 6	3 Jul 1990 (for purposes of s 13) (SI 1990/1383) 1 Dec 1990 (otherwise) (SI 1990/2372)
7(1), (2)	1 Jan 1991 (SI 1990/2372)
(3)	3 Jul 1990 (for purposes of s 13) (SI 1990/1383) 1 Jan 1991 (otherwise) (SI 1990/2372)
8–12	1 Jan 1991 (SI 1990/2372)
13	29 Jun 1990 (s 60(2))
14, 15	1 Jan 1991 (SI 1990/2372)
16(1), (2)	1 Dec 1990 (SI 1990/2372)
(3)	See Sch 1 below
(4), (5)	1 Dec 1990 (SI 1990/2372)
17–19	1 Dec 1990 (SI 1990/2372)
20	3 Jul 1990 (for purposes of s 13) (SI 1990/1383) 1 Jan 1991 (otherwise) (SI 1990/2372)
21(1)	3 Jul 1990 (for purposes of s 13) (SI 1990/1383) 1 Jan 1991 (otherwise) (SI 1990/2372)
(2)–(4)	1 Jan 1991 (SI 1990/2372)
(5), (6)	3 Jul 1990 (for purposes of s 13) (SI 1990/1383) 1 Jan 1991 (otherwise) (SI 1990/2372)
22	3 Jul 1990 (for purposes of s 13) (SI 1990/1383) 1 Jan 1991 (otherwise) (SI 1990/2372)
23, 24	1 Jan 1991 (SI 1990/2372)
25, 26	1 Dec 1990 (SI 1990/2372)
27(1)	1 Jan 1991 (SI 1990/2372)

Food Safety Act 1990 (c 16)—*cont*

s 27(2)	1 Dec 1990 (SI 1990/2372)
(3), (4)	1 Jan 1991 (SI 1990/2372)
(5)	1 Dec 1990 (SI 1990/2372)
28(1)	1 Jan 1991 (SI 1990/2372)
(2)	1 Dec 1990 (SI 1990/2372)
29	3 Jul 1990 (for purposes of s 13) (SI 1990/1383) 1 Jan 1991 (otherwise) (SI 1990/2372)
30, 31	1 Dec 1990 (SI 1990/2372)
32–36	3 Jul 1990 (for purposes of s 13) (SI 1990/1383) 1 Jan 1991 (otherwise) (SI 1990/2372)
37–39	1 Jan 1991 (SI 1990/2372)
40	1 Dec 1990 (SI 1990/2372)
41, 42	3 Jul 1990 (for purposes of s 13) (SI 1990/1383) 1 Jan 1991 (otherwise) (SI 1990/2372)
43	1 Jan 1991 (SI 1990/2372)
44	3 Jul 1990 (for purposes of s 13) (SI 1990/1383) 1 Jan 1991 (otherwise) (SI 1990/2372)
45	1 Dec 1990 (SI 1990/2372)
46	3 Jul 1990 (for purposes of s 13) (SI 1990/1383) 1 Jan 1990 (otherwise) (SI 1990/2372)
47	1 Jan 1991 (SI 1990/2372)
48(1)–(3)	3 Jul 1990 (for purposes of s 13) (SI 1990/1383) 1 Dec 1990 (otherwise) (SI 1990/2372)
(4), (5)	1 Dec 1990 (SI 1990/2372)
49(1)	3 Jul 1990 (for purposes of s 13) (SI 1990/1383) 1 Jan 1991 (otherwise) (SI 1990/2372)
(2)	1 Dec 1990 (SI 1990/2372)
(3)–(5)	3 Jul 1990 (for purposes of s 13) (SI 1990/1383) 1 Jan 1991 (otherwise) (SI 1990/2372)
50	3 Jul 1990 (for purposes of s 13) (SI 1990/1383) 1 Jan 1991 (otherwise) (SI 1990/2372)
51	29 Jun 1990 (s 60(2))
52	See Sch 2 below
53(1)	3 Jul 1990 (for purposes of ss 13, 51) (SI 1990/1383) 1 Dec 1990 (otherwise) (SI 1990/2372)
(2)–(4)	3 Jul 1990 (for purposes of s 13) (SI 1990/1383) 1 Dec 1990 (otherwise) (SI 1990/2372)
(5)	1 Dec 1990 (SI 1990/2372)
54	1 Apr 1992 (SI 1990/2372)
55(1)	1 Jan 1991 (SI 1990/2372)
(2)–(6)	Repealed
56	1 Jan 1991 (SI 1990/2372)
57(1)	3 Jul 1990 (for purposes of s 13) (SI 1990/1383) 1 Dec 1990 (otherwise) (SI 1990/2372)
(2)	3 Jul 1990 (for purposes of s 13) (SI 1990/1383) 1 Dec 1990 (otherwise) (SI 1990/2372)
58(1)	3 Jul 1990 (for purposes of s 13) (SI 1990/1383) 1 Jan 1991 (otherwise) (SI 1990/2372)
(2)–(4)	1 Jan 1991 (SI 1990/2372)
59(1)	See Sch 3 below
(2)	1 Dec 1990 (SI 1990/2372)
(3)	See Sch 4 below
(4)	See Sch 5 below
60	1 Jan 1991 (SI 1990/2372)
Sch 1	1 Dec 1990 (SI 1990/2372)
2, para 1–11	1 Jan 1991 (SI 1990/2372)

Food Safety Act 1990 (c 16)—*cont*

Sch 2, para	12–15	29 Jun 1990 (s 60(2))
	16	1 Jan 1991 (SI 1990/2372)
3, para	1–13	1 Jan 1991 (SI 1990/2372)
	14	Repealed
	15–28	1 Jan 1991 (SI 1990/2372)
	29, 30	13 Jul 1990 (for purposes of s 51) (SI 1990/1383) 1 Jan 1991 (otherwise) (SI 1990/2372)
	31–38	1 Jan 1991 (SI 1990/2372)
4		1 Dec 1990 (SI 1990/2372)
5		1 Dec 1990 (so far as relates to Public Analysts (Scotland) Regulations 1956, SI 1956/1162 or Public Analysts Regulations 1957, SI 1957/237, repeals of or in Food and Drugs (Scotland) Act 1956, ss 27, 29, 56 and Food Act 1984, ss 76(2), 79(5)) (SI 1990/2372) 1 Jan 1991 (all repeals so far as not already in force except those of or in Food Act 1984, s 13 so far as relating to regulations (see following notes), ss 16–20, 62–67, ss 92, 93 (so far as relate to ss 16 and 18), s 132(1) so far as relates to regulations (see following notes)) (SI 1990/2372) 1 Apr 1991 (repeals of Food Act 1984, ss 13, 132(1), so far as relate to Food Hygiene (Amendment) Regulations 1990, SI 1990/1431 (except reg 3(b), Sch 1 thereof)) (SI 1990/2372) 1 Apr 1992 (repeals of Food Act 1984, ss 13, 132(1), so far as relate to Food Hygiene (Amendment) Regulations 1990, reg 3(b), Sch 1) (SI 1990/2372) 3 Apr 1992 (repeals of or in Food Act 1984, ss 16–20, Pt IV (ss 62–67), ss 92 (so far as relates to s 16(2)), 93 (so far as relates to s 18(4))) (SI 1992/57)

Gaming (Amendment) Act 1990 (c 26)

RA: 13 Jul 1990

Commencement provisions: s 2(2), (3); Gaming (Amendment) Act 1990 (Commencement) Order 1991, SI 1991/59

s 1		See Schedule below
2		13 Sep 1990 (s 2(2))
Schedule,		
para	1, 2	13 Sep 1990 (s 2(2))
	3, 4	1 Apr 1991 (SI 1991/59)
	5–10	13 Sep 1990 (s 2(2))

Government Trading Act 1990 (c 30)

RA: 26 Jul 1990

Commencement provisions: s 4(3); Government Trading Act 1990 (Appointed Day) Order 1991, SI 1991/132

s 1	26 Jul 1990 (RA)

Government Trading Act 1990 (c 30)—*cont*

s 2	See Sch 1 below
3	26 Jul 1990 (RA)
4	See Sch 2, Pt I below
5	See Sch 2, Pt II below
Sch 1	26 Jul 1990 (RA)
2, Pt I	11 Feb 1991 (SI 1991/132)
II	26 Jul 1990 (RA)

Greenwich Hospital Act 1990 (c 13)

RA: 29 Jun 1990

29 Jun 1990 (RA)

Horses (Protective Headgear for Young Riders) Act 1990 (c 25)

RA: 13 Jul 1990

Commencement provisions: s 5(2); Horses (Protective Headgear for Young Riders) Act 1990 (Commencement) Order 1992, SI 1992/1200

s 1–3	30 Jun 1992 (SI 1992/1200)
4, 5	13 Jul 1990 (s 5(2))

Human Fertilisation and Embryology Act 1990 (c 37)

RA: 1 Nov 1990

Commencement provisions: s 49(2); Human Fertilisation and Embryology Act 1990 (Commencement No 1) Order 1990, SI 1990/2165; Human Fertilisation and Embryology Act 1990 (Commencement No 2 and Transitional Provision) Order 1991, SI 1991/480; Human Fertilisation and Embryology Act 1990 (Commencement No 3 and Transitional Provisions) Order 1991, SI 1991/1400; Human Fertilisation and Embryology Act 1990 (Commencement No 4—Amendment of Transitional Provisions) Order 1991, SI 1991/1781; Human Fertilisation and Embryology Act 1990 (Commencement No 5) Order 1994, SI 1994/1776

s 1	1 Aug 1991 (SI 1991/1400)[1]
2(1)	7 Nov 1990 (so far as relates to the definition of 'the Authority') (SI 1990/2165)
	1 Aug 1991 (otherwise) (SI 1991/1400)[1]
(2), (3)	1 Aug 1991 (SI 1991/1400)[1]
3	1 Aug 1991 (SI 1991/1400)[1]
3A	Inserted by Criminal Justice and Public Order Act 1994, s 156(1), (2) (qv)
4	1 Aug 1991 (SI 1991/1400)[1]
5(1), (2)	7 Nov 1990 (SI 1990/2165)
(3)	See Sch 1 below
6, 7	7 Nov 1990 (SI 1990/2165)
8	1 Aug 1991 (SI 1991/1400)[1]
9(1)–(4)	1 Aug 1991 (SI 1991/1400)[1]
(5)	8 Jul 1991 (for purpose of making regulations) (SI 1991/1400)
	1 Aug 1991 (otherwise) (SI 1991/1400)[1]

Human Fertilisation and Embryology Act 1990 (c 37)—*cont*

s 9(6)–(11)	1 Aug 1991 (SI 1991/1400)[1]
10	8 Jul 1991 (for purpose of making regulations) (SI 1991/1400)
	1 Aug 1991 (otherwise) (SI 1991/1400)[1]
11–13	1 Aug 1991 (SI 1991/1400)[1]
14(1)–(4)	1 Aug 1991 (SI 1991/1400)[1]
(5)	8 Jul 1991 (for purpose of making regulations) (SI 1991/1400)
	1 Aug 1991 (otherwise) (SI 1991/1400)[1]
15	1 Aug 1991 (SI 1991/1400)[1]
16(1)	8 Jul 1991 (for purpose of requiring that an application for a licence be made in an approved form and be accompanied by the initial fee) (SI 1991/1400)
	1 Aug 1991 (otherwise) (SI 1991/1400)[1]
(2)–(5)	1 Aug 1991 (SI 1991/1400)[1]
(6)	8 Jul 1991 (for purpose of fixing the amount of the initial fee) (SI 1991/1400)
	1 Aug 1991 (otherwise) (SI 1991/1400)[1]
(7)	1 Aug 1991 (SI 1991/1400)[1]
17–25	1 Aug 1991 (SI 1991/1400)[1]
26	7 Nov 1990 (SI 1990/2165)
27–29	1 Aug 1991 (SI 1991/1400)[1]
30(1)–(8)	1 Nov 1994 (SI 1994/1776)
(9), (10)	5 Jul 1994 (SI 1994/1776)
(11)	1 Nov 1994 (SI 1994/1776)
31, 32	1 Aug 1991 (SI 1991/1400)[1]
33(1)	7 Nov 1990 (SI 1990/2165)
(2)(a)	1 Aug 1991 (SI 1991/1400)[1]
(b)	7 Nov 1990 (SI 1990/2165)
(3)	1 Aug 1991 (SI 1991/1400)[1]
(4)	7 Nov 1990 (SI 1990/2165)
(5), (6)	1 Aug 1991 (SI 1991/1400)[1]
(6A)–(6G)	Inserted by Human Fertilisation and Embryology (Disclosure of Information) Act 1992, s 1(1), (3) (qv)
(7), (8)	1 Aug 1991 (SI 1991/1400)[1]
(9)	Added by Human Fertilisation and Embryology (Disclosure of Information) Act 1992, s 1(1), (4) (qv)
34, 35	1 Aug 1991 (SI 1991/1400)[1]
36	7 Nov 1990 (SI 1990/2165)
37	1 Apr 1991 (subject to transitional provisions) (SI 1991/480)
38, 39	1 Aug 1991 (SI 1991/1400)[1]
40	7 Nov 1990 (SI 1990/2165)
41(1), (2)	1 Aug 1991 (SI 1991/1400)[1]
(3)	8 Jul 1991 (SI 1991/1400)
(4)	8 Jul 1991 (so far as relates to s 41(3)) (SI 1991/1400)
	1 Aug 1991 (otherwise) (SI 1991/1400)[1]
(5)	7 Nov 1990 (so far as relates to s 33(1), (2)(b), (4)) (SI 1990/2165)
	1 Aug 1991 (otherwise) (SI 1991/1400)[1]
(6)	7 Nov 1990 (so far as relates to s 40) (SI 1990/2165)
	1 Aug 1991 (otherwise) (SI 1991/1400)[1]
(7), (8)	1 Aug 1991 (SI 1991/1400)[1]

Human Fertilisation and Embryology Act 1990 (c 37)—*cont*

s 41(9)	7 Nov 1990 (so far as relates to s 40) (SI 1990/2165)
	1 Aug 1991 (otherwise) (SI 1991/1400)[1]
(10), (11)	1 Aug 1991 (SI 1991/1400)[1]
42	7 Nov 1990 (SI 1990/2165)
43(1)	8 Jul 1991 (for purpose of making regulations) (SI 1991/1400)
	1 Aug 1991 (otherwise) (SI 1991/1400)[1]
(2), (3)	1 Aug 1991 (SI 1991/1400)[1]
44	1 Aug 1991 (SI 1991/1400)[1]
45	8 Jul 1991 (SI 1991/1400)
46, 47	1 Aug 1991 (SI 1991/1400)[1]
48(1)	7 Nov 1990 (so far as relates to provisions brought into force by SI 1990/2165) (SI 1990/2165)
	1 Apr 1991 (so far as relates to provisions brought into force by SI 1991/480) (SI 1991/480)
	8 Jul 1991 (so far as relates to provisions brought into force by SI 1991/1400) (SI 1991/1400)
	1 Aug 1991 (otherwise, except so far as relates to s 30) (SI 1991/1400)[1]
	5 Jul 1994 (so far as relates to s 30(9), (10)) (SI 1994/1776)
	1 Nov 1994 (so far as relates to s 30(1)(8), (11)) (SI 1994/1776)
(2)	1 Aug 1991 (SI 1991/1400)[1]
49(1), (2)	7 Nov 1990 (SI 1990/2165)
(3), (4)	1 Aug 1991 (SI 1991/1400)[1]
(5)	See Sch 4 below
(6), (7)	7 Nov 1990 (SI 1990/2165)
Sch 1	7 Nov 1990 (SI 1990/2165)
2–4	1 Aug 1991 (SI 1991/1400)[1]

[1] subject to transitional provisions set out in SI 1991/1400, arts 3, 4, as amended by SI 1991/1781, art 2

Import and Export Control Act 1990 (c 45)

RA: 6 Dec 1990

6 Dec 1990 (RA)

Landlord and Tenant (Licensed Premises) Act 1990 (c 39)

RA: 1 Nov 1990

Commencement provisions: s 2(3)

s 1(1)	1 Jan 1991 (s 2(3))
(2), (3)	1 Jan 1991 (subject to transitional provisions) (s 2(3))
(4)	1 Jan 1991 (s 2(3))
2	1 Jan 1991 (s 2(3))

Law Reform (Miscellaneous Provisions) (Scotland) Act 1990 (c 40)

RA: 1 Nov 1990

Commencement provisions: s 75(2)–(4); Law Reform (Miscellaneous Provisions) (Scotland) Act 1990 Commencement (No 1) Order 1990, SI 1990/2328; Law Reform (Miscellaneous Provisions) (Scotland) Act 1990 (Commencement No 2) Order 1990, SI 1990/2624; Law Reform (Miscellaneous Provisions) (Scotland) Act 1990 (Commencement No 3) Order 1991, SI 1991/330; Law Reform (Miscellaneous Provisions) (Scotland) Act 1990 (Commencement No 4) Order 1991, SI 1991/822; Law Reform (Miscellaneous Provisions) (Scotland) Act 1990 (Commencement No 5) Order 1991, SI 1991/850; Law Reform (Miscellaneous Provisions) (Scotland) Act 1990 (Commencement No 6) Order 1991, SI 1991/1252; Law Reform (Miscellaneous Provisions) (Scotland) Act 1990 (Commencement No 7) Order 1991, SI 1991/1903; Law Reform (Miscellaneous Provisions) (Scotland) Act 1990 (Commencement No 8) Order 1991, SI 1991/2151; Law Reform (Miscellaneous Provisions) (Scotland) Act 1990 (Commencement No 9) Order 1991, SI 1991/2862; Law Reform (Miscellaneous Provisions) (Scotland) Act 1990 (Commencement No 10) Order 1992, SI 1992/1599; Law Reform (Miscellaneous Provisions) (Scotland) Act 1990 (Commencement No 11) Order 1993, SI 1993/641; Law Reform (Miscellaneous Provisions) (Scotland) Act 1990 (Commencement No 12) Order 1993, SI 1993/2253; Law Reform (Miscellaneous Provisions) (Scotland) Act 1990 (Commencement No 13) Order 1995, SI 1995/364

s 1, 2	27 Jul 1992 (SI 1992/1599)
3(1)	4 Jul 1992 (for purpose of power to make order) (SI 1992/1599)
	27 Jul 1992 (otherwise) (SI 1992/1599)
(2)–(4)	27 Jul 1992 (SI 1992/1599)
4(1)–(3)	30 Sep 1992 (SI 1992/1599)
(4)	4 Jul 1992 (SI 1992/1599)
5(1), (2)	30 Sep 1992 (SI 1992/1599)
(3)	4 Jul 1992 (SI 1992/1599)
(4)	30 Sep 1992 (SI 1992/1599)
(5)	4 Jul 1992 (SI 1992/1599)
(6)–(14)	30 Sep 1992 (SI 1992/1599)
6	27 Jul 1992 (SI 1992/1599)
7(1)–(4)	27 Jul 1992 (SI 1992/1599)
(5)	4 Jul 1992 (for purpose of power to make regulations) (SI 1992/1599)
	27 Jul 1992 (otherwise) (SI 1992/1599)
(6)–(12)	27 Jul 1992 (SI 1992/1599)
8	27 Jul 1992 (SI 1992/1599)
9(1)–(4)	27 Jul 1992 (SI 1992/1599)
(5)	4 Jul 1992 (for purpose of power to make orders) (SI 1992/1599)
	27 Jul 1992 (otherwise) (SI 1992/1599)
(6), (7)	27 Jul 1992 (SI 1992/1599)
10–12	15 Sep 1993 (SI 1993/2253)
13, 14	27 Jul 1992 (SI 1992/1599)
15(1)–(4)	27 Jul 1992 (SI 1992/1599)
(5)(a)	27 Jul 1992 (SI 1992/1599)
(b)	4 Jul 1992 (for purpose of power to make orders) (SI 1992/1599)
	27 Jul 1992 (otherwise) (SI 1992/1599)
(c)	27 Jul 1992 (SI 1992/1599)

Law Reform (Miscellaneous Provisions) (Scotland) Act 1990 (c 40)—*cont*

s 15(5)(d)	4 Jul 1992 (for purpose of power to make orders) (SI 1992/1599)
	27 Jul 1992 (otherwise) (SI 1992/1599)
(6)–(10)	27 Jul 1992 (SI 1992/1599)
(11)	4 Jul 1992 (SI 1992/1599)
16(1)–(3)	1 Apr 1991 (SI 1991/822)
(4)	See Sch 1, Pt I below
17(1), (2)	Not in force
(3)	30 Sep 1991 (SI 1991/2151)
(4)–(10)	*Not in force*
(11)–(15)	30 Sep 1991 (SI 1991/2151)
(16)–(24)	*Not in force*
18(1)–(9)	*Not in force*
(10), (11)	30 Sep 1991 (SI 1991/2151)
(12)–(15)	*Not in force*
19	*Not in force*
20(1)–(11)	*Not in force*
(12)	See Sch 1, Pt II below
(13)–(17)	*Not in force*
21, 22	*Not in force*
23	1 Apr 1991 (SI 1991/822)
24	3 Jun 1991 (SI 1991/1252)
25(1)–(5)	*Not in force*
(6)	See Sch 2 below
26–29	*Not in force*
30	3 Jun 1991 (SI 1991/1252)
31	17 Mar 1993 (SI 1993/641)
32	17 Mar 1993 (for purpose of provisions relating to making of rules and orders in Solicitors (Scotland) Act 1980, s 60A(2), (3), (5)–(8)) (SI 1993/641)
	Not in force (otherwise)
33	3 Jun 1991 (SI 1991/1252)
34(1)	1 Apr 1991 (SI 1991/822)
(2)–(8)	3 Jun 1991 (SI 1991/1252)
(9)(a)–(c)	1 Apr 1991 (SI 1991/822)
(d)–(h)	*Not in force*
(10)	See Sch 3 below
35	1 Apr 1991 (SI 1991/822)
36(1)	20 Jul 1992 (SI 1992/1599)
(2)	4 Jul 1992 (for purpose of power to make act of sederunt) (SI 1992/1599)
	20 Jul 1992 (otherwise) (SI 1992/1599)
(3)	4 Jul 1992 (for purpose of power to make act of sederunt under Solicitors' (Scotland) Act 1980, s 61A) (SI 1992/1599)
	20 Jul 1992 (otherwise) (SI 1992/1599)
(4)	*Not in force*
37	20 Jul 1992 (SI 1992/1599)
38, 39	30 Sep 1991 (SI 1991/2151)
40–42	*Not in force*
43	3 Jun 1991 (SI 1991/1252)
44	1 Apr 1991 (SI 1991/822)
45–48	1 Jan 1991 (s 75(3)(a))
49(1)–(7)	1 Jan 1991 (s 75(3)(a))
(8)	See Sch 5 below
(9)–(11)	1 Jan 1991 (s 75(3)(a))

Law Reform (Miscellaneous Provisions) (Scotland) Act 1990 (c 40)—*cont*

s 50–55	1 Jan 1991 (s 75(3)(a))
56, 57	Repealed
58, 59	30 Sep 1991 (for purposes of proceedings in any sheriff court in the sheriffdom of Glasgow and Strathkelvin or Lothian and Borders) (SI 1991/2151)
	3 Apr 1995 (so far as not already in force) (SI 1995/364)
60	30 Sep 1991 (SI 1991/2151)
61	1 Apr 1991 (SI 1991/850)
62	Repealed
63	1 Dec 1990 (SI 1990/2328)
64, 65	1 Jan 1991 (SI 1990/2624)
66	See Sch 7 below
67	1 Jan 1991 (s 73(3)(b))
68	1 Apr 1991 (SI 1991/330)
69	1 Mar 1991 (SI 1991/330)
70, 71	1 Jan 1991 (s 75(3)(b))
72	Repealed
73(1)(a)	17 Mar 1993 (SI 1993/641)
(b)–(e)	1 Apr 1991 (SI 1991/822)
(2)	17 Mar 1993 (SI 1993/641)
74(1)	See Sch 8 below
(2)	See Sch 9 below
75	1 Nov 1990 (RA)
Sch 1, Pt I	1 Apr 1991 (SI 1991/822)
II	*Not in force*
2	*Not in force*
3, 4	1 Apr 1991 (SI 1991/822)
5	1 Jan 1991 (s 75(3)(a))
6	Repealed
7	1 Jan 1991 (s 75(3)(a))
8, Pt I, para 1–18	31 Dec 1991 (SI 1991/2892)
II, para 19, 20	*Not in force*
21	1 Jan 1991 (s 75(3)(b))
22	*Not in force*
23	1 Apr 1991 (SI 1991/822)
24, 25	*Not in force*
26	1 Jan 1991 (SI 1990/2624)
27(1), (2)	3 Jun 1991 (SI 1991/1252)
(3)	1 Nov 1990 (s 75(4))
28	1 Apr 1991 (SI 1991/850)
29(1)–(4)	3 Jun 1991 (SI 1991/1252)
(5)(a), (b)	*Not in force*
(c)	17 Mar 1993 (SI 1993/641)
(d)	*Not in force*
(6)(a), (b)	1 Jan 1991 (SI 1990/2624)
(c)	*Not in force*
(7)	1 Jan 1991 (SI 1990/2624)
(8)–(14)	3 Jun 1991 (SI 1991/1252)
(15)(a)	3 Jun 1991 (SI 1991/1252)
(b)–(d)	17 Mar 1993 (SI 1993/641)
(e)	3 Jun 1991 (SI 1991/1252)
(f)	17 Mar 1993 (SI 1993/641)

Law Reform (Miscellaneous Provisions) (Scotland) Act 1990 (c 40)—*cont*

Sch 8, Pt II, para 29(16),(17)	3 Jun 1991 (SI 1991/1252)
30	20 Jul 1992 (SI 1992/1599)
31, 32	1 Jan 1991 (SI 1990/2624)
33	Repealed
34	1 Jan 1991 (s 75(3)(b))
35	1 Dec 1990 (SI 1990/2328)
36(1)	*Not in force*
(2)–(5)	30 Sep 1991 (SI 1991/2151)
(6)	26 Aug 1991 (SI 1991/1903)
(7)–(9)	*Not in force*
(10)–(15)	30 Sep 1991 (SI 1991/2151)
(16)	*Not in force*
37	1 Jan 1991 (SI 1990/2624)
38	3 Jun 1991 (SI 1991/1252)
39	1 Jan 1991 (SI 1990/2624); prospectively repealed by Antarctic Act 1994, s 33, Schedule; any orders made under s 35 of that Act bringing the prospective repeal into force will be noted to that Act in the service to this work
9	1 Dec 1990 (repeals of or in Companies Act 1985, ss 38(1), 39(3), 186, 188(2), 462(2); Insolvency Act 1986, s 53(3); Companies Act 1989, s 130(3), Sch 17, paras 1(2), 2(4), 8, 10) (SI 1990/2328)
	1 Jan 1991 (repeals of or in Matrimonial Homes (Family Protection) (Scotland) Act 1981, ss 6(3)(e), 8; Representation of the People Act 1983, s 42(3)(b)) (SI 1990/2624)
	1 Apr 1991 (repeals of or in Unfair Contract Terms Act 1977, ss 15(1), 25(3)(d), (4)) (SI 1991/330)
	3 Jun 1991 (repeals of or in Solicitors (Scotland) Act 1980, ss 20(1), 31(3), 63(1), Sch 4, paras 1, 17) (SI 1991/1252)
	15 Aug 1991 (repeals of or in House of Commons Disqualification Act 1975, Sch 1; Solicitors (Scotland) Act 1980, ss 49, 65(1), Sch 5) (SI 1991/1252)
	30 Sep 1991 (repeals of or in Solicitors (Scotland) Act 1980, s 29; Legal Aid (Scotland) Act 1986, s 13(2)) (SI 1991/2151)
	17 Mar 1993 (repeals of or in Licensing (Scotland) Act 1976, ss 6, 18(1), 55, 61, 97(2), 131, 132, 133(4), Sch 4, paras 1, 12–17, 19–22; Solicitors (Scotland) Act 1980, s 27; Family Law (Scotland) Act 1985, s 8(1)(a); Law Reform (Miscellaneous Provisions) (Scotland) Act 1985, Sch 1, Pt I, para 5) (SI 1993/641)
	Not in force (otherwise)

Licensing (Low Alcohol Drinks) Act 1990 (c 21)

RA: 13 Jul 1990

Commencement provisions: s 3(2)

Licensing (Low Alcohol Drinks) Act 1990 (c 21)—*cont*

1 Jan 1994 (s 3(2)) (no day prior to that date was appointed by the Secretary of State)

Marriage (Registration of Buildings) Act 1990 (c 33)

RA: 26 Jul 1990

Commencement provisions: s 2(2)

26 Sep 1990 (s 2(2))

National Health Service and Community Care Act 1990 (c 19)

RA: 29 Jun 1990

Commencement provisions: s 67(2); National Health Service and Community Care Act 1990 (Commencement No 1) Order 1990, SI 1990/1329 (as amended by SI 1990/2511); National Health Service and Community Care Act 1990 (Commencement No 2) (Scotland) Order 1990, SI 1990/1520; National Health Service and Community Care Act 1990 (Commencement No 3 and Transitional Provisions) (Scotland) Order 1990, SI 1990/1793 (as amended by SI 1990/2510, SI 1992/799); National Health Service and Community Care Act 1990 (Commencement No 4 and Transitional Provision) Order 1990, SI 1990/2218; National Health Service and Community Care Act 1990 (Commencement No 5 and Revocation) (Scotland) Order 1990, SI 1990/2510; National Health Service and Community Care Act 1990 (Commencement No 6—Amendment, and Transitional and Saving Provisions) Order 1990, SI 1990/2511; National Health Service and Community Care Act 1990 (Commencement No 7) Order 1991, SI 1991/388; National Health Service and Community Care Act 1990 (Commencement No 8 and Transitional Provisions) (Scotland) Order 1991, SI 1991/607; National Health Service and Community Care Act 1990 (Commencement No 9) Order 1992, SI 1992/567; National Health Service and Community Care Act 1990 (Commencement No 3 and Transitional Provisions) (Scotland) (Amendment) Order 1992, SI 1992/799 (amending SI 1990/1793); National Health Service and Community Care Act 1990 (Commencement No 10) Order 1992, SI 1992/2975; National Health Service and Community Care Act 1990 (Commencement No 11) (Scotland) Order 1994, SI 1994/2658

s 1(1), (2)	Repealed
(3)	See Sch 1, Pt III below
(4), (5)	Repealed
2	Repealed
3(1)	Substituted by Health Authorities Act 1995, ss 2(1), Sch 1, Pt II, paras 65, 67(a) (qv)
(2)	1 Apr 1991 (SI 1990/1329)
(3), (4)	Repealed
(5), (6)	1 Apr 1991 (SI 1990/1329)
(6A)	Inserted (1 Apr 1991) by Health and Personal Social Services (Northern Ireland Consequential Amendments) Order 1991, SI 1991/195, art 7(1), (2)
(7), (8)	1 Apr 1991 (SI 1990/1329)
4(1), (2)	6 Mar 1991 (so far as relate to a reference under s 4(4)) (SI 1991/388)
	1 Apr 1991 (otherwise) (SI 1990/1329)
(3)	1 Apr 1991 (SI 1990/1329)

National Health Service and Community Care Act 1990 (c 19)—*cont*

s 4(4)	6 Mar 1991 (SI 1991/388)
(5), (6)	6 Mar 1991 (so far as relate to a reference under s 4(4)) (SI 1991/388)
	1 Apr 1991 (otherwise) (SI 1990/1329)
(7), (8)	1 Apr 1991 (SI 1990/1329)
(9)	6 Mar 1991 (so far as relates to a reference under s 4(4)) (SI 1991/388)
	1 Apr 1991 (otherwise) (SI 1990/1329)
(10)	Added (1 Apr 1991) by Health and Personal Social Services (Northern Ireland Consequential Amendments) Order 1991, SI 1991/195, art 7(1), (5)
5	See Sch 2 below
6–8	5 Jul 1990 (SI 1990/1329)
9	See Sch 3 below
10, 11	5 Jul 1990 (SI 1990/1329)
12(1)	17 Sep 1990 (subject to transitional provisions) (SI 1990/1329)
(2)	Repealed
(3)	17 Sep 1990 (subject to transitional provisions) (SI 1990/1329)
(4)	1 Oct 1991 (subject to savings) (SI 1990/2511)
(5)	Repealed
13	Repealed
14	17 Sep 1990 (SI 1990/1329)
15–18	1 Apr 1991 (SI 1990/1329)
19	Repealed
20(1)	See Sch 4 below
(2), (3)	1 Oct 1990 (SI 1990/1329)
(4)–(7)	5 Jul 1990 (SI 1990/1329)
21	17 Sep 1990 (SI 1990/1329)
22	1 Jan 1991 (SI 1990/1329)
23(1)–(3)	1 Jan 1991 (subject to transitional provisions) (SI 1990/1329, as amended by SI 1990/2511)
(4)	1 Jan 1991 (except so far as repeals second paragraph of National Health Service Act 1977, s 33(5)) (subject to transitional provisions) (SI 1990/1329, as amended by SI 1990/2511)
	Not in force (exception noted above)
(5)	Repealed
(6)–(8)	1 Jan 1991 (subject to transitional provisions) (SI 1990/1329)
24	17 Sep 1990 (SI 1990/1329)
25	1 Apr 1991 (SI 1990/1329)
26(1)	5 Jul 1990 (SI 1990/1329)
(2)(a)	5 Jul 1990 (SI 1990/1329)
(b)	Repealed
(c)	5 Jul 1990 (SI 1990/1329)
(d)	5 Jul 1990 (so far as relates to definition of 'National Health Service trust') (SI 1990/1329)
	1 Apr 1991 (otherwise) (SI 1990/1329)
(e)	5 Jul 1990 (SI 1990/1329)
(f)	17 Sep 1990 (SI 1990/1329)
(g)	5 Jul 1990 (SI 1990/1329)
(h)	1 Apr 1991 (SI 1990/1329)
(i)	5 Jul 1990 (SI 1990/1329)

National Health Service and Community Care Act 1990 (c 19)—*cont*

s 27(1), (2)	31 Mar 1991 (so far as have effect in relation to members of a Health Board or the management committee of the Common Services Agency for the Scottish Health Service) (SI 1990/1793)
	30 Jun 1992 (otherwise) (SI 1990/1793, as amended by SI 1992/799)
(3)	See Sch 5 below
28	17 Sep 1990 (SI 1990/1793)
29(1), (2)	17 Sep 1990 (SI 1990/1793)
(3)(a)	24 Jul 1990 (subject to a transitional provision and saving) (SI 1990/1520)
(b), (c)	24 Jul 1990 (SI 1990/1520)
(4)	24 Jul 1990 (SI 1990/1520)
30	1 Apr 1991 (SI 1990/1793)
31	24 Jul 1990 (SI 1990/1520)
32	See Sch 6 below
33	24 Jul 1990 (SI 1990/1520)
34	17 Sep 1990 (so far as relates to provisions of ss 87A, 87B(1) (so far as s 87B(1) provides for meaning of 'recognised fund holding practice' and 'allotted sum'), to be inserted into the National Health Service (Scotland) Act 1978) (SI 1990/1793)
	1 Apr 1991 (otherwise) (SI 1990/1793)
35	1 Apr 1992 (SI 1990/1793)
36(1)	See Sch 7 below
(2)–(8)	17 Sep 1990 (SI 1990/1793)
37	17 Sep 1990 (SI 1900/1793)
38	1 Apr 1991 (SI 1991/607)
39(1)–(3)	1 Apr 1991 (subject, in the case of s 39(2), to transitional provisions) (SI 1991/607)
(4)	1 Apr 1991 (except repeal in second paragraph of National Health Service (Scotland) Act 1978, s 23(5)) (SI 1991/607)
	Not in force (exception noted above)
(5)–(8)	1 Apr 1991 (SI 1991/607)
40, 41	17 Sep 1990 (SI 1990/1793)
42(1)	1 Apr 1993 (SI 1992/2975)
(2)	Repealed
(3)–(5)	1 Apr 1993 (SI 1992/2975)
(6), (7)	1 Apr 1991 (SI 1990/2218)
43, 44	1 Apr 1993 (SI 1992/2975)
45	12 Apr 1993 (SI 1992/2975)
46	1 Apr 1991 (SI 1990/2218)
47	1 Apr 1993 (SI 1992/2975)
48	1 Apr 1991 (SI 1990/2218)
49	10 Dec 1992 (SI 1992/2975)
50	1 Apr 1991 (SI 1990/2218)
51–54	1 Apr 1991 (SI 1990/2510)
55	1 Apr 1993 (SI 1992/2975)
56	1 Apr 1991 (so far as relates to insertion of Social Work (Scotland) Act 1968, s 13B) (SI 1990/2510)
	1 Apr 1993 (otherwise) (SI 1992/2975)
57	1 Apr 1993 (SI 1992/2975)
58	1 Apr 1991 (SI 1990/2510)
59(1)	Repealed
(2)	5 Jul 1990 (SI 1990/1329)
(3)	1 Apr 1991 (SI 1991/607)

National Health Service and Community Care Act 1990 (c 19)—*cont*

s 60	See Sch 8 below
61, 62	17 Sep 1990 (SI 1990/1329)
63	1 Apr 1991 (SI 1990/1329)
64, 65	5 Jul 1990 (SI 1990/1329)
66(1)	See Sch 9 below
(2)	See Sch 10 below
67	29 Jun 1990 (s 67(2))
Sch 1, Pt I, II	Repealed
III, para 6	Repealed
7	26 Jul 1990 (so far as has effect in relation to Regional Health Authorities) (SI 1990/1329) 17 Sep 1990 (otherwise) (SI 1990/1329)
8, 9	26 Jul 1990 (SI 1990/1329)
10	26 Jul 1990 (so far as has effect in relation to Regional Health Authorities) (SI 1990/1329) 17 Sep 1990 (otherwise) (SI 1990/1329)
2, 3	5 Jul 1990 (SI 1990/1329)
4, para 1–3	1 Oct 1990 (SI 1990/1329)
4	5 Jul 1990 (SI 1990/1329)
5–24	1 Oct 1990 (SI 1990/1329)
5	17 Sep 1990 (SI 1990/1793)
6	24 Jul 1990 (SI 1990/1520)
7, para 1	See paras 213 below
2	1 Dec 1994 (SI 1994/2658)
3(1)	See sub-paras (2)(7) below
(2)(a)–(c)	1 Dec 1994 (SI 1994/2658)
(d)	24 Oct 1994 (SI 1994/2658)
(3), (4)	1 Apr 1995 (SI 1994/2658)
(5)	1 Dec 1994 (SI 1994/2658)
(6)	24 Oct 1994 (SI 1994/2658)
(7)	1 Apr 1995 (SI 1994/2658)
4–12	1 Apr 1995 (SI 1994/2658)
13	1 Dec 1994 (SI 1994/2658)
14	1 Apr 1995 (SI 1994/2658)
15	1 Dec 1994 (SI 1994/2658)
8	1 Apr 1991 (SI 1990/1329)
9, para 1	24 Jul 1990 (SI 1990/1520)
2	5 Jul 1990 (SI 1990/1329)
3, 4	24 Jul 1990 (SI 1990/1520)
5(1)–(3)	1 Apr 1993 (SI 1992/2975)
(4)	5 Jul 1990 (SI 1990/1329)
(5)	1 Apr 1993 (SI 1992/2975)
(6), (7)	1 Apr 1991 (SI 1990/2218)
(8)	1 Apr 1991 (SI 1990/2218; SI 1990/2510)
(9)(a)	1 Apr 1993 (SI 1992/2975)
(b)	1 Apr 1991 (SI 1990/2510)
6–9	5 Jul 1990 (SI 1990/1329)
10(1)	*Not in force*
(2)–(6)	1 Apr 1991 (SI 1990/2510)
(7), (8)	1 Apr 1993 (SI 1992/2975)
(9)–(11)	1 Apr 1991 (SI 1990/2510)
(12)	24 Jul 1990 (SI 1990/1520)
(13)	1 Apr 1991 (SI 1990/2510)
(14)(a)	1 Apr 1991 (SI 1990/2510)
(b)	24 Jul 1990 (SI 1990/1520)
11(a)	1 Apr 1993 (SI 1992/2975)

National Health Service and Community Care Act 1990 (c 19)—*cont*

Sch 9, para 11(b)	1 Apr 1991 (SI 1990/2218)
(c)	1 Apr 1991 (so far as relates to s 46) (SI 1990/2218)
	1 Apr 1993 (otherwise) (SI 1992/2975)
12	1 Apr 1991 (SI 1990/2218)
13	5 Jul 1990 (SI 1990/1329)
14	24 Jul 1990 (SI 1990/1520)
15	Repealed
16	10 Dec 1992 (SI 1992/2975)
17	5 Jul 1990 (SI 1990/1329)
18(1)(a)	17 Sep 1990 (SI 1990/1329)
(b)	Repealed
(c)	17 Sep 1990 (SI 1990/1329)
(2)	17 Sep 1990 (SI 1990/1329)
(3)–(9)	5 Jul 1990 (SI 1990/1329)
(10), (11)	Repealed
(12), (13)	5 Jul 1990 (SI 1990/1329)
(14)	1 Apr 1993 (SI 1992/2975)
19(1)–(3)	17 Sep 1990 (SI 1990/1793)
(4), (5)	24 Jul 1990 (SI 1990/1520)
(6)	17 Sep 1990 (SI 1990/1793)
(7)(a)(i)	17 Sep 1990 (SI 1990/1793)
(ii)	24 Jul 1990 (SI 1990/1520)
(iii), (iv)	17 Sep 1990 (SI 1990/1793)
(b)–(d)	17 Sep 1990 (SI 1990/1793)
(8)	17 Sep 1990 (SI 1990/1793)
(9)–(14)	24 Jul 1990 (SI 1990/1520)
(15)	17 Sep 1990 (SI 1990/1793)
(16), (17)	24 Jul 1990 (SI 1990/1520)
(18)	Repealed
(19)	24 Jul 1990 (SI 1990/1520)
(20)	17 Sep 1990 (SI 1990/1793)
(21)	24 Jul 1990 (SI 1990/1520)
(22)(a)	17 Sep 1990 (SI 1990/1793)
(b)	24 Jul 1990 (SI 1990/1520)
(c)	24 Jul 1990 (so far as relates to definition 'National Health Service trust') (SI 1990/1520)
	1 Apr 1991 (otherwise) (SI 1990/1793)
(d)	24 Jul 1990 (SI 1990/1520)
(e)	17 Sep 1990 (SI 1990/1793)
(23)	1 Apr 1991 (SI 1990/1793)
(24)	24 Jul 1990 (SI 1990/1520)
20	5 Jul 1990 (SI 1990/1329)
21(a), (b)	5 Jul 1990 (SI 1990/1329)
(c)	24 Jul 1990 (SI 1990/1520)
22	Repealed
23	5 Jul 1990 (SI 1990/1329)
24(1), (2)	5 Jul 1990 (SI 1990/1329)
(3)(a), (b)	5 Jul 1990 (SI 1990/1329)
(c)	17 Sep 1990 (SI 1990/1329)
(4)	Repealed
(5)	5 Jul 1990 (SI 1990/1329)
(6)	Repealed (never in force)
(7)–(9)	5 Jul 1990 (SI 1990/1329)
25(1)	1 Apr 1993 (SI 1992/2975)
(2)	12 Apr 1993 (SI 1992/2975)
26, 27	5 Jul 1990 (SI 1990/1329)
28	24 Jul 1990 (SI 1990/1520)

National Health Service and Community Care Act 1990 (c 19)—*cont*

Sch 9, para 29	Repealed
30(1)(a)	5 Jul 1990 (SI 1990/1329)
(b), (c)	*Not in force*
(2)	5 Jul 1990 (SI 1990/1329)
31–33	5 Jul 1990 (SI 1990/1329)
34	17 Sep 1990 (SI 1990/1329)
35–37	5 Jul 1990 (SI 1990/1329)
10	5 Jul 1990 (repeals of or in National Health Service Act 1977, ss 8(5), 10(7)) (SI 1990/1329)
	17 Sep 1990 (repeals of or in National Health Service Act 1977, ss 8(1)–(3), 11(1), 12(a), 13(1), 14, 16, 18(3), 41(b), 55, 91(3)(b), 97(6), 99(1)(b), Sch 5, para 8; Health Services Act 1980, s 22, Sch 1; Public Health (Control of Disease) Act 1984) (SI 1990/1329)
	17 Sep 1990 (repeals of or in National Health Service (Scotland) Act 1978, ss 5, 6, 10(4), 85(1)(a), 108(1), Sch 3; Health and Medicines Act 1988, Sch 2, para 11) (SI 1990/1793)
	1 Oct 1990 (repeals of or in National Health Service Act 1977, s 98(1)(b), (3); Local Government and Housing Act 1989) (SI 1990/1329)
	1 Jan 1991 (repeals of or in National Health Service Act 1977, s 33(7)) (SI 1990/1329)
	1 Jan 1991 (repeals of National Health Service (Scotland) Act 1978, s 23(7)) (SI 1990/1793)
	1 Apr 1991 (repeals of or in Nursing Homes Registration (Scotland) Act 1938; Fire Precautions Act 1971; Health Services Act 1976; National Health Service Act 1977, Sch 5, para 15(2); National Health Service (Scotland) Act 1978; Employment Protection (Consolidation) Act 1978; Health Services Act 1980, ss 12–15, Schs 2–4; Registered Homes Act 1984; National Health Service (Amendment) Act 1986) (SI 1990/1329)
	1 Apr 1991 (repeals of or in National Health Service (Scotland) Act 1978, ss 7(2), 57(3)) (SI 1990/1793)
	1 Apr 1991 (repeals of or in National Assistance Act 1948, ss 35(2), (3), 36, 54 (so far as s 54 relates to England and Wales, and subject to a transitional provision (see SI 1990/2218, art 3)); Health Services and Public Health Act 1968, s 45(5); Chronically Sick and Disabled Persons Act 1970, s 2(1) (so far as relates to England and Wales)) (SI 1990/2218)
	1 Apr 1991 (so far as they apply to Scotland, repeals of or in National Assistance Act 1948, s 54; Social Work (Scotland) Act 1968, s 1(4); National Health Service (Scotland) Act 1978, ss 13A, 13B, Sch 15, para 15; Mental Health (Scotland) Act 1984, s 13(1)(c)) (S) (SI 1990/2510)
	6 Apr 1992 (repeal of National Assistance Act 1948, s 22(7)) (EW) (SI 1992/567)
	10 Dec 1992 (repeal in Children Act 1975, s 99(1)(b)) (SI 1992/2975)
	1 Apr 1993 (repeals of or in National Assistance Act 1948, ss 21(8), 26; National Health Service Act

National Health Service and Community Care Act 1990 (c 19)—*cont*

Sch 10—*cont*	1977, Sch 8, para 2; Mental Health Act 1983, ss 124(3), 135(6); Social Security Act 1986, Sch 10, para 32(2); Local Government Act 1988, Sch 1, para 2(4)(b); Local Government Finance Act 1988, Sch 1, para 9(2)(b)) (SI 1992/2975)
	1 Apr 1995 (repeals of National Health Service (Scotland) Act 1978, s 86(2); National Health Service and Community Care Act 1990, s 36(5)) (SI 1994/2658)
	Not in force (otherwise)

Pakistan Act 1990 (c 14)

RA: 29 Jun 1990

Commencement provisions: s 2(3)

1 Oct 1989 (retrospective; s 2(3))

Pensions (Miscellaneous Provisions) Act 1990 (c 7)

RA: 24 May 1990

Commencement provisions: ss 1(8), 14(3)

s 1(1)	24 Jul 1990 (s 14(3))
(2)(a)	24 Jul 1990 (s 14(3))
(b)	1 Jan 1992 (s 1(8))
(3)	24 Jul 1990 (s 14(3))
(4)	1 Jan 1993 (s 1(8))
(5)–(8)	24 Jul 1990 (s 14(3))
2–11	24 Jul 1990 (s 14(3))
12	24 May 1990 (RA)
13	24 Jul 1990 (s 14(3))
14	24 May 1990 (RA)

Planning (Consequential Provisions) Act 1990 (c 11)

RA: 24 May 1990

Commencement provisions: s 7(2), Sch 4, para 1(3), (4); Planning (Consequential Provisions) Act 1990 (Appointed Day No 1 and Transitional Provisions) Order 1991, SI 1991/2698[1]

24 Aug 1990 (s 7(2))

[1] This order appointed 2 Jan 1992 as the appointed day under Sch 4, para 1(3)(a) for the purposes of paras 3–16 of that Schedule (transitory modifications), but only for the purposes of awards of costs in relation to proceedings which give rise to a hearing

---

Planning (Hazardous Substances) Act 1990 (c 10)

RA: 24 May 1990

Commencement provisions: s 41(2), (3); Planning (Hazardous Substances) Act 1990 (Commencement and Transitional Provisions) Order 1992, SI 1992/725

11 Mar 1992 (so far as provisions of this Act confer on the Secretary of State a power, or impose upon him a duty, to make regulations, or make provision with respect to the exercise of any such power or duty, for the purpose only of enabling or requiring the Secretary of State to make regulations) (SI 1992/725)

1 Jun 1992 (otherwise) (SI 1992/725)

See, for transitory provisions, Planning (Consequential Provisions) Act 1990, s 6, Sch 4; those transitory provisions partially ceased to have effect on 2 Jan 1992 (SI 1991/2698), so that on that day para 6(8) of the Schedule to this Act came partially into force

---

Planning (Listed Buildings and Conservation Areas) Act 1990 (c 9)

RA: 24 May 1990

Commencement provisions: s 94(2)

24 Aug 1990 (s 94(2))

See, for transitory provisions, Planning (Consequential Provisions) Act 1990, s 6, Sch 4; those transitory provisions partially ceased to have effect on 2 Jan 1992 (SI 1991/2698), so that on that day, Sch 3, para 6(8) to this Act came partially into force

---

Property Services Agency and Crown Suppliers Act 1990 (c 12)

RA: 29 Jun 1990

29 Jun 1990 (RA)

Representation of the People Act 1990 (c 32)

RA: 26 Jul 1990

Commencement provisions: s 2(2); Representation of the People Act 1990 (Commencement No 1) Order 1991, SI 1991/1244; Representation of the People Act 1990 (Commencement No 2) Order 1991, SI 1991/1686

10 Jun 1991 (EW, S) (SI 1991/1244)

7 Aug 1991 (NI) (SI 1991/1686)

Rights of Way Act 1990 (c 24)

RA: 13 Jul 1990

Commencement provisions: s 6(2)

13 Aug 1990 (s 6(2))

Social Security Act 1990 (c 27)

RA: 13 Jul 1990

Commencement provisions: s 23(2), (3); Social Security Act 1990 (Commencement No 1) Order 1990, SI 1900/1446; Social Security Act 1990 (Commencement No 2) Order 1990, SI 1990/1942; Social Security Act 1990 (Commencement No 3) Order 1991, SI 1991/558; Social Security Act 1990 (Commencement No 4) Order 1992, SI 1992/632; Social Security Act 1990 (Commencement No 5) Order 1992, SI 1992/1532

s 1–5	Repealed
6(1)–(3)	Repealed
(4), (5)	13 Jul 1990 (s 23(2), (3))
7	See Sch 1 below
8–14	Repealed
15(1)–(10)	13 Jul 1990 (s 23(2), (3))
(11)	*Not in force*
16	Repealed
17(1)–(9)	Repealed
(10)	6 Apr 1992 (SI 1992/632)
18–20	13 Jul 1990 (s 23(2), (3))
21(1)	See Sch 6 below
(2)	See Sch 7 below
(3)	13 Jul 1990 (s 23(2), (3))
22	Repealed
23	13 Jul 1990 (s 23(2), (3))

Sch 1, para 1–4	Repealed
5(1), (2)	Repealed
(3)	13 Jul 1990 (s 23(2), (3))
(4)	Repealed
6	Repealed
7	13 Jul 1990 (s 23(2), (3))
2–5	Repealed
6, para 1	Repealed
2	13 Jul 1990 (s 23(2), (3))
3	Repealed
4(1), (2)	Repealed
(3)	13 Jul 1990 (s 23(2), (3))
5–7	Repealed
8(1)	Repealed
(2)	Spent
(3)	Repealed
(4)	13 Jul 1990 (s 23(2), (3))
(5)	Repealed
(6)	Spent
(7), (8)	Repealed
(9), (10)	13 Jul 1990 (s 23(2), (3))
(11)	Repealed
(12)	13 Jul 1990 (s 23(2), (3))
9–12	Repealed
13	13 Jul 1990 (s 23(2), (3))
14–26	Repealed
27	13 Jul 1990 (s 23(2), (3))
28	Repealed

Social Security Act 1990 (c 27)—*cont*

Sch 6, para 29	13 Jul 1990 (so far as consequential on any preceding provision brought into force on 13 Jul 1990) (s 23(2), (3))
	Not in force (otherwise)
30	Repealed
31(a), (b)	Repealed
(c)–(e)	1 Oct 1990 (SI 1990/1942); now superseded
7	13 Jul 1990 (so far as consequential on any preceding provision brought into force on 13 Jul 1990) (s 23(2), (3))
	1 Oct 1990 (repeals of or in Social Security Act 1975, ss 59B(1), (3), (4), (7)(b), (8) and s 152(6); Social Security Pensions Act 1975, ss 33(2), 56B–56D, 56E(1)(c), 56F–56K, 56L(1)(a), (5)(b), (c), 56M, 56N; Social Security and Housing Benefits Act 1982, s 46(3); Social Security Act 1985, s 31(1), Sch 5, para 35; Social Security Act 1986, s 85(4)(a); Social Security Act 1988, s 2(8), (8A); Social Security Act 1989, Sch 1, para 8(3), (4), (7), Sch 2, Pt II, para 1(2), 4(b)) (SI 1990/1942)
	21 Oct 1990 (repeals of or in Social Security Act 1986, s 79) (SI 1990/1942)
	28 Feb 1991 (repeals in Social Security Pensions Act 1975, Sch 1A, paras 1, 2, 11, 12) (SI 1990/1942)
	Not in force (otherwise)

Terms and Quarter Days (Scotland) Act 1990 (c 22)

RA: 13 Jul 1990

Commencement provisions: s 3(2)

s 1(1)–(4)	13 Jul 1991 (s 3(2))
(5), (6)	13 Jul 1990 (RA)
(7)	13 Jul 1991 (s 3(2))
2	13 Jul 1991 (s 3(2))
3	13 Jul 1990 (RA)

Town and Country Planning Act 1990 (c 8)

RA: 24 May 1990

Commencement provisions: s 337(2)

24 Aug 1990 (s 337(2))

See, for transitory provisions, Planning (Consequential Provisions) Act 1990, s 6, Sch 4; those transitory provisions partially ceased to have effect on 2 Jan 1992 (SI 1991/2698), so that on that day, s 322 of, and Sch 6, para 6(5) to, this Act came partially into force

1991

Age of Legal Capacity (Scotland) Act 1991 (c 50)

RA: 25 Jul 1991

Commencement provisions: s 11(2)

25 Sep 1991 (s 11(2))

Agricultural Holdings (Scotland) Act 1991 (c 55)

RA: 25 Jul 1991

Commencement provisions: s 89(2)

25 Sep 1991 (s 89(2))

Agriculture and Forestry (Financial Provisions) Act 1991 (c 33)

RA: 25 Jul 1991

Commencement provisions: ss 1(2)–(5), 5(2); Agricultural Mortgage Corporation (Specified Day for Repeals) Order 1991, SI 1991/1937; Scottish Agricultural Securities Corporation (Specified Day for Repeals) Order 1991, SI 1991/1978

s 1(1)	See Schedule below
(2)–(7)	25 Jul 1991 (RA)
2	25 Sep 1991 (s 5(2))
3–5	25 Jul 1991 (RA)
Schedule,	
Pt I	25 Sep 1991 (SI 1991/1937)
II	25 Sep 1991 (by virtue of s 1(3), SI 1991/1937)
III	25 Sep 1991 (SI 1991/1978)
IV	25 Sep 1991 (by virtue of s 1(5), SI 1991/1978)

Appropriation Act 1991 (c 32)

Whole Act repealed

Armed Forces Act 1991 (c 62)

RA: 25 Jul 1991

Commencement provisions: s 27(2)–(4); Armed Forces Act 1991 (Commencement No 1) Order 1991, SI 1991/2719

s 1	25 Jul 1991 (RA)
2–5	1 Jan 1992 (SI 1991/2719)

Armed Forces Act 1991 (c 62)—*cont*

s 6	1 Jan 1992 (with effect in relation to reception orders made after 31 Dec 1991) (SI 1991/2719)
7–16	1 Jan 1992 (SI 1991/2719)
17–23	*Not in force*
24(1), (2)	1 Jan 1992 (SI 1991/2719)
(3)	*Not in force*
(4), (5)	1 Jan 1992 (SI 1991/2719)
25	25 Jul 1991 (RA)
26(1)	See Sch 2 below
(2)	See Sch 3 below
27	25 Jul 1991 (RA)
Sch 1	1 Jan 1992 (SI 1991/2719)
2, para 1, 2	1 Jan 1992 (SI 1991/2719)
3	Repealed
4–6	1 Jan 1992 (SI 1991/2719)
7	1 Jan 1992 (with effect in relation to offences committed after 31 Dec 1991) (SI 1991/2719)
8	1 Jan 1992 (with effect in relation to appeals lodged after 31 Dec 1991) (SI 1991/2719)
9–11	1 Jan 1992 (SI 1991/2719)
3	1 Jan 1992 (repeal of Armed Forces Act 1986, s 1) (s 27(4))
	1 Jan 1992 (repeals of or in Naval and Marine Pay and Pensions Act 1865, ss 4, 5; Naval Forces (Enforcement of Maintenance Liabilities) Act 1947, ss 1(3), (5), 2; Army Act 1955, ss 71A(1B)(a), 71AA(1), (1A), (2), 93, 122(1), 127(2), 131(1), 145(1)(b), 150(1)(a), (5), 225(1), Sch 5A, paras 2, 6–9, 10(1A), 11(4), 15(3); Air Force Act 1955, ss 71A(1B)(a), 71AA(1), (1A), (2), 93, 122(1), 127(2), 131(1), 145(1)(b), 150(1)(a), (5), 223(1), Sch 5A, paras 2, 6–9, 10(1A), 11(4), 15(3); Naval Discipline Act 1957, ss 43A(1B)(a), 43AA, 60, 129(2), Sch 4A, paras 2, 69, 10(1A), 11(4), 15(3); Courts-Martial (Appeals) Act 1968; Rehabilitation of Offenders Act 1974; Rehabilitation of Offenders (Northern Ireland) Order 1978; Reserve Forces Act 1980; Reserve Forces Act 1982; Armed Forces Act 1986, Sch 1, para 12(3), (5); Children Act 1989) (SI 1991/2719)
	Not in force (otherwise)

Arms Control and Disarmament (Inspections) Act 1991 (c 41)

RA: 25 Jul 1991

Commencement provisions: s 6(2); Arms Control and Disarmament (Inspections) Act 1991 (Commencement) Order 1992, SI 1992/1750

s 1–5	17 Jul 1992 (SI 1992/1750)
6	25 Jul 1991 (RA)
Schedule	17 Jul 1992 (SI 1992/1750)

Atomic Weapons Establishment Act 1991 (c 46)

RA: 25 Jul 1991

Commencement provisions: s 6(2)

25 Sep 1991 (s 6(2))

Badgers Act 1991 (c 36)

Whole Act repealed

Badgers (Further Protection) Act 1991 (c 35)

Whole Act repealed

Breeding of Dogs Act 1991 (c 64)

RA: 25 Jul 1991

Commencement provisions: s 3(2)

25 Sep 1991 (s 3(2))

British Railways Board (Finance) Act 1991 (c 63)

RA: 25 Jul 1991

25 Jul 1991 (RA)

British Technology Group Act 1991 (c 66)

RA: 22 Oct 1991

Commencement provisions: ss 1(1), 11(2), 18(2)–(4); British Technology Group Act 1991 (Appointed Day) Order 1991, SI 1991/2721

s 1(1)–(5)	22 Oct 1991 (s 18(3))
(6)	See Sch 1 below
2	22 Oct 1991 (s 18(3))
3–6	6 Jan 1992 (ss 1(1), 18(2); SI 1991/2721)
7	22 Oct 1991 (s 18(3))
8–13	6 Jan 1992 (ss 1(1), 18(2); SI 1991/2721)
14	22 Oct 1991 (s 18(3))
15	6 Jan 1992 (ss 1(1), 18(2); SI 1991/2721)
16(1)	22 Oct 1991 (s 18(3))
(2)	6 Jan 1992 (ss 1(1), 18(2); SI 1991/2721)
17(1)	6 Jan 1992 (ss 1(1), 18(2); SI 1991/2721)
(2)	See Sch 2 below
(3)	See Sch 3 below
18	22 Oct 1991 (s 18(3))
Sch 1, para 1	22 Oct 1991 (s 18(3))
2–5	6 Jan 1992 (ss 1(1), 18(2); SI 1991/2721)
2, Pt I	6 Jan 1992 (ss 1(1), 18(2); SI 1991/2721)
II, III	*Not in force*
3	6 Jan 1992 (ss 1(1), 18(2); SI 1991/2721)

Caravans (Standard Community Charge and Rating) Act 1991 (c 2)

RA: 12 Feb 1991

12 Feb 1991 (RA)

Care of Churches and Ecclesiastical Jurisdiction Measure 1991 (No 1)

RA: 25 Jul 1991

Commencement provisions: s 33(2)

1 Mar 1993 (the day appointed by the Archbishops of Canterbury and York under s 33(2))

Census (Confidentiality) Act 1991 (c 6)

RA: 7 Mar 1991

7 Mar 1991 (RA)

Child Support Act 1991 (c 48)

RA: 25 Jul 1991

Commencement provisions: s 58(2)–(7); Child Support Act 1991 (Commencement No 1) Order 1992, SI 1992/1431; Child Support Act 1991 (Commencement No 2) Order 1992, SI 1992/1938; Child Support Act 1991 (Commencement No 3 and Transitional Provisions) Order 1992, SI 1992/2644, as amended by SI 1993/966; Child Support Act 1991 (Commencement No 3 and Transitional Provisions) (Amendment) Order 1993, SI 1993/966 (amending SI 1992/2644, Schedule, which contains transitional provisions)

s 1, 2	5 Apr 1993 (SI 1992/2644)
3(1), (2)	5 Apr 1993 (SI 1992/2644)
(3)(a), (b)	5 Apr 1993 (SI 1992/2644)
(c)	17 Jun 1992 (SI 1992/1431)
(4)–(7)	5 Apr 1993 (SI 1992/2644)
4(1)–(3)	5 Apr 1993 (subject to transitional provisions) (SI 1992/2644, as amended by SI 1993/966)
(4)	17 Jun 1992 (SI 1992/1431)
(5), (6)	5 Apr 1993 (subject to transitional provisions) (SI 1992/2644, as amended by SI 1993/966)
(7), (8)	17 Jun 1992 (SI 1992/1431)
(9)	5 Apr 1993 (subject to transitional provisions) (SI 1992/2644, as amended by SI 1993/966)
(10), (11)	Added by Child Support Act 1995, s 18(1) (qv)
5(1), (2)	5 Apr 1993 (SI 1992/2644)
(3)	17 Jun 1992 (SI 1992/1431)
6(1)	17 Jun 1992 (so far as confers power to prescribe kinds of benefit for purposes of s 6(1)) (SI 1992/1431) 5 Apr 1993 (otherwise) (SI 1992/2644)
(2)–(8)	5 Apr 1993 (SI 1992/2644)
(9), (10)	17 Jun 1992 (SI 1992/1431)
(11), (12)	5 Apr 1993 (SI 1992/2644)
(13)	17 Jun 1992 (SI 1992/1431)

Child Support Act 1991 (c 48)—*cont*

s 6(14)	5 Apr 1993 (SI 1992/2644)
7(1)–(4)	5 Apr 1993 (subject to transitional provisions) (SI 1992/2644, as amended by SI 1993/966)
(5)	17 Jun 1992 (SI 1992/1431)
(6), (7)	5 Apr 1993 (subject to transitional provisions) (SI 1992/2644, as amended by SI 1993/966)
(8), (9)	17 Jun 1992 (SI 1992/1431)
(10)	Added by Child Support Act 1995, s 18(2) (qv)
8(1)–(3)	5 Apr 1993 (subject to transitional provisions) (SI 1992/2644, as amended by SI 1993/966)
(3A)	Inserted by Child Support Act 1995, s 18(3) (qv)
(4)	5 Apr 1993 (subject to transitional provisions) (SI 1992/2644, as amended by SI 1993/966)
(5)	17 Jun 1992 (SI 1992/1431)
(6)–(8)	5 Apr 1993 (SI 1992/2644)
(9)	17 Jun 1992 (SI 1992/1431)
(10)	5 Apr 1993 (SI 1992/2644)
(11)(a)–(e)	5 Apr 1993 (SI 1992/2644)
(f)	17 Jun 1992 (SI 1992/1431)
9	5 Apr 1993 (subject to transitional provisions) (SI 1992/2644, as amended by SI 1993/966)
10	17 Jun 1992 (SI 1992/1431)
11(1)	5 Apr 1993 (SI 1992/2644)
(1A)–(1C)	Inserted by Child Support Act 1995, s 19 (qv)
(2), (3)	See Sch 1 below
12(1), (1A)	Substituted (for sub-s (1)) by Child Support Act 1995, s 11 (qv)
(2), (3)	17 Jun 1992 (SI 1992/1431)
(4)	5 Apr 1993 (SI 1992/2644)
(5)	17 Jun 1992 (SI 1992/1431)
13	1 Sep 1992 (SI 1992/1938)
14(1)	17 Jun 1992 (SI 1992/1431)
(1A)	Inserted by Child Support Act 1995, s 30(5), Sch 3, paras 2, 3(1) (qv)
(2)	5 Apr 1993 (SI 1992/2644)
(2A)	Inserted by Child Support Act 1995, s 30(5), Sch 3, paras 2, 3(2) (qv)
(3)	17 Jun 1992 (SI 1992/1431)
(4)	See Sch 2 below
15	5 Apr 1993 (SI 1992/2644)
16(1), (2)	17 Jun 1992 (SI 1992/1431)
(3), (4)	5 Apr 1993 (subject to transitional provisions) (SI 1992/2644)
(5), (6)	17 Jun 1992 (SI 1992/1431)
17(1), (2)	5 Apr 1993 (subject to transitional provisions) (SI 1992/2644)
(2A)	Inserted by Child Support Act 1995, s 12(1), (2) (qv)
(3)	5 Apr 1993 (subject to transitional provisions) (SI 1992/2644)
(4)	17 Jun 1992 (SI 1992/1431)
(4A)	Inserted by Child Support Act 1995, s 12(1), (4) (qv)
(5)	Substituted by Child Support Act 1995, s 12(1), (5) (qv)
(6)(a)	5 Apr 1993 (subject to transitional provisions) (SI 1992/2644)
(b)	17 Jun 1992 (SI 1992/1431)
(7), (8)	Added by Child Support Act 1995, s 12(1), (7) (qv)

Child Support Act 1991 (c 48)—*cont*

s 18(1)–(6)	5 Apr 1993 (subject to transitional provisions) (SI 1992/2644)
(6A)	Inserted by Child Support Act 1995, s 13 (qv)
(7)	5 Apr 1993 (subject to transitional provisions) (SI 1992/2644)
(8)	17 Jun 1992 (SI 1992/1431)
(9), (10)	5 Apr 1993 (subject to transitional provisions) (SI 1992/2644)
(10A)	Inserted by Child Support Act 1995, s 14(1) (qv)
(11)	17 Jun 1992 (SI 1992/1431)
(12)	5 Apr 1993 (subject to transitional provisions) (SI 1992/2644)
19	Substituted by Child Support Act 1995, s 15 (qv)
20	5 Apr 1993 (SI 1992/2644)
20A	Inserted by Child Support Act 1995, s 16 (qv)
21(1)	1 Sep 1992 (SI 1992/1938)
(2), (3)	17 Jun 1992 (SI 1992/1431)
(4)	See Sch 3 below
22(1), (2)	1 Sep 1992 (SI 1992/1938)
(3), (4)	17 Jun 1992 (SI 1992/1431)
(5)	See Sch 4 below
23	1 Sep 1992 (SI 1992/1938)
24(1)	5 Apr 1993 (SI 1992/2644)
(1A)	Prospectively inserted by Child Support Act 1995, s 30(5), Sch 3, paras 2, 7(1), (2)[1]
(2)–(5)	5 Apr 1993 (SI 1992/2644)
(6), (7)	17 Jun 1992 (SI 1992/1431)
(8)	5 Apr 1993 (SI 1992/2644)
(9)	1 Sep 1992 (SI 1992/1938)
25(1)	5 Apr 1993 (SI 1992/2644)
(2)(a)	17 Jun 1992 (SI 1992/1431)
(b)	5 Apr 1993 (SI 1992/2644)
(3)(a), (b)	5 Apr 1993 (SI 1992/2644)
(c)	17 Jun 1992 (SI 1992/1431)
(3A), (3B)	Inserted by Child Support Act 1995, s 30(5), Sch 3, paras 2, 8(1) (qv)
(4)	5 Apr 1993 (SI 1992/2644)
(5), (6)	17 Jun 1992 (SI 1992/1431)
26, 27	5 Apr 1993 (SI 1992/2644)
27A	Inserted by Child Support Act 1995, s 21 (qv)
28	5 Apr 1993 (SI 1992/2644)
28A–28H	Prospectively inserted by Child Support Act 1995, ss 1(1), 2-5, 6(1), 7, 8[1]
28I(1)–(3)	Prospectively inserted by Child Support Act 1995, s 9[1]
(4)	Inserted by Child Support Act 1995, s 9 (qv)
(5)	Prospectively inserted by Child Support Act 1995, s 9[1]
29(1)	5 Apr 1993 (SI 1992/2644)
(2), (3)	17 Jun 1992 (SI 1992/1431)
30(1)	17 Jun 1992 (SI 1992/1431)
(2)	*Not in force*
(3)	5 Apr 1993 (SI 1992/2644)
(4), (5)	17 Jun 1992 (SI 1992/1431)
(5A)	Prospectively added by Child Support Act 1995, s 30(5), Sch 3, paras 2, 9[1]
31(1)–(7)	5 Apr 1993 (SI 1992/2644)

Child Support Act 1991 (c 48)—*cont*

s 31(8)	17 Jun 1992 (SI 1992/1431)
32(1)–(5)	17 Jun 1992 (SI 1992/1431)
(6)	5 Apr 1993 (SI 1992/2644)
(7)–(9)	17 Jun 1992 (SI 1992/1431)
(10)–(11)	5 Apr 1993 (SI 1992/2644)
33	5 Apr 1993 (SI 1992/2644)
34(1)	17 Jun 1992 (SI 1992/1431)
(2)	*Not in force*
35(1)	5 Apr 1993 (SI 1992/2644)
(2)(a)	5 Apr 1993 (SI 1992/2644)
(b)	17 Jun 1992 (SI 1992/1431)
(3)–(6)	5 Apr 1993 (SI 1992/2644)
(7), (8)	17 Jun 1992 (SI 1992/1431)
36	5 Apr 1993 (SI 1992/2644)
37(1)	5 Apr 1993 (SI 1992/2644)
(2), (3)	*Not in force*
38	5 Apr 1993 (SI 1992/2644)
39	17 Jun 1992 (SI 1992/1431)
40(1)–(3)	5 Apr 1993 (SI 1992/2644)
(4)(a)(i)	5 Apr 1993 (SI 1992/2644)
(ii)	17 Jun 1992 (SI 1992/1431)
(b)	5 Apr 1993 (SI 1992/2644)
(5)–(7)	5 Apr 1993 (SI 1992/2644)
(8)	17 Jun 1992 (SI 1992/1431)
(9), (10)	5 Apr 1993 (SI 1992/2644)
(11)	17 Jun 1992 (SI 1992/1431)
(12)–(14)	5 Apr 1993 (SI 1992/2644)
41(1)	5 Apr 1993 (SI 1992/2644)
(2), (2A)	Substituted (for sub-s (2)) by Child Support Act 1995, s 30(5), Sch 3, paras 2, 11 (qv)
(3), (4)	17 Jun 1992 (SI 1992/1431)
(5), (6)	5 Apr 1993 (SI 1992/2644)
41A	Prospectively inserted by Child Support Act 1995, s 22[1]
41B	Inserted by Child Support Act 1995, s 23 (qv)
42	17 Jun 1992 (SI 1992/1431)
43(1)(a)	5 Apr 1993 (SI 1992/2644)
(b)	17 Jun 1992 (SI 1992/1431)
(2)(a)	17 Jun 1992 (SI 1992/1431)
(b)	5 Apr 1993 (SI 1992/2644)
44(1), (2)	5 Apr 1993 (SI 1992/2644)
(3)	17 Jun 1992 (SI 1992/1431)
45	17 Jun 1992 (SI 1992/1431)
46(1)–(10)	5 Apr 1993 (SI 1992/2644)
(11)	17 Jun 1992 (SI 1992/1431)
47	17 Jun 1992 (SI 1992/1431)
48	5 Apr 1993 (SI 1992/2644)
49	17 Jun 1992 (SI 1992/1431)
50(1)–(4)	5 Apr 1993 (SI 1992/2644)
(5)	17 Jun 1992 (SI 1992/1431)
(6)	5 Apr 1993 (SI 1992/2644)
(7)(a)–(c)	5 Apr 1993 (SI 1992/2644)
(d)	17 Jun 1992 (SI 1992/1431)
(8)	5 Apr 1993 (SI 1992/2644)
51, 52	17 Jun 1992 (SI 1992/1431)
53	5 Apr 1993 (SI 1992/2644)
54, 55	17 Jun 1992 (SI 1992/1431)

Child Support Act 1991 (c 48)—*cont*

s 56(1)	25 Jul 1991 (s 58(2))
(2)–(4)	17 Jun 1992 (SI 1992/1431)
57	17 Jun 1992 (SI 1992/1431)
58(1)–(11)	25 Jul 1991 (s 58(2))
(12)	*Not in force*
(13)	See Sch 5 below
(14)	25 Jul 1991 (s 58(2))
Sch 1, para 1(1), (2)	5 Apr 1993 (SI 1992/2644)
(3)	17 Jun 1992 (SI 1992/1431)
(4)	5 Apr 1993 (SI 1992/2644)
(5)	17 Jun 1992 (SI 1992/1431)
2(1)	17 Jun 1992 (SI 1992/1431)
(2), (3)	5 Apr 1993 (SI 1992/2644)
3	5 Apr 1993 (SI 1992/2644)
4(1)	17 Jun 1992 (SI 1992/1431)
(2)	5 Apr 1993 (SI 1992/2644)
(3)	17 Jun 1992 (SI 1992/1431)
5(1), (2)	17 Jun 1992 (SI 1992/1431)
(3)	5 Apr 1993 (SI 1992/2644)
(4)	17 Jun 1992 (SI 1992/1431)
6(1)	5 Apr 1993 (SI 1992/2644)
(2)–(6)	17 Jun 1992 (SI 1992/1431)
(7)–(11)	5 Apr 1993 (SI 1992/2644)
7–9	17 Jun 1992 (SI 1992/1431)
10	5 Apr 1993 (SI 1992/2644)
11	17 Jun 1992 (SI 1992/1431)
12, 13	5 Apr 1993 (SI 1992/2644)
14	17 Jun 1992 (SI 1992/1431)
15	5 Apr 1993 (SI 1992/2644)
16(1)–(4)	5 Apr 1993 (SI 1992/2644)
(4A)	Inserted by Child Support Act 1995, s 14(2) (qv)
(5)	17 Jun 1992 (SI 1992/1431)
(6)–(9)	5 Apr 1993 (SI 1992/2644)
(10), (11)	17 Jun 1992 (SI 1992/1431)
2, para 1	5 Apr 1993 (SI 1992/2644)
2(1)–(3)	5 Apr 1993 (SI 1992/2644)
(4)	17 Jun 1992 (SI 1992/1431)
3, para 1, 2	1 Sep 1992 (SI 1992/1938)
3(1), (2)	1 Sep 1992 (SI 1992/1938)
(3)	17 Jun 1992 (SI 1992/1431)
4–8	1 Sep 1992 (SI 1992/1938)
4	1 Sep 1992 (SI 1992/1938)
4A	Prospectively inserted by Child Support Act 1995, s 1(2), Sch 1[1]
4B	Prospectively inserted by Child Support Act 1995, s 6(2), Sch 2[1]
5, para 1	Repealed
2–4	1 Sep 1992 (SI 1992/1938)
5–8	5 Apr 1993 (SI 1992/2644)

[1] Orders made under Child Support Act 1995, s 30(4), bringing the prospective amendments into force will be noted to that Act in the service to this work

Children and Young Persons (Protection from Tobacco) Act 1991 (c 23)

RA: 27 Jun 1991

Commencement provisions: s 8(2); Children and Young Persons (Protection from Tobacco) Act 1991 (Commencement No 1) Order 1991, SI 1991/2500; Children and Young Persons (Protection from Tobacco) Act 1991 (Commencement No 2) Order 1992, SI 1992/332; Children and Young Persons (Protection from Tobacco) Act 1991 (Commencement No 3) Order 1992, SI 1992/3227

s 1–3	1 Mar 1992 (SI 1992/332)
4(1), (2)	20 Feb 1993 (SI 1992/3227)
(3)	17 Dec 1992 (SI 1992/3227)
(4)–(8)	20 Feb 1993 (SI 1992/3227)
(9)	17 Dec 1992 (SI 1992/3227)
5–7	1 Mar 1992 (SI 1992/332)
8(1)	1 Mar 1992 (SI 1992/332)
(2)	27 Jun 1991 (RA)
(3)–(5)	1 Mar 1992 (SI 1992/332)
(6), (7)	11 Nov 1991 (NI) (SI 1992/2500)
	1 Mar 1992 (otherwise) (SI 1992/332)

Civil Jurisdiction and Judgments Act 1991 (c 12)

RA: 9 May 1991

Commencement provisions: s 5(3); Civil Jurisdiction and Judgments Act 1991 (Commencement) Order 1992, SI 1992/745

1 May 1992 (SI 1992/745)

Coal Mining Subsidence Act 1991 (c 45)

RA: 25 Jul 1991

Commencement provisions: s 54(2), (3); Coal Mining Subsidence Act 1991 (Commencement) Order 1991, SI 1991/2508 30 Nov 1991 (subject to transitional provision with respect to s 34(1)(a)) (SI 1991/2508)

Community Charges (General Reduction) Act 1991 (c 9)

RA: 28 Mar 1991

28 Mar 1991 (RA)

Community Charges (Substitute Setting) Act 1991 (c 8)

Whole Act repealed

Consolidated Fund Act 1991 (c 7)

Whole Act repealed

Consolidated Fund (No 2) Act 1991 (c 10)

Whole Act repealed

Consolidated Fund (No 3) Act 1991 (c 68)

Whole Act repealed

Criminal Justice Act 1991 (c 53)

RA: 25 Jul 1991

Commencement provisions: s 102(2), (3); Criminal Justice Act 1991 (Commencement No 1) Order 1991, SI 1991/2208; Criminal Justice Act 1991 (Commencement No 2 and Transitional Provisions) Order 1991, SI 1991/2706; Criminal Justice Act 1991 (Commencement No 3) Order 1992, SI 1992/333 (as amended by SI 1992/2118); Criminal Justice Act 1991 (Commencement No 3 (Amendment) and Transitional Provisions and Savings) (Scotland) Order 1992, SI 1992/2118 (amending SI 1992/333); Criminal Justice Act 1991 (Commencement No 4) Order 1994, SI 1994/3191

s 1–7	1 Oct 1992 (SI 1992/333)
8(1), (2)	1 Oct 1992 (SI 1992/333)
(3)(a)	See Sch 1, Pt I below
(b)–(d)	1 Oct 1992 (SI 1992/333)
9(1)	1 Oct 1992 (SI 1992/333)
(2)	See Sch 1, Pt II below
10, 11	1 Oct 1992 (SI 1992/333)
12, 13	9 Jan 1995 (SI 1994/3191)
14(1)	See Sch 2 below
(2)	1 Oct 1992 (SI 1992/333)
15, 16	1 Oct 1992 (SI 1992/333)
17	1 Oct 1992 (but does not apply in relation to any offence committed before 1 Oct 1992) (SI 1992/333, as amended by SI 1992/2118)
18	Substituted by Criminal Justice Act 1993, s 65(1) (qv)
19	Repealed
20	1 Oct 1992 (SI 1992/333)
20A	Inserted by Criminal Justice and Public Order Act 1994, s 168(1), Sch 9, para 43 (qv)
21	Substituted by Criminal Justice Act 1993, s 65(3), Sch 3, para 3 (qv)
22	Repealed
23–25	1 Oct 1992 (SI 1992/333)
26(1), (2)	1 Oct 1992 (SI 1992/333)
(3)	Repealed
(4), (5)	31 Oct 1991 (SI 1991/2208)
27, 28	1 Oct 1992 (SI 1992/333)
29	Substituted by Criminal Justice Act 1993, s 66(6) (qv)
30, 31	1 Oct 1992 (SI 1992/333)
32(1)	1 Oct 1992 (SI 1992/333); prospectively substituted by Criminal Justice and Public Order Act 1994, s 149[1]
(2)–(6)	1 Oct 1992 (SI 1992/333)
(7)	See Sch 5 below
33–52	1 Oct 1992 (SI 1992/333)
53(1)–(4)	1 Oct 1992 (SI 1992/333)

Criminal Justice Act 1991 (c 53)—*cont*

s 53(5)	See Sch 6 below
(6), (7)	1 Oct 1992 (SI 1992/333)
54–59	1 Oct 1992 (SI 1992/333)
60(1)	1 Oct 1992 (SI 1992/333)
(2)(a)	1 Oct 1992 (SI 1992/333)
(b), (c)	*Not in force* (due to come into force on day appointed by order made by Secretary of State under s 62(1)) (SI 1992/333)
(3)	14 Oct 1991 (SI 1991/2208)
61	1 Oct 1992 (SI 1992/333)
61A	Prospectively inserted by Criminal Justice and Public Order Act 1994, s 21[1]
62, 63	1 Oct 1992 (SI 1992/333)
64	Repealed
65	1 Oct 1992 (SI 1992/333)
66	See Sch 7 below
67	1 Oct 1992 (SI 1992/333)
68	See Sch 8 below
69, 70	1 Oct 1992 (SI 1992/333)
71	See Sch 9 below
72	1 Oct 1992 (SI 1992/333)
73–75	Repealed
76–78	1 Apr 1992 (SI 1992/333)
79	1 Apr 1992 (SI 1992/333); repealed, partly prospectively, by Police and Magistrates' Courts Act 1994, s 93, Sch 9, Pt II (qv)
80–82	31 Oct 1991 (SI 1991/2208)
83, 84	Substituted by Criminal Justice and Public Order Act 1994, ss 95, 96 (qv)
85–88	31 Oct 1991 (SI 1991/2208)
88A	Inserted by Criminal Justice and Public Order Act 1994, s 99 (qv)
89(1)	31 Oct 1991 (SI 1991/2208)
(2)	See Sch 10 below
(3)	31 Oct 1991 (SI 1991/2208)
90, 91	31 Oct 1991 (SI 1991/2208)
92(1)	31 Oct 1991 (SI 1991/2208)
(1A)	Inserted by Criminal Justice and Public Order Act 1994, s 98 (qv)
(2)	1 Apr 1992 (SI 1992/333)
(3)	*Not in force* (due to come into force on day appointed by order made by Secretary of State under s 62(1)) (SI 1992/333)
(4)	Added by Criminal Justice and Public Order Act 1994, s 93(7) (qv)
93	31 Oct 1991 (SI 1991/2208)
94	Repealed
95	31 Oct 1991 (SI 1991/2208)
96, 97	Repealed
98	31 Oct 1991 (SI 1991/2208)
99(1)	14 Oct 1991 (except definitions 'child' and 'young person') (SI 1991/2208) 1 Oct 1992 (exceptions noted above) (SI 1992/333)
(2)	1 Oct 1992 (SI 1992/333)
100	See Sch 11 below
101(1)	See Sch 12 below
(2)	See Sch 13 below

Criminal Justice Act 1991 (c 53)—*cont*

s 102	14 Oct 1991 (SI 1991/2208)
Sch 1–4	1 Oct 1992 (SI 1992/333)
5	1 Oct 1992 (SI 1992/333); prospectively substituted by Criminal Justice and Public Order Act 1994, s 168(2), Sch 10, para 70[1]
6, 7	1 Oct 1992 (SI 1992/333)
8, para 1(1)	*Not in force*
(2)	1 Oct 1992 (SI 1992/333)
(3)	1 Oct 1992 (except to the extent that would otherwise apply to Children and Young Persons Act 1933, s 34) (SI 1992/333)
	Not in force (exception noted above)
2–6	1 Oct 1992 (SI 1992/333)
9	1 Oct 1992 (SI 1992/333)
10	31 Oct 1991 (SI 1991/2208)
11, para 1	1 Oct 1992 (SI 1992/333)
2(1)	1 Oct 1992 (SI 1992/333)
(2)(a)	1 Oct 1992 (SI 1992/333)
(b)	*Not in force* (due to come into force on day appointed by order made by Secretary of State under s 62(1)) (SI 1992/333)
(3)	1 Oct 1992 (SI 1992/333)
(4)(a), (b)	1 Oct 1992 (SI 1992/333)
(c)	*Not in force* (due to come into force on day appointed by order made by Secretary of State under s 62(1)) (SI 1992/333)
3–8	1 Oct 1992 (SI 1992/333)
9	Repealed
10–16	1 Oct 1992 (SI 1992/333)
17	Repealed
18	1 Apr 1992 (SI 1992/333)
19–23	1 Oct 1992 (SI 1992/333)
24	Repealed
25–28	1 Oct 1992 (SI 1992/333)
29	1 Apr 1992 (SI 1992/333)
30–35	1 Oct 1992 (SI 1992/333)
36	14 Oct 1991 (SI 1991/2208)
37–41	1 Oct 1992 (SI 1992/333)
12, para 1–6	1 Oct 1992 (SI 1992/333)
7	25 Oct 1991 (SI 1991/2208)
8–14	1 Oct 1992 (SI 1992/333)
15(1), (2)	1 Oct 1992 (SI 1992/333)
(3)–(5)	*Not in force* (due to come into force on day appointed by order made by Secretary of State under s 62(1)) (SI 1992/333)
16(1)	1 Oct 1992 (SI 1992/333)
(2)–(4)	*Not in force* (due to come into force on day appointed by order made by Secretary of State under s 62(1)) (SI 1992/333)
17–22	1 Oct 1992 (SI 1992/333)
23	14 Oct 1991 (SI 1991/2208)
24	1 Oct 1992 (SI 1992/333)
13	31 Oct 1991 (repeal of Metropolitan Police Act 1839, s 11) (SI 1991/2208)
	1 Oct 1992 (otherwise, except repeal in Criminal Justice Act 1967, s 67(6)) (SI 1992/333)

Criminal Justice Act 1991 (c 53)—*cont*

Sch 13—*cont*	*Not in force* (exception noted above) (due to come into force on day appointed by order made by Secretary of State under s 62(1)) (SI 1992/333)

[1] Orders made under Criminal Justice and Public Order Act 1994, s 172, bringing the prospective amendments into force will be noted to that Act in the service to this work

---

Criminal Procedure (Insanity and Unfitness to Plead) Act 1991 (c 25)

RA: 27 Jun 1991

Commencement provisions: s 9(2); Criminal Procedure (Insanity and Unfitness to Plead) Act 1991 (Commencement) Order 1991, SI 1991/2488 1 Jan 1992 (SI 1991/2488)

Crofter Forestry (Scotland) Act 1991 (c 18)

Whole Act repealed

Dangerous Dogs Act 1991 (c 65)

RA: 25 Jul 1991

Commencement provisions: s 10(4); Dangerous Dogs Act 1991 (Commencement and Appointed Day) Order 1991, SI 1991/1742

s 1–7	12 Aug 1991 (SI 1991/1742)
8	25 Jul 1991 (s 10(4))
9, 10	12 Aug 1991 (SI 1991/1742)

Deer Act 1991 (c 54)

RA: 25 Jul 1991

Commencement provisions: s 18(3)

25 Oct 1991 (s 18(3))

Development Board for Rural Wales Act 1991 (c 1)

RA: 12 Feb 1991

12 Feb 1991 (RA)

Diocesan Boards of Education Measure 1991 (No 2)

RA: 12 Jul 1991

Commencement provisions: s 13(3)

1 Aug 1991 (the day appointed by the Archbishops of Canterbury and York under s 13(3))

Disability Living Allowance and Disability Working Allowance Act 1991 (c 21)

RA: 27 Jun 1991

Commencement provisions: s 15(2), (3); Disability Living Allowance and Disability Working Allowance Act 1991 (Commencement No 1) Order 1991, SI 1991/1519; Disability Living Allowance and Disability Working Allowance Act 1991 (Commencement No 2) Order 1991, SI 1991/2617

s 1	Repealed
2(1)	Repealed
(2), (3)	6 Apr 1992 (SI 1991/2617)
3	Repealed
4(1)	Repealed
(2)	See Sch 2 below
5, 6	Repealed
7(1)	Repealed
(2)	See Sch 3 below
8, 9	Repealed
10	See Sch 4 below
11–14	Repealed
15	27 Jun 1991 (s 15(2), (3))
Sch 1	Repealed
2, para 1–5	Repealed
6, 7	3 Feb 1992 (for purposes of making claims for, and determination of claims and questions relating to, disability living allowance, or for purposes of making by persons who will have attained the age of 65 on 6 Apr 1992 of claims for, and determination of claims and questions relating to, attendance allowance) (SI 1991/2617) 6 Apr 1992 (otherwise) (SI 1991/2617)
8–11	Repealed
12	3 Feb 1992 (for purposes noted to Sch 2, paras 6, 7 above) (SI 1991/2617)
13	Repealed
14	3 Feb 1992 (for purposes noted to Sch 2, paras 6, 7 above) (SI 1991/2617) 6 Apr 1992 (otherwise) (SI 1991/2617)
15–17	Repealed
18	3 Feb 1992 (for purposes noted to Sch 2, paras 6, 7 above) (SI 1991/2617) 6 Apr 1992 (otherwise) (SI 1991/2617)
19	Repealed
20, 21	3 Feb 1992 (for purposes noted to Sch 2, paras 6, 7 above) (SI 1991/2617) 6 Apr 1992 (otherwise) (SI 1991/2617)
22	3 Feb 1992 (for purposes noted to Sch 2, paras 6, 7 above) (SI 1991/2617) 6 Apr 1992 (otherwise) (SI 1992/2617)
3, Pt I, para 1–8	Repealed
II, para 9–15	19 Nov 1991 (for purposes of making regulations expressed to come into force on or after 3 Feb 1992) (SI 1991/2617) 10 Mar 1992 (for purposes of making claims for, and determination of claims and questions

Disability Living Allowance and Disability Working Allowance Act 1991 (c 21)—*cont*

Sch 3, Pt II, para 9–15—*cont*	relation to, disability working allowance) (SI 1991/2617)
	6 Apr 1992 (otherwise) (SI 1991/2617)
4	6 Apr 1992 (SI 1991/2617)

Export and Investment Guarantees Act 1991 (c 67)

RA: 22 Oct 1991

Commencement provisions: s 15(6); Export and Investment Guarantees Act 1991 (Commencement) Order 1991, SI 1991/2430

23 Oct 1991 (SI 1991/2430)

Finance Act 1991 (c 31)

RA: 25 Jul 1991

See the note concerning Finance Acts at the front of this book

---

Football (Offences) Act 1991 (c 19)

RA: 27 Jun 1991

Commencement provisions: s 6(2); Football (Offences) Act 1991 (Commencement) Order 1991, SI 1991/1564

10 Aug 1991 (SI 1991/1564)

Foreign Corporations Act 1991 (c 44)

RA: 25 Jul 1991

Commencement provisions: s 2(3)

25 Sep 1991 (s 2(3))

Forestry Act 1991 (c 43)

RA: 25 Jul 1991

Commencement provisions: s 2(2)

25 Sep 1991 (s 2(2))

Land Drainage Act 1991 (c 59)

RA: 25 Jul 1991

Commencement provisions: s 76(2)

1 Dec 1991 (s 76(2))

Local Government Finance and Valuation Act 1991 (c 51)

Whole Act repealed

Local Government Finance (Publicity for Auditors' Reports) Act 1991 (c 15)

RA: 27 Jun 1991

Commencement provisions: s 2(2)

27 Aug 1991 (s 2(2))

Maintenance Enforcement Act 1991 (c 17)

RA: 27 Jun 1991

Commencement provisions: s 12(2); Maintenance Enforcement Act 1991 (Commencement No 1) Order 1991, SI 1991/2042; Maintenance Enforcement Act 1991 (Commencement No 2) Order 1992, SI 1992/455

s 1–8	1 Apr 1992 (SI 1992/455)
9	Repealed
10	See Sch 1 below
11(1)	See Sch 2 below
(2)	See Sch 3 below
12	27 Jun 1991 (RA)
Sch 1, para 1–14	1 Apr 1992 (SI 1992/455)
15–17	Repealed
18, 19	1 Apr 1992 (SI 1992/455)
20	Repealed
21	1 Apr 1992 (SI 1992/455)
2, para 1–10	1 Apr 1992 (SI 1992/455)
11	14 Oct 1991 (SI 1991/2042)
3	1 Apr 1992 (SI 1992/455)

Medical Qualifications (Amendment) Act 1991 (c 38)

RA: 25 Jul 1991

Commencement provisions: s 2(2); Medical Qualifications (Amendment) Act 1991 (Commencement) Order 1992, SI 1992/804

s 1	30 Mar 1992 (SI 1992/804)
2	25 Jul 1991 (RA)

Mental Health (Detention) (Scotland) Act 1991 (c 47)

RA: 25 Jul 1991

Commencement provisions: s 4(2); Mental Health (Detention) (Scotland) Act 1991 (Commencement) Order 1992, SI 1992/357

9 Mar 1992 (SI 1992/357)

Ministerial and other Pensions and Salaries Act 1991 (c 5)

RA: 28 Feb 1991

28 Feb 1991 (RA)

Motor Vehicles (Safety Equipment for Children) Act 1991 (c 14)

RA: 27 Jun 1991

27 Jun 1991 (RA)

Namibia Act 1991 (c 4)

RA: 28 Feb 1991

Commencement provisions: s 2(2)

21 Mar 1990 (s 2(2))

Natural Heritage (Scotland) Act 1991 (c 28)

RA: 27 Jun 1991

Commencement provisions: s 28(2); Natural Heritage (Scotland) Act 1991 (Commencement No 1) Order 1991, SI 1991/2187; Natural Heritage (Scotland) Act 1991 (Commencement No 2) Order 1991, SI 1991/2633

s 1	27 Nov 1991 (SI 1991/2633)
2(1)	27 Nov 1991 (SI 1991/2633)
(2)	1 Apr 1992 (SI 1991/2633)
3	27 Nov 1991 (SI 1991/2633)
4–7	1 Apr 1992 (SI 1991/2633)
8	27 Nov 1991 (SI 1991/2633)
9	1 Apr 1992 (SI 1991/2633)
10, 11	27 Nov 1991 (SI 1991/2633)
12, 13	1 Apr 1992 (SI 1991/2633)
14(1), (2)	27 Nov 1991 (SI 1991/2633)
(3), (4)	1 Apr 1992 (SI 1991/2633)
(5)	27 Nov 1991 (SI 1991/2633)
15–26	1 Oct 1991 (SI 1991/2187)
26A	Prospectively inserted by Environment Act 1995, s 120(1), Sch 22, para 96(1), (6)[1]
27(1)	See Sch 10 below
(2)	See Sch 11 below
28	27 Nov 1991 (SI 1991/2633)
Sch 1	27 Nov 1991 (SI 1991/2633)
2, 3	1 Apr 1992 (SI 1991/2633)
4	27 Nov 1991 (SI 1991/2633)
5–9	1 Oct 1991 (SI 1991/2187)
10, para 1	1 Oct 1991 (SI 1991/2187); prospectively repealed by Environment Act 1995, s 120(3), Sch 24[1]
2	27 Nov 1991 (so far as inserts reference to Scottish Natural Heritage in Superannuation Act 1965, s 39(1), para 7) (SI 1991/2633)
	1 Apr 1992 (otherwise) (SI 1991/2633)

Natural Heritage (Scotland) Act 1991 (c 28)—*cont*

Sch 10, para 3	27 Nov 1991 (SI 1991/2633)
4	1 Apr 1992 (SI 1991/2633)
5	1 Oct 1991 (SI 1991/2187)
6	1 Oct 1991 (SI 1991/2187); prospectively repealed by Environment Act 1995, s 120(3), Sch 24[1]
7	1 Oct 1991 (SI 1991/2187)
8	1 Apr 1992 (SI 1991/2633)
9	1 Oct 1991 (SI 1991/2187)
10	27 Nov 1991 (SI 1991/2633)
11–13	1 Apr 1992 (SI 1991/2633)
11	1 Oct 1991 (repeals of or in Spray Irrigation (Scotland) Act 1964; Water (Scotland) Act 1980, ss 77–79, Schs 5, 6) (SI 1991/2187) 1 Apr 1992 (otherwise) (SI 1991/2633)

[1] Any orders made under Environment Act 1995, s 125(3), bringing the prospective amendments into force will be noted to that Act in the service to this work

New Roads and Street Works Act 1991 (c 22)

RA: 27 Jun 1991

Commencement provisions: s 170(1); New Roads and Street Works Act 1991 (Commencement No 1) (Scotland) Order 1991, SI 1991/2286; New Roads and Street Works Act 1991 (Commencement No 1) Order 1991, SI 1991/2288; New Roads and Street Works Act 1991 (Commencement No 4) (Scotland) Order 1992, SI 1992/1671; New Roads and Street Works Act 1991 (Commencement No 3) Order 1992, SI 1992/1686; New Roads and Street Works Act 1991 (Commencement No 5 and Transitional Provisions and Savings) Order 1992, SI 1992/2984; New Roads and Street Works Act 1991 (Commencement No 6 and Transitional Provisions and Savings) (Scotland) Order 1992, SI 1992/2990

s 1–5	1 Nov 1991 (SI 1991/2288)
6(1), (2)	1 Nov 1991 (SI 1991/2288)
(3)	See Sch 2 below
(4)–(6)	1 Nov 1991 (SI 1991/2288)
7–26	1 Nov 1991 (SI 1991/2288)
27–42	21 Oct 1991 (SI 1991/2286)
43, 44	1 Nov 1991 (SI 1991/2286)
45–47	21 Oct 1991 (SI 1991/2286)
48, 49	14 Jul 1992 (SI 1992/1686)
50(1)–(3)	1 Jan 1993 (SI 1992/2984)
(4)	See Sch 3 below
(5)–(7)	1 Jan 1993 (SI 1992/2984)
51	1 Jan 1993 (SI 1992/2984)
52	14 Jul 1992 (SI 1992/1686)
53(1)–(3)	28 Nov 1992 (SI 1992/2984)
(4)–(6)	14 Jul 1992 (SI 1992/1686)
54	14 Jul 1992 (SI 1992/1686)
55	28 Nov 1992 (for purpose of making regulations) (SI 1992/2984) 1 Jan 1993 (otherwise) (SI 1992/2984)
56	14 Jul 1992 (SI 1992/1686)
57, 58	28 Nov 1992 (SI 1992/2984)
59(1), (2)	1 Jan 1993 (SI 1992/2984)
(3)	14 Jul 1992 (SI 1992/1686)

New Roads and Street Works Act 1991 (c 22)—*cont*

s 59(4)–(6)	1 Jan 1993 (SI 1992/2984)
60(1)	1 Jan 1993 (SI 1992/2984)
(2)	14 Jul 1992 (SI 1992/1686)
(3)	1 Jan 1993 (SI 1992/2984)
61	1 Jan 1993 (SI 1992/2984)
62	14 Jul 1992 (SI 1992/1686)
63(1)	See Sch 4 below
(2)–(4)	14 Jul 1992 (SI 1992/1686)
64	14 Jul 1992 (SI 1992/1686)
65(1), (2)	1 Apr 1993 (SI 1992/2984)
(3)	14 Jul 1992 (SI 1992/1686)
(4)–(6)	1 Apr 1993 (SI 1992/2984)
66	1 Jan 1993 (SI 1992/2984)
67	14 Jul 1992 (SI 1992/1686)
68, 69	1 Jan 1993 (SI 1992/2984)
70(1)–(3)	1 Jan 1993 (SI 1992/2984)
(4)	14 Jul 1992 (SI 1992/1686)
(5)–(7)	1 Jan 1993 (SI 1992/2984)
71	14 Jul 1992 (SI 1992/1686)
72–74	1 Jan 1993 (SI 1992/2984)
75	14 Jul 1992 (SI 1992/1686)
76–78	1 Jan 1993 (SI 1992/2984)
79, 80	*Not in force*
81(1), (2)	1 Jan 1993 (SI 1992/2984)
(3), (4)	14 Jul 1992 (SI 1992/1686)
(5)–(7)	1 Jan 1993 (SI 1992/2984)
82, 83	1 Jan 1993 (SI 1992/2984)
84(1)	1 Jan 1993 (SI 1992/2984)
(2)	14 Jul 1992 (SI 1992/1686)
(3), (4)	1 Jan 1993 (SI 1992/2984)
85–87	14 Jul 1992 (SI 1992/1686)
88–96	1 Jan 1993 (SI 1992/2984)
97–99	14 Jul 1992 (SI 1992/1686)
100–103	1 Jan 1993 (SI 1992/2984)
104–106	14 Jul 1992 (SI 1992/1686)
107, 108	14 Jul 1992 (SI 1992/1671)
109, 110	1 Jan 1993 (SI 1992/2990)
111	14 Jul 1992 (SI 1992/1671)
112(1)–(3)	30 Nov 1992 (SI 1992/2990)
(4)	14 Jul 1992 (SI 1992/1671)
(4A)	Inserted by Local Government etc (Scotland) Act 1994, s 149(b) (qv)
(5), (6)	14 Jul 1992 (SI 1992/1671)
113	14 Jul 1992 (SI 1992/1671)
114	30 Nov 1992 (for purpose of making regulations) (SI 1992/2990)
	1 Jan 1993 (otherwise) (SI 1992/2990)
115	14 Jul 1992 (SI 1992/1671)
116, 117	30 Nov 1992 (SI 1992/2990)
118(1), (2)	1 Jan 1993 (SI 1992/2990)
(3)	14 Jul 1992 (SI 1992/1671)
(4)–(6)	1 Jan 1993 (SI 1992/2990)
119(1)	1 Jan 1993 (SI 1992/2990)
(2)	14 Jul 1992 (SI 1992/1671)
(3)	1 Jan 1993 (SI 1992/2990)
120	1 Jan 1993 (SI 1992/2990)
121	14 Jul 1992 (SI 1992/1671)

New Roads and Street Works Act 1991 (c 22)—*cont*

s 122(1)	See Sch 6 below
(2)–(5)	14 Jul 1992 (SI 1992/1671)
123	14 Jul 1992 (SI 1992/1671)
124(1), (2)	1 Apr 1993 (SI 1992/2990)
(3)	14 Jul 1992 (SI 1992/1671)
(4)–(6)	1 Apr 1993 (SI 1992/2990)
125	1 Jan 1993 (SI 1992/2990)
126	14 Jul 1992 (SI 1992/1671)
127, 128	1 Jan 1993 (SI 1992/2990)
129(1)–(3)	1 Jan 1993 (SI 1992/2990)
(4)	14 Jul 1992 (SI 1992/1671)
(5)–(7)	1 Jan 1993 (SI 1992/2990)
130	14 Jul 1992 (SI 1992/1671)
131–133	1 Jan 1993 (SI 1992/2990)
134	14 Jul 1992 (SI 1992/1671)
135–137	1 Jan 1993 (SI 1992/2990)
138, 139	*Not in force*
140(1), (2)	1 Jan 1993 (SI 1992/2990)
(3), (4)	14 Jul 1992 (SI 1992/1671)
(5)–(7)	1 Jan 1993 (SI 1992/2990)
141, 142	1 Jan 1993 (SI 1992/2990)
143(1)	1 Jan 1993 (SI 1992/2990)
(2)	14 Jul 1992 (SI 1992/1671)
(3), (4)	1 Jan 1993 (SI 1992/2990)
144–146	14 Jul 1992 (SI 1992/1671)
147–155	1 Jan 1993 (SI 1992/2990)
156–158	14 Jul 1992 (SI 1992/1671)
159–162	1 Jan 1993 (SI 1992/2990)
163–165	14 Jul 1992 (SI 1992/1671)
166(1)	21 Oct 1991 (so far as relates to offence committed under Pt II (ss 27–47)) (S) (SI 1991/2286) 1 Nov 1991 (EW) (SI 1991/2288) 1 Jan 1993 (otherwise) (S) (SI 1992/2990)
(2)	21 Oct 1991 (so far as relates to offence committed under Pt II (ss 27–47)) (SI 1991/2286) 1 Jan 1993 (otherwise) (SI 1992/2990)
167(1)–(3)	21 Oct 1991 (so far as relate to Pt II (ss 27–47)) (S) (SI 1991/2286) 1 Nov 1991 (EW) (SI 1991/2288) *Not in force* (otherwise) (S)
(4), (5)	14 Jul 1992 (S) (SI 1992/1671) 14 Jul 1992 (EW) (SI 1992/1686)
(6)	21 Oct 1991 (so far as relates to Pt II (ss 27–47)) (S) (SI 1991/2286) 1 Nov 1991 (EW) (SI 1991/2288) *Not in force* (otherwise) (S)
168(1)	See Sch 8 below
(2)	See Sch 9 below
169(1)	1 Nov 1991 (SI 1991/2288)
(2)	14 Jul 1992 (SI 1992/1671)
(3)	*Not in force*
170, 171	1 Nov 1991 (SI 1991/2288)
Sch 1, 2	1 Nov 1991 (SI 1991/2288)
3	1 Jan 1993 (SI 1992/2984)
4	14 Jul 1992 (SI 1992/1686)
5	1 Jan 1993 (SI 1992/2984)

New Roads and Street Works Act 1991 (c 22)—*cont*

Sch 6	14 Jul 1992 (SI 1992/1671)
7	1 Jan 1993 (SI 1992/2990)
8, Pt I, para 1–16	1 Jan 1993 (SI 1992/2984)
II, para 17–25	1 Nov 1991 (SI 1991/2286; SI 1991/2288)
26	Repealed
27–78	1 Nov 1991 (SI 1991/2286; SI 1991/2288)
79	Repealed
80	1 Nov 1991 (SI 1991/2286; SI 1991/2288)
III, para 81–92	1 Jan 1993 (SI 1992/2990)
93(a)	21 Oct 1991 (SI 1991/2286)
(b)	1 Jan 1993 (SI 1992/2990)
(c)	21 Oct 1991 (SI 1991/2286)
94(a)	1 Jan 1993 (SI 1992/2990)
(b)	21 Oct 1991 (SI 1991/2286)
95	1 Jan 1993 (SI 1992/2990)
96, 97	21 Oct 1991 (SI 1991/2286)
IV, para 98	Repealed
99(1), (2)	1 Nov 1991 (SI 1991/2286; SI 1991/2288)
(3)(a)	1 Nov 1991 (SI 1991/2288)
(b)	1 Jan 1993 (SI 1992/2990)
100, 101	1 Jan 1993 (SI 1992/2984; SI 1992/2990)
102	1 Nov 1991 (SI 1991/2286)
103	1 Jan 1993 (SI 1992/2990)
104(a)	1 Nov 1991 (SI 1991/2286)
(b)	1 Jan 1993 (SI 1992/2990)
105	1 Jan 1993 (SI 1992/2990)
106	1 Jan 1993 (SI 1992/2984)
107	1 Nov 1991 (SI 1991/2288)
108	1 Jan 1993 (SI 1992/2990)
109	1 Jan 1993 (SI 1992/2984; SI 1992/2990)
110	Repealed
111	1 Jan 1993 (SI 1992/2984; SI 1992/2990)
112	1 Nov 1991 (SI 1991/2288)
113–115	1 Jan 1993 (SI 1992/2984; SI 1992/2990)
116	1 Nov 1991 (SI 1991/2288)
117	1 Nov 1991 (SI 1991/2286; SI 1991/2288)
118(1),(2)	1 Nov 1991 (SI 1991/2286; SI 1991/2288)
(3)	1 Jan 1993 (SI 1992/2984; SI 1992/2990)
119(1)–(6)	1 Jan 1993 (SI 1992/2984; SI 1992/2990)
(7)	1 Jan 1993 (SI 1992/2990)
120(1),(2)	1 Jan 1993 (SI 1992/2984; SI 1992/2990)
(3)	1 Jan 1993 (SI 1992/2990)
	Para prospectively repealed by Gas Act 1995, s 17(5), Sch 6[1]
121(1)	1 Nov 1991 (SI 1991/2286; SI 1991/2288)
(2)	1 Jan 1993 (SI 1992/2984; SI 1992/2990)
(3)	1 Nov 1991 (SI 1991/2286; SI 1991/2288)
(4)	1 Nov 1991 (SI 1991/2288)
122	Repealed
123	1 Jan 1993 (SI 1992/2984; SI 1992/2990)
124	1 Jan 1993 (SI 1992/2990)
125	1 Jan 1993 (SI 1992/2984; SI 1992/2990)
126(1),(2)	1 Nov 1991 (SI 1991/2288)
(3)	1 Jan 1993 (SI 1992/2984)
127	1 Jan 1993 (SI 1992/2990)
	21 Oct 1991 (repeal in Roads (Scotland) Act 1984, s 143(2)(b)(ii)) (SI 1991/2286)

New Roads and Street Works Act 1991 (c 22)—*cont*

Sch 8, Pt IV, para 127—*cont*	1 Nov 1991 (repeals of or in Road Traffic Regulation Act 1984, ss 1(2), (4), (5), 3(1), 5(2), 16(3), (4), 17(6), 19(3), 23(5), 34(1), 55(5), 68(1)(a), 86(4), 91, 106(8), 124(2), 132(6), 132A, Sch 9, paras 20(1), 21, 27(1); Roads (Scotland) Act 1984, s 127, Sch 7, paras 2, 3(a), (b), 4, Sch 9, paras 93(2)–(22), (23)(a), (24)–(38), (40), (42), (44)(a), (b), (d), (e), (45)(b); Transport Act 1985, s 137(1); Road Traffic Offenders Act 1988, Sch 3 (the entry relating to the Road Traffic Regulation Act 1984, s 29(3)); Environmental Protection Act 1990, Sch 8, para 7) (S) (SI 1991/2286)
	1 Nov 1991 (repeals of or in Road Traffic Regulation Act 1984; Transport Act 1985; Road Traffic Offenders Act 1988; Environmental Protection Act 1990) (EW) (SI 1991/2288)
	1 Nov 1991 (repeals in Local Government Act 1985, Sch 5) (SI 1991/2288)
	1 Jan 1993 (otherwise) (SI 1992/2984; 1992/2990)

[1] Orders made under Gas Act 1995, 18(2)–(4), bringing the prospective repeal into force will be noted to that Act in the service to this work

---

Northern Ireland (Emergency Provisions) Act 1991 (c 24)

RA: 27 Jun 1991

Commencement provisions: s 69(1); Northern Ireland (Emergency Provisions) Act 1991 (Commencement) Order 1992, SI 1992/1181

Continuance orders: Northern Ireland (Emergency Provisions) Act 1991 (Continuance) Order 1992, SI 1992/1390; Northern Ireland (Emergency and Prevention of Terrorism Provisions) (Continuance) Order 1992, SI 1992/1413; Northern Ireland (Emergency and Prevention of Terrorism Provisions) (Continuance) Order 1993, SI 1993/1522; Northern Ireland (Emergency and Prevention of Terrorism Provisions) (Continuance) Order 1994, SI 1994/1569; Northern Ireland (Emergency and Prevention of Terrorism Provisions) (Continuance) Order 1995, SI 1995/1566

s 1–33	27 Aug 1991 (s 69(1))
34	See Sch 3 below
35–46	27 Aug 1991 (s 69(1))
47, 48	1 Jun 1992 (SI 1992/1181)
48A, 48B	Inserted by Criminal Justice Act 1993, s 37 (qv)
49–52	1 Jun 1992 (SI 1992/1181)
52A	Inserted by Criminal Justice Act 1993, s 39 (qv)
52B	Inserted by Criminal Justice Act 1993, s 42 (qv)
53, 54	1 Jun 1992 (SI 1992/1181)
54A	Inserted (UK) by Criminal Justice Act 1993, s 48 (qv)
55	See Sch 4 below
55A	Inserted (UK) by Criminal Justice Act 1993, s 77, Sch 4, para 6 (qv)
56	1 Jun 1992 (SI 1992/1181)
57–59	27 Aug 1991 (s 69(1))
60(1), (2)	27 Aug 1991 (s 69(1))
(3)	See Sch 6 below
(4)–(6)	27 Aug 1991 (s 69(1))

Northern Ireland (Emergency Provisions) Act 1991 (c 24)—*cont*

s 61–69	27 Aug 1991 (s 69(1))
70(1), (2)	27 Aug 1991 (s 69(1))
(3)	See Sch 7 below
(4)	See Sch 8 below
71	27 Aug 1991 (s 69(1))
Sch 1, 2	27 Aug 1991 (s 69(1))
3	27 Aug 1991 (s 69(1), but note s 69(3), (4) which provide that s 34 and Sch 3 are deemed to have ceased to have effect immediately after coming into force)
4	1 Jun 1992 (SI 1992/1181)
5–8	27 Aug 1991 (s 69(1))

S 34 and Sch 3 are brought into force again immediately before the end of 15 Jun 1992, continued in force from the beginning of 16 Jun 1992, and then cease to be in force immediately after the coming into effect of their continuance (SI 1992/1390)

Note that the temporary provisions of this Act (Pts IV–III except ss 7, 63, 64, Sch 1, Pt III, Sch 4, para 20, and, so far as they relate to offences which are scheduled offences by virtue of Sch 1, Pt III, ss 3, 9, 10), except s 34 and Sch 3, are continued in force for twelve months from 16 Jun 1995 (SI 1995/2695, superseding SI 1994/1569)

Oversea Superannuation Act 1991 (c 16)

RA: 27 Jun 1991

Commencement provisions: s 3(2)

27 Aug 1991 (s 3(2))

Planning and Compensation Act 1991 (c 34)

RA: 25 Jul 1991

Commencement provisions: s 84(2)–(4); Planning and Compensation Act 1991 (Commencement No 1 and Transitional Provisions) Order 1991, SI 1991/2067; Planning and Compensation Act 1991 (Commencement No 2 and Transitional Provisions) (Scotland) Order 1991, SI 1991/2092; Planning and Compensation Act 1991 (Commencement No 3) Order 1991, SI 1991/2272; Planning and Compensation Act 1991 (Commencement No 4 and Transitional Provisions) Order 1991, SI 1991/2728; Planning and Compensation Act 1991 (Commencement No 5 and Transitional Provisions) Order 1991, SI 1991/2905; Planning and Compensation Act 1991 (Commencement No 6) (Scotland) Order 1992, SI 1992/71; Planning and Compensation Act 1991 (Commencement No 7 and Transitional Provisions) Order 1992, SI 1992/334; Planning and Compensation Act 1991 (Commencement No 8) Order 1992, SI 1992/665; Planning and Compensation Act 1991 (Commencement No 9 and Transitional Provision) Order 1992, SI 1992/1279; Planning and Compensation Act 1991 (Commencement No 10 and Transitional Provision) Order 1992, SI 1992/1491; Planning and Compensation Act 1991 (Commencement No 11 and Transitional Provisions) Order 1992, SI 1992/1630; Planning and Compensation Act 1991 (Commencement No 12 and Transitional Provisions) (Scotland) Order 1992, SI 1992/1937; Planning and Compensation Act 1991 (Commencement No 13

Planning and Compensation Act 1991 (c 34)—*cont*

and Transitional Provision) Order 1992, SI 1992/2413; Planning and Compensation Act 1991 (Commencement No 14 and Transitional Provision) Order 1992, SI 1992/2831; Planning and Compensation Act 1991 (Commencement No 15) (Scotland) Order 1993, SI 1993/275; Planning and Compensation Act 1991 (Commencement No 16) (Scotland) Order 1994, SI 1994/398; Planning and Compensation Act 1991 (Commencement No 17 and Transitional Provision) (Scotland) Order 1994, SI 1994/3292; Planning and Compensation Act 1991 (Commencement No 18 and Transitional Provision) (Scotland) Order 1995, SI 1995/2045

Abbreviation: "rules, etc" means "so much of the provision as enables provision to be made by rules of court, confers on the Secretary of State a power or imposes on him a duty to make or to make provision by development order or other order or regulations or to give or revoke directions, or makes provision with respect to the exercise of any such power or performance of any such duty, is brought into force on the specified date"

s 1	2 Jan 1992 (SI 1991/2905)
2	27 Jul 1992 (SI 1992/1630)
3	25 Nov 1991 (rules, etc) (SI 1991/2728)
	2 Jan 1992 (otherwise) (SI 1991/2905)
4	2 Jan 1992 (except so far as relates to breach of condition notices) (SI 1991/2905)
	27 Jul 1992 (exception noted above) (SI 1992/1630)
5	25 Nov 1991 (rules, etc) (SI 1991/2728)
	2 Jan 1992 (otherwise) (SI 1991/2905)
6(1)–(4)	2 Jan 1992 (SI 1991/2905)
(5)	25 Nov 1991 (rules, etc) (SI 1991/2728)
	2 Jan 1992 (otherwise) (SI 1991/2905)
(6)	13 Oct 1991 (SI 1991/2272)
7–9	2 Jan 1992 (SI 1991/2905)
10	25 Nov 1991 (rules, etc) (SI 1991/2728)
	27 Jul 1992 (otherwise) (SI 1992/1630)
11	2 Jan 1992 (SI 1991/2905)
12(1)	25 Oct 1991 (so far as substitutes Town and Country Planning Act 1990, s 106) (SI 1991/2272)
	25 Nov 1991 (so far as substitutes Town and Country Planning Act 1990, ss 106A, 106B) (rules, etc) (SI 1991/2728)
	9 Nov 1992 (otherwise) (SI 1992/2831)
(2), (3)	25 Oct 1991 (SI 1991/2272)
13(1)	27 Jul 1992 (SI 1992/1279)
(2)	25 Nov 1991 (rules, etc) (SI 1991/2728)
	27 Jul 1992 (otherwise) (SI 1992/1279)
(3)	27 Jul 1992 (SI 1992/1279)
14	2 Jan 1992 (SI 1991/2905)
15	25 Sep 1991 (SI 1991/2067)
16	25 Nov 1991 (rules, etc) (SI 1991/2728)
	17 Jul 1992 (otherwise) (SI 1992/1491)
17, 18	25 Sep 1991 (SI 1991/2067)
19	25 Nov 1991 (rules, etc) (SI 1991/2728)
	2 Jan 1992 (otherwise, except so far as relates to Town and Country Planning Act 1990, Sch 1, para 4(1), as it concerns applications for consent to the display of advertisements) (SI 1991/2905)
	6 Apr 1992 (exception noted above) (SI 1992/665)

Planning and Compensation Act 1991 (c 34)—*cont*

s 20	25 Nov 1991 (rules, etc) (SI 1991/2728) 17 Jul 1992 (otherwise) (SI 1992/1491)
21	See Sch 1 below
22	25 Sep 1991 (SI 1991/2067)
23(1)–(6)	2 Jan 1992 (SI 1991/2905)
(7)	25 Nov 1991 (so far as relates to Town and Country Planning Act 1990, s 214A(2)) (rules, etc) (SI 1991/2728) 2 Jan 1992 (otherwise) (SI 1991/2905)
(8)	2 Jan 1992 (SI 1991/2905)
24	6 Apr 1992 (SI 1992/665)
25	See Sch 3 below
26	25 Sep 1991 (SI 1991/2067)
27	See Sch 4 below
28	See Sch 5 below
29	25 Sep 1991 (SI 1991/2067)
30	2 Jan 1992 (subject to certain exceptions and savings; see SI 1991/2728, arts 3, 4) (SI 1991/2728) *Not in force* (exceptions referred to above)
31(1)	25 Sep 1991 (SI 1991/2067)
(2), (3)	25 Jul 1991 (s 84(4))
(4)	See Sch 6 below
(5), (6)	25 Sep 1991 (SI 1991/2067)
(7), (8)	25 Jul 1991 (s 84(4))
32	See Sch 7 below
33	26 Mar 1992 (SI 1992/334)
34	10 Aug 1992 (so far as inserts definition of breach of condition notice into Town and Country Planning (Scotland) Act 1972) (SI 1992/1937) 25 Sep 1992 (otherwise) (SI 1992/1937)
35	26 Mar 1992 (SI 1992/334)
36	26 Mar 1992 (except so far as relates to breach of condition notices) (SI 1992/334) 25 Sep 1992 (exception noted above) (SI 1992/1937)
37	24 Feb 1992 (for purpose of enabling Secretary of State to make regulations under Town and Country Planning (Scotland) Act 1972, s 84AA(10)) (SI 1992/334) 26 Mar 1992 (otherwise) (SI 1992/334)
38–41	26 Mar 1992 (SI 1992/334)
42	10 Aug 1992 (for purpose of enabling Secretary of State to make regulations or development order under Town and Country Planning (Scotland) Act 1972, s 90B) (SI 1992/1937) 25 Sep 1992 (otherwise) (SI 1992/1937)
43	26 Mar 1992 (SI 1992/334)
44	3 Feb 1995 (subject to a transitional provision) (SI 1994/3292)
45	10 Aug 1992 (SI 1992/1937)
46	3 Feb 1995 (SI 1994/3292)
47, 48	25 Sep 1991 (SI 1991/2092)
49	24 Jan 1992 (SI 1992/71)
50	25 Sep 1991 (SI 1991/2092)
51	See Sch 8 below
52, 53	24 Jan 1992 (SI 1992/71)
54	26 Mar 1992 (SI 1992/334)
55	10 Aug 1992 (SI 1992/1937)

Planning and Compensation Act 1991 (c 34)—*cont*

s 56	26 Mar 1992 (SI 1992/334)
57	See Sch 10 below
58	7 Mar 1994 (SI 1994/398)
59	See Sch 11 below
60(1)	25 Sep 1991 (SI 1991/2092)
(2), (3)	25 Jul 1991 (s 84(4))
(4)	25 Sep 1991 (SI 1991/2092)
(5)	25 Jul 1991 (s 84(4))
(6)	See Sch 12 below
(7), (8)	25 Sep 1991 (SI 1991/2092)
61	See Sch 13 below
62–69	25 Sep 1991 (SI 1991/2067)
70	See Sch 15 below
71–78	25 Sep 1991 (SI 1991/2092)
79	See Sch 17 below
80	25 Sep 1991 (except in relation to entries noted to Sch 18 below) (EW) (SI 1991/2067)
	25 Sep 1991 (except in relation to entries noted to Sch 18 below) (S) (SI 1991/2092)
	2 Jan 1992 (otherwise) (EW) (SI 1991/2728)
	30 Aug 1995 (otherwise) (S) (SI 1995/2045)
81	25 Sep 1991 (SI 1991/2067)
82	26 Mar 1992 (SI 1992/334)
83	25 Oct 1991 (SI 1991/2272)
84(1)–(5)	25 Jul 1991 (RA)
(6)	See Sch 19 below
(7)–(9)	25 Jul 1991 (RA)
Sch 1, 2	25 Sep 1991 (SI 1991/2067)
3, para 1	25 Sep 1991 (SI 1991/2067)
2–6	2 Jan 1992 (SI 1991/2905)
7	25 Nov 1991 (rules, etc) (SI 1991/2728)
	2 Jan 1992 (otherwise) (SI 1991/2905)
8–14	2 Jan 1992 (SI 1991/2905)
15	25 Nov 1991 (rules, etc) (SI 1991/2728)
	2 Jan 1992 (otherwise) (SI 1991/2905)
16–32	2 Jan 1992 (SI 1991/2905)
4, para 1, 2	25 Nov 1991 (rules, etc) (SI 1991/2728)
	10 Feb 1992 (otherwise) (SI 1991/2905)
3	10 Feb 1992 (SI 1991/2905)
4–25	25 Nov 1991 (rules, etc) (SI 1991/2728)
	10 Feb 1992 (otherwise) (SI 1991/2905)
26	10 Feb 1992 (SI 1991/2905)
27–38	25 Nov 1991 (rules, etc) (SI 1991/2728)
	10 Feb 1992 (otherwise) (SI 1991/2905)
39	25 Nov 1991 (rules, etc) (SI 1991/2728)
	10 Feb 1992 (otherwise) (SI 1991/2905)
	Prospectively repealed by Environment Act 1995, s 120(3), Sch 24[1]
40–51	25 Nov 1991 (rules, etc) (SI 1991/2728)
	10 Feb 1992 (otherwise) (SI 1991/2905)
5	25 Nov 1991 (rules, etc) (SI 1991/2728)
	9 Nov 1992 (otherwise; but note that amendments do not apply with respect to proposals which are or have been made available for inspection in accordance with Town and Country Planning Act 1990, Sch 7, para 5 or 6 before 12 Oct 1992

Planning and Compensation Act 1991 (c 34)—*cont*

Sch 5—*cont*	but simplified planning zone scheme had not yet come into operation on that date) (SI 1992/2413)
6, para 1	25 Jul 1991 (s 84(4))
2–4	25 Sep 1991 (SI 1991/2067)
5	25 Jul 1991 (s 84(4))
6–12	25 Sep 1991 (SI 1991/2067)
13	25 Jul 1991 (s 84(4))
14–49	25 Sep 1991 (SI 1991/2067)
7, para 1	27 Jul 1992 (SI 1992/1630)
2	2 Jan 1992 (SI 1991/2905)
3	27 Jul 1992 (SI 1992/1630)
4	2 Jan 1992 (SI 1991/2905)
5	2 Jan 1992 (except so far as relates to reference to s 187A) (SI 1991/2905)
	27 Jul 1992 (exception noted above) (SI 1992/1630)
6	25 Oct 1991 (SI 1991/2272)
7	2 Jan 1992 (SI 1991/2905)
8	25 Sep 1991 (SI 1991/2067)
9(1)	2 Jan 1992 (SI 1991/2905)
(2)(a)	10 Feb 1992 (SI 1991/2905)
(b)	27 Jul 1992 (SI 1992/1630)
(c)	25 Sep 1991 (SI 1991/2067)
(d)	2 Jan 1992 (so far as relates to reference to s 171C) (SI 1991/2905)
	9 Nov 1992 (otherwise) (SI 1992/2831)
(e)	2 Jan 1992 (SI 1991/2905)
(f)	2 Jan 1992 (so far as relates to reference to s 187B) (SI 1991/2905)
	27 Jul 1992 (otherwise) (SI 1992/1630)
(g)	2 Jan 1992 (SI 1991/2905)
(h)	25 Oct 1991 (SI 1991/2272)
(i)	2 Jan 1992 (except so far as relates to substitution of reference to 'section 316(1) to (3)' by reference to 'section 316') (SI 1991/2905)
	17 Jul 1992 (exception noted above) (SI 1992/1491)
10(1)	25 Sep 1991 (SI 1991/2067)
(2)	27 Jul 1992 (SI 1992/1279)
11	2 Jan 1992 (SI 1991/2905)
12	27 Jul 1992 (SI 1992/1630)
13	2 Jan 1992 (SI 1991/2905)
14, 15	17 Jul 1992 (SI 1992/1491)
16	2 Jan 1992 (SI 1991/2905)
17	17 Jul 1992 (SI 1992/1491)
18, 19	2 Jan 1992 (so far as relate to inclusion in Town and Country Planning Act 1990, ss 77(4), 79(4), of reference to s 73A) (SI 1991/2905)
	17 Jul 1992 (otherwise) (SI 1992/1491)
20–23	2 Jan 1992 (SI 1991/2905)
24(1)(a)	2 Jan 1992 (SI 1991/2905)
(b)	27 Jul 1992 (SI 1992/1630)
(2), (3)	2 Jan 1992 (SI 1991/2905)
25	2 Jan 1992 (SI 1991/2905)
26	2 Jan 1992 (except so far as relates to breach of condition notices) (SI 1991/2905)
	27 Jul 1992 (exception noted above) (SI 1992/1630)
27–29	2 Jan 1992 (SI 1991/2905)
30	27 Jul 1992 (SI 1992/1630)

Planning and Compensation Act 1991 (c 34)—*cont*

Sch 7, para 31	2 Jan 1992 (SI 1991/2905)
32, 33	27 Jul 1992 (SI 1992/1630)
34	17 Jul 1992 (SI 1992/1491)
35	2 Jan 1992 (SI 1991/2905)
36	25 Sep 1991 (SI 1991/2067)
37	17 Jul 1992 (SI 1992/1491)
38	6 Apr 1992 (SI 1992/665)
39–41	27 Jul 1992 (SI 1992/1630)
42	2 Jan 1992 (SI 1991/2905)
43, 44	27 Jul 1992 (SI 1992/1630)
45(1)	2 Jan 1992 (SI 1991/2905)
(2)	2 Jan 1992 (except so far as relates to reference to s 187A) (SI 1991/2905)
	27 Jul 1992 (exception noted above) (SI 1992/1630)
46	27 Jul 1992 (SI 1992/1630)
47	2 Jan 1992 (SI 1991/2905)
48	25 Nov 1991 (rules, etc) (SI 1991/2728)
	17 Jul 1992 (otherwise) (SI 1992/1491)
49	25 Nov 1991 (rules, etc) (SI 1991/2728)
	27 Jul 1992 (otherwise) (SI 1992/1630)
50	2 Jan 1992 (SI 1991/2905)
51	25 Sep 1991 (SI 1991/2067)
52(1)	2 Jan 1992 (SI 1991/2905)
(2)(a)	2 Jan 1992 (except so far as relates to definition 'breach of condition notice') (SI 1991/2905)
	27 Jul 1992 (exception noted above) (SI 1992/1630)
(b)	2 Jan 1992 (SI 1991/2905)
(c)	27 Jul 1992 (but not relating to demolition of building on land where, before 27 Jul 1992, planning permission has been granted under Town and Country Planning Act 1990, Pt III, or has been deemed to have been granted under that Part of that Act, for the redevelopment of the land) (SI 1992/1279)
(d)	27 Jul 1992 (SI 1992/1630)
(e)	17 Jul 1992 (SI 1992/1491)
(f), (g)	2 Jan 1992 (SI 1991/2905)
(3)	17 Jul 1992 (SI 1992/1491)
(4)	2 Jan 1992 (SI 1991/2905)
53(1)	See sub-paras (2)–(9) below
(2)	27 Jul 1992 (SI 1992/1630)
(3)	2 Jan 1992 (except so far as relates to applications for consent to the display of advertisements) (SI 1991/2905)
	6 Apr 1992 (exception noted above) (SI 1992/665)
(4)	17 Jul 1992 (SI 1992/1491)
(5)	2 Jan 1992 (so far as confers on the Secretary of State a power to make provision by development order) (SI 1991/2905)
	9 Nov 1992 (otherwise; but note that does not apply to application for planning permission or application for approval of matter reserved under outline planning permission (within meaning of Town and Country Planning Act 1990, s 92, made before 6 Nov 1992 nor to any alteration to that application accepted by the authority) (SI 1992/2831)

Planning and Compensation Act 1991 (c 34)—*cont*

Sch 7, para 53(6)	2 Jan 1992 (so far as relates to insertion of the words 'planning contravention notices under s 171C or') (SI 1991/2905)
	27 Jul 1992 (otherwise) (SI 1992/1630)
(7), (8)	2 Jan 1992 (SI 1991/2905)
(9)	25 Oct 1991 (SI 1991/2272)
54(1)	25 Sep 1991 (SI 1991/2067)
(2)	9 Nov 1992 (SI 1992/2831)
(3)(a)	25 Sep 1991 (SI 1991/2067)
(b)	9 Nov 1992 (SI 1992/2831)
(c)	2 Jan 1992 (SI 1991/2905)
(d)	27 Jul 1992 (SI 1992/1630)
(e)	2 Jan 1992 (SI 1991/2905)
(f)	9 Nov 1992 (SI 1992/2831)
(g)	27 Jul 1992 (SI 1992/1630)
(4)	17 Jul 1992 (SI 1992/1491)
55	17 Jul 1992 (SI 1992/1491)
56	25 Sep 1991 (SI 1991/2067)
57(1)	25 Sep 1991 (SI 1991/2067)
(2)(a)	2 Jan 1992 (so far as relates to omission of reference to s 63) (SI 1991/2905)
	27 Jul 1992 (otherwise) (SI 1992/1630)
(b)	25 Sep 1991 (SI 1991/2067)
(c)	2 Jan 1992 (SI 1991/2905)
(d), (e)	17 Jul 1992 (SI 1992/1491)
(f)	9 Nov 1992 (SI 1992/2831)
(g)	2 Jan 1992 (so far as relates to references to ss 196A–196C) (SI 1991/2905)
	27 Jul 1992 (otherwise) (SI 1992/1630)
(h), (i)	2 Jan 1992 (SI 1991/2905)
(j), (k)	17 Jul 1992 (SI 1992/1491)
(3)(a)	17 Jul 1992 (SI 1992/1491)
(b)	25 Sep 1991 (SI 1991/2067)
(c)	2 Jan 1992 (SI 1991/2905)
(d)	2 Jan 1992 (except so far as relates to s 187A) (SI 1991/2905)
	27 Jul 1992 (exception noted above) (SI 1992/1630)
(4)	25 Sep 1991 (SI 1991/2067)
(5)	17 Jul 1992 (except so far as relates to omission of reference to Part IV) (SI 1992/1491)
	27 Jul 1992 (exception noted above) (SI 1992/1630)
(6)(a), (b)	17 Jul 1992 (SI 1992/1491)
(c)	27 Jul 1992 (SI 1992/1630)
(d)	17 Jul 1992 (SI 1992/1491)
58–61	2 Jan 1992 (SI 1991/2905)
8, 9	24 Jan 1992 (SI 1992/71)
10, para 1, 2	25 Sep 1991 (SI 1991/2092)
3	18 Feb 1993 (SI 1993/275)
4–8	26 Mar 1992 (SI 1992/334)
9	18 Feb 1993 (SI 1993/275)
10	26 Mar 1992 (SI 1992/334)
11	1 May 1993 (SI 1993/275)
12, 13	26 Mar 1992 (SI 1992/334)
11	30 Aug 1995 (subject to a transitional provision) (SI 1995/2045)
12	25 Sep 1991 (SI 1991/2092)
13, para 1	25 Sep 1992 (SI 1992/1937)

Planning and Compensation Act 1991 (c 34)—*cont*

Sch 13, para 2	25 Sep 1991 (SI 1991/2092)
3, 4	7 Mar 1994 (SI 1994/398)
5, 6	25 Sep 1991 (SI 1991/2092)
7(a)(i)	3 Feb 1995 (SI 1994/3292)
(ii), (iii)	25 Sep 1991 (SI 1991/2092)
(b)	25 Sep 1991 (SI 1991/2092)
8	26 Mar 1992 (SI 1992/334)
9	25 Sep 1991 (SI 1991/2092)
10(a)	26 Mar 1992 (so far as relates to substitution of reference to '27(1), 27A, 28A and 29') (SI 1992/334)
	3 Feb 1995 (otherwise) (SI 1994/3292)
(b)	3 Feb 1995 (SI 1994/3292)
11(a)	25 Sep 1991 (SI 1991/2092)
(b)(i), (ii)	3 Feb 1995 (SI 1994/3292)
(iii)	26 Mar 1992 (SI 1992/334)
(iv)	3 Feb 1995 (SI 1994/3292)
(c)	25 Sep 1991 (SI 1991/2092)
12	25 Sep 1991 (SI 1991/2092)
13	26 Mar 1992 (SI 1992/334)
14	25 Sep 1991 (SI 1991/2092)
15	3 Feb 1995 (SI 1994/3292)
16	26 Mar 1992 (SI 1992/334)
17, 18	25 Sep 1992 (SI 1992/1937)
19	26 Mar 1992 (SI 1992/334)
20(a), (b)	26 Mar 1992 (SI 1992/334)
(c)	26 Mar 1992 (except so far as para 20(c)(ii) relates to substitution of Town and Country Planning (Scotland) Act 1972, s 85(5)(d)) (SI 1992/334)
	25 Sep 1992 (exception noted above) (SI 1992/1937)
(d)	25 Sep 1992 (SI 1992/1937)
(e)–(g)	26 Mar 1992 (SI 1992/334)
21	26 Mar 1992 (SI 1992/334)
22	10 Aug 1992 (SI 1992/1937)
23, 24	26 Mar 1992 (SI 1992/334)
25	26 Mar 1992 (except so far as substituted s 89A relates to breach of condition notice) (SI 1992/334)
	25 Sep 1992 (exception noted above) (SI 1992/1937)
26	25 Sep 1992 (SI 1992/1937)
27	26 Mar 1992 (SI 1992/334)
28	25 Sep 1991 (SI 1991/2092)
29, 30	26 Mar 1992 (SI 1992/334)
31–34	25 Sep 1992 (SI 1992/1937)
35	26 Mar 1992 (SI 1992/334)
36	25 Sep 1991 (SI 1991/2092)
37	26 Mar 1992 (except insertion of reference to s 87AA) (SI 1992/334)
	25 Sep 1992 (exception noted above) (SI 1992/1937)
38(a)–(d)	26 Mar 1992 (SI 1992/334)
(e)	25 Sep 1991 (SI 1991/2092)
(f)	26 Mar 1992 (SI 1992/334)
39	26 Mar 1992 (SI 1992/334)
40(1)(a)	26 Mar 1992 (so far as inserts definition 'breach of planning control') (SI 1992/334)
	10 Aug 1992 (otherwise) (SI 1992/1937)
(b), (c)	3 Feb 1995 (SI 1994/3292)
(d)	25 Sep 1992 (SI 1992/1937)
(e), (f)	26 Mar 1992 (SI 1992/334)

Planning and Compensation Act 1991 (c 34)—*cont*

Sch 13, para 40(2)	30 Aug 1995 (SI 1995/2045)
41(1)	25 Sep 1991 (SI 1991/2092)
(2)	26 Mar 1992 (SI 1992/334)
(3), (4)	3 Feb 1995 (SI 1994/3292)
42	3 Feb 1995 (SI 1994/3292)
43(a)(i)	25 Sep 1991 (SI 1991/2092)
(ii)	25 Sep 1992 (SI 1992/1937)
(iii)	26 Mar 1992 (except insertion of reference to 'section 90A') (SI 1992/334)
	25 Sep 1992 (exception noted above) (SI 1992/1937)
(iv)	26 Mar 1992 (SI 1992/334)
(b)(i)	25 Sep 1991 (SI 1991/2092)
(ii)	26 Mar 1992 (SI 1992/334)
(iii)	25 Sep 1992 (SI 1992/1937)
(c)	26 Mar 1992 (SI 1992/334)
44	*Not in force*; prospectively repealed by Local Government etc (Scotland) Act 1994, s 180(2), Sch 14[2]
45	13 Oct 1991 (SI 1991/2272; but note that SI 1992/334 also purports to bring this provision into force on 26 Mar 1992)
46	26 Mar 1992 (except insertion of reference to 'section 87AA') (SI 1992/334)
	25 Sep 1992 (exception noted above) (SI 1992/1937)
47	25 Sep 1992 (SI 1992/1937)
14	25 Sep 1991 (SI 1991/2067)
15, para 1–31	25 Sep 1991 (SI 1991/2067)
32	2 Jan 1992 (SI 1991/2728)
16, 17	25 Sep 1991 (SI 1991/2092)
18, Pt I	25 Sep 1991 (except entries relating to Planning (Hazardous Substances) Act 1990) (EW) (SI 1991/2067)
	25 Sep 1991 (except entries relating to Town and Country Planning (Scotland) Act 1972, ss 56J(8), 56K(12)) (S) (SI 1991/2092)
	2 Jan 1992 (exception noted above) (EW) (SI 1991/2728
	30 Aug 1995 (exception noted above) (S) (SI 1995/2045)
II	25 Sep 1991 (SI 1991/2067; SI 1991/2092))
19, Pt I	25 Sep 1991 (repeals of or in Town and Country Planning Act 1990, ss 55(6), 97(5), 219(6), 336(1) (definitions of 'development consisting of the winning and working of minerals', 'mineral compensation modifications', 'relevant order', 'restriction on the winning and working of minerals' and 'special consultations'), Sch 1, para 1(2), Sch 5, para 1(6), Sch 11, Sch 16, Pt III (entries relating to ss 312(2), 324(4)); Planning (Listed Buildings and Conservation Areas) Act 1990, s 9(5)) (SI 1991/2067)
	2 Jan 1992 (repeals of or in Town and Country Planning Act 1990, ss 63, 69(1), (3), 178(2), 186(1)(c), 190(4), 210(3), (5), 285(1), (2), (5), (6), 324(1)(b), (c), (2), 336(1) (definition of 'planning permission'), Sch 1, para 4(1) (except so far as concerns applications for consent to the display of

Planning and Compensation Act 1991 (c 34)—*cont*

Sch 19, Pt I—*cont* advertisements), Sch 16 (entry relating to s 285); Planning (Listed Buildings and Conservation Areas) Act 1990, ss 38(2), 39(7), 42(7), 55(6), 88(6), 90(6)(b), 92(2)(b); Planning (Hazardous Substances) Act 1990, ss 25(1)(c), 36(5); Planning (Consequential Provisions) Act 1990, Sch 2, para 38) (SI 1991/2905)

10 Feb 1992 (repeals of or in Town and Country Planning Act 1990, ss 12(4)(a), 14(3), 21(2), 22, 23(2)–(4), (9), (10), 49, 50, 51(1), 52(2), (3), 53(1), (2)(b), (g), (5), 284(1)(a), 287(1)(3), (5), 306(2), Sch 2, Pt I, paras 3, 5, 6, Pt II, paras 316, 18, Sch 13; Planning (Consequential Provisions) Act 1990, Sch 4) (SI 1991/2905)

6 Apr 1992 (repeal of Town and Country Planning Act 1990, Sch 1, para 4(1) (so far as not already in force)) (SI 1992/665)

17 Jul 1992 (repeals of or in Town and Country Planning Act 1990, ss 74(2), 198(4)(a), 220(3)(a), 336(1), (9), Sch 16, Pt I, entries relating to ss 77, 78, 79, Pt V) (SI 1992/1491)

27 Jul 1992 (repeals of or in Local Government (Miscellaneous Provisions) Act 1976, s 7(5)(a)(iii); Town and Country Planning Act 1990, ss 64, 188(1), 196, 250(2), 266(3), 284(3)(g), 286(1)(b), 290, 336(1), Sch 6, para 2(1)(c), (8), Sch 16, Pt IV; Planning (Consequential Provisions) Act 1990, Sch 2, paras 3(2), 35(1)(b)) (SI 1992/1630)

9 Nov 1992 (repeals of or in Town and Country Planning Act 1990, Sch 1, para 9(2), (3), Sch 7, para 13(2)(e)) (SI 1992/2831)

II 25 Jul 1991 (repeals of Land Compensation Act 1961, s 15(4)(a), (b); Land Compensation Act 1973, s 5(3)(a), (b); Town and Country Planning Act 1990, s 114; Planning (Listed Buildings and Conservation Areas) Act 1990, s 27) (s 84(4))

25 Sep 1991 (otherwise) (SI 1991/2067)

III 25 Sep 1991 (SI 1991/2067)

IV 25 Jul 1991 (repeals of Town and Country Planning (Scotland) Act 1972, ss 158, 160) (s 84(4))

25 Sep 1991 (repeal in Land Compensation (Scotland) Act 1973, Sch 2, Pt II) (SI 1991/2067)

25 Sep 1991 (repeals of or in Land Compensation (Scotland) Act 1963, ss 12, 23(4)(a), (b), 25(8), 30(3); Gas Act 1965, Sch 3, para 3; Public Expenditure and Receipts Act 1968, Sch 3, para 7(a); Town and Country Planning (Scotland) Act 1972, ss 19(5), 35, 36, 58(2)(a), 106, Pt VII (except s 145), 155(5), (6), 156, 157(1), (3), (4), 158, 160, 169(3), 231(3)(c), 244(2), 245, 246, 248, 249, 263, 264, 265, 275(1) (definitions of 'new development' and 'previous apportionment'), Sch 6, paras 3 9, 12, Sch 19, Pt I; Land Compensation (Scotland) Act 1973, ss 5(3)(a), (b), 27(1), (5), 31(6), 48(9)(b); Local Government, Planning and Land Act 1980, s 114(2); Civil Aviation Act 1982, s 53(1)(a); Airports Act 1986, s 61(1)(a)) (SI 1991/2092)

Planning and Compensation Act 1991 (c 34)—*cont*

Sch 19, Pt IV—*cont*	26 Mar 1992 (repeals of or in Town and Country Planning (Scotland) Act 1972, ss 85(5), (11), 88(1), (2), 93(1)(k), (5), 98(1), (3), 166(2)(c), 265(1)(b), (2A)(a), (4), 275(1) (in definition 'planning permission', words from 'and in construing' to the end)) (SI 1992/334)
	25 Sep 1992 (repeals of or in Town and Country Planning (Scotland) Act 1972, ss 51, 91(3), (5), 201(5), 214(3), 234, 275(1)) (subject to transitional provisions) (SI 1992/1937)
	3 Feb 1995 (repeal in Town and Country Planning (Scotland) Act 1972, s 28(1)) (SI 1994/3292)
	30 Aug 1995 (repeals of or in Town and Country Planning (Scotland) Act 1972, s 61(6), Sch 6A, para 12(2)(e), Sch 7, para 2(1)(c), Schs 12–15) (SI 1995/2045)
	Not in force (otherwise)
V	25 Sep 1991 (SI 1991/2067)

Note: the orders bringing this Act into force, as noted above, contain numerous transitional and saving provisions which are too complex to set out in this work

[1] Any order made under Environment Act 1995, s 125(3), bringing the prospective repeal into force will be noted to that Act in the service to this work

[2] Any order made under Local Government etc (Scotland) Act 1994, s 184(2), (3), bringing the prospective repeal into force will be noted to that Act in the service to this work

Ports Act 1991 (c 52)

RA: 25 Jul 1991

Commencement provisions: ss 32(8), 42(2); Ports Act 1991 (Transfer of Local Lighthouses: Appointed Day) Order 1992, SI 1992/2381

s 1–15	25 Jul 1991 (RA)
15A	Inserted by Finance Act 1995, s 159(1)
16–30	25 Jul 1991 (RA)
31–34	Repealed
35–42	25 Jul 1991 (RA)
Sch 1, 2	25 Jul 1991 (RA)

Property Misdescriptions Act 1991 (c 29)

RA: 27 Jun 1991

27 Jun 1991 (RA)

Radioactive Material (Road Transport) Act 1991 (c 27)

RA: 27 Jun 1991

Commencement provisions: s 9(3)

s 1–7	27 Aug 1991 (s 9(3))
8	27 Jun 1991 (RA)
9(1)	27 Aug 1991 (s 9(3))
(2)	See Schedule below
(3), (4)	27 Aug 1991 (s 9(3))
Schedule	27 Aug 1991 (s 9(3))

Registered Homes (Amendment) Act 1991 (c 20)

RA: 27 Jun 1991

Commencement provisions: s 2(2); Registered Homes (Amendment) Act 1991 (Commencement) Order 1992, SI 1992/2240

1 Apr 1993 (SI 1992/2240)

Representation of the People Act 1991 (c 11)

RA: 9 May 1991

Commencement provisions: s 3(2); Representation of the People Act 1991 (Commencement) Order 1991, SI 1991/1634

22 Jul 1991 (SI 1991/1634)

Road Traffic Act 1991 (c 40)

RA: 25 Jul 1991

Commencement provisions: s 84(1); Road Traffic Act 1991 (Commencement No 1) Order 1991, SI 1991/2054; Road Traffic Act 1991 (Commencement No 2) Order 1992, SI 1992/199; Road Traffic Act 1991 (Commencement No 3) Order 1992, SI 1992/421; Road Traffic Act 1991 (Commencement No 4 and Transitional Provisions) Order 1992, SI 1992/1286 (as amended by SI 1992/1410); Road Traffic Act 1991 (Commencement No 4 and Transitional Provisions) (Amendment) Order 1992, SI 1992/1410 (amending SI 1992/1286); Road Traffic Act 1991 (Commencement No 5 and Transitional Provisions) Order 1992, SI 1992/2010; Road Traffic Act 1991 (Commencement No 6) Order 1993, SI 1993/975; Road Traffic Act 1991 (Commencement No 6 and Transitional Provisions) Order 1993, SI 1993/1461, as amended by SI 1993/1686, SI 1993/2229; Road Traffic Act 1991 (Commencement No 6 and Transitional Provisions) (Amendment) Order 1993, SI 1993/1686; Road Traffic Act 1991 (Commencement No 7 and Transitional Provisions) Order 1993, SI 1993/2229; Road Traffic Act 1991 (Commencement No 8 and Transitional Provisions) Order 1993, SI 1993/2803; Road Traffic Act 1991 (Commencement No 9 and Transitional Provisions) Order 1993, SI 1993/3238, as amended by SI 1994/81; Road Traffic Act 1991 (Commencement No 10 and Transitional Provisions) Order 1994, SI 1994/81 (amending SI 1993/3238); Road Traffic Act 1991 (Commencement No 11 and Transitional Provisions) Order 1994, SI 1994/1482;

Road Traffic Act 1991 (c 40)—*cont*

Road Traffic Act 1991 (Commencement No 12 and Transitional Provisions) Order 1994, SI 1994/1484

s 1–21	1 Jul 1992 (SI 1992/1286)
22	See Sch 1 below
23–25	1 Jul 1992 (SI 1992/1286)
26	See Sch 2 below
27–34	1 Jul 1992 (SI 1992/1286)
35(1)	1 Oct 1991 (so far as relates to s 35(2), (5)) (SI 1991/2054) 2 Mar 1992 (otherwise) (SI 1992/199)
(2)	1 Oct 1991 (SI 1991/2054)
(3), (4)	2 Mar 1992 (SI 1992/199)
(5)	1 Oct 1991 (SI 1991/2054)
(6)	2 Mar 1992 (SI 1992/199)
36	1 Jul 1992 (SI 1992/1286)
37	1 Jul 1992 (SI 1992/1286); prospectively repealed by Criminal Justice (Scotland) Act 1995, s 117, Sch 6, Pt II, para 192, Sch 7, Pt II[1]
38–40	1 Jul 1992 (SI 1992/1286)
41, 42	5 Jul 1993 (EW) (SI 1993/1461, as amended by SI 1993/1686) *Not in force* (S)
43	1 Oct 1991 (EW) (SI 1991/2054) *Not in force* (S)
44	1 Oct 1991 (SI 1991/2054)
45, 46	1 Jul 1992 (SI 1992/1286)
47	1 Apr 1992 (SI 1992/421)
48	See Sch 4 below
49	1 Jul 1992 (SI 1992/1286)
50, 51	1 Oct 1991 (SI 1991/2054)
52(1)	1 Oct 1991 (SI 1991/2054)
(2)	See Sch 5 below
(3)–(9)	1 Oct 1991 (SI 1991/2054)
53–63	1 Oct 1991 (SI 1991/2054)
64(1)	Ss 64(1), 65, 66(1)(6), 67(4), (6), 68(2)(b), 69, 81 (so far as relates to Sch 7 as noted below), Sch 7, para 5(2), (3), brought into force, subject to transitional provisions relating to ss 66(2), 67(4), (6), 68(2)(b), on various dates and in respect of various London boroughs as follows— 5 Jul 1993 (only in London borough of Wandsworth) (subject to transitional provisions) (SI 1993/1461) 4 Oct 1993 (only in London boroughs of Bromley, Hammersmith and Fulham and Lewisham) (SI 1993/2229) 6 Dec 1993 (only in London boroughs of Camden, Hackney and Hounslow) (SI 1993/2803) 31 Jan 1994 (only in London borough of Richmond upon Thames) (SI 1993/3238, as amended by SI 1994/81) 5 Apr 1994 (only in London borough of Southwark) (SI 1994/81) 4 Jul 1994 (only in City of London and London boroughs of Barking and Dagenham, Barnet, Brent, Croydon, Ealing, Enfield, Greenwich,

Road Traffic Act 1991 (c 40)—*cont*

s 64(1)—*cont*	Haringey, Harrow, Havering, Hillingdon, Islington, Royal borough of Kensington and Chelsea, Royal borough of Kingston upon Thames, Lambeth, Merton, Newham, Redbridge, Sutton, Tower Hamlets, Waltham Forest, City of Westminster) (SI 1994/1482)
	4 Jul 1994 (only in London borough of Bexley, and not in relation to ss 67(4), (6), 68(2)(b), 69) (SI 1994/1484)
	Not in force (otherwise)
(2)	1 Oct 1991 (SI 1991/2054)
65	See note to s 64
66(1)–(4)	See note to s 64
(4A)	Inserted in relation to Common Council of the City of London and council of any London borough other than Tower Hamlets, by London Local Authorities Act 1995, s 8
(5), (6)	See note to s 64
(7)	See Sch 6 below
67(1)–(3)	5 Jul 1993 (subject to transitional provisions) (SI 1993/1461)
(4)	See note to s 64
(5)	5 Jul 1993 (subject to transitional provisions) (SI 1993/1461)
(6)	See note to s 64
(7)	5 Jul 1993 (subject to transitional provisions) (SI 1993/1461)
68(1)	5 Jul 1993 (subject to transitional provisions) (SI 1993/1461)
(2)(a)	5 Jul 1993 (subject to transitional provisions) (SI 1993/1461)
(b)	See note to s 64
(3), (4)	5 Jul 1993 (subject to transitional provisions) (SI 1993/1461)
69	See note to s 64
70–72	5 Jul 1993 (SI 1993/1461)
73–78	1 Oct 1991 (SI 1991/2054)
79	5 Jul 1993 (SI 1993/1461)
80	1 Oct 1991 (SI 1991/2054)
81	See Sch 7 below
82	1 Oct 1991 (SI 1991/2054)
83	See Sch 8 below
84–87	25 Jul 1991 (RA)
Sch 1, 2	1 Jul 1992 (SI 1992/1286)
3	1 Oct 1991 (SI 1991/2054)
4, para 1	Repealed
2, 3	1 Jul 1992 (SI 1992/1286)
4, 5	Repealed
6–26	1 Jul 1992 (SI 1992/1286)
27, 28	1 Oct 1991 (SI 1991/2054)
29, 30	1 Jul 1992 (SI 1992/1286)
31–35	1 Oct 1991 (SI 1991/2054)
36	1 Apr 1992 (SI 1992/421)
37–49	1 Jul 1992 (SI 1992/1286)
50	1 Apr 1992 (SI 1992/421)
51–72	1 Jul 1992 (SI 1992/1286)

Road Traffic Act 1991 (c 40)—*cont*

Sch 4, para 73(1)	1 Apr 1992 (so far as relates to para 73(2), (3)) (SI 1992/421) 1 Jul 1992 (otherwise) (SI 1992/1286)
(2), (3)	1 Apr 1992 (SI 1992/421)
(4)–(6)	1 Jul 1992 (SI 1992/1286)
74	1 Jul 1992 (SI 1992/1286)
75	1 Apr 1992 (SI 1992/421)
76–78	1 Jul 1992 (SI 1992/1286)
79	Repealed
80–84	1 Jul 1992 (SI 1992/1286)
85	1 Apr 1993 (for purposes of summary criminal proceedings in Scotland commenced on or after that date) (SI 1993/975) *Not in force* (otherwise)
86–101	1 Jul 1992 (SI 1992/1286)
102	1 Apr 1992 (but does not apply to offence alleged to have been committed before 1 Apr 1992) (SI 1992/199)
103–105	1 Jul 1992 (SI 1992/1286)
106	1 Oct 1991 (SI 1991/2054)
107–114	1 Jul 1992 (SI 1992/1286)
5	1 Oct 1991 (SI 1991/2054)
6	5 Jul 1993 (SI 1993/1461)
7, para 1	Repealed
2	1 Jul 1992 (SI 1992/1286)
3, 4	1 Oct 1991 (SI 1991/2054)
5(1)	1 Oct 1991 (SI 1991/2054)
(2), (3)	See note to s 64
(4)	1 Oct 1991 (SI 1991/2054)
6	*Not in force*
7	1 Oct 1991 (SI 1991/2054)
8	1 Sep 1992 (subject to transitional provisions with respect to a notice of a proposal to exercise a power to which the Local Government Act 1985, Sch 5, para 5(2), applies, given before 1 Sep 1992) (SI 1992/2010)
9–11	1 Oct 1991 (SI 1991/2054)
12	*Not in force*
8	1 Oct 1991 (repeals of or in Chronically Sick and Disabled Persons Act 1970, s 21(5); Road Traffic Regulation Act 1984, ss 35(9), 51(5), 55(4)(c), 99(2), 104(10), 105(3)(b), 106(2)–(6), (9), (10), 117(3)) (SI 1991/2054) 1 Apr 1992 (repeal of Road Traffic Act 1988, s 41(3)(b), (c)) (SI 1992/421) 1 Jul 1992 (otherwise, except repeals in Public Passenger Vehicles Act 1981, s 66A; Road Traffic Regulation Act 1984, s 102) (SI 1992/1286) 5 Jul 1993 (repeals in Road Traffic Regulation Act 1984, s 102) (SI 1993/1461) *Not in force* (repeal in Public Passenger Vehicles Act 1981, s 66A)

[1] Any order made under Criminal Justice (Scotland) Act 1995, s 118(2), bringing the prospective repeal into force will be noted to that Act in the service to this work

Road Traffic (Temporary Restrictions) Act 1991 (c 26)

RA: 27 Jun 1991

Commencement provisions: s 2(7); Road Traffic (Temporary Restrictions) Act 1991 (Commencement) Order 1992, SI 1992/1218

1 Jul 1992 (SI 1992/1218)

School Teachers' Pay and Conditions Act 1991 (c 49)

RA: 25 Jul 1991

Commencement provisions: s 6(5); School Teachers' Pay and Conditions Act 1991 (Commencement No 1) Order 1991, SI 1991/1874; School Teachers' Pay and Conditions Act 1991 (Commencement No 2 and Transitional Provision) Order 1992, SI 1992/532; School Teachers' Pay and Conditions Act 1991 (Commencement No 3) Order 1992, SI 1992/988; School Teachers' Pay and Conditions Act 1991 (Commencement No 4) Order 1992, SI 1992/3070

s 1	22 Aug 1991 (SI 1991/1874)
2(1)–(6)	6 Mar 1992 SI 1992/532)
(7)	4 Dec 1992 (SI 1992/3070)
(8)	6 Mar 1992 (SI 1992/532)
(9)	30 Mar 1992 (SI 1992/988)
3	6 Mar 1992 (SI 1992/532)
3A	Inserted by Education Act 1993, s 289 (qv)
4, 5	22 Aug 1991 (SI 1991/1874)
6(1), (2)	22 Aug 1991 (SI 1991/1874)
(3)	See Sch 2 below
(4), (5)	22 Aug 1991 (SI 1991/1874)
Sch 1	22 Aug 1991 (SI 1991/1874)
2	6 Mar 1992 (SI 1992/532)

Smoke Detectors Act 1991 (c 37)

RA: 25 Jul 1991

Commencement provisions: s 7(3)

Not in force

Social Security (Contributions) Act 1991 (c 42)

Whole Act repealed

Statute Law Revision (Isle of Man) Act 1991 (c 61)

RA: 25 Jul 1991

25 Jul 1991 (RA)

Statutory Sick Pay Act 1991 (c 3)

RA: 12 Feb 1991

Commencement provisions: s 4(2); Statutory Sick Pay Act 1991 (Commencement) Order 1991, SI 1991/260

s 1, 2	Repealed
3(1)	12 Feb 1991 (s 4(2))
(2)	See Schedule below
(3)–(5)	Repealed
(6)	12 Feb 1991 (s 4(2))
4	12 Feb 1991 (s 4(2))
Schedule	6 Apr 1991 (SI 1991/260)

Statutory Water Companies Act 1991 (c 58)

RA: 25 Jul 1991

Commencement provisions: s 17(2)

1 Dec 1991 (s 17(2))

War Crimes Act 1991 (c 13)

RA: 9 May 1991

Commencement provisions: s 3(4)

s 1(1)–(3)	9 May 1991 (s 3(4))
(4)	See Schedule below
2, 3	9 May 1991 (s 3(4))
Schedule	*Not in force* (Pt I prospectively repealed by Criminal Justice and Public Order Act 1994, ss 44(3), 168(3), Sch 4, Pt II, para 72(b), Sch 11; any order made under s 172 of that Act bringing the repeal into force will be noted to that Act in the service to this work)

Water Consolidation (Consequential Provisions) Act 1991 (c 60)

RA: 25 Jul 1991

Commencement provisions: s 4(2)

1 Dec 1991 (s 4(2))

Water Industry Act 1991 (c 56)

RA: 25 Jul 1991

Commencement provisions: s 223(2)

1 Dec 1991 (s 223(2))

Water Resources Act 1991 (c 57)

RA: 25 Jul 1991

Commencement provisions: s 225(2)

1 Dec 1991 (s 225(2))

Welfare of Animals at Slaughter Act 1991 (c 30)

RA: 27 Jun 1991

Commencement provisions: s 7(2)

27 Aug 1991 (s 7(2))

Welsh Development Agency Act 1991 (c 69)

RA: 19 Dec 1991

19 Dec 1991 (RA)

Wildlife and Countryside (Amendment) Act 1991 (c 39)

RA: 25 Jul 1991

Commencement provisions: s 3(3)

25 Sep 1991 (s 3(3))

1992

Access to Neighbouring Land Act 1992 (c 23)

RA: 16 Mar 1992

Commencement provisions: s 9(2); Access to Neighbouring Land Act 1992 (Commencement) Order 1992, SI 1992/3349

31 Jan 1993 (SI 1992/3349)

Aggravated Vehicle-Taking Act 1992 (c 11)

RA: 6 Mar 1992

Commencement provisions: s 4(2); Aggravated Vehicle-Taking Act 1992 (Commencement) Order 1992, SI 1992/764

1 Apr 1992 (SI 1992/764)

Appropriation Act 1992 (c 22)

Whole Act repealed

Appropriation (No 2) Act 1992 (c 47)

Whole Act repealed

Army Act 1992 (c 39)

RA: 16 Mar 1992

Commencement provision: s 5

1 Jul 1992 (s 5)

Bingo Act 1992 (c 10)

RA: 6 Mar 1992

Commencement provision: s 2(2)

6 May 1992 (s 2(2))

Boundary Commissions Act 1992 (c 55)

RA: 12 Nov 1992

12 Nov 1992 (RA)

Car Tax (Abolition) Act 1992 (c 58)

RA: 3 Dec 1992

Commencement provision: s 5

13 Nov 1992 (s 5)

Carriage of Goods by Sea Act 1992 (c 50)

RA: 16 Jul 1992

Commencement provision: s 6(3)

16 Sep 1992 (s 6(3))

Charities Act 1992 (c 41)

RA: 16 Mar 1992

Commencement provisions: s 79(2); Charities Act 1992 (Commencement No 1 and Transitional Provisions) Order 1992, SI 1992/1900; Charities Act 1992 (Commencement No 2) Order 1994, SI 1994/3023

s 1	1 Sep 1992 (except definitions 'financial year', 'independent examiner' and 'special trust' in sub-s (1), and except sub-s (3) (now repealed)) (SI 1992/1900)
	Not in force (exception noted above)
2–28	Repealed
29, 30	1 Sep 1992 (SI 1992/1900)
31–35	Repealed
36	1 Jan 1993 (SI 1992/1900)
37–48	Repealed
49, 50	1 Sep 1992 (SI 1992/1900)
51–57	Repealed
58	1 Mar 1995 (SI 1994/3023)
59	28 Nov 1994 (regulations, etc) (SI 1994/3023)
	1 Mar 1995 (otherwise) (SI 1994/3023)
60–63	1 Mar 1995 (SI 1994/3023)
64	28 Nov 1994 (regulations, etc) (SI 1994/3023)
	1 Mar 1995 (otherwise) (SI 1994/3023)
65–74	*Not in force*
75–79	1 Sep 1992 (SI 1992/1900)
Sch 1–4	Repealed
5	1 Sep 1992 (SI 1992/1900)
6, para 1	1 Jan 1993 (SI 1992/1900)
2	1 Sep 1992 (SI 1992/1900)
3–8	1 Jan 1993 (SI 1992/1900)
9	*Not in force*

Charities Act 1992 (c 41)—*cont*

Sch 6, para 10(a)	1 Sep 1992 (SI 1992/1900)
(b)	*Not in force*
11, 12	1 Sep 1992 (SI 1992/1900)
13(1)	1 Jan 1993 (SI 1992/1900)
(2)	Repealed (never in force)
(3)	1 Jan 1993 (SI 1992/1900)
14–17	1 Sep 1992 (SI 1992/1900)
7	1 Sep 1992 (repeals of or in War Charities Act 1940; National Assistance Act 1948, s 41; Trading Representations (Disabled Persons) Act 1958, s 1(2)(b); Mental Health Act 1959, s 8(3); Charities Act 1960, ss 4(6), 6(6), (9) (subject to transitional provisions), 7(4), 16(2), 19(6), 22(6), (9), 30C(1)(c), 31, 45(3), 46, Sch 1, para 1(3), Sch 6; Local Government Act 1966, Sch 3, Pt II, column 1, para 20; Local Authority Social Services Act 1970, Sch 1; Local Government Act 1972, s 210(8); Health and Social Services and Social Security Adjudications Act 1983, s 30(3); National Heritage Act 1983, Sch 4, paras 13, 14; Companies Consolidation (Consequential Provisions) Act 1985, Sch 2; Charities Act 1985 (except s 1) (subject to transitional provisions); Finance Act 1986, s 33) (SI 1992/1900)
	1 Jan 1993 (repeals of or in Charitable Trustees Incorporation Act 1872, ss 2, 4, 5, 7, Schedule; Charities Act 1960, ss 27 (subject to transitional provisions), 29, 44) (SI 1992/1900)
	Not in force (otherwise)

Cheques Act 1992 (c 32)

RA: 16 Mar 1992

Commencement provision: s 4(2)

16 Jun 1992 (s 4(2))

Church of England (Miscellaneous Provisions) Measure 1992 (No 1)

RA: 6 Mar 1992

Commencement provision: s 19(2)

The provisions of this Measure were brought into force on the following dates by instruments made by the Archbishops of Canterbury and York, and dated 27 May 1992 and 11 Jul 1992 (made under s 19(2))

s 1	1 Jun 1992
2, 3	11 Jul 1992
4	*Not in force*
5–14	1 Jun 1992
15	11 Jul 1992
16–19	1 Jun 1992
Sch 1	*Not in force*

Church of England (Miscellaneous Provisions) Measure 1992 (No 1)—*cont*

Sch 2	1 Jun 1992
3, para 1	11 Jul 1992
2–4	1 Jun 1992
5	11 Jul 1992
6–11	1 Jun 1992
12	11 Jul 1992
13–27	1 Jun 1992
4, Pt I	1 Jun 1992
II	1 Jun 1992 (except entry relating to Cremation Act 1902, s 11)
	11 Jul 1992 (exception noted above)

Civil Service (Management Functions) Act 1992 (c 61)

RA: 17 Dec 1992

17 Dec 1992 (RA)

Coal Industry Act 1992 (c 17)

RA: 6 Mar 1992

Commencement provisions: s 3(4); Coal Industry Act 1992 (Commencement) Order 1993, SI 1993/2514

s 1	6 Mar 1992 (RA)
2	20 Nov 1993 (SI 1993/2514)
3(1), (2)	6 Mar 1992 (RA)
(3)	See Schedule below
(4), (5)	6 Mar 1992 (RA)
Schedule,	
Pt I	6 Mar 1992 (RA)
II	20 Nov 1993 (SI 1993/2514)

Whole Act repealed by Coal Industry Act 1994, s 67(8), Sch 11, Pt III, as from a day to be appointed by order under s 68(4), (5) of that Act; any such order bringing the prospective repeal into force will be noted to that Act in the service to this work

Community Care (Residential Accommodation) Act 1992 (c 49)

RA: 16 Jul 1992

Commencement provisions: s 2(2); Community Care (Residential Accommodation) Act 1992 (Commencement) Order 1992, SI 1992/2976

s 1	1 Apr 1993 (SI 1992/2976)
2	16 Jul 1992 (RA)

Competition and Service (Utilities) Act 1992 (c 43)

RA: 16 Mar 1992

Commencement provisions: s 56(2); Competition and Service (Utilities) Act 1992 (Commencement No 1) Order 1992, dated 29 May 1992 (note that, due to a drafting error, commencement orders under this Act are not made by statutory instrument)

Abbreviation: "No 1" means the Competition and Service (Utilities) Act 1992 (Commencement No 1) Order 1992

s 1–4	1 Jul 1992 (No 1)
5	1 Sep 1992 (No 1)
6(1)	1 Jul 1992 (except so far as inserts Telecommunications Act 1984, s 27G(8)) (No 1)
	Not in force (exception noted above)
(2)	1 Jul 1992 (No 1)
7	1 Jul 1992 (except so far as inserts Telecommunications Act 1984, s 27H(4)) (No 1)
	Not in force (exception noted above)
8–14	1 Jul 1992 (No 1)
15	1 Jul 1992 (No 1); prospectively repealed by Gas Act 1995, s 17(5), Sch 6[1]
16	1 Sep 1992 (No 1); prospectively repealed by Gas Act 1995, s 17(5), Sch 6[1]
17	*Not in force*
18	1 Jul 1992 (No 1)
19	1 Jul 1992 (No 1); prospectively repealed by Gas Act 1995, s 17(5), Sch 6[1]
20–22	1 Jul 1992 (No 1)
23	*Not in force*
24–33	1 Jul 1992 (No 1)
34, 35	1 Sep 1992 (No 1)
36	*Not in force*
37	30 May 1992 (No 1)
38	1 Jul 1992 (No 1); prospectively repealed by Gas Act 1995, s 17(5), Sch 6[1]
39–50	1 Jul 1992 (No 1)
51	1 Sep 1992 (No 1)
52, 53	1 Jul 1992 (No 1)
54	16 Mar 1992 (s 56(2))
55	30 May 1992 (No 1)
56(1)–(5)	16 Mar 1992 (s 56(2))
(6)	See Sch 1 below
(7)	See Sch 2 below
Sch 1, para 1–4	1 Jul 1992 (No 1)
5, 6	1 Jul 1992 (No 1); prospectively repealed by Gas Act 1995, s 17(5), Sch 6[1]
7–30	1 Jul 1992 (No 1)
31	1 Sep 1992 (No 1)
2	1 Jul 1992 (No 1)

[1] Any order(s) made under Gas Act 1995, s 18(2), bringing the prospective repeals into force will be noted to that Act in the service to this work

Consolidated Fund Act 1992 (c 1)

Whole Act repealed

Consolidated Fund (No 2) Act 1992 (c 21)

Whole Act repealed

Consolidated Fund (No 3) Act 1992 (c 59)

Whole Act repealed

Education (Schools) Act 1992 (c 38)

RA: 16 Mar 1992

Commencement provisions: s 21(3); Education (Schools) Act 1992 (Commencement No 1) Order 1992, SI 1992/1157; Education (Schools) Act 1992 (Commencement No 2 and Transitional Provision) Order 1993, SI 1993/1190; Education (Schools) Act 1992 (Commencement No 3) Order 1993, SI 1993/1491

s 1(1)–(4)	16 May 1992 (SI 1992/1157)
(5), (6)	31 Aug 1992 (SI 1992/1157)
2(1), (2)	31 Aug 1992 (SI 1992/1157)
(3)(a), (b)	31 Aug 1992 (SI 1992/1157)
(c), (d)	*Not in force*
(e)	31 Aug 1992 (SI 1992/1157)
(4)–(6)	31 Aug 1992 (SI 1992/1157)
3(1)	31 Aug 1992 (SI 1992/1157)
(2)	*Not in force*
(3)–(5)	31 Aug 1992 (SI 1992/1157)
4	31 Aug 1992 (SI 1992/1157)
5(1)–(4)	16 May 1992 (SI 1992/1157)
(5), (6)	31 Aug 1992 (SI 1992/1157)
6(1), (2)	31 Aug 1992 (SI 1992/1157)
(3)(a), (b)	31 Aug 1992 (SI 1992/1157)
(c), (d)	*Not in force*
(e)	31 Aug 1992 (SI 1992/1157)
(4)–(6)	31 Aug 1992 (SI 1992/1157)
7(1)	31 Aug 1992 (SI 1992/1157)
(2)	*Not in force*
(3)–(5)	31 Aug 1992 (SI 1992/1157)
8	31 Aug 1992 (SI 1992/1157)
9(1)–(6)	12 Jun 1993 (SI 1993/1491)
(7)	See Sch 2 below
10(1)–(3)	31 Aug 1992 (SI 1992/1157)
(4)(a)	31 Aug 1992 (SI 1992/1157)
(b)	16 May 1992 (SI 1992/1157)
(5)–(9)	31 Aug 1992 (SI 1992/1157)
11, 12	31 Aug 1992 (SI 1992/1157)
13	12 Jun 1993 (SI 1993/1491)
14	1 May 1993 (SI 1993/1190) (note that SI 1993/1491 purports to bring this section into force on 12 Jun 1993)
15	1 Sep 1993 (in relation to secondary schools) (SI 1993/1491)
	1 Sep 1994 (in relation to other schools) (SI 1993/1491)
16	16 May 1992 (SI 1992/1157)
17	1 May 1993 (SI 1993/1190)
18(1)	16 May 1992 (SI 1992/1157)
(2), (3)	31 Aug 1992 (SI 1992/1157)

Education (Schools) Act 1992 (c 38)—*cont*

s 18(4)	16 May 1992 (SI 1992/1157)
19, 20	16 May 1992 (SI 1992/1157)
21(1)–(6)	16 Mar 1992 (s 21(3))
(7)	See Sch 4 below
(8)	See Sch 5 below
Sch 1, para 1–6	31 Aug 1992 (SI 1992/1157)
7–9	31 Aug 1992 (EW) (SI 1992/1157) 1 May 1993 (S) (SI 1993/1190)
2, Pt I, para 1–3	1 May 1993 (SI 1993/1190)
4, 5	31 Aug 1992 (SI 1992/1157)
6–8	12 Jun 1993 (SI 1993/1491)
9–9C	Substituted for original para 9 by Education Act 1993, s 307(1), Sch 19, para 173(5) (qv)
10–12	Substituted by Education Act 1993, s 307(1), Sch 19, para 173(6), (7) (qv)
II, para 13–15	31 Aug 1992 (SI 1992/1157)
3	31 Aug 1992 (SI 1992/1157)
4, para 1	*Not in force*
2, 3	Repealed
4	1 May 1993 (subject to a transitional provision) (SI 1993/1190)
5, 6	16 May 1992 (SI 1992/1157)
7	31 Aug 1992 (SI 1992/1157)
5	16 May 1992 (repeals in Education Reform Act 1988, s 22) (SI 1992/1157) 12 Jun 1993 (repeal of Education Act 1944, s 77(6)) (SI 1993/1491) 1 Sep 1993 (in relation to secondary schools, repeals of or in Education Act 1944, s 77(1), (5)) (SI 1993/1491) 1 Sep 1994 (in relation to schools other than secondary schools, repeals of or in Education Act 1944, s 77(1), (5)) (SI 1993/1491) *Not in force* (repeal of Education Reform Act 1988, Sch 1, para 5)

Finance Act 1992 (c 20)

Budget Day: 10 Mar 1992

RA: 16 Mar 1992

See the note concerning Finance Acts at the front of this book

Finance (No 2) Act 1992 (c 48)

Budget Day: 10 Mar 1992

RA: 16 Jul 1992

See the note concerning Finance Acts at the front of this book

Firearms (Amendment) Act 1992 (c 31)

RA: 16 Mar 1992

16 Mar 1992 (RA)

Friendly Societies Act 1992 (c 40)

RA: 16 Mar 1992

Commencement provisions: s 126(2); Friendly Societies Act 1992 (Commencement No 1) Order 1992, SI 1992/1325; Friendly Societies Act 1992 (Commencement No 2) Order 1992, SI 1992/3117; Friendly Societies Act 1992 (Commencement No 3 and Transitional Provisions) Order 1993, SI 1993/16; Friendly Societies Act 1992 (Commencement No 4) Order 1993, SI 1993/197; Friendly Societies Act 1992 (Commencement No 5 and Savings) Order 1993, SI 1993/1186; Friendly Societies Act 1992 (Commencement No 6 and Transitional Provisions) Order 1993, SI 1993/2213; Friendly Societies Act 1992 (Commencement No 7 and Transitional Provisions and Savings) Order 1993, SI 1993/3226; Friendly Societies Act 1992 (Commencement No 8) Order 1994, SI 1994/2543

s 1–4	8 Jun 1992 (SI 1992/1325)
5(1)–(5)	1 Feb 1993 (SI 1993/16)
(6)	See Sch 3 below
(7)	1 Feb 1993 (SI 1993/16)
6–26	1 Feb 1993 (SI 1993/16)
27(1)–(4)	13 Jan 1993 (for purpose of management and administration of incorporated friendly societies) (SI 1993/16)
	1 Jan 1994 (otherwise) (SI 1993/2213)
(5)	See Sch 11 below
28, 29	13 Jan 1993 (for purpose of management and administration of incorporated friendly societies) (SI 1993/16)
	1 Jan 1994 (otherwise) (subject to transitional provisions) (SI 1993/2213)
30	See Sch 12 below
31	13 Jan 1993 (for purpose of carrying on business by incorporated friendly societies) (SI 1993/16)
	1 Jan 1994 (in relation to registered friendly societies the value of whose specified income for the relevant year exceeded £3,000 and which do not apply for authorisation before 1 Jan 1994) (SI 1993/2213)
	1 Jan 1994 (for purpose of carrying on by a registered friendly society of insurance business in respect of which the society is deemed to be granted authorisation under s 32(7)) (SI 1993/2213)
	1 Jul 1994 (in relation to registered friendly societies the value of whose specified income for the relevant year exceeded £3,000 and which apply for authorisation before 1 Jan 1994) (SI 1993/2213)
	1 Nov 1994 (in relation to carrying on of any insurance business or non-insurance business by a registered friendly society (other than one to which SI 1993/2213, art 2(2), (3) or (4) applies) which does not duly apply to the Commission

Friendly Societies Act 1992 (c 40)—*cont*

s 31—*cont*	before 1 Nov 1994 under s 32 or 33 for authorisation to carry on or continue to carry on any class or part of a class of insurance business or any description of non-insurance business) (SI 1994/2543)
	1 Jan 1995 (in relation to carrying on of any insurance or non-insurance business by a friendly society to which s 96(2) of this Act applies) (SI 1993/3226)
	1 Apr 1995 (all remaining purposes) (SI 1994/2543)
32(1)–(3)	13 Jan 1993 (for purpose of authorisation of incorporated friendly societies following application from such societies and from registered friendly societies seeking to be incorporated under this Act) (SI 1993/16)
	13 Sep 1993 (otherwise) (SI 1993/2213)
(4)	Substituted (1 Sep 1994) by Friendly Societies Act 1992 (Amendment) Regulations 1994, SI 1994/1984, reg 4
(5)	13 Jan 1993 (for purpose of authorisation of incorporated friendly societies following application from such societies and from registered friendly societies seeking to be incorporated under this Act) (SI 1993/16)
	13 Sep 1993 (otherwise) (SI 1993/2213)
(6)	See Sch 13 below
(7)	13 Jan 1993 (for purpose of authorisation of incorporated friendly societies following application from such societies and from registered friendly societies seeking to be incorporated under this Act) (SI 1993/16)
	1 Jan 1994 (otherwise) (SI 1993/2213)
(8), (9)	13 Jan 1993 (for purpose of authorisation of incorporated friendly societies following application from such societies and from registered friendly societies seeking to be incorporated under this Act) (SI 1993/16)
	13 Sep 1993 (otherwise) (SI 1993/2213)
33	13 Jan 1993 (for purpose of applications from registered friendly societies seeking to be incorporated under this Act and from incorporated friendly societies for authorisation to carry on existing business as incorporated friendly societies) (SI 1993/16)
	13 Sep 1993 (otherwise) (SI 1993/2213)
34, 35	13 Jan 1993 (for purpose of grant and extension of authorisation of incorporated friendly societies following applications from incorporated friendly societies and from registered friendly societies seeking to be incorporated under Friendly Societies Act 1992) (SI 1993/16)
	13 Sep 1993 (otherwise) (SI 1993/2213)
36	13 Jan 1993 (for purpose of control of conduct of business by incorporated friendly societies) (SI 1993/16)
	13 Sep 1993 (otherwise) (SI 1993/2213)

Friendly Societies Act 1992 (c 40)—*cont*

s 36A	Inserted (1 Jan 1994) by Friendly Societies (Amendment) Regulations 1993, SI 1993/2519, reg 2(1)
37–43	13 Jan 1993 (for purpose of control of conduct of business by incorporated friendly societies) (SI 1993/16) 13 Sep 1993 (otherwise) (SI 1993/2213)
44(1)–(7)	13 Jan 1993 (for purpose of regulation of business of incorporated friendly societies) (SI 1993/16) 1 Jan 1994 (otherwise) (SI 1993/2213)
(8)	13 Jan 1993 (for purpose of regulation of business of incorporated friendly societies) (SI 1993/16) 13 Sep 1993 (otherwise) (SI 1993/2213)
45	13 Jan 1993 (for purpose of regulation of business of incorporated friendly societies) (SI 1993/16) 13 Sep 1993 (otherwise) (SI 1993/2213)
46(1)	13 Jan 1993 (for purpose of regulation of business of incorporated friendly societies) (SI 1993/16) 13 Sep 1993 (otherwise) (SI 1993/2213)
(2)	13 Jan 1993 (for purpose of regulation of business of incorporated friendly societies) (SI 1993/16)[1] 1 Jan 1994 (otherwise) (SI 1993/2213)
(3)	13 Jan 1993 (for purpose of regulation of business of incorporated friendly societies) (SI 1993/16) 13 Sep 1993 (otherwise) (SI 1993/2213)
(4)–(7)	13 Jan 1993 (for purpose of regulation of business of incorporated friendly societies) (SI 1993/16) 1 Jan 1994 (otherwise) (SI 1993/2213)
(8)	13 Jan 1993 (for purpose of regulation of business of incorporated friendly societies) (SI 1993/16) 13 Sep 1993 (otherwise) (SI 1993/2213)
47	13 Jan 1993 (for purpose of regulation of business of incorporated friendly societies) (SI 1993/16)[1] 1 Jan 1994 (otherwise) (SI 1993/2213)
48(1), (2)	13 Jan 1993 (for purpose of regulation of business of incorporated friendly societies) (SI 1993/16) 13 Sep 1993 (so far as confers powers to make regulations for purposes of section) (SI 1993/2213) 1 Jan 1994 (otherwise) (SI 1993/2213)
(3)–(5)	13 Jan 1993 (for purpose of regulation of business of incorporated friendly societies) (SI 1993/16) 1 Jan 1994 (otherwise) (SI 1993/2213)
(6), (7)	13 Jan 1993 (for purpose of regulation of business of incorporated friendly societies) (SI 1993/16) 13 Sep 1993 (so far as confers powers to make regulations for purposes of section) (SI 1993/2213) 1 Jan 1994 (otherwise) (SI 1993/2213)
49(1)	13 Jan 1993 (for purpose of regulation of business of incorporated friendly societies) (SI 1993/16) 13 Sep 1993 (otherwise) (SI 1993/2213)
(2), (3)	13 Jan 1993 (for purpose of regulation of business of incorporated friendly societies) (SI 1993/16) 1 Jan 1994 (otherwise) (SI 1993/2213)
49A	Inserted (1 Sep 1994) by Friendly Societies Act 1992 (Amendment) Regulations 1994, SI 1994/1984, reg 9

Friendly Societies Act 1992 (c 40)—*cont*

s 49B	Inserted (1 Sep 1994) by Friendly Societies Act 1992 (Amendment) Regulations 1994, SI 1994/1984, reg 10
50	13 Jan 1993 (for purpose of regulation of business of incorporated friendly societies) (SI 1993/16) 13 Sep 1993 (otherwise) (SI 1993/2213)
51, 52	13 Jan 1993 (for purpose of regulation of business of incorporated friendly societies) (SI 1993/16) 28 Apr 1993 (otherwise) (SI 1993/1186)
52A	Inserted (1 Sep 1994) by Friendly Societies Act 1992 (Amendment) Regulations 1994, SI 1994/1984, reg 13
53, 54	13 Jan 1993 (for purpose of regulation of business of incorporated friendly societies) (SI 1993/16) 28 Apr 1993 (otherwise) (SI 1993/1186)
55	13 Jan 1993 (for purpose of regulation of business of incorporated friendly societies) (SI 1993/16) 1 Jan 1994 (otherwise) (SI 1993/2213)
55A	Inserted (1 Sep 1994) by Friendly Societies Act 1992 (Amendment) Regulations 1994, SI 1994/1984, reg 14(1)
56	13 Jan 1993 (for purpose of regulation of business of incorporated friendly societies) (SI 1993/16) 28 Apr 1993 (otherwise) (SI 1993/1186)
57	Substituted (1 Sep 1994) by Friendly Societies Act 1992 (Amendment) Regulations 1994, SI 1994/1984, reg 15(1)
57A	Inserted (1 Jan 1994) by Friendly Societies (Amendment No 2) Regulations 1993, SI 1993/2519, reg 4(2); substituted (1 Sep 1994) by Friendly Societies Act 1992 (Amendment) Regulations 1994, SI 1994/1984, reg 16
58–61	13 Jan 1993 (SI 1993/16)
62–67	13 Jan 1993 (for purpose of regulation of business of incorporated friendly societies) (SI 1993/16) 28 Apr 1993 (otherwise) (SI 1993/1186)
67A	Inserted (1 Sep 1994) by Friendly Societies Act 1992 (Amendment) Regulations 1994, SI 1994/1984, reg 21(1)
67B	Inserted (1 Sep 1994) by Friendly Societies Act 1992 (Amendment) Regulations 1994, SI 1994/1984, reg 22
67C	Inserted (1 Sep 1994) by Friendly Societies Act 1992 (Amendment) Regulations 1994, SI 1994/1984, reg 23
67D	Inserted (1 Sep 1994) by Friendly Societies Act 1992 (Amendment) Regulations 1994, SI 1994/1984, reg 24
68, 69	13 Jan 1993 (for purpose of accounts and audit of incorporated friendly societies) (SI 1993/16) 1 Jan 1994 (otherwise) (SI 1993/2213)
70(1)–(4)	13 Jan 1993 (for purpose of accounts and audit of incorporated friendly societies) (SI 1993/16) 1 Jan 1994 (otherwise) (SI 1993/2213)
(5)–(7)	13 Jan 1993 (for purpose of accounts and audit of incorporated friendly societies) (SI 1993/16) 13 Sep 1993 (otherwise) (SI 1993/2213)

Friendly Societies Act 1992 (c 40)—*cont*

s 70(8)–(11)	13 Jan 1993 (for purpose of accounts and audit of incorporated friendly societies) (SI 1993/16) 1 Jan 1994 (otherwise) (SI 1993/2213)
71(1), (2)	13 Jan 1993 (for purpose of accounts and audit of incorporated friendly societies) (SI 1993/16) 13 Sep 1993 (so far as confers powers to make regulations for purposes of section) (SI 1993/2213) 1 Jan 1994 (otherwise) (SI 1993/2213)
(3)	13 Jan 1993 (for purpose of accounts and audit of incorporated friendly societies) (SI 1993/16) 1 Jan 1994 (otherwise) (SI 1993/2213)
72(1)	13 Jan 1993 (for purpose of accounts and audit of incorporated friendly societies) (SI 1993/16) 1 Jan 1994 (otherwise) (SI 1993/2213)
(2)	See Sch 14 below
73–79	13 Jan 1993 (for purpose of accounts and audit of incorporated friendly societies) (SI 1993/16) 1 Jan 1994 (otherwise) (SI 1993/2213)
80	13 Jan 1993 (subject to transitional provisions) (SI 1993/16)
81	13 Jan 1993 (SI 1993/16)
82(1)–(4)	13 Jan 1993 (SI 1993/16)
(5)	1 Jan 1994 (SI 1993/3226)
83	13 Jan 1993 (SI 1993/16)
84	1 Jan 1993 (subject to transitional provisions) (SI 1992/3117)
85–90	13 Sep 1993 (subject to transitional provisions) (SI 1993/2213)
90A	Inserted (1 Sep 1994) by Friendly Societies Act 1992 (Amendment) Regulations 1994, SI 1994/1984, reg 28
91, 92	13 Sep 1993 (subject to transitional provisions) (SI 1993/2213)
93(1)–(4)	1 Feb 1993 (SI 1993/16)
(5)–(15)	1 Jan 1994 (SI 1993/2213)
94	1 Feb 1993 (SI 1993/16)
95	See Sch 16 below
96	1 Jan 1994 (SI 1993/3226)
97	*Not in force*
98	See Sch 18 below
99	1 Feb 1993 (SI 1993/16)
100	See Sch 19 below
101	Substituted (1 Jan 1994) by Friendly Societies (Amendment) Regulations 1993, SI 1993/2519, reg 6(1)
102–113	1 Feb 1993 (SI 1993/16)
114	13 Jan 1993 (SI 1993/16)
115	1 Feb 1993 (SI 1993/16)
116–119	8 Jun 1992 (SI 1992/1325)
119A	Inserted (1 Sep 1994) by Friendly Societies Act 1992 (Amendment) Regulations 1994, SI 1994/1984, reg 31
119B	Inserted (1 Sep 1994) by Friendly Societies Act 1992 (Amendment) Regulations 1994, SI 1994/1984, reg 32
120(1)	See Sch 21 below
(2)	See Sch 22 below

Friendly Societies Act 1992 (c 40)—*cont*

s 121–123	8 Jun 1992 (SI 1992/1325)
124	1 Jan 1994 (SI 1993/3226)
125	1 Feb 1993 (SI 1993/16)
126	8 Jun 1992 (SI 1992/1325)
Sch 1	8 Jun 1992 (SI 1992/1325)
2	1 Feb 1993 (SI 1993/16)
3, para 1–8	1 Feb 1993 (SI 1993/16)
9(1)	1 Feb 1993 (SI 1993/16)
(2)	*Not in force*
(3)–(7)	1 Feb 1993 (SI 1993/16)
10–15	1 Feb 1993 (SI 1993/16)
4–10	1 Feb 1993 (SI 1993/16)
11, para 1–15	13 Jan 1993 (for purpose of committee of management of incorporated friendly societies) (SI 1993/16) 1 Jan 1994 (otherwise) (SI 1993/2213)
16	13 Jan 1993 (for purpose of committee of management of incorporated friendly societies) (SI 1993/16) 13 Sep 1993 (otherwise) (SI 1993/2213)
12, para 1–6	13 Jan 1993 (for purpose of meetings and resolutions of incorporated friendly societies) (SI 1993/16) 1 Jan 1994 (otherwise) (SI 1993/2213)
7	13 Jan 1993 (for purpose of meetings and resolutions of incorporated friendly societies) (SI 1993/16) 13 Sep 1993 (otherwise) (SI 1993/2213)
8, 9	13 Jan 1993 (for purpose of meetings and resolutions of incorporated friendly societies) (SI 1993/16) 1 Jan 1994 (otherwise) (SI 1993/2213)
13	13 Jan 1993 (for purpose of authorisation of incorporated friendly societies and applications for authorisation from registered friendly societies to carry on business as incorporated friendly societies) (SI 1993/16) 13 Sep 1993 (otherwise) (SI 1993/2213)
13A	Inserted (1 Sep 1994) by Friendly Societies Act 1992 (Amendment) Regulations 1994, SI 1994/1984, reg 14(2), Sch 1
13B	Inserted (1 Sep 1994) by Friendly Societies Act 1992 (Amendment) Regulations 1994, SI 1994/1984, reg 15(2), Sch 2
13C	Inserted (1 Sep 1994) by Friendly Societies Act 1992 (Amendment) Regulations 1994, SI 1994/1984, reg 21(2), Sch 3
14, para 1–6	13 Jan 1993 (for purpose of auditors of incorporated friendly societies) (SI 1993/16) 1 Jan 1994 (otherwise) (SI 1993/2213)
7(1)–(3)	1 Jan 1994 (SI 1993/2213)
(4)	13 Sep 1993 (SI 1993/2213)
(5)–(7)	1 Jan 1994 (SI 1993/2213)
8–16	13 Jan 1993 (for purpose of auditors of incorporated friendly societies) (SI 1993/16) 1 Jan 1994 (otherwise) (SI 1993/2213)
17	13 Jan 1993 (for purpose of auditors of incorporated friendly societies) (SI 1993/16) 13 Sep 1993 (otherwise) (SI 1993/2213)

Friendly Societies Act 1992 (c 40)—*cont*

Sch 15	13 Sep 1993 (SI 1993/2213)
16, para 1	See paras 252 below
2(1)(a)	13 Jan 1993 (SI 1993/16)
(b)	1 Jan 1994 (SI 1993/3226)
(2)	1 Jan 1994 (SI 1993/3226)
(3)	13 Jan 1993 (SI 1993/16)
3	28 Apr 1993 (SI 1993/1186)
4(a)	1 Feb 1993 (SI 1993/16)
(b)	1 Jan 1994 (subject to transitional provisions) (SI 1993/2213)
(c)	1 Feb 1993 (SI 1993/16)
5–7	1 Feb 1993 (SI 1993/16)
8, 9	1 Jan 1994 (SI 1993/2213)
10	1 Feb 1993 (SI 1993/16)
11, 12	1 Jan 1994 (subject to transitional provisions) (SI 1993/2213)
13, 14	1 Jan 1994 (SI 1993/3226)
15	1 Jan 1994 (SI 1993/2213)
16	1 Feb 1993 (SI 1993/16)
17	1 Jan 1994 (SI 1993/2213)
18(a)	1 Jan 1994 (SI 1993/2213)
(b)	1 Jan 1994 (SI 1993/3226)
19	1 Feb 1993 (SI 1993/16)
20, 21	1 Jan 1994 (SI 1993/3226)
22, 23	1 Jan 1994 (subject to transitional provisions) (SI 1993/2213)
24	1 Feb 1993 (so far as repeals Friendly Societies Act 1974, ss 7073, 75) (subject to transitional provisions) (SI 1993/16)
	Not in force (repeal of Friendly Societies Act 1974, s 74)
25, 26	13 Jan 1993 (subject to transitional provisions) (SI 1993/16)
27	1 Jan 1994 (SI 1993/3226)
28	13 Jan 1993 (SI 1993/16)
29	13 Sep 1993 (subject to transitional provisions) (SI 1993/2213)
30	1 Jan 1994 (SI 1993/3226)
31	13 Sep 1993 (SI 1993/2213)
32	1 Feb 1993 (insertion of Friendly Societies Act 1974, s 84A(1)–(7)) (SI 1993/16)[2]
	1 Jan 1994 (insertion of Friendly Societies Act 1974, s 84A(8)) (SI 1993/3226)
33	13 Sep 1993 (subject to transitional provisions) (SI 1993/2213)
34–36	28 Apr 1993 (SI 1993/1186)
37	1 Feb 1993 (SI 1993/16)
38(a)	1 Feb 1993 (subject to transitional provisions) (SI 1993/16)
(b)	28 Apr 1993 (SI 1993/1186)
(c)	28 Apr 1993 (so far as relates to Friendly Societies Act 1974, s 93(3)(a), (b)) (SI 1993/1186)
	1 Jan 1994 (so far as relates to Friendly Societies Act 1974, s 93(3)(c)) (SI 1993/3226)
39–41	28 Apr 1993 (SI 1993/1186)
42(a)	1 Feb 1993 (SI 1993/16)
(b), (c)	1 Jan 1994 (SI 1993/3226)

Friendly Societies Act 1992 (c 40)—*cont*

Sch 16, para 43	1 Jan 1994 (SI 1993/2213)
44	1 Jan 1994 (SI 1993/3226)
45	1 Feb 1993 (SI 1993/16)
46	1 Jan 1994 (SI 1993/3226)
47	1 Feb 1993 (SI 1993/16)
48(a)	1 Jan 1994 (SI 1993/3226)
(b)	1 Feb 1993 (SI 1993/16)
(c), (d)	1 Jan 1994 (SI 1993/3226)
(e)	1 Feb 1993 (SI 1993/16)
49, 50	1 Jan 1994 (SI 1993/3226)
51	1 Jan 1994 (SI 1993/2213)
52	1 Feb 1993 (SI 1993/16)
17	*Not in force*
18, Pt I, para 1, 2	1 Feb 1993 (for purpose of application of Financial Services Act 1986 to incorporated friendly societies) (SI 1993/16)
	1 Jan 1994 (otherwise) (SI 1993/2213)
3	1 Feb 1993 (for purpose of application of Financial Services Act 1986 to incorporated friendly societies) (SI 1993/16)
	28 Apr 1993 (otherwise) (SI 1993/1186)
4–9	1 Feb 1993 (for purpose of application of Financial Services Act 1986 to incorporated friendly societies) (SI 1993/16)
	1 Jan 1994 (otherwise) (SI 1993/2213)
II, para 10–12	1 Feb 1993 (for purpose of application of Financial Services Act 1986 to incorporated friendly societies) (SI 1993/16)
	1 Jan 1994 (otherwise) (SI 1993/2213)
13	1 Feb 1993 (for purpose of application of Financial Services Act 1986 to incorporated friendly societies) (SI 1993/16)
	1 Jan 1994 (otherwise) (SI 1993/3226)
14–22	1 Feb 1993 (for purpose of application of Financial Services Act 1986 to incorporated friendly societies) (SI 1993/16)
	1 Jan 1994 (otherwise) (SI 1993/2213)
19, Pt I, para 1	See paras 2–16 below
2(1)	1 Feb 1993 (SI 1993/16)
(2)	1 Feb 1993 (in relation to incorporated friendly societies and industrial assurance companies) (SI 1993/16)
	28 Apr 1993 (otherwise) (SI 1993/1186)
3	1 Feb 1993 (in relation to incorporated friendly societies and industrial assurance companies) (SI 1993/16)[3]
	28 Apr 1993 (otherwise) (SI 1993/1186)
4	1 Feb 1993 (in relation to incorporated friendly societies and industrial assurance companies) (SI 1993/16)
	28 Apr 1993 (otherwise) (SI 1993/1186)
5(1)(a), (b)	1 Feb 1993 (in relation to incorporated friendly societies and industrial assurance companies) (SI 1993/16)
	28 Apr 1993 (otherwise) (SI 1993/1186)
(c)	1 Jan 1994 (SI 1993/2213)

Friendly Societies Act 1992 (c 40)—*cont*

Sch 19, Pt I, para 5(1)(d),(e)	1 Feb 1993 (in relation to incorporated friendly societies and industrial assurance companies) (SI 1993/16)
	28 Apr 1993 (otherwise) (SI 1993/1186)
(2)(a)	1 Feb 1993 (in relation to incorporated friendly societies and industrial assurance companies) (SI 1993/16)
	28 Apr 1993 (otherwise) (SI 1993/1186)
(b)	1 Jan 1994 (SI 1993/2213)
6	1 Feb 1993 (SI 1993/16)
7	1 Jan 1994 (SI 1993/2213)
8	*Not in force*
9	13 Jan 1993 (SI 1993/16)
10	*Not in force*
11	1 Feb 1993 (in relation to incorporated friendly societies and industrial assurance companies) (SI 1993/16)
	28 Apr 1993 (otherwise, subject to a saving) (SI 1993/1186)
12	1 Feb 1993 (SI 1993/16)
13	1 Feb 1993 (in relation to incorporated friendly societies and industrial assurance companies) (SI 1993/16)
	28 Apr 1993 (otherwise) (SI 1993/1186)
14	1 Feb 1993 (in relation to incorporated friendly societies and industrial assurance companies) (subject to transitional provisions) (SI 1993/16)
	13 Sep 1993 (otherwise) (subject to transitional provisions) (SI 1993/2213)
15, 16	1 Feb 1993 (in relation to incorporated friendly societies and industrial assurance companies) (SI 1993/16)
	28 Apr 1993 (otherwise) (SI 1993/1186)
II, para 17	See paras 18–32 below
18–25	1 Jan 1994 (subject to savings) (SI 1993/3226)
26	*Not in force*
27	1 Jan 1994 (SI 1993/3226)
28	*Not in force*
29–32	1 Jan 1994 (SI 1993/3226)
20, Pt I	1 Feb 1993 (SI 1993/16)
II	Added (1 Jan 1994) (and original Sch 20 renumbered as Sch 20, Pt I) by Friendly Societies (Amendment) Regulations 1993, SI 1993/2519, reg 6(3)(a), (4)
21, Pt I, para 1	1 Feb 1993 (SI 1993/16)
2–4	1 Jan 1993 (SI 1992/3117)
5–11	1 Feb 1993 (SI 1993/16)
12–17	Repealed
18, 19	1 Jan 1994 (SI 1993/3226)
II	1 Jan 1994 (SI 1993/3226)
22, Pt I	13 Jan 1993 (repeals of or in Friendly Societies Act 1974, ss 76(1)(c), (d), (e), (5), 77, 78(1), (2), (3), 79(1), 80(1)) (subject to transitional provisions) (SI 1993/16)
	1 Feb 1993 (repeals of or in Industrial Assurance Act 1923, ss 2(1) (words "and anything which under" to the end), 4, 7, 8(3), Sch 1; Industrial Assurance and Friendly Societies Act 1948, ss 6, 7, 10(1)(b), (c)

Friendly Societies Act 1992 (c 40)—*cont*

Sch 22, Pt I—*cont*

(and words from "and shall, on demand" to the end of sub-s (1)), (2), (3), 11, Sch 1; Friendly Societies Act 1974, ss 8, 11(1), 13(2), 15 (words "society or", in each place they appear[4]), 17, 70–73, 75) (subject to transitional provisions) (SI 1993/16)

1 Feb 1993 (in relation to incorporated friendly societies which are collecting societies, repeals of or in: Industrial Assurance Act 1923, ss 8(2), (4), 15, 16, 18, 19(1)–(3), 35; Industrial Assurance and Friendly Societies Act 1948, s 13(3)) (SI 1993/16)

5 Feb 1993 (repeals of Industrial Assurance Act 1923, s 8(1)(b), in relation to collecting societies (as defined by s 1(1A) thereof) to which the criteria of prudent management described in Friendly Societies Act 1992, s 50(3) apply; Friendly Societies Act 1974, Sch 5) (SI 1993/197)

28 Apr 1993 (in relation to incorporated friendly societies, repeals of or in Financial Services Act 1986, ss 139(3)–(5), 207(1), Sch 11, paras 1, 26(1), (3), 27, 38(1)(a), 43, Sch 15, para 14(1), (3)) (SI 1993/1186)

28 Apr 1993 (repeals of or in Friendly Societies Act 1974, ss 6(2), 16, 88, 89, 106; Industrial Assurance Act 1948, s 17A(2)) (SI 1993/1186)

13 Sep 1993 (repeals of or in Industrial Assurance Act 1923, ss 36, 38; Friendly Societies Act 1974, s 82, Sch 9, para 5) (subject to transitional provisions) (SI 1993/2213)

1 Jan 1994 (so far as not brought into force on 1 Feb and 28 Apr 1993 by SI 1993/16, SI 1993/1186) (repeals of or in Industrial Assurance Act 1923, ss 8(2), (4), 15, 16, 18, 19(1)–(3), 35; Industrial Assurance and Friendly Societies Act 1948, s 13(3); Financial Services Act 1986, ss 139(3)–(5), 207(1), Sch 11, paras 1, 26(1), (3), 27, 38(1)(a), 43, Sch 15, para 14(1), (3) (SI 1993/2213)

1 Jan 1994 (repeals of or in Loan Societies Act 1840; Friendly Societies Act 1896; Industrial Assurance Act 1923, ss 20(1)(b), 31, 44, 45(2); Industrial Assurance and Friendly Societies Act 1929; Industrial Assurance and Friendly Societies Act 1948, ss 1, 4, 23(1), Schs 2, 3; Friendly Societies Act 1955, s 3(2); Industrial Assurance Act 1948 (Amendment) Act 1958; Friendly Societies Act 1974, ss 9(2), (3), 27, 28, 30(5), 46, 53(3), 107(1), Schs 1, 2, 3, Sch 9, paras 2, 6, 8, 10(1); Banking Act 1987, s 84(1); Income and Corporation Taxes Act 1988; Companies Act 1989) (subject to transitional provisions) (SI 1993/2213)

1 Jan 1994 (repeals of or in Industrial Assurance and Friendly Societies Act 1948, ss 2, 10(1)(a) (words "signed by two of the committee of management and by the secretary" only); Consumer Credit Act 1974, s 189(1); Friendly Societies Act 1974, ss 98, 111(6), 115, 117(3), Sch 3; Finance Act 1984; Friendly Societies Act 1984, s 3; Companies

Friendly Societies Act 1992 (c 40)—*cont*

Sch 22, Pt I—*cont*	Act 1985, s 449; Building Societies Act 1986, s 7; Banking Act 1987, s 96, Sch 2) (SI 1993/3226)
	1 Nov 1994 (repeal of Industrial Assurance Act 1923, s 2(1) (so far as not already in force), (2)) (SI 1994/2543)
	Repealed (repeal of Trade Union and Labour Relations (Consolidation) 1992, s 19(2))
	Not in force (otherwise)
II	1 Jan 1994 (except so far as repeals Industrial Assurance (Northern Ireland) Order 1979, SI 1979/1574, arts 4(1) (other than words "and in the exercise and performance of his powers and duties as Registrar under the Friendly Societies Act in relation to collecting societies" which are repealed), (3), 5, 9(1)(a) (other than words "signed by two of the committee of management and by the secretary" which are repealed)) (subject to transitional provisions) (SI 1993/3226)
	1 Nov 1994 (revocation of Industrial Assurance (Northern Ireland) Order 1979, SI 1979/1574, art 4(1) (so far as not already in force), (3)) (SI 1994/2543)
	Not in force (repeal of Industrial Assurance (Northern Ireland) Order 1979, SI 1979/1574, arts 5, 9(1)(a) (part))

[1] For transitional provisions (in respect of ss 46(2)(a)(ii), (c), 47(1)(a), (b)), see the Friendly Societies Act 1992 (Transitional and Consequential Provisions and Savings) Regulations 1993, SI 1993/932, regs 3–5

[2] Note that SI 1993/16 purports to bring into force Sch 16, para 32 (except sub-para (8)). As para 32 contains no sub-paragraphs, it is thought that it was intended to bring into force s 84A(1)–(7) of the 1974 Act, but not sub-s (8) thereof. Note also that SI 1993/2213 purports to bring Sch 16, para 32 (except s 84A(8)) into force for all remaining purposes on 13 Sep 1993

[3] For a saving in respect of the amendment made by Sch 19, Pt I, para 3, see the Friendly Societies Act 1992 (Transitional and Consequential Provisions and Savings) Regulations 1993, SI 1993/932, reg 10

[4] Note that the repeal of those words by the Friendly Societies Act 1992, s 120(2), Sch 22, Pt I, is made to the Friendly Societies Act 1974, s 16, and not to s 15 thereof

---

Further and Higher Education Act 1992 (c 13)

RA: 6 Mar 1992

Commencement provisions: s 94(3); Further and Higher Education Act 1992 (Commencement No 1 and Transitional Provisions) Order 1992, SI 1992/831 (as amended by SI 1992/2041); Further and Higher Education Act 1992 (Commencement No 1 and Transitional Provisions) (Amendment) Order 1992, SI 1992/2041 (amending SI 1992/831); Further and Higher Education Act 1992 (Commencement No 2) Order 1992, SI 1992/2377; Further and Higher Education Act 1992 (Commencement No 2) Order 1992, SI 1992/3057

s 1	6 May 1992 (SI 1992/831)
2–4	1 Apr 1993 (SI 1992/831)
5(1), (2)	1 Apr 1993 (SI 1992/831)
(3)	30 Sep 1992 (SI 1992/831)
(4)	1 Apr 1993 (SI 1992/831)

Further and Higher Education Act 1992 (c 13)—*cont*

s 5(5)–(7)	6 May 1992 (SI 1992/831)
(7A), (7B)	Prospectively inserted by Disability Discrimination Act 1995, s 30(3)[1]
(8)	6 May 1992 (SI 1992/831)
6(1)	1 Apr 1993 (SI 1992/831)
(2)–(4)	6 May 1992 (SI 1992/831)
(5), (6)	30 Sep 1992 (SI 1992/831)
7, 8	6 May 1992 (SI 1992/831)
9(1)–(3)	1 Apr 1993 (SI 1992/831)
(4)	1 Apr 1993 (SI 1992/2377)
(5)	1 Apr 1993 (SI 1992/831)
10, 11	1 Apr 1993 (SI 1992/831)
12	1 Aug 1993 (SI 1992/831)
13	Repealed
14(1)–(4)	6 May 1992 (for purposes of provisions brought into force on 6 May 1992 by SI 1992/831, art 2, Sch 1) (SI 1992/831) 30 Sep 1992 (for purposes of provisions brought into force on 30 Sep 1992 by SI 1992/831, art 2, Sch 2) (SI 1992/831) 1 Apr 1993 (otherwise) (SI 1992/831)
(5)	1 Apr 1993 (SI 1992/831)
(6)	1 Aug 1993 (SI 1992/831)
15(1)–(3)	6 May 1992 (SI 1992/831)
(4)	30 Sep 1992 (SI 1992/831)
(5)–(7)	6 May 1992 (SI 1992/831)
16	30 Sep 1992 (SI 1992/831)
17	6 May 1992 (SI 1992/831)
18–25	30 Sep 1992 (SI 1992/831)
26	30 Sep 1992 (except in respect of persons employed by a local authority to work solely at the institution the corporation is established to conduct and who are so employed in connection with an arrangement for the supply by that local authority of goods or services for the purposes of that institution in pursuance of a bid prepared under Local Government Act 1988, s 7) (SI 1992/831, as amended by SI 1992/2041) *Not in force* (exception noted above)
27	30 Sep 1992 (SI 1992/831)
28–33	6 May 1992 (SI 1992/831)
34, 35	1 Apr 1993 (SI 1992/831)
36	30 Sep 1992 (SI 1992/831)
37, 38	1 Apr 1993 (SI 1992/831)
39–43	6 May 1992 (SI 1992/831)
44	1 Apr 1993 (in respect of institutions which, before they became institutions within the further education sector, were schools maintained by a local education authority or grant-maintained schools) (SI 1992/831) *Not in force* (otherwise)
45	1 Apr 1993 (in respect of institutions which, before they became institutions within the further education sector, were schools maintained by a local education authority or grant-maintained schools) (SI 1992/831) *Not in force* (otherwise)

Further and Higher Education Act 1992 (c 13)—*cont*

s 46–50	1 Apr 1993 (SI 1992/831)
51	30 Sep 1992 (SI 1992/831)
52	1 Apr 1993 (SI 1992/831)
53	30 Sep 1992 (SI 1992/831)
54(1)	6 May 1992 (SI 1992/831)
(2)	1 Apr 1993 (SI 1992/831)
55(1)–(3)	1 Apr 1993 (E) (SI 1992/831) *Not in force* (W)
(4)–(6)	1 Apr 1993 (SI 1992/831)
(7)(a)	1 Apr 1993 (SI 1992/831)
(b)	*Not in force*
(c)	1 Apr 1993 (SI 1992/831)
56	6 May 1992 (SI 1992/831)
57(1), (2)	1 Apr 1993 (SI 1992/831)
(3)–(6)	6 May 1992 (so far as apply to the Further Education Funding Councils) (SI 1992/831) 1 Apr 1993 (otherwise) (SI 1992/831)
58	30 Sep 1992 (SI 1992/831)
59(1), (2)	30 Sep 1992 (SI 1992/831)
(3), (4)	6 May 1992 (SI 1992/831)
(5)	Repealed
60	1 Apr 1993 (SI 1992/831)
61, 62	6 May 1992 (SI 1992/831)
63	1 Apr 1993 (SI 1992/831)
64	6 May 1992 (SI 1992/831)
65, 66	1 Apr 1993 (SI 1992/831)
67(1)	1 Apr 1993 (SI 1992/831)
(2)–(5)	6 May 1992 (SI 1992/831)
68–73	6 May 1992 (SI 1992/831)
74	1 Apr 1993 (SI 1992/831)
75–84	6 May 1992 (SI 1992/831)
85	1 Apr 1993 (SI 1992/831)
86	6 May 1992 (SI 1992/831)
87	30 Sep 1992 (SI 1992/831)
88–92	6 May 1992 (SI 1992/831)
93(1)	See Sch 8 below
(2)	See Sch 9 below
94	6 May 1992 (SI 1992/831)
Sch 1	6 May 1992 (SI 1992/831)
2	30 Sep 1992 (SI 1992/831)
3	6 May 1992 (SI 1992/831)
4, 5	30 Sep 1992 (SI 1992/831)
6	6 May 1992 (SI 1992/831)
7	30 Sep 1992 (SI 1992/831)
8, Pt I, para 1	6 May 1992 (SI 1992/831)
2–5	1 Apr 1993 (SI 1992/831)
6	1 Apr 1993 (SI 1992/831); prospectively repealed by Education Act 1993, s 307(3), Sch 21, Pt II[2] (qv)
7, 8	1 Apr 1993 (SI 1992/831)
9	6 May 1992 (SI 1992/831)
10	1 Sep 1992 (so far as relates to institutions within the PCFC funding sector) (E) (SI 1992/831) 1 Sep 1992 (so far as relates to institutions within the PCFC funding sector) (W) (SI 1992/2377) 7 Dec 1992 (otherwise) (E) (SI 1992/3057) 1 Apr 1993 (otherwise) (W) (SI 1992/2377)

Further and Higher Education Act 1992 (c 13)—*cont*

Sch 8, Pt I, para	11, 12	1 Apr 1993 (SI 1992/831)
	13(1)	6 May 1992 (SI 1992/831)
	(2)(a)	6 May 1992 (in relation to references to 'further education' in provisions of this Act as they are brought into force) (SI 1992/831)
		1 Apr 1993 (otherwise) (SI 1992/831)
	(b), (c)	1 Apr 1993 (SI 1992/831)
	(d)	1 Aug 1993 (SI 1992/831)
	(e)–(g)	1 Apr 1993 (SI 1992/831)
	(3), (4)	1 Apr 1993 (SI 1992/831)
	14–16	1 Apr 1993 (SI 1992/831)
	17	1 Aug 1993 (SI 1992/831)
	18	Repealed
	19, 20	1 Apr 1993 (SI 1992/831)
	21	30 Sep 1992 (SI 1992/831)
	22, 23	1 Apr 1993 (SI 1992/831)
	24	1 Apr 1993 (note that amendments made by para 24(a) do not have effect in relation to provision for further education made by a local education authority before 1 Apr 1993) (SI 1992/831)
	25, 26	1 Apr 1993 (SI 1992/831)
	27	6 May 1992 (SI 1992/831)
	28	1 Apr 1993 (SI 1992/831)
	29	Repealed
	30	1 Apr 1993 (SI 1992/831)
	31	6 May 1992 (SI 1992/831)
	32(a)	1 Apr 1993 (SI 1992/831)
	(b)	6 May 1992 (SI 1992/831)
	33	1 Apr 1993 (SI 1992/831)
	34	6 May 1992 (SI 1992/831)
	35	1 Apr 1993 (SI 1992/831)
	36(a)	6 May 1992 (SI 1992/831)
	(b)	1 Apr 1993 (SI 1992/831)
	37(a)	1 Apr 1993 (SI 1992/831)
	(b)	6 May 1992 (SI 1992/831)
	38	6 May 1992 (SI 1992/831)
	39–42	1 Apr 1993 (SI 1992/831)
	43	6 May 1992 (SI 1992/831)
	44–47	1 Apr 1993 (SI 1992/831)
	48	6 May 1992 (SI 1992/831)
	49	1 Apr 1993 (SI 1992/831)
	50	6 May 1992 (so far as relates to Education Reform Act 1988, s 219(2)(e)) (SI 1992/831)
		1 Apr 1993 (otherwise) (SI 1992/831)
	51	6 May 1992 (SI 1992/831)
	52, 53	1 Apr 1993 (SI 1992/831)
	54	6 May 1992 (SI 1992/831)
	55	1 Apr 1993 (SI 1992/831)
	56(a)	1 Apr 1993 (SI 1992/831)
	(b), (c)	6 May 1992 (SI 1992/831)
	57, 58	1 Apr 1993 (SI 1992/831)
	59	6 May 1992 (SI 1992/831)
	60	1 Apr 1993 (SI 1992/831)
	61–65	6 May 1992 (subject to saving in relation to any matter notified to the Secretary of State by the Education Assets Board pursuant to Education

Further and Higher Education Act 1992 (c 13)—*cont*

Sch 8, Pt I, para 61–65—*cont*	Reform Act 1988, Sch 10, para 3, before 6 May 1992) (SI 1992/831)
66, 67	1 Apr 1993 (SI 1992/831)
8, Pt II, para 68	6 May 1992 (SI 1992/831)
69	Repealed
70–74	1 Apr 1993 (SI 1992/831)
75, 76	6 May 1992 (SI 1992/831)
77	1 Aug 1993 (SI 1992/831)
78, 79	6 May 1992 (SI 1992/831)
80	1 Aug 1993 (SI 1992/831)
81–83	1 Apr 1993 (SI 1992/831)
84, 85	6 May 1992 (SI 1992/831)
86	1 Aug 1993 (SI 1992/831)
87, 88	6 May 1992 (SI 1992/831)
89	30 Sep 1992 (SI 1992/831)
90–92	1 Apr 1993 (SI 1992/831)
93(a)	1 Apr 1993 (SI 1992/831)
(b)	6 May 1992 (SI 1992/831)
94, 95	1 Apr 1993 (SI 1992/831)
9	6 May 1992 (repeals of or in Education Reform Act 1988, ss 122(2)–(5), 129(3), (4), 136(3)–(7), 137(2) (expression 'or 129(3)'), 156 (so far as relates to institutions designated under Education Reform Act 1988, s 129), 219(2)(e), 227(2)–(4), 232(3) (expression 'or 227'), 232(4)(b) (expression '227'), Sch 7, para 19) (SI 1992/831)
	1 Apr 1993 (repeals of or in Education Act 1944, ss 8(3), 67(4A), 85(2), (3), 114(1), (1A), (1B), (1C); Education (Miscellaneous Provisions) Act 1948, s 3(3); Superannuation Act 1972, Sch 1; House of Commons Disqualification Act 1975, Sch 1, Pt III; Education (No 2) Act 1986, ss 43(5)(c), (7), 49(3)(d), (da), 51(2)(b), (5), (6), 58(3), (4), (5)(a), (ab); Education Reform Act 1988, ss 120, 124(4), 131, 132, 134, Pt II, Chapter III (ss 139–155), s 156 (so far as still in force), ss 157, 158(2), 159(2)(b), 161(1)(c), 205(6), 211(c), 218(10)(b), 219, 221(1)(c), (3), 222(2)(b), (3)(c), 230(1), (3)(c)(ii), 232(2), 234(2)(b), 235(2)(a), (h), Sch 12, paras 68, 69(2), 70, 100(2), 101(4); Environmental Protection Act 1990, s 98(2)(a)) (SI 1992/831)
	1 Aug 1993 (repeal in Education Reform Act 1988, s 105(2)(b)) (SI 1992/831)

[1] Any order made under Disability Discrimination Act 1995, s 70(3), bringing the prospective insertion into force will be noted to that Act in the service to this work

[2] Any order made under Education Act 1993, s 308(3), bringing the prospective repeal into force will be noted to that Act in the service to this work

---

Further and Higher Education (Scotland) Act 1992 (c 37)

RA: 16 Mar 1992

Commencement provisions: s 63(2); Further and Higher Education (Scotland) Act 1992 (Commencement No 1 and Saving Provisions) Order 1992, SI 1992/817

Further and Higher Education (Scotland) Act 1992 (c 37)—*cont*

s 1(1), (2)	1 Apr 1993 (SI 1992/817)
(3)–(5)	16 May 1992 (SI 1992/817)
(6)	1 Apr 1993 (SI 1992/817)
2	1 Apr 1993 (SI 1992/817)
3(1)–(4)	1 Apr 1993 (SI 1992/817)
(5)	16 May 1992 (SI 1992/817)
(6)	1 Apr 1993 (SI 1992/817)
4, 5	1 Apr 1993 (SI 1992/817)
6	16 May 1992 (SI 1992/817)
7–10	*Not in force*
11, 12	16 May 1992 (SI 1992/817)
13, 14	1 Apr 1993 (SI 1992/817)
15	16 May 1992 (SI 1992/817)
16	1 Sep 1992 (SI 1992/817)
17	1 Apr 1993 (SI 1992/817)
18	16 May 1992 (SI 1992/817)
19–25	1 Apr 1993 (SI 1992/817)
26–36	16 May 1992 (SI 1992/817)
37	1 Jun 1992 (SI 1992/817)
38	16 May 1992 (SI 1992/817)
39	1 Jun 1992 (so far as relates to institutions for whose activities the Council are considering providing financial support) (SI 1992/817)
	1 Apr 1993 (otherwise) (SI 1992/817)
40, 41	1 Apr 1993 (SI 1992/817)
42(1)	1 Jun 1992 (SI 1992/817)
(2), (3)	1 Apr 1993 (SI 1992/817)
(4)	1 Jun 1992 (SI 1992/817)
43(1)	1 Jun 1992 (SI 1992/817)
(2)	1 Apr 1993 (SI 1992/817)
(3)–(8)	1 Jun 1992 (SI 1992/817)
44	25 Apr 1992 (for purpose of authorising the making under s 44 of an Order which is expressed to come into force on or after 16 May 1992) (SI 1992/817)
	16 May 1992 (otherwise) (SI 1992/817)
45–49	16 May 1992 (SI 1992/817)
50, 51	1 Jun 1992 (SI 1992/817)
52	16 May 1992 (SI 1992/817)
53	1 Apr 1993 (SI 1992/817)
54(1), (2)	1 Jun 1992 (SI 1992/817)
(3)	1 Apr 1993 (SI 1992/817)
55–61	16 May 1992 (SI 1992/817)
62(1)	See Sch 8 below
(2)	See Sch 9 below
(3)	See Sch 10 below
63	25 Apr 1992 (SI 1992/817)
Sch 1	*Not in force*
2	16 May 1992 (SI 1992/817)
3, 4	1 Sep 1992 (SI 1992/817)
5, 6	16 May 1992 (SI 1992/817)
7	1 Jun 1992 (SI 1992/817)
8	16 May 1992 (SI 1992/817)
9, para 1	16 May 1992 (SI 1992/817)
2(a)	1 Apr 1993 (SI 1992/817)

Further and Higher Education (Scotland) Act 1992 (c 37)—*cont*

Sch 9, para	2(b), (c)	16 May 1992 (SI 1992/817)
	3	16 May 1992 (SI 1992/817)
	4(1), (2)	16 May 1992 (SI 1992/817)
	(3)	1 Jun 1992 (so far as relates to the Scottish Higher Education Funding Council) (SI 1992/817) *Not in force* (otherwise)
	(4)–(6)	16 May 1992 (SI 1992/817)
	5(1), (2)	16 May 1992 (SI 1992/817)
	(3)	1 Jun 1992 (so far as relates to the Scottish Higher Education Funding Council) (SI 1992/817) *Not in force* (otherwise)
	(4), (5)	16 May 1992 (SI 1992/817)
	6	16 May 1992 (SI 1992/817)
	7(1)	16 May 1992 (SI 1992/817)
	(2)–(6)	1 Apr 1993 (SI 1992/817)
	(7)	16 May 1992 (SI 1992/817)
	8(1), (2)	16 May 1992 (SI 1992/817)
	(3)	1 Apr 1993 (SI 1992/817)
	9	1 Apr 1993 (SI 1992/817)
	10	1 Jun 1992 (SI 1992/817)
	11	1 Apr 1993 (SI 1992/817)
	12(1), (2)	16 May 1992 (SI 1992/817)
	(3)	1 Apr 1993 (SI 1992/817)
	13(a)	1 Apr 1993 (SI 1992/817)
	(b), (c)	16 May 1992 (SI 1992/817)
10		16 May 1992 (repeals of or in Employment Protection (Consolidation) Act 1978, s 29; Education (Scotland) Act 1980, ss 3, 7, 77, 135(1)) (SI 1992/817) 1 Apr 1993 (repeals of or in School Boards (Scotland) Act 1988, ss 8, 22; Self-Governing Schools etc (Scotland) Act 1989, ss 54–66, 80) (SI 1992/817)

Human Fertilisation and Embryology (Disclosure of Information) Act 1992 (c 54)

RA: 16 Jul 1992

16 Jul 1992 (RA)

Licensing (Amendment) (Scotland) Act 1992 (c 18)

RA: 6 Mar 1992

Commencement provisions: s 2(2); Licensing (Amendment) (Scotland) Act 1992 (Commencement and Savings) Order 1992, SI 1992/819

s 1	15 Apr 1992 (subject to savings with respect to any licence temporarily transferred under the Licensing (Scotland) Act 1976, s 25(1), before 15 Apr 1992) (SI 1992/819)
2	6 Mar 1992 (RA)

Local Government Act 1992 (c 19)

RA: 6 Mar 1992

Commencement provisions: s 30(2), (3); Local Government Act 1992 (Commencement No 1) Order 1992, SI 1992/2371; Local Government Act 1992 (Commencement No 2) Order 1992, SI 1992/3241; Local Government Act 1992 (Commencement No 3) Order 1993, SI 1993/3169; Local Government Act 1992 (Commencement No 4) Order 1994, SI 1994/1445

s 1–7	6 May 1992 (s 30(2))
8	*Not in force*
9	4 Jan 1993 (SI 1992/3241)
10	14 Feb 1993 (SI 1992/3241)
11	See Sch 1 below
12–23	6 Mar 1992 (RA)
24	31 Oct 1992 (SI 1992/2371)
25–30	6 Mar 1992 (RA)
Sch 1, para 1	14 Feb 1993 (SI 1992/3241)
2(1)	13 Jun 1994 (SI 1994/1445)
(2), (3)	14 Mar 1994 (SI 1992/3241)
3–5	13 Jun 1994 (SI 1994/1445)
6, 7	4 Jan 1993 (SI 1992/3241)
8	14 Mar 1994 (SI 1992/3241)
9, 10	13 Jun 1994 (SI 1994/1445)
11	14 Feb 1993 (SI 1992/3241)
12	6 Jan 1994 (SI 1993/3169)
13, 14	4 Jan 1993 (SI 1992/3241)
2	6 Mar 1992 (RA)
3	31 Oct 1992 (SI 1992/2371)
4, Pt I	6 May 1992 (repeal in Local Government Finance Act 1982, s 15(1)) (s 30(2))
	Not in force (otherwise)
II	31 Oct 1992 (SI 1992/2371)

Local Government Finance Act 1992 (c 14)

RA: 6 Mar 1992

Commencement provisions: s 119(2); Local Government Finance Act 1992 (Commencement No 1) Order 1992, SI 1992/473; Local Government Finance Act 1992 (Commencement No 2) Order 1992, SI 1992/818; Local Government Finance Act 1992 (Commencement No 3) Order 1992, SI 1992/1460; Local Government Finance Act 1992 (Commencement No 4) Order 1992, SI 1992/1755; Local Government Finance Act 1992 (Commencement No 5 and Transitional Provisions) Order 1992, SI 1992/2183; Local Government Finance Act 1992 (Commencement No 6 and Transitional Provisions) Order 1992, SI 1992/2454, as amended by SI 1993/194; Local Government Finance Act 1992 (Commencement No 7 and Amendment) Order 1993, SI 1993/194 (amending SI 1992/2454); Local Government Finance Act 1992 (Commencement No 8 and Transitional Provisions) Order 1993, SI 1993/575; Local Government Finance Act 1992 (Commencement No 9 and Transitional Provision) Order 1994, SI 1994/3152

s 1–22	6 Mar 1992 (RA)

Local Government Finance Act 1992 (c 14)—*cont*

s 22A	Inserted by Local Government (Wales) Act 1994, s 36 (qv)
23–94	6 Mar 1992 (RA)
94A	Inserted (S) by Local Government etc (Scotland) Act 1994, s 24 (qv)
95	6 Mar 1992 (RA); prospectively repealed by Local Government etc (Scotland) Act 1994, s 180(2), Sch 14[1]
96–98	6 Mar 1992 (RA)
99(1)	6 Mar 1992 (RA)
(2)	1 Apr 1993 (SI 1993/575)
(3)	6 Mar 1992 (RA)
100–103	6 Mar 1992 (RA)
104	See Sch 10 below
105, 106	6 Mar 1992 (RA)
107	See Sch 11 below
108	6 Mar 1992 (RA)
108A	Inserted (S) by Local Government etc (Scotland) Act 1994, s 167 (qv)
109	6 Mar 1992
110(1)	1 Oct 1992 (subject to transitional provisions in relation to any financial year beginning before 1 Apr 1993) (SI 1992/2183)
(2), (3)	31 Mar 1995 (subject to a saving) (SI 1994/3152)
(4)	1 Oct 1992 (subject to transitional provisions in relation to any financial year beginning before 1 Apr 1993) (SI 1992/2183)
111	1 Apr 1993 (SI 1993/575)
112–116	6 Mar 1992 (RA)
117(1)	See Sch 13 below
(2)	See Sch 14 below
118, 119	6 Mar 1992 (RA)
Sch 1–9	6 Mar 1992 (RA)
10, para 1	18 Jun 1992 (SI 1992/1460)
2	7 Mar 1992 (SI 1992/473)
3	1 Apr 1992 (SI 1992/473)
4	7 Mar 1992 (so far as enables provision to be made by regulations) (SI 1992/473)
	1 Apr 1992 (otherwise) (SI 1992/473)
5–24	6 Mar 1992 (RA)
11, para 1–27	6 Mar 1992 (RA); prospectively repealed by Local Government etc (Scotland) Act 1994, s 180(2), Sch 14[1]
28	6 Mar 1992 (RA)
29(a)	1 Apr 1993 (SI 1993/575)
(b)	6 Mar 1992 (RA)
30	1 Apr 1993 (SI 1993/575)
31(a)	6 Mar 1992 (RA); prospectively repealed by Local Government etc (Scotland) Act 1994, s 180(2), Sch 14[1]
(b)	1 Oct 1992 (subject to transitional provisions in relation to any financial year beginning before 1 Apr 1993) (SI 1992/2183)
32–34	1 Apr 1993 (SI 1993/575); prospectively repealed by Local Government etc (Scotland) Act 1994, s 180(2), Sch 14[1]

Local Government Finance Act 1992 (c 14)—*cont*

Sch 11, para 35	1 Apr 1993 (SI 1993/575)
36	1 Apr 1993 (SI 1993/575); prospectively repealed by Local Government etc (Scotland) Act 1994, s 180(2), Sch 14[1]
37	1 Oct 1992 (subject to transitional provisions in relation to any financial year beginning before 1 Apr 1993) (SI 1992/2183); prospectively repealed by Local Government etc (Scotland) Act 1994, s 180(2), Sch 14[1]
38(a)	1 Oct 1992 (subject to transitional provisions in relation to any financial year beginning before 1 Apr 1993) (SI 1992/2183); prospectively repealed by Local Government etc (Scotland) Act 1994, s 180(2), Sch 14[1]
(b)	1 Apr 1993 (SI 1993/575); prospectively repealed by Local Government etc (Scotland) Act 1994, s 180(2), Sch 14[1]
(c)	1 Oct 1992 (subject to transitional provisions in relation to any financial year beginning before 1 Apr 1993) (SI 1992/2183); prospectively repealed by Local Government etc (Scotland) Act 1994, s 180(2), Sch 14[1]
(d)	6 Mar 1992 (RA)
(e)	1 Apr 1993 (SI 1993/575); prospectively repealed by Local Government etc (Scotland) Act 1994, s 180(2), Sch 14[1]
(f)	6 Mar 1992 (RA)
12	6 Mar 1992 (RA)
13, para 1	1 Apr 1993 (SI 1993/194)
2	1 Apr 1993 (SI 1993/575)
3–5	1 Apr 1993 (SI 1992/2454)
6–8	2 Nov 1992 (SI 1992/2454)
9	1 Apr 1993 (SI 1993/575)
10, 11	1 Apr 1992 (SI 1992/818)
12–14	2 Nov 1992 (SI 1992/2454)
15–25	6 Mar 1992 (RA)
26	2 Nov 1992 (SI 1992/2454)
27, 28	1 Apr 1993 (SI 1993/194)
29, 30	2 Nov 1992 (SI 1992/2454)
31	Repealed
32	1 Feb 1993 (SI 1993/194, amending SI 1992/2454)
33	*Not in force*
34	1 Apr 1993 (SI 1992/2454)
35	1 Apr 1993 (SI 1993/575)
36	1 Oct 1992 (subject to transitional provisions in relation to any financial year beginning before 1 Apr 1993) (SI 1992/2183)
37(1)	1 Apr 1995 (SI 1994/3152); prospectively repealed by Local Government etc (Scotland) Act 1994, s 180(2), Sch 14[1]
(2)	1 Apr 1993 (SI 1993/575); prospectively repealed by Local Government etc (Scotland) Act 1994, s 180(2), Sch 14[1]
38	1 Oct 1992 (so far as relates to Local Government (Scotland) Act 1973, s 110A) (subject to transitional provisions in relation to any financial year beginning before 1 Apr 1993) (SI 1992/2183)

Local Government Finance Act 1992 (c 14)—*cont*

Sch 13, para	38—*cont*	1 Apr 1993 (otherwise) (SI 1993/575)
	39	*Not in force*
	40	1 Apr 1993 (SI 1993/575)
	41	1 Apr 1992 (SI 1992/818)
	42	6 Mar 1992 (RA)
	43	1 Oct 1992 (subject to transitional provisions in relation to any financial year beginning before 1 Apr 1993) (SI 1992/2183)
	44(a), (b)	1 Apr 1993 (SI 1993/575); prospectively repealed by Local Government etc (Scotland) Act 1994, s 180(2), Sch 14[1]
	(c)	6 Mar 1992 (RA)
	(d)	1 Apr 1993 (SI 1993/575); prospectively repealed by Local Government etc (Scotland) Act 1994, s 180(2), Sch 14[1]
	45–47	6 Mar 1992 (RA)
	48	2 Nov 1992 (SI 1992/2454)
	49	1 Oct 1992 (subject to transitional provisions in relation to any financial year beginning before 1 Apr 1993) (SI 1992/2183)
	50–52	2 Nov 1992 (SI 1992/2454)
	53–56	1 Apr 1993 (SI 1993/575)
	57	1 Apr 1993 (SI 1992/2454)
	58	Repealed
	59–74	6 Mar 1992 (RA)
	75	Repealed
	76–88	6 Mar 1992 (RA)
	89	1 Apr 1992 (SI 1992/818)
	90, 91	2 Nov 1992 (SI 1992/2454)
	92	6 Mar 1992 (RA)
	93	1 Apr 1993 (SI 1993/575); prospectively repealed by Local Government etc (Scotland) Act 1994, s 180(2), Sch 14[1]
	94	1 Apr 1993 (SI 1993/194)
	95	1 Aug 1992 (subject to transitional provisions in relation to any financial year beginning before 1 Apr 1993) (SI 1992/1755); prospectively repealed by Environment Act 1995, s 120(3), Sch 24[2]
	96–98	1 Aug 1992 (subject to transitional provisions in relation to any financial year beginning before 1 Apr 1993) (SI 1992/1755)
	99, 100	6 Mar 1992 (RA)
14[3]		6 Mar 1992 (repeals of or in Local Government Finance Act 1988 (except Sch 12); Social Security Contributions and Benefits Act 1992; Social Security Administration Act 1992) (RA)
		1 Apr 1992 (repeals of or in Local Government (Financial Provisions) (Scotland) Act 1963, s 10; Local Government (Scotland) Act 1975, s 37(1); Local Government, Planning and Land Act 1980, s 46; Abolition of Domestic Rates etc (Scotland) Act 1987, Sch 1, para 19; Local Government Finance Act 1988, Sch 12, para 5; Local Government and Housing Act 1989, Sch 6, para 8) (SI 1992/818)
		1 Aug 1992 (repeals of or in Local Government and

Local Government Finance Act 1992 (c 14)—*cont*

Sch 14[3]—*cont*

Housing Act 1989, Sch 5, para 30(4); Water Resources Act 1991, ss 11, 135, 136 (subject to transitional provisions)) (SI 1992/1755)

1 Oct 1992 (repeals of or in Local Government (Scotland) Act 1973, s 110A; Abolition of Domestic Rates Etc (Scotland) Act 1987, ss 3A, 9, 10(7A), 11B, 28, Sch 2, paras 1(2), 2(1), Sch 5, paras 2–5, 9, 10, 14, 15, 17–19, 21, 25; Local Government Finance Act 1988, Sch 12, paras 10, 13) (subject to transitional provisions in relation to any financial year beginning before 1 Apr 1993)) (SI 1992/2183)

1 Apr 1993 (repeals of or in Education Reform Act 1988, s 81(8A); Local Government and Housing Act 1989, s 146 (subject to transitional provisions), Sch 5, paras 2–18, 43, 49–54, 55(3), 56, 58, 59, 61, 63–65, 70, 71, 73, 74, 76(3), 77, 78, Sch 11, para 98; Community Charges (Substitute Setting) Act 1991) (SI 1992/2454)

1 Apr 1993 (repeal of Local Government Finance and Valuation Act 1991) (SI 1993/194)

1 Apr 1993 (repeals of or in Registration of Births, Deaths and Marriages (Scotland) Act 1965, s 28B; Local Government (Scotland) Act 1966, Sch 1, Pt I, para 2A; Local Government (Scotland) Act 1973, ss 110, 118(1)(b); Local Government (Scotland) Act 1975, Sch 3, para 31; Water (Scotland) Act 1980, ss 41(2), (2A), 54(3)(b), 109(1); Debtors (Scotland) Act 1987, s 106; Abolition of Domestic Rates Etc (Scotland) Act 1987, ss 1–7, 14, 18(2A), 20(10), 25(1), (3), 26(1), (2), 27, 33, Sch 1, Sch 3, paras 1–4, 5(1), 7, Sch 5, paras 1, 6, 12, 13, 16, 19A, 20, 22 24, 26–49; Local Government Finance Act 1988, Sch 12, paras 8, 15, 17, 23, 27; Local Government and Housing Act 1989, ss 140, 141, Sch 6, paras 20, 21; Environmental Protection Act 1990, Sch 15, para 1; Caravans (Standard Community Charge and Rating) Act 1991, s 2) (subject to transitional provisions) (SI 1993/575)

Not in force (otherwise)

[1] Any orders made under Local Government etc (Scotland) Act 1994, s 184(2), (3), bringing the prospective repeal into force will be noted to that Act in the service to this work

[2] Any orders made under Environment Act 1995, s 125(3), bringing the prospective repeal into force will be noted to that Act in the service to this work

[3] For savings in relation to the repeals of Abolition of Domestic Rates (Scotland) Act 1987, Sch 2, para 7A, and Local Government Finance Act 1988, Sch 4, para 6, see Local Government Finance Act 1992 (Recovery of Community Charge) Saving Order 1993, SI 1993/1780

Maintenance Orders (Reciprocal Enforcement) Act 1992 (c 56)

RA: 12 Nov 1992

Commencement provisions: s 3; Maintenance Orders (Reciprocal Enforcement) Act 1992 (Commencement) Order 1993, SI 1993/618

5 Apr 1993 (SI 1993/618)

Mauritius Republic Act 1992 (c 45)

RA: 18 Jun 1992

18 Jun 1992 (RA; but note that s 1 deemed to have come into force on 12 Mar 1992 (s 1(4))

Medicinal Products: Prescription by Nurses etc Act 1992 (c 28)

RA: 16 Mar 1992

Commencement provisions: s 6(2); Medicinal Products: Prescription by Nurses etc Act 1992 (Commencement No 1) Order 1994, SI 1994/2408

s 1, 2	3 Oct 1994 (SI 1994/2408)
3	*Not in force*
4–6	16 Mar 1992 (RA)

Museums and Galleries Act 1992 (c 44)

RA: 16 Mar 1992

Commencement provisions: s 11(4); Museums and Galleries Act 1992 (Commencement) Order 1992, SI 1992/1874

s 1–8	1 Sep 1992 (SI 1992/1874)
9	1 Apr 1993 (SI 1992/1874)
10, 11	1 Sep 1992 (SI 1992/1874)
Sch 1–7	1 Sep 1992 (SI 1992/1874)
8, para 1(1)–(6)	1 Sep 1992 (SI 1992/1874)
(7)	Repealed
(8), (9)	1 Sep 1992 (SI 1992/1874)
2	Repealed
3	1 Sep 1992 (SI 1992/1874)
4	Repealed
5–9	1 Sep 1992 (SI 1992/1874)
10	Repealed
11–14	1 Sep 1992 (SI 1992/1874)
9	1 Sep 1992 (except repeal of Charities Act 1960, Sch 2, paras (da)–(dd)[1]) (SI 1992/1874)

[1] Entry relating to Charities Act 1960, Sch 2, paras (da)–(dd) (never in force) now repealed by Charities Act 1993, s 98(2), Sch 7

Non-Domestic Rating Act 1992 (c 46)

RA: 18 Jun 1992

Commencement provisions: s 10(2); Non-Domestic Rating Act 1992 (Commencement No 1) Order 1992, SI 1992/1486; Non-Domestic Rating Act 1992 (Commencement No 2) Order 1992, SI 1992/1642

s 1–4	16 Jul 1992 (SI 1992/1642)
5(1)	16 Jul 1992 (SI 1992/1642)
(2)	23 Jun 1992 (SI 1992/1486)
6	16 Jul 1992 (SI 1992/1642)
7	23 Jun 1992 (SI 1992/1486)
8	16 Jul 1992 (SI 1992/1642)
9	23 Jun 1992 (SI 1992/1486)
10	18 Jun 1992 (RA)

Nurses, Midwives and Health Visitors Act 1992 (c 16)

RA: 6 Mar 1992

Commencement provisions: s 17(3); Nurses, Midwives and Health Visitors Act 1992 (Commencement No 1) Order 1993, SI 1993/588

s 1(1)	1 Apr 1993 (SI 1993/588)
(2)	See Sch 1 below
2	6 Mar 1992 (RA)
3	1 Apr 1993 (SI 1993/588)
4	1 Apr 1993 (except so far as substitutes Nurses, Midwives and Health Visitors Act 1979, s 5(8)(e) and s 5(9) (so far as that substitution consists of removal of that provision in its application to Sch 2, para 7 to the 1979 Act)) (SI 1993/588) *Not in force* (exceptions noted above)
5(1)	1 Apr 1993 (SI 1993/588)
(2)	1 Apr 1993 (except in Northern Ireland) (SI 1993/588) *Not in force* (exception noted above)
(3)–(5)	1 Apr 1993 (SI 1993/588)
6–14	1 Apr 1993 (SI 1993/588)
15	6 Mar 1992 (RA)
16(1)	See Sch 2 below
(2)	See Sch 3 below
17(1), (2)	1 Apr 1993 (SI 1993/588)
(3)	6 Mar 1992 (RA)
(4)	1 Apr 1993 (except so far as applies to s 5(2)) (SI 1993/588) *Not in force* (exception noted above)
Sch 1, 2	1 Apr 1993 (SI 1993/588)
3	1 Apr 1993 (except repeal of Nurses, Midwives and Health Visitors Act 1979, Sch 2, para 7) (SI 1993/588) *Not in force* (exception noted above)

Offshore Safety Act 1992 (c 15)

RA: 6 Mar 1992

Commencement provisions: s 7(3); Offshore Safety Act 1992 (Commencement No 1) Order 1993, SI 1993/2406

s 1	6 Mar 1992 (RA)
2(1), (2)	6 Mar 1992 (RA)
(3)(a)	6 Mar 1992 (RA)
(b), (c)	*Not in force*
(4)	6 Mar 1992 (RA)
3(1)(a)	30 Nov 1993 (SI 1993/2406)
(b)–(d)	6 Mar 1992 (RA)
(e)	30 Nov 1993 (SI 1993/2406)
(2)	30 Nov 1993 (SI 1993/2406)
(3)(a)	6 Mar 1992 (RA)
(b)	*Not in force*
(c), (d)	6 Mar 1992 (RA)
(4)	6 Mar 1992 (RA)
4–6	6 Mar 1992 (RA)
7(1)	6 Mar 1992 (RA)
(2)	See Sch 2 below
(3), (4)	6 Mar 1992 (RA)
Sch 1	30 Nov 1993 (SI 1993/2406)
2	6 Mar 1992 (except repeals in Continental Shelf Act 1964; Gas Act 1986, s 47(5)) (RA)
	30 Nov 1993 (repeal in Continental Shelf Act 1964) (SI 1993/2406)
	Not in force (repeal, for certain purposes, of Gas Act 1986, s 47(5))

Offshore Safety (Protection Against Victimisation) Act 1992 (c 24)

Whole Act repealed

Parliamentary Corporate Bodies Act 1992 (c 27)

RA: 16 Mar 1992

16 Mar 1992 (RA)

Prison Security Act 1992 (c 25)

RA: 16 Mar 1992

Commencement provision: s 3(2)

16 May 1992 (s 3(2))

Protection of Badgers Act 1992 (c 51)

RA: 16 Jul 1992

Commencement provision: s 15(3)

16 Oct 1992 (s 15(3))

Sea Fish (Conservation) Act 1992 (c 60)

RA: 17 Dec 1992

Commencement provision: s 11(1), (2)

s 1(1)	17 Dec 1992 (RA)
(2)	17 Jan 1993 (except in relation to vessels of an overall length of 10 metres or less until such day as may be appointed) (s 11(1), (2))
	Not in force (exception noted above)
(3)	17 Dec 1992 (RA)
(4), (5)	17 Jan 1993 (s 11(1))
2	17 Dec 1992 (RA)
3	17 Jan 1993 (s 11(1))
4	17 Dec 1992 (RA)
5	17 Jan 1993 (s 11(1))
6–13	17 Dec 1992 (RA)

Sea Fisheries (Wildlife Conservation) Act 1992 (c 36)

RA: 16 Mar 1992

Commencement provision: s 2(2)

16 May 1992 (s 2(2))

Severn Bridges Act 1992 (c 3)

Local application only

Sexual Offences (Amendment) Act 1992 (c 34)

RA: 16 Mar 1992

Commencement provisions: s 8(3)–(5); Sexual Offences (Amendment) Act 1992 (Commencement) Order 1992, SI 1992/1336

s 1–7	1 Aug 1992 (SI 1992/1336)
8	16 Mar 1992 (s 8(3))

Social Security Administration Act 1992 (c 5)

RA: 13 Feb 1992

Commencement provision: s 192(4)

1 Jul 1992 (s 192(4); but note transitory modifications in Social Security (Consequential Provisions) Act 1992, Sch 4)

Social Security Administration (Northern Ireland) Act 1992 (c 8)

RA: 13 Feb 1992

Commencement provision: s 168(4)

1 Jul 1992 (s 168(4); but note transitory modifications in Social Security (Consequential Provisions) (Northern Ireland) Act 1992, Sch 4)

Social Security (Consequential Provisions) Act 1992 (c 6)

RA: 13 Feb 1992

Commencement provision: s 7(2), Sch 4, para 1(3); Social Security (Consequential Provisions) Act 1992 Appointed Day Order 1993, SI 1993/1025[1]

1 Jul 1992 (s 7(2))

[1] This order appointed 19 Apr 1993 as the appointed day in respect of Sch 4, paras 8, 9

Social Security (Consequential Provisions) (Northern Ireland) Act 1992 (c 9)

RA: 13 Feb 1992

Commencement provision: s 7(2)

1 Jul 1992 (s 7(2))

Social Security Contributions and Benefits Act 1992 (c 4)

RA: 13 Feb 1992

Commencement provision: s 177(4)

1 Jul 1992 (s 177(4); but note transitory modifications in Social Security (Consequential Provisions) Act 1992, Sch 4; those transitory modifications partially ceased to have effect on 19 Apr 1993 (SI 1993/1025) so that, on that day, Sch 2, para 6(2) to this Act came into force)

Social Security Contributions and Benefits (Northern Ireland) Act 1992 (c 7)

RA: 13 Feb 1992

Commencement provision: s 173(4)

1 Jul 1992 (s 173(4); but note transitory modifications in Social Security (Consequential Provisions) (Northern Ireland) Act 1992, Sch 4)

Social Security (Mortgage Interest Payments) Act 1992 (c 33)

RA: 16 Mar 1992

16 Mar 1992 (RA; but note that s 1(1) ceased to have effect on 1 Jul 1992, by virtue of s 1(2))

Sporting Events (Control of Alcohol etc) (Amendment) Act 1992 (c 57)

RA: 3 Dec 1992

3 Dec 1992 (RA)

Stamp Duty (Temporary Provisions) Act 1992 (c 2)

RA: 13 Feb 1992

Commencement provision: s 1(4)

s 1	16 Jan 1992 (s 1(4))
2, 3	13 Feb 1992 (RA)

Still-Birth (Definition) Act 1992 (c 29)

RA: 16 Mar 1992

Commencement provision: s 4(2)

s 1, 2	1 Oct 1992 (s 4(2))
3	16 Mar 1992 (RA)
4	1 Oct 1992 (s 4(2))

Taxation of Chargeable Gains Act 1992 (c 12)

RA: 6 Mar 1992

Commencement provision: s 289

Except where the context otherwise requires, this Act has effect in relation to tax for the year 1992–93 and subsequent years of assessment, and tax for the accounting periods of companies beginning on or after 6 Apr 1992 (s 289)

Timeshare Act 1992 (c 35)

RA: 16 Mar 1992

Commencement provisions: s 13(2); Timeshare Act 1992 (Commencement) Order 1992, SI 1992/1941 12 Oct 1992 (SI 1992/1941)

Tourism (Overseas Promotion) (Wales) Act 1992 (c 26)

RA: 16 Mar 1992

Commencement provision: s 3

16 May 1992 (s 3)

Trade Union and Labour Relations (Consolidation) Act 1992 (c 52)

RA: 16 Jul 1992

Commencement provision: s 302

16 Oct 1992 (s 302)

Traffic Calming Act 1992 (c 30)

RA: 16 Mar 1992

Commencement provision: s 3

16 May 1992 (s 3)

Transport and Works Act 1992 (c 42)

RA: 16 Mar 1992

Commencement provisions: s 70; Transport and Works Act 1992 (Commencement No 1) Order 1992, SI 1992/1347; Transport and Works Act 1992 (Commencement No 2) Order 1992, SI 1992/2043; Transport and Works Act 1992 (Commencement No 3 and Transitional Provisions) Order 1992, SI 1992/2784; Transport and Works Act 1992 (Commencement No 4) Order 1992, SI 1992/3144; Transport and Works Act 1992 (Commencement No 5 and Transitional Provisions) Order 1994, SI 1994/718

s 1–25	1 Jan 1993 (SI 1992/2784)
26–40	7 Dec 1992 (SI 1992/2043)
41, 42	31 Jan 1993 (SI 1992/3144)
43, 44	*Not in force*
45, 46	15 Jul 1992 (SI 1992/1347)
47(1)	See Sch 2 below
(2)	31 Jan 1993 (SI 1992/3144)
48	31 Jan 1993 (SI 1992/3144)
49	15 Jul 1992 (SI 1992/1347)
50	*Not in force*
51	31 Jan 1993 (SI 1992/3144)
52–56	*Not in force*
57–60	15 Jul 1992 (SI 1992/1347)
61	31 Jan 1993 (SI 1992/3144)
62	*Not in force*
63	15 Jul 1992 (subject to transitional provisions with respect to certain Harbour Revision Orders and Harbour Empowerment Orders) (SI 1992/1347)
64	31 Jan 1993 (SI 1992/3144)
65(1)(a)	15 Jul 1992 (SI 1992/1347)
(b)	1 Jan 1993 (except words "in section 25, the words 'and shall not be opened' onwards,"; and "section 48,") (SI 1992/2784)
	5 Apr 1994 (words "in section 25, the words 'and shall not be opened' onwards,") (subject to transitional provisions) (SI 1994/718)
	Not in force (words "section 48,")
(c), (d)	1 Jan 1993 (SI 1992/2784)
(e)	15 Jul 1992 (SI 1992/1347)
(f)	1 Jan 1993 (SI 1992/2784)

Transport and Works Act 1992 (c 42)—*cont*

s 65(2)	15 Jul 1992 (SI 1992/1347)
66, 67	15 Jul 1992 (SI 1992/1347)
68(1)	See Sch 4 below
(2)	*Not in force*
69	15 Jul 1992 (SI 1992/1347)
70–72	16 Mar 1992 (s 70)
Sch 1	1 Jan 1993 (SI 1992/2784)
2	22 Dec 1992 (for purpose of conferring on Secretary of State power to make regulation in relation to rail crossing extinguishment orders or rail crossing diversion orders) (SI 1992/3144)
	31 Jan 1993 (otherwise) (SI 1992/3144)
3	15 Jul 1992 (subject to transitional provisions with respect to certain Harbour Revision Orders and Harbour Empowerment Orders) (SI 1992/1347)
4, Pt I	15 Jul 1992 (repeals of or in British Railways Act 1965; London Transport Act 1965; Criminal Justice Act 1967; London Transport Act 1977; British Railways Act 1977) (subject to transitional provisions with respect to certain Harbour Revision Orders and Harbour Empowerment Orders) (SI 1992/1347)
	7 Dec 1992 (repeal in Railway Regulation Act 1842) (SI 1992/2043)
	1 Jan 1993 (repeals of or in Tramways Act 1870 (except words 'and shall not be opened' onwards in s 25, and s 48); Municipal Corporations Act 1882; Military Tramways Act 1887; Light Railways Act 1896; Railways (Electrical Power) Act 1903; Light Railways Act 1912; Railways Act 1921; Transport Act 1962; Administration of Justice Act 1965; Transport Act 1968 (expect ss 124, 125(4)); Local Government Act 1972; Supply Powers Act 1975; Administration of Justice Act 1982; Telecommunications Act 1984; Roads (Scotland) Act 1984; Insolvency Act 1986) (subject to transitional provisions) (SI 1992/2784)
	31 Jan 1993 (repeals of or in Regulation of Railways Act 1871, s 3; Highways Act 1980) (SI 1992/3144)
	5 Apr 1994 (repeals of Tramways Act 1870, s 25 (words and shall not be opened onwards); Road and Rail Traffic Act 1933, s 41; Transport Act 1968, s 125(4)) (subject to transitional provisions) (SI 1994/718)
	Not in force (otherwise)
II	15 Jul 1992 (subject to transitional provisions with respect to certain Harbour Revision Orders and Harbour Empowerment Orders) (SI 1992/1347)

Tribunals and Inquiries Act 1992 (c 53)

RA: 16 Jul 1992

Commencement provision: s 19(2)

1 Oct 1992 (s 19(2))

1993

Agriculture Act 1993 (c 37)

RA: 27 Jul 1993

Commencement provisions: ss 1(2)–(4), 21(2), (3), 26(2)–(4), 54(2), 55(3), 65(2), (3); Agriculture Act 1993 (Commencement No 1) Order 1993, SI 1993/2038

s 1(1)	Milk Marketing Scheme (Substitution of Date of Revocation) Order 1994, SI 1994/282, substituted the date 1 Jan 1995 for the date 1 Oct 1994 in s 1(2)(b), with the effect that s 1(1)(a) was to come into force on 1 Jan 1995; Milk Marketing Schemes (Substitution of Date of Revocation) (Scotland) Order 1994, SI 1994/685, substituted the date 1 Jan 1995 for the date 1 Apr 1994 in s 1(2)(a), with the effect that s 1(1)(b)(d) were to come into force on 1 Jan 1995; however, by the Milk Marketing Scheme (Certification of Revocation) (Scotland) Order 1994, SI 1994/2900, and the Milk Marketing Scheme (Certification of Revocation) Order 1994, SI 1994/2921, the date of transfer of the property, rights and liabilities of the Milk Marketing Boards under s 11 of this Act was 1 Nov 1994, thus bringing sub-s (1) into force on that date
(2)–(5)	27 Jul 1993 (RA)
2–11	27 Jul 1993 (RA)
12	See Sch 2 below
13–20	27 Jul 1993 (RA)
21(1)	Day on which s 1(1) comes into force completely (ie 1 Nov 1994) (s 21(2), (3), SI 1994/2922)
(2), (3)	27 Jul 1993 (RA)
22–25	27 Jul 1993 (RA)
26(1)	*Not in force*
(2)–(5)	27 Jul 1993 (RA)
27–35	27 Jul 1993 (RA)
36	See Sch 4 below
37–49	27 Jul 1993 (RA)
50–53	27 Sep 1993 (s 65(2))
54	27 Jul 1993 (RA)
55	4 Aug 1993 (SI 1993/2038)
56–58	27 Jul 1993 (RA)
59	4 Aug 1993 (SI 1993/2038)
60–65	27 Jul 1993 (RA)
Sch 1–4	27 Jul 1993 (RA)
5	27 Jul 1993 (except so far as repeals relate to potatoes and revocation of Potato Marketing Scheme, para 67) (RA)
	4 Aug 1993 (exceptions noted above) (SI 1993/2038)

Appropriation Act 1993 (c 33)

Whole Act repealed

Asylum and Immigration Appeals Act 1993 (c 23)

RA: 1 Jul 1993

Commencement provisions: s 14; Asylum and Immigration Appeals Act 1993 (Commencement and Transitional Provisions) Order 1993, SI 1993/1655

s 1	1 Jul 1993 (except so far as relates to ss 4–11) (RA)
	26 Jul 1993 (exception noted above) (SI 1993/1655)
2, 3	1 Jul 1993 (RA)
4–7	26 Jul 1993 (SI 1993/1655)
8–11	26 Jul 1993 (subject to savings) (SI 1993/1655)
12–16	1 Jul 1993 (RA)
Sch 1, 2	26 Jul 1993 (SI 1993/1655)

Bail (Amendment) Act 1993 (c 26)

RA: 20 Jul 1993

Commencement provisions: s 2(2); Bail (Amendment) Act 1993 (Commencement) Order 1994, SI 1994/1437

s 1	27 Jun 1994 (SI 1994/1437)
2	20 Jul 1993 (s 2(2))

Bankruptcy (Scotland) Act 1993 (c 6)

RA: 18 Feb 1993

Commencement provisions: s 12(3)–(6); Bankruptcy (Scotland) Act 1993 Commencement and Savings Order 1993, SI 1993/438

s 1–7	1 Apr 1993 (SI 1993/438)
8, 9	18 Feb 1993 (s 12(3))
10	1 Apr 1993 (SI 1993/438)
11(1), (2)	1 Apr 1993 (SI 1993/438)
(3)	See Sch 1 below
(4)	See Sch 2 below
12	18 Feb 1993 (s 12(3))
Sch 1, para 1–21	1 Apr 1993 (SI 1993/438)
22(1)–(4)	1 Apr 1993 (SI 1993/438)
(5)	18 Feb 1993 (s 12(3))
23	18 Feb 1993 (s 12(3))
24–30	1 Apr 1993 (SI 1993/438)
31(1)–(3)	1 Apr 1993 (SI 1993/438)
(4), (5)	18 Feb 1993 (s 12(3))
32	1 Apr 1993 (SI 1993/438)
2	1 Apr 1993 (SI 1993/438)

British Coal and British Rail (Transfer Proposals) Act 1993 (c 2)

RA: 19 Jan 1993

19 Jan 1993 (RA); whole Act prospectively repealed in relation to British Railways Board by Railways Act 1993, s 152(1), Sch 12, para 32; whole Act also

British Coal and British Rail (Transfer Proposals) Act 1993 (c 2)—*cont*
prospectively repealed by Coal Industry Act 1994, s 67(8), Sch 11, Pt III. Any order(s) made under those Acts bringing the prospective repeal into force will be noted to those Acts in the service to this work

Cardiff Bay Barrage Act 1993 (c 42)

Local application only

Carrying of Knives etc (Scotland) Act 1993 (c 13)

Whole Act repealed

Charities Act 1993 (c 10)

RA: 27 May 1993

Commencement provision: s 99; Charities Act 1993 (Commencement and Transitional Provisions) Order 1995, SI 1995/2695

s 1–4	1 Aug 1993 (s 99(1))
5(1)	1 Aug 1993 (subject to transitional provisions) (s 99(1), (4))
(2)	1 Aug 1993 (s 99(1))
(2A)	Inserted by Welsh Language Act 1993, s 32(3) (qv)
(3)–(6)	1 Aug 1993 (s 99(1))
6–40	1 Aug 1993 (s 99(1))
41–49	15 Oct 1995 (for purposes of making orders or regulations) (SI 1995/2695)
	1 Mar 1996 (otherwise, subject to a transitional provision) (SI 1995/2695)
50–68	1 Aug 1993 (s 99(1))
69	1 Mar 1996 (SI 1995/2695)
70–73	1 Aug 1993 (s 99(1))
74(1)(a)	1 Aug 1993 (subject to transitional provisions) (s 99(1), (4))
(b)	1 Aug 1993 (s 99(1))
(2)–(12)	1 Aug 1993 (s 99(1))
75(1)(a)	1 Aug 1993 (s 99(1))
(b)	1 Aug 1993 (subject to transitional provisions) (s 99(1), (4))
(2)–(10)	1 Aug 1993 (s 99(1))
76–97	1 Aug 1993 (s 99(1))
98(1)	See Sch 6 below
(2)	See Sch 7 below
99, 100	1 Aug 1993 (s 99(1))
Sch 1–5	1 Aug 1993 (s 99(1))
6, para 1–20	1 Aug 1993 (s 99(1))
21(1), (2)	1 Aug 1993 (s 99(1))
(3)	1 Mar 1996 (SI 1995/2695)
(4), (5)	1 Aug 1993 (s 99(1))
22–30	1 Aug 1993 (s 99(1))
7	1 Aug 1993 (subject to transitional provisions) (s 99(1)–(3))
8	1 Aug 1993 (s 99(1))

Clean Air Act 1993 (c 11)

RA: 27 May 1993

Commencement provision: s 68(2)

27 Aug 1993 (s 68(2))

Consolidated Fund Act 1993 (c 4)

Whole Act repealed

Consolidated Fund (No 2) Act 1993 (c 7)

Whole Act repealed

Consolidated Fund (No 3) Act 1993 (c 52)

Whole Act repealed

Criminal Justice Act 1993 (c 36)

RA: 27 Jul 1993

Commencement provisions: s 78; Criminal Justice Act 1993 (Commencement No 1) Order 1993, SI 1993/1968; Criminal Justice Act 1993 (Commencement No 2 Transitional Provisions and Savings) (Scotland) Order 1993, SI 1993/2035; Criminal Justice Act 1993 (Commencement No 3) Order 1993, SI 1993/2734; Criminal Justice Act 1993 (Commencement No 4) Order 1994, SI 1994/71; Criminal Justice Act 1993 (Commencement No 5) Order 1994, SI 1994/242; Criminal Justice Act 1993 (Commencement No 6) Order 1994, SI 1994/700; Criminal Justice Act 1993 (Commencement No 7) Order 1994, SI 1994/1951; Criminal Justice Act 1993 (Commencement No 8) Order 1995, SI 1995/43; Criminal Justice Act 1993 (Commencement No 9) Order 1995, SI 1995/1958

s 1–6	*Not in force*
7–16	Repealed
17	15 Feb 1994 (SI 1994/71)
18	Repealed
19	1 Apr 1994 (SI 1994/700)
20–23	1 Dec 1993 (SI 1993/2734)
24(1)–(11)	Repealed
(12)–(15)	3 Feb 1995 (SI 1995/43)
25	Repealed
26	1 Apr 1994 (SI 1994/700)
27, 28	3 Feb 1995 (SI 1995/43)
29–31	15 Feb 1994 (SI 1994/71)
32	1 Apr 1994 (SI 1994/700)
33	15 Feb 1994 (SI 1994/71)
34, 35	1 Dec 1993 (SI 1993/2734)
36–43	3 Feb 1995 (SI 1995/43)
44–46	1 Dec 1993 (SI 1993/2734)
47	15 Feb 1994 (SI 1994/71)
48	1 Apr 1994 (SI 1994/700)
49	15 Feb 1994 (SI 1994/71)
50, 51	1 Apr 1994 (SI 1994/700)
52–64	1 Mar 1994 (SI 1994/242)

Criminal Justice Act 1993 (c 36)—*cont*

s 65	20 Sep 1993 (SI 1993/1968)
66	16 Aug 1993 (SI 1993/1968)
67(1)	16 Aug 1993 (EW) (SI 1993/1968)
	16 Aug 1993 (S) (subject to savings) (SI 1993/2035)
(2)	Repealed
68, 69	Repealed
70, 71	27 Sep 1993 (s 78(1))
72	22 Aug 1994 (SI 1994/1951)
73	1 Dec 1993 (SI 1993/2734)
74	15 Feb 1994 (SI 1994/71)
75, 76	27 Jul 1993 (s 78(2))
77	1 Apr 1994 (SI 1994/700)
78	27 Jul 1993 (partly) (RA)
	15 Feb 1994 (otherwise) (SI 1994/71)
79(1)–(12)	27 Jul 1993 (s 78(2))
(13)	See Sch 5 below
(14)	See Sch 6 below
Sch 1, 2	1 Mar 1994 (SI 1994/242)
3	20 Sep 1993 (SI 1993/1968)
4	1 Apr 1994 (SI 1994/700)
5, para 1	14 Aug 1995 (SI 1995/1958)
2	Repealed
3	3 Feb 1995 (SI 1995/43)
4	1 Mar 1994 (SI 1994/242)
5, 6	Repealed
7–13	1 Mar 1994 (SI 1994/242)
14	15 Feb 1994 (SI 1994/71)
15	1 Apr 1994 (SI 1994/700)
16	1 Mar 1994 (SI 1994/242)
17(1)	1 Apr 1994 (SI 1994/700)
(2), (3)	3 Feb 1995 (SI 1995/43)
(4), (5)	1 Apr 1994 (SI 1994/700)
(6), (7)	3 Feb 1995 (SI 1995/43)
18–22	1 Mar 1994 (SI 1994/242)
6, Pt I	27 Jul 1993 (repeals in Criminal Procedure (Scotland) Act 1975; Prisoners and Criminal Proceedings (Scotland) Act 1993) (s 78(2))
	20 Sep 1993 (repeals in Magistrates' Courts Act 1980; Criminal Justice Act 1991) (SI 1993/1968)
	15 Feb 1994 (repeals of or in Drug Trafficking Offences Act 1986, ss 1(5)(b)(iii), 27(5); Criminal Justice Act 1988, ss 48 (EW only), 98; Prevention of Terrorism (Temporary Provisions) Act 1989; Criminal Justice (International Co-operation) Act 1990; Northern Ireland (Emergency Provisions) Act 1991, ss 50(2), 67(6)) (SI 1994/71)
	1 Mar 1994 (repeals of or in Company Securities (Insider Dealing) Act 1985; Financial Services Act 1986; Banking Act 1987; Criminal Justice Act 1987; Companies Act 1989) (SI 1994/242)
	3 Feb 1995 (repeals of or in Northern Ireland (Emergency Provisions) Act 1991, ss 48(3), 51(3)) (SI 1995/43)
	Not in force (otherwise)
II	1 Mar 1994 (SI 1994/242)

Crofters (Scotland) Act 1993 (c 44)

RA: 5 Nov 1993

Commencement provisions: ss 28(17), 64(2)

s 1–27	5 Jan 1994 (s 64(2))
28	*Not in force*
29–64	5 Jan 1994 (s 64(2))
Sch 1–7	5 Jan 1994 (s 64(2))

Damages (Scotland) Act 1993 (c 5)

RA: 18 Feb 1993

Commencement provision: s 8(3)

18 Apr 1993 (s 8(3))

Disability (Grants) Act 1993 (c 14)

RA: 27 May 1993

27 May 1993 (RA)

Education Act 1993 (c 35)

RA: 27 Jul 1993

Commencement provisions: s 308(3); Education Act 1993 (Commencement No 1 and Transitional Provisions) Order 1993, SI 1993/1975; Education Act 1993 (Commencement No 2 and Transitional Provisions) Order 1993, SI 1993/3106, as amended by SI 1994/436; Education Act 1993 (Commencement No 3 and Transitional Provisions) Order 1994, SI 1994/507; Education Act 1993 (Commencement No 4) Order 1994, SI 1994/1558; Education Act 1993 (Commencement No 5 and Transitional Provisions) Order 1994, SI 1994/2038, as amended by SI 1994/2248

s 1, 2	1 Oct 1993 (SI 1993/1975)
3, 4	1 Apr 1994 (SI 1994/507)
5	1 Sep 1993 (SI 1993/1975)
6–21	1 Apr 1994 (SI 1994/507)
22(1)	1 Jan 1994 (SI 1993/3106)
(2)(a)	1 Jan 1994 (SI 1993/3106)
(b)	1 Jan 1994 (for purpose of defining expression "proposals for the establishment of a new grant-maintained school") (SI 1993/3106)
	1 Apr 1994 (otherwise) (SI 1994/507)
(c)	1 Apr 1994 (SI 1994/507)
(3)	1 Jan 1994 (SI 1993/3106)
(4)	1 Apr 1994 (SI 1994/507)
23	1 Jan 1994 (subject to transitional provisions) (SI 1993/3106)
24	9 Dec 1993 (SI 1993/3106)
25–30	1 Jan 1994 (subject to transitional provisions) (SI 1993/3106)

Education Act 1993 (c 35)—*cont*

s 31(1), (2)	1 Jan 1994 (subject to transitional provisions) (SI 1993/3106)
(3)	1 Jan 1994 (subject to transitional provisions) (SI 1993/3106, as amended by SI 1994/436)
32–35	1 Jan 1994 (subject to transitional provisions) (SI 1993/3106)
36(1), (2)	1 Jan 1994 (subject to transitional provisions) (SI 1993/3106)
(3)–(5)	1 Apr 1994 (SI 1994/507)
37–46	1 Jan 1994 (subject to transitional provisions) (SI 1993/3106)
47(1)–(4)	1 Apr 1994 (SI 1994/507)
(5)–(9)	1 Jan 1994 (subject to transitional provisions) (SI 1993/3106)
48–54	1 Apr 1994 (SI 1994/507)
55–58	1 Jan 1994 (SI 1993/3106)
59–67	1 Jan 1994 (subject to transitional provisions) (SI 1993/3106)
68–70	1 Apr 1994 (SI 1994/507)
71–77	1 Jan 1994 (subject to transitional provisions) (SI 1993/3106)
78	1 Apr 1994 (SI 1994/507)
79, 80	1 Jan 1994 (SI 1993/3106)
81–91	1 Apr 1994 (SI 1994/507)
92	1 Jan 1994 (SI 1993/3106)
93–135	1 Apr 1994 (subject to transitional provisions relating to ss 96(3), 96(6)(a), 99(1), 104(2)) (SI 1994/507)
136(1)	1 Jan 1994 (SI 1993/3106)
(2)	1 Apr 1994 (SI 1994/507)
(3)	1 Jan 1994 (SI 1993/3106)
137	1 Jan 1994 (SI 1993/3106)
138–151	1 Apr 1994 (subject to transitional provisions relating to s 147(1)) (SI 1994/507)
152	1 Jan 1994 (SI 1993/3106)
153(1), (2)	1 Jan 1994 (SI 1993/3106)
(3)	1 Apr 1994 (SI 1994/507)
(4)	1 Jan 1994 (SI 1993/3106)
(5)	1 Apr 1994 (SI 1994/507)
154	1 Apr 1994 (SI 1994/507)
155–158	1 Jan 1994 (SI 1993/3106)
159	1 Apr 1994 (SI 1994/507)
160	1 Sep 1994 (SI 1994/2038)
161(1)–(4)	1 Apr 1994 (SI 1994/507)
(5)	1 Jan 1994 (SI 1993/3106)
(6), (7)	Prospectively added by Disability Discrimination Act 1995, s 29(2)[1]
162, 163	1 Apr 1994 (SI 1994/507)
164, 165	1 Sep 1994 (SI 1994/2038)
166(1)–(3)	1 Sep 1994 (SI 1994/2038)
(4)	1 Apr 1994 (SI 1994/507)
(5)	1 Sep 1994 (SI 1994/2038)
167(1)–(4)	1 Sep 1994 (SI 1994/2038)
(5)	See Sch 9 below
(6)	1 Sep 1994 (subject to transitional provisions) (SI 1994/2038, as amended by SI 1994/2248)

Education Act 1993 (c 35)—*cont*

s 168(1)–(6)	1 Sep 1994 (subject to transitional provisions) (SI 1994/2038, as amended by SI 1994/2248)
(7)	See Sch 10 below
169–171	1 Sep 1994 (subject to transitional provisions) (SI 1994/2038, as amended by SI 1994/2248)
172(1)	3 Mar 1994 (SI 1994/507)
(2)–(5)	1 Sep 1994 (SI 1994/2038)
(6)	3 Mar 1994 (SI 1994/507)
173–176	1 Sep 1994 (SI 1994/2038)
177(1)	1 Sep 1994 (SI 1994/2038)
(2)–(6)	1 Jan 1994 (SI 1993/3106)
178, 179	1 Jan 1994 (SI 1993/3106)
180(1), (2)	1 Jan 1994 (SI 1993/3106)
(3)	1 Sep 1994 (SI 1994/2038)
(4)	1 Apr 1994 (SI 1994/507)
(5), (6)	1 Sep 1994 (SI 1994/2038)
181	1 Jan 1994 (SI 1993/3106)
182(1)–(3)	3 Mar 1994 (for purpose of defining "special school", "maintained special school" and "grant-maintained special school" in relation to regulations made under Pt III and s 228) (SI 1994/507)
	1 Apr 1994 (otherwise) (SI 1994/507)
(4)	See Sch 11 below
183–185	1 Apr 1994 (subject to transitional provisions) (SI 1994/507)
186(1), (2)	3 Mar 1994 (SI 1994/507)
(3)	1 Apr 1994 (SI 1994/507)
(4)	3 Mar 1994 (SI 1994/507)
187	3 Mar 1994 (SI 1994/507)
188, 189	1 Apr 1994 (SI 1994/507)
190	*Not in force*
191	1 Apr 1994 (SI 1994/507)
192(1)–(5)	1 Oct 1993 (SI 1993/1975)
(6), (7)	1 Oct 1993 (for purposes of school attendance orders with respect to children other than those for whom a statement is maintained under the Education Act 1981, s 7) (SI 1993/1975)
	1 Sep 1994 (otherwise) (SI 1994/2038)
(8)	1 Oct 1993 (SI 1993/1975)
193(1)	1 Oct 1993 (subject to transitional provisions) (SI 1993/1975)
(2)–(6)	1 Oct 1993 (SI 1993/1975)
194(1)	1 Oct 1993 (SI 1993/1975)
(2)	1 Oct 1993 (subject to transitional provisions) (SI 1993/1975)
(3)–(8)	1 Oct 1993 (SI 1993/1975)
195(1)	1 Oct 1993 (subject to transitional provisions) (SI 1993/1975)
(2)–(4)	1 Oct 1993 (SI 1993/1975)
196	1 Sep 1994 (subject to transitional provisions) (SI 1994/2038)
197(1)–(4)	1 Oct 1993 (SI 1993/1975)
(5)	1 Sep 1994 (SI 1994/2038)
(6)	1 Oct 1993 (SI 1993/1975)
198–203	1 Oct 1993 (SI 1993/1975)

Education Act 1993 (c 35)—*cont*

s 204–212	1 Sep 1993 (subject to transitional provisions) (SI 1993/1975)
213–216	1 Jan 1994 (SI 1993/3106)
217(1)	1 Jan 1994 (SI 1993/3106)
(2)	1 Apr 1994 (SI 1994/507)
218–223	1 Jan 1994 (subject to transitional provisions) (SI 1993/3106)
224–226	1 Dec 1994 (SI 1994/2038)
227	1 Jan 1994 (SI 1993/3106)
228(1)–(3)	1 Jan 1994 (SI 1993/3106)
(4)	1 Dec 1994 (SI 1994/2038)
229(1)	1 Oct 1993 (so far as amends Education Act 1980, s 12(1)(d) (insertion of words "or to transfer a county school to a new site in the area")) (SI 1993/1975)
	1 Apr 1994 (otherwise) (subject to transitional provisions) (SI 1994/507)
(2)	1 Apr 1994 (subject to transitional provisions) (SI 1994/507)
(3)	1 Apr 1994 (SI 1994/507)
230(1)	1 Oct 1993 (so far as amends Education Act 1980, s 13(1)(b) (insertion of words "or to transfer the school to a new site")) (SI 1993/1975)
	1 Apr 1994 (otherwise) (subject to transitional provisions) (SI 1994/507)
(2)	1 Apr 1994 (subject to transitional provisions) (SI 1994/507)
(3)–(5)	1 Oct 1993 (SI 1993/1975)
(6)	1 Apr 1994 (SI 1994/507)
231–237	1 Apr 1994 (SI 1994/507)
238, 239	1 Jan 1994 (SI 1993/3106)
240	27 Jul 1993 (RA)
241	1 Sep 1994 (SI 1994/2038)
242–245	1 Oct 1993 (SI 1993/1975)
246	1 Jan 1994 (SI 1993/3106)
247–251	1 Oct 1993 (SI 1993/1975)
252	3 Mar 1994 (SI 1994/507)
253–258	1 Apr 1994 (SI 1994/507)
259(1)	1 Oct 1993 (SI 1993/1975)
(2)	1 Oct 1993 (subject to transitional provisions) (SI 1993/1975)
(3)	1 Oct 1993 (SI 1993/1975)
260	1 Oct 1993 (SI 1993/1975)
261, 262	1 Sep 1994 (SI 1994/2038)
263–265	1 Oct 1993 (SI 1993/1975)
266–268	1 Jan 1994 (subject to transitional provisions) (SI 1993/3106)
269	1 Oct 1993 (subject to transitional provisions) (SI 1993/1975)
270	1 Oct 1993 (SI 1993/1975)
271	1 Jan 1994 (SI 1993/3106)
272, 273	1 Apr 1994 (SI 1994/507)
274–276	1 Jan 1994 (subject to transitional provisions) (SI 1993/3106)
277	*Not in force*
278(1)–(5)	3 Mar 1994 (SI 1994/507)

Education Act 1993 (c 35)—*cont*

s 278(6)	1 Apr 1994 (subject to transitional provisions) (SI 1994/507)
279	15 Jun 1994 (for purposes of enabling regulations to be made under Education (No 2) Act 1986, s 51(1)–(4)) (SI 1994/1558)
	1 Apr 1995 (otherwise) (SI 1994/1558)
280	1 Oct 1993 (SI 1993/1975)
281	1 Jan 1994 (SI 1993/3106)
282–286	1 Oct 1993 (SI 1993/1975)
287, 288	1 Jan 1994 (SI 1993/3106)
289	1 Apr 1994 (SI 1994/507)
290–292	1 Jan 1994 (SI 1993/3106)
293, 294	1 Oct 1993 (SI 1993/1975)
295–297	1 Apr 1994 (SI 1994/507)
298(1)	1 Sep 1994 (SI 1994/2038)
(2)	1 Aug 1994 (for purpose of defining "pupil referral unit" in relation to regulations made under Sch 18, para 3) (SI 1994/2038)
	1 Sep 1994 (otherwise) (SI 1994/2038)
(3)–(7)	1 Sep 1994 (SI 1994/2038)
(8)	See Sch 18 below
299, 300	1 Jan 1994 (SI 1993/3106)
301–303	27 Jul 1993 (RA)
304	1 Apr 1994 (SI 1994/507)
305, 306	27 Jul 1993 (RA)
307(1)	See Sch 19 below
(2)	See Sch 20 below
(3)	See Sch 21 below
308	27 Jul 1993 (RA)
Sch 1, 2	1 Apr 1994 (SI 1994/507)
3, Pt I	1 Jan 1994 (subject to transitional provisions) (SI 1993/3106)
II	1 Apr 1994 (SI 1994/507)
4–7	1 Jan 1994 (subject to transitional provisions) (SI 1993/3106)
8	1 Apr 1994 (SI 1994/507)
9, para 1, 2	1 Sep 1994 (subject to transitional provisions) (SI 1994/2038, as amended by SI 1994/2248)
3	1 Apr 1994 (SI 1994/507)
4, 5	1 Sep 1994 (subject to transitional provisions) (SI 1994/2038, as amended by SI 1994/2248)
10, para 1–4	1 Sep 1994 (subject to transitional provisions) (SI 1994/2038, as amended by SI 1994/2248)
5(1), (2)	1 Sep 1994 (subject to transitional provisions) (SI 1994/2038, as amended by SI 1994/2248)
(3)	1 Apr 1994 (SI 1994/507)
(4)	1 Sep 1994 (subject to transitional provisions) (SI 1994/2038, as amended by SI 1994/2248)
6	1 Sep 1994 (SI 1994/2038)
7	1 Apr 1994 (SI 1994/507)
8(1)–(4)	1 Sep 1994 (SI 1994/2038)
(5)	1 Apr 1994 (SI 1994/507)
(6)	1 Sep 1994 (SI 1994/2038)
9–11	1 Sep 1994 (subject to transitional provisions) (SI 1994/2038, as amended by SI 1994/2248)
11, para 1–13	1 Apr 1994 (SI 1994/507)

Education Act 1993 (c 35)—*cont*

Sch 11, para 14	1 Jan 1994 (SI 1993/3106)
12	1 Jan 1994 (SI 1993/3106)
13	1 Jan 1994 (subject to transitional provisions) (SI 1993/3106)
14	1 Oct 1993 (SI 1993/1975)
15	1 Apr 1994 (SI 1994/507)
16, 17	1 Jan 1994 (SI 1993/3106)
18, para 1, 2	1 Sep 1994 (SI 1994/2038)
3	1 Aug 1994 (SI 1994/2038)
4–14	1 Sep 1994 (SI 1994/2038)
19, para 1	1 Oct 1993 (SI 1993/1975)
2	*Not in force*
3–5	1 Oct 1993 (SI 1993/1975)
6	1 Apr 1994 (subject to transitional provisions) (SI 1994/507)
7	1 Jan 1994 (SI 1993/3106)
8	1 Oct 1993 (SI 1993/1975)
9	1 Apr 1994 (SI 1994/507)
10	*Not in force*
11	1 Oct 1993 (SI 1993/1975)
12, 13	1 Apr 1994 (SI 1994/507)
14, 15	1 Oct 1993 (SI 1993/1975)
16	1 Sep 1994 (SI 1994/2038)
17	*Not in force*
18, 19	1 Apr 1994 (SI 1994/507)
20(a)	1 Oct 1993 (SI 1993/1975)
(b)	1 Apr 1994 (SI 1994/507)
21	1 Apr 1994 (SI 1994/507)
22	1 Jan 1994 (SI 1993/3106)
23(a)(i)	1 Oct 1993 (so far as amends Education Act 1944, s 105(2)(c)(i) (insertion of words "or on a transfer of the school to a new site")) (SI 1993/1975) 1 Jan 1994 (otherwise) (SI 1993/3106)
(ii)–(iv)	1 Jan 1994 (SI 1993/3106)
(b)	1 Apr 1994 (SI 1994/507)
24(a)(i)	*Not in force*
(ii), (iii)	1 Oct 1993 (SI 1993/1975)
(iv)	1 Jan 1994 (SI 1993/3106)
(b)	1 Jan 1994 (subject to transitional provisions) (SI 1993/3106)
25	1 Oct 1993 (SI 1993/1975)
26, 27	1 Apr 1994 (SI 1994/507)
28	1 Oct 1993 (SI 1993/1975)
29	1 Jan 1994 (SI 1993/3106)
30	1 Oct 1993 (SI 1993/1975)
31(a)	1 Sep 1994 (SI 1994/2038)
(b)–(f)	*Not in force*
32	1 Oct 1993 (SI 1993/1975)
33	*Not in force*
34	1 Oct 1993 (so far as relates to the Curriculum Council for Wales and the School Curriculum and Assessment Authority) (SI 1993/1975) 1 Apr 1994 (otherwise) (SI 1994/507)
35	1 Oct 1993 (SI 1993/1975)
36	*Not in force*; prospectively repealed by Children (Scotland) Act 1995, s 105(5), Sch 5[2]
37	*Not in force*

Education Act 1993 (c 35)—*cont*

Sch 19, para	38	1 Apr 1994 (SI 1994/507)
	39	1 Jan 1994 (SI 1993/3106)
	40–43	1 Oct 1993 (SI 1993/1975)
	44	1 Sep 1994 (SI 1994/2038)
	45	*Not in force*
	46–52	1 Apr 1994 (subject to transitional provisions relating to paras 49, 50) (SI 1994/507)
	53	*Not in force*
	54(a)	1 Sep 1994 (SI 1994/2038)
	(b)	*Not in force*
	55(a)	1 Apr 1994 (SI 1994/507)
	(b)	1 Jan 1994 (SI 1993/3106)
	56	1 Oct 1993 (SI 1993/1975)
	57	1 Apr 1994 (SI 1994/507)
	58	*Not in force*
	59	1 Apr 1994 (SI 1994/507)
	60	*Not in force*
	61, 62	1 Apr 1994 (SI 1994/507)
	63	*Not in force*
	64	1 Oct 1993 (SI 1993/1975) (also purported to be brought into force on 1 Apr 1994 by SI 1994/507)
	65, 66	1 Apr 1994 (SI 1994/507)
	67	*Not in force*
	68, 69	1 Oct 1993 (SI 1993/1975)
	70	1 Apr 1994 (SI 1994/507)
	71	*Not in force*
	72	1 Oct 1993 (SI 1993/1975)
	73	1 Apr 1994 (SI 1994/507)
	74	1 Sep 1994 (SI 1994/2038)
	75	1 Oct 1993 (SI 1993/1975)
	76	1 Apr 1994 (SI 1994/507)
	77(a)	1 Oct 1993 (SI 1993/1975)
	(b)	1 Apr 1994 (SI 1994/507)
	78	1 Oct 1993 (SI 1993/1975)
	79	1 Apr 1994 (SI 1994/507)
	80	1 Oct 1993 (SI 1993/1975)
	81	1 Apr 1994 (SI 1994/507)
	82	1 Jan 1994 (so far as repeals Education Act 1981, s 1) (SI 1993/3106)
		3 Mar 1994 (so far as repeals Education Act 1981, s 7(10)) (subject to a saving) (SI 1994/507)
		1 Apr 1994 (so far as repeals Education Act 1981, ss 2(4)–(7), 3, 11(2), (3), 12, 13, 14, Sch 1, paras 1(3), 4, Sch 3, paras 1, 2, 10, 13) (subject to transitional provisions and savings) (SI 1994/507)
		1 Sep 1994 (otherwise) (subject to transitional provisions and savings) (SI 1994/2038, as amended by SI 1994/2248)
	83	1 Jan 1994 (SI 1993/3106)
	84	1 Oct 1993 (SI 1993/1975)
	85, 86	1 Apr 1994 (SI 1994/507)
	87(a)	1 Sep 1994 (SI 1994/2038)
	(b)	1 Apr 1994 (SI 1994/507)
	(c)	1 Sep 1994 (SI 1994/2038)
	88	1 Sep 1994 (SI 1994/2038)
	89	1 Apr 1994 (SI 1994/507)

Education Act 1993 (c 35)—*cont*

Sch 19, para 90		1 Jan 1994 (so far as provides for Education (No 2) Act 1986, s 9(5), to have effect as if the transfer of a school to a new site in pursuance of Education Act 1980, s 16(1A)(c) were an alteration of the kind mentioned in sub-s (5) of that section) (SI 1993/3106)
		1 Apr 1994 (otherwise) (SI 1994/507)
	91–94	1 Apr 1994 (SI 1994/507)
	95, 96	1 Sep 1994 (SI 1994/2038)
	97(a)	1 Aug 1994 (for purpose of prescribing the period within which, under the articles of government for county, voluntary controlled and maintained special schools, the governing body are to be required to express their views to the local education authority as to the reinstatement of a permanently excluded pupil) (SI 1994/2038)
		1 Sep 1994 (otherwise) (SI 1994/2038)
	(b)–(d)	1 Sep 1994 (SI 1994/2038)
	98(a)	1 Aug 1994 (for purpose of prescribing the period within which, under the articles of government for voluntary aided and special agreement schools, the governing body are to be required to express their views to the local education authority as to the reinstatement of a pupil excluded for a fixed period) (SI 1994/2038)
		1 Sep 1994 (otherwise) (SI 1994/2038)
	(b)	1 Sep 1994 (SI 1994/2038)
	99, 100	1 Apr 1994 (SI 1994/507)
	101(a)	1 Sep 1994 (SI 1994/2038)
	(b)	1 Apr 1994 (SI 1994/507)
	102	1 Apr 1994 (subject to transitional provisions) (SI 1994/507)
	103, 104	1 Apr 1995 (SI 1994/1558)
	105, 106	1 Apr 1994 (SI 1994/507)
	107	1 Apr 1995 (SI 1994/1558)
	108	1 Apr 1994 (SI 1994/507)
	109(a)	1 Jan 1994 (SI 1993/3106)
	(b)(i)	1 Jan 1994 (SI 1993/3106)
	(ii)	1 Apr 1994 (SI 1994/507)
	(c), (d)	1 Apr 1994 (SI 1994/507)
	(e)	1 Jan 1994 (SI 1993/3106)
	110, 111	1 Apr 1994 (subject to transitional provisions) (SI 1994/507)
	112	1 Oct 1993 (SI 1993/1975)
	113(a)	1 Apr 1994 (SI 1994/507)
	(b)	*Not in force*
	114–117	1 Apr 1994 (SI 1994/507)
	118(a)	1 Jan 1994 (SI 1993/3106)
	(b)–(d)	1 Oct 1993 (subject to transitional provisions) (SI 1993/1975)
	(e)	1 Jan 1994 (SI 1993/3106)
	119	1 Oct 1993 (SI 1993/1975)
	120, 121	1 Sep 1994 (SI 1994/2038)
	122	1 Oct 1993 (SI 1993/1975)
	123	1 Jan 1994 (SI 1993/3106)
	124	1 Oct 1993 (SI 1993/1975)
	125(a)	3 Mar 1994 (SI 1994/507)

Education Act 1993 (c 35)—*cont*

Sch 19, para 125(b)	1 Apr 1994 (SI 1994/507)
126	1 Jan 1994 (so far as repeals Education Reform Act 1988, ss 52(3)–(9), 53–56, 58–72, 74–78, 104(1)(a), (b), (f)(h), (2), (3) (definition "incorporation date" only)) (subject to transitional provisions) (SI 1993/3106)
	1 Apr 1994 (otherwise) (subject to transitional provisions and savings) (SI 1994/507)
127–129	1 Apr 1994 (SI 1994/507)
130	1 Jan 1994 (so far as repeals reference to "52(4)" in Education Reform Act 1988, s 119(2)) (subject to transitional provisions) (SI 1993/3106)
	1 Apr 1994 (otherwise) (SI 1994/507)
131, 132	1 Oct 1993 (SI 1993/1975)
133–135	1 Jan 1994 (subject to transitional provisions) (SI 1993/3106)
136	1 Apr 1994 (SI 1994/507)
137	1 Jan 1994 (so far as repeals words "section 74 (taken with Schedule 10)" in Education Reform Act 1988, s 230(1)) (subject to transitional provisions) (SI 1993/3106)
	1 Apr 1994 (otherwise) (SI 1994/507)
138(a)	1 Jan 1994 (SI 1993/3106)
(b)(i)	1 Jan 1994 (so far as repeals references to "58(2), 59(1)" and "102" in Education Reform Act 1988, s 232(2)) (SI 1993/3106)
	1 Apr 1994 (otherwise) (SI 1994/507)
(ii)	1 Jan 1994 (SI 1993/3106)
139(a)(i)	1 Sep 1994 (SI 1994/2038)
(ii)	1 Jan 1994 (subject to transitional provisions) (SI 1993/3106)
(b), (c)	1 Jan 1994 (subject to transitional provisions) (SI 1993/3106)
140	1 Apr 1994 (SI 1994/507)
141	1 Oct 1993 (SI 1993/1975)
142	1 Apr 1994 (SI 1994/507)
143, 144	1 Jan 1994 (subject to transitional provisions) (SI 1993/3106)
145	1 Apr 1994 (so far as repeals Education Reform Act 1988, Sch 12, paras 26, 33) (SI 1994/507)
	1 Sep 1994 (otherwise) (SI 1994/2038)
146	*Not in force*
147, 148	1 Sep 1994 (SI 1994/2038)
149	1 Oct 1993 (SI 1993/1975)
150	1 Jan 1994 (SI 1993/3106)
151	1 Sep 1994 (SI 1994/2038)
152	1 Oct 1993 (SI 1993/1975)
153	1 Jan 1994 (SI 1993/3106)
154	1 Oct 1993 (so far as relates to Children Act 1989, Sch 12, para 4) (SI 1993/1975)
	1 Sep 1994 (otherwise) (SI 1994/2038)
155	1 Oct 1993 (SI 1993/1975)
156–159	1 Apr 1994 (subject to transitional provisions relating to para 156(a), (b), (d)) (SI 1994/507)
160	1 Sep 1994 (SI 1994/2038)
161	1 Apr 1994 (SI 1994/507)
162	1 Jan 1994 (SI 1993/3106)

Education Act 1993 (c 35)—*cont*

Sch 19, para 163(a)		1 Jan 1994 (subject to transitional provisions) (SI 1993/3106)
	(b)	1 Apr 1994 (SI 1994/507)
	(c)	1 Jan 1994 (subject to transitional provisions) (SI 1993/3106)
164		1 Jan 1994 (subject to transitional provisions) (SI 1993/3106)
165, 166		1 Jan 1994 (SI 1993/3106)
167(a)		1 Apr 1994 (SI 1994/507)
	(b)	1 Jan 1994 (SI 1993/3106)
168, 169		1 Apr 1994 (SI 1994/507)
170		1 Oct 1993 (SI 1993/1975)
171, 172		1 Apr 1994 (SI 1994/507)
173(1)(a)		1 Apr 1994 (SI 1994/507)
	(b)	1 Oct 1993 (SI 1993/1975)
	(c)	1 Sep 1993 (SI 1993/1975)
	(2)	1 Aug 1993 (for purpose of prescribing matters which fall to be prescribed under Education (Schools) Act 1992, Sch 2) (SI 1993/1975) 1 Sep 1993 (otherwise) (SI 1993/1975)
	(3)	1 Aug 1993 (for purpose of prescribing matters which fall to be prescribed under Education (Schools) Act 1992, Sch 2) (SI 1993/1975) 1 Sep 1993 (otherwise) (SI 1993/1975)
	(4)	1 Sep 1993 (SI 1993/1975)
	(5)	1 Aug 1993 (for purpose of prescribing matters which fall to be prescribed under Education (Schools) Act 1992, Sch 2) (subject to transitional provisions) (SI 1993/1975) 1 Sep 1993 (otherwise) (subject to transitional provisions) (SI 1993/1975)
	(6)	1 Aug 1993 (for purpose of prescribing matters which fall to be prescribed under Education (Schools) Act 1992, Sch 2) (subject to transitional provisions) (SI 1993/1975) 1 Sep 1993 (otherwise) (subject to transitional provisions) (SI 1993/1975)
	(7)	1 Sep 1993 (SI 1993/1975)
	(8)(a)	1 Aug 1993 (for purpose of prescribing matters which fall to be prescribed under Education (Schools) Act 1992, Sch 2) (SI 1993/1975) 1 Oct 1993 (otherwise) (SI 1993/1975)
	(b)	1 Oct 1993 (SI 1993/1975)
	(9)(a)	1 Aug 1993 (for purpose of prescribing matters which fall to be prescribed under Education (Schools) Act 1992, Sch 2) (SI 1993/1975) 1 Oct 1993 (otherwise) (SI 1993/1975)
	(b)	1 Oct 1993 (SI 1993/1975)
174		1 Jan 1994 (SI 1993/3106)
175		1 Oct 1993 (SI 1993/1975)
20, para 1		1 Jan 1994 (SI 1993/3106)
2		1 Apr 1994 (SI 1994/507)
3		1 Jan 1994 (SI 1993/3106)
4		1 Apr 1994 (SI 1994/507)
5–7		1 Jan 1994 (SI 1993/3106)
21		1 Oct 1993 (repeals of or in Children and Young Persons Act 1933, s 10; Education Act 1944, ss 1,

Education Act 1993 (c 35)—*cont*

Sch 21—*cont*

6, 16, 37, 39, 40, 114, Sch 8; Education (Miscellaneous Provisions) Act 1948, s 9; Education (Miscellaneous Provisions) Act 1953, s 10; Criminal Justice Act 1967; Education Act 1968, s 3, Sch 1, para 1; Children and Young Persons Act 1969; Criminal Law Act 1977; Education Act 1980, ss 10, 11, Sch 1, para 10; Education Reform Act 1988, ss 14(4), (5), 25, Sch 2, para 18; Children Act 1989, s 36, Sch 13) (SI 1993/1975)

1 Jan 1994 (repeals of or in Education Act 1944, ss 102, 103, 105(2); Education Act 1967, s 1; Superannuation Act 1972, Sch 1; House of Commons Disqualification Act 1975, Sch 1; Education Act 1981, s 1; Education Reform Act 1988, ss 14(1), 42, 52(3)–(9), 53–56, 58–72, 74–78, 102, 103, 104(1)(a), (b), (f)–(h), (2), (3) (definition "incorporation date" only), 119(2) (reference to "52(4)" only), 198(1), 200, 230(1) (words "section 74 (taken with Schedule 10)" only), 232(2) (references to "58(2), 59(1)" and "102" only), (4)(b), 235 (except definition "the 1981 Act" in sub-s (1)), Sch 2, paras 1, 9 (entries relating to membership of the National Curriculum Council and the School Examinations and Assessment Council only), 10(5) (entries relating to National Curriculum Council and the School Examinations and Assessment Council only), Sch 4, para 2, Sch 5; Children Act 1989, Sch 12, para 4; Diocesian Boards of Education Measure 1991, s 3(6)) (subject to transitional provisions) (SI 1993/3106)

3 Mar 1994 (repeals of or in Education Act 1981, s 7(10); Education (Grants and Awards) Act 1984) (subject to a saving) (SI 1994/507)

1 Apr 1994 (repeals of or in Education Act 1944, ss 9(5), 50(1), 52(1), Sch 1, Pts I, II, Sch 5, para 13; Local Government Act 1972; Education Act 1973, s 1; Education Act 1980, ss 12(3), 13(1), (3), 14(4), Sch 2, para 1, Sch 3, paras 4, 13; Education Act 1981, ss 2(4)–(7), 3, 11(2), (3), 1214, Sch 1, paras 1(3), 4, Sch 3, paras 1, 2, 10, 13; Education (No 2) Act 1986, ss 5(4), 9(5), 11, 12(3), 13(2), 38, 50, 54(12), 65(1), Sch 2; Local Government Act 1988; Education Reform Act 1988, ss 52(1), (2), 57, 73, 79–101, 104(1)(c), (d), (e), (i), (j), (3) (except definition "incorporation date"), (4), 111, 119(2) (so far as repeals in that section not already in force), 230 (so far as repeals in that section not already in force), 232 (so far as repeals in that section not already in force), Sch 1, para 9, Sch 2, paras 9, 10, Sch 12, paras 26, 33; Local Government and Housing Act 1989; Planning (Consequential Provisions) Act 1990; Further and Higher Education Act 1992, ss 13, 59(5), Sch 8, paras 18, 29; Local Government Finance Act 1992) (subject to savings and transitional provisions) (SI 1994/507)

Education Act 1993 (c 35)—*cont*

Sch 21—*cont*	1 Sep 1994 (repeals of or in Education Act 1944, s 56; Education Act 1981, ss 2(2), (3), 3A, 4, 5, 6, 7(1)–(9), (11), 8, 9, 10, 15, 16, 18, 19, 20(1) (other than definition "principal Act"), Sch 1, paras 1(1), (2), 2, 3, 5–7, Sch 2, paras 2–8, Sch 3, paras 8(2)(a), (c), 9, 15, 16; Education (No 2) Act 1986, ss 23, 24, 25; Education Reform Act 1988, s 235(1) (definition "the 1981 Act"), Sch 12, paras 27, 28, 83–85; Children Act 1989, s 27(4), Sch 12, para 36; National Health Service and Community Care Act 1990) (subject to transitional provisions and savings) (SI 1994/2038, as amended by SI 1994/2248))
	1 Apr 1995 (repeals of Education (No 2) Act 1986, ss 51(9), (13), 63(4)) (SI 1994/1558)
	Not in force (otherwise)

[1] Any orders made under Disability Discrimination Act 1995, s 70(3), bringing the prospective addition into force will be noted to that Act in the service to this work

[2] Any orders made under Children (Scotland) Act 1995, s 105, bringing the prospective repeal into force will be noted to that Act in the service to this work

---

European Communities (Amendment) Act 1993 (c 32)

RA: 20 Jul 1993

Commencement provision: s 7

23 Jul 1993 (s 7)

European Economic Area Act 1993 (c 51)

RA: 5 Nov 1993

5 Nov 1993 (RA)

European Parliamentary Elections Act 1993 (c 41)

RA: 5 Nov 1993

Commencement provisions: s 3(3); European Parliamentary Elections Act 1993 (Commencement) Order 1994, SI 1994/1089

s 1	1 May 1994 (SI 1994/1089)
2, 3	5 Nov 1993 (RA)
Schedule	5 Nov 1993 (RA)

Finance Act 1993 (c 34)

RA: 27 Jul 1993

See the note concerning Finance Acts at the front of this book

---

Foreign Compensation (Amendment) Act 1993 (c 16)

RA: 27 May 1993

Commencement provision: s 3(1)

27 Jul 1993 (s 3(1))

Gas (Exempt Supplies) Act 1993 (c 1)

RA: 19 Jan 1993

Commencement provisions: s 4(2); Gas (Exempt Supplies) Act 1993 (Commencement) Order 1994, SI 1994/2568

31 Oct 1994 (SI 1994/2568)

Health Service Commissioners Act 1993 (c 46)

RA: 5 Nov 1993

Commencement provision: s 22(4)

5 Feb 1994 (s 22(4))

Incumbents (Vacation of Benefices) (Amendment) Measure 1993 (No 1)

RA: 27 Jul 1993

Commencement provision: s 16(2)

The provisions of this Measure are brought into force on 1 Sep 1994 by an appointed day notice signed by the Archbishops of Canterbury and York and dated 25 Jul 1994 (made under s 16(2))

Judicial Pensions and Retirement Act 1993 (c 8)

RA: 29 Mar 1993

Commencement provision: s 31(2); Judicial Pensions and Retirement Act 1993 (Commencement) Order 1995, SI 1995/631

31 Mar 1995 (SI 1995/631)

Leasehold Reform, Housing and Urban Development Act 1993 (c 28)

RA: 20 Jul 1993

Commencement provisions: ss 138(2), 188(2), (3); Leasehold Reform, Housing and Urban Development Act 1993 (Commencement and Transitional Provisions No 1) Order 1993, SI 1993/2134; Leasehold Reform, Housing and Urban Development Act 1993 (Commencement No 2) (Scotland) Order 1993, SI 1993/2163; Leasehold Reform, Housing and Urban Development Act 1993 (Commencement and Transitional Provisions No 3) Order 1993, SI 1993/2762;

Leasehold Reform, Housing and Urban Development Act 1993 (c 28)—*cont*

Leasehold Reform, Housing and Urban Development Act 1993 (Commencement No 4) Order 1994, SI 1994/935

s 1–25	1 Nov 1993 (SI 1993/2134)
26(1)–(8)	1 Nov 1993 (SI 1993/2134)
(9)	2 Sep 1993 (SI 1993/2134)
27–66	1 Nov 1993 (SI 1993/2134)
67, 68	1 Nov 1993 (subject to savings) (SI 1993/2134)
69–74	1 Nov 1993 (SI 1993/2134)
75	2 Sep 1993 (so far as confers on Secretary of State a power to make orders, regulations or declarations) (SI 1993/2134)
	1 Nov 1993 (otherwise) (SI 1993/2134)
76–84	1 Nov 1993 (SI 1993/2134)
85, 86	1 Nov 1993 (subject to savings) (SI 1993/2134)
87	1 Nov 1993 (SI 1993/2134)
88	2 Sep 1993 (so far as confers on Secretary of State a power to make orders, regulations or declarations) (SI 1993/2134)
	1 Nov 1993 (otherwise) (SI 1993/2134)
89, 90	1 Nov 1993 (SI 1993/2134)
91	2 Sep 1993 (so far as confers on Secretary of State a power to make orders, regulations or declarations) (SI 1993/2134)
	1 Nov 1993 (otherwise) (SI 1993/2134)
92–97	1 Nov 1993 (SI 1993/2134)
98	2 Sep 1993 (SI 1993/2134)
99	2 Sep 1993 (so far as confers on Secretary of State a power to make orders, regulations or declarations) (SI 1993/2134)
	1 Nov 1993 (otherwise) (SI 1993/2134)
100	2 Sep 1993 (SI 1993/2134)
101–103	1 Nov 1993 (SI 1993/2134)
104–107	11 Oct 1993 (subject to savings) (SI 1993/2134)
108	2 Sep 1993 (so far as confers on Secretary of State a power to make orders, regulations or declarations) (SI 1993/2134)
	11 Oct 1993 (otherwise) (subject to savings) (SI 1993/2134)
109–120	11 Oct 1993 (subject to savings) (SI 1993/2134)
121	1 Dec 1993 (subject to transitional provisions) (SI 1993/2762)
122	1 Feb 1994 (subject to transitional provisions) (SI 1993/2762)
123	11 Oct 1993 (SI 1993/2134)
124, 125	11 Oct 1993 (subject to savings) (SI 1993/2134)
126, 127	20 Jul 1993 (RA)
128, 129	11 Oct 1993 (SI 1993/2134)
130	11 Oct 1993 (subject to savings) (SI 1993/2134)
131	11 Oct 1993 (SI 1993/2134)
132	10 Nov 1993 (so far as confers on the Secretary of State a power to make regulations) (SI 1993/2762)
	1 Apr 1994 (otherwise) (SI 1994/935)
133, 134	11 Oct 1993 (subject to savings) (SI 1993/2134)
135–137	20 Jul 1993 (RA)
138	1 Jan 1993 (s 138(2))
139, 140	20 Jul 1993 (RA)

Leasehold Reform, Housing and Urban Development Act 1993 (c 28)—*cont*

s 141–145	27 Sep 1993 (SI 1993/2163)
146, 147	1 Apr 1994 (SI 1993/2163)
148	27 Sep 1993 (SI 1993/2163)
149–151	20 Jul 1993 (RA)
152, 153	1 Apr 1994 (SI 1993/2163)
154–157	27 Sep 1993 (SI 1993/2163)
158–173	10 Nov 1993 (SI 1993/2762)
174	11 Oct 1993 (SI 1993/2134)
175	10 Nov 1993 (SI 1993/2762)
176	11 Oct 1993 (SI 1993/2134)
177	10 Nov 1993 (SI 1993/2762)
178	11 Oct 1993 (subject to savings) (SI 1993/2134)
179	11 Oct 1993 (SI 1993/2134)
180	11 Oct 1993 (except so far as relates to insertion of s 165A(2) of the 1980 Act) (SI 1993/2134)
	10 Nov 1993 (otherwise) (SI 1993/2762)
181(1), (2)	20 Jul 1993 (RA)
(3)	10 Nov 1993 (SI 1993/2762)
(4)	20 Jul 1993 (RA)
182	11 Oct 1993 (SI 1993/2134)
183	10 Nov 1993 (SI 1993/2762)
184	1 Apr 1994 (subject to transitional provisions) (SI 1994/935)
185	10 Nov 1993 (SI 1993/2762)
186	20 Jul 1993 (RA)
187(1)	See Sch 21 below
(2)	See Sch 22 below
188	20 Jul 1993 (RA)
Sch 1–15	1 Nov 1993 (SI 1993/2134)
16	11 Oct 1993 (subject to savings) (SI 1993/2134)
17–20	10 Nov 1993 (SI 1993/2762)
21, para 1	1 Nov 1993 (SI 1993/2134)
2	*Not in force*
3	10 Nov 1993 (SI 1993/2762)
4	2 Sep 1993 (SI 1993/2134)
5	1 Nov 1993 (subject to savings) (SI 1993/2134)
6	10 Nov 1993 (SI 1993/2762)
7	2 Sep 1993 (SI 1993/2134)
8	10 Nov 1993 (SI 1993/2762)
9	1 Nov 1993 (SI 1993/2134)
10	11 Oct 1993 (SI 1993/2134)
11–25	11 Oct 1993 (subject to savings) (SI 1993/2134)
26	1 Nov 1993 (SI 1993/2134)
27	2 Sep 1993 (SI 1993/2134)
28, 29	10 Nov 1993 (SI 1993/2762)
30	1 Nov 1993 (SI 1993/2134)
31, 32	10 Nov 1993 (SI 1993/2762)
22	20 Jul 1993 (repeal in Local Government and Housing Act 1989, s 80(1)) (RA)
	2 Sep 1993 (repeals of Housing Act 1988, s 41(1); Local Government and Housing Act 1989, Sch 11, para 51) (SI 1993/2134)
	27 Sep 1993 (repeals in Housing Scotland Act 1987) (SI 1993/2163)

Leasehold Reform, Housing and Urban Development Act 1993 (c 28)—*cont*

Sch 22—*cont*

11 Oct 1993 (repeals in Local Government, Planning and Land Act 1980; Housing Act 1988, s 69(2)) (SI 1993/2134)

11 Oct 1993 (repeals of or in Housing Act 1985, ss 124(3), 128(6), 132–135, 137, 138(1), 139(3), 140(5), 142, 153A(1), 153B(1), 164(6), 166(6), 169(3), 171C(2), 171H, 177, 180, 181(1), 182(1), 187, 188, Schs 6, 7–9; Housing and Planning Act 1986, Sch 5, para 5; Housing Act 1988, s 79; Local Government and Housing Act 1989, s 164) (subject to savings) (SI 1993/2134)

1 Nov 1993 (repeals in Housing Act 1980; Housing (Consequential Provisions) Act 1985) (SI 1993/2134)

1 Nov 1993 (repeals in Landlord and Tenant Act 1987) (subject to savings) (SI 1993/2134)

10 Nov 1993 (repeal in Land Compensation Act 1961) (SI 1993/2762)

1 Apr 1994 (repeal of English Industrial Estates Corporation Act 1981) (subject to transitional provisions) (SI 1994/935)

Not in force (otherwise)

Licensing (Amendment) (Scotland) Act 1993 (c 20)

RA: 1 Jul 1993

1 Jul 1993 (RA)

Local Government (Amendment) Act 1993 (c 27)

RA: 20 Jul 1993

Commencement provision: s 3(2)

20 Sep 1993 (s 3(2))

Local Government (Overseas Assistance) Act 1993 (c 25)

RA: 20 Jul 1993

Commencement provision: s 2(2)

20 Sep 1993 (s 2(2))

Merchant Shipping (Registration, etc) Act 1993 (c 22)

Whole Act repealed

National Lottery etc Act 1993 (c 39)

RA: 21 Oct 1993

Commencement provisions: s 65; National Lottery etc Act 1993 (Commencement No 1 and Transitional Provisions) Order 1993, SI 1993/2632; National Lottery etc

National Lottery etc Act 1993 (c 39)—*cont*

Act 1993 (Commencement No 2 and Transitional Provisions) Order 1994, SI 1994/1055; National Lottery etc Act 1993 (Commencement No 3) Order 1994, SI 1994/2659

s 1–15	25 Oct 1993 (SI 1993/2632)
16	21 Dec 1993 (SI 1993/2632)
17	25 Oct 1993 (SI 1993/2632)
18	21 Dec 1993 (subject to transitional provisions) (SI 1993/2632)
19, 20	25 Oct 1993 (SI 1993/2632)
21–25	21 Dec 1993 (SI 1993/2632)
26(1)	25 Oct 1993 (SI 1993/2632)
(2)	21 Dec 1993 (SI 1993/2632)
(3)–(5)	25 Oct 1993 (SI 1993/2632)
27–39	21 Dec 1993 (SI 1993/2632)
40–44	25 Oct 1993 (SI 1993/2632)
45–47	21 Dec 1993 (SI 1993/2632)
48, 49	3 May 1994 (subject to transitional provisions relating to s 48(3)) (SI 1994/1055)
50	3 Oct 1994 (SI 1994/1055)
51–55	3 May 1994 (subject to transitional provisions relating to s 52(4), (7), (8)) (SI 1994/1055)
56–59	14 Nov 1994 (SI 1994/2659)
60–63	25 Oct 1993 (SI 1993/2632)
64	See Sch 10 below
65, 66	25 Oct 1993 (SI 1993/2632)
Sch 1–3	25 Oct 1993 (SI 1993/2632)
4, 5	21 Dec 1993 (SI 1993/2632)
6	25 Oct 1993 (SI 1993/2632)
7, 8	3 May 1994 (subject to transitional provisions relating to Sch 7, Pt I, para 7) (SI 1994/1055)
9	3 Oct 1994 (SI 1994/1055)
10	21 Dec 1993 (repeals in Revenue Act 1898; National Heritage Act 1980) (SI 1993/2632)
	3 May 1994 (otherwise) (SI 1994/1055)

Noise and Statutory Nuisance Act 1993 (c 40)

RA: 5 Nov 1993

Commencement provision: s 12

s 1–5	5 Jan 1994 (s 12(1))
6	5 Jan 1994 (s 12(1)); prospectively repealed by Environment Act 1995, s 120(3), Sch 24[1]
7, 8	5 Jan 1994 (s 12(1))
9	*Not in force*
10–14	5 Jan 1994 (s 12(1))
Sch 1	5 Jan 1994 (s 12(1)); prospectively repealed by Environment Act 1995, s 120(3), Sch 24[1]
2	5 Jan 1994 (s 12(1))
3	*Not in force*

[1] Any orders made under Environment Act 1995, s 125(3), bringing the prospective repeals into force will be noted to that Act in the service to this work

Non-Domestic Rating Act 1993 (c 17)

RA: 27 May 1993

Commencement provisions: s 6(2); Non-Domestic Rating Act 1993 (Commencement No 1) Order 1993, SI 1993/1418; Non-Domestic Rating Act 1993 (Commencement No 2) Order 1993, SI 1993/1512

s 1(1)	6 Jul 1993 (SI 1993/1512)
(2)	4 Jun 1993 (SI 1993/1418)
(3)–(5)	6 Jul 1993 (SI 1993/1512); sub-ss (3), (4) superseded by Non-Domestic Rating Act 1994, s 1(2), (3)
2, 3	6 Jul 1993 (SI 1993/1512)
4	4 Jun 1993 (SI 1993/1418)
5, 6	6 Jul 1993 (SI 1993/1512)

Ordination of Women (Financial Provisions) Measure 1993 (No 3)

RA: 5 Nov 1993

5 Nov 1993 (RA)

Osteopaths Act 1993 (c 21)

RA: 1 Jul 1993

Commencement provision: s 42(2)–(5)

Not in force

Pension Schemes Act 1993 (c 48)

RA: 5 Nov 1993

Commencement provisions: s 193(2), (3); Pension Schemes Act 1993 (Commencement No 1) Order 1994, SI 1994/86

s 1	7 Feb 1994 (SI 1994/86)
2–5	7 Feb 1994 (SI 1994/86); prospectively repealed by Pensions Act 1995, ss 151, 177, Sch 5, paras 18, 19, Sch 7, Pt III[1]
6–12	7 Feb 1994 (SI 1994/86)
12A–12D	Prospectively inserted by Pensions Act 1995, s 136(5)[1]
13–21	7 Feb 1994 (SI 1994/86)
22	7 Feb 1994 (SI 1994/86); prospectively repealed by Pensions Act 1995, ss 151, 177, Sch 5, paras 18, 30, Sch 7, Pt III[1]
23	7 Feb 1994 (SI 1994/86)
24	7 Feb 1994 (SI 1994/86); prospectively repealed by Pensions Act 1995, ss 151, 177, Sch 5, paras 18, 32, Sch 7, Pt III[1]
25–28	7 Feb 1994 (SI 1994/86)
28A, 28B	Prospectively inserted by Pensions Act 1995, s 143[1]
29–32	7 Feb 1994 (SI 1994/86)
32A	Prospectively inserted by Pensions Act 1995, s 146(1)[1]

Pension Schemes Act 1993 (c 48)—*cont*

s 33	7 Feb 1994 (SI 1994/86)
33A	Prospectively inserted by Pensions Act 1995, s 147[1]
34	7 Feb 1994 (SI 1994/86)
35, 36	7 Feb 1994 (SI 1994/86); prospectively repealed by Pensions Act 1995, ss 151, 177, Sch 5, paras 18, 38, Sch 7, Pt III[1]
37	7 Feb 1994 (SI 1994/86); prospectively substituted by Pensions Act 1995, s 151, Sch 5, paras 18, 39[1]
38–42	7 Feb 1994 (SI 1994/86)
42A, 42B	Prospectively inserted by Pensions Act 1995, s 137(5)[1]
43–45	7 Feb 1994 (SI 1994/86)
45A, 45B	Prospectively inserted by Pensions Act 1995, s 138(5), 139[1]
46–48	7 Feb 1994 (SI 1994/86)
48A	Prospectively inserted by Pensions Act 1995, s 140(1)[1]
49	Substituted by Pensions Act 1995, s 126(c), Sch 4, Pt III, para 16 (qv)
50–58	7 Feb 1994 (SI 1994/86)
59	7 Feb 1994 (SI 1994/86); prospectively repealed by Pensions Act 1995, ss 151, 177, Sch 5, paras 18, 53, Sch 7, Pt III[1]
60–63	7 Feb 1994 (SI 1994/86)
64	7 Feb 1994 (SI 1994/86); prospectively repealed by Pensions Act 1995, ss 151, 177, Sch 5, paras 18, 58, Sch 7, Pt III[1]
65	7 Feb 1994 (SI 1994/86); prospectively repealed by Pensions Act 1995, ss 151, 177, Sch 5, paras 18, 59, Sch 7, Pt III[1]
66	7 Feb 1994 (SI 1994/86); prospectively repealed by Pensions Act 1995, ss 151, 177, Sch 5, paras 18, 60, Sch 7, Pt III[1]
67–76	7 Feb 1994 (SI 1994/86)
77–80	7 Feb 1994 (SI 1994/86); prospectively repealed by Pensions Act 1995, ss 122, 177, Sch 3, paras 22, 24, Sch 7, Pt I[1]
81–93	7 Feb 1994 (SI 1994/86)
93A	Prospectively inserted by Pensions Act 1995, s 153[1]
94–101	7 Feb 1994 (SI 1994/86)
102–108	7 Feb 1994 (SI 1994/86); prospectively repealed by Pensions Act 1995, ss 122, 177, Sch 3, paras 22, 25, Sch 7, Pt I[1]
109–111	7 Feb 1994 (SI 1994/86)
112	7 Feb 1994 (SI 1994/86); prospectively repealed by Pensions Act 1995, ss 122, 177, Sch 3, paras 22, 26, Sch 7, Pt I[1]
113	7 Feb 1994 (SI 1994/86)
114	7 Feb 1994 (SI 1994/86); prospectively repealed by Pensions Act 1995, ss 122, 177, Sch 3, paras 22, 27, Sch 7, Pt I[1]
115	7 Feb 1994 (SI 1994/86)
116	7 Feb 1994 (SI 1994/86); prospectively repealed by Pensions Act 1995, ss 122, 177, Sch 3, paras 22, 28, Sch 7, Pt I[1]
117	7 Feb 1994 (SI 1994/86)

Pension Schemes Act 1993 (c 48)—*cont*

s 118	7 Feb 1994 (SI 1994/86); prospectively repealed by Pensions Act 1995, ss 122, 177, Sch 3, paras 22, 29, Sch 7, Pt I[1]
119–122	7 Feb 1994 (SI 1994/86); prospectively repealed by Pensions Act 1995, ss 122, 177, Sch 3, paras 22, 30, Sch 7, Pt I[1]
123–132	7 Feb 1994 (SI 1994/86)
133–135	7 Feb 1994 (SI 1994/86); prospectively repealed by Pensions Act 1995, ss 151, 177, Sch 5, paras 18, 64, Sch 7, Pt III[1]
136–143	7 Feb 1994 (SI 1994/86); prospectively repealed by Pensions Act 1995, ss 161, 177, Sch 7, Pt IV[1]
144	7 Feb 1994 (SI 1994/86); prospectively repealed by Pensions Act 1995, ss 122, 177, Sch 3, paras 22, 38, Sch 7, Pt I[1]
145–151	7 Feb 1994 (SI 1994/86)
151A	Prospectively inserted by Pensions Act 1995, s 160[1]
152–158	7 Feb 1994 (SI 1994/86)
158A	Prospectively inserted by Pensions Act 1995, s 173, Sch 6, paras 2, 9[1]
159–167	7 Feb 1994 (SI 1994/86)
168	7 Feb 1994 (SI 1994/86); prospectively substituted (by ss 168, 168A) by Pensions Act 1995, ss 155(1)[1]
169–171	7 Feb 1994 (SI 1994/86)
172, 173	7 Feb 1994 (SI 1994/86); prospectively repealed by Pensions Act 1995, ss 151, 177, Sch 5, paras 18, 72, Sch 7, Pt III[1]
174	7 Feb 1994 (SI 1994/86)
175	7 Feb 1994 (SI 1994/86); prospectively substituted by Pensions Act 1995, ss 165[1]
176–187	7 Feb 1994 (SI 1994/86)
188(1), (2)	See Sch 5 below
(3)	7 Feb 1994 (SI 1994/86)
189	7 Feb 1994 (SI 1994/86)
190	See Schs 7, 8 below
191–193	7 Feb 1994 (SI 1994/86)
Sch 1	7 Feb 1994 (SI 1994/86); prospectively repealed by Pensions Act 1995, ss 151, 177, Sch 5, paras 18, 83, Sch 7, Pt III[1]
2–4	7 Feb 1994 (SI 1994/86)
5, Pt I	7 Feb 1994 (SI 1994/86)
II	*Not in force*
III, IV	7 Feb 1994 (SI 1994/86)
6	7 Feb 1994 (SI 1994/86)
7	*Not in force*
8, 9	7 Feb 1994 (SI 1994/86)

[1] Any orders made under Pensions Act 1995, s 180, bringing the prospective amendments into force will be noted to that Act in the service to this work

Pension Schemes (Northern Ireland) Act 1993 (c 49)

RA: 5 Nov 1993

Commencement provisions: s 186(2), (3); Pension Schemes (1993 Act) (Commencement No 1) Order (Northern Ireland) 1994, SR 1994/17

Pension Schemes (Northern Ireland) Act 1993 (c 49)—*cont*

s 1–181	7 Feb 1994 (SR 1994/17)
182(1), (2)	See Sch 4 below
(3)	7 Feb 1994 (SR 1994/17)
183	7 Feb 1994 (SR 1994/17)
184	See Schs 6, 7 below
185, 186	7 Feb 1994 (SR 1994/17)
Sch 1–3	7 Feb 1994 (SR 1994/17)
4, Pt I	7 Feb 1994 (SR 1994/17)
II	*Not in force*
III	7 Feb 1994 (SR 1994/17)
5	7 Feb 1994 (SR 1994/17)
6	*Not in force*
7, 8	7 Feb 1994 (SR 1994/17)

Priests (Ordination of Women) Measure 1993 (No 2)

RA: 5 Nov 1993

Commencement provision: s 12(2)

The provisions of this Measure are brought into force on 1 Feb 1994 by an appointed day notice signed by the Archbishops of Canterbury and York and dated 31 Jan 1994 (made under s 12)

Prisoners and Criminal Proceedings (Scotland) Act 1993 (c 9)

RA: 29 Mar 1993

Commencement provisions: s 48(2)–(4); Prisoners and Criminal Proceedings (Scotland) Act 1993 Commencement, Transitional Provisions and Savings Order 1993, SI 1993/2050

s 1–5	1 Oct 1993 (SI 1993/2050)
6(1), (2)	1 Oct 1993 (SI 1993/2050)
(3)	18 Aug 1993 (for purpose of enabling orders to be made so as to come into force on or after 1 Oct 1993) (SI 1993/2050) 1 Oct 1993 (otherwise) (SI 1993/2050)
7(1)	1 Oct 1993 (SI 1993/2050)
(1A), (1B)	Inserted by Criminal Justice and Public Order Act 1994, s 130(1) (qv)
(2)–(5)	1 Oct 1993 (SI 1993/2050)
(6)	18 Aug 1993 (for purpose of enabling orders to be made so as to come into force on or after 1 Oct 1993) (SI 1993/2050) 1 Oct 1993 (otherwise) (SI 1993/2050)
(7)	1 Oct 1993 (SI 1993/2050)
8	Repealed
9–19	1 Oct 1993 (SI 1993/2050)
20(1), (2)	1 Oct 1993 (SI 1993/2050)
(3)	18 Aug 1993 (for purpose of enabling orders to be made so as to come into force on or after 1 Oct 1993) (SI 1993/2050) 1 Oct 1993 (otherwise) (SI 1993/2050)

Prisoners and Criminal Proceedings (Scotland) Act 1993 (c 9)—*cont*

s 20(4), (5)	18 Aug 1993 (for purpose of enabling rules to be made, and directions to be given, so as to come into force on or after 1 Oct 1993) (SI 1993/2050)
	1 Oct 1993 (otherwise) (SI 1993/2050)
(6)	1 Oct 1993 (SI 1993/2050)
21–23	1 Oct 1993 (SI 1993/2050)
24, 25	18 Aug 1993 (SI 1993/2050)
26	1 Oct 1993 (SI 1993/2050)
27(1)–(3)	18 Aug 1993 (for purpose of enabling an order to be made so as to come into force on or after 1 Oct 1993) (SI 1993/2050)
	1 Oct 1993 (otherwise) (SI 1993/2050)
(4)–(7)	1 Oct 1993 (SI 1993/2050)
28–35	Repealed
36	18 Sep 1993 (subject to a saving) (SI 1993/2050)
37–43	Repealed
44	1 Oct 1993 (SI 1993/2050)
45, 46	18 Aug 1993 (SI 1993/2050)
47(1)	See Sch 5 below
(2)	See Sch 6 below
(3)	See Sch 7 below
48	29 Mar 1993 (s 48(4))
Sch 1, 2	1 Oct 1993 (subject to a saving) (SI 1993/2050)
3, 4	Repealed
5, para 1	Repealed
2–4	1 Oct 1993 (SI 1993/2050)
5	29 Mar 1993 (s 48(4))
6(1)–(4)	18 Aug 1993 (SI 1993/2050)
(5)	1 Oct 1993 (SI 1993/2050)
(6)	18 Aug 1993 (SI 1993/2050)
(7)	1 Oct 1993 (SI 1993/2050)
(8)	18 Aug 1993 (SI 1993/2050)
(9)	1 Oct 1993 (SI 1993/2050)
6	1 Oct 1993 (SI 1993/2050)
7	18 Sep 1993 (repeals of or in Criminal Procedure (Scotland) Act 1975, ss 108, 289D, 328; Criminal Justice (Scotland) Act 1980, Sch 3; Criminal Justice (Scotland) Act 1987, s 62) (subject to savings) (SI 1993/2050)
	1 Oct 1993 (otherwise) (subject to savings) (SI 1993/2050)

[1] Any orders made under Criminal Justice (Scotland) Act 1995, s 118, bringing the prospective amendments into force will be noted to that Act in the service to this work

---

Probation Service Act 1993 (c 47)

RA: 5 Nov 1993

Commencement provision: s 33(2)

5 Feb 1994 (s 33(2))

Protection of Animals (Scotland) Act 1993 (c 15)

RA: 27 May 1993

Commencement provision: s 2(2)

27 Jul 1993 (s 2(2))

Radioactive Substances Act 1993 (c 12)

RA: 27 May 1993

Commencement provision: s 51(2)

27 Aug 1993 (s 51(2))

Railways Act 1993 (c 43)

RA: 5 Nov 1993

Commencement provisions: s 154(2); Railways Act 1993 (Commencement No 1) Order 1993, SI 1993/3237; Railways Act 1993 (Commencement No 2) Order 1994, SI 1994/202; Railways Act 1993 (Commencement No 3) Order 1994, SI 1994/447; Railways Act 1993 (Commencement No 4 and Transitional Provision) Order 1994, SI 1994/571; Railways Act 1993 (Commencement No 5 and Transitional Provisions) Order 1994, SI 1994/1648; Railways Act 1993 (Commencement No 6) Order 1994, SI 1994/2142

s 1	5 Nov 1993 (s 154(2))
2, 3	1 Apr 1994 (SI 1994/571)
4(1)	24 Dec 1993 (for purposes of functions of Secretary of State under s 33) (SI 1993/3237)
	22 Feb 1994 (for purpose of functions of Regulator under s 70) (SI 1994/447)
	21 Mar 1994 (otherwise) (SI 1994/571)
(2)	22 Feb 1994 (for purpose of functions of Regulator under s 70) (SI 1994/447)
	21 Mar 1994 (otherwise) (SI 1994/571)
(3)	24 Dec 1993 (for purposes of functions of Secretary of State under s 33) (SI 1993/3237)
	22 Feb 1994 (for purpose of functions of Regulator under s 70) (SI 1994/447)
	21 Mar 1994 (otherwise) (SI 1994/571)
(4)	21 Mar 1994 (SI 1994/571)
(5), (6)	22 Feb 1994 (for purpose of functions of Regulator under s 70) (SI 1994/447)
	21 Mar 1994 (otherwise) (SI 1994/571)
(7)	24 Dec 1993 (for purposes of functions of Secretary of State under s 33) (SI 1993/3237)
	21 Mar 1994 (otherwise) (SI 1994/571)
(8)	21 Mar 1994 (SI 1994/571)
(9)	24 Dec 1993 (for purposes of definitions "environment" and "through ticket") (SI 1993/3237)
	21 Mar 1994 (otherwise) (SI 1994/571)
5	21 Mar 1994 (SI 1994/571)

Railways Act 1993 (c 43)—*cont*

s 6(1)	1 Apr 1994 (SI 1994/571)
(2)	6 Jan 1994 (SI 1993/3237)
(3), (4)	1 Apr 1994 (SI 1994/571)
7–16	1 Apr 1994 (SI 1994/571)
17–22	2 Apr 1994 (SI 1994/571)
23(1), (2)	1 Apr 1994 (SI 1994/571)
(3), (4)	6 Jan 1994 (SI 1993/3237)
24	1 Apr 1994 (SI 1994/571)
25(1), (2)	6 Jan 1994 (for purpose of providing definition "public sector operator") (SI 1993/3237)
	1 Apr 1994 (otherwise) (SI 1994/571)
(3)–(9)	1 Apr 1994 (SI 1994/571)
26–28	1 Apr 1994 (SI 1994/571)
29(1)–(7)	1 Apr 1994 (SI 1994/571)
(8)	6 Jan 1994 (SI 1993/3237)
30, 31	1 Apr 1994 (SI 1994/571)
32, 33	24 Dec 1993 (SI 1993/3237)
34–51	1 Apr 1994 (SI 1994/571)
52	21 Mar 1994 (SI 1994/571)
53	1 Apr 1994 (SI 1994/571)
54(1)	1 Apr 1994 (SI 1994/571)
(2)	21 Mar 1994 (SI 1994/571)
(3)	21 Mar 1994 (for purpose of definitions "franchising functions", in relation to the Franchising Director, and "railway investment") (SI 1994/571)
	1 Apr 1994 (otherwise) (SI 1994/571)
55–69	1 Apr 1994 (SI 1994/571)
70	22 Feb 1994 (SI 1994/447)
71–80	1 Apr 1994 (SI 1994/571)
81, 82	24 Dec 1993 (SI 1993/3237)
83(1)	24 Dec 1993 (for purposes of definitions "goods", "light maintenance services", "locomotive", "network", "network services", "premises", "passenger service operator", "railway", "railway services", "railway vehicle", "rolling stock", "station", "station services", "track", "train" and "vehicle" (SI 1993/3237)
	6 Jan 1994 (for purposes of definitions "additional railway asset", "the Director", "franchise agreement", "franchise operator", "franchise term", "franchised services", "franchisee", "information", "licence" and "licence holder", "light maintenance depot", "operator", "passenger licence", "private sector operator", "public sector operator", "railway asset", "railway passenger service", "records" and "station licence") (SI 1993/3237)
	22 Feb 1994 (for purposes of definitions "network licence" and "railway facility") (SI 1994/447)
	1 Apr 1994 (otherwise) (SI 1994/571)
(2)	24 Dec 1993 (SI 1993/3237)
84, 85	6 Jan 1994 (SI 1993/3237)
86	1 Apr 1994 (SI 1994/571)
87(1)	6 Jan 1994 (for purpose of enabling Secretary of State to transfer functions to himself) (SI 1993/3237)
	1 Apr 1994 (otherwise) (SI 1994/571)

Railways Act 1993 (c 43)—*cont*

s 87(2)	6 Jan 1994 (SI 1993/3237)
(3), (4)	1 Apr 1994 (SI 1994/571)
(5)	6 Jan 1994 (SI 1993/3237)
88–92	6 Jan 1994 (SI 1993/3237)
93(1), (2)	6 Jan 1994 (SI 1993/3237)
(3)(a)	6 Jan 1994 (SI 1993/3237)
(b)	1 Apr 1994 (SI 1994/571)
(4)–(13)	6 Jan 1994 (SI 1993/3237)
94–116	6 Jan 1994 (SI 1993/3237)
117	2 Feb 1994 (SI 1994/202)
118–121	8 Mar 1994 (SI 1994/571)
122–125	1 Apr 1994 (SI 1994/571)
126–128	6 Jan 1994 (SI 1993/3237)
129	1 Apr 1994 (SI 1994/571)
130, 131	6 Jan 1994 (SI 1993/3237)
132(1)–(4)	8 Mar 1994 (SI 1994/571)
(5)	Repealed
(6), (7)	8 Mar 1994 (SI 1994/571)
(8)	See Sch 10 below
(9), (10)	8 Mar 1994 (SI 1994/571)
133	8 Mar 1994 (SI 1994/571)
134(1)	See Sch 11 below
(2), (3)	6 Jan 1994 (SI 1993/3237)
135–137	1 Apr 1994 (SI 1994/571)
138	21 Mar 1994 (SI 1994/571)
139, 140	15 Jul 1994 (subject to transitional provisions) (SI 1994/1648)
141(1)	6 Jan 1994 (except para (a)) (SI 1993/3237) 1 Apr 1994 (para (a)) (SI 1994/571)
(2)–(5)	6 Jan 1994 (SI 1993/3237)
142–144	24 Dec 1993 (SI 1993/3237)
145(1)–(6)	24 Dec 1993 (except for purposes of sub-s (5)(a), (b)(i)) (SI 1993/3237) 1 Apr 1994 (exceptions noted above) (SI 1994/571)
(7)	1 Apr 1994 (SI 1994/571)
146–149	24 Dec 1993 (SI 1993/3237)
150(1)–(3)	24 Dec 1993 (SI 1993/3237)
(4)	1 Apr 1994 (SI 1994/571)
151(1)	24 Dec 1993 (for purposes of definitions "the Board", "body corporate", "company", "contravention", "the Franchising Director", "functions", "local authority", "the Monopolies Commission", "notice", "the Regulator", "subsidiary" and "wholly owned subsidiary") (SI 1993/3237) 6 Jan 1994 (otherwise) (SI 1993/3237)
(2)–(4)	6 Jan 1994 (SI 1993/3237)
(5)	24 Dec 1993 (SI 1993/3237)
(6)–(9)	6 Jan 1994 (SI 1993/3237)
152(1)	See Sch 12 below
(2)	See Sch 13 below
(3)	See Sch 14 below
153	6 Jan 1994 (SI 1993/3237)
154	24 Dec 1993 (SI 1993/3237)
Sch 1	5 Nov 1993 (s 154(2))

Railways Act 1993 (c 43)—*cont*

Sch 2, 3	1 Apr 1994 (SI 1994/571)
4	2 Apr 1994 (SI 1994/571)
5–7	1 Apr 1994 (SI 1994/571)
8, 9	6 Jan 1994 (SI 1993/3237)
10, para 1, 2	8 Mar 1994 (subject to transitional provisions) (SI 1994/571)
3(1)	8 Mar 1994 (so far as repeals Transport Act 1962, ss 69, 71) (SI 1994/571) *Not in force* (otherwise)
(2), (3)	8 Mar 1994 (SI 1994/571)
11, para 1–8	6 Jan 1994 (SI 1993/3237)
9(1), (2)	6 Jan 1994 (SI 1993/3237)
(3)	6 Jan 1994 (for purpose of inserting Transport Act 1980, s 52D(6)–(8)) (SI 1993/3237) 16 Aug 1994 (otherwise) (SI 1994/2142)
(4)	6 Jan 1994 (SI 1993/3237)
10	6 Jan 1994 (SI 1993/3237)
11	16 Aug 1994 (SI 1994/2142)
12–14	6 Jan 1994 (SI 1993/3237)
12, para 1–3	1 Apr 1994 (SI 1994/571)
4, 5	6 Jan 1994 (SI 1993/3237)
6(1)–(5)	6 Jan 1994 (SI 1993/3237)
(6)	1 Apr 1994 (SI 1994/571)
(7)	6 Jan 1994 (SI 1993/3237)
7, 8	6 Jan 1994 (SI 1993/3237)
9	1 Apr 1994 (SI 1994/571)
10–13	6 Jan 1994 (SI 1993/3237)
14(1)–(3)	6 Jan 1994 (SI 1993/3237)
(4)–(6)	1 Apr 1994 (SI 1994/571)
15–22	1 Apr 1994 (SI 1994/571)
23, 24	6 Jan 1994 (SI 1993/3237)
25	1 Apr 1994 (SI 1994/571)
26	6 Jan 1994 (SI 1993/3237)
27	1 Apr 1994 (SI 1994/571)
28	6 Jan 1994 (SI 1993/3237)
29	1 Apr 1994 (SI 1994/571)
30, 31	6 Jan 1994 (SI 1993/3237)
32	*Not in force*
13	1 Apr 1994 (SI 1994/571)
14	6 Jan 1994 (repeals of or in British Transport Commission Act 1950, s 43; Transport Act 1962, ss 4, 5, 13, 53; Transport Act 1968, ss 42, 45, 50, 137) (SI 1993/3237) 8 Mar 1994 (repeals of Transport Act 1962, ss 54(1)(b), (2), 69, 71) (SI 1994/571) 31 Mar 1994 (repeal of Transport Act 1981, Pt I, Sch 1) (SI 1994/571) 1 Apr 1994 (all repeals so far as not already in force except repeals of Transport Act 1962, s 70, Railways Act 1974, s 8, Transport Act 1981, s 36) (SI 1994/571) 15 Jul 1994 (repeals of Railways Act 1974, s 8, Transport Act 1981, s 36) (subject to transitional provisions) (SI 1994/1648) *Not in force* (repeal of Transport Act 1962, s 70)

Reinsurance (Acts of Terrorism) Act 1993 (c 18)

RA: 27 May 1993

27 May 1993 (RA)

Representation of the People Act 1993 (c 29)

RA: 20 Jul 1993

20 Jul 1993 (RA)

Road Traffic (Driving Instruction by Disabled Persons) Act 1993 (c 31)

RA: 20 Jul 1993

Commencement provision: s 7(2)

Not in force

Scottish Land Court Act 1993 (c 45)

RA: 5 Nov 1993

Commencement provision: s 2(3)

5 Jan 1994 (s 2(3))

Sexual Offences Act 1993 (c 30)

RA: 20 Jul 1993

Commencement provision: s 2(2)

20 Sep 1993 (s 2(2))

Social Security Act 1993 (c 3)

RA: 29 Jan 1993

29 Jan 1993 (RA; but note s 5(2))

Statute Law (Repeals) Act 1993 (c 50)

RA: 5 Nov 1993

Commencement provision: s 4(2), (3)

s 1(1)	See Sch 1 below
(2)	See Sch 2 below
2–4	5 Nov 1993 (RA)

Statute Law (Repeals) Act 1993 (c 50)—*cont*

Sch 1	5 Nov 1993[1] (except so far as repeals Shipbuilding (Redundancy Payments) Act 1978, Shipbuilding Act 1985, s 1) (RA)
	Not in force (exceptions noted above)
2	5 Nov 1993 (RA)

[1] By s 4(2), repeals of National Loans Act 1939, Sch 2, para 5, Bank of England Act 1946, Sch 1, para 10, Coal Industry Nationalisation Act 1946, s 33(8), have effect, so far as relating to stock registered in the National Savings Stock Register, on the coming into force of the first regulations made by virtue of National Debt Act 1972, s 3(1)(bb)

Trade Union Reform and Employment Rights Act 1993 (c 19)

RA: 1 Jul 1993

Commencement provisions: ss 7(4), 52; Trade Union Reform and Employment Rights Act 1993 (Commencement No 1 and Transitional Provisions) Order 1993, SI 1993/1908; Trade Union Reform and Employment Rights Act 1993 (Commencement No 2 and Transitional Provisions) Order 1993, SI 1993/2503; Trade Union Reform and Employment Rights Act 1993 (Commencement No 3 and Transitional Provisions) Order 1994, SI 1994/1365

s 1, 2	30 Aug 1993 (subject to transitional provisions) (SI 1993/1908)
3	See Sch 1 below
4–6	30 Aug 1993 (subject to transitional provisions) (SI 1993/1908)
7(1)	1 Apr 1996 (s 7(4))
(2)–(4)	1 Apr 1996 (SI 1993/1908)
8, 9	1 Jan 1994 (SI 1993/1908)
10–12	30 Aug 1993 (SI 1993/1908)
13	30 Aug 1993 (subject to transitional provisions) (SI 1993/1908)
14	30 Nov 1993 (SI 1993/1908)
15, 16	30 Aug 1993 (SI 1993/1908)
17	30 Aug 1993 (subject to transitional provisions) (SI 1993/1908)
18(1)	30 Aug 1993 (SI 1993/1908)
(2)	30 Aug 1993 (subject to transitional provisions) (SI 1993/1908)
19–21	30 Aug 1993 (subject to transitional provisions) (SI 1993/1908)
22	30 Aug 1993 (SI 1993/1908)
23	10 Jun 1994 (SI 1994/1365)[1]
24(1)	10 Jun 1994 (SI 1994/1365)[1,2]
(2), (3)	30 Aug 1993 (except for purpose of giving effect to s 60(a)–(f) of the 1978 Act) (subject to transitional provisions) (SI 1993/1908)
	10 Jun 1994 (otherwise) (SI 1994/1365)[1,2]
(4)	10 Jun 1994 (SI 1994/1365)[1,2]
25	10 Jun 1994 (SI 1994/1365)[1]
26	30 Nov 1993 (SI 1993/2503)
27	Repealed
28	See Sch 5 below
29, 30	30 Aug 1993 (subject to transitional provisions) (SI 1993/1908)

Trade Union Reform and Employment Rights Act 1993 (c 19)—*cont*

s 31	*Not in force*
32	30 Nov 1993 (SI 1993/2503)
33	30 Aug 1993 (SI 1993/1908)
34	30 Aug 1993 (subject to transitional provisions) (SI 1993/1908)
35	30 Aug 1993 (SI 1993/1908)
36(1), (2)	30 Nov 1993 (subject to transitional provisions) (SI 1993/2503)
(3)	30 Aug 1993 (for purpose of inserting s 128(5) of the 1978 Act) (SI 1993/1908)
	30 Nov 1993 (otherwise) (subject to transitional provisions) (SI 1993/2503)
37	30 Nov 1993 (SI 1993/2503)
38	30 Aug 1993 (SI 1993/1908)
39(1)	30 Aug 1993 (SI 1993/1908)
(2)	See Sch 6 below
40, 41	30 Aug 1993 (SI 1993/1908)
42	30 Nov 1993 (SI 1993/2503)
43, 44	30 Aug 1993 (SI 1993/1908)
45	30 Nov 1993 (so far as substitutes s 10(7) of the 1973 Act) (SI 1993/2503)
	1 Apr 1994 (otherwise) (ES) (SI 1993/2503)
	1 Apr 1995 (otherwise) (SI 1993/2503)
46	1 Apr 1994 (ES) (SI 1993/2503)
	1 Apr 1995 (otherwise) (SI 1993/2503)
47, 48	30 Aug 1993 (SI 1993/1908)
49(1)	See Sch 7 below
(2)	See Sch 8 below
50	See Sch 9 below
51	See Sch 10 below
52–55	1 Jul 1993 (RA)
Sch 1	30 Aug 1993 (subject to transitional provisions) (SI 1993/1908)
2, 3	10 Jun 1994 (SI 1994/1365)[1]
4	30 Nov 1993 (SI 1993/2503)
5	30 Aug 1993 (subject to transitional provisions) (SI 1993/1908)
6	30 Aug 1993 (SI 1993/1908)
7, para 1, 2	30 Aug 1993 (SI 1993/1908)
3(a)	30 Nov 1993 (SI 1993/2503)
(b)	30 Nov 1993 (except so far as relates to s 60 of the 1978 Act) (SI 1993/2503)
	10 Jun 1994 (exception noted above) (SI 1994/1365)[1]
4	30 Nov 1993 (SI 1993/2503)
5	30 Nov 1993 (except so far as relates to s 60 of the 1978 Act) (SI 1993/2503)
	10 Jun 1994 (exception noted above) (SI 1994/1365)[1]
6(a)	30 Nov 1993 (SI 1993/2503)
(b)	30 Nov 1993 (except so far as relates to s 60 of the 1978 Act) (SI 1993/2503)
	10 Jun 1994 (exception noted above) (SI 1994/1365)[1]
7	15 Oct 1993 (SI 1993/2503)
8–12	30 Nov 1993 (SI 1993/2503)
13–27	30 Aug 1993 (SI 1993/1908)
8, para 1	1 Apr 1994 (ES) (SI 1993/2503)
	1 Apr 1995 (otherwise) (SI 1993/2503)

Trade Union Reform and Employment Rights Act 1993 (c 19)—*cont*

Sch 8, para 2	30 Aug 1993 (SI 1993/1908)
3–5	1 Apr 1994 (ES) (SI 1993/2503)
	1 Apr 1995 (otherwise) (SI 1993/2503)
6, 7	30 Aug 1993 (SI 1993/1908)
8, 9	1 Apr 1994 (ES) (SI 1993/2503)
	1 Apr 1995 (otherwise) (SI 1993/2503)
10	30 Nov 1993 (SI 1993/2503)
11	30 Aug 1993 (SI 1993/1908)
12, 13	10 Jun 1994 (SI 1994/1365)[1]
14	30 Aug 1993 (SI 1993/1908)
15	10 Jun 1994 (SI 1994/1365)[1]
16	30 Aug 1993 (so far as relates to s 60A(1) of the 1978 Act) (SI 1993/1908)
	10 Jun 1994 (otherwise) (SI 1994/1365)[1]
17–19	10 Jun 1994 (SI 1994/1365)[1]
20(a)	30 Aug 1993 (SI 1993/1908)
(b)	10 Jun 1994 (SI 1994/1365)[1]
21	30 Aug 1993 (SI 1993/1908)
22, 23	30 Nov 1993 (SI 1993/2503)
24	30 Aug 1993 (SI 1993/1908)
25(a)	10 Jun 1994 (SI 1994/1365)[1]
(b)	30 Nov 1993 (SI 1993/2503)
26(a)(i)	30 Aug 1993 (SI 1993/1908)
(ii), (iii)	10 Jun 1994 (SI 1994/1365)[1]
(b)–(e)	10 Jun 1994 (SI 1994/1365)[1]
27	10 Jun 1994 (SI 1994/1365)[1]
28(a)	10 Jun 1994 (SI 1994/1365)[1]
(b), (c)	15 Oct 1993 (SI 1993/2503)
29	30 Aug 1993 (SI 1993/1908)
30	15 Oct 1993 (SI 1993/2503)
31	10 Jun 1994 (SI 1994/1365)[1]
32(a)	10 Jun 1994 (SI 1994/1365)[1]
(b)	30 Aug 1993 (SI 1993/1908)
33, 34	1 Apr 1994 (ES) (SI 1993/2503)
	1 Apr 1995 (otherwise) (SI 1993/2503)
35	10 Jun 1994 (SI 1994/1365)[1]
36–41	30 Aug 1993 (SI 1993/1908)
42	1 Jan 1994 (SI 1993/1908)
43(a)	1 Jan 1994 (SI 1993/1908)
(b)	30 Aug 1993 (SI 1993/1908)
44, 45	1 Jan 1994 (SI 1993/1908)
46, 47	30 Aug 1993 (SI 1993/1908)
48	30 Nov 1993 (SI 1993/1908)
49	30 Aug 1993 (SI 1993/1908)
50, 51	30 Nov 1993 (SI 1993/1908)
52–61	30 Aug 1993 (SI 1993/1908)
62(a)	1 Jan 1994 (SI 1993/1908)
(b)	30 Aug 1993 (SI 1993/1908)
63	30 Aug 1993 (SI 1993/1908)
64(a)	1 Jan 1994 (SI 1993/1908)
(b), (c)	30 Aug 1993 (SI 1993/1908)
65	30 Aug 1993 (SI 1993/1908)
66(a)	1 Jan 1994 (SI 1993/1908)
(b)	30 Aug 1993 (SI 1993/1908)
67–75	30 Aug 1993 (SI 1993/1908)

Trade Union Reform and Employment Rights Act 1993 (c 19)—*cont*

Sch 8, para 76, 77	30 Aug 1993 (so far as relate to s 57A of the 1978 Act) (SI 1993/1908) 10 Jun 1994 (otherwise) (SI 1994/1365)1
78–84	30 Aug 1993 (SI 1993/1908)
85	30 Nov 1993 (SI 1993/2503)
86–89	30 Aug 1993 (SI 1993/1908)
9, para 1	30 Aug 1993 (SI 1993/1908)
2	30 Aug 1993 (subject to transitional provisions) (SI 1993/1908)
3	30 Nov 1993 (SI 1993/2503)
4, 5	30 Aug 1993 (SI 1993/1908)
10	30 Aug 1993 (repeals of or in Factories Act 1961; Contracts of Employment and Redundancy Payments Act (Northern Ireland) 1965; Transport Act 1968; House of Commons Disqualification Act 1975; Northern Ireland Assembly Disqualification Act 1975; Industrial Relations (Northern Ireland) Order 1976; Employment Protection (Consolidation) Act 1978, ss 18, 53, 55, 64A, 93–95, 100, 123, 149, Schs 12, 13; Employment Act 1980, s 8, Sch 1; Transfer of Undertakings (Protection of Employment) Regulations 1981; Wages Act 1986; Income and Corporation Taxes Act 1988; Enterprise and New Towns (Scotland) Act 1990; Offshore Safety (Protection Against Victimisation) Act 1992; Trade Union and Labour Relations (Consolidation) Act 1992, ss 24, 34, 43, 52, 65, 74, 78, 118, 135, 154, 188, 190, 209, 246, 249, 256, 273, 283, 299, Sch 2, paras 15, 34) (SI 1993/1908) 15 Oct 1993 (repeal in Employment Protection (Consolidation) Act 1978, Sch/9, para 1A) (SI 1993/2503) 30 Nov 1993 (repeals in Trade Union and Labour Relations (Consolidation) Act 1992, ss 67, 288, 290, 291) (SI 1993/1908) 30 Nov 1993 (repeals of or in Employment Protection (Consolidation) Act 1978, ss 11(3), (7), 128(4), 133(1), 138(1), (2) (so far as words repealed relate to sub-ss (4), (5)), 139(1), 146(4), Sch 9, para 8; Employment Act 1982; Dock Work Act 1989; Employment Act 1989; Trade Union and Labour Relations (Consolidation) Act 1992, s 277(2), Sch 2, para 24(3)) (SI 1993/2503) 1 Jan 1994 (repeal in Trade Union and Labour Relations (Consolidation) Act 1992, s 32) (SI 1993/1908) 1 Apr 1994 (ES) and 1 Apr 1995 (otherwise) (repeals in Finance Act 1969; Chronically Sick and Disabled Persons Act 1970; Employment and Training Act 1973; Education (Scotland) Act 1980; Agricultural Training Board Act 1982; Industrial Training Act 1982) (SI 1993/2503) 10 Jun 1994 (so far as not already in force, except repeal of words "subject to subsections (3)–(5)" in Employment Protection (Consolidation) Act

Trade Union Reform and Employment Rights Act 1993 (c 19)—*cont*

Sch 10—*cont*	1978, s 138, so far as they relate to sub-s (3)) (SI 1994/1365)[1]
	1 Apr 1996 (repeals of Trade Union and Labour Relations (Consolidation) Act 1992, ss 115, 116) (SI 1993/1908)
	Not in force (otherwise)

[1] By SI 1994/1365, art 3(1), the amendments and repeals made by provisions of this Act brought into force by that Order have effect only in relation to women whose expected week of childbirth begins on or after 16 Oct 1994

[2] By SI 1994/1365, art 3(2), the amendments made by s 24 of this Act (so far as brought into force by that Order) apply to any dismissal where the effective date of termination in relation to that dismissal falls on or after 10 Jun 1994

Video Recordings Act 1993 (c 24)

RA: 20 Jul 1993

Commencement provision: s 6(2)

20 Sep 1993 (s 6(2))

Welsh Language Act 1993 (c 38)

RA: 21 Oct 1993

Commencement provisions: s 36; Welsh Language Act 1993 (Commencement) Order 1994, SI 1994/115

s 1–29	21 Dec 1993 (s 36(1))
30(1)	See sub-ss (2)–(6) below
(2)–(5)	1 Feb 1994 (SI 1994/115)
(6)	25 Jan 1994 (so far as enables prescription of descriptions of documents for purpose of s 710B(3)(a) of the 1985 Act and so far as enables prescription of manner in which a translation is to be certified for purpose of s 710B(8) of the 1985 Act) (SI 1994/115)
	1 Feb 1994 (otherwise) (SI 1994/115)
31	1 Feb 1994 (SI 1994/115)
32–34	21 Dec 1993 (s 36(1))
35(1)	See Sch 2 below
(2)	1 Feb 1994 (SI 1994/115)
(3)–(5)	21 Dec 1993 (s 36(1))
36, 37	21 Dec 1993 (s 36(1))
Sch 1	21 Dec 1993 (s 36(1))
2	21 Dec 1993 (except repeals in Companies Act 1985) (s 36(1), (2))
	1 Feb 1994 (exception noted above) (SI 1994/115)

1994

Antarctic Act 1994 (c 15)

RA: 5 Jul 1994

Commencement provision: s 35; Antarctic Act 1994 (Commencement) Order 1995, SI 1995/2748

s 1, 2	1 Nov 1995 (SI 1995/2748)
3–7	*Not in force*
8–32	1 Nov 1995 (SI 1995/2748)
33	See Schedule below
34–36	1 Nov 1995 (SI 1995/2748)
Schedule	1 Nov 1995 (except repeals of Antarctic Treaty Act 1967, ss 6, 7(2)(b), (7), 8, 9, 10, 11) (SI 1995/2748) *Not in force* (exceptions noted above)

Appropriation Act 1994 (c 24)

RA: 21 Jul 1994

21 Jul 1994 (RA)

Care of Cathedrals (Supplementary Provisions) Measure 1994 (No 2)

RA: 21 Jul 1994

Commencement provision: s 11(2)

The provisions of this Measure are brought into force on 1 Oct 1994 by an appointed day notice signed by the Archbishops of Canterbury and York and dated 25 Jul 1994 (made under s 11(2))

Chiropractors Act 1994 (c 17)

RA: 5 Jul 1994

Commencement provisions: s 44(2)(6)

s 1–41	*Not in force*
42	See Sch 2 below
43	*Not in force*
44	5 Jul 1994 (for purpose of bringing into force s 42, Sch 2) *Not in force* (otherwise)
Sch 1	*Not in force*
2	5 Jul 1994 (s 44(2))

Church of England (Legal Aid) Measure 1994 (No 3)

RA: 21 Jul 1994

Commencement provision: s 8(2)

The provisions of this Measure are brought into force on 1 Sep 1994 by an appointed day notice signed by the Archbishops of Canterbury and York and dated 25 Jul 1994 (made under s 8(2))

Coal Industry Act 1994 (c 21)

RA: 5 Jul 1994

Commencement provisions: s 68(2)–(6); Coal Industry Act 1994 (Commencement No 1) Order 1994, SI 1994/2189; Coal Industry Act 1994 (Commencement No 2 and Transitional Provision) Order 1994, SI 1994/2552; Coal Industry (Restructuring Date) Order 1994, SI 1994/2553; Coal Industry Act 1994 (Commencement No 3) Order 1994, SI 1994/3063; Coal Industry Act 1994 (Commencement No 4) Order 1995, SI 1995/159; Coal Industry Act 1994 (Commencement No 5) Order 1995, SI 1995/273; Coal Industry Act 1994 (Commencement No 6) and Membership of the British Coal Corporation (Appointed Day) Order 1995, SI 1995/1507

s 1	19 Sep 1994 (SI 1994/2189)
2, 3	31 Oct 1994 (SI 1994/2552)
4–6	19 Sep 1994 (SI 1994/2189)
7–9	5 Jul 1994 (s 68(4), (6))
10, 11	31 Oct 1994 (SI 1994/2553)
12–14	5 Jul 1994 (s 68(4), (6))
15, 16	31 Oct 1994 (SI 1994/2552)
17	5 Jul 1994 (s 68(4), (6))
18	31 Oct 1994 (SI 1994/2553)
19, 20	31 Oct 1994 (SI 1994/2552)
21	19 Sep 1994 (SI 1994/2189)
22(1)	31 Oct 1994 (SI 1994/2552)
(2)	*Not in force*
(3)	31 Oct 1994 (SI 1994/2552)
23	31 Oct 1994 (SI 1994/2553)
24	31 Jan 1995 (SI 1995/159)
25–30	31 Oct 1994 (SI 1994/2552)
31–34	31 Oct 1994 (SI 1994/2553)
35	31 Oct 1994 (SI 1994/2552)
36	31 Oct 1994 (SI 1994/2553)
37	31 Oct 1994 (SI 1994/2552)
38–44	31 Oct 1994 (SI 1994/2553)
45–47	31 Oct 1994 (SI 1994/2552)
48–53	31 Oct 1994 (SI 1994/2553)
54	5 Jul 1994 (s 68(4), (6))
55	31 Oct 1994 (SI 1994/2553)
56–61	31 Oct 1994 (SI 1994/2552)
62–66	5 Jul 1994 (s 68(4), (6))
67(1)	See Sch 9 below
(2)–(6)	5 Jul 1994 (s 68(4), (6))
(7)	See Sch 10 below
(8)	See Sch 11 below
68	5 Jul 1994 (s 68(4), (6))

Coal Industry Act 1994 (c 21)—*cont*

Sch 1	19 Sep 1994 (SI 1994/2189)
2	5 Jul 1994 (s 68(4), (6))
3	31 Oct 1994 (SI 1994/2552)
4	19 Sep 1994 (SI 1994/2189)
5	31 Oct 1994 (SI 1994/2552)
6–8	31 Oct 1994 (SI 1994/2553)
9, para 1–6	31 Oct 1994 (SI 1994/2553)
7	*Not in force*
8	31 Oct 1994 (SI 1994/2552)
9, 10	31 Oct 1994 (SI 1994/2553)
11(1)(a)	31 Oct 1994 (SI 1994/2553)
(b)	31 Oct 1994 (SI 1994/2552)
(2)(a)	31 Oct 1994 (SI 1994/2553)
(b)	31 Oct 1994 (SI 1994/2552)
(3)–(5)	31 Oct 1994 (SI 1994/2553)
12	31 Oct 1994 (SI 1994/2552)
13(1), (2)	31 Oct 1994 (SI 1994/2553)
(3)	1 Nov 1994 (SI 1994/2552)
14–23	31 Oct 1994 (SI 1994/2553)
24	*Not in force*
25–28	31 Oct 1994 (SI 1994/2553)
29, 30	*Not in force*
31–38	31 Oct 1994 (SI 1994/2553)
39(1)	31 Oct 1994 (SI 1994/2553)
(2), (3)	1 Nov 1994 (SI 1994/2552)
(4)	31 Oct 1994 (SI 1994/2553)
40–44	31 Oct 1994 (SI 1994/2553)
45	*Not in force*
10	31 Oct 1994 (SI 1994/2552)
11, Pt I	5 Jul 1994 (s 68(4), (6))
II	31 Oct 1994 (SI 1994/2553)
III	31 Oct 1994 (repeals of or in Coal Act 1938; Coal Act 1943; Coal Industry Nationalisation Act 1946, ss 52, 57, 58, 63(2); Opencast Coal Act 1958; Land Commission Act 1967; Electricity Act 1989) (SI 1994/2552)
	1 Nov 1994 (repeals in Town and Country Planning (Scotland) Act 1972; Town and Country Planning Act 1990) (SI 1994/2552)
	24 Dec 1994 (repeals of or in Coal Industry Nationalisation Act 1946, s 45 (for purposes specified in sub-s (1) thereof); Housing and Planning Act 1986, Sch 8, para 8; Coal Industry Act 1987, Sch 1, paras 9, 17, 20) (SI 1994/3063)
	1 Mar 1995 (repeals of or in Coal Industry Nationalisation Act 1946, s 4 (subject to a saving in relation to sub-s (6)); Coal Consumers' Councils (Northern Irish Interests) Act 1962 (subject to a saving in relation to s 2); Chronically Sick and Disabled Persons Act 1970, s 14(1)) (SI 1995/273)
	30 Jun 1995 (repeals of or in Coal Industry Nationalisation Act 1946, s 2(2), (3), (5); Coal Industry Act 1949, s 1(2), (4)) (SI 1995/1507)
	Not in force (otherwise)
IV	*Not in force*

Consolidated Fund Act 1994 (c 4)

RA: 24 Mar 1994

24 Mar 1994 (RA)

Consolidated Fund (No 2) Act 1994 (c 41)

RA: 16 Dec 1994

16 Dec 1994 (RA)

Criminal Justice and Public Order Act 1994 (c 33)

RA: 3 Nov 1994

Commencement provisions: ss 82(3), 172(2)–(4), (6); Criminal Justice and Public Order Act 1994 (Commencement No 1) Order 1994, SI 1994/2935; Criminal Justice and Public Order Act 1994 (Commencement No 2) Order 1994, SI 1994/3192; Criminal Justice and Public Order Act 1994 (Commencement No 3) Order 1994, SI 1994/3258; Criminal Justice and Public Order Act 1994 (Commencement No 4) Order 1995, SI 1995/24; Criminal Justice and Public Order Act 1994 (Commencement No 5 and Transitional Provisions) Order 1995, SI 1995/127; Criminal Justice and Public Order Act 1994 (Commencement No 6) Order 1995, SI 1995/721; Criminal Justice and Public Order Act 1994 (Commencement No 7) Order 1995, SI 1995/1378; Criminal Justice and Public Order Act 1994 (Commencement No 8 and Transitional Provision) Order 1995, SI 1995/1957

s 1–4	*Not in force*
5–15	3 Nov 1994 (s 172(4))
16	9 Jan 1995 (SI 1994/3192)
17, 18	3 Feb 1995 (subject to a saving relating to s 17) (SI 1995/127)
19	30 May 1995 (SI 1995/1378)
20–22	*Not in force*
23, 24	3 Feb 1995 (subject to a saving relating to s 23) (SI 1995/127)
25–30	10 Apr 1995 (SI 1995/721)
31–33	3 Feb 1995 (subject to a saving relating to s 31) (SI 1995/127)
34–39	10 Apr 1995 (SI 1995/721)
40–43	3 Feb 1995 (SI 1995/127)
44	*Not in force*
45	See Sch 5 below
46–51	3 Feb 1995 (subject to a saving relating to s 50) (SI 1995/127)
52	11 Jan 1995 (SI 1994/3258)
53	2 Feb 1995 (SI 1995/24)
54–60	10 Apr 1995 (SI 1995/721)
61	3 Nov 1994 (s 172(4))
62	10 Apr 1995 (SI 1995/721)
63	3 Nov 1994 (s 172(4))
64(1)–(3)	3 Feb 1995 (so far as relating to powers conferred on a constable by s 63) (SI 1995/127)
	Not in force (otherwise)
(4)–(6)	10 Apr 1995 (SI 1995/721)

Criminal Justice and Public Order Act 1994 (c 33)—*cont*

s 65	3 Nov 1994 (s 172(4))
66(1)–(5)	10 Apr 1995 (SI 1995/721)
(6)	3 Feb 1995 (SI 1995/127)
(7)–(9)	10 Apr 1995 (SI 1995/721)
(10)–(13)	3 Feb 1995 (SI 1995/127)
67(1), (2)	10 Apr 1995 (SI 1995/721)
(3)–(5)	3 Feb 1995 (SI 1995/127)
(6), (7)	10 Apr 1995 (SI 1995/721)
(8), (9)	3 Feb 1995 (SI 1995/127)
68–71	3 Nov 1994 (s 172(4))
72–74	3 Feb 1995 (SI 1995/127)
75, 76	24 Aug 1995 (SI 1995/1957)
77–81	3 Nov 1994 (s 172(4))
82	3 Jan 1995 (s 82(3))
83	3 Nov 1994 (s 172(4))
84–88	3 Feb 1995 (subject to a saving relating to s 88) (SI 1995/127)
89	1 Nov 1995 (subject to a transitional provision) (SI 1995/1957)
90	3 Nov 1994 (s 172(4))
91, 92	3 Feb 1995 (SI 1995/127)
93–101	3 Nov 1994 (s 172(4))
102–117	3 Feb 1995 (SI 1995/127)
118–125	10 Apr 1995 (SI 1995/721)
126–128	3 Nov 1994 (s 172(4))
129–131	3 Feb 1995 (subject to savings relating to s 129) (SI 1995/127)
132	Repealed
133–141	3 Feb 1995 (though note that s 134(3) only comes into force on that date for purpose of making rules under Prisons (Scotland) Act 1989, s 18(3A(s 134(3) otherwise comes into force on 1 Jun 1995) (subject to savings relating to s 134(3)) (SI 1995/127)
142–148	3 Nov 1994 (s 172(4))
149	*Not in force*
150	3 Nov 1994 (s 172(4))
151	9 Jan 1995 (SI 1994/3192)
152–155	3 Feb 1995 (SI 1995/127)
156	10 Apr 1995 (SI 1995/721)
157	3 Feb 1995 (subject to a saving) (SI 1995/127)
158(1)	3 Nov 1994 (s 172(4))
(2)	*Not in force*
(3), (4)	3 Nov 1994 (s 172(4))
(5)–(8)	*Not in force*
159(1), (2)	19 Dec 1994 (SI 1994/2935)
(3)	*Not in force*
(4)	19 Dec 1994 (SI 1994/2935)
(5)	*Not in force*
160–164	3 Feb 1995 (SI 1995/127)
165	*Not in force*
166, 167	3 Nov 1994 (s 172(4))
168(1)	See Sch 9 below
(2)	See Sch 10 below
(3)	See Sch 11 below
169, 170	3 Feb 1995 (SI 1995/127)
171, 172	3 Nov 1994 (s 172(4))

Criminal Justice and Public Order Act 1994 (c 33)—*cont*

Sch 1, 2	3 Nov 1994 (s 172(4))
3	10 Apr 1995 (SI 1995/721)
4	*Not in force*
5	4 Sep 1995 (SI 1995/1957)
6	3 Feb 1995 (SI 1995/127)
7	10 Apr 1995 (SI 1995/721)
8	3 Feb 1995 (subject to a saving) (SI 1995/127)
9, para 1–27	3 Feb 1995 (subject to a saving relating to para 15) (SI 1995/127)
28	Repealed
29–33	3 Feb 1995 (subject to a saving relating to para 33) (SI 1995/127)
34	9 Jan 1995 (SI 1994/3192)
35–37	3 Feb 1995 (save for para 37(3)) (SI 1995/127) 10 Apr 1995 (para 37(3)) (SI 1995/721)
38	*Not in force*
39	3 Feb 1995 (subject to a saving relating to para 40) (SI 1995/127); prospectively repealed by Police (Amendment) (Northern Ireland) Order 1995, SI 1995/2993 (NI 17), art 32(2), Sch 2
40	3 Feb 1995 (subject to a saving relating to para 40) (SI 1995/127)
41	9 Jan 1995 (SI 1994/3192)
42–45	3 Feb 1995 (SI 1995/127)
46	3 Nov 1994 (s 172(4))
47–53	3 Feb 1995 (subject to a saving relating to para 50) (SI 1995/127)
10, para 1–3	10 Apr 1995 (SI 1995/721)
4	*Not in force*
5, 6	10 Apr 1995 (SI 1995/721)
7, 8	3 Feb 1995 (SI 1995/127)
9	*Not in force*
10	10 Apr 1995 (SI 1995/721)
11	3 Feb 1995 (SI 1995/127)
12	*Not in force*
13, 14	3 Feb 1995 (SI 1995/127)
15	10 Apr 1995 (SI 1995/721)
16	*Not in force*
17, 18	3 Feb 1995 (SI 1995/127)
19–23	10 Apr 1995 (SI 1995/721)
24	*Not in force*
25	3 Feb 1995 (SI 1995/127)
26	3 Nov 1994 (s 172(4), (6))
27–29	3 Feb 1995 (SI 1995/127)
30	*Not in force*
31	3 Feb 1995 (SI 1995/127)
32–34	10 Apr 1995 (SI 1995/721)
35, 36	3 Nov 1994 (s 172(4), (6))
37, 38	3 Feb 1995 (SI 1995/127)
39	*Not in force*
40	9 Jan 1995 (SI 1994/3192)
41–44	10 Apr 1995 (SI 1995/721)
45	3 Feb 1995 (SI 1995/127)
46	*Not in force*
47	3 Feb 1995 (SI 1995/127); prospectively repealed by Criminal Justice (Scotland) Act 1995, s 117(2), Sch 7, Pt I[1]

Criminal Justice and Public Order Act 1994 (c 33)—*cont*

Sch 10, para 48	10 Apr 1995 (SI 1995/721)
49, 50	*Not in force*
51	10 Apr 1995 (SI 1995/721)
52	3 Feb 1995 (SI 1995/127)
53	24 Aug 1995 (SI 1995/1957)
54–58	10 Apr 1995 (SI 1995/721)
59, 60	3 Nov 1994 (s 172(4), (6))
61, 62	10 Apr 1995 (SI 1995/721)
63(1)	3 Nov 1994 (s 172(4), (6))
(2)	3 Feb 1995 (SI 1995/127)
(3)–(5)	3 Nov 1994 (s 172(4), (6))
64	9 Jan 1995 (so far as substitutes for reference to s 41 references to ss 41 and 41B in Prisons (Scotland) Act 1989, s 19(4)) (SI 1994/3192) 3 Feb 1995 (so far as not already in force) (SI 1995/127)
65	4 Sep 1995 (SI 1995/1957)
66	*Not in force*
67	10 Apr 1995 (SI 1995/721)
68	3 Feb 1995 (SI 1995/127)
69	9 Jan 1995 (SI 1994/3192)
70	*Not in force*
71	10 Apr 1995 (SI 1995/721)
72, 73	*Not in force*
11	3 Nov 1994 (repeals in Sexual Offences Act 1967; Caravan Sites Act 1968; Sexual Offences (Amendment) Act 1976; Public Order Act 1986; Criminal Justice (Scotland) Act 1980; Homosexual Offences (Northern Ireland) Order 1982, SI 1982/1536) (s 172(4))[2] 9 Jan 1995 (repeals of or in Magistrates' Courts Act 1980, s 24; Criminal Justice Act 1988, s 126; Criminal Justice Act 1991, s 64; Criminal Justice Act 1993, s 67(2)) (SI 1994/3192) 3 Feb 1995 (repeals of or in Indictable Offences Act 1848; Sexual Offences Act 1956; Children and Young Persons Act 1963; Police (Scotland) Act 1967; Children and Young Persons Act 1969; Police Act 1969; Police Act (Northern Ireland) 1970; Juries Act 1974; Rehabilitation of Offenders Act 1974; Criminal Law Act 1977, s 38; Protection of Children Act 1978; Magistrates' Courts Act 1980, ss 22(1), 38(2)(b); Criminal Justice Act 1982, s 12(6), (7), (11); Video Recordings Act 1984; Prisons (Scotland) Act 1989; Broadcasting Act 1990; Northern Ireland (Emergency Provisions) Act 1991; Criminal Justice Act 1991 (so far as not already in force); Parole Board (Transfer of Functions) Order 1992, SI 1992/1829; Video Recordings Act 1993; Criminal Justice Act 1993 (so far as not already in force)) (SI 1995/127) 10 Apr 1995 (repeals in Criminal Evidence Act 1898; Criminal Evidence Act (Northern Ireland) 1923; Bail Act 1976; Police and Criminal Evidence Act 1984; Criminal Evidence (Northern Ireland) Order 1988, SI 1988/1987) (SI 1995/721) 4 Sep 1995 (repeals in Prosecution of Offences Act

Criminal Justice and Public Order Act 1994 (c 33)—*cont*

Sch 11—*cont*	1985, Criminal Justice Act 1988, ss 25, 34, 160) (SI 1995/1957)
	Not in force (otherwise)

[1] Any orders made under Criminal Justice (Scotland) Act 1995, s 118, bringing the prospective repeal into force will be noted to that Act in the service to this work

[2] In relation to repeal of Criminal Justice Act 1991, s 50(4), note that s 150 of this Act (which also effects that repeal) is brought into force on 3 Nov 1994 as noted above

Deregulation and Contracting Out Act 1994 (c 40)

RA: 3 Nov 1994

Commencement provisions: s 82(2)–(7); Deregulation and Contracting Out Act 1994 (Commencement No 1) Order 1994, SI 1994/3037; Deregulation and Contracting Out Act 1994 (Commencement No 2) Order 1994, SI 1994/3188; Industrial Relations (Deregulation and Contracting Out Act 1994) (Commencement) Order (Northern Ireland) 1994, SR 1994/488; Deregulation and Contracting Out Act 1994 (Commencement No 3) Order 1995, SI 1995/1433; Deregulation and Contracting Out Act 1994 (Commencement No 4 and Transitional Provisions) Order 1995, SI 1995/2835

s 1–6	3 Nov 1994 (s 82(3))
7	3 Jan 1995 (s 82(2))
8	3 Jan 1995 (SI 1994/3188)
9, 10	3 Jan 1995 (s 82(2))
11	3 Jan 1995 (SI 1994/3188)
12	3 Jan 1995 (s 82(2))
13(1)	See Sch 5 below
(2)	See Sch 6 below
14	3 Nov 1994 (s 82(3))
15–17	3 Jan 1995 (s 82(2))
18	3 Nov 1994 (s 82(3))
19	3 Jan 1995 (SI 1994/3188)
20, 21	3 Jan 1995 (s 82(2))
22–24	1 Dec 1994 (SI 1994/3037)
25–30	3 Nov 1994 (s 82(3))
31	3 Jan 1995 (s 82(2))
32–34	3 Nov 1994 (s 82(3))
35	See Sch 10 below
36(1)	3 Jan 1995 (subject to transitional provisions) (SI 1994/3188)
(2)	3 Jan 1995 (subject to transitional provisions) (SR 1994/488)
37	3 Nov 1994 (s 82(3))
38	1 Jan 1996 (SI 1995/2835)
39	See Sch 11 below
40	3 Nov 1994 (s 82(3))
41–57	Repealed
58	3 Jan 1995 (SI 1994/3188)
59	1 Jan 1996 (subject to transitional provisions) (SI 1995/2835)
60	1 Apr 1995 (subject to transitional provisions) (SI 1994/3188)
61	1 Jan 1996 (subject to transitional provisions) (SI 1995/2835)

Deregulation and Contracting Out Act 1994 (c 40)—*cont*

s 62	3 Jan 1995 (SI 1994/3188)
63	1 Jan 1996 (subject to transitional provisions) (SI 1995/2835)
64	3 Jan 1995 (SI 1994/3188)
65, 66	1 Jan 1996 (subject to transitional provisions) (SI 1995/2835)
67	3 Jan 1995 (SI 1994/3188)
68	See Sch 14 below
69–79	3 Jan 1995 (s 82(2))
80	1 Jan 1996 (subject to transitional provisions) (SI 1995/2835)
81	See Sch 17 below
82	3 Nov 1994 (s 82(3))
Sch 1	3 Nov 1994 (s 82(3))
2–4	3 Jan 1995 (s 82(2))
5	1 Jul 1995 (SI 1995/1433)
6, para 1, 2	1 Jul 1995 (so far as enables regulations to be made under Companies (Northern Ireland) Order 1986, SI 1986/1032, arts 603B(6)(f), 603C(2)(f)) (SI 1995/1433)
	1 Nov 1995 (otherwise) (SI 1995/1433)
3, 4	1 Nov 1995 (SI 1995/1433)
7	3 Jan 1995 (SI 1994/3188)
8, 9	3 Jan 1995 (s 82(2))
10	3 Jan 1995 (SI 1994/3188)
11	3 Nov 1994 (amendments relating to Road Traffic Regulation Act 1984; Charities Act 1993) (s 82(3))
	3 Jan 1995 (amendments relating to Fair Trading Act 1973, ss 93A, 133; Energy Act 1976; Competition Act 1980; Building Societies Act 1986; Financial Services Act 1986; Companies Act 1989; Companies (Northern Ireland) Order 1990) (s 82(2))
	3 Jan 1995 (amendments relating to Licensing Act 1964; Fair Trading Act 1973, s 77) (SI 1994/3188)
	1 Jul 1995 (amendment relating to Company Directors Disqualification Act 1986, s 2(1)) (SI 1995/1433)
	1 Nov 1995 (amendment relating to Companies (Northern Ireland) Order 1989, SI 1989/2404, art 5(1)) (SI 1995/1433)
	Not in force (otherwise)
12, 13	Repealed
14, para 1	See paras 2–8 below
2	1 Jan 1996 (subject to transitional provisions) (SI 1995/2835)
3	3 Jan 1995 (SI 1994/3188)
4	1 Jan 1996 (subject to transitional provisions) (SI 1995/2835)
5(1)	1 Jan 1996 (subject to transitional provisions) (SI 1995/2835)
(2)(a)	1 Jan 1996 (subject to transitional provisions) (SI 1995/2835)
(b)	3 Jan 1995 (SI 1994/3188)
6–8	1 Jan 1996 (subject to transitional provisions) (SI 1995/2835)

Deregulation and Contracting Out Act 1994 (c 40)—*cont*

Sch 15, 16	3 Jan 1995 (s 82(2))
17	3 Nov 1994 (repeals in Road Traffic Regulation Act 1984; Weights and Measures Act 1985; Charities Act 1992; Charities Act 1993) (s 82(3))
	1 Dec 1994 (repeals of or in Shops Act 1950; Shops (Airports) Act 1962; Shops (Early Closing Days) Act 1965; Local Government Act 1972; Local Government (Scotland) Act 1973; Cinemas Act 1985; Employment Act 1989; Sunday Trading Act 1994) (SI 1994/3037)
	3 Jan 1995 (repeals in Fair Trading Act 1973; Competition Act 1980; Telecommunications Act 1984; Gas Act 1986; Building Societies Act 1986; Financial Services Act 1986; Electricity Act 1989; Companies Act 1989; Companies (Northern Ireland) Order 1990; Electricity (Northern Ireland) Order 1992; Railways Act 1993) (s 82(2))
	3 Jan 1995 (repeals of or in Merchant Shipping Act 1894; Licensing Act 1964; Employment Agencies Act 1973; House of Commons Disqualification Act 1975; Employment Protection Act 1975; Employment Protection (Consolidation) Act 1978; Merchant Shipping Act 1979; Public Passenger Vehicles Act 1981, ss 14A(3), 17(2)(b), 27; Employment (Miscellaneous Provisions) (Northern Ireland) Order 1981, SI 1981/839; Income and Corporation Taxes Act 1988) (SI 1994/3188)
	1 Jan 1996 (so far as not already in force) (SI 1995/2835)

Drug Trafficking Act 1994 (c 37)

RA: 3 Nov 1994

Commencement provisions: s 69(2)

3 Feb 1995 (s 69(2))

Education Act 1994 (c 30)

RA: 21 Jul 1994

Commencement provisions: s 26; Education Act 1994 (Commencement) Order 1994, SI 1994/2204

s 1–21	21 Sep 1994 (SI 1994/2204)
22(1), (2)	21 Sep 1994 (SI 1994/2204)
(3)–(5)	1 Apr 1995 (SI 1994/2204)
(6)–(9)	21 Sep 1994 (SI 1994/2204)
23–27	21 Sep 1994 (SI 1994/2204)
Sch 1, 2	21 Sep 1994 (SI 1994/2204)

European Union (Accessions) Act 1994 (c 38)

RA: 3 Nov 1994

3 Nov 1994 (RA)

Finance Act 1994 (c 9)

RA: 3 May 1994

See the note concerning Finance Acts at the front of this book

---

Firearms (Amendment) Act 1994 (c 31)

RA: 21 Jul 1994

Commencement provision: s 4(2)

21 Sep 1994 (s 4(2))

Inshore Fishing (Scotland) Act 1994 (c 27)

RA: 21 Jul 1994

Commencement provisions: s 5(1); Inshore Fishing (Scotland) Act 1994 (Commencement) Order 1994, SI 1994/2124

8 Aug 1994 (SI 1994/2124)

Insolvency Act 1994 (c 7)

RA: 24 Mar 1994

24 Mar 1994 (RA; but note ss 1(7), 2(4), 3(5), Sch 1, para 3)

Insolvency (No 2) Act 1994 (c 12)

RA: 26 May 1994

Commencement provision: s 6(2)

26 Jul 1994 (s 6(2))

Intelligence Services Act 1994 (c 13)

RA: 26 May 1994

Commencement provisions: s 12(2); Intelligence Services Act 1994 (Commencement) Order 1994, SI 1994/2734

15 Dec 1994 (SI 1994/2734; though note that for purposes of making any Order in Council under s 12(4) it is brought into force on 2 Nov 1994)

Land Drainage Act 1994 (c 25)

RA: 21 Jul 1994

Commencement provision: s 3(2)

21 Sep 1994 (s 3(2))

Law of Property (Miscellaneous Provisions) Act 1994 (c 36)

RA: 3 Nov 1994

Commencement provision: s 23; Law of Property (Miscellaneous Provisions) Act 1994 (Commencement No 1) Order 1995, SI 1995/145; Law of Property (Miscellaneous Provisions) Act 1994 (Commencement No 2) Order 1995, SI 1995/1317

s 1–20	1 Jul 1995 (SI 1995/1317)
21(1)	See Sch 1 below
(2)–(4)	1 Jul 1995 (SI 1995/1317)
22–24	1 Jul 1995 (SI 1995/1317)
Sch 1, para 1	1 Jul 1995 (SI 1995/1317)
2	15 Feb 1995 (SI 1995/145)
3–12	1 Jul 1995 (SI 1995/1317)
2	1 Jul 1995 (SI 1995/1317)

Local Government etc (Scotland) Act 1994 (c 39)

RA: 3 Nov 1994

Commencement provisions: s 184(2), (3); Local Government etc (Scotland) Act 1994 (Commencement No 1) Order 1994, SI 1994/2850, as amended by SI 1994/3150; Local Government etc (Scotland) Act 1994 (Commencement No 2) Order 1994, SI 1994/3150; Local Government etc (Scotland) Act 1994 (Commencement No 3) Order 1995, SI 1995/702; Local Government etc (Scotland) Act 1994 (Commencement No 4) Order 1995, SI 1995/1898; Local Government etc (Scotland) Act 1994 (Commencement No 5) Order 1995, SI 1995/2866; Local Government etc (Scotland) Act 1994 (Commencement No 6 and Saving) Order 1995, SI 1995/3326

s 1	8 Nov 1994 (SI 1994/2850)
2–4	6 Apr 1995 (SI 1995/702)
5	8 Nov 1994 (SI 1994/2850)
6	*Not in force*
7	8 Nov 1994 (SI 1994/2850)
8–11	4 Jan 1995 (SI 1994/2850)
12	8 Nov 1994 (SI 1994/2850)
13–17	4 Jan 1995 (SI 1994/2850)
18, 19	6 Apr 1995 (SI 1995/702)
20	1 Apr 1996 (SI 1995/702)
21, 22	*Not in force*
23	6 Apr 1995 (SI 1995/702)
24	4 Jan 1995 (SI 1994/2850)
25–29	6 Apr 1995 (SI 1995/702) (but note s 29(1) effective from 1 Apr 1996)
30–32	*Not in force*

Local Government etc (Scotland) Act 1994 (c 39)—*cont*

s 33	1 Apr 1996 (SI 1995/702)
34	4 Jan 1995 (SI 1994/2850)
35	*Not in force*
36	6 Apr 1995 (subject to a transitional provision) (SI 1995/702)
37	*Not in force*; prospectively repealed by Environment Act 1995, s 120(3), Sch 24[1]
38	4 Jan 1995 (SI 1994/2850)
39	6 Apr 1995 (SI 1995/702)
40	4 Jan 1995 (SI 1994/2850)
41	*Not in force*
42, 43	6 Apr 1995 (SI 1995/702)
44	4 Jan 1995 (SI 1994/2850)
45, 46	*Not in force*
47	4 Jan 1995 (SI 1994/2850)
48	*Not in force*
49, 50	4 Jan 1995 (SI 1994/2850)
51(1), (2)	*Not in force*
(3)	4 Jan 1995 (SI 1994/2850)
(4), (5)	*Not in force*
52	1 Apr 1996 (SI 1995/702)
53, 54	*Not in force*
55, 56	6 Apr 1995 (SI 1995/702)
57	8 Nov 1994 (SI 1994/2850)
58	1 Aug 1995 (so far as enables a new local authority to enter into an agreement with any other new local authority for carrying out an activity or service on and after 1 Apr 1996) (SI 1995/702)
	Not in force (otherwise)
59	6 Apr 1995 (SI 1995/702)
60	4 Jan 1995 (SI 1994/2850)
61	8 Nov 1994 (SI 1994/2850)
62–64	17 Jul 1995 (SI 1995/1898)
65(1)	*Not in force*
(2)	17 Jul 1995 (SI 1995/1898)
66	17 Jul 1995 (SI 1995/1898)
67	30 Oct 1995 (SI 1995/2866)
68(1)	30 Oct 1995 (SI 1995/2866)
(2), (3)	*Not in force*
(4), (5)	30 Oct 1995 (SI 1995/2866)
69–71	30 Oct 1995 (SI 1995/2866)
72	*Not in force*
73, 74	17 Jul 1995 (SI 1995/1898)
75	*Not in force*
76, 77	17 Jul 1995 (SI 1995/1898)
78	*Not in force*
79(1)–(3)	17 Jul 1995 (SI 1995/1898)
(4)	*Not in force*
(5)	17 Jul 1995 (SI 1995/1898)
80	*Not in force*
81	17 Jul 1995 (SI 1995/1898)
82	*Not in force*
83–90	17 Jul 1995 (SI 1995/1898)
91–96	10 Mar 1995 (SI 1995/702)
97(1)–(5)	4 Jan 1995 (SI 1994/2850)
(6)	8 Nov 1994 (SI 1994/2850)
(7), (8)	4 Jan 1995 (SI 1994/2850)

Local Government etc (Scotland) Act 1994 (c 39)—*cont*

s 98	17 Jul 1995 (SI 1995/1898)
99, 100	*Not in force*
101	4 Jan 1995 (subject to a transitional provision) (SI 1994/2850)
102, 103	*Not in force*
104	4 Jan 1995 (SI 1994/2850)
105–112	*Not in force*
113–115	4 Jan 1995 (SI 1994/2850)
116	17 Jul 1995 (SI 1995/1898)
117	*Not in force*
118(1)	17 Jul 1995 (SI 1995/1898)
(2), (3)	*Not in force*
119	*Not in force*
120(1)	17 Jul 1995 (SI 1995/1898)
(2)	*Not in force*
121	*Not in force*
122, 123	17 Jul 1995 (SI 1995/1898)
124	4 Jan 1995 (SI 1994/2850)
125	8 Nov 1994 (SI 1994/2850)
125A	Prospectively inserted by Environment Act 1995, s 116, Sch 21, para 6[1]
126	4 Jan 1995 (SI 1994/2850)
127–131	6 Apr 1995 (except so far as s 127(1) provides for the transfer of functions referred to therein or repeals Social Work (Scotland) Act 1968, s 36(1)) (SI 1995/702)
	Not in force (exceptions relating to s 127(1) noted above)
132	*Not in force*
133–136	6 Apr 1995 (SI 1995/702)
137(1)	8 Nov 1994 (so far as applies to s 12) (SI 1994/2850)
	4 Jan 1995 (otherwise) (SI 1994/2850)
(2)–(5)	4 Jan 1995 (SI 1994/2850)
138	6 Apr 1995 (SI 1995/702)
139	*Not in force*; prospectively repealed by Children (Scotland) Act 1995, s 105(5), Sch 5[2]
140	*Not in force*
141	4 Jan 1995 (SI 1994/2850)
142	*Not in force*
143	4 Jan 1995 (SI 1994/2850)
144, 145	*Not in force*
146–151	4 Jan 1995 (SI 1994/2850)
152	1 Apr 1995 (SI 1994/3150)
153	4 Jan 1995 (SI 1994/3150)
154–156	1 Apr 1995 (SI 1994/3150)
157	8 Nov 1994 (SI 1994/2850)
158, 159	1 Apr 1995 (SI 1994/3150)
160, 161	4 Jan 1995 (SI 1994/3150)
162(1)	1 Apr 1995 (SI 1994/3150)
(2)	*Not in force*
163	3 Nov 1994 (RA)
164(1), (2)	1 Apr 1995 (SI 1995/702)
(3)–(5)	*Not in force*
165–167	4 Jan 1995 (SI 1994/2850)
168	1 Apr 1995 (subject to a transitional provision) (SI 1995/702)
169	6 Apr 1995 (SI 1995/702)

Local Government etc (Scotland) Act 1994 (c 39)—*cont*

s 170	4 Jan 1995 (SI 1994/2850)
171	30 Oct 1995 (so far as enables a local authority to comply with their duties under the Local Government (Scotland) Act 1973, s 171A(5) before the beginning of the financial year commencing 1 Apr 1996, and so far as enables the Secretary of State to approve under s 171A(6) of the 1973 Act the proposals submitted by the local authority under sub-s (5) of that section) (SI 1995/2866)
	1 Apr 1996 (otherwise) (SI 1995/2866)
172, 173	4 Jan 1995 (SI 1994/2850)
174	*Not in force*
175	4 Jan 1995 (SI 1994/2850)
176	1 Apr 1996 (SI 1995/2866)
177(1)	See sub-ss (2), (3) below
(2)	6 Apr 1995 (so far as relates to entry in House of Commons Disqualification Act 1975, Sch 1, Pt II, concerning Scottish Children's Reporter Administration) (SI 1995/702)
	17 Jul 1995 (so far as relates to entry in House of Commons Disqualification Act 1975, Sch 1, Pt II, concerning East of Scotland Water Authority, North of Scotland Water Authority and West of Scotland Water Authority) (SI 1995/1898)
	30 Oct 1995 (otherwise) (SI 1995/2866)
(3)	8 Nov 1994 (so far as relates to entry in House of Commons Disqualification Act 1975, Pt III, concerning any member of the staff commission) (SI 1994/2850)
	6 Apr 1995 (so far as not already in force) (SI 1995/702)
178	8 Nov 1994 (SI 1994/2850)
179	4 Jan 1995 (SI 1994/2850)
180(1)	See Sch 13 below
(2)	See Sch 14 below
181(1), (2)	8 Nov 1994 (SI 1994/2850)
(3)–(7)	6 Apr 1995 (SI 1995/702)
(8), (9)	8 Nov 1994 (SI 1994/2850)
182	4 Jan 1995 (SI 1994/2850)
183(1)	8 Nov 1994 (SI 1994/2850)
(2)	*Not in force*
(3)	6 Apr 1995 (SI 1995/702)
(4), (5)	*Not in force*
(6)	6 Apr 1995 (SI 1995/702)
184	8 Nov 1994 (SI 1994/2850)
Sch 1, 2	8 Nov 1994 (SI 1994/2850)
3	6 Apr 1995 (SI 1995/702)
4	1 Apr 1996 (SI 1995/702)
5	4 Jan 1995 (SI 1994/2850)
6	1 Apr 1996 (SI 1995/702)
7, 8	17 Jul 1995 (SI 1995/1898)
9	30 Oct 1995 (SI 1995/2866)
10	*Not in force*
11	10 Mar 1995 (SI 1995/702)
12	6 Apr 1995 (SI 1995/702)

Local Government etc (Scotland) Act 1994 (c 39)—*cont*

Sch 13, para 1, 2	*Not in force*
3	4 Jan 1995 (SI 1994/2850)
4(1)	4 Jan 1995 (SI 1994/2850)
(2)	*Not in force*
(3)	4 Jan 1995 (SI 1994/2850)
5–16	*Not in force*
17	*Not in force*; prospectively repealed by Merchant Shipping Act 1995, s 314(1), Sch 12[3]
18–26	*Not in force*
27(1), (2)	4 Jan 1995 (SI 1994/2850)
(3)(a)(i)	4 Jan 1995 (SI 1994/2850)
(ii)	*Not in force*
(b)–(o)	*Not in force*
(p)	6 Apr 1995 (SI 1995/702)
(q)	*Not in force*
(4)	*Not in force*
28–56	*Not in force*
57	1 Apr 1995 (SI 1994/3150)
58, 59	*Not in force*
60(1)	4 Jan 1995 (SI 1994/2850)
(2)	*Not in force*
(3)(a)–(c)	4 Jan 1995 (SI 1994/2850)
	Not in force
(4)	1 Apr 1995 (SI 1994/3150)
(5)	*Not in force*
61–66	*Not in force*
67(1), (2)	1 Apr 1995 (SI 1994/3150)
(3), (4)	*Not in force*
(5)	1 Apr 1995 (SI 1994/3150)
68–70	*Not in force*
71(1)	4 Jan 1995 (SI 1994/2850)
(2)–(5)	*Not in force*
(6)	4 Jan 1995 (SI 1994/2850)
(7)–(17)	*Not in force*
72(1), (2)	1 Apr 1995 (SI 1995/702)
(3)–(9)	*Not in force*
73, 74	*Not in force*
75(1)	4 Jan 1995 (SI 1994/2850)
(2)(a)	*Not in force*
(b)	4 Jan 1995 (subject to a transitional provision) (SI 1994/2850)
(c)	*Not in force*
(d)	4 Jan 1995 (subject to a transitional provision) (SI 1994/2850)
(e)	4 Jan 1995 (SI 1994/2850)
(3)–(12)	*Not in force*
(13)(a)(i)	*Not in force*
(ii)	4 Jan 1995 (SI 1994/2850)
(b), (c)	*Not in force*
(14)	4 Jan 1995 (subject to a transitional provision) (SI 1994/2850)
(15), (16)	*Not in force*
(17)(a)–(c)	*Not in force*
(d)	4 Jan 1995 (subject to a transitional provision) (SI 1994/2850)
(18)(a), (b)	*Not in force*
(c)	4 Jan 1995 (SI 1994/2850)

Local Government etc (Scotland) Act 1994 (c 39)—*cont*

Sch 13, para 75(19)(a)	*Not in force*
(b)	4 Jan 1995 (subject to a transitional provision) (SI 1994/2850)
(20)	4 Jan 1995 (subject to a transitional provision) (SI 1994/2850)
(21)–(23)	*Not in force*
(24)	4 Jan 1995 (subject to a transitional provision) (SI 1994/2850)
(25)(a)	*Not in force*
(b)	17 Jul 1995 (SI 1995/1898)
(26)–(28)	*Not in force*
76–91	*Not in force*
92(1)	4 Jan 1995 (SI 1994/2850)
(2)–(19)	*Not in force*
(20)	4 Jan 1995 (SI 1994/2850)
(21)	*Not in force*
(22)	4 Jan 1995 (SI 1994/2850)
(23), (24)	*Not in force*
(25)	1 Apr 1995 (SI 1995/702)
(26), (27)	4 Jan 1995 (SI 1994/2850)
(28)–(33)	*Not in force*
(34), (35)	*Not in force*; prospectively repealed by Environment Act 1995, s 120(3), Sch 24[1]
(36)–(59)	*Not in force*
(60)	Repealed
(61)–(69)	*Not in force*
(70)	4 Jan 1995 (SI 1994/2850)
(71)–(74)	*Not in force*
93, 94	*Not in force*
95(1)	4 Jan 1995 (SI 1994/2850)
(2)(a)	4 Jan 1995 (SI 1994/2850); prospectively repealed by Environment Act 1995, s 120(3), Sch 24[1]
(b)	4 Jan 1995 (subject to a transitional provision) (SI 1994/2850); prospectively repealed by Environment Act 1995, s 120(3), Sch 24[1]
(c)	*Not in force*; prospectively repealed by Environment Act 1995, s 120(3), Sch 24[1]
(d)	4 Jan 1995 (SI 1994/2850); prospectively repealed by Environment Act 1995, s 120(3), Sch 24[1]
(e)	*Not in force*; prospectively repealed by Environment Act 1995, s 120(3), Sch 24[1]
(3)–(7)	*Not in force*
(8), (9)	*Not in force*; prospectively repealed by Environment Act 1995, s 120(3), Sch 24[1]
(10)	*Not in force*
96–99	*Not in force*
100(1)	4 Jan 1995 (SI 1994/2850)
(2)	1 Apr 1995 (SI 1994/3150)
(3)	*Not in force*
(4), (5)	1 Apr 1995 (SI 1994/3150)
(6)(a)(i)	6 Apr 1995 (SI 1995/702)
(ii)	*Not in force*
(b)	*Not in force*
(7), (8)	*Not in force*
(9)(a)–(e)	*Not in force*
(f), (g)	4 Jan 1995 (SI 1994/2850)
(h)–(j)	*Not in force*

Local Government etc (Scotland) Act 1994 (c 39)—*cont*

Sch 13, para 101, 102	*Not in force*
103	*Not in force*; prospectively repealed by Children (Scotland) Act 1995, s 105(5), Sch 5[2]
104–118	*Not in force*
119(1)	4 Jan 1995 (SI 1994/2850)
(2)–(4)	*Not in force*
(5)(a)–(c)	*Not in force*
(d)	4 Jan 1995 (SI 1994/2850)
(e)	*Not in force*
(6)	*Not in force*
(7)(a), (b)	*Not in force*
(c)(i)	*Not in force*
(ii)	4 Jan 1995 (SI 1994/2850)
(d)	*Not in force*
(8)–(33)	*Not in force*
(34)	4 Jan 1995 (SI 1994/2850)
(35)	*Not in force*
(36)	4 Jan 1995 (SI 1994/2850)
(37)–(41)	*Not in force*
(42)–(45)	4 Jan 1995 (SI 1994/2850)
(46)	4 Jan 1995 (so far as relates to definition "wholesome" in Water (Scotland) Act 1980, s 76L(1)) (SI 1994/2850) *Not in force* (otherwise)
(47)–(50)	*Not in force*
(51)	4 Jan 1995 (SI 1994/2850)
(52)	*Not in force*
(53)(a)(i)–(iii)	*Not in force*
(iv)	4 Jan 1995 (SI 1994/2850)
(v)	*Not in force*
(vi)	4 Jan 1995 (SI 1994/2850)
(b)	*Not in force*
(54)–(58)	*Not in force*
120–128	*Not in force*
129(1)	4 Jan 1995 (SI 1994/2850)
(2)–(19)	*Not in force*
(20)(a)	*Not in force*
(b)	4 Jan 1995 (SI 1994/2850)
(21), (22)	*Not in force*
130–148	*Not in force*
149	*Not in force*; prospectively repealed by Gas Act 1995, s 17(5), Sch 6[4]
150–155	*Not in force*
156(1)	4 Jan 1995 (SI 1994/2850)
(2)	*Not in force*
(3), (4)	4 Jan 1995 (SI 1994/2850)
(5), (6)	*Not in force*
157–161	*Not in force*
162(1), (2)	22 Dec 1995 (subject to a saving) (SI 1995/3326)
(3), (4)	1 Apr 1996 (SI 1995/3326)
163–175	*Not in force*
176(1)	31 Dec 1994 (SI 1994/3150)
(2)–(18)	*Not in force*
(19)(a)	*Not in force*
(b)	31 Dec 1994 (subject to a transitional provision) (SI 1994/3150)

Local Government etc (Scotland) Act 1994 (c 39)—*cont*

13, para	176(19)(c), (d)	4 Jan 1995 (SI 1994/2850)
	177	4 Jan 1995 (SI 1994/2850)
	178–184	*Not in force*
14		4 Jan 1995 (repeals of or in Burial Grounds (Scotland) Act 1855; Fire Services Act 1947, ss 15(2), 36(2); Local Government (Scotland) Act 1973, s 84(2), (4); Water (Scotland) Act 1980, ss 6467, 76H(8), 76L(1) (definition "wholesome" only), 109(1) (definition "owner" only); Civic Government (Scotland) Act 1982, s 121) (SI 1994/2850)
		4 Jan 1995 (repeals of Local Government (Scotland) Act 1973, s 116(6); Local Government (Miscellaneous Provisions) (Scotland) Act 1981, Sch 2, paras 41, 42; Water Act 1989, Sch 25, para 60(2)) (SI 1994/3150)
		1 Apr 1995 (repeals of or in Sporting Lands Rating (Scotland) Act 1886; Local Government (Scotland) Act 1947, ss 243, 243A, 243B, 244; Valuation and Rating (Scotland) Act 1956, s 22A; Local Government and Miscellaneous Financial Provisions (Scotland) Act 1958, s 7; Local Government (Scotland) Act 1966; Town and Country Planning (Scotland) Act 1972, Sch 21; Local Government (Scotland) Act 1973, Sch 9, para 11; Local Government (Scotland) Act 1975, Sch 6, Pt II, paras 6, 13, 34; Local Government Planning and Land Act 1980, Sch 32 para 33 (except repeal of definition "rates" in sub-para (4)); Local Government (Miscellaneous Provisions) (Scotland) Act 1981, s 6, Sch 3, para 26; Local Government and Planning (Scotland) Act 1982, s 4; Rating and Valuation (Amendment) (Scotland) Act 1984, ss 6, 7, Sch 2, para 7; Local Government Finance Act 1988, s 128, Sch 12, Pt II, para 6; Water Act 1989, Sch 25, para 22; Local Government and Housing Act 1989, Sch 6, para 7; Local Government Finance Act 1992, Sch 13, para 75) (SI 1994/3150)
		1 Apr 1995 (repeals of or in Local Government (Scotland) Act 1973, ss 83(4B)(d), 96(5), 100(3); Criminal Procedure (Scotland) Act 1975, Sch 7D, para 59; Local Government (Scotland) Act 1975, Sch 3, para 22(1), head (c) and para 24A; Local Government Act 1988, Sch 6, para 11; Local Government Finance Act 1992, Sch 7, para 1(6)) (SI 1995/702)
		1 Apr 1996 (repeals in Prisons (Scotland) Act 1989, ss 14(2), 16(2)) (SI 1995/3326)
		Not in force (otherwise)

[1] Any orders made under Environment Act 1995, s 125(3), bringing the prospective amendments into force will be noted to that Act in the service to this work

[2] Any orders made under Children (Scotland) Act 1995, s 105(1), (2), bringing the prospective repeals into force will be noted to that Act in the service to this work

[3] Any orders made under Merchant Shipping Act 1995, s 314(3), Sch 14, para 5(2),

Local Government etc (Scotland) Act 1994 (c 39)—*cont*

bringing the prospective repeal into force will be noted to that Act in the service to this work

[4] Any orders made under Gas Act 1995, s 18(2), bringing the prospective repeal into force will be noted to that Act in the service to this work

---

Local Government (Wales) Act 1994 (c 19)

RA: 5 Jul 1994

Commencement provisions: s 66(2)–(4); Local Government (Wales) Act 1994 (Commencement No 1) Order 1994, SI 1994/2109; Local Government (Wales) Act 1994 (Commencement No 2) Order 1994, SI 1994/2790; Local Government (Wales) Act 1994 (Commencement No 3) Order 1995, SI 1995/546, as amended by SI 1995/851; Local Government (Wales) Act 1994 (Commencement No 4) Order 1995, SI 1995/852; Local Government (Wales) Act 1994 (Commencement No 5) Order 1995, SI 1995/2490; Local Government (Wales) Act 1994 (Commencement No 6) Order 1995, SI 1995/3198

s 1(1), (2)	5 Jul 1994 (s 66(2)(a))
(3)	See Sch 2 below
(4)	See sub-ss (5)–(8) below
(5), (6)	24 Oct 1994 (in relation to sub-ss (5), (6), for interpretation of Pt IV of Local Government Act 1972) (subject to a saving) (SI 1994/2790)
	20 Mar 1995 (in relation to sub-s (5), for interpretation of Local Government Act 1972, ss 21, 25, 26, 79, 80, 270(1), (3) and s 17 of this Act) (subject to a saving) (SI 1995/546)
	3 Apr 1995 (in relation to sub-ss (5), (6), for interpretation of provisions of Local Government Act 1972 falling to be applied in consequence of SI 1995/852) (subject to a saving) (SI 1995/852)
	1 Oct 1995 (in relation to sub-s (5), for interpretation of Local Government Finance Act 1982, Pt III) (subject to a transitional provision) (SI 1995/2490)
	1 Apr 1996 (otherwise) (SI 1995/3198)
(7)	5 Jul 1994 (s 66(2)(a))
(8)	24 Oct 1994 (for interpretation of Pt IV of Local Government Act 1972) (subject to a saving) (SI 1994/2790)
	20 Mar 1995 (for interpretation of Local Government Act 1972, ss 21, 25, 26, 79, 80, 270(1), (3) and s 17 of this Act) (subject to a saving) (SI 1995/546)
	3 Apr 1995 (for interpretation of provisions of Local Government Act 1972 falling to be applied in consequence of SI 1995/852) (subject to a saving) (SI 1995/852)
	1 Oct 1995 (for interpretation of Environment Act 1995, s 65(4), Sch 7, para 2) (SI 1995/2490)
	1 Apr 1996 (otherwise) (SI 1995/3198)
2	20 Mar 1995 (subject to a saving) (SI 1995/546)
3	5 Jul 1994 (s 66(2)(a))
4	20 Mar 1995 (subject to a saving) (SI 1995/546)
5	3 Apr 1995 (subject to a saving) (SI 1995/852)

Local Government (Wales) Act 1994 (c 19)—*cont*

s 6, 7	5 Jul 1994 (s 66(2)(a))
8–13	1 Apr 1996 (SI 1995/3198)
14, 15	3 Apr 1995 (SI 1995/852)
16	1 Apr 1996 (SI 1995/3198)
17	20 Mar 1995 (only for purposes of legislative provisions specified in SI 1995/546, art 5, and subject to a transitional provision) (SI 1995/546, as amended by SI 1995/851)
	Not in force (otherwise)
18(1)–(6)	3 Apr 1995 (for purposes specified in SI 1995/852, art 4(2), and subject to savings) (SI 1995/852)
	1 Apr 1996 (otherwise) (SI 1995/852)
(7)	1 Apr 1996 (SI 1995/3198)
19	3 Apr 1995 (SI 1995/852)
20(1)–(3)	1 Apr 1996 (SI 1995/3198)
(4)	See Sch 6 below
21	*Not in force*
22	See Schs 7–11 below
23(1)	1 Apr 1996 (SI 1995/3198)
(2)–(6)	3 Apr 1995 (SI 1995/852)
24	Repealed
25–38	3 Apr 1995 (subject to a saving relating to s 35) (SI 1995/852)
39, 40	5 Jul 1994 (s 66(2)(a))
41	15 Aug 1994 (SI 1994/2109)
42	3 Apr 1995 (SI 1995/852)
43	5 Jul 1994 (s 66(2)(a))
44, 45	3 Apr 1995 (SI 1995/852)
46–48	5 Jul 1994 (s 66(2)(a))
49, 50	1 Apr 1996 (SI 1995/3198)
51	3 Apr 1995 (SI 1995/852)
52	15 Aug 1994 (SI 1994/2109)
53	3 Apr 1995 (SI 1995/852)
54, 55	5 Jul 1994 (s 66(2)(a))
56–60	3 Apr 1995 (SI 1995/852)
61	*Not in force*
62	1 Apr 1996 (SI 1995/3198)
63, 64	5 Jul 1994 (s 66(2)(a))
65	15 Aug 1994 (SI 1994/2109)
66(1)–(4)	5 Jul 1994 (s 66(2)(c))
(5)	See Sch 15 below
(6)	See Sch 16 below
(7)	See Sch 17 below
(8)	See Sch 18 below
(9)	5 Jul 1994 (s 66(2)(c))
Sch 1	5 Jul 1994 (s 66(2)(b))
2, para 1–3	1 Apr 1996 (SI 1995/3198)
4, 5	24 Oct 1994 (subject to a saving) (SI 1994/2790)
6, 7	1 Apr 1996 (SI 1995/3198)
8, 9	3 Apr 1995 (SI 1995/852)
10–12	1 Apr 1996 (SI 1995/3198)
13	1 Oct 1995 (SI 1995/2490)
3	5 Jul 1994 (s 66(2)(b))
4, 5	1 Apr 1996 (SI 1995/3198)
6, para 1	*Not in force*
2	3 Apr 1995 (SI 1995/852)

Local Government (Wales) Act 1994 (c 19)—*cont*

Sch 6, para 3, 4	3 Apr 1995 (SI 1995/852); prospectively repealed by Environment Act 1995, s 120(3), Sch 24[1]
5–10	*Not in force*; prospectively repealed by Environment Act 1995, s120(3), Sch 24[1]
11, 12	3 Apr 1995 (subject to a saving) (SI 1995/852); prospectively repealed by Environment Act 1995, s120(3), Sch 24[1]
13–17	*Not in force*
18	*Not in force*; prospectively repealed by Environment Act 1995, s120(3), Sch 24[1]
19, 20	*Not in force*
21	3 Apr 1995 (SI 1995/852)
22	*Not in force*
23	3 Apr 1995 (SI 1995/852); prospectively repealed by Environment Act 1995, s120(3), Sch 24[1]
24(1)(a)	*Not in force*; prospectively repealed by Environment Act 1995, s 120(3), Sch 24[1]
(b)	3 Apr 1995 (SI 1995/852); prospectively repealed by Environment Act 1995, s120(3), Sch 24[1]
(2)–(9)	*Not in force*
(10)(a)	*Not in force*
(b)	1 Oct 1995 (SI 1995/2490)
(11)–(16)	*Not in force*
(17)(a)	1 Oct 1995 (SI 1995/2490)
(b)	*Not in force*
(18), (19)	*Not in force*
25–27	*Not in force*
28, 29	*Not in force*; prospectively repealed by Environment Act 1995, s 120(3), Sch 24[1]
7, para 1	3 Apr 1995 (for purposes specified in SI 1995/852, art 4(5), and subject to a transitional provision) (SI 1995/852)
2–26	*Not in force*
27(1)–(3)	*Not in force*
(4)	1 Oct 1995 (SI 1995/2490)
28–43	*Not in force*
8, para 1, 2	*Not in force*
3(1)	*Not in force*
(2)	1 Oct 1995 (for purposes specified in SI 1995/2490, art 4(2), and subject to a transitional provision) (SI 1995/2490) 1 Apr 1996 (otherwise) (SI 1995/2490)
(3)–(5)	*Not in force*
4–11	*Not in force*
9	*Not in force*
10, para 1–13	*Not in force*
14	3 Apr 1995 (SI 1995/852)
11	*Not in force*
12	3 Apr 1995 (subject to savings) (SI 1995/852)
13, 14	5 Jul 1994 (s 66(2)(b))
15, para 1	24 Oct 1994 (SI 1994/2790)
2	*Not in force*
3	3 Apr 1995 (SI 1995/852)
4, 5	*Not in force*
6	20 Mar 1995 (SI 1995/546)
7	24 Oct 1994 (subject to a saving) (SI 1994/2790)
8(1)–(4)	*Not in force*

Local Government (Wales) Act 1994 (c 19)—*cont*

Sch 15, para 8(5)	24 Oct 1994 (subject to a saving) (SI 1994/2790)
9(1)–(3)	*Not in force*
(4)(a)	*Not in force*
(b)	24 Oct 1994 (subject to a saving) (SI 1994/2790)
10(1)	1 Oct 1995 (SI 1995/2490)
(2), (3)	*Not in force*
11(1)	*Not in force*
(2)	24 Oct 1994 (subject to a saving) (SI 1994/2790)
12(a)	*Not in force*
(b)	24 Oct 1994 (subject to a saving) (SI 1994/2790)
13–17	*Not in force*
18, 19	24 Oct 1994 (subject to a saving) (SI 1994/2790)
20	3 Apr 1995 (subject to a saving) (SI 1995/852)
21, 22	*Not in force*
23	3 Apr 1995 (SI 1995/852)
24, 25	*Not in force*
26	3 Apr 1995 (subject to a saving) (SI 1995/852)
27–51	*Not in force*
52	1 Oct 1995 (SI 1995/2490)
53, 54	*Not in force*
55	3 Apr 1995 (subject to a saving) (SI 1995/852)
56	*Not in force*
57	24 Oct 1994 (subject to a saving) (SI 1994/2790)
58–61	1 Oct 1995 (SI 1995/2490)
62–66	*Not in force*
16, para 1–11	*Not in force*
12	1 Oct 1995 (for purposes specified in SI 1995/2490, art 5(2), and subject to a transitional provision) (SI 1995/2490)
	1 Apr 1996 (otherwise) (SI 1995/2490)
13–25	*Not in force*
26	1 Oct 1995 (for purposes specified in SI 1995/2490, art 5(4), and subject to a transitional provision) (SI 1995/2490)
	1 Apr 1996 (otherwise) (SI 1995/2490)
27–53	*Not in force*
54(1)	*Not in force*
(2)	1 Jan 1996 (subject to a saving) (SI 1995/3198)
55, 56	*Not in force*
57(1)–(5)	3 Apr 1995 (subject to a saving) (SI 1995/852)
(6)	*Not in force*
58–67	*Not in force*
68(1)–(5)	*Not in force*
(6)	20 Mar 1995 (subject to savings and transitional provisions) (SI 1995/546)
(7)	20 Mar 1995 (but not in respect of Representation of the People Act 1983, s 35(1A)(b)) (subject to a saving) (SI 1995/546)
(8), (9)	20 Mar 1995 (subject to savings and transitional provisions in respect of sub-para (8)) (SI 1995/546)
(10)–(12)	*Not in force*
(13)–(16)	20 Mar 1995 (subject to transitional provisions in respect of sub-para (16)) (SI 1995/546)
(17), (18)	*Not in force*
(19)	20 Mar 1995 (SI 1995/546)
(20)	*Not in force*
69–77	*Not in force*

Local Government (Wales) Act 1994 (c 19)—*cont*

Sch 16, para 78		*Not in force*; prospectively repealed by Gas Act 1995, s 17(5), Sch 6[2]
	79–81	*Not in force*
	82(1)–(3)	3 Apr 1995 (for purposes of orders made under Coroners Act 1988, s 4A, and subject to transitional provisions) (SI 1995/852)
		1 Apr 1996 (otherwise) (SI 1995/852)
	(4)	3 Apr 1995 (subject to transitional provisions) (SI 1995/852)
	(5)	3 Apr 1995 (only in respect of Coroners Act 1988, s 4A(1), (2), (7), (9), (10)) (SI 1995/852)
		Not in force (otherwise)
	(6)–(10)	*Not in force*
	83	*Not in force*
	84–86	3 Apr 1995 (SI 1995/852)
	87	*Not in force*
	88	3 Apr 1995 (SI 1995/852)
	89–95	*Not in force*
	96, 97	3 Apr 1995 (SI 1995/852)
	98	1 Oct 1995 (to have effect only in relation to any financial year beginning on or after 1 Apr 1996) (SI 1995/2490)
	99–105	*Not in force*
	106	3 Apr 1995 (SI 1995/852)
	107–109	*Not in force*
17, para	1	5 Jul 1994 (s 66(2)(b))
	2, 3	3 Apr 1995 (SI 1995/852)
	4	5 Jul 1994 (s 66(2)(b))
	5	3 Apr 1995 (SI 1995/852)
	6	5 Jul 1994 (s 66(2)(b))
	7, 8	20 Mar 1995 (SI 1995/546)
	9	5 Jul 1994 (s 66(2)(b))
	10–12	3 Apr 1995 (SI 1995/852)
	13	3 Apr 1995 (SI 1995/852); prospectively repealed by Environment Act 1995, s120(3), Sch 24[1]
	14	3 Apr 1995 (SI 1995/852)
	15	1 Apr 1996 (SI 1995/3198)
	16	*Not in force*
	17	1 Apr 1996 (SI 1995/3198)
	18–23	3 Apr 1995 (SI 1995/852)
18		24 Oct 1994 (repeals in Local Government Act 1972, ss 55(5)(a), 59(2), 72(2)) (subject to a saving) (SI 1994/2790)
		20 Mar 1995 (repeals in Representation of the People Act 1983, ss 35(1), 36(3)(b)) (SI 1995/546)
		3 Apr 1995 (repeals in Local Government Act 1972, 74(3), (4); Local Government, Planning and Land Act 1980, ss 4(7), 20(1); Town and Country Planning Act 1990, ss 1(3), 2(1)) (SI 1995/852)
		1 Oct 1995 (repeals of or in Local Government Act 1972, Sch 4, Pt IV, Sch 8, para 8, Sch 10, Sch 11, para 3(2)(b), (c)) (SI 1995/2490)
		1 Jan 1996 (subject to a saving) (repeal in European Parliamentary Elections Act 1978, Sch 2, para 5A(4)(a)) (SI 1995/3198)
		Not in force (otherwise)

Local Government (Wales) Act 1994 (c 19)—*cont*

[1] Any orders made under Environment Act 1995, s 125(3), bringing the prospective repeals into force will be noted to that Act in the service to this work

[2] Any orders made under Gas Act 1995, s 18(2), bringing the prospective repeal into force will be noted to that Act in the service to this work

---

Marriage Act 1994 (c 34)

RA: 3 Nov 1994

Commencement provisions: s 3(2); Marriage Act 1994 (Commencement No 1) Order 1994, SI 1994/3116; Marriage Act 1994 (Commencement No 2) Order 1995, SI 1995/424

s 1(1)	1 Apr 1995 (SI 1995/424)
(2)	24 Feb 1995 (so far as inserts Marriage Act 1949, ss 46A, 46B(2)) (SI 1995/424)
	1 Apr 1995 (otherwise) (SI 1995/424)
(3)	See Schedule below
2(1)	1 Jan 1995 (so far as inserts Marriage Act 1949, s 35(2A)) (SI 1994/3116)
	1 Apr 1995 (so far as not already in force) (SI 1995/424)
(2)	1 Jan 1995 (SI 1994/3116)
3	1 Jan 1995 (SI 1994/3116)
Schedule	
para 1	See paras 2–8 below
2–4	1 Apr 1995 (SI 1995/424)
5	24 Feb 1995 (SI 1995/424)
6–9	1 Apr 1995 (SI 1995/424)

Mental Health (Amendment) Act 1994 (c 6)

RA: 24 Mar 1994

Commencement provision: s 2(3)

14 Apr 1994 (s 2(3))

Merchant Shipping (Salvage and Pollution) Act 1994 (c 28)

Whole Act repealed

New Towns (Amendment) Act 1994 (c 5)

RA: 24 Mar 1994

24 Mar 1994 (RA)

Non-Domestic Rating Act 1994 (c 3)

RA: 24 Feb 1994

24 Feb 1994 (RA)

Parliamentary Commissioner Act 1994 (c 14)

RA: 5 Jul 1994

Commencement provision: s 3(2)

5 Sep 1994 (s 3(2))

Pastoral (Amendment) Measure 1994 (No 1)

RA: 24 Mar 1994

Commencement provision: s 15(2)

The provisions of this Measure are brought into force on 1 Apr 1994 by an appointed day notice signed by the Archbishops of Canterbury and York and dated 25 Mar 1994 (made under s 15(2))

Police and Magistrates' Courts Act 1994 (c 29)

RA: 21 Jul 1994

Commencement provisions: s 94; Police and Magistrates' Courts Act 1994 (Commencement No 1 and Transitional Provisions) Order 1994, SI 1994/2025; Police and Magistrates' Courts Act 1994 (Commencement No 2) Order 1994, SI 1994/2151; Police and Magistrates' Courts Act 1994 (Commencement No 3 and Transitional Provisions) Order 1994, SI 1994/2594; Police and Magistrates' Courts Act 1994 (Commencement No 4 and Transitional Provisions) (Scotland) Order 1994, SI 1994/3075; Police and Magistrates' Courts Act 1994 (Commencement No 5 and Transitional Provisions) Order 1994, SI 1994/3262, as amended by SI 1995/246 and SI 1995/899; Police and Magistrates' Courts Act 1994 (Commencement No 5 and Transitional Provisions) (Amendment) Order 1995, SI 1995/246, and Police and Magistrates' Courts Act 1994 (Commencement No 5 and Transitional Provisions) (Amendment No 2) Order 1995, SI 1995/899 (both amending transitional provisions set out in SI 1994/3262); Police and Magistrates' Courts Act 1994 (Commencement No 6 and Transitional Provisions) Order 1995, SI 1995/42; Police and Magistrates' Courts Act 1994 (Commencement No 7 and Transitional Provisions) (Scotland) Order 1995, SI 1995/492, as amended by SI 1995/3003; Police and Magistrates' Courts Act 1994 (Commencement No 8 and Transitional Provisions) Order 1995, SI 1995/685; Police and Magistrates' Courts Act 1994 (Commencement No 9 and Amendment) Order 1995, SI 1995/3003

s 1(1)	Ss 1, 2 (so far as substitutes new s 3 of Police Act 1964), 3, 44 (so far as relates to Sch 5, paras 5, 15), 93 (so far as relates to repeal in Sch 9, Pt I of Police Act 1964, s 25(5)), Schs 1, 2 all brought into force on 8 Aug 1994 by SI 1994/2025, for purposes specified in art 4(1) of that Order and subject to modifications specified in art 4(3)–(6) of that Order. Those provisions (ie ss 1, 2, 3, 44 (so far as relates to Sch 5, paras 5, 15), 93 (so far as relates to repeal in Sch 9, Pt I of Police Act 1964, s 25(5)), Schs 1, 2) are brought into force, subject to transitional provisions, for all remaining purposes on 1 Apr 1995 by SI 1994/3262, as amended by SI 1995/246
(2)	See Sch 1 below

Police and Magistrates' Courts Act 1994 (c 29)—*cont*

s 2	See note to s 1
3(1)	21 Jul 1994 (for purpose of power to make orders under Police Act 1964, s 3A) (s 94(3)(a)(i)) See note to s 1 otherwise
(2)	See Sch 2 below
4	Ss 4 (except so far as substitutes new s 4(1) of the Police Act 1964 and inserts new s 4C thereof), 8, 10, 11, 15 (except so far as substitutes new s 28D of the 1964 Act), 16, 31, 43 (so far as relates to Sch 4, except paras 1–4, 15(2), 42 thereof), 45 all brought into force on 1 Oct 1994 by SI 1994/2025, for purposes specified in art 6(1) of that Order and subject to modifications specified in art 6(3)–(6) of that Order. Those provisions (ie ss 4, 8, 10, 11, 15, 16, 31, 43 (so far as relates to Sch 4, except paras 1–4, 15(2), 42 thereof), 45) are brought into force, subject to transitional provisions, for all remaining purposes on 1 Apr 1995 by SI 1994/3262, as amended by SI 1995/246
5–7	1 Apr 1995 (SI 1994/3262)
8	See note to s 4
9	1 Apr 1995 (SI 1994/3262)
10, 11	See note to s 4
12	1 Apr 1995 (SI 1994/3262)
13	21 Jul 1994 (s 94(3)(b))
14	1 Oct 1994 (so far as substitutes new ss 21A, 21C of Police Act 1964) (SI 1994/2025) 1 Apr 1995 (otherwise) (SI 1994/3262)
15, 16	See note to s 4
17	1 Nov 1994 (for purposes of any financial year beginning on or after 1 Apr 1995, and subject to SI 1994/2025, art 7(3), (4)) (SI 1994/2025)
18	8 Aug 1994 (except so far as sub-s (3) inserts Police Act 1964, s 33(3)) (SI 1994/2025) *Not in force* (exception noted above)
19	*Not in force*
20, 21	1 Apr 1995 (subject to a transitional provision in respect of s 21) (SI 1994/3262)
22	1 Oct 1994 (SI 1994/2025)
23, 24	1 Apr 1995 (SI 1994/3262)
25	1 Oct 1994 (SI 1994/2025)
26	21 Jul 1994 (so far as relates to service in accordance with arrangements made under Police Act 1964, s 15A(2)) (s 94(3)(c)) 1 Apr 1995 (otherwise) (SI 1994/3262)
27, 28	1 Nov 1994 (for purposes of any financial year beginning on or after 1 Apr 1995, and subject to SI 1994/2025, art 7(3), (4)) (SI 1994/2025)
29	1 Apr 1995 (SI 1994/3262)
30	15 Mar 1995 (for purposes of issuing a basic credit approval under the Local Government and Housing Act 1989, s 53, to a new police authority in respect of the financial year beginning on 1 Apr 1995) (SI 1994/3262) 1 Apr 1995 (otherwise) (SI 1994/3262)
31	See note to s 4

Police and Magistrates' Courts Act 1994 (c 29)—*cont*

s 32	1 Oct 1994 (only in respect of new police authorities which have come into existence) (SI 1994/2025)
	Not in force (otherwise)
33	1 Oct 1994 (SI 1994/2025)
34–38	*Not in force*
39(1)	1 Oct 1994 (SI 1994/2025)
(2), (3)	1 Apr 1995 (SI 1994/3262)
(4)–(7)	1 Oct 1994 (SI 1994/2025)
40	1 Apr 1995 (SI 1994/3262)
41	8 Aug 1994 (SI 1994/2025)
42	1 Oct 1994 (SI 1994/2025)
43	See Sch 4 below
44	See Sch 5 below
45	See note to s 4
46	8 Aug 1994 (SI 1994/2025)
47(1)	13 Dec 1995 (SI 1995/3003)[1]
(2)(a)	1 Apr 1995 (subject to transitional provisions) (SI 1995/492)
(b)	13 Dec 1995 (SI 1995/3003)[1]
(3)	1 Apr 1996 (SI 1995/492)
(4), (5)	13 Dec 1995 (SI 1995/3003)[1]
48	1 Jan 1995 (for purpose of regulations under Police (Scotland) Act 1967, Pt II, relating to appointments and promotions to rank of assistant chief constable) (SI 1994/3075)
	1 Apr 1995 (so far as not already in force) (SI 1995/492)
49	1 Apr 1996 (SI 1995/492)
50	21 Jul 1994 (s 94(3)(b))
51(a)	1 Jan 1996 (subject to a transitional provision) (SI 1994/3075)
(b)	1 Jan 1995 (SI 1994/3075)
(c)	1 Jan 1996 (subject to a transitional provision) (SI 1994/3075)
52(1)	See sub-ss (2)(4) below
(2)	*Not in force*
(3)	8 Aug 1994 (so far as inserts Police (Scotland) Act 1967, s 26(2B)) (SI 1994/2025)
	1 Jan 1995 (for purpose of regulations under Police (Scotland) Act 1967, s 26, for purposes mentioned in sub-ss (2A), (2C) thereof) (SI 1994/3075)
	Not in force (otherwise)
(4)	*Not in force*
53(1)	1 Jan 1995 (SI 1994/3075)
(2)	1 Apr 1995 (SI 1995/492)
54	1 Apr 1996 (SI 1995/492)
55(1)	1 Jan 1995 (for purpose of rules under Police (Scotland) Act 1967, s 30(3), (4), (6)) (SI 1994/3075)
	Not in force (otherwise)
(2)	*Not in force*
56–58	1 Jan 1995 (SI 1994/3075)
59	1 Jan 1995 (for purpose of substitution of Police (Scotland) Act 1967, s 36(1), in relation to consultation by Secretary of State with the Joint Central Committee etc, and for purpose of power to make regulations or orders under s 36) (SI 1994/3075)

Police and Magistrates' Courts Act 1994 (c 29)—*cont*

s 59—*cont*	1 Apr 1995 (otherwise) (SI 1994/3075, but see further SI 1995/492 below)
	1 Apr 1995 (so far as not already in force (though already brought fully into force by SI 1994/3075)) (SI 1995/492)
60	21 Jul 1994 (so far as relates to service in accordance with arrangements made under Police (Scotland) Act 1967, s 12A(2)) (s 94(3)(c))
	1 Apr 1995 (so far as not already in force) (SI 1995/492)
61	*Not in force*
62	1 Jan 1995 (SI 1994/3075)
63(1)	1 Jan 1995 (SI 1994/3075)
(2)	1 Apr 1995 (SI 1995/492)
(3)	*Not in force*
(4)	21 Jul 1994 (so far as relates to service in accordance with arrangements made under Police (Scotland) Act 1967, s 12A(2)) (s 94(3)(c))
	1 Apr 1995 (so far as not already in force) (SI 1995/492)
(5)	1 Apr 1995 (SI 1995/492)
(6)	1 Jan 1995 (SI 1994/3075)
(7)(a)	21 Jul 1994 (so far as relates to service in accordance with arrangements made under Police (Scotland) Act 1967, s 12A(2)) (s 94(3)(c))
	1 Apr 1995 (so far as not already in force) (SI 1995/492)
(b)	1 Jan 1995 (SI 1994/3075)
(8)	*Not in force*
(9)(a)	13 Dec 1995 (SI 1995/3003)[1]
(b)	1 Jan 1995 (SI 1994/3075)
(10)	*Not in force*
64	1 Apr 1996 (SI 1995/492)
65	8 Aug 1994 (SI 1994/2025)
66	23 Aug 1994 (SI 1994/2151)
67	23 Aug 1994 (SI 1994/2151); prospectively repealed by Police (Amendment) (Northern Ireland) Order 1995, SI 1995/2993 (NI 17), art 32(2), Sch 2
68	23 Aug 1994 (SI 1994/2151)
69–71	1 Nov 1994 (subject to transitional provisions and savings relating to ss 70, 71) (SI 1994/2594)
72(1)–(5)	1 Apr 1995 (subject to transitional provisions) (SI 1995/685)
(6)	1 Apr 1995 (in relation to magistrates' courts committee for inner London area) (SI 1995/685)
	1 Oct 1995 (so far as inserts Justices of the Peace Act 1979, s 22(9)–(11), except in relation to magistrates' courts committee for inner London area) (SI 1995/685)
	1 Jan 1996 (so far as inserts Justices of the Peace Act 1979, s 22(8), except in relation to magistrates' courts committee for inner London area) (SI 1995/685)
73	1 Apr 1995 (SI 1995/685)
74	1 Nov 1994 (SI 1994/2594)
75	1 Apr 1995 (except so far as inserts Justices of the Peace Act 1979, s 24D(5), in relation to

Police and Magistrates' Courts Act 1994 (c 29)—*cont*

s 75—*cont*	appointments of justices' chief executives by magistrates' courts committees for Hampshire, Kent and Lincolnshire) (SI 1995/685)
	Not in force (exception noted above)
76, 77	1 Apr 1995 (SI 1995/685)
78	1 Nov 1994 (SI 1994/2594)
79	1 Nov 1994 (for purpose only of enabling a magistrates' courts committee for inner London area to be constituted in accordance with regulations made under s 21 of the 1979 Act as amended by s 71 of this Act) (SI 1994/2594)
	1 Apr 1995 (so far as not already in force) (SI 1995/685)
80, 81	1 Apr 1995 (SI 1995/685)
82	*Not in force*
83(1)	1 Apr 1995 (except in relation to inner London area) (SI 1995/685)
	Not in force (exception noted above)
(2)	1 Apr 1995 (so far as applies to Justices of the Peace Act 1979, s 57) (SI 1995/685)
	Not in force (otherwise)
84	1 Apr 1995 (SI 1995/685)
85–87	1 Nov 1994 (SI 1994/2594)
88(1)–(5)	1 Nov 1994 (SI 1994/2594)
(6)	1 Apr 1995 (SI 1995/685)
89, 90	1 Nov 1994 (SI 1994/2594)
91(1)	See Sch 8 below
(2), (3)	1 Apr 1995 (SI 1995/685)
92	1 Nov 1994 (SI 1994/2594)
93	See Sch 9 below
94–97	21 Jul 1994 (RA)
Sch 1	See note to s 1
2	21 Jul 1994 (for purpose of power to make regulations under Police Act 1964, Sch 1C, para 11) (s 94(3)(a)(ii))
	See note to s 1 otherwise
3	*Not in force*
4, para 1–4	1 Apr 1995 (SI 1994/3262)
5–14	See note to s 4
15(1)	See note to s 4
(2)	1 Apr 1995 (SI 1994/3262)
(3), (4)	See note to s 4
16–24	See note to s 4
25	See note to s 4 (and see also SI 1994/3262, art 4(8), providing that Sch 4, para 25 comes into force on 15 Jan 1995 for purposes of a direction under Local Government Act 1992, s 1)
26–41	See note to s 4
42	1 Apr 1995 (SI 1994/3262)
43–63	See note to s 4
5, para 1	31 Dec 1994 (subject to a transitional provision in respect of para 1(2)(a)) (SI 1994/3262)
2–4	1 Apr 1995 (SI 1994/3262)
5	See note to s 1
6, 7	1 Apr 1995 (SI 1994/3262)

Police and Magistrates' Courts Act 1994 (c 29)—*cont*

Sch 5, para 8	31 Dec 1994 (subject to a transitional provision in respect of para 8(3)) (SI 1994/3262)
9	1 Apr 1995 (SI 1994/3262)
10(1)	1 Oct 1994 (SI 1994/2025)
(2)	1 Apr 1995 (SI 1994/3262)
(3)	1 Oct 1994 (SI 1994/2025)
11, 12	*Not in force*
13, 14	1 Apr 1995 (SI 1994/3262)
15	See note to s 1
16	1 Oct 1994 (SI 1994/2025)
17–20	21 Jul 1994 (so far as relate to service in accordance with arrangements made under Police Act 1964, s 15A(2), Police (Scotland) Act 1967, s 12A(2)) (s 94(3)(c))
	1 Apr 1995 (otherwise) (SI 1994/3262)
21	1 Oct 1994 (SI 1994/2025)
22, 23	1 Apr 1995 (SI 1994/3262)
24(a)	1 Apr 1995 (SI 1994/3262)
(b)	*Not in force*
25–28	*Not in force*
29, 30	1 Apr 1995 (SI 1994/3262)
31–34	*Not in force*
35–38	1 Apr 1995 (SI 1994/3262)
39, 40	*Not in force*
6, 7	*Not in force*
8, Pt I, para 1	*Not in force*
2–4	1 Nov 1994 (SI 1994/2594)
5	1 Apr 1995 (SI 1995/685)
6–9	1 Nov 1994 (SI 1994/2594)
10–16	1 Apr 1995 (SI 1995/685)
17	1 Nov 1994 (SI 1994/2594)
18	1 Apr 1995 (SI 1995/685)
19(1)	See sub-paras (2), (3) below
(2)	3 Feb 1995 (subject to a saving) (SI 1995/42)
(3)	1 Apr 1995 (except so far as definition "responsible authority" relates to inner London area) (SI 1995/685)
	Not in force (exception noted above)
20, 21	1 Apr 1995 (SI 1995/685)
22	1 Nov 1994 (subject to a saving) (SI 1994/2594)
23	*Not in force*
II, para 24	*Not in force*
25–32	1 Apr 1995 (SI 1995/685)
33(1)–(4)	1 Apr 1995 (SI 1995/685)
(5)	*Not in force*
(6)	1 Apr 1995 (SI 1995/685)
34	1 Apr 1995 (SI 1995/685)
35	*Not in force*
9, Pt I	8 Aug 1994 (repeals in Metropolitan Police Act 1856; Police Act 1964, s 33(5); Drug Trafficking Offences Act 1986) (SI 1994/2025)
	In relation to repeal of Police Act 1964, s 25(5), see note to s 1
	23 Aug 1994 (repeals in Police Act (Northern Ireland) 1970) (SI 1994/2151)

Police and Magistrates' Courts Act 1994 (c 29)—*cont*

Sch 9, Pt I—*cont*

1 Oct 1994 (repeals in Licensing Act 1902; Police Negotiating Board Act 1980; Local Government Act 1985, s 30(2)) (SI 1994/2025)

31 Dec 1994 (repeals in Police Act 1964, s 12) (SI 1994/3262)

1 Jan 1995 (repeals of or in Police (Scotland) Act 1967, ss 24(3), 38(1)–(3), (5), Sch 4) (SI 1994/3075)

1 Apr 1995 (all entries so far as relate to enactments as they apply in England and Wales, except those in respect of Metropolitan Police Act 1856; Licensing Act 1902; Police Act 1964, ss 12, 33(5), 53(1), 60; Police Negotiating Board Act 1980; Police and Criminal Evidence Act 1984, ss 67(8), 85(8), 90(3), (4), (6), (8), 91, 92, 94, 97(4), 99(2), 101, 103, 104(1), (2), 105, Sch 4; Local Government Act 1985, s 30(2); Drug Trafficking Offences Act 1986; Courts and Legal Services Act 1990; Police Act (Northern Ireland) 1970) (SI 1994/3262)

1 Apr 1995 (S) (repeals in Police (Overseas Service) Act 1945; Police Act 1969; Police Pensions Act 1976; Overseas Development and Cooperation Act 1980) (SI 1995/492)

1 Apr 1995 (repeals in Police (Scotland) Act 1967, ss 6(2), 7(1), 31(2), (4)) (subject to transitional provisions) (SI 1995/492)

13 Dec 1995 (repeals of or in Police (Scotland) Act 1967, ss 7(2), 14(1), 26(2)(d), 51(1); Police and Criminal Evidence Act 1984, Sch 4, para 11) (SI 1995/3003)[1]

1 Apr 1996 (repeal in Police (Scotland) Act 1967, s 8(1)) (SI 1995/492)

Not in force (otherwise)

II

1 Nov 1994 (repeals of or in Justices of the Peace Act 1979, ss 12(7), 18(2), 19(3), (4), 21(1), 23(1), 24(1)(a), (2), (5), 24A(1), 70 (definition "joint committee area" only) and (for purpose specified in entry to s 79 of this Act above), repeal of s 35 of the 1979 Act) (SI 1994/2594)

1 Apr 1995 (repeals of or in Reserve and Auxiliary Forces (Protection of Civil Interests) Act 1951, s 48; Administration of Justice Act 1964, Sch 3, Pt II, para 29; Gaming Act 1968, Sch 2, para 2(2); Juries Act 1974, Sch 1, Pt I, Group B; Justices of the Peace Act 1979, ss 22(2), 26(1), (2), (4), (5), 27(1)–(5), (7), (9), 28(1A), 30(1), 35 (so far as not already in force), 36–38, 53(6), 57, 63(2), (4); Magistrates' Courts Act 1980, ss 68(7), 141(3), 145(1)(d); Local Government Act 1985, s 12; the Criminal Justice Act 1988, ss 164(3), 165; Courts and Legal Services Act 1990, s 10(3)–(5), Sch 18, para 25; Criminal Justice Act 1991, s 76(3), 79 (so far as applies to Justices of the Peace Act 1979, s 55(2)), 93(1), Sch 11, paras 40(2)(k), 41(2)(c)) (subject to transitional provisions) (SI 1995/685)

Police and Magistrates' Courts Act 1994 (c 29)—*cont*

Sch 9, Pt II—*cont*	*Not in force* (otherwise)

[1] Note that these provisions were to come into force on 1 Apr 1996 by virtue of SI 1995/492, which was subsequently amended by SI 1995/3003.

Race Relations (Remedies) Act 1994 (c 10)

RA: 3 May 1994

Commencement provision: s 3(3)

3 Jul 1994 (s 3(3))

Road Traffic Regulation (Special Events) Act 1994 (c 11)

RA: 3 May 1994

3 May 1994 (RA)

Sale and Supply of Goods Act 1994 (c 35)

RA: 3 Nov 1994

Commencement provision: s 8(2)

3 Jan 1995 (s 8(2))

Sale of Goods (Amendment) Act 1994 (c 32)

RA: 3 Nov 1994

Commencement provision: s 3(3)

3 Jan 1995 (s 3(3))

Social Security (Contributions) Act 1994 (c 1)

RA: 10 Feb 1994

10 Feb 1994 (RA; but note ss 1(2), 2(3), 3(2))

Social Security (Incapacity for Work) Act 1994 (c 18)

RA: 5 Jul 1994

Commencement provisions: s 16(2), (3); Social Security (Incapacity for Work) Act 1994 (Commencement) Order 1994, SI 1994/2926

s 1	13 Apr 1995 (SI 1994/2926)
2(1)	18 Nov 1994 (for purpose of authorising the making of regulations expressed to come into force on 13 Apr 1995) (SI 1994/2926) 13 Apr 1995 (otherwise) (SI 1994/2926)

Social Security (Incapacity for Work) Act 1994 (c 18)—*cont*

s 2(2)	13 Apr 1995 (SI 1994/2926)
(3)	18 Nov 1994 (SI 1994/2926)
(4)	13 Apr 1995 (SI 1994/2926)
(5)	18 Nov 1994 (for purpose of authorising the making of regulations expressed to come into force on 13 Apr 1995) (SI 1994/2926) 13 Apr 1995 (otherwise) (SI 1994/2926)
(6)	13 Apr 1995 (SI 1994/2926)
(7)	18 Nov 1994 (SI 1994/2926)
3(1)	18 Nov 1994 (for purpose of authorising the making of regulations expressed to come into force on 13 Apr 1995) (SI 1994/2926) 13 Apr 1995 (otherwise) (SI 1994/2926)
(2)	13 Apr 1995 (SI 1994/2926)
4	18 Nov 1994 (SI 1994/2926)
5, 6	18 Nov 1994 (for purpose of authorising the making of regulations expressed to come into force on 13 Apr 1995) (SI 1994/2926) 13 Apr 1995 (otherwise) (SI 1994/2926)
7	18 Nov 1994 (SI 1994/2926)
8(1)	6 Apr 1995 (SI 1994/2926)
(2)	18 Nov 1994 (SI 1994/2926)
(3), (4)	6 Apr 1995 (SI 1994/2926)
9(1)–(3)	18 Nov 1994 (for purpose of authorising the making of regulations expressed to come into force on 13 Apr 1995) (SI 1994/2926) 13 Apr 1995 (otherwise) (SI 1994/2926)
(4)	18 Nov 1994 (SI 1994/2926)
10(1)	18 Nov 1994 (for purpose of authorising the making of regulations expressed to come into force on 13 Apr 1995) (SI 1994/2926) 13 Apr 1995 (otherwise) (SI 1994/2926)
(2)	13 Apr 1995 (SI 1994/2926)
(3)	18 Nov 1994 (for purpose of authorising the making of regulations expressed to come into force on 13 Apr 1995) (SI 1994/2926) 13 Apr 1995 (otherwise) (SI 1994/2926)
11	13 Apr 1995 (SI 1994/2926)
12	18 Nov 1994 (SI 1994/2926)
13	13 Apr 1995 (SI 1994/2926)
14–16	5 Jul 1994 (s 16(2))
Sch 1, 2	13 Apr 1995 (SI 1994/2926)

State Hospitals (Scotland) Act 1994 (c 16)

RA: 5 Jul 1994

Commencement provisions: s 3(2), (3); State Hospitals (Scotland) Act 1994 Commencement Order 1995, SI 1995/576

1 Apr 1995 (SI 1995/576)

Statutory Sick Pay Act 1994 (c 2)

RA: 10 Feb 1994

Commencement provision: s 5(2)

s 1	6 Apr 1994 (s 5(2))
2–5	10 Feb 1994 (s 5(2))

Sunday Trading Act 1994 (c 20)

RA: 5 Jul 1994

Commencement provisions: ss 1, 9(3); Sunday Trading Act 1994 Appointed Day Order 1994, SI 1994/1841

s 1	5 Jul 1994 (RA)
2–5	26 Aug 1994 (SI 1994/1841)
6–8	5 Jul 1994 (RA)
9(1)	5 Jul 1994 (RA)
(2)	26 Aug 1994 (SI 1994/1841)
(3), (4)	5 Jul 1994 (RA)
Sch 1–5	26 Aug 1994 (SI 1994/1841)

Trade Marks Act 1994 (c 26)

RA: 21 Jul 1994

Commencement provisions: s 109; Trade Marks Act 1994 (Commencement) Order 1994, SI 1994/2550 31 Oct 1994 (SI 1994/2550; though note that, for certain purposes relating to the making of subordinate legislation, ss 4(4), 13(2), 25(1), (5), (6), 34(1), 35(5), 38(1), (2), 39(3), 40(4), 41(1), (3), 43(2), (3), (5), (6), 44(3), 45(2), 63(2), (3), 64(4), 65(1), (3)–(5), 66(2), 67(1), (2), 68(1), (3), 69, 76(1), 78, 79, 80(3), 81, 82, 88, 90, Sch 1, para 6(2), Sch 2, para 7(2), Sch 3, paras 10(2), 11(2), 12, 14(5) are brought into force on 29 Sep 1994, and note that ss 66(1), 80(1), (3) are brought into force on that date for certain purposes relating to the exercise of the registrar's powers)

Transport Police (Jurisdiction) Act 1994 (c 8)

RA: 24 Mar 1994

Commencement provision: s 2(2)

1 Apr 1994 (s 2(2))

Value Added Tax Act 1994 (c 23)

RA: 5 Jul 1994

Commencement provision: s 101(1)

1 Sep 1994 (s 101(1))

Vehicle Excise and Registration Act 1994 (c 22)

RA: 5 Jul 1994

Commencement provisions: s 66, Sch 4, para 9

1 Sep 1994 (s 66; though note that by Sch 4, para 9 to the Act, s 20 and the references thereto in ss 45(1)(b), 57(5) do not come into force until a day to be appointed by the Secretary of State)

1995

Activity Centres (Young Persons' Safety) Act 1995 (c 15)
RA: 28 Jun 1995

Commencement provision: s 5

28 Aug 1995 (s 5)

Agricultural Tenancies Act 1995 (c 8)
RA: 9 May 1995

Commencement provision: s 41(2)

1 Sep 1995 (s 41(2))

Appropriation Act 1995 (c 19)
RA: 19 Jul 1995

19 Jul 1995 (RA)

Atomic Energy Authority Act 1995 (c 37)
RA: 8 Nov 1995

8 Nov 1995 (RA)

Building Societies (Joint Account Holders) Act 1995 (c 5)
RA: 1 May 1995

1 May 1995 (RA) (and see s 2(2))

Carers (Recognition and Services) Act 1995 (c 12)
RA: 28 Jun 1995

Commencement provision: s 5(2)

1 Apr 1996 (s 5(2))

Charities (Amendment) Act 1995 (c 48)
RA: 8 Nov 1995

8 Nov 1995 (RA)

Child Support Act 1995 (c 34)

RA: 19 Jul 1995

Commencement provisions: s 30(3), (4); Child Support Act 1995 (Commencement No 1) Order 1995, SI 1995/2302; Child Support Act 1995 (Commencement No 2) Order 1995, SI 1995/3262

s 1–8	*Not in force*
9	22 Jan 1996 (in respect of insertion of Child Support Act 1991, s 28I(4)) (SI 1995/3262) *Not in force* (otherwise)
10	*Not in force*
11	22 Jan 1996 (SI 1995/3262)
12(1)	See sub-ss (2)–(7) below
(2)–(4)	22 Jan 1996 (SI 1995/3262)
(5)	1 Oct 1995 (for the purpose of regulations under Child Support Act 1991, s 17(5)) (SI 1995/2302) 22 Jan 1996 (otherwise) (SI 1995/3262)
(6)	22 Jan 1996 (SI 1995/3262)
(7)	1 Oct 1995 (for the purpose of regulations under Child Support Act 1991, s 17(7)) (SI 1995/2302) 22 Jan 1996 (otherwise) (SI 1995/3262)
13–15	22 Jan 1996 (SI 1995/3262)
16, 17	18 Dec 1995 (SI 1995/3262)
18–21	4 Sep 1995 (SI 1995/2302)
22	*Not in force*
23	4 Sep 1995 (so far as inserts Child Support Act 1991, s 41B(1), (2), (7)) (SI 1995/2302) 1 Oct 1995 (otherwise) (SI 1995/2302)
24, 25	1 Oct 1995 (SI 1995/2302)
26(1)–(3)	4 Sep 1995 (SI 1995/2302)
(4)(a)	*Not in force*
(b)	4 Sep 1995 (SI 1995/2302)
(c)	1 Oct 1995 (SI 1995/2302)
(5), (6)	4 Sep 1995 (SI 1995/2302)
27, 28	4 Sep 1995 (SI 1995/2302)
29	19 Jul 1995 (s 30(3))
30(1)–(4)	19 Jul 1995 (s 30(3))
(5)	See Sch 3 below
(6)	19 Jul 1995 (s 30(3))
Sch 1, 2	*Not in force*
3, para 1	1 Oct 1995 (so far as inserts Income and Corporation Taxes Act 1988, s 617(2)(ae)) (SI 1995/2302) *Not in force* (otherwise)
2	4 Sep 1995 (SI 1995/2302)
3(1)	1 Oct 1995 (SI 1995/2302)
(2)	4 Sep 1995 (SI 1995/2302)
4	4 Sep 1995 (SI 1995/2302)
5–7	*Not in force*
8	4 Sep 1995 (SI 1995/2302)
9	*Not in force*
10	4 Sep 1995 (SI 1995/2302)
11, 12	1 Oct 1995 (SI 1995/2302)
13	*Not in force*
14–16	4 Sep 1995 (SI 1995/2302)
17	*Not in force*

Child Support Act 1995 (c 34)—*cont*

Sch 3, para 18	18 Dec 1995 (SI 1995/3262)
19	4 Sep 1995 (SI 1995/2302)
20	*Not in force*

Children (Scotland) Act 1995 (c 36)

RA: 19 Jul 1995

Commencement provisions: s 105(1), (2); Children (Scotland) Act 1995 (Commencement No 1) Order 1995, SI 1995/2787

s 1(1)–(3)	1 Nov 1995 (for purpose of bringing into force ss 15, 103, Sch 4, para 12) (SI 1995/2787) *Not in force* (otherwise)
(4)	*Not in force*
2–14	*Not in force*
15	1 Nov 1995 (SI 1995/2787)
16–34	*Not in force*
35	1 Nov 1995 (SI 1995/2787)
36	*Not in force*
37	1 Nov 1995 (SI 1995/2787)
38–48	*Not in force*
49	Repealed
50–98	*Not in force*
99	1 Nov 1995 (SI 1995/2787)
100–102	*Not in force*
103, 104	1 Nov 1995 (SI 1995/2787)
105(1), (2)	19 Jul 1995 (RA)
(3)	*Not in force*
(4)	See Sch 4 below
(5)	See Sch 5 below
(6)–(10)	19 Jul 1995 (RA)
Sch 1–3	*Not in force*
4, para 1–11	*Not in force*
12, 13	1 Nov 1995 (SI 1995/2787)
14–17	*Not in force*
18(1)	See sub-paras (2), (3) below
(2)	1 Nov 1995 (SI 1995/2787)
(3)	*Not in force*
19–23	*Not in force*
24	Repealed
25, 26	*Not in force*
27	Repealed
28	*Not in force*
29	Repealed
30–39	*Not in force*
40(a)	*Not in force*
(b)	1 Nov 1995 (SI 1995/2787)
41–44	*Not in force*
45	1 Nov 1995 (SI 1995/2787)
46–52	*Not in force*
53(1)	See sub-paras (2)(5) below
(2)	*Not in force*
(3)	1 Nov 1995 (SI 1995/2787)
(4), (5)	*Not in force*
54–60	*Not in force*

Children (Scotland) Act 1995 (c 36)—*cont*

Sch 5	1 Nov 1995 (repeals in Registration of Births, Deaths and Marriages (Scotland) Act 1965, s 43) (SI 1995/2787)
	Not in force (otherwise)

Church of England (Miscellaneous Provisions) Measure 1995 (No 2)

RA: 19 Jul 1995

Commencement provision: s 15(2)

Not in force

Civil Evidence Act 1995 (c 38)

RA: 8 Nov 1995

Commencement provision: s 16(2)

Not in force

Civil Evidence (Family Mediation) (Scotland) Act 1995 (c 6)

RA: 1 May 1995

Commencement provisions: s 3(3); Civil Evidence (Family Mediation) (Scotland) Act 1995 (Commencement and Transitional Provision) Order 1996, SI 1996/125

19 Feb 1996 (but Act not to apply to any civil proceedings in which any evidence has been given or heard (in whole or in part) at any time prior to that date) (SI 1996/125)

Commonwealth Development Corporation Act 1995 (c 9)

RA: 28 Jun 1995

28 Jun 1995 (RA)

Consolidated Fund Act 1995 (c 2)

RA: 23 Mar 1995

23 Mar 1995 (RA)

Criminal Appeal Act 1995 (c 35)

RA: 19 Jul 1995

Commencement provisions. s 32; Criminal Appeal Act 1995 (Commencement No 1 and Transitional Provisions) Order 1995, SI 1995/3061

s 1, 2	1 Jan 1996 (subject to transitional provisions) (SI 1995/3061)
3	*Not in force*

Criminal Appeal Act 1995 (c 35)—*cont*

s 4	1 Jan 1996 (subject to transitional provisions) (SI 1995/3061)
5	*Not in force*
6	1 Jan 1996 (subject to transitional provisions) (SI 1995/3061)
7	1 Jan 1996 (subject to transitional provisions, and except in so far as relating to references by the Criminal Cases Review Commission) (SI 1995/3061)
	Not in force otherwise
8–25	*Not in force*
26–28	1 Jan 1996 (subject to transitional provisions) (SI 1995/3061)
29	See Schs 2, 3 below
30	1 Jan 1996 (subject to transitional provisions) (SI 1995/3061)
31(1)(a)	*Not in force*
(b)	1 Jan 1996 (subject to transitional provisions) (SI 1995/3061)
(2)	1 Jan 1996 (subject to transitional provisions) (SI 1995/3061)
32–34	1 Jan 1996 (subject to transitional provisions) (SI 1995/3061)
Sch 1	*Not in force*
2, para 1, 2	1 Jan 1996 (subject to transitional provisions) (SI 1995/3061)
3	*Not in force*
4(1)–(3)	1 Jan 1996 (subject to transitional provisions) (SI 1995/3061)
(4)	*Not in force*
(5)	1 Jan 1996 (subject to transitional provisions) (SI 1995/3061)
5, 6	1 Jan 1996 (subject to transitional provisions) (SI 1995/3061)
7–11	*Not in force*
12(1)–(4)	1 Jan 1996 (subject to transitional provisions) (SI 1995/3061)
(5)	*Not in force*
(6)	1 Jan 1996 (subject to transitional provisions) (SI 1995/3061)
13, 14	*Not in force*
15	1 Jan 1996 (subject to transitional provisions) (SI 1995/3061)
16	*Not in force*
17	1 Jan 1996 (subject to transitional provisions) (SI 1995/3061)
18, 19	*Not in force*
3	1 Jan 1996 (so far as relates to repeals of or in the Criminal Appeal Act 1968, s 23(3), the Courts-Martial (Appeals) Act 1968, the Criminal Law Act 1977, the Magistrates' Courts Act 1980, the Criminal Appeal (Northern Ireland) Act 1980, ss 16(1), 25(3), the Supreme Court Act 1981, the Criminal Justice Act 1988, the Criminal Procedure (Insanity and Unfitness to Plead) Act

Criminal Appeal Act 1995 (c 35)—*cont*

Sch 3—*cont* 1991, Sch 3, para 3(1), and subject to transitional provisions) (SI 1995/3061)
Not in force (otherwise)

Criminal Injuries Compensation Act 1995 (c 53)

RA: 8 Nov 1995

8 Nov 1995 (RA)

Criminal Justice (Scotland) Act 1995 (c 20)

Whole Act repealed by Criminal Procedure (Consequential Provisions) Act 1995, s 6(1), Sch 5, as from 1 Apr 1996, subject to savings for prospective amendments; see s 4, Sch 3, paras 3, 16 thereto

Commencement provisions: s 118(2), (3) (repealed as noted above); Criminal Justice (Scotland) Act 1995 (Commencement No 1, Transitional Provisions and Savings) Order 1995, SI 1995/2295

Criminal Law (Consolidation) (Scotland) Act 1995 (c 39)

RA: 8 Nov 1995

Commencement provision: s 53(2)

1 Apr 1996 (s 53(2)), subject to transitional provisions and savings in Criminal Procedure (Consequential Provisions) (Scotland) Act 1995, in particular for consolidated provisions which are not in force at that date; see s 4, Sch 3 thereto

Criminal Procedure (Consequential Provisions) (Scotland) Act 1995 (c 40)

RA: 8 Nov 1995

Commencement provision: s 7(2)

1 Apr 1996 (s 7(2)), subject to transitional provisions and savings, in particular for amendments by consolidated enactments which are not in force at that date; see s 4, Sch 3 thereto

Criminal Procedure (Scotland) Act 1995 (c 46)

RA: 8 Nov 1995

Commencement provision: s 309(2)

1 Apr 1996 (s 309(2)), subject to transitional provisions and savings in Criminal Procedure (Consequential Provisions) (Scotland) Act 1995, in particular for consolidated provisions which are not in force at that date; see s 4, Sch 3 thereto

Crown Agents Act 1995 (c 24)

RA: 19 Jul 1995

19 Jul 1995 (RA) (note that certain provisions of this Act have effect as from "the appointed day" or as from the dissolution of the Crown Agents—as at 1 February 1996 no such day had been appointed under s 1(1) and no such dissolution order had been made under s 8(4))

Disability Discrimination Act 1995 (c 50)

RA: 8 Nov 1995

Commencement provisions: s 70(2), (3); Disability Discrimination Act 1995 (Commencement No 1) Order 1995, SI 1995/3330; Disability Discrimination Act 1995 (Commencement No 1) Order (Northern Ireland) 1996, SR 1996/1

s 1–49	*Not in force*
50–52	1 Jan 1996 (EW, S) (SI 1995/3330); 2 Jan 1996 (NI) (SR 1996/1)
53–69	*Not in force*
70(1)–(3)	8 Nov 1995 (s 70(2))
(4), (5)	*Not in force*
(6)	8 Nov 1995 (s 70(2))
(7)	*Not in force*
(8)	8 Nov 1995 (s 70(2))
Sch 1–4	*Not in force*
5	1 Jan 1996 (EW, S) (SI 1995/3330); 2 Jan 1996 (NI) (SR 1996/1)
6, 7	*Not in force*
8	8 Nov 1995 (s 70(2))

Environment Act 1995 (c 25)

RA: 19 Jul 1995

Commencement provisions: s 125(2)–(5); Environment Act 1995 (Commencement No 1) Order 1995, SI 1995/1983; Environment Act 1995 (Commencement No 2) Order 1995, SI 1995/2649; Environment Act 1995 (Commencement No 3) Order 1995, SI 1995/2765; Environment Act 1995 (Commencement No 4 and Saving Provisions) Order 1995, SI 1995/2950

s 1	28 Jul 1995 (SI 1995/1983)
2	*Not in force*
3(1)	*Not in force*
(2)–(8)	28 Jul 1995 (SI 1995/1983)
4	28 Jul 1995 (SI 1995/1983)
5, 6	*Not in force*
7	28 Jul 1995 (SI 1995/1983)
8	*Not in force*
9	28 Jul 1995 (SI 1995/1983)
10, 11	*Not in force*
12	28 Jul 1995 (SI 1995/1983)
13–19	*Not in force*
20–23	12 Oct 1995 (SI 1995/2649)
24–29	*Not in force*
30–32	12 Oct 1995 (SI 1995/2649)
33–35	*Not in force*

Environment Act 1995 (c 25)—*cont*

s 36	12 Oct 1995 (SI 1995/2649)
37(1), (2)	28 Jul 1995 (SI 1995/1983)
(3)–(8)	*Not in force*
(9)	28 Jul 1995 (SI 1995/1983)
38–40	28 Jul 1995 (SI 1995/1983)
41	21 Sep 1995 (so far as confers power to make schemes imposing charges) (SI 1995/1983) *Not in force* (otherwise)
42	21 Sep 1995 (SI 1995/1983)
43–52	28 Jul 1995 (SI 1995/1983)
53–55	*Not in force*
56	28 Jul 1995 (SI 1995/1983)
57, 58	21 Sep 1995 (so far as confer power on Secretary of State to make regulations or orders, give directions or issue guidance, or so far as make provision with respect to the exercise of any such power) (SI 1995/1983) *Not in force* (otherwise)
59	12 Oct 1995 (so far as confers power on Secretary of State to make regulations) (SI 1995/2649) *Not in force* (otherwise)
60	*Not in force*
61–73	19 Sep 1995 (s 125(2))
74	19 Jul 1995 (s 125(3))
75–77	19 Sep 1995 (s 125(2))
78	See Sch 10 below
79	19 Sep 1995 (s 125(2))
80–92	*Not in force*
93–95	21 Sep 1995 (SI 1995/1983)
96(1)	See Schs 13, 14 below
(2)	1 Nov 1995 (SI 1995/2765)
(3)	*Not in force*
(4)	1 Nov 1995 (so far as repeals Town and Country Planning Act 1990, s 105) (SI 1995/2765) *Not in force* (otherwise)
(5), (6)	1 Nov 1995 (EW) (SI 1995/2765) *Not in force* (S)
97–103	21 Sep 1995 (SI 1995/1983)
104	*Not in force*
105	See Sch 15 below
106–114	*Not in force*
115(1)	1 Apr 1996 (so far as relates to other provisions of this section brought into force by SI 1995/2950) (SI 1995/2950) *Not in force* (otherwise)
(2)	1 Apr 1996 (so far as relates to Pt III of this Act) (SI 1995/2950) *Not in force* (otherwise)
(3), (4)	1 Apr 1996 (so far as relates to provisions of sub-s (2) brought into force by SI 1995/2950) (SI 1995/2950) *Not in force* (otherwise)
(5)	*Not in force*
(6)	1 Apr 1996 (so far as relates to provisions of sub-s (2) brought into force by SI 1995/2950) (SI 1995/2950) *Not in force* (otherwise)

Environment Act 1995 (c 25)—*cont*

s 116	See Sch 21 below
117–119	*Not in force*
120(1)	28 Jul 1995 (so far as confers powers to make regulations) (SI 1995/1983)
	See Sch 22 below (otherwise)
(2)	See Sch 23 below
(3)	See Sch 24 below
(4)–(6)	28 Jul 1995 (SI 1995/1983)
121–124	28 Jul 1995 (SI 1995/1983)
125	19 Jul 1995 (s 125(3))
Sch 1	28 Jul 1995 (SI 1995/1983)
2	28 Jul 1995 (so far as relates to s 3) (SI 1995/1983)
	Not in force (so far as relates to s 22)
3	28 Jul 1995 (SI 1995/1983)
4–6	*Not in force*
7, para 1–6	19 Sep 1995 (s 125(2))
7(1)	19 Sep 1995 (s 125(2))
(2)	*Not in force*
(3)–(5)	19 Sep 1995 (s 125(2))
8–20	19 Sep 1995 (s 125(2))
8, 9	19 Sep 1995 (s 125(2))
10, para 1	23 Nov 1995 (SI 1995/2950)
2(1)	23 Nov 1995 (SI 1995/2950)
(2)	1 Apr 1996 (SI 1995/2950)
(3)–(8)	23 Nov 1995 (SI 1995/2950)
(9)(a)	23 Nov 1995 (SI 1995/2950)
(b)	1 Apr 1996 (SI 1995/2950)
(c), (d)	23 Nov 1995 (SI 1995/2950)
3–7	23 Nov 1995 (SI 1995/2950)
8(1)	1 Apr 1996 (SI 1995/2950)
(2)	23 Nov 1995 (SI 1995/2950)
(3)	1 Apr 1996 (SI 1995/2950)
9	23 Nov 1995 (SI 1995/2950)
10(1)	23 Nov 1995 (SI 1995/2950)
(2)	*Not in force*
(3)	23 Nov 1995 (SI 1995/2950)
11, 12	23 Nov 1995 (SI 1995/2950)
13	1 Apr 1996 (SI 1995/2950)
14, 15	23 Nov 1995 (SI 1995/2950)
16	1 Apr 1996 (SI 1995/2950)
17–19	23 Nov 1995 (SI 1995/2950)
20	1 Apr 1996 (SI 1995/2950)
21	23 Nov 1995 (SI 1995/2950)
22(1), (2)	*Not in force*[1]
(3)	1 Apr 1996 (subject to a saving) (SI 1995/2950)
(4)(a), (b)	1 Apr 1996 (SI 1995/2950)
(c)	*Not in force*
(5)	1 Apr 1996 (subject to a saving) (SI 1995/2950)
(6)	*Not in force*
(7)	*Not in force*; prospectively repealed by s 120(3) of, Sch 24 to, this Act
23–26	23 Nov 1995 (SI 1995/2950)
27	*Not in force*
28–31	23 Nov 1995 (SI 1995/2950)
32(1)–(13)	23 Nov 1995 (subject to a saving in relation to sub-s (2)) (SI 1995/2950)

Environment Act 1995 (c 25)—*cont*

Sch 10, para 32(14)	*Not in force*
(15)–(18)	23 Nov 1995 (SI 1995/2950)
33(1)–(5)	23 Nov 1995 (SI 1995/2950)
(6)–(8)	*Not in force*
34	23 Nov 1995 (SI 1995/2950)
35	23 Nov 1995 (so far as adds the Local Government Finance Act 1992, s 35(5)(c) and the word "or" immediately preceding it) (SI 1995/2950)
	Not in force (otherwise)
36, 37	23 Nov 1995 (SI 1995/2950)
38(1)	23 Nov 1995 (SI 1995/2950)
(2)	*Not in force*
11, 12	*Not in force*
13, 14	1 Nov 1995 (EW) (SI 1995/2765)
	Not in force (S)
15, para 1–12	*Not in force*
13	1 Jan 1999 (SI 1995/1983)
14(1)	1 Jan 1999 (SI 1995/1983)
(2), (3)	*Not in force*
(4)	1 Jan 1999 (SI 1995/1983)
15, 16	*Not in force*
17	1 Jan 1999 (SI 1995/1983)
18, 19	*Not in force*
20	1 Jan 1999 (SI 1995/1983)
21–24	*Not in force*
25	21 Sep 1995 (SI 1995/1983)
26(1)	21 Sep 1995 (SI 1995/1983)
(2)	1 Jan 1999 (SI 1995/1983)
16–20	*Not in force*
21, para 1	*Not in force*
2(1)–(3)	21 Sep 1995 (SI 1995/1983)
(4)	*Not in force*
3–6	*Not in force*
22, para 1–3	*Not in force*
4	28 Jul 1995 (SI 1995/1983)
5–14	*Not in force*
15	12 Oct 1995 (SI 1995/2649)
16–18	*Not in force*
19–27	*Not in force*; prospectively repealed by s 120(3) of, Sch 24 to, this Act
28	*Not in force*
29(1)	See sub-paras (2)–(35) below
(2)–(21)	*Not in force*
(22)	12 Oct 1995 (so far as confers power on Secretary of State to make regulations) (SI 1995/2649)
	Not in force (otherwise)
(23)–(35)	*Not in force*
30	*Not in force*
31	28 Jul 1995 (SI 1995/1983)
32–36	*Not in force*
37(1)	21 Sep 1995 (SI 1995/1983)
(2), (3)	*Not in force*
(4)	21 Sep 1995 (SI 1995/1983)
(5)–(8)	*Not in force*
38, 39	21 Sep 1995 (SI 1995/1983)
40, 41	*Not in force*
42	28 Jul 1995 (SI 1995/1983)

Environment Act 1995 (c 25)—*cont*

Sch 22, para 43–50	*Not in force*
51(1)–(3)	12 Oct 1995 (SI 1995/2649)
(4)	*Not in force*
(5)	12 Oct 1995 (SI 1995/2649)
52	*Not in force*
53	12 Oct 1995 (SI 1995/2649)
54–75	*Not in force*
76(1)	21 Sep 1995 (SI 1995/1983)
(2)	*Not in force*
(3)	21 Sep 1995 (SI 1995/1983)
(4)–(7)	*Not in force*
(8)(a)	19 Jul 1995 (s 125(3))
(b)	*Not in force*
77–79	*Not in force*
80(1), (2)	21 Sep 1995 (SI 1995/1983)
(3)	*Not in force*
81	*Not in force*
82(1)	See sub-paras (2)–(5) below
(2)–(4)	*Not in force*
(5)	21 Sep 1995 (so far as confers power on Secretary of State to make regulations or makes provision with respect to the exercise of any such power) (SI 1995/1983)
	Not in force (otherwise)
83–132	*Not in force*
133(1)	21 Sep 1995 (SI 1995/1983)
(2)	*Not in force*
134	*Not in force*
135	19 Jul 1995 (s 125(3))
136	*Not in force*
137–139	21 Sep 1995 (SI 1995/1983)
140–146	*Not in force*
147	21 Sep 1995 (SI 1995/1983)
148–152	*Not in force*
153	21 Sep 1995 (SI 1995/1983)
154–161	*Not in force*
162	21 Sep 1995 (so far as confers power on Secretary of State to make regulations or makes provision with respect to the exercise of any such power) (SI 1995/1983)
	Not in force (otherwise)
163–181	*Not in force*
182	21 Sep 1995 (SI 1995/1983); prospectively repealed by s 120(3) of, Sch 24 to, this Act
183–186	*Not in force*
187(1)	21 Sep 1995 (SI 1995/1983)
(2)	*Not in force*
188–191	*Not in force*
192	21 Sep 1995 (SI 1995/1983)
193–212	*Not in force*
213(1)	28 Jul 1995 (SI 1995/1983)
(2)(a)	*Not in force*
(b)	28 Jul 1995 (SI 1995/1983)
(3)	28 Jul 1995 (SI 1995/1983)
(4), (5)	*Not in force*
214–222	*Not in force*
223(1)(a), (b)	*Not in force*

Environment Act 1995 (c 25)—*cont*

Sch 22, para 223(1)(c)	28 Jul 1995 (SI 1995/1983)
(2)	*Not in force*
224–230	*Not in force*
231	*Not in force*; prospectively repealed by s 120(3) of, Sch 24 to, this Act
232, 233	*Not in force*
23, para 1–13	*Not in force*
14(1)–(4)	*Not in force*
(5), (6)	1 Jan 1999 (SI 1995/1983)
(7)	*Not in force*
(8)	1 Jan 1999 (definitions "grating" and "the substitution date") (SI 1995/1983) *Not in force* (otherwise)
15–24	*Not in force*
24	21 Sep 1995 (repeal of Water Resources Act 1991, ss 68, 69(5), 126(6), 129(4)) (SI 1995/1983) 1 Jan 1999 (repeals in Salmon and Freshwater Fisheries Act 1975, ss 30, 41(1)) (SI 1995/1983) 1 Nov 1995 (repeal of Town and Country Planning Act 1990, s 105) (SI 1995/2765) *Not in force* (otherwise)

[1] Sch 10, para 22(1) repealed as from coming into force of repeal by Sch 24 to this Act of Wildlife and Countryside Act 1981, s 39(5)(a) (ss 120(3), 125(3), Sch 10, para 22(7), Sch 24)

European Communities (Finance) Act 1995 (c 1)

RA: 16 Jan 1995

16 Jan 1995 (RA)

Finance Act 1995 (c 4)

RA: 1 May 1995

See the note concerning Finance Acts at the front of this book

Gas Act 1995 (c 45)

RA: 8 Nov 1995

Commencement provisions: s 18(2)(4)

s 1–7	*Not in force*
8(1)	*Not in force*
(2)	8 Nov 1995 (RA)
9, 10	*Not in force*
11(1)–(5)	8 Nov 1995 (RA)
(6), (7)	*Not in force*
12	*Not in force*
13	8 Nov 1995 (RA)
14–16	*Not in force*
17(1), (2)	8 Nov 1995 (RA)
(3), (4)	*Not in force*
(5)	See Sch 6 below
18	8 Nov 1995 (RA)

Gas Act 1995 (c 45)—*cont*

Sch 1–4	*Not in force*
5	8 Nov 1995 (RA)
6	8 Nov 1995 (RA) (so far as relating to Gas Act 1986, s 62(7))
	Not in force (otherwise)

Geneva Conventions (Amendments) Act 1995 (c 27)

RA: 19 Jul 1995

Commencement provision: s 7(2)

Not in force

Goods Vehicles (Licensing of Operators) Act 1995 (c 23)

RA: 19 Jul 1995

Commencement provisions: ss 50(2), 61; Goods Vehicles (Licensing of Operators) Act 1995 (Commencement and Transitional Provisions) Order 1995, SI 1995/2181

s 1–49	1 Jan 1996 (subject to transitional provisions) (SI 1995/2181)
50	*Not in force*
51–62	1 Jan 1996 (SI 1995/2181)
Sch 1–4	1 Jan 1996 (SI 1995/2181)
5	*Not in force*
6–8	1 Jan 1996 (SI 1995/2181)

Health Authorities Act 1995 (c 17)

RA: 28 Jun 1995

Commencement provisions: ss 1(2), 2(3), 4(2), 5(2), 8(1)

s 1(1)	28 Jun 1995 (regulations etc)[1] (s 8(1))
	1 Apr 1996 (otherwise) (s 1(2))
(2)	28 Jun 1995 (RA)
2(1)	See Sch 1 below
(2), (3)	28 Jun 1995 (RA)
3	28 Jun 1995 (RA)[2]
4(1)	See Sch 2 below
(2)	28 Jun 1995 (RA)
5(1)	See Sch 3 below
(2)	28 Jun 1995 (RA)
6–10	28 Jun 1995 (RA)
Sch 1	28 Jun 1995 (regulations etc)[1] (s 8(1))
	1 Apr 1996 (otherwise) (s 2(3))
2	28 Jun 1995 (regulations etc)[1] (s 8(1))
	1 Apr 1996 (otherwise) (s 4(2))
3	28 Jun 1995 (repeal in National Health Service Act 1977, s 18(3)) (RA)
	1 Apr 1996 (otherwise) (s 5(2))

Health Authorities Act 1995 (c 17)—*cont*

[1] "regulations etc" means "so far as is necessary for enabling the making of any regulations, orders, directions, schemes or appointments" (s 8(1))

[2] whole section (apart from sub-s (8)) repealed as from 1 Apr 1996 (s 3(10))

Home Energy Conservation Act 1995 (c 10)

RA: 28 Jun 1995

Commencement provisions: s 9(2), (3); Home Energy Conservation Act 1995 (Commencement) Order (Northern Ireland) 1995, SR 1995/455; Home Energy Conservation Act 1995 (Commencement No 2) (England) Order 1995, SI 1995/3340

s 1, 2	1 Apr 1996 (NI, E) (SR 1995/455; SI 1995/3340); *not in force* (W, S)
3(1)	1 Jan 1996 (NI) (SR 1995/455); 15 Jan 1996 (E) (SI 1995/3340); *not in force* (W, S)
(2)–(4)	1 Apr 1996 (NI, E) (SR 1995/455; SI 1995/3340); *not in force* (W, S)
4(1), (2)	1 Jan 1996 (NI) (SR 1995/455); 15 Jan 1996 (E) (SI 1995/3340); *not in force* (W, S)
(3)	1 Apr 1996 (NI, E) (SR 1995/455; SI 1995/3340); *not in force* (W, S)
5–9	1 Apr 1996 (NI, E) (SR 1995/455; SI 1995/3340); *not in force* (W, S)

Insurance Companies (Reserves) Act 1995 (c 29)

RA: 19 Jul 1995

Commencement provision: s 4(2)

s 1	*Not in force*
2	19 Jul 1995 (RA)
3	*Not in force*
4	19 Jul 1995 (RA)

Jobseekers Act 1995 (c 18)

RA: 28 Jun 1995

Commencement provisions: s 41(2), (3); Jobseekers Act 1995 (Commencement No 1) Order 1995, SI 1995/3228

s 1	*Not in force*
2(1)(a), (b)	*Not in force*
(c)	12 Dec 1995 (for purpose of authorising regulations to be made) (SI 1995/3228)
	Not in force (otherwise)
(d)	*Not in force*
(2), (3)	*Not in force*
(4)(a)	*Not in force*
(b)	12 Dec 1995 (for purpose of authorising regulations to be made) (SI 1995/3228)
	Not in force (otherwise)
(c)	*Not in force*
3(1)(a)–(e)	*Not in force*

Jobseekers Act 1995 (c 18)—*cont*

s 3(1)(f)(i), (ii)	*Not in force*
(iii)	12 Dec 1995 (for purpose of authorising regulations to be made) (SI 1995/3228) *Not in force* (otherwise)
(2)–(4)	12 Dec 1995 (for purpose of authorising regulations to be made) (SI 1995/3228) *Not in force* (otherwise)
4(1)(a)	*Not in force*
(b)	12 Dec 1995 (for purpose of authorising regulations to be made) (SI 1995/3228) *Not in force* (otherwise)
(2)	12 Dec 1995 (for purpose of authorising regulations to be made) (SI 1995/3228) *Not in force* (otherwise)
(3)	*Not in force*
(4), (5)	12 Dec 1995 (for purpose of authorising regulations to be made) (SI 1995/3228) *Not in force* (otherwise)
(6)–(11)	*Not in force*
(12)	12 Dec 1995 (for purpose of authorising regulations to be made) (SI 1995/3228) *Not in force* (otherwise)
5(1), (2)	*Not in force*
(3)	12 Dec 1995 (for purpose of authorising regulations to be made) (SI 1995/3228) *Not in force* (otherwise)
6(1)	*Not in force*
(2)–(5)	12 Dec 1995 (for purpose of authorising regulations to be made) (SI 1995/3228) *Not in force* (otherwise)
(6)	*Not in force*
(7), (8)	12 Dec 1995 (for purpose of authorising regulations to be made) (SI 1995/3228) *Not in force* (otherwise)
(9)	*Not in force*
7(1)	*Not in force*
(2)–(6)	12 Dec 1995 (for purpose of authorising regulations to be made) (SI 1995/3228) *Not in force* (otherwise)
(7)	*Not in force*
(8)	12 Dec 1995 (for purpose of authorising regulations to be made) (SI 1995/3228) *Not in force* (otherwise)
8	12 Dec 1995 (for purpose of authorising regulations to be made) (SI 1995/3228) *Not in force* (otherwise)
9(1)	12 Dec 1995 (for purpose of authorising regulations to be made) (SI 1995/3228) *Not in force* (otherwise)
(2)–(7)	*Not in force*
(8)	12 Dec 1995 (for purpose of authorising regulations to be made) (SI 1995/3228) *Not in force* (otherwise)
(9)	*Not in force*
(10)–(12)	12 Dec 1995 (for purpose of authorising regulations to be made) (SI 1995/3228) *Not in force* (otherwise)

Jobseekers Act 1995 (c 18)—*cont*

s 9(13)	12 Dec 1995
10(1)	12 Dec 1995 (for purpose of authorising regulations to be made) (SI 1995/3228) *Not in force* (otherwise)
(2)–(5)	*Not in force*
(6)(a), (b)	*Not in force*
(c)	12 Dec 1995 (for purpose of authorising regulations to be made) (SI 1995/3228) *Not in force* (otherwise)
(d)	*Not in force*
(7)	12 Dec 1995 (for purpose of authorising regulations to be made) (SI 1995/3228) *Not in force* (otherwise)
(8)	*Not in force*
11(1)	*Not in force*
(2)	12 Dec 1995 (for purpose of authorising regulations to be made) (SI 1995/3228) *Not in force* (otherwise)
(3), (4)	*Not in force*
(5)	12 Dec 1995 (for purpose of authorising regulations to be made) (SI 1995/3228) *Not in force* (otherwise)
(6)	*Not in force*
(7), (8)	12 Dec 1995 (for purpose of authorising regulations to be made) (SI 1995/3228) *Not in force* (otherwise)
(9)	*Not in force*
12, 13	12 Dec 1995 (for purpose of authorising regulations to be made) (SI 1995/3228) *Not in force* (otherwise)
14	*Not in force*
15(1)	12 Dec 1995 (for purpose of authorising regulations to be made) (SI 1995/3228) *Not in force* (otherwise)
(2)(a)–(c)	*Not in force*
(d)	12 Dec 1995 (for purpose of authorising regulations to be made) (SI 1995/3228) *Not in force* (otherwise)
(3), (4)	*Not in force*
(5), (6)	12 Dec 1995 (for purpose of authorising regulations to be made) (SI 1995/3228) *Not in force* (otherwise)
(7)–(10)	*Not in force*
16	*Not in force*
17(1)	12 Dec 1995 (for purpose of authorising regulations to be made) (SI 1995/3228) *Not in force* (otherwise)
(2)–(5)	*Not in force*
18	*Not in force*
19(1)	*Not in force*
(2)	12 Dec 1995 (for purpose of authorising regulations to be made) (SI 1995/3228) *Not in force* (otherwise)
(3)	*Not in force*
(4)	12 Dec 1995 (for purpose of authorising regulations to be made) (SI 1995/3228) *Not in force* (otherwise)

Jobseekers Act 1995 (c 18)—*cont*

s 19(5), (6)	*Not in force*
(7), (8)	12 Dec 1995 (for purpose of authorising regulations to be made) (SI 1995/3228) *Not in force* (otherwise)
(9)	*Not in force*
(10)(a)	12 Dec 1995 (SI 1995/3228)
(b)	*Not in force*
(c)	12 Dec 1995 (for purpose of authorising regulations to be made) (SI 1995/3228) *Not in force* (otherwise)
20(1), (2)	*Not in force*
(3)–(8)	12 Dec 1995 (for purpose of authorising regulations to be made) (SI 1995/3228) *Not in force* (otherwise)
21, 22	12 Dec 1995 (for purpose of authorising regulations to be made) (SI 1995/3228) *Not in force* (otherwise)
23(1)	12 Dec 1995 (for purpose of authorising regulations to be made) (SI 1995/3228) *Not in force* (otherwise)
(2)	*Not in force*
(3), (4)	12 Dec 1995 (for purpose of authorising regulations to be made) (SI 1995/3228) *Not in force* (otherwise)
(5)	*Not in force*
25	*Not in force*
26	12 Dec 1995 (for purpose of authorising regulations to be made) (SI 1995/3228) *Not in force* (otherwise)
27	12 Dec 1995 (for purpose of authorising regulations to be made) (SI 1995/3228) 6 Apr 1996 (otherwise) (SI 1995/3228)
28	12 Dec 1995 (for purpose of authorising regulations to be made) (SI 1995/3228) 1 Apr 1996 (otherwise) (SI 1995/3228)
29	1 Jan 1996 (SI 1995/3228)
30	1 Apr 1996 (SI 1995/3228)
31	12 Dec 1995 (for purpose of authorising regulations to be made) (SI 1995/3228) *Not in force* (otherwise)
32	*Not in force*
33	6 Apr 1996 (SI 1995/3228)
34(1), (2)	6 Apr 1996 (SI 1995/3228)
(3)	12 Dec 1995 (for purpose of authorising regulations to be made) (SI 1995/3228) 6 Apr 1996 (otherwise) (SI 1995/3228)
(4)–(6)	6 Apr 1996 (SI 1995/3228)
(7)	12 Dec 1995 (for purpose of authorising regulations to be made) (SI 1995/3228) 6 Apr 1996 (otherwise) (SI 1995/3228)
35–37	12 Dec 1995 (SI 1995/3228)
38(1)(a)	*Not in force*
(b)	6 Apr 1996 (SI 1995/3228)
(2)–(4)	*Not in force*
(5)	6 Apr 1996 (SI 1995/3228)
(6)–(8)	*Not in force*
39	28 Jun 1995 (s 41(2))

Jobseekers Act 1995 (c 18)—*cont*

s 40	12 Dec 1995 (for purpose of authorising regulations to be made) (SI 1995/3228)
	Not in force (otherwise)
41(1)–(3)	28 Jun 1995 (s 41(2))
(4)	See Sch 2 below
(5)	See Sch 3 below
(6)	28 Jun 1995 (s 41(2))
Sch 1	12 Dec 1995 (for purpose of authorising regulations to be made) (SI 1995/3228)
	Not in force (otherwise)
2, para 1–29	*Not in force*
30(1)–(4)	*Not in force*
(5)	12 Dec 1995 (for purpose of authorising regulations to be made) (SI 1995/3228)
	Not in force (otherwise)
31–40	*Not in force*
41	6 Apr 1996 (SI 1995/3228)
42–76	*Not in force*
3	1 Apr 1996 (repeals of Supplementary Benefits Act 1976, s 30, Sch 5) (SI 1995/3228)
	Not in force (otherwise)

Land Registers (Scotland) Act 1995 (c 14)

RA: 28 Jun 1995

Commencement provisions: s 2(2); Land Registers (Scotland) Act 1995 (Commencement) Order 1996, SI 1996/94

1 Apr 1996 (SI 1996/94)

Landlord and Tenant (Covenants) Act 1995 (c 30)

RA: 19 Jul 1995

Commencement provisions: s 31; Landlord and Tenant (Covenants) Act 1995 (Commencement) Order 1995, SI 1995/2963

1 January 1996 (SI 1995/2963)

Law Reform (Succession) Act 1995 (c 41)

RA: 8 Nov 1995

8 Nov 1995 (RA)

Licensing (Sunday Hours) Act 1995 (c 33)

RA: 19 Jul 1995

Commencement provisions: s 5; Licensing (Sunday Hours) Act 1995 (Commencement) Order 1995, SI 1995/1930

6 Aug 1995 (SI 1995/1930)

Medical (Professional Performance) Act 1995 (c 51)

RA: 8 Nov 1995

Commencement provision: s 6

Not in force

Mental Health (Patients in the Community) Act 1995 (c 52)

RA: 8 Nov 1995

Commencement provision: s 7(2)

1 Apr 1996 (s 7(2))

Merchant Shipping Act 1995 (c 21)

RA: 19 Jul 1995

Commencement provision: s 316(2), Sch 14, para 5

s 1–59	1 Jan 1996 (s 316(2))
60	*Not in force*
61–79	1 Jan 1996 (s 316(2))
80(1)	1 Jan 1996 (s 316(2))
(2)	*Not in force*
(3)	1 Jan 1996 (s 316(2))
(4)	*Not in force*
81–110	1 Jan 1996 (s 316(2))
111	*Not in force*
112–114	1 Jan 1996 (s 316(2))
115, 116	*Not in force*
117	1 Jan 1996 (s 316(2))
118	*Not in force*
119(1)	1 Jan 1996 (s 316(2))
(2), (3)	*Not in force*
120–126	1 Jan 1996 (s 316(2))
127	*Not in force*
128–313	1 Jan 1996 (s 316(2))
314(1)	See Sch 12 below
(2)–(4)	1 Jan 1996 (s 316(2))
315, 316	1 Jan 1996 (s 316(2))
Sch 1–11	1 Jan 1996 (s 316(2))
12	1 Jan 1996 (except repeals in Aliens Restriction (Amendment) Act 1919, Local Government etc (Scotland) Act 1994) (s 316(2), Sch 14, para 5) *Not in force* (exceptions noted above)
13, 14	1 Jan 1996 (s 316(2))

National Health Service (Amendment) Act 1995 (c 31)

RA: 19 Jul 1995

Commencement provisions: s 14(3), (4); National Health Service (Amendment) Act 1995 (Commencement No 1 and Saving) Order 1995, SI 1995/3090; National

National Health Service (Amendment) Act 1995 (c 31)—*cont*

Health Service (Amendment) Act 1995 (Commencement No 2 and Saving) (Scotland) Order 1995, SI 1995/3214

s 1, 2	21 Dec 1995 (subject to transitional provisions) (for the purposes of amending the National Health Service Act 1977 in relation to general medical services and general dental services only) (SI 1995/3090) *Not in force* (otherwise)
3–6	21 Dec 1995 (subject to transitional provisions) (SI 1995/3090)
7, 8	1 Jan 1996 (subject to transitional provisions) (for the purposes of amending the National Health Service (Scotland) Act 1978 in relation to general medical services and general dental services only) (SI 1995/3214) *Not in force* (otherwise)
9–12	1 Jan 1996 (subject to transitional provisions) (SI 1995/3214)
13	19 Jul 1995 (RA)
14(1)	19 Jul 1995 (RA)
(2)	See Schedule below
(3)–(6)	19 Jul 1995 (RA)
Schedule	21 Dec 1995 (subject to transitional provisions) (repeals in National Health Service Act 1977, Health Authorities Act 1995) (SI 1995/3090) 1 Jan 1996 (subject to transitional provisions) (repeals in National Health Service (Scotland) Act 1978) (SI 1995/3214)

Northern Ireland (Remission of Sentences) Act 1995 (c 47)

RA: 8 Nov 1995

Commencement provisions: s 2; Northern Ireland (Remission of Sentences) Act 1995 (Commencement) Order 1995, SI 1995/2945

17 November 1995 (SI 1995/2945)

Olympic Symbol etc (Protection) Act 1995 (c 32)

RA: 19 Jul 1995

Commencement provisions: s 19(2); Olympic Symbol etc (Protection) Act 1995 (Commencement) Order 1995, SI 1995/2472

20 Sep 1995 (SI 1995/2472)

Pensions Act 1995 (c 26)

RA: 19 Jul 1995

Commencement provisions: ss 135, 150(2), 180, Sch 4; Pensions Act 1995 (Commencement No 1) Order 1995, SI 1995/2548; Pensions Act 1995 (Commencement No 2) Order 1995, SI 1995/3104

Pensions Act 1995 (c 26)—*cont*

s 1–38	*Not in force*
39	1 Jan 1996 (SI 1995/3104)
40–61	*Not in force*
62–66	4 Dec 1995 (for purpose of authorising the making of regulations under ss 63(5), 64(2), (3), 66(4)) (SI 1995/3104)
	1 Jan 1996 (otherwise) (SI 1995/3104)
67–89	*Not in force*
90	2 Oct 1995 (SI 1995/2548)
91–116	*Not in force*
117	1 Jan 1996 (so far as relates to s 39) (SI 1995/3104)
	4 Dec 1995 and 1 Jan 1996 (so far as relates to ss 62–66) (SI 1995/3104)
	Not in force (otherwise)
118, 119	*Not in force*
120	4 Dec 1995 and 1 Jan 1996 (so far as relates to ss 62–66) (SI 1995/3104)
	Not in force (otherwise)
121	1 Jan 1996 (so far as relates to s 39) (SI 1995/3104)
	4 Dec 1995 and 1 Jan 1996 (so far as relates to ss 62–66) (SI 1995/3104)
	Not in force (otherwise)
122	See Sch 3 below
123	*Not in force*
124	1 Jan 1996 (so far as relates to s 39) (SI 1995/3104)
	4 Dec 1995 and 1 Jan 1996 (so far as relates to ss 62–66) (SI 1995/3104)
	Not in force (otherwise)
125	*Not in force*
126	See Sch 4 below
127–134	19 Jul 1995 (s 180(2))
135–155	*Not in force*
156	2 Oct 1995 (SI 1995/2548)
157–167	*Not in force*
168	19 Jul 1995 (s 180(2))
169	2 Oct 1995 (SI 1995/2548)
170, 171	19 Jul 1995 (s 180(2))
172	2 Oct 1995 (SI 1995/2548)
173	See Sch 6 below
174, 175	2 Oct 1995 (so far as they relate to s 172) (SI 1995/2548)
	4 Dec 1995 and 1 Jan 1996 (so far as relates to ss 62–66) (SI 1995/3104)
	Not in force (otherwise)
176	*Not in force*
177	See Sch 7 below
178	*Not in force*
179	19 Jul 1995 (s 180(2))
180, 181	See ss 1179 above
Sch 1, 2	*Not in force*
3, para 1–28	*Not in force*
29	1 Jan 1996 (SI 1995/3104)
30, 31	*Not in force*
32–37	1 Jan 1996 (SI 1995/3104)
38	*Not in force*
39(a)	*Not in force*

Pensions Act 1995 (c 26)—*cont*

Sch 3, para 39(b)	1 Jan 1996 (SI 1995/3104)
(c), (d)	*Not in force*
40, 41	*Not in force*
42	1 Jan 1996 (SI 1995/3104)
43	*Not in force*
44(a)(i)	1 Jan 1996 (SI 1995/3104)
(ii)	*Not in force*
(b)	*Not in force*
45, 46	*Not in force*
47	1 Jan 1996 (SI 1995/3104)
4	19 Jul 1995 (s 180(2))[1]
5	*Not in force*
6, para 1	2 Oct 1995 (SI 1995/2548)
2–16	*Not in force*
7, Pt I	*Not in force*
II	Has effect in accordance with Sch 4 (s 180(2))
III	*Not in force*
IV	19 Jul 1995 (repeal in Pensions (Increase) Act 1971) (s 180(2))
	Not in force (otherwise)

[1] Certain provisions of Sch 4 have effect as followspara 2 has effect on or after 6 Apr 2010 (para 2(2)); para 4 has effect in relation to any person attaining pensionable age on or after 6 Apr 2010 (para 4(2)); para 6(1) comes into force on 6 Apr 2010; and para 6(2)–(4) have effect in relation to incremental periods beginning on or after that date (para 6(5)); paras 18, 19 have effect on or after 6 Apr 2010 (para 20)

Prisoners (Return to Custody) Act 1995 (c 16)

RA: 28 Jun 1995

Commencement provisions: s 3(2); Prisoners (Return to Custody) Act 1995 (Commencement) Order 1995, SI 1995/2021

5 Sep 1995 (SI 1995/2021)

Private International Law (Miscellaneous Provisions) Act 1995 (c 42)

RA: 8 Nov 1995

Commencement provision: s 16

s 1–4	*Not in force*
5–8	8 Jan 1996 (s 16(2))
9–15	*Not in force*
16–19	8 Nov 1995 (RA)
Schedule	8 Jan 1996 (s 16(2))

Proceeds of Crime Act 1995 (c 11)

RA: 28 Jun 1995

Commencement provisions: s 16(3)–(6); Proceeds of Crime Act 1995 (Commencement) Order 1995, SI 1995/2650

s 1–13	1 Nov 1995 (SI 1995/2650)
14	28 Jun 1995 (s 16(4))
15	1 Nov 1995 (SI 1995/2650)
16	28 Jun 1995 (s 16(4))
Sch 1, 2	1 Nov 1995 (SI 1995/2650)

Proceeds of Crime (Scotland) Act 1995 (c 43)

RA: 8 Nov 1995

Commencement provision: s 50(2)

1 Apr 1996 (s 50(2)), subject to transitional provisions and savings in Criminal Procedure (Consequential Provisions) (Scotland) Act 1995, in particular for consolidated provisions which are not in force at that date; see s 4, Sch 3 thereto

Requirements of Writing (Scotland) Act 1995 (c 7)

RA: 1 May 1995

Commencement provision: s 15(2)

1 Aug 1995 (s 15(2))

Road Traffic (New Drivers) Act 1995 (c 13)

RA: 28 Jun 1995

Commencement provisions: s 10(2), (3)

Not in force

Sale of Goods (Amendment) Act 1995 (c 28)

RA: 19 Jul 1995

Commencement provision: s 3(2)

19 Sep 1995 (s 3(2))

Shipping and Trading Interests (Protection) Act 1995 (c 22)

RA: 19 Jul 1995

Commencement provision: s 9(4)

1 Jan 1996 (s 9(4))

South Africa Act 1995 (c 3)

RA: 23 Mar 1995

23 Mar 1995 (RA)

Statute Law (Repeals) Act 1995 (c 44)

RA: 8 Nov 1995

8 Nov 1995 (RA)

Team and Group Ministries Measure 1995 (No 1)

RA: 28 Jun 1995
Commencement provision: s 20(2)

s 1	*Not in force*
2	28 Jun 1995 (s 20(2))
3–19	*Not in force*
20	See ss 1–19 above
Sch 1, 2	*Not in force*

Town and Country Planning (Costs of Inquiries etc) Act 1995 (c 49)

RA: 8 Nov 1995

8 Nov 1995 (RA)